P9-CQR-392

THE GLOBAL ENCYCLOPEDIA OF
Wine

THE GLOBAL ENCYCLOPEDIA OF

Wine

REBECCA CHAPA, CATHERINE FALLIS MS, PATRICK FARRELL MW
AND 33 ADDITIONAL WINE EXPERTS

PETER FORRESTAL, *Editor*

Foreword by JAMES HALLIDAY

THE WINE APPRECIATION GUILD

PUBLISHER	Gordon Cheers
ASSOCIATE PUBLISHER	Margaret Olds
FOREWORD BY	James Halliday
TEXT MANAGING EDITOR	Mary Halbmeyer
PHOTOGRAPHY MANAGING EDITOR	Anna Cheifetz
EDITORS	Tricia Bancroft
	Lynn Cole
	Fiona Doig
	Scott Forbes
	Sue Grose-Hodge
	Shelley Kenigsberg
	Rowena Lennox
	Merry Pearson
	Frank Povah
	Ann Savage
	Sarah Shrubb
ART DIRECTOR	Stan Lamond
COVER DESIGN	Bob Mitchell
	Stan Lamond
PAGE LAYOUT	Cathy Campbell
	Moyna Smeaton
	Robert Taylor
	Veronica Varetsa
CARTOGRAPHER	John Frith
MAP EDITORS	Derek Barton
	Merry Pearson
MAP CONSULTANT	Valerie Marlborough
PICTURE RESEARCH	Gordon Cheers
TYPESETTING	Dee Rogers
INDEX	Glenda Browne
PUBLISHING ASSISTANT	Erin King
PRODUCTION	Rosemary Barry
	Bernard Roberts

First published in North America 2001 by
THE WINE APPRECIATION GUILD LTD
360 Swift Avenue
South San Francisco CA 94080
800 231-9463

ISBN 1-891267-38-8

Produced by Global Book Publishing Pty Ltd
1/181 High Street, Willoughby, NSW Australia 2068
Phone 61 2 9967 3100 fax 61 2 9967 5891

Printed in Hong Kong by Sing Cheong Printing Co. Ltd,
Film separation Pica Digital Pte Ltd, Singapore

CAPTIONS

pages 2-3: Vineyards, La Rioja, Spain.
page 4: Rows of vines, Barbaresco, Piedmont, Italy.
page 7: Gibbston Valley cellar, Central Otago, New Zealand.
page 9: Harvesting chasselas grapes, Geneva, Switzerland.
page 10: See p. 912; top to bottom refer to pp. 62, 222, 334, 376, 278.
page 11: See p. 912; top to bottom refer to pp. 454, 488, 500, 576, 654.
page 12: Merlot grapes.
pages 14-15: Vineyards and winery buildings, Te Mata Estate, Hawkes Bay, New Zealand.

All captions for pictures found in the introductions to each chapter can be located on page 912 (the last page of the book).

Note on abbreviation used in this book: NA in the Producer listings denotes that the relevant information was Not Available from the producer at time of going to press.

Contributors

Maureen Ashley MW started tasting wine as a hobby in the 1970s and entered the wine trade in 1979. She became a Master of Wine in 1984, also attaining the Tim Derouet Award for the excellence of her results. She became a freelance writer in 1986. One of the foremost Italian wine experts, she now lives in Rome. Maureen has written three books in the *Touring in Wine Country* series as well as *Italian Wines*, in the Sainsbury's Regional Wine Guides series. She writes widely for international audiences, leads wine tours in Italy, and gives talks and tutored tastings.

Tony Aspler, based in Toronto, is the editor of *Winetidings* magazine, wine columnist for the *Toronto Star* and creator of the Air Ontario Wine Awards. He is a member of the Advisory Board for Masters of Wine (North America). Tony contributed to Jancis Robinson's *Oxford Companion To Wine* and the *Larousse Encyclopedia of Wine*. He is himself the author of several books on wine, including *Guide to New World Wines*, *Vintage Canada*, *Travels With My Corkscrew*, *The Wine Lover's Companion* and *The Wine Lover Dines*. He also writes murder mysteries about a wine writer detective. His website is at www.tonyaspler.com.

James Aufenast and writes for *Harpers Wine & Spirit Weekly*, the UK's major wine trade magazine, on emerging wine areas including the south of France, Israel and Canada. He specializes in Eastern Europe, and has visited Romania and Bulgaria to investigate the wine industries in those countries. He also writes for *The Times* Weekend section on food and drink and reviews restaurants for the *Who Drinks Where Crushguide*, a London restaurant guide. James has written a cocktail book for Quarto Publishing. He lives in London.

Helena Baker, a native of Prague, holds a Diploma from the Wine & Spirit Education Trust in London, is one of the founders of the Prague Wine Society and the Slow Food Convivium of Prague, a freelance wine writer, columnist, wine taster at international wine competitions, consultant and lecturer. She has translated the *Encyclopedia of Czech and Moravian Wines*, by professor Vilém Kraus, and published her own *Pocket Guide 2000 to the Wines and Winemakers of the Czech Republic*, which she is currently translating into English. She lives in a country house just outside Prague.

Jeffrey Benson spent the last 30 years traveling to virtually every wine growing country in the world as buying director for a large wine importing company. Specializing in wines from outside Europe, he was instrumental in developing new export markets for such countries as India, Canada and Zimbabwe. He has coauthored three books on his favorite wines, *Sauternes*, *Saint Emilion/Pomerol* and *The Sweet wines of Bordeaux*. He is now a wine consultant to various hotel groups around the world and travels extensively lecturing, and contributing articles to various international wine publications.

Stephen Brook worked as an editor in the United States and Britain before becoming a freelance writer specializing in travel and wine. His *Liquid Gold: Dessert Wines of the World* won the Andre Simon Award in 1987. Other awards include the Bunch Award for wine writer of the year in 1996. He is the author of *Sauvignon Blanc and Semillon* and the *Wine Companion to Southern France*, *Sauternes and the Other Sweet Wines of Bordeaux*, and *The Wines of California*. He lives in London, where he is a regular contributing editor for *Decanter* and writes on wine for *Conde Nast Traveller*.

Jim Budd started writing about wine in 1988, having previously taught English in London. He contributes to a number of specialist drinks magazines, including *Wine & Spirit International, Decanter* and *Harpers Wine & Spirit*

Weekly, and contributes to a number of internet sites including decanter.com, madaboutwine.com and wineplanet.com. He wrote *Appreciating Fine Wines*, and contributed to *Oz Clarke's Pocket Wine Book*, the Oz Clarke CD ROM and *Oz Clarke's Encyclopedia of Wine*. In 1997 he won Le Prix du Champagne Lanson Noble Cuvée for investigating on bogus Champagne investment schemes and now has a website (www.investdrinks.org) about drinks investments.

Rebecca Chapa is a San Francisco-based wine consultant whose clients include some major hotels. She is a contributing editor for *Wine & Spirits* and writes freelance for *Santé*, SpiritsUSA.com, and has a bimonthly column in *SOMA* magazine. She was co-program chair of the Society of Wine Educators Conference in San Jose, California, in August 2000. She has completed the Higher Certificate towards the Master of Wine degree given by the Wine and Spirits Education Trust in England and is one of a handful of Americans to have completed the Diploma course of study.

Steve Charters MW qualified as a lawyer in the UK, but was seduced by the allure of wine, and worked in retail and wine education in both London and Sydney. He is one of only 240 members of the Institute of Masters of Wine in the world, and one of only 12 in Australia, having passed its rigorous theory and tasting examination in 1997. Steve now lectures in Wine Studies at Edith Cowan University, in Perth, Australia. His courses cover the understanding and appreciation of wine, its varying worldwide styles, and marketing and selling wine.

Catherine Fallis MS is the fifth woman in the world to have earned the title of Master Sommelier; she is also a student in the UK-based Master of Wine program. In January 2000, she opened PlanetGrape.com, a wine writing and consulting service and website. She is wine editor of SpiritsUSA.com, and has recently co-authored a wine encyclopedia. Her articles on wines, spirits, cigars, food, travel, and lifestyle appear regularly in a variety of trade and consumer publications and websites including *Epicurean*, Foofoo.com, *Restaurant Hospitality*, *Santé*, Smartwine.com, and *Wine Business Monthly*.

Dr Patrick Farrell MW, a medical doctor by training, is one of a handful of masters of wine living in the United States. He has followed California's wine-producing regions carefully since moving to the golden state in 1988. He is a past program and professional session chairman of the Society of Wine Educators and actively teaches about wine. Patrick has judged wine competitions internationally and keeps a busy schedule visiting the world's wine regions. He is currently combining his wine and medical training in writing a book on wine and health.

Peter Forrestal (Consultant Editor) was the founding editor of *The Wine Magazine* and is now its associate editor. As a freelance wine and food writer, he has written *A Taste of the Margaret River*, co-authored *The Western Table*, and edited *Discover Australia: Wineries*. He is a former president of the Wine Press Club of Western Australia, a member of the Circle of Wine Writers and the Australian Society of Wine Educators. He has been wine correspondent for the *West Australian*, the *Western Review* and the *Perth Weekly*.

Michael Fridjhon is chairman of the South African Wine Industry Trust and an international wine judge. He is the convenor of the South African Airways selection panel, a regular columnist for *Business Day*, and a contributor to the *Financial Mail*, *Wine, Wine & Spirit (UK)*, and *Decanter*. He wrote *The Penguin Book of South African Wine*, is coauthor of *Conspiracy of Giants—An Analysis of the South African Liquor Industry*, a contributor to the *John Platter South Africa Wine Guide*, *The Complete Book of South African Wine*, the *Hugh Johnson Wine Companion* and new *Oxford Companion to Wine*.

Ken Gargett, based on the Gold Coast in Queensland, Australia, is a practicing lawyer as well as a senior writer

for *Vine, Wine & Cellar* and a contributor to *The Wine Magazine*, *Discover Australia: Wineries* and other publications. He is a wine educator for the Wine Society in Queensland and conducts training and consults within the industry, as well as judging. He was the 1993 winner of the Vin de Champagne Award and has conducted numerous Australian wine promotions, seminars and master of wine classes internationally.

Harold Heckle pursued his love of romance languages and literature at the universities of Bristol and King's College (England). After working with the British Council in Perú and a subsidiary of the Bank of England, he became a theatre producer, then went on to research, write and broadcast for BBC Radio. One feature, *The Grape Debate*, led to wine journalism. He has chaired The Wine Club since its inception. Today, Harold writes for *Wine & Spirit International* and *Decanter*, and is columnist for the Spanish newspaper, *El Mundo*. He lives in England and grows his own organic vegetables.

Brian Jordan became interested in wine in the early 1980s when he purchased a hotel restaurant in Britain's west country, and subsequently was twice winner and twice runner-up for the best wine list in the UK. He began writing about wine in the 1990s, subsequently expanding into international judging, consultancy, photography, lecturing, broadcasting and organizing wine competitions. As a freelance wine writer, his articles have appeared in every significant wine-oriented magazine in the UK as well as several in other countries.

James Lawther MW, based in Bordeaux, France, cut his teeth in the wine trade retailing wine at Steven Spurrier's Caves de la Madeleine in Paris and as a lecturer at the Académie du Vin. He was the first Englishman to pass the Master of Wine examination while resident in France (1993). He is now an independent wine consultant, writer and contributing editor to *Decanter*. He is the author of the *Bordeaux Wine Companion* and has contributed to the recent edition of *The Wine Atlas of France*. He also leads tours in the French wine regions.

Alex Liddell has lived in France, Portugal and Italy and travels the wine countries of the world for six months of the year. He is the author of *Port Wine Quintas of the Douro* and *Madeira* and is currently working on a book about the wines of Hungary. He is a member of the Circle of Wine Writers and contributes to Australia's *The Wine Magazine*.

Wink Lorch has worked in the world of wine for over 20 years, in the last 15 as a writer and educator. She was one of the two contributing editors for Williams-Sonoma's *The Wine Guide* published by Time-Life in 1999 and she writes for trade and consumer magazines in the UK. Wink is a founding member of the Association of Wine Educators in the UK and regularly leads tutored tastings and wine courses. She divides her time between her chalet in the French Alps (close to Savoie, Jura and Swiss vineyards) and a *pied-a-terre* in England.

Nico Manessis, born on the island of Corfu, has been active in the international wine business for over 20 years in Europe and the USA. His first book, *The Greek Wine Guide*, published in 1994, has been instrumental in bringing quality Greek wine to international attention. More recently, he has written *The Illustrated Greek Wine Book*. He also regularly contributes to newspapers and *Decanter* and lectures frequently on the new wines of his native country, appearing often at the Université de Vin in France. He is a member of l'Académie Internationale du Vin and lives in Geneva, Switzerland.

Sally Marden is a professionally trained journalist who cut her writing teeth on regional UK newspapers. She turned to drink in 1990 when she joined leading trade publication *Off Licence News*. She has traveled extensively to wine regions throughout Europe, the USA, Chile and Australia, and, as well as writing for a range of wine publications in the UK, has co-presented a food and drink television series for Channel 4. In 1998 she moved to the Barossa, where she now writes and consults for a specialist wine marketing company, as well as contributing regularly to publications including *The Wine Magazine* and *Le Vigneron*.

Giles MacDonogh is a historian and the author of several books on Germany, including lives of Frederick the Great and the Kaiser and histories of Prussia and Berlin. He is also a wine writer, contributing a regular column to the *Financial Times* and *Punch*, as well as writing occasional articles for *Decanter*, *Wine* and other specialized magazines. He is the author of three books on wine, two of them on Austria: *The Wine and Food of Austria* and *New Wines from the Old World*. He is currently writing a book on Portuguese wines.

Kate McIntyre learned first hand about vineyards and wineries growing up from the age of nine on her family's estate on Victoria's Mornington Peninsula, and began her career in the wine industry at Philip Murphy Wine and Spirits in 1996. In 1998 she was the inaugural winner of the Negociants Working with Wine Fellowship. She is now studying for the Master of Wine exam and is a regular contributor to *The Wine Magazine*. In 1999 she was wine writer for *Women's Weekly* and is an occasional contributor to *Divine* magazine. She was also a contributor to *Discover Australia: Wineries*.

Alex Mitchell credits her involvement in the 1998 Negociants Working With Wine program as being the turning point in her career in wine. It exposed her to an unprecedented range of imported wines and winning its prestigious Wine Writing Prize has led to her writing regularly for *The Wine Magazine*. After many years of nursing and four years in wine retail, she now has her own business. She has taught wine studies at Swinburne University and has contributed to two books. She plans to complete a Bachelor of Oenology and intends to become a winemaker.

Jasper Morris MW joined the UK wine trade in 1979 and founded his company, Morris & Verdin Ltd, two years later. The plan was to import wines from all over France but he rapidly developed a heavy bias towards Burgundy. He has also developed a strong second string in Californian wines. Since becoming a Master of Wine in 1985, he has been much in demand as a writer and lecturer. He regularly contributes to *Decanter* magazine and was responsible for the Burgundy entries in the *Oxford Companion to Wine*.

Jeremy Oliver is an independent Australian wine writer, broadcaster, author and speaker. Since 1984, when he became the world's youngest published wine author, he has written nine books and has contributed wine columns to dozens of magazines and newspapers. In addition to his self-published annual guide to Australian wine, *The OnWine Australian Wine Annual*, and his bi-monthly newsletter, *Jeremy Oliver's OnWine Report*, his current contributions include *The Wine Magazine*, *Personal Investment* and *The Australian Way*. He is also a speaker and master of ceremonies at wine presentations and has a comprehensive and independent wine website at www.onwine.com.au.

Anthony Peregrine, who comes from Lancashire in Northern England, studied political sciences before working as a teacher in Mexico City. On his return to England, he wrote for several newspapers before moving to France in 1988. He now lives near Montpellier in the Languedoc region from where he freelances for the general and specialist British press, covering wine, food and travel. His work appears in the *Daily Telegraph*, the *Daily Mail*, *Decanter*, *Wine & Spirit International* and on BBC Radio 4.

John Radford has been writing about wine professionally since 1977, after an earlier career in the wine trade. He has a special interest in the wines Spain and Portugal and contributed chapters on Iberia to the *Larousse Encyclopedia of Wine* and *Hugh Johnson's Wine Companion*. His book, *The New Spain*, won the Glenfiddich, Lanson, and Versailles Cookbook Fair prizes in 1999. He co-wrote the *Mitchell Beazley Pocket Guide to Fortified and Sweet Wines* and also writes for *Decanter*, *Wine* and other specialist magazines in the UK. He lives on the south coast of England.

Margaret Rand has been writing about wine for 18 years. She has edited *Wine* and *Wine & Spirit International*, is wine editor of *Oz Clarke's Wine Guide* and was founding editor of *Whisky Magazine*. She contributes to a wide range of publications including *The Sunday Times*, the *Daily Telegraph*, *Wine* and winetoday.com. She wrote the audio guide for Vinopolis, London's major wine exhibit, and is currently working with Oz Clarke on a book about grape varieties. Other forthcoming publications include an introductory guide to wine, with Robert Joseph.

Michele Round was an art teacher before pursuing her fascination for food and wine as a consultant, writer and commentator. She is a regular contributor to *The Wine Magazine*, writes a weekly food column for a Tasmanian newspaper and has written about wine for a variety of national publications. Through her work in gastronomy as a cook, writer and teacher, she is passionate about the synergy between food and wine. Born and raised in Tasmania, Michele became well known as a champion of the developing island wine industry through a weekly ABC Radio wine segment.

Joanna Simon is an award-winning wine writer for *The Sunday Times* (UK), for which she writes a weekly column, and a contributor to many other publications worldwide. She is a former editor of two leading UK wine magazines, *Wine* and *Wine & Spirit International*, and is author of *Wine with Food* and the best-selling *Discovering Wine*. She is also a broadcaster, presenting "The Bottle Uncorked" in 1999, BBC Radio 4's first series devoted to wine. When not writing, tasting, talking about wine or visiting the world's vineyards, she escapes from London to a beautiful and remote part of France.

Marguerite Thomas is the author of *Wineries of the Eastern States*. She is travel editor of *The Wine News* and she writes "Tastings," a food and wine column for the Los Angeles Times International Syndicate. She is a regular contributor on food and wine to various US publications, including *Saveur*, *Country Home* and *Time Out New York*. She was raised in France and California, and now resides in New York, where she has been nominated to recieve the prestigious James Beard Award for wine journalism.

Joelle Thomson is a freelance wine writer in Auckland, New Zealand. She started writing about wine for the weekly arts newspaper, *Capital Times*, in the mid-1990s and worked full-time in food and design magazines in New Zealand prior to her freelance career. She published her first book, *Joelle Thomson's Under $15 Wine Guide*, in 1999 and has since written *Weekends for Wine Lovers*. She is currently wine writer for the *Christchurch Press*, *Grocer's Review*, *SHE* and *NZ Home & Entertaining* and a regular contributor to *The Wine Magazine* and the Wine Planet website.

Roger Voss, one of Britain's leading wine and food writers, is European editor for the New York-based *Wine Enthusiast* magazine and writes for UK magazines such as *Decanter* and *Harpers Wine & Spirit Weekly*. For four years editor of the Consumers' Association's *Which? Wine Guide*, he has also written guides to port and sherry, to the chardonnay and cabernet sauvignon grapes, *Wine and Food of France* and *The Wines of the Loire*. Up-coming publications include a fifth edition of his guide to the wines of the Loire, Alsace and the Rhône. He lives in the Bordeaux region of France.

Dr Paul White, originally from Oregon in the USA, captained the Oxford University Blind Wine Tasting Team while completing a doctorate at Oxford University and developed his analytical skills further as a judge at London's International Wine Challenge. Based in Wellington, he is currently a columnist for the *New Zealand Herald* and contributes to the *Oregonian* and other media throughout Australasia, USA and Europe. He also publishes an online wine tasting guide at www.winesense.co.nz. His senior judging credits include London's International Wine Challenge, the Sydney International Top 100, and Sydney Royal Easter Show.

Simon Woods, a former electronics design engineer, picked up the wine bug while traveling in Australia in 1988 and has hardly put a glass down since. He spent the early 1990s coordinating London's International Wine Challenge, the world's largest wine competition, and is now co-editor of *Which? Wine Guide*, as well as being a regular columnist for *Wine*. He has judged at wine competitions in England, France and Australia, and has also appeared on radio and television both at home and abroad. He lives in the Pennines in the North of England.

C o n t

ents

Foreword

The title says it all: a global encyclopedia covering every aspect of wine from its history to its making and enjoyment; from Burgundy to Zimbabwe, from Turkmenistan to Uruguay. When I first heard of the project, its sheer audacity took my breath away, for the text is one thing, but maps another thing altogether. I have been the author of several atlases, and have first-hand experience of the painstaking, if not downright painful, care and skill which are needed to produce maps which are accurate, legible and esthetically pleasing.

Another feature of this massive book is that it is up to date. Wherever you have a work that involves authors from every corner of the globe covering subjects ranging from the familiar to the arcane, it is all too easy to let the timelines run wildly out of control. The consequence is that the material submitted becomes stale by the time the laggards are finally rounded up and the editor breathes a huge sigh of relief.

This book has run to a tight schedule without compromising its integrity. Peter Forrestal has had to live in multiple time zones throughout its gestation, cajoling authors to meet deadlines and answer queries. In the end, it has all come together, and all of those involved in the production of such a major reference work can feel well pleased with their efforts. It is a benchmark publication in the world of wine.

The Global Encyclopedia of Wine will satisfy the most discerning reader. Those who know their local wine regions and appreciate their local product, will find a wealth of information to add to their knowledge. The comprehensive international coverage of the subject will empower any wine lover to taste beyond their boundaries.

James Halliday

The World of Wine

Steve Charters MW

The History of Wine

An ancient Minoan wine press from Crete. Grapes would have been pressed by foot.

Donkeys are still used as transport in some areas of Cyprus, an important commercial center of the wine trade in medieval times.

More than any other drink across the world, wine fascinates, entices and seduces. Tea and coffee have their rituals, beer and water quench the thirst, whisky and brandy intoxicate, but none of these attract so many connoisseurs, stimulate such fellowship, or even give so much pleasure as wine. More books are written about wine than any other drink, and more wine is tasted in the formalized rituals of sniff and slurp than any other beverage.

It is too easy, while we enjoy a glass of chilled chardonnay, to ignore where it came from, how it was made, or the cultural background that spawned it. However, wine is rooted in history, and it has a dynamic relationship to both those cultures who have drunk it for millennia and those who have enjoyed it for less than 100 years.

Wine was probably first made in the region of the Caucasus Mountains between Europe and Asia, roughly in present-day Georgia or Kurdistan. The current best evidence for its origin suggests that it was being made there perhaps 8,000 years ago. Some archeologists think beer was made before wine because barley, which is essential for making beer, was a key initial crop in the diet of our ancestors. Mead, made from honey, and palm wine were also important early beverages. Nevertheless, wine has a venerable history.

It is likely that the first winemaker would have been a woman, for women would probably have been responsible for gathering fruit and nuts in Neolithic society. The usual hypothesis is that a few bunches of wild grapes were stored in a clay pot and forgotten for a few days. They began to ferment, probably by carbonic maceration. As juice ran out, yeast fermentation may have begun. After a few days, the owner of the pot remembered the grapes and, perhaps feeling thirsty, she drank the juice that had accumulated at the bottom. Although it may not have been very pleasant, it made her feel strangely euphoric. Thus the first wine, and maybe the first alcoholic drink, was born.

At first, wine would have been made on a haphazard basis, probably from the wild vines of the region. Initially, its limited availability, depending on grapes occurring naturally, would have confined its use to special occasions. Later, when wine was made from cultivated grapes, its use would have become more widespread.

WINE AS A COMMODITY

As Neolithic society became more developed due to the more efficient cultivation of crops, so it started to create surplus product and afford certain individuals the opportunity to trade that surplus. Wine could not easily be produced everywhere. The climate around cities like Ur and Babylon, the earliest centers of civilization in the Middle East, was too hot to produce the balanced grapes needed for good wine, but these places had the wealth to purchase wine. Thus, wine became a commodity, with the power to make its traders rich.

The first wine trader might have lived in one of the cities of Sumer, in what is now southern Iraq. These cities were on major rivers, like the Tigris and Euphrates, which gave the cities their wealth. They not only irrigated the crops, but they were also arteries of trade. The rivers flow down from southeast Turkey, close to the original cradle of wine production. Wine producers there would load up reed boats with large pots of the magic liquid and float it downstream to the great metropolises of the south. There they could trade it for gold and jewels, and later for bronze weapons.

Wine spread through the Mediterranean world rapidly. It was produced by the Egyptians, though only for the rich, and then by the Greeks, who produced it for all classes. The austere early Romans were suspicious of it, but wine had become popular well before the time of Caesar, and was again a source of wealth for those who produced it (using slave labor) on a large scale.

The wine drunk in the ancient world would not have resembled most of the wines we drink today. The taste then was for sweeter wine. It may well have had a lower alcohol level, and would regularly have been mixed with other substances such as honey, spices or even seawater! The two wines we see today that most resemble the ancient styles are probably the dried-grape wines of northeast Italy, the *recioto*, and retsina, the Greek wine flavored with pine resin.

The peace established by the Roman Empire, and its efficient transport system, encouraged not only trade in wine but also the spread of the vine. Even before the Romans arrived, Greek traders had brought the vine to the south of France, but the *pax Romana* sent it out through France and Spain—and possibly encouraged the use of wild vines in Germany. By the end of the third century AD, wine was being made in many of the places we now see as its traditional home: Bordeaux, Burgundy, the Mosel valley and Jeréz. In time, these areas started to send wine back to Rome itself.

Critical to this spread was a revolution in the method of transporting wine. The early storage of all liquids, including wine, was in clay jars, usually long thin ones called *amphorae*. However, in the second century AD, a new form of container appeared from France.

Barrels, invented by the Celts, were probably being made in 500 BC. In the first century AD, they were generally used to transport wine, ultimately replacing *amphorae* as the preferred container. The coopers developed substantial skills in shaping and fitting the staves into watertight containers and, though despised as barbarians by their Roman overlords, they revolutionized the transport of wine. *Amphorae* are cumbersome, heavy,

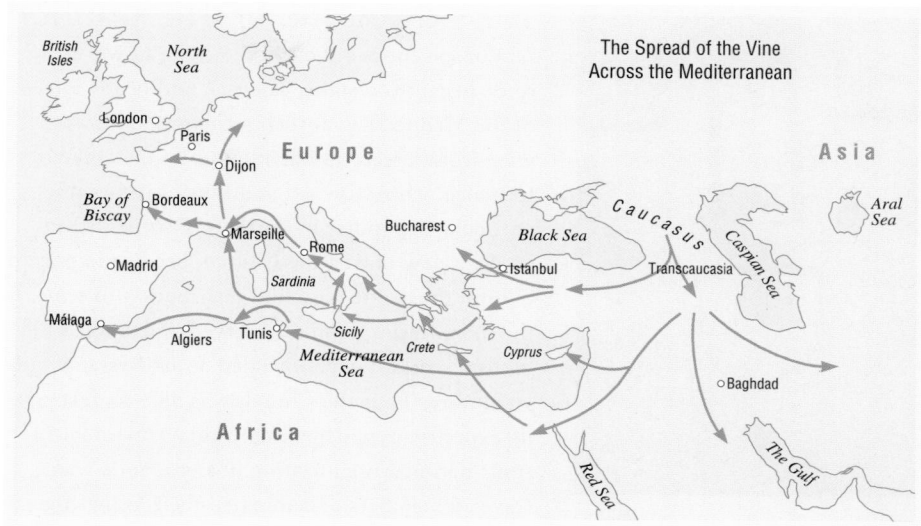

The Spread of the Vine Across the Mediterranean

unstackable and easily broken. Barrels, on the other hand, are resilient, hold more and are stackable—they were the technological change necessary to spread cheap mass-produced wine to the burgeoning masses of Rome. In one respect, however, the barrels had an adverse effect on wine. Clay pots could be made airtight, which meant that wine could mature in them for many years. Oak casks sped the oxidation process, so that wine aged, and spoiled, more rapidly.

The end of the Roman Empire in western Europe led to the period known as the Dark Ages. During this time, although there was a dramatic decline in the European wine trade, viticulture thrived in the eastern Mediterranean vineyards of Greece, Turkey and the Balkans in the Byzantine Empire for many centuries.

Above: *Recioto and retsina; modern wine styles that most resemble wines drunk in ancient times.*

Left: *Traditional Portuguese barcos rabelos, used to transport young port down the river Douro.*

Thirsty pilgrims can choose between wine or water at a monastery on the way to Santiago de Compostela in Galicia, Spain.

Gnarled old "mission" vines in South America.

THE INFLUENCE OF THE CHURCH

As Europe entered the Middle Ages, however, trade began to resume. The rich and heady wines of the Mediterranean such as malmsey, a sweet wine from Greece (made famous by the Duke of Clarence, who drowned in a butt of it) became particularly popular in northern Europe. Meanwhile, a new player, the Church, became important in both the production and distribution of wine. In the monasteries, monks observed and studied the natural world, which included an understanding of viticulture. Thus the Church was able to develop its expertise in winemaking. And as the only truly trans-national organization in Europe, its widely traveled members disseminated their knowledge, as did monasteries, acting as providers of hospitality.

The Abbey of Citeaux, founded in 1098 by the Cistercian order, sits just outside the Côte d'Or, the heartland of the Burgundy wine region. Originally seeking a simple, austere life, the monks later became wealthy as the laity, concerned for their souls in the afterlife, bequeathed property (including vineyards) to the abbey. By the end of the twelfth century the Church owned much of the land in the village of Vougeot. At the same time, the abbey became a major staging post for travelers. As a result, visitors sampled the wines and thus the monks' reputation spread, stimulating demand for their produce. Their influence lasted until 1789, when the French Revolution appropriated Church lands, although their direct control of the vineyards had ceased some time before then.

Perhaps the event that best symbolized the end of the Middle Ages was Columbus' voyage to the Americas in 1492. By the end of 1521, there were vineyards in Mexico, by 1548 they could be found in Chile and by 1769 in California. The Dutch made wine in the Cape of Good Hope in 1659, and vine cuttings were taken from there by the first European settlers of Australia and New Zealand.

Part of the reason for the spread of wine to Spain's new colonies in the Americas was the clergy, particularly the Jesuits, who came in the wake of the conquistadors, intent on saving the souls of the new subject peoples and requiring wine to celebrate the Eucharist. Initially, new plantings in the colonies were forbidden, to protect Spanish wine production. But exports could not keep up with demand, and the Church, among others, planted vineyards. One of the grapes now widely planted in South America is called the "mission," the name betraying its original use.

THE SCIENTIFIC REVOLUTION

The seventeenth and eighteenth centuries saw the scientific and industrial revolutions. In this period, empirical work allowed the development of the greatest sparkling wine in the world in Champagne, and yet more growth in the wine trade. At the same time, the rise of the middle classes provided a burgeoning market for what until then had been predominantly consumed by those who produced it. The influence of this nascent consumer revolution can be seen by the early nineteenth century, when the two most expensive wines in the world were tokay and constantia—not from France or Italy, but from Hungary and South Africa. Sixty years later, the spread of railways led to the next development. When wines from Italy or the south of France could be delivered in Berlin or London or Paris within 24 hours, producers no longer needed to seek a market only in the nearest town.

One other important legacy of the nineteenth century was the work of Louis Pasteur. Enology as a science is based on biochemistry, and was one of the later branches of science to develop. Louis Pasteur contributed substantially to our ability to control the processes involved in winemaking—and thus our ability to make good wine. He was a scientist of wide interests, and one who enjoyed wine as well. Pasteur didn't discover yeasts, but he showed that microscopic organisms were responsible for fermentations. When he was commissioned by the French government to investigate wine spoilage, he discovered the various bacteria that cause it and offered means of preventing their activity. It was due to this man more than any other that winemaking became a science, and that the drink we now enjoy can be produced so reliably and cheaply.

What had been a golden age came to an end in the 1860s when the pest phylloxera arrived from North America. It ravaged vineyards, first in France, then through the rest of Europe, until the solution of grafting was discovered. At the same time, the widening trade in wine provoked widespread fraud, as producers of cheap wine tried to pass their product off as *grand vin*. Then came war, and prohibition in the USA—and general depression to wine producers around the world.

The response to the fraud problem in Europe was to develop a system to protect the producers of quality wine by guaranteeing its origin. This process, which developed into the French Appellation system, also gave rise to the European idea

Laboratory analysis of wine, which still includes a tasting assessment.

of labeling "quality" wine, which has a specific demarcated origin, and "table" wine, which does not. The European system is the basis for all quality control systems—and is reflected in other parts of the world—as with American Viticultural Areas (AVAs) in the United States and Geographic Indicators (GIs) in Australia.

WINE TODAY

The last century has consolidated the impact of developments in the scientific, technological and transport worlds. Discoveries of the scientific basis for malolactic fermentation and for keeping oxygen away from wine have altered what we drink—as has the fact that Jacob's Creek Chardonnay can be shipped from Australia to the UK for less than 10p per bottle (US15¢). Perhaps the main change since the Second World War, however, has been in consumption practice. Mediterranean countries have traditionally consumed a lot of wine, but in England wine was considered a drink for the aristocrats, in Australia for alcoholics and in the US it had been banned under prohibition. However, the impact of war (during which many young men were introduced to wine), along with growing disposable income and the rapid development of technology (making cheap but fruity wine commonplace), all spread wine drinking. In the last decade, this has extended to include Japan, China and Southeast Asia. It is now normal for shoppers in a UK supermarket to pick up a bottle to drink with their evening meal—something their parents would never have done. The spread of wine consumption has spawned an industry of education in the subject. Writers like Hugh Johnson are owed a large debt by the wine industry for making this product so well understood.

Wine drinking the Spanish way!

WHY DO WE DRINK WINE?

Technically, alcohol is a depressant, acting on the nervous system in a similar way to some tranquilizers, and in moderate amounts creating a feeling of contentment and cheerfulness. But alcohol is also found—in stronger form—in spirits. So why do we not drink spirits exclusively? Because there are other reasons for drinking wine—magic, for example. In earlier times people did not understand the process of fermentation, and believed that when they drank wine, gods had taken over their bodies. The relationship between wine and ritual continues in the communion service of the Christian Church today.

Another reason was that wine was safer to drink than water. Until the development of pure water supplies 160 years ago, water carried all kinds of bacteria, causing dysentery, cholera and typhoid. The alcohol content of wine, however, sustains very few bacteria and none of them are harmful. So wine became the safe drink of choice in the Mediterranean countries, just as beer was in northern Europe.

As wine became the daily drink, a natural relationship grew between wine and different styles of food. In Spain, for instance, inland regions make full-bodied red wines to go with their heavy food, which is often based on lamb. Their white wines—rioja is a good example—are traditionally also full-bodied to match the fleshy river fish of the central areas. Coastal regions produce lighter wines. The crisp, fresh, albariño-based wines of Galicia in the northwest and the sparkling cava of Catalonia are classic examples which marry better with the seafood or shellfish of those areas.

We cannot avoid mentioning the relationship of wine to status. There has been a tension throughout history between wine as an elite beverage and wine for consumption by the masses. In ancient Egypt, wine tended to be the preserve of the rich. In Greece, it was everyone's everyday drink. From the eighteenth century on in the United Kingdom—later in other northern European and English-speaking countries—wine was associated with the

moneyed classes, while even the peasants drank it daily in southern countries. For the former it became associated with pretension and snobbery, giving rise to ideas of connoisseurship and "tasting"—concepts that would have been completely alien to most of the world's wine drinkers.

CULTURAL TASTES

National tastes vary, and there are even different cultural tastes within the same country. The volume of wine consumed also varies between countries; but these consumption patterns are subject to change. Since the mid-1980s, it has been clear that there is a process of "convergence," with respect to alcohol consumption, between different cultures. It has been found, for example, that beer drinkers have the occasional bottle of wine, confirmed wine-lovers take a beer now and then, both sometimes try spirits and spirit drinkers themselves may indulge in both wine and beer.

The chart detailing consumption trends in three different countries shows that, in a typical southern European wine-producing country such as Portugal, consumption has halved over about 35 years. In Germany, on the other hand, a country which makes and imports wine, there has been a steady growth in the amount drunk. From the small base in the United Kingdom, there has been rapid growth, particularly in the last ten years. Worldwide, in the long term, if markets in China and the United States grow, then overall consumption may increase. In the countries of Southeast Asia recently there has been a dramatic increase in the consumption of red wine.

Tastes in wine vary considerably. As a rule, Germans like their white wine light and slightly sweet. Italians enjoy their whites dry and rather neutral, to match but not dominate their food. Traditionally, the Portuguese and some eastern Europeans prefer their whites heavy and oxidized. Australians like very fruity wines, while the French opt for some restraint. All of this is good news for wine lovers, for it means there are many types of wine to explore and, for each style you dislike, there will be many others you will appreciate.

Winemakers are catering for different national tastes. An Australian producer of a large-consumption branded chardonnay can adjust the residual sugar levels in the drink so that it is comparatively sweet for the Japanese market, has some noticeable softness for the domestic or Scandinavian market, rather less for the United States and is fairly dry for the UK market.

WORLD WINE PRODUCTION AND CONSUMPTION [1]

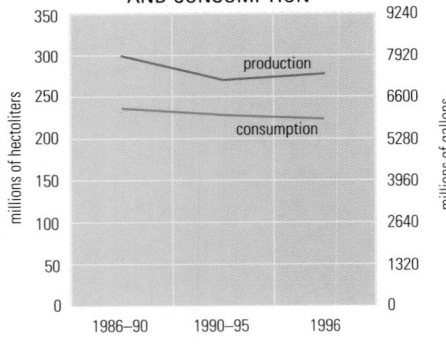

WINE CONSUMPTION TRENDS PER CAPITA IN THREE COUNTRIES [2]

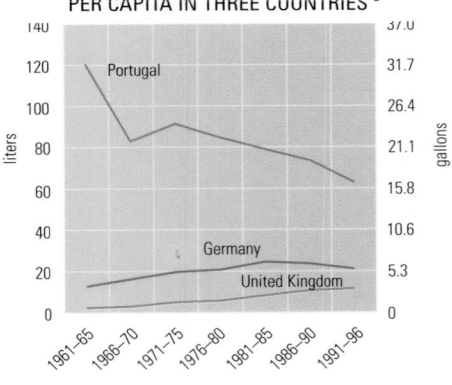

1 Figures from the Wine Institute, California, based on information from the Organisation for Wine and the Vine, Paris.
2 Based on Berger, Anderson and Stringer, "Trends in the World Wine Market," 1961–96, CIES, Adelaide, 1998.

The Wine Trade

The different origins of wine in diverse countries have given rise to different structures of production. Large companies dominate in the newer wine-producing countries, while small-scale producers are the norm in the more established regions. Essentially, the way wine industries organize themselves relates to the fact that grape growing—an agricultural activity—is often handled on a small scale, and wine production—a capital-intensive manufacturing activity—is often more effectively handled on a large scale.

PRODUCING WINE

The business of grape growing comes in all shapes and sizes. In much of southern Europe, grape growers often own small plots of vines which they farm along with other crops. In Burgundy, French inheritance laws mean that holdings have become smaller and smaller. Growers who make their living from grapes may own a few rows of vines in one vineyard, a few more in a second one, an acre somewhere else and so on. In Alsace in the early 1990s, the average holding of grape growers was less than 2.5 acres (1 ha) each. In vineyards in Monterey, California, on the other hand, 8,650 acres (3,500 ha) may be planted in one site.

What options are available to such small-scale, and even moderately sized, producers? In many parts of the world, they can sell to large wine production companies—this happens in much of northern Europe and the newer wine-producing countries. Another alternative, found in southern Europe particularly, is the local cooperative, owned by many local growers. It makes wine using all of their grapes, often at different quality levels. Traditionally, the wine from co-ops was often of poor quality. Now some cooperatives—such as "La Chablisienne" in Chablis—are actively pursuing quality and their wines can be both good and reasonably priced.

In some parts of the world a system of *négociants*, or brokers, evolved. They bought the grapes or wine of small producers, and then made larger scale blends under their own label. Often primarily merchants, *négociants* had

the resources to market the wines further afield than a small producer could. This system became particularly strong in Burgundy, where committed *négociants* could make some of the greatest wines, while those with less integrity got away with some of the most execrable. In time, these producers often bought land and grew grapes themselves.

The committed grape grower, who has enough land or who has little but high-quality terrain, can make wine either by making the capital investment to build their own winery, by using someone else's facilities or by paying a local winery to make the wine for them. The last two options save the expense of equipping a winery, but still allow a degree of control over how the grapes are used.

The non-European wine-producing countries are dominated by large producers. In New Zealand, two companies—Montana and Corbans—produce about 75 percent of all wine. In Australia, the top four companies—Southcorp, BRL Hardy, Orlando Wyndham and Simeon Wines—are responsible for about two-thirds of the grapes processed, and rather more of the wine sold. Meanwhile, the Gallo company in the United States makes more wine each year than the whole

Beautiful Rippon Vineyard, Otago. In New Zealand, two companies produce three-quarters of all wine.

Vineyards on slopes at Nuits-St-Georges, Burgundy. The vineyard could well be owned by a number of different grape-growers.

Above: *An Australian cellar-door tasting room with a few wines to taste, made by the producer.*

Top: *A Spanish food and wine store with a wide range for sale, from many different wine makers.*

of Australia produces. Countries with a well-established wine industry—including South Africa and Chile as well as European nations—have large companies (Louis Vuitton Moët Hennessey in France is an example), but none dominate the market in the same way.

Even the large companies rarely grow all their own grapes. From major champagne houses like Moët et Chandon to top Australian producers like Orlando Wyndham, the majority of grapes is bought in from external growers. This minimizes the company's need for investment to be tied up in land, and allows flexibility from year to year—especially important given the vagaries of climate and the changing preferences of the market.

DISTRIBUTING WINE

In most wine-producing countries, some wine is sold at the cellar door. Sometimes a producer may rely solely on cellar-door and mail-order sales, but that is rare. The cellar door has the advantage of allowing you to taste the wine before you buy, while enjoying the winery setting. Paradoxically, it may not always be much cheaper than in a shop, especially in popular tourist regions. It can, however, introduce you to little-known wine regions or to small producers of high-quality wine that is not easily available internationally. The disadvantage is the sense of guilt you can feel as you make your excuses and leave without buying a case.

A very large producer will probably establish its own distribution channels, but most producers rely on someone else to distribute, and sometimes market, their wine. A wholesaler can concentrate on obtaining exposure in the most appropriate stores and restaurants. This becomes particularly important for dealing with the language, law and culture of another country when exporting. US distribution is complicated by the fact that licensing is controlled by each of the 50 states.

The choice of wines you are able to buy will depend on whether or not you are in a wine-producing country. Sweden and Singapore, for instance, which don't produce wine, have a range of wines available from a number of countries. In France, however, you have to search very hard for a wine from Australia, though a token chianti or rioja might be available. In Australia, you might find chianti and bordeaux, but not much from Portugal or Spain. The advantage of buying in a wine-producing country is that the local wine should be comparatively cheap, though occasionally punitive tax regimes (as in Australia) are anomalies. The USA is the exception to the general rule, both producing wine and offering an excellent variety from overseas.

Most wine is still bought in shops, but the traditional, pompous wine merchant is becoming a creature of the past. In Europe, supermarkets have come to dominate sales over the last couple of decades. In 1997, in the United Kingdom, 60 percent of all sales were made in supermarkets, and 97 percent of sales there were under £5 (8 Euros; 85 percent are below US$8 in the USA). In France, sales are even more concentrated. The buying power of supermarkets means that they can keep prices down, often buying direct in bulk and bottling under their own labels. The downside of such mass selling is the restriction of choice. However, the supermarkets, particularly in France, may have regular "wine fairs" (*foires du vin*) which offer a wider range and particular bargains.

In other countries, wine retailing is also becoming more concentrated as the benefit of centralized buying power allows prices to be kept low. But retail chains in Australia and the United Kingdom are expanding at the expense of smaller outlets. Meanwhile, some countries have legislated for the introduction of this kind of concentration: Sweden and Canada, for example, both with a strong tradition of anti-alcohol campaigning, have long had state monopoly retail outlets.

For more choice and higher quality, seek out the smaller chains or independent retailers. Oddbins in the United Kingdom has long offered a wide range of excellent wines. A company called Nicholas, centered in France, sells very high-quality wines. Some independent merchants in all countries offer range and quality, and places like the *oenotecas* (local cafés/wine stores) in Italy may offer local wines at good prices.

One easy way to buy wine is via mail order from wine clubs. These may be stand-alone operations but are often linked to other organizations. The United Kingdom's largest wine retailer is now Bordeaux Direct, whose most well-known affiliate is the *Sunday Times* Wine Club. Wine clubs offer ease of access, and their size generally affords competitive prices but a comparatively restricted choice. They also tend to fill their "special offers" with wines that they have bottled directly under their own labels (on which the mark-up is substantial). Most offer a regular preselected dozen a few times a year—which can be a good way to taste new wines, but leaves you at the mercy of the club's selection panel.

The most venerable of the wine clubs are the wine societies, which are cooperative ventures requiring members to purchase a "share." There are wine societies in the United Kingdom and Australia, although they operate in slightly different ways. They may not be as cheap as their more recent rivals, but have a much wider selection, particularly of high-quality wines, and often cellar old stock that may become available to members. (These should not be confused with the American Wine Society, which is an organization dedicated to consumer education.)

Auctions were first used to sell wine in the mid-eighteenth century, and carried on until the Second World War. The trend re-emerged in the 1960s, when Christie's appointed Master of Wine Michael Broadbent to head its wine auction department. Sotheby's, now with renowned MW Serena Sutcliffe in charge, followed suit, and both companies have extended their operations to the North American market. Internationally, it dominates the fine wine market, but the emergence of Winebid.com online may also become important. Regionally, other auctioneers can be influential, such as Langton's in Australia, whose "class-ification of distinguished Australian wine" is the nearest the country has to a system of classed growths. Auctions tend to sell only the highest quality wine, and can offer bargains, as well as provide a snapshot of how wine prices are moving. At this point, however, wine can become an investment rather than just a drink.

The most recent development in the selling of wine has been on the Internet. A number of existing wine suppliers have developed web sites. Many producers are also offering their wines in this way, sometimes consolidating with their colleagues, as has happened with Australian Wine Online (www.winetitles.com.au). All countries where wine is sold now have at least one major online supplier who will deliver a wide range of wines to the door. These companies generally have a wider selection than the mail-order companies, plus easier access and often equally competitive prices. WinePlanet in Australia (www.wineplanet.com.au) and Chateau On Line in the United Kingdom (www.ChateauOnLine.co.uk) are examples. As more people become at ease with online buying, these companies may take over the bulk of non-supermarket retailing.

WINE EDUCATION

As the popularization of wine increases, the demand for education is spreading. A wide range of books is available, dealing with anything from the history of wine to details about a single producer, from the art of tasting to how wine is produced, often at quite a technical level.

Another good way of finding out more about wine is to subscribe to magazines. *Decanter* and *WINE* in the United Kingdom and the *Wine Spectator* in the United States are the most internationally renowned in the English-speaking world, but most countries have their own publications. There is *The Wine Magazine* in Australia, *Cuisine* in New Zealand and, for those who speak French, *Le Revue des Vins de France* is informative and wide-ranging. Most magazines offer articles about wine regions and other issues of interest, as well as tastings of current releases and quality older wines. However, it must be said that panel systems of tasting (like wine shows) do not always do justice to the higher quality but more subtle wines. Many newspapers also have regular columns about wine, although these vary in quality and are often not educative beyond telling you which are the

Below: *One of the most established wine auctions in the world, at Beaune, France.*

Bottom: *Wine education on the frontline. A class at the Golan Heights, Israel.*

Preparing for the festival of the new vintage, Alsace, France; a good way to promote the wines of an entire region.

A visitor gets a feel for traditional pressing at a Californian wine festival.

fruitiest chardonnays selling for less than $7 in the USA or £3.99 in the UK.

Wine infotainment has even spread to television, and some programs can be extremely informative. This version of wine education has a limited airtime, but videos allow the best of these series to remain accessible to the aficionado. Those by Jancis Robinson MW and Hugh Johnson are particularly recommended.

The Internet is another way to keep up with what is happening in the world of wine, although a general search against "wine" on the web will throw up over a million sites. While it is true that the Internet can provide a good general introduction to wine, it is of limited use to those seeking more detailed knowledge. Increasingly, owners of web sites are offering interactive options to subscribers. The *Wine Spectator* does this on a regular basis. The Australian company Penfolds has offered real-time tastings online, by advising participants in advance which wines to buy, then having an expert taste and give comments at a specified time on a chat line.

The main handicap to both magazines and the web is that, despite Penfolds' attempts, you won't benefit from the experience unless you buy the complete selection of the wines being discussed, which can be expensive, especially if you discover that you don't like some of them. One solution is to attend a wine course. These are often run by adult education providers, or by companies involved in the wine business (who may have a vested interest in the wines being displayed).

These courses may be offered by anyone from an interested amateur to a Master of Wine. While the style and content can vary greatly, they provide the chance to taste a number of wines and to compare more wines of a specific variety or region than most individuals' budgets normally allow. More complex, often technical, courses may be available to the public, sometimes at universities or technical colleges. The Wine and Spirit Education Trust runs industry training in the United Kingdom, and its courses are now offered to the public in many countries in the English-speaking world.

For those who enjoy that process, it is often possible to find a local wine club. These tend to be run voluntarily for willing accomplices and may involve presenters who are either immensely knowledgable or just sharing their ignorance. Critically, however, they also allow the chance to taste and compare a number of wines at one sitting—invaluable if one is to develop one's ability to distinguish and assess wines.

Most good wine stores will run occasional tastings, which could be just a couple of wines on the counter each Saturday, through to a tutored tasting run by a winemaker with a dinner attached. Sometimes more disinterested organizations, such as educational institutions or regional wine producers' federations, will arrange tastings that are open to the public. Often the most enjoyable way to learn more about your tastes in wine without spending too much is to get a group of like-minded friends together at home and split the cost of tasting a number of wines. This also avoids the sometimes starchy atmosphere of a more organized tasting, and you may feel more secure about venturing your own opinions about a wine.

One of the most exciting and interactive ways to learn more about wine is to go to a festival or show. This may feature local wines, or showcase those from a particular region or country. Often, the winemakers are present to answer questions. Classic examples of these are the Decanter Fine Wine Encounter in the United Kingdom, or the California Wine Experience in the United States. Vinopolis, a permanent wine show on the South Bank in London (which opened to mixed reviews in 1999) offers a guided tour of the whole world of wine with a chance to taste at the end. Other countries offer similar experiences, from the local Musée du Vin in regional France to the forthcoming National Wine Center in Adelaide, Australia—but these tend to be more parochial in their outlook.

Grapes and Viticulture

Terroir of Chablis, France; stones guarantee good drainage.

In producing wine, there's a perceived tension between what occurs "naturally" and what results from human intervention. Broadly, the debate is between the role of nature (environment and grape variety), and what the viticulturist and winemaker can do. In practice, this is a false dichotomy. For a commercial wine that is made on a large scale and sells for less than US$8, the essential element is the ability of the winemaker to maximize the character of the variety. For expensive, high-quality wines the varietal character should shine through, but the winemaker may also need enough restraint to reveal the environmental influences. In examining how wine is made, it becomes apparent that the relative importance of these factors will vary from wine to wine.

THE ENVIRONMENT FOR GROWING GRAPES

Vines need a temperate climate and generally flourish best between 30 and 50 degrees of latitude in the northern hemisphere and between 30 and 40 degrees in the southern hemisphere (because of its greater maritime influence). Altitude reduces the average temperature by 2°F (0.6°C) for each 330 feet (100 m), so vines tend to be planted at lower levels except in the warmest climates. Vines must also have access either to a reasonable rainfall, ideally concentrated in winter, or irrigation.

Before examining the various natural conditions that affect vines, it is useful to examine the concept of *terroir*. This French term, related to *terre*, the word for soil, is more correctly translated as "region." The term encompasses the entire natural environment of the vine—the climate, soil, site and topography of the vineyard where it grows. It is a useful concept for some wines, but it also provokes much meaningless debate. Diehard *terroiristes*, usually perceived to be extreme Europhiles, claim that wine must reflect the specific site on which the grapes are grown. Their opponents, crudely caricatured as technocrats, retort that all you need to grow wine grapes is a decent warm climate and a regular supply of water (from irrigation, if necessary).

Whatever the merits of either argument, the reality is that most winemakers don't limit their production to grapes from single regions. At the end of the 1990s, even in France—the bastion of *terroir*-based wines—50 percent of all wine sold was *vin de table*, which is not marketable under a region of

WORLD DISTRIBUTION OF VINEYARDS AND INFLUENCE OF CLIMATE

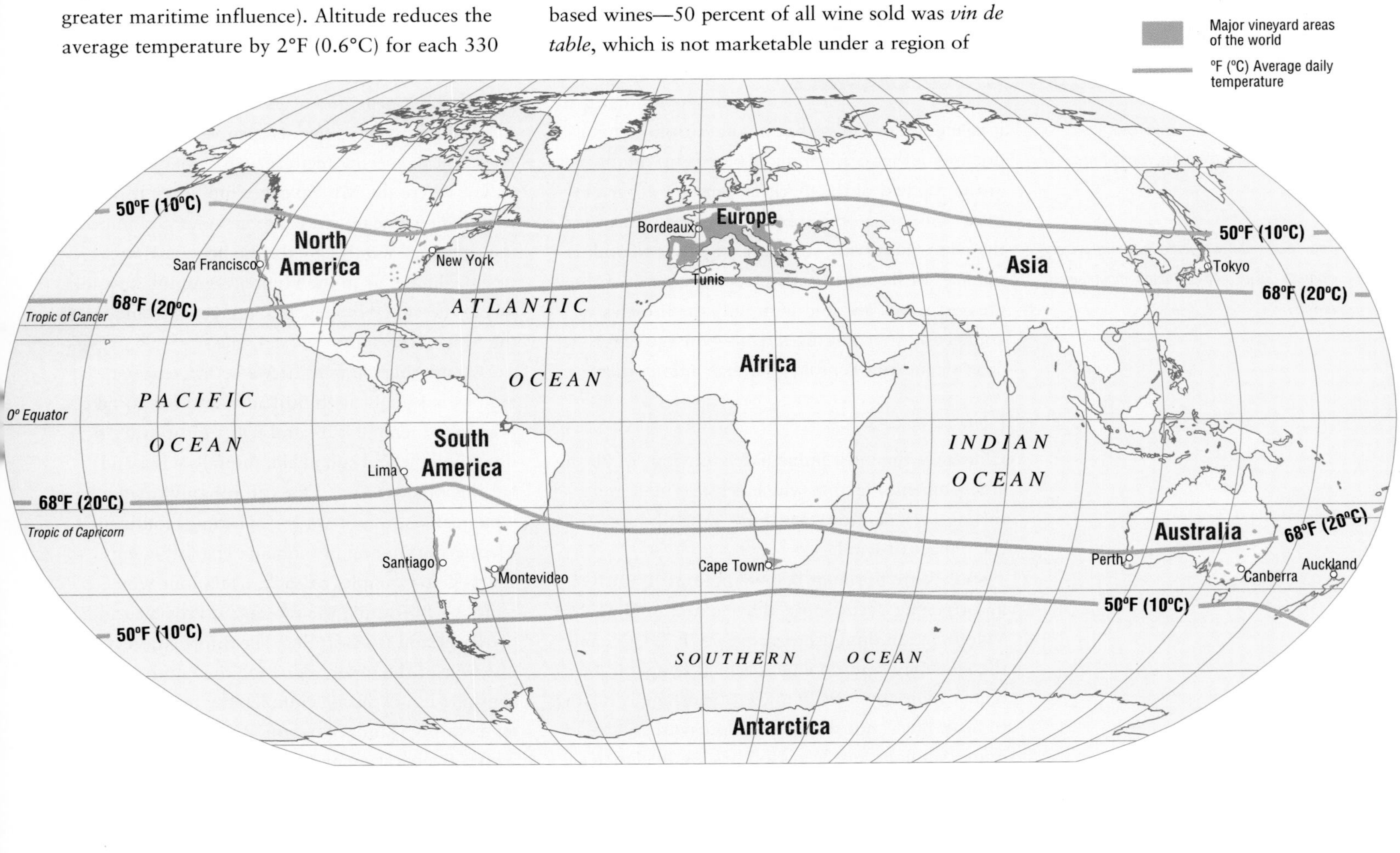

Major vineyard areas of the world

°F (°C) Average daily temperature

50°F (10°C)

68°F (20°C)

Tropic of Cancer

North America

San Francisco   New York

ATLANTIC

Bordeaux   Europe

Tunis

Asia

Tokyo

50°F (10°C)

68°F (20°C)

PACIFIC

OCEAN

0° Equator

OCEAN

Africa

INDIAN

OCEAN

South America

Lima

68°F (20°C)

Tropic of Capricorn

Santiago   Montevideo

Cape Town

Perth

Australia

68°F (20°C)

Canberra   Auckland

50°F (10°C)

50°F (10°C)

SOUTHERN   OCEAN

Antarctica

Above: *The vine in winter, Soave, Italy; snow is not a problem, but spring frosts can be.*

Top: *"God's Stairway," the Scala Dei winery, Priorato, Spain, in a protected, mountainous basin.*

origin. However, in California and the southern hemisphere, many wine producers continue to claim that the specific topographies and soils which characterize their own particular vineyards make their wines distinctive.

The average bottle of wine is sold for US$6 per bottle. At that price, it is enough to know that it comes from Languedoc or southeast Australia. There is no doubt that at the top end of the market—perhaps 1 percent of all wine sold—the specific site does influence the wine, modifying structure slightly and adding nuances of flavor. It is also true that some of the greatest wines are sold with only the broadest connection to a specific *terroir*—vintage port, champagne and Penfolds' Grange among them.

Climate

Climate is the most immediately obvious of all the environmental factors which affects vines, and includes temperature, sunshine, rainfall, frost and the impact of wind.

Vines are dormant below about 50°F (10°C), and ripening occurs only above about 63°F (17°C). Vine function diminishes above 75°F (24°C), and the vine may shut down entirely at temperatures higher than about 90°F (32°C). Sunshine is related to heat, but is not the same. Photosynthesis requires sunlight, not heat, so hot cloudy climates are not ideal for producing wine grapes. Sunny days well into fall are crucial, as harvest may take place late in September, or even into October (March or April in the southern hemisphere).

A vine needs about 20 inches (500 mm) of water per year in cool climates, rising to about 30 inches (750 mm) in the warmest regions, both for general functioning and to promote photosynthesis. In traditional regions where irrigation is banned, this may mean that it is difficult to obtain a good vintage in drought years (though most of the places that refuse to irrigate are temperate with a good rainfall). Where irrigation is practised, the level of rainfall becomes less important—as long as dam water levels or river flow are maintained.

Frost affects the quantity of wine more than the quality. Winter frosts are rarely a problem, but a frost late in spring can literally nip a crop in the bud by burning off the spring shoots. In 1991, the yields in Touraine in the Loire valley were about 10 percent of normal because a severe frost that struck on April 21–22 destroyed most shoots. The impact of frosts can be mitigated by good site selection, or by artificial means. The most basic of these is using hot braziers in the vineyards to raise the temperature, while one of the more technologically advanced ways is aspersion—spraying the shoots with water, which freezes and, paradoxically, insulates them against the worst of the cold.

Wind may cool the vines, or burn them when the wind is warm, and at its worst can rip leaves off. While it is not a general problem, it may be recurrent in specific regions such as the Rhône valley, where the Mistral can whip down towards the Mediterranean, stressing the vines and impeding ripening. Winds can also be beneficial in a warm climate, as in the Hunter region in Australia, where the valley funnels in sea breezes to moderate the heat of the sun.

Comparing climates between different wine regions is fraught with difficulty, and has to take account of temperature and temperature variability, sunlight and sun angle, rainfall, wind and various other factors. One can roughly categorize wine regions in four ways—maritime, continental, Mediterranean and hot inland. The following charts give examples of each, using four wine regions—Bordeaux, the Rheingau, Provence and the Riverland in Australia. The information covers just four of the many variables: the number of sunshine hours during summer, the mean July temperature (January for the Riverland), the mean winter temperature and the annual rainfall.

From this, it becomes apparent that Bordeaux and the Rheingau have broadly similar summer temperatures (the former is a bit hotter, and has marginally more sunshine), but the continental climate is markedly colder in winter. The Mediterranean and hot inland climates are both warmer in summer, and noticeably warmer in winter. The maritime climate, with its proximity to the ocean, is the wettest, but the Mediterranean is also quite wet (though it is in fact rather drier in summer, which is why it has the highest number of sunshine hours). The inland region has the least rainfall, and irrigation is essential here.

It is impossible to use climatic modeling to predict exactly what varieties will be used, and which wines will be made, but the wines of each of these nominated regions shows something about their climate:

Rheingau produces delicate, light but intensely flavorful white wines, based on riesling.

Bordeaux has a range of full whites, fine cabernet and merlot-based reds and dessert wines.

Provence boasts robust but flavorful reds, and some tasty rosés.

Riverland produces some good wines, but it concentrates on the production of bulk wine.

An important distinction must be made between the climate of a wine region and its weather. The climate is the average of all the weather factors over a long period. It allows one to predict what is likely to happen to a vineyard planted there and, therefore, is a key indicator of site selection. The weather is what happens in a particular year, and it will inevitably deviate from the climatic norms. Thus, 1987 in Bordeaux was wetter than normal, especially in autumn, so that cabernet sauvignon grapes did not ripen properly. On the other hand, 1990 in the same region was warmer and sunnier than usual, resulting in an early and large crop of high-quality grapes. That is how the impact of weather leads to vintage variation, though it is more of an issue in marginal climates. In warmer regions, there is likely to be less variation

CLIMATIC VARIABLES IN FOUR MAJOR WINE-GROWING REGIONS [3]

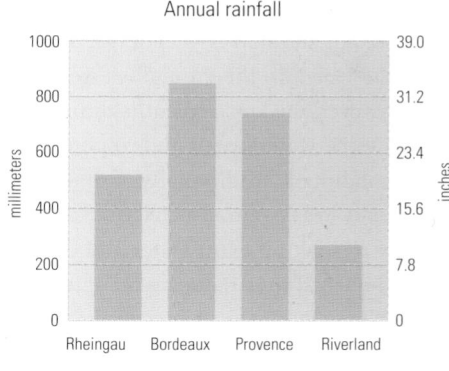
Annual rainfall

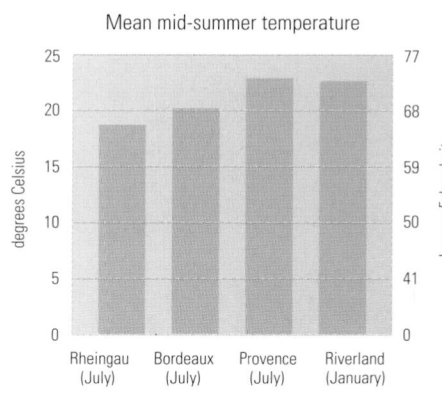
Mean mid-summer temperature

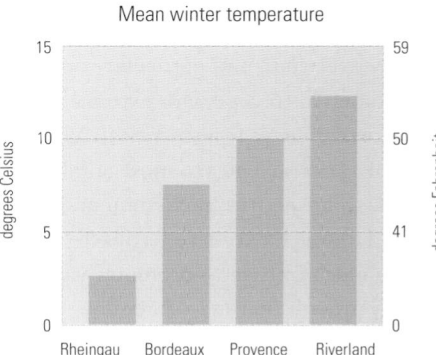
Mean winter temperature

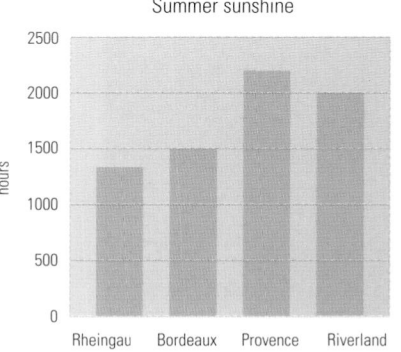
Summer sunshine

from one year to the next, with fewer poor crops and fewer pronounced high-quality vintages. Hail is an unpredictable weather condition that can devastate a vineyard—ripping leaves off and puncturing grapes in a matter of minutes, often on quite a localized basis.

3 Based on J. Gladstones, "Viticulture and Environment," Winetitles, Adelaide, 1992.

Clockwise from left: *German riverside vineyards; vines in maritime Bordeaux; flat vineyards in the hot south of California; bush vines in Mediterranean south France.*

Above: *Vineyards planted in sand in the Clarendon Hills, South Australia.*

Middle: *The world-famous "Terra Rossa" (red soil) of Coonawarra, Australia, provides excellent drainage.*

Top: *Soil profile showing different "horizons" in Costers del Segre, Spain.*

Soil

The most important benefit offered by soil is also the most overlooked, and that is anchorage. The ability to root the vine into the ground is essential. Beyond that, however, the key element is drainage. Vines don't like to be waterlogged and respond badly in those conditions. Additionally, if drainage is poor and there is heavy rain near harvest, the grapes are likely to soak up extra water and dilute their other components, thus reducing the quality of the resulting wine. Drainage can be modified.

Vines can tolerate quite a wide range of soil pH levels, from about 5.5 (acidic) to around 8.5 (alkaline), but it may be better to adjust the soil at either end of the spectrum, and particular rootstocks may be required to cope with extreme situations. Nutrient content is also critical. Vines need a supply of various elements, most notably nitrogen, but also phosphorus, potassium and various metals. However, excessive fertilizer—particularly too much nitrogen—promotes vigorous vine canopy growth that may shade the bunches of grapes and inhibit ripening. Likewise, too much potassium in the soil will reduce the acid level in juice—and consequently in the wine—making it less balanced and stable, and reducing its aging potential. This has been a major problem in the vineyards of Burgundy in the last few decades after intemperate use of fertilizer in the years following the Second World War.

Modern viticulturists monitor soil structure and composition, and moderate water supply and nutrient addition (which often come through the same pipe) accordingly. There is a view, however—though it is hard to adduce concrete evidence for it—that the best wine comes from the vineyards which are manipulated the least.

The ideal soil, therefore, has good drainage, with access to retained water at some depth if irrigation is not an option. It should have a balanced texture—neither too much clay, which will waterlog, nor too much sand, which drains well but does not retain nutrients. It has reasonable access to essential elements, but is not so fertile that it promotes luxuriant canopy growth. As well, it should not be overly limey or acidic. In many ways (except for the lime content), chalky soil is close to perfect, but the only substantial wine region where it predominates is Champagne.

One common myth needs to be nailed. There is no evidence that the soil in the vineyard conveys flavor to the wine. Mosel wines may be described as "slatey," or chablis as "flinty," but that is not because slate or flint in the soil imparts flavor. It is possible, though unproven, that chemical component of the soil may influence nuances of taste, but it is not true that soil conveys its flavor to the wine.

Site and topography

The site of a vineyard mediates between the predominant soil and the overall climate of the region. By dint of a particular aspect, the climate may have, say, a more south-facing aspect than is general, or the soil may be modified by erosion. The winding Mosel valley offers many sites; the best are those with a southerly aspect on a hillside. The flatter parts of the region make less fine, less intense wine.

Other factors can also be decisive. Isolated hills encourage airflow, thus reducing the chance of frosts in late spring. Rivers also reduce the likelihood of frosts because they tend to raise the prevailing temperature slightly through airflow. Altitude can also be decisive; a rise of 330 feet (100 m) reduces the average temperature by 2°F (0.6°C). Site can be modified by human intervention. Trees are often planted to act as wind-breaks. Eroded soil can be taken from the foot of a slope back up to the top.

THE RHEINGAU—A CLASSIC EXAMPLE OF THE IMPORTANCE OF SITE

Although it is quite a large region, the Rheingau in Germany is a good example of how site can modify the overall climate and situation of a wine region. In this case, it turns an area in what is a very marginal latitude into one of the country's prime wine regions. The site modifies the position in a number of ways:

- The river Rhine, which generally flows south–north through Germany, turns east–west at this point. This gives some riverside slopes a southerly aspect, maximizing sun exposure at the warmest part of the day.
- The Taunus Mountains to the north protect the vineyards from the cold winds that blow down from the Arctic.
- The river provides airflow, reducing air pockets, thus limiting the development of frosts.
- The river provides some reflected light onto the slopes, which is crucial to aid the final ripening in a cool northern fall.
- The river encourages mists in some years, which are necessary for the development of "noble rot" to make great botrytized sweet wines.

VINE AND VARIETY

The grape

The grape variety is of vital importance in shaping wine styles. At its most basic, it determines the color of the wine: you cannot get red wine from white grapes (although you can get white wine from red grapes). After that, choice of grape influences the levels of acidity, alcohol and (in red wines) tannin, as well as the body and style of the wine. The variety also determines how the winemaker will approach the wine. Few winemakers would age riesling in oak or put it through malolactic fermentation. Conversely, no winemaker is going to prevent the malolactic fermentation in cabernet sauvignon, and most will give it some oak treatment.

The typical wine grape is quite small. Even with white wines, some flavor comes from the skin, and a low juice-to-skin ratio enhances those characters. In black grapes (also known as red grapes), the skin gives the wine its tannin and color. Thicker skins and/or smaller grapes mean deeper color and more tannic wine.

The variety, of course, also gives the wine its core flavors. Each variety may have a range of typical aromas and tastes—its "flavor spectrum." No wine will display all of these flavors, but a reasonably good wine should show at least one or two flavors to give good varietal character, and a complex wine will display more.

The flavor spectrum for shiraz, for instance, includes herbs, mint, spice, pepper, raspberry, cherry, mulberry, blackberry, plum, cassis, black olives, aniseed, liquorice, prune, stewed plum, chocolate, jammy and raisin.[5] The primary fruit in shiraz develops, roughly, in that order, moving generally from fruit grown in a cool climate (or which may be underripe) to fruit from warm areas (which may be too ripe).

Though there may be some overlap between varieties, the flavor spectrum differs from variety to variety. Thus, shiraz may show a white pepper character, but cabernet sauvignon should not. Both types of wine, however, may display plummy or curranty flavors.

The condition of the fruit is also important. In cool regions, underripe fruit will give harsh green characters to the wine and, if it is damp, disease could dull or spoil the wine. In hot climates, the grapes may become overripe, giving hot alcohol and jammy flavors that lack balance and complexity.

While the variety shapes the style of wine, the climate modifies how each variety develops. Riesling grows well in a very cool climate because it can become flavor-ripe while it is barely physiologically ripe. Thus, intense rieslings are made in northern Germany with a potential alcohol content of about 9 percent—relatively speaking, a small amount on a world scale—and showing a comparatively low level of sugar content at ripeness. But the same variety also flourishes in the Clare valley—a warm, if not baking hot, region of South Australia—where it makes fuller but still intense styles of wines.

THE TYPICAL COMPOSITION OF A GRAPE[4]

Water	75.00%
Sugars	22.00%
Acids	
-Tartaric	0.6%
-Malic	0.5%
Total	1.10%
Nitrogenous matter	0.80%
Phenolics	0.05%
Minerals	0.50%
Other matter	0.55%

Note that this is for a grape of average ripeness, and will vary according to variety and location.

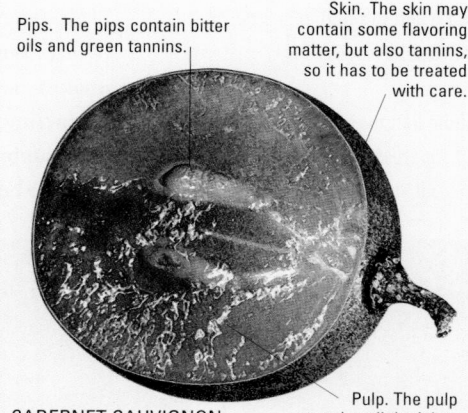

Pips. The pips contain bitter oils and green tannins.

Skin. The skin may contain some flavoring matter, but also tannins, so it has to be treated with care.

Pulp. The pulp contains all the juice.

CABERNET SAUVIGNON

4 Based on P. Iland and P. Gago, "Australian Wine—From the Vine to the Glass," Patrick Iland Promotions, Adelaide, 1997.
5 Based on Coombes and Dry, "Viticulture in Australia," Vol. 2, Winetitles, Adelaide, 1992.

Human modification to vineyard sites.
Below left: *Precipitous terraced slopes of the Mosel Valley, Germany;* **Below:** *Trees form windbreaks for angled vineyards in Yarra Valley, Australia.*

Red grape varieties

Barbera Widely planted in Italy and California but only makes characterful wines in Piedmont.

Cabernet franc Overlooked sibling of the next red variety, but contributes a lot to Bordeaux wines, and makes interesting, underrated wines in the Loire valley.

Cabernet sauvignon The most ubiquitous red variety in the world. Bordeaux is its heartland, but upstarts in California, Tuscany and Australia are staking a claim.

Gamay Makes fruity (and occasionally age-worthy) wines in Beaujolais, whose wines are much misunderstood.

Grenache The most planted red variety in the world, but concentrated in France and Spain. Only makes great wine in Châteauneuf-du-Pape, but is attracting some interest in Australia.

Lambrusco This can be better than you might expect, but you have to search out the best examples. Otherwise, it's a frothy, sweet, insubstantial wine for cola drinkers.

Malbec A minor player in southwest France (including Bordeaux), but malbec is the major player in Argentina.

Merlot The "other" great red variety of Bordeaux, but responsible for its priciest wines. Now relocating to California, but yet to be granted residency elsewhere in the world.

Mourvèdre Little-known grape from southern France and Spain that gives tannic backbone to blends. Attracting attention in Australia and California.

Nebbiolo High acid, high tannin variety which makes complex long-lived wines in Piedmont, but hasn't repeated the feat elsewhere in the world.

Petit verdot A minor but high-quality component in the bordeaux mix; also being investigated in emerging wine regions.

Pinotage South Africa's very own variety, a crossing of the productive cinsault and exacting pinot noir. Can make some good wines, but often results in jammy or tart nonentities.

Pinot meunier Least well known but most widely planted grape in Champagne. Traditionally treated as second rate, but Krug at least is proud of pinot meunier's role in its wine.

Pinot noir The classic red grape of Burgundy, but one of the fussiest varieties to manage. It has captivated obsessives across the world, but only New Zealand and parts of the USA seem to be making headway with it.

Sangiovese Widely planted in Italy, and capable of making great savory wines in Tuscany. Attracting cautious interest elsewhere.

Syrah/shiraz Makes stunning wines in the northern Rhône and Australia. An increasingly popular variety, sometimes to blend, in other parts of the world.

Tannat Hard tannic variety in southwest France that, with age, turns in some complex, interesting wines.

Tempranillo The great grape of Rioja, also producing good wines in other parts of Spain and northern Portugal.

Touriga naçional Portugal's great indigenous variety. A key component of port, but also used for increasingly good table wines.

Zinfandel California's own variety (though it also appears as the primitivo in southern Italy). Makes juicy, brambly, powerfully alcoholic wines.

Below (left to right): Cabernet franc—almost ripe. Cabernet sauvignon.

Middle (left to right): Grenache. Malbec. Petit verdot. Pinot noir.

Bottom (left to right): Hand picked syrah, awaiting crushing. Tannat. Tempranillo. Zinfandel.

White grape varieties

Chardonnay The most desired grape variety in the world, originating in Burgundy but now widespread. Makes full-bodied, potentially complex wines.

Chenin blanc Makes great wine in the Loire valley and much ordinary (but occasionally good) wine in South Africa.

Colombard A good workhorse variety in the south of France; it is also widely planted for making neutral wines in South Africa, California and Australia.

Furmint Described as "fiery," this grape is the great variety of Hungarian tokay and has potential for table wine.

Garganega Neutral variety, but can make wines of great texture and character in Soave.

Gewürztraminer A most distinctive variety, with lychee and rose-petal characters. At its best in Alsace. Planted widely but not densely elsewhere.

Malvasia Heavy but interesting variety, little known but widely planted in southern Europe.

Marsanne Mainstay of white wines in the northern Rhône valley, and surprisingly concentrated in central Victoria, Australia.

Melon de bourgogne The variety of muscadet. Neutral and light.

Müller-thurgau Widely planted, early ripening, but mediocre "flowery" variety. Planted mainly in Germany but with an outpost in New Zealand.

Muscadelle Generally a minor supporting variety, but the grape behind the great fortified tokays of Australia.

Muscat A wide family of grapes, but at its best (*muscat blanc à petits grains*) responsible for dry aromatic wines in Alsace, good sparkling wine in Asti and great fortified wines in southern France and Australia.

Palomino Boring variety, but it does make exciting sherry.

Pinot blanc Restrained variety, at its best in Alsace and Italy. The subject of interesting experiments in the United States.

Pinot gris Makes full-bodied, slightly aromatic wines. Best in Alsace, but also used in Italy and central Europe, and attracting attention elsewhere.

Riesling The world's greatest white variety, making stunning, focused wines (from dry to very sweet) in Germany, Alsace, Austria and Australia. Misunderstood and mistreated elsewhere.

Sauvignon blanc A classic in the central Loire and New Zealand. Other regions are still trying.

Sémillon Makes great wines in Bordeaux (especially botrytized dessert wines) and the Hunter valley. Ignored elsewhere.

Trebbiano The world's most widely planted and boring white grape variety. Ideal for cognac.

Viognier Makes full-bodied and aromatic white centered on the northern Rhône, but now attracting attention elsewhere in the world, especially in California.

Above (left to right): *Pink muscat grapes. Pinot gris. Riesling. Sémillon waiting to be processed. Viognier.*

Top (left to right): *Chardonnay. Furmint in Tokaji—yet to ripen fully. Dark tinted gewürztraminer. Hand-picking malvasia. Muscadelle.*

Lunch among the vines of Champagne, where chardonnay is a vital component of sparkling wine.

Chardonnay around the world

A good example of how one type of grape can make different styles of wine when grown in different surroundings is given by the most versatile of varieties, chardonnay, which is grown in a wide range of environments.

Adelaide Hills Good natural acidity combined with ripe fruit make a typical, comparatively ripe Australian wine with good aging potential.

Carneros The mists of the San Francisco Bay moderate what would otherwise be a hot climate, making for well-structured wines that still show some generosity of fruit.

Chablis The steely table wines of this cool region have a firm acidity that allows them to develop into some of the longest living whites available.

Champagne In this cool region of France, the grape makes acidic and delicate base wine for the greatest sparkling wines of the world.

Hunter valley One of the warmest regions of Australia produces big chardonnays with a typical "peaches and cream" character.

Languedoc In the south of France, the chardonnay grape produces melon and butter characters that reflect Burgundy without its great structural balance and intensity.

Marlborough In this dry region of New Zealand, chardonnay produces wines that may echo some of the Australian fruit styles, but with an extra vein of acidity.

Meursault In the Côte d'Or, the heartland of Burgundy, the grape produces buttery, nutty wines with a streak of acidity.

Napa valley Just 20 miles (32 km) north of Carneros, chardonnay becomes full, ripe and generous, but without the tautness of the wines from further south.

The vine

The grapevine *Vitis vinifera*, originally native to east Asia, is now the most commonly cultivated species across the world. Within the *vinifera* species are thousands of varieties, possibly as many as 10,000, although few of them are used to make wine. Only 200 are recorded as being significant in France.

The varieties commonly used for winemaking have developed over the centuries. Sometimes they have appeared naturally, sometimes encouraged by grape growers. The pinot family, for instance, is prone to mutation. Pinot meunier and pinot gris came from pinot noir, pinot blanc from pinot gris.

For the last century or so, it has been possible to create specific new varieties by taking the pollen from one and fertilizing the flower of another variety, and planting out the resulting seeds. The two most famous of these crossings are probably müller-thurgau, now the most widely planted grape in Germany, and pinotage in South Africa. Both will occasionally make good wine, but they are generally used as workhorse varieties. The problem with new varieties is that the viticulturists who produce them are searching for higher yields or early ripening rather than enhanced flavor, structure or quality in the resulting wine.

It is now also possible to produce hybrids—vines that have as their parents both a *Vitis vinifera* vine and another species, invariably one from North America. This is done to create vines with resistance to specific pests, diseases or weather conditions. Traditionally, hybrids are perceived to make poor wine and are prohibited for the production of "quality" wine in Europe. In practice, some of these grapes—seyval blanc in the United Kingdom is an example—can make fair, if not great, wine.

Most viticultural attention these days is focused not on new varieties, but on the genetic manipulation of existing varieties. It should be possible to exclude from chardonnay the genes that make it prone to rots and other fungal diseases, thus reducing the costs of growing the grapes and guaranteeing more regular quality. Inevitably, this raises the spectre of labeling problems, with consumers seeking information about genetically manipulated wine. Less acknowledged is the likelihood that, as with most other viticultural developments, modifications will be developed to aid the grape grower—primarily by encouraging larger yields—rather than the consumer, who would rather see the development of more intense, complex and harmonious wines.

The most important part of the vine's cycle is the process of ripening, which is what creates the final wine—and it is particularly important in the period following *véraison* (the key stage at which the grape skins begin to turn black, or to become translucent if they are white grapes). After *véraison*, when the vine normally has sufficient reserves of sugar, the surplus is sent into the grapes. This is eventually converted to alcohol, making grape juice into wine.

A YEAR IN THE LIFE OF A VINE

Left: *The pruned vine is dormant in winter, allowing it to preserve its strength for the next season.*

Below: *Budburst: the first obvious sign of life, and a dangerous time where late spring frosts occur.*

Left: *Spring growth: the vine is focusing its energies on the development of shoots and foliage.*

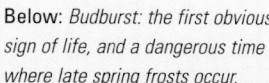

Left: *The apparently insignificant vine flowers.*

Above: *The "set": the flower heads form into nascent grapes. Poor weather can lead to the failure of bunches to form, or irregularly developing bunches.*

Above: *Grapes ripening on the vine following* veraison—*the point at which their color changes. Now the sugar levels in the bunches increase, and acidity becomes proportionately less important.*

Right: *A vineyard in late fall, following harvest, and just prior to leaf-fall.*

Above: *Planting a grafted vine in a stony Spanish vineyard.*

Top: *Newly planted vines, protected from damage in plastic tubes, with posts ready for trellis wires. It will take another two years before these vines bear usable fruit.*

Ripening, however, is crucial for more than just sugar accumulation. The acidity is very high in developing grapes, but the relative acid levels drop with the ripening process, allowing a balanced wine to develop. In cool grape-growing regions, poor weather during summer can limit ripening. If this happens, the resulting wines will be unbalanced or will have to be treated to reduce the acidity. Conversely, in hot regions, the acidity may drop too much and have to be replaced.

Ripening also allows the various flavor components of the grape to develop. At the same time, the phenolic compounds that give red wines their color and tannin also increase, with the tannins developing from green and coarse to ripe and smooth. Red wine made from insufficiently ripened grapes will be found to have a harsh, bitter, tannic structure.

IN THE VINEYARD

Site selection

Before a vine is even planted, the choice of site for the vineyard is crucial. In addition to the factors detailed previously (under site and topography), such as avoiding frosts and guaranteeing good drainage—there are economic factors to consider. Can a vineyard be harvested mechanically? Is there ready access to a market; or, if a cellar door is planned, will there be substantial passing trade? What does the land cost? In Champagne, for example, you will pay much more per acre than you would in Languedoc.

These factors have little importance in the classic regions of Europe. Here, vineyards have been planted for centuries—even millennia—and inherited land is the rule. But elsewhere in the world, including the distant reaches of the south of France or Spain and parts of eastern Europe, site selection for enterprising new grape growers is very relevant.

Many tests can be done before planting—for instance, to assess drainage, pH and nutrient content. When the tests are completed the land can be prepared—this might be deep ploughing to break up the soil, digging in lime or having the land treated for nematodes or other pests.

Rootstocks

In Europe and California, and often in other parts of the world, grapevines will invariably be grafted on to other rootstocks before planting. The technique of grafting has been known to horticulturists for centuries, and essentially is the insertion of the shoot of one species into the branch of another. This can be done to allow, for instance, two or three varieties of apple to grow out of one tree trunk. In viticulture, it allows shoots from *Vinifera* vines to be grafted onto the roots of another vine species, often in order to gain resistance to pests, disease or other conditions.

The main reason for grafting in viticulture is to avoid phylloxera (see below), but rootstocks can also benefit vines planted in soils with a high lime content by minimizing the effect of lime in inhibiting the uptake of some essential elements. Other rootstocks can help the vine to cope with summer aridity or high salinity.

Planting

The orientation within which vines will be planted is done with two—sometimes contradictory—aims. The first is to optimize the angle to sun; to be at 90° to the midday sun is generally considered to be ideal. However, it is also better to plant along a slope rather than down it, as rows of vines down a slope will facilitate erosion.

In Europe, vines are traditionally close-spaced, sometimes as many as 20,000 per acre (10,000 per ha). The theory is that this increases the pressure on the vines, limiting yields, and thus guaranteeing quality. In practice, much less dense planting is used in many regions, especially where machines are used for harvesting and other forms of vineyard management. It is also the case that, while dense planting is preferable in the poor vineyard soils of Europe, wider spacing will, in fact, induce the vine to give its best in high-potential soils.

Pruning and training

Pruning allows the viticulturist to determine how productive the vine is to be for the next season, offering the opportunity for a greater or lesser yield. It is also the precursor to training the vine, creating the "architecture" of the canopy to allow for various forms of management.

Training determines how the vine is to be shaped. It may be along a wire, with just one cane or cordon or a number of them, or it may be in bush form, which is excellent for conserving the vine's resources in arid regions, but not a good shape for a vineyard that is mechanized. Canopy management techniques are designed to open grapes up to sunlight, or to encourage airflow to inhibit diseases that stem from humidity.

Irrigation

As with the subject of *terroir*, irrigation is now very much a non-issue, despite the traditional resistance to it in Europe. Opponents of irrigation would argue the dangers of increasing yield excessively by using extra water, but supporters are aware that it needs to be controlled carefully according to the style of wine being made. It is also worth remembering that the regions in which irrigation is banned tend to be those with a temperate climate and regular, year-round rainfall. Much high-quality Australian and Chilean wine

would not exist substantially without irrigation. Interestingly, Spain has now relaxed its ban on irrigation, and the practice appears in other parts of the European Union.

The oldest method of irrigation, known since ancient times, was flood irrigation, which was later developed into irrigation by furrow, channelling water along rows by the vines. This system needs flattish land to work effectively, and vineyards are more often planted on slopes. Spray irrigation was developed over the last 40 years (often with mobile sprinklers), and then drip irrigation, with a pipe along each row of vines

Vines planted along the contours, to reduce erosion, high above a Basque village.

Pruning high-trained vines in the Vinho Verde region of northern Portugal. The high-training allows air-flow, reducing disease, but also makes it harder to ripen the vines.

Above: *Furrows offer a more basic form of irrigation in Chile, which is imprecise in its application.*

Top: *Overhead sprinklers irrigating vineyards in the Adelaide Hills, Australia.*

dropping water into the soil, was introduced. The advantages of this system are precision, simplicity and the ability to apply other products such as liquid fertilizer along with the water. It is very responsive, and can be used to a greater or lesser extent according to need.

Many grape growers—especially those committed to quality—would argue that they only resort to irrigation in the driest seasons, except in the first three years of the vine's life, when it is essential to establish the young plant. However, it remains a useful tool in the viticultural armory.

Soil management

Historically, the land between vine rows has been kept free of vegetation. This was useful in dry climates where grass and weeds would otherwise compete with the vines for limited water supplies. However, it has been found that a mid-row crop inhibits soil erosion and makes it easier to get mechanical access without churning up the soil. Careful choice of the crop (grass, clover or rye) allows cutting or digging-in the greenery to create a nutritious mulch. This is more natural than inorganic fertilizers, which are still widely used. Soil compacts with time, so it may be necessary to plough or even deep-rip it to facilitate airflow and drainage. Unfortunately, loosening the soil can also promote erosion.

Diseases and disorders

Much of the viticulturist's time is spent ensuring the good health of the vine. Four types of disease, as well as some disorders, can affect grape vines. The largest group, fungal disease, is caused by microscopic filament-shaped organisms. They include rots, oidium and peronospera.

Rots (especially grey rot) attack the whole vine and spread rapidly. Rot starts from dead material (often dead flowers from late spring) and needs humidity to develop. It reduces yields and can impair the color and flavor of wine. It spreads particularly fast when berries are split, which may result from bird activity or rapid berry growth after high autumn rainfall. It is controlled by sprays and pre-empted by good canopy management. Oidium is a powdery mildew that splits berries and inhibits bunch growth. Uniquely for fungal diseases, it does not need humidity, just warmth and shade. It is now easily inhibited by dusting with sulfur if caught early. Peronospera is a downy mildew that requires warm, humid conditions. A cottony growth appears on the underside of leaves and inhibits plant growth. It is easily controlled with copper-based sprays.

Bacterial diseases are few in number. The most virulent is Pierce's Disease, which kills vines and is incurable, and is a particular problem in the USA. Leaves develop dead spots, which enlarge, causing leaf fall. It is spread by small insects called leafhoppers and occurs especially in vineyards near streams (the bacteria grow in water).

Viral diseases, including fanleaf virus and leafroll virus, are of recent origin (from about 1890) when rootstocks began to be used. They tend to be spread by cuttings from infected plants, although insects like nematodes may pass them on. They do not necessarily kill, but may weaken vines and reduce yields. The only effective treatment is to heat-treat vine stock to create virus-free material. Fanleaf virus, which may be spread by nematodes, causes malformed growth in the form of fan-like deformed leaves that cause poor set and small bunches. Cabernet sauvignon vines are particularly sensitive to this disease. It is a major problem in the Napa valley and Burgundy. So far, the only cure that has been discovered is to uproot the whole vineyard, fumigate and replant it with virus-free stock. With the onset of leafroll virus, often spread by mealy bugs, leaves roll downwards and discolor. It is now widespread, especially in humid regions. Although it rarely kills vines, it reduces yields and delays ripening.

Vine disorders, including chlorosis, *coulure* and *millerandage*, also occur. These are not diseases, but environmental problems that can afflict vines. Chlorosis is common in chalky soils which inhibit iron uptake from the soil and limit the development of chlorophyll, causing yellowing leaves and poor photosynthesis. *Coulure* and *millerandage* refer to poor berry formation resulting from inadequate fertilization of flowers or poor fruit set. It results from poor carbohydrate supply due to inadequate photosynthesis at flowering, usually because of poor weather.

Vine pests

Vines are vulnerable to many animal and insect pests. Birds pick holes in fruit, rabbits and deer nibble shoots, and insects defoliate or attack berries and roots. Critically, pests can also act as vectors, or carriers, of a disease. Different pests are active in different countries and regions, but the one with a worldwide impact on the wine industry is phylloxera.

This small louse, native to North America, lives on the roots of American vine species. Here, vines have become tolerant to the insect and, as it feeds off the roots, they callous over with no lasting damage. However, in other parts of the world vines have no natural protection against this pest and it has caused great destruction.

Phylloxera spread to France in the early 1860s, probably from an imported vine from North America, starting in a vineyard in Marseilles. In searching for food, the American parasite had discovered *Vinifera* vines and started feeding from their roots. Its life-cycle—a single female can lay up to 20 million eggs in a season—was enough to ensure a rapid progress throughout the entire country (it had reached all parts within 30 years) and then on through Europe.

The French puzzled for years about how to deal with it. They discovered that phylloxera would not tolerate sandy soil, but in practical terms this knowledge was of little use. It could be dealt with by flooding a vineyard for 100 days, but again, that was rarely possible or practical. Certain chemicals injected into the soil would kill it—carbon disulfide was found to be the best— but they were expensive, dangerous and had only temporary impact. The solution was to graft scions of *Vitis vinifera* varieties onto rootstocks from native American vines. That way, growers were able to keep their syrah or chardonnay grapes but could now protect them from devastation.

In the interim, however, hundreds of thousands of acres of vine had been lost, never to be replanted, and the viticultural map of Europe changed. Old, often high-quality varieties, like carmenere in Bordeaux, disappeared because they could be replanted with more productive vines. Rigorous vineyard management also became the order of the

day. Phylloxera still exerts an influence in some regions of the world. It is active in New Zealand and in Victoria in Australia, though other parts of Australia are effectively quarantined. Paradoxically, it has also just run through the vineyards of California, causing complete replanting there.

Age of vines

As each viticulturist has decisions to make about the start of a vineyard's life, so he or she must determine when it should come to an end. Vines reach maximum productivity at about seven years. Productivity declines after 20 to 30 years. Regular replanting is necessary to maintain the yields for those making a mass-produced wine from high yields. On the other hand, a producer seeking high quality may welcome the lower yields of older vines, which offer more concentrated flavor and more depth in the resulting wine. In that case, they are more likely to just replace vines as they die rather than replant an entire vineyard, thus maintaining a high average age for the vineyard as a whole.

In some cases, the use of old vines (*veilles vignes*) is treated as a useful marketing tool. Chateau Tahbilk in Australia makes great play of their shiraz vineyard, planted in the 1860s and used to make a single special wine. With one grape variety, at least, old vines become essential. Carignan, in the south of France, makes undistinguished high-volume wine; however, occasionally, when the vines are allowed to age to 60 or 80 years and the yields drop, it can provide wine of interest and complexity.

Grapes growing at Chateau Tahbilk in Australia, where one vineyard dates back to the mid-nineteenth century.

Below: *Noble rot is a fungus that does not harm the grapes, but produces a complex and sweet wine.*

Bottom: *Cleaning buckets to prevent the spread of disease, Maximin Grünhäuser Estate, Saar, Germany.*

Winemaking

Mechanical harvesters straddle the vines, and rapidly vibrating beaters shake the plant's trunk, dislodging the grapes.

HARVEST AND CRUSHING

The first stage in the process of making wine is to harvest the grapes. This can be done either by machine or by hand. Neither of these methods is technically "better" than the other; it just depends on where you are and what kind of wine you choose to make.

Mechanical harvesting is usually fine on flat or undulating vineyard sites. It is quick (one person can do in four hours what may take six to ten days to complete if done by hand), and therefore cheaper. It allows you to harvest at night, which is useful in warm climates to minimize oxidation. It generally preserves the fruit quality almost as well as hand-picked fruit. Hand-picking does, however, allow more selectivity and can ensure that you pick whole bunches without any of the juice starting to run, which is all but inevitable with the vigorous harvesters.

The decision whether or not to pick by machine generally boils down to factors other than that of quality. Traditionally, grapes have been hand-picked in California because the availability of cheap Mexican labor has made the cost of investing in a mechanical harvester pointless. In the flat land of the Muscadet region, producing wines that generally sell in the £3.50–6.00 (US$5.50–9.50) bracket, most picking is by machine. Usually, vineyards in Australia are picked by machine, but a quality producer may hand-pick for that extra selectivity. In the steep parts of the Mosel valley, it is impossible to get machines on the slopes. In Champagne, where whole, unbroken bunches are essential for the sparkling wine, hand-picking is the order of the day.

The various types of mechanical harvesters all work by straddling the vines, while a number of vibrating beaters strike the vine trunks vigorously to dislodge the grapes. Generally, the bunch stalks remain on the plant. The grapes fall into trays under the beaters, and are then carried up into hoppers at the top of each side of the harvester. Every few rows, the hoppers are emptied into a trailer, which carries the grapes back to the winery.

PRESSES

Presses come in different forms. The most traditional type is the basket press, which is still used in Champagne, and by anyone who wants a fast but gentle press. A more recent development is the vaslin press, comprising a cylinder with plates at each end that are pulled together by metal chains, thus compressing the grapes. The movement of the heavy chains as the press compacts and opens breaks up the cake of skins, making repressing easier.

Today the most common style of press is probably the air-bag (bladder) press. A thick rubber membrane lies in a cylinder that is filled with grapes. The membrane is then blown up, compacting the grapes and extracting the juice. The advantage of this is that it is gentle—avoiding the extraction of bitter phenolics from the pips and stems—but it is also efficient. These days, the process is computerized, and the winemaker can preset the machine for a number of pressings at different pressures.

Below left: *A traditional "basket" press in Spain, with the marc (pressed grape skins and residue) spilling out after a pressing.*

Below: *Mats used to contain the grapes in a basket press, drying after use.*

Most vineyards are close to the wineries that serve them, but transporting the grapes becomes an issue when they are some distance away. Adding sulfur dioxide to inhibit the oxidation process, then blanketing them under an inert gas in a closed container allows them to be shipped over long distances without too much damage, although there could still be a quality problem with broken or rotten grapes. Often, large producers will have white grapes pressed and then transported to a winery as juice. In Champagne, where grapes need to be dealt with quickly to guarantee a good base wine, they are often pressed at press-houses in the middle of vineyards. At the winery, the grapes may be sorted (a process called *triage* in French) to eliminate rotten or unripe bunches. The appellation regulations in Chateauneuf-du-Pâpe make it compulsory to exclude 10 percent of the grapes to enhance quality.

The first stage at the winery is to destem and crush the grapes. Crushing does not press juice out of the grapes; it is merely designed to split open the skins to encourage some juice to run out naturally. Destemming is almost always carried out because the bunch stems carry tannins that may be quite green and could leach out into the juice and taint the wine. However, some of the stems are left in with some red wines. With wines that require whole-bunch pressing—as with sparkling wines, or some white wines where the winemaker wants to emphasize delicate fruit—the stems obviously remain, but a fast, gentle pressing precludes any phenolic uptake from them.

WHITE WINE FERMENTATION

White grapes are pumped from the crusher to the press, initially without any pressure. The grapes merely sit (or get turned if it is a rotary press) to encourage juice to flow out naturally. This is the "free-run juice" that provides the freshest, most delicate wine. After it has been allowed to run out, pressure is applied, and a number of pressings will probably be carried out. The pressed juice is fermented separately from the free-run juice to ensure that, if it is too harsh, it does not spoil the more elegant wine made from the free-run juice.

Often the grapes in a particular region will not have the necessary balance to give a wine the right structure. The juice, or must, can be modified to ensure that the resulting wine is well structured. This includes:

Enrichment This increases the sugar content of the must, which increases the final alcohol content of the wine. Generally, it is done by adding sugar to the ferment (chaptalization), but sometimes it is done by adding concentrated grape juice. Chaptalization is common in Europe—especially the cool north—and allowed in New Zealand, but banned in Australia. Enrichment doesn't sweeten the wine, it only increases its alcohol level.

Acidification In warm climates, the acid level of the grapes may drop to too low a level before the grapes have attained flavor ripeness. Therefore, acid can be added to the must, which both maintains its freshness and protects it from bacterial spoilage. Acidification is frequently practised in warm wine-producing areas such as Australia, but is rare in northern Europe.

Deacidification In cool areas, the process of ripening may not reduce acid levels sufficiently, and the resulting wine would be too searing. In that event acid can be removed from the must.

Above: *Getting hand-picked bunches into the crusher before pressing.*

Below: *Grapes need to be taken to the winery fast once picked: the Swiss way.*

WHITE WINE FERMENTATION

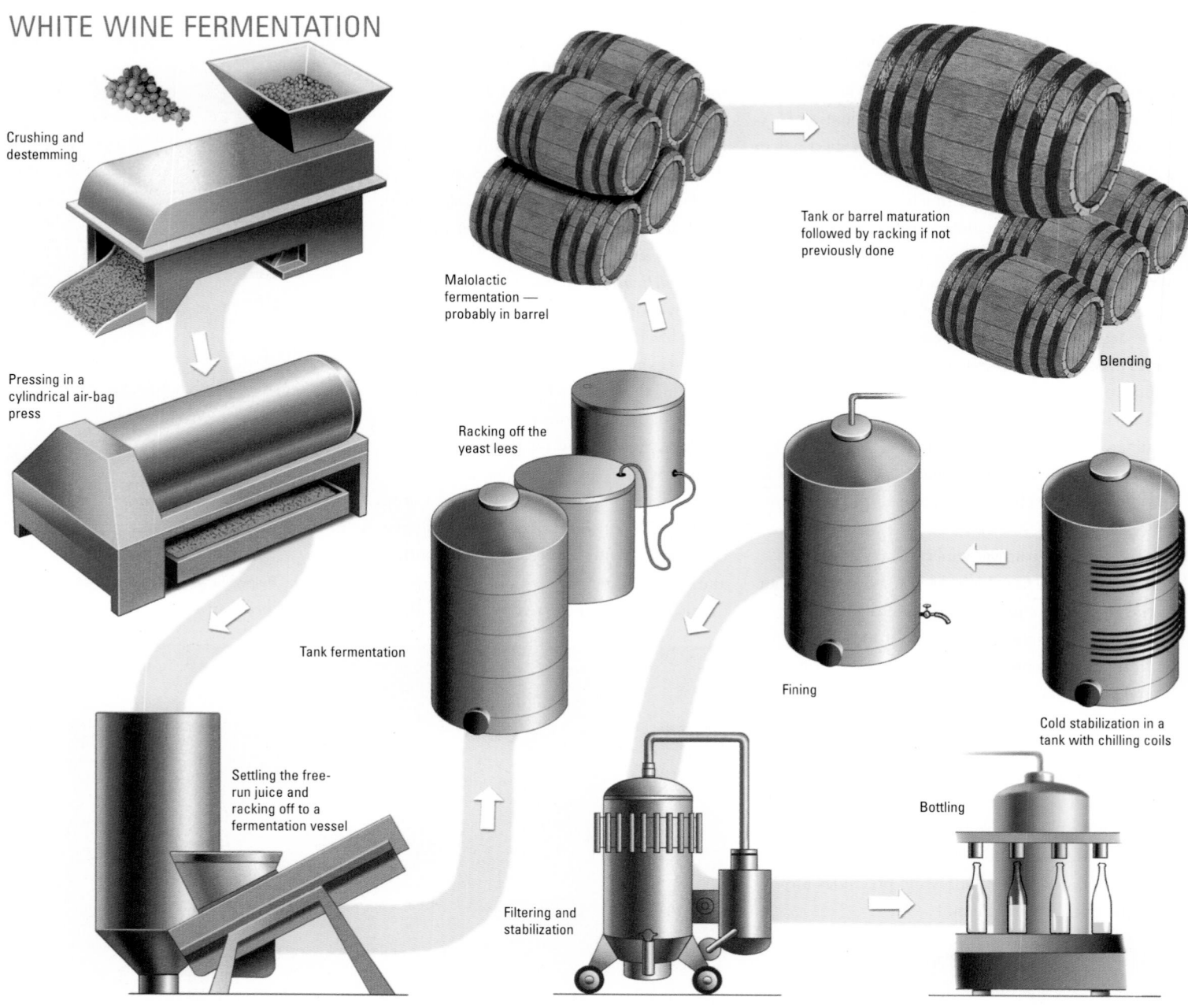

Crushing and destemming

Pressing in a cylindrical air-bag press

Settling the free-run juice and racking off to a fermentation vessel

Tank fermentation

Racking off the yeast lees

Malolactic fermentation — probably in barrel

Tank or barrel maturation followed by racking if not previously done

Blending

Fining

Cold stabilization in a tank with chilling coils

Filtering and stabilization

Bottling

Must adjustment is not designed to alter the taste of wine, but rather to modify its structure. In small amounts, it improves the wine without being detectable; but it is noticeable in higher amounts and can have a detrimental effect on the wine.

RED WINE FERMENTATION

A key element in the production of red wine is the extraction of the phenolics, a process which happens mainly during maceration of the grape must and skins. Generally, winemakers are looking for the presence of three factors: an appropriate color, the right amount of tannins and the suitable fineness of tannins. Red grape varieties that tend to have thicker skins are more likely to produce deeper color and firmer tannins in the wine,

although ripeness and the level of yield also affect this. The major difference between making red and white wine is, therefore, that the former includes skins in the fermentation process, while the latter relies on juice only.

The fermentation temperature for red wines is generally higher than that for whites. This is necessary to help extract the color and tannin from the skins, but the heat sacrifices some of the aromatic elements which are therefore less likely to show in red wines. The temperature varies from the low 70s F (20s C), which enhances the ripe primary fruit aromas of the wine up to 90°F (32°C), which evaporates some of the primary fruit characters, but offers more complexity and help in creating a finer structure in the wine.

RED WINE FERMENTATION

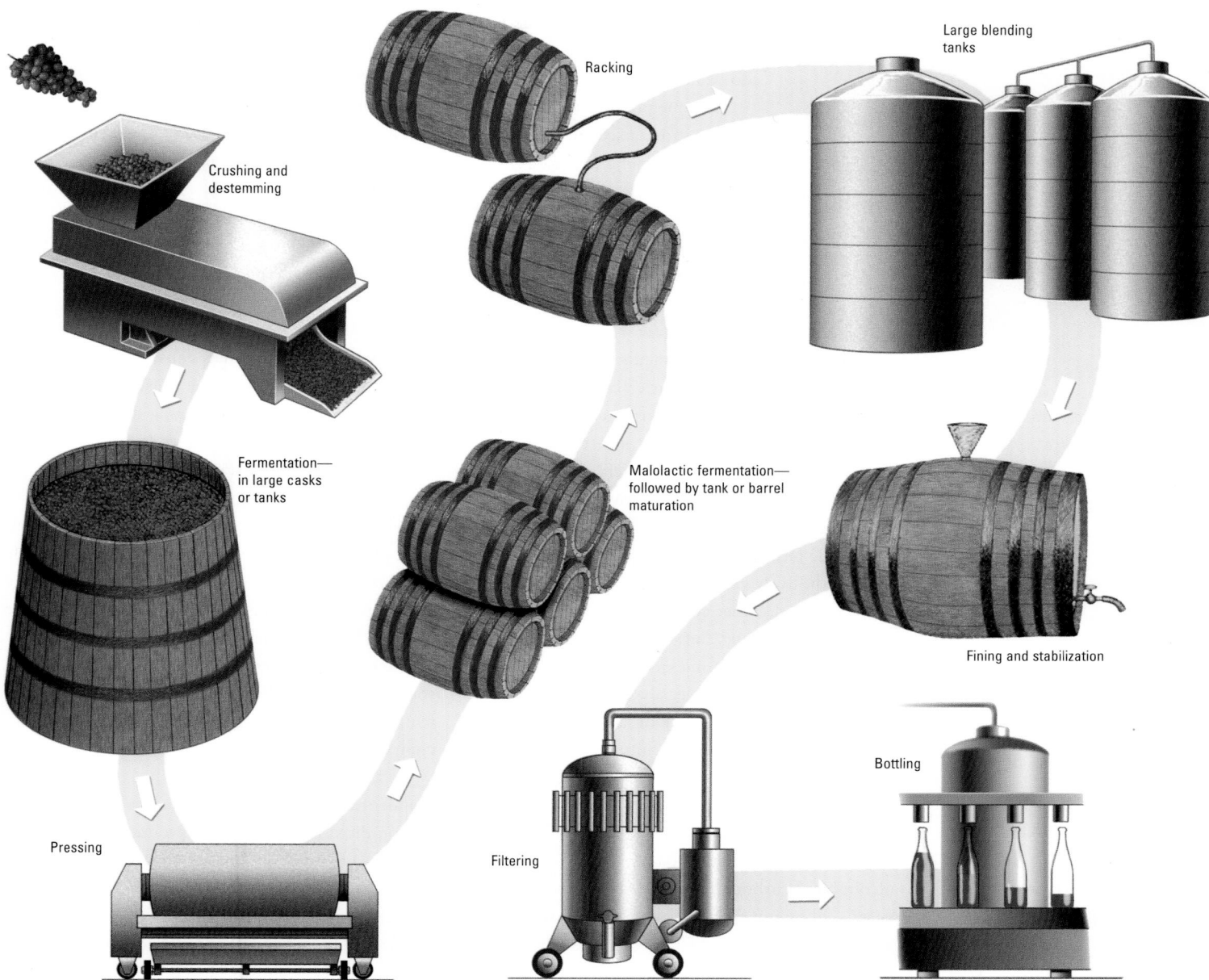

Crushing and destemming

Racking

Large blending tanks

Fermentation— in large casks or tanks

Malolactic fermentation— followed by tank or barrel maturation

Fining and stabilization

Pressing

Filtering

Bottling

Winemakers have several methods to aid the uptake of phenols in the wine, generally relying on the fact that the skins, stalks and other solid matter tend to form a "cap" on the top of the must in the fermentation tank:

Pumping must over This involves taking wine from the bottom of the fermentation tank and spraying it over the cap. Done vigorously, the action increases the extraction of phenolics.

Plunging Pushing the cap down into the must to enable more contact.

Header boards A series of boards at right angles to each other that is used to keep the cap constantly submerged below the top of the must.

Rotofermenting This is the modern method, and is essentially a fermentation tank tipped on its

side that can rotate occasionally to tumble the cap. Care has to be taken to ensure that this is not overdone, as this would over-extract phenolics.

Other methods can be adopted to increase phenolic content. The wine can be *saignéed*, which involves taking a small amount of juice off at the start of fermentation, thus increasing the skin-to-juice ratio. Outside Europe, tannin is also often added in powder form to improve the structure.

Following the end of fermentation, or sometimes just before it is completed, the red wine is pumped off the skins, which are then run into a press. Red press wine is generally much harsher than the other wine because the process of pressing extracts more tannins, although the resulting wine may be quite deep-colored and flavorful. As a

In hot climates it is difficult to control the temperature at the start of fermentation, sometimes leading to spillage.

result, only a portion may be added back to the final blend to avoid making the finished wine too coarse.

At some point after the end of fermentation, a second process—called "malolactic fermentation"—may also be used on the wine. Almost all red wines undergo this, as may some more full-bodied whites. This results from the activity not of yeasts, but of bacteria. New wine contains a number of acids; the most important is tartaric acid, but another is malic acid that is a green, sharp and apple-like. The activity of lactic bacteria converts the malic acid into softer, creamier lactic acid. Red wines do not need green acidity, which is why the process is encouraged for them. With some white wines, malolactic fermentation is discouraged to preserve their fresh, lively character, but with others, it may be encouraged, either completely or partially, because the creamier, buttery components it imparts give extra complexity to the wine. These days the winemaker can easily control the process, either inhibiting the activity of lactic bacteria, or adding them to the wine in cultured form if the procedure is desired.

How fermentation works

One of the procedures for monitoring fermentation: pinot noir nearing the end of the process in Burgundy, France.

Fermentation is the conversion of sugar into alcohol and carbon dioxide. It is catalyzed by yeast—minute microflora—which consume sugar as food and give out alcohol as a result. In the process, the yeast cells multiply rapidly, speeding up the process of fermentation so that, by the time it finishes, there may be hundreds of thousands of yeast cells per cubic inch of wine. The fermentation also creates a great deal of heat, which usually needs to be controlled because the yeasts may die if the temperature exceeds 95°F (35°C).

Fermentation ends naturally when either all the yeast nutrients (predominantly sugar) are used up, or when the alcohol level reaches a point where it poisons the yeasts—usually around 15 percent abv (alcohol by volume)—or when a combination of sugar and alcohol exhausts the yeasts. It can also be ended by heating the wine to kill the yeasts, by dosing them with very high levels of sulfur dioxide, or by filtering them out.

Historically, the ferment was started naturally by the yeast occurring naturally around wineries. Almost invariably today, the process is begun with the winemaker adding specially prepared yeast to the juice. This has the advantage of ensuring a quick start to the ferment, precluding spoilage and giving the winemaker more control over the process. Occasionally, winemakers use natural yeasts, which are sometimes considered to give more flavor complexity to the finished wines.

A key component in managing fermentation is the control of temperature which is crucial to the ultimate style of wine. White wines tend to be fermented at lower temperatures than red, to preserve their aromatic and fruity qualities, but the most aromatic of white varieties—like riesling and gewürztraminer—will be fermented at the very coolest temperatures, say 45–55°F (8–12°C). Other wines—classically, chardonnay—may be fermented at higher temperatures, up to 72°F (22°C) and sometimes even higher, which will lose some of the fruitiest characters, but may give them more complexity, with nutty or savory tones.

In the past, wine was generally aged in huge wooden vats, usually open-topped to let the carbon dioxide escape. Some producers seeking a more traditional style still opt for these. During the last century, other inert containers became common. Initially, these were lined concrete, but now are stainless steel, which is simply produced, can be kept clean easily, and can be cooled without difficulty during fermentation.

Sometimes the winemaker will opt for barrel fermentation. This involves the whole or, more commonly, the last part of fermentation in small barrels. This gives some of the character of oak to the wine—the oak flavors will be subtle and more completely integrated into the wine because the wine is fermented in and not just aged in oak. (There are a number of reasons for this, but it is due primarily to the action of yeasts on the oak aromatics, essentially muting them.) Given the difficulty of transferring red must—including skins—into barrels with small bung-holes, the practice is reserved for white wines. Some reds—especially pinots—may be pressed just before the completion of fermentation and then pumped into barrels, where the yeast cells finish the process.

MATURATION

Following fermentation, some wines are aged on their yeast lees—the yeast cells that have died at the end of fermentation and sink to the bottom of the tank or barrel. With white wines, where lees aging is most important, it adds a subtle flavor component, a hint of yeasty or bready character. Critically, however, for red wines also, lees aging affects the mouthfeel of the wine, making it richer and smoother. The process is adopted particularly for chardonnay, but most white varieties can have some lees aging. The lees also help to protect wines being aged in barrel against some of the effects of oxygen, such as loss of flavor or browning of color, during maturation.

All wine needs a period to settle down following fermentation, during which it may undergo some treatments. For light, fresh wines, this period of maturation may only be a few weeks, but it may last up to three years for some wines before bottling takes place. There are different ways in which maturation can occur.

Barrel For much of the last 2,000 years, this has been the most widespread way of storing, and thus aging, wine. Barrels come in all shapes and sizes, and may be made of oak (of various types) or chestnut—or occasionally of some other woods. Oak is comparatively inert, but it does allow minute oxygen contact with the wine through the staves. This both helps it to stabilize naturally and develops the flavor components. Traditionally, the oak was rarely new; barrels would have been used and reused many times, and it was oxygen that had the major impact.

Tank Today, it is possible to keep wine in large stainless steel tanks. These are completely inert (especially if filled to the brim, or if the headspace is filled with an inert gas), so the wine can be stored for a fairly long period without losing its freshness. However, most wines matured in tanks will be released onto the market within a few months—a year at the most—of the end of fermentation.

Bottle Wine is rarely stored for long in bottle. The economics of production mean that it is usually out on the wine store shelves as soon as possible after bottling. However, wines can suffer "bottle shock," so the better wines will be kept for a few weeks or months before release to settle them down. Some wine styles—late-disgorged champagnes, Hunter valley sémillons from Australia and red Rioja *gran reservas*—will have extended bottle aging.

Above: *Stainless steel containers are now used by many producers for the aging and fermentation of wine.*

Top: *A glass-fronted barrel being filled with new wine in Germany; the cloudiness is due to the yeast lees.*

Planks of oak for barrels are left to mature outside the factory for at least four to five years.

OAK

When wine-lovers talk about oak today, they are really referring to the impact of new oak barrels on the wine. Oak is an excellent wood for storing liquids: it is flexible and malleable and, crucially, it can be made watertight. For wine, it has the additional advantage of adding oak flavors—creamy, vanillin, cedary and spicy. This sometimes gives wine a desirable complexity. Oak contains tannins, so it also gives additional phenols to the wine, which is something makers of white wine in particular must treat with care.

The oak for barrels generally comes from two countries, France and the USA. The trees used are of different oak species, and there are often different methods of seasoning the wood, so the two types provide varying components to the wine. As a general rule, American oak offers more overt vanillin and coconut components to the wine, whereas French oak tends to be more restrained, with spicy, cedary characters predominating. The size of barrel also has an impact on this, with small barrels like the widely used Bordeaux barrique of 60 gallons (225 l) offering a greater surface-to-wine ratio than larger ones, and thus more easily imparting oak qualities to the wine. Winemakers these days tend to match oak type to wine. Rioja and Australian shiraz are often aged in American oak. Chardonnay and cabernet are more likely to be aged in French oak.

Assembling a barrel involves heating the inside of the staves, often with an open flame, to make them bend easily. This chars the insides of the barrel, and the level of charring can affect the wine. Thus, barrels come with a high, medium or low toast, with the high-toasted barrels tending to impart a distinctly smoky style to the wine.

Clearly, the longer that the wine is in the barrel, the higher the uptake of flavor and tannin. This part of the aging process has to be very carefully monitored by the winemaker to avoid the oak characters dominating the fruit aroma and flavor of the wine.

Above: *Chemical analysis is used to measure the development and composition of wine, and monitor the levels of additives.*

Top: *Blending port. This process is critical with the objective that the final wine must be more than the sum of its parts.*

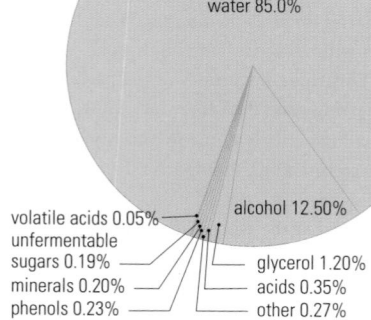

THE COMPONENTS
OF WINE[6]

water 85.0%

alcohol 12.50%

volatile acids 0.05%
unfermentable
sugars 0.19%
minerals 0.20%
phenols 0.23%

glycerol 1.20%
acids 0.35%
other 0.27%

6 There is no single, precise measurement of the composition of wine, but this gives an example of a typical, dry, European red wine.

Racking

Racking generally refers to the process of moving juice, must or wine from one container to another, which will probably happen a number of times to a wine in the course of its evolution. However, the term is also used explicitly in reference to wines that age for some time in the cellar. Racking is used to aerate the wine when a little oxygen contact is deemed beneficial. It also allows wine to be removed from any solid matter that has settled to the bottom of the container during the maturation period, thus encouraging natural clarification of the wine.

FINISHING

Wine goes through a number of processes before it is bottled. Critical to the final style of the wine is how it is blended. Almost all wines, including the most expensive vintages in the world, are blended in some form or other. What is essential is that any blend should be better balanced and more complex than the sum of its parts. Otherwise, the blend does not really succeed. Unfortunately, blending is sometimes carried out merely to stretch the quantity of the wine, with the result that the quality of the best constituents is reduced, not enhanced.

Most often, wine is blended from a number of vineyards and/or varieties. Different sites produce slight variations in the wine, even when the same variety is used. They may be more or less tannic or acidic and produce different flavor components so that structural balance and complexity can be improved by the blend. Different grape varieties may give complementary aspects. In both Bordeaux and outside Europe, sémillon, which gives weight, texture and aging ability, is regularly blended with sauvignon blanc, which gives acidity, freshness and fruit to the youthful incarnation of the wine. At this stage, some of the press wine may also be added. It may offer fuller flavors, but too much in the blend may provide unacceptably

coarse phenolics for either red or white wines, so it needs to be handled with discretion.

Less often, wine may be blended across vintages—tawny port and champagne are classic examples of this. Even for table wine, however, most countries allow other vintages to be blended into a wine; in Australia and South Africa, 15 percent of wine from a previous year can be used in this way.

It is critical to stabilize a wine; otherwise, the wine may become spoiled, develop haze or not show at its best. A number of operations may be included in this process.

Fining This process uses substances with one electrical charge (positive or negative) to attract substances that are suspended in the wine and have the opposite charge. Thus, bentonite (a powdered clay) may be added to white wines to attract and remove proteins that exist in the wine that could cause a haze after bottling. With red wine, a number of substances, including egg white, may be added to remove some of the xcoarser tannins or phenolic bitterness.

Filtration This extracts solids that may exist in the wine, often of minute size, including yeast cells and bacteria. A number of filtration methods may be adopted, including coarse filtration, which only extracts the largest particles, and centrifuging, spinning the wine at very high speed, to push solids out of the wine. Filtration is the subject of great debate. Opponents say it rips the guts out of the wine, and supporters claim it is essential to guarantee a stable, attractive drink. While it may modify some of the fine nuances of top-quality wine, as a general rule, it does nothing but ensure its drinkability.

Additives Like most food, almost all wine has some chemical addition to ensure its freshness, and sometimes to act against bacterial or yeast spoilage. The most common such additive is sulfur dioxide, which has been used at least since ancient Roman times to ward off oxidation and guarantee a lively, enjoyable wine. In most cases, sulfur dioxide is a perfectly safe substance, but chronic asthmatics may experience a reaction to it. Additionally, excessive quantities can dull wine and give it a "burnt match" smell. Generally today, precise measurement and using it in combination with forms of ascorbic acid (vitamin C, which also acts as a preservative) ensures freshness without detrimental effects.

Cold stabilization For complex chemical reasons, wine that is chilled tends to deposit crystals of potassium bitartrate. These are harmless, but consumers tend to find them unsightly and may even be concerned that they are fragments of glass. A number of treatments can be carried out to remove the tartrates. Most involve chilling the wine so the tartrates precipitate out so they can be filtered out of the finished product.

From all the foregoing information, it should be clear that effective analysis is a key tool in the winemaker's armory. Many simple tests are carried out—to obtain rough alcohol level, or to assess the progress of malolactic fermentation—in even the smallest winery. More complex tests may have to be done, or at least confirmed, by an external laboratory, although the largest companies have highly equipped in-house facilities. For many situations, both to satisfy domestic or export authorities, or to deal with subsequent problems, a winery has to obtain precise measurements of various components of the wine or additives to it.

BOTTLING

The final stage in the process is to get the drink into the bottle. This is generally done just after a final filtration and, ideally, is carried out in sterile conditions to ensure no damage to the wine occurs. These days, the whole process is mechanized, and large companies have their own bottling lines in constant use. Small companies may transport their wine to larger ones for bottling, or use a mobile bottling plant.

Bottles come in many shapes and sizes. The standard size is 28 fluid ounces (750 ml)—about 6–7 glasses. A half bottle is 14 fluid ounces (375 ml). Some wines have their own sized bottles—the *clavelin* for *vin jeaune* Jura wine is traditionally 24 fluid ounces (640 ml). A magnum is 56 fluid ounces (1.5 l)—an excellent size for the slow aging of wine. There are also larger—and more unwieldy—sizes.

There is currently much debate about how bottles are closed. Cork—a flexible and effective stopper—has been used for at least 300 years. Its problem is that it can cause cork taint, which at best dulls the wine and at worst makes it less attractive than ditch water.

Because it affects between 2 and 5 percent of wine bottled, potentially one bottle in each case of wine you buy could be tainted. To avert this, many wine companies are exploring other options, such as synthetic corks

and even crown seals. While these may be fine for short-term storage, no one is sure about their long-term impact on wine that is designed to age. They may be too effective at keeping out oxygen (a small amount passes by the cork, and helps to catalyze the necessary aging process in the bottle). It is possible that they could also add off flavors to the wine. Perhaps we will have a clearer idea of their effect in 25 years' time.

The chief problem with alternative closures may be rooted in ritual. Drawing a blue piece of plastic from a bottle—or pulling off a crown seal—doesn't have the same impact or drama as extracting a cork. Meanwhile, the cork industry is claiming to be tackling the issue.

A mechanical bottling line in process.

Different wine bottle shapes have a cultural, rather then practical significance.

Above: *Bunches of fruit are spread out on racks to produce the raisin-like grapes which make flavorful sweet wines.*

Below: *Riddling involves shaking bottles of sparkling wine to help remove yeast lees following second fermentation in bottle.*

Bottom: *Twenty-first century riddling. A "gyropalette" carries out the process mechanically, controlled by computer.*

OTHER WINE STYLES

Specific wine styles will be dealt with in subsequent text on specific wine regions—the entries on Champagne, for instance, will discuss sparkling wines, Tokay and Sauternes will examine sweet wines, and Port and Sherry will consider fortifieds. Nevertheless, it is useful to have a brief introduction to how each of these styles are made.

Sweet wine

Table wine is produced when yeasts ferment all the available sugar, creating a dry wine. Sweet wines occur when, either naturally or artificially, the yeast stops operating, and fermentation ceases with some unfermented sugar remaining (this is called "residual sugar").

Fermentation stops naturally when a high alcohol level poisons the yeasts, or a combination of high alcohol and the effort of fermenting an abundant quantity of sugar exhausts them. Such a high sugar level occurs when natural conditions, particularly the presence of the fungal disease *Botrytis cinerea*, conspire to produce it. It also arises from leaving grapes on the vine longer than normal (late harvest wines), which concentrates the sugars at the expense of water content, or when grapes are picked and left to shrivel (as with the reciotos and amarones of northeast Italy). Icewines, notably of Germany and Canada, also have this effect. These processes tend to produce the best and most complex sweet wines.

Fermentation can also be stopped artificially. Chilling the wines to suspend yeast activity and then filtering the yeasts out has this effect. High levels of sulfur dioxide will also inhibit yeast activity, but can also make the wine unpleasant.

Wine should never be sweetened merely by adding sugar, but in some countries a sweet wine can be made by adding grape juice or concentrate to a wine that has been fermented dry. Wines made in this way, however, are generally cheap and of little complexity.

Sparkling wine

Like cola, sparkling wine can be made by injecting carbon dioxide, but is of execrable quality and not worth further consideration. To achieve any kind of excellence, sparkling wine requires a second fermentation. When sugar and yeast are added to dry table wine (the base wine) in an enclosed container, there is a process of refermentation, which creates not just extra alcohol, but also extra carbon dioxide. The enclosed container keeps the carbon dioxide dissolved in the wine, and it only becomes gaseous when the container is opened. The best way to produce this effect is to put the base wine and yeast/sugar addition in a bottle, where the second fermentation takes place. This method was perfected in Champagne, and is now used throughout the world.

Sparkling wine can also be made in large tanks and then transferred into bottles under pressure so the gas does not escape. The wine made this way can be quite drinkable, but for various reasons rarely has the excitement or balance of bottle-fermented sparkling wine.

Fortified wine

One of the simplest wine styles to produce, fortified wines have extra alcohol added to them, usually in the form of grape spirits. Generally, this happens during the course of fermentation, and the total abv (alcohol by volume) of the wine becomes so high that the yeast is instantly killed and fermentation ceases. The resulting residual sugar leaves the wine sweet. Occasionally, the wine is fortified at the end of fermentation, leaving wine with a high-alcohol content but a dry finish. This method is used to produce certain sherry styles, principally *fino* and *amontillado*.

Fortified wines are fiery and unintegrated when young and, in the case of port, also very tannic. They usually need to go through a maturation process, which can take place either in wood or in bottle to make them drinkable. The more common process is wood aging, which is done in old oak barrels to gain the impact of the oxygen on the wine rather than the sweet oak flavors which younger wood would impart. The oxygen contact effects the integration of the wine and, with red wines, deposits some of the phenolics, allowing the wine to be drinkable from anywhere within two years (for a muscat de beaumes de venise) to ten or 20 years (for some tawny ports).

Alternatively, the wine can be aged in bottle, but a substantially longer time is required for maturation because the oxygen contact is much more limited and the processes much slower. Good vintage port generally needs 15 years or more before it is soft enough to drink and enjoy.

AGING

The final part of the process for any wine is its development in bottle. Most wines, whether red or white, are designed to be drunk young and, although a few months in bottle probably benefits their integration, they are best consumed within two years or so. Only a few wines will benefit obviously from aging.

The development of wine in bottle is still little understood. However, it can best be summarized as a slow oxidation. Once the oxygen is used up, other chemical changes take place in what is called a reductive environment. The danger in this is that the oxidizing process will reduce the wine to a dull liquid which will not be drunk (the ultimate fate of all lifeless wine), or even a vinegar. The first precondition for aging wine, therefore, is a component to slow down its oxidative development. With both white and red wines, but more essentially with whites, acidity performs this function by preserving freshness. In red wine, the phenolics also protect the wine because they tend to react with the oxygen before other flavorful components of the wine do. This means that the white wines which age the longest tend to be those with high acidity—rieslings, Loire chenin blancs and Hunter valley sémillons. With red wines, it follows that the more tannic varieties—cabernets and merlots, nebbiolo and syrah—age the longest. However, this may also be dependent on the style of wine. Many sweet, alcoholic dessert wines will age well, and madeira is possibly the longest lived of all.

With white wine, the impact of time is to deepen its color through lemon to gold and finally to amber. The reverse is true with red wine: with age, it moves from deep purple, via ruby and mahogany to tawny. In both cases, if the wine is brown the process has gone too far and the wine is oxidized, unless it is a fortified wine, in which case brown may be acceptable.

The second requirement for aging wine is that it has sufficient flavor complexity to make it worth keeping. A US$9 cabernet sauvignon from almost anywhere in the world may have enough tannin to allow it to age, but it will lose its fruitiness with time, and develop no interesting new flavors to make it enjoyable. Some quite expensive wines are deliberately made to be drunk young and are all the more enjoyable for it, for they will seem little different, and certainly no better, after some years.

Critically, with red wines, the process of aging causes the phenolics in the wine to polymerize—

that is, the tannin and coloring material form large chains of molecules. With time, these polymers become so large that they can no longer remain suspended in the liquid, so they fall out as deposits. This means that wines that may be astringent, or even unpleasant, when young soften with time and become much more attractive to drink. Youthful ports, barolos and many cabernet-based wines can seem horrible at two years of age, but sublime at 15. There is a tendency today to think that "real" red wine has to be chock-full of tannins to be taken seriously. However, most styles are designed to be aged and soft, and will be much more exciting and palatable for it.

The alcohol and sugar in sweet wines also acts as a preservative, and helps to allow them to age for a particularly long time. Sparkling wines can also age well because the pressure of carbon dioxide helps marginalize oxygen activity, and their particularly high acidity preserves freshness. With time, they acquire toasty, biscuity aromas, and ultimately even mushroom and truffle characters. While they may lose some of their fizz, they can remain exciting and fascinating wines.

Old bottles age in a cellar; the phenolics soften and the flavors should become more complex over time.

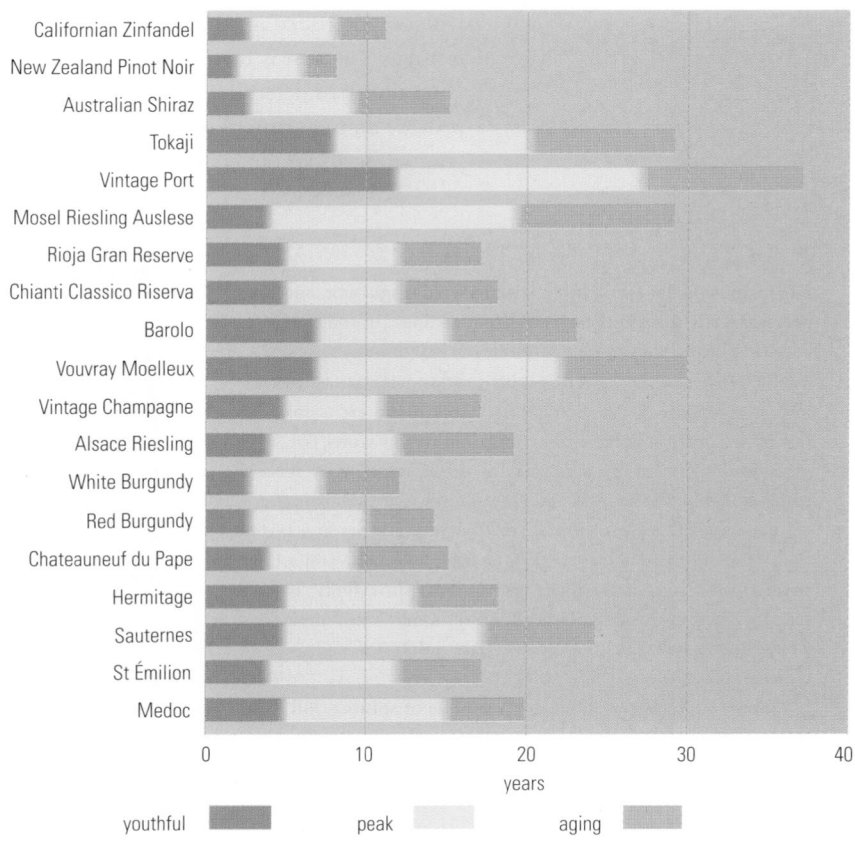

WINE STYLE MATURITY

Californian Zinfandel
New Zealand Pinot Noir
Australian Shiraz
Tokaji
Vintage Port
Mosel Riesling Auslese
Rioja Gran Reserve
Chianti Classico Riserva
Barolo
Vouvray Moelleux
Vintage Champagne
Alsace Riesling
White Burgundy
Red Burgundy
Chateauneuf du Pape
Hermitage
Sauternes
St Émilion
Medoc

0   10   20   30   40
years

youthful   peak   aging

Enjoying Wine

Sampling the local product in Slovakia.

Above all, wine is designed to be enjoyed, preferably with entertaining companions and good food. However, although wine is often drunk in copious quantities in those circumstances, the issue of "tasting" arises for anyone who develops more than a passing interest in the subject.

Tasting is not drinking—the situation is different. It is not primarily companionable (it can even be competitive) and ideally food should not be present, at least while tasting seriously. The purpose is also different. While drinking is for pleasure, tasting is primarily for assessment. It should have a pleasurable component, although if you have spent a day judging 150 oaked chardonnays you may begin to doubt that. Crucially, it allows you to widen your knowledge about wines and develop your skills in evaluating them.

There are two good reasons why consumers who are interested in wine should go to wine tastings. The first is that they actually improve your ability to determine what you like. They provide an opportunity to learn about quality, and you will begin to understand why and where it appears in wines. Attending a formal tasting allows you to compare a number of wines at one sitting, which would otherwise be prohibitively expensive for most of us. The second reason for tasting is to discover what you do and do not want to buy. If you are going to extend your purchasing beyond the cheapest bottles, it pays to know what you are getting: wine can be an easy way to waste your money. Learning to taste, and making use of the skill, gives opportunities to sample more expensive wines before committing yourself to buying them.

That does not alter the fact that there is a lot of mystique around the idea of tasting, with novices uncertain about why experts swirl wine around in the glass, slurp it and then spit it out. One of the reasons is that tasting has to be disciplined for the analysis to be effective and comparable, and drinking all the wines you taste will prevent you from carrying this out.

HOW TO TASTE WINE

Tasting is more than just swilling the liquid into your mouth. There are in fact four senses used: sight, smell, taste and touch. Wine jargon has arisen around the whole process and these are dignified with the terms "appearance," "nose" and "palate" (which covers both taste and touch). Before you even take a sip, you may, using these criteria, be able to determine the wine's likely age, possible origin and the grape variety used, as well as the climate the grapes were produced in and how the wine was made and stored. Critically, you should also be able to establish if the wine is faulty or too old.

Anyone can taste. Many wine drinkers think that their palate may be defective, or that they will never have the ability to become a good wine taster. It is not true. Anyone can become a first-rate taster if they practise enough. Even though each palate is different and we all react to varying components in the wine with diverse responses, no palate is worse than another.

A NOTE ABOUT SPITTING

For many wine-lovers, spitting is considered disgusting, and its practice tends to keep them away from tastings. In some cultures, it even breaks the conventions of polite society to be seen spitting in public. However, the sight of people spitting wine at tastings is normal to people in the wine industry and, if you are to take your tasting seriously, you have to be prepared to spit wines out. Even after drinking just a few sips of half a dozen wines, your senses begin to be dulled by the alcohol and your ability to make distinctions and see nuances is lessened. If there are 20 or more wines at a tasting, then drinking them all rather than spitting will make you a liability to all around you—and will ensure you have little ability to understand what is in the glass. Using a spittoon may seem unpleasant at first, but you will quickly overcome your inhibition and come to take it for granted.

Some people worry about the technique of spitting, but it isn't difficult. If you are uncertain about it, try it in the shower with a glass of water. Take a slurp and swoosh it out into the corner. You'll quickly become adept at getting it where you want it to go.

Learning to spit is an essential part of developing tasting skills—at least if you want to try more than a handful of wines at a go.

CHANGING COLOR WITH AGE

Above: Penfold's Grange 1993 (left) and 1981 (right). The young red wine (although actually comparatively old) has a deep plum color and vibrant pink-crimson rim. This is Australia's greatest red wine, Penfold's Grange, from the 1993 vintage. The color of the older vintage Grange (1981) is no longer as deep: the hue has changed more to ruby, and there is a distinct brick tone about the rim, a clear sign of age.

Below: Trimbach Riesling, cuvee "Frederic Emile" 1994 (left) and 1983 (right). The younger white wine has a very pale lemon hue, with a tinge of green (common in white wines from a cooler climate). This is the great Alsace riesling made by the house of Trimbach, cuvee "Frederic Emile" from the 1994 vintage. The older wine (1983) has developed a distinct gold-amber hue, betraying the impact of oxygen as it ages.

Sight

The first part of the process is to look carefully at the wine. Is its appearance cloudy or hazy? If it is, then it may be out of condition—although a slight haze on some red wines may merely mean that the winemaker has chosen not to filter too harshly and, in fact, the wine may be excellent. A deposit in the bottom of the glass, in the form of a sediment in older red wines and occasionally small crystals, does not count as a haze, and is a perfectly normal part of the development of the wine in the bottle.

The depth of color gives clues about the wine. A deep red suggests a thick-skinned variety like cabernet sauvignon or syrah. A paler color may imply a variety like pinot noir or gamay. As red wines get older their color also fades, so this will give you more information about the wine.

A pale, almost watery color with white wines points to grapes grown in a cool area. A deep gold could be the result of a warmer climate, though it can also suggest some age on the wine and/or the use of oak as part of the aging process.

The hue of the wine is also important. A youthful red wine will probably have a purple–crimson character. With age, the wine progresses through shades of cherry or plum (still revealing some youth), through ruby to garnet and tawny. With white wines the reverse is true: the older the wine, the deeper it becomes, and the lemon (and sometimes green) of youth becomes gold, then old-gold and amber. In any wine (other than fortified wines), a shade of brown shows the wine is too old.

Particularly useful in observing red wines is the hue of the wine's rim. (Hold it at a 45° angle against a white background and look at the edge of the wine.) A terracotta color is an early indication that the wine is developing some age.

With sparkling wines, it is also important to observe the bead (the bubbles) and the mousse (the foam on the surface). There should be multiple, persistent beads of small bubbles trailing up to the surface of the wine, forming a regular mousse. Large bubbles that fade quickly are a sign of lower quality.

Smell

Most novice drinkers make the mistake of thinking that the point of smelling wine is to come up with as many flowery descriptions of the aroma as possible, covering the widest available range of fruits and encompassing flowers, vegetables and some of the more inaccessible parts of the countryside. Aroma *is* important, but there are other equally crucial matters to consider. The first is the condition of the wine. Generally, if a wine is faulty or oxidized, it will be evident on the nose—and in the event of a serious problem, the taster will not even need to put the drink in their mouth.

Assessing sparkling wine—bubbles showing regular and persistent bead in a glass of Champagne.

Below: *Port as it ages. The color develops from ruby, through tawny, to a definite amber at 40 years of age.*

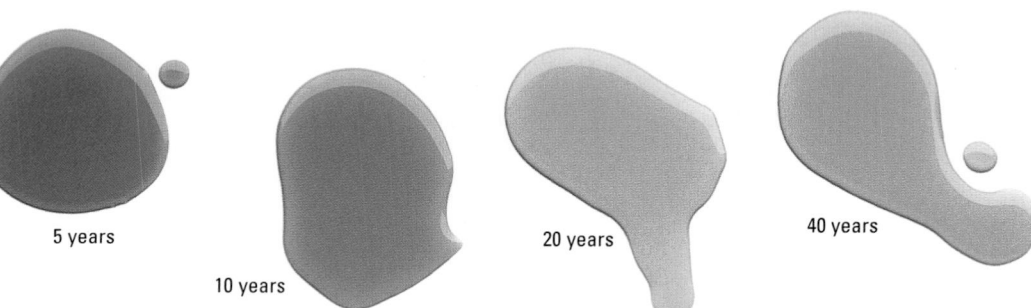

5 years
10 years
20 years
40 years

A big sniff gets the full aroma of the wine.

After that, the nose should give the taster a sense of the age and maturity of the wine. The two are not the same. A three-year-old sauvignon blanc may be getting a bit tired, whereas a three-year-old cabernet may be barely hitting its straps. Broadly, however, the fresher the wine smells, the younger it is. Wines can be classified as youthful, developing, mature (at their peak), tiring (often still quite enjoyable), or too old.

The terms aroma and bouquet are often used interchangeably, but they do not mean the same thing. There are a number of different definitions of them but, broadly, aroma is used to describe the smell of a young, fresh wine, whereas bouquet is a term for an older wine, one less fresh but possibly more complex. Another way of differentiating smell is between primary aroma—youthful, with lots of fresh fruit—and secondary or developed fruit—showing more age, with stewed or dried fruit and other smells also competing for attention.

Yet another key aspect of assessing wine is the intensity of the smell. Generally, the more intense the smell, the better the quality of the wine. Some wines have a fragrance that leaps from the glass; other wines, usually described as "dumb," have barely a whiff at all.

The aromas themselves come in myriad types. Many attempts to classify them have been made—and while various types of fruit predominate, flowers, woods, vegetables and other foods are all conjured into use at various times. Unfortunately, too much emphasis is placed on aromatic description, often by wine writers who think they are educating the consumer. What one person perceives as blackberry, another thinks is cherry and a third notes as blackcurrant. People unused to wine tasting can find this intimidating, whereas a diversity of response to smell is normal. On the other hand, the stress on aroma can hide the equal importance of the other elements of smelling wine. It is often better to give broad descriptors (black fruit, red fruit, citrus) than attempt to be so precise that you come to blows with fellow tasters.

A number of methods have been used to classify what we smell and taste in wine. The most widely accepted currently is the aroma wheel. This is undoubtedly helpful as a prompt when you are trying to work out what it is you are smelling. Its danger is that it makes tasters believe that they should all smell and taste exactly the same characters in a wine.

Taste

The final action in the process of tasting is to get the wine into the mouth. At this point, both the sense of taste and that of touch come into play.

Although many drinkers think that they can taste a number of complex characters when the wine gets on their tongue, in fact they cannot. Generally speaking, the tongue can only taste compounds that are sweet, sour (or acidic), salty and bitter. (There is evidence of a fifth taste sensation on the tongue, named *umami* by the Japanese, that may be a component in wine, but the arguments around this are complex and undecided at present.) All the other descriptors that are used for wine are an extension of the sense of smell, which is why smelling the wine is so important before drinking it—it tells you about three-quarters of what you are going to learn about the drink.

In the physiology of taste, the mouth and the nose are connected by the retronasal passage (the back of the nose passage), as shown in the diagram. When wine is drunk, the aromas waft up the retronasal passage until they reach the olfactory bulb, the bundle of nerves that transmit

THE AROMA WHEEL[7]

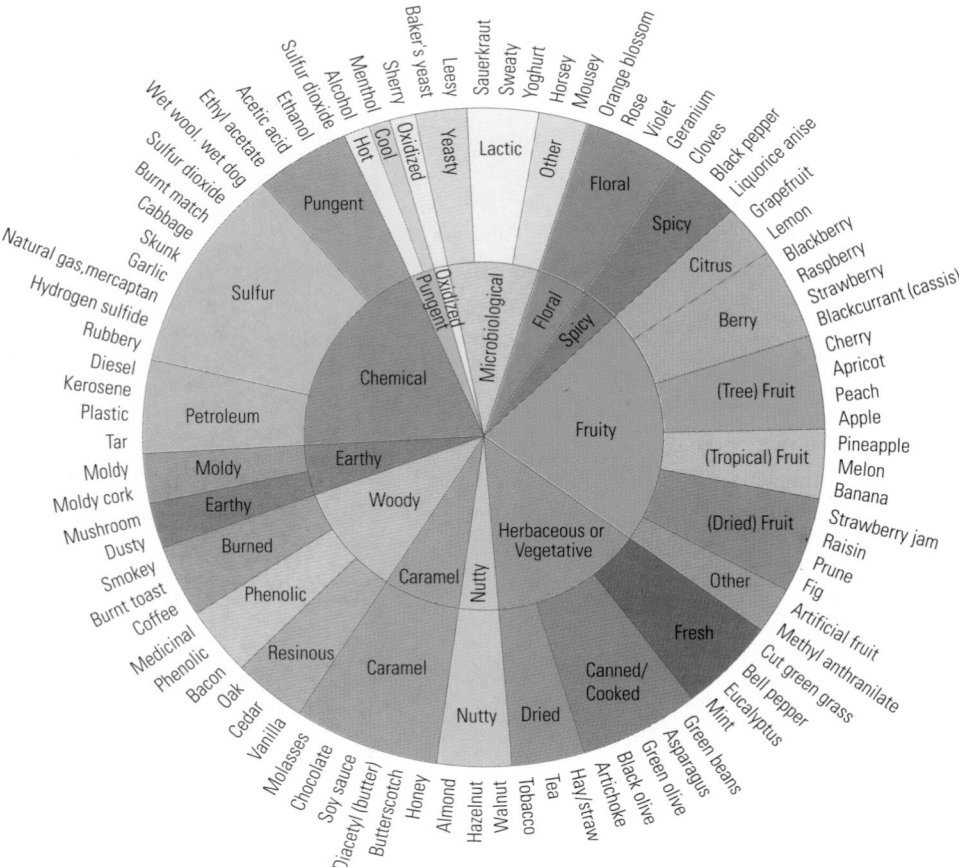

messages about smell to the brain. While we may think we can taste "blackberries with a dusting of icing sugar" when the wine is in the mouth, in fact, that sensation is being registered in the nose. Anything that accelerates the movement of the aromas up the retronasal passage will therefore improve tasting. It is for this reason that experienced tasters often open their mouth and slurp in air while they still have the wine in it; the air movement around the wine increases its vaporization and enhances the registration of the smell at the olfactory bulb.

SUGAR

One would guess that, logically, sugar is the component in wine that provides sweetness. For many people, sugar tends to be detected most strongly towards the tip of the tongue. Wines are classified as dry (with no detectable sugar) through to sweet, with gradations in between—from off-dry (for example, a cheaper Australian riesling), through medium-dry (a Californian blush wine, or a German kabinett), via medium-sweet (a demi-sec vouvray) through to sweet (sauternes) and luscious (an Australian botrytized wine or an Austrian trockenbeerenauslese). Sugar is not the only cause of sweetness in wine, however. Alcohol itself is a sweet liquid, so that wines with a higher alcohol level may give a hint of sweetness. This could apply to a chardonnay at 14 percent abv, even if analytically it had been fermented to dryness.

The detection of sugar in a wine depends on how much sugar from the grape juice has not been fermented into alcohol—the level of "residual sugar." However, many fruity wines, especially wines produced outside Europe, appear to be sweet without actually having any residual sugar. This is because the ripe, fruity flavor of the wine gives an impression of sweetness—of mangos, peaches, strawberries or other similarly luscious fruit. When tasting these wines it becomes important to distinguish the fruit sweetness from sugar sweetness.

ACIDITY

This is the tart character one can sense in food and drinks. A lemon is highly acidic. Acidity is generally sensed on the sides of the tongue, but not everyone may respond this way to it. All wines are acidic—because acidity is necessary to provide freshness and to protect the wine against bacterial damage and premature aging—but some have higher acidity levels than others. Fresh and delicate

white wines—rieslings, sauvignon blancs and chenin blancs—will have the highest levels of acidity. Red wines generally need less acid, and a fortified red wine, like a port, will have among the lowest acidity component.

BITTERNESS

Bitterness should only be present in wines in very limited amounts, and in white wines should ideally be avoided altogether. It tends to be sensed at the back of the tongue and the back of the throat, and is often associated with high tannin levels, especially "green" tannins from grapes which are not fully ripe. Bitterness can also appear with high acid levels, particularly when extra acidity has also been added.

SALT

In minute doses, salt may be noticed from the trace minerals in wine, but any wine that has an obviously salty character is unpleasant and likely to be badly made. Salt tends to be detected at the center of the tongue.

Touch

ALCOHOL

Although we register only four components of taste on the tongue, we also pick up other sensations in the mouth associated with what we feel. Alcohol is a key factor here. The warmth of the

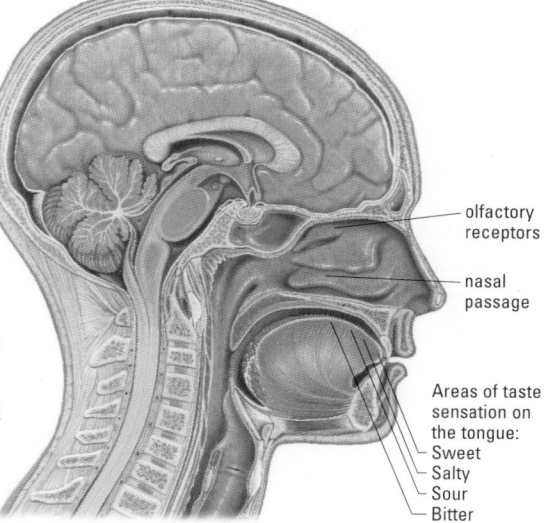

THE PHYSIOLOGY OF TASTE

olfactory receptors

nasal passage

Areas of taste sensation on the tongue:
Sweet
Salty
Sour
Bitter

The tongue can only detect four basic flavors—salty, sweet, sour, and bitter. However, aromas from (food and) wine rise into the nasal cavity where they are picked up by olfactory nerve receptors. These send messages directly to the brain and combined with the flavor messages from the tongue, comprise the overall sensation of taste.

Bottles designed specifically for tasting in Catalonia, Spain.

Buyers tasting wine before bidding at the most famous wine auction in the world, the Hospices de Beaune, in Burgundy.

teeth, cheeks and gums when red wine is swallowed. (It rarely appears as a major component in white wines and, if it appears in more than minute quantities, is the result of poor winemaking.) It's similar to the sensation of drinking tea that has stewed in the pot for 20 minutes, making the gums appear to "fur up" with the grainy, tannic character. Red wines have different levels of tannins: thicker-skinned varieties like cabernet sauvignon and syrah tend to have a lot; thinner-skinned varieties like grenache and pinot noir have less. Tannins also come in different forms. Some are coarse and sandy, which is not generally so attractive; some—even with wines that display high tannin levels—seem fine and smooth. Tannin is often, though not invariably, associated with bitterness in wine, and high tannin levels may make the sensation of bitterness more apparent.

TEXTURE

Wine also has mouthfeel, or texture. Again, this is connected to weight, but is not identical, and it is also related to acidity and the form of tannin. A big condrieu (a wine made from viognier grapes in the Rhône valley in France) will seem viscous, almost oily or buttery, in the mouth. A sancerre, made from sauvignon blanc, on the other hand, feels much less smooth.

Just as sparkling wines require attention to the appearance of the bead, so when tasting them it is necessary to think about the mousse in the mouth. The ideal mouthfeel should be smooth, almost creamy. A wine that has large bubbles that explode aggressively will be much less pleasant.

At most tastings, you will be given a list of the wines you are trying, and maybe details of the bottle in front of you. Others are blind tastings—when you do not know anything about the wine in the glass. This allows you to try the wine, and make judgments about it without the influence of any prejudices you might have about a particular wine. It also allows you to make a true test of your own abilities as a taster, for here you are having to form judgments independently—and if you are ever to have faith in your own skills as a taster, this is a key part of the process.

The visual assessment of wine can tell us about its likely "body" and tactile qualities.

alcohol rises in the throat when wine is spat or swallowed. Drinking a neat spirit such as whisky or brandy has a distinct warming effect because of its high alcohol level, but many people are barely aware of it in wines because the alcohol in most wines is integrated into the overall impression of the drink. It may, however, leave an unpleasantly hot sensation if the alcohol is excessive for the wine style. Occasionally, the alcohol level may be insufficient, and the wine will have too light a body. This is one reason why alcohol-free wines have failed to take off—the alcohol itself gives weight and body that is essential to the experience of drinking wine.

BODY

Body is the next tactile sensation. It is a quality that one feels as a sense of weight on the tongue. Just as olive oil feels fuller in the mouth than water, so different wine styles have different weights, from a light Mosel riesling to a weighty vintage port. Body is not identical to the impact of alcohol but is related, as alcohol is one of the heavier constituents of wine.

TANNIN

Tannin is also registered by what we feel in the mouth. Tannin can be difficult to understand when one is new to wine, but it is the drying sensation that covers the

The concept of structure

The components of taste and touch we have been discussing form what is known as the structure of the wine. They are the skeleton, with the flavors and aromas being the flesh which fill it out. When most people taste wine they think about, and enjoy, its aromatic and flavorsome qualities, and rarely think about the acidity or the alcohol level. However, the wine will seem flabby and lack freshness if the acidity is too low. It will seem unpleasantly hot if the alcohol is too high and if the structure does not hang together well, the wine drinker will be dissatisfied with it despite its flavor.

The structure of the wine includes acidity, sugar, bitterness (occasionally), tannin (in red wines), alcohol, weight and mouthfeel and mousse (in sparkling wines), as well as the intensity of the fruit flavor. All of these components should be in balance—they are not just viewed in isolation, but in relationship to each other. Thus, wines with high sugar levels need crisp acidity to avoid becoming too cloying. High tannins need a full body and overt alcohol to avoid being too aggressive. All the components must be in equilibrium with the intensity of the fruit flavor if the wine is to avoid being, literally, fruitless and uninteresting to drink. If balance is achieved, the wine is harmonious.

Making distinctions

The outline of the process of tasting summarizes how to examine a specific wine; however, if wine-lovers are to develop their skills, they also need to compare wines. Formal tastings where wines line up against each other are a great way to do this, but wines also need to be compared at different times. The more one tastes, the more one learns to recall past wines, but this palate memory can be slow for many of us to develop.

Only a few tasters seem to have an innate ability to recognize instantly wines they have tasted on a previous occasion. The best solution, which in itself develops a better memory, is to write notes about wines you've tasted. That allows for comparisons across time and, if you own a number of bottles of a particular wine, it allows you to see how your abilities are developing. A few scribbled comments that summarize the structure of the wine, its appearance and aromatic character will suffice.

Wine tasting is normally done in a controlled environment. It requires surprising concentration and, if one is to do it effectively, certain conditions need to be met. These are all part of the ritual of tasting and, although they may seem to be designed to intimidate the newcomer, there are good reasons for them.

While the quality of a wine is often referred to, it is rarely defined. There is an argument that claims there is no way to determine quality, other than by examining the purpose to which the wine is to be put and its value for money. However, that is of little help to someone embarking on tasting who wants to know how they should assess the worth of what they are drinking. Experienced tasters have their own varying ways of analyzing the excellence of what they drink, but the following is a good rule of thumb.

Intensity of flavor Ideally, a wine should have a good hit of fruit flavor on the palate, and that ought to be balanced by a concentrated aroma. Another way of expressing this is the idea of "concentration."

Balance The structural elements of a wine should be in balance. This is often—especially where the balance is particularly esthetically pleasing—referred to as "harmony."

Length How long can you taste the flavor of the wine after you have swallowed it? Mediocre and commercial wines will fade fast, but good wines have a flavor that will go on for 15 seconds or longer.

Complexity The most difficult of the quality components to understand, complexity is the one that is most often absent. Complexity refers to the layers of flavor in the wine. A simple syrah will only have one or two distinctive flavors—black fruit, for instance. A complex one could also exhibit spice, coffee, cedar, black olive and tar (this sounds a horrendous combination, but it actually makes the wine very exciting). Complex wines also tend to have flavor patterns that develop and change in the mouth, starting with fruit dominating, adding coffee and cedar, and ending on spice and tar without ever entirely losing the fruit.

Wine glasses ready for a tasting.

THE RULES FOR TASTING

- **DO NOT INTRODUCE INTRUSIVE SMELLS**
  No perfume or aftershave: it really can distract your and other people's ability to smell and assess wine.
- **ENSURE THERE IS GOOD LIGHTING**
  It is the only way to get a really good idea of the appearance of the wine.
- **BE QUIET**
  Talking may disturb others.
- **DO NOT DISCUSS THE WINES WITH OTHERS**
  This may prejudice them or you, and cause you to reach faulty conclusions. You can compare notes at the end.
- **WRITE NOTES**
  To aid memory.
  To act as a reminder—especially if later decisions have to be made about it.
  To monitor the progress of the wine.
- **ALWAYS SPIT IF TASTING MORE THAN A FEW WINES**
  To avoid getting drunk.
- **THINK CAREFULLY ABOUT THE WINE**
  Start by analyzing the structure.
  Don't get sidetracked by the fruit aromas and flavors.
  Evaluate the quality and maturity of the wine.
  This is not primarily a case of whether or not you like it, but how good it is.
- **KEEP YOUR GLASSES CLEAN**
  Even detergent may affect the character of the wine.

Unfortunately, the more complex a wine is, the harder it can be to separate and analyze all the component flavors, even for the most experienced taster.

Not every high-quality wine will have all of these—and all but the most dreadful of wines should show some attributes of quality—but all good wines should at least have balance, intensity and generally length. The best will also show some complexity of flavor. Ideas of quality are complicated by differing cultural approaches to what is in the glass. A French drinker may place a lot of emphasis on the structure of the wine, and less on intense, ripe fruit. An Australian seeks great intensity, but may look less for structural harmony. An American is probably halfway between the two.

Conveying critical information about a wine can be done in many ways. Traditionally, wines were merely discussed in words, but these days points or stars are often used. In Australia, it is common to mark wines out of 20 (in practice, however, all wines get at least 10). In the United States, marks out of 100 are given (except, again, that the marking starts from halfway, so in practice one is only marking out of 50). Marks can be a useful aid to a quick personal assessment of a wine, but the danger is that they supplant the more informative process of describing the wine. Knowing that a wine has balanced acidity, firm tannins, quite a full body and intense and long black fruit and cedar characters conveys more information than a wine score of 16/20 (or 80/100. A good taster can use numbers to support a judgment, and as a quick reminder of rough quality, but no one should use them to hide from the more rigorous but useful process of describing the wine.

In many parts of the world—both the traditional like France and the more recent wine-producing countries (as well as wine-consuming nations like the United Kingdom)—wine shows are regularly used as a means of assessing wines. These can be an excellent way of helping the consumer make decisions about purchases, as well as helping successful producers sell their wines (note the number of bottles decorated with gold or silver medals in your local wine store). Some shows require judges to assess large classes—150–200 wines or more—very rapidly. This can also skew the show results because wines that are bold and forward are more easily appreciated than subtle and delicate ones, even if the latter have more complexity and balance.

THE RITUALS OF WINE

Choosing wine

The key factors in choosing a wine are the setting and context in which it will be drunk. Is it a casual drinks party in the garden, a barbecue or a more formal situation? Will there be food? Do the guests want to have wines to sip and think about, or merely to quench their thirst? Will you be serving wine on a warm summer's evening or will there be snow on the ground?

Riesling, for example, makes a light, crisp white wine, sometimes with a little residual sugar. It is great summer drinking, or with lighter foods at any time of the year. It provides some of the greatest value for money in terms of taste per dollar of any white wine in the world. But it is also often subject to unsubstantiated prejudice from people who think it makes tasteless sugar water (it doesn't) or that it should be oaked (which would destroy it). It clearly has a place, but it is not invariably the best white wine to serve.

The subject of food and wine is much misunderstood. Historically, it has been hidebound with

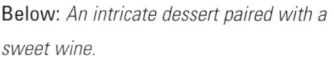

Below: *An intricate dessert paired with a sweet wine.*

Bottom: *Perhaps a less common choice: snails with red burgundy.*

rules about what can and cannot be eaten and drunk together. There is a very strong reaction against this currently, with some experts even saying that any food can go with any wine as long as the food itself is in balance. It is therefore clearly an area fraught with difficulty. A classic work on wine may suggest a good bordeaux or, possibly burgundy, for lamb, on the basis that the meat is roasted. But what if it is lamb tagine with quince? Or lamb daube, stewed in wine with herbs and olives? Or lamb curry? Each of those would probably clash with the traditional match, and if you had invested a lot of money in the wine you would probably be disappointed. The old adage that if you have a good wine you need a plain dish is probably the safest course.

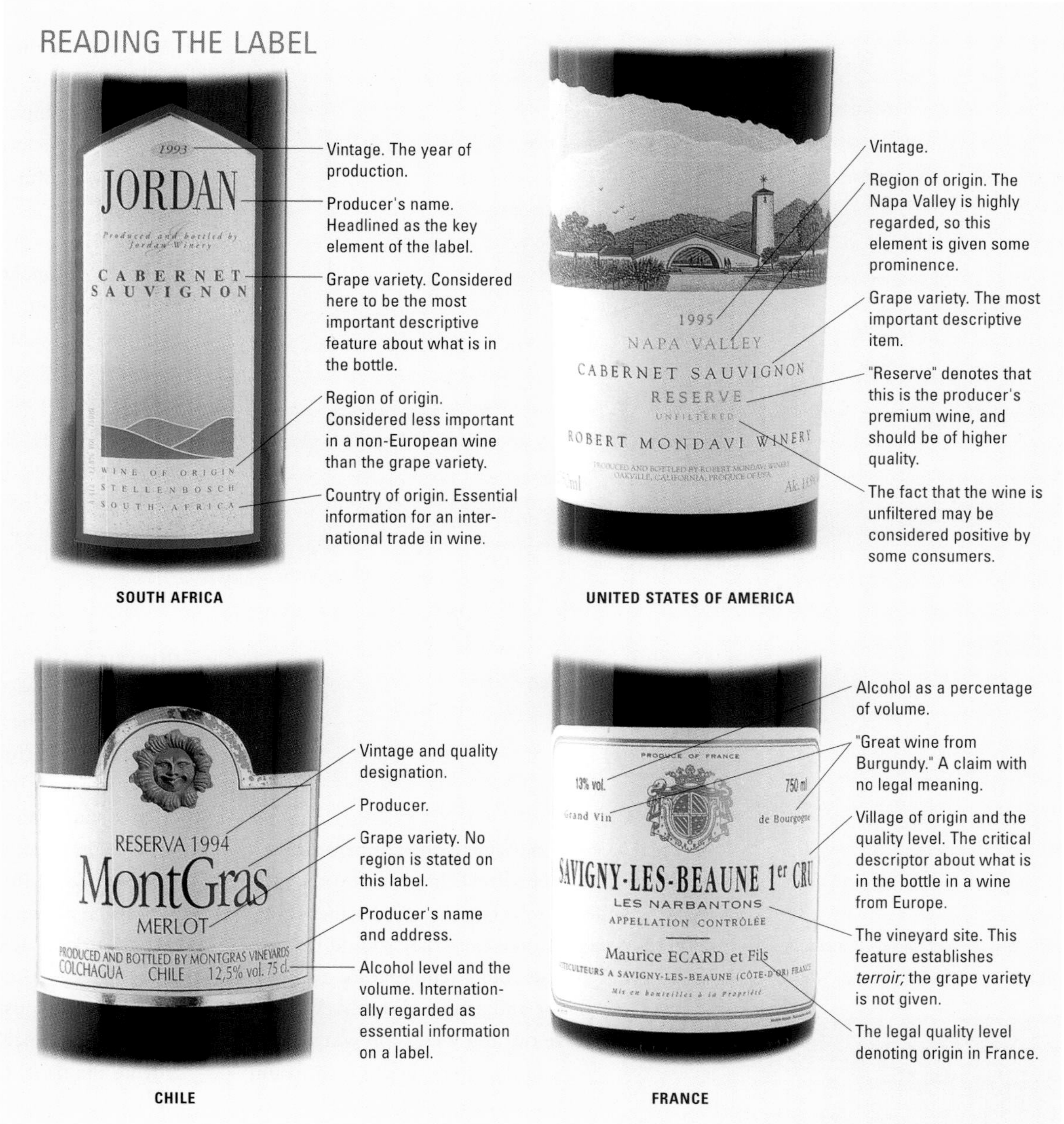
READING THE LABEL
1993
JORDAN
CABERNET SAUVIGNON
WINE OF ORIGIN STELLENBOSCH SOUTH AFRICA
Vintage. The year of production.
Producer's name. Headlined as the key element of the label.
Grape variety. Considered here to be the most important descriptive feature about what is in the bottle.
Region of origin. Considered less important in a non-European wine than the grape variety.
Country of origin. Essential information for an international trade in wine.
SOUTH AFRICA
1995
NAPA VALLEY
CABERNET SAUVIGNON
RESERVE
UNFILTERED
ROBERT MONDAVI WINERY
Vintage.
Region of origin. The Napa Valley is highly regarded, so this element is given some prominence.
Grape variety. The most important descriptive item.
"Reserve" denotes that this is the producer's premium wine, and should be of higher quality.
The fact that the wine is unfiltered may be considered positive by some consumers.
UNITED STATES OF AMERICA
RESERVA 1994
MontGras
MERLOT
PRODUCED AND BOTTLED BY MONTGRAS VINEYARDS
COLCHAGUA CHILE 12,5% vol. 75 cl.
Vintage and quality designation.
Producer.
Grape variety. No region is stated on this label.
Producer's name and address.
Alcohol level and the volume. Internationally regarded as essential information on a label.
CHILE
PRODUCE OF FRANCE
13% vol.
750 ml
Grand Vin
de Bourgogne
SAVIGNY-LES-BEAUNE 1er CRU
LES NARBANTONS
APPELLATION CONTRÔLÉE
Maurice ECARD et Fils
Alcohol as a percentage of volume.
"Great wine from Burgundy." A claim with no legal meaning.
Village of origin and the quality level. The critical descriptor about what is in the bottle in a wine from Europe.
The vineyard site. This feature establishes *terroir;* the grape variety is not given.
The legal quality level denoting origin in France.
FRANCE

Consequently, your paramount rule should be to drink what you want with whatever you choose to eat, as long as the wine is a good one. As noted Australian wine producer and expert Len Evans has said, "Life is too short to drink bad wine." I have drunk white wine with roast lamb, which goes against every rule of food and wine matching and, while it was not my normal choice, it was a perfectly palatable, if unexciting, match.

Another suggestion that may help match food and wine is to balance weight with weight. So a lighter-bodied wine will be preferable with seafood and very light cold meats, a medium-bodied wine will be better with fish and less fatty meats, and a full-bodied wine will complement heavier dishes such as casseroles and roasts. As for the color of the wine, some people will only drink red or white with their meal, and not both. Critically, however, it is often the sauce or key seasonings rather than the main component of the dish that should be considered when selecting the wine.

Wine and food pairing has evolved naturally in Europe over many millennia. The reason rosé wines are popular in Provence, for example, is because, despite the fact that region historically produces full-bodied red wines, the locals need something to go with their bouillabaisse.

Food and wine generally go together well. Wine is an aid to digestion, and its acidity and tannin can complement the process of eating. Some foods clash with certain wines, but often there is a general symbiosis between them. Yet the great matches—where the two just meld into each other—seem to happen by accident. You may have an idea that a particular dish and a selected wine will generally work together, but sometimes by chance they just seem predestined to go with each other. Enjoy it when it happens—it is serendipity.

Australian and New Zealand wines displaying their awards.

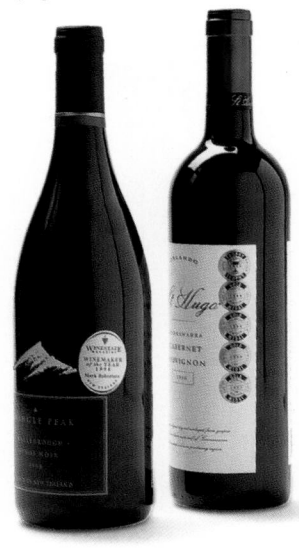

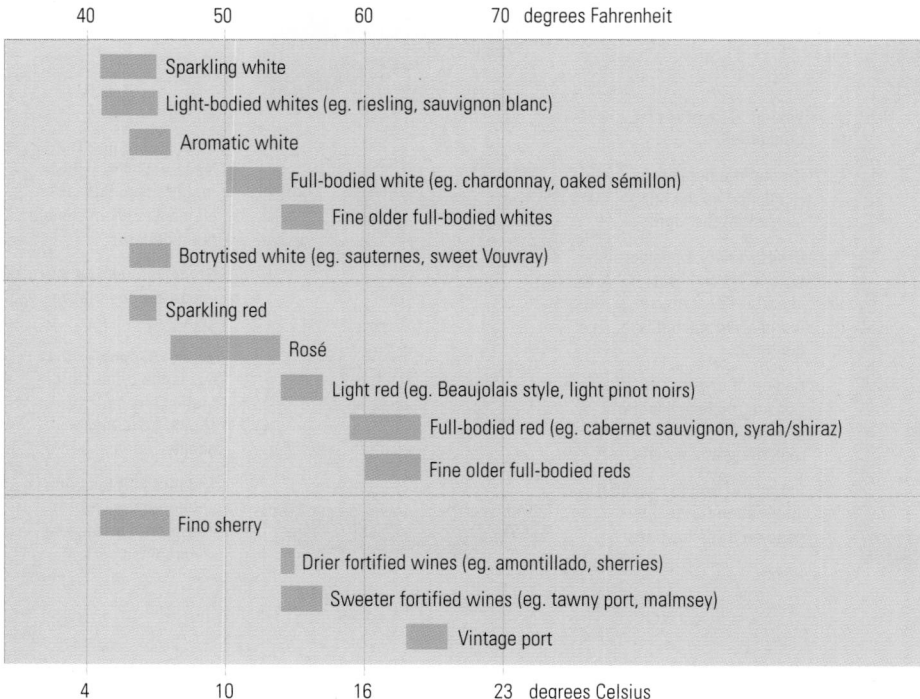

IDEAL TEMPERATURES FOR SERVING WINE

degrees Fahrenheit
40   50   60   70

Sparkling white
Light-bodied whites (eg. riesling, sauvignon blanc)
Aromatic white
Full-bodied white (eg. chardonnay, oaked sémillon)
Fine older full-bodied whites
Botrytised white (eg. sauternes, sweet Vouvray)

Sparkling red
Rosé
Light red (eg. Beaujolais style, light pinot noirs)
Full-bodied red (eg. cabernet sauvignon, syrah/shiraz)
Fine older full-bodied reds

Fino sherry
Drier fortified wines (eg. amontillado, sherries)
Sweeter fortified wines (eg. tawny port, malmsey)
Vintage port

degrees Celsius
4   10   16   23

Serving wine

CHILLING

Critical to enjoying wine is the temperature at which it should be served. In general today, we have a tendency to serve our white wines too cold on the basis that, like beer, they should refresh. Unfortunately, too cool a temperature deadens flavor and aroma. Conversely, we often serve our red wines too warm. The maxim that they should be at room temperature was established before the age of central heating or the move of the English-speaking world en masse into warm places like Australia. The following are the suggested ideal temperatures for the service of different wines. In the case of some of the red wines in particular, it means that 20 minutes in the refrigerator to take the warmth off may be a good idea.

Chilling wine in the refrigerator for too many days will dull its character. Keeping wine cool is important, but it should not be too cold. It can be returned to the refrigerator after opening, or an ice bucket or vacuum cooler will do the trick. As the wine warms up a little, the aromas are released, and the wine opens up. Too

Extracting the cork (though it is easier with the bottle on a table!).

warm, however, and the aromas dissipate too much because the alcohol is evaporating too readily. Chilling, meanwhile, reduces the apparent activity of acidity, as well as the activity of carbon dioxide, thus making sparkling wines appear less aggressive and maintaining their fizz for longer.

UNCORKING

The conventional corkscrew comes in all shapes and sizes. About the only rule is that it should be a complete spiral rather than a central column with a flanged screw around it because that will tend to push cork into the wine. "Waiters' friends" are simple, but not always the easiest to use. It is worth buying a corkscrew you feel happy with, even if it is a bit more expensive because you may be using it regularly for many years. A foil cutter that removes the capsule easily is also an excellent investment. For those whose bank balance allows them to drink older wines regularly, a corkscrew that can deal with decaying corks is helpful. The style which consists of two long thin metal blades that slip down between the cork and the neck of the bottle does this particularly well.

Surprisingly, many people do not know how to uncork sparkling wine. For safety, as well as wine enjoyment, never shake a bottle of sparkling wine before opening it: at best, you will waste what is in the bottle; at worst, you are increasing the pressure on the cork, which could be dangerous. Likewise, never pry the cork open and let it pop into the air: eyes have been lost in this way. Instead, having removed the muzzle, grip the cork and gently twist it from the neck. Conventional wisdom is to hold the base of the bottle, but it is often easier to grip the neck. Hold the bottle at a 45° angle while you do this and the cork should escape with the faintest hiss of escaping gas and no loss of precious liquid. (Note that the pressure on Australian sparkling red wines can be a bit higher, so take particular care with them.)

DECANTING

The next ritual of wine is decanting. Generally, one would only decant red wines, and mainly old red wines that have thrown a deposit or sediment. No one wants a glass tainted by gritty particles, so to pour off the wine carefully, leaving half an inch or so (a centimeter or two) in the bottom with the sediment. The bottle should be left to stand for a while to allow the deposit to collect at its base before you do this, and then opened very gently to avoid disturbance.

You do not need a cut-glass decanter for this operation. An empty bottle—well rinsed in hot but soapless water—will do. You can then empty and rinse the original bottle and return the wine to it for service.

Decanting also has the benefit of blowing off the wine the temporary "bottle stink" that many wines develop with age, making them more immediately attractive before they get to the glass.

With very old wines you should only decant immediately before service, otherwise what is left of the fruit aromas may dissipate very fast and the wine could lose its appeal. Wines of moderate age (say, six to 15 years old, depending on variety and vintage) will benefit from decanting about 30 minutes before service.

The second reason to decant wines attracts some controversy. A few wine lovers think that young red wines benefit from decanting an hour or so before drinking. This speeds the development of the wine by oxygen which normally takes some years in the bottle. Decanting in this way does not replicate the aging process precisely, but it does integrate and soften the wine, making it more attractive. However, the weight of expert opinion is against it, saying it is better to allow the wine to develop in the glass. What is of no use is pulling the cork and standing the bottle, allowing the wine to "breathe." This has been conclusively shown to have no impact on the wine, as the surface area of wine in the neck of the bottle is too small to change its character.

SAMPLING WINE

Commonly, before wine is shared, the person who is offering it will first pour a small sample and smell it. This is not a meaningless ritual, but essential to ensure the wine is in good condition—particularly that it is not maderized or subject to cork taint.

What happens if you do not finish the wine? It is not true that the alcohol in wine will keep it fresh for some time. Some wines (aromatic whites and *fino* sherries) may keep in the fridge for 24 hours, but no longer. Full-bodied whites and reds may keep for another day (some young reds actually improve if opened and kept overnight). More full-bodied fortified wines may keep for a few days, or maybe a week, but even a tawny port (made with long-term oxygen contact) will not remain fresh for long. If you like having a wine open to sip occasionally, then choose madeira. After the heating process, bacterial development

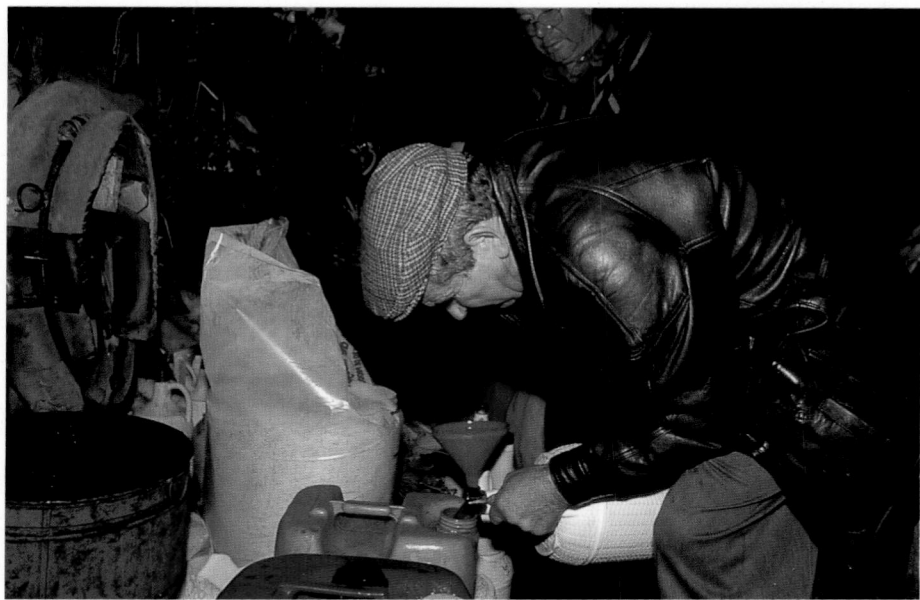

Traditional distribution methods. "Bottling" in plastic containers for home consumption from a small winery in Portugal.

and aging with air contact, no other "damage" can really occur. It is also a wonderful and much misunderstood drink.

Wine faults

Many faults can affect wine, though with modern methods of analysis, good hygiene and a careful scientific approach to winemaking these should now be minimized. It is worthwhile being aware of some of the major problems that occur so that, if faced with a bottle showing a fault, it can be replaced. Too many people drink faulty wines without enjoying them and without realizing it should be poured down the sink.

Cork taint This fault is entirely outside the control of winemakers and is the bane of their lives. Essentially, a mold that occasionally exists in the cork combines with chlorine compounds (which may come from the cork processor, or the winery, or may just be in the air). The resulting chemical gives the wine a moldy smell, like wet hessian or damp cardboard, and usually destroys its fruit flavors. Unfortunately, it does not always appear in a clear-cut form. It may occasionally just dull the wine, rather than completely ruin it, making it hard for even the most experienced taster to decide whether or not it is faulty.

Excess sulfur dioxide This used to plague many European wines, especially sweet ones. Sulfur dioxide is necessary to maintain freshness in the wine, but if added to excess it can give a burnt match character to the smell, and dull the fruit. A few minutes to let the wine breathe—especially by swirling it around in the glass—should help the fault blow off.

Wine paraphernalia & glassware

The glassware in which the wine is served is critical. There was a fashion a few years ago to serve wine in small heavy water glasses. Nothing could be more designed to spoil the effect. These days, many glass producers make a living persuading aficionados that their glass, or series of glasses, is essential to the better enjoyment of wine. Often they are right, but even for those who cannot afford US$50 for a single glass, it is possible to improve one's enjoyment of wine if you stick to a few simple rules.

The ideal glass should have a tapering shape, narrower at the top than the base, to concentrate the aromas. It should be comparatively wide for red wines, to let air contact develop the wine, but less so for whites, where preserving the delicate aromatic quality is essential

BORDEAUX GLASS

A tall glass with a large bowl, designed to aid air contact with the wine, which should enhance the development of the wine in the glass; ideal for big, tannic wines.

DRIP STOPPER

A metal ring with a felt lining, which fits over the neck of an opened bottle, catching any drops as the wine is poured.

WINE CRADLE

A container that holds a bottle at an angle, encouraging the deposit that forms in older red wines to settle at the bottom of the bottle.

WHITE BURGUNDY GLASS

Intended primarily for full-bodied whites, like chardonnay, it has a smaller bowl than a red wine glass, limiting air contact and preserving the wine's aromatic quality.

SYRAH/SHIRAZ GLASS

Similar to the bordeaux glass in size and purpose—the large bowl allows the wine to be swilled easily, making it easier to smell.

STOPPER

An elaborate cork with a crest intended to stopper bottles repeatedly. Of more design than functional importance.

WAITER'S FRIEND

A corkscrew that also has a foil cutter (and sometimes a bottle top remover). The corkscrew operates with a lever that clips over the top of the bottle giving leverage for extraction of the cork.

WINGED CORKSCREW

Designed with a central screw that twists into the cork easily, raising the "arms" of the corkscrew as it goes. The cork is then extracted by pulling the arms down.

to enjoying the wine. It should not be made of cut glass, which distorts the appearance of the wine, but otherwise it helps the process of enjoyment if it is esthetically appealing. The narrower the rim, the better the quality of glass and the delivery of wine to the mouth. For sparkling wines, the tall flute is ideal for preserving both their fizz and delicate aromas. Never use a flat coupe.

An efficient corkscrew and good glassware are essential items. A decanter and cooler are useful too, and a neck thermometer may be a help. Beyond that ice jackets, wine preservers, aerators and the like are only for the most dedicated.

BEAUJOLAIS GLASS
Intended for fruity, less tannic reds; curved so that little development occurs in the glass from air contact, and the aromatic nature of the wine is preserved.

DECANTER
An attractive cut-glass container into which older red wines can be poured, to allow them to breathe, and to leave gritty deposit in the bottle, so it does not get poured into glasses.

RED BURGUNDY GLASS
Half-way between the bordeaux glass (for big, tannic reds) and the beaujolais glass (fruity reds). This gives some air contact for older wines, but doesn't let the ethereal aromas be dissipated quickly.

SPARKLING WINE STOPPER
Designed to clip onto the flange at the top of a bottle of sparkling wine, so it is not blown off by the gas pressure. It inhibits fizz from escaping.

CHAMPAGNE FLUTE
Tall and thin, not to enhance the appearance of the bubbles, but to slow their dissipation into the air.

RIESLING GLASS
Small and narrow, to protect the aromas of the most delicate aromatic white wines.

CHAMPAGNE CORK EXTRACTOR
Intended to give a grip on stubborn corks in sparkling wine bottles and ease their removal.

SMALL TASTING GLASSES
Designed for taking small samples of wine purely for tasting purpose; but it could also double as a glass for fortified wines.

SPARKLING WINE STOPPER

Sulfur compounds These can form either from residual sulfur in the vineyard or, more usually, as part of the process of fermentation, giving a "rotten egg" stink from hydrogen sulfide. At that stage, the problem can be easily cured. Unfortunately, if it is allowed to continue in the closed environment of a barrel, mercaptans may develop. These impart a foul garlic smell to the wine that cannot be removed.

Volatile acidity Few bacteria can survive in wine, but one that can (so long as oxygen is present) is acetobacter. This creates acetic acid (vinegar) which will not harm a wine in small doses (it may even add to its complexity), but in larger amounts gives the wine a sharp smell and a hard, bitter acid finish. It is easy to prevent—good hygiene, keeping the wine away from oxygen and dosing with small amounts of sulfur dioxide will inhibit bacterial activity. Once it exists, however, it cannot be eradicated.

Caskiness Sometimes a wine will smell or taste (on the finish) a bit woody or casky. A slightly unclean barrel or a faulty filter pad are among the causes for this. But there is no excuse for poor winemaking, and the wine should be returned.

Storage

Sooner or later, anyone who develops a love for wine wants to keep a few bottles lying around. With time, those "few bottles" become a few cases—as we decide to buy wine young so that it can age, and we can see how it develops. When those few cases expand into a few more, the issue arises about where and how to store it. There are a few basic rules about storage:

Temperature Having a cool temperature to store wine is not as important as having a steady one, without much variation. Overt heat, and fluctuations, will accelerate the aging process and, at extremes, will damage the wine. A maximum temperature for mid-term storage is about 64°F (18°C); for the longer term, about 57°F (14°C) is best. Cellars are genuinely ideal, giving a constant cool, but not freezing, temperature. But even good wines have been kept for a few months in the heat of the Australian summer without undue harm.

Light Ultraviolet light can harm wines, giving it vegetal characters. For this reason, wine is usually bottled in green or brown glass, but even then it should be kept away from light sources for long-term storage.

Vibration Movement is thought to damage wine, though the scientific understanding of this is imperfect. However, it is best to minimize movement of wine that is stored.

Position Bottles should be stored horizontally to keep the cork moist. This stops the cork from shrinking, thus keeping out air that could accelerate the oxidization process. (This does not apply to sparkling wine.)

Meeting all these conditions can be difficult if you have limited space. One option is commercial storage facilities, which often have wine stores. There are also specially chilled storage chambers, much like fridges. Some providers will even build a cellar into your garage floor, based on a spiral stairway. Whatever you do, never buy expensive wine to age and keep it in warm conditions for years on end in the hope that it will survive. It won't, and you will have wasted a lot of money.

A FINAL WORD: VINTAGES AND VINTAGE CHARTS

The term "vintage" does not describe a special wine—it merely means the year the grapes were picked. Almost all wines (except blended champagne and fortified wines) are therefore likely to be vintage wine.

Given the impact of the weather on grape quality (especially in more marginal climates, like those of Germany, Burgundy, Oregon or Tasmania), and therefore on the resulting wine, it should be clear that some years will make better wine than others. Part of the lore of connoisseurship involves learning by rote the good and the bad years, to avoid making embarrassing mistakes.

It is customary in reference books on wine to publish a chart giving the best, worst and moderate years for many of the classic areas of wine production in the world. However, there are

Below: *Corks come from the bark of a species of oak tree mainly grown in Portugal, Spain and North Africa.*

Bottom: *Corks designed to hold sulphur pellets. The pellets burn in barrels to sterilize it, but the amount used has to be carefully controlled.*

problems with this. The main one is that such charts are so general that they ignore the particular details of a specific year or producer. Wine—and especially the production of quality wine—is nothing if not individual.

For example, the year 1983 in the Medoc is treated with reservation and graded as worse than 1982. However, apart from the south of the region, around Margaux, it was actually a rather better year than the previous one, with some very attractive wines. A simple vintage chart would fail to register this point. More particularly, even within a small area such as a *commune* like Margaux, whether because of site, mesoclimate or winemaking technique, there will be some producers who will make great wine in poor vintages, or fail in an otherwise great year.

Additionally, a broad approach of marking vintages fails to be precise about what went wrong or why. In the 1980s the two vintages of 1984 and 1987 are generally considered to be the poorest. In 1984 it was because of poor weather at flowering—which especially harmed the development of merlot. In 1987 it was because of rain late in the vintage which ruined the cabernet crop. However, some growers made fair, if not great wine in that year, with some ripe and fruity merlot. At the same time, because of the run of other excellent vintages in the early and mid-1980s some producers were now more capital-rich than three years earlier. Some of their money was invested in equipment which enabled them to mitigate the worst aspects of rot and underripeness. So although in climatic terms both years were bad, the wines made in 1987 were nevertheless drinkable over the short term.

Assessment of vintages also changes with time and it is usually wise to be cautious with any chart confidently detailing recent years. After a string of years with great summers at the end of the 1980s, the 1991 vintage in Bordeaux was declared a disaster. However, this perspective had to be modified a few years later when the even more variable 1992 and wet vintage of 1993 offered greener and less fruity wines. At the same time, to return to our initial caveat, there were some producers who made perfectly good wines, and therefore good-value wines, in both of these years.

Above: *Wines from the middle of the last century: 1951 in Burgundy was actually very poor and not worth keeping!*

Top: *Bottles being stored in the correct fashion as they age.*

France

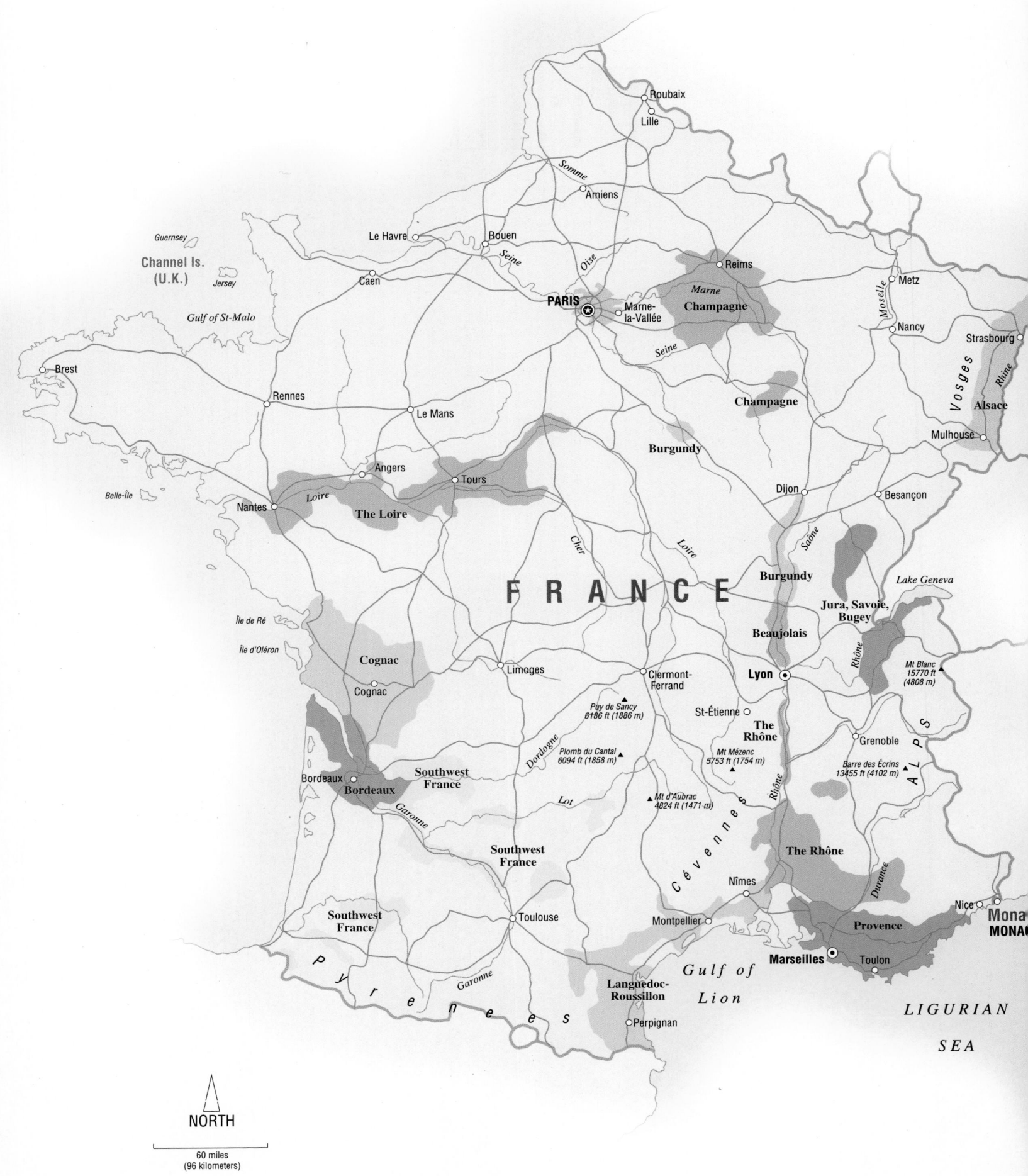

Roubaix
Lille
Somme
Amiens
Guernsey
Channel Is.
(U.K.)
Jersey
Le Havre
Rouen
Reims
Metz
Seine
Marne
Moselle
Caen
PARIS
Marne-
la-Vallée
Champagne
Nancy
Gulf of St-Malo
Seine
Strasbourg
Vosges
Rhine
Rennes
Le Mans
Champagne
Alsace
Mulhouse
Brest
Burgundy
Angers
Tours
Belle-Île
Loire
Dijon
Besançon
Nantes
The Loire
Saône
Cher
Loire
FRANCE
Burgundy
Lake Geneva
Jura, Savoie,
Bugey
Île de Ré
Beaujolais
Rhône
Île d'Oléron
Cognac
Limoges
Clermont-
Ferrand
Lyon
Mt Blanc
15770 ft
(4808 m)
Cognac
Puy de Sancy
6186 ft (1886 m)
St-Étienne
The
Rhône
Grenoble
Barre des Écrins
13455 ft (4102 m)
ALPS
Bordeaux
Plomb du Cantal
6094 ft (1858 m)
Mt Mézenc
5753 ft (1754 m)
Dordogne
Bordeaux
Southwest
France
Mt d'Aubrac
4824 ft (1471 m)
Cévennes
Rhône
Garonne
Lot
Durance
Southwest
France
The Rhône
Nice
Mona
Nîmes
Toulouse
MONA
Southwest
France
Montpellier
Provence
Pyrenees
Garonne
Languedoc-
Roussillon
Marseilles
Toulon
Gulf of
Lion
Perpignan
LIGURIAN
SEA

NORTH

60 miles
(96 kilometers)

France

Few would disagree that, when it comes to wine, France is pre-eminent. It produces more wine than any other country and, despite having the world's second-highest per-capita level of consumption, heads the league table of exporters. But there is more to its status than size.

France was pre-eminent when Italy's output was greater in the early 1990s, and it remains so even though Spain continues to have a larger acreage under vine. Its supremacy rests on the fact that it produces more great wines than any other country; as a consequence, its wines serve as a model for the rest of the world.

This doesn't mean that France produces only wines of enviable quality. Although winemaking standards have improved enormously in the last two decades—control of fermentation temperatures allowing the harvesting of riper grapes, for example— the French continue to be responsible for some very poor wines. This is partly the result of certain cultural factors—mainly the combined forces of complacency and ignorance—but also of the country's highly variable climate.

Corsica
Île de
Beauté
:cio

Appellation rules seek to maintain quality by controlling winemaking procedures.

Landscape and climate

The classic French wine regions—including Bordeaux, Burgundy and Champagne—are all close to the geographical limits of successful vine-growing. In poor years, the grapes just don't see enough sun and warmth to get perfectly ripe. In other years, all might be progressing well when devastating hail tears through the vineyards, as occurred in part of St-Émilion in September 1999, or torrential downpours arrive just before the harvest, as happened in much of the Médoc in the same year.

Yet, to talk of a marginal climate is misleading, for France encompasses an extraordinary range of terrain and weather patterns, which is precisely why its winemaking practices are so complex and its wines so diverse. Bordeaux, for example, on the west coast, has a maritime climate. The prevailing dampness means that disease is a perennial threat, but one such infestation, *Botrytis cinerea* (noble rot), is a boon for the sweet-wine producers of Sauternes. Burgundy, inland to the north and east, is cooler than Bordeaux; so much so that its continental climate, with relatively high rainfall, places it at the northern limit (in the northern hemisphere) for making red wines. But consider those wines: at their best, they have a fragrance, complexity of flavor and silkiness of texture that leaves normally voluble critics speechless. The Loire Valley lies even farther north, but vines still thrive there as a result of the moderating influences of moist Atlantic breezes and the expansive river and its tributaries. In France's most northerly wine region, Champagne, the grapes barely ripen each year, but that's rarely a cause for concern—high-acid, relatively low-sugar grapes are perfect raw material for the finest sparkling wines.

French producers rarely consider climate in isolation, however. What counts is *terroir*, the complete package of soil and subsoil, aspect and altitude, climate and mesoclimate—and any other natural feature that might affect the vines. The soils and geology of French vineyards are at least as varied as the climates. For instance, Burgundy and Jura have limestone, Beaujolais and the northern Rhône sit on granite, Champagne has chalk, the Médoc has gravel, and some of the vine-

yards in Châteauneuf-du-Pape are covered with huge, smooth stones for as far as the eye can see.

No single soil type produces the best wine, but if there is one characteristic that France's finer vineyards share, it is that they tend to be located on poor soils where little else will thrive—in particular, on poor soils on slopes that can retain some water without becoming waterlogged. Thus, in regions such as Alsace, Burgundy and Beaujolais, the best vineyards (often called *crus*) tend to be on the hillsides and the more ordinary vineyards on flatter ground. Similarly, the exciting new *domaines* that have made a name for themselves in Languedoc in the last 20 years are not located on the coastal plains but on the inland *coteaux*, or hills.

As any producer in any one of these regions would tell you, however, these are generalizations. There is no such thing as a single-soil region. As a result, most of the important French winegrowing areas have been divided into subregions based on the characteristics of their *terroirs*. Such distinctions form the basis of France's national classification system, known as *appellation d'origine contrôlée*, often abbreviated to AC or AOC.

Appellations and other classifications

The appellation system was created in 1935, after nearly 30 years of piecemeal and pragmatic legislation, to protect the authenticity of wines and the livelihoods of their producers. It does this by defining boundaries and, within each area, stipulating the permitted grape varieties, yields and alcohol content; cultivation, vinification and maturation practices; and labelling procedures.

Fine distinctions may result in a large number of subregions. In Bordeaux, for example, in addition to the generic Bordeaux appellation, there are 56 smaller appellations. Burgundy, which is less than a quarter the size of Bordeaux, has no fewer than 98 appellations, some of them tiny but nevertheless divided between many owners. That makes it probably the most complex of all French regions.

As far as the consumer is concerned, *appellation d'origine contrôlée* guarantees the origin and style of a wine—at least in theory. What it does not do, in theory or practice, is guarantee quality, and in many appellations, such as generic Bordeaux or Anjou Rosé, the standards are clearly inadequate.

In the past—as recently as ten years ago—it could be said that the tighter the specifications of an individual appellation, the better its wines would be. Now, anyone who toes that line does so with less conviction, simply because the appel-

Many French estates are known as châteaux, *whether or not they incorporate the grand style of residence that the term implies.*

lation authorities, often under the influence of local vested interests, have sometimes shown themselves to be pointlessly, even harmfully, intractable. In Provence, for example, the leading estate, Domaine de Trévallon, was refused appellation status on the grounds that its blend contained "too much" cabernet sauvignon.

Unless the authorities display some commonsense flexibility (as they have done recently in some places, such as Madiran), it can be difficult for dynamic, quality-conscious winemakers to innovate, improve their wines, or even just label them differently—labelling by grape variety, for example, is almost never permitted for appellation wines (with the exception of AC Alsace, where the practice is traditional and where there is only one principal appellation). This state of affairs has led some producers to opt for the less prestigious but much less restrictive *vin de pays* (VDP) classification. This was created in 1979 as an intermediate category between *vin de table*, the most basic of French wine, and AC. (There is also a small category called *vin délimité de qualité supérieure*, or VDQS, which was intended to be for novice or probationary appellations, but it

dwindles with every promotion to AC.) *Vin de pays* was introduced principally to encourage producers of *vins de table* to raise their standards, especially in the vast Languedoc-Roussillon area in the south, and overall it has worked extremely well, now accounting for three in every ten bottles of French wine. These include wines labelled by grape variety, or *vins de cépages* as they are known locally. The French tend to be dismissive of varietal wines, insisting that wine is much more than mere grapes—it is *terroir*—but recently they have had to acknowledge that these wines are commercially successful. So *vins de pays* such as Chardonnay Vin de Pays d'Oc now compete with varietal wines from countries like Australia, Chile and Argentina, and have become one of the recent success stories of French wine.

As complicated and absurd as it may sometimes appear, *appellation d'origine contrôlée* is not all bad. If it were, you can be sure it would not have spawned so many similar appellation systems around the world. Furthermore, it has played a critical role in protecting the identity and reputation of French wines, both at home and overseas.

Joanna Simon

France's wide range of climates and soil result in a diversity of wine styles.

A bottle of Veuve Clicquot La Grande Dame
sits on ice, in preparation for serving.

Champagne

Ken Gargett & Peter Forrestal

Champagne's effervescent charm has conquered the globe. Whenever a celebration of any sort takes place in the modern world, you can be certain that the sound of champagne corks popping will not be far away. Weddings, births, anniversaries, victories of any nature whatsoever—all call for a bottle of the world's best bubbly.

Champagne originates from the province of same name in northeastern France, which lies just 100 miles (160 km) east of Paris. It encompasses the five departments of Marne, Haute-Marne, Seine-et-Marne, Aisne and Aube, and centers on the towns of Reims and Épernay, where most of the champagne houses are based. This region has been producing wine for hundreds of years, but it was only in the seventeenth century that the natural process that gives rise to the bubbles began to be understood, and only in the nineteenth century that sparkling wine became Champagne's principal product. Over the past 300 years, the procedure for making champagne has evolved and gradually been refined. Today, only wines made following the local appellation laws and originating in the viticultural region of Champagne are allowed to use that name.

History

It is likely that wine was first made in Champagne during the Roman occupation of the region in the middle of the first century AD. Emperor Domitian perceived the local producers as such a threat to the vignerons of Italy that he ordered the vineyards of Gaul to be destroyed in AD 92. This ban on grape growing remained in place until AD 282, when it was lifted by the Emperor Probus. The vineyards of Champagne could not, therefore, have become well-established until the fourth century AD. Yet even at this early stage of the area's development, the wines were considered among the best in the Empire. The discovery of flute-like glasses (the shape best suited to retaining the bubbles) dating to Gallo-Roman times indicates that the early Champenois winemakers might have been used to a slight sparkle in their wines. However, even if this is true, it is unlikely that it was the result of any conscious effort.

The fall of the Roman Empire and the subsequent political instability in western Europe caused significant disruption to life in Champagne between the fifth and tenth centuries. In spite of this, the region's vineyards continued to build a reputation for quality wines, due in large part to the involvement of the monastries in the winegrowing industry. Pope Urban II, pontiff from 1088–99, declared that there was never a better wine than that produced in Aÿ—although, given that he was a Champenois, he might just have been a little biased. In the *Bataille des Vins*, written around 1200, Henri d'Andelys rated the wines of Épernay, Reims and Hautvillers among the best in Europe.

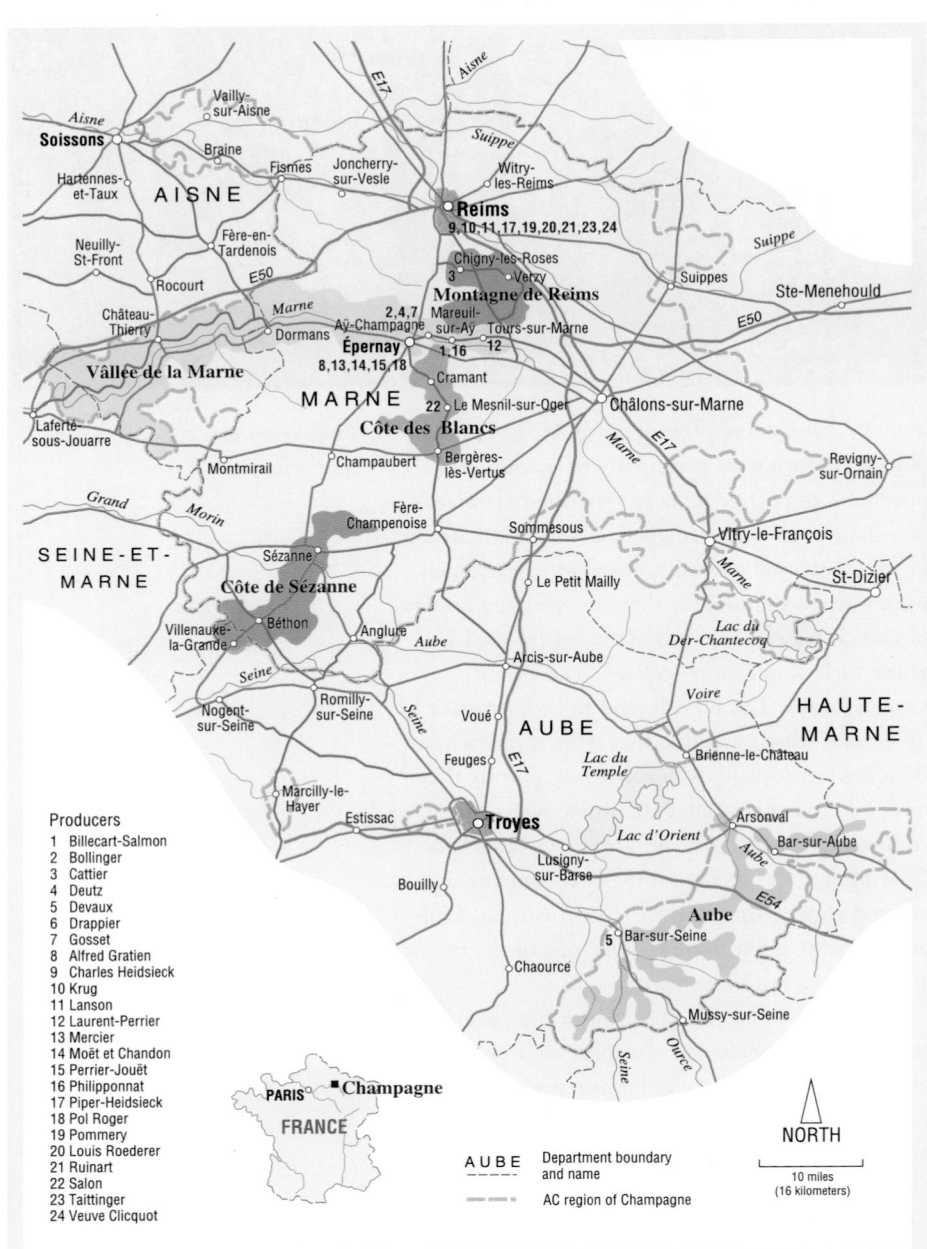

Producers
1 Billecart-Salmon
2 Bollinger
3 Cattier
4 Deutz
5 Devaux
6 Drappier
7 Gosset
8 Alfred Gratien
9 Charles Heidsieck
10 Krug
11 Lanson
12 Laurent-Perrier
13 Mercier
14 Moët et Chandon
15 Perrier-Jouët
16 Philipponnat
17 Piper-Heidsieck
18 Pol Roger
19 Pommery
20 Louis Roederer
21 Ruinart
22 Salon
23 Taittinger
24 Veuve Clicquot

AUBE   Department boundary and name

    AC region of Champagne

NORTH

10 miles
(16 kilometers)

In the first half of the sixteenth century, Pope Leo X, Charles V of Spain, François I of France and Henry VIII of England all owned vineyards in Champagne. A batch of *vin d'Aÿ* sent to Henry VIII's chancellor, Cardinal Wolsey, in 1518, was the first recorded shipment of wine from Champagne to England. Henri IV became the first French king to introduce wine from Champagne to his court. The export trade, which flourished during his reign (1589–1610), encouraged producers to improve their techniques of viticulture and vinification. At this time, the wines were mainly red table wines, similar to those of Burgundy but lighter in both body and color. Such was their reputation, however, that they commanded higher prices than Burgundy wines.

The first country to develop a taste for sparkling wine was England. During the period following the Restoration of 1660, the young wines of Champagne were much in demand there. They were usually shipped in barrels during winter, by which time the cold Champagne climate had arrested fermentation before the grape sugars converted to alcohol and before malolactic fermentation occurred. Once spring arrived, however, the wine, by now transferred to bottles, would warm again and the yeasts would be reactivated. Fermentation would then restart, producing carbonic gas. In France, this usually caused the bottle to open or shatter; in England, however, cork stoppers and much stronger glass were already in widespread use. The wine could therefore develop further, creating more gas—and a style of wine that was much appreciated by the locals.

It is likely that the process of secondary fermentation also began to be understood in France soon afterward, probably by several producers, although the discovery is traditionally attributed to one of the great figures in the history of wine, Dom Pérignon. Contrary to legend, he did not invent champagne; indeed, it is likely that he deliberately attempted to prevent his wine from bubbling. However, his contributions were highly significant. He introduced cork stoppers to France from Spain, and he may also have led the way in the use of strong English glass (*verre anglais*), a version of which was manufactured in his birthplace, Ste-Menehoulde. He also pioneered the art of blending and was the first to make a white wine from black grapes. The first notable producer of champagne, as we know it, was Ruinart, founded in 1729 (though Gosset had been producing still wine since at least 1584 and remains the oldest Champagne

Fall colors swathe the elegant exterior of a residence in the town of Épernay.

house operating today). Others were established soon afterward, including the houses now known as Taittinger in 1734, Moët et Chandon in 1743 and Veuve Clicquot in 1772.

Yet for a long period the still wines of Champagne remained in greater demand. This situation only changed following several technical innovations in the early nineteenth century. From 1806 onward, Madame Clicquot worked on the process of *remuage* (or riddling), which allowed producers to remove the sediment that forms during secondary fermentation without emptying the bottle—the bottles were held upside down so that the sediment collected in the neck and could be removed. In 1818, this procedure was refined by her cellar master Antoine Müller and came into general use. In 1836 and 1837, André François published two important papers describing a reliable method for measuring sugar left in the bottle after primary fermentation. This helped reduce the number of bottles broken by allowing producers to calculate how much sugar and yeast to add to control the development of bubbles. A regular supply of strong glass and good corks also reduced waste, which in turn restrained the selling price of the wine. Demand subsequently grew, and the late nineteenth century was a glorious time for Champagne.

Even when phylloxera struck in the 1890s, the Champenois' strong financial position allowed them to cope with replanting better than most.

The dawn of a new century saw unrest among growers from the Aube district, who had been excluded from Champagne by government decree in 1908 following protests by growers from the Marne region who considered the Aube grapes to be inferior. Simmering discontent erupted in 1911 when 5,000 Aube growers marched on Champagne. Violence ensued and troops had to be called in to restore order. The matter was eventually resolved in 1927 when the Aube was incorporated into the region of Champagne.

The post-phylloxera revival was cut short by the First World War, which ravaged the region; it was followed by the Depression and a second global conflict. One positive development during the middle of the century was the creation of the Comité Interprofessionel du Vin de Champagne (CIVC), which was set up in 1941—intriguingly, with the assistance of the occupying German army—to monitor production methods, implement quality control and eventually promote the local wines.

Since the Second World War, the region has prospered. Recently, the industry has been rationalized and there have been amazing improvements in the yield and quality of the harvest. Yet, at the same time, the distinctive character of champagne remains much as it was in the late nineteenth century.

Champagne bottles are stored in angled racks so that sediment falls into the bottle neck.

Landscape and Climate

Perhaps more than in any other winegrowing area, Champagne's *terroir*—its unique combination of geology, climate, hydrology and environment—directly determines the style of its wine. Champagne lies near the northern limits of the wine-producing world, where the mean annual temperature of 50°F (10°C) is barely sufficient to ripen grapes. Furthermore, Atlantic mildness and continental harshness interact here, creating a highly variable climate that is compounded by the undulating terrain. Only in certain areas do topography, aspect and other factors such as the presence of forests (which stabilize temperatures and supply moisture) create a *terroir* fit for ripening vines. At the same time, these marginal conditions have turned out to be highly appropriate for the production of champagne: the cool temperatures produce high levels of acidity that are perfect for sparkling wine, and subregional variations result in distinctive styles that lend themselves to blending.

By far the most significant influence on the character of the wine is the geological makeup of the soil. Champagne's chalk subsoils originally formed as the floor of an ancient ocean, which retreated about 70 million years ago. Earthquakes 20 and 10 million years ago pushed some of these marine sediments, known as belemnite chalk, to the surface, creating the area's undulating terrain. Most of the land now has a thin layer of surface soil over a deep layer of belemnite chalk (except in the Aube, where the soils are clay), which may be hundreds of feet thick in places.

Belemnite subsoils are thought to be the source of much of the fineness and lightness that characterize champagne. They provide excellent drainage, adequate moisture retention, and—critically in such a marginal climate—absorb heat from the sun by day and slowly release it at night, thereby warming the vines at the coldest time of day.

Vineyards and classifications

The Champenois' determination to protect their famous wine is legendary, and numerous restrictions have been placed on production processes and the use of the name. Recently, these have been tightened in response to challenges from other regions and to counter suggestions that not all champagne is what it should be.

The boundaries of the viticultural area of Champagne were legally defined in 1927. This allowed the appellation to have a size of 84,155 acres (34,057 ha), but in reality only about 76,600 acres (31,000 ha) were available for vineyards—roads, schools and housing occupied much of the rest. By the 1990s, around 71,660 acres (29,000 ha) were under cultivation—almost 2 percent of France's total vineyard area. Very little land suitable for vines now remains in Champagne.

There are five major wine-producing districts: Côte des Blancs, Montagne de Reims and Vallée de la Marne; Côte de Sézanne; and the Aube. These cover more than 300 villages, 261 houses, and 44 cooperatives. Around 5,000 growers make and sell their own wine; another 14,000 sell only grapes.

The top villages in Champagne are ranked as either Grand Cru or Premier Cru, from a system known as the *échelle des crus* ("cru ladder"), introduced in 1919. The very finest villages are deemed to be Grand Cru and awarded an *échelle* of 100 percent. Premier Cru villages receive an *échelle* of between 90 and 99 percent; others are rated as low as 50 percent, though this was modified in 1985 to a minimum of 80 percent. Villages can receive different ratings for different varieties. Following the 1985 reclassification, there were 17 Grand Cru and 38 Premier Cru villages,

although two of the Grand Cru villages were ranked as Premiers Crus for certain grape varieties.

The *échelle* system used to dictate growers' payments. A price would be struck and Grand Cru vineyards would receive 100 percent of that price; others would receive the percentage represented by their village's *échelle*. This method was eroded during the 1990s. A free-market system now operates, but the villages still retain their ratings.

In 1919, laws entitling the Champagne region to its own appellation were passed. Legislation in 1927 made Champagne one of the earliest appellations in France; it is still the only one permitted to omit the phrase *appellation d'origine contrôlée* or the initials AC or AOC from its labels.

Under Champagne appellation rules, up to 673 gallons (2,550 l) of juice from a pressing of 8,820 pounds (4,000 kg) can be used. The first 541 gallons (2,050 l) are the *cuvée*; the nest 132 gallons (500 l) are the *taille*. Till 1992, a second *taille* of a further 44 gallons (166 l) was permitted. Nonvintage wines must spend fifteen months on lees, vintage champagnes three years—better producers usually extend these periods to three and five years respectively. One hundred percent of a vintage wine must come from the stated vintage.

Vines and wines

Only three kinds of grape variety are permitted in Champagne: pinot noir, pinot meunier and chardonnay. Pinot noir makes up 38 percent of plantings. It gives champagne structure, weight, power and backbone, plus a richness of flavor. It does

The vineyards in the commune of Verzenay, near Verzy, are classified as Grand Cru.

Tall glasses known as flutes are designed to preserve the bubbles in champagne.

especially well in the Montagne de Reims and is the most planted variety in the Aube.

Pinot meunier covers 35 percent of the vineyards, and is dominant in the Vallée de la Marne. It is an undervalued grape that few houses admit to using (though most do); it provides fruit flavor in the mid-palate and sometimes a slightly earthy character. It is particularly useful in cold years due to its ripening ability, although there is justifiable concern that it matures too quickly. Chardonnay, which makes up 27 percent of the vineyard (though this percentage increases in the Grands Crus), is the only variety that is used regularly on its own in a champagne, the *blanc de blancs*. At is best, the grape is characterized by elegance, delicacy, finesse and refinement. It also contributes to the acidity of the wine and is essential to the length of the finish. The Côte des Blancs is almost entirely devoted to chardonnay.

Around 80 percent of champagnes are nonvintage blends—which is why the name of the producer rather than the vineyard appears on the label. The Champenois are master blenders, skillfully combining wines from different grapes, vineyards and vintages. This is a clear case of necessity being the mother of invention, as over the years local producers had to use blending to deal with the vagaries of the climate and the limited output of most growers. Wine from a poor vintage can be turned into an outstanding product by blending with wines from superior vintages. In doing so, the blenders add their own signatures to the wines and create house styles.

Because the *terroir* is so variable, grape varieties will have different characteristics when they are grown in different vineyards. This can be useful in creating a blend; for example, chardonnay grown on the Côte des Blancs has a steely backbone, yet on the Montagne de Reims and in some parts of the Vallée de Marne it produces a much fuller wine.

Around 1870, some houses started bottling particularly good years separately, thus creating

Only chardonnay, pinot noir and pinot meunier can be planted in Champagne.

vintage champagnes. Today, these are released, on average, four or five times a decade. Other styles of champagne include rosé, *blanc de blancs*, and the unusual *blanc de noirs*, which is made only from black grapes. Most houses also issue prestige *cuvées*, a practice that began when Moët et Chandon released the 1921 Dom Pérignon in 1937. The Champagne region also makes small quantities of still reds, rosés and whites, as well as ratafia and eaux-de-vie.

Winemaking

Each year, the CIVC declares the date when the harvest can commence, usually a day in the middle of September. Only handpicking is permitted, and presshouses are located near the vineyards to minimize oxidation. Whole grapes are pressed, often using traditional vertical presses, though more modern airbag presses are becoming more common. The juice then goes through *débourbage*, or settling out, normally achieved by cooling but sometimes involving filtration or centrifuging. This is followed by fermentation with natural or cultivated yeasts, either in stainless steel or oak. In most cases, the wine then undergoes malolactic fermentation, which softens its acidity.

After racking, the *assemblage*, or blending, takes place. To ensure that the nonvintage blend is consistent and reflects the house style, the cellar master will draw on a large supply of reserve wines from previous vintages stored for this purpose.

After the blend is bottled, the *liqueur de tirage* (a solution of yeast and sugar) is added to initiate secondary fermentation. The bottles are then sealed with a crown cap or the traditional agrafe cork and placed in cellars to spend time on lees and build complexity prior to *remuage* and disgorgement. During *remuage*, which may be carried out manually or using machines known as gyropalettes, the dead yeast cells are slowly worked down to the top of the inverted bottle, which is then dipped in freezing brine. As soon as the cap is removed, the frozen plug of sediment flies out (the *dégorgement*, or disgorgement). A small quantity of wine plus sugar (the *liqueur d'expedition*) is then added, with the amount of sugar determining the eventual sweetness of the champagne. Levels range from brut (very dry) through extra sec (dry), sec (semisweet, despite its name) and demisec (sweet) to doux (very sweet). Finally, the champagne cork is inserted—all this takes place very quickly—and the bottle is ready for labelling, transportation and sale.

Producers

BILLECART-SALMON

Established 1818 *Owner* NA *Production* 60,000 cases
Vineyard area 25 acres (10 ha)

Billecart-Salmon is a small house whose distinctive products have established a niche at the top end of the champagne market. The wines are fine and delicate, and age very well—the result of reducing the temperature during fermentation to prolong the process. The flagship Cuvée N. F. Billecart shows great finesse, subtlety and intensity, and a gentle, persistent finish. Billecart produces a greater percentage of rosé than most houses and its fresh, gentle style has proved highly successful.

BOLLINGER

Established 1829 *Owner* NA *Production* 100,000 cases
Vineyard area 356 acres (144 ha)

The favorite tipple of everyone from James Bond to the Ab Fab set, Bollinger champagnes are among the most impressive available. The style is distinctive: rich, complex and heavily reliant on pinot. The prestige R.D. (*récemment dégorgé*) is effectively the vintage wine (Grande Année) given additional time on lees to develop further complexity. The Grande Année is also mixed with still

pinot noir to produce a very powerful rosé that can sometimes, however, seem out of balance. The rare Vieilles Vignes Françaises is an exceptionally rich, powerful and complex 100 percent pinot noir made from nongrafted bush vines.

CATTIER

Established 1763 *Owner* NA *Production* 35,000 cases
Vineyard area 45 acres (18 ha)

For many years, this small Chigny-les-Roses producer sold its grapes to the major houses, but it has recently gained a strong reputation for its own charming wines. The Clos du Moulin, which comes from one of the few remaining *clos* (walled vineyards) in Champagne, is a blend of three vintages (indicated on the label). Because this wine is disgorged to order, it often sees up to ten years on lees; this contributes to its soft, toasty, warm-biscuit characters. The Brut and Rosé exhibit red berry flavors; the vintage wines are similar but fuller.

DEUTZ

Established 1838 *Owner* Louis Roederer *Production* 75,000 cases *Vineyard area* 104 acres (42 ha)

The Aÿ-based house of Deutz came under the control of Louis Roederer in 1993. Since then, it has curtailed much of its international expansion and

The house of Bollinger is the source of some of the world's most prestigious champagnes.

This monument at the house of Moët et Chandon commemorates one of the great figures in Champagne's history, Dom Pérignon.

DOM PERIGNON
1638 – 1715
CELLERIER DE L'ABBAYE D'HAUTVILLERS
DONT LE CLOITRE ET LES GRANDS VIGNOBLES
SONT LA PROPRIETE DE LA MAISON
MOËT CHANDON

concentrated on regaining its previously high standards. Deutz champagnes are mid-weight wines with great clarity of flavor. The vintage *blanc de blancs* exhibits a fresh citrus flavor when young, while the flagship wine, Cuvée William Deutz, which uses only the finest-quality fruit, displays greater complexity. The Cuvée William Deutz Rosé, considered one of the region's finest rosés, is full-flavored and especially well balanced.

DEVAUX

Established 1967 *Owner* Cooperative of 800 members
Production 200,000 cases *Vineyard area* 2,965 acres
(1,200 ha)

This massive cooperative, which formed when 12 smaller cooperatives merged, quickly established itself as the Aube's leading producer. It now operates out of immaculate facilities at Bar-sur-Seine. Although the wines usually reflect the ripeness that is a hallmark of Aube fruit, their quality has helped lift the area's profile. The range includes a vintage *blanc de blancs*, a rare, nonvintage *blanc de noirs* and one of the few Rosé des Riceys produced in the appellation. In 1987, Devaux was involved in setting up Yarrabank, a quality sparkling-wine producer in Australia's Yarra Valley.

DRAPPIER

Established 1808 *Owner* NA *Production* 60,000 cases
Vineyard area 87 acres (35 ha)

This small, independent Aube producer first came to notice when General De Gaulle declared its champagne to be his favorite. Today, Drappier's

fame is based solely on the quality of its output and its reasonable prices, which in turn have done much to improve the reputation of the Aube. Both the nonvintage and vintage champagnes bearing the Carte d'Or Brut label reflect the ripeness associated with the district. The single-vineyard, old-vine Grand Sendrée, is full-flavored and quickly builds in toasty richness; it is often the Aube's finest wine.

GOSSET

Established 1584 *Owner* Rémy-Cointreau *Production* 50,000 cases *Vineyard area* 30 acres (12 ha)

Gosset has an even longer history, albeit as a maker of still wines, than Ruinart (generally considered to be the oldest champagne producer) and remained in family hands until as recently as 1994, when it was sold to Rémy-Cointreau. The Grand Reserve shows more power and depth than the slightly sweet Brut Excellence, but the stars here are the vintage wines, including the recently introduced Célebris and the muscular Grand Millésime. Occasionally, Gosset produces special releases, such as the gloriously rich Quatrième Centenaire. The packaging is always fabulous.

ALFRED GRATIEN

Established 1864 *Owners* Gratien, Meyer, Seydoux and Cie
Production 12,000 cases *Vineyard area* None

Gratien wines tend to have higher acidity than most when young, and they develop complexity with age while retaining freshness. To achieve this, the winemakers ferment their wines in small barrels and avoid malolatic fermentation. The

Krug wines are fermented in large oak casks.

SEGUIN MOREAU
KRUG & Cᵒ REIMS
MA

recent addition of a flagship wine, Cuvée Paradis, reveals a change of direction for the house, with a higher percentage of chardonnay producing a more delicate style. Gratien also makes sparkling Saumur from the Loire Valley.

CHARLES HEIDSIECK

Established 1785 *Owner* Rémy-Cointreau *Production* 170,000 cases *Vineyard area* 74 acres (30 ha)

Substantial investment in a state-of-the-art winery and a far-sighted policy of building significant stocks of reserve wines (under the direction of winemaker, Daniel Thibault) have dramatically improved the quality of Charles Heidsieck produce during the past decade. The full-flavored and intense nonvintage wines are now labelled as "Mis en Cave" ("placed in cellar") and display the year in which they were bottled—for the first time anywhere, customers now know the bottle age of a nonvintage wine. Heidsieck's prestige champagne is now the intensely flavored, 100 percent chardonnay Blanc de Millénaires which is 12 to 15 years old on release yet displays a youthful vibrancy along with its more mature characters.

KRUG

Established 1843 *Owner* LVMH *Production* 50,000 cases *Vineyard area* 49 acres (20 ha)

Although ownership of this house passed from the family to Rémy-Cointreau and thence to LVMH (in 1999), the company is still managed by brothers Henri and Rémi Krug. The Krugs are traditionalists who ferment in 54-gallon (205-l) oak casks and allow no malolactic fermentation or filtration. Substantial reserves enable them to blend close to 50 wines from numerous vintages to produce their monumental Grande Cuvée. Vintage Krug is one of the world's great wines, exhibiting delicacy and finesse with a tight structure, steely backbone, great richness and depth of flavor, power and complexity. The classy and expensive 100 percent chardonnay Clos du Mesnil, with its creamy texture and underlying strength, is a rarity, as it comes from a single, walled vineyard.

LANSON

Established 1760 *Owner* Marne et Champagne *Production* 500,000 cases *Vineyard area* None

When LVMH sold Lanson in 1991, they retained its extensive vineyards, so this grand family business survives only as a label for the region's second-largest producer, Marne et Champagne. However, the quality of the wines remains impressive; in

fact, they are probably better than ever. Lanson wines do not go through malolactic fermentation and so may appear austere when young, but they develop complexity and power with time. Vintage Lanson has complex, nutty, yeasty characters, is full-bodied and firm on the finish.

LAURENT-PERRIER

Established 1812 *Owners* de Nonancourt family *Production* 500,000 cases *Vineyard area* 260 acres (105 ha)

At the end of the Second World War, Laurent-Perrier's output was insignificant, but following the arrival of Bernard de Nonancourt its fortunes improved dramatically. This is now not only one of the region's major producers, it also owns several other champagne houses including Salon (see below). The wines are superb: the nonvintage is crisp, clean and balanced; the Ultra Brut, which has gained a cult following, is searingly dry but softens significantly when accompanied by food. The flagship Grand Siècle (first released in 1957) is a blend of three outstanding vintages; it is fresh, fragrant, lively, powerful and steely, with impressive complexity and weight as well as great intensity and depth of flavor. A single-vintage Grand Siècle is occasionally released on the American market.

MERCIER

Established 1858 *Owner* LVMH *Production* 500,000 cases *Vineyard area* (225 ha)

It surprises many people to discover what a huge seller Mercier is in its homeland, for it is difficult to find outside France. Founder Eugene Mercier pioneered the marketing of champagne, developing the giant barrels used in his publicity and creating the world's first champagne film commercial. Mercier originally owned the Dom Pérignon label, but gave it to Moët et Chandon when a Mercier married a Chandon-Moët. Mercier wines tend to be at the ripe end of the spectrum and often represent excellent value. The Brut is an easy-drinking style, and the better vintages can be full-flavored.

MOËT ET CHANDON

Established 1743 *Owner* LVMH *Production* 2 million cases *Vineyard area* 1,520 (615 ha)

The is largest of the Champagne houses and was the first (in 1962) to

This intricately carved barrel graces the entrance hall in the house of Mercier.

Sealed with crown caps, bottles of Moët et Chandon undergo secondary fermentation.

be floated on the Paris stockmarket. Moët claims that a bottle of its champagne is popped somewhere in the world every couple of seconds. The nonvintage Brut Impérial may occasionally be inconsistent—hardly surprising given the vast quantities produced—but vintage Moët is admirable, its bold citrus flavors and strong acidity ensuring that it matures superbly. The flagship, Dom Pérignon, is also outstanding, displaying delicate, lemon citrus flavors; rich, creamy texture; great finesse and balance; and gentle, refreshing acidity.

PERRIER-JOUËT

Established 1811 *Owner* Seagram *Production* 250,000 cases *Vineyard area* 267 acres (108 ha)

First used in 1902, Émile Gallé's ornate floral design for Perrier-Jouët bottles was revived almost 70 years later for a prestige *cuvée*, La Belle Époque. This is a wine of great delicacy, finesse and elegance that often takes a decade to mature. Although the nonvintage Perrier-Jouët is good and the vintage even better, another prestige *cuvée*, Blason de France, has more power, a strong, yeasty, bready flavor, and an extra level of richness. For a nonvintage champagne, it shows remarkable quality.

PHILIPPONNAT

Established 1910 *Owner* Boizel Chanoine Champagne *Production* 40,000 cases *Vineyard area* 30 acres (12 ha)

Philipponnat's flagship wine, the Clos des Goisses, is sourced from the Marne Valley vineyard of the same name. Floral, almost tropical when young, it develops powerful, toasty flavors and a creamy, honeyed texture with age. Le Reflet is ripe and approachable and includes any fruit from the Clos des Goisses not used in the prestige wine. Both the Brut and Rosé are soft, easy-drinking wines. The sale of Philipponnat in 1997 has seen the dynamic Bruno Paillard take the helm, a move that is likely to result in further improvement in the wines.

PIPER-HEIDSIECK

Established 1834 *Owner* Rémy-Cointreau *Production* 420,000 cases *Vineyard area* 54 acres (22 ha)

This is one of three Heidsieck firms that can trace their roots back to the original house founded in 1785. Although Piper-Heidsieck, Charles Heidsieck and Heidsieck & Co. share the same ownership, state-of-the-art winery and outstanding winemaker (Daniel Thibault), their styles are poles apart. Piper wines have been transformed in the last decade as a result of Thibault's insistence that they undergo full malolactic fermentation. This has softened their hard acidic edge, making them more approachable—but still bold and lively—in their youth.

POL ROGER

Established 1849 *Owner* NA *Production* 110,000 cases *Vineyard area* 210 acres (85 ha)

This small, charming family establishment makes what were Winston Churchill's favorite champagnes, a connection that is commemorated in the name of the prestige *cuvée*, Sir Winston Churchill. Released in 1984, this displays power and finesse, accompanied by layers of flavor that linger on the palate and in the memory. The rest of the range is equally impressive. The White Foil is a medium-bodied nonvintage with some floral characters and persistent flavors; the vintage is pristine, intense and tightly structured when young, and develops a biscuity toastiness with age. The Blanc de Chardonnay combines lemony freshness, an exquisitely creamy texture and impressive intensity.

POMMERY

Established 1856 *Owner* LVMH *Production* 500,000 cases *Vineyard area* 759 acres (307 ha)

It's considered almost obligatory these days, when touring Champagne, to visit the remarkable chalk cellars and wall carvings at Pommery. Although he no longer owns the business, Prince Alain de Polignac, whose family assumed control in 1879, remains as winemaker and custodian of tradition. The company's greatest asset is its vineyard holdings (especially in Grand Cru villages), which enable it to control grape production for a higher percentage of its wines than most other houses. They also allow it to produce vintage wines in years when others are unable to do so. The house style tends towards finesse and delicacy, with the vintage wines notable for their body and depth of flavor. The prestige Cuvée Louise displays even greater intensity, a tighter structure and yet more power.

LOUIS ROEDERER

Established 1760 *Owners* Roederer family *Production* 220,000 cases *Vineyard area* 470 acres (190 ha)

Louis Roederer is undoubtedly one of the great houses of Champagne and its range of wines is superb. The Brut Premier, with its tight structure, power, and biscuity, yeasty flavors, is invariably one of the top nonvintage champagnes. Likewise, the vintage is outstanding, showing finesse, balance and intensity of flavor. For many people, however, the pinnacle, not only of the Roederer portfolio but of champagne, is the superb Cristal. Sold in a clear (though not crystal!) bottle wrapped in yellow cellophane to protect the wine from ultraviolet light, it is the embodiment of elegance—subtle, yet powerful; delicate, but intense; restrained, yet opulent. It also displays a soft, creamy texture and gentle, lingering acidity. A memorable drinking experience.

RUINART

Established 1729 *Owner* LVMH *Production* 160,000 cases
Vineyard area 37 acres (15 ha)

The oldest of Champagne houses boasts impressive early connections, as founder Nicholas Ruinart's uncle was a close friend of Dom Pérignon. Although now part of a worldwide enterprise, Ruinart retains its identity as a small, quality-orientated house. The flagship wine, Dom Ruinart, a *blanc de blancs*, is outstanding.

SALON

Established 1914 *Owner* Laurent-Perrier *Production* 10,000 cases *Vineyard area* 2.5 acres (1 ha)

Salon is unique in Champagne in that it offers only one wine, a vintage *blanc de blancs* from vineyards in Le Mesnil-sur-Oger. This receives no malolactic fermentation, extended time on lees, and little dosage. The result is a magnificent wine with great depth of flavor and elegance, and razor-sharp acidity; it also has perhaps the greatest potential for aging of all champagnes. The decisions to produce or not produce certain vintages have sometimes been puzzling, however: for example, no wine was made from the outstanding 1945 and 1975 vintages.

TAITTINGER

Established 1734 *Owners* Taittinger family *Production* NA
Vineyard area 633 acres (256 ha)

The prestige wines of Taittinger are the Comtes de Champagne, a 100 percent chardonnay wine, and the 100 percent pinot noir Comtes de Champagne Rosé. The former undergoes malolactic fermentation and, unusually for champagne, includes a portion of wine that has been matured in new oak; this gives it an enticing, creamy texture to match its delicacy and finesse. The rosé is fuller and more powerful. When youthful, the vintage wine has citrus and yeast flavors, and crisp, fresh acidity on the finish.

VEUVE CLICQUOT

Established 1772 *Owner* LVMH *Production* 750,000 cases
Vineyard area 702 acres (284 ha)

Madame Clicquot assumed control of this house in 1805 at the tender age of 27, following the death of her husband François (*veuve* means "widow" in French). During the next half-century, she transformed the company and the industry with her energy and innovations. Today, Veuve Clicquot is best known for its rich pinot-dominated champagnes, including the distinctive Yellow Label Brut nonvintage. The vintage is consistently excellent: delicate, yet intense; balanced, yet powerful; crisp and dry, yet soft and refreshing. The prestige cuvée, La Grande Dame is a wine of great finesse and balance with firm structure and biscuity, yeasty flavors; it comes within a hair's breath of the great champagnes.

The distinctive company seal adds a neat finishing touch to bottles of Veuve Clicquot.

Louis Roederer offers an outstanding range, including the famous prestige cuvée, Cristal.

The Loire

Roger Voss

The French have a saying: "The Loire is a queen and the kings of France have loved her." It's an accurate—if probably politically incorrect—description of the intimate relationship that France has with its longest and arguably most beautiful river.

For 620 miles (1,000 km), from the mountains of the Massif Central to the Atlantic Ocean, the Loire flows past some of the most stupendous and most characteristic French landscape. Once a major transport artery for French agricultural and industrial products, today it is quiet and peaceful, the last natural, undammed great river of Europe. Many French people feel a strong affinity for the Loire. The language spoken in the regions of Anjou and Touraine, through which the river flows, is regarded as the purest, clearest form of French. The great cities of Orléans, Tours, Nantes and Angers are some of the most historic in the country, and they, and their castles, the grand châteaux for which the Loire Valley is most famous, are a reminder of the country's glorious past.

The River Loire also provides a mild mesoclimate for wine production. While the country to the north and south is too inhospitable for the vine, the Loire Valley and the valleys of the river's main tributaries are just those few vital degrees warmer in summer and winter, allowing grapes to flourish. There are few hills in the region, so moist, warm air from the Atlantic Ocean can spread far up into the interior, moderating the climate, which is often described locally as *doux* (soft) or *humide* (damp). It is this special and privileged mesoclimate that is also responsible for the milky blue light that has made the Loire region such an inspiration for generations of painters and travelers alike.

History

As was so often the case in western Europe, it was the Romans who first planted vines in the Loire region. The name of Pouilly-sur-Loire is a corruption of the Latin name, *Paulica Villa*, the villa of Paulus. Just across the river, in Sancerre, is the Porte César, so-called, according to a local theory, because Julius Caesar himself used this hill as a viewing post during the Gallic wars.

Even after the Roman era, vines continued to be a prominent feature of local life, with the Church playing an important part in the early development of winemaking. Saint Martin of Tours (the fourth century saint who divided his cloak among the beggars) is credited with having created most of the vineyards in Touraine. From the eleventh century, the Abbey of St-Denis in Paris fostered viticulture on land it owned in Reuilly, and the thirsty monks of St-Satur stimulated the production of wine in Sancerre.

Above: *Some producers in Sancerre have begun to experiment with wood aging.*

Top: *The vineyards of Sancerre are renowned for their dry white wines.*

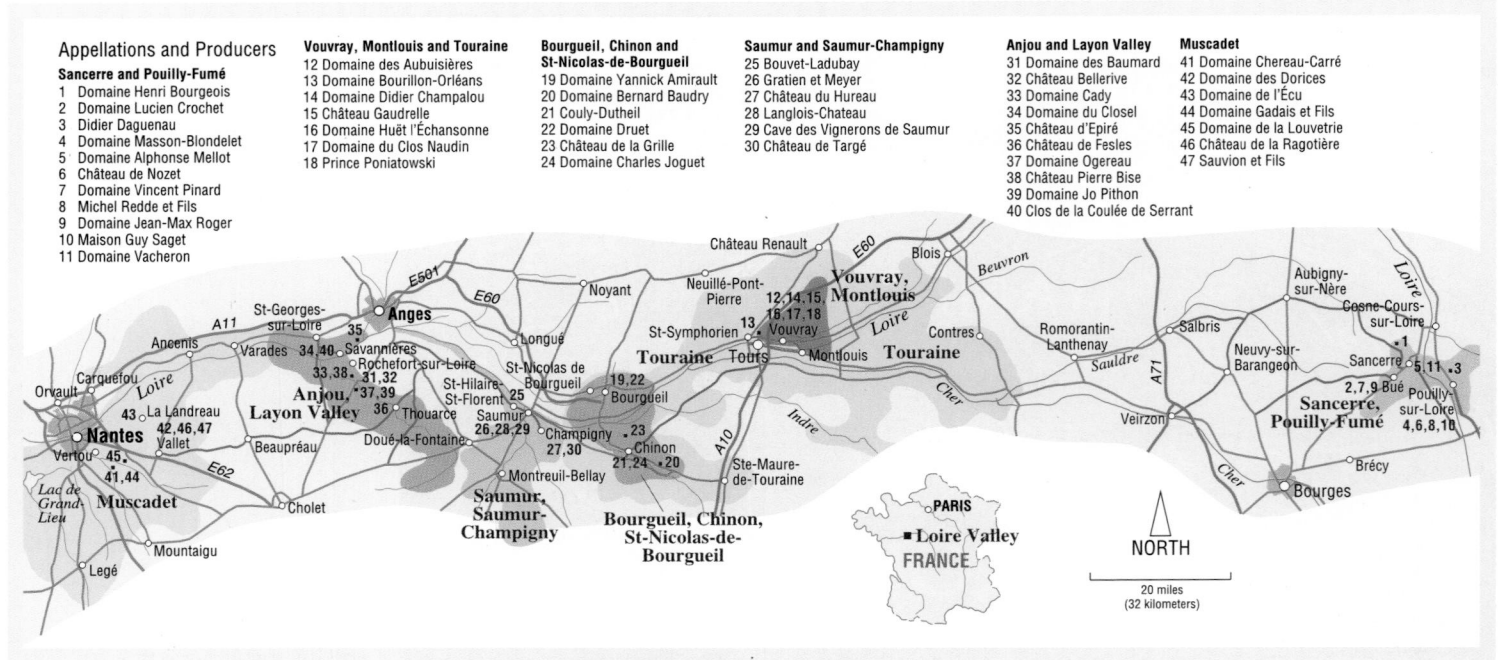

Appellations and Producers

Sancerre and Pouilly-Fumé
1 Domaine Henri Bourgeois
2 Domaine Lucien Crochet
3 Didier Dagueneau
4 Domaine Masson-Blondelet
5 Domaine Alphonse Mellot
6 Château de Nozet
7 Domaine Vincent Pinard
8 Michel Redde et Fils
9 Domaine Jean-Max Roger
10 Maison Guy Saget
11 Domaine Vacheron

Vouvray, Montlouis and Touraine
12 Domaine des Aubuisières
13 Domaine Bourillon-Orléans
14 Domaine Didier Champalou
15 Château Gaudrelle
16 Domaine Huët l'Échansonne
17 Domaine du Clos Naudin
18 Prince Poniatowski

Bourgueil, Chinon and St-Nicolas-de-Bourgueil
19 Domaine Yannick Amirault
20 Domaine Bernard Baudry
21 Couly-Dutheil
22 Domaine Druet
23 Château de la Grille
24 Domaine Charles Joguet

Saumur and Saumur-Champigny
25 Bouvet-Ladubay
26 Gratien et Meyer
27 Château du Hureau
28 Langlois-Chateau
29 Cave des Vignerons de Saumur
30 Château de Targé

Anjou and Layon Valley
31 Domaine des Baumard
32 Château Bellerive
33 Domaine Cady
34 Domaine du Closel
35 Château d'Epiré
36 Château de Fesles
37 Domaine Ogereau
38 Château Pierre Bise
39 Domaine Jo Pithon
40 Clos de la Coulée de Serrant

Muscadet
41 Domaine Chereau-Carré
42 Domaine des Dorices
43 Domaine de l'Écu
44 Domaine Gadais et Fils
45 Domaine de la Louvetrie
46 Château de la Ragotière
47 Sauvion et Fils

Later, in the Middle Ages, powerful barons and kings who set up court in the region also encouraged the development of vines. The vineyards of Vouvray, Montlouis and Vendôme owed their late-medieval and renaissance prosperity to their proximity to these châteaux.

In the nineteenth century, phylloxera dealt a particularly cruel blow to the vignerons in some of the more remote areas of the Loire. For instance, in the Auvergne, which once had 150,000 acres (60,000 ha) of vines, little more than 2,500 acres (1,000 ha) remain. Something similar occurred in the vineyards of Orléans and Châteaumeillant. Today, total plantings in the Loire are just over half of what they were before phylloxera struck.

Loire styles

The Loire wine region extends from Montbrison in the Côtes du Forez, just across the mountains from Beaujolais, all the way to the Atlantic Ocean. Throughout that region, vineyards line the river and its tributaries—the Allier, Cher, Indre, Vienne, Sèvre Nantaise and Loir. In total, approximately 120,000 acres (50,000 ha) of vines produce what can be described as Loire wines. These cover every style imaginable—dry and sweet white, light red and rich red, dry and sweet sparkling—and include 60 different appellations. But all share certain characteristics, including freshness, fruitiness and zing, and all are very much northern, cool-climate wines. The fact that so many wines and styles are made in the Loire is both confusing and challenging: confusing because it is difficult to remember all the names and permutations of names that the Loire has to offer, but, more importantly, challenging, because the more a wine-lover investigates the riches of the Loire, the more he or she is tempted to explore further.

Twenty years ago, the Loire was much less well-known than it is today. Now, wines such as the sauvignon blancs of Sancerre and Pouilly-Fumé are benchmarks for the rest of the world, and muscadet is every wine bar's house wine (or at least it was until the prices and aspirations of growers rose in parallel). Recent "discoveries" include the sweet wines of Anjou and the reds of Chinon and Bourgueil—and opportunities still exist to snap these up before prices go sky high. As for tomorrow, who knows: it could be the whites of Reuilly or Quincy, or the dry rosés of the Rosé de Loire, or the reds of Touraine Mesland.

Production standards have improved significantly in the Loire in recent years. Even vignerons with as little as 25 acres (10 ha) now have the necessary equipment to make good wine and, more importantly, many know how to use it. Most appellations—even some of the smallest—have their leading wine producers who set standards and attract attention and money. Increasingly, it is these growers, rather than the more conservative *négociants* that dominate production, who are showing the way ahead.

Grape varieties

If Loire wine styles are varied, so are the region's grape varieties. The list of obscure Loire grapes is

Magnificent Azay-le-Rideau is one of the Loire Valley's most splendid châteaux.

The town of Pouilly-sur-Loire, center of the world-famous Pouilly-Fumé appellation.

A vineyard worker marks vines that must be replaced before the next growing season.

fascinating and almost endless. The tressallier of Saint-Pourçain; the romorantin of Cour-Cheverny; the pineau d'aunis, pineau menu and groslot of Touraine; the gros plant of the Pays Nantais—all are rare species that make wines with unusual, sometimes exotic flavors. However, the finest wines in the Loire are produced from three grape varieties that never seem to achieve such quality elsewhere in France. Perhaps the fact that the Loire is at the limits of grape-growing brings out the best in chenin blanc, cabernet franc and sauvignon blanc.

The great whites of the Coteaux du Layon, Savennières, Vouvray and Montlouis are all based on chenin blanc. The intense acidity of the wines when young, whether sweet or dry, gives them an extraordinary ability to age. Low cropping, harvesting with several passes through the vineyard, the increased use of barrel aging and a succession of fine vintages (1988, 1989, 1990, 1994, 1995, 1996 and 1997) all contributed to the production of superb chenins in the late 1980s and 1990s.

Cabernet franc, which only ever plays a walk-on part in Bordeaux, is able to strut its stuff in the quartet of red-wine appellations of Saumur-Champigny, Bourgueil, St-Nicolas-de-Bourgueil and Chinon. The styles of these wines vary from the lighter produce of Saumur-Champigny to the velvet richness of great Chinon.

Sauvignon blanc's spiritual home is in the vineyards of Sancerre and Pouilly-sur-Loire. Here, the wines never have warm-climate, tropical-fruit flavors; instead they are crisper and more herbaceous. However, an increasing number of good producers are obtaining plenty of concentration, and some have even been experimenting with wood. Pouilly-Fumé tends to be softer and richer than Sancerre, and also ages better.

Of these three grapes, only one, chenin blanc, is native to the Loire. The theory is that it is a mutation of the pineau d'aunis, a native wild vine found in Anjou. The fact that the chenin is also called pineau de la Loire or pineau d'anjou lends some credence to this hypothesis. Cabernet franc and sauvignon blanc are both incomers from Bordeaux, and are related via cabernet sauvignon. Cabernet franc was originally called "the Breton," most probably because it was used for red wines that were sold to Brittany and thence to Britain. Sauvignon blanc was widely planted in the sixteenth century in the regions of Berry (Sancerre) and Nevers (Pouilly), where it is still encountered today.

Three other major grape varieties are encountered in the Loire: muscadet or melon de bourgogne, pinot noir and gamay—all imports from eastern France. Melon de bourgogne's arrival provides a fascinating perspective on the role of chance in the history of winemaking. In the seventeenth century, a devastating frost killed existing red vines in what is now the Muscadet region. The Dutch, who bought these thin wines for distillation, persuaded the local growers to plant white grapes that could be more easily distilled. Melon soon won favor as it was found to be the most resistant to frost. Its name was subsequently changed to muscadet, and the grape has been in the Pays Nantais ever since.

Made for aging

Just because Loire wines, when young, are fresh and fruity, doesn't mean that they do not age; on the contrary, most Loire white wines develop well. This is especially true of chenin-blanc-based wines from Savennières, the Coteaux du Layon (including Quarts de Chaume and Bonnezeaux) and Vouvray. Experts often suggest that, after an initial fruity spell, these wines go through a dumb period—when they do not show their best—between two and five years of age. After that, the best examples can be expected to age for upward of 20 years.

Other Loire white wines also have surprisingly long lives. The sauvignon-blanc-based wines of Pouilly-Fumé, for example, do not begin to show their true character until they are around three years old. Sancerre whites mature and fade more quickly, as does muscadet, although in the best vintages the top *cuvées* will develop and mature.

Loire reds can also develop well. The better wines from Chinon and Bourgueil age as well as many Bordeaux reds, and the lighter wines of Saumur-Champigny and St-Nicolas-de-Bourgueil will continue to develop for at least ten years, maybe more, depending on the vintage. The reds of Sancerre are less long-lived, although a few producers who have cut yields and wood-aged the wines can produce 10- or 15-year-old examples that still have youthful fruit.

APPELLATIONS AND PRODUCERS

The Loire's 60-odd appellations include some famous names and some rarities. Among the latter are the scattered VDQS areas of Châteaumeillant (red and rosé wines made near La Châtre in the Cher department), Coteaux di Giennois (red, rosé and white wines from just north of Pouilly-sur-Loire), Vin de l'Orléanais (red, rosé and white wines from around the city of Orléans—the closest Loire vineyards to Paris), and Vin du Thouarsais

(more red, rosé and white wines, this time made south of the main Anjou vineyards). Travelers to the region may, if they persevere, come across these and other remnants of what were often much larger vineyard areas until phylloxera and economic difficulties put paid to them.

There are two major Loire-wide appellations. Crémant de Loire applies to traditional method sparkling wines with a generally higher level of quality than those of Saumur, and Vin de Pays du Jardin de la France applies to varietally labeled wines (in particular chardonnay). Otherwise, the Loire's appellations can be conveniently grouped under the following headings.

Sancerre, Pouilly-Fumé and the vineyards of the Center

Sauvignon blanc and pinot noir are the two stars in these vineyards. The two principal appellations are Sancerre (whites, reds and rosés) and Pouilly-Fumé (whites only). Other lesser appellations are Menetou-Salon (whites, reds and rosés), Quincy (whites only) and Reuilly (whites, reds and rosés). All these wines combine richness, freshness and acidity. The whites have the characteristic goose-

Vineyards cover almost every hillside around the historic walled town of Sancerre.

The Loire's long, winding journey takes it through attractive towns such as Saumur.

Among Guy Saget's extensive range of Loire wines, those from Pouilly-Fumé stand out.

berry and grapefruit flavors of sauvignon blanc, those of Pouilly-Fumé being fuller, fatter and more long-lived than those of Sancerre, while those from Reuilly, Quincy and Menetou-Salon are generally soft and round. The reds, from pinot noir, are lightweight burgundy lookalikes, only rarely achieving more than passing attractiveness.

DOMAINE HENRI BOURGEOIS

Established Eighteenth century *Owners* Bourgeois family *Production* 43,000 cases *Vineyard area* 148 acres (60 ha)

Dynamism and the Bourgeois seem to go hand in hand. Not content with seeming to own every building on the main street of Chavignol, they have constructed an enormous, space-age cellar opposite the Mont Damnés vineyard, where they make an exemplary range of wines. The simpler Sancerres, La Vigne Blanche and Les Baronnes are fresh expressions of sauvignon blanc, while wines such as La Côte des Monts Damnés and La Bourgeoise (made from old vines) are complex and perfumed. The Bourgeois also make Pouilly-Fumé of similar quality, and own another *négociant* firm in Sancerre, Domaine Laporte.

DOMAINE LUCIEN CROCHET

Established NA *Owners* Crochet family *Production* 21,000 cases *Vineyard area* 84 acres (34 ha)

Gilles Crochet has taken over from his father Lucien as winemaker, but the family's Sancerres remain full-bodied and concentrated. Recently, the Crochets built a huge modern cellar and office in the middle of Bué, a sign of their importance and their success. The *négociant* wines, made from purchased grapes, are pleasant enough, but the emphasis is on the *domaine* wines, from vineyards that include parts of some of the best in Bué. The Le Chêne *cuvée* comes from the Chêne Marchand vineyard, whereas the Sancerre Prestige is a blend from the best lots.

DIDIER DAGUENEAU

Established 1980s *Owner* Didier Dagueneau *Production* 4,200 cases *Vineyard area* 28.4 acres (11.5 ha)

Didier Dagueneau is known as the wild man of Pouilly, not just because of his hirsute appearance and penchant for flying the American Confederate flag outside his house, but also for his stand against what he sees as much mediocre Pouilly-Fumé, derived from high yields and the overuse of sugar. Dagueneau's wines could never be called mediocre and are among the great white wines of France. The range of different *cuvées*, many of which are wood-aged, begins with Cailloux, named for the soil from which it comes, and moves through increasingly complex, long-lasting wines: Le Bois Renard (formerly known as Le Bois Menard), Silex (again named after the soil), Pur Sang and, most remarkable of all, Astéroïde.

DOMAINE MASSON-BLONDELET

Established Late nineteenth century *Owner* Masson family *Production* 10,000 cases *Vineyard area* 47 acres (19 ha)

Jean-Michel Masson's *domaine* is scattered across the appellations of Pouilly and Sancerre. His modern cellars in Pouilly produce a well-crafted range of wines, including the fruity Sancerre Thauvenay and the Pouilly-Fumé Les Angelots. The top-of-the-range wines include the serious, complex Villa Paulus, which is named for the Roman estate that provided Pouilly with its name; and Tradition Catulus, a rich, powerful, wood-aged wine made from old vines.

DOMAINE ALPHONSE MELLOT

Established Seventeenth century *Owners* Mellot family *Production* 25,000 cases *Vineyard area* 120 acres (50 ha)

There have been 18 Alphonses at the head of this family company, whose cellars and shop in the centre of Sancerre are among the most prominent of any Sancerrois producer. The current Alphonse has changed the whole nature of his wines in the last 15 years, reducing yields and pushing up quality to a remarkable extent. The wines from the Domaine la Moussière are top-quality Sancerre, the result of considerable research into the right clones and of picking superripe fruit at harvest-time. The nineteenth Alphonse, now in charge of winemaking, has even had a *cuvée* named after him, Sancerre Génération XIX.

CHÂTEAU DE NOZET

Established NA *Owners* de Ladoucette family *Production* 100,000 cases *Vineyard area* 257 acres (104 ha)

Based in their showpiece, nineteenth-century château, the de Ladoucettes are the biggest players in Pouilly and also own the firms of Comte Lafon in Sancerre, Marc Brédif in Vouvray and Albert Pic in Chablis. When Château du Nozet came out with its top *cuvée*, Pouilly-Fumé Baron de L, in 1973, it shone like a beacon among much second-rate Loire wine. If it no longer shines so brightly today, that is because standards have risen across the region. The rest of the Nozet range is made from purchased grapes and is generally of a good standard.

DOMAINE VINCENT PINARD

Established NA *Owner* Vincent Pinard *Production* 7,100 cases *Vineyard area* 32 acres (13 ha)

A serious, dedicated winemaker, Vincent Pinard makes an appealing range of Sancerres from his Bué vineyards, which include portions of Le Chêne Marchand and Le Grand Chemarin. Unlike some other local winegrowers, he doesn't indicate the vineyard origins on his labels, preferring to use more abstract names. Thus the lightest of his *cuvées* is called Florès, while the meatier, richer offerings from his old vines are called Cuvée Nuance and Cuvée Harmonie. Harmonie, especially, is an extraordinary, dense wine, aged in wood but bursting with ripe fruit.

MICHEL REDDE ET FILS

Established Nineteenth century *Owners* Redde family *Production* 21,000 cases *Vineyard area* 87 acres (35 ha)

The Reddes, father Michel and son Thierry, run a smart, modern operation that turns out a wide range of excellent-quality Pouilly-Fumé. The winery, on the main road that passes Pouilly, also acts as an attractive sales outlet for the family produce. The main part of the vineyard is on the slopes that face south onto the Loire. The top *cuvée*, Cuvée Majorum, made only in the best years, has excellent ripeness and depth, while the light *cuvée*, La Moynerie (named after the estate), is spicier and less complex. The Reddes also make Sancerre and Les Tuilières, as well as the rare, chasselas-based Pouilly-sur-Loire.

DOMAINE JEAN-MAX ROGER

Established NA *Owner* Jean-Max Roger *Production* 20,000 cases *Vineyard area* 67 acres (27 ha)

The Rogers have lived in the village of Bué since the sixteenth century, but it was the current head of the family, Jean-Max, who built up the estate's large landholding, which includes vines in neighboring Menetou-Salon. It now has vines in two of Bué's best vineyards, Le Grand Chemarin and Le Chêne Marchand, and makes two *cuvées*, G. C. and G. M., from these. The Roger white-wine style is rich and full-bodied, becoming approachable after a year. The red and rosé Sancerres are attractive wines but lack the elegance of the whites.

MAISON GUY SAGET

Established NA *Owner* NA *Production* 330,000 cases *Vineyard area* 94 acres (38 ha)

From the production figures above, it is easy to deduce that Guy Saget's main business is as a *négociant*. He

Bottom: *A crate of the 1997 Sancerre from Domaine Alphonse Mellot, ready for shipping.*

Below: *The nineteenth Alphonse Mellot examines some of the wine in his cellar.*

The gently sloping vineyards of Chinon produce some of the Loire's best reds.

produces a wide range of wines from most of the major appellations in the Loire; all are competent, and some better than that. But his starting point was Pouilly-Fumé, and that is where his winery is located. His three of Pouilly-Fumé *cuvées*—Chantalouette, Les Roches and Marie de Beauregard—have steadily improved in quality and now compare well with the appellation's top wines. Recently, Saget purchased Domaine de la Perrière in Sancerre, which also produces an attractive range of wines.

DOMAINE VACHERON

Established NA *Owners* Vacheron family *Production* 22,000 cases *Vineyard area* 89 acres (36 ha)

From the Vacheron cellars, in the heart of the town of Sancerre, issues a range that includes the best red *cuvée* in the area, a wine that is one of the few to justify the fuss made about Sancerre reds. Aged in barriques, it also develops well in bottle—10- and even 15-year-old examples are still in their early maturity. The whites shouldn't be forgotten either and are generally fresh, clean and minerally. The Vacherons have made wine for generations, and Jean-Louis, Denis and Jean-Dominique have continually updated their production methods, filling the ancient, rambling cellars, with stainless steel tanks and modern presses.

Some of the cellars in Touraine are hollowed out of the limestone hills that line the river.

Vouvray, Montlouis and Touraine

A wide variety of grapes is planted in the vineyards of Touraine including gamay, malbec, cabernet sauvignon and cabernet franc for red wines; pineau d'aunis, gamay, pinot gris and pinot noir for rosé wines; and, for whites, chenin blanc, sauvignon blanc and chardonnay.

The two principal village appellations are Vouvray and Montlouis, both of which are only for white wines produced from chenin blanc. Confusingly, since these wines can be made in any degree of sweetness from bone dry to ultra-botrytized, words such as *moelleux* (very sweet) and *sec* (dry) are often omitted from the label.

Several appellations are grouped under the Touraine name. The Touraine appellation itself covers the whole region; other Touraine wines (sauvignon blanc and gamay, in particular) are labelled varietally. Within the regional appellation, the following villages have the right to add their name to that of Touraine: Amboise, Azay-le-Rideau and Mesland.

To the north of the main Loire valley, the appellations of the Loir are Jasnières and Coteaux du Loir, where the principal grape is chenin blanc. In the eastern Touraine, Cheverny and Cour-Cheverny make whites, reds and rosés. The specialty wine here is white Cour-Cheverny, made from the very dry romorantin grape.

DOMAINE DES AUBUISIÈRES

Established NA *Owner* Bernard Fouquet *Production* 9,200 cases *Vineyard area* 54 acres (22 ha)

This estate on the *coteaux* (slopes) of Vouvray is well sited for south-facing exposure. Bernard Fouquet and his father, a nurseryman, clone their own vines and have developed a chenin that botrytizes easily. The Marigny *cuvée* is produced in both dry and sweet versions, depending on how well the grapes ripen each year, and both have great elegance. Another sweet *cuvée*, Alexandre, offers a much richer, fleshier wine that is opulent and full of botrytis. There is also a Vieilles Vignes, which needs long-term aging.

DOMAINE BOURILLON-ORLÉANS

Established 1875 *Owners* Bourillon family *Production* 6,500 cases *Vineyard area* 45 acres (18 ha)

Winemaker Frédéric Bourillon is the latest in a long line of growers that has worked in the family's ancient cellars beneath the town of Rochecorbon. Using these and the state-of-the-art winery recently built next door, Bourillon

produces some complex Vouvrays that also have considerable charm. However, his *demi-sec*, rich with apples and exotic fruits, is probably his classic wine. The sweet wines, such as the Trie Spéciale La Coulée d'Or, are hugely concentrated without ever losing a zingy acidity. The *domaine* also produces one of the most successful dry sparkling Vouvrays, Diamant Prestige.

DOMAINE DIDIER CHAMPALOU

Established 1984 *Owners* Didier and Catherine Champalou
Production 6,700 cases *Vineyard area* 47 acres (19 ha)

Didier and Catherine Champalou are both graduates of the local wine school of Montreuil-Bellay, and their training shows in the quality of their wines and the standards they have set themselves. Like a number of the other younger growers in Vouvray, they favor the *sec-tendre* style—off dry, with approximately 0.14–0.53 ounces (4–15 g) of residual sugar. They make two blends in this style: a standard *cuvée* and the superior Fondraux. Of course, they wouldn't be true Vouvray producers if they didn't also make some superb sweet botrytized wines (including Cuvée CC) as well as an excellent dry sparkling wine.

CHÂTEAU GAUDRELLE

Established NA *Owner* Alexander Monmousseau
Production 6,000 cases *Vineyard area* 35 acres (14 ha)

Alexander Monmousseau is a leading protagonist of the *sec-tendre* style of winemaking, which is much favored in Vouvray. This produces supple, ripely fruity wines that enhance the qualities of chenin blanc even when young, avoiding the almost obligatory five-year wait for drier and sweeter Vouvrays. Controlled temperature vinification in large wood casks gives concentration and depth. Monmousseau also makes sparkling wines and, in suitable years, produces a hugely syrupy Réserve.

DOMAINE HUËT L'ÉCHANSONNE (LE HAUT LIEU)

Established NA *Owner* Gaston Huët *Production*
12,500 cases *Vineyard area* 87 acres (35 ha)

This is the most famous vineyard in Vouvray. It was formerly run by owner and noted winemaker Gaston Huët, but with Huët well into his eighties, son-in-law Noël recently took charge. He has transformed the estate into an impressive biodynamic vineyard, and the wines, already great, have gone from strength to strength. The new approach produces a great purity of fruit and a

Bourgueil's vineyards occupy a sunny location, resulting in rich, firm red wines.

The red wines of St-Nicolas-de-Bourgueil
are produced mainly from cabernet franc.

In fall, this mansion in Saumur is transformed
daily as the leaves on its walls turn red.

fine expression of the *terroir*. Stars of the Huët range include the single-vineyard wines from the Clos du Bourg, which are made in dry, medium-dry and sweet styles. The *domaine* also makes one of the best sparkling wines in Vouvray.

DOMAINE DU CLOS NAUDIN

Established **NA** *Owner* **Philippe Foreau** *Production* **5,000 cases** *Vineyard area* **30 acres (12 ha)**

Philippe Foreau makes full-bodied, full-flavored fare that ages well. A fine cook, he also likes to create wines that will successfully accompany a wide variety of foods. His ability to pick the perfect moment for harvesting is legendary among Vouvray vignerons. In his cellar, he vinifies and ages in both stainless steel and wood. In great years, he makes a heavily botrytized *cuvée* called Réserve, and his sparkling wine is one of Vouvray's most satisfying: aged more than two years on lees, it also has a great ability to age in bottle.

PRINCE PONIATOWSKI

Established **1707** *Owners* **Poniatowski family** *Production* **3,000 cases** *Vineyard area* **30 acres (12 ha)**

The ancient Vouvray estate of Clos Baudoin has been in the Poniatowski family for about 70 years. The wines, which are on the dry side, emphasize elegance and finesse, and take several years to develop. Clos Baudoin is name of the main still wines, whereas the Aigle Blanc label is used for still and sparkling wines. Like many properties in

Vouvray, the Poniatowski winery is set into the cliff, so that part of the house is actually a cave.

Bourgueil, Chinon and St-Nicolas-de-Bourgueil

Although these appellations are also in Touraine, they form a red-wine (cabernet franc) enclave in a predominantly white-wine region. Of the three, Bourgueil produces the firmest and most tannic wines, St-Nicolas-de-Bourgueil the lightest; Chinon wines are rich, soft and velvety.

DOMAINE YANNICK AMIRAULT

Established **NA** *Owners* **Yannick and Nicole Amirault** *Production* **6,000 cases** *Vineyard area* **40 acres (16 ha)**

Yannick Amirault, who works alongside his wife Nicole, is a rising star in Bourgueil, but vinifies in a style that leaves commentators divided—is there too much new wood, or not enough? The outstanding Les Malgagnes Vieilles Vignes from St-Nicolas-de-Bourgueil and Petite Cave Vieilles Vignes from Bourgueil display just as much fruit as wood. Both need at least three years aging to achieve a balance, but then reveal splendid, ripe, sumptuous flavors.

DOMAINE BERNARD BAUDRY

Established **1975** *Owner* **NA** *Production* **9,000 cases** *Vineyard area* **69 acres (28 ha)**

Bernard Baudry has his vines in Cravant-les-Coteaux, to the east of Chinon, on the slopes above the river Vienne. This is the heart of the

appellation, with the village of Cravant having one-third of Chinon's vines. Baudry vinifies the grapes from each of his parcels of land separately. Those from the land nearer the river make the lighter Les Granges, whereas those from the plateau provide Le Domaine and La Croix Boissée, and the slope itself supplies Les Grezeaux. All Baudry wines are aged in a mix of old and new barrels, adding complexity to great fruit.

DOMAINE COULY-DUTHEIL

Established 1921 *Owners* Couly family *Production* 60,000 cases *Vineyard area* 210 acres (85 ha)

The *négociant* firm of Couly-Dutheil dominates winemaking in Chinon, both through its sheer size and, more recently, its increasing quality. Estate wines such as the single-vineyard Clos de l'Écho, Clos de l'Olive and Les Gravières are among the best wines in the appellation, full of super-mature fruit that provides great richness. Bertrand Couly, in charge of vinification on the estate, also makes the other *cuvées* such as Domaine René Couly, as well as the *négociant* wines that come from Chinon, Bourgueil and St-Nicolas-de-Bourgueil. Keeping it in the family, the firm introduced a range of special *cuvées* for the year 2000, with a bottle designed by Françoise Couly, wife of Jacques, the current director and Bertrand's uncle.

DOMAINE DRUET

Established 1980 *Owners* Druet family *Production* 10,000 cases *Vineyard area* 49 acres (20 ha)

Pierre-Jacques Druet is a winemaking perfectionist. His attention to detail, his technique of heating the must to obtain maximum color before fermentation, and his use of wood aging in new barrels all contribute to some of Bourgueil's finest wines. Though they are made in a modern style, Druet is also eager to emphasize vineyard differences. Two wines are matured only in stainless steel: Les Cent Boisselées and Clos de Danzay. Of his wood-aged *cuvées*, Beauvais is the lightest, while Le Grand Mont displays medium weight and longevity, and Vaumoreau is the most powerful.

CHÂTEAU DE LA GRILLE

Established Fifteenth century *Owners* Gosset family *Production* 14,000 cases *Vineyard area* 69 acres (28 ha)

Although the origins of the Château de la Grille date to the fifteenth century, the current building owes more to the nineteenth-century passion for mock-Gothic architecture. Now in the possession of the Gosset family, vignerons since 1584, the château contrasts with the modern winery next door. Its Chinon is made in the modern idiom, with new wood and ripe, opulent fruit. Tradition asserts itself in the elegant, skittle-shaped, eighteenth-century-style bottle, but otherwise the wine gives the lie to the idea that Chinons are merely lightweight reds.

Chinon includes a wide variety of soils, ranging from clay-gravel to limestone.

DOMAINE CHARLES JOGUET

Established NA *Owner* Charles Joguet *Production* 9,000 cases *Vineyard area* 91 acres (37 ha)

Although Charles Joguet himself has entered semi-retirement (perhaps to devote himself to his other interests, poetry and sculpture), the estate that bears his name continues to produce some of the best wines in Chinon. A dip in quality with the 1997 vintage, the result of local hailstorms, was followed by a return to form in 1998. In ascending order of power and richness, the Joguet *cuvées* are: Chinon Terroir, Cuvée du Clos de la Cure, Cuvée Clos du Chêne Vert, Les Varennes du Grand Clos and Clos de la Dioterie. The distinguishing characteristics of all Joguet wines, now made under the control of Alain Delaunay, are the suppleness and ripeness of the tannins.

Saumur and Saumur-Champigny

The westernmost vineyards of Anjou are normally treated separately from the rest of the province. The three principal appellations in this area are Saumur for white wines from chenin blanc and red wines from cabernet franc; Saumur-Champigny for quality red wines, similar to those of St-Nicolas-de-Bourgueil; and Saumur Mousseux for sparkling wines made mainly from chenin blanc. Saumur Mousseux is the second-largest sparkling wine appellation in France after Champagne, producing on average 12 million bottles a year.

BOUVET-LADUBAY

Established 1851 *Owner* Champagne Taittinger *Production* 275,000 cases *Vineyard area* None

This is certainly the most exciting of the Saumur sparkling-wine producers. With its wood-fermented Cuvée Trésor, Bouvet-Ladubay has created a wine that proves Saumur's potential to make great sparklers. The care that goes into this wine is

The wooded plateau above Bourgueil protects the vines from prevailing winds.

reflected in other aspects of the Bouvet-Ladubay range: the Saphir and the red Rubis Rouge, for example, represent excellent value at a lower price point. The recently introduced range of still wines, Les Non Pareils, shows the company using its expertise to expand the product line. Innovations include several specially selected *cuvées* from Saumur-Champigny and Anjou, a Vin de Pays des Deux Sèvres, and a red from the western Loire that is of excellent quality.

GRATIEN ET MEYER

Established 1864 *Owners* Gratien family *Production* 170,000 cases *Vineyard area* 49 acres (20 ha)

One of the largest producers of sparkling Saumur, Gratien et Meyer has recently shown a definite hike in quality. Wines such as Cuvée Flamme, the vintage Cuvée de Minuit and the Crémant de Loire Cuvée Royale are the result of two kinds of investment. The first was a significant financial investment in the creation of vast new cellars which were hollowed out of the rocks to the east of Saumur; the second involved working with contract growers to improve their viticulture and hence the quality of the fruit. A new departure for this company, which is under the same family ownership as Champagne Alfred Gratien, was the development of a range of still wines from the estate, under the name Château Gratien.

CHÂTEAU DU HUREAU

Established NA *Owners* Vatan family *Production* 10,000 cases *Vineyard area* 47 acres (19 ha)

The Vatans have owned the Château de Hureau for five generations, and throughout that time they have produced red Saumur-Champigny in the estate's thirteenth-century cellars. These wines have a structure that allows them to age well, although they start life attractively fruity and fresh. The Cuvée Lisagathe and the single-vineyard Cuvée des Fevettes are the most successful of the range. The Vatans also make tiny quantities of almost hand-made Saumur Brut, and, in good years, a rare sweet white Coteaux du Saumur.

LANGLOIS-CHATEAU

Established 1885 *Owner* Bollinger *Production* 70,000 cases *Vineyard area* 161 acres (65 ha)

Now owned by the Champagne firm of Bollinger, this company was originally founded by Edouard Langlois and Jeanne Chateau in the nineteenth century. Drawing on vineyards in Saumur, Saumur-Champigny and Sancerre, it makes a range of still wines, of which the most exciting are the red Saumur and Saumur-Champigny. Following the traditions of its parent company, the firm also makes sparkling wine, but instead of making the local Saumur, it produces Crémant de Loire to a high standard. The best is Cuvée Quadrille, a blend of chenin blanc, chardonnay, cabernet franc and cabernet sauvignon.

CAVE DES VIGNERONS DE SAUMUR

Established 1957 *Owner* Cooperative of 300 members *Production* 1 million cases *Vineyard area* 3,460 acres (1,400 ha)

The huge cellar complex of the Saumur cooperative at St-Cyr-en-Bourg is not only big, it is also one of the most modern in France. Using its 6 miles (10 km) of underground cellars, gravity-fed pumps and huge state-of-the-art vinification and press rooms, the cooperative makes a range of wines from all over the Saumur and Saumur-Champigny appellations, as well as Rosé de Loire and some sparkling wines. The most successful are the red and white Saumur, and the deliciously fruity rosés.

CHÂTEAU DE TARGÉ

Established 1655 *Owner* Edouard Pisani-Ferry *Production* 11,000 cases *Vineyard area* 59 acres (24 ha)

Firmly tannic wines are produced at this historic family estate, whose old cellars and house, like so many in the region, are hollowed out of the tufa rock. Up on top of the cliff, however, among the château's vines, lies a brand-new winery where the vinification takes place. Current proprietor Edouard Pisani-Ferry makes two Saumur-Champignys: a classic Château de Targé and the wood-aged Cuvée Ferry. Recently, he has also started making small quantities of white Saumur.

Anjou and the Layon valley

An enormous variety of wines comes under the Anjou banner. The two principal styles are whites (both dry and sweet) from chenin blanc and reds from cabernet franc. The jewels are the sweet-white-wine vineyards concentrated around the Layon valley in the following appellations: Bonnezeaux, Quarts de Chaume, Coteaux du Layon (including village appellations such as Coteaux du Layon Chaume, Coteaux du Layon St-Lambert-du-Lattay and Coteaux du Layon St-Aubin-de-Luigné) and Coteaux de l'Aubance. Across the Loire from the Layon vineyards lies the tiny enclave of Savennières, which produces dry white wines from chenin blanc, often seen as the purest expression of that grape variety.

The local reds are grouped under the Anjou Rouge and superior Anjou Villages appellations. Huge quantities of semisweet, generally indifferent Anjou Rosé have given a bad name to a region that can and does produce great wines.

DOMAINE DES BAUMARD

Established NA   *Owners* Baumard family   *Production* 15,000 cases   *Vineyard area* 99 acres (40 ha)

This *domaine* is at the top of the tree in the Layon valley. Other producers may make better individual wines, but Florent Baumard (who has taken over from his father Jean) makes the valley's best and most consistent range at the sixteenth-century family home in Rochefort-sur-Loire. The Quarts de Chaume has the characteristic intensity of this great sweet wine and develops beautifully after ten years in bottle. The two Savennières, Clos St-Yves and Clos du Papillon, are lighter than some wines from this appellation and therefore more appealing when young. Clos Ste-Catherine is a deliciously balanced Coteaux du Layon. The Baumards also make red Anjou and a Crémant de Loire.

CHÂTEAU BELLERIVE

Established NA   *Owners* Malinge family   *Production* 2,500 cases   *Vineyard area* 30 acres (12 ha)

Although inheritance laws forced Jacques Lalanne to sell this famous property to the Malinge family, it very sensibly kept him in charge. Lalanne's

Exceptional sweet white wines come from the vineyards of the Layon Valley in Anjou.

preferred techniques include low yields, removal of berry clusters, and a series of passes through the vineyard during harvest to find perfectly botrytized berries. The ultrarich, ultrasweet Quarts de Chaume is among the great wines of the Loire. Packed with a mélange of orange marmalade, quince and spices, recent vintages such as the 1995, 1996 and 1997 are sensual and opulent. At the very top of the range is Cuvée Quintessence, which is aged in old wood and lasts for years.

DOMAINE CADY

Established NA *Owner* Philippe Cady *Production* NA
Vineyard area 52 acres (21 ha)

Philippe Cady loves sweet wines; you can tell by the way he names them. Cuvée Volupté is the richest and most viscous, and one of the great sweet wines of the Layon valley. Then there are the special blends: the Coteaux du Layon Cuvée Alexandre and the Cuvée Eléonore, which are named after his children. These are certainly the stars of the Cady range, ultrarich but still with the essential acidity of a fine, sweet Loire chenin blanc. The rest of the range is more conventional: red Anjou Rouge and Anjou Villages, a well-balanced dry Anjou Blanc and a Rosé de Loire.

DOMAINE DU CLOSEL

Established 1820 *Owner* Madame de Jessey *Production* 7,500 cases *Vineyard area* 49 acres (20 ha)

The latest in a long line of owners of the Château de Vaulx and its Domaine du Closel, Madame de Jessey is the first woman to be in charge. She makes some of the most approachable Savennières in her Cuvée Classique, and also some of the most classic in her Clos du Papillon, which comes from

her portion of the vineyard of the same name and which spends a few months' aging in chestnut-wood casks. The Cuvée Speciale is a wine with slight residual sugar and therefore a soft finish. Du Closel also makes a red Anjou Villages.

CHÂTEAU D'EPIRÉ

Established NA *Owners* Bizard family *Production* 5,000 cases *Vineyard area* 25 acres (10 ha)

This *domaine* has been owned by the Bizard family for over a century. Based in a fine château in the village of Epiré, it includes 20 acres (8 ha) of chenin blanc for Savennières and 5 acres (2 ha) of cabernet franc for an Anjou Rouge, Clos de la Cerisaie. The traditional technique of using old wood for fermentation was abandoned here only in the early 1990s in favor of stainless steel, but much of the white wine is still aged in barrels. The wines are designed for long-term aging, and the Savennières is at its best after 10 years. The chateau also produces medium-dry and sweet wines in good years such as 1996 and 1997.

CHÂTEAU DE FESLES

Established NA *Owner* Bernard Germain *Production* 33,000 cases *Vineyard area* 87 acres (35 ha)

The benchmark *domaine* for the ultrasweet Bonnezeaux, Château de Fesles has undergone a series of changes in the past decade. From being owned by the Boivin family, with Jacques Boivin in charge of winemaking, it passed briefly through the hands of Parisian pâtissier Gaston Lenôtre (who spent millions renovating both the cellar and the château), before landing in the lap of Bernard Germain, whose family owns 11 estates in Bordeaux as well as others in the Coteaux du Layon. The Bonnezeaux of Château de Fesles is the star of the range, which also includes a Rosé d'Anjou, an Anjou Rouge and an Anjou Villages.

DOMAINE OGEREAU

Established Early twentieth century *Owner* Vincent Ogereau *Production* 5,800 cases *Vineyard area* 57 acres (23 ha)

Vincent Ogereau believes in making wines with balance. From his vineyards in the Coteaux du Layon village of St-Lambert-du-Lattay, he is able to conjure wines that combine lightness and elegance with sweet, sometimes botrytized flavors. Whole-cluster maceration before fermentation adds concentration to the likes of the Coteaux du Layon St-Lambert and the top-of-the-range Prestige. Half the production is good-quality Anjou Rouge and Anjou Villages.

Touraine's vines yield good-value varietals including fine sauvignon blanc and gamay.

CHÂTEAU PIERRE BISE

Established NA *Owner* Claude Papin *Production*
15,000 cases *Vineyard area* 124 acres (50 ha)

Among the leading handful of winemakers in
Anjou, Claude Papin has long been fascinated by
variations in his *terroirs*, from which he makes a
bewildering variety of wines that clearly express
the different soil types. A visit to the cellars of
Château Pierre Bise consists as much in handling
stones and rocks as in tasting wine. Although his
Quarts de Chaume is probably his greatest product, the Coteaux du Layon Beaulieu Anclaie
certainly runs it close. The beautifully balanced
Savennières Clos de Coulaine has less of that appellation's typically minerally character but every
bit of its elegance. Even the simple, fruity Anjou
Gamay attains the same high standards.

DOMAINE JO PITHON

Established NA *Owner* Jo Pithon *Production* 1,700 cases
Vineyard area 20 acres (8 ha)

From his small vineyard near St-Lambert-du-Lattay,
Jo Pithon produces tiny quantities of superrich,
superconcentrated sweet wines. He began to specialize in this style in 1991, when the frost of that
year made him realize that the only way forward
was to make wines of the highest quality. Some

people find his wines too rich, but others praise
them highly. The best include the Quarts de
Chaume and the St-Lambert Bonnes Blanches.
At the top of the range—and costing three times
the price of other wines from the village—is his
Coteaux du Layon St-Lambert Ambroisie.

CLOS DE LA COULÉE DE SERRANT

Established Twelfth century *Owners* Joly family
Production 1,700 cases *Vineyard area* 35 acres (14 ha)

Nicolas Joly, who manages his family's property,
is a passionate, articulate advocate for biodynamic
cultivation, and his ongoing attempts to promote
this practice regularly arouse controversy and debate in the Anjou area. In addition, Joly has to
deal with the responsibility of making wine in one
of just three single-vineyard appellations in the
whole of France (the other two are Romanée-
Conti in Burgundy and Château-Grillet in the
Rhône). The white wine, made from chenin blanc,
comes from a precipitous 17-acre (7-ha) slope in
the Savennières vineyards. Recent vintages have
revealed enormously rich, dry, full-bodied wines,
which last, seemingly, forever. Among the other
wines originating from the Joly family cellars, the
Savennières Roches aux Moines and the minerally
Savennières Becherelle stand out.

*A rainbow points to the pot of gold amid the
Quarts de Chaume vineyards in Anjou.*

Muscadet

The westernmost vineyards, in the Pays Nantais region around Nantes, are devoted almost entirely to white wines. There are four Muscadet appellations, all using the muscadet or melon de bourgogne grape. In order of importance, they are Muscadet de Sèvre et Maine, Muscadet Côtes de Grand Lieu, Muscadet des Coteaux de la Loire and Muscadet. Muscadet de Sèvre et Maine and Muscadet Côtes de Grand Lieu are bottled on lees, straight from the unracked, unfiltered cask or tank in which they were fermented, giving a slight prickle and extra freshness to the taste.

The other important appellation in the Pays Nantais is the ultradry, crisp, white Gros Plant, made from the grape of the same name.

DOMAINES CHEREAU-CARRÉ

Established 1412 *Owners* Chereau family *Production* 300,000 cases *Vineyard area* 297 acres (120 ha)

Négociant, estate owner, and a noted proponent of wood-aging top muscadet *cuvées*, the Chereau family is one of the leading producers in this region. Properties such as Château du Coing and Château de Chasseloir provide fine vines for their *domaine* wines. Top of the range is Comte Leloup de Chasseloir, a nonoaked *cuvée* of great intensity, far from the ordinary run of muscadets. Cuvée Comte de St-Hubert is aged in new wood, but the quality of the fruit limits the wood to its proper role: enhancing and balancing the wine. The *négociant* wines—the largest part of the business—are more conventional, but benefit from the *domaine*'s reputation and from the experience and expertise that it has accumulated.

DOMAINE DES DORICES

Established 1429 *Owners* Boullault family *Production* 17,000 cases *Vineyard area* 99 acres (40 ha)

The Boullault family estate is located just outside Vallet in the heart of Muscadet de Sèvre et Maine. Over 40 years ago, Léon Boullault converted the vineyards to organic farming, a revolutionary step in those days, and it is possible to detect the results of this decision in the intense fruit flavors of the wines. Cuvée Choisie is a selection of the best lots after the harvest; Cuvée Grande Garde is aged on lees for two winters before bottling, and spends a further year in bottle before release. Many of the wines carry the seal of approval of the Hermine d'Or, a local society that carries out blind tastings under the supervision of a top enologist.

Local producers sample each others' wares at an informal picnic in the Pays Nantais.

The Loire is at the limit of winegrowing in western France and winters can be chilly.

DOMAINE DE L'ÉCU

Established NA *Owner* Guy Bossard *Production*
11,000 cases *Vineyard area* 49 acres (20 ha)

Guy Bossard's estate is living proof that biodynamic methods of cultivation really do work. It
makes what are generally considered the best muscadets produced anywhere: wines with concentration, weight and a clear expression of *terroir*.
Terroir plays a further part in the Bossard range
of wines, since the muscadets go out under the
names of the soils in which the vines are planted:
Expression Granit, Expression Gneiss and
Expression Orthogneiss. For muscadets, normally
wines to be drunk young and forgotten, these are
serious wines that can age well. Look out, also,
for the sparkling muscadet, Cuvée Ludwig Hahn.

DOMAINE GADAIS ET FILS

Established 1950 *Owners* Gadais family *Production*
20,000 cases *Vineyard area* 62 acres (25 ha)

The dynamic Christophe Gadais recently took over
his family's property and is now making pure, elegant wines that are classics of their kind—full of
freshness but with some weight and depth. Gadais
produces three muscadet *cuvées*: Domaine de la
Tourmaline, Grande Réserve du Moulin and the

extraconcentrated Vieilles
Vignes. In addition, there is
a particularly good, superdry
Gros Plant du Pays Nantais.

DOMAINE DE LA LOUVETRIE

Established NA *Owner* Joseph
Landron *Production* 12,500 cases
Vineyard area 62 acres (25 ha)

Joseph Landron makes several
muscadets, each one from grapes
grown in a particular soil type.
The lightest and freshest, Cuvée
Amphibolite, is bottled without any chaptalization
or filtration. Hard, rocky orthogneiss soils are
used to produce the fatter Hermine d'Or, which
carries the seal of approval of the society of the
same name, and the old-vine Fief du Breuil wines.
The Landrons also own Clos du Château de la
Carizière, where equally fine muscadet is produced.

CHÂTEAU DE LA RAGOTIÈRE

Established NA *Owners* Couillaud brothers *Production*
40,000 cases *Vineyard area* 161 acres (65 ha)

The Couillaud brothers—Bernard, François and
Michel—own two Muscadet properties, Château
de la Ragotière and the much less well-known
Château la Morinière. From the first comes classic,
rich, fat muscadet, including one *cuvée*, Auguste
Couillaud, that is aged in wood. From the second
property issues a *vin de pays* made from chardonnay, which, in warm years, seems almost akin to
chablis. At the top of the range is a superb bottling
of the best selection from Château de la Ragotière,
which is aged on, and racked straight off, the lees.

SAUVION ET FILS

Established 1965 *Owners* Sauvion family *Production*
15,000 cases *Vineyard area* 74 acres (30 ha)

This is one of the best-known names in Muscadet,
partly as a result of assiduous marketing, but also
because of the quality of the wine. The vineyards
at the family property of Château du Cléray
Sauvion near Vallet produce a reserve wine. The
other top *cuvée* is Cardinal Richard, which is
made from wines selected by a panel of tasters
from the best lots during the spring following the
harvest. The Découverte range consists of *négociant* wines, again chosen by a tasting panel in
the spring after harvest. The Sauvions also make
Allégorie, a barrel-fermented muscadet, which has
the distinctive vanilla-and-toast taste that muscadet connoisseurs either love or loathe.

*A winemaker samples late-harvest grapes
that will be used to make sweet wine.*

Cognac

Anthony Peregrine

Cognac, the spirit with the highest self-esteem of any in the world, was in turmoil as the twenty-first century began. Export sales had plummeted from around 145 million bottles in 1990 to nearer 107 million by the end of the decade. Furthermore, a crisis atmosphere had spread across the region's 200,000 acres (81,000 ha) of low-lying vineyards, which roll westward from near Angoulême to the Atlantic coast. Overproduction was running at 25 percent, prices paid to grape growers had plunged, and government aid had been requested.

This was a sorry state of affairs for a drink that had long traded on its image of aristocratic sub-limity. Then again, the image itself was part of the problem. Quite simply, cognac producers had never got to grips with a modern era in which dark spirits are considered old hat. And their relentless attempts to promote cognac as evermore sophisti-cated, evermore ethereal (a key word in the cognac lexicon), simply put the drink even farther beyond most people's financial and aspirational reach.

Cognac vineyards are planted mainly with ugni blanc, France's most common variety.

The promotional attempts were, however, understandable. They were dictated by a tra-dition that began when Dutch traders pioneered distillation in Charentes in the early seven-teenth century. The Dutch had created a thriving trade in alco-holic drinks between France, Holland and other parts of northern Europe. They them-selves preferred their alcohol distilled and strong, and in Charentes they discovered not only vast tracts of vines but the supplies of timber necessary to fire stills. Moreover, it soon became clear that the local wine (now made overwhelmingly from ugni blanc) lent itself perfectly to double-distilling and oak-aging, whereas other wines required repeated distillation to remove unpleasant flavors. By 1700, "cogniack brandy," as it was known in England, was already outdistancing rivals.

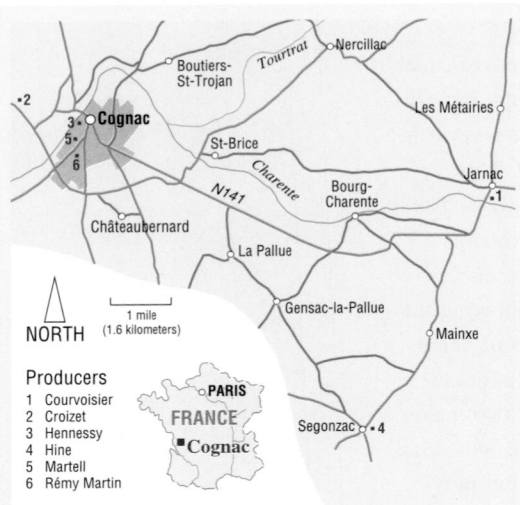

In the eighteenth century, the English and Irish came to the region to exploit cognac's potential, and Jean Martell (from Jersey), Thomas Hine (England) and James Hennessy (Ireland) all set up businesses that still exist today. In 1909, the pro-duction area was defined, and 25 years later the six constituent *crus* were recognized. This fuelled cognac's growing popularity which, in turn, in the late 1970s and 1980s, attracted the attention of the multinationals that now dominate the sector.

Production in the Cognac *crus*

The cognac production zone, which centers on the town of the same name, divides into six *crus* on the basis of climate and, especially, the concentra-tion of chalk in the soil. The soils with the heaviest concentrations resemble those of Champagne, and are therefore known as Grande Champagne and Petite Champagne. The former has the most chalk and provides the finest, most delicate cognacs. Cognac from the Petite Champagne tends to have a more floral bouquet and a touch less finesse. (Fine Champagne is a mix of these *crus*, including a minimum of 50 percent Grande Champagne.)

The smallest *cru* in size, though not production, is the Borderies. Its cognac is rounder and more robust than those of the Champagnes, with a dis-tinctive bouquet of violets, and ages more quickly. The Fins Bois is the largest producer, though quality varies; its cognac is marked by aromas of crushed grapes and is much used in blending. Encircling the other zones, the Bons Bois *cru* yields more rustic produce, while near the ocean the Bois Ordinaires/Communs supplies the most basic fare.

Once vinified, cognac wine is double-distilled in copper pot-stills. Afterward, it measures 70 percent alcohol, so it has to be diluted during aging, usually with distilled water. The length of aging varies, but can last for decades. As a result of evaporation dur-ing aging, each year about 2 percent of the cognac in the region's storehouses simply disappears into thin air—the equivalent of about 23 million bot-tles! Cognac folk call it "the angels' share."

Although single-vintage and single-*cru* cognacs are becoming fashionable, most cognacs are made from different *crus* and vintages. The traditional cognac classifications relate to the length of aging. VS (Very Special) or three stars means that the youngest brandy in the blend has been aged for at least two years; the youngest brandy in a VSOP (Very Superior Old Pale) blend has been aged for four years. A Napoléon has had a minimum aging of six years, though it is more usually seven to fifteen. This is the stepping stone from VSOP to XO (Extra Old), whose youngest component must have been aged for six years, though it is not unusual for the actual minimum to be nearer twenty-five years.

Almost all cognac is sold by *négociants*, who usually buy in grapes or eaux-de-vie, though some also have their own vineyards. The market is dominated by the "Big Four"—Hennessy, Rémy Martin, Martell and Courvoisier—which are responsible for 70 percent of sales. These companies have led the way in dealing with the recent crisis, mainly by producing new styles of cognac aimed at customers never considered before—women and the young. At the same time, the houses continue to make hugely expensive, antique fare to remind us that cognac retains a superb and, yes, ethereal, dimension. The requisite balancing act represents an enormous challenge to producers, but the cognac sector is all the more interesting for it.

COURVOISIER

Established 1805 *Owner* Allied Domecq *Production* 1 million cases

Napoleon visited Courvoisier's operation in 1811, thus initiating the link between the emperor and cognac. The house continues to justify its imperial connections with a range as fine and aromatic as any. From a VS with fruit and flower tones, it runs through the complexity of the flagship Napoleon to an XO Impérial of almost exotic character.

CROIZET

Established 1805 *Owners* Eymard family *Production* 45,000 cases

Croizet offers exceptional cognacs in the Napoleon category and above. It also has stocks from the era before phylloxera and is one of very few houses to sell single-vintage produce. If you're looking for a fine 1928 or 1944, this is a good place to start.

HENNESSY

Established 1765 *Owner* LVMH *Production* 3 million cases

Since Christophe Navarre took over in 1998, cognac's biggest producer has consolidated its hold in the US, created three single-distillery cognacs (Camp Romain, Izambard and Le Peu) and produced one of the most interesting of the "young-generation" cognacs, the Pure White. It has also

The vineyards of Biard are part of Cognac's most important cru, Grande Champagne.

enhanced its reputation for complex premium cognacs with the top-end Grande Champagne XO.

HINE

Established 1763 *Owner* LVMH *Production* 60,000 cases

This house retains its unbeatable reputation for cognacs of delicacy, elegance and great age. Rare & Delicate is as its name suggests, but rounded out with structured mellowness, while Antique balances light and shade, and displays floral notes as well as hints of leather.

MARTELL

Established 1715 *Owner* Seagram *Production* 1.25 million cases

Martell is best known for its longstanding Cordon Bleu blend, but has recently sought to attract young drinkers with the excellent Odys and Artys brands, as well as new-wave connoisseurs with the Réserve de J&F Martell, a flowery, restrained, single-growth cognac. Création and the infinitely subtle L'Art de Martell maintain the company's presence at the very top of the market.

RÉMY MARTIN

Established 1724 *Owner* Rémy Cointreau *Production* 1.5 million cases

The only house whose produce is all at least Fine Champagne, Rémy has nevertheless affixed its centaur emblem to new-era cognacs—notably, the floral and spicily fruity Trek. Meanwhile, Rémy Silver (cognac pre-mixed with vodka and a "secret ingredient") is a shot at the cocktail market. But Rémy's most notable achievement remains the Louis XIII: a Grande Champagne of astonishingly rich, concentrated aromas made from eaux-de-vie at least 50 and up to 100 years old. Purchasers will, of course, need deep pockets.

Below: *A distinctive style of glassware has been developed for serving cognac.*

Bottom: *Barrels of century-old eaux-de-vie, which is added to blends for XO cognacs.*

Bordeaux

James Lawther MW

A tower is the motif of Château Latour, one of Bordeaux's most prestigious estates.

Bordeaux has been synonymous with wine for centuries. The Romans sowed the seeds of an embryonic industry more than 2,000 years ago and since then Bordeaux has evolved into the largest fine wine region in the world. Today, approximately 284,050 acres (115,000 ha) are under production, and yearly sales of more than 600 million bottles provide an annual turnover of 14 billion francs (US$2 billion/2 billion Euros). Add to this a working and commercial force of 12,500 wine growers, 57 cooperatives, 400 trading companies or *négociants* and 130 brokers, and the concept of a vinous empire is complete. Wine is Bordeaux's *raison d'être*.

To the outside world, however, Bordeaux's reputation rests squarely on a group of illustrious châteaux and their highly sought-after and increasingly expensive wines. The likes of Margaux, Lafite and Pétrus certainly turn out benchmark products—firm, long-lived, finely balanced and for the most part red. But they are merely the tip of the iceberg, representing just 5 percent of Bordeaux's total production. Below the waterline lies a vast range of wines, including excellent-value offerings from the *petites appellations* as well as a large quantity of far-from-consistent generic bordeaux. About 85 percent of the region's output is red; the rest is mainly dry and sweet white, with a little rosé, *clairet* and sparkling *crémant*.

Bottles from the 1799 vintage are still held in the cellars of Château Lafite-Rothschild.

History

The Romans may have been the first to cultivate the vine in Bordeaux, but it was under English rule that trade in wine initially developed. In 1152, Eléanor, Duchess of Aquitaine, married Henry Plantagenet, the future King of England, thereby ceding her territories to England. As a result of various concessions offered by the English Crown in return, ships sailing from Bordeaux were exempted from export tax and wines from the region were excluded from restrictions placed on those from other areas such as the Haut Pays (Bergerac, Cahors and Gaillac), to the west. As a result, a flourishing trade in wine and other commodities grew between Bordeaux and Britain. Soon, vineyards in the Graves, Entre-Deux-Mers, Blaye, Bourg and St-Émilion developed; the port of Libourne was constructed (1270); seafaring trade routes opened; and Bordeaux established itself as a major commercial center for wine.

This golden period came to an end when the French army defeated the English at the Battle of Castillon in 1453. However, the links with England were not completely severed and trading continued, although other markets gradually gained in importance. The Dutch, in particular, became a major force during the seventeenth century, initiating a number of changes in wine styles and channels of distribution. Whereas the demand from the English was for the rather thin, light-red *clairet* (hence the term "claret" for red bordeaux), the Dutch taste ran to dry and semi-sweet white wines, both for general consumption and for distilling into brandy. From Holland, these products soon spread into other parts of northern Europe. The Dutch also introduced sulfur wicks for sterilizing barrels and, most notably, helped drain the marshland of the Médoc, enabling the region to develop as a major winegrowing district.

The eighteenth century provided Bordeaux's second golden era. Overseas commerce broadened to include lucrative trades in sugar, coffee, cotton and slaves with the French West Indies. This in turn gave rise to a new, powerful moneyed class, the *noblesse de robe*, who were keen to invest in vineyards and as members of the Bordeaux parliament had a direct say in the affairs of the region. One notable member of this class was Nicolas

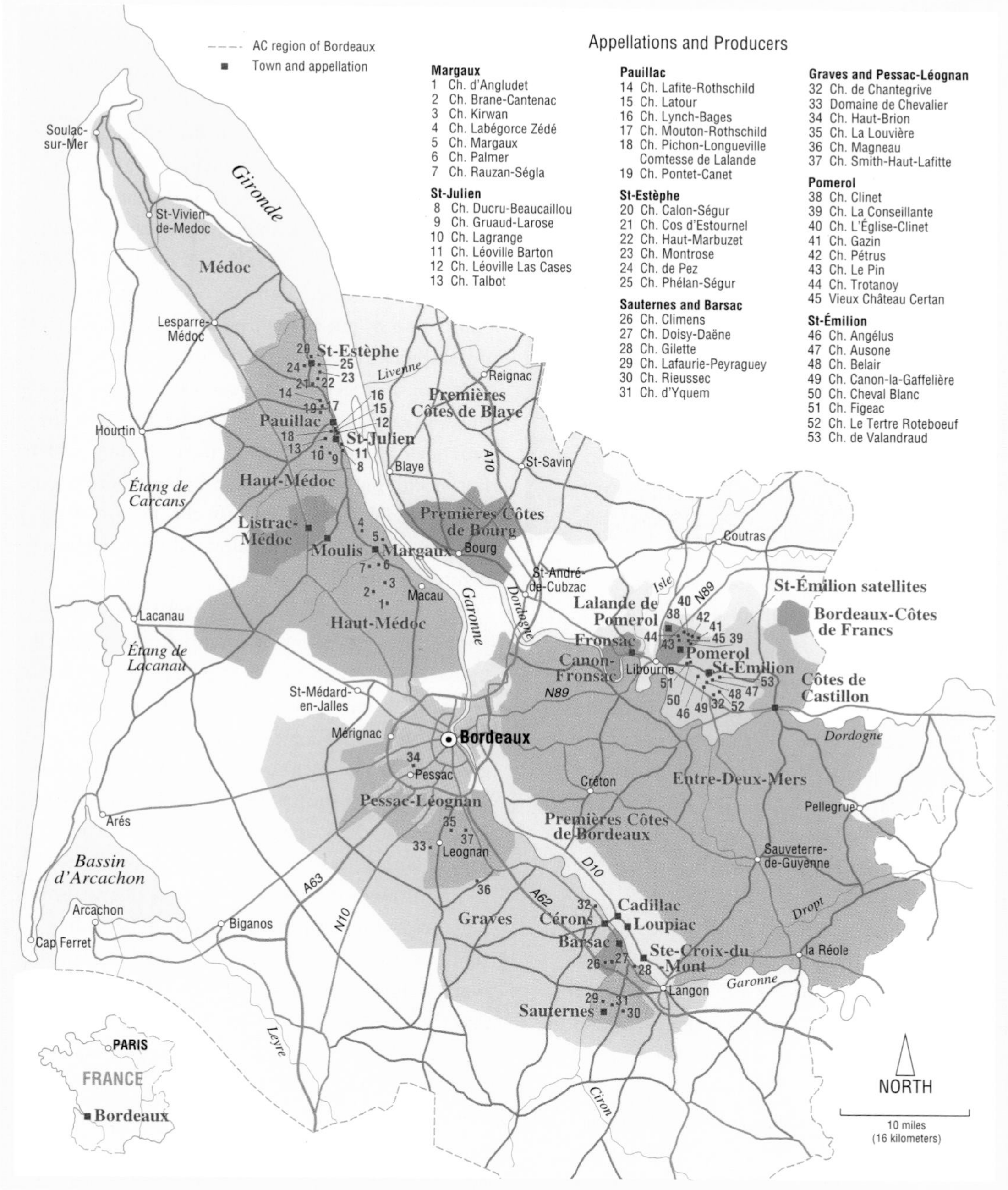
AC region of Bordeaux
Town and appellation
Appellations and Producers
Margaux
1 Ch. d'Angludet
2 Ch. Brane-Cantenac
3 Ch. Kirwan
4 Ch. Labégorce Zédé
5 Ch. Margaux
6 Ch. Palmer
7 Ch. Rauzan-Ségla
St-Julien
8 Ch. Ducru-Beaucaillou
9 Ch. Gruaud-Larose
10 Ch. Lagrange
11 Ch. Léoville Barton
12 Ch. Léoville Las Cases
13 Ch. Talbot
Pauillac
14 Ch. Lafite-Rothschild
15 Ch. Latour
16 Ch. Lynch-Bages
17 Ch. Mouton-Rothschild
18 Ch. Pichon-Longueville Comtesse de Lalande
19 Ch. Pontet-Canet
St-Estèphe
20 Ch. Calon-Ségur
21 Ch. Cos d'Estournel
22 Ch. Haut-Marbuzet
23 Ch. Montrose
24 Ch. de Pez
25 Ch. Phélan-Ségur
Sauternes and Barsac
26 Ch. Climens
27 Ch. Doisy-Daëne
28 Ch. Gilette
29 Ch. Lafaurie-Peyraguey
30 Ch. Rieussec
31 Ch. d'Yquem
Graves and Pessac-Léognan
32 Ch. de Chantegrive
33 Domaine de Chevalier
34 Ch. Haut-Brion
35 Ch. La Louvière
36 Ch. Magneau
37 Ch. Smith-Haut-Lafitte
Pomerol
38 Ch. Clinet
39 Ch. La Conseillante
40 Ch. L'Église-Clinet
41 Ch. Gazin
42 Ch. Pétrus
43 Ch. Le Pin
44 Ch. Trotanoy
45 Vieux Château Certan
St-Émilion
46 Ch. Angélus
47 Ch. Ausone
48 Ch. Belair
49 Ch. Canon-la-Gaffelière
50 Ch. Cheval Blanc
51 Ch. Figeac
52 Ch. Le Tertre Roteboeuf
53 Ch. de Valandraud
Soulac-sur-Mer
Gironde
St-Vivien-de-Medoc
Médoc
Lesparre-Médoc
St-Estèphe
Livenne
Reignac
Premières Côtes de Blaye
Pauillac
St-Julien
Hourtin
Blaye
St-Savin
A10
Haut-Médoc
Étang de Carcans
Premières Côtes de Bourg
Listrac-Médoc
Moulis
Margaux
Bourg
Coutras
St-André-de-Cubzac
Macau
Garonne
Dordogne
Isle
N89
St-Émilion satellites
Lalande de Pomerol
Bordeaux-Côtes de Francs
Lacanau
Haut-Médoc
Fronsac
Pomerol
Étang de Lacanau
Canon-Fronsac
Libourne
St-Émilion
Côtes de Castillon
St-Médard-en-Jalles
Mérignac
Bordeaux
Dordogne
Pessac
Créton
Entre-Deux-Mers
Pessac-Léognan
Pellegrue
Arès
Premières Côtes de Bordeaux
Léognan
Bassin d'Arcachon
Sauveterre-de-Guyenne
D10
A63
Arcachon
A62
Cadillac
Biganos
N10
Graves
Cérons
Loupiac
Dropt
Cap Ferret
Barsac
Ste-Croix-du-Mont
La Réole
Langon
Garonne
Sauternes
PARIS
FRANCE
Bordeaux
Leyre
Ciron
NORTH
10 miles (16 kilometers)

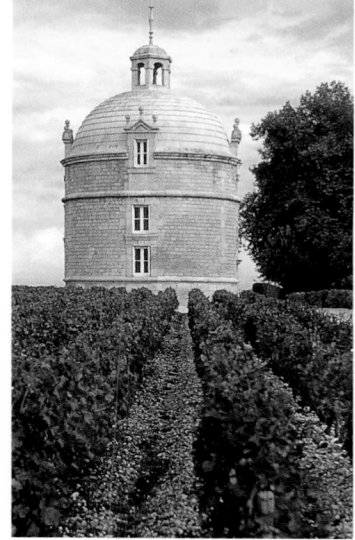

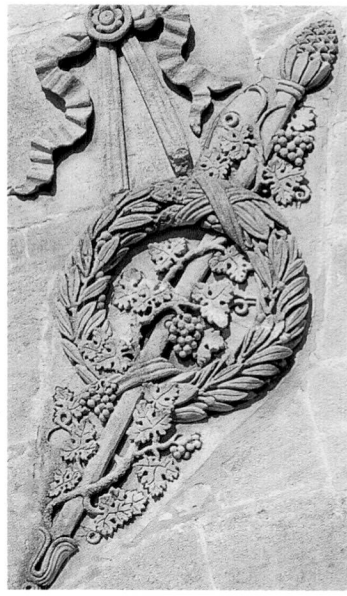

Alexandre, Marquis de Ségur, who in the early eighteenth century was president of the Bordeaux parliament and proprietor of Châteaux Latour, Lafite, Mouton and Calon-Ségur.

Wines from individual estates—a phenomenon first noted by the English diarist Samuel Pepys when he reported drinking "Ho Bryan" or Haut-Brion in a London tavern in 1663—were increasingly recognized and sought out by wealthy Europeans. Trade in these "new French clarets," as they were known, lured a different kind of merchant to Bordeaux. Originating mainly from Britain, Ireland, Holland and Germany, these entrepreneurs set up businesses in and around the Quai des Chartrons. Some of the merchant houses founded in this period, such as Johnson and Barton, exist to this day. Growing prosperity led to a spate of building in Bordeaux, and much of the city's imposing architecture dates from this period.

The early part of the nineteenth century saw a consolidation of the trends that had begun in the eighteenth century. The region of St-Émilion, where church control had inhibited the development of viticulture prior to the Revolution, now began to supply wines from individual estates and to build strong trading links with the Benelux countries. The overall number of *négociants* increased further, and although Britain once

Below: *The vineyards of Château Latour are crowned by this seventeenth-century tower.*

Bottom: *Carvings on the wall of the Château Cos d'Estournel in St-Estèphe.*

Fermentation tanks in the cellars of Château Mouton-Rothschild. The Rothschilds pioneered the practice of châteaux bottling.

Opposite page: The cool, humid St-Émilion region is best-suited to early-ripening grapes.

again became Bordeaux's best customer, new markets were developed in Russia and North and South America. In 1855, a classification system was introduced, which ranked the wines from the top châteaux in the Médoc and Sauternes according to their market price (see p. 106). The only setback during this period of prosperity was the arrival in 1851 of the vine disease oïdium, or powdery mildew; however, it was eventually brought under control in 1857 through the use of sulfur.

Unfortunately, it was followed shortly afterward by the arrival of phylloxera in the 1870s and downy mildew toward the end of the century. Both devasted the region's vineyards and heralded a period of severe economic depression. Viticulturalists used American rootstock to reconstruct phylloxera-damaged vineyards and the *bouille bordelaise* mixture of lime and copper sulfate to treat mildew. It was probably around this time that cabernet sauvignon, cabernet franc, merlot, sémillon, sauvignon blanc and muscadelle became the principal Bordeaux grape varieties. Pre-phylloxera, there were at least 20 different grape varieties under cultivation.

The beginning of the twentieth century was a difficult period for Bordeaux. Prices fell, vineyards were overcropped to compensate for the shortage of plants, and, worse still, wines from outside the region were fraudulently sold as bordeaux by local merchants. The First World War and the Depression of the 1930s prolonged the slump. Little finance was available for investment, and vineyards changed hands regularly and at derisory prices. Almost the only positive development

during this period was the establishment in 1936 of a system of *appellation contrôlée*, which delimited boundaries, defined work practices and, to a degree, set standards of quality.

A revival of Bordeaux's fortunes occurred only during the 1960s, when capital gradually became available for investment in vineyards, buildings and new technology, particularly stainless-steel fermentation tanks and cooling systems. During this period, châteaux owners and *négociants* also began to realize that they could finance development by selling wines as futures, or *en primeur*, a procedure that soon found favor with the American market in particular. In 1972, the practice of bottling wines at the châteaux, which Baron Philippe de Rothschild had introduced in 1924, became compulsory for the 1855-classed growths; this in turn encouraged other independent châteaux to follow suit.

In the early 1970s, the recovery came to a temporary halt following a market crash caused by overpricing and the 1973 energy crisis. However, it was kick-started by the qualitative and commercial success of the 1982 vintage, and given further momentum by a series of excellent vintages during the 1980s. Subsequently, important new markets opened in countries such as Japan, land prices increased, and there was a frenzy of investment in the region's vineyards and wineries, with institutional investors becoming significant new owners. Furthermore, a younger, more skilled generation arrived to fill technical and management positions.

Landscape and climate

The Bordeaux region is located in the Gironde department of southwestern France. It extends more than 95 miles (150 km) from the Pointe de Grave in the northwest to Langon in the southeast, and about 50 miles (75 km) from the city of Bordeaux in the west to Sainte-Foy-la-Grande in the east. It is crossed by the Dordogne and Garonne rivers, which meet at and flow into the great Gironde Estuary on the Atlantic coast. The vineyards are situated along these waterways or between the two rivers in an area known as the Entre-Deux-Mers. They are protected to some degree from strong Atlantic winds by the forests of the Landes, which lie to the southwest.

Most of Bordeaux is flat or undulating and there are no steep slopes; indeed, the highest point is only 430 feet (130 m) above sea level. Generally, soil types determine which variety

of grape is planted. On the "left bank" (the Médoc and the Graves), the soils are composed mainly of pebbles, gravel and sand carried down from the Pyrenees and the Massif Central by glaciers during the Quaternary ice age. These soils are generally poor, but retain heat and have good filtration properties, and are therefore ideal for late-ripening cabernet sauvignon.

On the "right bank" (St-Émilion, Pomerol and Fronsac), the soils are composed mainly of clay, limestone, sand and small pockets of gravel, and are significantly more humid and therefore cooler. This makes them more suited to early-ripening merlot. The terrain in the Entre-Deux-Mers varies considerably, from fertile alluvial river terraces (which are less well suited to the cultivation of the vine) to cool, moist, limestone-clay and clay soils, some of which are similar to those found on the right bank.

Bordeaux has a temperate maritime climate made milder by the warming influence of the Gulf Stream. Rainfall is generally abundant, with an annual average of 33 inches (840 mm), and there are approximately 2,150 hours of sunshine each year. Summers are warm, with temperatures reaching a peak of around 77°F (25°C) in August; winter temperatures rarely drop below 32°F (0°C). The absence of climatic extremes means that the grapes ripen only to a certain level of intensity, resulting in wines that are generally subtle and reserved rather than up-front and powerful.

However, as the great freeze of 1956 proved, winemakers have to be prepared for cold snaps in winter. Spring frosts are also a danger to budding vines in the early part of the year (although vineyard areas close to the Gironde are protected to some degree by the warming effects of the estuary.) In early June, when flowering usually takes place, cooler-than-average temperatures can result in bad fruit set. July to early September is the critical period for ripening; the harvest usually starts in early September for dry whites and finishes around mid-October for the last reds. Often it coincides with a rainy spell, creating a nail-biting finish to the growing season; fortunately, Bordeaux winegrowers have become increasingly adept at harvesting between bouts of rain. Violent hail-storms can sometimes be a problem in summer. In fall, morning mists caused by the mixing of the cool waters of the Ciron River with the

Regular early morning mists in Sauternes contribute to the formation of botrytis.

warmer waters of the Garonne benefit local producers of sweet white wines, as they provoke the onset of noble rot (*Botrytis cinerea*).

Vines and wines

Bordeaux has a number of distinctive grape varieties, but they are normally combined in blends rather than being used to make single-variety wines. This is in contrast to, say, Burgundy, where pinot noir holds sway. The makeup of each blend varies according to the zone of production, the plantings at individual châteaux and the relative success of each variety in a given vintage.

The production of red wines has increased dramatically over the last 30 years, with red grape varieties now covering 237,120 acres (96,000 ha) as opposed to 113,620 acres (46,000 ha) in 1970. Merlot is the most widely planted grape, occupying a total of 133,380 acres (54,000 ha). Its supple fruit and higher alcohol content add weight and substance to a blend, while its softness can make a wine more approachable. It is easier to ripen than cabernet sauvignon and adapts well to the cooler clay-limestone soils of the right bank and Entre-Deux-Mers, where it dominates.

Cabernet sauvignon is probably Bordeaux's most famous red variety, being firmly associated with the great wines of the Médoc and Graves: it may, for instance, constitute up to 80 percent of a Château Lafite, Mouton-Rothschild or Latour. Cabernet sauvignon is less sensitive to spring frosts than merlot and ripens later, but it needs the assistance of warmer soils to come to full maturity. Its small, thick-skinned grapes provide color, tannin and a firm but finely edged texture and bouquet. Currently, 66,690 acres (27,000 ha) are under production.

Cabernet franc is the third-most-planted grape variety. It plays a particularly significant role on the right bank, where it partners merlot in St-Émilion and Pomerol blends. When fully ripe, cabernet franc adds elegance and a fruity complexity. Other red varieties include petit verdot and malbec. The former, although difficult to ripen, has a following among producers in the communal appellations of the Médoc for its firm extract and acidity; the latter is found principally in the Côtes de Bourg and Premières Côtes de Blaye.

The great red wines of Bordeaux are capable of aging for several decades, and become gradually more harmonious and complex with time. In the past, they were rather austere and unyielding when young; however, a more consistent supply of riper

The pebbly soils of the Graves offer excellent drainage and heat retention.

fruit and a demand from consumers for more approachable young wines have encouraged the development of a more supple style during the last 20 years. Nowadays, generic bordeaux is drinkable after only two or three years in bottle.

White grape varieties now make up only about 15 percent of the vineyards compared with around 52 percent in 1970. Sémillon has suffered most in the swing to red wine but is still the principal white variety, particularly in the sweet-wine appellations. A productive grape, it makes wines with a citrus flavor and aroma when vinified dry; however, because it is particularly susceptible to noble rot, it is more widely used to make sweet wines that are rich, unctuous, and redolent of honey, raisins and tropical fruits.

Sauvignon blanc is the only white variety that is planted more widely now than in the past: there are over 12,350 acres (5,000 ha) today, compared with 4,421 acres (1,790 ha) in 1970. Small amounts are blended with sémillon in sweet wines to supply added zest and aroma. However, in areas such as the Entre-Deux-Mers, sauvignon blanc is used to create a crisp, dry, aromatic, single-variety wine. In the Graves, where it is normally blended with sémillon, it is given greater weight and complexity through barrel fermentation and lees stirring.

The other white varieties are now less significant. Muscadelle is used to create a more complex aroma in sweet wines such as Cadillac and Ste-Croix-du-Mont. Colombard and ugni blanc cover around 4,150 acres (1,680 ha) in total, mainly in

Bordeaux's harvest usually begins in early September and ends around mid-October.

A winemaker samples the new vintage at Château Léoville-las-Cases in the Médoc.

During winter, vineyard workers prune the vines and gather cuttings for grafting.

the Blaye, and are used in generic bordeaux blends. There are also some experimental plantings of sauvignon gris (thought to be a muscat clone), which producers use for its fruit and heady aroma.

Appellations and viticulture

Bordeaux's system of *appellation contrôlée* was established in 1936. As in other parts of France, each appellation is the subject of a ministerial decree that stipulates the geographical delimitation of the appellation, authorized grape varieties, methods of cultivation and vinification, base yield per hectare, minimum natural level of alcohol, minimum and maximum degrees of alcohol after fermentation, and labelling procedure (which is now controlled by European Union legislation).

While complying with these directives, the producer must apply for appellation status every year by declaring the harvest and requesting a certificate of approval. This is granted following the analysis and tasting of wines (which can involve two samplings separated by a set period of time). If the certificate is refused—a sensitive issue, as the tasting panels are usually made up of fellow winegrowers—the producer can submit the wine for approval in a lower-graded appellation.

If this too fails, the wine must be sold as a simple table wine (*vin de table*).

Virtually all of the 284,050 acres (115,000 ha) under vine in Bordeaux are delimited as *appellation contrôlée*, with less than 2 percent delimited as *vin de table*. There are 57 different appellations, ranging from regional (for example, Bordeaux and Bordeaux Supérieur) to subregional (Haut-Médoc, for instance) and communal or village (such as Pauillac and Fronsac). Each has its own set of directives and each has a winegrowers' association, or *syndicat viticole*, that defends and promotes the appellation.

Considerable progress has been made in viticulture over the last decade, with the more assiduous pro-

ducers realizing that good wine is made in the vineyard. There has been greater investment in planting, equipment and labor; fungal diseases have been better contained; and management has improved. The advances have been most evident during difficult vintages such as 1992, which 20 years ago would have been a total disaster. Overcropping is still a problem, but grapes are now allowed more time to ripen: traditionally, winegrowers waited 100 days after flowering before harvesting, but most now allow 110 days.

Vine density varies according to the soil type and the economic imperatives of the producer. In the Médoc, the density may be as high as 4,000 vines per acre (10,000 vines per ha), whereas in St-Émilion, between 2,000 and 2,400 vines per acre (5,000 and 6,000 vines per ha) is the norm. In the Entre-Deux-Mers, where economic difficulties resulted in the pulling up of rows of vines in the 1960s and 1970s, there are still some vineyards with as little as 800 vines per acre (2,000 per ha). However, the general tendency is to increase density to provide competition for the vine.

The majority of Bordeaux's vineyards are Guyot-trained, either to one or two canes. Cordon-training is used in some of the more mechanized vineyards, while the lyre system also has its advocates. Pruning is usually carried out by hand, although occasionally some mechanical prepruning occurs. Herbicides are still widely used for weed control, but chemical fertilizers are used less frequently and organic manuring has been reintroduced. Growers are once again working the soils and ploughing between rows of vines. At the same time, the use of grass cover between rows to regulate the water supply to the vines is favored in some regions, especially where erosion is a problem.

Bordeaux's damp climate means that fungal diseases are a perennial threat. Grey rot, oidium and mildew are the most common, but excoriose and eutypa dieback also attack susceptible varieties such as cabernet sauvignon. Other dangers include the animal parasites grape moth and red spidermite, and the viral disease known as *court-noué*, or fanleaf degeneration. Such environmental problems make a completely organic approach to viticulture difficult, but an increasing number of producers are embracing the idea of the "*lutte raisonnée*." This strategy involves limiting chemical spraying to periods when climatic conditions render it most effective, with the timing being based on local weather forecasts. Other innovations include the use of pheromone capsules that disorient the male grape moth, thus preventing the fertilization of eggs, and the introduction of a white spider-mite, the typhlodrome, to combat the red spider-mite.

Increased expenditure on labor has occurred mainly in the realm of canopy management. Although vine-trimming is normally mechanized, there has been an increase in shoot-thinning, the removal of excess buds and leaf-stripping, all of which are done by hand. Green harvesting to reduce the number of bunches per vine has also become a more common practice.

Winemaking

For many people, Bordeaux conjures up an image of hardy workers picking grapes by hand, but the reality is that 70–80 percent of the vineyard area is now harvested by machine. (However, hand-picking is still considered essential at the top châteaux and in sweet-wine appellations.)

Scientific methods now enable growers to time the harvest of various parcels of vines more precisely, and the wider use of sorting tables, which can be applied to both machine- and hand-picked grapes, has allowed winemakers to be more selective.

The procedure used at Bordeaux's top estates for making red wines has become a classic of its kind. It took on its present guise in the 1970s and has since been constantly refined on the basis of scientific research undertaken by the University of Bordeaux's Faculté d'Oenologie.

Each grape variety is vinified separately, as are grapes from different parcels of land if sufficient tank space is available. The fruit is destemmed and crushed, and then pumped or gravity-fed into fermentation tanks or *cuves*. The tanks may be made of cement, stainless steel or wood. Each material has its own attributes and champions: for example, Pétrus is vinified in cement, Haut-Brion

At most of Bordeaux's leading vineyards, grapes are normally harvested by hand.

The practice of ploughing between rows of vines has been reintroduced to many areas.

Clearing grape skins from the wine press at Château Cos d'Estournel in St-Estèphe.

in stainless steel and Margaux in wood. Sulfur dioxide (SO2) is widely used as an additive to protect against oxidation and bacteria.

Alcoholic fermentation is regulated at around 82–86°F (28–30°C) and lasts an average of eight to ten days. Natural yeasts are used and, if necessary, a yeast starter, or *pied de cuve*, may be taken from one tank and added to the others. Chaptalization is permitted, but only to increase the alcohol content by a maximum of 2 percent. The use of concentrators, involving either reverse osmosis or evaporation under vacuum, is tolerated rather than officially sanctioned. The cost of these machines means that only the top estates can afford them, but they are becoming more popular.

The level of extraction sought during fermentation is an issue that currently divides opinion in Bordeaux. On the one hand, men like enologist Michel Rolland argue that with riper grapes it is possible to push the extraction process farther to obtain greater color, tannin and weight. This requires higher fermentation temperatures, more regular pumping over of the grape must, and a longer period of post-fermentation maceration—anything up to 25 days. The opposing camp argues that this produces overdeveloped wines that lack the balance and finesse of traditional Bordeaux products; it proposes a less vigorous regime using only the press wine, if anything, to build structure.

Following fermentation and maceration, the free-run wine is drained off and the remaining marc pressed. The press wine is retained for blending purposes, with between 5 and 10 percent being used in the final blend. The wine then undergoes malolactic fermentation either in tank or, increasingly, in new oak barrels. The long-term benefits

After destemming, the harvested grapes are fed into large cylindrical wine presses.

of the latter are unclear; however, in the short-term the oak integrates better with the young wine, enhancing the flavor—and therefore gaining the plaudits of journalists and buyers at the tastings held early in the following year!

Once malolactic fermentation has been completed, the wine is aged for anything up to 24 months (although 16 to 18 months is now the norm) in classic 59-gallon (225-l) French oak barrels or *barriques*. A choice of oak is available (Limousin, Nièvre or Allier) and producers often buy from a number of cooperages, both to ensure supply and to increase complexity. American oak is used at some châteaux but rarely by the top producers. The percentage of new oak is determined by the cost and the quality of the wine, but it can be up to 100 percent. During the aging process, the wine is racked off its lees into a fresh barrel every three or four months. It is

also clarified or fined using egg whites or a similar albumin preparation. Prior to bottling, the wine normally undergoes a light filtration.

An important task during the early stages of barrel maturation is the selection and blending for the principal wine. The various batches of different grape varieties are tasted and a decision made as to the blend for a given year. Wines rejected from the *grand vin* may find their way into a second- or even third-label wine, or be sold in bulk to the *négociants*. In recent years, the selection process has become steadily more rigorous, with the *grand vin* now representing as little as 30 to 40 percent of total production at top estates.

The procedure for making dry white wines generally follows principles employed around the world (although European Union regulations dictate that dry wine should contain no more than 0.04 ounces per gallon [4 g per litre] of residual sugar.) Variations practiced in Bordeaux include hand harvesting into perforated plastic containers, and machine harvesting and barrel fermentation.

Normally, the grapes are lightly crushed (and sometimes destemmed), then pressed. A prefermentation maceration on the skins may be carried out, particularly with sauvignon blanc. The juice is allowed to settle, then racked off heavy lees. Fermentation is carried out at a temperature of around 64–68°F (18–20°C), and involves the use of cultured yeasts. Malolactic fermentation is usually prohibited in Bordeaux to preserve acidity. In the Graves and Pessac-Léognan appellations, and occasionally elsewhere, fermentation is carried out in oak barrels with lees stirring.

The sweet, rich wines of the best estates in Sauternes and Barsac, and occasionally across the river in Cadillac, Loupiac and Ste-Croix-du-Mont, are made from grapes affected by noble rot, or

During the maturation process, the cellar master selects wines for the blend.

Botrytis cinerea. Because the development of the rot is irregular, growers must make several selective harvests, collecting only fruit that has achieved around 20–21° alcohol potential.

The grapes are subsequently pressed and fermented, either in stainless steel or, increasingly at the top estates, in new or relatively new oak barrels. The fermentation process is necessarily long and slow. When the wine has reached the desired alcohol-sugar balance—ideally 13.5–14° alcohol and 6–7° (0.94–1.1 ounces per gallon [102–119 g per l]) residual sugar—the fermentation process is halted by reducing the temperature, racking and adding sulfur dioxide. Aging in barrel then continues for another two or three years. The process of cryoextraction, whereby sugars are concentrated by freezing the grapes, has been introduced at a number of châteaux to compensate for rainy vintages.

The Place de Bordeaux

The Bordeaux wine trade is unique in that it has its own marketplace, the Place de Bordeaux, where wines are sold in bulk and bottle, and as futures. Producers sell to *négociants*, who then sell to distributors in France or importers overseas. The transaction between producer and *négociant* is brokered by a middleman, the *courtier*, who receives a 2 percent commission on the price paid by the purchaser. About 400 *négociants* (including 150 of consequence) now handle 75 percent of the region's production, providing both châteaux wines and wines for commercial brands. The latter are purchased from producers and cooperatives, then blended and bottled in the merchants' cellars.

In the past, châteaux wines were also bought by the *négociants* and aged and bottled in their cellars. However, the growth of château bottling and the cost of holding inventory put an end to this tradition; wines from the top estates and less prestigious châteaux with a market rating are now sold mainly as futures, and dispatched to the purchaser 18 to 24 months after the transaction. The buoyancy of the futures market depends on the quality of the vintage, demand and the economic climate at the time. *Négociants* selling futures usually work on a minimum 12–15 percent margin but occasionally take a loss, as occurred following the overpriced 1997 vintage.

Regional cuisine

Like most of the cuisine of southwestern France, Bordeaux's regional fare is rich, warm and hearty. Red meat, duck and game figure heavily on Bordeaux menus, and are often served *à la bordelaise*—in a red or white wine sauce made with marrow and shallots. Typical dishes include *foie gras*, *entrecôte* (sirloin steak grilled over vine cuttings), milk-fed Pauillac lamb and *confit de canard* (duck cooked and preserved in its own fat). In autumn, *cèpe* mushrooms are particularly sought-after; in spring, market stalls are loaded with asparagus from Blaye. The Atlantic Ocean and Gironde Estuary are the source of a number of dishes: lampreys served *à la bordelaise* are a local specialty, as are oysters from the Bassin d'Arcachon served with flat, round sausages known as *crépinettes*. A crisp white wine from the Graves or Entre-Deux-Mers is the perfect accompaniment to these fish or seafood dishes, while red bordeaux, with its fresh, tannic edge, is a natural foil for the region's heartier cuisine.

The classifications

Several classification systems are in use in Bordeaux. The most famous is the 1855 classification for red wines of the Médoc and sweet white wines of Sauternes, but others operate in St-Émilion and the Graves. Even the Crus Bourgeois of the Médoc have a grading, although it is limited by a European Union directive to the use of that term. Pomerol is the only major appellation without a classification. Each ranking has its own history and set of controls; the most important are explained in the box features on the following pages.

MAJOR APPELLATIONS

Margaux

Margaux is the most southerly and extensive of the communal appellations in the Médoc, with approximately 3,340 acres (1,352 ha) under production. The vineyards are spread through five communes: Arsac, Labarde, Cantenac, Soussans and Margaux itself. Margaux's gravel and sand soils are poorer than those farther north, which accounts for the area's generally lighter-bodied and more fragrant style of red wine. The soils and warmer local climate suit late-ripening cabernet sauvignon and petit verdot.

Twenty-one Margaux châteaux were included in the 1855 classification, including Château Margaux, a Premier Cru which today supplies around 70 percent of production. Margaux has often been accused of underachieving, but since the 1990s a younger generation has come to the helm and there has been greater level of investment and commitment. As a result, this is once again an appellation to watch.

CHÂTEAU D'ANGLUDET

Owners Sichel family *Production* 15,000 cases
Vineyard area 79 acres (32 ha); 55 percent cabernet sauvignon, 35 percent merlot, 10 percent petit verdot

The wines from this Cru Bourgeois estate have been consistently supple and generous, and have gained a loyal following. Purchased in a run-down state by Peter Sichel in 1961, the vineyard was completely replanted the same year; it extends over one block on the sandy, gravel soils of the Grand Poujeau plateau in Cantenac. The wine is aged for 18 months in oak *barriques*, a third of which are renewed yearly. A second wine, La Ferme d'Angludet, was introduced in 1991.

CHÂTEAU BRANE-CANTENAC

Owner Henri Lurton *Production* 12,000 cases *Vineyard area* 210 acres (85 ha); 70 percent cabernet sauvignon, 20 percent merlot, 10 percent cabernet franc

Located on the poor, free-draining, gravel soils of the Cantenac plateau, this second growth is capable of producing wines of great finesse. The estate has a longstanding reputation but was put firmly on the map in the early nineteenth century by the Baron de Brane, a viticultural pioneer who gave his name to the property. In 1925, it was purchased by François Lurton and since 1992 has been owned

Grapes affected by noble rot produce the great sweet wines of Sauternes and Barsac.

Some of the top estates have their own cooperages where the barriques are made.

THE 1855 CLASSIFICATION

This classification was based on commercial considerations rather than any qualitative assessment. It was compiled in 1855, when wines from Bordeaux were presented at the Universal Exhibition in Paris and Emperor Napoleon III requested a classification. The listing was drawn up by the Union of Bordeaux Brokers and based on over 100 years of trading statistics (brokers may have been ranking wines unofficially since at least 1730). Sixty châteaux from the Médoc and one (Haut-Brion) from the Graves were classified in five different grades, while twenty-six from Sauternes and Barsac were presented in two grades. The châteaux were ranked according to the trading price they commanded at the time; this original order has been retained here. Only one change has been made to the list since it was compiled: in 1973, Mouton-Rothschild was upgraded from Deuxième Cru to Premier Cru.

THE MÉDOC

Premiers Crus (First Growths)

Château Lafite-Rothschild	Pauillac
Château Margaux	Margaux
Château Latour	Pauillac
Château Haut-Brion	Pessac-Léognan
Château Mouton-Rothschild (upgraded in 1973)	Pauillac

Deuxièmes Crus (Second Growths)

Château Rauzan-Ségla	Margaux
Château Rauzan-Gassies	Margaux
Château Léoville Las Cases	St-Julien
Château Léoville Poyferré	St-Julien
Château Léoville Barton	St-Julien
Château Durfort-Vivens	Margaux
Château Gruaud-Larose	St-Julien
Château Lascombes	Margaux
Château Brane-Cantenac	Margaux
Château Pichon-Longueville (Baron)	Pauillac
Château Pichon-Longueville Comtesse de Lalande	Pauillac
Château Ducru-Beaucaillou	St-Julien
Château Cos d'Estournel	St-Estèphe
Château Montrose	St-Estèphe

Troisièmes Crus (Third Growths)

Château Kirwan	Margaux
Château d'Issan	Margaux
Château Lagrange	St-Julien
Château Langoa Barton	St-Julien
Château Giscours	Margaux
Château Malescot-St-Exupéry	Margaux
Château Boyd-Cantenac	Margaux
Château Cantenac-Brown	Margaux
Château Palmer	Margaux
Château La Lagune	Haut-Médoc
Château Desmirail	Margaux
Château Calon-Ségur	St-Estèphe
Château Ferrière	Margaux
Château Marquis d'Alesme-Becker	Margaux

Quatrièmes Crus (Fourth Growths)

Château St-Pierre	St-Julien
Château Talbot	St-Julien
Château Branaire	St-Julien
Château Duhart-Milon	Pauillac
Château Pouget	Margaux
Château La Tour Carnet	Haut-Médoc
Château Lafon-Rochet	St-Estèphe
Château Beychevelle	St-Julien
Château Prieuré-Lichine	Margaux
Château Marquis de Terme	Margaux

Cinquièmes Crus (Fifth Growths)

Château Pontet-Canet	Pauillac
Château Batailley	Pauillac
Château Haut-Batailley	Pauillac
Château Grand-Puy-Lacoste	Pauillac
Château Grand-Puy-Ducasse	Pauillac
Château Lynch-Bages	Pauillac
Château Lynch-Moussas	Pauillac
Château Dauzac	Margaux
Château d'Armailhac	Pauillac
Château du Tertre	Margaux
Château Haut-Bages-Libéral	Pauillac
Château Pédesclaux	Pauillac
Château Belgrave	Haut-Médoc
Château Camensac	Haut-Médoc
Château Cos Labory	St-Estèphe
Château Clerc Milon	Pauillac
Château Croizet-Bages	Pauillac
Château Cantemerle	Haut-Médoc

SAUTERNES AND BARSAC

Premier Cru Supérieur (Superior First Growth)

Château d'Yquem	Sauternes

Premiers Crus (First Growths)

Château La Tour Blanche	Sauternes
Château Lafaurie-Peyraguey	Sauternes
Château Clos Haut-Peyraguey	Sauternes
Château Rayne Vigneau	Sauternes
Château Suduiraut	Sauternes
Château Coutet	Barsac
Château Climens	Barsac
Château Guiraud	Sauternes
Château Rieussec	Sauternes
Château Rabaud-Promis	Sauternes
Château Sigalas-Rabaud	Sauternes

Deuxièmes Crus (Second Growths)

Château de Myrat*	Sauternes
Château Doisy-Daëne*	Sauternes
Château Doisy-Dubroca*	Sauternes
Château Doisy-Védrines*	Sauternes
Château d'Arche	Sauternes
Château Filhot	Sauternes
Château Broustet	Barsac
Château Nairac	Barsac
Château Caillou	Barsac
Château Suau	Barsac
Château de Malle	Sauternes
Château Romer du Hayot	Sauternes
Château Lamothe	Sauternes
Château Lamothe Guignard	Sauternes

* Châteaux located in Barsac which use the Sauternes label

Traditional modes of transport are still in use on some of the region's estates.

and managed by his grandson, Henri. He has re-planted certain parcels of vines, improved canopy management, reintroduced hand harvesting and renovated the cellars. As a result, the cabernet-dominated wines are now richer and more precise.

CHÂTEAU KIRWAN

Owners Schÿler family *Production* 14,000 cases
Vineyard area 87 acres (35 ha); 40 percent cabernet sauvignon, 30 percent merlot, 20 percent cabernet franc, 10 percent petit verdot

Mark Kirwan, an Irish *négociant* from Galway, inherited this estate in 1760 and later gave his name to the property. The wines had a strong reputation in the nineteenth century and in 1855 Kirwan was classified as a Troisième Cru. At the beginning of the twentieth century, the merchant house of Schröder and Schÿler was contracted to handle the sale of the wines, which led to the purchase of the estate by Armand Schÿler in 1926. Kirwan has recently gained a new lease of life as a result of a renewed commitment from the Schÿler family and the hiring of consultant enologist Michel Rolland. The cellars have been renovated, a second wine, Les Charmes de Kirwan, intro-duced and the harvest is now riper and more selective, providing wines of greater intensity.

CHÂTEAU LABÉGORCE ZÉDÉ

Owner Luc Thienpont *Production* 15,000 cases
Vineyard area 69 acres (28 ha); 50 percent cabernet sauvignon, 35 percent merlot, 10 percent cabernet franc, 5 percent petit verdot

Located in Soussans, in the north of the Margaux appellation, this Cru Bourgeois was bought by the Thienpont family in 1979. Current owner Luc Thienpont has instigated a program of expansion, replanting and drainage that has transformed the property. The selection process has also been improved by hand-picking individual parcels of vines and by the introduction in 1984 of a second wine, Domaine Zédé, which now represents between 35 and 55 percent of the château's pro-duction. The wines, which are firm and richly textured, are aged in 50 percent new oak barrels. A separate 22-acre (9-ha) vineyard designated AC Bordeaux produces the label Z de Zédé.

CHÂTEAU MARGAUX

Owners Mentzelopoulos family and associates
Production 33,000 cases *Vineyard area* 193 acres (78 ha); 75 percent cabernet sauvignon, 20 percent merlot, 5 percent petit verdot and cabernet franc

This magnificent estate, with its nineteenth century colonnaded château, produced highly variable

The imposing façade of Château Margaux, the appellation's most productive winery.

The head winemaker outside the historic winery at Château Branaire, St-Julien.

After pruning, the canes that supported the previous year's vines are burned off.

wines during the 1960s and 1970s; however, since it was purchased by André Mentzelopoulos in 1977, it has probably been the most consistent of the Premiers Crus. The property is managed by André's daughter, Corinne, with the assistance of technical director Paul Pontallier. In recent years, the selection process has become more rigorous, with only 50 percent of the production going into the *grand vin* and the rest into the second wine, Pavillon Rouge. Both of these wonderful wines combine power and elegance with a purity of fruit and finely honed structure. The château also produces 3,300 cases of a white wine, Pavillon Blanc, made from 30 acres (12 ha) of barrel-fermented sauvignon blanc.

CHÂTEAU PALMER

Owner SCI Château Palmer *Production* 18,000 cases
Vineyard area 112 acres (45 ha); 55 percent cabernet sauvignon, 40 percent merlot, 5 percent petit verdot

Established in the early nineteenth century by Englishman General Charles Palmer, this estate has regularly surpassed its Troisième Cru classification. The wines have been remarkably consistent, and for a period in the 1960s and 1970s were probably the best in the Margaux appellation. The large quantity of merlot grown on the estate accounts for Château Palmer's famous velvety texture, and with only one-third new oak barrels used for aging, the oak always remains discreet.

Since 1938, the château has been owned by a consortium of French, English and Dutch families. A new vatroom with 33 conically shaped stainless-steel tanks was completed in 1995.

CHÂTEAU RAUZAN-SÉGLA

Owner Wertheimer family
Production 15,000 cases
Vineyard area 121 acres (49 ha);
61 percent cabernet sauvignon,
35 percent merlot, 4 percent petit verdot and cabernet franc

In 1855, Château Rauzan-Ségla was considered the appellation's leading producer after Château Margaux, and classified as a second growth. Although it regained form sporadi-

cally in the 1980s, it has only begun to realize its full potential since it was acquired by the Wertheimer family, owners of Chanel, in 1994. A massive program of investment has left no stone unturned: vineyards have been drained and replanted, cellars renovated, new equipment installed and the proportion of new oak barrels increased to around 70 percent. Production from the estate's younger vines now goes into a second wine called Ségla. The high percentage of merlot in the main blend (up to 40 percent) endows Rauzan-Ségla with the body and texture to complement its elegant bouquet.

Other Margaux producers of note include Bel Air Marquis d'Aligre, Cantenac-Brown, Dauzac, Durfort-Vivens, Ferrière, Giscours, La Gurgue, d'Issan, Labégorce, Lascombes, Malescot-St-Exupéry, Marquis de Terme, Monbrison, Prieuré-Lichine, Siran and du Tertre.

St-Julien

St-Julien can rightfully lay claim to having been the most consistent appellation in Bordeaux during the past 15 years. No fewer than 11 Classed Growths are found here, representing 80 percent of the appellation's production. But that is not the whole story: success requires a superior location and highly committed producers, and fortunately St-Julien has both. The appellation's 2,223 acres (900 ha) are situated on two plateaus located between Pauillac to the north and the Haut-Médoc to the south, and close to the warming influence of the waters of the Gironde Estuary. A southeasterly exposure and free-draining, gravelly soils enhance the ripening cycle, contributing to a mellow fruit character in the red wines that is backed by a firm, structure with great potential for aging. Since the 1980s, the appellation's châteaux owners have made the most of these conditions by investing heavily in their vineyards and cellars.

CHÂTEAU DUCRU-BEAUCAILLOU

Owner Borie family *Production* 18,000 cases
Vineyard area 123 acres (50 ha); 65 percent cabernet sauvignon, 25 percent merlot, 5 percent cabernet franc, 5 percent petit verdot

Owned by the Borie family since 1942, this Deuxième Cru occupies a prime location, close to the Gironde Estuary at the southern end of the appellation. It is named for the *"beaux cailloux"*— the coarse chunks of quartz, flint and other rocks that are clearly visible in the vineyard's soil.

The estate's fortunes were revived during the 1950s by Jean-Eugène Borie, with the assistance of enologist Émile Peynaud, and their work is now being continued by Borie's son, François-Xavier. Wood contamination in the cellars caused some irregularity in late-1980s vintages, but new cellars and improvements in the selection process have seen Ducru-Beaucaillou return to top form. The wines are rich, ripe and elegant but need at least ten years to develop.

CHÂTEAU GRUAUD-LAROSE

Owners Merlaut family *Production* 38,000 cases
Vineyard area 203 acres (82 ha); 55 percent cabernet sauvignon, 31 percent merlot, 10 percent cabernet franc, 2 percent petit verdot, 2 percent malbec

Gruaud Larose is probably the most full-bodied, fruity and muscular wine in St-Julien. This can be partly attributed to its location in the southern half of the appellation, where the soils are slightly heavier. Over the last 18 years the ownership has changed hands four times; the present owners, the Merlaut family, purchased the property from the industrial conglomerate Alcatel-Alstom in 1997. The latter was responsible for a massive program of investment in 1993, which included improved drainage, new machinery, the installation of a weather station and 14 new wooden vats. During vinification, the wines are pumped over and undergo a long period of maceration. The estate uses only 30 percent new oak barrels for aging.

CHÂTEAU LAGRANGE

Owner Suntory *Production* 55,000 cases
Vineyard area 279 acres (113 ha); 66 percent cabernet sauvignon, 27 percent merlot, 7 percent petit verdot

The Japanese beverage group Suntory came to the rescue of this Troisième Cru in 1983. At that point, the estate, the largest of the Classed Growths, was woefully run-down: the eighteenth century château had been gutted by fire and the vineyard had shrunk to 140 acres (57 ha). Under the direction of manager Marcel Ducasse, the property has since been rebuilt to include modern cellars and an extended vineyard with a higher percentage of cabernet sauvignon. The *grand vin* has gradually gained in depth and intensity and displays the mellow fruit character of the appellation. A second wine, Les Fiefs de Lagrange, was introduced in 1985 to take advantage of the high proportion of young plants, and now represents just over 50 per cent of production. A white wine, Les Arumes de Lagrange, was launched in 1996.

CHÂTEAU LÉOVILLE BARTON

Owner Anthony Barton *Production* 21,000 cases
Vineyard area 116 acres (47 ha); 72 percent cabernet sauvignon, 20 percent merlot, 8 percent cabernet franc

This Dexième Cru has been owned by the Barton family since 1826 and run by Anthony Barton since 1982. The vineyard, which at one time formed part of the vast Léoville estate, has a high percentage of old vines. The estate has no château or cellars, so the wine is made at Troisième Cru Château Langoa Barton, also owned by the Barton family. Wooden vats are used for vinification, and the wine is then aged in 50 percent new oak barrels. Anthony Barton and manager Michel Raoult have made the winemaking process steadily more rigorous, and the results are now rich, full and firmly structured.

CHÂTEAU LÉOVILLE LAS CASES

Owners Delon family *Production* 30,000 cases
Vineyard area 240 acres (97 ha); 65 percent cabernet sauvignon, 19 percent merlot, 13 percent cabernet franc, 3 percent petit verdot

This second growth was also once part of the Léoville estate. Its recent success owes much to the determination of owner Michel Delon, whose aim has always been parity with the Premiers Crus. A draconian selection process sees only 40 percent of production going into the *grand vin*. A large proportion of this comes from the walled Grand Enclos, 123 acres (50 ha) that lie immediately to

Tending to the vines on the estate of Château Léoville Las Cases, St-Julien.

St-Julien is best suited to red grape varieties.

Château Lafite's coarse gravel soils are typical of those of northern Pauillac.

the south of Château Latour and form the core of the Las Cases operation. The result is a deeply colored, immaculately honed, long-aging wine with a touch of Pauillac firmness and weight. The estate's second label is called Clos du Marquis.

CHÂTEAU TALBOT

Owners Mesdames Rustmann and Bignon *Production* 55,000 cases *Vineyard area* 252 acres (102 ha); 66 percent cabernet sauvignon, 26 percent merlot, 5 percent petit verdot, 3 percent cabernet franc

Château Talbot's extensive vineyard lies at the center of the St-Julien appellation. The property, a Quatrième Cru, was the pride of Jean Cordier and is now owned by his two daughters. The wines have always had plenty of fruit and charm but recently have also acquired greater weight and elegance as a result of improvements in vinification, selection and bottling. An aromatic dry white wine, Caillou Blanc, is also produced from barrel-fermented sauvignon blanc and sémillon.

Other St-Julien producers of note include Beychevelle, Branaire, La Bridane, Glana, Gloria, Lalande-Borie, Langoa Barton, Léoville Poyferré, and St-Pierre.

Pauillac

Pauillac, for many, provides the quintessential wine of the Médoc: firm and powerful, slightly austere in youth, made for aging, and with a distinct scent of blackcurrant and cigar box. Significantly, this appellation is home to three Premiers Crus—Lafite, Mouton-Rothschild and Latour—as well as 15 other classified estates.

Bounded by St-Estèphe to the north and St-Julien to the south, Pauillac's 2,890 acres (1,170 ha) of vineyard are divided into two zones. North of the town of Pauillac, where both Lafite and Mouton are located, the land is higher (80 feet [24 m]), the vineyards farther from the estuary, and the gravel soils rest on a bed of sandy marl and limestone. To the south, home of Latour among others, the land is significantly lower but closer to the estuary, and the gravel soils are somewhat heavier and deeper and contain some very large pebbles. While the characteristics of

each area add different nuances to the wines, both are ideal for cultivating the appellation's principal grape variety, cabernet sauvignon.

CHÂTEAU LAFITE-ROTHSCHILD

Owners Barons de Rothschild *Production* 20,000 cases *Vineyard area* 247 acres (100 ha); 72 percent cabernet sauvignon, 23 percent merlot, 3 percent cabernet franc, 2 percent petit verdot

The most northerly of Pauillac's three Premiers Crus, Lafite has been owned by the Rothschilds since 1868 and is presently run by Eric de Rothschild. Most of the vineyard is planted on an undulating gravel knoll which faces the Gironde Estuary to the east and extends toward the Breuil River in the north. Whether it is a result of the topography or the higher percentage of limestone in the subsoil, Lafite has always been lighter in style than either Mouton or Latour, and possessed

a greater elegance; it also has a huge capacity for aging. Since 1995, manager Charles Chevallier and his team have refined their viticulture, resulting in a wine of greater weight and structure. The estate's second wine is known as Carruades.

CHÂTEAU LATOUR

Owner François Pinault *Production* 33,000 cases
Vineyard area 160 acres (65 ha); 75 percent cabernet sauvignon, 20 percent merlot, 5 percent cabernet franc and petit verdot

Château Latour is the epitome of a classic Pauillac wine: deep color; blackcurrant, cedar and mineral bouquet; subdued power; and firm structure for long aging. The vineyard, too, has a classic profile with a high proportion of cabernet sauvignon, a southeasterly exposure, deep gravel soils, and close proximity to the warming influence of the Gironde Estuary. Its heart is the 116-acre (47-ha) Enclos,

which surrounds the château. Wines for the Grand Vin de Château Latour are produced from this area, while the excellent second wine, Les Forts de Latour, and a third wine, simply labelled Pauillac, are produced from other parcels.

Château Latour is named for a square-shaped, fourteenth-century fortification, but the present tower dates from the seventeenth century. After 30 years of British ownership, Latour was acquired by French businessman François Pinault in 1993.

CHÂTEAU LYNCH-BAGES

Owners Cazes family *Production* 45,000 cases
Vineyard area 222 acres (90 ha); 73 percent cabernet sauvignon, 15 percent merlot, 10 percent cabernet franc, 2 percent petit verdot

For a number of years, this Cinquième Cru has sold at the same level as the best Premiers Crus. The wine is distinctive and pleasing with deep

Exquisite Château Latour, with its extensive vineyards and seventeenth-century tower.

color, plenty of generous extract, fine tannins and a blackcurrant, minerally bouquet. Located on the Bages plateau, to the south of Pauillac, the estate was owned for three-quarters of a century prior to 1824 by the Lynch family, who were of Irish origin. In 1934, it was purchased by Jean-Charles Cazes and is today managed by his grandson, Jean-Michel.

The estate's second wine, Château Haut-Bages Averous, represents 25 percent of the production; a white wine, Blanc de Lynch-Bages, is also produced from sémillon, sauvignon blanc and muscadelle.

CHÂTEAU MOUTON-ROTHSCHILD

Owner Baronne Philippine de Rothschild
Production 25,000 cases *Vineyard area* 185 acres (75 ha); 80 percent cabernet sauvignon, 10 percent cabernet franc, 8 percent merlot, 2 percent petit verdot

In 1853, Baron Nathaniel de Rothschild purchased this vineyard and changed the name from Brane-Mouton to Mouton-Rothschild. Classified as a Deuxième Cru in 1855, it was eventually upgraded to Premier Cru in 1973. This was mainly due to the work and persistence of Baron Philippe de Rothschild, who took over the estate in 1922, introduced château bottling in 1924, initiated the idea of artist-designed labels in 1945, and generally improved the quality and dimensions of the wines. He was succeeded by his daughter, Philippine de Rothschild, in 1988.

Mouton has the power and concentration of Pauillac but an opulence and panache that sets it apart from Lafite, whose vineyard has the same geological profile. A second label, Le Petit Mouton, was introduced in the 1990s and a small quantity of white wine, L'Aile d'Argent, is also produced.

Château Mouton-Rothschild houses a range of artworks that take wine as their theme.

CHÂTEAU PICHON-LONGUEVILLE COMTESSE DE LALANDE

Owner Madame de Lencquesaing
Production 36,000 cases *Vineyard area* 185 acres (75 ha); 45 percent cabernet sauvignon, 35 percent merlot, 12 percent cabernet franc, 8 percent petit verdot

The original estate of Pichon-Longueville was subdivided in 1850, with three-fifths of the property becoming Pichon-Longueville Comtesse de Lalande. In 1925, Pichon Comtesse was bought by Bordeaux winebrokers Edouard and Louis Miailhe; since 1978 it has been owned and managed by Edouard's daughter, the redoubtable May-Eliane de Lencquesaing.

Two things about this estate are unique: the 27 acres (11 ha) of the vineyard are actually located in St-Julien, and the mix of grape varieties includes higher proportions of merlot and cabernet franc and a lower proportion of cabernet sauvignon than elsewhere in Pauillac. Consequently, the wines have a heightened fruit character that makes them attractive early on, as well as a supple texture and firm but fine structure that support aging.

CHÂTEAU PONTET-CANET

Owners Tesseron family *Production* 40,000 cases *Vineyard area* 195 acres (78 ha); 62 percent cabernet sauvignon, 32 percent merlot, 6 percent cabernet franc

The Tesseron family have completely overhauled this Cinquième Cru since purchasing it in 1975. The vineyard has been replanted, the cellars renovated and modernized, and the percentage of new oak barrels used for aging increased to around 50 percent. This drive for quality brought results in the 1990s, when the wines gained greater weight and distinction. A second wine, Les Hauts de Pontet, was introduced in 1982.

Other Pauillac producers of note include d'Armailhac, Batailley, Clerc Milon, Duhart-Milon, Fonbadet, Grand-Puy-Ducasse, Grand-Puy-Lacoste, Haut-Bages-Libéral, Haut-Batailley, La Fleur Milon, Pibran and Pichon-Longueville (Baron).

St-Estèphe

St-Estèphe is the most northerly of the Médoc's four principal communal appellations. Its varied soil structure includes gravel hillocks near the estuary; a bedrock of limestone, the *calcaire de St-Estèphe*, which outcrops in certain areas; and deposits of sand and clay, particularly in the west and north of the appellation. These variations influence the choice of grape varieties and add certain nuances to the wines. Cabernet sauvignon is still the most common variety but, given the preponderance of cooler soils, merlot has gained favor and now represents 35 percent of the 3,038 acres (1,230 ha) under production.

There are only five Classed Growths, which produce 20 percent of the total output. The lion's share of 54 percent is generated by the Crus

Bourgeois, with a further 17 percent coming from the local cooperative. St-Estèphe wines are generally fruity and full-bodied but with a firm tannic edge. This edge can be a little aggressive, though modern winemaking methods and grape selection have alleviated this problem.

CHÂTEAU CALON-SÉGUR

Owner Madame Capbern-Gasqueton *Production* 25,000 cases *Vineyard area* 136 acres (55 ha); 60 percent cabernet sauvignon, 30 percent merlot, 10 percent cabernet franc

The most northerly of the Classed Growths, Calon is also one of the appellation's oldest estates, its origins dating back to Gallo-Roman times. In the eighteenth century, it was owned by the powerful Ségur family, proprietors of Lafite and Latour. Georges Capbern-Gasqueton acquired the property in 1894 and it remains in the same family today.

The wines are firm, powerful and rich in the better vintages, but have tended toward leanness at other times. Fortunately, recent changes, including work in the vineyard, the inauguration of a new vatroom in 1999, the introduction of partial malolactic fermentation in barrel, and an increase in the percentage of new oak for aging have gone some way to remedying this problem.

CHÂTEAU COS D'ESTOURNEL

Owners Merlaut family and Cavas de Santa Maria *Production* 25,000 cases *Vineyard area* 161 acres (65 ha); 60 percent cabernet sauvignon, 40 percent merlot

Cos, which in the old Gascon tongue means "hill of pebbles," was founded in 1811 by Louis Gaspard d'Estournel, whose fascination with eastern Asia led to the construction of the distinctive pagoda-like winery. The recent success of Cos is mainly

Château Pichon-Longueville (Baron), with its elegant spires and ornamental lake.

Cos d'Estournel's unusual winery was inspired by Asian architecture.

due to coowner Bruno Prats, who managed the estate from 1970 until it was sold to the Merlaut family (in association with an Argentinian group, Cavas de Santa Maria) in 1998. Bruno Prats' son, Jean-Guillaume, remains as general manager.

The wines are dark, rich and opulent, the high percentage of merlot adding an uncharacteristic (for the appellation) suavity and the well-judged oak an exotic, spicy nuance. The second wine, Les Pagodes de Cos, was baptized in 1994. Previously, the young vines were vinified with those of a separate estate, Château de Marbuzet, and sold as the second label under this name.

CHÂTEAU HAUT-MARBUZET
Owner Henri Duboscq   *Production* 25,000 cases
Vineyard area 124 acres (50 ha); 50 percent cabernet sauvignon, 40 percent merlot, 10 percent cabernet franc

Henri Duboscq has succeeded in making this Cru Bourgeois into one of the most tempting wines in the Médoc. His approach is to create a robust wine that will age well, while masking the presence of tannin with ripe fruit and wood aromas. Yields are therefore kept low, the grapes are picked super-ripe, the percentage of merlot in the blend is high, malolactic fermentation is completed in barrel,

and 100 percent new oak barrels are used for aging, whatever the vintage. The resulting wines possess a voluptuous, exotic nature but also sufficient structure to age well. By 1994, Duboscq had extended the initial 17-acre (7-ha) holding his father, Hervé, bought in 1952 to around 124 acres (50 ha), all of which are located on the well-exposed, gravelly Marbuzet hill.

CHÂTEAU MONTROSE
Owner Jean-Louis Charmolüe   *Production* 27,000 cases
Vineyard area 168 acres (68 ha); 65 percent cabernet sauvignon, 25 percent merlot, 10 percent cabernet franc

The vineyard of this Deuxième Cru has exactly the same profile as that of Château Latour or the Grand Clos of Château Léoville Las Cases: deep gravel soils, southeasterly exposure and close proximity to the Gironde Estuary. Like those of Latour, Château Montrose's wines are firm and powerful, dominated by cabernet sauvignon, and have great potential for aging. In recent years, later picking of riper grapes has mellowed what used to be a rather tough exterior. The estate's second wine, La Dame de Montrose, is also worth seeking out. The property has been owned by the Charmolüe family since 1896.

CHÂTEAU DE PEZ

Owner Champagne Louis Roederer *Production* 11,000 cases
Vineyard area 60 acres (24 ha); 45 percent cabernet sauvignon, 44 percent merlot, 8 percent cabernet franc, 3 percent petit verdot

This Cru Bourgeois estate sits on a high plateau, just to the east of the town of St-Estèphe. The property dates from the fifteenth century, but the first vines were planted in the seventeenth century by the Pontac family, also owners of Château Haut-Brion. The wines are tannic, powerful and made for long aging. In 1995, Pez was acquired by the Champagne house Louis Roederer and an extra edge of fruit and finesse has since appeared in the wines. Vinification takes place in oak vats and the wines are then aged for 16–18 months in 40 percent new oak barrels.

CHÂTEAU PHÉLAN-SÉGUR

Owners Gardinier family *Production* 33,000 cases
Vineyard area 163 acres (66 ha); 60 percent cabernet sauvignon, 30 percent merlot, 10 percent cabernet franc

This Cru Bourgeois was created in the early nineteenth century as a result of the amalgamation of two separate estates by Irishman Frank Phelan. Much of its recent success can be attributed to the Gardinier family, who purchased the estate in 1985. Having survived an early disaster caused by the contamination of wines by chemical spray—the 1982 and 1983 vintages were recalled and no wine was made in 1984 and 1985—they have completely renovated the property and lifted the quality of their produce. The wines are now concentrated and possess great poise and finesse. A second wine, Frank Phélan, was introduced in 1986.

Other St-Estèphes producers of note include Le Boscq, Cos Labory, Haut-Beauséjour, Lafon-Rochet, Le Crock, Lilian-Ladouys, Marbuzet, Meyney, Les Ormes de Pez and Tour de Pez.

Sauternes and Barsac

Situated 25 miles (40 km) southeast of the city of Bordeaux and encircled by vineyards of the Graves, the five communes of Bommes, Fargues, Sauternes, Preignac and Barsac are authorized to make the rich, opulent wines known as Sauternes and Barsac. (Producers in the commune of Barsac can label wines either Barsac or Sauternes.) If ever there was a product of nature, it is these wines, for they are the direct result of a unique combination of climatic influences. In fall, as the cool waters of the Ciron run into the warmer Garonne, mists

form that provoke the onset of noble rot, or *Botrytis cinerea*. This fungal spore reduces the water content of the grape, increasing its sugar levels, acidity and flavor. The haphazard occurrence of this natural process means that the grapes have to be hand-picked selectively; this in turn means that the wines are costly to make and that in certain years the top châteaux are unable to declare a vintage. The success of several vintages in the 1980s and 1990s, however, has supplied funds for investment that were lacking in the past.

There are currently approximately 5,558 acres (2,250 ha) under production, with maximum yields restricted to 1.4 tons per acre (25 hl per ha). Sémillon is the principal grape variety; a little sauvignon blanc is normally added to increase aroma and acidity, and occasionally muscadelle is added too. The lower-lying land and higher limestone content in the soils generally make Barsac a lighter wine than Sauternes.

CHÂTEAU CLIMENS, BARSAC

Owner Bérénice Lurton *Production* 4,500 cases
Vineyard area 72 acres (29 ha); 100 percent sémillon

Climens is the quintessential Barsac: rich and concentrated, and displaying unparalleled finesse and delicacy as well as increasing complexity as it ages. The vineyard is located at the highest point of the Barsac plateau, on a soil composed of fissured limestone that provides good natural drainage. Lucien Lurton purchased this first growth in 1971 and provided the financial security that allowed the estate to return to a stricter system of grape selection; the property

The vineyards at Château Climens occupy the highest ground on the Barsac plateau.

Pressed grape skins may be used as fertilizer.

is now run by his daughter Bérénice. The wines, produced uniquely from sémillon, are fermented and aged in oak barrels, 50 percent of which are renewed yearly. In some years, a second wine, Les Cyprès de Climens, is produced.

CHÂTEAU DOISY-DAËNE, BARSAC

Owners Pierre and Denis Dubourdieu *Production* 4,200 cases *Vineyard area* 37 acres (15 ha); 80 percent sémillon, 20 percent sauvignon blanc

Deuxième Cru Doisy-Daëne is sold under the Sauternes label, but the vineyard is located on the upper Barsac plateau. Pierre Dubourdieu has been running the family property since 1945 and is now assisted by his son, Denis, a professor at Bordeaux's Faculté d'Oenologie.

The wines have a rich, creamy quality, balance and purity of fruit. They have been exceptional in the 1990s, although 1992 and 1993 were not declared. In 1990, 1996 and 1997 a tiny quantity of super-rich wine entitled Extravagant was produced. The estate is also known for its dry white wine, Vin Sec de Doisy-Daëne, made principally from barrel-fermented sauvignon blanc.

The vineyards and winery buildings of Château d'Yquem in Sauternes.

CHÂTEAU GILETTE, SAUTERNES

Owner Chistian Médeville *Production* 600 cases *Vineyard area* 11 acres (4.5 ha); 87 percent sémillon, 10 percent sauvignon blanc, 3 percent muscadelle

This remarkable wine is only placed on the market a minimum of 15 years after the vintage. Vinification takes place in temperature-controlled stainless steel tanks. The wines are then aged for 12–14 years in epoxy-lined concrete vats to reduce oxygen contact and subsequently bottled and stored in cellars for a further three to five years.

Château Gilette has a rich golden hue and retains the freshness of the fruit; yet it also has a complex aroma and a rich, unctuous texture. Two *cuvées* are produced, the Doux and richer Crème de Tête. The Médeville family has owned the property since the eighteenth century.

CHÂTEAU LAFAURIE-PEYRAGUEY, SAUTERNES

Owner Domaines Cordier *Production* 6,000 cases *Vineyard area* 99 acres (40 ha); 90 percent sémillon, 5 percent sauvignon blanc, 5 percent muscadelle

The property is situated on an exposed hillock in Haut-Bommes, and includes a château that dates

from the thirteenth century. In 1978, the estate began using oak casks again for fermentation; it has since increased the proportion of new oak to around 50 percent. In addition, the picking has become increasingly selective. Since the notable 1983 vintage, Lafaurie-Peyraguey has consistently turned out wines that are rich, full and balanced and have wonderful fruit expression.

CHÂTEAU RIEUSSEC, SAUTERNES

Owners Barons de Rothschild *Production* 7,500 cases
Vineyard area 185 acres (75 ha); 90 percent sémillon,
8 percent sauvignon blanc, 2 percent muscadelle

Rieussec is the one estate capable of rivaling its neighbour Yquem for the power and concentration of its wines. Since the Rothschilds of Château Lafite purchased this Premier Cru in 1985, a certain amount of fine-tuning has yielded greater finesse and fruit flavor. The selective harvesting has become more precise, the aging in barrel has been lengthened from 15 months to two-and-half years, and in 1996 the estate once again began fermenting the wines in barrel.

CHÂTEAU D'YQUEM, SAUTERNES

Owners Group LVMH and Lur-Saluces family
Production 7,500 cases *Vineyard area* 262 acres (106 ha);
80 percent sémillon, 20 percent sauvignon blanc

Singled out as a Premier Cru Supérieur in the 1855 classification, Yquem owes its celebrated status to the continuity provided by the Lur-Saluces family (owners since 1785), the precision with which the *domaine* is run, and its geographical situation—the vineyard is located in one block on a prominent knoll that provides excellent ripening conditions. Yields here rarely exceed 0.5 tons per acre (9 hl per ha), the equivalent of just one glass of wine per vine, and in certain difficult years (1910, 1915, 1930, 1951, 1952, 1964, 1972, 1974 and 1992) no Yquem was produced. The wines are fermented and aged for three-and-a-half years in 100 percent new oak barrels, and are the richest and most powerful in the appellation. Their capacity to age is legendary.

In 1996, the majority shareholding in Yquem was sold to the luxury group LVMH, but Comte Alexandre de Lur-Saluces retains an interest and remains as general manager.

Other Sauternes and Barsac producers of note include Bastor-Lamontagne, Clos Haut-Peyraguey, Coutet, Cru Barréjats, Doisy-Védrines, Fargues, Guiraud, Haut-Bergeron, les Justices, de Malle,

de Myrat, Nairac, Rabaud-Promis, Raymond-Lafon, Rayne Vigneau, Sigalas-Rabaud, Suduiraut and La Tour Blanche.

During fall, workers continue to tend the vines, trimming shoots prior to pruning.

The Graves and Pessac-Léognan

The Graves is Bordeaux's oldest viticultural zone, its vineyards dating back to at least the Middle Ages. It extends for 30 miles (50 km) southeast of the city of Bordeaux and is bounded to the east by the Garonne River and to the west by the Landes forest. The region takes its name from its gravel soils, which are particularly common around the fringes of the city.

In 1987, the northern sector of the Graves became a separate appellation, Pessac-Léognan. It now has 3,260 acres (1,320 ha) under vine and has seen considerable investment in the last ten years. Red wine represents 80 percent of production, and there is a limited output of top-quality white. The 1959 Graves Crus Classés are all located here.

The Graves appellation is more varied, both in terms of soil types and wine quality. It is also more extensive, with 5,410 acres (2,190 ha) under vine for red wines and 2,320 acres (940 ha) for dry white; a further 1,150 acres (465 ha) are allotted to sweet Graves Supérieur.

The red wines of the Graves and Pessac-Léognan are similar to those of the Médoc and just as impressive at the top level. Cabernet sauvignon is the dominant red variety, although merlot is on the increase in the Graves. The dry whites, made from sauvignon blanc and sémillon, have a citrus and mineral nuance but gain extra weight and finesse when barrel-fermented and aged on lees.

At first light, mist from the Garonne drifts across the vineyards of Pessac-Léognan.

THE 1959 CLASSIFICATION OF THE GRAVES

This classification was undertaken by the INAO (Institut National des Appellations d'Origine). It was first ratified in 1953 for red wines only; dry white wines were included in 1959. The system is simple and grants all 16 châteaux Cru Classé (Classed Growth) status. Some estates are classified for both red and white wines, others for only one kind. All the châteaux are located in the Pessac-Léognan appellation of the northern Graves, which only came into existence in 1987. Because the system has not been updated since 1959, it cannot be regarded as a fair reflection of the current market standing of these wines.

THE CRUS CLASSÉS (CLASSED GROWTHS) OF THE GRAVES

Château Bouscaut	(red and white)
Château Carbonnieux	(red and white)
Château Couhins	(white)
Château Couhins-Lurton	(white)
Château de Fieuzal	(red)
Château Haut-Bailly	(red)
Château Haut-Brion	(red)
Château Laville Haut-Brion	(white)
Château Malartic-Lagravière	(red and white)
Château La Mission Haut-Brion	(red)
Château Olivier	(red and white)
Château Pape Clément	(red)
Château Smith-Haut-Lafitte	(red)
Château La Tour Haut-Brion	(red)
Château La Tour-Martillac	(red and white)
Domaine de Chevalier	(red and white)

Because the whites are more signifcant in this region than elsewhere in Bordeaux, separate figures have been provided in the following entries for red and white wine production.

CHÂTEAU DE CHANTEGRIVE, GRAVES

Owners Françoise and Henri Lévèque *Production* 34,000 cases (17,000 red, 17,000 white) *Vineyard area* 106 acres (44 ha) of red (55 percent cabernet sauvignon, 35 percent merlot, 10 percent cabernet franc), 114 acres (46 ha) of white (50 percent sémillon, 40 percent sauvignon blanc, 10 percent muscadelle)

Françoise and Henri Lévèque built this estate from scratch in 1967 and have steadily expanded it to the point where it is now the largest in the Graves. The regular white wine is crisp and fruity, but of

most interest is the Cuvée Caroline, a special bottling of barrel-fermented sémillon and sauvignon blanc. In certain years it can stand alongside the best from Pessac-Léognan. The red has been of less interest, but in 1998 the yields were reduced and the wines now appear richer and riper.

DOMAINE DE CHEVALIER, PESSAC-LÉOGNAN

Owners Bernard family *Production* 13,500 cases (12,000 red, 1,500 white) *Vineyard area* 74 acres (30 ha) of red (65 percent cabernet sauvignon, 30 percent merlot, 5 percent cabernet franc), 10 acres (4 ha) of white (70 percent sauvignon blanc, 30 percent sémillon)

Domaine de Chevalier was improved during the postwar years by Claude Ricard and since 1983 has been astutely managed by Olivier Bernard. The estate vineyard, which is located southwest of Léognan, is surrounded by dense forest and part of it is subject to spring frosts. To counter this threat, four large wind machines have recently been installed. The elegant, sauvignon-dominated, dry white wine is taut and complex, and capable of aging for between 20 and 30 years. It is fermented in 100 percent new oak barrels and aged on lees for 18 months. The red wine has a deep color, and is full and firmly structured.

CHÂTEAU HAUT-BRION, PESSAC-LÉOGNAN

Owner Domaine Clarence Dillon *Production* 12,800 cases (12,000 red, 800 white) *Vineyard area* 106 acres (43 ha) of red (45 percent cabernet sauvignon, 37 percent merlot, 18 percent cabernet franc), 7.4 acres (3 ha) of white (63 percent sémillon, 37 percent sauvignon blanc)

Established in the sixteenth century and classified as a first growth in 1855, Haut-Brion is *the* great

The imposing metal gateway at the entrance to Château La Mission Haut-Brion.

estate of the Graves region. It was bought by the American Clarence Dillon in 1935 and is now administered by his granddaughter Joan, the Duchesse de Mouchy. The vineyard is situated on two southeast-facing gravel hills and surrounded by Bordeaux's suburban sprawl. Average temperatures are slightly higher here than in the Médoc, allowing the grapes to attain greater levels of maturity. They are then vinified in a modern *cuverie* that was purpose-built by manager Jean-Bernard Delmas and opened in 1991. The red wine is always finely textured with smooth tannins, ripe fruit and a slightly burnt, roasted note. The white is full and complex. The Dillon family also own Châteaux La Mission Haut-Brion, Laville Haut-Brion and La Tour Haut-Brion.

CHÂTEAU LA LOUVIÈRE, PESSAC-LÉOGNAN

Owner André Lurton *Production* 17,000 cases (13,500 red, 3,500 white) *Vineyard area* 82 acres (33 ha) of red (64 percent cabernet sauvignon, 30 percent merlot, 6 percent cabernet franc and petit verdot), 37 acres (15 ha) of white (85 percent sauvignon blanc, 15 percent sémillon)

André Lurton purchased this run-down estate in 1965 and has since turned it into one of the leading lights of the Pessac-Léognan appellation. Both the red and white wines are of a regularly high quality: the white rich and aromatic, and marked by the sauvignon, and the red full, firm and bal-

anced. André Lurton is also the owner of other properties in the Pessac-Léognan appellation, notably Couhins-Lurton, Cruzeau and Rochemorin.

CHÂTEAU MAGNEAU, GRAVES

Owners Ardurats family *Production* 19,000 cases (5,500 red, 13,500 white) *Vineyard area* 37 acres (15 ha) of red (50 percent merlot, 45 percent cabernet sauvignon, 5 percent cabernet franc), 62 acres (25 ha) of white (45 percent sauvignon blanc, 40 percent sémillon, 15 percent muscadelle)

This *domaine* in La Brède has been owned by the Ardurats for several generations. A phase of modernization that took place in the 1980s included the installation of temperature-control and airconditioning equipment as well as an increase in the number of new oak barrels. The emphasis is on white wine, including a fresh, fruity Graves and a more serious Cuvée Julien which is barrel fermented and aged on lees. The red is structured and firm and usually shows a good level of ripeness.

CHÂTEAU SMITH-HAUT-LAFITTE, PESSAC-LÉOGNAN

Owners Daniel and Florence Cathiard *Production* 11,000 cases (8,500 red, 2,500 white) *Vineyard area* 111 acres (45 ha) of red (55 percent cabernet sauvignon, 35 percent merlot, 10 percent cabernet franc), 25 acres (10 ha) of white (100 percent sauvignon blanc)

Following its purchase by Daniel and Florence Cathiard in 1990, this estate became one of the

Château Olivier, a Cru Classé, is classified for both its red and its white wines.

In recent years, most producers in the Graves have increased the proportion of new oak barrels in use in their cellars.

In fall, the rich colors of the vine leaves brighten the landscape of Bordeaux.

revelations of the 1990s. No expense has been spared to improve the wines: the vineyard has been reorganized, yields reduced and organic methods introduced; winemaking facilities have been modernized; and the percentage of new oak barrels has been increased—50 percent are now provided by the estate's own cooperage, which opened in 1995. The barrel-fermented white is rich and aromatic and contains a tiny percentage of sauvignon gris. Since 1994, the red has gained in both density and finesse.

Other Graves producers of note include Archambeau, d'Ardennes, Bichon-Cassignols, Brondelle, Clos Floridène, Le Bonnat, Léhoul, Rahoul, Respide Médeville, St-Robert, du Seuil, Vieux Château Gaubert and Villa Bel Air.

Other Pessac-Léognan producers of note include Carbonnieux, Les Carmes Haut-Brion, de Fieuzal, de France, La Garde, Haut-Bailly, Haut-Bergey, Larrivet Haut-Brion, Latour-Martillac, Laville Haut-Brion, Malartic-Lagravière, La Mission Haut-Brion, Olivier, Pape Clément, Le Thil Comte Clary and La Tour Haut-Brion.

Pomerol

The tiny appellation of Pomerol produces some of the finest and most sought-after wines in the world. Dominated by merlot, the best are rich, sweet and unctuous, the layered fruit extract adding gloss to a firm, tannic structure. Only 1,927 acres (780 ha) of Pomerol, located on a gently sloping plateau northeast of the town of Libourne, are under production. The clay and gravel soils of the center and east, the highest area, produce the richest wines, while the sandy soils to the west and south yield wines that are lighter in style. A ferruginous sand known as *crasse de fer*, which is found throughout the region, also provides added vigor. There is no official classification in Pomerol, but Pétrus heads the list of an unofficial hierarchy. The producers' properties are generally small and unassuming, the average holding no more than 12 acres (5 ha).

CHÂTEAU CLINET

Owners Jean-Michel Arcaute and associates *Production* 3,500 cases *Vineyard area* 22 acres (9 ha); 75 percent merlot, 15 percent cabernet sauvignon, 10 percent cabernet franc

Rich, powerful and intense, Clinet has been one of the outstanding producers in Pomerol during the last 15 years. Its style changed in the 1980s when Jean-Michel Arcaute, with the assistance of enologist Michel Rolland, imposed new work methods. The grapes are now picked extremely ripe and given a long period of maceration for maximum extract, and the wine is aged in new oak barrels for at least 24 months.

CHÂTEAU LA CONSEILLANTE

Owner Nicolas family *Production* 4,500 cases *Vineyard area* 30 acres (12 ha); 70 percent merlot, 25 percent cabernet franc, 5 percent malbec

La Conseillante is one of the most elegant Pomerols. Finely textured, it lacks the weight and power of Pétrus but retains an incredible complexity of aroma. The vineyard is located in a single block on the high plateau between Pétrus and Cheval Blanc and has a variety of clay, gravel and sand soils that contribute to the character of the wine. It has been owned by the Nicolas family since 1871.

CHÂTEAU L'ÉGLISE-CLINET

Owner Denis Durantou *Production* 2,000 cases *Vineyard area* 14 acres (5.5 ha); 80 percent merlot, 20 percent cabernet franc

L'Église-Clinet has enjoyed great success in recent years. In part, this is due to the large proportion of vines (one-third) that date back to the 1930s, but it also owes much to the winemaking skills of Denis Durantou, who took over management of the family-owned *domaine* in 1983. Modern practices such as the use of inert gas to prevent oxidation, careful temperature control and exacting standards of hygiene have been combined with traditional techniques. The resulting wines have a distinctive balance and refinement.

CHÂTEAU GAZIN

Owner Bailliencourt family *Production* 8,000 cases *Vineyard area* 59 acres (24 ha); 80 percent merlot, 15 percent cabernet franc, 5 percent cabernet sauvignon

Located just to the east of Pétrus, Château Gazin is the largest of the top estates in Pomerol. It is an ancient domain of the Knights of Malta and has been owned by the Bailliencourt family since the beginning of the twentieth century. Under the direction of Nicolas de Bailliencourt, the estate has had a succession of fine vintages and the wines have regained the allure they had been lacking since the late 1980s. Ripe and fleshy with notes of spice, they are typical of the full-blown Pomerol style.

CHÂTEAU PÉTRUS

Owners Ets Jean-Pierre Moueix and Madame Lily Lacoste *Production* 4,000 cases *Vineyard area* 27 acres (11 ha); 95 percent merlot, 5 percent cabernet franc

Pétrus was virtually unknown on the international market prior to the Second World War, but is now the outstanding estate in the Pomerol and Bordeaux's most expensive wine. Produced almost entirely from merlot, it is big, powerful and brooding, with layers of rich extract and firm but fine tannins, and it ages extremely well. Two factors contribute to the continuation of the Pétrus myth: the vineyard and *négociant* Jean-Pierre Moueix. The vineyard is located on the highest part of the Pomerol plateau on a unique deposit of ferruginous clay—the "Pétrus buttonhole" as it is known locally—on which merlot thrives. Moueix provides the marketing strategy and invaluable technical expertise: the merchant house's team of pickers is able to harvest the grapes at optimum ripeness in just half a day. The wines are then vinified in cement tanks and aged in 100 percent new oak barrels.

CHÂTEAU LE PIN

Owner Jacques Thienpont *Production* 700 cases *Vineyard area* 5 acres (2 ha); 92 percent merlot, 8 percent cabernet franc

Its limited volume, velvety texture and almost Burgundian intensity of raspberry and cherry fruit have made Le Pin one of the region's biggest sensations of the past 15 years. Occasionally, prices for Le Pin even surpass those for Pétrus—and this for a *domaine* created in 1979!

The vineyard is located on sand and gravel soils not far from Vieux Château Certan. The yields are kept low (2 tons per acre [35 hl per ha]), the grapes vinified in temperature-controlled stainless steel vats, and the wine run off into 100 percent new oak barrels, where it undergoes malolactic fermentation and matures for a period of up to 18 months.

CHÂTEAU TROTANOY

Owner Ets Jean-Pierre Moueix *Production* 3,000 cases *Vineyard area* 18.5 acres (7.5 ha); 90 percent merlot, 10 percent cabernet franc

Owned by merchant house Jean-Pierre Moueix since 1953, Trotanoy comes close to rivalling Pétrus for power and depth. The best vintages are

opaque in color and have a rich, layered fruit extract and finely integrated tannins. Replanting in the 1980s caused a dip in form, but the property is now back at its best. The vineyard is located on clay-gravel soils to the west of the high plateau.

VIEUX CHÂTEAU CERTAN

Owners Thienpont family *Production* 4,500 cases *Vineyard area* 33 acres (13.5 ha); 60 percent merlot, 30 percent cabernet franc, 10 percent cabernet sauvignon

The high percentage of cabernet in this wine provides a distinctive style that is more characteristic of the Médoc than Pomerol. The property, which dates to the sixteenth century, was acquired by

Bringing in the harvest by hand at the Château Certan-de-May in Pomerol.

Château Figeac's vineyards include a high proportion of cabernets sauvignon and franc.

Belgian wine merchant Georges Thienpont in 1924. It is ideally located on the high plateau, next to Pétrus, and has a complexity of soils that includes pure clay, gravel, clay-gravel and ancient sands. Each parcel of the vineyard is worked according to soil type, grape variety and age of vine.

Other Pomerol producers of note include Beauregard, Le Bon Pasteur, Bourgneuf-Vayron, Certan de May, Clos l'Église, La Croix de Gay, La Croix du Casse, L'Évangile, La Fleur-Pétrus, Gombaude-Guillot, Lafleur, Latour à Pomerol, Mazeyres, Montviel, Petit Village, La Pointe and de Sales.

St-Émilion

St-Émilion is Bordeaux's most historic wine region, and vine cultivation has occurred here since Gallo-Roman times. The zone is located around nine villages or communes, including the town of St-Émilion, which was granted administrative control over the region by Edward I of England in 1289. The whole area was declared a World Heritage site by UNESCO in 1999.

There are 13,340 acres (5,400 ha) under production and two appellations within the same region, St-Émilion and St-Émilion Grand Cru. The latter requires a higher minimum-alcohol content (11 percent), lower yields (3 tons per acre

[53 hl per ha]) and the approval of two tasting panels. It accounts for 40 percent of production and is obligatory for classified wines. The St-Émilion classification is reviewed every ten years and has two levels: the Premier Grand Cru Classé (13 wines) and the Grand Cru Classé (55 wines).

Merlot is the dominant grape variety followed by cabernet franc, but there is a wide variety of wine styles, defined mainly by site and winemaking philosophy. For example, in the northwest, adjacent to Pomerol, a pocket of gravelly soils provides elegant, cabernet-dominated wines, as exemplified by Châteaux Cheval Blanc and Figeac, while on the limestone plateau and *côtes*, the merlot-dominated wines are full-bodied, fresh and made for long aging. The properties are generally small family-run affairs, and, consequently, the local cooperative is also a major producer.

CHÂTEAU ANGÉLUS

Owner Boüard family *Production* 9,500 cases *Vineyard area* 58 acres (23 ha); 50 percent merlot, 47 percent cabernet franc, 3 percent cabernet sauvignon

Promoted to Premier Grand Cru Classé in 1996, Angélus is St-Émilion's modern success story. In the 1980s, Hubert de Boüard and his cousin Jean-Bernard Grenié took over the family property and introduced new practices in the vineyard (lower yields and a riper harvest) and cellars (the period of maceration was increased, a second wine, Carillon de l'Angélus, was launched to improve selection, and the proportion of new oak barrels was increased to 100 percent). This transformed the château from a middling Grand Cru Classé into a top estate, and set the standard for a more contemporary style of St-Émilion: deeper in color, richer and more concentrated.

CHÂTEAU AUSONE

Owner Vauthier family *Production* 2,000 cases *Vineyard area* 17 acres (7 ha); 50 percent merlot, 50 percent cabernet franc

Ausone and Cheval Blanc are the only two estates in the St-Émilion classification to have been designated Premier Grand Cru Classé A. The château takes its name from the fourth-century Roman poet Ausonius (Decimus Magnus), and is located on the steep southern slopes of St-Émilion. The

southeasterly exposure of the vineyard and the limestone, clay and sand soils shape the character of the wine—powerful but fine, and slow to mature. Since Alain Vauthier took charge of production in 1996, the wines have gained in color, weight and fruit expression.

CHÂTEAU BELAIR

Owner Madame Dubois-Challon *Production* 4,000 cases *Vineyard area* 32 acres (13 ha); 60 percent merlot, 40 percent cabernet franc

Château Belair epitomizes the style of wine produced on St-Émilion's rugged limestone plateau: pure, crisp fruit; lightness; vibrant structure; fine tannins; and fresh finish. For the last 20 years, the property has been run by manager and winemaker Pascal Delbeck; in 1998, the vineyard was fully converted to the biodynamic system of cultivation.

THE CLASSIFICATION OF ST-ÉMILION

The first classification in St-Émilion took place in 1955, 100 years after the introduction of the Médoc system. Unlike that of the Médoc, this system is revised every ten years or so, most recently in 1996. Modifications have been also made between reviews, as occurred in 1969 and 1985.

The classification consists of only two grades: Premier Grand Cru Classé (with an indicator of A or B status) and Grand Cru Classé. There are currently 13 of the former (Châteaux Angélus and Beau-Séjour-Bécot having been promoted in 1996) and 55 of the latter. To be considered for classification, a winery must already hold the St-Émilion Grand Cru appellation certificate. It must then make a presentation, including samples from the last ten vintages, for review by a commission nominated by the INAO.

THE 1996 CLASSIFICATION

Premiers Grands Crus Classés (First Great Classed Growths) A
Château Ausone
Château Cheval Blanc

Premiers Grands Crus Classés (First Great Classed Growths) B
Château Angélus
Château Beau-Séjour-Bécot
Château Beauséjour (Duffau-Lagarrose)
Château Belair
Château Canon
Château Figeac
Château La Gaffelière
Château Magdelaine
Château Pavie
Château Trottevieille
Clos Fourtet

Grands Crus Classés (Great Classed Growths)
Château L'Arrosée
Château Balestard-La-Tonnelle
Château Bellevue
Château Bergat
Château Berliquet
Château Cadet-Bon
Château Cadet-Piola
Château Canon-La-Gaffelière
Château Cap de Mourlin
Château Chauvin
Château La Clotte
Château La Clusière
Château Corbin
Château Corbin-Michotte
Château La Couspaude
Couvent des Jacobins
Château Curé-Bon

Château Dassault
Château La Dominique
Château Faurie-de-Souchard
Château Fonplégade
Château Fonroque
Château Franc-Mayne
Château Grand Mayne
Château Grandes-Murailles
Château Grand Pontet
Château Guadet St-Julien
Château Haut-Corbin
Château Haut-Sarpe
Château Lamarzelle
Château Laniote
Château Larcis-Ducasse
Château Larmande
Château Laroque
Château Laroze
Château Matras
Château Moulin-du-Cadet
Château Pavie-Decesse
Château Pavie-Macquin
Château Petit-Faurie-de-Soutard
Château Le Prieuré
Château Ripeau
Château St-Georges-Côte-Pavie
Château La Serre
Château Soutard
Château Tertre-Daugay
Château La Tour-Figeac
Château La Tour du Pin-Figeac (Giraud-Belivier)
Château La Tour du Pin-Figeac (Moueix)
Château Troplong-Mondot
Château Villemaurine
Château Yon-Figeac
Clos des Jacobins
Clos de l'Oratoire
Clos Saint-Martin

The unusual mix of gravel, sand and clay in the vineyard at Château Cheval Blanc contributes to a distinctive style of wine.

CHÂTEAU CANON-LA-GAFFELIÈRE

Owner Stephan von Neipperg *Production* 7,500 cases
Vineyard area 48 acres (19.5 ha); 50 percent merlot,
40 percent cabernet franc, 5 percent cabernet franc

This Grand Cru Classé is now one of the leading châteaux in the appellation. Acquired by Count Joseph-Hubert von Neipperg in 1971, it has been managed in an intuitive and innovative manner by his son Stephan since 1983. It is run on partly organic principles: the fruit is gently extracted in oak vats with a system of *pigeage* and the wines aged in 100 percent oak casks without racking but with the addition of oxygen. The wines are now less extracted than they were in the late 1980s and early 1990s, and have wonderful fruit expression, balance and harmony. Von Neipperg also owns and manages Clos de l'Oratoire and La Mondotte.

CHÂTEAU CHEVAL BLANC

Owners Albert Frère and Bernard Arnault *Production* 12,000 cases *Vineyard area* 89 acres (36 ha); 60 percent cabernet franc, 40 percent merlot

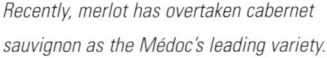
Recently, merlot has overtaken cabernet sauvignon as the Médoc's leading variety.

Known for its silky, elegant style and long aging potential, Cheval Blanc has been St-Émilion's top wine for the last 50 years. It owes its originality to the estate's soil types (ancient gravel, sand and clay) and the high percentage of cabernet franc in the blend. The vineyard was first cultivated in the eighteenth century and an extensive drainage system was installed in the late nineteenth century, around the time when the first cabernet franc grapes were planted. The estate was then owned by the Fourcaud-Laussac family, whose association with the property continued until 1998, when it was sold to businessmen Albert Frère and Bernard Arnault. Manager Pierre Lurton has ensured a high degree of continuity during the last decade. Yields are kept very low, and a second wine, Le Petit Cheval, permits further selection.

CHÂTEAU FIGEAC

Owner Thierry Manoncourt *Production* 10,000 cases
Vineyard area 99 acres (40 ha); 35 percent cabernet franc,
35 percent cabernet sauvignon, 30 percent merlot

The origins of Figeac date back to the Gallo-Roman period. In the eighteenth century, the estate comprised some 494 acres (200 ha), including what is now Château Cheval Blanc. A large part of the vineyard is located on ancient gravel soils, and when the present owner started replanting in

1947, the nature of the *terroir* led him to select an unusually high proportion of cabernet franc and cabernet sauvignon. These produce a wine that is more *Médocain* in style, displaying elegance, balance and depth of fruit in good years, a slight herbaceousness in mediocre vintages and a deceptive ability to age.

CHÂTEAU LE TERTRE ROTEBOEUF
Owner François Mitjavile *Production* 2,200 cases
Vineyard area 14 acres (5.7 ha); 80 percent merlot,
20 percent cabernet franc

François Mitjavile took over this tiny family *domaine*, located on southeast-facing slopes in the east of the appellation near St-Laurent-des-Combes, in 1977 and has since propelled it to the top of the appellation. The wines are not classified—a personal choice on the part of Mitjavile—but sell at the same price as the Premiers Grands Crus Classés. Harvesting the grapes at optimum ripeness and a well-judged period of aging in new oak barrels produce a wine that is rich, full-bodied and suave, with an almost exotic complexity of aroma.

CHÂTEAU DE VALANDRAUD
Owner Jean-Luc Thunevin *Production* 1,000 cases
Vineyard area 22 acres (9 ha); 75 percent merlot, 20 percent cabernet franc, 5 percent malbec

A pioneer in the development of "microwines" in the early 1990s, Thunevin created Château de Valandraud from three small parcels of vines located on the Dordogne plain and clay-limestone hillslopes, producing his first vintage in his garage in 1991. His aim was to create small quantities of dark, rich, concentrated, merlot-based wines. This required an obsessive attention to detail and a procedure involving tiny yields (1.1 tons per acre [20 hl per ha]), hand harvesting and destemming, cold prefermentation maceration, new oak vats for vinification and 100 percent new oak barrels for malolactic fermentation and maturation. The high selling price of the wines has provided ample reward. Recently, the vineyard has been expanded and cellars have been constructed.

Other St-Émilion producers of note include L'Arrosée, Balestard-la-Tonnelle, Beau-Séjour-Bécot, Canon, Clos Fourtet, La Dominique, Faugères, Fleur Cardinale, La Gaffelière, Grand Mayne, Grand Pontet, Larcis-Ducasse, Larmande, Laroze, Magdelaine, Monbousquet, La Mondotte, Moulin St-Georges, Pavie, Pavie-Decesse, Pavie-Macquin, Pipeau, Soutard, La Tour Figeac, Troplong-Mondot.

MINOR APPELLATIONS

Médoc
The Médoc (formerly Bas-Médoc) appellation is situated beyond St-Estèphe in the northern third of the Médoc peninsula. The region has a distinct rural feel, with undulating countryside and a mix of soils including clay-limestone, sand and gravel. Cabernet sauvignon used to be the dominant grape variety, but it has been gradually overtaken by merlot. There are more than 600 vine growers, two-thirds of whom belong to the cooperative system, cultivating 11,850 acres (4,800 ha). The wines, uniquely red, are generally fruity and forward, but a growing band of producers is using improved vineyard and cellar practices to create greater weight, fruit and style.

Médoc producers of note include La Cardonne, d'Escurac, Fontis, Les Grands Chênes, Greysac, Lacombe-Noaillac, Lafon, Loudenne, Les Ormes-Sorbet, Patache d'Aux, Potensac, Ramafort, Rollan de By, La Tour de By, Tour Haut-Caussan, Vieux Château Landon and Vieux Robin.

Haut-Médoc
This appellation covers designated viticultural land in the southern half of the Médoc peninsula that is not delimited within the six communal appellations of Margaux, Listrac, Moulis, St-Julien, Pauillac and St-Estèphe. The soils are predominantly gravel, and, with the requisite investment in skill, labor and materials, have the potential to produce red wines of Classed Growth standard, as demonstrated by Château Sociando-Mallet. In fact, five of the estates included in the 1855 classification are located within the appellation, although the bulk of the production from the 10,375 acres (4,200 ha) of vineyard is Crus Bourgeois.

Haut-Médoc producers of note include Beaumont, Belgrave, Camensac, Cantemerle, Charmail, Cissac, Citran, Coufran, La Lagune, Lanessan, Lestage Simon, Malescasse, Maucamps, Sociando-Mallet, La Tour Carnet, Tour du Haut-Moulin and Verdignan.

The vineyards at Château Loudenne, one of the top producers in the Médoc appellation.

Throughout Bordeaux, grapes and wine appear regularly in locally produced art.

THE CLASSIFICATION OF THE CRUS BOURGEOIS OF THE MÉDOC

The term Cru Bourgeois was first used in the Médoc in the 1920s to identify and help market châteaux ranked below the Classed Growths. The first classification, drawn up by Bordeaux wine brokers in 1932, listed 444 properties. This list gradually diminished as estates either amalgamated or ceased winemaking. In 1966, a reconstituted winegrowers association, the Syndicat des Crus Bourgeois du Médoc, published a new classification, which was revised in 1978. This ranked châteaux in three categories: Crus Bourgeois, Crus Grands Bourgeois and Crus Bourgeois Exceptionnels (although European Union legislation permits only the words "Cru Bourgeois" to appear on labels). The syndicat currently has 329 members, who produce wines of varying quality and price. It plans to introduce a new classification in the next few years that will reflect a more contemporary view of the quality of the wines.

The minor appellations of the Médoc almost exclusively plant red grape varieties.

Listrac-Médoc

Listrac-Médoc is one of the six communal appellations of the Médoc situated northwest of Margaux. Because it lies farther from the Gironde Estuary than its famous neighbor, its ripening cycle may take place as much as a week later. The soils are also cooler here, with a preponderance of clay and limestone. The wines of the Listrac-Médoc are firm and slightly austere, but the tendency of late has been to plant and use a higher proportion of merlot in order to soften them. A total of 1,580 acres (640 ha) are under production, and the local cooperative is an important producer.

Listrac producers of note include Cap Léon Veyrin, Clarke, Ducluzeau, Fourcas-Dupré, Fourcas-Hosten, Fourcas-Loubaney and Mayne Lalande.

Moulis

With only 1,358 acres (550 ha) under production, Moulis is the smallest of the Médoc's six communal appellations. It is situated to the northwest of Margaux, and also includes a ridge of gravel farther to the east near the Gironde Estuary. Several of the châteaux here produce cabernet sauvignon-dominated wines that are of a high quality and similar in style to those of St-Julien to the north. Farther inland, the soils are similar to those of neighboring Listrac-Médoc, with a high percentage of limestone and clay. Châteaux here have tended to plant more merlot and to produce wines that are light and fruity.

Moulis producers of note include Anthonic, Biston-Brillette, Brillette, Chasse-Spleen, Gressier-Grand-Poujeaux, Maucaillou and Poujeaux.

Cérons

Cérons is a sweet white wine appellation just to the north of Barsac, within the Graves area, which takes in the communes of Cérons, Podensac and Illats. Winegrowers within this zone can produce both red and white Graves and Cérons; however, production problems and low returns mean that very little Cérons is actually produced—only 180 acres (73 ha) were declared in 1998. The wine can be elegant and concentrated, although not to the same degree as Sauternes or Barsac.

Cérons producers of note include Cérons, Chantegrive, Grand Enclos du Château de Cérons, Haura and Seuil.

Premières Côtes de Bordeaux

The appellation stretches for 37 miles (60 km) along the right bank of the Garonne, from the city of Bordeaux to the village of St-Maixant, and is only 3 miles (5 km) across at its widest point. It has a total of 7,410 acres (3,000 ha) under production. Some sweet white wine is produced here, but of more interest are the merlot-dominated reds, which have a bright, aromatic fruit character and are either firm or lightly structured.

This is one of the most beautiful parts of Bordeaux, and it has attracted a regular stream of new investors, both French and foreign. This in turn has improved the quality of the wines, making the Premières Côtes de Bordeaux one of the best value-for-money appellations.

Premières Côtes de Bordeaux producers of note include Carignan, Carsin, Chelivette, Clos Ste-Anne, Constantin, Grand Mouëys, Jonchet, Lamothe de Haux, Malagar, Melin, Plaisance, Puy Bardens, Reynon, Le Sens and Suau.

Entre-Deux-Mers

The Entre-Deux-Mers region of Bordeaux is the enormous wedge of land that lies between the Dordogne and Garonne rivers. It is the source of a large volume of generic red bordeaux but also of the Entre-Deux-Mers appellation, a dry white wine produced from sauvignon blanc, sémillon and muscadelle. Modern vinification techniques make this a crisp and fruity offering suitable for early drinking. Approximately 4,446 acres (1,800 ha) are under white-wine production, although this figure is likely to decrease as producers continue to follow the current trend of turning their vineyards over to red varietals.

Entre-Deux-Mers producers of note include Bonnet, Castelneau, Castenet-Greffier, Fontenille,

Nardique La Gravière, Ste-Marie, Tour de Mirambeau, Toutigeac and Turcaud.

Cadillac

This rather amorphous sweet white wine appellation is delimited to 22 communes in the southern half of the Premières Côtes de Bordeaux, on the right bank of the Garonne. The quality and style of the wines yielded by the 543 acres (220 ha) under production varies considerably, from fresh, fruity and semisweet to richly botrytized. The relatively small return on investment for producing sweet white wines has stalled development, but the winegrowers' association is trying to improve the situation by tightening the rules of production and seeking to apply the title of Grains Nobles to richer, unchaptalized wines.

Cadillac producers of note include Carsin, Cayla, Juge, Manos, Mémoires and Ste-Catherine.

Loupiac

The 988 acres (400 ha) of this sweet white wine appellation lie on the opposite side of the Garonne from Barsac. The wines are consistent, fresh, fruity, and sweet rather than concentrated. Vinification usually occurs in tank with few producers using oak barrels for aging or fermentation. Sémillon, sauvignon and muscadelle are the main varieties.

Loupiac producers of note include Clos Jean, Cros, Loupiac-Gaudiet, Mémoires, Noble, Ricaud and Roques.

Ste-Croix-du-Mont

Historically, this is the most important of the three sweet white wine appellations on the right bank of the Garonne. Its 1,136 acres (460 ha) are located on slopes opposite Sauternes. The soils contain a significant percentage of gravel, which is beneficial for the onset of noble rot. Although the potential for rich, concentrated wines is strong, quality varies considerably. At the best *domaines*, the procedure is similar to that used in Sauternes, involving low yields, selective picking and the use of oak barrels for aging. The results can be equally good.

Ste-Croix-du-Mont producers of note include Crabitan Bellevue, Loubens, Mailles, Mont, Pavillon and La Rame.

Côtes de Castillon and Bordeaux-Côtes de Francs

The Côtes de Castillon was only granted appellation status in 1989. It takes its name from the town of Castillon-la-Bataille, where in 1453 the French army defeated the English, terminating three centuries of English rule in Aquitaine. Geographically, the region is the easterly prolongation of the St-Émilion hill-slopes; most of the 7,163 acres (2,900 ha) of vineyard lie on these clay-limestone slopes and the rest on the flat alluvial plain below. The rising cost of land in St-Émilion has recently attracted investors to Côtes de Castillon, traditionally an area of small family holdings. The appellation's merlot-based wines are solid and fruity.

Neighboring Bordeaux-Côtes de Francs to the north is considerably smaller, with only 1,160 acres (470 ha) under production. The region has one of the lowest levels of rainfall in Bordeaux and abundant sunshine. The involvement of the Thienpont family, who came to the area in 1946 and now own a number of properties, has contributed significantly to its success in recent years. Both red and dry white wines are produced, and standards are usually high.

Côtes de Castillon producers of note include d'Aiguilhe, Belcier, Cantegrive, Cap de Faugères, Côte Montpezat, La Clarière Laithwaite, Lapeyronie, Peyrou, Poupille, Robin and Vieux Château Champs de Mars.

Bordeaux-Côtes de Francs producers of note include Charmes-Godard, Francs, Laclaverie, Marsau, Moulin La Pitié, La Prade and Puygueraud.

St-Émilion satellites

The St-Émilion "satellites" are located to the north of the main appellation, on a continuation of the

Piles of wooden stakes lie ready to be used to support new plantations of vines.

Many of Bordeaux's finest vineyards occupy flat land along the region's waterways.

St-Émilion hillslopes. Four communes—Lussac, Montagne, Puisseguin and St-Georges—have the right to append St-Émilion to their communal names. Conditions throughout the satellites vary, but generally there is a high proportion of limestone and clay in the soil. Merlot is the most common grape variety. Overall, the wines are similar in style to St-Émilion, though a little rougher, and display plummy fruit and firm, slightly rustic tannins. A total of 9,633 acres (3,900 ha) are under production, with Montagne the largest appellation and the Puisseguin-Lussac cooperative a major force in the region.

Notable producers in the St-Émilion satellites include La Grenière and Lyonnat in Lussac; Calon and Faizeau in Montagne; Durand-Laplagne and Guibeau-La-Fourvieille in Puisseguin; and St-André Corbin and St-Georges in St-Georges.

Lalande de Pomerol

North of Pomerol, beyond the Barbanne River and surrounding the communes of Lalande and Néac, lie the 2,717 acres (1,100 ha) of Lalande de Pomerol. The soils here vary considerably, with silt and sand to the west, clay on hillier ground to the east, and gravel in the north. Consequently, the wines are not terribly consistent, despite merlot being the principal grape variety throughout the area. The best, however, possess a touch of the opulence found in Pomerol.

Lalande de Pomerol producers of note include Bertineau St-Vincent, Garraud, Fleur de Boüard, Fougeailles, Grand Ormeau, Haut-Chaigneau, Sergant and Viaud.

Fronsac and Canon-Fronsac

In the eighteenth and nineteenth centuries, Fronsac, particularly wines from the south-facing Côte Canon, sold at a higher premium than St-Émilion. The region is located to the west of the town of Libourne and forms a triangle bounded to the east by the river Isle and to the south by the Dordogne. There are two appellations: Fronsac with 2,038 acres (825 ha) under production and, to the south, the tiny 741-acre (300-ha) enclave of Canon-Fronsac. Only the higher ground with a bedrock of limestone, clay and sandstone is delimited for these appellations. Merlot is the predominant

A vineyard worker ties the vines to stakes in preparation for another long winter.

grape variety, with cabernet franc, cabernet sauvignon and malbec playing a supporting rôle.

Naturally vigorous and firm, the wines can be a little rustic, although improvements in winemaking and vineyard management in the 1990s have added fruit and refined tannins. A recent increase in investment and commitment on the part of producers also make this a region to watch. There is little difference between Fronsac and Canon-Fronsac, any contrasts being the result of good and bad winemaking.

Fronsac producers of note include Barrabaque, Canon, Canon de Brem, Canon-Moueix, Cassagne Haut-Canon, Dalem, La Fleur Cailleau, Fontenil, Grand Renouil, Haut Carles, Mayne-Vieil, Moulin Haut Laroque, Moulin Pey Labrie, La Rivière, Tour du Moulin, Les Trois Croix, La Vieille Cure, Villars and Vrai Canon Bouché.

Côtes de Bourg

The Romans were the first to cultivate the vine in the Côtes de Bourg. Later, in the Middle Ages, the port of Bourg became an important commercial center for the English. The appellation's proximity to the confluence of the Dordogne and the Garonne gives it a slightly warmer climate than other parts of Bordeaux and its average rainfall is also one of the lowest in the region.

The 9,139 acres (3,700 ha) of vineyard are planted in a hilly area that incorporates two ridges running parallel to the river. The soils are mainly clay and limestone: hence merlot is the dominant grape variety, followed by cabernet sauvignon, cabernet franc and malbec. The red wines are full-bodied with good color and structure; the best have a little more polish as a result of aging in oak barrels. A little dry white Côtes de Bourg is produced from sauvignon, sémillon and muscadelle.

Côtes de Bourg producers of note include Brulesécaille, Bujan, Falfas, Fougas, Garreau, Guerry, Haut-Macô, Macay, Mercier, Nodoz, Roc de Cambes, Rousset and Tayac.

Premières Côtes de Blaye

Red wines from the region of Blaye, on the right bank of the Gironde Estuary are all labelled Premières Côtes de Blaye, whereas the miniscule production of white wine is labelled Premières Côtes de Blaye, Côtes de Blaye or Blaye, depending on the proportions of sauvignon blanc, colombard and ugni blanc used in the blend. Blaye's 12,103 acres (4,900 ha) of red Premières Côtes de Blaye are scattered around three distinct zones within a block of 148,200 acres (60,000 ha) of mixed agricultural land. Merlot is the main grape variety; the wines are firm and fruity, but less substantial than those of neighboring Bourg. However, higher levels of investment and new contributions from a younger generation of producers have made this a more interesting appellation in recent years.

Premières Côtes de Blaye producers of note include Bel-Air La Royère, Charron, Haut Bertinerie, Haut-Grelot, Les Jonqueyres, Loumède, Mondésir-Gazin, La Raz Caman, Roland-la-Garde, Segonzac and Les Tourtes.

After mechanical harvesting, workers collect grapes that have been missed by hand.

Bordeaux and Bordeaux Supérieur

The Bordeaux and Bordeaux Supérieur appellations account for just over 50 percent of the production in the Bordeaux region and about the same proportion of the total area under plantation. The wines are produced throughout the Gironde, but the most important zone is the Entre-Deux-Mers. There are 145,730 acres (59,000 ha) under production.

The volume of red wine far outstrips that of white and rosé. Quality and style varies considerably, from light and fruity wines to richer, oak-aged offerings. A large percentage of red AC Bordeaux is commercialized under a brand name or as own-label supermarket wine. The market leader in this field is Mouton Cadet, with yearly sales of 13 million bottles. The Bordeaux Supérieur appellation requires an extra half degree minimum alcohol (10°), a slight reduction in yield and a longer period of maturation. About 75 percent of Bordeaux Supérieur is bottled at the property, in contrast to 25 percent of AC Bordeaux. In the northeastern corner of Entre-Deux-Mers, producers can use the Ste-Foy-Bordeaux label.

Bordeaux and Bordeaux Supérieur producers of note include Abbaye de St-Ferme, Les Arromans, Barreyre, Bonnet, Bouillerot, Bru, Courteillac, Cugat, Fontenille, Grand Verdus, Jonqueyres, Malromé, Marjosse, Méaume, Parenchère, Penin, Plaisance, Rauzan Despagne, Reignac, Roquefort, Seguin, Thieuley and Trocard.

In many wineries, an Archimedean screw is used to deliver the grapes to the crusher.

The Southwest

Jim Budd

The vineyards of southwestern France are dispersed over a wide area, stretching from the edge of Sauternes in Bordeaux to Toulouse in the southeast and the Spanish border in the far southwest. They encompass a wide variety of environments, including the Atlantic-influenced mesoclimates of the Dordogne and the Landes, the warmer river gorges of the Cevennes and the sheltered valleys of the Pyrenean foothills. There are around 30 appellations in all, but most form isolated pockets of vineyards, and the region has nothing like the vine monoculture found in Bordeaux. However, it does produce some of the most distinctive French wines, often using grape varieties found nowhere else.

Among the local white varieties are the petit manseng and gros manseng of Jurançon; petit courbu from Irouléguy, Jurançon and Pacherenc du Vic Bilh; mauzac from Gaillac; and loin-de-l'œil, also from Gaillac. The reds include duras from Gaillac; fer servadou, found in Madiran, Côtes de St-Mont, Irouléguy and several other appellations; and the negrette of the Côtes du Frontonnais. The once-rare tannat is the leading variety in Madiran, and has now spread overseas to Argentina and Uruguay. Malbec is the most significant variety in Cahors, where it is known as auxerrois.

Bordeaux's influence is particularly strong in neighboring appellations such as Bergerac and Buzet, and has had a significant and not always positive impact on the Southwest's wine production throughout history. In the Middle Ages, for example, Bordeaux merchants imposed taxes and shipping restrictions on the wines of Bergerac, Cahors and Gaillac, or the *Haut Pays* as they were then known, to advantage their own sales. Furthermore, more robust wines from Cahors were used to give color and body to weedy clarets, enhancing claret's reputation at the expense of Cahors'.

It could be said that Bordeaux continues to exert a negative influence, as many wine buyers judge the quality of local vintages by those of Bordeaux, failing to realize that what occurs in Bordeaux does not necessarily occur in neighboring regions. Indeed, as a result of variations in climate and the timing of the harvest, there is often a considerable difference in quality between bordeaux and wines from the Southwest. The 1987 and 1994 vintages, for instance, were considerably better in Madiran than in Bordeaux.

The Southwest can be divided into three main areas: the so-called "satellite" vineyards of Bordeaux; the vineyards of the upper Garonne

Winegrowing areas near the southwest coast tend to have mild, wet climates.

and its tributaries; and the southern appellations of the Landes, Gascogne and the Pays Basque.

The Bordeaux "satellites"

These areas lie close to the Bordeaux vineyards, grow a similar mix of grape varieties and make comparable wines that often represent better value than their Bordeaux equivalents. They include the various appellations around the town of Bergerac, in the Dordogne Valley; the Côtes de Duras, around the town of Duras, between the Dordogne and the Garonne; the Côtes de Marmandais, centered on the town of Marmande on the Garonne; and Buzet, between the towns of Damazan and Agen. Before the advent of *appellation contrôlée*, regions such as Bergerac and Buzet were permitted to label their wines Bordeaux.

The whites are made principally from sauvignon blanc, sémillon and a little muscadelle; the reds are normally a blend of merlot, cabernet sauvignon and cabernet franc, with the early-ripening merlot usually the most important component in the blend.

Approximately 31,200 acres (12,600 ha) are planted in the Bergerac area. The standard of the wines has improved considerably in recent years, although there remains a significant difference in quality between the best producers and the rest. As well as AC Bergerac (white, red and rosé), there is a bewildering number of other appellations here. Pécharmant, just to the northeast of Bergerac, is for reds only; these are some of the best in the region and will age well. Côtes de Bergerac doesn't relate to a particular area but is awarded to certain reds made from a restricted yield; these can often, but not invariably, be more concentrated and longer-lived than Bergerac, and tend to be more expensive. There is also a separate Côtes de Bergerac for sweet wines. Monbazillac is for sweet wines that involve selective picking and a high proportion of botrytized grapes; the best is a rich honeyed mouthful that will, in good vintages, last at least 50 years. Saussignac is also for sweet wines, with the best coming from Château Richard and Clos d'Yvigne. Montravel is mainly for dry whites, whereas Côtes de Montravel and Haut-Montravel are sweet-wine appellations. The rarely used Rosette appellation applies to mildly sweet wines.

The Côte de Duras lies in undulating country to the southeast of Bergerac and includes around 5,000 acres (2000 ha) of vines. The Landerrouat-Duras cooperative accounts for 50 percent of production, with much of the wine being sold under the Duc de Berticot brand. Duras seems to be best

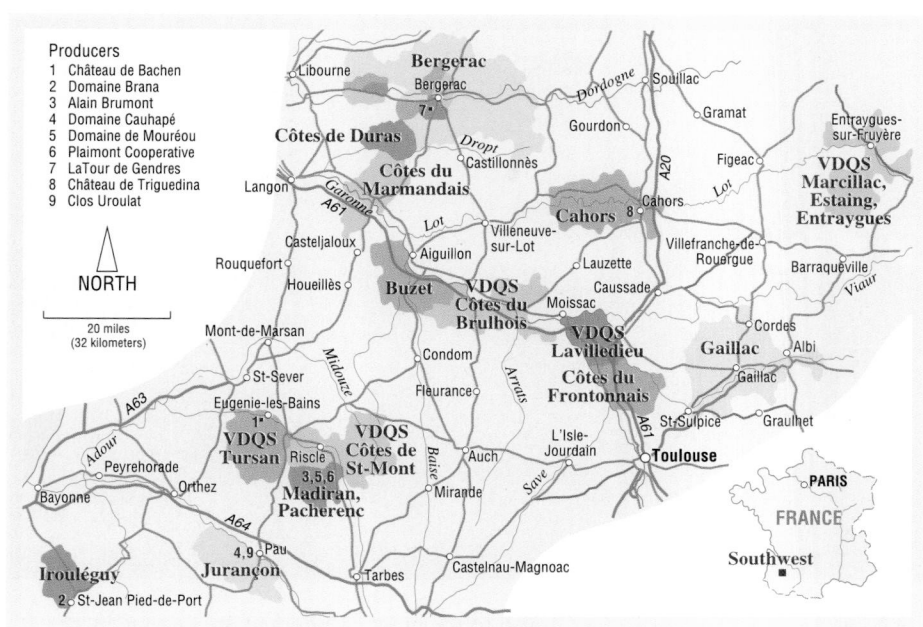

suited to dry whites, in particular sauvignon blanc, as well as sweet whites in exceptional years, but the appellation lacks a clear identity and the wines tend to be sound rather than exciting.

Côtes du Marmandais comes from around 4,500 acres (1,800 ha) of vineyards planted on both banks of the Garonne around the eponymous market town, 25 miles (40 km) east of Langon. Most of the production is red and comes from two cooperatives, Beaupuy and Cocumont. When Côtes de Marmandais was promoted from VDQS to AC status in 1990, the growers had to agree that Bordeaux varieties would not make up more than 75 percent of the blends and would be supplemented by fer servadou, gamay, malbec, syrah and the local red variety, abouriou.

Buzet's production is dominated by the well-run Cave Cooperative in Damazan, which makes more than 90 percent of the appellation's wines and even has its own cooperage. Red wines account for 90 percent of the cooperative's output; the rest is white and rosé. The range includes both generic wines—the top *cuvée* is Baron d'Ardeuil—and wines from individual estates, such as the Château de Gueyze, which are owned by the members.

The Garonne and its tributaries

Winemaking on the northernmost tributary of the Garonne, the Lot, centers on Cahors. Grape-growing dates back to the Roman era here, and by the Middle Ages the wines of Cahors had already gained widespread fame. In particular, the area was known for its "black wine," which owed its name to the dark auxerrois (malbec) grape and

Sheep's milk is used to make rich cheeses that are a fine match for the region's wines.

The mountainous Irouléguy appellation has potential for rapid growth in the near future.

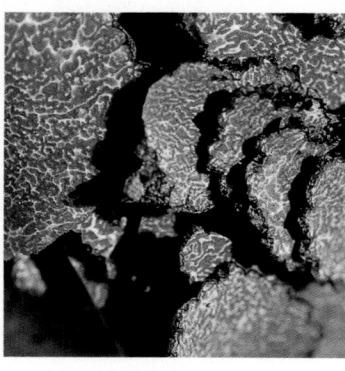

Fresh truffles are an expensive delicacy in many parts of the Southwest.

also to the practice, adopted at one time by the French Navy, of boiling the wine, which improved its keeping capacity but also deepened its color. In 1956, a severe frost almost brought production to a halt, but Cahors has now recovered and has 10,467 acres (4,236 ha). The appellation is for reds only; it permits up to 30 percent of merlot to be added to soften the auxerrois. Although Cahors produces some light, easy-drinking wines, the best producers favor concentrated, powerful fare that needs time in oak and then bottle.

Farther up the Lot Valley lie the vestiges of the vineyards of the Aveyron department. In 1835, 84,000 acres (34,000 ha) were planted here; all that's left are the small VDQSs of Estaing (17.3 acres [7 ha]) and Entraygues (22.2 acres [9 ha]), and Marcillac (346 acres [140 ha]), which produces powerful, rustic reds, mainly from fer servadou, and was recently promoted to appellation status.

Located north of Toulouse between the Garonne and the Tarn, the Côtes du Frontonnais appellation has around 5,000 acres (2,000 ha) under production, much of which is planted on gravel terraces laid down by the Garonne. The local grape is négrette, a red variety, which is blended with cabernet franc and cabernet sauvignon, gamay, malbec, mauzac and syrah. The wines range from soft and light to those that need two or three years' aging. The leading producers are Châteaux Baudare, Bellevue la Forêt, Ferran, Montauriol, Le Roc and the Cave de Fronton.

Northwest of Frontonnais there are two small VDQS appellations, Lavilledieu and Côtes du Brulhois, which produce mainly red wines. To the east lies Gaillac (6,200 acres [2,500 ha]), another area where grapes were first planted in Roman times. Gaillac is a curiously amorphous appellation and lacks a clear identity. This may be because it produces an enormous array of styles from a wide range of grapes. The area's most interesting producer is the Plageoles estate, which concentrates on mauzac, ondenc and duras.

The Landes, Gascogne and the Pays Basque

This area is home to some of the most dynamic producers in the Southwest. The best of the wines, particularly those from Madiran, are powerful and robust. The vineyards went into decline after the First World War—Madiran all but disappeared—but are now enjoying a renaissance.

One of the region's recent success stories is the Côtes de Gascogne *vin de pays*, which is now sold throughout northern Europe. It was chiefly created to find an outlet for the excess production resulting from the decline in sales of the local brandy, Armagnac. As a result, most of the production is white. Colombard is the principal variety but ugni blanc, chardonnay and gros manseng are also used. Generally, the *vin de pays* is light and citric, and made to be drunk young.

The nearby Tursan VDQS appellation has 1,137 acres (460 ha) under plantation. About 65 percent of production is red or rosé; the white is made from baroque, which is found only in Tursan. The principal producer is the Tursan Cooperative in Geaune. The presence of Michel Guérard, the famous French chef, at Château de Bachen, has brought the appellation welcome publicity.

To the southeast lie Madiran (3,460 acres [1,400 ha]), a red-wine appellation, and the much smaller dry- and sweet-wine appellation of Pacherenc (395 acres [160 ha]). The chief red grape here is the appropriately named tannat, a decidedly robust and tannic variety capable of producing complex, powerful wines; these need around a decade of aging to show their best and respond well to long-aging in oak. Somewhat oddly, the appellation laws officially prohibit wines made from 100 percent tannat, insisting on the addition of some cabernet franc, cabernet sauvignon or fer servadou. Recently, however, the top local producers, led by Alain Brumont, have ignored the regulations and made their best *cuvées* wholly from tannat. (The wines are nevertheless awarded appellation status—such is Brumont's reputation that the INAO would only look foolish if it refused to classify the wine.) Permitted varieties for Pacherenc include arrufiac, petit and gros manseng, bordelais, sauvignon and sémillon. Greater emphasis is now being placed on the local varieties, and some remarkable sweet wines are being made by growers who delay picking until December.

Côtes de St-Mont (2,500 acres [1,000 ha]) is often described as a junior Madiran because the red is made mainly from tannat and the appellation lies immediately to the north. However, these reds are considerably softer and need much less time to age. There is also a white made from local varieties, and a small amount of rosé. The Plaimont Cooperative is the chief producer.

The best Jurançon is one of the country's most elegant and complex whites, but as there are only (2,500 acres [1,000 ha]) of vineyards, it is not as widely known as it deserves to be. Fortunately, interest in the appellation is growing, especially in France. In the nineteenth century, there were some 7,400 acres (3,000 ha) here, but by the 1950s this had fallen to 740 acres (300 ha). Despite suitable land being available and a growing demand for Jurançon, the vineyards are unlikely to expand because EU restrictions prevent further planting.

Jurançon is made from three varieties: petit and gros manseng, and petit courbu. Traditionally, it was a sweet wine made from late-harvested grapes, mainly petit manseng, picked in November and December with the sweetness coming from *passerillage* rather than botrytis (neither the climate nor the thick skin of petit manseng favors the development of noble rot); but a dry wine, Jurançon sec, was created during the difficult years in the middle of the nineteenth century. Gros manseng is the chief variety used and it now accounts for 75 percent of the production. Partly as a result of its high level of acidity, both styles of Jurançon can age well. Unfortunately, as a result of the appellation's decline during the twentieth century, few old vintages are available for tasting.

The small Pyrenean appellation of Irouléguy went into a dramatic decline following the arrival of phylloxera in 1912 and the outbreak of the First World War, dwindling from nearly 1,240 acres (500 ha) at the beginning of the century to 740 acres (300 ha) by 1947, and then to just 160 acres (65 ha) in 1980. The last 20 years have seen a considerable revival and there are now around 500 acres (200 ha) in production, although the appellation has a potential area of 3,030 acres (1,226 ha). The reds and rosés are made from cabernet franc, cabernet sauvignon and tannat. They tend to be less muscular versions of Madiran and show their best after several years aging. The whites, which have

just been reintroduced following a gap of some 40 years, are made from petit courbu and gros and petit manseng, and are usually crisp and lemony.

Regional cuisine

The robust cuisine of the southwest is a good match for its usually sturdy wines. Generally, dishes are rich and display their rustic origins—this is not a land of sophisticated, prettified cuisine. Duck figures frequently on the menu, especially confit of duck, preserved in its own fat. The Gers is the foremost producer of foie gras in France, Bayonne is famous for both ham and chocolate, Agen for

In southwestern France, vineyards occupy less fertile pockets amid lush farmland.

Domaine Brana was the first producer to reintroduce white wines after the mid-twentieth-century crisis in Irouléguy.

The Southwest's vineyards are planted with many distinctive local grape varieties.

its prunes. A rich vegetable soup called *garbure* is one of Gascony's specialties, whereas the Pyrenees are best known for sheep's cheese, traditionally made by shepherds tending their flocks in summer on the high peaks. The eastern part of the region is home to the hearty and filling dish known as *cassoulet*, a stew of beans, confit of duck and sausage.

Producers

CHÂTEAU DE BACHEN, VDQS TURSAN
Established 1988 *Owner* Michel Guérard *Production* NA
Vineyard area 42 acres (17 ha)

Michel Guérard, one of France's best-known chefs, is the owner of a restaurant and hotel at Eugenie-les-Bains and an Armagnac vineyard and distillery near Cazaubon in the Bas Armagnac. He bought Château de Bachen in 1983, built an impressive winery in Palladian style and produced his first vintage in 1988. The wines include an unoaked Château de Bachen and the Baron de Bachen, which is fermented and aged in new oak. The latter is more concentrated, complex and benefits from two to three years in bottle. The former should be drunk young and goes well with shellfish.

DOMAINE BRANA, IROULÉGUY
Established 1985 *Owners* Brana family *Production* NA
Vineyard area 54 acres (22 ha)

The Brana family set up a *negoçiant* business at Ustaritz in 1897, moving to St-Jean Pied de Port in 1920. In 1974, Étienne Brana started to distill high-quality fruit *eaux de vies* and began to plan a vineyard. The first wines were made in 1989, and a winery was then built. When Étienne died in 1992, his son Jean took over the winemaking, and his daughter Martine became the distiller. Both red and white Irouléguy are made. The red is a blend of cabernet franc, cabernet sauvignon and tannat and is aged in oak for 12 months. The white is made from petit courbu and gros manseng.

ALAIN BRUMONT, MADIRAN
Established 1980 *Owner* Alain Brumont *Production* NA *Vineyard area* 195 acres (79 ha)

Alain Brumont has played a leading role in the revival of the fortunes of the Southwest.

A visit to his properties at Domaine Bouscassé and Château Montus is now more akin to a visit to a well-heeled classed growth in the Médoc rather than an estate in what was considered a rural backwater. Brumont made his name with his Montus Prestige and Bouscassé Vieilles Vignes. Both are 100 percent tannat and aged in new oak for at least a year. His Montus Pacherenc, made from 100 percent petit courbu fermented in new oak, is also notable for its quality—it will keep for ten years while growing in complexity. There is also a series of progressively richer *moelleux*, and a range of *vin de pays* from the Côtes de Gascogne.

DOMAINE CAUHAPÉ, JURANÇON
Established 1980 *Owner* Henri Ramonteau *Production* NA
Vineyard area 62 acres (25 ha)

Henri Ramonteau has done much to raise the international profile of Jurançon with his excellent range of wines. There are four dry whites: three from 100 percent gros manseng (one of which is made from old vines) and one from 100 percent petit manseng fermented in new oak. The sweet-wine range is headed by Noblesse de Petit Manseng and Quintessence, which are made exclusively from petit manseng, and the Vieilles Vignes, which is half petit manseng and half gros manseng.

DOMAINE DE MOURÉOU, MADIRAN
Established 1968 *Owner* Patrick Ducorneau *Production* NA
Vineyard area 35 acres (14 ha)

Patrick Ducournau makes elegant, powerful and well-balanced wines, especially Chapelle Lenclos, which is made from pure tannat and ages well—at least ten to fifteen years after good vintages. But he is likely to be best remembered as the inventor of the micro-oxygenation system. This feeds a minute but continuous dose of oxygen to a wine as it matures in vat. It is of particular use in stainless steel vats, as it keeps the level of oxygen constant and reduces the need for racking. Initially developed to help soften tannat's powerful tannins, it is being used increasingly in France and elsewhere to soften and round out wines without using costly barrels.

PLAIMONT COOPERATIVE, MADIRAN
Established 1970 *Owner* Plaimont Producteurs *Production* NA *Vineyard area* NA

This cooperative in the Adour Valley has done much, under the leadership of André Dubosc, to develop both VDQS Côtes de St-Mont and VDP des Côtes de Gascogne. It was Dubosc who foresaw the decline of Armagnac and realized that

Gascogne could yield easy-drinking, everyday white wines. More recently, as well as investing in vinification centers, the cooperative has helped growers to improve viticultural practices and hence the quality of their grapes. The Plaimont range includes some Madiran, but it's the red Côtes de St-Monts that offer the greatest interest and value, particularly the top of the range, Château de Sabrezan.

LA TOUR DE GENDRES, BERGERAC
Established NA *Owner* SCEA de Conti *Production* NA
Vineyard area 100 acres (40 ha)

Luc de Conti is one of a number of producers who have shown that Bergerac can at times outshine Bordeaux. His vineyards, which lie to the south of Monbazillac, are run mainly on organic principles and planted with sauvignon blanc, sémillon, merlot and cabernet sauvignon. The white wines range from La Tour de Gendres, a good-value, pure sémillon, to Moulin des Dames, a blend of sémillon and sauvignon, and the rich, barrel-fermented Anthologia, which is mainly sauvignon blanc and always expensive. The red wines include La Gloire de Mon Père, which is chiefly merlot, and Moulin des Dames, a blend of cabernet sauvignon, cabernet franc and merlot.

CHÂTEAU DE TRIGUEDINA, CAHORS
Established 1830 *Owners* Baldès family *Production* NA
Vineyard area 99 acres (40 ha)

This was one of the few producers, along with the late Jean Jouffreau at Clos de Gamot, to keep the appellation alive during the dark days of the mid-twentieth century. The vineyards are planted on gravel with 70 percent auxerrois, 20 percent merlot and 10 percent tannat. The wines, made by Jean-Luc Baldès, are among the best in Cahors. Prince Probus comes from old vines and is aged in new oak. Deep-colored when young, its concentration and power usually require a good five years in bottle. It is named for the Roman emperor Probus, who allowed vines to be planted in Quercy in AD 280.

CLOS UROULAT, JURANÇON
Established 1983 *Owner* Charles Hours *Production* NA
Vineyard area 18.5 acres (7.5 ha)

Charles Hours contents himself with making just two wines: Cuvée Marie, a Jurançon sec, and the sweet Clos Uroulat; both are fermented in barrel. The vineyard is planted with petit courbu and the two mansengs, and yields are kept low, which explains the concentration and complexity that supports a thrilling purity of flavor in all Hours' wines.

Viewed from Massat, parallel ranges rise toward the heights of the Pyrenees.

Languedoc-Roussillon

Jim Budd

The city of Carcassonne was first fortified by the Romans almost 2,000 years ago.

Although some 370,000 acres (150,000 ha) of vines have been pulled up in the past decade, Languedoc-Roussillon remains the world's largest wine region. About 620,000 acres (250,000 ha) of vines lie between the Rhône delta and the Spanish border at Banyuls—nearly two and half times the area of vines currently planted in Australia and just a little less than the entire US vineyard. After 150 years devoted to producing mainly cheap red table wines, the last 15 years has seen a shift toward Mediterranean specialties and major international varietals. In the process, Languedoc-Roussillon has become France's most dynamic and exciting wine region.

Landscape and climate

Although lumped together administratively, Languedoc and Roussillon are two distinct areas, historically and geographically. Roussillon was part of Spain from the thirteenth century until the Treaty of the Pyrenees in 1659 when it was ceded to France, and has strong links with Catalonia across the border. Its geography is dominated by the Pyrenees, in particular by the Canigou mountain massif, and its vineyards are located mainly in narrow valleys. In contrast, Languedoc's vines are planted mainly on the broad coastal plains, although some of the higher-quality wines come from the inland hills, or *coteaux*.

Languedoc-Roussillon has a Mediterranean climate, with most of its rain falling in winter and very little occurring between the beginning of May and mid-August. The plains are the hottest and most arid areas of France, with an average annual temperature of 57°F (14°C), and the dry climate is often accentuated by the *tramontane*, an inland wind that blows from the northwest. Indeed, parts of Languedoc are so arid that vines and olives are the only viable crops.

Throughout Languedoc-Roussillon, drought can be a problem in summer, particularly as French and EU regulations do not allow appellation vines to be irrigated. Rains in late August and early September can make the harvest difficult, and winter storms sometimes damage vines: in mid-November, 1999, the equivalent of an average year's rain fell in just 36 hours, causing widespread flooding and destruction in the vineyards of Corbières and Minervois. Violent hailstorms also occur: parts of Roussillon were badly hit in May 1999.

Generally, Languedoc-Roussillon remains best suited to the production of red wines, as well as rosés for summer drinking. Despite modern methods, whites still tend to lack acidity and freshness.

History

Along with those of Provence, the vineyards of Languedoc-Roussillon are the oldest in France. Vines were first planted here by the Greeks near Narbonne during the fifth century BC and have been an important part of the regional economy ever since. During the eighteenth and early nineteenth centuries, the area had a reputation for quality wine, most of which came from the *coteaux*, or hillsides, where the soils are poorer and the temperatures more moderate than elsewhere in the region.

In the mid-nineteenth century, several factors combined to transform the Languedoc-Roussillon wine industry and the regional economy as a whole. The development of heavy industry in the northeast created a substantial thirst among workers—by mid-century, annual French wine consumption per capita was around 32 gallons (120 l)—and the opening of a railroad link to Paris in 1850 allowed southern produce to more readily reach the capital and the industrial north. Soon, Languedoc began to supply northern France with cheap red wine—known as *le gros rouge*—made principally from aramon and alicante bouchet. As the yields were

Vines and typical Mediterranean scrubland surround a ruined castle at Tuchan in Fitou.

high, the wine was usually thin and had to be bolstered by more full-bodied reds from Algeria.

The destruction of the region's vineyards by phylloxera during the latter half of the nineteenth century merely accelerated the decline of the *coteaux* and the move to producing high-volume, low-quality *vin de table* on the plains. The American rootstock used to reconstruct the vines did not grow well in the limestone soils on the hillsides, and this coupled with the markedly higher costs of growing vines on the *coteaux* gave the plains a significant economic advantage.

Wine production continued to focus on *le gros rouge* until the late twentieth century. Then, in 1962, Algeria gained independence, and the supply of powerful red wines was cut off. More significantly, various changes in French lifestyle during the 1970s caused the demand for cheap red wine to collapse. These included the decline of heavy industry; the development of a more sophisticated taste among the broad population—drinkers were now consuming smaller quantities of better wines; and a growing fashion for drinking whisky rather than wine as an aperitif. These trends have continued: by 1998, per capita consumption of wine in France had declined to around 16 gallons (60 l) from around 30 gallons (112 l) in 1970.

Vines and wines

With the cheap table wine market in terminal decline, Languedoc-Roussillon has been forced to change course, and in the past 15 years there has been a dramatic move toward higher-quality produce. This change has been driven both by far-sighted local producers and by newcomers and investors from other parts of France, Europe and even Australia and California.

The change has taken two main forms: the plains that used to produce the oceans of *gros rouge* are now planted with international varieties, and the vineyards on the *coteaux* have been revived. The shift to international varieties, which include cabernet sauvignon, chardonnay, merlot and syrah, is partly the result of the introduction of the *vin de pays* classification which, unlike local appellation laws, permits usage of these grapes (see p. 218). Varietal *vins de pays* from the plains of Languedoc-Roussillon have been very successful on export markets, especially in northern Europe.

On the *coteaux*, where wines were traditionally made mainly from carignan, new grape varieties, mainly from the Rhône, such as syrah, grenache, mourvèdre, vermentino and viognier, have been

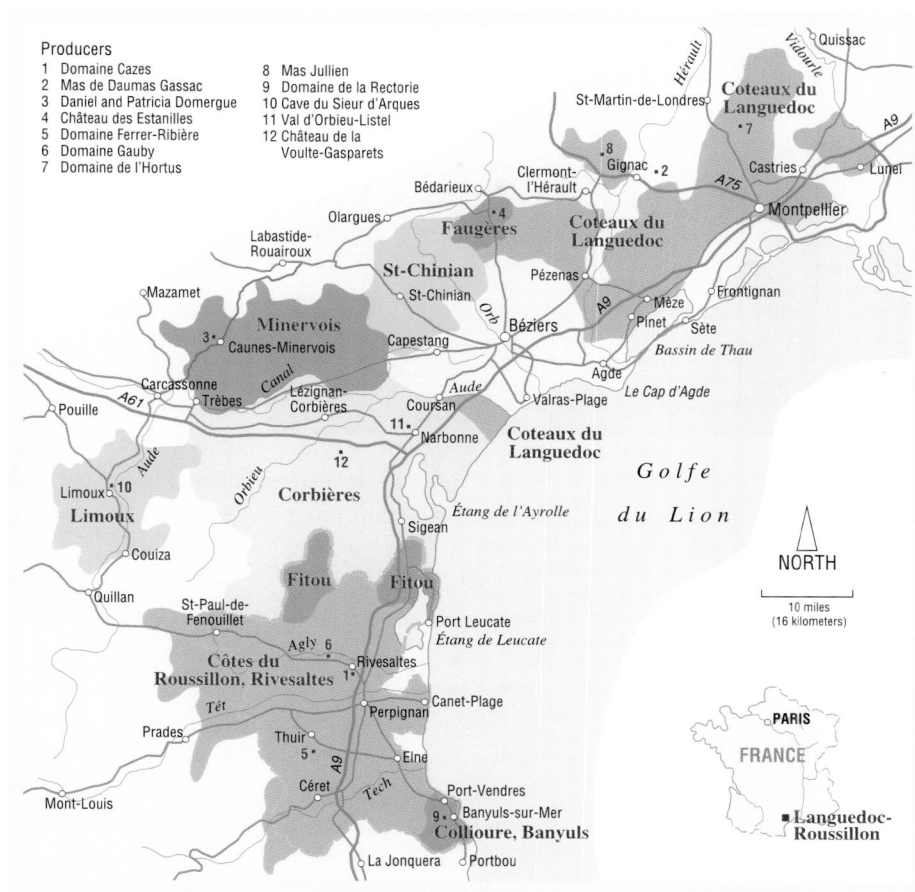

Producers
1 Domaine Cazes
2 Mas de Daumas Gassac
3 Daniel and Patricia Domergue
4 Château des Estanilles
5 Domaine Ferrer-Ribière
6 Domaine Gauby
7 Domaine de l'Hortus
8 Mas Jullien
9 Domaine de la Rectorie
10 Cave du Sieur d'Arques
11 Val d'Orbieu-Listel
12 Château de la
   Voulte-Gasparets

planted for use as flavor boosters (*cépages améliorateurs*) in blends. These varieties once grew in Languedoc-Roussillon, but were wiped out by phylloxera and largely replaced with aramon, alicante bouchet and carignan. There is now also a growing acceptance that carignan is worth cultivating; but unfortunately a lot of old carignan vines were pulled out in the late 1980s and early 1990s, and replaced with new varieties such as syrah. Because growers have to wait at least 40 years for carignan to produce satisfactory juice, no one is replanting it.

The enormous potential of the *coteaux* has, however, been realized over the past decade, with producers now turning out wines of concentration and character, often interwoven with the scents—especially rosemary and thyme—of the region's characteristic vegetation, the scrubby *garrigue*. Notable wine-producing regions on the hillsides include the Pic St-Loup, some 15 miles (25 km) north of Montpellier; the schistose hills of Faugères; and nearby St-Chinian. To the west,

The port of Sète in Languedoc was a wine-trading center during the Roman era.

The Banyuls appellation, near the Spanish border, is noted for its fortified wines.

Few crops other than vines flourish in the region's generally arid, gravelly soils.

significant areas include the terraces of the Minervois, which overlook the Valley of the Aude, and the vineyards of the dramatically varied Corbières region, which extends from the shores of the Mediterranean to the gentle slopes of the Aude Valley and upward into the mountains. Another important area is the coastal bluff of La Clape, close to Narbonne.

Appellations

The improved standard of Languedoc-Roussillon's wines has resulted in many producers being promoted to *appellation contrôlée*. Most of the appellation wines are red and tend to be blends chosen from carignan, grenache, syrah, mourvèdre and occasionally cinsault. For many years, Fitou, created in 1948, was the region's sole red-wine appellation, but in 1982 it was joined by Faugères and St-Chinian, and in 1985 by Coteaux du Languedoc, Corbières and Minervois.

The imposition of *appellation contrôlée* has not been entirely successful. This is because the system is designed for areas, such as Bordeaux, Burgundy and Champagne, where there is widespread, longstanding agreement on which grape varieties best suit each area. This is certainly not the case in Languedoc-Roussillon; but given that for some 120 years the region specialized in producing the cheapest possible reds, it would be astonishing if growers had been able to arrive at a consensus after only 15 years.

Although appellation restrictions have limited the excessive planting of cabernet sauvignon, chardonnay and merlot, they have, at the same time, prevented growers experimenting with different varieties of grapes. The reluctance of producers from other French wine regions to permit their grape varieties to be approved for use in Languedoc-Roussillon appellations has also been a hindrance in this respect. The constraints of appellation laws have encouraged many growers to opt for *vin de pays* classification.

Roussillon is also noted for its fortified wines, known locally as *vins doux naturels*. This is somewhat of a misnomer because the sweetness of these wines is not natural but due to the addition of

pure alcohol to halt fermentation and leave some residual sugar. Among the most important fortified-wine appellations are Rivesaltes and Muscat de Rivesaltes; however, Banyuls, which comes from the steep hillside vineyards around the town of the same name and the fishing port of Collioure, is the best known. At one time, the production of various proprietary brands of aperitif, such as Dubonnet, was a significant activity, but this business has declined as these drinks have gone out of fashion.

Regional cuisine

The major influences on the cuisine of Languedoc-Roussillon are olive oil, of which the region is a major producer, Mediterranean fish and seafood, and the intense summer heat.

Generally, the climate is not suited to heartier dishes, although there is a need for them in winter, particularly in the hills away from the sea—Carcassonne and Limoux, for example, are just on the eastern edge of *cassoulet* (stew) country. Fishing is a major industry in the region, and fish that feature prominently on local menus include lotte (monkfish), racasse, red mullet, sea bass, sea bream, squid and sardines. Fish soups are a specialty, as is creamed salt cod, *brandade de morue*. Game is eaten when in season, and vegetables, particularly aubergines, peppers and tomatoes, are important year-round. Meat and fish are usually grilled.

There are some notable differences between the cuisines of Languedoc and Roussillon. In particular, Roussillon displays a strong Catalan influence, with grilled pepper salad and *crème catalan*, a form of crème brulée, among the local specialties.

Producers

DOMAINE CAZES, RIVESALTES, ROUSSILLON
Established NA *Owners* André and Bernard Cazes
Production 66,700 cases *Vineyard area* 395 acres (160 ha)

This estate has recently begun converting its entire vineyard to the biodynamic system. Once this is completed, Domaine Cazes may be the largest biodynamic winemaker in the world. It currently produces some 20 different wines, ranging from *vins de pays* through Côtes du Roussillon and Côtes du Roussillon Villages to some very fine *vins doux naturels*. Aimé Cazes, their top fortified wine, is made from grenache blanc and is aged for more than 20 years before it is released. Although it is a *vin de pays*, Le Credo is the estate's top red; it is made from cabernet sauvignon, merlot and syrah planted on appellation land.

MAS DE DAUMAS GASSAC, VDP DE L'HÉRAULT, LANGUEDOC

Established 1974 *Owners* Aimé and Véronique Guibert
Production 15,000 cases *Vineyard area* 87 acres (35 ha)

Whether Mas de Daumas Gassac is really the best wine produced in Languedoc-Roussillon is open to debate; however, there is no doubt that it was the wines made here during the 1980s that alerted enthusiasts to the remarkable developments taking place in, and the enormous potential of, the Midi.

When Aimé and Véronique Guibert bought this property in 1970, they had no intention of making wine; it was only when the special qualities of the soil were pointed out to them that they decided to plant vines. These produced their first vintage in 1978. The red is mainly cabernet sauvignon, malbec, merlot and syrah; the white, introduced later, is mainly viognier, chardonnay and muscat. The Guiberts also collaborate with their local cooperative to produce ranges of cheaper wines sold under names such as Figaro and Terrasses de Guilheim.

DANIEL AND PATRICIA DOMERGUE, MINERVOIS, LANGUEDOC

Established NA *Owners* Daniel and Patricia Domergue
Production 6,250 cases *Vineyard area* 25 acres (10 ha)

Daniel Domergue and his wife Patricia make both fine Minervois and intriguing *vin de pays* from regional grape varieties grown mainly in vineyards located close to Caunes-Minervois. The Domergues' preference for the cinsault grape, which has a poor reputation with the INAO, has brought them into conflict with the authorities. Their top wine, the impressively concentrated Clos de Centeilles, is made from syrah, mourvèdre and grenache. Others include the Capitelle de Centeilles, produced from 100 percent cinsault, and the Carignanissime, which is 100 percent carignan. Campagne de Centilles is mainly cinsault with a little syrah, whereas Guiniers is made from pinot noir and displays true varietal character with a clear southern influence.

CHÂTEAU DES ESTANILLES, FAUGÈRES, LANGUEDOC

Established NA *Owner* Michel Louison *Production* 11,000 cases *Vineyard area* 87 acres (35 ha)

Michel Louison insists that top-quality wine is created in the vineyard and has long railed against neighbors who don't look after their vines properly. One hundred percent of Louison's top red *cuvée* comes from his most impressive site, Clos de Feu, which is planted with syrah; yet, bizarrely, the local appellation regulations do not allow him to state this on the label. Other Château des Estanilles wines include an aged rosé that is fermented in wood, an excellent Coteaux du Languedoc white, and a very good pure viognier.

DOMAINE FERRER-RIBIÈRE, CÔTES DU ROUSSILLON, ROUSSILLON

Established Fifteenth century *Owners* Denis Ferrer and Bruno Ribière *Production* NA *Vineyard area* NA

The Ferrers have been growing vines at Terrats, southwest of Perpignan, for 600 years. But until Bruno Ribière persuaded the family to form a part-

REGIONAL DOZEN

Domaine Borie de Maurel
  Cuvée Sylla Minervois red
Aimé Cazes Domaine Cazes
  Rivesaltes fortified
Château des Estanilles
  Faugères red
Domaine de la Coste Cuvée
  Selectionnée Coteaux du
  Languedoc St-Christol red
Domaine Ferrer-Ribière
  Empreinte des Temps Côtes
  du Roussillon red
Domaine Gauby La Muntada
  Côtes du Roussillon
  Villages red
Domaine de l'Hortus Grande
  Cuvée Coteaux du
  Languedoc Pic St-Loup red
Mas Jullien Les Vignes
  Oubliées Coteaux du
  Languedoc white
Domaine de la Rectorie Cuvée
  Léon Parcé Collioure red
Cellier des Templiers Cuvée
  Président Henry Vidal
  Banyuls fortified
Domaine de la Tour Vieille
  Puig Ambeille Collioure red
Château de la Voulte-
  Gasparets Cuvée Romain
  Pauc Corbières red

The Castle of Puilaurens in the high Corbières was once a refuge for Cathar "heretics."

Minerve in the Minervois appellation occupies an elevated position above the River Cesse.

nership, the grapes were sent to the local cooperative. Now Domaine Ferrer-Ribière is among the brightest stars in Roussillon, offering remarkably complex wines made from old vines. The range includes three *vin de pays*: Catalan, a muscat; a grenache blanc made from vines that are more than 70 years old; and Cuvée Centenaire, made from carignan planted in 1878. Another outstanding offering is the remarkably concentrated Côtes du Roussillon, Empreinte des Temps.

DOMAINE GAUBY, CÔTES DU ROUSSILLON VILLAGES, ROUSSILLON

Established NA *Owner* Gérard Gauby *Production* 6,700 cases *Vineyard area* 87 acres (35 ha)

In the early 1990s, Domaine Gauby wines were rather severe, with hard tannins overwhelming the fruit. More recently, however, they have softened, allowing the fruit to come to the fore. The transformation is mainly the result of improvements in the vineyards, which are run on organic principles. For example, yields are always kept low, and in 1999 all the lateral roots of the vines in the best-sited vineyards were cut off to encourage the lower

roots to grow downward rather than outward. The pick of the range are a powerful Côtes de Roussillon Villages; the white Cuvée Centenaire, a rich wine made from grenache blanc which displays fruit and honey flavors; and La Muntada, made from syrah. Most Gauby whites are now designated *vin de pays* as they invariably exceed the low 12.5 percent limit set for Côtes du Roussillon.

DOMAINE DE L'HORTUS, COTEAUX DU LANGUEDOC (PIC ST-LOUP), LANGUEDOC

Established 1981 *Owner* Jean Orliac *Production* NA *Vineyard area* 74 acres (30 ha)

Jean Orliac is among the top producers in the Pic St-Loup. He and his wife Marie-Thérèse began in 1981 and bottled their first vintage in 1990. Their vineyards are mainly planted with mourvèdre, syrah and grenache. The Cuvée Classique, a blend of these three red varieties, is matured in stainless steel vats, whereas the Grande Cuvée is made from mourvèdre and syrah, and spends 15 months or so in new oak. Orliac also makes a promising barrel-fermented white (Grande Cuvée), a blend of chardonnay and viognier. Pic St-Loup's high-altitude location means that acidity levels remain high, making it well suited to white-wine production.

MAS JULLIEN, COTEAUX DU LANGUEDOC, LANGUEDOC

Established NA *Owner* Olivier Jullien *Production* 6,500 cases *Vineyard area* 42 acres (17 ha)

Olivier Jullien uses traditional local grapes to make some of the most exciting wines in France; these are now in such demand that prospective purchasers have to join a long waiting list. The vineyard contains carignan, cinsault, grenache, mourvèdre and syrah for the reds, and chenin blanc, clairette, grenache blanc, viognier and other varieties for the whites. The reds include Les Cailloutis and Les Depierre. The white, Les Vignes Oubliées, made with terret bouret, carignan and grenache, is outstanding. Jullien also makes a late-harvest Clairette Beaudille from vines that are over 70 years old.

DOMAINE DE LA RECTORIE, COLLIOURE AND BANYULS, ROUSSILLON

Established NA *Owners* Marc and Thierry Parcé *Production* NA *Vineyard area* 54 acres (22 ha)

At one time, the fame of the wines of Banyuls and Collioure rested almost entirely upon the efforts of the late Dr André Parcé at Domaine de Mas Blanc. His relatives Marc and Thierry Parcé at Domaine de la Rectorie have recently taken over the mantle; they produced their first wine in 1984, and are now established as the area's top winemakers. Their Banyuls Cuvée Parcé Frères can be enjoyed young, but the impressive Collioure will repay long aging. The Cuvée Leon Parcé, which is aged in oak for 18 months, has a robust structure and also ages well. An outstanding *vin de pays*, Cuvée l'Argile, is made from grenache gris.

CAVE DU SIEUR D'ARQUES, LIMOUX, LANGUEDOC

Established 1946 *Owner* Cooperative of 500 members *Production* 1.6 million cases *Vineyard area* 12,350 acres (5,000 ha)

One of the most efficient cooperatives in France, Sieur d'Arques is responsible for around 90 percent of all the wine made in the Limoux area. It has surveyed all of its members' vineyards and divided them into four zones based on variations in climate and growing seasons. For example, higher, and therefore cooler, areas in the southwest have a longer growing season than warmer, low-lying land around Carcassonne. This information helps the cooperative decide when to give the go-ahead for the harvest in each area.

Sieur d'Arques makes a wide range of varietal *vin de pays* from chardonnay, chenin, mauzac, cabernet sauvignon and merlot. It also produces a barrel-fermented Toques et Clochers Chardonnay from the four zones, as well as individual-vineyard, barrel-fermented AC Limoux chardonnays. In addition, it makes 90 percent of all sparkling Blanquette de Limoux and Crémant de Limoux, plus small quantities of *méthode ancestrale*.

VAL D'ORBIEU-LISTEL, LANGUEDOC-ROUSSILLON

Established 1967 *Owner* Val d'Orbieu-Listel *Production* 7 million cases *Vineyard area* 34,600 acres (14,000 ha)

This association of cooperatives and individual producers is the largest winemaker in Languedoc-Roussillon, the second-largest wine group in France, and the country's largest exporter of wines by volume. It now includes 17 cooperatives, about 180 wineries and 4,000 vine growers. In 1995, Val d'Orbieu acquired Listel, which owned extensive vineyards near the Languedoc coast and in Provence; in 1997, Val d'Orbieu-Listel took a controlling interest in the *négociant* side of Domaines Cordier in Bordeaux. As a result, the association now markets wines from Banyuls to Provence. Output includes an intriguing range of blends made with local and international varieties.

CHÂTEAU DE LA VOULTE-GASPARETS, CORBIÈRES, ROUSSILLON

Established NA *Owner* Patrick Reverdy *Production* NA cases *Vineyard area* 114 acres (46 ha)

This vineyard has long been one of the leading estates in the Corbières. It lies in the commune of Boutenac, which is located on the gently undulating hills at the edge of the Aude Valley and is recognized as one of the best areas in the appellation. The generic *cuvée* is for early drinking. The two best reds are made from 60 percent carignan, 30 percent grenache and 10 percent syrah: the Cuvée Reservée is made from vines that are between 20 and 40 years old, while the prestige *cuvée*, Romain Pauc, is made from 90-year-old vines; it also spends longer in a higher proportion of new oak. The château also produces some Corbières Blanc, which should be drunk young.

The less fertile soils of the coteaux are better suited to viticulture than those of the plains.

Winemakers on the plains have recently begun to use international grape varieties.

Provence

Anthony Peregrine

Increasingly fine red wines, capable of long aging, are being produced in Provence.

Provence is one of France's prettiest playgrounds and for years its mainly rosé wines had a merely playful reputation. No one, least of all the producers, took them very seriously; they were light fare for sundrenched vacationers. There is, though, another, deeper side to Provence and some wines are now reflecting this. Without sacrificing any of their characteristic freshness, the rosés (which make up 75 percent of production) have gained a gastronomic legitimacy—most notably within the context of high-tone Provençal cuisine, but also as accompaniments to East Asian dishes. Meanwhile, the improvement in red wines has spread outward from the Bandol appellation over much of the region, and a few terrific whites have even emerged. Provençal wines remain fun, but now display far greater depth, substance and consistency.

History

You don't have to spend long in Provence before someone tells you that this is France's oldest wine region, that vines were first planted here by the Greeks 2,600 years ago. Although this is interesting, it is largely irrelevant, for when the Romans turned up later, they ordered all the Provençal vines to be ripped out, thereby eliminating any producers that might compete with Rome's own industry.

Winegrowing didn't get underway again until the Middle Ages, when the region's production achieved fleeting renown as a result of Eléonore of Provence's marriage to Henry III of England—a useful PR coup. But the wines were unremarkable and remained so until the nineteenth century, when phylloxera all but destroyed the local industry.

Replanting was of prolific carignan and aramon, which reflected the region's concern with quantity rather than quality. Then in the 1930s— an era that saw the advent of paid leave in France—producers suddenly had droves of undemanding customers arriving on their doorstep, happy to be there and ready to drink anything. And for a while that's what the locals were happy to serve them. It's only in the last two decades that producers have felt the need to improve standards—with excellent results that the wine world has, frankly, been slow to acknowledge.

This could be because winegrowing in Provence is, and has always been, geographically and politically fractured. The region boasts eight appellations, few of which get along with each other, and none of which shares any common ground with local *vins de pays* administrators. In total, the appellations make approximately 29 million gallons (110 million l) each year. *Vin de pays* accounts for 11.6 million gallons (44 million l), and the regional *vins de table* 10.6 million gallons (40 million l).

Landscape and climate

Warm summers and relatively mild winters provide 3,000 hours of sun a year—good conditions for grape-growing overall. But there are many nuances, for Provence is a disparate region. In the Alpine foothills, for instance, winters can be tough; and the mistral wind whistling down the Rhône Valley can bend strong men in two. Yet it can also be a godsend: after short, violent Mediterranean storms, the blasting wind quickly dries vines, keeping them disease-free. Summers can be very hot, particularly in the inland areas, though nearer the coast, the torrid conditions are softened by moist sea breezes.

If the Provençal climate is varied, its *terroirs* are more so. Though mainly limestone and arid, they range from the beautiful terraced slopes overlooking the sea at Bandol and Cassis to the Var uplands, where vines dispute space with lavender and *garrigue*, and the pebbly soil is colored red by iron oxide. The Côtes de Provence appellation alone has four distinct zones: the coast, the inland valley, the Var hills and, off to the west, the Ste-Victoire district, dominated by the mountain of the same name that so enchanted local lad Paul Cézanne.

Wines and vines

Although most of Provence's production is fresh, fruity rosé—the Var department is the world's number-one pink-wine region—it also includes dry, aromatic whites from areas such as Cassis, and elegant, powerful reds, capable of long aging, from Bandol and, increasingly, other zones. Even the

A wide range of mesoclimates and soils allows local farmers to grow diverse crops.

Producers
1 Domaine de la Bastide Neuve
2 Mas de Cadenet
3 Domaines Ott
4 Château de Pibarnon
5 Domaine Rabiéga
6 Château Roubine
7 Domaine St-André-de-Figuière
8 Châteaux Elie Sumeire
9 Domaine de Trévallon
10 Château Vignelaure

rosé producers are now looking for greater structure, finesse, freshness and fruit in their wines.

The range of quality produce is now huge, as is the permitted range of grape varieties. The Côtes de Provence appellation, for instance, allows 13. Across the region, the main rosé and red varieties are grenache, mourvèdre, cinsault, carignan, the local tibouren and syrah. Of late, cabernet sauvignon has also crept in, though it remains a suspect outsider to more puritanical producers. White wine, which makes up 5 per cent of the total comes mainly from clairette, ugni blanc, the wonderfully aromatic rolle, bourboulenc, sémillon and sauvignon.

Appellations and classifications

There are eight Provençal wine appellations, many the outcome of political bickering rather than genuine differences in winemaking styles. In descending order of size, they are as follows:

Côtes de Provence, which was declared in 1977, covers 47,000 acres (19,000 ha) and produces 100 million bottles a year. It is the region's locomotive in terms of quantity and, increasingly, quality. Rosé is kingpin, accounting for up to 80 percent of production, but there are remarkable reds, too.

Coteaux d'Aix-en-Provence, an appellation since 1985, includes 8,650 acres (3,500 ha) around the town of Aix-en-Provence. These produce underrated rosés and reds, some of them extraordinary.

Coteaux Varois, declared an appellation in 1993, covers 4,450 acres (1,800 ha). It is establishing a good name, especially for its middle-market pinks.

Bandol produces the region's finest red wines, mainly from mourvèdre grown on 3,460 acres (1,400 ha) of steep terraces. Declared in 1941, the appellation demands a minimum of 18 months in oak. It produces excellent, structured rosés, too.

Les Baux-de-Provence broke away from Coteaux d'Aix after a tiff in 1995. Its 800 acres (325 ha) surround the citadel town of Les Baux and produce good reds and rosés.

Cassis is Provence's oldest appellation, dating from 1936. It produces lively whites from 430 acres (175 ha) around the eponymous coastal village.

Bellet, a microappellation of 79 acres (32 ha) on the outskirts of Nice, produces all three colors in classy style—reds include local fuella and braquet grape varieties. However, the wines tend to be expensive and are usually found only in Nice.

Palette, a miniscule microappellation, covers barely 25 acres (10 ha). It was once the estate of Good King René, Count of Provence. Fittingly, its wines seem to come from another time: the reds are full-bodied and dark to the point of tarriness, the rosés solidly structured and the whites aromatic.

Provence is also home to many *vin de pays* classifications, the biggest being those covering the Var and Bouches-du-Rhône departments (see p. 218).

The local fishing industry provides a rich variety of seafood to accompany Provence's much-improved rosé and white wines.

Eighteen Provençal estates have the right to call their wines Crus Classés. They gained this privilege in 1955, after petitioning the authorities. Much to the annoyance of other producers who have been denied access to the classification, none of these *domaines* is subject to any form of quality control. Certain of the better Crus Classés recently agreed to monitor each other's standards and thereby prove that they merit their status. The truth is that many do, some don't: here, at least, Cru Classé is still not the guarantee it should be.

Viticulture and winemaking

The impact of outside investment in Provençal vineyards and cellars since the late 1970s should not be underestimated. Although certain large family businesses such as Ott and Elie Sumeire have always kept up with advances in viticulture, other, smaller concerns have lacked the will or financial resources to adapt to the modern era. Supplying money and motivation, the outsiders—mainly Swiss financiers, French industrialists and British businessfolk—have offered a lead that has been followed eagerly.

Increasingly, organic methods are being used in the vineyards, while in the cellars, temperature control, which was rare 15 years ago and is vital for rosés, is now standard. Most producers of red wines can now afford new oak barrels, though the question of whether or not they should use them—do they distort Provençal typicity, for example?—remains charged with a degree of emotion that only the French can generate for such issues.

Producers

DOMAINE DE LA BASTIDE NEUVE

Established 1988 *Owners* Wiestner family *Production* 8,300 cases *Vineyard area* 42 acres (17 ha)

On purchasing this estate, Swiss financier Hugo Wiestner installed Jérome Paquette, one of the area's brightest young innovators, as director. Since then, Bastide Neuve's range has become infinitely more interesting. The Cuvée d'Antan red is fine and aromatic, yet with the concentration to age well; the Cuvée des Anges is Paquette's entirely successful attempt to prove that a rosé can be a substantial and impressive wine.

Stricter controls in cellars have greatly improved standards across the region.

MAS DE CADENET

Established 1813 *Owners* Négrel family *Production* 25,000 cases *Vineyard area* 99 acres (40 ha)

Guy Négrel has been at the forefront of the battle to have the Ste-Victoire zone recognized as a distinct *cru* within Côtes de Provence. His own wines are his best argument, especially the Mas Négrel Cadenet Cuvée Prestige range. Reds and rosés (*both* raised in wood) have an earthy side to their elegance that makes them utterly distinctive, and even the rosé has the structure and staying power for summer *and* winter drinking.

DOMAINES OTT

Established 1912 *Owners* Ott family *Production* 52,000 cases *Vineyard area* 420 acres (170 ha)

Marcel Ott, from Alsace, bought the Château de Selle at Taradeau in the Côtes de Provence in 1912, thus founding one of the region's finest family-run winemaking empires. Subsequently, the Otts added the white-producing Clos Mireille (also Côtes de Provence) and Château Romassan in Bandol to the stable, while building an unbeatable reputation for quality and consistency. The rosé, Cœur de Grain, has been their worldwide calling card, and the Blanc de Blancs and Bandol reds justify prices somewhat above the Provençal average.

CHÂTEAU DE PIBARNON

Established 1978 *Owners* de St-Victor family *Production* 20,000 cases *Vineyard area* 111 acres (45 ha)

If Bandol is the most prestigious of Provençal appellations, it's because it is known for red wines (which are taken far more seriously than rosés by wine folk) and has benefited from the presence of a small group of quality-minded trailblazers keen to restore mourvèdre to primacy. Among their leaders is Henri de St-Victor, who resculpted the terraced coastal vineyard of Château Pibarnon. The limestone soils now harness the power of mourvèdre to the cause of finesse and structure; the resulting wines represent an exemplary combination of *terroir*, grape variety and exceptional winemaking. The rosé is powerful, spicy and fresh, and quite the equal of the outstanding reds.

DOMAINE RABIÉGA

Established 1986 *Owner* Vin&Sprit *Production* 13,000 cases *Vineyard area* 119 acres (48 ha)

The Swedish company Vin&Sprit bought this Côtes de Provence estate in the mid-1980s and installed Lars Torstensson as manager and winemaker. This proved to be an inspired move as

In Bandol, vineyards climb rugged ranges just a short distance from the ocean.

Torstensson has brought great imagination and typically Swedish meticulousness to red-wine production in particular. His Clos d'Ière Cuvées I and II are as classy as any Provençal wine, and led to him twice being named French Winemaker of the Year. The syrah-based Cuvée I is particularly opulent, full of fruit with old-vine intensity and tannic finesse, and remains his finest achievement.

DOMAINE ST-ANDRÉ-DE-FIGUIÈRE

Established 1992 *Owners* Combard family *Production* 30,000 cases *Vineyard area* 104 acres (42 ha)

Benefiting from old vines, including carignan nearing its centenary, Alain Combard's range mixes accessibility with power and elegance, notably in his red Cuvée Spéciale. The Cuvée des Princes rosé is light and full of fresh flavor, and as bright as Provençal rosés should be, and the Vieilles Vignes rosé has power and structure underpinning the fruit.

CHÂTEAUX ELIE SUMEIRE

Established 1900 *Owners* Sumeire family *Production* 125,000 cases *Vineyard area* 741 acres (300 ha)

Dating back to the 1500s and including nine châteaux and estates, Elie Sumeire is Provence's oldest and largest family concern; it is also among the very best. Its leading châteaux, including Coussin in the Ste-Victoire zone, L'Afrique at Cuers, and de Maupague in Puyloubier, produce especially fine reds, Coussin's Rouge de Garde being a real gem. The rosés are also outstanding, the sophisticated pale color providing no warning of the impact of the full-fruit bouquet and good citrus-fruit length on the tastebuds.

DOMAINE DE TRÉVALLON

Established 1973 *Owners* Durrbach family *Production* 4,200 cases *Vineyard area* 49 acres (20 ha)

Eloi Durrbach fashioned his vineyard from the limestone *garrigue* of the northern Alpilles hills and has since followed an idiosyncratic, organic-influenced path to create rich, tannic but wonderfully elegant wines that age for years. Made with low-yielding cabernet sauvignon and syrah, fermented for an extended period (without temperature control) and aged for 18-22 months, these are world-class reds. Yet they fall foul of the Les Baux appellation rules—too much cabernet, no grenache—and have to be sold as *vin de pays*. Durrbach should worry: not only are the wines the undoubted stars of Provence (indeed, of the whole of southern France), but they also command the highest prices in the region.

CHÂTEAU VIGNELAURE

Established 1995 *Owners* O'Brien family *Production* 30,000 cases *Vineyard area* 148 acres (60 ha)

After a halcyon period in the 1970s and 1980s, Vignelaure was trading mainly on its reputation when Irish racehorse trainer David O'Brien (son of Vincent) and his wife Catherine took over the estate. Aided by Hugh Ryman, they have restored and enhanced its reputation for bordeaux-tinged reds. These incorporate beautifully balanced cabernet sauvignon, syrah and grenache, and are barrel-aged for 18 months, creating a concentrated wine that will age splendidly beyond ten years. The headline wine is AC, but due to their high cabernet content the other *cuvées* are classified VDP Côteaux du Verdon. Vignelaure also produces a fine rosé.

REGIONAL BEST

QUALITY WINES

Mas Négrel Cadenet rosé
Château de Pibarnon rosé
Domaine Rabiéga Clos d'Ière
 Cuvée I red
Domaine de Trévallon red

BEST VALUE WINES

Château Coussin rosé
Domaine St-André de Figuière
 Cuvée des Princes rosé
Château Vignelaure red

The Rhône

Simon Woods

A wine book that appeared in 1995 described the Rhône Valley as an "up-and-coming region packed with the newly sexy grenache, syrah and viognier." In the same year, in his introduction to Remington Norman's *Rhône Renaissance,* Hugh Johnson wrote, "Winegrowing in the Rhône Valley is probably the oldest established in France." While these two statements appear to be at odds with each other, anyone familiar with the Rhône would agree with both. For the Rhône Valley is an area of contrasts, of ancient and modern, of classical French rural scenery and industrial sprawl, of steep, stark slopes in the north and generous rolling hills in the south, of the splendor of outstanding estate-grown Châteauneuf-du-Pape and the shame of mass-produced, inferior examples.

Until comparatively recently, wine lovers have been somewhat reticent in embracing this fascinating area. If their experience of the region is based on that staple of French café life, Côtes du Rhône, it's not hard to see why. But taste the finest wines from Châteauneuf and from other appellations such as Côte Rôtie and Hermitage, and it is not possible to deny that the Rhône deserves the same recognition as France's other great red-wine regions, Bordeaux and Burgundy. Indeed, at its best, the Rhône offers the authority and longevity of the former with the sensual pleasures of the latter, and usually undercuts both in price.

Geographical pedants may say that the Rhône Valley actually starts at Lake Geneva in Switzerland and runs through some of the winegrowing districts of Savoie. But from a winemaking point of view, the region known as the Rhône begins in eastern central France near Vienne to the south of Lyon and then spreads southward toward the Mediterranean, finishing in a rather sprawling fashion around Avignon. The region splits conveniently, both geographically and in terms of the wines produced, into two distinct subregions: the northern and southern Rhône.

The northern Rhône runs from Vienne, home of Côte Rôtie, southward to St-Péray, which lies just across the river from the town of Valence. The steep slopes overlooking the river are home to red wines of power and elegance made from the syrah grape. Whites are very much in the minority here, but the best, made from viognier, marsanne and rousanne, can be every bit as compelling as the reds. From just south of Montélimar, the start of the southern Rhône, the air gradually fills with the aromas of herbs, the valley flattens out, and the vines stretch away from the river, mainly to the east. Here, as in the north, red wines vastly outnumber whites, although grenache is the principal variety. Although whites, with a few notable exceptions, seldom approach the reds in quality, this is the home of France's best and most famous *vin doux naturel,* Muscat de Beaumes de Venise.

The town of Tain, on the Rhône River, from among the adjoining vineyards.

Most wines labelled simply Côtes du Rhône also hail from this southern sector.

What makes the Rhône one of the most exciting wine regions in the world is the progress that was made during the last part of the twentieth century, and the potential for further improvement in the twenty-first. Both the Californians and Australians may have played a large part in making grenache, syrah and viognier "newly sexy," but it is the Rhône producers who still create the benchmarks for these varieties and who are making better examples with each vintage. And, most refreshingly, in a wine world where too many vignerons think nothing of slapping exorbitant price-tags on their wines, the Rhône Valley remains a happy hunting ground for those who are guided by value for money rather than the whims of fashion.

History

Wine has played an important part in the history of the Rhône not just for centuries but for millennia. In the time of Julius Caesar, if not earlier, the river was used by the expanding Roman Empire as a means of transporting wine from the province of Narbonensis along the Mediterranean coast to parts of what was then Gaul. Once Gaul had been conquered, it was only a matter of time before the Romans thought about planting vines, especially in the warm southern reaches, where the vegetation matched that of their homeland.

The area to the north was the home of the Allobroges tribe, whose territory stretched from the Rhône eastward to Lake Geneva. The Romans found grapes already growing here on sites such as the slope of Côte Rôtie and the hill of Hermitage; in both cases, the aspect and orientation of the land provided excellent growing conditions. The wine made in Vienna (modern-day Vienne) by the Allobroges was praised in AD 71 by Pliny the Elder. Pliny called the red grape used for this wine allobrogica and described it as being resistant to cold. This makes it highly unlikely that allobrogica was the syrah grape found in the northern Rhône today. However, one theory says that it could have been an ancestor, either the dureza of the nearby Ardèche or a member of the mondeuse family from Savoie, farther upstream.

Another explanation for syrah's presence in the Rhône is that the vine was brought from Shiraz in Persia by Phocaeans, the Greeks of Asia Minor, at the time they established Marsilia (Marseilles), around 600 BC. Yet another is that syrah takes its name from Syracuse in Sicily, and that the Romans

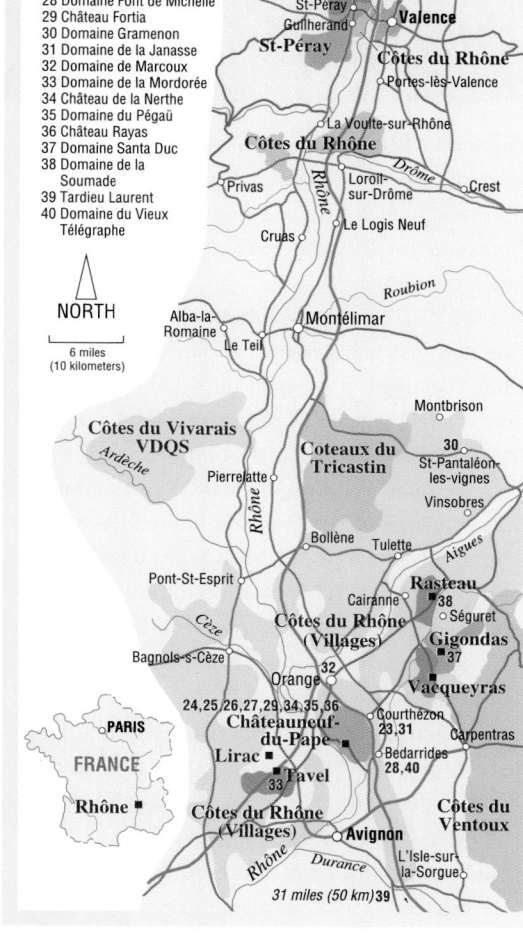

Producers
1 Chapoutier
2 Chave
3 Clape
4 Clusel-Roch
5 Jean-Luc Colombo
6 Yves Cuilleron
7 Delas Frères
8 Pierre Dumazet
9 Bernard Faurie
10 Jean-Michel Gerin
11 Alain Graillot
12 Jean-Louis Grippat
13 Guigal
14 Paul Jaboulet Aîné
15 Jean-Paul & Jean-Luc Jamet
16 André Perret
17 René Rostaing
18 Marc Sorrel
19 Georges Vernay
20 Noel Verset
21 François Villard
22 Alain Voge
23 Château de Beaucastel
24 Henri Bonneau
25 Les Cailloux
26 Domaine de la Charbonnière
27 Clos des Papes
28 Domaine Font de Michelle
29 Château Fortia
30 Domaine Gramenon
31 Domaine de la Janasse
32 Domaine de Marcoux
33 Domaine de la Mordorée
34 Château de la Nerthe
35 Domaine du Pégaü
36 Château Rayas
37 Domaine Santa Duc
38 Domaine de la Soumade
39 Tardieu Laurent
40 Domaine du Vieux Télégraphe

Hermitage, both red and white, produced by the Chapoutier winery.

under Emperor Probus took the grape from there to the Rhône in the third century AD, along with viognier, which had originated in Dalmatia.

After the Romans, there is little history of winemaking in the Rhône until 1157, when Bishop Geoffroy of Avignon planted an estate there. The Church continued its involvement in winemaking in the fourteenth century when Clément V, who founded Château Pape-Clément in Bordeaux, became Pope and transferred the papacy to

Winery and vineyards near Tain, in the Rhône Valley.

An ornate gate set in an old wall, Châteauneuf-du-Pape, Rhône Valley.

Avignon in 1309. Clément is reputed to have ordered vines to be planted nearby, but it was his successor, John XXII, who built a new castle—*château neuf*—between 1318 and 1333 and established a vineyard.

However, we know nothing about the type of wine that was being made for the papal court, which remained in Avignon until 1378. Indeed, there are few records of the precise flavor of any Rhône wines from the time of Pliny until 1787, when Thomas Jefferson, then US Ambassador to France, eulogised both red and white Hermitage. He praised the red for its "full body, dark purple color … exquisite flavor and perfume which is … compared to that of raspberry," and he thought the white was the finest white wine in the world "without a single exception."

Hermitage of both colors had risen in popularity throughout Europe, partly due to a visit to Tain by Louis XIII. The red wine was also much in demand in Bordeaux for "improving" the local produce, and wines that had been *Hermitagé* ("Hermitaged") sold for higher prices than unblended clarets. Farther up the Rhône, Côte Rôtie also enjoyed considerable acclaim in the eighteenth century, while at the same time farther south, the Vin du Pape from the village of Châteauneuf-Calcernier was beginning to make a name for itself.

The advent of phylloxera at the end of the nineteenth century caused havoc in both northern and southern vineyards. This, combined with the two world wars that followed and the Great Depression of the 1930s, meant that the Rhône entered the last half of the twentieth century in a pitiful state. The castle at Châteauneuf had been destroyed by the retreating Germans, many of the young men of the region had been killed in the wars, and many landowners found it more profitable to plant fruit trees than vines. The north, in particular, was badly affected: in 1956, there were just 119 acres (48 ha) of vineyards left in Côte Rôtie, while Condrieu boasted less than 25 acres (10 ha).

If Châteauneuf-du-Pape was in slightly better shape, it was largely thanks to the efforts of Baron Pierre Le Roy de Boiseaumarie of Château Fortia. In 1923, in an effort to preserve the reputation the wines had enjoyed prior to phylloxera, Baron Le Roy drew up a set of regulations stipulating what was permissible for the local wines. Among other things, this placed limits on the zones of production, grape varieties and yields. The scheme proved so successful that it became the blueprint for France's national appellation system. Yet despite these rules, by the second half of the century the average Châteauneuf, while drinkable, was still not exactly inspiring.

So when did the Rhône become the vibrant and exciting region it is today and what triggered its rise in fortunes? No event can be singled out as *the* turning point, but 1978 proved to be a very significant vintage. First, it was a great year for both the northern and southern Rhône, and several wines from that year still have plenty of life ahead of them more than two decades later. In Châteauneuf, it was the year that Jacques Perrin died, leaving Château de Beaucastel in the very capable hands of his sons François and Jean-Pierre; the standards they have since set have served as reference points for many vignerons in the south.

In the north, 1978 saw the first release of Marc Guigal's Côte Rôtie La Landonne, arguably the finest of the company's stunning trio of single-vineyard wines from the appellation (La Mouline and La Turque being the others). These wines set new standards for the Rhône as a whole, both in terms of quality and for the prices they commanded, and established the Rhône as a fully fledged fine wine region.

Since then, there have been further developments and other mold breakers. In 1988, for example, the firm of Chapoutier, which had been trading on its historical reputation for several years, received an injection of new blood when Marc and Michel Chapoutier took the reins of the company. Today, Chapoutier's prestige *cuvées* (blends) are every bit as good as those of Guigal.

When it comes to seminal forces, mention must be made of the influential American wine writer Robert Parker. Many people associate Parker with Bordeaux, but his enthusiasm for the Rhône is, if anything, greater and his comments on the southern Rhône in particular have hit home with many producers. Are they making wines just to please Parker? Maybe, but a more pertinent question would be are the wines they make now better than they used to be? The answer is "yes." Thanks largely to Parker, many *domaines* have cut their yields, reduced or eliminated fining and filtration, and are now bottling in one batch rather than over a period of months or even years. And, encouraged by the success of others, several growers who traditionally sold their grapes or must to local cooperatives have now begun producing their own wines, often with excellent results.

The effect of Parker's comments has not been entirely positive, however. For example, a number of *domaines* now produce two *cuvées*, one of which is unfined and unfiltered, and destined primarily for the American market, where most of Parker's readers buy their wines. A more desirable outcome would be for there to be just one superior *cuvée* available to everyone.

Looking to the future, the major change is likely to be the continuing rise in prominence of the southern Rhône. Châteauneuf-du-Pape has almost ten times as much vineyard area as Côte Rôtie and Hermitage put together, and only a relatively small number of producers are currently taking full advantage of its *terroir*.

Gigondas will also become a serious wine village, and neighbors such as Vacqueyras, Cairanne and Séguret could also rise to prominence. Those who now look outside Europe for exciting new finds would do well to turn their gaze back to a region that has being making memorable wine for at least 2,000 years.

Landscape and climate

Visitors to the Rhône Valley don't have to be wine experts to observe that the vine-growing regions in the northern sector, the *Septentrionale* as the French call it, are generally cooler, wetter and steeper than those of the southern sector, the *Méridionale*. Indeed, the only common factors

Built of local stone, the village of Côtes du Rhône seems to grow out of the landscape.

Hillside terraces are angled to protect the vines from the ferocity of the winds.

in the two regions are the river itself and the often vicious winds. The climate in the north is continental, with cold winters and generally warm summers. July temperatures can be high, but not all sites are suitable for viticulture—at least viticulture aimed at producing high-quality fruit. The best sites, such as those in Côte Rôtie and Hermitage, are steep slopes angled south or southeast and often overlooking the river so that the vines benefit from reflected as well as direct heat. The finest vineyards in Cornas aren't especially close to the river, but their situation, in the lee of a hill, means that they are sheltered from the north winds. In vineyards with more northerly aspects and at the highest altitudes there can be problems ripening grapes in some vintages.

The subsoils on the slopes of the northern Rhône are mainly granite (which retains daytime heat and so promotes ripening) with pockets of schist, while the topsoils are based on sand and/or limestone. As you travel toward St-Péray, the incidence of limestone outcrops increases. The steepness of the slopes and their exposure mean that soil erosion is an ever-present problem. To combat this, some sites are terraced, providing convenient retaining walls on which the owners—most visibly Chapoutier and Jaboulet in Hermitage—are not averse to promoting their wares.

Not all the northern vineyards are on slopes. Large parts of the appellations of St-Joseph and Crozes-Hermitage adjoin the river, where the land is flat enough to allow the fruit to be picked by machine. The rich alluvial soils here, often with a high clay content, are not ideal for vines, although when cultivated well, the soft, easy-drinking wines they produce serve as a gentle and affordable introduction to the northern Rhône.

In the scattered winegrowing areas along the Drôme, the climate and countryside are more alpine than anything else, and the soil is clay and limestone over hard rock. Beyond Montélimar, in the southern Rhône, rainfall is lower than in the north—27 inches (700 mm) a year in Orange as opposed to 35 inches (900 mm) in Valence—and the average temperature is about 2°F (1°C) higher. The land is more undulating and, at least in those parts not given over to vineyards and other agriculture, covered with the scrubby but highly scented southern vegetation known as the *garrigue*.

Of the several severe winds that affect the Rhône the most aggressive is the mistral, which originates in eastern France and funnels down the narrow valley of the northern Rhône, emerging near Montélimar at speeds as high as 90 miles per hour (145 km per hour). Such winds can rip branches from vines, so cypress and poplar trees are often planted as windbreaks. Grim as these winds can be—they occur on one day in every three in parts of the southern Rhône—they do have their advantages, most notably that they dry the vines and protect them from spring frosts.

In the southern vineyards, which lie mostly to the east of the river (Tavel and Lirac are exceptions), there is no such thing as a typical soil. The limestone outcrops in evidence at the lower end of the northern Rhône are more common here, but there are also pockets of clay—very welcome for its water-retaining properties in the arid climate—weathered sand, ironstone, marl and pebbles. The topsoil is stonier than farther north and, in certain vineyards, most famously those of Châteauneuf-du-Pape, the stones can be as much as 10 inches (250 mm) across.

The accepted wisdom is that such stones store heat during the day and release it to the vines at night. In a warm climate, this may be too much of a good thing; indeed, some of the best vineyards, most noticeably those of Château Rayas, not only have no pebbles but also face partly north. The most useful function of the stones may well be to help the soil retain moisture that would otherwise evaporate. Tractor-friendly they are not.

Some southern vineyards are located at relatively high elevations. For example, in Gigondas, Vacqueyras and some of the villages entitled to use the Côtes du Rhône-Villages appellation, such as Rasteau and Séguret, vineyards lie at all altitudes from 300 feet (90 m) up to 1,850 feet (550 m). On the higher sites, the harvest can be as much as two weeks later, which can cause problems in poorer vintages. Although these vineyards are generally planted with a high proportion of grenache, it will be interesting to see if their owners decide in future that syrah is a more appropriate variety.

Viticulture

If a nineteenth-century vigneron from the Rhône were to visit the region's vineyards and cellars today, there would be some in which he would feel immediately at home. On the other hand, there would be others that would be so far removed from his realm of experience that he might think he was on another planet. Both styles of operation are capable of turning out high-class wines.

The northern and southern sectors of the valley produce very different styles of wine, so it's no surprise that the vineyards are quite different. Vines are much more densely planted in the north—Hermitage is typically planted at 3,000 or more

to the acre (7,500 per ha), which is two to three times what you will find in Châteauneuf-du-Pape, for example. The training systems also differ. The favored grape in the north, syrah, requires trellising of some sort. On flatter ground this can be done with wires, but on steeper slopes winegrowers often use elaborate wigwam-like constructions made from chestnut twigs to support the vines and provide protection from the mistral and other winds. In contrast, grenache and other southern varieties are typically grown low as bush vines. The mistral blows with even more force here, but because the vines grow close to the ground, it has little effect.

Old-fashioned hand plows are still used among the vines on this difficult terrain.

In both north and south, improved viticulture means that fruit can be picked riper than was once the case. The north's erratic weather means that chemical fertilizers and sprays are still used by most producers, albeit in decreasing quantities. An exception is the Chapoutier *domaine*, where biodynamic viticulture is the order of the day. The drier, windier conditions in the south mean that the need to treat vineyards against pests and diseases is greatly reduced. Many *domaines* are, to all intents, organically farmed, although few promote themselves as such, preferring to hold onto their chemicals in case of adverse weather.

If our ancient vigneron had lived in the southern Rhône, he would have had several varieties planted willy-nilly on his *domaine*. Such vineyards still exist, but many are now established with a view to matching particular varieties to particular sites. For example, of the two varieties increasingly being planted in the south, syrah often appears on cooler, north-facing slopes, while mourvèdre is being planted on warmer south-facing plots. But the major difference our vigneron would note in the vineyards generally would be the use of machinery. In the flatter parts of Crozes-Hermitage, for example, mechanical harvesters are a common sight, and helicopters are often used for spraying at certain times of year.

In the cellars, the differences would be even more striking. Some wineries are still lined with ancient oak casks, but others are full of gleaming stainless steel and sophisticated, computer-controlled equipment. Generalizations

Vineyards of Châteauneuf-du-Pape.

Marc barrel at Chapoutier winery.

concerning methods of winemaking can be misleading, but producers fall roughly into three camps. Traditionalists do things as they have always been done, modernists use the latest gizmos and techniques, and pragmatists weigh up the pros and cons of each approach and use what they think will work best for them. The only principle on which they all agree is that the lower the yields in the vineyards, the better the quality of the wine. The pragmatists may be the ones showing the way for the future, but the truth is that good and great wines emerge from all three camps.

One issue that divides local winemakers is whether or not to destem. Traditionally, neither syrah in the north nor grenache in the south was destemmed, resulting in firm, tannic wines with the structure to age for years, even decades. Modernists criticize such an approach, saying that wine should be made from grapes, not stalks, that the broken stalks release unripe green tannins into the wine and that, without stems, the maceration period can be extended. Pragmatists look at the attributes of particular vintages and destem accordingly. In ripe years, when the wood is less green and astringent, they include more stems; in lesser vintages, they exclude most or even all of them. If they are also taking lower yields, there is a greater likelihood that their stems will be riper, in which case they can follow either approach.

Stainless steel, old wooden vats and concrete are all used for fermenting syrah in the north, the choice being a personal preference on the part of the producer. Fermentation temperatures are generally high, while total maceration times vary from a few days to up to three weeks after fermentation has stopped. Traditional southern producers follow a similar method, but others prefer to put

some or all of the fruit through carbonic maceration, which produces lighter and fruitier wines. Château de Beaucastel in Châteauneuf-du-Pape is unusual in that it performs an operation known as *vinification à chaud*, in which the grapes are heated to 82°F (30°C) for about a minute and a half before cooling them back down to 64°F (20°C). According to the owners, the Perrins, this enhances color extraction, limits oxidation, prolongs fermentation and reduces the need for sulfur.

Traditionalists age their wines in large, old barrels; modernists often prefer new oak, although thankfully few do so to the degree that occurs in other parts of the world. The pragmatists look at the quality of just-fermented wine, and apportion the new oak accordingly: a higher percentage for above-average years, a lower proportion for poor ones. Again, good viticulture gives riper, richer fruit, leaving the winemaker with more options.

Commercial pressures often mean that wines are bottled earlier than a producer would prefer. Also, while quantities produced in most northern Rhône cellars allow wines to be bottled in just one batch, this is not the case at many southern *domaines*, where some wines are still bottled to order over a period that could extend over some 18 months. Clearly, the wines from the first batch will differ from the final bottling, yet there is no indication of this on the labels. Such practices have attracted plenty of criticism from commentators such as Robert Parker, and the comments have prompted many *domaines* to adjust their bottling schedules. Furthermore, thanks to Parker and others, many *domaines* have now reduced or even eliminated the processes of fining and filtration, and the wines are fuller and richer as a result.

Advances in vinification technology have had a particularly beneficial effect on Rhône white wines. Temperature-controlled fermentation, the ability to suppress malolactic fermentation—especially important in the low-acid south—and early bottling mean that dull, heavy, oversulfured and downright faulty whites are disappearing. Similarly, improved standards of hygiene mean that there is less risk now of bacterial spoilage in the cellars, which is particularly significant for those with loftier ambitions, who like to ferment and age their wines in cask.

Some producers now choose to make different batches of wine and blend them. So a fresh, aromatic, fruity portion that has been fermented at a low temperature in stainless steel might be blended with a barrel-fermented and aged *cuvée* that has

Traditional farm buildings, Rhône Valley.

less fruitiness but greater weight and more complex, nutty flavors.

Great Rhône wines have existed for centuries, but as a result of advances in both viticulture and winemaking, there are now many more. Our nineteenth-century vigneron might have produced good wine despite his efforts rather than because of them; in contrast, virtually all the modern winemakers, whether traditionalist, modernist or pragmatist, have a greater awareness of what they are doing and why they are doing it in that way. The improvement in the wines provides the eloquent and very enjoyable evidence.

No flying saucers

While Châteauneuf-du-Pape provided the model for France's *appellation contrôlée* system, not all laws passed in the district have achieved universal circulation. In 1954, the wine producers issued an extraordinary decree, which was translated by John Livingstone-Learmonth in his *The Wines of the Rhône* (Faber & Faber, 1992) as follows: "Article 1. The flying overhead, landing and taking off of aeronautical machines called 'flying saucers' or 'flying cigars', of whatever nationality they may be, is strictly forbidden on the territory of the commune of Châteauneuf-du-Pape. "Article 2. Any aeronautical machine—'flying saucer' or 'flying cigar'—that lands on the territory of the commune will be immediately taken off to the pound."

Classifications

Unlike France's other great red-wine regions of Burgundy and Bordeaux, the Rhône has no system for rating its best vineyard sites. Cases could be made for certain sites to be Premiers Crus—for example, Les Bessards in Hermitage and La Landonne in Côte Rôtie—but although wines from such vineyards are able to command a premium price, there is no official statute that confirms their superior status.

The Côtes du Rhône appellation covers the entire region, and growers in other appellations, such as Cornas or Gigondas, can downgrade their wines to Côtes du Rhône if they so wish. Sixteen villages are entitled to label their wines Côtes du Rhône-Villages, and if a wine comes from just one of these villages, the name can be appended to the appellation. Thus, you find wines labelled Côtes du Rhône-Villages Cairanne, Côtes du Rhône-Villages Rasteau, and so on. Something of an oddity is Brézème-Côtes du Rhône, which comes

from a single vineyard at Livron-sur-Drôme, close to where the Drôme meets the Rhône. Brézème is not one of the 16 villages but is allowed to put its name before the Côtes du Rhône appellation. In addition to Côtes du Rhône, there are numerous smaller, and in many cases more significant, appellations, the most important of which are indicated on the map and described in more detail below.

Northern appellations and producers

The Chave family has plantings of zinfandel on the hill of Hermitage, and Californian Jim Clendenen of Au Bon Climat feels that the *terroir* of Crozes-Hermitage is ideally suited for the Italian grape teroldego. But, in the main, red wine from the northern Rhône means syrah.

A number of the red-wine appellations do, however, permit white grapes to be included in the blend. Marsanne and roussanne can be used in Hermitage, Crozes-Hermitage (both up to 15 percent) and St-Joseph (up to 10 percent), although few producers make use of such an allowance. Côte Rôtie can contain up to 20 percent viognier, and although its use is not widespread, several versions still include at least 5 percent to add a perfumed note to the wines.

Côte Rôtie is the most northerly of the appellations. The aspect and incline of the slopes (in the best vineyard sites at least) ensure that the grapes ripen satisfactorily more often than not. Yet, while no one would describe the wines as lightweights, they seldom achieve the muscle of those 25 miles (40 km) or so downstream at Hermitage. They do, however, tend to be more elegant, and are marked by a heady perfume, sometimes of violets, sometimes of blossom. Where viognier has been used

Fall sunset in Rasteau, one of the 16 villages in the Côtes du Rhône appellation.

Wine bottle with its wax capping intact.

Lush vineyards with stone building, near Tain, in the Rhône Valley.

A glass bung in an oak barrel.

in the blend, its aromas are always secondary to those of syrah, although it does bring a softness to the wines that helps them to mature faster.

Soils in the vineyards north of the town of Ampuis, in what is known as the Côte Brune, have more clay and iron, whereas those of the Côte Blonde, to the south, tend to be sandier. As a consequence, Côte Brune wines tend to be sturdier than the more refined offerings from the Côte Blonde. A worthwhile if expensive comparison is to try Marcel Guigal's La Landonne (Côte Brune) alongside his La Mouline (Côte Blonde).

Thanks in no small part to Guigal, new small barrels are today more frequently found in the cellars of Côte Rôtie. Even so, most of the growers here (and indeed throughout the Rhône) come from a long winemaking tradition, and wood is, for the most part, used with a sensitivity born from generations of experience. A three-year-old wine may have the toasty, vanilla flavors of new oak, but it will seldom be dominated by them. The style of a wine also depends on factors such as the calibre of the vintage and the influence of the winemaker, but good young Côte Rôtie should be reasonably full-bodied, packed with the smoky plum, berry, blackcurrant and orange-peel characters of syrah, and may display an aroma reminiscent of lamb fat.

Côte Rôtie can be quite seductive at a tender age, but drinking it on release is a mistake. Even poorer vintages need five years before they begin to show their mettle, while with great vintages, a

decade of patience pays off and, thanks to the tannin and acidity, the wines can happily be kept for much longer. With time, more gamey characters emerge and the flavors become mellower, yet somehow the perfume remains.

Côte Rôtie's rival for top spot in the northern Rhône is the majestic Hermitage. Côte Rôtie is the queen to Hermitage's king and, at their best, both are superlative wines. As in Côte Rôtie, there is considerable difference between the various parts of the appellation. The two best vineyards are the granite-based Les Bessards, which yield sturdy, spicy reds, and the limestone soil of Le Méal, the source of more perfumed supple wines. You can now find single-vineyard *cuvées* bearing these names, as well as those of other plots, such as Les Greffieux and L'Hermite. However, many producers still consider that the best Hermitage is a blend of grapes from various sites. The vogue for new oak found in Côte Rôtie is less apparent in Hermitage, perhaps because by the time the wines are ready to drink, the impact of the oak will largely have subsided.

Overall, it's warmer on the hill of Hermitage than on the slopes above Ampuis, and this is reflected in richer, fuller, more tannic wines. There are some of the same smoky fruit flavors, but there are also more spicy, cedary notes, which with bottle age can make the wines seem similar to the cabernet-sauvignon-based wines of Bordeaux. Although red Hermitage may lack the perfume of Côte Rôtie, it is certainly not an uncouth brute of a wine; however, it does require plenty of time in bottle to unravel before you'll get a glimpse of its finesse. Wines from a great vintage, such as 1978, can still taste as if they are some way from their peak, and the top 1990s seem to be evolving in a similar fashion. Given the price Hermitage now commands, it makes sense to give it the time it needs, a minimum of eight years from vintage and, for the good years, considerably longer.

Hermitage may not be a brute, but Cornas can be. The granite soils in this appellation on the west bank of the Rhône are the same as those found in Hermitage but, thanks to its sheltered situation, Cornas is considerably warmer and drier. The best vineyards are on terraced south- to southeast-facing slopes, and are home to vines whose considerable age and, hence, deep roots are a boon in a district where drought can cause problems during hot vintages.

This combination of heat, old vines and rustic winemaking has traditionally resulted in massive, black wines with undoubted concentration of baked black-fruit flavor, but often with palate-numbing levels of tannin. The typical old-fashioned Cornas remains a wine whose pleasures are still accompanied by a certain amount of pain. Providing you can cope with this, and don't mind the ten years that even an average vintage takes to mature, traditional Cornas can be a very worthwhile and sensibly priced wine.

In recent years, however, a more user-friendly style of Cornas has emerged, thanks largely to the effort of enologist Jean-Luc Colombo. A combination of techniques, including picking riper fruit, destemming all grapes prior to fermentation, lengthy maceration and aging in new oak has resulted in wines that seem to have the intensity of flavor of the traditional style without the rough edges. Debate rages as to whether such wines are quintessential Cornas. Both types at their best—Clape in the old style, Colombo's Les Ruchets in the new—are excellent, even if neither achieves the class of top-notch Hermitage.

Crozes-Hermitage is the largest of the northern appellations by a considerable margin. The diversity of *terroir* within its boundaries means that there's no such thing as a typical Crozes. The finest wines, from the granite-rich vineyards around the village of Gervans or the stony plateau around Les Chassis and Les Sept Chemins, have very little in common with those from the flat, alluvial plains south of the town of Tain l'Hermitage, where the machine-harvesters roam. Unfortunately, vineyard designation has still to take off here, so pick your producer with care. A bottle labelled Crozes-Hermitage could contain a wine with much the same flavors and finesse as Hermitage itself, albeit one that is ready to drink somewhat sooner; it could also contain something not far removed from basic Beaujolais.

Diversity of *terroir* is also an issue in St-Joseph. The appellation used to consist of about 222 acres (90 ha) of vineyards mostly on terraced, granite-rich slopes between the towns of Mauves and Vion. However, in 1969 it was extended to a whopping 17,300 acres (7,000 ha) running along the west bank of the Rhône from just south of the village of Condrieu all the way to the boundary with Cornas. Much of the new land was unsuitable for quality wine and remained unplanted, but the appearance of vines in such places prompted the local growers' syndicate to apply for another boundary change in 1994, which reduced the area by more than half. Many of the best wines still come from the original pre-1969 core of vineyards, although some of the new sites in the northern reaches that overlap part of the Condrieu appellation are showing promise.

The style of St-Joseph wines varies enormously. Some are light, fresh and full of raspberry flavors, intended for early drinking and almost capable of taking a light chill. Others are more powerful and tannic, with the raspberry joined by blackcurrant, cherry and plum, and need five years to show their best, although it is a rare St-Joseph that will last beyond ten years.

Gathering the harvest on the terraces near Cornas, Rhône Valley.

White wines are in a minority in the northern Rhône and fall into two distinct camps. Condrieu and Château Grillet are made entirely from the viognier grape, while Hermitage, Crozes-Hermitage, St-Joseph and St-Péray use marsanne and roussanne. "Exotic" is the tired cliché most often used for Condrieu, but exotic it undoubtedly is— or should be. Making great viognier is a tricky business, and not all succeed. The grapes need to be ripe enough for the development of the tell-tale musky perfume, yet not so ripe that sugar levels— and therefore alcohol levels—soar while acidity all but disappears.

Picked too early, Condrieu is just another white wine. Picked too late, it can become an ungainly, overweight caricature. Picked just right, it is a heady delight, rich and redolent of dried apricots, peaches and pears with perhaps a dollop of honey, and with a heavenly scent—gewürztraminer in silk stockings. When used judiciously, oak can enhance the richness without making the wine overtly woody. Condrieu is at its best in its youth, so aim to drink it before its fourth birthday.

The famous estate of Château Grillet lies close to the village of Condrieu and, unusually, has its own appellation. Given the superbly sited vineyards and the prices the wine manages to command, it really should be better. There were signs of improvement in the mid-1990s, but the wine is still not as ripe and concentrated as it should be, and Château Grillet still has some way to go to catch up with the star performers of Condrieu.

White Hermitage stands as one of the world's least well-known great wines. Marsanne is the preferred grape, although the use of roussanne is increasing, perhaps because of the success that Château de Beaucastel in Châteauneuf-du-Pape has enjoyed with this variety. A young white Hermitage is full-bodied and creamy, packed with honeyed peach and apricot flavors. An adolescent white Hermitage can be something of a disappointment: an eight-year-old wine, for example, can often seem to have lost its fruit without gaining any extra complexity. Patience is all that is required, as white Hermitage can last as long as the red, and needs a similar sojourn in bottle. From 15 years onward, aromas and flavors of nuts, flowers, toast and more appear, and the wine can then survive happily for at least another decade.

A few estates produce a Hermitage *vin de paille* ("straw wine"), made by drying whole bunches of grapes on straw mats before crushing and fermenting. These wines have intense flavors of butter, orange marmalade, nuts, apricots, peaches and more, and will outlast even the regular *cuvées* of white Hermitage.

The other whites of the northern Rhône— Crozes-Hermitage, St-Joseph and St-Péray—only seldom approach the quality of Hermitage. Crozes is the most promising of the trio, offering wines with weight and flavor that can age well for five or six years. Chapoutier's St-Joseph Les Granits serves as a stunning reminder of what is possible. Clape's St-Péray is the best still wine in this lackluster appellation. Of its *méthode champenoise* wines, also made from marsanne and roussanne, sparkling-wine authority Tom Stevenson says they are "… made from the wrong grapes grown on the wrong soil." We won't disagree.

CHAPOUTIER

Established 1808 *Owners* Chapoutier family *Production* 30,000 cases *Vineyard area* 173 acres (70 ha)

Since Max Chapoutier handed over the reins of the family business to his sons in 1989, this has become arguably the most dynamic company in the whole of the Rhône Valley. Viticulture and winemaking are in the capable hands of the outspoken Michel Chapoutier. One of his most drastic measures has been to institute biodynamic farming throughout the extensive family *domaines*, which include as much as 25 percent of the total Hermitage appellation. The prestige *cuvées* made today, Ermitage Le Pavillon (red), Hermitage Cuvée de l'Orée (white), St-Joseph Les Granits (red and white), Crozes-Hermitage Les Varonniers (red), Côte Rôtie La Mordorée and Châteauneuf-du-Pape Barbe Rac, are each among the top halfdozen wines made in each appellation. And if you can't find these limited-production wines, the regular releases from Côtes du Rhône and Côtes du Ventoux levels upward are also reliably good.

CHAVE

Established 1481 *Owners* Gérard and Jean-Louis Chave *Production* 4,000 cases *Vineyard area* 37 acres (15 ha)

A Rhône institution, the Chave family has been growing vines in Hermitage "depuis 1481," according to the sign on the door of the *domaine*. Aided by old, low-yielding vines, Gérard Chave and his well-traveled son Jean-Louis make exemplary Hermitage, both red and white, with each

Below: *Preparing brandy for topping up the barrels at Chapoutier winery.*

Bottom: *In front of the winery.*

being capable of lasting for 20 years or longer. Since 1990, good vintages have seen a small parcel of the wine being given a sojourn in new oak and the result is the superb but rare Cuvée Cathelin. There are also small quantities of a ripe, supple St-Joseph and, from the 1997 vintage onward, rather larger amounts of a distinctly affordable Côtes du Rhône called Mon Cœur.

CLAPE

Established Early eighteenth century *Owners* Auguste and Pierre-Marie Clape *Production* 2,570 cases *Vineyard area* 16 acres (6.5 ha)

When people refer to textbook Cornas they usually have Auguste and Pierre-Marie Clape's version in mind. Just one Cornas is made: a rich, smoky, tannic but fruit-packed wine that typically needs ten years to settle down and will happily keep for another ten years after that. The bargains are the red and white Côtes du Rhône—the red being in effect a declassified Cornas—and the 100 percent syrah *vin de table* called Vin des Amis. In addition, Clape also produces one of the few commendable versions of St-Péray, made like the winery's Côtes du Rhône from 100 percent marsanne.

CLUSEL-ROCH

Established 1980 *Owners* Gilbert Clusel and Brigitte Roch *Production* 1,300 cases *Vineyard area* 8.7 acres (3.5 ha)

Since the mid-1980s, Gilbert Clusel and his wife Brigitte Roch, proprietors of this blossoming Côte Rôtie *domaine*, have shown an increasingly deft hand, turning out concentrated but elegant wines. The prestige *cuvée*, Les Grandes Places, is made from vines that are more than 60 years old. It spends two years in oak (as opposed to the 18 months the regular Côte Rôtie receives). A small amount of Condrieu is also made.

JEAN-LUC COLOMBO

Established 1987 *Owner* Jean-Luc Colombo *Production* NA *Vineyard area* 12 acres (5 ha)

This Cornas-based consultant enologist isn't afraid to ruffle a few feathers in the Rhône. Critics say his wines are formulaic; fans, in growing numbers, disagree. Colombo encourages the *domaines* he works with—among them Château Fortia, Jean-Michel Gérin and Domaine de la Soumade—to pick only very ripe fruit and destem the grapes. At his own *domaine* in Cornas, the Les Ruchets *cuvée*, made from old hillside vines, is every bit

Intricate terracing exposes the vines to the maximum possible warmth and sunlight.

Fall colors start to tint the vine leaves.

the cellars, there has been a much-needed surge in quality. The Hermitage Les Bessards remains the finest wine, but whereas it used to be necessary to choose carefully from the rest of the range, everything is now of a high standard.

PIERRE DUMAZET

Established 1880 *Owner* Pierre Dumazet *Production* 400 cases *Vineyard area* 3 acres (1.2 ha)

Pierre Dumazet makes a number of reds from northern Rhône appellations using bought-in fruit, but it is for his plump, spicy Condrieus from the southern reaches of the appellation that he is best known. He uses more wood than is the norm in Condrieu, with his top-of-the-range *cuvée* Côte Fournet being entirely aged in oak, 20 percent of it new. Bargain hunters should seek out Dumazet's Côtes du Rhône and Vin de Pays des Collines Rhodaniennes, both 100 percent viognier and both of which put many a Condrieu to shame.

BERNARD FAURIE

Established Late nineteenth century *Owner* Bernard Faurie
Production 1,500 cases *Vineyard area* 8.7 acres (3.5 ha)

This source of increasingly compelling yet quite traditional Hermitage and St-Joseph is not the best known of producers. It makes small amounts of white Hermitage and two *cuvées* of red, the finer of which is that from the Le Méal vineyard.

JEAN-MICHEL GERIN

Established 1990 *Owner* Jean-Michel Gerin *Production* 2,700 cases *Vineyard area* 20 acres (8 ha)

Although the Gerin family has been well known in Côte Rôtie for several years, this *domaine* was established only in 1990. With the help of Jean-Luc Colombo, Jean-Michel Gerin makes full-flavored yet relatively forward wines. Champin Le Seigneur is the basic *cuvée*, Le Champin Junior comes from young vines, and Les Grandes Places and the recently introduced La Landonne sit at the top of the range. Other wines include a rather oaky Condrieu and a lovely red Côtes du Rhône made from vines located just outside the Côte Rôtie boundary.

ALAIN GRAILLOT

Established 1985 *Owner* Alain Graillot *Production* 10,000 cases *Vineyard area* 53 acres (21.5 ha)

With no previous winemaking experience, Alain Graillot left the agro-chemical industry to make his own wine, and within a few vintages was producing some of the finest reds and whites in

as dark and concentrated as Clape's, but more supple in structure, and marked by the influence of new wood. Colombo also makes wines using bought-in fruit, including a Châteauneuf made with grapes from Château Fortia.

YVES CUILLERON

Established Late nineteenth century *Owner* Yves Cuilleron
Production 10,000 cases *Vineyard area* 64 acres (26 ha)

Since Yves Cuilleron took charge of the family estate in 1986, he has made some of the most exciting wines in the northern Rhône. While his Côte Rôtie has yet to convince, his red and white St-Josephs are among the best in the appellation. But it is with his wines from Condrieu, where his 22 acre (9 ha) *domaine* is one of the largest in the district, that he excels. All are rich and full-bodied yet have the generous, sumptuous texture and perfume of fine viognier. La Côte is his regular bottling, while Les Chaillets is his *vieilles vignes cuvée*, "*vieilles*" in this instance meaning at least 30 years old. There is also a small amount of the Vendange Tardive Les Eguets, a heady, incredibly concentrated wine that is the essence of viognier.

DELAS FRÈRES

Established 1835 *Owner* Louis Roederer *Production* 121,000 cases *Vineyard area* 35 acres (14 ha)

This long-established company is now owned by the Champagne house Louis Roederer, which acquired the previous owner Champagne Deutz in 1993. Wine quality prior to the 1997 vintage was frustratingly erratic, given the quality of the vineyard sites, especially those in Hermitage, Condrieu and Côte Rôtie. However, with Jacques Grange (ex-Chapoutier and Colombo) now in charge of

Crozes-Hermitage. Although he was initially purchasing grapes, he now has his own *domaine*, which includes small parcels in Hermitage and St-Joseph. Yet the red Crozes remains the star, with rich fruit intensity and a structure that helps it age for up to a decade. The top *cuvée* La Guiraude is a selection of the best barrels rather than a wine from a single vineyard.

JEAN-LOUIS GRIPPAT

Established 20 generations ago *Owner* Jean-Louis Grippat *Production* 40,000 cases *Vineyard area* 20 acres (8 ha)

Jean-Louis Grippat is a master of St-Joseph. His white, made from 100 percent marsanne, is rich and peachy and, unlike many whites from the district, does well with a few years of bottle age. His reds, from the same granite soils, can be slightly vegetal in their youth, the result of leaving the stems on the grapes. But they also possess plenty of rich blackcurrant fruit and age well, especially the Hospices *cuvée*, which spends time in a proportion of new oak. Given this success in the relatively lowly appellation of St-Joseph, it's a surprise that the wines from his small plot of Hermitage are not better.

GUIGAL

Established 1946 *Owner* Marcel Guigal *Production* 340,000 cases *Vineyard area* 35 acres (14 ha)

If any person can claim to have dragged the Rhône into the modern era, it is Marcel Guigal. With his three single-vineyard Côte Rôties, he showed that the northern Rhône could make wines as fine as any in the world—and command prices to match. Of this majestic trio, La Mouline has the most viognier and is the lightest and most perfumed, La Turque still has the perfume but has more muscle, and La Landonne is the massive tannic monster built for the very long haul. Each receives 42 months in new oak barrels, and the fact that they emerge without excessively woody flavors is testimony to their concentration. If you can't find (or afford) these, try the Côte Brune et Blonde *cuvée*, which is still a lovely wine and which makes up around 40 percent of the total annual production of Côte Rôtie. The recently introduced Château d'Ampuis *cuvée* sits between this and the grand trio in terms of price, quantity and quality.

Guigal also has holdings in Condrieu, from which he produces delicious wine, with the partly barrel-fermented and aged La Doriane *cuvée* ranking as one of the stars of the appellation. Of the other Guigal wines blended from bought-in grapes and wines, the Côtes du Rhône stands out for its reliability and value for money, and the Châteauneuf also merits attention.

PAUL JABOULET AÎNÉ

Established 1834 *Owner* Jaboulet family *Production* 50,000 cases *Vineyard area* 260 acres (105 ha)

One of the great names of French winemaking, Jaboulet makes an extensive selection from throughout the Rhône Valley. However, the company's reputation rests on the high quality of its northern Rhône wines, especially the monumental Hermitage La Chapelle. This wine, which with a couple of decades age can begin to resemble a Bordeaux cabernet, is not a single-vineyard wine but a selection of the best of the vintage from Jaboulet's extensive holdings in Hermitage (the remainder now appears in a wine called La Pied de la Côte). The other stars of the portfolio are the Crozes-Hermitage from Domaine de Thalabert— "poor man's La Chapelle," as some call it—and the Domaine St-Pierre Cornas, which first made its appearance in 1994.

JEAN-PAUL AND JEAN-LUC JAMET

Established 1950 *Owners* Jamet family *Production* 1,300 cases *Vineyard area* 15 acres (6 ha)

The Jamet brothers make just one wine, assembled from nearly 20 separate sites in Côte Rôtie. Some new wood is used for aging, but the brothers are against destemming their grapes, which can seem short-sighted in less favorable vintages. In good years, however, the wines are rich, powerful and long-lived, and among the finest in the appellation.

ANDRE PERRET

Established 1985 *Owner* Andre Perret *Production* 3,500 cases *Vineyard area* 25 acres (10 ha)

A master with viognier, Andre Perret makes two *cuvées* of superb Condrieu. Clos Chanson, grown on clay-rich soils, is the more aromatic of the pair and shows well when young. In contrast, Coteau de Chery, from the sandy, flint- and chalk-rich soils known as arzelle, can be quite dumb on release and needs about two years to show its intense and fragrant best. This is also a

Gleaming wine glasses.

The Jaboulet family vineyard.

source of fine red and white St-Joseph, Les Grisières being the top red *cuvée*.

RENÉ ROSTAING

Established 1971 *Owner* René Rostaing *Production* 3,250 cases *Vineyard area* 20 acres (8 ha)

Although he started his *domaine* in 1971, René Rostaing's Côte Rôties are only now beginning to get the attention they deserve. His enterprise received two very welcome bonuses in the early 1990s when first his father-in-law Albert Dervieux-Thaize and then his uncle Marius Gentaz-Dervieux retired and handed over the running of virtually all their Côte Rôtie holdings to René. From a selection of vineyards, which includes vines more than 80 years old, he makes four *cuvées*: regular, Côte Blonde, La Viallière and La Landonne—all richly fruited and supple. Rostaing also produces small amounts of fine Condrieu.

MARC SORREL

Established 1928 *Owner* Marc Sorrel *Production* 1,600 cases *Vineyard area* 10 acres (4 ha)

Not to be confused with his brother Jean-Michel, who also has holdings in a number of the same vineyards, Marc Sorrel makes fine and underrated Hermitage, as well as some delicious Crozes-Hermitage. The top red is the dense, sweet Hermitage Le Gréal, made from a mixture of fruit (including some marsanne) from the Le Méal and Les Greffieux vineyards. The top white is the powerful, alcoholic and long-lived, 100 percent marsanne Hermitage Les Rocoules.

GEORGES VERNAY

Established 1953 *Owner* Christine Vernay *Production* 8,000 cases *Vineyard area* 40 acres (16 ha)

The standard of this estate's red wines from Côte Rôtie and St-Joseph seems to have risen since Georges Vernay's daughter Christine took over the winemaking responsibilities. But this is still first and foremost a reference point for Condrieu, of which Georges Vernay has been a leading producer since the 1950s. The family's aim is to accentuate viognier's peach and apricot characters, so the harvest tends to take place as late as possible. A mixture of stainless steel and oak, some of it new, is used for fermentation and aging of the wines. A regular *cuvée* is bottled when young, but the two top wines, Les Chaillées de l'Enfer ("The Terraces of Hell") and Coteau de Vernon, spend extra time in cask on their lees. Both emerge in fat, aromatic splendor, and drink well for up to five years from vintage.

Vines in the southern Rhône Valley.

NOEL VERSET

Established NA *Owner* Noel Verset *Production* 900 cases
Vineyard area 5 acres (2 ha)

Theoretically in retirement, Noel Verset still turns
out small quantities of quintessential Cornas from
vineyards that include a plot of vines that are
nearly 100 years old in the Sabarottes vineyard.
These aged vines plus low yields, ripe fruit and
minimal intervention in the cellar are the keys to
this rich, spicy and very long-lived wine.

FRANÇOIS VILLARD

Established NA *Owners* François Villard *Production*
900 cases *Vineyard area* 9 acres (3.6 ha)

An up-and-coming producer, Villard makes good
Côte Rôtie and admirable St-Joseph, with the
white impressing as much as the red. The top
wines, however, are those from Condrieu, all of
which undergo long lees contact and some of
which are fermented and aged in new oak.
Coteaux de Poncin is the best of the dry *cuvées*.
When vintage circumstances permit, Villard also
produces a tiny amount of unctuously sweet,
botrytis-affected Quintessence.

ALAIN VOGE

Established 1958 *Owner* Alain Voge *Production*
3,400 cases *Vineyard area* 27 acres (11 ha)

From one of the largest holdings in Cornas, Alain
Voge makes wines that are packed with so much
ripe berry fruit that you tend not to notice the firm
structure underneath. As well as regular and
vieilles vignes bottlings, in exceptional years Voge
makes a wine called La Vieille Fontaine, solely
from a plot planted in the 1920s. The St-Péray is
one of the better versions available.

Up the Drôme

On the Drôme, Brézème-Côtes du Rhône is a one-
man-band appellation near Livron-sur-Drôme.
Here Jean-Marie Lombard makes syrah reds and
marsanne and roussanne whites that are as good
as many in more famous northern Rhône appellations. Farther upstream are some appellations that
have little in common with other Rhône wines.
Châtillon-en-Diois is another appellation dominated by one producer, in this instance the Cave
Cooperative de Die. Its Aligoté and Chardonnay
are better than the gamay-based red and rosé, but
none of the wines can be recommended. The
sparkling wine formerly called Clairette de Die and
now known as Crémant de Die is slightly better,
but being made from the lackluster clairette, it

*The ruins of a fort in the southern Rhône
Valley—the Romans were the first to grow
wine here, after conquering the Gauls.*

lacks style. Clairette de Die Tradition, or Clairette
de Die Méthode Dioise Ancestrale as it is now
sold, must include at least 75 percent muscat blanc
à petits grains and is far more interesting. The
méthode dioise ancestrale involves halting fermentation partway through and bottling the wine with
residual sugar. The fermentation continues in
bottle, producing the bubbles; subsequently, the
wine is filtered to remove the yeast before being
transferred to a fresh bottle, still with some residual sweetness. The result is France's answer to
Italy's Asti Spumante, a delicious, frothy wine with
a peachy, grapey flavor.

Southern appellations and producers

Wines such as Côte Rôtie, Hermitage and Condrieu ensure that the northern Rhône enjoys great
prestige. However, its production is dwarfed by
that of the southern sector of the valley, which
makes more than 95 percent of all Rhône wines,
the vast majority of them red. If syrah dominates
the north, then the south is emphatically grenache
country. One explanation for its ubiquity is that
the beefy, high-alcohol wines it produces were
much in demand until as recently as the 1960s for
bolstering the wines of chilly Burgundy.

Ripening grenache in the southern warmth is
seldom a problem, but making high-quality wine
from this variety presents more of a challenge.
When overcropped, it produces wines that have
a reasonable level of alcohol, but not much color
or flavor. Color and slightly jammy, berry flavors
start to appear as the yield decreases, but since
grenache doesn't have especially high levels of
tannin in its skins, by that time the wine often

*Château de Saint Cosme Gigondas 1998,
and Châteauneuf-du-Pape 1997 from
Southern producer Domaine de la Janasse.*

Vines trained on wires, Gigondas AC.

REGIONAL DOZEN

SOUTHERN RHÔNE
Château de Beaucastel
  Châteauneuf-du-Pape
Château de Beaucastel
  Châteauneuf-du-Pape
  Roussanne Vieilles Vignes
Henri Bonneau Châteauneuf-
  du-Pape Réserve des
  Célestins
Chapoutier Châteauneuf-du-
  Pape Barbe Rac
Domaine Fonsalette Côtes du
  Rhône Syrah
Domaine Gramenon Côtes du
  Rhône Ceps Centenaire
Domaine de la Mordorée
  Châteauneuf-du-Pape Cuvée
  de la Reine des Bois
Domaine Pégaü Châteauneuf-
  du-Pape Cuvée Réservée
Château Rayas Châteauneuf-
  du-Pape
Domaine Santa Duc Gigondas
  Les Hautes Garrigues Cuvée
  Prestige
Tardieu Laurent Vacqueyras
  Vieilles Vignes
Domaine du Vieux Télégraphe
  Châteauneuf-du-Pape

lacks the structure to support them. There are two ways of providing grenache with backbone. One is to slash yields even further to levels where the sheer strength of flavor carries the wines along. The other is to blend it with other grapes such as syrah and mourvèdre. This method has an additional advantage: grenache by itself is prone to oxidation, and both syrah and mourvèdre act as antioxidants to counter this.

Both methods have their adherents in this most famous appellation of the southern Rhône, Châteauneuf-du-Pape. As well as as grenache, 12 other grape varieties are allowed for Châteauneuf, namely syrah, mourvèdre, cinsault, counoise, vaccarèse, terret noir and muscardin (all red grape varieties); and clairette, bourboulenc, roussanne, picpoul and picardan (all white). This extensive list simply reflects what was in the vineyards when the appellation laws were drawn up, rather than being an indication of what the quintessential Châteauneuf-du-Pape should contain.

In the early twentieth century, Commander Joseph Ducos, whose property included Château la Nerte (today known as Château de la Nerthe, see p.169), devised a formula for the ideal Châteauneuf. This contained 20 percent cinsault and grenache for "warmth, liqueur-like sweetness and mellowness;" 40 percent syrah, mourvèdre, muscardin and vaccarèse for "solidity, durability and color, accompanied by a straightforward, almost thirst-quenching flavor;" 30 percent counoise and picpoul for "vinosity, charm, freshness and accentuation of bouquet;" and 10 percent clairette and bourboulenc for "finesse, fire and sparkle."

Today, few producers make use of all 13 varieties, Château de Beaucastel being a notable exception. A normal Châteauneuf would be 70 percent grenache, with syrah and mourvèdre making up most of the remainder and the other varieties being used only in minute amounts. Some producers exclude other grapes entirely, while others include less than one-third grenache.

Lusty fruit infused with the character of thyme, bay and other southern herbs is found in most Châteauneuf but, thanks to the many permutations of grape varieties and variations in winemaking styles, there is no such thing as a textbook wine. And for every quality-minded producer of Châteauneuf, there are are several more for whom quantity is more important. Disappointing as this can be, it does highlight the vast and still largely untapped potential of the appellation.

Châteauneufs made using a proportion of carbonic maceration are ready to drink sooner than traditionally fermented versions and tend to be less intensely flavored. In contrast, old-fashioned versions, aged in large, old wooden casks and often made with a high proportion of fruit from old vines and not destemmed are massive beasts packed with herby, spicy red- and black-fruit flavors. These need ten years or so in bottle before they show their warm, welcoming side.

Many of the best wines combine old-vine fruit with high-class winemaking techniques (both ancient and modern) to produce solid sumptuous wines that are less rustic than traditional Châteauneuf but no less concentrated or long-lived. Where a larger than normal amount of syrah is used in the blend, the wine can have a peppery, orange-peel character that is pleasant in small doses but can occasionally be overwhelming. Mourvèdre—ripe mourvèdre at least—brings more earthy, animal aromas, and flavors such as mushrooms and leather.

Châteauneuf's increasing popularity has prompted many producers to release prestige *cuvées*. Here again, the range of styles is enormous. There's a world of difference between Chapoutier's 100 percent Grenache Barbe Rac and Beaucastel's Hommage à Jacques Perrin, which can be as much as 70 percent mourvèdre with only 15 percent grenache. Pleasingly, few suffer from excessive levels of new oak; indeed, overoaking hardly ever occurs in Châteauneuf. Prices for such wines may seem high, but not when compared with those for top burgundy and bordeaux, and the quality is usually excellent.

Châteauneuf is, without doubt, the finest appellation in the southern Rhône, but it no longer has a monopoly on quality. Gigondas, which has had its own appellation since 1971, is the most successful of the pretenders to Châteauneuf's throne. The range of grapes permitted here is even wider than in Châteauneuf. In practice, the blends tend to be similar, with a large proportion of grenache (but no more than 80 percent according to the appellation rules) bolstered by at least 15 percent syrah and mourvèdre. While Gigondas includes a variety of growing conditions in its 2,500 acres (1,000 ha), it's generally cooler here than in Châteauneuf, so syrah can make up a higher proportion of the blend without dominating. The flipside of the coin is that it is more difficult to ripen mourvèdre here.

Although the finest Gigondas can be mistaken for good Châteauneuf, the wines tend to be less full-bodied, with sweeter fruit, and take a shorter time to reach their peak. They are still broad-shouldered though, and most can safely be kept for ten years at least. Cash-strapped wine lovers looking for gutsy reds to replenish their stocks couldn't do much better than a few cases of 1998 Gigondas from a top *domaine*. However, here, as in Châteauneuf (and indeed throughout the southern Rhône), the diversity of styles and blends is huge, and it is important to pick your producer with care. The number of those who have the inclination (not to mention the francs) to raise quality levels is rising, but too much potentially good wine still deteriorates in the large, musty old barrels of the town's many cellars.

Neighboring Vacqueyras formerly came under the Côtes du Rhône-Villages appellation but was elevated to full AC status in 1990. Vacqueyras is to Gigondas as Gigondas is to Châteauneuf—based on roughly similar blends, but more rustic, ready to drink sooner, and cheaper. Top wines will last into their second decade, but most are at their best at around five to seven years old.

Lirac lies across the Rhône from Châteauneuf and is the least well-known of the main southern-Rhône appellations. A few wines, especially those of Domaine de la Mordorée, show that this appellation could be capable of taking on Vacqueyras and even Gigondas, but few producers are as yet fully exploiting its potential.

Most wines labelled as Côtes du Rhône hail from the southern Rhône. Ninety-six percent of them are red, and these range from insipid to inspiring, from bland table wine to declassified Côte Rôtie or Châteauneuf-du-Pape. A simple and effective rule of thumb is that producers who make good wines in a loftier appellation generally make the best Côtes du Rhône. Domaines Gramenon and Réméjeanne, which don't have vineyards elsewhere and make only Côtes du Rhône, are excellent exceptions to this rule. They and a number of other estates now produce *cuvées* that are 100 percent syrah, and the quality being achieved is increasingly impressive. We're still not talking Hermitage or Côte Rôtie, but the best can stand comparison with wines from St-Joseph and Crozes-Hermitage.

The 16 southern villages that are considered to be superior to the general standard and are entitled to append their name to the Côtes du Rhône-Villages appellation are Beaumes de Venise, Cairanne, Chusclan, Laudun, Rasteau, Roaix, Rochegude, Rousset-les-Vignes, Sablet, St-Gervais, St-Maurice-sur-Eygues, St-Pantaléon-les-Vignes, Séguret, Valréas, Vinsobres and Visan. The wines follow the general grenache-based trend of southern Rhône wines and, once again, quality and style vary enormously. On current form, the villages of Beaumes de Venise, Cairanne, Rasteau, Sablet and Séguret are the best of the 16, but the wines cannot be recommended unconditionally. When wines from two or more of the villages are blended, they are labelled simply as Côtes du Rhône-Villages.

The other red-wine appellations of the greater Rhône Valley, namely Coteaux du Pierrevert, Coteaux du Tricastin, Côtes du Luberon, Côtes du Ventoux and Côtes du Vivarais, produce wines very much in the style—or styles—of Côtes du Rhône. Few of these are remarkable, but the wines from such well-known Rhône producers as Chapoutier and the Perrins of Château de Beaucastel (under the La Vieille Ferme label) can

The steep hillsides of the Rhône Valley turn brown as winter approaches.

be excellent value. With the exception of Châteauneuf-du-Pape, all the southern Rhône red-wine appellations are allowed to make rosé wine using the same grape varieties. In addition, Tavel, Lirac's neighbor, is a rosé-only district. Rhône rosés have plenty of guts and can be wonderfully juicy and fresh, packed with thirst-quenching raspberry and strawberry flavors. Unfortunately, most are spoiled by clumsy vinification and lose the joy of youth that is the essence of rosé. Quite why Tavel has a reputation as a wine that can be aged escapes most sane wine drinkers.

The majority of white wines from the southern Rhône are also best in the flush of youth. The most widely planted varieties are grenache blanc, which produces rich, full-bodied wines with a floral hint; the softer, lighter clairette; and bourboulenc, which provides body and acidity. The early harvesting and modern winemaking that many estates now employ result in fairly full-bodied but not especially intensely flavored wines that are best drunk within a year of release.

Finer white Rhônes with greater potential for aging do exist, and the vast majority are to be found in the appellation of Châteauneuf-du-Pape. Many include large proportions of roussanne, a variety that is prone to oxidation but is slowly gaining popularity among vignerons for its full-fleshed wines with aromas and flavors of flowers, nuts, peaches and cream. Some producers ferment and age some of their wine in new oak barrels, and then blend with unoaked *cuvées* to excellent effect. Such wines buck the southern white trend in that they keep happily for eight years or more.

Quality whites are quite hard to find outside Châteauneuf. The Côtes du Rhône and Côtes du Rhône-Villages can provide happy hunting grounds, not least because viognier, outlawed in Châteauneuf, is permitted here. But once again, the best advice is try before you buy. Perhaps the best-known white wine of the southern Rhône, and arguably the most consistent, is Muscat de Beaumes de Venise, made from the muscat blanc à petits grains. This is a *vin doux naturel*,

Vineyards near Tavel, in the southern Rhône.

made by adding grape spirit to a partly fermented wine, resulting in a heady concoction with a minimum of 15 percent alcohol and 14.6 ounces per gallon (110 g per l) of unfermented sugar. It's wonderfully rich and floral, with flavors of apricot, marmalade and barley sugar, and although certainly sweet, it is seldom cloying.

The region's other *vin doux naturel* is Rasteau, made from at least 90 percent grenache. Grenache comes in both red and white forms, so Rasteau appears in various colors, and there is also a separate appellation, Rasteau Rancio, for wines that have been aged for longer periods. Port-like these are not: they are raw, sweet, fiery wines to warm you up on a cold day. Age mellows them slightly, but none approaches the quality of Muscat de Beaumes de Venise.

CHÂTEAU DE BEAUCASTEL

Established 1909 *Owner* Perrin family *Production* 32,500 cases *Vineyard area* 232 acres (94 ha)

This innovative estate, one of the few to utilize all 13 permitted varieties for its Châteauneuf, produces a red in which mourvèdre rather than grenache is often the dominant grape. This makes for a distinctive style of wine with feral, gamey overtones, which can seem disjointed when young but which shines from eight years of age onward. The top *cuvée*, Hommage à Jacques Perrin, has even more mourvèdre.

For the impressive whites, roussanne is the preferred grape, and the Roussanne Vieilles Vignes, as well as being the best white in the southern Rhône, is a rarity among white Châteauneufs in that it takes very kindly to bottle age. The red and white Coudoulet de Beaucastels—humble Côtes du Rhônes due to the location of the vineyards—receive almost as much attention, and outshine many a Châteauneuf. Look out too for the wines sold under the Perrin and La Vieille Ferme labels from the Côtes du Ventoux and Côtes du Luberon.

HENRI BONNEAU

Established 12 generations ago *Owner* Henri Bonneau *Production* 1,500 cases *Vineyard area* 15 acres (6 ha)

Old grenache vines and low yields are just two of the factors that make this one of the best addresses for fans of Châteauneuf, but Henri Bonneau is not likely to divulge the other secrets of his huge, sumptuous and long-lived wines. For a fabulous tasting begin with the (far from) basic *cuvée* then work up through the Cuvée Marie Beurrier to the stupendous Réserve des Célestins.

LES CAILLOUX

Established Nineteenth century *Owner* André Brunel
Production 8,000 cases *Vineyard area* 52 acres (21 ha)

Partly as a result of following advice from Jean-
Luc Colombo concerning destemming and the
cuvaison (the length of time a fermenting wine
spends on skins), Andre Brunel's Châteauneufs
have been in fine form since the mid-1980s.
Grenache is the dominant variety used, although
the percentage of mourvèdre in the blend is
increasing. The regular release is deep and fruity,
while the Cuvée Centenaire, introduced in 1989 to
celebrate the 100th birthday of the vines, and
made only in good years, is immensely powerful
yet still wonderfully silky.

DOMAINE DE LA CHARBONNIÈRE

Established 1912 Owner Michel Maret Production
5,000 cases Vineyard area 54 acres (22 ha)

Michel Maret sprang to prominence in the 1990s
for his ripe, herby Châteauneufs. Mourvèdre plays
a prominent part—as much as 25 percent—in
most of his wines, although the finest *cuvée*, the
Vieilles Vignes, is mostly grenache. The *domaine*
also makes fine Vacqueyras.

CLOS DES PAPES

Established 1880 *Owner* Paul Avril *Production* 10,000
cases *Vineyard area* 87 acres (35 ha)

Paul Avril and son Vincent make one of the most
long-lived of the Châteauneufs from vineyards
dotted around the appellation. The sole red produced is an intense, chewy wine that needs time
to show at its best. The white is spicy and floral,
acquiring richness and nutty characters with a
few years of bottle aging.

DOMAINE FONT DE MICHELLE

Established 1950 *Owners* Jean and Michel Gonnet
Production 10,000 cases *Vineyard area* 74 acres (30 ha)

The late Étienne Gonnet, brother-in-law of Henri
Brunier of Vieux Télégraphe, worked hard during
the 1950s to expand his family *domaine* in
Châteauneuf from 25 acres (10 ha) to 59 acres
(24 ha). His sons Jean and Michel now run the
estate and make a crisp, fruity white and a
modern-style, smoky, spicy red with cherry and
berry flavors. In homage to their father, they make
Cuvée Étienne Gonnet, the red a deliciously aromatic and full-bodied wine, the white fleshy and
perhaps slightly overoaked.

*The substantial Château des Fines Roches,
Châteauneuf-du-Pape appellation.*

Cultivating between the rows with a light horse-drawn plow.

CHÂTEAU FORTIA

Established Eighteenth century *Owner* Baron Le Roy de Boiseaumarie *Production* 6,000 cases *Vineyard area* 67 acres (27 ha)

It was Baron Pierre Le Roy de Boiseaumarie of Château Fortia who in 1923 drew up the rules concerning production of Châteauneuf-du-Pape which eventually developed into France's system of *appellation contrôlée*. The wines he made established Fortia's reputation, but several of those made by his son Henri, who took over in 1967, were not up to the same standard. This gave other *domaines* the opportunity to catch up and even overtake the estate in quality terms. Henri's son Bruno has been in charge since 1994, and with help from Jean-Luc Colombo is making ripe, concentrated but supple wines that have swiftly put Fortia back on track.

DOMAINE GRAMENON

Established 1979 *Owners* Philippe and Michèle Laurent *Production* 8,000 cases *Vineyard area* 54 acres (22 ha)

Philippe Laurent acquired his vineyards in 1979, but for several years sold the fruit to the likes of Jaboulet and Guigal. He bottled his first wines during the excellent 1990 vintage and since then has made his name as one of the finest producers of Côtes du Rhône. Several red *cuvées* are made, all of them rich, concentrated and far superior to the average Châteauneuf-du-Pape. The finest are Les Ceps Centennaires (from a 100-year-old grenache vineyard) and Cuvée des Laurentides (grenache plus 30 percent syrah). Gramenon recently introduced a late-harvest Cuvée Pascal and a full-bodied white, heavy with viognier.

DOMAINE DE LA JANASSE

Established 1973 *Owners* Aimé and Christophe Sabon *Production* 2,500 cases *Vineyard area* 74 acres (30 ha)

Rising stars of the southern Rhône, Aimé Sabon and son Christophe make three *cuvées* of Châteauneuf-du-Pape and some of the finest Côtes du Rhône available. With the exception of one of the Côtes du Rhônes that contains a high proportion of old-vine carignan, grenache is the mainstay variety, the Vieilles Vignes being 90 percent from 80-plus-year-old vines, and the Cuvée Chaupin, from a vineyard planted in 1912, 100 percent. The wines are concentrated yet surprisingly elegant, beginning life quietly and then opening out with time in bottle to reveal their glories. The white Châteauneuf is good too, with barrel-fermented roussanne becoming an increasingly important component in the blend.

DOMAINE DE MARCOUX

Established Thirteenth century *Owner* SCEA Armenier *Production* 3,300 cases *Vineyard area* 45 acres (18 ha)

Philippe Armenier runs one of the finest estates in Châteauneuf-du-Pape. He began experimenting with biodynamic viticulture in 1990, and now the whole estate is run on these principles. Maybe this, combined with the old vines and low yields, is what gives his wines such intensity of spicy, plummy, blackcurrant-and-cherry flavors, even in less than favorable vintages. The Vieilles Vignes *cuvée* is spectacularly good, while the white, in which the fleshy roussanne makes its presence felt, is also excellent.

DOMAINE DE LA MORDORÉE

Established 1989 *Owner* Christophe Delorme *Production* 12,500 cases *Vineyard area* 94 acres (38 ha)

Christophe Delorme's best wines are his rich, sweet and complex Châteauneufs, especially the Cuvée de la Reine des Bois. It is remarkable that he has achieved such very high standards in such a very short time—his first vintage was only in 1989. Yet even more impressive are the wines he produces in such less exalted appellations as Lirac (with a red, a white and a rosé), Tavel and Côtes du Rhône. In particular, his top Lirac, also called Cuvée de la Reine des Bois, knocks spots of most of the commonly found Châteauneufs.

CHÂTEAU DE LA NERTHE

Established 1785 *Owner* S. C. Château de la Nerthe
Production 31,000 cases *Vineyard area* 225 acres (90 ha)

With a history stretching back to 1560, and an
imposing château built in 1760, La Nerthe (or La
Nerte, as it was once known) is an institution in
Châteauneuf-du-Pape. Formerly one of the best
estates in the area, by the 1980s the wines had
deteriorated. The Ricaud family took over in 1985
and installed Alain Dugas as manager. The reds
are now bottled without fining or filtration and
the estate is again near the top of the Châteauneuf
tree. The best wines are the Cuvée des Cadettes
Red and Clos de Beauvenir white.

DOMAINE DU PÉGAÜ

Established Late seventeenth century *Owners* Paul and
Laurence Feraud *Production* 5,500 cases *Vineyard area*
45 acres (18 ha)

Paul and Laurence Feraud make traditional Châteauneuf from scattered vineyards (some plots date
back to 1902). The reds are fermented and aged
in large old oak *foudres*—two years for the Cuvée
Réservée and up to six years for Cuvée Laurence.
These thick, spicy, fruity wines need eight years to
show their best and will drink well for at least a
decade after that. New wood is used with a portion
of the rich, waxy grenache-blanc-based white.

CHÂTEAU RAYAS

Established 1890 *Owner* Emmanuel Reynaud *Production*
1,000 cases *Vineyard area* 30 acres (12 ha)

It's too early to say how well the sister and nephew of the late Jacques Reynaud are following in
his eccentric but compelling footsteps. His policy
of miserly yields and almost 100 percent grenache
created the sweet and stylish Rayas, in the top
league of Châteauneufs. Pignan, from a separate
vineyard, is a fine wine, and much cheaper; the
two Côtes du Rhônes from Domaine Fon salette,
one a blend of 50 percent grenache with mourvèdre and syrah, the other a thick, smoky, long-lived
100 percent syrah, are also relative bargains.

DOMAINE SANTA DUC

Established NA *Owner* Yves Gras *Production* 7,000 cases
Vineyard area 47 acres (19 ha)

The Gigondas appellation has a growing reputation, partly thanks to the work done by Yves Gras
at this estate. Old vines, low yields and ultraripe
fruit are the secrets, and the result is wines with
powerful structures and fruit flavors; they need
several years in bottle to soften. In good vintages,
Santa Duc produces a Cuvée Prestige des Hautes
Garrigues which spends time in new oak and contains a high proportion of mourvèdre. Bargain
hunters should look for the Côtes du Rhône.

DOMAINE DE LA SOUMADE

Established 1979 *Owner* André Romero *Production*
10,000 cases *Vineyard area* 64 acres (26 ha)

A self-taught winemaker, André Romero is the star
producer in Rasteau. He makes two *cuvées* of the
vin doux naturel for which the village is renowned,
but it is his three Côtes du Rhône-Villages reds
that really merit attention. The basic wine is soft
and friendly and is best drunk in the first five years
of its life, whereas the Cuvée Prestige, from vines
averaging 45 years of age, is a more serious, full-
bodied and slightly leathery wine. The top wine is
Cuvée Confiance, a wonderfully juicy blend of
ancient grenache with about 20 percent syrah.

TARDIEU LAURENT

Established 1996 *Owner* Michel Tardieu *Production*
5,000 cases *Vineyard area* None

A recent arrival, this estate is the brainchild of
Dominique Laurent and Michel Tardieu. Although
based in Lourmarin in the southern Rhône, the
company sources wine from throughout the Rhône
Valley. Quantities are small but quality is high, as
are prices. The Côtes du Rhône Cuvée Guy Louis
is an admirable introduction to a fine range.

DOMAINE DU VIEUX TÉLÉGRAPHE

Established 1900 *Owners* Daniel and Frédéric Brunier
Production 22,000 cases *Vineyard area* 178 acres (72 ha)

This well-known estate produces one of the more
restrained Châteauneufs, a wine with lovely cherry
and raspberry fruit infused with the aromas of
Provençal herbs. It
doesn't demand exten-
sive bottle age, but it
doesn't object, either,
holding its fresh fruiti-
ness. The 1993 vintage
saw a new second
label, Vieux Mas des
Papes; a rare prestige
cuvée (Hippolyte) ap-
peared in 1994. Vieux
Télégraphe, a white, is
a fresh, floral wine
best drunk young. A
Hippolyte white was
first made in 1997.

Wine aging in the cellars of Château de la Nerthe, Châteauneuf-du-Pape.

The church of the village of Fleurie occupies a prominent position amid local vineyards.

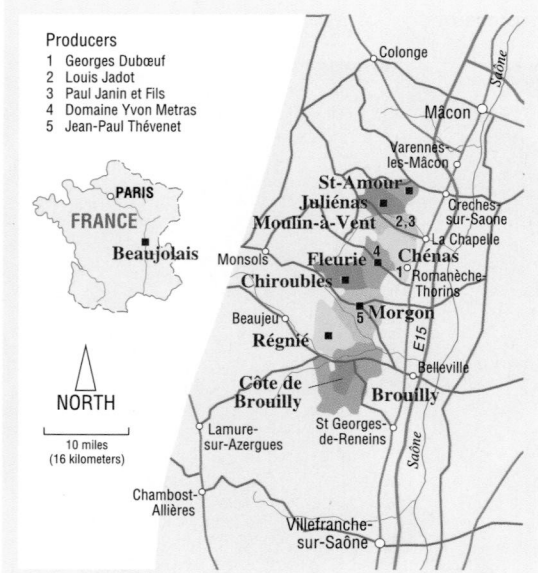

Producers
1 Georges Dubœuf
2 Louis Jadot
3 Paul Janin et Fils
4 Domaine Yvon Metras
5 Jean-Paul Thévenet

Beaujolais

Catherine Fallis MS

From the gluggable, tooth-staining *nouveau* wines dispatched to the far reaches of the globe each November, to the serious, cellarworthy selections from the region's best *crus*, Beaujolais wines are, almost without exception, red, soft, fruit-driven and light—truly, wines with universal appeal.

Although classified as a part of Burgundy, the wines and residents of Beaujolais are vastly different from their northern neighbours. On a cusp between the serious, cold north and the precocious sunny Mediterranean, their personalities, lifestyle, climate, soils, principal grape variety, viticulture, production and marketing are all unique.

History

Vineyards were first planted in Beaujolais during the Roman occupation, and Benedictine Monks tended vineyards here in the seventh century. Wine-growing continued under the Dukes of Beaujeu, who ruled from town of the same name from the tenth century.

In 1395, Philip the Bold, Duke of Burgundy issued an edict forbidding the use of the gamay grape in the Cote d'Or. This enabled Beaujolais to distinguish itself from Burgundy by specializing in wine made mainly from gamay. This affordable quaff soon found favor with thrifty Lyonnais and by the mid-twentieth century had seduced even the haughtiest of Parisians. By the 1970s, the British had been charmed, and in the 1980s, Americans, Japanese and Europeans were won over. Beaujolais gained a following in Asia in the 1990s, where consumers were drawn to red wine by reports of its health benefits.

Today, Germany is the leading importer (taking 26 percent of production), Switzerland is the second-largest customer and Japan the third-largest. Exports to the UK have declined, but sales to North America, the Netherlands and Italy are stable.

Landscape and climate

French wine authorities divide Burgundy into four departments: the Yonne (Chablis), the Côte d'Or (Côte de Nuits and Côte de Beaune), the Saone-et-Loire (Côte Chalonnaise and Maconnais regions), and the Rhône department (Beaujolais)—not to be confused with the Rhone Valley. Considered part of Burgundy, Beaujolais is the region's largest producer, yielding 40 percent of its output from 54,000 acres (22,000 ha) in the flatter southernmost district of Beaujolais, which is known as Beaujolais Bas. Here, boatloads of simple AC Beaujolais, the basic appellation, and Beaujolais Supérieur, which has an extra 0.5 percent of alcohol, are sold most often as Beaujolais Nouveau, the simple, grapey wine that is rushed to market 60 days after the just-fermented juice hits the bottle. This area's rich soils don't favor the production of high-quality gamay, but the warm climate helps the grapes ripen to maturity.

Haut Beaujolais, to the north, is hillier, with granite-based subsoils and easy-draining sandy topsoils, on which gamay thrives. Its climate is generally temperate and sunny, though summer hailstorms occasionally wreak havoc. Thirty-nine communes, or villages, in the area qualify for the superior Beaujolais-Villages appellation, and an additional ten communes are singled out as *crus*. Like the Premier and Grand Crus of Burgundy, these are considered the jewels of the region.

Winemaking and wine styles

Ninety-eight percent of Beaujolais is planted with gamay noir à jus blanc, a gamay not grown elsewhere. Two percent is planted with chardonnay, used mainly for Beaujolais Blanc. Aligoté is also allowed, but rarely planted. After ten years, vines are left to develop independently without training or trellising. Grapes are usually harvested by hand.

Small growers are the dominant source of fruit, which they sell to *negoçiants*. Few contracts exist, and each year the growers have an anxious wait to see if their crop is up to snuff. Major buyers can make or break an entire year's worth of work.

The grapes are normally fermented by carbonic maceration. The maceration time is minimal—four days for Beaujolais Nouveau and up to ten days for a *cru* wine. The juice is run off immediately, then blended with the press wine. Chaptalization is widely employed, especially in low-quality wines.

Beaujolais is a good introduction to red wines. Fans of whites and rosés enjoy this fruity, smooth, silky, perfumed wine, especially chilled. Beaujolais Nouveau is best known (but least impressive)—it has to be drunk young. Beaujolais-Villages can be good, and keeps for up to two years. The most characterful wines are from the *crus*. Differing *terroirs* alter the character of similar wines: Chiroubles is delicate, Brouilly is full-flavored, Côte-de-Brouilly is earthy, Julienas has wild aromatics, Fleurie is elegant and full-bodied, St-Amour is less fruity, Chenas is ageworthy, and Morgon and Moulin-à-Vent are powerful, solid, and ageworthy. Regnie is still establishing its identity. After 3–5 years, the top *crus* take on the characteristics of well-aged softer Rhône or Cotes de Beaune wines.

Recently, demand for *cru* wines has increased as interest in Beaujolais Nouveau has dwindled. This is understandable as the *cru* wines are usually a bargain and almost guaranteed to give pleasure, while the quality of the *nouveau* wines is highly variable.

Producers

GEORGES DUBŒUF

Established 1964 *Owners* Georges Dubœuf and family
Production 2.6 million cases *Vineyard area* NA

The king of Beaujolais, Georges Dubœuf works with over 600 growers to produce a dizzying array of wines—always around, affordable, and reliable. His *cru* bottlings are at the top of their class; the Morgon, for example, is lean and juicy with cranberry and licorice flavors, becoming softer and more subtle after three to four years in bottle.

LOUIS JADOT

Established 1859 *Owner* Kobrand *Production* NA
Vineyard area NA

For many, the wines of Jacques Lardiere are the first taste of Burgundy on their lips. Jadot's wines are good value and reliable. Lardière's passion comes through in the Château des Jacques' Moulin-à-Vent —it has great intensity of fruit when young and ages superbly. His trusty Beaujolais-Villages should be on the required drinking list of every blossoming youth.

PAUL JANIN ET FILS

Established 1925 *Owners* Paul Janin and family
Production 1,200 cases *Vineyard area* 25 acres acres (10 ha)

Janin's vineyard, Domaine des Vignes du Tremblay, is located on granite-based hillsides in Moulin-à-

Vent and was planted by his grandparents; it is now farmed biodynamically. The wine is bold and characterful: after four to five years it displays aromas and flavors of incense, cigar box, cranberries and orange rind; a lithe, soft texture; and a long finish.

DOMAINE YVON METRAS

Established NA *Owner* Yvon Metras *Production* 600 cases
Vineyard area 3.75 acres (1.5 ha)

Metras' vineyard is known locally as Grille Midi, or "roasting at midday," a reference to its sunny location. It produces inky, concentrated Fleurie, which is rarely chaptalized. Metras belongs to a group of growers known as the Gang of Four. It follows organic principles and avoids using sulfur or yeasts during fermentation. His Fleurie shows floral, raspberry, and cherry flavors and a lush texture, with enough acid and tannins for aging.

JEAN-PAUL THÉVENET

Established 1870 *Owner* Jean-Paul Thévenet *Production* 2,000 cases *Vineyard area* 13 acres (5 ha)

Another member of the Gang of Four, Jean-Paul Thévenet produces two Morgon *cuvées*: Tradition and Vieilles Vignes. The latter is made from 70-year-old vines and aged in oak for six to eight months. Intense, cedary and grapey when young, it softens and becomes even more elegant over two to three years.

Beaujolais is named for the town of Beaujeu, which was founded in the tenth century.

After three to five years in bottle, top cru wines become seamless, rich and velvety, and display distinctive earthy characters.

A floral display in the streets of Beaune, the center of winemaking in Burgundy.

Burgundy

Jasper Morris MW

Burgundy produces some of the greatest red and white wines of the world, mostly from two grape varieties, pinot noir and chardonnay. It is a region full of paradox: steeped in tradition yet equipped with modern research stations; simple to comprehend in some respects (there are only two main grapes), yet complex in others (many hundreds of individually named vineyards are divided up between many thousands of producers). The word itself is tremendously evocative, suggesting a deep red color (though many of the wines are a light,

bright cherry red), a sense of winter warmth, an almost imperial majesty. It conjures up images of cobwebbed stone cellars with high, vaulted ceilings; tiled roofs on imposing bourgeois mansions; small villages dominated by churches; and gnarled peasants working among the vines all hours of the day—one such worker, the late, widely respected André Mussy, whose working life as a vigneron in Pommard lasted more than 70 years, started at the age of thirteen with a 72-hour working week and never grew out of the habit.

When all is well, the wines of Burgundy can be the most majestic of all—Le Chambertin delights in the cliché of "The King of Wines; The Wine of Kings"—yet disappointments have been all too frequent. In 1869, the *Blue Guide* to the wines of the department of the Côte d'Or reproached the local winemakers for apathy, resistance to new ideas and healthy methods of cultivation, and a preference for quantity over quality. A century later, Anthony Hanson, in the first edition of his book on Burgundy, wrote in much the same language. Fortunately, Burgundy is currently enjoying a golden age, and the region has never been in better hands than today. More producers, whether growers or merchants, are making fine wine than ever before. This resurgence of quality is particularly noticeable in the region's red wines.

Burgundy was once a great independent duchy, nearly a separate kingdom, that stretched from the foothills of the Alps to Flanders. Today, it is a province of France, where it is known as Bourgogne (*la Bourgogne* refers to the region of Burgundy; *le Bourgogne* to the wine, burgundy). The four departments that make up administrative Burgundy are the Yonne, Nièvre, Côte d'Or and Saône et Loire. Although there are vineyards in the Nièvre, notably at Pouilly-Fumé, from a winemaking point of view they are considered part of the Loire.

The vineyards of Burgundy are usually divided into five groups. Those of the Yonne department are the farthest north; they include the appellations of Chablis, Sauvignon-de-St-Bris and generic Bourgogne, and some recently restored outlying vineyards near the towns of Joigny and Vézelay. Most of the wines produced here are white. To the south, in the department of the Côte d'Or are the Côte de Nuits and the Côte de Beaune. The former

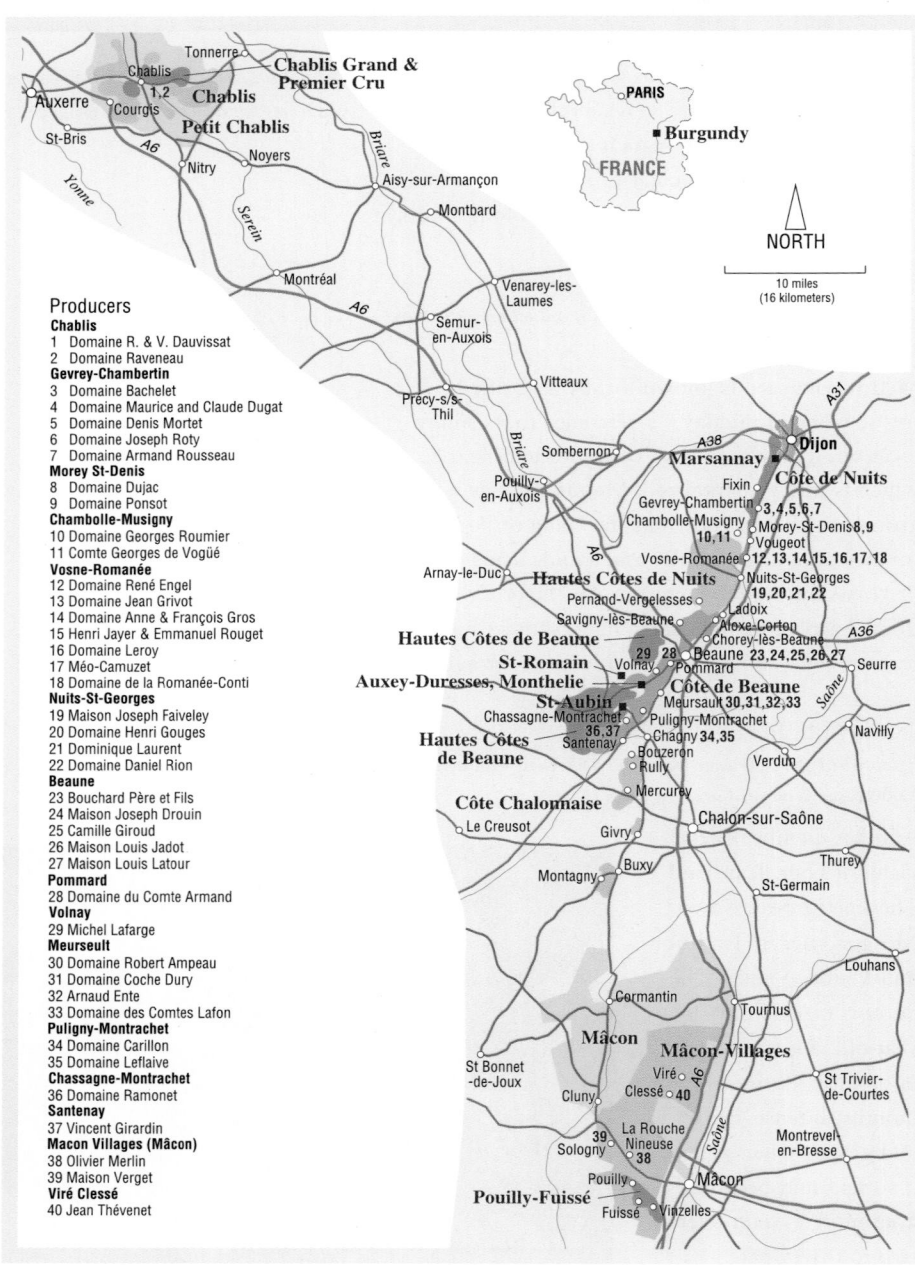

Producers

Chablis
1 Domaine R. & V. Dauvissat
2 Domaine Raveneau
Gevrey-Chambertin
3 Domaine Bachelet
4 Domaine Maurice and Claude Dugat
5 Domaine Denis Mortet
6 Domaine Joseph Roty
7 Domaine Armand Rousseau
Morey St-Denis
8 Domaine Dujac
9 Domaine Ponsot
Chambolle-Musigny
10 Domaine Georges Roumier
11 Comte Georges de Vogüé
Vosne-Romanée
12 Domaine René Engel
13 Domaine Jean Grivot
14 Domaine Anne & François Gros
15 Henri Jayer & Emmanuel Rouget
16 Domaine Leroy
17 Méo-Camuzet
18 Domaine de la Romanée-Conti
Nuits-St-Georges
19 Maison Joseph Faiveley
20 Domaine Henri Gouges
21 Dominique Laurent
22 Domaine Daniel Rion
Beaune
23 Bouchard Père et Fils
24 Maison Joseph Drouin
25 Camille Giroud
26 Maison Louis Jadot
27 Maison Louis Latour
Pommard
28 Domaine du Comte Armand
Volnay
29 Michel Lafarge
Meurseult
30 Domaine Robert Ampeau
31 Domaine Coche Dury
32 Arnaud Ente
33 Domaine des Comtes Lafon
Puligny-Montrachet
34 Domaine Carillon
35 Domaine Leflaive
Chassagne-Montrachet
36 Domaine Ramonet
Santenay
37 Vincent Girardin
Macon Villages (Mâcon)
38 Olivier Merlin
39 Maison Verget
Viré Clessé
40 Jean Thévenet

runs from the southern outskirts of Dijon to just beyond the town of Nuits-St-Georges; the latter takes over north of Beaune and continues southward through Chassagne-Montrachet, Santenay and Maranges. In both cases, the vineyards lie in a narrow strip that runs along the east-facing hillsides.

South of the market town of Chagny is a handful of villages that forms a loose grouping named the Côte Chalonnaise. The fifth and final region is the Mâconnais, where the hillsides are planted with vines and the valleys are used for growing corn or grazing Charollais cattle and sheep. Here, more than 40 widely scattered villages produce the largest volume of white wine in the whole of Burgundy.

For reasons of commercial expediency, the Beaujolais (see p. 170), most of which falls in the department of the Rhône, is considered to be part of Burgundy by some. But the soil is quite different (granite as opposed to limestone), the principle grape variety is gamay, and the wines bear no resemblance to those of Burgundy.

The cities of Burgundy—Dijon, Auxerre, Chalon-sur-Saône and Mâcon—show little evidence of being winemaking centers. It is rather to the smaller towns, such as Beaune and Nuits-St-Georges, and certain large villages that the wine seeker must go. Beaune is the capital of vinous Burgundy, with scores of wine shops, cafés, restaurants and museums, as well as the medieval grandeur of the Hôtel Dieu, the headquarters of the Hospices de Beaune. This institution was founded in the mid-fifteenth century by the Chancellor of the Duchy of Burgundy, Nicolas Rolin, to care for the poor and needy of Beaune. Though the hospice has now moved to modern premises, the charitable foundation still derives some of its income from the sale of wines made in vineyards that have been bequeathed to it over the centuries.

For all its pageantry, Burgundy remains a proud and private place. This is above all a rural area where the inhabitants are attached to the land and their small communities. Vineyards seldom come up for sale, except as a result of hardship or an absence of heirs. The producers, even those with titled names, owe their fortunes to the soil, not the city. Men in suits are happily rare.

History

We do not know exactly when, but at some point during the Roman period, between 52 BC, when Julius Caesar defeated Vercingetorix at Alésia, and AD 312, when one Eumenius made a political

speech during which he complained about the dilapidated state of local vineyards, the vine was introduced to Burgundy—or Gallia Lugdunensis as it was known at the time. The name Burgundy only came into being with the arrival of the Burgondes in the fifth century. Originally from the Danish island of Burgundarholm (now Bornholm), this Scandinavian people first migrated to the Danube basin but were forced to move on by the Huns and Vandals. Subsequently, they were sucked into the vacuum created by the collapse of the Roman Empire, ending up in what is now eastern France.

The Bourgondes in turn were overrun by the Franks under Clovis. The Franks were Christians, and there is evidence that under their rule the church began to play a significant role in developing vineyards. For instance, in AD 775, Charlemagne, the great Frankish leader, who is immortalized in the Grand Cru Corton-Charlemagne, donated a parcel of vines in Aloxe-Corton to the Abbey of St-

The picturesque village of Nuits-St-Georges in the appellation of the same name.

Burgundy is home to numerous cooperages offering a wide choice of barrel types.

The colorful rooftop of the Hôtel Dieu, headquarters of the Hospice de Beaune.

Andoche. The Church's role became even more significant following the founding of the monasteries. The Cistercian monks of Cîteaux developed the vineyard now known as Clos de Vougeot and enclosed it within a wall (the *clos*) as early as the fourteenth century. Around the same time, the Abbeys of St-Vivant and Bèze were also cultivating vineyards in Vosne-Romanée and Gevrey-Chambertin respectively, and these are now enshrined in the Grands Crus of Romanée St-Vivant and Chambertin Clos de Bèze.

The Burgundian state enjoyed its most glorious period under the Valois Dukes of Burgundy (1364–1477). Their courts, based in Dijon and Beaune, were among the finest and richest in Europe. Though it never quite became a kingdom, Burgundy was a state in its own right, an independent duchy that was at times more powerful than the neighboring kingdom of France. It came to an end with the death of Charles the Rash and Burgundy's absorption into France.

In the eighteenth century, much-improved transport systems, especially new canals, created potential for exporting wines, and many merchant houses, the ancestors of today's *négociants*, were founded. Most of the vineyards remained in the hands of the church and nobility, but the professional middle classes were also becoming landowners. Significantly, they were keen to sell their produce, in contrast to the nobility who tended to keep their wine for their own enjoyment.

Radical changes took place following the French Revolution in 1789. Church and nobility were dispossessed of their property and many famous vineyards were sold at auction. Perhaps more significantly, the Napoleonic Code changed the laws of inheritance so that all children had to receive equal shares of a family property. Thus began the fragmentation of the vineyards that has made the Burgundian wine scene such a hotchpotch today.

The eighteenth century also saw the appearance of the first wine book on Burgundy, which was written by the Abbé Claude Arnoux in 1728 as a textbook for an English pupil. More compre-

hensive studies were published in the nineteenth century, by Dr Morelot in 1831 and Dr Lavalle in 1855; the latter included a detailed classification of contemporary Burgundian vineyards which still looks fairly accurate today.

Toward the end of the nineteenth century, Burgundy was hit by the multiple scourges of oidium, mildew, phylloxera, and economic depression; these were quickly followed in 1914 by the First World War, which decimated the male population. Further economic depression in the 1920s and 1930s saw the emergence of the cooperative movement and estate bottling as alternative sources of supply to the *négociants*. In 1935, the system of *appellation d'origine contrôlée* and the official classification of vineyards into village, Premier Cru and Grand Cru were introduced.

The burgundy of the 1930s was not as we know it now. Because pinot noir did not ripen every year, and since it is not naturally a deeply colored grape, the wines were often supplemented by darker, fuller-bodied wines from the south and even from Algeria. Some of these dubious blends continued to be shipped as late as the 1970s.

In the 1980s, winemakers attempted to return to a purer burgundy; unfortunately, they didn't have the expertise that is available today and the resulting wines, as well as being pale, lacked depth and concentration. Now, many different styles of burgundy are available, some pale but fine, others darker and more extracted. Never before have there been so many competent, quality-driven producers of this wonderful wine.

Landscape and climate

Located in eastern central France, Bugundy has a generally continental climate, with cold winters, warm summers and short autumns. Overall, the temperature is cooler than in maritime Bordeaux, especially in autumn, so Burgundy is very much at the northern limit of red-wine-producing regions in the northern hemisphere. Rainfall is fairly high, averaging 28.6 inches (732 mm) per annum in the 30 years to 1992. Its presence is usually more problematic than its absence, even though, as in the rest of France, irrigation is not permitted. September rainfall adversely affected, to at least a minor degree, the harvests of 1991, 1992, 1993, 1994, 1995, 1998 and 1999.

The prevailing wind is a southwesterly, which brings wet, blustery conditions—what's left of Atlantic fronts. The southerlys are hot, heavy winds that are usually the precursors of storms;

the northeasterly brings bright, cool weather, as does the gentler north wind, known locally as *la bise (du nord)*. The locals also have a saying that "the wind on Palm Sunday will be the wind for the year." Certainly, this was the case in 1996, when the northeasterly wind that prevailed on Palm Sunday blew throughout the crucial month of September.

Most of Burgundy is underpinned by limestone soils. During the Jurassic period (195 to 135 million years ago), central France was under ocean. The Lower Jurassic deposited clays, the Middle Jurassic limestone and the Upper Jurassic limestone, marl and clay. The exact types of limestone found in different parts of Burgundy today vary according to the period of formation and the types of marine life they contain. Some of the best from a winemaking point of view are the Kimmeridgian limestones of the Upper Jurassic period, found in Chablis, and the oolitic limestones of the Middle Jurassic, which appear in the Côte d'Or.

The vineyards of the Côte d'Or, the heartland of Burgundy, are situated on a fault line that runs between the Morvan plateau in the west and the fertile Saône valley in the east. This fault exposes different types of rock in different places. The great vineyards of the Côte de Nuits are situated mostly on Bajocian and Bathonian limestone from the Middle Jurassic period, whereas those of the Côte de Beaune, which formed a little later, have soils that contain a higher level of marlstone. The best vineyards of the Mâconnais are found where Bajocian and Bathonian limestone crop up again.

It is not just the mother rock that influences the soil. For example, the escarpment on which the vineyards of the Côte d'Or are planted is cut through with streams, including the Avant Dheune (in Santenay), the Dheune (Pommard), the Rhoin (Savigny-lès-Beaune), the Meuzin (Nuits-St-Georges) and the Vouge (Vougeot), all of which carry eroded soils from the hills. It is no coincidence that the appellations through which these streams flow tend to make some of the region's heaviest wines, as the proportions of clay deposit to limestone rock are higher in these areas than in, say, stream-free Volnay or Chambolle-Musigny.

The extraordinary complexity of soil types throughout Burgundy accounts for the wonderful diversity of flavor profiles found in individual vineyards. Burgundy is perhaps the region that best exemplifies the French concept of *terroir*, and it is fascinating to taste regularly with a top producer and sample the difference between one vineyard and another only 50 yards (46 m) away—a difference that is reproduced year in and year out despite variations in vintages. Yet the makeup of the soil is not the only determinant of the wine's flavor. Other factors include the vineyard's exact exposure to the sun; how steep the slope is; whether it faces due east or east-southeast; whether the ground is in a little dip or on an exposed mound; what the drainage is like—all these variables play a part in creating a wine even before human intervention, in the form of varying viticultural practices, shapes the style further.

Monitoring the vineyards in winter at Domaine Dujac in the Côte de Nuits.

Mist shrouds the vineyards surrounding the village of Fuissé in the Mâconnais.

The shops of Beaune offer an extensive range of produce from local winemakers.

Many Burgundy vineyard names give an indication of their *terroir*. Thus Les Perrières, a vineyard name in several villages including Meursault, Puligny-Montrachet and Nuits-St-Georges, indicates a stony soil, as does Les Caillerets in Chassagne-Montrachet, Puligny-Montrachet, Meursault and Volnay. On the other hand, Lavières (Savigny and Nuits-St-Georges) and Argillières (also Nuits-St-Georges) indicate clay soil.

The best way to comprehend the layout of the Côte d'Or vineyards is to stand by the side of the main road, the RN74, which links the wine villages from Dijon through Beaune and on to Chagny in the south, and look up to the top of the hill to the west. The summits are rather too exposed to cool winds for ideal grape production and the soil is too thin or nonexistent; as a result, they are generally bare land or forest. It is the hillsides below that produce the best wine. Sloping steeply in some places and more gently in others, they have excellent exposure to the sun, good drainage and relatively thin soil. Where the slope flattens out, the vineyards have to compete for space with the buildings of the district's compact villages. Behind you, on the other side of the main road you will see other vineyards, planted for generic burgundy production, but the soil here is thick and fertile and the grapes soon give way to an agricultural plain that stretches away toward the River Saône.

Vines and wines

The two great grapes of Burgundy are chardonnay for white wines and pinot noir for reds, both of which have an affinity for the local limestone soils. A village called Chardonnay exists near Mâcon, though it is not clear whether the grape or the village was first to bear this name. Though by no means the most widely planted white grape in the world, chardonnay is certainly the most sought-after and Burgundy is its home. Chardonnay has many advantages: it is relatively easy to grow, can set a reasonable crop without obvious detriment to quality, ripens more often than not, produces a full-bodied wine that appeals to expert and beginner alike, and can be made in a variety of styles.

The Kimmeridgian soils of Chablis impart a minerally character to the area's wines.

The average annual production of white burgundy is 19.2 million gallons (72.6 million l)—about 100 million bottles—so although Burgundy may be the home of the chardonnay grape, production is insignificant compared to California or Australia. The department of the Yonne accounts for just under a third of Burgundy's whites, most of which is Chablis. That far north the wines are leaner, with a strong mineral character; they are usually vinified in stainless steel. To the south, the Saône et Loire, which incorporates the Côte Chalonnaise and the Mâconnais is the biggest producer, with over half of total white wine production. The most famous part of Burgundy, the Côte d'Or, represents only 15 percent of white-wine production, but as well as some generic wines it supplies the great white wines of Burgundy: Meursault, Puligny-Montrachet, Chassagne-Montrachet and Corton-Charlemagne.

Much white burgundy is made for early drinking, but the great wines of the Côte d'Or, as well as some Chablis or Pouilly-Fuissé, can age extremely well—for example, a well-made and well-stored 1959 should still be a great bottle of wine today. However, most other wines from the 1960s, 1970s and early 1980s should have been drunk up by now, as should 1987. Wines from 1985, 1986 and vintages between 1988 and 1994 inclusive should mostly be ready to drink, the best years being 1989, 1990 and 1992.

Between 1995 and 1997, Burgundy enjoyed a trio of very good white-wine vintages whose lesser wines should be drunk now but whose better wines need keeping. The 1995 vintage was a smallish crop, ripe yet with decent acidity; the wines were quite firm from the start and may prove to be the best of the trio in due course.

The next two vintages both enjoyed dry and sunny Septembers but are completely different in style: 1996 was cool and sunny, creating adequate sugar levels but leaving a marked acidity—these wines have a wonderful, crystal-clear purity, but the best will take years to mature—whereas 1997 was hot and sunny, giving high sugar levels and low acidity, which in turn resulted in rich, fat wines for relatively early consumption.

In 1998, growers had a difficult vintage, with a short harvest of mostly modest quality. However, the vines made up for it in 1999 with a bumper crop of very good wines, though the size of the yield indicates that most should be drunk young.

Other white grapes are used in Burgundy, of which the most important is aligoté. It is also

The historic town of Chablis, which has given its name to a type of white wine.

grown widely in Romania, but has attained no great distinction anywhere in the world. In Burgundy, it has traditionally been used to make a wine that is served by the *pichet* (jug) in cafés. This wine is light and tart, with a little too much acidity for its body to be of any interest except as a refreshing, lowish-alcohol drink or as the main component in *vin blanc cassis* (dry white wine mixed with blackcurrant liqueur), also known as *kir* for the Canon of Dijon, who made it famous.

Another minor white grape variety that you can still come across in the Yonne is sacy, which is lightish and thinnish and of only historical interest. Yet another, which used to be prevalent in the region and has even been replanted recently near Vézelay, is the melon de bourgogne, a hardy, frost-resistant grape variety which now thrives most notably near the mouth of the River Loire, where it goes under the name of muscadet.

After chardonnay, however, the most significant white-wine grapes are members of the pinot family, particularly pinot gris—including the local version known as pinot beurot—and pinot blanc. These are mutations of the original red grape (pinot noir), so some pinot gris grapes may have a pinkish tinge while others are more obviously

white. Tradition, now enshrined in appellation laws, allows these grapes to be used where they have always been grown. A certain amount of pinot blanc especially can be found scattered throughout the famous, theoretically chardonnay vineyards of the Côte de Beaune, even in Grand Cru vineyards such as Corton-Charlemagne. In the Côte de Nuits, particularly in Nuits-St-Georges, a few white-wine vineyards have been deliberately planted with pinot blanc.

While chardonnay is highly adaptable, producing great wine in many different parts of the world, pinot noir is much more difficult to grow. Burgundy is generally though to be ideal for pinot as its south-east-facing slopes provide sufficient exposure to the sun to ripen the fruit yet seldom experience the extreme heat that tends to scorch the thin-skinned grape in other parts of the world. But, even here, despite improvements in viticultural techniques and, to a lesser extent, equipment, success is not guaranteed. Often, for example, September rainfall takes the edge off a potentially fine vintage, as occurred in 1986, 1992 and 1994.

Because pinot skins are relatively thin, tannin generally plays a lesser part in burgundy's ability to age than acidity. Certain years do have high

A vineyard worker trimming chardonnay vines following the annual harvest.

The nozzle of a pipette used to extract wine from barrels for sampling.

tannin levels—notably 1976, 1983 and 1988—but in some instances (the first two years, for example) the fruit never comes into balance with the dryness of the tannin. Underripe vintages, when the acidity levels are high, can produce excellent wines, as occurred in 1980 and 1993. Some hot vintages have provided fleshy, fruity wines without enormous structure—1989 and 1997, for example. In recent decades, only the vintages of 1959, 1978 and 1990 offered the perfect combination of rich, fully ripe fruit and a decent structure for long-term aging.

Since a wine's color is in part derived from the grape's skin, red burgundy tends to be pale. Winemakers who macerate for maximum color often extract coarser tannins as well. The ideal color for burgundy has long been a source of debate. In the eighteenth century, when it was very light, the Abbé Tainturier thought it should not be. For much of the twentieth century it has been deeper—often as a result of the addition of Algerian or southern French wine—but purists felt it should not be. Today the debate continues, with one school seeking the depth of color and apparent concentration derived from the use of new oak and heavy extraction, and the other placing greater emphasis on the wine's purity.

Either way, the hallmark of great pinot noir is its beguiling fragrance which, when the wines are young, covers a whole register of red fruits, from cherries of different sorts through red currants to raspberries, strawberries and plums. As the wines age, the details of the fragrance emerge. At Premier Cru level or above, it should be multilayered: just as a rosebud gradually opens out to reveal its petals, so a wonderful bouquet should slowly unfold, its core of fruit edged by a decadent leafy,

gamey or truffley aroma of decay. Above all, there should be a long, graceful, lingering finish.

The minor red grapes of Burgundy are gamay and césar (although another ancient variety, tréssot, may also still exist). The latter is found only in the Yonne department and makes a coarse, rustic red whose value is to impart color in a district where the pinot can be pale and uninteresting. Gamay is more significant. It thrives on the acidic granite and sandy soils of the Beaujolais but produces indifferent quality on the alkaline soils of Burgundy. It sets and can ripen a sizeable crop, so in periods when quantity was more sought-after than quality, it was widely planted—Duke Philip of Burgundy famously tried to outlaw this "bad and disloyal plant" in 1395. Nowadays, it is grown in the least interesting vineyards at the foot of the slopes of the Côte d'Or, to be used in a blend with pinot noir in Bourgogne Passetoutgrains or occasionally on its own as Bourgogne Grande Ordinaire.

An irritating and unnecessary anomaly allows for any of the 10 *crus* of Beaujolais, which have to be made from gamay, to be declassified into Bourgogne Rouge. Wines from villages such as Chiroubles and Chénas, which have not been particularly successful in the Beaujolais market, are frequently declassified in this way. (Otherwise, one would expect a bottle labeled Bourgogne Rouge to be made from pinot noir.)

Appellations and classifications

Almost all the vineyards of Burgundy fall within *appellation contrôlée* regulations. In theory, each department can also produce *vin de pays*, but in practice little is made. The region also has one VDQS, Sauvignon-de-St-Bris. There are various levels of appellations and classifications. At the bottom level are the generic appellations— Bourgogne Blanc and Rouge, Bourgogne Aligoté and Passetoutgrains, Hautes Côtes de Nuits and Côtes de Beaune, and Mâcon—which between them account for just over 50 percent of all burgundy. At the next level are the communal or village appellations, which extend from Chablis in the north to Pouilly-Fuissé in the south and include such famous names of the Côte d'Or as Gevrey-Chambertin and Puligny-Montrachet. Excepting the Mâconnais district, the best vineyards of each village are classified as Premiers Crus. At last count, there were 571 Premiers Crus, which gives an indication of the complexity of the region.

The very best Côte d'Or vineyards are classified as Grand Cru. There are 33 of these in all, including recently promoted La Grande Rue in Vosne-Romanée. There have been occasional promotions to Premier Cru status as well, but by and large the classification has not been changed significantly since it was introduced in 1935. Nor are there many obvious injustices.

However, the status of any given wine depends not on the owner, nor even on how good the actual wine may be, but on the potential quality of the patch of vineyard from which it came; and many producers own a range of vineyards with different classifications. So there are many simple wines that outperform their lowly status thanks to the diligence and skills of the winemaker; and sadly some unworthy bottles of Grand Cru burgundy are made by the incompetent and greedy.

The following list indicates the different classification levels that are possible within the village of Gevrey-Chambertin:

Bourgogne Rouge	Generic burgundy
Gevrey-Chambertin	Village wine
Gevrey-Chambertin Clos de la Justice	Village wine + vineyard name
Gevrey-Chambertin Premier Cru	Premier Cru wine (may be from more than one vineyard)
Gevrey-Chambertin Clos St-Jacques Premier Cru	Premier Cru from named vineyard
Chambertin Clos de Bèze	Grand Cru wine

Appellation laws specify where vines can be planted, which grape varieties are allowed, how they must be pruned, what yields are permitted and minimum sugar levels. The most important issue is yield, especially for pinot noir. The following maximum levels are stipulated, although for each vintage a tolerance, usually of 20 percent, is allowed. Wines produced between the regular limit and the upper one (known as the PLC or *plafond limite de classement*) are required to undergo a tasting test. In high-yielding vintages, the tolerance may be set at a higher level: thus, some villages asked for a tolerance of 30 percent in 1996 and all the villages of the Côte d'Or were granted a 40 percent tolerance for the abundant 1999 crop. This allowed for 3.6 tons per acre (63 hl per ha) for white wines and 3.2 tons per acre (56 hl per ha) for red wines.

Bourgogne Blanc	3.4 tons per acre (60 hl per ha)
Chablis	2.8 tons per acre (50 hl per ha)
Chablis Grand Cru	2.6 tons per acre (45 hl per ha)
Village wines (white)	2.6 tons per acre (45 hl per ha)
Grand Cru (white)	2.3 tons per acre (40 hl per ha)
Bourgogne Rouge	3.2 tons per acre (55 hl per ha)
Village wines (red)	2.3 tons per acre (40 hl per ha)
Grand Cru (red)	2.0 tons per acre (35 hl per ha)

Viticulture and winemaking

The vineyards of Burgundy are densely planted—usually 3.3 feet (1 m) by 3.3 feet (1 m) for each vine—giving 1,620 vines to the acre (10,000 plants per ha), which equates to about half a bottle of

Made mainly from chardonnay, white burgundy typically has a golden hue.

Vineyards in the Côte de Beaune appellation.

Once the vines have shed their leaves, they are cut back to encourage new growth.

wine per vine. Some older vineyards are planted even more densely, with 3.3 feet (1 m) by 3 feet (0.9 m) spacing. Training and pruning is by the single-cane guyot method, leaving six or, more greedily, eight bunches per vine. Slightly different training methods are used in the Mâconnais and also in the Hautes Côtes de Beaune and de Nuits, where the cooler sites require a higher canopy.

Vines are always grafted onto rootstocks. Producers vary in their preference either for planting clones—the research center at Dijon has produced ranges for both chardonnay and pinot noir that are becoming the industry standards throughout the world—or for selecting cuttings from the best of their established vines. There has been no rush to replant currently healthy vineyards, and there are many examples of vineyards with 60- or 80-year-old vines in fruitful production.

Viticultural practices vary. The traditional method was to spray chemically against weeds, pests and diseases while adding fertilizer. This resulted in sterile soils and excessive levels of potassium, which in turn led to dangerously low acidity levels. Many growers have therefore switched to organic methods. Some are certified as organic producers, whereas others follow broadly organic lines without looking for certification. A handful of estates, including some of the region's flagship names (Lafon, Leflaive and Leroy), have espoused biodynamic principles.

The harvest takes place between mid-September and early October, Chablis and the Hautes Côtes picking later than the Mâconnais and the Côte d'Or. In the Côte d'Or, harvesting is carried out almost entirely by hand, though machines are common in

Chablis and the Mâconnais. A policy of strict sorting either in the vineyard or on a table or belt at the winery is essential for red grapes as the relatively high humidity can cause problems with rot.

After harvest, the white grapes are pressed, left overnight to settle (a process known in French as *débourbage*), then run off into tanks or barrels for fermentation. Most Chablis and Mâconnais wines are fermented in tanks, whereas most Côte d'Or whites are fermented in barrels, of which a percentage will be new. Côte Chalonnaise wines may be tank or barrel fermented, though the use of older barrels is probably most typical. Throughout the region, white wines are still allowed to ferment using natural yeasts rather than the juice being cleaned up and inoculated with cultured yeasts. Most cellars are warmed slightly to encourage fermentation, which, despite this, may take several months.

In the last few years, most producers have returned to the formerly standard practice of lees stirring (*bâtonnage*), which nourishes the wine, fleshes it out a bit, and ensures the natural antioxidant function of the yeast cells acts on all the wine.

White wines almost always undergo malolactic fermentation, again using natural bacteria, although a few producers prefer to partially block the process, especially in very ripe, low-acid years. After malolactic fermentation, the wines are racked and then left on fine lees in barrel or tank until bottling. With generic white burgundy, Mâconnais wines and some Chablis, bottling starts in the spring after the harvest; most other whites are bottled in August or September, to make way for the new harvest. A few of the finer wines, especially in Meursault, where cellars are deep and cool, will spend a second winter in barrel, during which time tartrates, proteins and other unstable impurities are likely to precipitate out; this minimizes the treatments needed to prepare the wine for bottling.

Red grapes may be lightly sulfured when they leave the vineyard, and in warm years may need to be cooled on arrival at the cellar so that the juice can macerate on the skins for a few days before fermentation begins. (One extreme version of this technique, propounded by local enologist Guy Accad, recommends heavy sulfuring and cooling to a very low temperature prior to prolonged maceration, but few people now follow this route.) Fermentation usually takes place in open-topped vats and is accompanied by regular punching down (*pigeage*). Some producers pump the juice over; others use horizontal vats with mechanical arms that perform this task automatically.

Many vineyard managers now use organic methods, though not all seek certification.

The wine remains in vat for fermentation and maceration for between one and four weeks, although 14 to 21 days is most typical. It is then run off into barrel, where malolactic fermentation takes place, for further maturation. One racking is performed after the malolactic fermentation, another if the wine needs subsequent aeration. Barrels vary in age and provenance depending on the winemaker and the quality of the wine: Grand Cru Burgundy may require 50–100 percent new wood, Premier Cru from one third to a half, and village Côte d'Or wine 10–50 percent. Lesser red wines go into older barrels.

Burgundian winemakers have an excellent range of barrels to choose from as the region is home to more than 30 different coopers (*tonneliers*) who not only provide for their domestic market but also export their barrels to all parts of the world where top-quality chardonnay and pinot noir are grown. The best-known names include François Frères, who provide barrels for the Hospices de Beaune and Domaine de la Romanée-Conti; Damy, whose barrels seem to suit white burgundy particularly well; and the Tonnellerie de Mercurey. Further variations in barrel quality may depend on the forest used to source the wood and to what extent the barrels are toasted.

Growers, cooperatives and merchants

The label on a bottle of burgundy will tell you the name of the producer, but you may have to dig a little deeper to find out if the wine has come from an individual grower, cooperative or merchant (*négociant*). Growers' wines are normally identified by words such as *propriétaire-récoltant* (owner-grower) or *mise en bouteilles au domaine* (bottled at the estate), whereas a merchant's wines usually bear the words *négociant-éleveur*. Wines from co-operatives are sometimes disguised as if they were from individual producers, but normally the label will refer to a *cave cooperative*, *producteurs réunis* or *groupement de producteurs*.

As a result of the introduction of the Napoleonic code in the eighteenth century, the production scene in Burgundy is enormously fragmented. Currently, 4,422 producers own 67,020 acres (27,123 ha) between them—making the average holding just 15 acres (6 ha) per producer. Fifty percent of producers own less than 12.4 acres (5 ha) and only 4 percent own more than 49 acres (20 ha). All of which might raise an eyebrow or two in other parts of the world—Australia's Riverina, for instance.

This situation came about because all inheritances must be divided equally between all of the deceased's children. Thus, if Monsieur Dupont has three acres each of three different vineyards and three children, each child will inherit one-third share (one acre) of each of the three vineyards. The children may then marry into other local landowning families, adding morsels of other vineyards to their holding. Within only a few generations a vigneron might have a holding of, say, ten acres spread over a dozen separate vineyards. This does not happen in Bordeaux, where the land holdings are kept together under the name of the château and shares in the château are divided between the children. This practice is now becoming more common in Burgundy, but it can also result in complications, as after a few generations a large number of shareholders may have conflicting expectations; furthermore, heavy inheritance taxes apply from generation to generation.

Just to complicate the grower scene and naming practices further, many families in Burgundy

Mechanical harvesters are now widely used, particularly in Chablis and the Mâconnais.

A cellar-hand records fluctuations in temperature on the outside of a barrel.

use double-barrelled names, especially if the bride brings her own vineyards to the marriage. Thus, when a Monsieur Machin marries a Mademoiselle Truc, they may become known as Monsieur and Madame Machin-Truc. If the succession passes down the female line, this can become more complicated. For example, the late Edmond Delagrange-Bachelet in Chassagne-Montrachet had a daughter who married Jacques Gagnard, thus changing the name of the *domaine* to Gagnard-Delagrange. They in turn produced two daughters, who subsequently married men with the surnames of Blain and Fontaine; so within just a couple of generations what had been Domaine Delagrange-Bachelet was divided between Domaines Blain-Gagnard and Fontaine-Gagnard. Look under "wine producers" in the Meursault telephone book and you'll find five different members of the Bouzereau family, four Buissons, four Jobards, three Coches and three Millots, most of whom are cousins. Neighboring Puligny-Montrachet has four Chavys, while Chassagne-Montrachet has four Moreys, five Pillots and numerous members of the Gagnard tribe.

A great deal more burgundy is now marketed by cooperatives and *négociants* than by individual growers. The cooperative movement got under way in the 1920s when economic depression forced winegrowers in the less fashionable parts of Burgundy such as the Mâconnais and Chablis to group together in order to capture some sort of market. Today, the best cooperatives are flourishing, most notably those of Lugny and Viré in the Mâconnais, Buxy in the Chalonnais, and La Chablisienne in Chablis.

The first *négociants*, or merchant houses, were established in the eighteenth century—beginning with Champy in 1720 and Bouchard in 1731—to sell Burgundian wares into the Netherlands and farther afield. The forerunners of Maison Louis Latour and Maison Louis Jadot were established soon afterward, and other classic houses, such as Drouhin, were founded in the nineteenth century. The leading *négociants* sell Burgundian wines made with fruit from their own vineyards and with grapes and wine bought from other suppliers. Recently, a new wave of merchants, led by J-C Boisset and selling a wider range of wines than just the classic Burgundian appellations, has swallowed up less successful established houses and significantly altered the shape of the market.

During the 1980s and 1990s, a new breed of *mini-négociants* also emerged. Many are individual

The view across the vineyards to the town of Nuits-St-Georges in the Côte de Nuits.

growers who decided to expand their ranges of wines a little; others are specialists in one color, such as Olivier Leflaive or Verget for white wines and Nicolas Potel or Dominique Laurent for reds.

In the 1930s, sales collapsed as a result of the Depression and merchants stopped buying wine, even from winegrowers in the heartland of the Côte d'Or. As a result, several producers, notably Henri Gouges of Nuits-St-Georges and Marquis d'Angerville of Volnay, began to bottle and market their own wine. Thus the practice of *domaine* bottling was born, and although it remained a minority activity until the burgundy boom of the 1980s, it is now widespread.

Burgundian food

Burgundy has a wonderful tradition of rich food and great chefs to match its wine. Some, including Lameloise in Chagny and Loiseau in Saulieu, have received French cuisine's highest accolade, three stars in the Michelin guide; others content themselves with simpler renditions of classic Burgundian cuisine. Signature Burgundian dishes include *pochouse*, a rich fish stew with white wine, bacon and onions; *oeufs en meurette*, eggs poached in a red wine, bacon, onion and mushroom sauce; snails, of course; *boeuf bourguignon* and *coq au vin*; and richly flavored local cheeses such as Epoisses, L'Ami de Chambertin and Cîteaux.

As this list indicates, Burgundian cuisine is rich even to the point of being heavy. This makes it a successful match for the heady white wines of the region or the richer reds when they are mature; it is less well suited to vibrant young red burgundy, which can be paired more successfully with modern chargrilled dishes.

Festivals: Les Trois Glorieuses

Burgundy is also famous for its festivals, most notably Les Trois Glorieuses, the "Three Glorious Feasts," which take place during the weekend of the Hospices de Beaune charity auction, held on the third Sunday in November.

The first feast is the Saturday-night celebration organized by the Chevaliers de Tastevin in their headquarters, the Clos de Vougeot. Guests enjoy abundant food, plenty of wine, rather too many speeches, and some cheerful singing from a local group called "Les Joyeux Bourguignons."

On the Sunday, the auction itself takes place in Les Halles, the covered market opposite the Hôtel Dieu. This is a long, drawn-out affair in which barrels of new wine from the vineyards belonging

to the Hospices de Beaune are sold off at relatively elevated prices (reflecting the charitable purpose of the auction) which, however, provide some indication of the price levels that can be expected in the new season. Another formal dinner follows, and is again washed down with much wine and song.

The third and most entertaining feast is the Paulée de Meursault, held in the Château de Meursault at lunchtime on the Monday. A substantial meal is served to 600-odd guests, who each bring bottles (or cases) of their own wines, both recent vintages and old. As the bottles are passed up and down the tables, "Les Joyeux Bourguignons" once more provide the musical accompaniment. Afterward, many of the cellars in the village are opened so that revellers can continue to explore the merits of Meursault wines.

Above: *Wine from the Hospices de Beaune vineyards on display on the day of the auction.*

Top: *Burgundy's hearty cuisine includes local specialties such as seasoned pork sausages.*

The benefits of burgundy

Researchers at Dijon university have been at the forefront of studies into the relationship between wine and cholesterol. In particular, they have pioneered the study of resveratrol, one of a number of types of molecules called phytoalexins produced by grapes as a defence against rot. Grapes generate resveratrol when rot threatens but before it actually occurs; as a result, levels of these molecules are especially high when an attack of rot is averted (if rot occurs, the resveratrol supplies are used up). The 1985 vintage was unique in that there was never any threat of rot and no resveratrol was produced.

Resveratrol turns out to have some useful side effects from the point of view of health: it keeps blood fluid and blocks the transfer of "good" cholesterol into "bad" cholesterol, and its antioxidant character makes it anticarcinogenic. Early research, admittedly by Burgundians, indicates that there is more resveratrol in burgundy than in bordeaux. All red wine should be beneficial, however.

Valmur is one of only seven Chablis Grand Cru vineyards. Note the chalky soil.

THE YONNE

The most northerly of Burgundy's departments, the Yonne rarely experiences enough warmth to ripen red grapes, but it is home to one of the most famous of all white wines, Chablis. Its location also makes it the most logical place in Burgundy for a major production center of sparkling wine. The principal producer, Caves de Bailly, possesses beautiful cellars carved out of the rock above the banks of the Yonne, just south of Auxerre.

Chablis

There must be something magical about the name of Chablis for it to have spawned so many imitators. Yet the real thing nearly died out in the 1950s, when little more than 1,250 acres (500 ha) were still under vine. Fortunately, there are now 10,000 acres (4,000 ha) of vines and many more are likely to be planted in the near future.

The key to Chablis is its Kimmeridgian soil. This limestone-clay mix, which is full of tiny marine fossils, seems to give the wine its energetic, flinty character. Another soil type found locally called Portlandian does not contain the marine fossils, and, according to one point of view, wines from this soil do not have the authentic Chablis character. There was almost civil war in Chablis in the early 1970s when a group of vignerons suggested expanding the appellation to include some slopes on Portlandian soil. The purists were horrified, but eventually the expansionists won out— and there are now signs that the battle is to be fought all over again in the first years of the new century, with some producers campaigning for more Portlandian land to be designated as Petit Chablis or upgraded from that lesser appellation to Chablis or even Chablis Premier Cru.

The classifications used here are as follows: Petit Chablis, Chablis, Chablis Premier Cru and Chablis Grand Cru. The name of Petit Chablis is used for wines from less-favored, mostly outlying vineyards; these can be delicious in their first year or two. Most straight Chablis wines can be drunk fairly young though some producers make them to keep; producers are not permitted to specify a vineyard name, although they can add brand names or use the term *vieilles vignes* on old-vine *cuvées*. Better sites are designated as Premier Cru vineyards. There are more than 40 of these, accounting for just over 20 percent of production; the best known are Mont de Milieu, Montée de Tonnerre, Fourchaume, Vaillons and Montmains. These wines usually benefit from two or three years in bottle, during which the details of their flavor profiles emerge.

The highest classification is Chablis Grand Cru which is shared by seven contiguous vineyards located on the same steep slope overlooking the River Serein. They are Blanchot, Bougros, Les Clos, Grenouilles, Preuses, Valmur and Vaudésir. Chablis Grand Cru wines are powerful and concentrated, and need to be kept for five or more years—not something you usually think of doing with Chablis.

DOMAINE R. & V. DAUVISSAT

Owner Vincent Dauvissat *Production* 4,500 cases *Vineyard area* 24 acres (9.5 ha)

A cousin of the Raveneaus (see below), Vincent Dauvissat is considered by many to have jumped to the top of his league. The wines are made in a similar style to Raveneau wines and you will still see old-style Chablis *feuillettes* (132-l [34.5-gallon] oak barrels) at this estate. Wines to look out for include the delicious Premiers Crus Vaillons, Séchet and Fourchaumes, along with the Grands Crus Les Clos and Les Preuses.

DOMAINE RAVENEAU

Owner Jean-Marie Raveneau *Production* 4,000 cases *Vineyard area* 20 acres (8 ha)

François Raveneau, now retired, established this *domaine* as the greatest name in Chablis, and his son Jean-Marie is continuing the good work. Old barrels are still used to make fascinating, rich, complex Chablis from the Grands Crus of Valmur, Les Clos and Blanchots, and Premiers Crus such as Chapelots and Fôrets. Twenty- or thirty-year-old wines from Raveneau *père* are still fabulous.

Other reliable Chablis producers include Domaines Adhémar Boudin, Defaix, Droin, Grossot, Laroche, Michel, Picq and Vocoret, as well as the cooperative La Chablisienne.

Bourgogne

In the area surrounding Chablis, usually called the Auxerrois after the nearest big city, there are scattered vineyards, the remnants of a much wider industry that once supplied Paris with enormous quantities of cheap table wine before the advent of railways made it possible to bring wine to the capital from further south. The best areas are currently enjoying something of a renaissance. They are, for reds only, Irancy, and, for reds and whites, Côtes d'Auxerre, Epineuil, Coulanges-La-Vineuse, Chitry, and a bit farther afield, Vézelay and Côte St-Jacques. The village of Chitry is also locally well known for its Bourgogne Aligoté.

Sauvignon-de-St-Bris

Sauvignon-de-St-Bris is the only wine in Burgundy that has VDQS status; it is also the only wine in the region that is made from sauvignon blanc (St-Bris is not far from and on similar soil to the vineyards of Sancerre and Pouilly-Fumé, where sauvignon reigns supreme). The best grower is J.-H. Goisot.

CÔTE DE NUITS

The department of the Côte d'Or (the Slope of Gold) is somewhat romantically named for the vine-covered escarpment that rises from the valley of the Saône below. By custom, this is divided into two halves (the boundary is in fact the ancient dividing line between the bishoprics of Langres and Autun): the Côte de Nuits and the Côte de Beaune. As well as the major appellations described below, numerous vineyards in the Côte d'Or are located wherever favorable sites can be found in the hills and valleys of the plateau behind the famous slope. These sites are considerably cooler than the escarpment vineyards, so the grapes ripen later and less reliably. The wines are given the generic appellations of Bourgogne Hautes Côtes de Nuits or

Bourgogne Hautes Côtes de Beaune, which together cover about 2,500 acres (1,000 ha) of red grapes and 500 acres (200 ha) of white.

The Côte de Nuits makes Burgundy's greatest red wines from villages such as Gevrey-Chambertin, Vosne-Romanée and Nuits-St-Georges, and the Grands Crus of Chambertin, Musigny and La Romanée-Conti—all located in a narrow band of vineyards rarely more than half a mile (1 km) wide.

Côte de Nuits Villages

Although many villages in the Côte de Beaune can market their wines either under their own village name or as Côte de Beaune Villages, the less-favored communes of the Côte de Nuits are permitted to use only the general appellation of Côte de Nuits Villages. These communes are Fixin (in part) and Brochon (in part) at the northern end of the Côte de Nuits, along with Prémeaux-Prissey (in part), Corgoloin and Comblanchien to the south. There is a tiny amount of white Côte de Nuits Villages, but the vast majority is a light, refreshing red wine made for early drinking.

Marsannay

The vineyards in Marsannay are increasingly in danger of being overwhelmed by the urban sprawl of Dijon. The appellation covers all three colors, though the whites are modest and the reds usually on the light side; there are no Premier or Grand Cru vineyards. Originally, Marsannay's reputation, uniquely in Burgundy, was built on its rosé wines. The best grower in the village is Bruno Clair, who has vineyards up and down the Côte. Other good

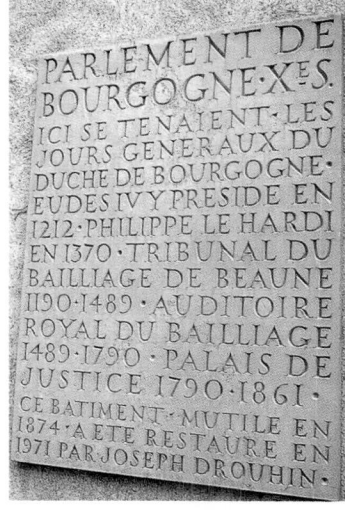

Above: *Domaine Laroche is one of the leading producers in Chablis.*

Top: *This plaque outside the cellars of Joseph Drouhin commemorates the long and distinguished history of the building.*

The town of Chablis viewed from Valmur.

Speed is of the essence at harvest time.

sources for Marsannay are Domaines Charlopin, Coillot, Collotte, Guyard and Naddef.

Fixin

The wines of Fixin are much more substantial than those of Marsannay—deeper in color, with greater depth of fruit and noticeably more tannin, which means they need three to five years in bottle before drinking. They resemble Gevrey-Chambertin, but cost substantially less. The best vineyards are the Premiers Crus of Les Arvelets, Les Hervelets, Clos de la Perrière, Clos du Chapitre and Clos Napoleon, and the most interesting growers are Berthaut and Gelin. Not much Fixin is exported.

Gevrey-Chambertin

Traveling south from Dijon, the first of the famous Burgundy villages, and the biggest, is Gevrey-Chambertin. Its size and fame are such that producers have been able trade on its reputation alone, and a good deal of substandard wine has been made here in recent years. Fortunately, a younger generation has done much to improve the quality of the village's output in recent years.

The wines of Gevrey-Chambertin, when properly made, are among the longest-lived burgundies. Deeper in color than most, they are not immediately appealing and do not display the soft red fruit one might expect; instead, they are more full-bodied and the fruit is sometimes masked by a fair dose of tannin. After several years in bottle, however, the classical, autumnal, gently decaying flavors of great burgundy usually develop. Good vintages should be kept for at least five years.

Gevrey-Chambertin is blessed with eight Grands Crus: Chambertin and Chambertin Clos de Bèze lead the pack, making majestic, powerful, profound wines that require between 15 and 30 years maturation in the best vintages. Ruchottes-Chambertin and Griotte-Chambertin have very thin soils, so the wines are lighter in color but wonderfully perfumed. Latricières-Chambertin and Mazis- (or Mazy-) Chambertin are a touch fuller and richer. The most seductive is Charmes-Chambertin, although it can disappoint—as Chapelle-Chambertin usually does. The eight vine-

A sign marks one of the boundaries of the Grand Cru vineyards of Chambertin.

yards lie alongside the Route des Grands Crus, halfway up the gentle slope south of the village.

The best Premier Cru, which some think better than all but the top two Grands Crus, is Clos St-Jacques, which lies on a separate slope. Other good Premier Cru vineyards are Cazetiers, Lavaux St-Jacques, Estournelles St-Jacques and Combottes.

DOMAINE BACHELET

Owner Denis Bachelet *Production* 1,200 cases *Vineyard area* 8 acres (3 ha)

Denis Bachelet is currently trying to buy more vineyards to increase the size of his tiny but beautifully run estate. It benefits from a high proportion of old vines, especially in the village Gevrey-Chambertin, the Premier Cru Les Corbeaux and a superbly perfumed Charmes-Chambertin.

DOMAINE MAURICE AND CLAUDE DUGAT

Owner Claude Dugat *Production* 1,600 cases *Vineyard area* 10 acres (4 ha)

This tiny *domaine* produces deep-colored wines of impeccable class and concentration. Scarcity adds to the value of the Charmes-Chambertin, Griotte-Chambertin, Gevrey-Chambertin Lavaux St-Jacques and Gevrey-Chambertin, all of which have become collectors' items. The wines have a very tight structure when young, which reins in an exuberant concentration of fruit that takes time to develop.

DOMAINE DENIS MORTET

Owner Denis Mortet *Production* 4,000 cases *Vineyard area* 25 acres (10 ha)

Despite having inherited a *domaine* with a modest reputation, Denis Mortet has risen to fame with his deeply colored, quite heavily extracted wines made from a range of village Gevrey-Chambertin vineyards and a tiny bit of Le Chambertin. The most recent vintages indicate that he is searching for a touch more refinement along with the power.

DOMAINE JOSEPH ROTY

Owner Joseph Roty *Production* 3,200 cases *Vineyard area* 20 acres (8 ha)

Joseph Roty's forceful personality shows through in the character of his wines, which were dark, concentrated and oaky even in the early 1980s when such a style was rare in Burgundy. Roty's range of single-vineyard Gevrey-Chambertin wines is supplemented by tiny amounts of Griottes-Chambertin, Mazy-Chambertin and a wonderful Charmes-Chambertin made from very old vines and labelled *très vieilles vignes*.

DOMAINE ARMAND ROUSSEAU
Owner **Charles Rousseau** *Production* **5,500 cases**
Vineyard area **36 acres (14.5 ha)**

The leading estate in Gevrey-Chambertin, Armand
Rousseau has been run for the last 40 years by
Charles Rousseau, who is now making way for his
son and daughter. The wines are produced in a classical manner from great sites, including the Grands
Crus of Chambertin and Chambertin Clos de Bèze,
the outstanding Premier Cru of Clos St-Jacques, and
other Grands Crus such as Mazis-Chambertin,
Charmes-Chambertin and Clos de la Roche. They
are rarely deeply colored but have an ethereal grace,
lingering perfume and every bit as much power and
persistence as more obviously concentrated wines.

Other recommended producers include Bernard
Dugat-Py, Alain Burguet, Philippe Charlopin, Michel
Esmonin et Fille, Dominique Gallois, Géantet-
Pansiot, Domaine Hereszytn and Christian Serafin.

Morey St-Denis

In times past, the wines of Morey St-Denis were
often sold as either Chambolle-Musigny or Gevrey-
Chambertin, and even today the appellation lacks
a strong identity. The wines are usually described
as having the elegance of Chambolle with the
structure of Gevrey-Chambertin, but do have not
quite as much of either. Certainly, a Morey St-
Denis in a line-up of Chambolle-Musignys will
seem somewhat more *sauvage*, a touch more rustic.

   Good Premier Cru vineyards include Clos de la
Bussière (Roumier), Clos des Ormes (Lignier) and
Les Millandes (Amiot), but the pride of the village
is its range of Grands Crus. Two of these are monopolies: Clos de Tart belongs exclusively to the
Mommessin family and makes worthy wine in
great vintages, slightly dull wine in other years;
the Saier family's Clos des Lambrays, on the other
hand, seems to be returning to consistent form.
The others are Clos St-Denis and Clos de la Roche,
plus a part of Bonnes Mares that is mostly in
Chambolle-Musigny. It was from Clos St-Denis
that Morey derived part of its name.

DOMAINE DUJAC
Owner **Jacques Seysses** *Production* **4,500 cases** *Vineyard
area* **28 acres (11.5 ha)**

A *domaine* put together by Jacques Seysses since
1968, consisting of Clos de la Roche, Clos St-
Denis, Bonnes Mares, Charmes-Chambertin,
Echézeaux, Chambolle-Musigny Les Gruenchers,
Vosne-Romanée Les Beauxmonts, Gevrey-

Chambertin Les Combottes and Morey St-Denis.
Dujac's controversial wines are frequently light
in color when young and carry the aroma of the
stalks, which are not removed—a rarity nowadays.
After a few years in bottle, however, a magnificent
perfume transcends any youthful awkwardness.

DOMAINE PONSOT
Owner **Laurent Ponsot** *Production* **2,500 cases** *Vineyard
area* **22 acres (8.75 ha)**

For many, Domaine Ponsot qualifies as a blue-chip
producer on the basis of its Clos de la Roche
Vieilles Vignes, Clos St-Denis, Griotte-Chambertin

Vineyards stretch to the horizon in Chablis.

Vineyard managers carry out winter maintenance work at Domaine Dujac.

and various *cuvées* of Morey St-Denis, including an unusual white from the Premier Cru Monts Luisants. For others, these wines are pallid catastrophies. Certainly, the policy of late picking, almost no sulfuring and long maturation with minimum handling is a high-risk strategy. Lesser vintages appear very fragile when young, though they often seem to regain color and body as they age. But the great vintages are stupendous, with an extraordinary depth of flavor and many layers of richly detailed fruit. Oddly, Ponsot's greatest successes have not been in the classic Burgundy vintages such as 1978, 1990 and 1996, but in offbeat years such as 1980, 1991 and 1997.

Other sound bets in Mory St-Denis include Domaines Perrot-Minot, Hubert Lignier, Georges Lignier and Jean Raphet.

Chambolle-Musigny

A typical Chambolle-Musigny is the most elegant wine in Burgundy. The soil in this appellation incudes a high proportion of active chalk and not much clay, so the wines tend not to be deep-colored nor especially full-bodied; however, they make up for this with an exquisite, lacy delicacy and a sublime fragrance.

There are two Grands Crus, Musigny and Bonnes Mares, and some outstanding Premier Cru vineyards. Le Musigny harnesses all of the fragrance that typifies Chambolle to sumptuous weight and body. This is one of Burgundy's most majestic wines, conjuring up the image of an iron fist in a velvet glove. Such wines need to age for a minimum of 15 years. De Vogüé, Mugnier, Drouhin

and Jadot are the finest producers. Bonnes Mares, on the Morey St-Denis side of the village, is relatively full-bodied and structured and will develop some of the untamed characteristics of Morey. De Vogüé, Roumier, Groffier and Jadot are the leading producers of the wine, which again should be kept for a decade or more.

The Premier Cru Les Amoureuses is the sensual understudy to Le Musigny. Every bit as seductive, it matures more quickly and can thrill the palate even in its first five years. Once again, the best sources are de Vogüé, Roumier, Mugnier, Groffier, Drouhin and Jadot. Les Charmes comes close behind Les Amoureuses, followed by Les Cras, Les Sentiers, Les Feussellotes and Les Fuées. The best producers of village Chambolle-Musigny are Roumier, Mugnier, Groffier, Ghislaine Barthod, Pierre Bertheau and Patrice Rion.

DOMAINE GEORGES ROUMIER
Owner Christophe Roumier ***Production*** 4,500 cases
Vineyard area 35 acres (14 ha)

This *domaine* expresses the essence of Chambolle-Musigny with wines that are only moderately deep in color yet superbly perfumed, full of subtlety and delicacy, and amazingly long-lived. As well as Chambolle-Musigny, the Premier Cru Les Amoureuses, and the Grands Crus Bonnes Mares and Le Musigny, Roumier produces a characterful Morey-St-Denis Clos de la Bussière, exemplary Ruchottes-Chambertin and even a very few barrels of white Grand Cru Corton-Charlemagne.

COMTE GEORGES DE VOGÜÉ
Owner Baronne de Ladoucette ***Production*** 3,600 cases
Vineyard area 30 acres (12 ha)

This impressive *domaine* is to Chambolle-Musigny what Domaine de la Romanée-Conti is to Vosne-Romanée. It makes grand Le Musigny, Bonnes Mares, Chambolle-Musigny Les Amoureuses, Chambolle-Musigny and a little white Musigny. Nowadays the reds have immense concentration of fruit, which seems to come from the vineyard—there is no sense of overextraction or of coarse use of oak here. Naturally massive, they should be kept for many years. Avoid most vintages of the 1970s and 1980s, but even the lesser vintages of the 1990s have been most impressive.

Vougeot

There are only 166 acres (66 ha) under vine in Vougeot. Of these, 12 acres (4.8 ha) are village Vougeot, 29 acres (11.7 ha) are Premier Cru (Les

Cras, Le Clos Blanc, Les Petits Vougeots and Clos de la Perrière), and 125 acres (51 ha) constitute the single Grand Cru, Clos de Vougeot (usually pronounced and sometimes spelled without the "de").

Cistercian monks identified this as prime vineyard land as early as the twelfth century, and in the fourteenth century they enclosed the land with a stone wall, or *clos*. It was said that the perfect wine consisted of a blend from the top, middle and bottom parts of the *clos*. Today, there are at least 80 different proprietors and quality varies widely from producer to producer, depending on their winemaking skills and the location of their holdings. The bottom of the *clos*, abutting the main RN74 road, is low-lying land with soil that is really too heavy to produce Grand-Cru-quality wine. Whether the best plots are in the middle or the top of the *clos* is open to discussion.

Clos de Vougeot is not a seductive wine when young. It is deep in color, powerful and concentrated, with a fairly tannic structure. Rather than red fruits, it displays black fruits, chocolate and even coffee. Good examples will age for up to 50 years, but this is more of a blockbuster than a subtly suggestive wine.

The best producers are Anne Gros, René Engel, Méo-Camuzet, Jadot, Leroy and Faiveley. Look out also for the wines of Domaine de la Vougeraie, owned by Jean-Claude Boisset and made from the 1999 vintage onward by Pascal Marchand.

Vosne-Romanée

If Chambolle-Musigny epitomises finesse and Gevrey-Chambertin *gravitas*, only Vosne-Romanée can combine the two qualities. The wines have a striking elegance on top of a brilliantly concentrated structure, without ever seeming heavy. Village-level Vosne-Romanée is fine, balanced and attractive quite early; the Grands Crus are exceptionally long-lived. Four are owned entirely by single *domaines*: La Romanée-Conti and La Tâche by Domaine de la Romanée-Conti; La Grande Rue (promoted from Premier Cru in 1992) by Domaine Lamarche; and La Romanée by the Liger-Belair family, though the house of Bouchard Père et Fils is responsible for bottling and marketing.

The Grand Cru vineyards of Richebourg, whose 20 acres (8 ha) make a wonderfully rich, profound wine, and Romanée-St-Vivant, whose 23 acres (9.3 ha) yield a wine that is a touch lighter and very stylish, both have a variety of owners. Domaine de la Romanée-Conti, Leroy and Hudelot-Noellat produce both wines. Anne Gros, Grivot and

Méo-Camuzet produce excellent examples of Richebourg; very fine Romanée-St-Vivant can be found *chez* Drouhin and Arnoux.

By convention, the only two vineyards in the commune of Flagey-Echézeaux are considered part of Vosne-Romanée. They are both Grands Crus, Echézeaux and Grands Echézeaux, though the former with 93 acres (38 ha) is a little too large to be consistently worthy of this status. However, reliable, often exciting wines from these vineyards are made by Domaine de la Romanée-Conti (both vineyards), René Engel (both), Drouhin (Grands Echézeaux), Rouget, Dujac, Grivot and Confuron-Cotétidot (all Echézeaux).

The outstanding Premier Cru vineyards here, with the leading exponents given in brackets, are: Malconsorts (Hudelot-Noellat, Thomas-Moillard), Clos de Réas (Michel Gros), Cros Parentoux (Méo-Camuzet, Henri Jayer, Emmanuel Rouget), Les Brulées (Engel, Grivot, Leroy, Méo-Camuzet), Beauxmonts (Leroy, Rouget, Rion, Jadot), and Suchots (Arnoux, Grivot, Jadot).

All of the above producers, plus Domaines Cathiard, Clavelier, Confuron-Cotétidot, Forey and various Mugnerets, also make outstanding village Vosne-Romanée.

DOMAINE RENÉ ENGEL

Owner Philippe Engel *Production* 2,500 cases *Vineyard area* 17 acres (7 ha)

Over the past ten years, Philippe Engel, grandson of René, has turned a competent *domaine* into a leading producer. The wines in his limited range—Vosne-Romanée, Premier Cru Les Brûlées, Grands Crus Echézeaux and Clos de Vougeot—are always

Pinot noir is the ideal red grape for Burgundy's cool, sunny climate.

The entrance to one of the many holdings in the historic Clos de Vougeot Grand Cru.

elegant, balanced and classy. His holding of Clos de Vougeot is particularly well situated and is usually among the best examples.

DOMAINE JEAN GRIVOT
Owner Etienne Grivot *Production* 5,500 cases *Vineyard area* 36 acres (14.5 ha)

After a few anxious years looking for the right approach, Étienne Grivot, son of Jean, has been making first-class reds since 1993. The wines have fleshed out, regained equilibrium and developed the almost ethereal fragrance typical of the finest red burgundy. The *domaine* is equally well served in Premier Crus from Nuits-St-Georges and Vosne-Romanée, along with the Grands Crus of Clos de Vougeot, Echézeaux and Richebourg.

DOMAINE ANNE & FRANÇOIS GROS
Owner Anne Gros *Production* 2,000 cases *Vineyard area* 12 acres (5 ha)

So many members of the Gros family are involved in the winemaking business that it is easy to get confused. They include Jean (father), Michel (son), (Bernard, another son), Anne-Francoise (daughter) and Anne (cousin), who has taken over her father François' land and is currently making the best wines of the family. Her Village Vosne-Romanée and Chambolle-Musigny are both beautifully elegant, the Clos de Vougeot as good as it gets, and the Richebourg sublime.

HENRI JAYER & EMMANUEL ROUGET
Owner Emmanuel Rouget *Production* 2,500 cases *Vineyard area* 17 acres (7 ha)

Now in retirement, Henri Jayer became the most famous of all growers for his wonderfully rich, perfumed and marvellously harmonious red wines. His nephew, Emmanuel Rouget, is his heir both to the vineyards and the style. The wines include Echézeaux, Vosne-Romanée Les Beaumonts, Vosne-Romanée Cros Parentoux, Vosne-Romanée and Nuits-St-Georges.

Bottom: A sign indicates an outer limit of the town of Nuits-St-Georges.

Below: Vineyards at Nuits-St-Georges.

DOMAINE LEROY
Owner Lalou Bize-Leroy *Production* 5,000 cases *Vineyard area* 56 acres (22.5 ha)

In 1998, Domaine Leroy purchased Domaine Charles Noellat, which included Richebourg, Romanée-St-Vivant, Clos de Vougeot, Vosne-Romanée Beauxmonts, Vosne-Romanée Les Brulées and Nuits-St-Georges Boudots. More recent acquisitions have added Le Musigny, Le Chambertin, Latricières Chambertin, Clos de la Roche and Volnay-Santenots. The Leroy estate is run biodynamically with tiny yields; the wines have extraordinary concentration and longevity—and astronomical prices.

MÉO-CAMUZET
Owner Jean and Jean-Nicolas Méo *Production* 6,000 cases *Vineyard area* 37 acres (15 ha)

This estate produces Corton Clos Rognet, Clos de Vougeot, Richebourg, Vosne-Romanée Cros Parantoux, Vosne-Romanée Les Brulées, Vosne-Romanée Les Chaumes, Nuits-St-Georges Aux Boudots, Nuits-St-Georges Aux Murgers, Vosne-Romanée and Nuits-St-Georges. The wines have gained great acclaim for their power and structure, although for some people the oak is a little too dominant. Formerly, much of the *domaine* was worked by the legendary Henri Jayer (see above).

DOMAINE DE LA ROMANÉE-CONTI
Owners de Villaine and Leroy families *Production* 6,500 cases *Vineyard area* 63 acres (25.5 ha)

This is the grandest *domaine* of them all, making nothing but Grand Cru wines, including those from two vineyards that it owns outright, La Romanée-Conti and La Tâche. The other wines are Richebourg, Romanée-St-Vivant, Grands Echézeaux, Echézeaux and Le Montrachet. Yields are kept low and less-than-perfect grapes are eliminated during the harvest, which usually takes place later than in neighboring vineyards. The stems are left on during vinification, a practice that is now rare and can give the wines a slightly austere edge when young, but seems to provide structure for the long term. Even the most modest of the wines is wonderfully perfumed, silky and gracious. The top wines have the same delicacy, to which they add a massive, powerful framework that requires years of bottle age to reach perfection.

Nuits-St-Georges
The capital of the Côte de Nuits, Nuits-St-Georges is home to a number of the region's *négociants*, notably Faiveley and Boisset, as well as all the houses that have been taken over by the latter. The village has no Grands Crus, although Les St-Georges would be promoted by some and Les Vaucrains and Les Cailles are of comparable quality. The

Nuits-St-Georges appellation extends south to include much of the commune of Prémeaux.

The soil in Nuits-St-Georges is richer than in
neighboring Vosne-Romanée, with a higher clay
content. As a result, the wines are deeper-colored,
full-bodied, sturdy, a little more tannic and a little
less fine. All are worth aging for the medium term,
and in the case of traditionalist producers such as
Gouges, for several decades.

Half a dozen *domaines* produce white Nuits-
St-Georges, which was first made by Henri Gouges
from pinot noir that had degenerated into pinot
blanc. Domaine de l'Arlot and Domaine Daniel
Rion also make interesting examples.

MAISON JOSEPH FAIVELEY
Owner François Faiveley *Production* NA *Vineyard area*
285 acres (115 ha)

Though technically a *négociant*, Faiveley has sufficient vineyards of its own to supply most of its
needs. The red wines are deep in color and sometimes quite tannic, making them a trifle ungainly
in their youth but capable of long aging. The range
includes a fine selection of Grands Crus, a bevy of
Nuits-St-Georges including the whole production
of Clos de la Maréchale, and a major holding of

Mercurey in the Côte Chalonnaise. A handful of
white wines are produced, including Mercurey
Blanc and a little exquisite Corton-Charlemagne.

DOMAINE HENRI GOUGES
Owners Christian and Pierre Gouges *Production*
5,500 cases *Vineyard area* 36 acres (14.5 ha)

Following a less impressive spell, the grandsons of
the original Henri Gouges have carefully nurtured
this *domaine* back to the top league. Even now,
Gouge wines are not always appreciated because
they are made for the long term and sometimes
lack youthful appeal. But the superb range of
Nuits-St-Georges Premiers Crus, notably Les St-
Georges, Vaucrains, Clos des Porrets St-Georges
and Pruliers, will reward long aging. The *domaine*
also makes a small quantity of interesting white
Nuits-St-Georges from pinot blanc.

DOMINIQUE LAURENT
Owner Dominique Laurent *Production* NA *Vineyard
area* None

This former pastry chef turned *mini-négociant*
specializes in small batches of red wines sourced
from low-yielding, old vines. Laurent is a devotee
of new oak, and has been celebrated by some for

*The historic Clos de Vougeot Grand Cru
vineyard has at least 80 registered owners.*

A farmhouse and vineyards near Beaune.

Vineyard workers are used to long hours, even in winter, outside the growing season.

using what has been described as "200 percent new wood"—meaning that he racks his wine from one new barrel into another brand new one. The wines are certainly concentrated and can be fabulous, but sometimes the taste of the vineyard is lost behind the style of vinification and maturation.

DOMAINE DANIEL RION
Owners Patrice Rion and brothers *Production* 8,000 cases
Vineyard area 46 acres (18.5 ha)

This steadily developing *domaine* in Prémeaux makes comparatively modern, structured wines from Hauts Pruliers, Clos des Argillières and Vignes Rondes in Nuits-St-Georges, plus several *cuvées* of Vosne-Romanée and some Grand Cru Echézeaux and Clos de Vougeot. In recent years, the quality of the fruit has blossomed, the better to support the wines' firm structures.

Other top producers include Robert Chevillon (fruity wines from eight Premier Cru vineyards including Les St-Georges, Les Cailles and Vaucrains), Robert Arnoux (full, oaky Les Corvées-Pagets and Les Procès), Domaine de l'Arlot (fine, perfumed Clos de l'Arlot and Clos des Forêts St-Georges), and, from neighboring Vosne-Romanée, Grivot (Les Boudots, Les Pruliers and Les Roncières).

CÔTE DE BEAUNE
The Côte de Beaune begins northwest of the town of Beaune and stretches southwest into the northern Sâone et Loire near the town of Chagny. This is again an excellent source of red wines, although none can match the greatest reds of the Côte de Nuits. However, the outstanding wines here are the whites from the Montrachet vineyards, Meursault and Corton-Charlemagne.

Côte de Beaune Villages
This is a catch-all appellation for red wines coming from 14 villages within the Côte de Beaune. These are either major white-wine producers (Meursault, Puligny-Montrachet, Chassagne-Montrachet) that also make some red wine, or else villages of lesser fame (north of Beaune: Ladoix, Pernand-Vergelesses, Savigny-lès-Beaune and Chorey-lès-Beaune; to the south: Monthelie, Auxey-Duresses, Blagny, St-Aubin, St-Romain, Santenay and Maranges) whose own names, which they can opt to use, are not strong brands. Confusingly, there is also a small appellation (for both colors) called Côte de Beaune, which covers a handful of vineyards rather too high up on the hillside above Beaune to yield top wine.

Ladoix
The Ladoix vineyards are located on the eastern slope of the hill of Corton and indeed almost all the vineyards of merit are classified as Corton, including Rognets and Vergennes, or as Corton-Charlemagne. Some village and Premier Cru vineyards are classified as Ladoix, but these are rarely seen. The best-known growers are Prince de Mérode, Domaines Capitain-Gagnerot, Edmond Cornu, Maldant, Mallard and Nudant.

Pernand-Vergelesses

This village is easy to overlook, being set back in a side valley behind Aloxe-Corton. Yet it has two vineyards of note. The first is the "En Charlemagne" part of the Grand Cru Corton-Charlemagne, which produces one of Burgundy's most thrilling white wines and is located, unusually for the region, on a southwest-facing slope. The outstanding producer in the village is Bonneau du Martray; Dubreuil Fontaine, Marey, Rollin and Rapet also make good wine. The second significant vineyard, the Premier Cru Les Vergelesses, which lies across the valley and faces due east, is the source of the best red wines. Chandon de Briailles makes the best example. Otherwise, the red and white wines of Pernand Vergelesses can be rather angular.

Aloxe-Corton

The village and Premier Cru wines of Aloxe-Corton are a little expensive for their quality—perhaps the Corton suffix is to blame. Aloxe is the headquarters for the *négociants* Louis Latour and La Reine Pedauque as well as Domaines Senard, Voarick and Follin-Arvelet. However, the local jewels are the Grands Crus Corton-Charlemagne (white) and Corton (mostly red), though both are shared with neighboring Pernand-Vergelesses and Ladoix.

Domaine Bonneau du Martray, Maison Louis Latour and Maison Louis Jadot produce the most impressive Corton-Charlemagne in reasonable quantity; smaller quantities from Michel Juillot, Coche-Dury, Tollot-Beaut, Faiveley and Roumier can also be excellent. A great Corton-Charlemagne, best drunk after a decade or more in bottle, will combine a scintillating mineral quality with depth of flavor and Grand Cru richness.

The red Grand Cru, Corton, covers a number of subdivisions and it could be argued that these should either become Grands Crus in their own right or else be demoted. The best of them are Le Corton (Bonneau du Martray and Méo-Camuzet), Corton-Bressandes (Prince de Mérode and Comte Senard) and Corton Clos du Roi (Prince de Mérode and Comte Senard), along with the Corton-Pougets of Maison Louis Jadot, Corton Clos des Cortons of Maison Joseph Faiveley and the Corton Clos de la Vigne au Saint of Maison Louis Latour. A bottle labelled simply Corton, without the "Le," could be from one or more of the subdivisions.

Savigny-lès-Beaune

Savigny is a sound bet for good-quality red burgundy at an affordable price. The wines are attractive when young (especially those from Premier Cru vineyards such as Lavières), yet sturdy enough to age well (particularly Peuillets and Dominodes). The best producers in the village are Domaine Chandon de Briailles, Simon Bize et Fils, Jean-Marc Pavelot, Jean-Jacques and Philippe Girard, and Luc Camus-Brochon. The Savigny Narbantons of Leroy and the Savigny Dominodes of Bruno Clair are also excellent. The small quantity of white Savigny is of less interest.

Chorey-lès-Beaune

This is almost a forgotten village, as most of the vineyards lie on the wrong side of the RN74, on the flat land of the plain. Single-vineyard wines are rarely if ever encountered here. Most of the production is red, and consists of a fruity, Côte-de-Beaune-style burgundy best drunk quite young. The leading growers in the village are Tollot-Beaut, Jacques Germain at the Château de Chorey-lès-Beaune and Arnoux Père et Fils.

Beaune

The capital of winegrowing Burgundy, Beaune is home to most of the major *négociants*, as well as the Hôtel Dieu, headquarters of the Hospices de Beaune. The vineyards themselves are not among the most distinguished of the Côte: there is a fair amount of sand in the soil, especially in the northern part of the appellation, so the grapes tend to mature fairly quickly. The wines are sound, middle-of-the-road examples of red burgundy. There are no Grands Crus but a plethora of Premiers Crus (44 of them), among which Grèves, Fèves, Clos du Roi, Bressandes and Teurons stand out. The four great

The village of Pernand-Vergelesses is tucked into a side valley off the main slope.

Beaune's wine cellars form a labyrinth of tunnels covering around 3 acres (1.2 ha).

A cellar-hand cleans the barrels at Maison Joseph Drouhin in the Côte de Beaune.

négociant houses of Beaune are Bouchard Père et Fils, Joseph Drouhin, Louis Jadot and Louis Latour.

BOUCHARD PÈRE ET FILS
Owner Joseph Henriot *Production* NA *Vineyard area* 230 acres (93 ha)

No Bouchards, neither *père* nor *fils*, have been involved in this company since 1995, when it was purchased by Joseph Henriot of Champagne. He has since restored the quality that was missing in the 1970s and 1980s. Bouchard's best Beaune *cuvée* is Vigne de l'Enfant Jésus; its top whites include Corton-Charlemagne and Chevalier-Montrachet.

MAISON JOSEPH DROUHIN
Owner Drouhin family *Production* NA *Vineyard area* 156 acres (63 ha)

Drouhin wines are fine and perfumed, never the deepest in color nor the weightiest, but long-lived nonetheless. A specialty is their heady, dramatic Beaune Clos des Mouches *blanc*; the red version is also attractive. Other excellent reds include Le Musigny, Griottes-Chambertin, Grands Echézeaux, Chambolle-Musigny Les Amoureuses and Vosne-Romanée Les Petits Monts. In the field of white wines, Drouhin are strong in Chablis and are also responsible for the Marquis de Laguiche wines, including the famous Montrachet.

CAMILLE GIROUD
Owners Bernard and François Giroud *Production* NA *Vineyard area* 1 acre (0.4 ha)

This small *négociant* house was founded in Beaune in 1865 and is currently run by the founder's daughter-in-law(!) and her sons. Deliberately old-

fashioned—it adopts nineteenth-century methods whenever possible—Giroud makes solid, long-lived wines. They may display a toughness that is an acquired taste, but 50-year-old examples can be sublime. Most of the stock is released at maturity, so very old bottles can be found here.

MAISON LOUIS JADOT
Owner Kopf family *Production* NA *Vineyard area* 148 acres (60 ha)

Maison Louis Jadot makes powerful wines including very good Beaune Clos des Ursules, Beaune Grèves and Beaune Boucherottes and Corton-Pougets, plus such Grands Crus from the Côte de Nuits as Chambertin Clos de Bèze and Le Musigny. The estate's white wines are unusual in that the malolactic fermentation is often deliberately blocked. Particularly impressive are their Chevalier-Montrachet Les Demoiselles, Corton-Charlemagne, Chassagne-Montrachet and, at an inexpensive level, Rully.

MAISON LOUIS LATOUR
Owner Louis Latour *Production* NA *Vineyard area* 111 acres (45 ha)

The Maison Latour red wines have an indifferent reputation here and seem a little lacklustre in their youth, although older bottles can be extremely good. However, the white wines at both ends of the price spectrum are much more impressive, ranging from Mâcon Lugny and Montagny up to a powerful Corton-Charlemagne.

Other leading Beaune *négociants* include the oldest, Champy (founded 1720), makers of a fine Beaune Avaux; Chanson, owners of a range of Beaune vineyards; Bouchard Aîné, which is part of the Boisset group; Albert Bichot; Patriarche; and Remoissenet. The best Beaune made by individual growers comes from Albert Morot and François Germain in Chorey-lès-Beaune—both of whom have a good range of vineyards—and Michel Lafarge in Volnay, particularly his Beaune Grèves.

Pommard
Pommard wines fetch the highest prices in the Côte de Beaune after Corton, despite the fact that their relatively high tannin content, which requires substantial aging, makes them unfashionable. They are firm, deep wines that are slow to mature and have little immediate charm.

The best vineyards are Les Rugiens, south of the village, whose stony red soil produces a Pommard with great depth of flavor, and the various

Epenots vineyards to the north: Grands Epenots, Petits Epenots and the Clos des Epeneaux. Here the slope is gentler and the wines finer, if less rich.

DOMAINE DU COMTE ARMAND
Owner **Comte Armand** *Production* **NA** *Vineyard Area* **NA**
Comte Armand is noted for its immensely rich, black, tannic Pommard Clos des Epeneaux, to which it has sole rights and which for a long period was its only wine. Now, it has additional red wines from Auxey-Duresses and Volnay, along with a little white wine. Between 1985 and 1998, the wines were made by the talented Pascal Marchand; his successor, Benjamin Leroux, looks set to maintain or even improve his high standards.

Other leading sources are Domaine de Courcel (Pommard Rugiens and Pommard Grands Epenots), Domaine Coste-Caumartin (Clos des Boucherottes), Domaine Parent (Epenots, Pézerolles) and Jean-Marc Boillot (fine Pommard from Rugiens, Saussilles and Jarolières), who is possibly better known for his range of white wines. Outside the village Michel Lafarge, Marquis d'Angerville and Hubert de Montille in Volnay are also all excellent sources of Premier Cru Pommard.

Volnay

The Côte de Beaune's most elegant wines are produced in Volnay, which is totally different from neighboring Pommard. Comparisons can more easily be drawn with Chambolle-Musigny in the Côte de Nuits: in both cases, the wines lack deep color but are wonderfully perfumed, subtle and complex, and, despite their appeal when young, can age very well. In the best examples, a fine structure is overlaid with the gorgeous, velvety texture of ripe red fruit.

There are no Grands Crus in Volnay, but half a dozen Premiers Crus stand out: Les Caillerets (including the Clos des 60 Ouvrées belonging to Domaine de la Pousse d'Or), Clos des Chênes (outstanding examples come from Michel Lafarge as well as Comtes Lafon), Taillepieds (the best come from Marquis d'Angerville, Hubert de Montille and Carré Courbin), and Champans (especially de Montille and Lafon). The other leading vineyard, Santenots, is in fact over the border in Meursault but is allowed to use the name of Volnay. Here, there is more clay in the soil, producing slightly richer wines—notably those from Lafon and Leroy.

The Grand Cru vineyards of Aloxe-Corton.

Bidders at the Hospices de Beaune auction.

Burning off the dead wood in fall at
Domaine Robert Ampeau, Côte de Beaune.

MICHEL LAFARGE

Owner Michel Lafarge *Production* 4,000 cases *Vineyard Area* 25 acres (10 ha)

Michel Lafarge has now handed over to his son Frédéric, and the wines here continue to be the finest in Volnay—perhaps in the Côte de Beaune. They are not overextracted or overoaked, yet are dark in color and intense in flavor. Lafarge produces Beaune Grèves and Pommard Les Pézérolles, plus a fine range of Volnays, topped by a superb Clos des Chênes, a benchmark for Volnay.

Monthelie

This village sits on the hill above Meursault. The local reds have a slightly harder edge and not quite the same depth of fruit as Volnays. The best examples come from Darviot-Perrin, de Suremain and Garaudet, and from Lafon in Meursault. Les Duresses is the best vineyard.

Auxey-Duresses

"Duresses" (which is derived from Les Duresses in Monthelie) refers to a certain hardness found in both red and white wines of the village. The wines are good value only in warm years. Jean-Pierre Diconne, the Prunier family, various Lafouges and Maison Leroy are all worth investigating.

St-Romain

The vineyards of St-Romain are significantly higher than the rest of the Côte, so ripeness is harder to achieve and the style tends to be lean. There are no Premier or Grand Cru vineyards here; production is divided fairly equally between reds and whites. The leading winegrower is Alain Gras.

Meursault

The largest great white-wine village of the Côte d'Or, Meursault produces over 150,000 cases of full-bodied, round, satisfying wine each year. There may be no Grands Crus, but there are many excellent vineyards and more competent growers than either Puligny- or Chassagne- Montrachet can boast. Mature Meursault (five to ten years old) is buttery and nutty; when younger, it is rounded and weighty—the full bouquet needs time to develop.

Three of Meursault's Premier Cru vineyards stand out. Genevrières has light, stony soil that yields wines with a thrilling, racy, mineral quality, abundant finesse and not too much weight. Try those made by Lafon, François Jobard and Rémi Jobard. Charmes has a soft, rich texture. Look for the same producers plus Ampeau, Roulot and Darviot-Perrin. Perrières combines the best of both the others, but outdoes both. The top producers are Lafon, Coche-Dury, Grivault (for their Clos des Perrières), Morey and Roulot. Other good Premier Cru vineyards are Poruzot and Goutte d'Or.

One of Meursault's great strengths is its village wine: try Tesson (from Bouzereau, Fichet, Roulot and Pierre Morey), Chevalières (Coche-Dury and Fichet), Narvaux (Coche Dury, Javillier and Leroy) and Clos de la Barre (Lafon).

Most Meursault producers have underground cellars where they keep their wine in barrel for two winters (bottling normally occurs after 18 months). These wines often settle during the second winter, and require little (if any) stabilization before bottling; they also seem to gain in richness and longevity. Soem red is produced, mostly for local consumption. Santenots is the red vineyard of real quality—it uses the name Volnay-Santenots.

At the southern end of Meursault lies Blagny. The white wines produced here are designated as Meursault Blagny Premier Cru, a status they generally do not deserve, and the red wines, which are

mostly light and austere and sometimes have a delicious cherry perfume, are called Blagny.

DOMAINE ROBERT AMPEAU
Owner Michel Ampeau *Production* 5,000 cases *Vineyard area* 25 acres (10 ha)

Michel Ampeau does not have much to do with other Meursault producers and it is difficult to compare his wines with theirs, largely because he prefers to release only mature wines. The whites come from Meursault and Puligny-Montrachet, the reds from Volnay, Pommard and Savigny-lès-Beaune. They are not the most elegant wines of their appellations, but are frequently satisfying.

DOMAINE COCHE DURY
Owner Jean-François Coche Dury *Production* 3,500 cases *Vineyard area* 22 acres (9 ha)

Dury makes hyper-elegant, fine and exciting Meursault from Les Perrières (Premier Cru), Les Narvaux, Les Rougeots and other vineyards, in addition to a tiny amount of Grand Cru Corton-Charlemagne. These wines have a near-perfect de-lineation of detail and much more power than the attractive floral bouquet would suggest. Domaine Coche Dury also makes some some increasingly good reds, mostly from lesser appellations.

ARNAUD ENTE
Owner Arnaud Ente *Production* 1,500 cases *Vineyard area* 10 acres (4 ha)

Arnaud Ente is one of the region's most meticulous producers. His small *domaine* makes Meursault, Meursault Goutte d'Or, Puligny-Montrachet Les Referts and Volnay-Santenots, as well as impressive generic wines. All are pure, deep and concentrated, the Meursault including the fruit of ancient vines in the Ormeau vineyard.

DOMAINE DES COMTES LAFON
Owner Lafon family *Production* 5,000 cases *Vineyard area* 33 acres (13 ha)

Lafon produce unsurpassed, rich, long-lived white burgundy from Meursault, Meursault Clos de la Barre, Meursault Goutte d'Or, Meursault Charmes, Meursault Genevrières, Meursault Perrières and Le Montrachet, and very fine, full-bodied yet subtle reds (which have been top-class since 1989) from Monthelie Les Duresses, Volnay Santenots-du-Milieu, Volnay Clos des Chênes and Volnay-Champans. The vineyards are now farmed biodynamically. The family has also just bought a property in the Mâconnais (the first vintage was 1999).

Some of the finest reds in the Côte de Beaune come from the Meursault area.

Other Meursault producers include Roulot, Fichet, Pierre Morey, Boyer-Martenot, Grivault, François Jobard, Rémi Jobard, Michel Bouzereau, Patrick Javillier and Henri Germain.

Puligny-Montrachet
The most famous of the white wine villages is Puligny, which, since the late nineteenth century, has been allowed to append the noble name of Montrachet. The Grand Cru Montrachet vineyard, only 20 acres (8 ha) in size, has been considered the most sublime of Burgundy's white-wine vineyards since the early eighteenth century. The soil is poor and stony, but the critical factor is probably the vineyard's aspect: forming a slight saddle, it is exposed to both east and south, which provides maximum sunlight, and it is also very well drained. To recommend producers is really just to tease, since only the extraordinarily rich can afford a bottle, but the wines of Lafon, Ramonet, Domaine de la Romanée-Conti, Leflaive, Marquis de Laguiche, Baron Thénard and Bouchard Père et Fils, should live up to the vineyard's reputation. Do not be in a hurry to drink a fine vintage—any time in its first 50 years will do.

Just uphill from Le Montrachet is the Grand Cru of Chevalier-Montrachet, where the soil is thinner and the wines not quite so opulent; however, they can still be enormously impressive, particularly those from Domaine Leflaive, Michel Niellon, Louis Jadot and Louis Latour. The last two producers share a special and much sought-after patch known as Les Demoiselles. Just below Le

REGIONAL DOZEN

CÔTE DE BEAUNE (WHITE)
Domaine Carillon Puligny-Montrachet
Coche-Dury Meursault Perrières
Jean-Philippe Fichet Bourgogne Blanc
Alain Gras St-Romain
Maison Louis Jadot Chevalier Montrachet les Demoiselles
Rémi Jobard Meursault Chevalières
Domaine des Comtes Lafon Meursault Perrières
H. & O. Lamy St-Aubin-en-Remilly
Domaine Leflaive Puligny-Montrachet les Pucelles
Bonneau du Martray Corton-Charlemagne
Domaine Ramonet Le Montrachet
Guy Roulot Meursault Le Tesson

Keeping the vineyards clear of leaves and debris is an ongoing task in fall.

Montrachet are the Grands Crus of Bâtard-Montrachet, Bienvenues-Bâtard-Montrachet and Criots-Bâtard-Montrachet. The last-named is in fact entirely in the commune of Chassagne-Montrachet; Le Montrachet and Bâtard-Montrachet are shared between the two villages. The wines of the various Bâtards are a little more approachable than Chevalier-Montrachet, but also slightly less fine. Give them a decade of bottle age before opening.

Most consumers look to Puligny-Montrachet for more affordable Premier Cru and village wines. Puligny has a fine range of the former: Les Caillerets (particularly from Hubert de Montille and Michel Bouzereau), Les Pucelles (especially from Domaine Leflaive), Les Combettes (Leflaive and Sauzet), Les Folatières (Leflaive, Chavy and Pernot) and Les Demoiselles. In these vineyards, the wines combine a marvellous floral perfume and elegance with a steely backbone that promises both concentration and longevity.

The village wines have some flowery elegance but less concentration. The water table is much higher here than in Meursault; this prevents the growers digging out the deep cellars that are ideal for long barrel maturation. Carillon and Jean-Marc Boillot are among the most reliable sources of fine Puligny-Montrachet village wines. Good *négociant* selections are available from Jadot, Drouhin and Leflaive.

DOMAINE CARILLON

Owner Louis Carillon *Production* 5,000 cases *Vineyard Area* 30 acres (12 ha)

The Carillons have been a reliable source of Puligny-Montrachet for several generations (since at least 1632, they claim), but over the last 15 years they have risen to close to the top of the pile thanks to their fine, pure, white wines, which typify the respective vineyard sites—from village Puligny through the Premier Crus Les Combettes, Champs-Canet, Champ-Gain, Perrières and Referts, to the Grand Cru Bienvenues-Bâtard-Montrachet. The wines are delicious to drink quite young, yet hold together well for a decade.

DOMAINE LEFLAIVE

Owner Leflaive family *Production* NA *Vineyard area* NA

Vincent Leflaive and his daughter Anne-Claude have produced great whites—sensual yet refined, concentrated yet appealing—from Le Montrachet, Chevalier-Montrachet, Bâtard-Montrachet, Bienvenues-Bâtard-Montrachet, Puligny-Montrachet Les Pucelles, Puligny-Montrachet Les Combettes, Puligny-Montrachet Folatières, Puligny-Montrachet Clavoillon and Puligny-Montrachet. They are. There was a weak period in the late 1980s and early 1990s. The recent introduction of biodyamic methods has helped the *domaine* return to top form.

St-Aubin

This village is best known for its white wines, which are similar to a lesser Puligny-Montrachet. But the fruity, if sometimes lean, red wines account for more than half the total production. Look out for the Premiers Crus En Remilly, Murgers Dents de Chien, La Chatenière and (for reds) Les Frionnes. Notable growers include Marc Colin, Hubert Lamy, Gérard Thomas and Dominique Derain.

Chassagne-Montrachet

The international fame of Chassagne-Montrachet rests on its white wines and stems from the Grands Crus Le Montrachet, Bâtard-Montrachet and Criots-Bâtard-Montrachet, which lie partly or (in the case of the last) wholly within Chassagne-Montrachet. There is also a handful of top Premiers Crus—Les Caillerets, Les Chaumées, Remilly, Blanchot, Vergers and Chenevottes—which make excellent white wine. Fine white Chassagne-Montrachet has the steely backbone of Puligny-Montrachet and slightly more weight, but lacks the floral character and, often, the elegance.

It is only recently that production of white Chassagne-Montrachet has overtaken that of red. Much pinot noir area has been replanted with chardonnay, even though most of the soil is more suited to red wine production. The problem is that the reds, even when good, do not come close to the best whites. Red Chassagne-Montrachet can be beautifully colored and fruity in cask, but in bottle tannins seem to remove the charm. The best vineyards for reds are Clos St-Jean and Morgeots.

DOMAINE RAMONET

Owner Ramonet family *Production* 7,000 cases *Vineyard area* 42 acres (17 ha)

Now run by the late Pierre Ramonet's grandsons, wines here develop outstanding concentration and complexity with bottle age: whites from Le Montrachet, Bâtard-Montrachet, Bienvenues-Bâtard-Montrachet; Premier Cru Chassagne-Montrachet from Les Ruchottes, Les Caillerets, Les Chaumées and Morgeot; and the red Premiers Crus Morgeot, Clos de la Boudriotte and Clos St-Jean.

Other good Chassagne-Montrachet producers include families with multiple *domaines* (Gagnards, Colins, Moreys, Pillots, Jouards and Coffinets) and some smaller producers, such as Michel Niellon and Guy Amiot-Bonfils.

Santenay

Geologists have identified rock strata in Santenay that are similar to those of the Côte de Nuits, but the red wines, while generally full-bodied, tend toward the rustic. The best vineyards are Les Gravières, La Comme, Clos des Tavannes and Clos Rousseau. White Santenay can be interesting.

VINCENT GIRARDIN

Owner Vincent Girardin *Production* NA *Vineyard area* NA

Having established a reputation for the quality of his red and white wines, mostly in Santenay,

Vincent Girardin has set satisfied growing demand by setting up as a *négociant* as well. The wines, which are generally oaky but still full of fruit, include an impressive Chassagne-Montrachet.

Other Santenay producers include Lucien Muzard et Fils and Claude Maréchal.

Maranges

Three communes—Cheilly, Dezize and Sampigny—share the Premier Cru Maranges, and their former appellations have been grouped together under this name. Most of the wine is red; it can be deep in color and full of fruit but is usually tannic and somewhat rustic. A little white is also made.

CÔTE CHALONNAISE

South of Chagny, the escarpment that provides the great wines of the Côte d'Or peters out and the vineyards become more fragmented. Five villages make up the area called the Côte Chalonnaise, named for the nearest large town, Chalon-sur-Saône. Both red and white wines are produced here, mostly for early consumption. As yet, there are not enough good growers with proper investment be-

In the Côte Chalonnaises, as in most of Burgundy, limestone soils predominate.

Southern Burgundy, where temperatures are generally higher than in the north.

Chardonnay grapes ripening on the vine.

hind them to put this region squarely on the map, and the best wines often come from the *négociants*. Wines produced outside the five villages are sold under the name of Bourgogne Côte Chalonnaise.

Bouzeron

This small village is noted for its aligoté, the lesser and thinner of the Burgundian white grapes, which is, however, attractive in its youth for its firm, tangy character. Having first been allowed to add its name to a label alongside Bourgogne Aligoté, Bouzeron now has its own appellation, but only for this grape. Aubert de Vilaine is the best producer.

Rully

The first major village south of Chagny is Rully, where red and white wines are produced in equal quantities along with some sparkling wine. The white wines are light and fruity but generally do not age well beyond two or three years. The red wines are also no more than medium-bodied and rely on fruit rather than structure; yet they can be extremely pleasing. Good addresses for Rully include the Château de Rully, Jacqueson, and *négociants* such as Olivier Leflaive and Louis Jadot.

Mercurey

The best and most ageworthy red wines of the Côte Chalonnaise are to be found in Mercurey, though they need a soft hand during vinification to produce sufficient fruit without too much tannin. Two *négociants* have major holdings in Mercurey: Faiveley, which produces several high-quality *cuvées* such as La Croix Jacquelet and La

The vineyards of the plains tend to yield less impressive wines than those on the slopes.

Framboisière; and Rodet, which makes and distributes the Mercurey wines of the Château de Chamirey. Among the growers, various members of the Juillot family have impressed, but they could do with more rivals. White Mercurey accounts for just 10 percent of production but should not be ignored. The white wines can be quite full-bodied, with an attractive hint of licorice.

Givry

This was favorite wine of King Henri IV of France, doubtless because his mistress came from Givry. The reds usually have good fruit backed by a reasonably tannic structure and can age for three to five years. The best vineyards are Clos Jus, Clos de la Servoisine and Clos Salomon. The best producers are Joblot, François Lumpp, Vincent Lumpp, Ragot, Mouton, Sarrazin and Chofflet-Valdenaire. A small amount of attractive white wine is made.

Montagny

Only white wines are produced in Montagny. They can be brisk and steely rather than soft and round, and should usually be drunk young. Louis Latour's Montagny is extremely reliable, and Stephane Aladame is clearly a rising star. In addition, the de Buxy cooperative has long been a fine source, along with Domaines Michel, Roy and Vachet.

MÂCONNAIS

The limestone hills west of the city of Mâcon are given over to arable and livestock farming, but the most suitable slopes are reserved for vineyards. Most of the production is white and inexpensive, save for fashionable Pouilly-Fuissé, and made from chardonnay. Red Mâcon and Mâcon Supérieur, both of which may be followed on labels by the name of the village of production, are made from the gamay grape, which has infiltrated from Beaujolais, while wines made from pinot noir are labeled Bourgogne Rouge.

Mâcon Villages

The vast majority of white Mâcon wines—over two million cases per year—are labeled Mâcon Villages. Producers also have the option of using the name of whichever of the 41 specified villages their wine comes from. Those most commonly seen are Mâcon Lugny (from the cooperative and Louis Latour), La Roche Vineuse (Merlin), Chaintré (Valette), Chardonnay and Prissé.

Most Mâcon Villages is made from high yields, vinified in stainless steel and bottled early, provid-

ing inexpensive but unremarkable chardonnay that struggles to compete in the international market. However, a group of growers led by Jean Thévenet and Olivier Merlin has shown that the soils of the best villages can produce fine white burgundy if yields are restricted and skillful barrel fermentation and maturation are applied. Such wines can age for up to ten years, whereas normal Mâcon Villages should be drunk in the first year or two.

OLIVIER MERLIN

Established 1987 *Owner* Olivier Merlin *Production* NA
Vineyard area NA

Olivier Merlin, based in La Roche Vineuse, has established a reputation as one of the most serious producers of high-quality, barrel-aged Mâcon. In order to make some Pouilly-Fuissé, the top appellation in this area, he took out a *négociant* licence in 1997 which allows him to buy in grapes. The wines are gently oaky after up to 18 months in barrel, yet always showing refinement and balanced acidity. His principal wine is an excellent Mâcon La Roche Vineuse Vielles Vignes.

MAISON VERGET

Owner Jean-Marie Guffens Heynen *Production* NA
Vineyard area NA

Jean-Marie Guffens Heynen has a tiny *domaine* of his own in the Mâconnais but most of his production is through his *négociant* business, Maison Verget, based in Sologny. His ego does not distract him from making excellent wines, though it may diminish the appreciation of his efforts by others. Prices are generally high, though the wines vary from very good and inexpensive Mâcon through concentrated, expensive Chablis Grand Cru to the top appellations of the Côte d'Or, painstakingly sourced from the best growers. Some seem to suffer from too much oak.

Viré-Clessé

The adjacent villages of Viré and Clessé used to be part of Mâcon Villages, but as of the 1998 vintage were promoted to appellation status. Both have long been known for making some of the richest and most appealing of Mâcon wines, especially those from the excellent cooperative and such growers as Bonhomme and Thévenet.

JEAN THÉVENET

Owner Jean Thévenet *Production* NA *Vineyard area* NA

Clessé-based Thévenet's specialty is late-picked wines, sometimes botrytis affected, as in the Cuvée

The Mâconnais produces mainly white wines.

Levroutée. The residual sugar in his wines is deliberate rather than accidental, and should not be seen as an underhand way of ensuring mass appreciation of his very limited stock of wines. Not everybody approves locally and the rules for the new appellation of Viré-Clessé forbid residual sugar.

St-Véran

This appellation was only created in 1973, taking in vineyards on both sides of Pouilly-Fuissé. Those to the north are mostly on classical Burgundian limestone soils. Those to the south are on red, sandy, granitic soils more typical of Beaujolais and much less suited to chardonnay—so choose carefully. Domaine des Deux Roches and Domaine Corsin are excellent sources.

Pouilly-Fuissé

This is the top appellation in the Mâconnais. It covers the communes of Chaintré, Vergisson and Solutré as well as the two villages that make up its name. The wines are generally rich, full-bodied, heady and powerful, especially those from the south-facing vineyards of Chaintré or the sun-trap of Fuissé. Those from Vergisson ripen less easily, as the vineyards are less well exposed, but this can provide balance in a hot year.

Wines (and prices) vary enormously from some fairly ordinary cooperative *cuvées* to the best selections of leading growers such as Château de Fuissé, Michel Forest, Robert Denogent, Gérard Valette and Madame Ferret. The two satellite appellations of Pouilly-Loché and Pouilly-Vinzelles are of lesser quality and importance, together producing no more than 50,000 cases of wine a year.

REGIONAL DOZEN

CÔTE CHALONNAISE & MÂCONNAIS

Stéphane Aladame Montagny Les Coères
Cave de Buxy Montagny
Château de Chamirey Mercurey (red and white)
Michel Forest Pouilly-Fuissé Les Crays
Château de Fuissé Pouilly-Fuissé Vieilles Vignes
Domaine Guffens-Heynen Pouilly-Fuissé Les Petits Croux
Maison Louis Jadot Rully Blanc
Domaine Joblot Givry Clos de la Servoisine (red)
Michel Juillot Mercurey Clos des Barraults (red)
Mâcon la Roche Vineuse vieilles vignes
Gérard Valette Pouilly-Fuissé le Clos de Mr Noly Vieilles Vignes
Maison Verget Mâcon Villages Tête de Cuvée

Jura, Savoie & Bugey

Wink Lorch

Many Jura reds are suitable for long aging.

Located on the eastern fringes of France, in the foothills of the Alps, the wine regions of Jura, Savoie and Bugey are somewhat out on a limb. Yet their isolation is at least in part responsible for the distinctive and intriguing nature of their wines.

JURA

The vineyards of Jura, for example, produce one of France's most curious, sought-after wines, the sherry-like *vin jaune* ("yellow wine"), as well as luscious, sweet *vin de paille* ("straw-wine"), and dry whites, reds and sparkling wines from both burgundian and rare, indigenous grape varieties. Today, the industry centers on the town of Arbois, once home to Louis Pasteur, widely acknowledged as the "father" of the modern wine industry for his work on fermentation. Revived interest in preserving local winemaking traditions has led to a recent, steady increase in the vineyard area to 4,570 acres (1,850 ha), which currently produce around 2.64 million gallons (10 million l). However, this is less than one-tenth of the size of the vineyard before phylloxera struck in the late nineteenth century.

Jura is both the name of the department and of the mountain range that straddles France and Switzerland. It is also the derivation of the term "Jurassic", and both Jurassic and Triassic limestone form the basis of the local geology. The landscape is both dramatic and gentle, with curiously shaped mountains, walls and ridges rising up from rolling hillsides. Vineyards are sited, sometimes quite steeply, on the southern and southwestern slopes, at altitudes similar to those in Burgundy—between 650 and 1,300 feet (200 and 400 m). The soils are characterized by pebbled marl with some calcareous deposits (notably tiny, star-shaped fossils in the aptly named L'Étoile appellation). With a continental climate bringing warm summers and cold winters, there is some risk of frosts hitting older and more sensitive vines, both in winter and spring.

The winegrowing region, a northeast–southwest strip of vineyards, lies 50 miles (80 km) east of, and runs almost parallel to, Burgundy's Côte d'Or. The two largest appellations are the Côtes du Jura, which covers almost the whole strip, and, in the north, Arbois, with its subappellation Arbois-Pupillin. Côtes du Jura and Arbois may be produced as white, rosé, or red wines, as well as *vin jaune* and *vin de paille*. To the south, the tiny L'Étoile appellation (198 acres [80 ha]) can be used for white wine only, including *vin jaune* or *vin de paille*; the even smaller, more famous Château-Chalon appellation (124 acres [50 ha]) can only be used for *vin jaune*. Increasing quantities of *méthode traditionelle* sparkling wines are made and given the appellation Crémant du Jura. There is also an appellation called Macvin du Jura for a liqueur made from local marc mixed with unfermented grape juice.

Vines and wines

Links with Burgundy resulted in chardonnay and pinot noir reaching Jura several centuries ago. Both continue to be important, with chardonnay taking up 45 percent of the vineyard area. The white savagnin grape, a local specialty, is most famous for *vin jaune*, but is used in other whites too. It has a quite different character from its distant relative, traminer: it lacks that grape's typical aromatic notes and although it displays hazelnut and almond flavors, it shows greater acidic bite. The thin-skinned, early-ripening, indigenous poulsard is the most widely planted red grape (making up 25 percent of the total), followed by pinot noir and the rare local variety, trousseau, which is planted mainly in Arbois.

Traditionally, Jura red wines were blends, but today many are single varietals. Poulsard is vinified warm, undergoes several days skin maceration and is matured as a red wine, yet is sometimes marketed as rosé due to its very pale color. Combined with

Outside of the growing season, Jura producers must protect vines against frost.

the right dish (such as the local smoked Morteau sausage), it can be surprisingly good. Typically, reds are stored for a year or two in old wooden barrels or vats. Pinot noir may spend some time in newer oak, but this is rare and generally there is a certain rusticity to Jura Pinot. Trousseau provides the most interesting red, displaying structure and almost animal flavors combined with dark red fruits. For all red wines, producers recommend aging for several years, and only market the wines when two or three years old.

Most Jura winemakers eschew the modern, fresh, fruity style of dry whites, preferring to make wines that have the slightly oxidized or nutty flavors associated with aging in old wood. Some barrels are deliberately not topped up, allowing oxidation to occur. Wines are usually varietal chardonnays or savagnins, or a blend. The savagnins can be highly acidic, but those from older vines show better balance and concentration. Like the reds, whites are sold with at least two years' cellar aging. Crémant du Jura is usually made with chardonnay and is similar to a delicate Crémant de Bourgogne, the best being creamy and fruity with well-integrated bubbles.

Vin de paille may be made from any of the five varieties but is usually chardonnay with savagnin and some red poulsard. How much of the last is in the blend determines how much pink there is in the otherwise amber-colored wine. The grapes are harvested early in September, at the start of the harvest, and must be free of rot. The bunches are then laid in boxes or suspended from rafters to dry, until January. Once pressed and fermented, the wine is transferred to old barrels for two to three years. The result is a wine of at least 15 percent alcohol with high acid and high residual sugar levels. Good examples rate among the finest sweet wines, and are a great match for foie gras or desserts.

Vin jaune is the apogee of Jura winemaking, with Château-Chalon the best-known example. Savagnin is a late ripener and when used for *vin jaune* is left on the vine as late as possible. After fermentation, the wine is put into old wooden barrels, which are not completely filled. It must then stay in barrel for a minimum of six years and three months without topping up or racking. A film of yeast called a *voile* or veil, similar to a sherry's *flor*, develops and protects the wine from the worst of oxidation. After the prescribed time, the *vin jaune* is clarified and bottled in a special 62-cl (22-ounce) bottle called a *clavelin*. This is the only nonstandard size permitted in the EU, and is said to represent the amount remaining from one liter of wine

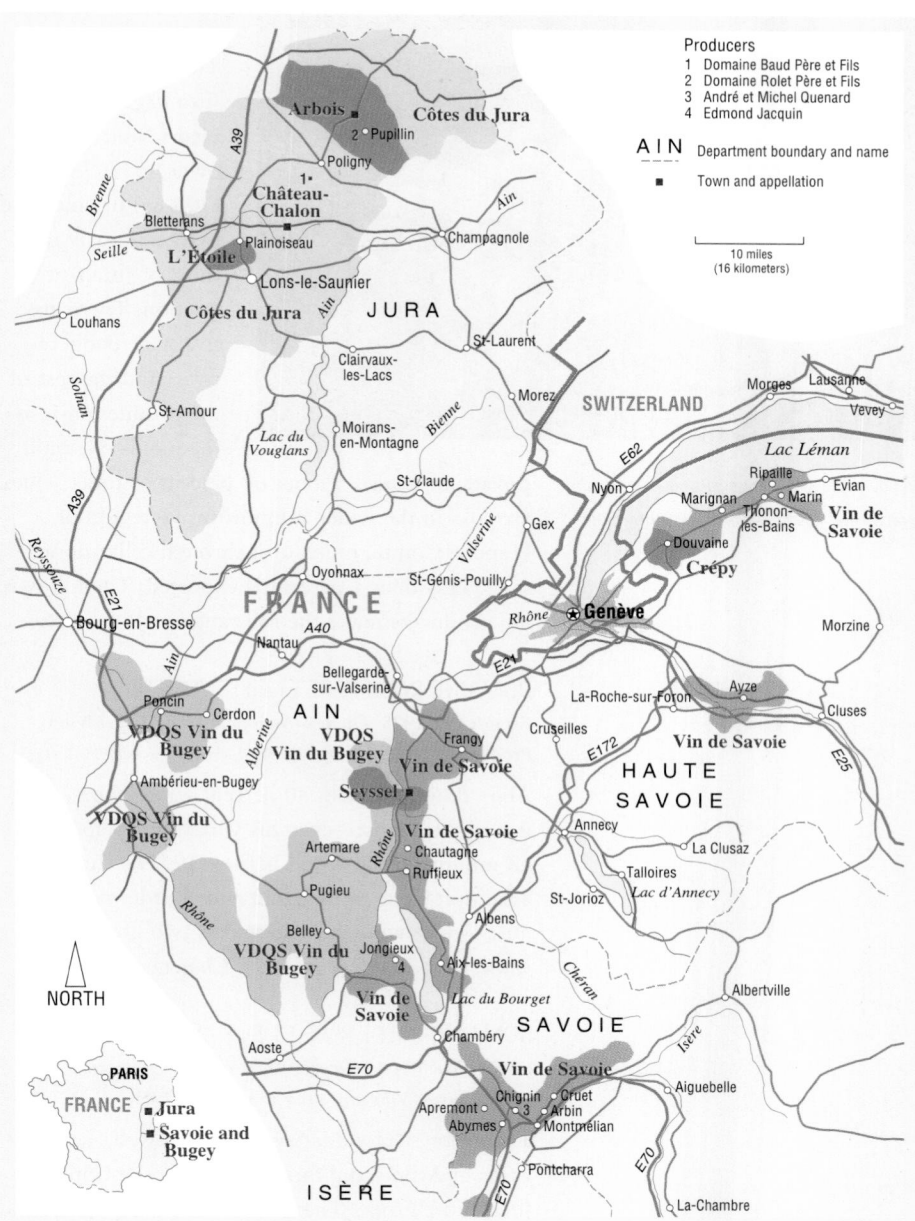

following the evaporation that takes place during the specified aging period. The wine is distinctly yellow, dry, and concentrated, with flavors of spice and nuts and sometimes even a cheesy or fungal character—it can resemble old dry sherry, though being unfortified is usually only about 14 percent alcohol. *Vin jaune* ages well for decades and stays in perfect condition for several weeks once opened. It should be served just above cellar temperature.

Such wines demand food and Jura has a strong gastronomic tradition that has been integral to the success of its wines. Comté, the region's best-known cheese is similar to Switzerland's Gruyère, with a strong, nutty flavor that is a perfect match for *vin jaune*. The Bresse area, just to the south, produces France's best chickens; Bresse chicken in a cream and *vin jaune* sauce with morels is a local specialty.

Vin de paille, *a Jura specialty, is made from grapes that have been dried on straw mats.*

Producers

The largest of the Jura *négociants* is Henri Maire, who owns about 740 acres (300 ha) of vines and markets nearly one-third of Jura's production. There are five wine cooperatives, and the rest of the production is in the hands of small, private *domaines*. About 60 percent of Jura's wines are sold in the wider, administrative region of Franche-Comté, much of it through cellar-door sales. Less than 5 percent is exported. The following producers make the full range of Jura wines:

DOMAINE BAUD PÈRE ET FILS, VOITEUR
Established 1978 *Owners* Alain and Jean-Michel Baud *Production* 8,000 cases *Vineyard area* 40 acres (16 ha)

Alain Baud produces 80 percent white wines. He is a traditionalist—even his Chardonnay spends 18 months in old wood before sale. His Cuvée Tradition blend of savagnin and chardonnay is a nutty white wine; he also makes two great *vins jaunes*: a Côtes du Jura and a Château-Chalon.

DOMAINE ROLET PÈRE ET FILS, ARBOIS
Established 1940s *Owners* Rolet family *Production* 30,000 cases *Vineyard area* 153 acres (62 ha)

The region's second-largest producer, Rolet has vineyards in Arbois and farther south in the Côtes du Jura and L'Étoile. The trousseau variety now provides its most successful red, the Arbois Trousseau, notable for its powerful structure. The whites are of a traditional style, and the *vin jaune* is exemplary.

SAVOIE AND BUGEY

Savoie wines are inextricably linked with images of snow-capped mountains and wooden chalets. Yet the region's vineyards, on south-facing slopes, are in fact confined to altitudes where snow is rare. Indeed, some enjoy an almost Mediterranean climate—peach and almond trees thrive in the area. The lower Alpine pastures also abound with herbs, which are used in the wine-based dry French vermouth made in and named Chambéry.

The increase in ski and summer tourism in Savoie after the Second World War revived the fortunes of the local vineyards. Around 5,000 acres (2,000 ha) are now planted, producing around 3.4 million gallons (13 million l) each year. Only about 10 percent is sold outside the area.

Bugey, whose vineyards lie west of the River Rhône in the Ain department, is less influenced by Alpine weather. With no large cities or tourist industry, it has had a harder time establishing a market for its wines. It currently produces about 530,000 gallons (2 million l) from 1,235 acres (500 ha).

Appellations and wines

Savoie's wine zones are scattered across a large area from just outside Geneva, Switzerland, southward almost toGrenoble. Most lie within the departments of Savoie and Haute Savoie, with a few in nearby Ain and Isère. The soils vary, but a high percentage are of glacial origin and alluvial deposits are common. The mesoclimates are also varied; growers plant according to the *terroir*.

Savoie is planted with 80 percent white grapes, the most important of which is jacquère. Other white varieties grown are altesse (also called roussette, believed to originate from Cyprus), chasselas, chardonnay (also widespread in Bugey), roussanne (here called bergeron), gringet (related to Jura's savagnin) and molette. The reds are gamay, pinot noir and the exciting local variety, mondeuse.

The main Vin de Savoie appellation is given to white, red or rosé wines from the whole area; the label may include one of 17 designated *crus* and, sometimes, the grape variety. The Roussette de Savoie appellation is for white wines made from altesse. Two other appellations exist for Crépy, a small area near Lake Geneva planted exclusively with chasselas, and Seyssel, by the River Rhône, which makes still and sparkling white wines. Vin du Bugey is VDQS (again, certain *crus* may add their names to the label).

The vineyard areas and major *crus* of Savoie are as follows, starting in the north:

The crus of Ripaille, Marin and Marignan and the Crépy appellation are near Lake Geneva. Chasselas is grown exclusively.

Ayze is a tiny *cru* in the Arve valley. Gringet is the main variety here for sparkling and still wines.

Frangy, an isolated *cru* northwest of Annecy, makes wines from the altesse grape and uses the Roussette de Savoie appellation.

Seyssel appellation vineyards, located on the banks of the Rhône, grow altesse and molette for both sparkling and still wines.

Chautagne is a large *cru* located north of Aix-les-Bains and Lake Bourget. It is best known for gamay, but also produces other whites and reds.

Jongieux, a village and *cru* between Lake Bourget and the Rhône, is famed for altesse, particularly from the tiny Marestel *cru*. The area also produces reds from all three varieties.

Apremont and Abymes, *crus* close to Chambéry, form the largest area. Both grow jacquère on stony hillsides near the foot of Mont Granier.

The Combe de Savoie is the second-largest area. The vineyards, planted with jacquère, altesse and mondeuse, include the *crus* of Chignin, Montmélian, Arbin and Cruet. Chignin also grows roussanne for Chignin Bergeron. The Combe de Savoie is a center of vine propagation and grafting.

Jacquère whites are fresh, with a flowery fruitiness, and should be drunk young. The chasselas rarely have the power of Swiss chasselas, but do have some of the same dry, stony character and will develop for two or three years. Chignin Bergeron can be delicious, with its residual sugar and rich apricot or peachy fruit balanced by firm acidity; it ages well. The best Savoie white is altesse, sold as Roussette de Savoie. With a similar structure to chardonnay, it is made in various styles: with residual sugar, old-oak aging, or dry and fresh with a nutty, fruity character. A couple of producers vinify in oak; the best such wines age very well. In Bugey, chardonnay is the most successful white; some is light and fresh, some is vinified in oak.

Most Savoie reds are simple and fruity, particularly those from gamay and pinot noir; the best come from Chautagne and Jongieux. Mondeuse provides more interesting reds, and some producers are now recognizing the value of older vines and lower yields, as well as longer skin maceration and oak maturation. Mondeuse has an earthy flavor, allied with blackberry and blueberry, and a spicy touch not unlike syrah, even when unoaked. Most is best drunk within two to three years of harvest; the more structured can cope with five to ten years aging. Vin du Bugey reds—generally made from gamay, pinot noir or mondeuse—are light, early-drinking fare.

Sparkling wines have long been made in Savoie, especially in Seyssel. Outside Seyssel, chardonnay and/or jacquère are the main varieties and the wines are usually made using the *méthode traditionnelle*. In the *cru* of Ayze, gringet provides a more aromatic sparkling wine. Bugey sparklers include *méthode traditionnelle* wines made from chardonnay and labelled Bugey Brut, and some good rosés made from gamay and poulsard grown in the Cerdon area. Some Cerdon sparklers are made in a semisweet style, using the *méthode ancestrale*.

Producers

Savoie and Bugey have several *négociants*, some good cooperatives and a number of *domaines* that produce and bottle their own wine. The following have good ranges from different grapes.

EDMOND JACQUIN ET FILS, JONGIEUX

Established NA *Owners* Jacquin family *Production* NA
Vineyard area 47 acres (19 ha)

Both Jacquin sons have studied enology and are totally committed to the family estate. Roussette is a specialty, and their Marestel is a concentrated, fruity style balanced by lively acidity.

ANDRÉ & MICHEL QUENARD, CHIGNIN

Established 1960s *Owners* André and Michel Quenard
Production 12,000 cases *Vineyard area* 49 acres (20 ha)

André and son Michel are consistently good producers of Chignin Bergero. They also make reds from mondeuse, which generally require a couple of years in bottle to soften the tannins.

Savoie's growers plant mainly white varieties, with jacquère being the most significant.

Alsace

Roger Voss

When you sample Alsatian wines, you feel as though you are getting a snapshot of central European history in a glass. There is the Germanic bottle, tall and fluted. There are the Germanic grape varieties: riesling, gewürztraminer and sylvaner. And there are the German surnames: Hugel, Dopff, Humbrecht. Yet, the addresses on the labels are French. The language is French. And so is the style of the wine.

This is a reflection of Alsace's status as a long-disputed territory, caught in a perpetual tug-of-war between Germany and France. Four times in the past 140 years the region has changed hands, and although it has been resolutely French since the Second World War, from a winemaking point of view the stylistic conundrum remains. This is the only part of France that is permitted to plant riesling, for example, even though it is obvious that this is a great grape variety that could prosper in many other French wine regions.

Partly as a result of its Germanic heritage and partly because of its climate, Alsace is predominantly a white-wine region. It is, in fact, the most important white-wine region in France, with an astonishing 32,000 acres (13,000 ha) of vines and an average annual production of approximately 143 million bottles. That should place it at least as high in the white-wine stakes as Burgundy or Sancerre (and many wine conoisseurs would argue that Alsatian wines are better and more interesting than either of these popular styles). Yet, Alsace is curiously neglected, even by the French,

Delightful timbered houses line the Lauch River in the winemaking center of Colmar.

and, probably as result of the stylistic confusion, nobody is quite sure how to rank the wines.

There are two essential things to remember about Alsace. The first is that the vast majority of its wines are dry. They may have Germanic grape names, but the sugar in the wonderfully ripe Alsatian grapes is all converted into alcohol. That means that some of the wines—gewürztraminer and the tokay pinot gris for example—are relatively high in alcohol, at around 13.5 or 14 percent. Only the superripe Vendange Tardive and Sélection des Grains Nobles (SNG) wines (see below) are likely to be sweet, and even then the sweetness often takes third place to the weight and richness of the wine.

The second thing to remember is that Alsatian wines are labelled varietally. Appellation laws stipulate that they must be 100 per cent of one variety (the only exceptions being miscellaneous blends called Edelzwickers and wines labelled Klevener which are blends of pinot blanc and pinot auxerrois). In this respect, Alsace is both being consumer-friendly in a wine world dominated by varietal wines, and flying in the face of every other French wine appellation, where varietal labelling is frowned upon, if not banned.

Landscape and climate

Alsace's situation makes it perfect for grape growing. Facing east and south across the Rhine toward Germany, the vineyards lie on the leeward side of the Vosges Mountains. This lofty range, which runs from north to south and reaches its highest point of 4,272 feet (1,424 m) at Grand Ballon, shields Alsace from the Atlantic weather systems that spread eastward across France. Consequently, Alsace's rainfall is among the lowest in the country, ranging from 58.5–78 inches (1,500–2,000 mm) a year on the western side of the mountains to just 25.4 inches (650 mm) on the eastern side where the vineyards are located. Rainclouds can be seen over the Vosges at almost any time, but rarely over the Alsatian vines.

The best vineyards are located on the mountainsides, either on the flanks of the steep valleys that run deep into the range or on the gentler slopes that face outward onto the flat, alluvial plain that extends toward the Rhine. The higher vineyards are composed of volcanic and schist soils and produce some of the most complex wines with higher acidity when young. The sandstone soils on the lower slopes make fuller wines that can be long-lasting. A number of vineyards are now planted on the rich soils of the plain, but these rarely produce anything other than simple, fruity wines.

Alsatian producers have long recognized that certain vineyards have especially fine sites, and in 1983 some of these were formally classified as Grand Crus. This occurred despite considerable local opposition, not surprisingly from growers who did not own vines in the favored vineyards.

The Alsatian wine country is a picture-book landscape and traveling the region's wine route, which runs in a straight line from north to south with detours into several of the the side-valleys, is an enchanting experience. Half-timbered medieval houses cluster at the base of the hills, and are surrounded by vines that climb up the slopes and tumble down to the plains. Above the vines, the heavily wooded slopes of the lower Vosges stretch up toward towering peaks.

Alsace's winegrowing areas are located in two departments: to the north, the Bas-Rhin ("Low Rhine"—but "lower" only in that it is farther down the Rhine), and, to the south, the Haut-Rhin ("High Rhine"). The latter, where the mountains are higher and therefore afford greater protection from the worst of the weather, has the finest vineyards and most picturesque villages. To walk the narrow streets of Riquewihr, Ribeauvillé, Bergheim or Eguisheim is to experience the quaintness and charm of the medieval world without any of its squalor. Even Colmar, the department's principal town, has retained its picturesque historic quarters, including a cluster of charming canals called La Petite Venise (Little Venice).

As you travel through these towns, you'll notice that their names, architecture and institutions all reflect the contrasting influences of French and German culture. This cultural mix is also evident in the region's gastronomy. The local cuisine, with its emphasis on sausage, foie gras, rich stews and *choucroute* (the equivalent of German sauerkraut, though less acidic) is a blend of German heartiness and French refinement.

Vines and wines

Alsatian grape varieties are divided into two categories: the noble varieties—gewürztraminer, riesling, tokay pinot gris and muscat—and the lesser varieties. Apart from pinot noir, all are white.

Gewürztraminer has brought more fame to the region than any other grape variety. In Alsace, the wine has high alcohol and a distinctive, spicy, full, oily taste. Sometimes it also has a bitter finish, and there is a dryness in even the sweetest examples. Because it ripens easily, gewürztraminer is the grape most frequently used in late-picked Vendange Tardive and Sélection des Grains Nobles wines. Although Alsatian gewürztraminers are not the kind of wines that you would drink in large quantities, they are excellent with many of the rich local dishes such as *choucroute*, spicy sausages and Munster cheese.

By common consent, riesling provides the finest wine in Alsace and epitomizes the clear differences between Alsatian and German wine-making. In Alsace, it makes a wine that has medium alcohol and is bone dry, with a flinty, steely taste; it is usually very fresh and frequently acidic when young, but softens with age, developing into a superb wine with a minerally taste. During outstanding vintages, riesling is used to make sweeter wines which, however, still retain a certain dryness and firmness that no German winemaker would ever seek to achieve.

Above: *Partly because Alsace wines suit the local cuisine so well, winemakers regularly hold tastings in restaurants.*

Top: *The Bourse aux Vins (Wine Exchange), a trading center in Colmar, was built in 1609.*

Producers
1 Jean-Baptiste Adam
2 Domaine Allimant-Laugner
3 Léon Beyer
4 Domaine Paul Blanck
5 Domaine Léon Boesch
6 Domaine Albert Boxler
7 Domaine Marcel Deiss
8 Domaine Jean-Pierre Dirler
9 Dopff au Moulin
10 Dopff et Irion
11 Domaine Hering
12 Hugel et Fils
13 Roger Jung et Fils
14 Kuentz-Bas
15 Domaine Seppi Landmann
16 Domaine des Marroniers
17 Domaine Meyer-Fonné
18 Domaine René Muré
19 Domaine Gérard Neumeyer
20 Domaine Ostertag
21 Cave Vinicole de Pfaffenheim et Gueberschwihr
22 Domaines Schlumberger
23 Domaine Jean Sipp
24 Domaine Bruno Sorg
25 Pierre Sparr et Ses Fils
26 Maison Trimbach
27 Cave Vinicole de Turckheim
28 Domaine Weinbach
29 Domaine Zind-Humbrecht

Tokay pinot gris, also known as tokay d'Alsace, is no relation to the Tokay or Tokaji wine of Hungary (which is made with a different grape variety, furmint), but is related to Austria's grauer burgunder, Hungary's szürkebarát and Italy's pinot grigio. The name Tokay, although formally banned outside Hungary by the EU, is still widely used in Alsace—in fact, most producers refer to the local wine as tokay pinot gris. Many Alsatians would choose this as their favorite style of wine: it is full, rich, soft and well-balanced, with high acidity, a touch of pepper, moderately high alcohol and an ability to age over a long period. It is often drunk with foie gras, which it complements perfectly.

In Alsace, muscat makes a wine that is dry, yet with a honeyed tone. A perfect combination of sweetness and lightness, it is absolutely delicious as an aperitif wine. Unfortunately, there is very little of this variety in Alsace, mainly because it is difficult to grow so far north and growers are therefore reluctant to devote valuable space to it. Two types are used: muscat blanc à petits grains, or muscat d'Alsace, and muscat ottonel. The latter is easier to grow, but the former produces finer wine.

Among the other grape varieties grown in Alsace, pinot blanc, which is also known locally as klevner or clevner, produces some of the region's most drinkable wines. These are relatively low in alcohol, fresh-tasting and soft, and have a pleasing touch of acidity and not too pronounced a character. Two forms of pinot blanc are grown in Alsace: pinot blanc itself and pinot auxerrois. The two are normally blended and sold under the name Pinot Blanc (or Klevner), or further blended with other varieties and sold as Edelzwicker or simply under a brand name.

Sylvaner is widely planted in Alsace and produces a neutral, reliable wine that is good for quaffing and is often used as a component in Edelzwicker blends. Plantings are, however, decreasing as producers turn increasingly to noble varieties. Chasselas was also once widely planted, but is now down to about 3.5 percent of the vineyard and usually appears only in blends. When tasted by itself, it has a smoky, herby taste and a soft, low-acid, fruit flavor.

In Alsace, red and rosé wines are all made from pinot noir. Until recently—within the last dozen years or so—the reds displayed little color, and their aromas and flavors were equally pale and uninteresting. With the arrival of modern techniques, however, greater color and tannin extraction have become possible and some respectable reds are now being made (although some suffer from too much wood aging).

In Alsace, the harvest usually lasts from mid-September until mid-November.

The Trois Châteaux d'Eguisheim crown the hill above Husseren-les-Châteaux.

ALSACE GRANDS CRUS

The first list of 25 Grand Cru vineyards was created in 1983, and producers were allowed to add the term "Grand Cru" to the vineyard names from the 1985 vintage onward. At that point, production of Alsace Grand Cru became 15 percent of total Alsace production. A second list of another 25 vineyards was created in December 1992.

The following lists give the name of the Grand Cru followed by the commune and department, and the size of the vineyard.

THE 1983 CLASSIFICATION

Altenberg de Bergbieten, Bergbieten, Bas-Rhin	72 acres (29 ha)
Altenberg de Bergheim, Bergheim, Haut-Rhin	87 acres (35 ha)
Brand, Turckheim, Haut-Rhin	141 acres (57 ha)
Eichberg, Eguisheim, Haut-Rhin	143 acres (58 ha)
Geisberg, Ribeauvillé, Haut-Rhin	21 acres (8.5 ha)
Gloeckelberg, Rodern and St-Hippolyte, Haut-Rhin	57 acres (23 ha)
Goldert, Gueberschwihr, Haut-Rhin	111 acres (45 ha)
Hatschbourg, Hattstatt and Voegtlinshoffen, Haut-Rhin	116 acres (47 ha)
Hengst, Wintzenheim, Haut-Rhin	188 acres (76 ha)
Kanzlerberg, Bergheim, Haut-Rhin	7.4 acres (3 ha)
Kastelberg, Andlau, Bas-Rhin	15 acres (6 ha)
Kessler, Guebwiller, Haut-Rhin	69 acres (28 ha)
Kirchberg de Barr, Barr, Bas-Rhin	99 acres (40 ha)
Kirchberg de Ribeauvillé, Ribeauvillé, Haut-Rhin	27 acres (11 ha)
Kitterlé, Guebwiller, Haut-Rhin	64 acres (26 ha)
Moenchberg, Andlau and Eichhoffen, Bas-Rhin	30 acres (12 ha)
Ollwiller, Wuenheim, Haut-Rhin	89 acres (36 ha)
Rangen, Thann and Vieux Thann, Haut-Rhin	47 acres (19 ha)
Rosacker, Hunawihr, Haut-Rhin	64 acres (26 ha)
Saering, Guebwiller, Haut-Rhin	67 acres (27 ha)
Schlossberg, Kaysersberg and Kientzheim, Haut-Rhin	198 acres (80 ha)
Sommerberg, Niedermorschwihr and Katzenthal, Haut-Rhin	69 acres (28 ha)
Sonnenglanz, Beblenheim, Haut-Rhin	82 acres (33 ha)
Spiegel, Bergholtz and Guebwiller, Haut-Rhin	45 acres (18 ha)
Wiebelsberg, Andlau, Bas-Rhin	30 acres (12 ha)

THE 1993 CLASSIFICATION

Altenberg de Wolxheim, Wolxheim, Bas-Rhin	69 acres (28 ha)
Bruderthal, Molsheim, Bas-Rhin	47 acres (19 ha)
Engelberg, Dahlenheim, Bas-Rhin	27 acres (11 ha)
Florimont, Ingersheim, Haut-Rhin	37 acres (15 ha)
Frankstein, Dambach-la-Ville, Bas-Rhin	131 acres (53 ha)
Froehn, Zellenberg, Haut-Rhin	32 acres (13 ha)
Furstentum, Kientzheim and Sigolsheim, Haut-Rhin	69 acres (28 ha)
Kaefferkopf, Ammerschwihr, Haut-Rhin	148 acres (60 ha)
Mambourg, Sigolsheim, Haut-Rhin	161 acres (65 ha)
Mandelberg, Mittelwihr, Haut-Rhin	30 acres (12 ha)
Markrain, Bennwihr, Haut-Rhin	111 acres (45 ha)
Muenchberg, Nothalten, Bas-Rhin	45 acres (18 ha)
Osterberg, Ribeauvillé, Haut-Rhin	59 acres (24 ha)
Pfersigberg, Eguisheim, Haut-Rhin	138 acres (56 ha)
Pfingstberg, Orschwihr, Haut-Rhin	69 acres (28 ha)
Praelatenberg, Orschwiller and Kintzheim, Bas-Rhin	30 acres (12 ha)
Schoenenbourg, Riquewihr, Haut-Rhin	99 acres (40 ha)
Sporen, Riquewihr, Haut-Rhin	54 acres (22 ha)
Steinert, Pfaffenheim, Haut-Rhin	94 acres (38 ha)
Steingrubler, Wettolsheim, Haut-Rhin	47 acres (19 ha)
Steinklotz, Marlenheim, Bas-Rhin	59 acres (24 ha)
Vorbourg, Rouffach and Westhalten, Haut-Rhin	178 acres (72 ha)
Wineck-Schlossberg, Katzenthal and Ammerschwihr, Haut-Rhin	59 acres (24 ha)
Winzenberg, Blienschwiller, Bas-Rhin	12.4 acres (5 ha)
Zinnkoepflé, Westhalten and Soultzmatt, Haut-Rhin	153 acres (62 ha)
Zotzenberg, Mittelbergheim, Bas-Rhin	84 acres (34 ha)

Appellations and classifications

Alsace's appellation system is relatively simple, but was once even simpler: formerly, all wine came under the single Alsace appellation. Today, the general *appellation contrôlée* covers all vineyards save those that are designated Alsace Grand Cru or Crémant. Any of the permitted grape varieties grown in any village in any vineyard can qualify for the Alsace appellation, making it the largest white-wine appellation in France.

Alsace Grand Cru covers specified vineyards for particular grape varieties. In other words, if Grand Cru vineyard X is designated as Grand Cru only for riesling, any gewürztraminer produced by that vineyard will be simple AC Alsace. Grand Cru wines can be either 100 percent from one vineyard (in which case the vineyard will be named on the label) or from a number of Grand Cru vineyards (in which case it will simply be called Alsace Grand Cru). All Alsace Grand Cru wines must be 100 percent from one grape variety, and only the noble varieties can be used. Permitted yields are lower than for AC Alsace, at 3.7 tons per acre (65 hl per ha).

Crémant d'Alsace is an appellation for sparkling wine. It must be made by the classic method of secondary fermentation in the bottle, using grapes grown only in the Alsace appellation area. The permitted varieties are pinot blanc, pinot auxerrois, pinot noir, pinot gris, riesling and chardonnay, although Crémant d'Alsace is normally made from pinot blanc and pinot auxerrois.

Sweeter wines made from bunches or selected berries that have particularly high levels of sugar and potential alcohol are classified as Vendange Tardive or Sélection des Grains Nobles, the former

The Alsace Wine Route extends 112 miles (180 km) from Marlenheim to Thann.

REGIONAL DOZEN

being whole bunch, the latter single berry. These categories correspond to the German categories of Beerenauslese and Trockenbeerenauslese, with the vital difference that they are richer and never as sweet as their German equivalents. Both wines, but particularly Sélection des Grains Nobles, may contain botrytis-affected grapes.

Producers

JEAN-BAPTISTE ADAM

Established 1614 *Owners* Adam family *Production* 80,000 cases *Vineyard area* 37 acres (15 ha)

The Adam family has been making wine in Ammerschwihr since the seventeenth century. The winery has its own vineyard but also buys in grapes from another 198 acres (80 ha) or so. The style, up-front and fruity, is immediately attractive at all levels, from the basic wines through the Sigillé *cuvées*, which are tasted and approved by the local Confrérie de St-Etienne (an Alsatian promotional organization founded in 1440), up to the top Jean-Baptiste Adam *cuvées*. Traditional large oak casks with interior temperature control are still used for fermentation, although more modern techniques and facilities, such as a pneumatic press and a new bottling hall, have also been introduced. For their quality, the wines are reasonably priced and always a pleasure. Look out, also, for Adam's second label, Pfister.

DOMAINE ALLIMANT-LAUGNER

Established 1724 *Owner* Hubert Laugner *Production* 6,000 cases *Vineyard area* 25 acres (10 ha)

This small producer has made a big name for itself with light, elegant wines that go well with food. There are, however, exceptions to this style, such as a powerful Tokay Pinot Gris and a suitably rich Gewürztraminer Sélection des Grains Nobles. Lovers of sparkling Alsace will appreciate Laugner's vintage Crémant d'Alsace.

LÉON BEYER

Established 1867 *Owners* Beyer family *Production* 60,000 cases *Vineyard area* 173 acres (70 ha)

This *négociant* firm continues the wine activities of the Beyer family, who first arrived in Eguisheim in 1580. Directed today by Léon Beyer and his son Marc, it is best known for its dry, elegant style of wine, expressed both in the top Cuvée des Comtes d'Eguisheim and in the well-made Léon Beyer and Réserve ranges. The firm is particularly noted for its Gewürztraminer as well as its Vendange Tardive wines. After a brief spell in the early 1990s when some of the wines were inconsistent, Beyer seemed to return to top form with the 1997 vintage.

DOMAINE PAUL BLANCK

Established 1922 *Owners* Blanck family *Production* 20,000 cases *Vineyard area* 84 acres (35 ha)

With Grand Cru vineyards in Furstentum, Mambourg, Schlossberg and Sommerberg, the Blanck family makes an extensive variety of produce, including a good range of single-vineyard wines. All benefit from rigorous vineyard techniques, which include low yields and an almost biodynamic attitude to pesticides and fertilizers. The wines from the Furstentum vineyard— Riesling, Gewürztraminer and Tokay Pinot Gris— are outstanding. At a less exclusive level, the Specialité range includes some notable curiosities such as a Pinot Blanc aged in wood, a Pinot Auxerrois from old vines and a bone-dry Brut Sauvage Crémant d'Alsace.

DOMAINE LÉON BOESCH

Established 1832 *Owners* Boesch family *Production* 6,500 cases *Vineyard area* 25 acres (10 ha)

The Boesch family vineyards are spectacularly sited in a natural amphitheater just beneath the highest peaks of the Vosges, in the village of Soultzmatt. The vines are cultivated with a minimum of chemicals, and in the Grand Cru Zinnkoepflé vineyard feromones are used to protect against insects. This degree of care continues in the cellar, where the winemaker, Gérard Boesch, aims for a style marked by purity and balance. This is especially true of his Gewürztraminer, which has suprising freshness for this varietal. The rieslings, on the other hand, need considerable aging before developing a fine, nutty character.

DOMAINE ALBERT BOXLER

Established 1946 *Owner* Jean-Marc Boxler *Production* 5,000 cases *Vineyard area* 26 acres (10.5 ha)

Jean-Marc Boxler uses his two main vineyards to produce two contrasting wines. The Grand Cru Sommerberg Tokay Pinot Gris is particularly rich and smoky, whereas the Grand Cru Brand Riesling

In most Alsatian cellars, the wine is aged in large, old barrels; new wood is rarely used.

reflects the granite soils in its steely, almost re-strained style. Now that Boxler's son Jean is involved in the family business, the future of this small producer seems assured.

DOMAINE MARCEL DEISS

Established 1949 *Owner* Marcel Deiss *Production* 10,000 cases *Vineyard area* 49 acres (20 ha)

The extravagant, flamboyant Marcel Deiss makes equally extravagant wines from a fine collection of vineyards around Bergheim. The best way to describe them is as perfect expressions of their *terroir*—Deiss's obsession with his vines ensures that consumers receive nothing less. Although his greatest success is his Riesling, Deiss has also gone way outside Alsatian conventions in creating his Grand Vin d'Altenberg de Bergheim, a blended wine that, for Deiss, encapsulates the vineyard rather than any particular grape variety. Deiss's next move is difficult to predict: suffice to say that the wines will be exciting and out of the ordinary.

DOMAINE JEAN-PIERRE DIRLER

Established 1871 *Owners* Dirler family *Production* 5,000 cases *Vineyard area* 20 acres (8 ha)

Jean-Pierre Dirler, who works alongside his son Jean, possesses some fine Grand Cru vineyards around Guebwiller in southern Alsace. Rieslings from the Kessler, Spiegel and Saering vineyards epitomize his search for dry wines with no residual sugar. Another star in the Dirler range is the Muscat, which is produced from superripe grapes and consequently has great concentration. In 1880, the family became the first producer to make sparkling wine in Alsace, but with the advent of Second World War, production came to a halt and has not resumed.

DOPFF AU MOULIN

Established 1574 *Owners* Dopff family *Production* 275,000 cases *Vineyard area* 180 acres (75 ha)

One of the largest of the *négociant* firms in Alsace, this is one of two Dopff companies based in Riquewihr, and the only one still in the hands of the Dopff family. It is named for the windmill that acts as the company symbol. This branch of the Dopff family virtually invented sparkling Crémant d'Alsace, and its Cuvée Julien is still one of the region's benchmarks. The importance of sparkling wine to this *domaine* makes it easy to overlook the still wines, which come from a rich clutch of vineyards in Riquewihr and in neighboring villages. The Tokay Pinot Gris de Riquewihr, Riesling

Alsace's top vineyards are located on the lower slopes of the Vosges Mountains.

Grand Cru Schoenenbourg and Riesling de Riquewihr are among the best of a wide range.

DOPFF ET IRION

Established 1945 *Owner* Chateaux & Terroirs Holdings *Production* 160,800 cases *Vineyard area* 77 acres (32 ha)

Following the sale of this estate by the Dopff family in 1990, a lack of investment saw Dopff et Irion wines hit a dull patch, but the quality has recently recovered. The range of varietals that goes out under the Domaines du Château de Riquewihr label comes from the firm's own vineyards and includes the stars of the portfolio: the Les Sorcières Gewürztraminer and Tokay Pinot Gris Les Maquisards are particularly succcessful. The Cuvée René Dopff range,

Discarded wine barrels are regularly used for promotional purposes.

named for the firm's founder, is typical of the company's understated style. Although perfect for the table, it often performs less well in tastings.

DOMAINE HERING

Established 1858　*Owners* Pierre and Jean-Daniel Hering　*Production* 7,000 cases　*Vineyard area* 22 acres (9 ha)

This small *domaine* is located in the northern part of Alsace and its production centers on vineyards in the Grand Cru of Kirchberg de Barr. Two specialty wines are also made: a Riesling from a tiny vineyard in the town of Barr called Le Clos de la Folie, and a floral Muscat from another small vineyard, Le Clos Feyel. The style is very open, with an emphasis on fruit—which may be explained by the fact that Jean-Daniel Hering, the winemaker, spent some time working in Australia's Yarra Valley.

HUGEL ET FILS

Established 1639　*Owners* Hugel family　*Production* 110,000 cases　*Vineyard area* 62 acres (25 ha)

A major name in Alsace, Hugel is also highly respected outside the region. From its winery in Riquewihr, the family has helped shape Alsatian wine styles. Most recently, it lobbied hard for the creation of the superrich Vendange Tardive and Sélection des Grains Nobles categories. Although Hugel is no longer at the very pinnacle of Alsatian winemaking, its top wines are still among the best. The other wines are more variable, particularly the range of varietals named Hommage à Jean Hugel (in tribute to the flamboyant Johnny Hugel, who recently retired). The Tradition range, however, provides excellent wines, especially the Tokay Pinot Gris and Riesling.

ROGER JUNG ET FILS

Established 1961　*Owners* Jung family　*Production* 8,000 cases　*Vineyard area* 32 acres (13 ha)

Roger Jung's winery lies on the edge of the picture-book village of Riquewihr and his vines are on some of the best sites in the neighborhood: riesling comes from the Schoenenbourg and Rosacker vineyards and gewürztraminer from Sporen. The wines gain much of their intense expressiveness from Jung's practice of leaving the grapes hanging as long as possible. The Pinot Blanc is particularly attractive, and, at the other end of the spectrum, the Riesling Sélection des Grains Nobles is outstanding.

KUENTZ-BAS

Established 1795　*Owners* Bas and Weber families　*Production* 30,000 cases　*Vineyard area* 41 acres (17 ha)

This medium-sized *négociant* firm is based in an attractive, rambling cellar complex in Husseren-les-Châteaux. It owns vines in two Grands Crus in Eguisheim—Pfersigberg and Eichberg—but buys in grapes for about half of its production. Under the control of Christian Bas and Jacques Weber, Kuentz-Bas makes some of the most reliable, appealing wines in Alsace. The style is rich, often opulent, particularly in the Gewürztraminer and the wonderful muscats. The top-range Réserve Personelle wines are especially ageworthy.

DOMAINE SEPPI LANDMANN

Established 1982　*Owner* Seppi Landmann　*Production* 5,400 cases　*Vineyard area* 21 acres (8.5 ha)

Since he appeared on the scene in the early 1980s, Seppi Landmann has been a powerful force in Alsatian winemaking. His personality, sometimes described as Rabelaisian, made that inevitable, and his wines certainly reflect his character. They are powerful and concentrated, especially the Riesling and Gewürztraminer from the Grand Cru Zinnkoepflé vineyard. His less expensive Vallée Noble range, named for the valley in which the vines are situated, is well-priced, and his Sylvaner is a cut above most other sylvaners in Alsace. He also produces an excellent Crémant d'Alsace.

DOMAINE DES MARRONIERS

Established 1888　*Owner* Guy Wach　*Production* 3,700 cases　*Vineyard area* 17 acres (7 ha)

By far the best producer in the village of Andlau, Guy Wach has vineyards in the Grands Crus of Kastelberg and Moenchberg. His family has been in the wine business since 1748, first as barrel-makers, and then, from 1888, as vineyard owners. His crisp Riesling Grand Cru Kastelberg is racy and fresh, and his more modest wines, such as the Sylvaner, are equally modestly priced. Guy Wach's aim is to obtain maximum varietal character, and the estate is now run on organic lines.

DOMAINE MEYER-FONNÉ

Established 1961 *Owners* François and Félix Meyer
Production 6,000 cases *Vineyard area* 25 acres (10 ha)

One of a young generation of vignerons that has pushed up the quality of Alsatian wines by restricting yields, Félix Meyer makes dense, concentrated wines which are attractive when young and—especially the Tokay Pinot Gris from the Kaefferkopf vineyard—age well. Good-value pinot blanc is something of a specialty with this producer, and Meyer manages to coax great richness from this generally underrated variety. But Meyer-Fonné's outstanding wines are probably the Gewürztraminer and Riesling from the Grand Cru of Wineck-Schlossberg.

DOMAINE RENÉ MURÉ

Established 1630 *Owner* René Muré *Production* 25,000 cases *Vineyard area* 54 acres (22 ha)

René Muré is a fortunate man. With the 40-acre (16-ha) vineyard of Clos St-Landelin at its heart, his *domaine* is able to produce some of the most impressive riesling in Alsace, as well as a highly successful Pinot Noir. The wines of Clos St-Landelin, which is classified as Grand Cru Vorbourg, come from steep, south-facing slopes of stony limestone, and are rich and complex, even when dry. Other Muré wines from less steeply sloping vineyards go out under the Côte de Rouffach label. Another Muré specialty is the

riesling-based Crémant d'Alsace, which successfully retains its aromatic character after bottle aging.

DOMAINE GÉRARD NEUMEYER

Established NA *Owner* Gérard Neumeyer *Production* 9,000 cases *Vineyard area* 37 acres (15 ha)

This young, dynamic producer is based in Molsheim, due west of Strasbourg in the Bas-Rhin department. His pride and joy is his vineyard in the Grand Cru of Bruderthal, from which he produces fine Tokay Pinot Gris and Gewürztraminer. Other stars in his firmament are the Tokay Pinot Gris from the Coteau des Chartreux and the special *cuvée* he produces for the Hospices de Strasbourg.

DOMAINE OSTERTAG

Established 1966 *Owners* Ostertag family *Production* 7,000 cases *Vineyard area* 30 acres (12 ha)

Yes, André Ostertag writes publications such as *The Riesling Manifesto*, a collection of panegyrics for the grape, in collaboration with Californian winemaker Randall Grahm and German Johannes Selbach. Yes, he has easter lambs on his label as a play on the family name of "Easter Day." But his fame rests principally on his wines, which sometimes achieve greatness and sometimes fall flat on their faces. The successes include the complex Riesling Grand Cru Moenchberg and the Riesling Fronholz. The Tokay Pinot Gris is made in a dense style that is more Burgundian than Alsatian and

One of the region's most common varieties, gewürztraminer gives relatively low yields.

The steep slopes of Clos St-Landelin provide Domaine René Muré with superb fruit.

Unusually for an area dominated by white grape varieties, the Pfaffenheim vineyards include significant plantings of pinot noir.

Maison Trimbach produces some of Alsace's best rieslings and gewürztraminers.

has its detractors. One thing is sure, however: an Ostertag wine can never be ignored.

CAVE VINICOLE DE PFAFFENHEIM ET GUEBERSCHWIHR

Established 1957 *Owners* 220 members of cooperative *Production* 210,000 cases *Vineyard area* 580 acres (235 ha)

One of the top cooperatives in Alsace, this establishment specializes in wines from pinot blanc, tokay pinot gris and pinot noir—in fact, it is one of the very few wineries in Alsace to make a success of red wines. It also makes an excellent tokay-pinot-gris-based Crémant d'Alsace, which, like all its sparkling wines, goes under the Hartenberger label. The cooperative has vines in three Grand Crus: Goldert, Steinert and Hatschbourg. A number of estate bottlings, including Les Aubépines and Clos des Amandiers (both from tokay pinot gris) are outstanding.

DOMAINES SCHLUMBERGER

Established 1810 *Owners* Schlumberger family *Production* 85,000 cases *Vineyard area* 346 acres (140 ha)

The largest estate in Alsace was put together by Nicolas Schlumberger in the early years of the nineteenth century from land around the town of Guebwiller, in what are now the Grands Crus of Saering, Kessler, Kitterlé and Spiegel, as well as at other sites such as Heissenstein and Schimberg. The Grands Crus provide the top of the range wines, while other wines go under the brand name of Les Vins des Princes Abbés. The minerally character of many of these wines, derived from the local soil, is a hallmark of the Schlumberger style. The two famous *cuvées* (Cuvée Christine, a Vendange Tardive, and Cuvée Anne, a Sélection des Grains Nobles) are triumphs, although both tend to be rich and full-bodied rather than sweet. The company is currently managed by seventh-generation Eric Beydon-Schlumberger.

DOMAINE JEAN SIPP

Established 1654 *Owner* Jean Sipp *Production* 12,000 cases *Vineyard area* 57 acres (23 ha)

The Sipp family estate traces its origins back to 1654, when another Jean Sipp set up as a vigneron. The premises in which the current Jean Sipp works are even older than that, dating from 1416. Sipp's wines are generally characterized by their attractiveness when young, but that doesn't prevent them aging well. With Grand Cru land in Kirchberg de Ribeauvillé and Osterberg, Sipp has some fine vineyards at his disposal. The Kirchberg, in fact, produces his best wine, the Riesling Grand Cru, which develops to give a wonderful minerally character. Other house specials are the Pinot Auxerrois, made from old vines and the Tokay Pinot Gris Clos Ribeaupierre, a properly rich, concentrated wine.

DOMAINE BRUNO SORG

Established 1965 *Owners* Sorg family *Production* 6,200 cases *Vineyard area* 25 acres (10 ha)

Rightly feted for the consistency and the quality of its wines, this small *domaine* is unusual in Alsace for being only in its second generation. Bruno Sorg himself is still in charge, but son François is now winemaker and he has pushed the quality to new levels. His finest wines are probably the Muscat Grand Cru Pfersigberg, which remains terrific value, and the Riesling Grand Cru Pfersigberg Vieilles Vignes, which needs many years of cellaring before revealing its true, rich character. Other fine wines include a Riesling from Grand Cru Florimont and a huge Gewürztraminer Sélection des Grains Nobles.

PIERRE SPARR ET SES FILS

Established 1680 *Owners* Sparr family *Production* 126,000 cases *Vineyard area* 79 acres (33 ha)

This sizeable *négociant* firm also has significant holdings of vineyards in Sigolsheim and Turckheim, including parts of the Grand Crus of Mambourg and Brand. From these vineyards and purchased grapes, it produces an enormous range of wines, of which the Sélection Réserve and Sparr Prestige labels are the most successful. These have, however, recently been rivalled by the Crémant d'Alsace Glorious 2000, which was launched for the Millennium and enjoys both gaudy packaging and ripe flavors derived from long bottle-aging. The house style generally veers towards richness, which is best experienced in the likes of the Tokay Pinot Gris Grand Cru Mambourg.

MAISON TRIMBACH

Established 1626 *Owners* Trimbach family *Production* 100,000 cases *Vineyard area* 65 acres (27 ha)

If you want to taste classic Alsatian riesling, you need look no further than Trimbach. Its range of this varietal starts with a basic, pure wine made from bought-in grapes and called simply Trimbach Riesling. Above this are two superb *cuvées*: Cuvée Frédéric Émile, named after the family member who brought the firm to prominence in the nineteenth century, and the single-vineyard Clos Ste-Hune—for many this 3.2-acre (1.3-ha) vineyard is the best place in Alsace for riesling. There is not a trace of residual sugar in these expensive, rare and beautifully balanced wines, both of which demand long aging. With such excellent rieslings on offer, it is easy to overlook the wonderful Gewürztraminer Cuvée des Seigneurs de Ribeaupierre and the Tokay Pinot Gris Réserve Personelle. All these wines put Trimbach at the top of the Alsatian hierarchy.

CAVE VINICOLE DE TURCKHEIM

Established 1955 *Owners* 230 members of cooperative *Production* 525,000 cases *Vineyard area* 815 acres (330 ha)

This is one of a group of dynamic cooperatives that maintains a high standard of quality for basic AC Alsace. With its four ranges of wine—the simple Cave Tradition, the Cave Réserve, the Prestige Range and the Grands Crus—and a special blend, Alsace Decapole, Turckheim is one of the most important suppliers to the UK market, with around 30 per cent of all sales. It also produces one of the biggest-selling Crémant d'Alsaces, Mayerling, made from pinot blanc, and owns the long-established *négociant* firm of Preiss-Zimmer.

DOMAINE WEINBACH

Established 1898 *Owners* Madame Théo Faller and daughters *Production* 15,000 cases *Vineyard area* 59 acres (24 ha)

Based in a former capuchin monastery surrounded by walled vineyards, Colette Faller, widow of Théo Faller, and her two daughters Catherine and Laurence farm some fine riesling and produce a bewildering array of wines. The Cuvée Théo, Cuvée Catherine and Cuvée Laurence ranges include various late-harvest wines, Sélections des Grains Nobles, and something even more concentrated called Quintessence. Then there are the dry wines: the Riesling from the Grand Cru of Schlossberg and the Gewürztraminer from the Grand Cru of Furstentum. The concentration and purity of fruit in these wines is the result of severe green harvests and almost organic viticulture.

DOMAINE ZIND-HUMBRECHT

Established 1620 *Owners* Humbrecht family *Production* 15,000 cases *Vineyard area* 99 acres (40 ha)

The father-and-son team of Léonard and Olivier Humbrecht is currently the finest producer of great Alsatian wines. Wonderful vineyards in some of the best Grands Crus, which are managed by Léonard, and the winemaking skills of Olivier, France's first Master of Wine, combine to produce an enormous range of stunning produce. The style is rich, but never sweet (except of course for the Vendange Tardive and Sélection des Grains Nobles wines). Possibly the finest wines of a consistently great range are those from the Grands Crus of Brand and Hengst and those from the Clos St-Urbain in Thann. The estate recently converted to biodynamic methods, so it will be fascinating to see if the already superb fruit becomes even purer.

Grand Cru vineyards surround the small town of Niedermorschwihr.

Corsica

Anthony Peregrine

Corsican wines have come a long way in a short time. Barely 20 years ago, they were predominantly rustic items, the products of a mountainous Mediterranean island with a reputation for beautiful, rugged scenery, political instability and endless vendettas. In recent years, however, the wines have improved significantly, becoming increasingly worthy of a viticultural tradition that stretches back approximately 2,500 years.

Corsicans both ancient and modern have benefited from the Mediterranean's climate—warm sunshine and maritime humidity. And although the wild, tortuous terrain, which was perfect for the bandits of Corsican folklore, is mainly granitic (especially in the south and west) there is also some schistose land to the northeast and some limestone in between.

Corsica's most interesting white wines are made from vermentino, an Italian variety.

Two-thirds of Corsica's vineyards have been restructured under a replanting program. Although this has included international varieties such as cabernet sauvignon and chardonnay, the emphasis has generally been on traditional grapes. The dense, tannic nielluccio (known as sangiovese in Tuscany) and the more supple, sophisticated (and indigenous) sciacarello have reassumed their primacy in Corsican reds and rosés, while vermentino once again characterizes the ample dry whites. Simultaneously, winemaking techniques have developed immeasurably, so that even the more modest wines—which once either descaled the throat or passed down it unnoticed—generally, these days, boast freshness and balance.

The overall effects of these developments have been twofold. Firstly, the island now produces an improving range of *vins de pays*, classified as VDP de l'Île de Beauté. These account for 54 percent of Corsica's annual production of 9.24 million gallons (35 million l), and are usually at least honest, consistent and refreshing. They include a good selection of varietal wines, notably those made from the traditional grapes mentioned above, and an interesting range of double-variety wines. Cabernet sauvignon and nielluccio may appear to be unlikely partners but can work well together.

Secondly, and more importantly, the island's appellation wines (26 percent of total production) now proudly embody the often craggy hillside *terroirs*, the grape varieties grown there, and the local cultures. Some of the reds are darkly robust (generally those with nielluccio to the fore), others are lighter and spicier (usually those made with sciacarello), and the best rosés marry fruitiness and structure. Whites are in the minority but can range from the fruity and nervous to the more aromatically complex.

Corsica's appellation structure is complex, reflecting the diversity of its vineyards and terrain. *Vin de Corse* is the generic, catch-all category, though, in practice, its supple reds and racy rosés come mainly from the cooperatives on the east coast. It accounts for 56 percent of Corsican AOCs.

Within the *Vin de Corse* are five subregional classifications: Calvi, with supple, sunny wines; Sartène, which offers characterful reds and rosés; Figari, whose dry, windy granite plateau produces well-structured fare; Porto-Vecchio, with elegant reds and aromatic rosés; and tiny Coteaux du Cap Corse, whose whites have very floral aromas.

In addition, the island boasts two independent *crus*. Ajaccio is the home territory of the sciacarello grape and makes silky wines which can age well. Patrimonio is perhaps the best-known of Corsican appellations; the nielluccio grape here produces rich, powerful red wines and the district's rosés are among the classiest on the island.

Producers

CLOS CAPITORO

Established 1856 *Owners* Bianchetti family *Production* 22,000 cases *Vineyard area* 120 acres (50 ha)

Jacques Bianchetti currently directs the family estate near Ajaccio. The sciacarello grape is king here, so the red wines are lighter in color than others. However, they lack nothing in structure or staying power. Bianchetti's rosés combine sophistication and festive fruitiness.

DOMAINE FUIMICICOLI

Established 1962 *Owners* Andréani family *Production* 20,000 cases *Vineyard area* 108 acres (45 ha)

Félix Andréani has had control of what is now the dominant property in the Sartène appellation since 1962, and now has a top-line reputation. In collaboration with his son Simon, he produces reds (from sciacarello, nielluccio and grenache) which have spicy elegance, strength and length, and rosés that demonstrate how intense sciacarello can be.

DOMAINE DE TANELLA

Established 1850 *Owners* De Perretti della Rocca family *Production* 22,000 cases *Vineyard area* 144 acres (60 ha)

The leading producer in the Figari appellation is restructuring, but the quality of its Cuvée Alexandra range has not suffered. Named after the daughter of the house, the *cuvée* comes in all three colors, all of which are regularly cited among the island's top wines. The outstanding red, in which syrah has been added to the two traditional Corsican varieties, is a wine of real breeding; it displays structured elegance and is at once deeply aromatic and built to last.

DOMAINE DE TORRACCIA

Established 1964 *Owner* Christian Imbert *Production* 22,200 cases *Vineyard area* 103 acres (43 ha)

After a varied early career, Christian Imbert landed on the coast near Porto-Vecchio 36 years ago. Since then, he's been a leader in the island's viticulture. His own wines all speak forcefully of their *terroir*—and of Imbert's dedication. The red, a mixture of (mainly) nielluccio and some sciacarello, develops richness and power without losing finesse or balance—with potential to age for years.

Fall leaves create a colorful contrast with empty wine bottles.

Nielluccio, Corsica's most planted grape variety, is a type of sangiovese.

Vins de Pays

Jim Budd

In areas such as Languedoc-Roussillon, vin de pays *allows producers greater freedom.*

Introduced in September 1979, the *vin de pays* (VDP) classification added another layer to the pyramid of categories used to define wine quality in France. *Vin de pays*—literally "country wine"—occupies a position above basic *vin de table* but below VDQS and *appellation contrôlée*.

Found throughout France—with the notable exceptions of Bordeaux, the Côte d'Or, Champagne and Alsace—*vins de pays* are classified as departmental, regional, or zonal. Thirty-nine denominations cover departments. In four areas, neighboring departments have agreed to group together to form a regional denomination. The four areas are Vin de Pays d'Oc, covering Languedoc-Roussillon; Vin de Pays du Jardin de la France, covering the Loire Valley; Vin de Pays du Comté Tolosan, covering the Midi-Pyrénées region; and Vin de Pays des Comtés Rhodaniens, covering the Rhône-Alps region. Conversely, some smaller denominations have been established within departments. These are the 95 zonal *vin de pays*, which vary enormously in size and importance, from major denominations such as the Côtes de Gascogne and the Coteaux de l'Ardèche to little-known *vin de pays* such as Côtes de Montestruc in the Gers.

Producers in the Minervois can opt to use VDP d'Oc or departmental VDP classifications.

The classification regulations include an overall yield limit of 5.1 tons per acre (90 hl per ha), although individual regions can specify lower yields; a natural minimum alcohol level of 9 percent (10 percent for the Mediterranean region); and a maximum alcohol content of 15 percent, although individual regions may set lower limits. Each department has its own list of permitted grapes, normally including local varieties plus some international ones. Generally, this allows producers much greater freedom than the appellation rules.

There are some constraints, however. Certain seemingly appropriate varieties are banned—viognier cannot be used in the Loire, for example. The words "château" or "*clos*" cannot be used on the label, nor can an individual vineyard be mentioned. Furthermore, in some regions, such as the Loire, the maximum alcohol permitted is 12.5 percent. This can be difficult to achieve in ripe years (such as 1997), particularly for producers who want to keep their yields low or pick their fruit at the optimum time. In 1996, the naming of a second grape variety on the label was permitted; yet it is still illegal to name a third or a fourth and the French wine establishment remains dismissive of varietal wines (*vins de cépage*).

For the most part, however, producers have taken to the *vin de pays* classification with relish, and it has grown rapidly in importance in recent years. Today, almost 30 percent of French wine is *vin de pays*; about 65 percent of this is red, 17 percent rosé and 18 percent white.

Few *vin de pays* have attained the status of Italy's so-called "super *vini da tavola*", which have been awarded the IGT (Indicazione Geographica Tipica) denomination and are now among the country's most expensive wines. But this situation could change, especially in southern France where strict appellation laws have encouraged a number of leading producers to adopt the new classification. For example, since 1994 wine from Eloi Dürrbach's Domaine de Trévallon in Provence (see p. 147) has been sold as a VDP des Bouches-du-Rhône instead of AC Les Baux-de-Provence, because its high proportion of cabernet sauvignon disqualifies it from the appellation. Dürrbach is probably the most high-profile producer to opt for *vin de pays* status, but others in the Midi, such as Gérard Gauby and Domaine Cazes in the Roussillon and Daniel and Patricia Domergue in the Minervois, are following suit (see pp. 140–42).

Vin de pays areas

ANIVIT, the French association of *vin de pays* producers, divides the country into a number of areas as follows:

The Loire produces some 15.8 million gallons (60 million l) each year. Although it includes 19 denominations, the regional VDP du Jardin de la France accounts for 94 percent of production,

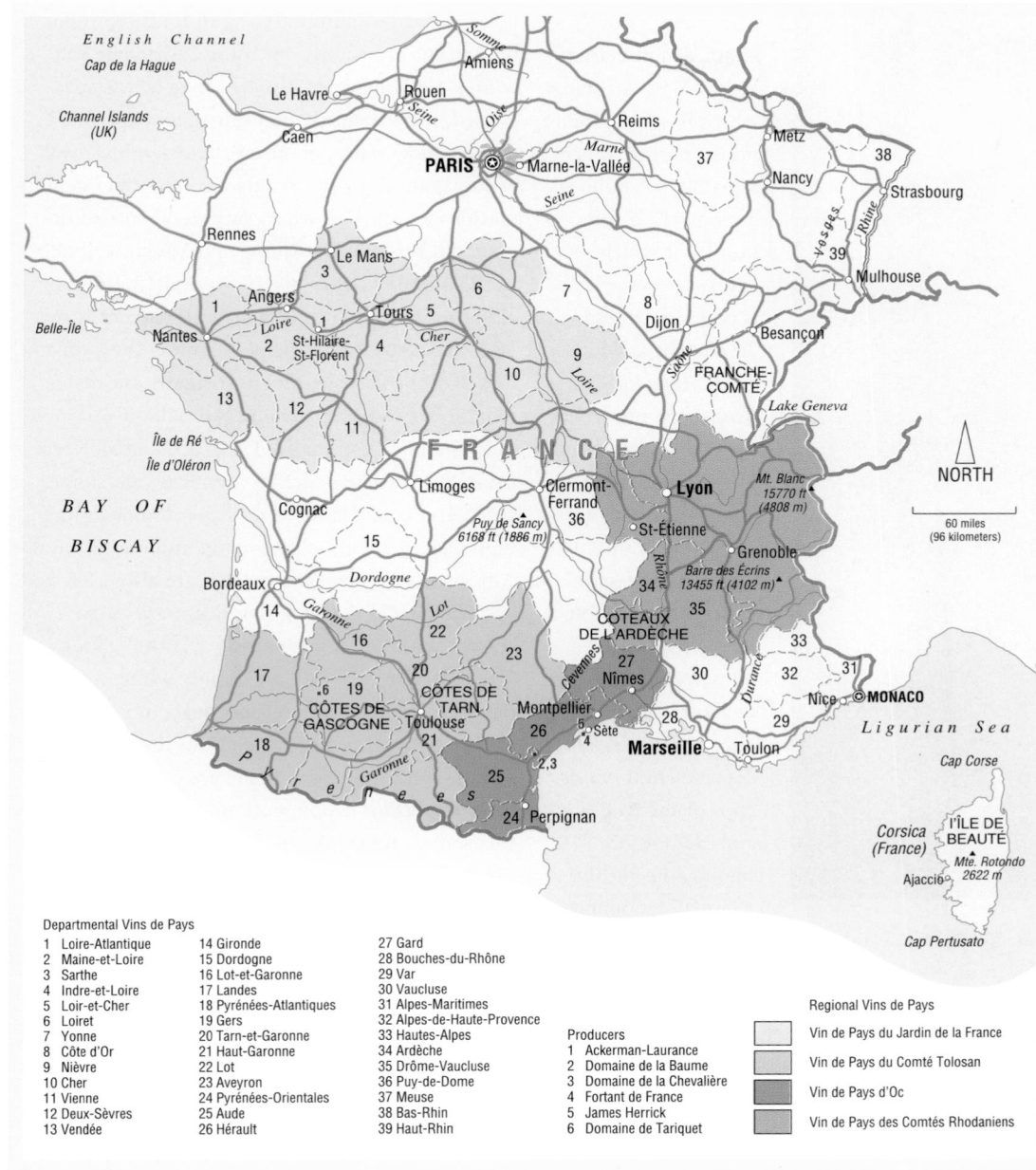

English Channel
Cap de la Hague
Channel Islands (UK)

Le Havre
Rouen
Caen
Amiens
Somme
Seine
Oise

PARIS
Marne-la-Vallée
Marne
Reims
Metz
Nancy
Strasbourg

Rennes
Le Mans
3
6
7
Seine
37
38
39
Mulhouse

Angers
1
Loire
Tours
5
St-Hilaire-St-Florent
4
Cher
8
Dijon
Besançon

Nantes
2
FRANCHE-COMTÉ

Belle-Île
13
10
9
Loire
Seine
Lake Geneva

12
11
FRANCE

Île de Ré
Île d'Oléron
Limoges
Clermont-Ferrand
36
Lyon
Mt. Blanc 15770 ft (4808 m)
NORTH

BAY OF BISCAY
Cognac
15
Puy de Sancy 6168 ft (1886 m)
St-Étienne
Grenoble
Barre des Écrins 13455 ft (4102 m)
60 miles (96 kilometers)

Bordeaux
Dordogne
Rhône
34
35
Bordeaux
14
Garonne
Lot
COTEAUX DE L'ARDÈCHE
33

16
22
23
27
30
32
31

17
20
Nîmes
Nice
MONACO

.6 19
CÔTES DE TARN
Montpellier
28
29
Ligurian Sea
Cap Corse

CÔTES DE GASCOGNE
Toulouse
21
26
5
4
Sète
Marseille
Toulon

18
Garonne
25
.2,3
Corsica (France)
I'ÎLE DE BEAUTÉ

24
Perpignan
Ajaccio
Mte. Rotondo 2622 m

Cap Pertusato

Departmental Vins de Pays

1 Loire-Atlantique	14 Gironde	27 Gard	
2 Maine-et-Loire	15 Dordogne	28 Bouches-du-Rhône	
3 Sarthe	16 Lot-et-Garonne	29 Var	
4 Indre-et-Loire	17 Landes	30 Vaucluse	
5 Loir-et-Cher	18 Pyrénées-Atlantiques	31 Alpes-Maritimes	
6 Loiret	19 Gers	32 Alpes-de-Haute-Provence	
7 Yonne	20 Tarn-et-Garonne	33 Hautes-Alpes	
8 Côte d'Or	21 Haute-Garonne	34 Ardèche	
9 Nièvre	22 Lot	35 Drôme-Vaucluse	
10 Cher	23 Aveyron	36 Puy-de-Dome	
11 Vienne	24 Pyrénées-Orientales	37 Meuse	
12 Deux-Sèvres	25 Aude	38 Bas-Rhin	
13 Vendée	26 Hérault	39 Haut-Rhin	

Producers
1 Ackerman-Laurance
2 Domaine de la Baume
3 Domaine de la Chevalière
4 Fortant de France
5 James Herrick
6 Domaine de Tariquet

Regional Vins de Pays
Vin de Pays du Jardin de la France
Vin de Pays du Comté Tolosan
Vin de Pays d'Oc
Vin de Pays des Comtés Rhodaniens

REGIONAL DOZEN

QUALITY WINES

Domaine de l'Aigle Pinot Noir Haute Vallée de l'Aude
Cuvée l'Argile Frères Parcé VDP des Côtes Catalanes
Domaine Cazes Le Credo VDP des Côtes Catalanes
Mas de Daumas Gassac Haute Vallée du Gassac VDP de l'Hérault
Domaine de Moulines Viognier, VDP de l'Hérault
Domaine de Trévallon VDP des Bouches du Rhône

BEST VALUE WINES

Les Vignerons Ardechois Syrah Cuvée Prestige VDP des Coteaux de l'Ardeche
Domaine de Bachellery Cabernet Sauvignon VDP d'Oc
Les Vignerons de Branceilles Mille et une Pierres VDP de Corrèze
Domaine Couillaud, Chardonnay, VDP du Jardin de la France
Domaine des Hauts de Seyr Le Montaillant Chardonnay VDP des Coteaux Charitois
James Herrick Syrah Mille Passum VDP d'Oc

---

with Maine-et-Loire being the only VDP other yielding more than 260,000 gallons (1 million l) a year. Approximately 45 percent of production is white and most are varietal wines. In the Pays Nantais, for example, some growers have decided not to rely solely on muscadet (melon de bourgogne), the appellation's only permitted variety, and have instead diversified into chardonnay, creating wines in a crisp, lemony, unoaked style. It has been suggested that all the smaller denominations should be subsumed into Jardin de la France. Although this makes commercial sense for producers in appellation areas, it is much less attractive to those working where no appellation exists.

Aquitaine-Charente produces around 23.7 million gallons (90 million l), with three zonal denom-

inations, L'Agenais, Pays Charentais and Terroirs Landais accounting for 80 percent of production. Pays Charentais is by far the most important and represents 57 percent of the total production; because it is a major producer of white wine, more than half of the region's output is white. The current slump in the sales of Cognac makes it likely that more of the vineyards of the Charente will convert to producing *vin de pays* wine.

The Midi-Pyrénées is the third-most important area, mainly as a result of the large amount of *vin de pays* produced in the Côtes de Gascogne. Its annual output is currently around 18.5 million gallons (70 million l), with white accounting for more than 75 percent; more than 13.2 million gallons (50 million l) of the total comes from Gascogne.

Abroad, the most successful vin de pays *have been international varietals from the south.*

The region's other major denomination is the Côtes de Tarn, which has an annual production of approximately 4.6 million gallons (17.5 million l), of which nearly 50 percent is red and around 30 percent is white.

Languedoc-Roussillon producers saw the introduction of the *vin de pays* classification as an ideal opportunity to upgrade the region's vast vineyards; consequently, nearly 80 percent of all *vins de pays* is now produced here. Certain departmental *vin de pays* of the Aude and Hérault are significant, but the regional denomination, VDP d'Oc, established in 1987, is the most important. It now accounts for 33 percent of the area's output and 24 percent of the total French production of *vin de pays*. There is no doubt that it has become the major driving force behind the rise in the quality of Midi wine and of the *vin de pays* category as whole. Red wine accounts for 60 percent of VDP d'Oc, white 24 percent and rosé 16 percent. Varietal wines, especially those made from international varieties, are highly significant, particularly because grapes such as cabernet, merlot and chardonnay are rarely permitted in appellation wines (see p. 138).

Corsica is the name used for appellation wines on the island, so all *vin de pays* is labelled with the much more evocative "l'Île de Beauté." Corsica's annual production of *vin de pays* is around 4.2 million gallons (16 million l), 43 percent of which is red, 32.5 percent rosé and 24.5 percent white. Many of the varieties grown here are Italian or native Corsican grapes, such as nielluccio and sciacarello, but international varieties are also being cultivated on a small but increasing scale.

Provence-Côte d'Azur is the second-largest producer of *vin de pays*, turning out around 21 million gallons (80 million l) a year. Reds represent 65 percent of production, rosés 27 percent and whites just 8 percent. A wide range of varieties is used, including cabernet sauvignon, carignan, merlot, mourvèdre, pinot noir and syrah, as well as local oddities such as caladoc. The chief denominations are du Var, which produces most of the rosé, des Bouches du Rhône and Vaucluse.

The Rhône-Alpes makes around 13.2 million gallons (50 million l), of which 80 percent is red, 12 percent rosé and 8 percent white. The Coteaux de l'Ardèche is easily the most significant denomination, producing around 8.6 million gallons (32.5 million l) annually. The grapes include typical Rhône varieties such as grenache, marsanne, syrah and viognier, as well as chardonnay, pinot noir, gamay, cabernet sauvignon and merlot; in the Alps, varieties such as mondeuse are also cultivated.

The East is the least significant *vin de pays* region, with an output of only 185,000 gallons (700,000 l). The wines are mainly white, and the majority are made with chardonnay, though aligoté, auxerrois (a white variety and not the auxerrois of Cahors) and sauvignon blanc are also used. The most important denominations are Franche-Comté, the Yonne and the Meuse. The wines reflect their northerly climes with vibrant fruit and acidity.

Producers

ACKERMAN-LAURANCE, VDP DU JARDIN DE LA FRANCE, LOIRE

Established 1811 *Owner* Rémy Pannier Group *Production* NA *Vineyard area* NA

Founded in 1811, this is the oldest sparkling-wine house in Saumur and one of the biggest of the Loire *négociants*. Ackerman and sister company Rémy Pannier used to be known for the poor quality of their still wines. Fortunately, during the last decade they have recognized their shortcomings and changed policy. Increasingly, the wine is made by the company in its own wineries; as a result, quality has improved dramatically. VDP du Jardin de la France now accounts for 25 percent of production; the principal varieties are chardonnay, chenin, and cabernet franc.

DOMAINE DE LA BAUME, VDP D'OC, LANGUEDOC

Established 1989 *Owner* BRL Hardy *Production* NA *Vineyard area* 45 acres (18 ha)

Located just east of Beziers, this estate was purchased by Australian company BRL Hardy in 1990 and subsequently renovated. Capacity is now up to 400,000 gallons (1.6 million l). The estate produces two ranges of varietal wines: La Baume and Domaine de la Baume. The La Baume range is made from fruit purchased from a number of growers, and includes five wines: Chardonnay, Sauvignon Blanc, Cabernet Sauvignon, Merlot and Syrah. Wines produced from the estate's own vineyards are sold as Domaine de la Baume; currently, they include a merlot and a chardonnay viognier.

DOMAINE DE LA CHEVALIÈRE, VDP D'OC, LANGUEDOC
Established 1995 *Owner* Michel Laroche *Production* NA *Vineyard area* 15 acres (6 ha)

Michel Laroche, one of the leading Chablis producers, bought this property just to the west of Béziers in 1995. He subsequently renovated the estate and constructed a new winery. The majority of the grapes are sourced from 740 acres (300 ha) owned by a number of growers in various parts of Languedoc. Laroche is convinced that blending is the key to success here, and thus believes that even a pure varietal should come from several sites with varying soils and climates. The 1996 Merlot, for instance, was sourced from eight different areas. The small vineyard at the property has been planted with chardonnay, roussanne, vermentino, viognier, cabernet sauvignon, merlot and syrah, which will eventually be used for prestige *cuvées*.

FORTANT DE FRANCE, VDP D'OC, LANGUEDOC
Established 1974 *Owner* Robert Skalli *Production* 1.5 million cases *Vineyard area* None

Led by Robert Skalli, owner of the St Supéry estate in California's Napa Valley, Fortant was one of the first companies to recognize the potential of varietal wines from the Languedoc. As early as 1982, it began to offer growers attractive, long-term agreements to provide international red and white varieties, and it now has approximately 17,300 acres (7,000 ha) under contract.

The heart of the operation is in Sète, the site of extensive barrel-aging facilities, a modern bottling line and a visitor center. There are three product ranges: an unoaked range, a lightly oaked middle range, and a premium range, Fortant F (Chardonnay, Cabernet Sauvignon and Merlot) which was launched in 1998. In 1999, Skalli introduced three AC wines from Corbières, Minervois and Coteaux du Languedoc, despite having criticized appellation regulations. Although it is now immensely productive, Fortant has also experienced failure: for example, an extensive range of varietals introduced in 1996 was a flop.

JAMES HERRICK, VDP D'OC, LANGUEDOC
Established 1989 *Owner* Southcorp *Production* 170,000 cases *Vineyard area* 445 acres (180 ha)

James Herrick and his fellow-Australian business partners began planting chardonnay here in 1989, introducing techniques, such as neat trellises and drip-feed irrigation, that were entirely foreign to the locals. The resulting wine has fruit to the fore, yet retains French finesse. Herrick also introduced a red wine, Cuvée Simone, made from grenache, syrah and cabernet sauvignon, in 1997, and in 1999 launched a premium range of three single-vineyard chardonnays and four reds called the Roman Collection. In September 1999, following an unsatisfactory joint venture with Val d'Orbieu (see p. 143), Australian company Southcorp acquired the estate as part of its plan to expand its overseas operations.

DOMAINE DE TARIQUET, VDP CÔTES DE GASCOGNE, SOUTHWEST
Established NA *Owners* Grassa family *Production* NA *Vineyard area* 618 acres (250 ha)

Along with the Plaimont Cooperative, the Grassas were pioneers of VDP des Côtes de Gascogne. They bought Tariquet, near the town of Eauze in the heart of Armagnac country, after the Second World War, when it consisted of only 12.4 acres (5 ha) planted with the hybrid noah, and subsequently built up the estate to its current size; now Yves and Maité, their children, have taken over. The Tariquet range runs through crisp dry whites with a colombard base to an attractive and complex Chardonnay/Sauvignon and a late-harvest Gros Manseng. The estate also produces Domaine de La Jalousie, Domaine de Plantérieu and Domaine de Rieux, as well as a fine range of Armagnacs.

Viognier grapes, which make a full-bodied and aromatic white wine, are grown in many areas of France.

Regional, departmental and zonal vin de pays classifications are all used in the Rhône.

Germany

Kiel

Rostock

Lübeck

Wilhelmshaven

Bremerhaven

Hamburg

Schwerin

Lake Müritz

Elbe

Oder

Oldenburg

Bremen

Weser

G E R M A N Y

◉ **BERLIN**

Potsdam

Ems

Osnabrück

Hanover

Wolfsburg

Braunschweig

Magdeburg

Hildesheim

Salzgitter

Münster

Bielefeld

Cottbus

Dessau

Elbe

Hamm

Paderborn

▲ *Mt Brocken*
3746 ft (1142 m)

Gelsenkirchen

Dortmund

Duisburg

Bochum

Göttingen

Halle

Leipzig

S A C H S E N

Krefeld

Essen

Hagen

Mönchen-
Gladbach

Düsseldorf

Wuppertal

Solingen

Kassel

Saale-Unstrut

Naumberg

Sachsen

Leverkusen

Cologne

Siegen

Fulda

Erfurt

Dresden

Aachen

Bonn

Mittelrhein

Gera

Chemnitz

Dresden

Ahr

Rhine

Zwickau

E r z g e b i r g e

Koblenz

Mittelrhein

Frankfurt am Main

Main

**Mosel-Saar-
Ruwer**

Mosel

Rheingau

Wiesbaden

Bernkastel

Nahe

Mainz

Offenbach

Franken

Würzburg

Trier

Nahe

Rheinhessen

Darmstadt

B ö h m e r w a l d

Kaiserslautern

Ludwigshafen

Hessische-Bergstrasse

Mannheim

Nuremburg

Saarbrücken

Heidelberg

Pfalz

Baden

Heilbronn

Regensburg

Karlsruhe

Württemberg

Rhine

Pforzheim

Stuttgart

Danube

Passau

Augsburg

◉ **Munich**

Baden

Freiburg

*Lake
Constance*

↑
NORTH

50 miles
(80 kilometers)

Germany

Stephen Brook

A century ago German wine was as highly prized as the finest Bordeaux. Prestigious merchants' wine lists offered bottles from the top vineyards and villages of Germany—Rüdesheim, Marcobrunn, Piesport—at prices comparable to, and sometimes even higher than, first-growth Bordeaux.

Nowadays most people find this hard to believe, a sad reflection on the decline in reputation of German wine as a whole. There remains a following for the high-priced and rare specialties—eiswein and trockenbeerenauslesen from the finest estates—but no wine-producing country can base a reputation, or indeed an industry, on a relatively small quantity produced in exceptional vintages.

Some of the long-term factors that provoked this slump in reputation will be examined in the sections that follow, but the main reason has been the connivance of the regulatory authorities with the production and promotion of dilute sugary wines of poor quality, which at one time captured a size-able proportion of the world market for cheap wines, but at terrible cost.

An old oak barrel decorated with carved motifs in a winemaking theme.

The magnificent twelfth-century cellars of Kloster Eberbach, Rheingau.

In the minds of the general public, German wine became associated not with its glorious rieslings, its stern sylvaners, its robust pinot blancs and its exquisite sweet wines, but with sugar-water. Despite the best efforts of the good German wine producers and of importers and wine writers fully aware of how marvelous the best wines from Germany can be, this damage to Germany's reputation has yet to be reversed.

But no one should be in any doubt that Germany remains fully capable of producing some of the world's great white wines. The mainstay of this greatness is the versatile riesling grape, which in the eyes of many connoisseurs is the greatest white wine grape in the world, despite the continued rapture with which chardonnay is acclaimed. Other countries produce fine riesling—France, Austria, Australia, New Zealand—but no other country or region has been able to replicate the ethereal delicacy, the mouth-watering freshness and grapiness of a Mosel kabinett from a top estate. Riesling, especially from the cooler regions of northern Germany, where it attains its greatest intensity, is still Germany's trump card, still its unique feature. There are excellent wines from other regions, as the country is blessed with considerable climatic and cultural diversity, but for the foreseeable future, riesling will surely remain its crowning glory.

History

In the cellars of the town hall of Bremen—for centuries a center of the German wine trade in the north—repose some large old casks. Nothing remarkable in that, except that the casks contain wine dating back to the seventeenth century. The oldest, which a select few are allowed to taste on occasion, contains a wine made when Oliver Cromwell was still ruling England. When the guardians of this historic cellar feel it is time to refresh the evaporating wine with something younger, they top up with wine taken from casks of eighteenth-century wine that rest nearby.

These ancient wines, now as dry and pungent as a venerable madeira, are testimony to the long history of German wine production. In the Mosel there is archaeological evidence from Roman times. In Brauneberg and Piesporter are vestiges of Roman wineries and other artifacts, and in other parts of Germany there is archeological confirmation that vineyards have been present for 2,000 years or more. It seems likely that the styles of wine varied considerably, from very dry to unctuously sweet. The Germans date the "invention" of late-harvested sweet wines from 1775, when the messenger bringing authorization to begin the harvest to the Schloss Johannisberg estate in the Rheingau was delayed. The grapes had began to raisin on the vine, but when they were eventually picked, they made astonishingly delicious sweet wine, despite their unwholesome appearance.

It's just a legend, as there is documentary evidence of late-harvested wines throughout Europe since the seventeenth century. But it's the great sweet-wine vintages that mark the progress of German wine through the past two centuries: 1893 and 1921 were both outstanding years, and bottles of beerenauslese or trockenbeerenauslese from these vintages still surface from time to time, or are sold at auction for astronomical sums.

German wine was always expensive, though, and demand for it during periods of pre-1914 prosperity kept prices buoyant. It also encouraged counterfeiters, just as in France, where the amount of Châteauneuf-du-Pape available before strict regulations were introduced always exceeded the quantity of wine the region could conceivably have produced. Wine laws were introduced in 1901 to combat fraud. During the same period, the wines of the Mosel began to challenge the supremacy of the wines from the Rheingau and Pfalz, which, with their large estates, many in aristocratic hands, had long dominated the market for premium German wine. Many Mosel estates had once been owned by the Church—a history still reflected in the names of estates and vineyards—but have been under secular ownership, for the most part, since the early nineteenth century.

The two world wars and the dire economic and social troubles of the intervening years inevitably had an adverse effect on German wine, although Prohibition in the United States had little impact, as comparatively little wine was exported. The domestic wine trade was, however, dealt a very specific blow as a consequence of anti-semitism. Many leading and well-respected figures in the trade were Jewish and, after their imprisonment, expulsion or murder, their acumen was sorely missed. Despite the collapse of the international wine trade and the lack of men to work the vines and harvest the grapes, 1945, surprisingly, turned out to be an exceptional vintage, as also was 1949.

The postwar years saw a revival of the German wine industry and the introduction of practices that may have seemed sensible at the time but have had unsatisfactory long-term consequences. Vineyard reorganization imposed German logic on a fairly chaotic system, but the primary goal was not so much to improve the quality of viticulture as to lessen the costly dependence on manual labor. Previously, vineyards had been planted where nothing else would grow, on steep, often stony slopes that were hard to cultivate but yielded grapes of tremendous intensity and quality. New vineyards were planted on flatter land, where the more fertile soils often yielded four times more grapes than hillside sites—good news for growers, bad news for quality-conscious consumers.

New grape varieties—generated by crossing existing varieties—were part of the same movement. Postwar Europe was thirsty for sweet wines, for nutritional as well as gustatory reasons, but good sweet wines, made from late-harvested riesling on good sites, were costly to make. The new crossings, however, ripened early and were genetically selected to produce high sugar levels. It was a grape-grower's dream: large, very large crops of very sweet wines. Unfortunately, most of them were heavy and sickly and the proliferation of wines from these new varieties—such as ortega, optima, bacchus and siegerrebe—did nothing for the reputation of German sweet wine. Of the new varieties kerner could produce decent dry or off-dry wine, and rieslaner could, and still does, produce sweet wine with a bracing balancing acidity. Scheurebe, too, can be excellent.

Together with advances in viticulture, there were innovations in winery equipment. The traditional large oak casks found in every German cellar—beautiful to look at but expensive and time-consuming to maintain in sound condition—were often replaced, especially at the larger estates, by stainless-steel tanks. This caused no problems in itself, but along with the tanks came batteries of filters and centrifuges, which, if coarsely handled, could strip the wines of their individuality. Sterile filtration encouraged the production of *süss-reserve*, stable grape must that could be used to sweeten wines without the risk of further fermentation. Whereas sweet wine in German had traditionally been the consequence of incomplete fermentations that left residual sugar in the wine, now the taste could be replicated by technology. The worst of the innovations, however, has

The church steeple dominates the township of Zeltingen, in Mosel.

Grapes do well beside the Mosel River where the banks plunge steeply down to the water's edge.

Spätburgunder grapes, Germany's pinot noir.

proved to be the German wine law of 1971, well-intentioned, but disastrous in the long term. It has defined the commercial history of German wine ever since and is dealt with later (see p. 233).

In the 1980s and 1990s there has been a trend toward greater diversity in the wines of Germany. Dry white wines, even from regions better suited to off-dry or sweet wines, became extremely fashionable, as growers sought to meet the demands of wine writers for a native equivalent to, say, chablis. Although warm regions such as the Pfalz proved well-suited to the production of dry rieslings, more northerly regions such as the Mosel were more likely to produce tart green wines that gave pleasure, it seemed, only to German gastronomes. Export markets, unused to the flavor of unripe grapes, could not abide them. The vogue for such wines has diminished, although they remain a feature of domestic wine production.

Much German red wine, even the highly praised spätburgunders from the Rheingau and Ahr, strikes outsiders as thin and weedy, although there were exceptions in ripe vintages. But the

Germans have always lamented the seeming inability of their climate to yield stylish fruity red wines and set about finding ways to correct this. From the 1980s some good, if rarely world-class, red wines, usually from spätburgunder but also from new varieties such as the juicy dornfelder, began to be produced in warmer regions such as the southern Pfalz, Württemberg and Baden.

At the same time the worldwide fashion for barrique-aged wines hit Germany, with some disastrous consequences—barrique-fermented rieslings. Fortunately, the trend was short-lived. Today there are some very good barrique-aged wines, especially from southern Germany, notably from the pinot family of grapes and chardonnay.

At the dawn of the twenty-first century the best wines of Germany are surely as good as they have ever been. Estates such as Breuer, Robert Weil, Müller-Catoir, von Buhl, J. J. Prüm and Dr Loosen—and perhaps two dozen more—release wines of stunning quality in a wide range of styles. The choice of styles today is greater than it would have been a century ago and the experimentation of the 1980s has settled down to a steady exploitation of appropriate grapes in appropriate sites. Overall, yields remain far too high and the crisis for the German wine industry continues, but at the top end, German wine is of brilliant quality.

Landscape and climate

German wine, good German wine, is enormously site-sensitive. Just as in Burgundy the wine produced on one patch of land can differ markedly from the wine made from identical grape varieties planted just a short distance away, so in Germany the nuances of site and microclimate count for a great deal. This was, undoubtedly, why certain sites have always been acclaimed as especially fine. Except in the Pfalz and Baden, the German climate is cool, so every nuance of exposition and climate must be exploited to the maximum. This explains why only certain slopes along the Mosel's banks are planted with vines; along the opposite side the sunshine is too patchy to allow the grapes to ripen. The best vineyards in the Rheingau face due south and are often planted on the steepest slopes.

With variations in location and altitude come nuances in taste and structure. In the Middle Mosel, the wines of Graach are usually identifiable as a touch broader and more ample than those from neighboring Wehlen. Within the large Brauneberger Juffer vineyard is a central patch that, it has long been acknowledged, usually provides better wines than the rest of the site: this is the parcel honored with its own name of Brauneberger Juffer-Sonnenuhr. The reflection of sunshine off the river, as well as the moderating climatic effect of the river-flow, are crucial factors affecting quality; the altitude and exposition of the vines is also of great consequence. It was Thomas Jefferson, in the late eighteenth century, who declared that the wines emanating from Schloss Johannisberg in the Rheingau were the finest of the region and anyone who looks down on that majestic vineyard soon understands why.

Because the German climate is, in viticultural terms, either marginal or extreme, it is not always easy to ripen the grapes. Many German red wines could easily be mistaken for rosés, though less so now than in the past. Without some balancing residual sugar, the rieslings of the Saar and Ruwer can be uncompromisingly harsh and tart, except in the very hottest years. The müller-thurgaus from the former eastern German regions are also prone to flavors that suggest severe underripeness. The acidity that can be so refreshing and zesty in a well-balanced riesling can be tooth-achingly unpleasant in a wine made from unripe grapes.

The greatest wines have always been made on the climatic edges. Burgundy has a less than ideal climate, but few would deny that when grapes grown there ripen fully, its pinot noir is the greatest in the world. Likewise in Germany, there are occasional disastrous vintages (though the past decade has been uncharacteristically warm, perhaps the consequence of global warming). But a great vintage, especially in the riesling zone, gives wines of unique quality and distinction that perform a near-miraculous balancing act between fruitiness and acidity.

The eastern regions can be as climatically challenging as the northern ones. Both Franken and Württemberg enjoy a continental climate. Summers can be very warm, but winters can be bitterly cold; thus the extremes of temperature are greater than in the Mosel, Rhine or Baden regions. If the vines survive unscathed through the ravages of winter, then the warm summer can deliver wines of great ripeness and body.

Even in the more southerly regions landscape plays its part. In Baden, the Kaiserstuhl region, focused around some volcanic slopes, is the hottest in Germany, giving wines that could easily be mistaken for their Alsatian counterparts from the opposite bank of the Rhine. In Franken, the supremacy of the Würzburger Stein, facing onto the great baroque city from across the river, is unchallenged. In the Pfalz, the Haardt mountains protect the vineyards from rain and cold and a few estates demonstrate their bravado by planting

The gutedel grape grown in southern Baden is the same as the Swiss chasselas variety.

Perfectly geometrical terraced plantings of vines at Oberrotweil, Kaiserstuhl, Baden.

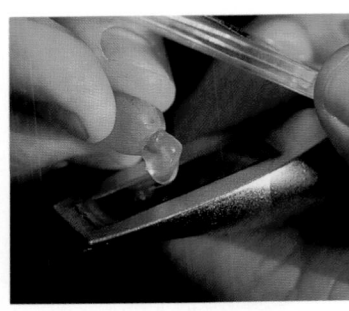

A refractometer is used to establish the level of natural sugar in the grapes.

lemon trees as proof of the exceptional micro-climate of their villages.

It would be foolish to try to single out the precise consequences of all these factors, but there can be no doubt that this singular cocktail of soil, exposition, altitude and steepness makes a vital contribution to the character and personality of the best German wines.

In 1997 the area planted with vineyards stood at 259,455 acres (105,000 ha) so the wine region is not that large when compared with the USA (778,365 acres/315,000 ha) or Italy (2,258,500 acres/914,000 ha). Rheinhessen and Pfalz are the largest regions, with well over 49,500 acres (20,000 ha) each, followed by Baden and the Mosel–Saar–Ruwer.

Vines and wines

By now it should be apparent that as far as Germany is concerned, riesling is king. Although its late-ripening character can cause problems when inclement weather dogs the fall months, the long growing season riesling craves can yield wines of superlative structure. The grapes can be physiologically ripe without attaining exceptional sugar levels. A great Mosel may have no more than 7° (or 7 percent) of alcohol; a Rheingau or Nahe wine perhaps 10° of alcohol. Yet this low alcohol does not entail any loss of intensity.

As long as yields are kept to a sensible level so that there is no trace of dilution or unripeness, that intensity is provided by the racy acidity allied to the mouthwatering fruitiness of the riesling grape. There is no white variety quite as versatile

Plastic sheeting protects these riesling grapes from birds until picking time.

as riesling. In warmer regions it can produce rich dry wines of considerable power. The mighty dry rieslings of Alsace and the Wachau in Austria show this to be so, though in some vintages dry rieslings from the Pfalz can come close to matching their power. But the German dry rieslings are more graceful and elegant than those from elsewhere in the world, with far greater emphasis on finesse rather than power.

In the more northerly regions, the wines need some balancing residual sugar. In the Rheingau the estates that formed the Charta Association in the 1970s promoted an off-dry style (known as halb-trocken in German). This wine was intended to be better adapted to consumption with food than the sweeter styles of riesling. Although German wine producers are fond of quoting analyses of sugar and acidity levels to demonstrate the excellence of their wines (tasting them should do the trick for most of us), figures alone tell us little. Good white wine is all about balance. For example, some rieslings from the Mosel–Saar–Ruwer have surprisingly high levels of residual sugar, yet the wine does not taste especially sweet; this is because of the equally high levels of acidity and extract. The precise balance of any wine is partly the result of the attributes of the grapes when harvested, but is also subject to the choices made by the producer.

Where riesling astonishes most is in its capacity to produce very long-lived and unashamedly sweet wines. It's a risky business, but the top estates will leave grapes on the vine until perilously late in the fall. If they are lucky, the grapes will have shriveled or become botrytised, provoking a concentration of sugar as well as the production of other chemical compounds such as glycerol. These very late-harvested wines, beerenauslese or trockenbeerenauslese, are so high in sugar that they ferment with difficulty and are often even lower in alcohol than traditional riesling styles. Their acidity is very high too, allowing them to age for decades, becoming gradually more honeyed and unctuous. A great beerenauslesen or trockenbeerenauslesen from a classic vintage, even at 50 or 100 years old, can be a mind-blowing experience, with an infinitely complex range of aromas and flavors. Even a more modest riesling of kabinett quality, if well made, can easily age (and improve) over 20 years.

Eiswein (ice wine) is a relatively new phenomenon and was a great rarity, a freak of nature, until the 1970s, when certain estates began to go out of their way to produce such wines. They left parcels of vines untouched in some corners of the

Looking down on the town of Oberrotweil,
Kaiserstuhl, Baden.

vineyard that were most prone to frost; often they would cover them with nets to protect them from the pecking beaks of sugar-addicted birds. Strict regulations dictated the depth and longevity of the frost required before the resulting wine could be classified as eiswein. Often the required conditions never arrived, or by the time they did the grapes had been too ravaged by insects or mold to be serviceable. Nonetheless, eiswein has been produced in reasonable quantities in most parts of Germany and this style of wine has remained fashionable, despite very high production costs.

The more traditional, and indeed more complex, beerenauslese and trockenbeerenauslese are often produced in tiny quantities—no more than token—and most estates regard them as showcases rather than as commercial ventures. They might be poured for honored guests, or conserved for decades in the estate cellars to amaze a future generation. Sometimes they are offered at auction where high prices win recognition for the estate.

Riesling is planted in most German wine regions, even on the Ihringer Winklerberg, said to

be the hottest single vineyard in all of Germany. Naturally styles differ greatly, but there are few areas to which riesling is positively unsuited. Müller-thurgau has become Germany's workhorse grape. A crossing bred in 1882, its merits were not recognized for many decades. Now widely planted, it is lower in acidity than riesling and delivers large vintages of vaguely fruity, reasonably fresh wine. If yields are kept fairly low, müller-thurgau wines can be enjoyable, especially those from Franken, with its bracing continental climate. An alternative name for müller-thurgau is rivaner, and the presence of that name on a label sometimes, but not always, denotes, a barrel-aged wine.

Sylvaner has quite a distinguished pedigree in Germany, despite its lowly reputation. It thrives best in Rheinhessen, especially close to the Rheinfront, and in Franken. Although sweetish versions exist, it is best as a somewhat earthy, vigorous, dry wine, which can be well suited to accompany food. It is traditional (and very satisfactory) served with asparagus. In southern Germany the pinot varieties do well: spätbur-

Trollinger grapes, common in Württemberg.

Bins of spätburgunder, ready for collection.

gunder (pinot noir), weissburgunder (pinot blanc) and grauer burgunder (pinot gris). They are ubiquitous in Baden, but even as far north as the Rheinhessen grauer burgunder can be a good wine. Spätburgunder and weissburgunder are well adapted to oak-aging, though various styles exist.

Grauer burgunder is rarely improved by aging in barriques, but the German consumer is quite keen on the style. When vinified as a sweet wine, especially in Baden, grauer burgunder is often known as ruländer and can give extremely fat, unctuous, figgy wines at beerenauslese and trockenbeerenauslese levels. At some of the more old-fashioned estates in Baden, especially cooperatives, spätburgunder is sometimes produced in a lightly sweet style (as spätlese or auslese), which only local wine drinkers find palatable.

There have been misguided attempts to produce cabernet sauvignon in the Pfalz, with dismal results. The newish red grape dornfelder, with its deep color and gamay-like exuberance, is far more successful, filling the niche for a grapey red that can be enjoyed young. In Württemberg, lemberger (known in Austria as blaufränkisch) has been grown since the seventeenth century and can make a lively cherryish wine of considerable character.

The other common red variety in this part of Germany is trollinger, which gives pallid wines that appeal mostly to local consumers. Pinot meunier, known in Germany as schwarzriesling, is also found in Württemberg and Baden, but as a dry red wine it can be somewhat neutral. There are swathes of portugieser in many southern vineyards; its wine is light, fruity and innocuous.

The new white varieties have already been mentioned. Now that the market for soupy sweet wines is on the wane, some vineyards planted with optima, ortega and the like have been grubbed up and replanted with more noble varieties. There are some good crossings, however. Rieslaner, which, unlike most other crossings, has high acidity, makes brilliant sweet wines, very close in character to riesling, in regions such as Franken and the Pfalz. Scheurebe, which has been around for many decades, yields a somewhat grapefruity dry wine, especially in the Pfalz, and can make exceedingly good sweet wines.

The remaining white varieties are marginal. The gutedel of southern Baden is the same as the chasselas of Switzerland and the wines tend to be equally boring: pleasant quaffing wines on a summer picnic, but little more than that.

Muskateller can be good in southern Germany, both in dry and very sweet styles. Chardonnay is a relative newcomer to Germany, to the dismay of traditionalists, but it can give quite good wines in the Pfalz and Baden as long as makers resist the tendency to smother it in new oak.

Sparkling wine, known as sekt, has a strong presence on the domestic market, although international drinkers reared on champagne rarely find sekt particularly palatable. However, quite a few producers have, over the past decade, sought to make more serious méthode champenoise wines, either from riesling or from the pinot varieties. Some of these sparkling wines—from Breuer in the Rheingau, Lindenhof in the Nahe and Koehler-Ruprecht in the Pfalz, among many others—are of very acceptable quality.

In regions producing red wine, rosé is made under the name of weissherbst. Although many of these wines are intended to be simple thirst-quenchers, there is also a vogue for late-harvest rosés up to trockenbeerenauslese level, which can be much better than they sound.

Wine laws

The wine regulations that have bedeviled the industry came into force in 1971. Some form of regulation was undoubtedly necessary, but the laws put in place were broad and open to abuse. The 1971 wine law placed German wine production into three roughly equal categories: Tafelwein (the most basic), Qualitätswein (QbA) and the superior Qualitätswein mit Prädikat (QmP). The "Prädikat" consisted of further quality categories, rising from kabinett to trockenbeerenauslese. The sole criterion for inclusion in any category was grape sugar at harvest and therein lay the fatal flaw. The boundaries between the sub-categories of kabinett, spätlese, auslese, beerenauslese and trockenbeerenauslese were, it's true, adjusted according to the wine region. Thus higher grape sugars were required for a wine from warm Baden than from cool Nahe. But the levels were generous, thanks to the lobbying of the cooperatives and *négociants*, and among the better estates declassi-fication has become routine. A typical explanation would be: "It's better to offer a terrific kabinett than a mediocre spätlese." And so on up the scale.

At the same time as the wine laws were being promulgated, the new early-ripening varieties were coming into production and it became a simple task to produce auslese or beerenauslese from ortega, bacchus and the like. In earlier times, auslese on the

Oak barrels in the cellars of Weingut Bercher Burkheim, Kaiserstuhl, Baden.

label implied a high degree of selection in the vine-yard and correspondingly high quality—at least from the best growers, but after 1971 sugar level alone determined what was labeled auslese. Moreover, it remains perfectly legal to blend some blowsy ortega auslese into a vat of riesling auslese and still bottle the wine as a riesling. The potential abuses were endless and the fine name that once attached to the notion of "auslese" was degraded. Nor was it necessarily the case that a QbA was inferior to a QmP, since it was legal to chaptalise the former but not the latter. In years when ripeness was a problem, such as 1987 in the Mosel–Saar–Ruwer, many a lightly chaptalised QbA proved a more enjoyable and better-balanced wine than a thin kabinett.

The wine laws permit the unrestricted use of harvesting machines, so it is perfectly legal to machine-harvest trockenbeerenauslese, which is hardly a way to ensure high quality. There is also no limitation on yields. Many growers, hoping for an easy living, pushed their vines to yield the maximum quantity of grapes to qualify for Qualitätswein. In 1989, for example, the average yield throughout Germany was 8 tons per acre (140 hl per ha) and as recently as 1998 the average yield for the Mosel was 6.9 tons per acre (121 hl per ha). Despite this, only the tiniest proportion of Germany's wine production emerged from its wineries as Tafelwein, which meant that vast amounts of undistinguished wine could proudly carry the label Qualitätswein. This dross, often dolled up in fancy bottles with fancy names, including the now infamous Liebfraumilch, ended up on supermarket shelves in Britain and else-where and the consumer began to associate German "quality wine" with the sugar-water on

A mechanical harvester at work in the Bercher Burkheim vineyards.

Two ways of harvesting: top, by mechanical means, and below, by hand, the preferred way to produce top-quality wines.

which sites were the finest and what their particular characteristics were. To some extent this understanding survived and a premium was placed on wines from the most famous vineyards, Erbach, Marcobrunn, Bernkastel Doctor and the like. But as far as the law was concerned all of Germany's many thousands of named vineyards were equal. Even worse, new appellations came into being: the Bereich and the Grosslage. This allowed large producers to blend wines from various districts within a region and sell them under a regional or district name. Unfortunately, the Grosslagen were named after the most famous village in the district. Notorious examples include Piesporter Michelsberg and Niersteiner Gute Domtal, and wines carrying those names on the label were under no legal obligation to include a single drop of wine (let alone riesling wine) from those famous villages, whose reputations have yet to recover from their degradation.

Most wine producers in Germany will admit to the failings of the wine law, but the main regulatory and marketing bodies are dominated, certainly financially, by the big players in the industry, who have no short-term interest in reforming the system. Pressure to reform has come from the leading estates, which have grouped together to form associations (such as the VDP or Charta) and demand far stricter quality controls than the feeble wine laws. Other estates have simply imposed tough self-regulation, ensuring that anything offered under their label to the consumer is of good quality.

Grosslagen are at last on their way out and there are moves in many regions toward vineyard classification. Twenty years ago leading north German estates might have produced wines from 10 different vineyards; today those same estates will use a single-vineyard name only for wines from its top sites, while the rest of the production will be blended to form a "gutsriesling" or estate blend, which may be of excellent quality but will not have the pretensions to site specificity of the leading sites.

As in other parts of the grape-growing world, the name of the estate has become the best guarantee of quality. It is scarcely conceivable that properties such as Robert Weil or Maximin Grünhaus will market a mediocre wine and the shrewd consumer should opt for a modest category from a top estate in preference to a grander appellation from an unknown grower, whose yields may be three times as high.

offer. And since it was usually the cheapest wine on the shelves, the consumer couldn't see the point in paying two or three times as much for some other "quality wine" from Germany. Whereas the French wine industry had led proudly from the top, boasting of its great crus from Bordeaux and Burgundy, the German industry made the disastrous mistake of leading from the bottom. By the 1990s many growers in the more prolific wine regions, such as the Pfalz and Rheinhessen, were on the brink of ruin, as grape prices plummeted and pressure grew from the EU to remove the most undistinguished industrial-scale vineyards.

Nor was there any attempt at vineyard classification. At the turn of the century everyone knew

There is great debate within Germany as to the best way forward. Vineyard classification benefits the well-established estates with holdings in the best sites, whereas a conscientious producer with no exceptional vineyards but a good track record for quality may feel himself penalized by such a classification. No doubt these debates will continue. Meanwhile, the gradual process of undoing the worst damage inflicted by the 1971 wine laws and those who abused them is getting underway.

These long-term abuses as well as climatic variations between regions make generalizations about style very tricky. The hierarchy of spätlese, auslese and so forth does, of course, relate to sweetness, but should also have to do with quality and this is not necessarily the case. A spätlese from the Saar would, because of climatic differences, bear little relation to a much weightier spätlese from Franken. The vogue for dry wines has seen the introduction of the words trocken or halbtrocken. Trocken has up to 9 grams of residual sugar which, given the generally high acidity in German wines, still leaves the wine tasting dry. Halbtrocken, with between 9 and 18 grams, is a style well suited to the wines of the Rheingau. Although the Charta Association's wines are not labeled as such, they are in effect halbtrocken. Fewer producers are using the term, which they see as unhelpful to the consumer. (Some have adopted the term feinherb to denote an off-dry wine.)

To confuse matters further, some top growers, who routinely make several forays through their vineyards seeking out only the best grapes, may produce more than one auslese from a particular site. These are differentiated by the "AP" number (assigned to every wine approved by the regional tasting panels) or by length or color of the lead capsule. Thus an estate may release, from the same vintage, an Auslese, an Auslese Goldkapsel and an Auslese Lange Goldkapsel. Price will be an indication of the value placed on each by the grower.

Viticultural practices

These are often a function of terrain. The steep sites, from which most of the best wine emanates, have to be cultivated and harvested manually. On flatter land, especially in the Rheinhessen and the Pfalz, mechanization is usual. Green-harvesting and other post-pruning measures intended to reduce yields are relatively new in Germany and there is much debate as to the appropriate yields for, say, a good-quality riesling. Whereas yields of 1,600 gallons per acre (150 hl per ha) are perfectly feasible, most growers would see yields of 650 to 750 gallons (6,000–7,000 l) as more compatible with decent quality, although some would argue for considerably lower yields. In some vineyards green cover has been planted, either to combat erosion or to provide competition for the hungry vine roots and so reduce yield.

Given the marginal climate of many of Germany's wine regions, it is not surprising that organic or biodynamic viticulture has made little headway. The strong possibility of cool rainy spells also increases the likelihood of rot and disease and few growers are prepared to eliminate spraying or other treatments from their vineyards. However, there are estates, such as Heyl zu Herrnsheim and Graf von Kanitz, that are wholly or partly committed to organic viticulture.

Winemaking procedures are relatively uncontroversial. There is near-universal agreement that for varieties such as riesling, müller-thurgau and sylvaner, barriques are anathema. Many traditional estates retain their large oval casks, often up to 100 years old, in which all their wines are fermented and aged. They argue that these large casks allow the wine to breathe and mature gracefully without imparting any trace of oakiness. Other producers favor a more reductive approach and have banished wood in favor of stainless steel, which is also easier and less costly to maintain. There are outstanding producers in both camps and many employ both tanks and casks.

The pinot varieties and red wines, most growers acknowledge, benefit from some wood-aging, but the kind of aging varies greatly. In Baden new barriques enjoy a strong following, sometimes with coarse results, but styles of oak-aging vary as much in Germany as they do in France or Italy. There were some ghastly barrique-aged wines made 15 years ago, when oak was little understood, but such wines are rarely seen nowadays, as producers have honed their skills in this respect.

The presence of residual sugar in many wines means that technical options such as chilling, sterile filtration or centrifuging are still employed. But dependence on technology is less unquestioning than it would have been 20 years ago and German wine from top estates is a product of considerable purity.

Grape juice fermenting in glass.

Science lends winemakers a hand at the Department of Viticulture's State Research Institute in Geisenheim, Rheingau.

Mosel–Saar–Ruwer

This elaborate old fountain in Bernkastel celebrates the bounty of the vine.

The Mosel River twists and turns on its leisurely way from Koblenz toward Luxembourg. Vineyards are planted on the best-exposed nearby slatey slopes—and, regrettably, on some flat land stretching away from the river. More thrive along the slopes beside its two tributaries, the Saar and Ruwer, which have been tossed into the administrative region of the Mosel–Saar–Ruwer.

Despite the size of the region, there is surprising homogeneity in the character of its riesling wines. Although half the vineyards are planted with other varieties, mostly müller-thurgau, the Mosel–Saar–Ruwer is, or should be, pre-eminently riesling territory. Nowhere else in the world does riesling display such razor-sharp intensity of flavor. Although the noble wines from the Rheingau may dispute the claim, many would argue that Mosel rieslings are the finest of all.

The Mosel River itself is divided into the Lower, Middle and Upper Mosel—and the greatest of these is the Middle or Mittelmosel (M-M). Most of the estates, especially in the Lower Mosel, are small, and the largest properties were formerly ecclesiastical or educational foundations, which used their vineyard profits to fund charitable activities. Instead of aristocratic estates that once

dominated the Rheingau, many of the Mosel's best vineyards have been in the hands of clans such as the Prüms or Pauly-Bergweilers for generations.

The Lower Mosel encompasses the stretch of the river between Koblenz and Zell and has less of the slate that characterizes the Middle Mosel. Its wines rarely ascend the heights scaled by those from the Middle Mosel, but some villages produce high-quality riesling, notably Zell, Cochem and Bullay. The wines tend to be light and delicate, without the steeliness of the finest rieslings.

The wine heartland lies in the Middle Mosel, a succession of river bends from Zell to just north of Trier, with a succession of celebrated villages, of which the best known are Wehlen, Bernkastel and Piesport. Here the slatey soils perform their dual function of imbuing the wines with a characteristic mineral tang and of reflecting the warmth of the day back onto the vines as daylight fades.

The Lower Mosel is a more amorphous region, following the river south from Trier. Riesling is less dominant here than in other sections of the Mosel, and müller-thurgau and elbling are commonly encountered. Although some good wines emanate from Trier itself and Konz, both along the Mosel, the best rieslings from the region come from the two tributaries: the Ruwer, flowing into the Mosel just north of Trier, and the Saar, entering at Konz southwest of Trier.

These are chilly valleys, especially the Saar, so the nuances of exposition and incline become even more important than in the Middle Mosel. In some years the grapes struggle to reach ripeness, but when they do, they give the most elegant and racy wines of the entire region.

Despite the northerly climate, sublime sweet rieslings can be produced in certain vintages. These great rarities fetch very high prices at auction.

Villages of Middle Mosel

Bernkastel's busy streets don't encroach on the slatey vineyards towering above it. Doctor is the best-known site and its wines are the most expensive, but others, such as Lay, come close in quality with steely, fruity, quintessential Mosel riesling.

Brauneberg was made famous by winemaker Fritz Haag, but its celebrity is ancient. Powerful, long-lived wines. Best site: Juffer-Sonnenuhr.

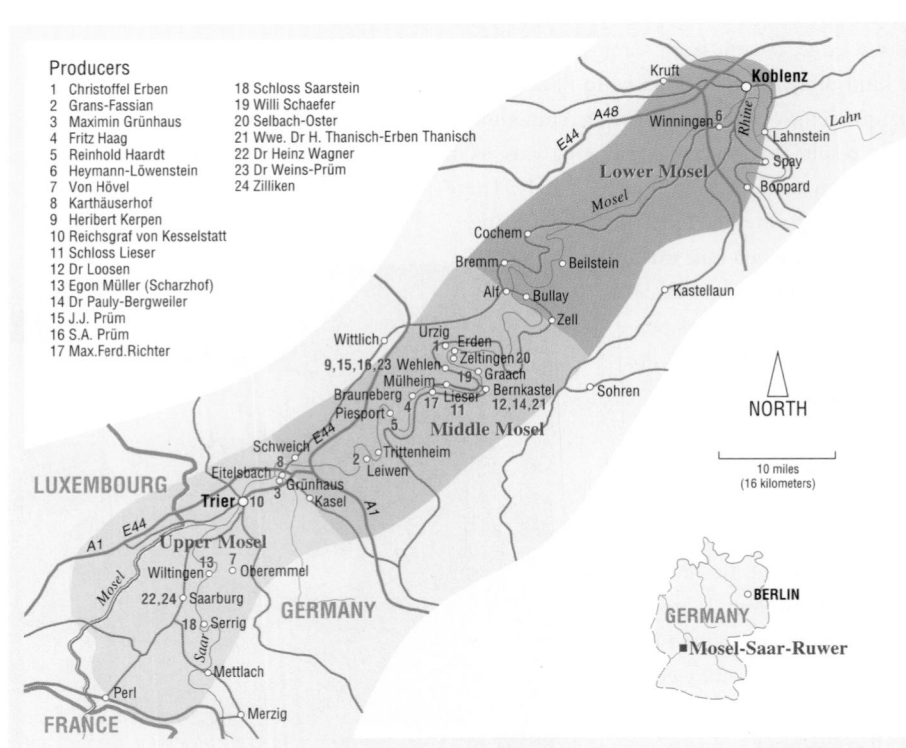

Producers

1 Christoffel Erben
2 Grans-Fassian
3 Maximin Grünhaus
4 Fritz Haag
5 Reinhold Haardt
6 Heymann-Löwenstein
7 Von Hövel
8 Karthäuserhof
9 Heribert Kerpen
10 Reichsgraf von Kesselstatt
11 Schloss Lieser
12 Dr Loosen
13 Egon Müller (Scharzhof)
14 Dr Pauly-Bergweiler
15 J.J. Prüm
16 S.A. Prüm
17 Max.Ferd.Richter
18 Schloss Saarstein
19 Willi Schaefer
20 Selbach-Oster
21 Wwe. Dr H. Thanisch-Erben Thanisch
22 Dr Heinz Wagner
23 Dr Weins-Prüm
24 Zilliken

Erden faces Urzig and is best known for its rich and long-lived rieslings from Prälat vineyard.

Graach has a broad band of superb vineyards between Bernkastel and Wehlen, producing wines a tad richer but less elegant than its neighbors. Best sites: Himmelreich and Josephshöfer.

Piesport comprises a succession of vineyards facing south across the river. Goldtröpfchen is best known but its neighbors produce a similar standard. Many wines have a mineral, aniseed quality.

Trittenheim's mostly steep vineyards give its wines delicacy and finesse. Best site: Apotheke.

Urzig's slatey soil is mixed with red clay, giving wines of unusual spiciness and exotic flavor.

Wehlen is perfectly exposed, and Wehlener Sonnenuhr is one of the classic sites of the region, producing the most exquisite rieslings.

Zeltingen, a neighbor of Wehlen, produces wines of comparable finesse, especially from its best vineyard, the Sonnenuhr.

Kasel, Ruwer, is the home of the Nies'chen vineyard, which regularly delivers rieslings with enticing delicacy and elegance.

Saarburg, Saar, is the source of good steely wines, especially from its top vineyard, Rausch.

Serrig, Saar, south of Saarburg, produces lean, tight rieslings that need years to evolve.

Wiltingen, Saar, has many good sites, but the most celebrated, justly, is the great hill of the Scharzhofberg, source of the Saar's most ethereal rieslings and most intense eisweins.

Producers

CHRISTOFFEL ERBEN, URZIG
Owner Hans Leo Christoffel *Production* 1,600 cases *Vineyard area* 5 acres (2 ha)

This small, highly traditional estate still ages all its wines in old casks, which doesn't prevent them from reaching the highest levels of elegance. Christoffel is fortunate to have a fine parcel of carefully nurtured vines in the superlative Urziger Würzgarten vineyard, the source of ravishingly sweet wines in top vintages. Kabinetts and drier wines from Erdener Treppchen can also be very good.

GRANS-FASSIAN, LEIWEN
Owner Gerhard Grans *Production* 5,000 cases *Vineyard area* 20 acres (8 ha)

Leiwen is one of the lesser-known villages of the Middle Mosel, which has certainly hampered its best growers in achieving the reputation they deserve. Gerhard Grans is the clear exception to this. As well as sound bottles from Leiwen, he also produces delicious and vigorous wines from two other top sites: Trittenheimer Apotheke and Piesporter Goldtröpfchen. Get to know his wines at the family's bar and restaurant in Trittenheim.

A vineyard worker tastes a bunch of freshly picked grapes.

Looking across the Mosel River toward Trittenheim, in the southern Mittelmosel.

The church at Piesport. The town itself sits in a great amphitheater of vineyards.

generate the most excitement. Von Schubert bottles auslese from individual casks under a rather confusing cask number. Price indicates quality.

FRITZ HAAG, BRAUNEBERG

Owner **Wilhelm Haag** *Production* **5,000 cases** *Vineyard area* **17 acres (7 ha)**

Wilhelm Haag produces some of the most powerful wines of the Middle Mosel—not powerful in alcohol, but in intensity of flavor and long complex aftertastes. All his best wines come from the Juffer-Sonnenuhr vineyard. The Fritz Haag name on the label has become a guarantee of classic, long-lived riesling. And the sweet wines—sometimes three or more auslesen in any vintage—are sensational, if increasingly unaffordable.

REINHOLD HAART, PIESPORT

Owner **Theo Haart** *Production* **3,500 cases** *Vineyard area* **13 acres (5 ha)**

The degrading of the once-great name of Piesport has meant that some wine fanciers dismiss its wines as less fine than those of Bernkastel or Wehlen, but Haart can prove them wrong. His small property is now the top estate in Piesport. These are wines of pungency and elegance, and sometimes they have a delicate hint of aniseed. The top wines come from Piesporter Goldtröpfchen, but there are also excellent and less expensive bottles from the Wintricher Ohligsberg vineyard.

HEYMANN-LÖWENSTEIN, WINNINGEN

Owner **Reinhard Löwenstein** *Production* **3,500 cases** *Vineyard area* **15 acres (6 ha)**

While Winningen, just south of Koblenz, does not have the reputation of the villages in the Middle Mosel, Reinhard Löwenstein has in recent years shown their striking potential. The dry wines are good examples of the style, but it's the sweeter ones that show how fine the wines of the Upper Mosel can be, if vinified with skill and dedication.

MAXIMIN GRÜNHAUS, GRÜNHAUS

Owner **Dr Carl Von Schubert** *Production* **9,000 cases** *Vineyard area* **84 acres (34 ha)**

This famous property is a living model of German ecclesiastical history. Originally a monastic estate dating from the tenth century, its top site is the Abtsberg (abbot's hill), followed by the Herrenberg (lord's hill) and Brudersberg (brothers' hill). The Brudersberg has been replanted so the vines are fairly young and, at present, the best wines come from the other sites. The estate is admired within Germany for its dry rieslings, but for everyone else it is the marvelous auslesen and eisweins that

VON HÖVEL, OBEREMMEL

Owner **Eberhard von Kunow** *Production* **3,500 cases** *Vineyard area* **22 acres (9 ha)**

Jovial von Kunow is sole proprietor of Oberemeller Hütte, from which he makes a range of impeccable wines. Like others from the Saar, these are delicate and racy. In outstanding vintages the Hütte site delivers finely tuned and hauntingly sweet wines and eiswein. Von Kunow also makes wines from the celebrated Scharzhofberg vineyard, but those from the Hütte are usually just as fine.

KARTHÄUSERHOF, EITELSBACH
Owner Christoff Tyrell *Production* 12,500 cases *Vineyard area* 47 acres (19 ha)

Sturdy Christoff Tyrell sometimes gives the impression that he'd as soon be out hunting as making wine, but he has brought this Ruwer estate to the top ranks. The once-segmented vineyards, all owned by Tyrell, have been reunited under the mouth-filling name Eitelsbacher Karthäuserhofberg. The wines can be austere when young and benefit from bottle age. The estate has a fine reputation for dry wines, but its intense and ethereal sweet wines are well appreciated abroad.

HERIBERT KERPEN, WEHLEN
Owners Kerpen family *Production* 3,500 cases *Vineyard area* 13 acres (5 ha)

Less well known than some of the dynastic estates of Wehlen, Kerpen is nonetheless very reliable. The property is now run by the engaging Martin Kerpen, who is keen on drier-style wines. The sweet wines are often sensational and different strata of spätlesen and auslesen are distinguished, somewhat confusingly, by a star system on the label.

REICHSGRAF VON KESSELSTATT, TRIER
Owner Annegret Reh-Gartner *Production* 33,000 cases *Vineyard area* 141 acres (57 ha)

In 1978 the Reh family bought this large and ancient estate and many feared the worst, since the family was associated with some very large commercial wine-producing companies. But Annegret Reh-Gartner has put all those fears to rest, having rationalized the cumbersome estate (only wines from outstanding sites are now bottled under the vineyard name) and imposed high standards in the vineyard and winery. Kesselstatt owns vineyards throughout the Mosel–Saar–Ruwer, and wines from Kaseler Nies'chen, Scharzhofberg, Josephshöfer, Piesporter Goldtröpfchen and Bernkasteler Doctor can be recommended without hesitation.

SCHLOSS LIESER, LIESER
Owner Thomas Haag *Production* 3,500 cases *Vineyard area* 16 acres (6.5 ha)

Although Lieser lies midway between Bernkastel and Brauneberg, it has never enjoyed the high reputation of its neighbors. Since 1992, when Thomas Haag, son of the great Wilhelm Haag, took over the winemaking at this estate, a new star is rising. Wilhelm now owns the property, formerly known as the Schorlemer property and is turning out vibrant and concentrated wines.

DR LOOSEN, BERNKASTEL
Owner Ernst Loosen *Production* 6,000 cases *Vineyard area* 25 acres (10 ha)

In the late 1990s the dynamic Ernst Loosen took over the running of this old property, which owns superb sites in Wehlen, Urzig and Erden. Loosen openly expresses his view that the German wine laws of 1971 have allowed the largest and most cynical producers to exploit and traduce the names associated with the finest German wines. He is focused on quality above all else, ruthlessly cutting yields and harvesting as late as possible. Other estates may sometimes surpass Loosen in finesse, but few can match the sheer brilliance and concentration of his wines, from the humblest kabinett to his majestic sweet wines.

EGON MÜLLER (SCHARZHOF), WILTINGEN
Owners Egon Müller family *Production* 4,000 cases *Vineyard area* 20 acres (8 ha)

This is surely the most legendary estate in Germany, distinguished by the astonishing quality of its wines and the even more astonishing prices obtained for them. Based in a beautiful old manor house at the foot of the Scharzhofberg, the Egon Müllers, father and son, coax the utmost complexity and refined structure from their incomparable and indestructible sweet wines, although the QbA and kabinett are usually of lesser interest.

DR PAULY-BERGWEILER, BERNKASTEL
Owner Dr Peter Pauly *Production* 6,000 cases *Vineyard area* 35 acres (14 ha)

Dr Peter Pauly is a proud and rather prickly man, which may have prevented his wines from winning the acclaim they deserve. With fine vineyards located throughout the Middle Mosel (Bernkastel, Graach, Erden, Würzig, Wehlen—he has them all), he is able to offer a wide range of wines (including a pinot noir), but his strength lies in superb sweet wines, including trockenbeerenauslese and eiswein.

J. J. PRÜM, WEHLEN
Owner Manfred Prüm *Production* 10,000 cases *Vineyard area* 35 acres (14 ha)

The grandest of the Prüm estates in Wehlen, this is run with fastidious attention to detail by Dr Manfred Prüm. Thanks to the gentle prickle of natural carbon dioxide in the wine, they can be deceptively youthful and can age for decades. In great vintages these can be the finest expressions of the Middle Mosel, supremely elegant distillations of the steep slaty soils of the Wehlener Sonnenuhr.

Harvest time at the Maximin Grünhaus vineyard in the Saar Valley.

REGIONAL DOZEN

QUALITY WINES

Brauneberger Juffer-Sonnenuhr Riesling Beerenauslese (Fritz Haag)

Eitelsbacher Karthäuserhof Riesling Auslese (Karthäuserhof)

Erden Prälat Riesling Auslese (Dr Loosen)

Maximin Grünhauser Abtsberg Riesling Eiswein (Maximin Grünhaus)

Scharzhofberger Riesling Beerenauslese (Egon Müller)

Wehlener Sonnenuhr Riesling Auslese (J. J. Prüm)

BEST VALUE WINES

Erdener Treppchen Riesling Kabinett (Dr Loosen)

Scharzhofberger Riesling Kabinett (Kesselstatt)

Serriger Schloss Saarsteiner Riesling Auslese (Schloss Saarstein)

Wehlener Sonnenuhr Riesling Kabinett (Kerpen)

Wintricher Ohligsberg Riesling Spätlese (Haart)

Zeltinger Sonnenuhr Riesling Spätlese (Selbach-Oster)

A wine tasting at S. A. Prüm's winery in Wehlen, in the Mosel.

S. A. PRÜM, WEHLEN

Manager Raimund Prüm *Production* 4,000 cases *Vineyard area* 25 acres (10 ha)

This property is no longer owned by the Prüm family, but Raimund Prüm is still in charge of the winemaking. If the wines rarely reach the heights attained by J. J. Prüm, they are still extremely good, especially from Wehlener Sonnenuhr. The vines are very old, yielding wines of impeccable concentration and fruitiness.

MAX. FERD. RICHTER, MÜLHEIM

Owner Dr Dirk Richter *Production* 10,000 cases *Vineyard area* 35 acres (14 ha)

This ancient property, run for many years by the dynamic Dr Dirk Richter, is a *négociant* as well as an estate, and the former wines carry yellow labels to distinguish them from estate-bottlings. The best estate vineyards are in Brauneberg and the wines are very well made and always reliable. The house specialty is the eiswein, made almost every year from a special parcel of vines in the Mülheimer Helenkloster vineyard.

SCHLOSS SAARSTEIN, SERRIG

Owner Christian Ebert *Production* 5,000 cases *Vineyard area* 25 acres (10 ha)

Christian Ebert has been coaxing racy and elegant wines from this estate for 15 years. Since it is located in the Saar, it is not surprising that the wines are characterized by prominent acidity and some vintages need several years in bottle to become harmonious. Prices are reasonable.

WILLI SCHAEFER, GRAACH

Owner Willi Schaefer *Production* 2,000 cases *Vineyard area* 6 acres (2.5 ha)

Although the Schaefers have owned vineyards in Wehlen and Graach since the sixteenth century, the smallness of the property and the natural diffidence of the Schaefer family has meant that the outstanding quality of the wines only became widely recognized in the 1990s. The sweet wines are often the best, marrying grace and elegance with understated power and purity of fruit.

SELBACH-OSTER, ZELTINGEN

Owner Johannes Selbach *Production* 6,500 cases *Vineyard area* 25 acres (10 ha)

Johannes Selbach is a shrewd *négociant* as well as an estate owner. All his wines are of good quality, but those from his own vineyards in Zeltingen, Wehlen and Graach are often outstanding. Selbach-Oster demonstrates the high quality of the Zeltingen sites, which can rival those of neighboring Wehlen. The wines are accessible young, but age well.

WWE. DR H. THANISCH—ERBEN THANISCH, BERNKASTEL

Owner Sofia Thanisch Spier *Production* 4,000 cases *Vineyard area* 15 acres (6 ha)

Maddeningly, there are two estates with almost identical names and with almost identical labels. This, the better of the two, is run by Sofia Spier and sports the VDP logo on its label. Although the estate owns vines in the excellent Brauneberger Juffer-Sonnenuhr, it is best known for rich, firm wines of great distinction from the Bernkasteler Doctor vineyard. Buyers pay a handsome premium for the illustrious name.

DR HEINZ WAGNER, SAARBURG

Owner Dr Heinz Wagner *Production* 5,000 cases *Vineyard area* 22 acres (9 ha)

Wagner owns excellent steep sites in Ayl and Ockfen, but his best wines usually come from the Saarburger Rausch vineyard. Despite the austere climate of the Saar, Wagner makes some pungently fruity dry and off-dry wines, as well as some lovely elegant sweeter wines balanced by the racy acidity typical of the region. His eiswein can be magical.

DR WEINS-PRÜM, WEHLEN

Owner Bert Selbach *Production* 3,200 cases *Vineyard area* 10 acres (4 ha)

The taciturn Bert Selbach inhabits another of the proud riverbank mansions built by the Prüms in Wehlen. Although quite small, the Weins-Prüm estate owns a wide spectrum of vineyards and, in addition to fruity, stylish and dependable wines from Wehlener Sonnenuhr, there are some succulent sweet wines from Erdener Prälat.

ZILLIKEN, SAARBURG

Owner Hans-Joachim Zilliken *Production* 4,000 cases *Vineyard area* 25 acres (10 ha)

The cellars beneath the Zilliken residence are three storys deep and bottles resting in the lowest level, where the humidity is so high the walls ooze with condensation, scarcely seem to age at all. Hans-Joachim Zilliken is proud of the longevity of his wines, which have the steely acidity typical of the Saar, as well as great concentration of flavor. His wines from Ockfener Bockstein can be very good but his masterpieces come from Saarburger Rausch, notably his breathtaking eiswein.

Nahe

The Nahe, named after a tributary of the Rhine, is one of Germany's more amorphous regions. Whereas the Mosel and Rheingau are geographically focused, the vineyards of the Nahe are more dispersed. Nor is there much uniformity of style, which is hardly surprising given the geological variation within the region. Some of the best wines, with fine extract and raciness, come from the volcanic and slatey soils around Niederhausen and Schlossböckelheim. The best wines, inevitably, are rieslings, but this variety accounts for less than one third of the area planted. Many other varieties are grown here, including almost as much müller-thurgau as riesling, as well as sylvaner, grauer burgunder and more recent varieties such as kerner. A little red wine is produced in the Nahe, usually from spätburgunder or portugieser, but general standards are not very high.

So it's riesling that's king here, as in the rest of the more northerly wine regions. At their best, Nahe rieslings have the verve and raciness of good Mosel combined with the weightier structure of the Rheingau. Equally important, the Nahe has some very singular vineyards with remarkable and distinctive soils; when yields are kept low, these vineyards produce wines with a strong personality.

Compared with wines from the Rheingau or Mosel, prices remain very reasonable and there are bargains to be found, but the growing reputation of the Nahe for stunning eiswein and other very sweet styles may prompt an upward movement in prices. However, it is clear that at many estates, often with fine vineyards, the full potential for high-quality wines has yet to be realized.

Villages of the Nahe

Bad Kreuznach is an attractive spa town, fringed with good vineyards such as Kahlenberg and Brücke.

Dorsheim, in the hilly northern sector of the Nahe, has two outstanding vineyards, Goldloch and Pittermänchen.

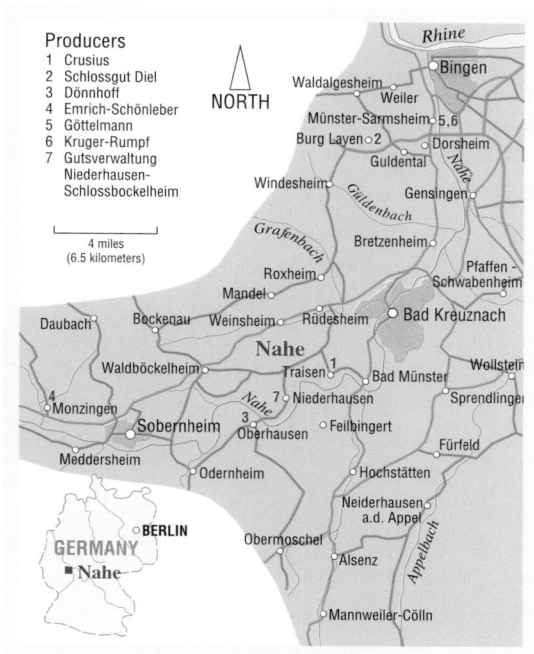

Niederhausen has exceptional vineyards near the river, notably Hermannsberg and Hermannshöhle, producing wines for the State Domaine.

Schlossböckelheim is best known for its Kupfergrube site, a former copper mine planted with vines by the State Domaine. After the sale of State Domaine, other growers have purchased portions of this great site.

Traisen shelters the tiny Bastei vineyard on a strip of land beneath awesome porphyry cliffs.

Riesling grapes in frost-prone corners are protected from birds and later made into the stunning eisweins for which Nahe is famous.

REGIONAL DOZEN

QUALITY WINES

Dorsheimer Pittermännchen
  Riesling Auslese (Diel)
Monzinger Frühlingsplätzchen
  Riesling Auslese (Emrich-
  Schönleber)
Münsterer Dautenpflänzer
  Riesling Auslese (Kruger-
  Rumpf)
Niederhäuser Hermannsberg
  Riesling Eiswein (Gutsver-
  waltung Niederhausen-
  Schlossböckelheim)
Oberhäuser Brücke Riesling
  Eiswein (Dönnhoff)
Traiser Bastei Riesling Spätlese
  (Crusius)

BEST VALUE WINES

Monzinger Frühlingsplätzchen
  Riesling Kabinett (Emrich-
  Schönleber)
Münsterer Pittersberg Riesling
  Spätlese Trocken (Kruger-
  Rumpf)
Münsterer Rheinberg Riesling
  Spätlese (Göttelmann)
Niederhäuser Hermannshöhle
  Riesling Spätlese (Dönnhoff)
Norheimer Dellchen Riesling
  Auslese (Lötzbeyer)
Schlossböckelheimer Kupfer-
  grube Riesling Spätlese
  (Gutsverwaltung Nieder-
  hausen-Schlossböckelheim)

Villages dot the river banks throughout the wine regions of Germany.

Producers

CRUSIUS, TRAISEN

Owner Dr Peter Crusius *Production* 6,500 cases *Vineyard area* 30 acres (12 ha)

After a brief somnolent period, this highly regarded estate is back on form. Its top wine is invariably the riesling from Traiser Bastei, which has a distinctive earthy mineral tone allied to vivacity and finesse. Almost as fine are the wines from Traiser Rotenfels, named after the huge red porphyry cliffs that tower above the Bastei and the river, and from Schlossböckelheimer Felsenberg.

SCHLOSSGUT DIEL, BURG LAYEN

Owner Armin Diel *Production* 7,500 cases *Vineyard area* 37 acres (15 ha)

Armin Diel is a respected food and wine critic as well as a wine producer. The Diel wines can be prone to waves of fashion and went through a phase of being vinified in an assertively dry style. More recently, while not abandoning his fondness for dry wines, Diel has also been making wines in a more classic style from his Dorsheim sites, but devotees of barrique-aged burgundian varieties will find them here, too. The range is topped by some exceptional but very pricy sweet wines.

DÖNNHOFF, OBERHAUSEN

Owner Helmut Dönnhoff *Production* 7,000 cases *Vineyard area* 32 acres (13 ha)

The unassuming Helmut Dönnhoff has for some years been the Nahe's most outstanding producer. Although some dry wines are produced—from pinot blanc and pinot gris as well as riesling—the glory of this estate is its riesling, which comes from some of the top vineyards in the Nahe. These wines show an exceptional balance of fruit and acidity and develop considerable complexity as they mature. In suitable vintages, Dönnhoff also produces an extraordinary range of dazzling sweet wines that are worth searching for.

EMRICH-SCHÖNLEBER, MONZINGEN

Owner Werner Schönleber *Production* 9,000 cases *Vineyard area* 35 acres (14 ha)

Although this estate is in the less well regarded western sector, it has, during the past decade, established an enviable reputation for fruity and zesty rieslings from its principal sites, Monzinger Halenberg and Monzinger Frühlingsplätzchen.

GÖTTELMANN, MÜNSTER-SARMSHEIM

Owners Ruth Göttelmann and Götz Blessing *Production* 5,000 cases *Vineyard area* 25 acres (10 ha)

Münster-Sarmsheim is the most northerly vineyard area in the Nahe, lying close to Bingen and the Rhine. The Göttelmann estate is typical of the Nahe in that although riesling is the dominant variety, many wines are made from other varieties such as sylvaner and even chardonnay. The wines may not be the Nahe's most dazzling, but they are sound and consistent and offer excellent value.

KRUGER-RUMPF, MÜNSTER-SARMSHEIM

Owner Stefan Rumpf *Production* 10,000 cases *Vineyard area* 40 acres (16 ha)

Dry styles dominate production, not only from riesling but from the burgundian varieties. A house specialty here is the excellent sylvaner, traditionally enjoyed as an accompaniment (a very successful one) to the new season's asparagus. The Rumpfs own an informal restaurant, where the suggestion can easily be put to the test. The rieslings are both fruity and elegant.

GUTSVERWALTUNG NIEDERHAUSEN-SCHLOSSBÖCKELHEIM, NIEDERHAUSEN

Owner Erich Maurer *Production* 17,000 cases *Vineyard area* 84 acres (34 ha)

In the 1970s and 1980s this large and magnificent estate, then the State Domaine, was probably the finest in the region. But despite the possession of superb sites such as the Kupfergrube, quality faltered in the early 1990s and the Domaine was subsequently privatized. The new owners, the Maurer family, seem determined to turn things around and appear to be succeeding in their goal of restoring this *domaine* to its former glory.

Rheingau

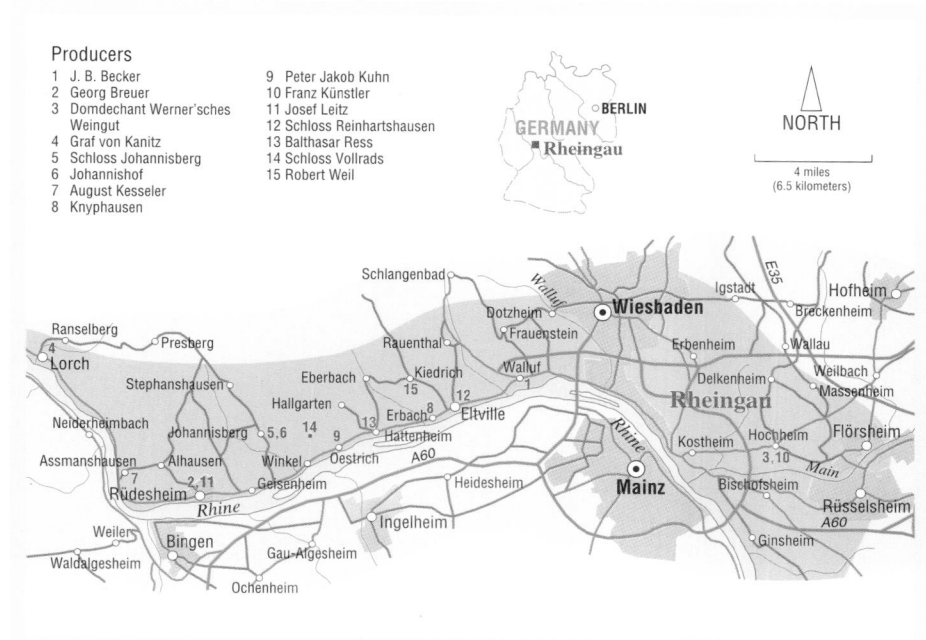

West of the twin cities of Mainz and Wiesbaden, the northern banks of the Rhine are swathed in an almost uninterrupted band of vineyards for about 22 miles (35 km) as far as the picturesque village of Rüdesheim, with its exceptionally steep vineyards. The vineyards of Hochheim, just east of Mainz, are also part of the Rheingau. This sector is regarded with affection by an older generation of British wine-lovers, since the word Hock was a term used for wine from Hochheim and, by extension, from the Rheingau in general. Beyond Rüdesheim the river turns north and the vineyards peter out a short way on in the village of Lorch. The vineyards closest to the river are gently sloping, but there are many steeper patches rising into the Taunus mountains and, after about 2.5 miles (4 km), the height and exposure become unsuitable for viticulture. The lower sites benefit from richer soils, but the higher vineyards enjoy more sunshine than the sometimes mist-shrouded riverbanks.

The Rheingau is, by German standards, a small region, about 7,900 acres (3,200 ha). It has become synonymous with riesling, which is by far the dominant variety, although around the village of Assmannshausen spätburgunder (pinot noir) is a highly regarded local specialty. Historically, the Rheingau is a more important flagship for fine riesling than any other German wine region, but in recent decades it has been eclipsed by the best Mosel and Saar estates; the warmer Pfalz has also provided strong competition.

Village of Rüdesheim, near Bad Kreuznach, is overlooked by steep vineyards.

From historic Schloss Johannisberg the vines run down to the river in orderly rows.

Kloster Eberbach's twelfth-century cellar is part of a former Cistercian monastery.

It is widely accepted that the Rheingau is continuing to suffer from a long-term identity crisis. The fame of the region led to some complacency and many of the wines, including those from very well-known estates, were not as good as their proprietors liked to think they were. There was also some stylistic confusion, shared by several other regions. While the domestic market, urged on by German wine and food writers, favored increasingly dry styles of wine, even at the price of fierce acidity levels, the export market continued to favor wines with some residual sugar to balance the sometimes corrosive acidity.

The solution was a compromise and for once compromise proved to be a sensible choice. Even producers personally devoted to drier styles admitted that a fully dry Rheingau riesling was only enjoyable in very ripe years. The sweeter styles, however, were, with rare exceptions, not ideal food wines. The compromise took the form of the Charta Association, founded by, among others, Bernhard Breuer and the late Graf Matuschka-Greiffenclau of Schloss Vollrads in Oestrich.

The estates who signed up to Charta committed themselves to far higher quality—notably by reducing yields and declassifying modest examples of, say, technically acceptable spätlesen to kabinett—and to a style that was, in fact, halb-trocken, with a level of residual sugar lying between 8 and 15 grams per liter. In well-structured wines with sound acidity this was barely perceptible as sweetness but did give the wine an impression of greater body and roundness.

Charta promoted its wines, dressed up in a special bottle, assiduously, touting them as the German answer to chablis: basically dry wines

with fruit and raciness that would be admirable accompaniments to a wide range of dishes. Moreover, its members insisted, the style was a return to an authentic form of Rheingau Riesling, more typical of the region's traditions than the sweeter soupier style. The wines enjoyed considerable success within Germany, but never really caught on widely in other countries, despite great promotional efforts in the form of banquets accompanied by a large number of Charta wines. Today Charta-style wines coexist with the slightly sweeter kabinett and spätlese wines revered by riesling fanciers worldwide. And in exceptional vintages there are the stunning nobly sweet wines from botrytised riesling, wines that evolve for many decades.

In 1999 Charta ceased to exist after it amalgamated with the VDP. Leading players in the region, such as Bernhard Breuer, who were keen to move toward a vineyard classification as the next step to improving quality found themselves sharing the same ground as major figures within the VDP. The amalgamation prevented duplication of effort. Any vineyard classification is fraught with political difficulties. Many of the universally recognized top growths—Erbacher Marcobrunn, Rüdesheimer Berg Schlossberg, Kiedricher Gräfenberg and many others—are largely owned by a handful of the best-known estates, who thus stand to gain more (financially as well as in renown) than smaller growers not blessed with parcels in the very best sites but nonetheless with a fine track record as good wine producers. Discussions will continue.

The Rheingau's flagship is the magnificent Kloster Eberbach, buried in the forests just behind the most northerly band of vineyards and long in use as a cultural and educational center. The accessibility of the region from some of Germany's largest and most prosperous cities has made it a focus for gastronomic festivals, held in some of the Rheingau's magnificent cellars and monasteries.

Villages of the Rheingau

Assmannshausen is a special case in the Rheingau, as the most widely planted grape here is red, spät-burgunder (pinot noir). For all its celebrity the wine can be light, even weedy, and often disappoints, but quality has been improving. In ripe years it can be surprisingly structured and subtle and capable of benefiting from barrique-aging.

Erbach is deservedly renowned for its great Marcobrunn vineyard, low-lying but located where it enjoys maximum sunshine. The wines are sumptuous and very long-lived.

Hattenheim is home to one of the celebrated Steinberg, solely owned by the Staatsweingut. Nussbrunnen and Wisselbrunnen often come close in quality. The wines tend to be rich and powerful.

Hochheim's best-known site is the Königin Victoria Berg. The wines are sturdy, built to last, but can lack the elegance of the best Rheingaus.

Johannisberg is dominated by lordly Schloss Johannisberg, but wines from the Schloss are often eclipsed by those from smaller estates in the village.

Kiedrich's vineyards have long had a fine reputation, but it is the success of Robert Weil in the 1990s that has really put them on the map—the Gräfenberg can deliver great sweet wines.

Lorch, just around the corner from the Rheingau, produces spicy rieslings that can be bargains compared with their illustrious cousins to the east.

Oestrich has more vineyard area than other Rheingau villages. Its wines can be patchy, but the sweet wines from the Lenchen site are exquisite.

Rauenthal's best vineyard is Baiken. The Staatsweingut, in an old monastery at Kloster Eberbach, is the principal producer.

Rüdesheim's vineyards are among the finest in the Rheingau—powerful, extracted wines that can be the epitome of Rheingau Riesling.

Winkel, gateway to Schloss Vollrads, produces lovely wines from sites such as Hasensprung.

Producers

J. B. BECKER, WALLUF

Owner Hans-Josef Becker *Production* 7,500 cases *Vineyard area* 30 acres (12 ha)

Hans-Josef Becker is a winemaker of firm and fixed opinions. Not everyone admires his wines, but they do have a strong personality. Predominantly dry, they are well structured and can be intimidating in their youth. His best wines, from the Wallufer Walkenberg, include a creditable spätburgunder. His nobly sweet wines can be very high in alcohol, but that is what Becker prefers.

GEORG BREUER, RÜDESHEIM

Owner Bernhard Breuer *Production* 7,000 cases *Vineyard area* 57 acres (23 ha)

Bernhard Breuer, a wine historian and author as well as producer, was the man behind the Charta Association and the attempt to restore the reputation of the Rheingau as a great white-wine region. A fervent advocate of vineyard classification, he uses only the names of the top Rüdesheim vineyards on his labels. Anything from less than first-rate sites is bottled under the estate name. His dry wines are exemplary, never showing harshness or lack of ripeness. And his nobly sweet wines can be extraordinary—and understandably expensive.

DOMDECHANT WERNER'SCHES WEINGUT, HOCHHEIM

Owner Dr Franz-Werner Michel *Production* 7,500 cases *Vineyard area* 30 acres (12 ha)

For many years Dr Franz-Werner Michel was the urbane head of the German Wine Institute. As he was busy running this complex organization, it was perhaps not surprising that quality has been inconsistent. Nonetheless, the wines can be excellent, especially from the Domdechaney vineyard. They tend to be made in a richly fruity style typical of the village.

GRAF VON KANITZ, LORCH

Owner Carl Albrecht Graf von Kanitz *Production* 6,500 cases *Vineyard area* 35 acres (14 ha)

This organic estate has long focused on riesling wines. Lorch is as close in microclimate to the Mittelrhein as the Rheingau, and there is a strong slate component in the soils. All this shows in the wines, which combine vivid fruit with lively acidity. The Renaissance Hilchenhaus on the property is now the estate's restaurant, and a good place in which to enjoy the wines with food in a stylish setting.

SCHLOSS JOHANNISBERG, JOHANNISBERG

Owner Fürst von Metternich *Production* 20,000 cases *Vineyard area* 86 acres (35 ha)

One of the largest and most historic estates in the Rheingau, the *domaine* is dominated by its large Schloss, visible from miles around; the cellars beneath the castle are equally magnificent. The grapes, all riesling, are grown on the bank of vineyards spreading down from the castle terraces to the river. However, the wines are not as splendid as the setting. The quality is sound and at the

At wine auctions held in Kloster Eberbach's cellars, the finest wines from Rheingau estates are sold.

The last bottle of riesling from the great 1917 vintage at Kloster Eberbach.

Schloss Vollrads has substantial vineyards and buildings in the hills above Winkel.

top level of eiswein or beerenauslese can be outstanding, but given the high prices charged across the board for the Schloss wines, they hardly represent good value.

JOHANNISHOF, JOHANNISBERG

Owner Johannes Eser *Production* 10,000 cases *Vineyard area* 44 acres (18 ha)

For some years this property has been one of the top estates in Johannisberg, often outshining the quality achieved by its more illustrious neighbor at the Schloss. In recent years the estate has expanded by acquiring vineyards in Rüdesheim, which should further enhance quality as well as quantities of wine available. The style of the wines is quite steely and they benefit from some bottle age before they show at their best.

AUGUST KESSELER, ASSMANNSHAUSEN

Owner August Kesseler *Production* 7,500 cases *Vineyard area* 40 acres (16 ha)

Based in Assmannshausen, it is not surprising that Kesseler has focused on red wines. Indeed, spätburgunder constitutes half the vineyards on this estate. These are not the watery pallid reds that were common here 20 years ago, but well-structured barrique-aged wines that command high prices.

Kesseler also makes luscious rieslings from excellent sites in Rüdesheim.

KNYPHAUSEN, ERBACH

Owner Gerko Freiherr zu Knyphausen *Production* 10,000 cases *Vineyard area* 54 acres (22 ha)

Gerko zu Knyphausen is such a charming man and his ancient home so beautiful that it is impossible to visit the estate without conceiving a great affection for the wines. Produced from a range of good sites in Erbach, Kiedrich and Hattenheim, the wines are not in the very first rank, but are invariably elegant and shapely. These are classic examples of firm Rheingau Riesling.

PETER JAKOB KUHN, OESTRICH

Owner Peter Jakob Kuhn *Production* 7,000 cases *Vineyard area* 30 acres (12 ha)

Kuhn has quickly made a reputation for himself with his skilfully made dry rieslings, which have proved immensely popular in Germany. He also produces sweet wines that manage to be both rich and bracing. Unlike the dry wines, which all originate in Oestricher Doosberg or Lenchen, the sweet styles are bottled without a vineyard designation, which gives Kuhn more flexibility as well as simplifying life for the consumer.

FRANZ KÜNSTLER, HOCHHEIM
Owner Gunter Künstler *Production* 12,000
bottles *Vineyard area* 59 acres (24 ha)

Once perceived as a rising star, Gunter
Künstler now ranks with Rheingau's
elite producers. He is a master of all
styles, from dry to ultra-sweet. In
1996 Künstler bought the well-known
Aschrott estate, also in Hochheim,
and this led to an expansion of his
production facilities and he now offers
a broader range of wines.

JOSEF LEITZ, RÜDESHEIM
Owner Johannes Leitz *Production* 3,000
cases *Vineyard area* 15 acres (6 ha)

Johannes Leitz is a well-traveled and
widely experienced winemaker, so it is
not surprising that he is up with the
latest winemaking trends. The use of
indigenous yeasts is rare among German wine estates, which prefer technological
certainties to the vagaries of nature, but their use
is routine practice here. Nor should one discount
the splendid potential of his vineyards, which lie in
some of the steepest sections of Rüdesheim.

SCHLOSS REINHARTSHAUSEN, ELTVILLE-ERBACH
Manager August Kesseler *Production* 40,000 cases
Vineyard area 250 acres (100 ha)

This enormous estate has been owned since the
1850s by the royal house of Prussia, but for many
years quality was lackluster. Now, while still under
royal ownership, the estate has been rejuvenated
by dedicated management and considerable investment, including the conversion of the Schloss into
a luxury hotel. With outstanding sites such as
Erbacher Marcobrunn at its disposal, Reinharts-
hausen is, under the new regime, producing wines
of superb quality, a standard reflected in prices.

BALTHASAR RESS, HATTENHEIM
Owner Stefan Ress *Production* 18,000 cases *Vineyard area*
82 acres (33 ha)

The engaging Stefan Ress has never faltered in his
enthusiasm for spreading the good word about
Rheingau wines wherever he travels. With several
outstanding sites in Oestrich, Rüdesheim and
Hattenheim, he can produce a large range of
wines, which, if rarely in the very top rank, are
consistent, well-made and capable of giving great
drinking pleasure. His sweeter wines often show
wonderful delicacy as well as richness of fruit.

The beautiful old cellars of Kloster Eberbach.

SCHLOSS VOLLRADS, OESTRICH-WINKEL
Manager Dr Rowald Hepp *Production* 32,000 cases
Vineyard area 119 acres (48 ha)

The inclusion of Schloss Vollrads here is an act of
faith rather than a celebration of achievement. The
recent history of this splendid estate, exclusively
dedicated to riesling grown entirely on the property, is tragic. Owner Graf Matuschka, who has
done as much as anybody to rescue the reputation
of Rheingau wines through the Charta Association
and the VDP, ran into financial difficulties and
took his own life. Yet despite his commitment to
the cause of Rheingau Riesling, his own wines
were very hit and miss. After years of uncertainty,
the estate is now under new management and first
signs are encouraging. Only time will tell whether
Vollrads can regain its place as one of the Rheingau's leading wine estates.

ROBERT WEIL, KIEDRICH
Manager Wilhelm Weil *Production* 30,000 cases *Vineyard
area* 131 acres (53 ha)

The rise to stardom of this estate has been spectacular. Its vineyards, most notably the Kiedricher
Gräfenberg, are outstanding. Wilhelm Weil has
also insisted on ripeness levels far above the minimum prescribed by the wine laws, so his auslesen
are more likely to be declassified beerenauslesen.
All the wines are good, even the modest kabinett,
but it's at the top of the range that Weil excels,
with a simply breathtaking range of nobly sweet
wines. Prices are as staggering as quality.

REGIONAL DOZEN
Erbacher Marcobrunn Riesling
  Spätlese (Schloss Reinharts-
  hausen)
Hochheimer Kirchenstück
  Riesling Spätlese (Künstler)
Johannisberger Goldatzel
  Riesling Kabinett
  (Johannishof)
Johannisberger Klaus Riesling
  Spätlese (Prinz von Hessen)
Kiedricher Gräfenberg Riesling
  Trockenbeerenauslese (Weil)
Kiedricher Sandgrub Riesling
  Spätlese (Knyphausen)
Lorcher Krone Riesling
  Spätlese (von Kanitz)
Oestricher Doosberg Riesling
  Beerenauslese (Ress)
Riesling Eiswein (P. J. Kuhn)
Rüdesheimer Berg Rottland
  Riesling Auslese Trocken
  (Leitz)
Rüdesheimer Berg Rottland
  Riesling Spätlese (Kesseler)
Rüdesheimer Berg Schlossberg
  Riesling "Erstes Gewächs"
  (Breuer)

Rheinhessen

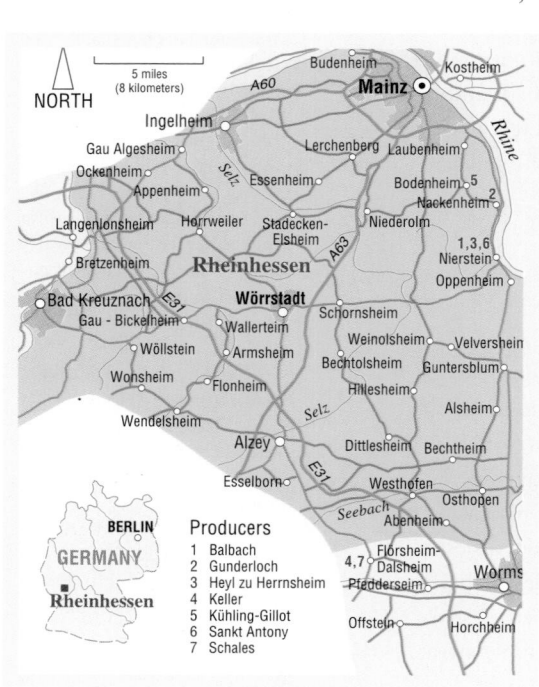

The ornate cathedral at Worms. The town marks the southern limit of the Rheinhessen wine region.

The vineyards of Rheinhessen cover more than 64,000 acres (26,000 ha), making it nine times larger than the Rheingau and the source of one quarter of all German wine production. And there lies the problem. The overall quality of wines from Rheinhessen is distressingly low and much of the blame for the decline in Germany's international reputation as a great wine-producing country lies at its door. There are excellent producers and vineyards on the eastern fringes of Rheinhessen, but the vast swathes of vineyards in the central and western parts of the zone are mostly dedicated to cheap mass-produced wine.

Riesling is a minor player here, accounting for less than 10 percent of plantings. About a quarter of the vineyards are stocked with the often neutral müller-thurgau; sylvaner, which can deliver very good wines if grown in the right site, is also widely planted. Elsewhere, Rheinhessen is home to the crossings developed some years ago (bacchus, kerner, huxelrebe and many others) to generate high yields of early-ripening grapes; some of these varieties are also frost-resistant, enabling them to be planted in very fertile soils that are better suited to potatoes. A little red wine, usually undistinguished, is also produced.

Nonetheless, excellent wine can be found in Rheinhessen, much of it sensibly priced, perhaps reflecting the low esteem in which the region as a whole is regarded. In the north, near Bingen, are some good riesling sites. The most distinctive wines come from the so-called Rhinefront, the string of riverside villages south of Mainz: Nackenheim, Nierstein and Oppenheim. Some of the vineyards here have reddish loam soil, which gives the wines a bracing earthiness that can be very appealing. Sylvaner can be delicious here. The notorious Niersteiner Grosses Domtal Grosslage has done great damage to the district's reputation.

Rheinhessen is also the birthplace of Liebfraumilch, although legally a wine bearing that label can be produced from other northern regions, too. Made entirely for export markets, Liebfraumilch must be produced from müller-thurgau, sylvaner and kerner, but riesling can also be used in the blend (although few growers would want to use this noble variety in such a low-priced wine). The historic Liebfrau vineyards in the center of Worms once had a good reputation. The firm of Valckenberg, present owner of the vineyards, is making a gallant attempt to rescue its good name.

For years growers of the Rheinhessen interior made a good living from their overcropped vineyards, but bulk wine prices tumbled in the 1990s and some growers are now losing money, however high their yields. Some of the over-production disappears into "Euro-blends," but it is increasingly clear that the market for insipid, sugary wine is dwindling. This will mean short-term pain for many growers, but perhaps the overall consequences for the German industry will be beneficial. As in other regions, there is a move, spearheaded by the VDP, to institute a vineyard classification.

Villages of the Rheinhessen

Bingen's rieslings bear some resemblance to those from the Rheingau, just across the river from Rüdesheim, but they rarely attain the same finesse.

Nackenheim's best site is Rothenberg, blessed with the zone's famous red soils. Gunderloch is the best-known producer in this Rhinefront village.

Nierstein is famous, but most bottles labeled Nierstein don't contain a single drop from this village. Authentic Nierstein riesling or sylvaner can be excellent, so look for the top vineyard names of Oelberg, Hipping, Brudersberg and Pettental.

Oppenheim's chalky soils are well adapted to riesling, which is well represented in this Rhinefront village. Only a few of the steepest vineyards are of outstanding quality.

Producers

BALBACH, NIERSTEIN
Manager/lessor Fritz Hasselbach *Production* 8,000 cases
Vineyard area 32 acres (13 ha)

Balbach went into a gradual decline in the early 1990s, but in 1996 the estate was leased by Fritz

---

NORTH
5 miles (8 kilometers)

Budenheim
Kostheim
Mainz
A60
Rhine
Ingelheim
Lerchenberg
Laubenheim
Gau Algesheim
Essenheim
Ockenheim
Bodenheim
Appenheim
Nackenheim
Selz
Horrweiler
Stadecken-Elsheim
Niederolm
Langenlonsheim
A63
1,3,6
Bretzheim
Rheinhessen
Nierstein
Oppenheim
Bad Kreuznach
Wörrstadt
Gau - Bickelheim
Schornsheim
Wallertem
Weinolsheim
Velvershein
Wöllstein
Armsheim
Bechtolsheim
Guntersblum
Wonsheim
Flonheim
Hillesheim
Selz
Alsheim
Wendelsheim
Dittlesheim
Bechtheim
Alzey
Esselborn
Westhofen
Osthofen
Seebach
Abenheim
BERLIN
Flörsheim-
Dalsheim
4,7
GERMANY
Pfeddersheim
Worms
Rheinhessen
Offstein
Horchheim

Producers
1 Balbach
2 Gunderloch
3 Heyl zu Herrnsheim
4 Keller
5 Kühling-Gillot
6 Sankt Antony
7 Schales

Hasselbach of the Gunderloch *domaine* (see below). He has taken advantage of the excellent vineyards owned by Balbach to revive the reputation of the property. Hasselbach will probably purchase the vineyards eventually. Riesling is the dominant variety and Hasselbach has rightly focused on it, producing a fine range of fairly broad, succulent wines in the late 1990s.

GUNDERLOCH, NACKENHEIM
Owner Fritz Hasselbach *Production* 7,000 cases *Vineyard area* 32 acres (13 ha)

The Hasselbachs have done wonders at this property. Although the estate owns vineyards in Nierstein, its top wines come from the reddish soil of the Nackenheimer Rothenberg site. The standard, off-dry riesling is labeled "Jean-Baptiste" and offers good value, but the top wines are the sweeter styles from Rothenberg. The wines are well-structured and require a few years to open up.

HEYL ZU HERRNSHEIM, NIERSTEIN
Owner Markus Ahr *Production* 17,000 cases *Vineyard area* 92 acres (37 ha)

Once the most celebrated estate in the Rheinhessen, it was brought to its best by Peter von Weymarn. An enthusiast for dry, often austere wines, mostly from riesling and sylvaner, he also released sweeter styles. In the mid-1990s the property was bought by the Ahr family, who have been vigorously building on von Weymarn's firm foundations. The top site is usually the Brudersberg, but there are also outstanding wines from Pettental and Oelberg.

KELLER, FLÖRSHEIM–DALSHEIM
Owner Klaus Keller *Production* 8,000 cases *Vineyard area* 30 acres (12 ha)

This long-established estate is based on Dalsheim. Although not one of the most renowned villages in Rheinhessen, lying just west of Worms, the Kellers have won an enviable reputation for producing intense, succulent sweet rieslings.

KÜHLING-GILLOT, BODENHEIM
Owners the Gillot family *Production* 6,500 cases *Vineyard area* 22 acres (9 ha)

The Gillot family's vineyards lie mostly in Oppenheim, just south of Nierstein. The top site is often the well-known Sackträger. A wide range of wines is produced, but the best tend to be the rieslings, which are made in a full range of styles. The sweeter wines are quite opulent and lush, with a slight suggestion of tropical fruits.

SANKT ANTONY, NIERSTEIN
Owner MAN Corporation *Production* 12,000 cases *Vineyard area* 57 acres (23 ha)

This is a large estate owned by a Munich corporation. Sankt Antony has recently made some excellent rieslings from its best vineyards, notably Pettental and Oelberg. Many of the Sankt Antony wines are aged in large casks in the traditional manner. It has enjoyed considerable success with its drier wine styles.

SCHALES, FLÖRSHEIM-DALSHEIM
Owners the Schales family *Production* 25,000 cases *Vineyard area* 119 acres (48 ha)

Although not in the very first rank, the estate is typical of the best of the *domaines* inland from the Rhine. The Schales cultivate a huge range of grape varieties and vinify them in many different styles. Although a bit hit-and-miss, there is good rieslaner and a bizarre sparkling eiswein. The estate has a small but interesting wine museum.

REGIONAL DOZEN

Binger Scharlachberg Riesling Spätlese (Villa Sachsen)
Dalsheimer Hubacker Riesling Eiswein (Keller)
Nackenheimer Rothenberg Riesling Auslese (Gunderloch)
Niersteiner Auglangen Riesling Spätlese (Sankt Antony)
Niersteiner Hipping Riesling Auslese (Balbach)
Niersteiner Hipping Riesling Spätlese (Schneider)
Niersteiner Pettental Riesling Auslese (Franz Karl Schmitt)
Niersteiner Pettental Riesling Auslese (Heyl zu Herrnsheim)
Oppenheimer Herrenberg Riesling Spätlese (Kühling-Gillot)
Riesling Kabinett Halbtrocken "Jean Baptiste" (Gunderloch)
Rieslaner Auslese (Schales)
Westhofener Aulerde Chardonnay Trockenbeerenauslese (Wittmann)

The town of Westhofen among vine-covered slopes.

Pfalz

Riesling grapes, prized for their versatility.

Although the Pfalz (formerly known as the Rhein-pfalz, or the Palatinate) runs in an almost continuous 50-mile (80-km) band of vineyards from Kindenheim to just beyond Neustadt, it is a varied wine region, united principally by its sheltered location to the east of the Haardt Mountains. These protect it from cold and wet and ensure an exceptionally warm microclimate in which even fig trees can flourish. Soils vary remarkably, which partly explains the diversity of wines.

The quality heart of the region lies in the stretch of vineyards just south of Bad Dürkheim, through the villages of Wachenheim, Forst,

Deidesheim and Ruppertsberg. Here are the great estates of the Pfalz and the source of most of the area's greatest wines. Other excellent vineyards can be found just north of Bad Dürkheim in the villages of Kallstadt and Ungstein.

But whereas 20 years ago few would have paid much attention to the other sectors of the Pfalz, today there is wide recognition that these other parts, notably in the Südliche Weinstrasse in the south around Landau, are capable of producing wines of high quality, although not all are in the classic riesling mold. In the past the southern part of the Pfalz was dominated by cooperatives; they still exist, but many growers have broken away and set up, with increasing success, on their own. Nonetheless, average yields in the south remain high and there is ample room for improvement.

The Pfalz is the largest German wine region after Rheinhessen, with 58,000 acres (23,500 ha) under vine. Not surprisingly, a good deal of mediocre wine is produced in the less-favored localities and for much the same reasons as in Rheinhessen: large vineyards on essentially flat land are planted with high-yielding and early-ripening varieties best suited to bulk wines. Even before the planting of those varieties, much of the Pfalz was regarded primarily as a source of cheap blending wine and the reputation of the region was far from distinguished. Even so, there is a far higher proportion of fine wine made in the Pfalz than in its northern neighbor.

Riesling is more significant here than in Rheinhessen, although with only 20 percent of plantings it is still not a major player. On the other hand, there is no doubt that the southern sector in particular is well suited to the classic Burgundian varieties, for which the potential has yet to be fully expressed. Since 1992 chardonnay has been permitted as a commercial variety and quite a few estates have planted it, to the dismay of some traditionalists. The best reds are spätburgunder, although the grape is still not as widely planted as portugieser or dornfelder. Portugieser rarely yields wine of much interest or structure and is often vinified as a rosé, but dornfelder can be as enjoyable as a ripe Beaujolais-type as long as yields are kept under control. There is also a smattering of cabernet sauvignon, but growing it remains an

Producers

1 Bassermann-Jordan
2 Friedrich Becker
3 Josef Biffar
4 Von Buhl
5 Bürklin-Wolf
6 Christmann
7 Kurt Darting
8 Knipser
9 Koehler-Ruprecht
10 Mosbacher
11 Müller-Catoir
12 Pfeffingen
13 Rebholz
14 J.L. Wolf

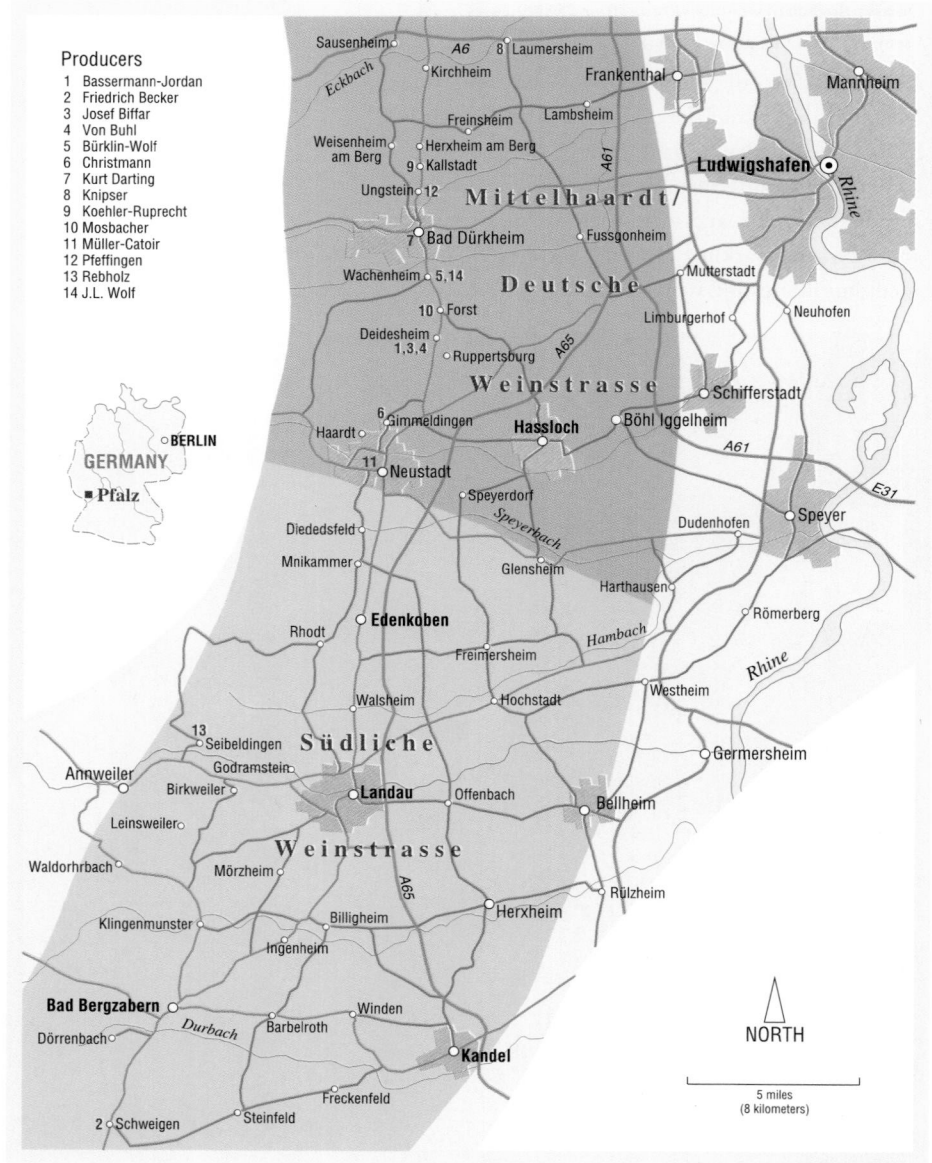

NORTH

5 miles
(8 kilometers)

exercise in perversity, since there is no evidence that the Pfalz is well suited to this variety.

The climatic conditions that make the Pfalz so appropriate for Burgundian varieties also means that rieslings here have a different structure from those found farther north. The grapes mature at higher must weights, making it feasible to produce fully dry rieslings with no hint of tartness. Levels of acidity are not as fierce as in the Mosel or the Mittelrhein, so the wines tend to taste broader and fleshier. Throughout the region riesling combines fruitiness, opulence and stylishness, especially in its sweeter manifestations. Top producers avoid flabbiness by maintaining lower yields and an impressive concentration of fruit. In some years, sweet wines of the most astounding syrupy richness can be made.

Fifteen years ago the Pfalz, for all its potential, produced far too many disappointing wines. That has all changed and many observers now find it the country's most exciting wine region. Formerly somnolent great estates such as von Buhl and Bassermann-Jordan have bounced back, once again producing a wide range of stimulating wines. Other estates that were little known in previous decades—Knipser, Christmann, Mosbacher, Biffar and Rebholz—are now well established and reli-

able sources of excellent wines. One innovative estate, Müller-Catoir, has for some years been showing what a remarkable winemaker can do even with vineyards that are rated in the top rank.

As in other regions, there is much talk about vineyard classification, although this is a sensitive issue in the Südliche Weinstrasse, where there is a lack of celebrated sites. In regions such as Rheingau, any classification applies only to riesling, but in a more-varied region such as the Pfalz this would be too limiting. Some estates, such as von Buhl and Bürklin-Wolf, have devised their own internal classification system, but any proliferation of such schemes, however intrinsically worthy, may prove confusing to consumers.

Villages of the Pfalz

Deidesheim, just south of Forst, is a handsome town with a clutch of fine vineyards that are marginally warmer than those of its neighbor to the north, including Herrgottsacker, Mäushöhle and Leinhöhle.

Forst has a complex palette of soils—basalt as well as loam—which gives distinctive wines of remarkable elegance and richness. The best sites include Jesuitengarten, Ungeheuer, Pechstein and Kirchenstück. Von Buhl is a major proprietor here.

The village of Ranschbach with some of its sloping vineyards in the foreground.

Vines trained on wires—a labor-intensive but often necessary task.

J. L. Wolf 1996 and 1997 Rieslings; the first vintages under the management of

Kallstadt, north of Bad Dürkheim, is best known for the range of wines made from its best site, the chalky Saumagen, by Koehler-Ruprecht.

Ruppertsberg is essentially a satellite of Deidesheim. It is a good source of riesling, especially from top sites Reiterpfad and Gaisböhl. Some detect an earthiness in the wines from this village.

Ungstein, south of Kallstadt, has some steep sites such as the excellent Herrenberg. Both riesling and scheurebe deliver exceptional results here.

Wachenheim, just south of Bad Dürkheim, has vineyards that deliver exceptionally ripe and full-bodied rieslings with considerable elegance. Top sites include Goldbächel and Gerümpel.

Producers

BASSERMANN-JORDAN, DEIDESHEIM
Owner Margrit von Bassermann-Jordan *Production* 30,000 cases *Vineyard area* 104 acres (42 ha)

Still owned by the founding family after almost three centuries, this grand estate has not truck with grape varieties other than riesling. Although based in Deidesheim, its best vineyards are in Forst and Ruppertsberg. The wines were decidedly dull in the 1980s, but have improved since the arrival of a new winemaker.

FRIEDRICH BECKER, SCHWEIGEN
Owner Friedrich Becker *Production* 8,000 cases *Vineyard area* 32 acres (13 ha)

Becker is one of a new breed of growers making a name for themselves in the southern sector of the Pfalz in the 1990s. He makes dry white wines from a range of varieties—riesling, but also chardonnay, and grauer and weisser burgunder. He is deservedly best known for spätburgunder, which he has been aging in small oak since 1989. It may be because of the vagaries of the climate that his red wines are somewhat inconsistent, but when he gets it right they are among Germany's best.

JOSEF BIFFAR, DEIDESHEIM
Owner Gerhard Biffar *Production* 7,000 cases *Vineyard area* 30 acres (12 ha)

It may be the departure in 1996 of the winemaker, but this once-notable estate seems to have slightly lost its way. Its record with stylish, usually understated but well-structured rieslings leaves hope that Biffar wines will soon recover their verve.

VON BUHL, DEIDESHEIM
Owner Reichsfreiherr Georg Enoch von und zu Gutenberg *Production* 30,000 cases *Vineyard area* 141 acres (57 ha)

Like Bassermann-Jordan (see above), this estate, with vineyards in Forst, Ruppertsberg and Deidesheim, was in the doldrums for much of the 1970s and 1980s, but von Buhl is once again in the forefront of Pfalz estates. A new winemaker, Frank John, was taken on in the mid-1990s. He has produced some dazzling wines, from dry rieslings to sumptuous trockenbeerenauslesen. John's main change is to harvest fruit later—this ensures high levels of ripeness, but can mean smaller crops.

BÜRKLIN-WOLF, WACHENHEIM
Owner Bettina Bürklin-Wolf Guradze *Production* 60,000 cases *Vineyard area* 235 acres (95 ha)

Bürklin-Wolf has never let its standards slip. Its top wines are made by whole-cluster pressing, which delivers cleaner, more aromatic and more elegant fruit. A very large property, it can produce wines in a variety of styles. Its dry wines have quite a following, but its sweeter styles are more popular outside Germany. In exceptional vintages, its nobly sweet wines and eisweins are sensational. Riesling dominates, but there are also decent reds made from spätburgunder and dornfelder.

CHRISTMANN, GIMMELDINGEN
Owner Karl-Friedrich Christmann *Production* 8,000 cases *Vineyard area* 32 acres (13 ha)

Christmann estate's best wines come from its holdings in Deidesheim and Ruppertsberg. The Christmanns maintain fastidiously high standards in the vineyards and winery, which show in the fine purity and complexity of their rieslings.

KURT DARTING, BAD DÜRKHEIM
Owner Helmut Darting *Production* 12,000 cases *Vineyard area* 40 acres (16 ha)

A disciple of Hans-Gunter Schwartz at Müller-Catoir (see below), Helmut Darting has shown himself as versatile as his master, although his wines rarely reach the mind-blowing levels of concentration shown at Müller-Catoir. His vineyards are a mixed bag and not all the sites are top quality. Nonetheless, he makes an impressive range of wines from a clutch of grape varieties and, given the quality, they remain remarkably inexpensive. Riesling is not the strong point here, but rieslaner, muskateller and weissburgunder can be very good; there are some splendid sweet wines.

KNIPSER, LAUMERSHEIM
Owner Werner Knipser *Production* 10,000 cases *Vineyard area* 50 acres (20 ha)

Werner Knipser is a devotee of barriques, using them for his red wines as well as for dry whites. Spätburgunder is the most important red variety here, but Knipser also cultivates lemberger and, with patchy success, the Bordeaux varieties. In general, the red wines are of greater interest than the whites, but they are quite expensive and not always harmonious.

KOEHLER-RUPRECHT, KALLSTADT
Owner Bernd Philippi *Production* 6,000 cases *Vineyard area* 25 acres (10 ha)

Bernd Philippi, an international wine consultant as well as a winemaker, is an individualist. The core of his production remains rieslings from the splendid Saumagen vineyard, made in every conceivable style according to the vintage. They are powerfully structured wines capable of great longevity. But Philippi also makes a range of barrique wines, including chardonnay, spätburgunder, and weisser and grauer burgunder, and his sweet wines—such as the occasional spätburgunder eiswein—can be extraordinary. To avoid confusion, barrique wines are sold under the Philippi rather than the estate label. Sample the wines in the Weincastell, the family's fine restaurant adjoining the winery.

MOSBACHER, FORST
Owner Richard Mosbacher *Production* 8,500 cases *Vineyard area* 27 acres (11 ha)

Only since the 1990s have admirers of Pfalz rieslings come to realize how impeccable are the wines from this estate, now in the first rank of Forst properties under the management of Jürgen Düringer. The dry rieslings are very fine, full of fruit and beautifully balanced, and the sweeter styles are stylish and never overblown. The vines from Forster Pechstein give wines with a pronounced mineral character that require a few years to develop. The top bottlings are indicated by three stars on the label.

MÜLLER-CATOIR, NEUSTADT
Owner Jakob Heinrich Catoir *Production* 11,000 cases *Vineyard area* 50 acres (20 ha)

The estate's vineyards in Mussbach and Gimmeldingen are not in the top tier of Pfalz growths, yet winemaker Hans-Gunter Schwartz routinely produces exceptional wines. Riesling is the dominant grape, but Schwartz also works his magic with grauer burgunder, muskateller and scheurebe. His rieslaner is surely the finest in Germany. Yields are low, which accounts for their concentration, but another part of the formula is Schwartz's willingness to trust the wine to make itself and his unwillingness to use the usual technical battery.

PFEFFINGEN, UNGSTEIN
Owner Doris Eymael *Production* 7,500 cases *Vineyard area* 27 acres (11 ha)

Doris Fuhrmann-Eymael runs this well-regarded estate. After a bad patch while its vineyards, replanted in the late 1980s, were attaining maturity, Pfeffingen is back on form. As well as rich spicy riesling from Ungsteiner Herrenberg, the estate produces robust sylvaner and plump, sappy scheurebe. A little spätburgunder and dornfelder have been planted and they will be barrique-aged.

REBHOLZ, SIEBELDINGEN
Owner Hansjörg Rebholz *Production* 6,000 cases *Vineyard area* 25 acres (10 ha)

This estate in the depths of the Südliche Weinstrasse has defied convention by refusing to produce the light fruity wines typical of the region and focusing instead on intense and fully dry wines, mostly white, but with a fair amount of spätburgunder, too. The rieslings can be too austere for some palates, but the Burgundian varieties, including chardonnay, show more roundness. Labels with "R" signify barrique-aged wines, often extremely powerful and of high quality.

J. L. WOLF, WACHENHEIM
Owners the Sturm family (Ernst Loosen, manager) *Production* 4,000 cases *Vineyard area* 25 acres (10 ha)

This was one of the more lackluster estates in the core of the Pfalz until Ernst Loosen of Bernkastel and a partner took it over in 1996. Its sites include such prime vineyards as Forster Ungeheuer and Jesuitengarten and Wachenheimer Gerümpel. Riesling is by far the most important variety. Initial vintages have been sound rather than brilliant, but Loosen is unlikely to rest until he has restored the estate to its proper rank.

Hotel sign with a grape theme.

REGIONAL DOZEN

QUALITY WINES
Chardonnay Spätlese Trocken "R" (Rebholz)
Forster Ungeheuer Riesling Trockenbeerenauslese (von Buhl)
Mussbacher Eselshaut Rieslanre Auslese (Müller-Catoir)
Ruppertsberger Reiterpfad Riesling Spätlese Trocken (von Buhl)
Ruppertsberger Reiterpfad Riesling Trockenbeerenauslese (Bassermann-Jordan)
Wachenheimer Gerümpel Riesling Eiswein (Bürklin-Wolf)

BEST VALUE WINES
Forster Pechstein Riesling Auslese (Mosbacher)
Kallstadter Saumagen Riesling Spätlese (Koehler-Ruprecht)
Ruppertsberger Reiterpfad Riesling Spätlese Trocken (Christmann)
Ungsteiner Herrenberg Riesling Auslese (Darting)
Wachenheimer Gerümpel Riesling Eiswein (Bürklin-Wolf)
Wachenheimer Goldbächel Riesling Spätlese (Biffar)

Franken

Many of the great vineyards in Franken grow on very steep sites.

Franken (or Franconia) is a Bavarian region surrounding the splendid baroque city of Würzburg. The River Main loops through the region, with most vineyards on steep sites overlooking the river and benefiting from the warmth reflected by it. The soils are varied, but fall into three main types: sandstone, limestone and marl. These soils influence the varieties planted and the flavor and structure of the wines.

Franken enjoys an essentially continental climate: winters are cold and prolonged, bringing a risk of spring frosts; summers can be blisteringly hot. Harvesting rarely begins before October and often continues until the end of November.

At 14,825 acres (6,000 ha), Franken is a medium-size region by German standards. Müllerthurgau is the most widely planted variety, delivering fresh, straightforward wines that can have a light mineral tone and a refreshing acidity, according to where it is planted. But Franken's specialty is sylvaner, originally brought here from Austria in the seventeenth century. Overcropped sylvaner can be neutral in character, but in Franken it can have a fine mineral edge. Inevitably it is at its best and most enjoyable when yields are kept low. Riesling can also be delicious here, but it can be planted only in the best sites because it ripens so late.

Over past decades there has been considerable vineyard expansion and, sadly, it is the lesser varieties, such as kerner and bacchus, that have been planted. More resistant to frost than riesling and sylvaner, they have been employed in flatter sites previously rejected as unsuitable for viticul-ture. Surprisingly, bacchus can deliver quite good results here and the off-dry aromatic wine it produces is popular locally.

For centuries Franken wine has been consigned to a dumpy bottle called the *bocksbeutel*. The Franconians are fiercely proud of it, despite the fact that in export markets it is associated with Mateus Rosé. There can be little doubt, however, that its near-universal use has severely hampered the wine's international reputation. This is a shame, since the quality of the best wines is extremely high. Most are dry, but have the body and structure to keep any harshness at bay. They have an almost earthy mineral quality that is directly derived from the splendid vineyards.

There are also some magnificent sweet wines, intense, structured and long-lived. The rieslaner grape is planted by only the most ambitious estates, since its yields are low and it doesn't always ripen sufficiently, but it can deliver exceptional nobly sweet wines.

Parts of Franken, especially in the western zones, are also well-suited to red wines. Spätburgunder is the principal grape, but a new variety, domina, is also popular. The best red wines are aged in barriques and command high prices. White Burgundian varieties are also grown and these, too, are often fermented and aged in barriques, with considerable success.

Villages of Franken

Burgstadt, in western Franken, has an outstanding vineyard in Centgrafenberg. Grapes grown on its red sandstone soils produce excellent red wines.

Castell is the almost feudal headquarters of the princely Castell family, and its best sites, such as Schlossberg, have been owned by the family for centuries. It produces good sylvaner and rieslaner.

Escherndorf is dominated by one superb site that glories in the name of Lump.

Homburg's great site is Kallmuth, originally planted on stone terraces constructed by monks about 1,000 years ago.

Iphofen has one supreme site, the Julius-Echter-Berg, on which Juliusspital and Wirsching are the major proprietors.

Randersacker, just south of Würzburg, has an outstanding site in Pfülben.

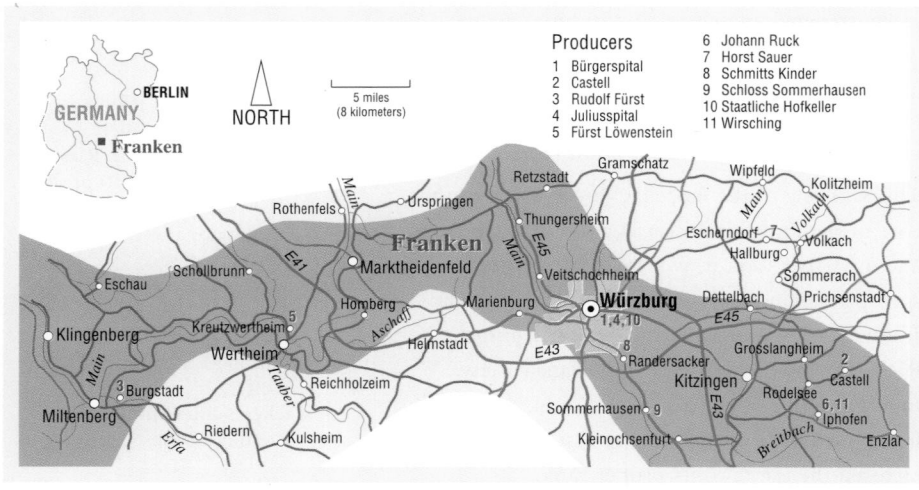

Producers
1 Bürgerspital
2 Castell
3 Rudolf Fürst
4 Juliusspital
5 Fürst Löwenstein
6 Johann Ruck
7 Horst Sauer
8 Schmitts Kinder
9 Schloss Sommerhausen
10 Staatliche Hofkeller
11 Wirsching

Würzburg is no mere village, but a stately baroque city on the banks of the Main. Within its boundaries are some of Franken's best vineyards. The large Stein, with a reputation centuries old, overlooks the river and city.

Producers

BÜRGERSPITAL, WÜRZBURG

Manager **Rudolf Friess** *Production* **85,000 cases** *Vineyard area* **356 acres (144 ha)**

Established in 1319 as a charitable institution, its activities are funded by selling wines from its vast estate. One third of the vineyards are planted with riesling, which is not typical of Franken. This was also the first large estate to specialize in weissburgunder. The wines, as always in Franken, are predominantly dry. There are some outstanding sweet wines from sylvaner, grauer burgunder and other varieties. Reds are undistinguished and quality has been far from exceptional, but the appointment in 1999 of a new cellarmaster may help to improve performance.

CASTELL, CASTELL

Owner **Ferdinand Erbgraf zu Castell** *Production* **50,000 cases** *Vineyard area* **161 acres (65 ha)**

Until 1806 Castell was the fiefdom of a family that has lived there since the eleventh century and still inhabits the Schloss. Family members still run the winery and a chain of banks. Production is supplemented with grapes bought from growers in the village and there is a complex hierarchy according to the quality and provenance of the wines; the very finest come from Casteller Schlossberg. At the top level the rieslings, sylvaners and rieslaners are first-rate. The former long-term cellarmaster liked to make wines that were sound rather than exciting, but in 1997 a new team was installed and quality is showing exciting signs of improvement.

RUDOLF FÜRST, BURGSTADT

Owner **Paul Fürst** *Production* **8,000 cases** *Vineyard area* **37 acres (15 ha)**

The reserved but self-confident Rudolf Fürst makes a range of wines from the Centgrafenberg vineyard, mostly delicious dry wines from sylvaner and riesling and vibrant sweet rieslaner. But he is best known for his sophisticated and expensive reds, most of which are aged in small oak barrels. Most of the reds are spätburgunder, but he also offers a popular blend called Parzifal, made from spätburgunder and domina.

Huge bunches of spätburgunder grapes.

JULIUSSPITAL, WÜRZBURG

Manager **Horst Kolesch** *Production* **80,000 cases** *Vineyard area* **250 acres (100 ha)**

Run with great aplomb by Horst Kolesch, the ancient Juliusspital is currently the best of the large Würzburg estates. Like Bürgerspital, this is primarily a charitable foundation, supported by its wine production. It has extensive holdings in almost all the best sites in Franken and glories in its 64 acres (26 ha) in Würzburger Stein. It is a conservative estate, having no truck with blends or brands, but there is no question that the quality of the wines is brilliant. Riesling and sylvaner are the star turns, but there are also exceptional wines from weissburgunder and rieslaner. Nobly sweet wines are rarities here, but when they are made they are magnificent.

FÜRST LÖWENSTEIN, KREUZWERTHEIM

Owner **Alois Konstantin Fürst zu Löwenstein** *Production* **18,000 cases** *Vineyard area* **67 acres (27 ha)**

Since the mid-1990s a determined attempt has been made to improve the performance of a once lackluster estate. Richly earthy sylvaner comes from the great Homburger Kallmuth site, but this princely estate has good vineyards in many other parts of Franken, as well as in Baden. Other than the rare sweet wines, all varieties are vinified in a totally dry style and the top range is bottled under

Collecting the grapes along steep terraces.

REGIONAL DOZEN

Bürgstadter Centgrafenberg
Spätburgunder Trocken
(Fürst)

Bürgstadter Centgrafenberg
Weisser Burgunder Spätlese
Trocken (Fürst)

Casteller Kugelspiel Sylvaner
Eiswein (Castell)

Escherndorfer Lump Riesling
Beerenauslese (Sauer)

Homburger Kallmuth Sylvaner
Spätlese Trocken
(Löwenstein)

Iphofer Julius-Echter-Berg
Sylvaner Kabinett Trocken
(Ruck)

Iphofer Julius-Echter-Berg
Sylvaner Spätlese Trocken
(Wirsching)

Randersackerer Pfülben
Rieslaner Beerenauselse
(Bürgerspital)

Randersackerer Pfülben
Riesling Kabinett Trocken
(Schmitts Kinder)

Sommerhäuser Steinbach
Riesling Spätlese Trocken
(Schloss Sommerhausen)

Würzburger Stein Riesling
Beerenauslese (Juliusspital)

Würzburger Stein Sylvaner
Spätlese Trocken
(Staatlicher Hofkeller)

In the western parts of Franken the main grape variety grown is spätburgunder.

the Asphodel label, referring to the rare flower that grows in the sheltered Kallmuth. There is also some good spätburgunder that is aged in mostly new barriques.

JOHANN RUCK, IPHOFEN

Owners Ruck family *Production* 7,000 cases *Vineyard area* 35 acres (14 ha)

Johann Ruck traces his family way back to 945, but they think of themselves as relative newcomers to Iphofen, having arrived in 1839. He produces classic Franken wines, taut, elegant and mostly dry. Yields are kept low, so the wines are finely concentrated. No wood is used, except for Ruck's pride and joy, a parcel of weissburgunder vines that are 40 years old. He handles this wine with special care and vinifies it in small oak.

HORST SAUER, ESCHERNDORF

Owner Horst Sauer *Production* 6,000 cases *Vineyard area* 22 acres (9 ha)

Sauer is a rising star, producing impeccable riesling and sylvaner from his vineyards in the outstanding Escherndorfer Lump site near Würzburg. His harvesters check through the vineyards repeatedly to ensure that only the ripest fruit is picked. The wines are all aged on the fine lees in steel tanks to retain their freshness and purity of fruit. Sauer also makes nobly sweet wines of sensational quality, but they are hard to come by as, sadly, he makes only very tiny quantities.

SCHMITTS KINDER, RANDERSACKER

Owner Karl Martin Schmitt *Production* 10,000 cases *Vineyard area* 35 acres (14 ha)

Sylvaner is the main variety here, but Schmitt also does well with riesling, rieslaner and even bacchus. For his top wines and for the sweet wines, he likes to use barriques, although oaked müller-thurgau is not a great success. Nor are the red wines, since the soils here are not suited to red varieties, but the dry white wines are of the highest quality.

SCHLOSS SOMMERHAUSEN, SOMMERHAUSEN

Owners Steinmann family *Production* 13,000 cases *Vineyard area* 50 acres (20 ha)

Owned since 1968 by the same family, the Schloss estates produce very good sylvaner and riesling and a wide range of Burgundian varieties, as well as a well-known range of sparkling wines. The best of these are produced from riesling and auxerrois. In top years there are superb nobly sweet wines from chardonnay, rieslaner and scheurebe.

STAATLICHE HOFKELLER, WÜRZBURG

Owners Bavarian government *Production* 85,000 cases *Vineyard area* 371 acres (150 ha)

Until 1803 the winery belonged to the prince-bishops of Würzburg and it has magnificent candle-lit cellars beneath the city's palatial Residenz. The mostly dry white wines are very good, but a touch broad in style. A change in director and cellarmaster in early 2000 should signal an improvement in quality and perhaps greater concentration in the wines. The Hofkeller has also been making some robust red wines, which have proved successful despite their high prices.

WIRSCHING, IPHOFEN

Owner Dr Heinrich Wirsching *Production* 36,000 cases *Vineyard area* 173 acres (70 ha)

After some disappointing years, this large private estate is returning to form under the direction of oenologist Uwe Mateus. The winemaking is less interventionist than at most other large estates and this allows spicy complex fruitiness to shine forth. Sylvaner and riesling are very good dry wines and there is attractive traminer and rieslaner in a sweeter style. Wirsching is rightly proud of its low-yielding grauer burgunder, aged for 15 months in barriques. The reds are also of above-average quality.

Baden

Baden is a state, not a wine region. Its microclimates and soils are so diverse that it is futile to seek a characteristic that unites this region of 39,535 acres (16,000 ha). The northern sector, which accounts for only 20 percent of production, lies north of Heidelberg; some scattered vineyards lie between Heidelberg and Karlsruhe. A more southerly band, known as the Ortenau, flanks the Black Forest between the spa town of Baden-Baden and Offenburg and vineyards continue as far south as Freiburg. The hill called Tuniberg to the west of Freiburg is dominated by müller-thurgau, while north of Tuniberg is the volcanic Kaiserstuhl, usually Germany's hottest wine district and the natural home of burgundian varieties. These produce wines that can resemble those from Alsace, which, after all, lies a just a short distance away on the other side of the Rhine. Incongruously, the distant vineyards on the shores of Lake Constance also belong to Baden.

Not surprisingly, wine styles vary enormously. In the far north you can find sylvaners sold in *bocksbeutel*, the squat bottles of Franken, which is not far away; in the Ortenau Rhine-style rieslings dominate. To the south the Burgundian varieties thrive, especially spätburgunder, but even on the baking Kaiserstuhl there are rows of riesling and sylvaner vines. Although the climate encourages the production of dry wines, there are areas, such as the Kaiserstuhl, where it is often possible to make botrytis wines of excellent quality. Rich and figgy, they tend to mature much more rapidly than the equivalent wines from the Mosel or Rhine.

This vast range of wines is perpetuated by the 120 cooperatives that dominate Baden's wine production. Some are of very high quality, but even the best offer a huge variety of wines and styles to satisfy local demand. The effect is to rob the region of any strong regional identity, and this has hampered the occasional attempts to increase the renown of Baden wines outside Germany and stimulate exports. A handful of excellent private estates are able to sell all their wines within Germany at gratifyingly high prices.

As in Württemberg, a selection of best villages is not feasible, but the names to look for include Neuweier, Durbach, Sasbach, Ihringen, Oberrotweil and Königschaffhausen.

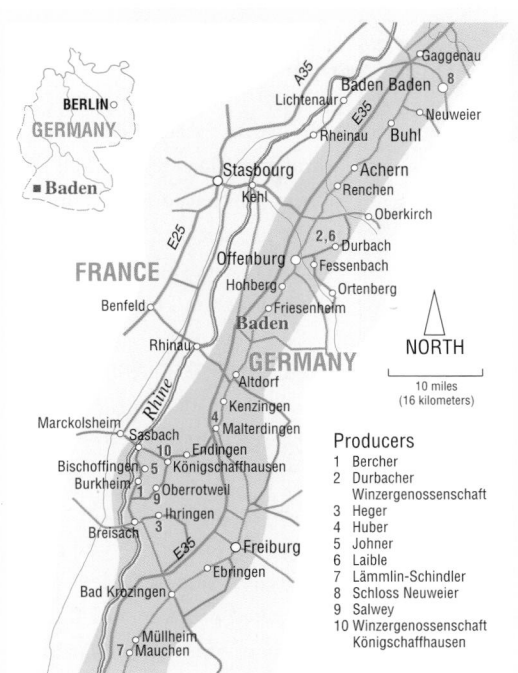

Producers
1 Bercher
2 Durbacher
   Winzergenossenschaft
3 Heger
4 Huber
5 Johner
6 Laible
7 Lämmlin-Schindler
8 Schloss Neuweier
9 Salwey
10 Winzergenossenschaft
   Königschaffhausen

South from Freiburg to the Swiss border the dominant grape is gutedel (Swiss chasselas).

Producers

BERCHER, BURKHEIM

Owners Eckhard and Rainer Bercher *Production* 12,000 cases *Vineyard area* 52 acres (21 ha)

The Berchers' winery is as impressive as the wines. As expected from the Kaiserstuhl, these are quite powerful wines, almost invariably dry and quite high in alcohol. The burgundian varieties are foremost, among them excellent chardonnay. The spätburgunder is often outstanding. The best, and most expensive, bottlings have "SE" on the label.

DURBACHER WINZERGENOSSENSCHAFT, DURBACH

Manager Konrad Geppert (Cooperative) *Production* 250,000 cases *Vineyard area* 800 acres (320 ha)

This excellent cooperative dominates the village of Durbach, with its very steep slopes. Riesling is the specialty here, although the burgundian varieties also do well. The rieslings, in good years, have exceptional raciness and extract, dry or sweet.

HEGER, IHRINGEN

Owner Joachim Heger *Production* 8,000 cases *Vineyard area* 37 acres (15 ha)

Given the vast range of varieties grown by Joachim Heger and the very low yields he insists upon, it is remarkable how many wines he manages to produce each year. The range is extraordinary: crisp dry rieslings, powerful dry muskatellers, broad spicy grauer burgunder and the most sumptuous nobly sweet wines. One outstanding site, the

REGIONAL DOZEN

Achkarrer Schlossberg Sylvaner Spätlese Trocken (Dr Heger)

Blauer Spätburgunder Trocken "SJ" (Johner)

Burkheimer Feuerberg Grauer Burgunder Auslese Trocken "SE" (Bercher)

Chardonnay Spätlese Trocken (Lämmlin-Schindler)

Durbacher Plauelrain Riesling Auslese Trocken (Durbacher Winzergenossenschaft)

Durbacher Plauelrain Riesling Spätlese Trocken (Laible)

Ihringer Winklerberg Muskateller Trockenbeerenauslese (Dr Heger)

Königschaffhauser Hasenberg Ruländer Trockenbeerenauslese (Winzergenossenschaft Königschaffhausen)

Königschaffhauser Hasenberg Weisser Burgunder Auslese Trocken (Winzergenossenschaft Königschaffhausen)

Neuweierer Mauerberg Riesling Spätlese Trocken "Alte Reben" (Schloss Neuweier)

Oberrotweiler Henkenberg Grauer Burgunder Spätlese Trocken "Alte Reben" (Salwey)

Spätburgunder Trocken Reserve (Huber)

Extensive vineyards near Offenburg.

Neat rows of gutedel grapes grown on wires to allow maximum penetration of sunshine to ripen the fruit.

Ihringer Winklerberg, is almost solely responsible for this array of glorious wines. Wines from the Heger estate are bottled under the Dr Heger label; those from purchased grapes or lesser sites are released as cheaper varietal wines under the Weinhaus Joachim Heger label.

HUBER, MALTERDINGEN
Owner Bernhard Huber *Production* 8,000 cases *Vineyard area* 37 acres (15 ha)

Bernhard Huber left the local cooperative in 1987 and rapidly became one of Baden's most respected producers of Burgundian wines. The chardonnay has sometimes been over-oaked, and a similar defect has marred the otherwise excellent spätburgunder, especially the sumptuous Reserve bottling. With each successive vintage Huber manages to fine-tune the wines and they now show more finesse as well as richness and power.

JOHNER, BISCHOFFINGEN
Owner Karl-Heinz Johner *Production* 8,500 cases *Vineyard area* 42 acres (17 ha)

Given the extremely fragmented nature of his vineyard holdings, Karl-Heinz Johner decided long ago to sidestep the complex German wines laws. All his wines are plain varietals and all are aged in barriques. The top bottlings carry the "SJ" label. These are rich, full-bodied wines typical of the Kaiserstuhl and the oak is extremely well handled. The spätburgunder is usually the star turn.

LAIBLE, DURBACH
Owner Andreas Laible *Production* 2,500 cases *Vineyard area* 15 acres (6 ha)

These are the finest rieslings of Baden, although the Durbach cooperative can run Andreas Laible close. Made from low-yielding grapes grown on steep rocky slopes, these are wines of great fire and extraction. Gewürztraminer and grauer burgunder can also be excellent, but riesling is definitely the specialty of the house.

LÄMMLIN-SCHINDLER, MAUCHEN
Owner Gerd Schindler *Production* 11,000 cases *Vineyard area* 50 acres (20 ha)

Although based in the Markgräflerland, gutedel constitutes only a quarter of the estate. The wines, from a range of white varieties as well as spätburgunder, are delicate and lively, crisp rather than fat, elegant rather than structured. The weisser burgunder and grauer burgunder are usually the most successful and have more weight than the slightly anemic reds.

SCHLOSS NEUWEIER, BADEN-BADEN
Owner Gisela Joos *Production* 5,500 cases *Vineyard area* 25 acres (10 ha)

This grand castle has been restored by the Joos family, who have also improved the quality of the wine. Almost all the wines are produced from riesling grapes and the style is generally dry. These wines can be quite austere in their youth and are not to everyone's taste, but they are quite impressive, with shapely acidity, great elegance and fine concentration. They can be sampled with good food in the castle's restaurant.

SALWEY, OBERROTWEIL
Owner Wolf-Dietrich Salwey *Production* 13,000 cases *Vineyard area* 50 acres (20 ha)

The easygoing Wolf-Dietrich Salwey makes a wide range of wines, mostly in a dry style, from riesling, sylvaner and the burgundian varieties. They can be a bit hit-and-miss and the red wines, from spätburgunder, are sometimes disappointing. But Salwey excels with grauer burgunder and sylvaner, and if the wines fail to excite for any reason, make a beeline for his marvelous fruit schnapps.

WINZERGENOSSENSCHAFT KÖNIGSCHAFFHAUSEN, KÖNIGSCHAFFHAUSEN
Manager Edmund Schillinger (Cooperative) *Production* 100,000 cases *Vineyard area* 408 acres (165 ha)

This cooperative produces wines of better quality than many private estates in Baden. Its subtly oaked weisser burgunder is exemplary and there is a fine range of oaked spätburgunder, too. The cooperative also produces some of the most sumptuous and brilliant nobly sweet wines in Baden, often from the grauer burgunder grape (known when vinified sweet as ruländer).

Other German Regions

Trollinger grapes, Württemberg's most commonly planted red variety.

WÜRTTEMBERG

Of all the major German wine regions, Württemberg is the least known. Hardly any of its wines are exported and much of what is produced is consumed by the wealthy local population, whose annual wine consumption is double the national average. Its vineyards are scattered, nestling on a handful of well-exposed slopes, usually close to the River Neckar or its tributaries. Because of its geography, it is a more difficult area for tourists to explore, although many of the best vineyards actually lie within or between the region's major cities of Stuttgart and Heilbronn. Although some good, even exceptional, riesling is produced, especially around Stuttgart, this is essentially red-wine country. One leading grower, Ernst Dautel, points out that the northern European climate gives wines of aroma and finesse, rather than body and richness. Curiously, Württemberg's least impressive red grape, trollinger, is the most popular. This gives a pale red that is easily mistaken for rosé. Thirst-quenching it may be, but distinguished it definitely is not.

Other varieties cultivated are spätburgunder (pinot noir), schwarzriesling (pinot meunier), lemberger (identical to Austria's blaufränkisch and often delicious) and the mutation of schwarzriesling known as samtrot. The top growers take

A bend in the River Neckar, with the town of Neckarsulm in the background.

Pickers eat lunch in the vineyards.

all these varieties seriously and many of the best examples are aged in small oak barrels and can have surprising richness and extraction, which makes the popularity of the trollinger grape all the more mysterious.

Cooperatives are important here, but their influence is gradually waning, as some ambitious growers extract themselves and set up as individual producers and bottlers. In the 1980s cooperatives accounted for 85 percent of production; today it is closer to 70 percent. Many of the largest private estates have been in the hands of the same noble families for centuries.

Because the wine-growing area is fragmented, there is little point in listing the individual villages and vineyards. In each zone there are, inevitably, one or two sites deemed superior to the rest, but the names of the best—Stettener Pulvermächer, Schwaigerner Ruthe—have only local renown.

Best producers

GRAF ADELMANN, KLEINBOTTWAR
Owner Michael Graf Adelmann *Production* 10,000 cases *Vineyard area* 44 acres (18 ha)

Based in the exquisite Schaubeck castle, this has been one of the region's leading estates for several decades. Adelmann harvests as late as possible, so these are wines of richness and great concentration. The dry rieslings are excellent and there is some lovely traminer and muskateller, but the best wines are oak-aged red cuvées. 'Herbst im Park' is intended to be drunk with game and is supple and lush. More structured is 'Vignette', an exceptionally elegant blend of lemberger and samtrot.

DAUTEL, BÖNNIGHEIM.
Owner Ernst Dautel *Production* 6,000 cases *Vineyard area* 25 acres (10 ha)

This excellent producer is equally competent at all styles of wine. His rieslings are spicy and tangy and there is rich, toasty, barrique-aged weissburgunder. But it is with red wines, mostly oak-aged, that Dautel's undoubted skill shows through. The best of them, bottled under the designation "S", are usually wines of power and density. "Kreation," a blend of merlot, cabernet sauvignon and lemberger, provides irrefutable proof that the Bordeaux varieties can do well here.

KARL HAIDLE, KERNEN-STETTEN
Owner Hans Haidle *Production* 12,000 cases *Vineyard area* 42 acres (17 ha)

Hans Haidle's estate is unusual in that a great deal of riesling is grown here. These rieslings, as well as the weissburgunders, are excellent, but Haidle prides himself on his range of reds. As well as the traditional local varieties, he produces a plummy red from the Austrian variety zweigelt. The style is overtly fruity and jammy, hedonistic rather than subtle or structured.

NEIPPERG, SCHWAIGERN
Owner Karl Eugen Erbgraf zu Neipperg *Production* 20,000 cases *Vineyard area* 77 acres (31 ha)

The vineyards are clustered around the ancient Schloss Neipperg. Although riesling is made here, this is not Neipperg's strength. Instead, Graf von Neipperg prefers to produce varietal red wines and has little interest in the fashionable blended reds. An enthusiast for local traditions, he also ages his best reds in barrels crafted from oak trees grown in the family's own forests. The top wines are usually lemberger and samtrot.

WÖHRWAG, UNTERTÜRKHEIM
Owner Hans-Peter Wöhrwag *Production* 12,000 cases *Vineyard area* 42 acres (17 ha)

Hans-Peter Wöhrwag is probably Württemberg's finest riesling producer. These are lean elegant wines, quite close in style to Rheinland wines. His best rieslings are from 40-year-old vines and have delicious, powerful flavor. In most vintages he is also able to produce sensational riesling eiswein. Wöhrwag does not neglect red wines and produces two cuvées, named after his sons Moritz and Philipp. The latter is the better of the two, a blend of lemberger and spätburgunder, with a dash of cabernet sauvignon.

HESSISCHE BERGSTRASSE

This very small region of just over 1,112 acres (450 ha)—no longer Germany's smallest since the reunification—is clustered around the small town of Bensheim. It's a fairly warm region and has much in common with northern Baden, a short distance to the south. When the wine laws were put in place in 1971, the Bergstrasse was offered to other regions for incorporation, but Rheingau declined (for good reasons), as did Baden (for perhaps less good reasons). So Hessische Bergstrasse was left on its own.

Nonetheless it has prospered, and for three reasons. First, it is planted mostly with riesling, which in these steep sites is bound to deliver wines of fairly good, if not very good, quality. Second, in the Staatsweingut it has an exceptionally consistent producer. And third, its proximity to Darmstadt (north) and Heidelberg (south) guarantees a steady stream of local visitors, so almost all the wine is bought and drunk locally.

The Staatsweingut is a *domaine* of 89 acres (36 ha), including the solely owned Heppenheimer Centgericht from which its best wines emerge. Riesling is the leading variety, but the Burgundian varieties all do well here. The winery specializes in eiswein, from both riesling and spätburgunder. Another reliable estate is Simon-Bürkle, which offers a wide range, red as well as white, at very reasonable prices. The town of Bensheim also has its own winery, making good riesling and burgundian wines from its chalky Kalkgasse site.

AHR

The River Ahr flows into the Rhine at Linz to the northwest of Koblenz. Where the river turns and twists for some 15 miles (25 km), its terraced rocky slopes are planted with vines. What is surprising is that this most northerly of German wine regions is best known for red wines that are particularly popular within Germany, in large part because the zone of production is exceedingly pretty and studded with inns and watering holes where day-trippers can sip the local produce with a platter of cold cuts.

More than half of the 1,285 acres (520 ha) of vines are planted with spätburgunder (pinot noir) and there is also some riesling. The other red variety is portugieser, but serious growers are focusing their attention, and rightly so, on spätburgunder. The reason the valley was first thought suitable for viticulture lies in the warming reflections off its craggy cliffs, which helps bring the grapes to maturity. The impression of mediocrity that characterized the region until the 1990s may have stemmed from the domination of cooperatives that were not quality-conscious. Today there is a handful of estates eager to take advantage of the propitious microclimates of the valley to make pinot noirs that are increasingly rich and Burgundian in style. The best wines are expensive and would not be regarded as good value by most foreign visitors to the region.

Best producers

DEUTZERHOF, MAYSCHOSS
Owner Wolfgang Hehle *Production* 4,000 cases *Vineyard area* 20 acres (8 ha)

Wolfgang Hehle releases his best spätburgunder under the imposing name of "Grand Duc Select," while wines made from less exceptional grapes are bottled as "Caspar C." The ducal wines are, in terms of German classification, Auslese Trocken and display considerable and unexpected power

REGIONAL BEST

Spätburgunder Auslese
  Trocken No 1 (Adeneuer)
Spätburgunder Auslese
  Trocken "Grand Duc
  Select" (Deutzerhof)
Spätburgunder Trocken "B-
  52" (Nelles)
Spätburgunder Trocken
  "Futura" (Nelles)
Spätburgunder Trocken "S"
  (Meyer-Näkel)
Spätburgunder Trocken
  "Signatur" (Burggarten)

Vineyards rise steeply behind the town of Besigheim, near Stuttgart.

Pickers hard at work in Martin Able's vineyard outside Heilbronn.

and richness, although they lack finesse. Prices, however, are at Burgundy Premier Cru levels.

NELLES, HEIMERSHEIM

Owner Thomas Nelles *Production* 3,000 cases *Vineyard area* 12 acres (5 ha)

Although spätburgunder is planted in only half the Nelles vineyards, they are the base of the best wines. Bottled without vineyard designation but with an arcane numbering system, these are pinot noirs of substance and elegance. The "B-52" is often the best wine in the range. The prices are less extravagant than those of Deutzerhof and the "Rubis" bottling offers a lively, simple pinot noir at an affordable price.

MITTELRHEIN

Many visitors are attracted to the Mittelrhein as much for its dazzling scenery as for the quality of its wines. Riverside villages crouch beneath steep vineyards and castle-capped cliffs, and visitors enjoy sampling the wines in the many inns. The 1,480 acres (600 ha) of vineyards are strung out along the Rhine both north and, more importantly, south of Koblenz, the city that also marks the most northerly part of the Mosel at its confluence with the Rhine. Riesling is the dominant variety, but the wines have less body and complexity than those from the Rheingau. Bacharach, in the far south part of the region, is the best-known wine-producing village and often its wines, from vines grown on slatey soils, are among the best the Mittelrhein has to offer. Boppard is the other

leading village, capable in certain vintages of producing notable sweet wines.

The Mittelrhein offers a racy styles of riesling that can give great pleasure. Their marked acidity gives them a freshness that is appealing when young and helps the wines to age quite well, although most of them are consumed while very young and fruity by avid tourists. The prices remain very reasonable.

Best producers

TONI JOST, BACHARACH

Owner Peter Jost *Production* 4,500 cases *Vineyard area* 22 acres (9 ha)

Long the leader of the pack, Peter Jost remains the leading grower, although his pre-eminence is increasingly being challenged by other quality-conscious estates. Jost makes a full range of wines, from dry to very sweet, and all are of reliable quality. He is best known for his amazingly sumptuous dessert wines, especially the Riesling Trockenbeerenauslese from Bacharacher Hahn.

WEINGART, SPAY

Owner Florian Weingart *Production* 6,500 cases *Vineyard area* 15 acres (6 ha)

Florian Weingart supplements his estate-grown grapes with fruit purchased from his neighbors, but that entails no compromises on quality. The wines are fresh and zesty and especially successful when crafted in a lightly sweet style balanced by the natural lively acidity so typical of the region.

SAALE-UNSTRUT

Named after the two rivers that flow through it, this 1,235-acre (500-ha) wine region has the dubious distinction of being the most northerly in continental Europe. It lies to the west of Leipzig. The climate can be harsh here, so early-ripening varieties dominate, not a recipe for high quality. Devastating spring frosts are a hazard and in some years yields are greatly reduced, making it exceedingly difficult for growers to earn any kind of living. Nor has there ever been much of a tradition of fine wine production here, even though vineyards have been widely established since medieval times. As early as the sixteenth century commentators were complaining of the wine's sourness and not much has changed. Müller-thurgau is the dominant variety. Astonishingly, the leading estate, Lützkendorf, occasionally succeeds in producing a beerenauslese from sylvaner grapes.

SACHSEN

The Sachsen wine region lies at roughly the same latitude as Saale-Unstrut but is considerably farther east, compounding the climatic difficulties of growing grapes in this part of Germany. Here, too, frosts in spring can cause major headaches and slash yields to uneconomic levels. With 865 acres (350 ha) under vine, it is slightly smaller than Saale-Unstrut and müller-thurgau is again the dominant variety. The greatest difference between the two regions is that riesling is a significant variety in Sachsen and the white Burgundian varieties, as well as traminer, are also quite widely encountered. Sachsen has yet to establish any reputation for quality, despite investments made in recent years by private estates such as Schloss Proschwitz. The Zimmerling estate bottles all its production as dry table wine and this has the merit of simple varietal labeling. In Meissen, which lies in the center of the vineyard region, there is a "Weingalerie" near the cathedral where many of the wines can be sampled.

Pickers arrive at Heilbronn, where many of Württemberg's best vineyards are found.

Austria

Giles MacDonogh

A small, but significant wine producer, Austria makes about the same amount of wine as the Bordeaux region. It is now producing some of the most exciting sweet and dry white wines in Europe, as well as increasingly interesting reds, which make up 20 percent of the output. Grapes

were planted in the area we now call Austria as early as Celtic times and wine received another fillip from the Romans. It was the wine-loving Emperor Probus who first encouraged vine-growing in the area when idle soldiers were set to work planting vines on the warm Pannonian plain in the east. The Barbarian invasions naturally set back developments, but by the end of the first millennium Charlemagne's armies had established Christianity on both sides of the Danube. In their wake came the great monasteries and with the monks came the vineyards.

Vineyard scenes such as this at Grinzing, outside Vienna, attract many visitors.

Grüner veltliner grapes, are Austria's most widely planted cultivar. This remarkably versatile grape accounts for a little more than a third of the area under vine.

As the Hapsburg Empire grew to take in much of what we now know as Hungary, Czecho-Slovakia, Poland, Slovenia, Croatia and northern Italy, the emperors and nobility could choose their wines from a vast number of sources. Austria was not always their first choice. On the other hand, the steep, south-facing hills to the west of Vienna enjoyed a huge reputation until the popularity of local inns or Heurigen led local growers to concentrate more on bulk than quality.

Austria was shorn of its many dependencies after 1945. Between the two world wars the country established a reputation for hospitality and good cheer that appealed chiefly to the Germans to the north. Sweet, or off-dry wines were the rule, but in the 1970s and 1980s the Wachau and South Styria took a lead in developing completely dry white wines, while Burgenland proved its ability to make convincing reds. Production of sweet wines is now chiefly limited to the area around the shallow Neusiedlersee, where autumnal mists encourage the spread of *Botrytis cinerea*, particularly near Rust and Illmitz.

Landscape and climate

Those unfamiliar with Austria imagine it to be more mountainous than it is. Most of the vineyards of Lower Austria are found close to the River Danube, taking advantage of the ridges of loess and volcanic rock that provide relief to a largely flat region. The Wachau and parts of the Kremstal are composed of steep primary rock soils where grapes grown on horizontal terraces produce racy wines. The same dramatic hills occur west of the capital, Vienna.

The warmest regions are Burgenland, Styria and Thermenregion to the south and west. In Burgenland black grapes, such as cabernet sauvignon, merlot, syrah and nebbiolo, have little problem achieving good levels of ripeness when grown close to the warm Neusiedler Lake. The Leitha Hills to the north and west are chalky and both chardonnay and pinot noir have been successfully cultivated here.

Central and Southern Burgenland are predominantly red-wine areas. The chief grape is the blaufränkisch. In the eastern parts of Styria wine is made on a series of volcanic knolls. In the south of the region, on the Slovenian border, mostly white grapes are grown on rolling hills that provide excellent exposure to long hours of sunshine.

With a continental climate, Austria has a long growing season. Top growers in the Wachau, for example, may still be picking at the end of November. The northern Weinviertel, on the Czech border, is particularly arid, and the Pulkatal has been used for black grapes for about 200 years. Recent experiments have shown that syrah and gamay do well there. High levels of ripeness can be a problem now that Austria has opted for dry whites rather than the semi-sweet styles of the past. Fermented out, these wines often nudge 15° of alcohol, which can make them difficult to match with food and sometimes hard to sell.

Vines and wines

Austria's numerous indigenous varieties provide a welcome distraction from the globalization of tastes that has taken place in the past generation. On the other hand international competitions and an ingrained inferiority complex have led many to plant varieties that have been most successful in France, America and Australia. Some have been highly successful, others less so. On heavy soils in traditional areas such as the Weinviertel, grüner veltliner produces sappy, refreshing wines with a distinctly peppery bouquet ideally suited to the local diet. On the primary rock soils of the Wachau, however, it takes on another character altogether and has often misled experienced tasters into believing they were drinking top white burgundies. Riesling, with just 2.5 percent of the area planted, is the most important white grape, after the huge success of the top wines of the Wachau. Chardonnay, known as "morillon," has a long tradition in Styria, but more recently it has shown its mettle best as a non-oaked wine, demonstrating refreshing "Austrian" acidity. Others have succeeded in making it in a more international idiom. Weiss- and grauburgunder, or pinots blanc and gris, have a longer tradition and often produce better results.

Neuburger is sometimes claimed as a pinot. Its ability to make semi-sweet wines has made it unfashionable recently, but vinified dry or affected by botrytis it can be superb. Rarer are grapes such as white roter veltliner (black grapes are called "blau" or blue), traminer (red or yellow), sylvaner, and the Thermenregion specialties of rotgipfler and zierfandler (spätrot). In Burgenland and Styria the workhorse grape is welschriesling, which can be excellent when well-vinified and in sweeter styles.

The most widely planted red grape is zweigelt, a crossing of St laurent and blaufränkisch. If yields are kept low it can produce stunning results. Blaufränkisch is seen as the number-one quality cultivar, but it tends to dry out in barriques.

St laurent has affinities with pinot noir, but is unpopular because the flowers set poorly in spring. In West Styria there is blauer wildbacher, which is generally vinified as an acid rosé called "Schilcher." Every now and then a proper red wine that tastes a little like merlot is made.

Wine laws

In 1985, after some producers were found to have been adding diethylene glycol (anti-freeze) to their wines to make them taste sweeter, a new wine law was promulgated (and adapted in 1991) to limit yields to 3.4 tons per acre (60 hl per ha) for whites and 4.3 tons per acre (75 hl per ha) for reds. Wine is graded by "'Prädikat," that is, by levels of natural residual sweetness. Above common or garden Tafel and Landwein comes Qualitätswein. Unlike Germany this is not a Prädikat level and may therefore be chaptalized. The first Prädikat level is Kabinett. Again the difference from Germany is striking. Kabinett wine must have 84 Oechsle (a measure of grape sugar) and a mininum 12.7° (or 12.7 percent) of alcohol. Dry wines must be under 9 grams residual sugar per liter with a balancing acidity. This highish level was proposed by the EU to fit with norms in Germany and was formerly 4 grams. Most spätlese and much auslese is dry in Austria, spätlese with a minimum of 94 Oechsle, auslese 105. Straw wine, eiswein and beerenauslese all come in at 127 Oechsle. The sweetness must be natural, with no interference to nature's workings.

Ausbruch (138 Oechsle) is Austria's special grade of Prädikat. This style brought fame to Rust in Burgenland and denotes a sweet wine high in

Wine grapes are very different from table grapes, but an experienced winemaker may taste them to assess their readiness.

Picking riesling grapes by hand at Wolkersdorf.

Winery workers take a lunch break in the cellars of Weingut Ing, Heiligenstadt.

Schnapps is distilled from grape skins at W. Klaus Wolkersdorf's winery.

veltliner are generally thought not to need it. In Styria the classical style with sauvignon blanc or morillon (chardonnay) has been to vinify in large oak, concrete or stainless steel. There are also oaky cuvées, made in imitation of wines from France or elsewhere. Many reds are also "oak aged."

Austrian wine today

The glycol scandal damaged the Austrian wine trade to such a degree that there are now very few firms able to supply a large amount of wine of consistent quality. Companies such as FWW, Lenz Moser and Dinstlgut Loiben, or the larger cooperatives in Central Burgenland, are the nearest thing there is to a reliable source of bulk wine. Austria's strength now lies in high-quality niche products. Demand is very high at the top and prices, too. With the average size of a holding less than 5 acres (2 ha), and a great many well-known, talented growers providing for their families on less than 17 acres (7 ha), most Austrians cannot hope to lay hands on some of the more highly rated wines.

Even with as little as 15 acres (6 ha), a grower will make up to half a dozen wines, ranging from dry whites to reds and botrytis-affected whites or eiswein. The need to offer all styles sometimes leads to folly: most Styrian reds are a case in point; a Viennese cabernet sauvignon is another.

The Heurige or Buschenschank (as it is generally known in the countryside), where wine was drunk very young, has been seen as the enemy of quality. Wine is cheap and the atmosphere cheerful and these places often make such a good profit that there is little incentive to labor over making good wine. On the other hand some makers reinvest their profits in properly made wines. To balance this rustic charm, Austria has some of the best restaurants in the German-speaking world, most clustered in Vienna. But in touristy regions such as the Wachau you have the advantage of choosing from a range of growers and not merely being restricted to the wines made by your host.

Vienna

FRITZ WIENINGER, WIEN STAMMERSDORF
Owner Fritz Wieninger *Production* 7,220 cases *Vineyard area* 32 acres (13 ha)

Vienna's best winemaker, Fritz Wieninger, harvests his grapes on perfect south-facing slopes rising steeply from the river on the loess soils of the Bisamberg. Although his family runs a profitable Heurige, he makes few concessions to the traditional offering, "Mischsatz"—a sort of vinous

alcohol like a French sauternes. It should be made from fruit affected by noble rot, but this is not always the case. Trockenbeerenauslese is the highest grade (156 Oechsle) although some growers have toyed with making Essencia.

In some areas there are informal classifications of vineyards on the basis of the French "cru" system, but they have yet to be recognized by the state. Grapes are regulated by the different federal governments. If the variety has not been approved, the grower may not call it anything other than "Landwein" and must not use a standard bottle.

Viticulture and winemaking

Austrians like wines with a refreshing acidity. Flavors tend to be more angular than those produced, say, in Australia. Good Austrian wine is unashamedly refreshing, for drinking, rather than winning competitions. That said, competitive growers often set out to prove they can produce wines with impressive levels of sugar, tannin, alcohol or new oak flavorings. Oaking, in particular, became very common in the late eighties and barriques were often used to vinify quite light, unsuitable wines. There is less of this now, but Austria has yet to determine the levels of oaking required for blaufränkisch, where the fruit is fragile and can be overpowered by new wood.

Most of the oak was once bought in France, but Austrians have now discovered that their own oak works well. The forests of Mannhartsberg and Glaswein are well known. Some growers use oak from their own woods. Many of Austria's best growers never use barriques. Riesling and grüner stew. After training in California, Wieninger is keen to show he can make new-wave chardonnay, pinot noir and cabernet within Vienna's walls.

Thermenregion
KARL ALPHART, TRAISKIRCHEN
Owner Karl Alphart *Production* 4,445 cases *Vineyard area* 25 acres (10 ha)

The Thermenregion derives its name from its warm springs and spas. It is a little suntrap protected by the last outriders of the Alps and grapes ripen a little too well here, meaning either too much sugar, or too much alcohol. Despite the difficulties, Alphart makes it seem easy to make great wine. His first loves are the curious duo of zierfandler and rotgipfler, two local grapes found pretty well nowhere else. He vinifies them together and apart, always imbuing them with an exciting spiciness. But that is not the end of the story, and there is exciting riesling from the steep slopes, good chardonnay and, once in a while, marvelous beerenauslesen and trockenbeerenauslesen.

Carnuntum
HANS PITNAUER, GÖTTLESBRUNN
Owner Hans Pitnauer *Production* 3,900 cases *Vineyard area* 23 acres (9.5 ha)

Carnuntum is named after the old Roman city east of Vienna. It benefits from the Pannonian climate with its warm winds, and black grapes ripen well here. In Göttlesbrunn, zweigelt tends to be the favored grape. Elsewhere it is the Burgenland specialty of blaufränkisch. Pitnauer is a great experimenter who always has something new to offer: a vermouth, a grappa. But his great wines are the pure zweigelt bienenfresser (bee-eater), with its exemplary soft tannins, and Franz Josef, a new-wave cocktail of cabernet, zweigelt and St laurent. He has planted syrah, too, so don't be surprised if that surfaces in the next batch.

Donauland
KARL FRITSCH, KIRCHBERG AM WAGRAM
Owners Fritsch family *Production* 2,500 cases *Vineyard area* 17 acres (7 ha)

The Wagram, a long, south-facing, loess ridge overlooking the Danube, produces some exemplary grüner veltliner. The Fritsches, father and son, have built up a huge reputation over the past few years for their whites. They also make a few red wines, but the joy is still a wine like the Schlossberg with its redolence of pineapples and grapefruit; or Perfektion (a name that might be

asking for trouble), which is a silent Auslese, up to 14 percent alcohol, with a huge bouquet of pepper and angelica.

Weinviertel
HELMUT TAUBENSCHUSS, POYSDORF
Owner Helmut Taubenschuss *Production* 5,550–6,650 cases *Vineyard area* 25 acres (10 ha)

Poysdorf on the Brünn Road provides the base wine for much of Austria's sparkling sekt. While some local is very sour, Helmut seems to have no trouble at all making well-rounded balanced wines here on the Czech border. He makes lovely grüner veltliners bursting with flavor, but his best wines are weissburgunders. They can be massive, but they are massively good, too.

Kamptal
WILLI BRÜNDLMAYER, LANGENLOIS
Owners Bründlmayer family *Production* 21,000 cases *Vineyard area* 123 acres (50 ha)

By Austrian terms Bründlmayer's estate is vast, yet there is very little wine you might disdain. It ranges from national to international in style; from super-concentrated grüner veltliner and riesling to an exemplary chardonnay with barrique aging but no malolactic; to a wonderful, buttery, barrique-aged grauburgunder, a trio of reds and one of Austria's best champagne-style sparklers. When the year is up to it, he makes glorious dessert wines.

Kremstal
MARTIN NIGL, SENFTENBERG
Owner Martin Nigl *Production* 3,900–5,000 cases *Vineyard area* 23 acres (9.5 ha)

Nigl is typical of modern Austria: a decade ago he was unknown. He is still very young and yet he has already established a reputation as one of the country's best winemakers. His grapes grow on the best land in the Krems Valley, on primary rock soils that produce the raciest grüner veltliners and rieslings imaginable. Most of it is bone-dry, but every now and then out comes a trockenbeeren-auslese or an eiswein. He makes two wines with less appeal: a semi-sweet chardonnay, and a trendy, but misguided, sauvignon blanc.

After 1945 most of Austria gradually went over to the high-training methods advocated by Lenz Moser III to maximise exposure to warmth and sunlight. The grüner veltliner grape, above, adapted well to being trained on wires, but sylvaner, once widely grown, fell by the wayside.

Many producers shun mechanical harvesting, preferring to use grapes picked by hand.

REGIONAL BEST

Bela Rex, Engelbert
     Gesellmann
Franz Josef, Hans Pitnauer
Grand Select Chardonnay,
     Fritz Wieninger
Grassnitzberg Weissburgunder,
     Erich and Walter Polz
Grüner Veltliner, Willi
     Bründlmayer
Loibner Berg Grüner Veltliner,
     F. X. Pichler
Marienthal Blaufränkisch,
     Ernst Triebaumer
Olivin, Georg Winkler-
     Hermaden
Perfektion Grüner Veltliner,
     Karl Fritsch
Perwolf, Krutzler
Riesling, Martin Nigl
Spätrot-Rotgipfler, Karl
     Alphart
Weissburgunder, Ludwig
     Neumayer
Weisser Berg Weissburgunder,
     Helmut Taubenschuss
Zwischen den Seen, Luis
     Kracher

Wachau

F. X. PICHLER, LOIBEN

Owner F. X. Pichler *Production* 5,550 cases *Vineyard area*
18 acres (7.5 ha)

Austrian winelovers would almost certainly cite
F. X. as their greatest winemaker, yet he makes so
little wine that very few of them would be speaking from experience. F. X. makes great riesling
and grüner veltliner on steep sites in the beautiful
Wachau. He is an austere, unrelenting man, but his
determination shows in the great concentration of
the wines. The best of a great year is marked "M"
for "monumental." These wines are rarest of all.

Traisental

LUDWIG NEUMAYER, INZERSDORF OB DER TRAISEN

Owner Ludwig Neumayer *Production* 3,000 cases *Vineyard
area* 18 acres (7.5 ha)

Traisental is Austria's newest region. Its best winemaker, Ludwig Neumayer, took up the challenge
just after the glycol scandal and began by making
concentrated white wines from weissburgunder,
riesling and grüner veltliner on his rocky soils. He
also makes an old-fashioned cuvée from a promis-
cuous vineyard containing a few throwbacks to
the years before phylloxera. Most recently he has
experimented with sauvignon blanc, but he will
release nothing until he has got it right.

Neusiedlersee

LUIS KRACHER, ILLMITZ

Owner Luis Kracher *Production* NA *Vineyard area*
18 acres (7.5 ha), plus purchased grapes in good years

Now that he has turned his hand to production in
California, Luis Kracher is the Austrian winemaker

*The historical association between the
Church and wine-producing remains strong.*

best-known abroad. He is the pope of Austrian
sweet wine and in some years he makes more
trockenbeerenauslesen than the rest of Germany.
He has not only his skill to thank, but also the
special conditions around his home village, where
the mists settle on the stagnant ponds and botrytis
sets in most years. The wines divide into new-oak
fermented Nouvelle Vague, and the Zwischen den
Seen range, made in traditional acacia wood casks.

Neusiedlersee–Hügelland

ERNST TRIEBAUMER, RUST

Owners Triebaumer family *Production* 4,600 cases
Vineyard area 27 acres (11 ha)

Rust is the home of Ausbruch, but there is more to
it than great sweet wines. On its warm soils black
grapes ripen superbly, producing good dry whites.
E. T. is the broadest brush in Rust. He makes
superb Ausbruch, often with high alcohol levels,
but in the Marienthal he also makes Austria's best
blaufränkisch, a barrel-fermented chardonnay and
a lovely traminer (made at the insistence of his
wife). Ernst shares his cellars with his son Herbert,
who is now also making fine Ausbruch.

Central Burgenland

ENGELBERT GESELLMANN, DEUTSCHKREUZ

Owners Gesellmann family *Production* 8,900 cases
Vineyard area 44 acres (18 ha)

Grim Deutschkreuz is the home of Engelbert
Gesellmann and his son Albert. This is the red
wine belt of Austria, chiefly flat, gravelly soils
where blaufränkisch feels most at home but where
there is now also a fair smattering of cabernet.
Albert learned how to handle it in South Africa
and California and his Bela Rex, bordeaux blend is
about the best Austria has to offer. There are other
"cuvées" in the stable: Greitzer and Opus Exim-
ium, which are based on blaufränkisch. Gesellmann makes exemplary St laurent and zweigelt,
some good dry whites and the occasional sticky.

Southern Burgenland

KRUTZLER, DEUTSCH SCHÜTZEN

Owners Krutzler family *Production* 4,220 cases *Vineyard
area* 16 acres (6.5 ha), plus purchased grapes

Wild and remote, Southern Burgenland is the
home of uhudler (wines made from American
vines and reputed to provoke madness). But there
is nothing mad about the Krutzlers. The father,
Hermann, is in local politics and the sons look
after the wine. The best is Perwolf, a blend of
blaufränkisch and cabernet that works extremely

Sidestreet in the village of Heiligenstadt.

well. The cabernet covers the crumbly blaufränkisch fruit. There is good welschriesling, too.

Southeast Styria
GEORG WINKLER-HERMADEN, KAPFENSTEIN

Owners Winkler-Hermaden family *Production* 6,000 cases
Vineyard area 30 acres (12 ha), plus some purchased grapes

The family seat of the Winkler von Hermadens (as they were) is now a fine hotel and restaurant, the best in the area, and the slopes below the castle are Georg's province. He makes the wine, the most famous of which is Olivin, a fantastically concentrated zweigelt grown on olivine rock. Other wines are more approachable: the burgunder-based Caphenstein, a big weissburgunder, a lovely sauvignon blanc, an oaky grauburgunder and a traminer that occasionally sufaces as a beerenauslese.

South Styria
ERICH AND WALTER POLZ, SPIELFELD

Owners Polz family *Production* 12,000 cases *Vineyard area*
43 acres (17.5 ha), plus 20 acres (8 ha) from Aubell and
some purchased grapes

The Polz brothers now have plenty of wine to sell, but there is never enough to satisfy the demand for their hauntingly sappy muskateller, their weissburgunder from the Grassnitzberg and the morillon (chardonnay) and sauvignon blanc from the Hochgrassnitzberg. The brothers have adhered more to a supple Styrian style, preferring not to broaden the flavors with new oak as some other producers do. They make one oaky wine, the morillon Obegg. There is also a lovely welschriesling and possibly Styria's best riesling.

West Styria
DOMAINE MÜLLER, GROSS ST FLORIAN

Owner Günter Müller *Production* 20,000 cases *Vineyard
area* 50 acres (20 ha), plus 60 acres (25 ha) rented

Günter Müller is the giant of West Styria. Not only is his production huge by Austrian standards, but he is also the importer of some of the best French wines, such as Pétrus, DRC and Bollinger. West Styria is best known for its acid, thin rosé wine—Schilcher. It is an acquired taste. Müller has found an excellent commercial formula: he makes it into a very good sparkler. His vineyards are not confined to West Styria and from neighboring South Styria he produces sauvignon blanc and chardonnay and a few experimental red wines.

Schnapps can be a profitable sideline.

Switzerland

Wink Lorch

The most mountainous country in Europe finds space for more than 37,000 acres (15,000 ha) of vineyards in its valleys and foothills. Surprisingly, few cling to the sides of mountains and most are planted at altitudes common in Alsace and Burgundy. Switzerland has borders with Alsace, Haute Savoie and Jura in France, with Baden in southern Germany, with western Austria and with northern Italy, so a number of wine styles are produced. Some grape types that survive

from ancient times have names of Latin origin, such as amigne and arvine. The Romans cultivated vines in the canton of Valais on the shores of lakes Geneva, Neuchâtel, Zürich and Constance, where vineyards still thrive.

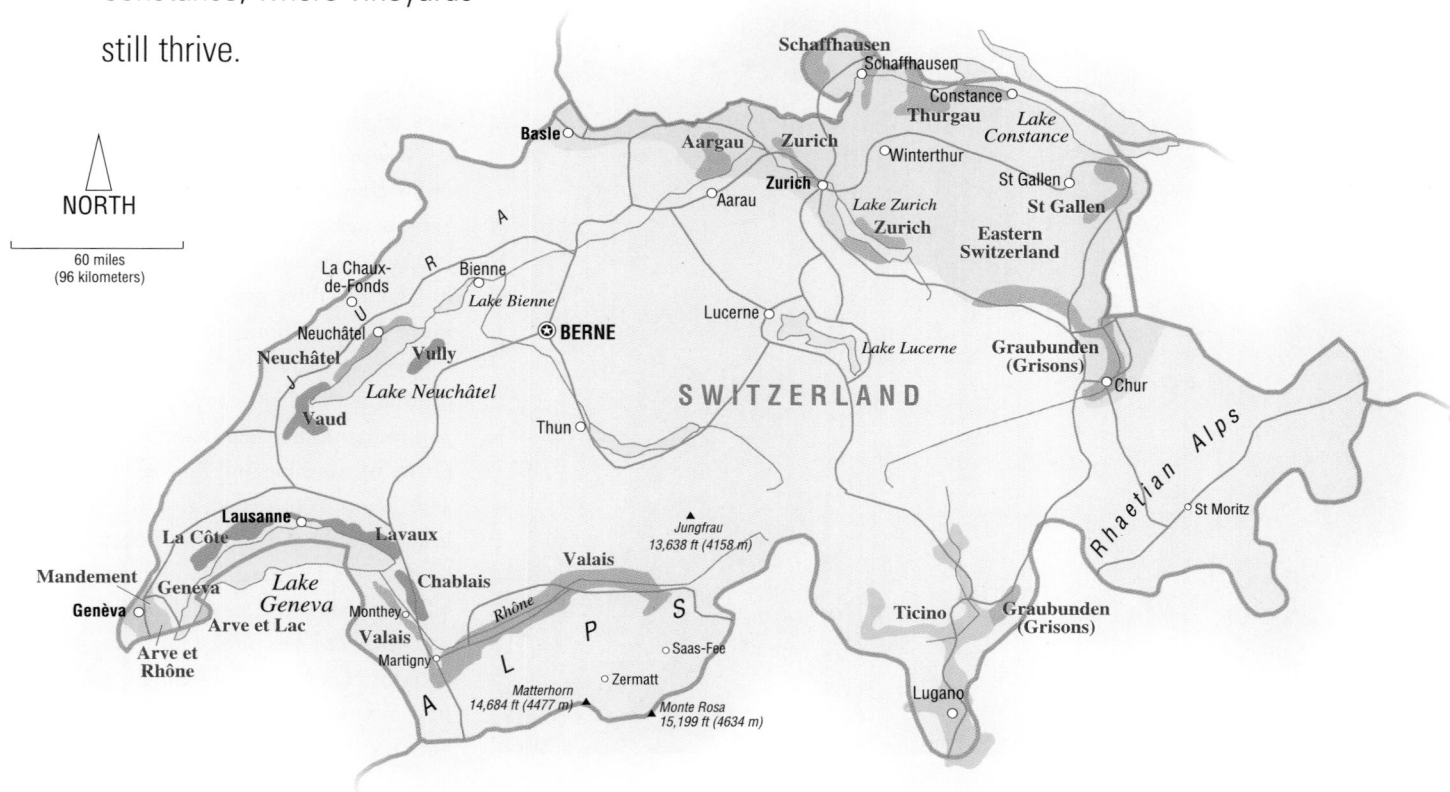

Wine production flourished in Switzerland from the seventeenth century and by the time phylloxera arrived vineyards covered twice the area they now do. As in other European areas, there was a dramatic decline when imports became cheaper and fewer people wanted to work such difficult terrain.

Landscape and climate

Switzerland's vineyards lie between the 45° and 47°N latitude, potentially ideal for quality viticulture. Generally the climate is temperate or continental, with plenty of sunshine and rainfall at the right time of year, cold winters and warm summers, though with considerable vintage variation. The appearance in some valleys of the Foehn (or Föhn), a warm alpine wind, can hasten ripening dramatically. Many soils are of glacial origin and broken-up slate, schist and large stones are very common. The variety of soil types accounts for marked differences in character in chasselas wines.

Vaud's Lavaux region on the slopes above Lake Geneva, where the vines are said to receive three suns—from the sky, and reflected off the lake and stone walls.

Wine regions

Wine regions in Switzerland are divided, first into the three main language divisions, French, German and Italian, and then further into cantons. French-speaking Switzerland accounts for about 28,320 acres (11,460 ha) of vines, 77 percent of the total, from which about 83 percent of Switzerland's wine is produced. The most important cantons, in size order, are Valais, Vaud, Geneva and Neuchâtel.

Valais is the most prolific wine canton and it also has some of the most picturesque vineyards. Protected by high alpine ranges, they include some of Europe's highest vineyards at 3,600 feet (1,100 m). This area is in the Haut-Valais at Visperterminen (a German-speaking part of Valais), below the ski resorts of Zermatt and Saas-Fee. However, the greatest density of vineyards is on the south-facing slopes of the upper Rhône Valley, which runs east–west between Leuk (Loèche) and Martigny with vineyard altitudes between 1,475 and 2,460 feet (450 m and 750 m). The wine center and capital of the canton is Sion. Sunshine hours are high but rainfall is the lowest in Switzerland, so some drip irrigation is necessary.

Vaud has four main vineyard regions, the three largest close to Lake Geneva, named from the west La Côte, Lavaux and, toward Valais, Chablais (not to be confused with Chablis). The smallest region, linking three separate areas, Bonvillars, Côtes-de-l'Orbe and Vully, is close to Lake Neuchâtel. The lakes have a most important climatic influence, regulating temperature and increasing the effect of the sun by reflection. Toward the east, closer to the Alps, rainfall increases and the Chablais area may be affected by the Foehn.

Geneva's city center is just 6 miles (10 km) east of Switzerland's largest grape-growing community, Satigny, with nearly 1,235 acres (500 ha) of vineyards. This is the heart of Mandement, the largest of Geneva's three growing areas, the others being Entre Arve et Rhône (between the Arve and Rhône rivers) and Entre Arve et Lac. Viticulture in this canton, with a landscape of rolling hills, is easier and more mechanized than elsewhere. There is plenty of sunshine and the nearby Jura mountains and the pre-Alps deflect clouds, giving relatively low rainfall. Lake Geneva protects the vineyards from spring frost and the best vineyards are on hillsides that warm rapidly in morning sunshine.

Neuchâtel lies on the northern shores of the lakes of Neuchâtel and Bienne and south of the Jura mountains. This area has a fairly dry climate, but lacks the intensity and amount of sunshine enjoyed by more southerly cantons. Vineyard altitudes vary from 1,400–2,000 feet (430–600 m) and have some Jurassic limestone, as found in France's Jura and Burgundy vineyards on the other side of the mountains. Topsoils are very diverse.

German-speaking Switzerland has vineyards scattered across 18 cantons, with significant plantings in Zürich, Schaffhausen, Aargau, Graubünden (Grisons), Thurgau and St Gallen (by Lake Constance). The climate is marginal for viticulture, though proximity to the Rhine River in the north, to various lakes, and the influence of the Foehn in the east, help certain vineyards.

Almost all the vineyards in Italian-speaking Switzerland are in Ticino, the fourth-largest wine-producing canton. Sopraceneri and Sottoceneri, north and south of Monte Ceneri, have scattered plots, mostly on terraces, many currently being reconstructed to aid mechanization. With the climate influenced by the Mediterranean, there are more sunshine hours than anywhere in Switzerland, but rainfall is higher, too, mostly in dramatic spring storms that can bring hail.

Wine laws

These are set both at federal and cantonal level. Changes to federal wine law were made in 1992 and generally fall in line with EU law, with provision for a system of controled appellation of origin (AOC). The most important change was to bring in a maximum-yield requirement, although at current levels this is too high to assure quality. However, several cantons impose lower yields. The four major French-speaking cantons all have an AOC system in place, but each works differently. There is some movement toward harmonization. Most wines are labeled with the canton, some with the village, too, and usually the grape variety, unless the wine is marketed under a one of several "stylistic" appellations, in use for many years.

Vines and wines (white)

Chasselas is grown widely in the French-speaking cantons, notably in Vaud, where it dominates the vineyards. The wine's character derives much more from the soil type than from the grape. Malolactic fermentation is used to lower acidity and create a softer, creamier mouth-feel. Almost all chasselas is dry and fendant from the Valais can vary from soft and fruity (sometimes lacking in acidity) to a much more intense, mineral or stony flavor.

The Grand Crus of Dézaley and Calamin provide intensity in the first and elegance in the

second, but nearby villages of Epesses and Saint-Saphorin can produce equally good, structured and honeyed wines. Yvorne and Aigle with steep vineyards in Chablais also produce excellent chasselas. Young chasselas often has a slight spritz and good examples benefit from two or more years aging.

Riesling-sylvaner, known elsewhere as müller-thurgau, is the first recorded vine crossing. It was made by Dr Müller of Thurgau, to suit marginal climates. It is most prevalent in German-speaking parts where it produces a dry or medium-dry, flowery wine to drink young. When yields are well controlled, the wines have good aromatic flavor.

Sylvaner thrives on steep, stony sites and produces grapes with considerably higher natural sugar levels than chasselas. In Valais, where it has always been revered, sylvaner wines are labeled, Johannisberg. Sylvaner can be made into a dry, medium or perfumed late-harvest wines.

Chardonnay, although widely planted in Valais during the 1970s, does better in Geneva and Neuchâtel where both dry light and elegant styles are made and, less successfully, oak-matured wines.

Pinot gris has long been grown in Valais, where sweeter styles are called malvoisie. It does well in the warmer parts of German Switzerland.

Marsanne has thrived for years in the Upper Rhône Valley yielding wines labeled Ermitage (or Hermitage). Highly alcoholic, these dry or sweet wines, develop vivid dried apricot or peach tones.

The village of Féchy, Vaud, beside Lake Geneva. Half of Vaud's production comes from La Côte, a concentrated vineyard area on gentle slopes following the lake around from Nyon, northeast of Geneva, to Morges, west of Lausanne.

Vineyard labor costs in Switzerland are probably the highest in the world. Pulley systems help at harvest time, but pickers often carry boxes of grapes up or down impossibly steep paths and stone steps between the terraces.

Old drystone walled terracing near Sion,
the capital of the canton of Valais.

REGIONAL BEST

Aigle "Les Murailles," Henri
  Badoux & Fils, Vaud
Chamoson Pinot Noir
  "Rénommée de Saint-Pierre,"
  René Favre et Fils, Valais
Chamoson Petite Arvine, René
  Favre et Fils, Valais
Château Lichten, Rouvinez,
  Valais
Dardagny Le Bertholier Rouge
  Domaine Les Hutins, Geneva
Dardagny Pinot Noir Reserve,
  Domaine Les Hutins, Geneva
Dézaley L'Arbalette, Jean et
  Pierre Testuz, Vaud
Dézaley-Marsens "De La Tour,"
  Les Frères Dubois, Vaud
Epesses "Clos du Boux," Luc
  Massy, Vaud
Heida "Gletscherwein," Oskar
  Chanton, Valais
Johannisberg Moelleux,
  Domaine du Mont d'Or,
  Valais
Merlot del Ticino "Riflessi
  d'Epoca," I Vini di Guido
  Brivio, Ticino
Petite Arvine "Sous l'Escalier,"
  Domaine du Mont d'Or,
  Valais
Syrah "Cayas," Bon Père
  Germanier, Valais
Vétroz Amigne "Mitis," Bon
  Père Germanier, Valais

Vines and wines (red)

Pinot noir is especially favored in German Switzerland, where it accounts for 70 percent of plantings.
Thermo-vinification is widely practiced to give
color but no tannin and this means most wines
are rather lacking in flavor. Where producers with
good sites treat pinot better, results are good. Also
important in French Switzerland, it is Neuchâtel's
only permitted red grape giving, notably, an excellent dry rosé, Oeil de Perdrix. It is gaining ground
in Vaud, especially in La Côte and is the most-
planted red in Valais, where much goes into the
dôle and goron blends.

Gamay is grown widely in French Switzerland
and used almost exclusively for blends in Valais,
but Geneva successfully produces a characteristic
fruity varietal with good acid balance.

Merlot is now the principal variety in Ticino.
Good Ticino merlots show lively acidity, soft
tannins and succulent fruit flavors, but many are
light, fruity and rather thin. Several producers are
making structured merlot, some with oak aging.

Syrah is causing excitement in Valais. Small
quantities have been grown there for many years,
but not given much attention. There are now
about 125 acres (50 ha), mostly in Valais, on
prime, steep slopes for maximum sunshine.

Gamaret and *garanoir* are two red wine crossings with white reichensteiner (itself a crossing)
and red gamay in their parentage. They have
proved remarkably successful, particularly in
Geneva and Vaud. Used sometimes in blends and

sometimes pure, they can
produce deep-colored reds
with good black fruit character and structure to cope with
oak aging. In the Valais the
crossing diolinoir is also
gaining ground.

Specialty grapes

More than 50 varieties grow
in the varied topography and
soils of Valais, several ancient
and found nowhere else.
Exciting white obscurities
include petite arvine (also
grown in Aosta, Italy), amigne
(only 50 acres/20 ha in the
world, all in Valais) and païen
or heida (probably the savagnin from Jura). Both petite
arvine and amigne can be
made dry or medium-sweet to sweet, described as
"mi-flétri" or "flétri" meaning "shriveled on the
vine." Petite arvine, grown across Valais, has crisp
acidity, good fruit concentration and an almost
salty flavor. Amigne, almost all grown in Grand
Cru vineyards of Vétroz, can show an attractive
mandarin flavor and has proved particularly good
when vinified sweet. Heida is grown in the high
vineyards of Visperterminen and on these steep
vineyard slopes it produces a dry wine of astonishing power with strong aromatic flavors. Now,
plantings of païen (as it is called in the French
part) are being developed elsewhere in Valais. For
reds, the most interesting obscurities making a
comeback are cornalin and humagne.

Producers

Switzerland has several thousand vineyard owners,
many with tiny plots. Most are either part of a
wine cooperative, or pass their crop over to a local
négociant. In Valais alone about 700 producers
make and sell their own wine. The following producers make a range that can be recommended.

BON PÈRE GERMANIER, VALAIS

Established 1896 *Owners* Bon Père Germanier S. A. (owned
by Germanier family) *Production* 40,000 cases *Vineyard
area* 27 acres (11 ha), plus some purchased grapes

Based close to Vétroz, near Sion, in modern cellars, Jean-René Germanier's nephew Gilles Bess
makes all the Valais varieties, including Cayas, a
superbly deep barrique-aged syrah. However, it is

the elegant sweet wine Mitis from the rare amigne grapes that stands out. Made from part-frozen and part-botrytised fruit and aged in new oak, it has the concentration and acidity to last many years.

RENÉ FAVRE & FILS, VALAIS

Established 1978 *Owners* Mike and Jean-Charles Favre *Production* 6,500 cases *Vineyard area* 27 acres (11 ha)

The Favre brothers produce a vast range from this small domaine. Their whites are good, especially a petite arvine, partly from 70-year-old vines, but pinot noir is Mike's passion. The best of the three pinots made is Renommée de St Pierre. This barrel-aged wine from vines more than 40 years old has superb balance with fruit flavors reminiscent of good California pinot noir.

DOMAINE LES HUTINS, GENEVA

Established 1976 *Owners* Jean and Pierre Hutin *Production* 12,000 cases *Vineyard area* 44 acres (18 ha)

Based in Dardagny, close to the French border, Jean and Pierre Hutin were among the first Swiss to plant sauvignon blanc. They produce both non-oaked and barrique versions of sauvignon blanc, chardonnay and pinot noir, the latter most successfully. Their best chasselas, Le Bertholier, is fresh and creamy. Le Bertholier Rouge, 80 percent gamaret with cabernet sauvignon, is aged partly in new barriques giving fabulous depth and complexity. Viognier and merlot are the latest challenge.

DOMAINE DU MONT D'OR, VALAIS

Established 1848 *Owners* Domaine du Mont d'Or S. A. (majority Schenk S. A.) *Production* 16,000 cases *Vineyard area* 50 acres (20 ha)

This famous old domaine has vineyards in prime south-facing, steep sites. It has always made reliable fendant and dôle, but its specialty is late-harvest wine, from several varieties, wherever possible from botrytised grapes. Its signature wine is Johannisberg from sylvaner, which shows a tropical fruit character. The fine Petite Arvine Sous L'Escalier ("below the steps") ages superbly.

JEAN & PIERRE TESTUZ, VAUD

Established 1845 *Owners* J & P Testuz S. A. (100% owned by Testuz family) *Production* 200,000 cases *Vineyard area* 147 acres (60 ha) (some leased)

A large firm of growers and *négociants* based in the Grand Cru vineyards of Dézaley in Lavaux, Testuz specializes in chasselas, but also produces a range of other varietals. Run by Jean-Philippe, a thirteenth-generation Testuz, the firm takes its chasselas seriously. A wine with a subtly different character, reflecting various soil types and aspects, is produced from each major Lavaux appellation.

Wine tastings attract both locals and tourists to visit the wineries.

Many vineyards, like these near Lake Geneva, benefit from particular micro-climates, provided by proximity to water.

Italy

Matterhorn
14,684 ft (4477 m)

Mt Rosa
15,199 ft (4634 m)

Mt Bianco
15,770 ft (4808 m)

Valle d'Aosta

Piedmont

ALPS

Lake
Maggiore

Lake Como

Bolzano

Trentino-
Alto Adige

Trento

DOLOMITES

Udine

Franciacorta
Bergamo

Lake
Garda

Valpolicella
Soave

Vicenza

Friuli-Venezia
Giulia

Trieste

Novara

Monza
Milan

Brescia

Lugana

Verona

Mestre

Padua

Venice

Gulf of Venice

Turin

Po

Piacenza

Adige

Po

Asti

Emilia-
Romagna

Parma

Ferrara

Emilia-
Romagna

Piedmont

Reggio nell'Emilia

Modena

Bologna

Genoa

APENNINES

Emilia-
Romagna

Savona

Liguria

Liguria

La Spézia

Rimini

SAN MARINO

ADRIATIC

Prato

Florence

Pisa

Ancona

Livorno

Tuscany

Arezzo

Tevere

Marche

Siena

Lake
Trasimeno

Perugia

SEA

Elba

Tuscany

Umbria

Orvieto

Teramo

Terni

Pescara

Corsica
(France)

Lazio

L'Aquila

Abruzzo

Monti dei Frentani

ROME

Lazio

Molise

Campobasso

Foggia

Campania

Bari

TYRRHENIAN

Mt Vesuvius
4201 ft (1281 m)

Basilicata

Puglia

Sardinia

Naples

Torre del Greco

Sassari

SEA

Ischia

Campania

Potenza

Brindi

Sardinia

Salerno

Taranto

Campania

Mt del Papa
6576 ft (2005 m)

Appennino Lucano

Punta La Marmora
6015 ft (1834 m)

Calabria

Sardinia

Mt Botte Donato
6323 ft (1928 m)

Cagliari

Cosenza

Calabria

Calabria

Catanzaro

Lipari Islands

Calabria

Messina

Trapani

Palermo

Sicily

Reggio
di Calabria

Bianco

Sicily

NORTH

Sicily

Mt Etna
10,899 ft (3323 m)

Catania

60 miles
(96 kilometers)

Sicily

Siracuse

Sicily

Pantelleria

Italy

Maureen Ashley MW

If it's true that good things come in small packages then Italy, with its multiplicity of often pocket handkerchief-sized wine zones, must have good things in plenty. The profusion of its wines and the abundance of the grape varieties making them are both Italy's glory and its downfall, however. For some the country's wines are a treasure trove, for others they are just complicated and confusing.

Italy is geographically complex, too. To the north, the well-drained lower slopes of the bordering Alps provide prime grape-growing territory before they give way to the plainlands of the Po valley, about the only part of Italy where grapes are not consistently grown. This entire northern part has a gently continental climate with marked inconsistencies from year to year giving pronounced vintage variations.

The long, narrow peninsular part of the country is defined by the Apennine mountain chain that forms its spine. There are numerous hill ranges and comparatively little flat ground. In some places the mountains fall right to the sea, creating the most dramatic of scenery and growing conditions.

While Italy's climate is naturally categorized as Mediterranean, the great variety of altitudes and exposures gives a far greater spread of climatic conditions than might be expected.

Much of the glorious lack of consistency in Italy's wine production derives from its history. Wine has been produced on its lands for several thousand years, at least since the time of the Phoenicians and Greeks. Yet Italy has been united politically only since the 1860s, and socially only since the arrival of television half a century or so ago. Even now a journey of just 50 miles can seem like 500, so frequent are the changes in dialects and eating habits.

Italy's wine scene today is principally the result of two major, comparatively recent movements. The first followed the devastation of the Second World War; in the economic boom that accompanied reconstruction, partly from necessity the wine producers' motto appeared to become "more is better," and the industry was aimed firmly at ever greater quantities, with hardly a thought given to quality. The second was the realization that this path was dreadfully flawed and that survival lay in high quality. This change, often called the Italian wine renaissance, started in the mid-1970s and hit its peak in the late 1980s, although it must be said that a few corners of the country are learning the lesson only now; it left its mark mainly in the vineyards, where mediocre but high-producing varieties sometimes squeezed out the more characterful, and in complex wine laws.

Italy has a vast heritage of grape varieties, possessing a wealth of indigenous vines as well as the varieties more often seen worldwide. What ended up where hundreds of years ago depended not only on the suitability of growing conditions but also on how well the wines made from a particular variety suited the local diet.

The rediscovery and repropagation of the less well-known varieties, many of them rendered almost extinct during the quantity-driven days, is now in full swing. Often these are "troublesome" varieties, in the sense that they are naturally low-yielding, ripen with difficulty or are prone to disease. In compensation they may well give wines of incomparable flavor or, used in a blend, turn a good wine into an exciting one.

Dozens of varieties can be considered emblematic of one or more regions—Piedmont's nebbiolo, the tocai of Friuli–Venezia Giulia, nero d'avola in Sicily, for example. In general the only varieties found nationwide are what the Italians call the innovative varieties and what we would term the classics, cabernet and chardonnay leading the field. There is a strong penchant for varietal wines in the northeast; in the rest of the country the attitude is more pragmatic, making both varietals and blends. Italians become a little coy about revealing the make-up of their wines only in those cases where they have added a small amount of chardonnay to an indigenous variety to make it more international in taste; they prefer you to think that such a wine comes from a pure indigene.

In the early stages of the quantity-to-quality shift the emphasis was on winemaking, a vast amount of investment going into cellar equipment and the acquisition of technical know-how. Out went the old concrete vats and other rudimentary bits of equipment and in came stainless steel vats, automatic temperature control, oxygen-free systems, cold sterile bottling, air-conditioned storage areas and all the other baggage of the standard modern winemaking plant. On most estates the changeover took no more than a year or two, and while it was achieved with little interruption to production, there were huge effects on the wines produced. Some altered so much they became almost unrecognizable.

The next stage reached to the core of the matter: the vineyards. Revamping a vineyard is a much longer and more complicated procedure. Most estates have had to start from scratch to find the best combinations of rootstock and variety for their heterogeneous terrains, the most suitable clones and optimal planting density. Such research can take years and the vineyard must be replanted

The Italian climate, broadly categorized as Mediterranean, has great regional variation.

Fertile valleys set among rugged mountains are typical of the vine-growing regions in Tuscany, central Italy.

in stages to avoid massive interruptions to production. The improvements this stage brings will no doubt continue to emerge over the next decade. One thing is clear, however. The direction in vineyard plantings is towards high density. A few wine producers have taken the "more is better" theory to the extreme, planting up to 25,000 vines or more per acre (62,000 vines per ha), regardless of the cost or the effect on cultivation efficiency.

REGIONS AND STYLES

Italy's wine laws follow the standard European Community breakdown into "quality wine" and "table wine." Within quality wine Italy has two categories, DOC (*denominazione di origine controllata*) and the higher-level DOCG (*denominazione di origine garantita*). At the beginning of 2000 there were over 300 DOCs, wines with basic controls on origin, grape varieties and style, and several cultivation and winemaking parameters. Increasingly, larger DOCs are becoming nested with, for example, a DOC zone containing one or more subzonal DOCs which have tighter production constraints (and, therefore, presumably higher quality). In theory the nesting can continue right down to single-vineyard DOCs, but it will be quite some time before this level is reached.

DOCG was conceived as a class apart to represent the top wines. Currently either an entire zone may gain the additional qualification or at some stage along the nesting process a subzone can move from DOC to DOCG. Originally, though, zones had to be promoted whole or not at all and this caused some undeserving wines to gain their *garantita* along with other, more worthy ones.

Perhaps the best—or worst—example is that of Chianti. Good wines from the Classico heartland and the higher quality subzones, lesser wines from the lower quality subzones and poor stuff from the periphery, became DOCG together. This means that the G does not guarantee very much, although producers still cherish the qualification and keenly seek promotion to it.

At the table wine end of the spectrum, simple VdT (*vino da tavola*) is about as basic as you can get. A large and increasing number of wines fall into the higher subcategory, IGT (*indicazione geografica tipica*). Conceived to offer broadly regional wine styles, which to some extent it does (although there are regional DOCs too), just as often it is used as a sort of catch-all category, especially for wines that don't fit into their DOC for some reason (usually the grape varieties used). Hence the quality can be anything from mundane to marvellous. The only sensible advice is to ignore the category and go by the name of the producer.

Italy is a country that changes rapidly, sometimes breathtakingly so. Wine trends perforce come and go a little slower but there are always talking points which, given the impassioned nature of most Italian discussion, often become the subject of intense debate. Recently the use of the classic varieties provoked argument. On one side were those who saw use of the innovative varieties as a way of making Italian wines more readily acceptable on the international market; on the other were those who saw them as compromising Italy's unique wine styles, leading to homogeneity of tastes. The fence-sitters argued that innovative varieties were useful initially to gain entrance to

Vineyards framed by a tower window at Cantine F. Oddero, Piedmont.

The ancient small town of Poggio Lavarino in Umbria, Italy's only landlocked region.

Early stone carving held in the wine museum in Torgiano, Umbria.

foreign markets; once there, classic Italian styles could take over. It is now generally accepted that international varieties have their place but that the future of Italian wine lies in the individuality provided by the indigenous grapes.

The use of the *barrique* is a current talking point. Traditionally, Italian wines, if aged at all, were put in large wooden barrels (*botti*), which were used for decades. These were most commonly made of oak from the forests of Slavonia. Today there is scarcely an estate that hasn't replaced or supplemented its *botti* stock with *barriques*—here used to mean small casks of new oak, usually but not always French. While most winemakers seem convinced that they are needed to produce high-quality wines, a growing voice holds that many Italian grape varieties are not well-suited to the *barrique* treatment. Even with those that are, say dissenters, the *barrique* tends to homogenize styles, squashing individuality with its oaky overlay.

There is also discussion about roving enologists. Producers of all sizes are increasingly placing their trust in well-known, highly skilled contract winemakers to guide production. While this does ensure that a wine is competently made, producers risk their wines reflecting their enologist's ideas on style and character rather than their own—and resembling others made by him. Worse, the enologists most in demand are taking on dozens of estates and cannot possibly give detailed personal attention to each one. It must be admitted, however, that scores of estates have seen their wines improve out of all recognition.

Even sweet wines have come under the microscope. The classic method for creating the additional grape sugar necessary to produce a sweet (or strong) wine is to pick the grapes when normally ripe (sometimes even slightly underripe) and leave them to dry out until sufficient concentration has been reached. In the north the bunches are either hung from hooks or laid out on shallow racks in airy indoor locations. The drying process, called *appassimento*, is slow, lasting up to four months. In the hotter south the grapes are laid out on racks out of doors, and the *appassimento* is much faster, sometimes lasting just two to three weeks. The resulting *passito* wines can be delicately or richly sweet but they retain freshness and rarely cloy. Increasing numbers of producers, however, lured by the siren song of "renowned international style," are turning to late harvesting to ensure high sugar content, and once more the local traditional methods are having to fight for their place.

One thing does not brook debate, however. In Italy wine is conceived and made as a food accompaniment. Drinking wine on its own is a habit for foreigners, not Latins. As a result, many wines that taste disappointingly harsh or neutral when unaccompanied suddenly spring into life when drunk with food, so hasty judgments at a tasting bench are not always wise.

Italy is split into 20 administrative regions. While these do not often tally with viticultural zones it has become customary to use the regional breakdown when discussing Italian wines and this convention is followed here, if loosely.

Piedmont and Northwest Italy

The northwest of Italy is well-known to skiers (Courmayeur, Cervinia), car buffs (Turin, home of Fiat), supporters of the football giant Juventus and wine enthusiasts. The heart of the northwest is the Piedmont region and at Piedmont's heart are the zones of Barolo and Barbaresco, names that for many represent the peak of Italian winemaking.

Landscape and climate

Parts of Piedmont are mountainous but the main wine zones cluster to the south and east of Turin, an area of sharply defined hilly outcrops intersected by flat river valleys. The northwest also comprises the regions of Valle d'Aosta, which borders France and Switzerland; Liguria, a narrow mountain-ringed arc adjacent to the French Riviera and centered on Genoa; and the western part of Lombardy. Valle d'Aosta is almost completely mountainous, with no more than the occasional patch of terraced vineyard lying close to the main Dora Baltea River valley, sited wherever the twists of the land enable enough sun to penetrate the mountain barrier. Viticulture in Liguria is similarly marginal, with tiny plots of vines hugging the midground between the lower slopes, which are used as nurseries, and the olive-bedecked upper slopes.

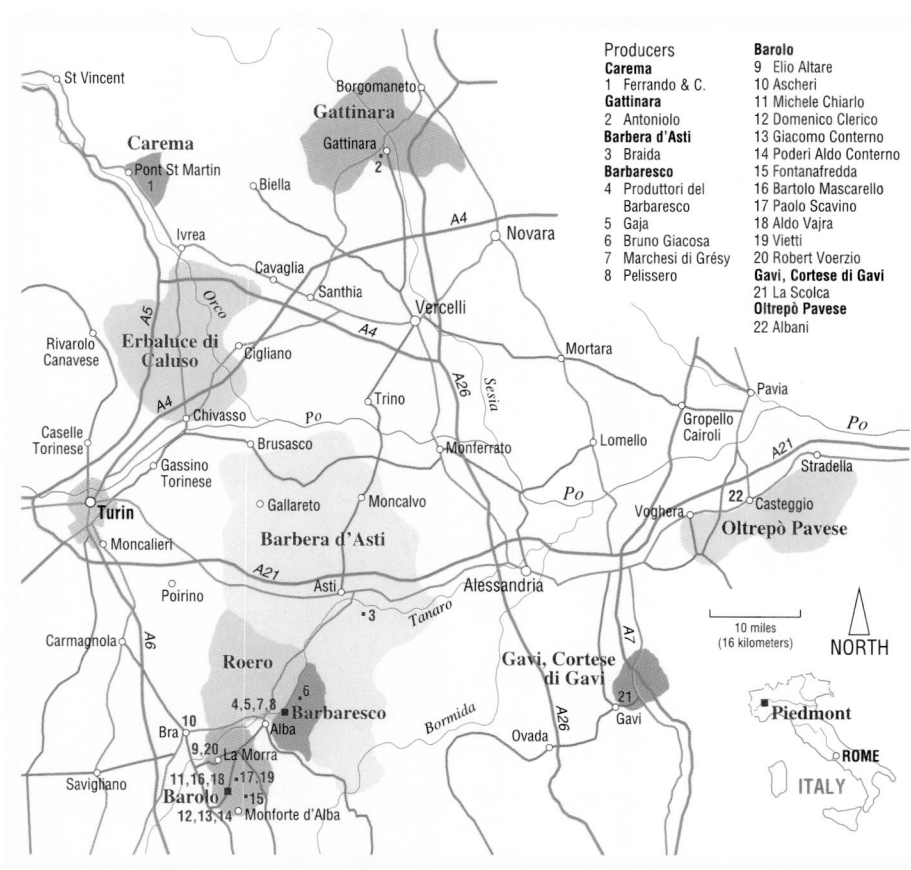

Producers

Carema
1 Ferrando & C.

Gattinara
2 Antoniolo

Barbera d'Asti
3 Braida

Barbaresco
4 Produttori del Barbaresco
5 Gaja
6 Bruno Giacosa
7 Marchesi di Grésy
8 Pelissero

Barolo
9 Elio Altare
10 Ascheri
11 Michele Chiarlo
12 Domenico Clerico
13 Giacomo Conterno
14 Poderi Aldo Conterno
15 Fontanafredda
16 Bartolo Mascarello
17 Paolo Scavino
18 Aldo Vajra
19 Vietti
20 Robert Voerzio

Gavi, Cortese di Gavi
21 La Scolca

Oltrepò Pavese
22 Albani

The shuttered winery building on the estate of the Marchesi di Grésy, Piedmont.

Winemaker Clerico Francesco tastes some of his own very good product.

Throughout the northwest, winters are cold (except on the coastal side of Liguria) and summers reasonably hot. In Piedmont winters are marked by fog in the valleys whenever the high pressure weather systems set in. Spring and fall are very changeable, causing producers great anxiety and creating notable vintage variations.

Vines and wines

In the Piedmont heartland, most wines are single varietals. Three varieties, all red, stand out, nebbiolo being the most illustrious—for many, Piedmont means nebbiolo. Late-ripening and very sensitive to weather variations, nebbiolo makes slow-developing wines of intensity, austerity and refinement. It can also make wines that, while still punchy, are more fruit-forward and can be drunk sooner. Those grown away in the zones of Barolo and Barbaresco are somewhat lighter. Nebbiolo shows a strong swathe of acidity and tannin that can mask the underlying dense, complex fruit. In its proper place, with robust red meat or game dishes, the fruit trickles through as an intriguing mix of savory, spicy (licorice, tar, meat juices), and floral (roses and violets).

Nebbiolo needs plentiful fall sun, so plantings are concentrated on south-facing slopes. Vineyards with good exposure to the sun are greatly prized and often given the prefix Sorì, "sun-drenched",

to emphasize their importance. Hilltop sites are honored in Piedmontese by the prefix Bricco.

Beyond Barolo and Barbaresco and the lands between them south of the Tanaro River, nebbiolo is grown north of the Tanaro in the Roero; in the east in the small zone of Gattinara and on the foothills beyond Novara and Vercelli; and on the Valle d'Aosta border in the northwest, in the zone of Carema. It also grows, just, in the Valtellina, a slim ribbon of land in northern Lombardy; "just" because all depends on being close to the Adda River, which reflects light and warmth onto the south-facing slopes on its northern bank. Even within this limited area there are four subzones, Sassella, Grumello, Inferno and Valgella, each with clearly recognizable styles of wine. There is also a style called Sfursat (or Sforzato) produced from lightly dried nebbiolo grapes; the drying increases the strength of the wine to at least 14.5 percent.

Barbera is Piedmont's Cinderella grape—once despised, it is now extensively planted. In theory, barbera produces unbalanced wines with very high acidity but very little tannin. Many believe the solution is to age the wine in *barrique*, attenuating the perception of acidity and allowing the oak pick-up to compensate for the lack of tannin. The result has been some top-quality wines—but they lack the vibrancy of unbarriqued barbera. Most of the rest use large, old *botti* to soften the wine a little without losing its zip. Some leave barbera completely unoaked. Surprisingly, if there is enough flavor in the grapes, the resultant wine is wonderful, if rather shocking. It certainly provides the perfect foil for salami. Barbera is found throughout southern Piedmont. The most typical Barberas come from near Asti; those who prefer a fuller, richer Barbera rate the area nearer Alba as superior. There are also a few who think that Barbera should be light and easy drinking, and prefer the wines from the Basso Monferrato area.

The third grape is dolcetto. The wines are mid-weight, less austere than those from nebbiolo and barbera, and are usually best drunk fairly young. Dolcetto's role in Piedmont's rich, meat-based diet is either as the starter red at more important meals or as the sole red at family meals. Dolcetto is grown fairly widely in southeast Piedmont, but the finest wines come from around Alba.

Other indigenous red grapes of note include grignolino, a strange variety producing lightweight but incisive wines with a remarkable affinity for the full range of Piedmont cuisine; freisa, fresh, raspberry-like and sometimes made a little sweet

Vineyards and winery buildings set in the landscape typical of Piedmont.

or lightly sparkling; and brachetto, with aromas of strawberries and fresh grapes as if it were a red moscato, well-suited to still and sparkling wines of lowish alcohol, both dry and sweet.

Another red grape of importance in northwest Italy is often overlooked since its homeland is western Lombardy rather than Piedmont: croatina, also known as bonarda and grown mainly in the Oltrepò Pavese area. Traditionally it is vinified into a lightweight, lightly sparkling, off-dry wine, but much of it is blended with barbera to great effect. Croatina can also produce serious wines of notable refinement.

Leading the white grapes is moscato bianco, the white muscat that here produces the lightest, freshest, grapiest wine imaginable. More serious debate arises over the qualities of cortese. Grown mainly in the southeast of the region, in and around the zone of Gavi, there are as many who think it overrated and underperforming as there are those who admire its steely restraint and its aging potential. Certainly it rarely produces more than a "fair-enough" impression when drunk young, but those with the patience to see it past its first year or two are often amply rewarded. Opinions are similarly mixed over arneis: for some it leads to a refined, perfumed wine that gives Piedmont a white to be proud of, for others it needs a percentage of chardonnay to liven it up. Favorita, when handled with skill, gives comparatively light, floral wines of great charm. The rare erbaluce, grown only in a small zone near the Valle d'Aosta border, can make a rich, well-fruited wine of firm acidity but comes into its own when the grapes are dried after picking and vinified sweet. The acidity gives the perfect lift to the rich sweetness and the wine often has remarkable longevity.

Wine nomenclature in Piedmont is in most cases comparatively simple, with the name of the grape and the zone it comes from forming the denomination: Dolcetto d'Alba, Barbera d'Asti, Erbaluce di Caluso, for example. A few wines, such as Barolo, Barbaresco, Roero, Gattinara, Gavi and Carema, give only the location.

Barolo and Barbaresco

Nowhere does nebbiolo show its class as much as in the two zones of Barolo and Barbaresco. And nowhere else in Italy is there such a tight mesh of small vineyards, each vineyard firmly stamping its personality onto its wines.

Barolo is a rough horseshoe made up of two ridges which almost meet. The western ridge is of a clay-rich calcareous marl with plentiful magnesium and manganese; in the east the marl has more sand and chalk as well as iron, potassium and phosphorus. The wines from the west, marked by greater aroma and finesse, develop quicker, while those from the east have greater structure, body, power and longevity. The zone embraces 11 communes of which five are important: La Morra and Barolo itself (west), Serralunga, Monforte and Castiglione Falletto (east).

The smaller zone of Barbaresco comprises three communes: Neive, Treiso and Barbaresco itself. Here too there is considerable variation, but in general the hills are a little lower and less steep, and the soil somewhat lighter. There is also a little more warmth to speed ripening, from the zone's proximity to the Tanaro river.

A further layer of variation comes from the grapes themselves. Although both Barolo and Barbaresco come exclusively from nebbiolo the three main subvarieties grown (lampia, michet and rosé) each supply certain characteristics. Then comes the producer element. Traditionally Barolo and Barbaresco underwent extremely long maceration periods—sometimes upwards of 40 days—and some producers still prefer extended maceration. Others keep it as short as possible, sometimes down to a couple of days, while the rest stick to more conventional timings. Differences occur in the length of time the wines spend in oak, and the *barrique/botti* argument rages fiercely here also.

All this makes it difficult to discuss a "typical" Barolo style, but overall Barolo is considered a

Italy's wines are made to accompany food. Cotechino sausages decorate a wall in the Piedmont region.

Vineyards at Montforte d'Alba in the Barolo zone, northwest Italy.

The entrance gate to the winery buildings at Cantine F. Oddero, Piedmont.

little chunkier and fuller, more powerful and slower-aging than the more refined Barbaresco.

Moscato wines

Regrettably the word *spumante*, which simply means "sparkling," has acquired a pejorative connotation outside Italy, and even more so when linked with the name Asti. Whatever the reasons for this and however bad some examples may once have been, most Asti Spumante made today suffers nothing more than prejudice. It is a dessert wine, fresh, light, sweet and frothy, produced from moscato bianco grapes grown in a rectangle stretching east from the Tanaro River to Acqui Terme.

Asti is made, unlike most sparking wine, from a single fermentation. The moscato must begins the fermentation normally; when the residual sugar drops to a predetermined point, the tanks are sealed. Fermentation continues until the trapped carbon dioxide gas reaches sufficient pressure, at which stage it is halted. Some unfermented grape sugars remain, hence the delicate grapey sweetness that is neither sugary nor cloying. Unfermented sugars also result in a lowish alcohol: between 7 and 9.5 percent.

Asti needs to be drunk as fresh as possible. At its best it is sheer joy, not only to give a lift at the end of a meal but also to partner the richest of desserts, desserts that other sweet wines would compete with rather than complementing.

An even lighter, more elegant, more delicate and classy version is Moscato d'Asti. Also the product of a stopped fermentation, the wine is still or has at most a gentle beading of bubbles and alcohol is even lower than sparkling Asti, at 4.5 to 6.5 percent. This is the dessert wine of choice.

REGIONAL DOZEN

Barbaresco "Sori San Lorenzo" (Gaja)
Barbaresco "Vigneti in Rio Sordo" (Produttori del Barbaresco)
Barbera d' Alba "Vittoria" (Gianfranco Alessandria)
Barbera d' Asti Superiore "Montruc" (Franco M. Martinetti)
Barolo (Bartolo Mascarello)
Barolo "Vigneto Arborina" (Elio Altare)
Barolo Riserva "Gran Bussia" (Poderi Aldo Conterno)
Brachetto d' Acqui (Braida)
Dolcetto d' Alba "Barturot" (Ca' Viola)
Gavi dei Gavi "Etichetta Nera" (La Scolca)
Langhe Rosso "Monpra" (Conterno Fantino)
Roero Arneis "Bricco delle Ciligie" (Almondo)

REPRESENTATIVE PRODUCERS

Carema

FERRANDO & C.

Established 1900 *Owners* Ferrando family *Production* 4,500 cases *Vineyard area* 7.5 acres + 10 leased (3 + 4 ha)

Luigi Ferrando, practically the only commercial producer of Carema, has been influential in preventing other growers abandoning the area's traditions. Now working increasingly in Caluso, he has three still versions of Erbaluce di Caluso; a brut sparkling wine from erbaluce; a late harvest, lightly sweet Erbaluce and a Caluso Passito.

Gattinara

ANTONIOLO

Established 1949 *Owners* Antoniolo family *Production* 5,000 cases *Vineyard area* 37 acres (15 ha)

Rosella Antoniolo and her children Alberto and Lorella are sharpening up the rather tired image of Gattinara by concentrating on wines from nebbiolo that do not require long aging to be enjoyable. Coste della Sesia Nebbiolo Juvenia typifies their approach. The estate's leading wine, the Gattinara *cru* Osso San Grato, has plentiful, soft, red-berried fruitiness to offset its natural austerity.

Barbera d'Asti

BRAIDA

Established 1961 *Owners* Bologna family *Production* 25,000 cases *Vineyard area* 50 acres + 20 leased (20 + 8 ha)

The estate was founded by Giuseppe Bologna, a larger-than-life character in all respects and the pioneer of Barbera in *barrique*. The result, Barbera d'Asti Bricco dell'Uccellone, a fat, deep, spicy wine, brought him to prominence although some prefer the estate's tighter-knit Bricco della Bigotta or the late-harvested Ai Suma. Young, lively Barbera La Monella and finely balanced Moscato d'Asti show the breadth of the range. Since the death of Giacomo in 1990 his wife and children have shared responsibility for the estate.

Barbaresco

PRODUTTORI DEL BARBARESCO

Established 1958 *Owners* Cooperative *Production* 3,300 cases *Vineyard area* 220 acres (90 ha)

With cellars right in the village of Barbaresco, this is one of the most surprising cooperatives in Italy.

Not only do its 60-odd members have vineyards on some of the zone's best sites but a forward-looking management team and the technical expertise of the young and quality directed Dr Vacca ensure well-structured, rounded, classically styled wines of a quality far above the output of most cooperatives. Only nebbiolo is vinified. Depending on grape quality up to nine Barbaresco *crus* may be produced each year: Asili, Rabajà, Pora, Ovello, Pajé, Montestefano, Montefico, Moccagatta and Rio Sordo.

GAJA

Established 1859 *Owner* Angelo Gaja *Production* 20,000 cases *Vineyard area* 135 acres (55 ha)

Angelo Gaja's contribution to the wine scene, and not just in Barbaresco, is almost impossible to summarize in a few words. An acute brain, an enquiring mind, an uncompromising attitude to quality and a keenly directed sense of marketing have brought his wines head and shoulders above the competition and made him one of the most respected and sought-after characters in Italy. The wines are duly expensive but the combination of balance, complexity and class is unparalleled.

BRUNO GIACOSA

Established 1900 *Owner* Bruno Giacosa *Production* 37,000–42,000 cases *Vineyard area* 37 acres (15 ha)

This family-run estate is now in its third generation. Wines were sold in bulk until bottling started in the 1960s. Giacosa's philosophy was always to seek the best growers from the best sites and buy in grapes, but his ideas have now softened a little and he has bought 22 acres (9 ha) of vineyard in Serralunga (Barolo). The complex, floral, spicy, firm Barbaresco *cru* Santo Stefano di Neive is exemplary and stands out in a fairly large range.

MARCHESI DI GRÉSY

Established 1973 *Owner* Alberto di Grésy *Production* 13,500 cases *Vineyard area* 72 acres (29 ha)

While the di Grésy family settled in Piedmont in the seventeenth century and have been grape growers ever since, it was only in 1973 that the estate started to vinify. Now the energetic Alberto di Grésy, assisted by winemakers Piero Ballario and Marco Dotta, makes highly individual, light, graceful wines from well-sited vineyards. *Crus* Gaiun, Camp Gros and Martinenga are highly acclaimed and a good Moscato d'Asti, La Serra, is made but di Grésy is now investing extra effort in chardonnay, sauvignon and cabernet sauvignon.

Alberto di Grésy with a magnum of wine from his estate.

PELISSERO

Established 1960 *Owner* Giorgio Pelissero *Production* 8,500 cases *Vineyard area* 37 acres (15 ha)

This small, family-run estate is now in the third generation of winemakers. It produces finely honed, well-typed, refined Barbaresco, notable among them being the *cru* Vanotu. There is also good Dolcetto d'Alba and Barbera d'Alba, and examples of Freisa and Grignolino.

Barolo

ELIO ALTARE

Established 1948 *Owner* Elio Altare *Production* 3,000 cases *Vineyard area* 11 acres (4.5 ha)

Elio Altare represents one of the peaks of the short-maceration school in Barolo and his estate, though small, is highly influential. Ownership passed to Elio, the third generation, in 1976, 15 years after the first bottlings. The wines are supple, complex, well-fruited and refined. Top of the range is the *cru* Barolo Vigneto Arborina (not to be confused with Vigna Arborina, a non-Barolo Nebbiolo). Barbera d'Alba and Dolcetto d'Alba are also fruit-forward and attractively balanced.

Part of Vila Giulia, a nineteenth century hunting lodge in Barbaresco, Piedmont.

ASCHERI

Established 1880 *Owners* Ascheri family *Production* 11,000 cases *Vineyard area* 62 acres (25 ha)

Matteo Ascheri's wines in the past few years have undergone something of a transformation in that

The colorful chapel of Santissima Madonna delle Grazie, Barolo, Piedmont.

Signor Gianfranco Barile seeks out truffles with his canine assistant Stella, Barolo.

they have made a complete turnaround to riper, fleshier, more concentrated and classically styled wines. This has been achieved partly by buying vineyard wherever possible and also by imposing severe viticultural controls on the other growers who supply his needs. The estate is based in Bra, which is outside of the main growing areas, but the vineyards lie mainly within the Barolo zone. On those vineyards that are situated closer to home, viognier and syrah have been planted, to noticeably fine effect.

MICHELE CHIARLO

Established 1956 *Owners* Chiarlo family *Production* 85,000 cases *Vineyard area* 125 acres + 140 acres leased (50 + 55 ha)

This large, family-owned company with cellars in Barolo, Gavi and Monferrato makes a vast range of wines from all the major wine-growing areas of southeast Piedmont. The quality throughout is at the least sound and often very good, as is the value for money. Although Michele Chiarlo is, rightly, most proud of his Barolo *crus*, his Barberas, from vine-yards recently bought in the prime barbera area of Agliano, are the wines to watch.

DOMENICO CLERICO

Established 1977 *Owner* Domenico Clerico *Production* 5,500 cases *Vineyard area* 37 acres (15 ha)

Before 1977, the beginning of vinification, the Clerico family were growers, selling grapes first privately and later to the Barolo cooperative. Domenico Clerico, regarded as a forward-thinking modernist, is primarily known for Arte, a richly perfumed, rounded, mouth-filling wine made from 90 percent nebbiolo and 10 percent barbera.

GIACOMO CONTERNO

Established prior to 1700 *Owner* Giovanni Conterno *Production* 4,000–6,500 cases *Vineyard area* 37 acres (15 ha)

This ancient estate has been passed down from father to son for many generations and was first documented in 1700. In 1969 the estate was divided between Giovanni, the current owner and one of the best of the traditionally minded producers, and his brother Aldo. Unusually for the area all the grapes come from one contiguous, southwest-facing plot. The Conterno wines have wonderful structure, power and complexity. Barolo Monfortino, made from selected grapes, is the flagbearer for the estate.

PODERI ALDO CONTERNO

Established 1969 *Owner* Aldo Conterno *Production* 10,000–12,500 cases *Vineyard area* 55 acres (23 ha)

Aldo Conterno is a prickly character, sometimes expansive, sometimes reclusive. Like his brother he calls himself a traditionalist, although he is not averse to experimentation and some innovation. There is nothing contradictory about his wines, however—they are quite simply stunning, with a wealth of ripe fruit throughout the range that balances perfectly the classic barolo astringency and acts as counterpoint to the classic barbera acidity. Wines from this concern are, it must be said, in very high demand.

FONTANAFREDDA

Established 1878 *Owners* Amministrazione Immobiliare SpA *Production* 600,000 cases *Vineyard area* 170 acres (68 ha)

This large, well-known estate, originally owned by an offshoot of Italy's royal family and practically a hamlet in its own right, is today a major landmark in Barolo. The wines are not overly intense but are well-typed and very good value, providing an excellent introduction to the type (notably Barolo Serralunga d'Alba, blended from the products of several vineyards), especially for those wary of more austere versions. Barolo *crus* La Delizia, La Villa, Lazzarito, Gattinera and La Rosa are at the top of a fairly long list.

BARTOLO MASCARELLO

Established 1918 *Owner* Bartolo Mascarello *Production* 2,000–2,500 cases *Vineyard area* 12 acres (5 ha)

Bartolo Mascarello, among the fiercest of adherents to traditional winemaking practices in Barolo, refuses to admit *barriques* into his cellar and has no intention of following any Californian winemaking model. He also eschews the idea of *cru* wines, preferring to blend the grapes from his own vineyards to create balance. His stunning Barolo, muscular, intense, rich and long-lived, proves the wisdom of this "folly." Excellent Barbera d'Alba and Dolcetto d'Alba are also made.

PAOLO SCAVINO

Established 1921 *Owner* Enrico Scavino *Production* 5,000 cases *Vineyard area* 22 acres (9 ha)

The minute attention paid to detail in the Scavino vineyards is what gives these wines their edge. Dense and elegantly perfumed, they have a broad-based appeal. Scavino owns plots situated on some of Barolo's best sites: Bric del Fiasc (Castiglione Falletto), Cannubi (Barolo) and also at Rocche dell'Annunziata (La Morra).

ALDO VAJRA

Established 1972 *Owners* Vajra family *Production* 7,500 cases *Vineyard area* 50 acres (20 ha)

Aldo Vajra produces some of Barolo's most elegant, refined and stylish wines, lacking in neither intensity nor longevity. The beautifully constructed Barolo *cru* Bricco delle Viole leads a fine range of reds from nebbiolo, barbera and dolcetto, while Kié is undoubtedly one of the best examples of Freisa to be found.

VIETTI

Established 1905 *Owners* Corrado e Alfredo Vietti & C. *Production* 7,000 cases (+ 4,500 from bought-in grapes) *Vineyard area* 55 acres (22 ha)

This fourth-generation, family-run estate was the first in recent times to see the potential of arneis, and actively sought out plots of the variety. The wines produced here are beautifully balanced, well-typed and elegant and are led by Barolo *crus* Rocche, Brunate, Lazzarito, Villero and Castiglione. Well-structured Barbera and Dolcetto and finessed Moscato d'Asti also feature.

ROBERTO VOERZIO

Established 1986 *Owner* Roberto Voerzio *Production* 2,500–3,300 cases *Vineyard area* 25 acres (10 ha)

Roberto Voerzio began winemaking on his father's estate but became independent in 1986 when the property was divided between himself and his brother. He pares yields down to incredibly low levels to get highly concentrated grapes and, as a consequence, very intense, richly fruited wines. Barolo *cru* Cerequio is undoubtedly his finest, closely followed by *crus* Brunate and La Serra, two versions of Barbera d'Alba and a Dolcetto d'Alba.

Gavi, Cortese di Gavi

LA SCOLCA

Established 1919 *Owner* Giorgio Soldati *Production* 16,500–21,000 cases *Vineyard area* 86 acres (35 ha)

The emergence of Gavi as a wine of note derives from the efforts of this estate, which launched the wine in the 1950s and skillfully marketed it as Gavi dei Gavi, in the sense of "the Gavi of all the Gavis" (a nomenclature no longer permitted). Scolca's Gavi does remain well ahead of the brood though, especially the version with the black label known as Etichetta Nera, from selected grapes. Like most Gavis it is rather inexpressive when young but matures into a firm, fleshy, spicily fruity wine of good structure: a red-wine drinker's white. From the rest of La Scolca's large range a finely tuned brut sparkling wine stands out.

Oltrepò Pavese

ALBANI

Established 1992 *Owner* Riccardo Albani *Production* 4,500–5,300 cases *Vineyard area* 37 acres (15 ha)

Riccardo Albani's carefully nurtured estate, though a new arrival in Oltrepò Pavese, has eclipsed the competition with its superbly refined wines of sheer class. There are just three wines: a slightly sparkling, off-dry, all-too-drinkable but not simplistic Bonarda; a stylish, slow-developing, varietally pure Rhine Riesling; and Vigna della Casona, mainly from barbera, a wine that balances intensity and elegance with aplomb.

Vineyards seen through a decorated casement at Cantine F. Oddero, Piedmont.

Snowcapped mountains form a stunning backdrop to this estate in Piedmont.

North Central Italy

Imposing colonaded buildings lining a street in Traviso, northern Italy.

The focal points of the central part of northern Italy are Milan and Lake Garda. Milan and its hinterland occupy much of central Lombardy, with viticulture relegated to outcrops of hilly country toward the edges of the region, away from the slumbrous Po River and its flat, humid valley to the southeast. Lake Garda, Italy's largest lake, separates Lombardy from the more rural region of Veneto to the east, with its major vineyard areas of Valpolicella and Soave.

Lake Garda, 30-odd miles (50 km) long and up to 11 miles (17 km) wide, has a noticeable impact on local climate. Skies are usually clearer in its vicinity, the light brighter, the air clearer. The lake is often regarded as a huge "lung," especially since convection currents cause a daily on-shore/off-shore breeze known as the *ora di Garda*. The warmth Lake Garda creates supports considerable olive cultivation, otherwise impossible at this latitude (the lake's southern extremity lies at about 45°30′N).

Vineyards appear sporadically on the west bank but the important areas are situated to its south and southeast.

The white wine zone of Lugana spreads southward from the lake where the effect of the *ora di Garda* is most marked. The grape grown there, usually called trebbiano di lugana, or simply lugana, is quite distinct from the more neutral trebbiano widespread in central Italy and possibly more akin to the verdicchio grown along the Adriatic coast. The wine is usually unoaked and drunk young and crisp, but can repay aging for a few years, when its fleshy green nuts character softens and takes on depth and breadth.

Nudging the lake to the north of Lugana is the Bianco di Custoza zone where an intriguing mix of grapes gives zip to a gently fruited white. The base is trebbiano (the central Italy version this time) and garganega, the grape responsible for Soave. Admixtures of tocai friulano, cortese and one or two others make the difference.

The northern sector of Bianco di Custoza overlaps the southern part of Bardolino, which comes from the same grape mix as Valpolicella and is very similar in style, a little lighter, more linear and more herbaceous. Bardolino also lends itself to vinification as a pale rosé called Bardolino Chiaretto, a sheer delight, yet poorly known.

Valpolicella lies just east of Bardolino, with Soave just east again. Past these two major zones the style of wine production begins to align more with practices in northeast Italy, where single-varietal wines are the norm. The most prominent is Breganze, which has varietal wines from cabernet sauvignon, pinot nero, marzemino (native to Trentino), pinot bianco, pinot grigio, vespaiolo (local variety), chardonnay and sauvignon. There is also Breganze Bianco, made from tocai friulano (native to Friuli), Breganze Rosso, from merlot, and the sweet wine Torcolato, from vespaiolo grapes dried after picking. Similarly long lists of varieties are also found in Colli Euganei and Colli Bericiano, still further east, and in Piave and Lison–Pramaggiore.

Colli Trevigiani, north of Venice, is the small but influential realm of the prosecco grape. Prosecco wines are most frequently sparkling, the style

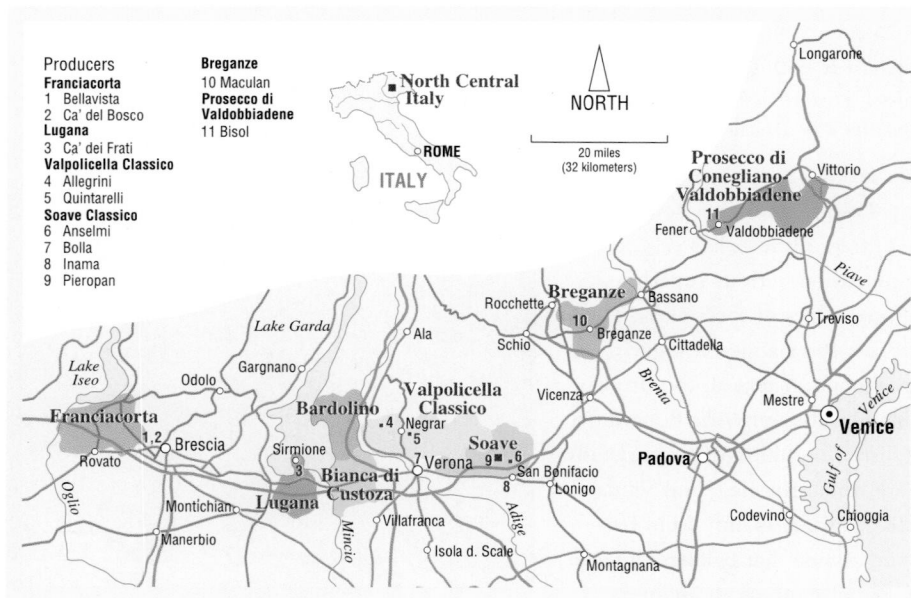

Producers
Franciacorta
1 Bellavista
2 Ca' del Bosco
Lugana
3 Ca' dei Frati
Valpolicella Classico
4 Allegrini
5 Quintarelli
Soave Classico
6 Anselmi
7 Bolla
8 Inama
9 Pieropan

Breganze
10 Maculan
Prosecco di Valdobbiadene
11 Bisol

a deliberately light, youthful fruitiness more reminiscent of the base wine than the yeasty richness sought in most sparklers. The natural aperitif throughout Italy, it somehow appeals equally to all palates. The wine can be anything from bone-dry to fairly sweet. There are also a fair number of *frizzante* (lightly sparkling) versions and some completely still. The grapes grow on steep hills to either side of the Soligo stream, Prosecco di Conegliano to the east and Prosecco di Valdobbiadene to the west. In theory, Conegliano's wines are softer, Valdobbiadene's tighter and more elegant, but differences are not marked. In the far west is a subzone of particularly steep slopes called Cartizze, where without dispute the wines are finer; a significant majority of these wines are made semi-sweet.

The other important sparkling wine of the central north is Franciacorta, from the hills north of Brescia in Lombardy, undisputedly the zone that produces Italy's classiest sparkling wines from the classic varieties chardonnay, pinot bianco and pinot nero. Production is a postwar phenomenon, making Franciacorta a mere babe by Italian standards, led by the new breed of outward-looking, quality-committed, entrepreneurial types who have colonized the area and openly sought to emulate Champagne—with remarkable success. The still wines from the area, called Terre di Franciacorta, also usually acquit themselves with aplomb.

Soave and Valpolicella

Soave and Valpolicella are two of the best-known Italian wine names and, like most of the big names, are normally regarded as also-ran wines, fine to drink if nothing better is available. That reputation is no longer justified as there has been a sharp upturn in the quality of the wine.

The Valpolicella heartland, a series of four roughly parallel valleys north of Verona, is ventilated by air currents from Lake Garda and the Po Valley. The wine is from a three-plus grape blend of which corvina is the most important. Versatile in style, Valpolicella can as easily be made for drinking as a young, fresh, vibrant red as a fuller, rounder, longer-aged wine. In either case it has a clear vein of red-cherry fruit with spice, pepper and a slightly medicinal edge. In addition there is Amarone della Valpolicella, a highly traditional wine made from grapes dried for around three months after picking, crushed and fermented slowly to dryness, the wine bottled after a period in oak. Amarone retains the cherry-like character-

istics of basic Valpolicella but is far stronger in alcohol (14 percent minimum, often exceeded) and somewhat port-like. *Amarone* means "strongly bitter" but there is only an edge of bitterness on the aftertaste. Indeed the first, fleeting, impression on the palate is of possible sweetness, despite the wine being dry. Producers are increasingly turning to a wine halfway between "normal" Valpolicella and Amarone by bringing the former to referment on the lees of the latter, a style called *ripasso*.

A further variant, Recioto della Valpolicella, also comes from dried grapes but the fermentation does not go to completion and the wine is sweet.

Vineyards near the town of Montebelluna in North Central Italy.

Snow dusts the vines near the winery at Monteforte Soave Classico, Veneto region.

has now been working with him for almost 20 years. Both have cast more than a passing glance over Champagne for inspiration and are following several of its precepts. The Bellavista sparkling wines are silky, graceful, supremely elegant and very long—equal in quality but different in style from Ca' del Bosco. They also produce a top-rate range of still wines using cabernet sauvignon, chardonnay and pinot nero.

CA' DEL BOSCO
Established 1968 *Owners* Maurizio Zanella/Santa Margherita *Production* 50,000 cases *Vineyard area* 250 acres (100 ha)

The most opulent wines of Franciacorta, some of its most prized and most costly. They are produced in immaculate, cathedral-like, underground cellars with perfect aging conditions. The spotlight falls naturally on the sparkling wines, the Dosage Zéro, the Brut, the Crémant (now Satèn) and the high-quality Cuvée Annamaria Clementi. Their still wines, Chardonnay, Maurizio Zanella (the wine, from cabernet sauvignon, and maker) and Pinèro (pinot nero) have also caused something of a stir.

Lugana

CA' DEI FRATI
Established 1956 *Owners* Pietro Dal Cero and Sons *Production* 21,000 cases *Vineyard area* 90 acres (36 ha)

Beginning as grape growers, the estate has evolved into the prime exponent of Lugana with elegant full wines of youthful charm but evident staying power, especially the Lugana Brolettino from late-picked grapes given *barrique* aging. This is complemented by the oak-free and beautifully crafted Lugana I Frati. The estate is also gaining plaudits for Pratto, a barriqued wine from a blend of trebbiano di lugana, chardonnay and sauvignon.

Valpolicella Classico

ALLEGRINI
Established 1920 *Owners* Allegrini family *Production* 30,000 cases *Vineyard area* 60 acres (24 ha)

Giovanni Allegrini set the tone of the estate by his tireless attention to detail. His three children now divide the work: Walter oversees the vineyards, Franco the cellars, Marilisa the administrative and commercial aspects. They acquired the La Grola vineyard, one of Valpolicella's top sites, around a decade ago and make a warm, spicy, full but supple wine from it. They also make an excellent

Practicing a craft almost as old as wine-making, a cooper in the Veneto region marks his raw materials with wooden dividers.

The sweetness is classically achieved by drying the grapes for longer than for Amarone, creating such a concentration of sugars that the yeasts are unable to ferment to dryness, although it is not unheard of for producers to halt the fermentation. Recioto is a niche wine, produced in small quantities. The name itself derives from *recie*, a dialect word for the "ears" of the grape bunch, the part that ripens most fully.

Soave also has its Recioto, at its best giving a floral, gently honeyed sweetness of finesse but this too is a tiny proportion of the normal dry type. It is made predominantly from garganega grapes with, optionally, a small proportion of trebbiano di soave and others. Soave's heartland lies on the steep slopes to the north and east of the castellated village of Soave itself.

In the case of both Soave and Valpolicella, their popularity has caused vineyards to spread beyond the heartland Classico areas out onto the surrounding plains. These non-Classico wines generally have far less to offer; the rule of thumb is to always stick to the Classico wines.

REPRESENTATIVE PRODUCERS

Franciacorta

BELLAVISTA
Established 1977 *Owner* Vittorio Moretti *Production* 62,500 cases *Vineyard area* 290 acres (117 ha)

Bellavista is the dream child of industrialist Vittorio Moretti. His fortune was to find an enologist of the caliber of Mattia Vezzola, who single varietal corvina, La Poja. Allegrini wines in general are marked by great vibrancy linked to textbook Valpolicella typing.

QUINTARELLI

Established early 1900s *Owner* Giuseppe Quintarelli
Production 4,500 cases *Vineyard area* 30 acres (12 ha)

Quintarelli is often termed Valpolicella's magician. His approach is strongly traditionalist with few concessions to modernity. Although his wines, technically, can display faults—and bottle-to-bottle variance—they are so weighty, multi-layered, full of personality and, well, unique that any faults seem to enhance their character rather than detract from it. The "standard" Valpolicella is a *ripasso*, the Amaroneis nothing short of stellar.

Soave Classico

ANSELMI

Established 1980 *Owner* Roberto Anselmi *Production* 30,000 cases *Vineyard area* 86 acres (35 ha)

When Roberto Anselmi took over from his father he turned the enterprise from a bottling and selling organisation into one of Soave's top estates. He is the counterpoint to his father, Pieropan. While the latter is quiet and introspective, Anselmi is the jovial extrovert and his wines reflect his character. From top sites, rich, ripe and sometimes skillfully oaked, they express the essence of Soave.

BOLLA

Established 1883 *Owners* Bolla family *Production* 2,500,000 cases *Vineyard area* Grapes mostly bought in

This enormous merchant house is known worldwide for its Soave but also makes Valpolicella and a significant range of other wines. The quality is always at least reliable, sometimes surprisingly good, and improving annually.

PIEROPAN

Established 1876 *Owner* Leonildo Pieropan *Production* 18,500 cases *Vineyard area* 74 acres (30 ha)

The name of Pieropan has long been synonymous with meticulous care and considered research to achieve the highest quality. The wines are beautifully crafted and well-knit, giving texture and depth to the Soave character. Pieropan has a firm belief in trebbiano di soave and was primarily responsible for saving it from extinction. He also believes strongly in the individual personalities that wines from single vineyards can achieve, as borne out by the two *cru* Soaves, Vigneto Calvarino and

Vigneto La Rocca, slow-developing, concentrated, complex wines of great class. The Recioto di Soave is considered archetypal.

INAMA

Established 1960 *Owners* Giuseppe and Stefano Inama
Production 20,000 cases *Vineyard area* 70 acres (28 ha)

Inama has leapt to prominence in the past few years as Soave's great innovator. Italian commentators have been very impressed by their work with sauvignon and chardonnay but the core remains Soave Classico. The base wine is round, well-fruited and excellent value, while single-vineyard and oaked versions have great style and character.

Breganze

MACULAN

Established 1933 *Owner* Fausto Maculan *Production* 30,000 cases *Vineyard area* 173 acres (70 ha) part owned, part leased, part other arrangements with growers

Maculan brought the wines of Breganze to public notice and keeps them there by means of a large range of characterful wines in combination with his own strong personality. At first gaining fame for the sweet Torcolato and, later, for the even sweeter, late-harvested Acini Nobili and the more delicately sweet Dindarello, from moscato fior d'arancia, the leaders of the Maculan range are now the hefty Ferrata Cabernet Sauvignon and Ferrata Chardonnay.

Prosecco di Valdobbiadene

BISOL

Established 1875 *Owners* Bisol family *Production* 40,000 cases *Vineyard area* 114 acres (46 ha)

The history of the Bisol family as winemakers can be traced back to the mid-sixteenth century though the current regime was established as recently as 1875. This is one of the area's larger producers with a carefully honed array of immaculate wines. The estate's range is a wide one, with both tank-method and classic-method sparklers produced, and Prosecco ranging from sweet to dry, from still to fully sparkling.

Wine bottles and their protective straw pictured in Verona, Veneto region.

Trentino—Alto Adige

Verdant vineyards in dramatic contrast to snow-covered mountains, Barolo, Piedmont.

The region of Trentino–Alto Adige is Italy's northernmost, bordering Austria. It links two provinces, Trento (Trentino) and the more northerly Bolzano (Alto Adige) but the dash joining them represents a barrier as much as a tie and coexistence between the two is anything but easy.

Although both provinces were part of Austria until 1918, Trentino had historically been more closely related to Italy and returned happily to Italian rule. Alto Adige, on the other hand, had been firmly connected with Austria. More than 80 years on, Alto Adige remains predominantly German-speaking—although officially bilingual—separatist in attitude and distinctly disinclined to collaborate with Trentino any more than is absolutely necessary.

The region is mountainous and the winelands cling closely to the low hills beside the Adige river and its tributaries. The river valley is gorge-like in its northern, upper reaches and grape growing is spasmodic, the siting of vineyards heavily dependent on both the amount of sunlight that peeks between the mountains and reflected warmth from the rivers. As the valley gradually broadens and the altitude drops vines become more prolific. The valley floor, though, is nearly always reserved for orchards, the provinces being Italy's major producers of apples. The climate is marked by extreme diurnal temperature swings, with Bolzano being one of Italy's hottest cities by day (despite the latitude) and one of its coldest by night. Lower down the valley temperature changes become less severe and the climate a little warmer overall.

Nearly all the wines are single-varietals and most producers make a large number, sometimes as many as 20 or more. The varieties grown fall into three main groups: those of French origin (chardonnay, sauvignon, cabernet franc, cabernet sauvignon, pinot nero), those of German origin (müller-thurgau, rhine riesling, sylvaner) and those of Italian or local origin (pinot bianco, malvasia, pinot grigio, moscato giallo, moscato rosa, rebo, schiava, lagrein, marzemino, nosiola, traminer aromatico, teroldego). Placing traminer aromatico, known elsewhere as gewürztraminer, among the grapes of "Italian or local" origin may cause a few raised eyebrows, but there is good evidence the variety originated in the Alto Adige village of Termeno (Tramin in German).

The local variety schiava is the most prolific and is particularly widely diffused in Alto Adige. It makes a lightish-colored, fresh, lightweight wine reminiscent of raspberry yoghurt, an ideal foil for the substantial Germanic foods of the zone. It not only furnishes much of the local drinking but has a significant export market in the neighboring countries: Austria, Switzerland and Germany. It shows at its best in the small, completely vine-clad area of Santa Maddalena adjacent to the town of Bolzano, and in the larger area of Caldaro. Lagrein, also more widespread in Alto Adige than Trentino, also finds its ideal growing conditions near Bolzano but is in much more serious vein, lean and firm with plentiful fruit and good aging potential, although it is sometimes made as an easy-drinking rosé.

On the Trentino side marzemino springs into prominence. It makes a midweight red for simple quaffing but can give greater satisfaction, and this is especially so when the grapes are grown in the Vallagarina, in the southern part of the region. Teroldego is somewhat different, seemingly thriving only on the Rotaliano Plain, a small triangle of flinty gravel soil in the north of Trentino. The plain is bordered to the north and southwest by steep mountain walls that protect it from cold winds and river-borne air-streams. Teroldego makes a deep, firm, well-structured wine of good acidity, richly berried with a herbal tang. Good examples are amenable to *barrique* aging and have not inconsiderable longevity.

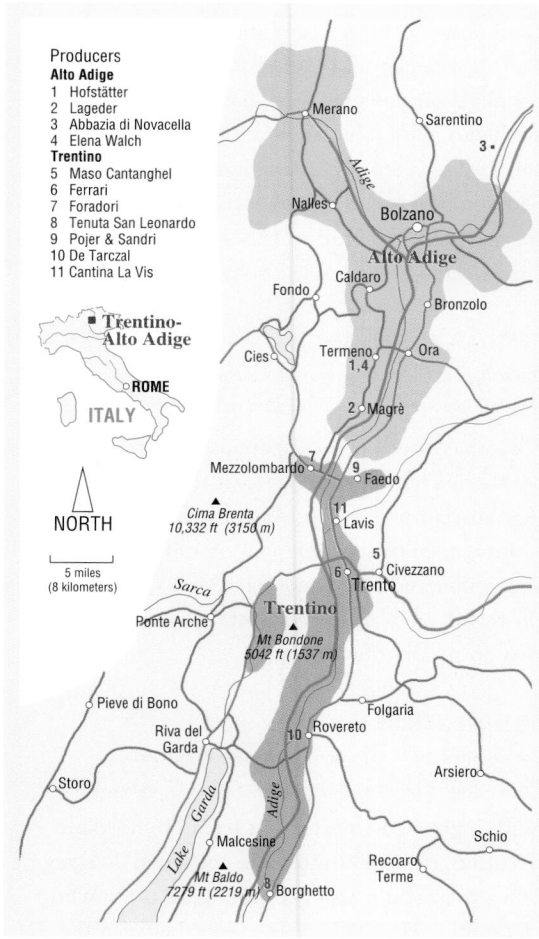

Producers
Alto Adige
1 Hofstätter
2 Lageder
3 Abbazia di Novacella
4 Elena Walch
Trentino
5 Maso Cantanghel
6 Ferrari
7 Foradori
8 Tenuta San Leonardo
9 Pojer & Sandri
10 De Tarczal
11 Cantina La Vis

The image of the region comes from its whites, however. These are pure-toned, with varietal character that can be piercingly fresh and with more penetrating perfume than most Italian whites. These wines have the potential for even more overt aroma but, according to Italian thinking, this would render them less suitable for drinking with food. Hardly surprisingly, given its world-wide fame, chardonnay is now capturing the largest slice of the vineyard area.

Trentino is also important for sparkling wine production, mostly from chardonnay, pinot bianco, pinot nero and pinot meunier, ranging in quality from adequate to excellent. Confusingly, although most wine from Trentino comes under the DOC "Trentino," the DOC for sparkling wine is "Trento." There is additionally a small but prized production of Vino Santo, similar to Tuscany's Vin Santo but made from nosiola grapes.

An unusually high proportion of the wines comes from cooperative wineries, an increasing number of which have abandoned the rather lax attitudes of the past and embraced a quality regime. Bottles stating they come from a Cantina Sociale should not be dismissed out of hand.

REPRESENTATIVE PRODUCERS

Alto Adige

HOFSTÄTTER

Established 1907 *Owners* Foradori–Hofstätter family
Production 50,000 cases *Vineyard area* 110 acres (45 ha)

Founded early in the twentieth century by Josef Hofstätter, the estate eventually passed to his granddaughter. She married Paolo Foradori, who took over the running and enlarged the estate with vineyards in his family's possession, several in prime sites. Although the estate produces roughly a dozen varietals, all well-rated, it is primarily known for its Pinot Nero, easily the best in the area. The *cru* version, Sant'Urbano, from high-density plantings of 2,630 vines per acre (6,500 per ha) is outstanding.

LAGEDER

Established 1855 *Owner* Alois Lageder *Production* 80,000 cases *Vineyard area* 42 acres (17 ha) + bought-in grapes

Now at the fourth generation of winemakers, this large merchant house is moving steadily towards vineyard holdings and has several of note, the best known being Löwengang. There has also been investment in Casòn Hirschprunn, a separate estate. The estate wines have great individuality of character; the rest of the range, comprising over 20 wines, is well-typed and of good quality.

ABBAZIA DI NOVACELLA

Established 1142 *Owner* Canonici Regolari Agostiniani di Novacella *Production* 37,500 cases *Vineyard area* 45 acres (18 ha)

From its foundation in the middle of the twelfth century the work of the Abbey of Novacella has included grape cultivation and winemaking. Situated in the north, in the Valle Isarco, it is the prime exponent of the purity of aroma and freshness that Alto Adige wines can achieve. As well as being the focal point for research and development in Valle Isarco, this winery is the only commercial producer of any size in the north of the valley.

ELENA WALCH

Established 1869 *Owners* Walch family *Production* 25,000 cases *Vineyard area* 59 acres (24 ha)

Elena Walch, an architect by profession, represents the new generation of go-ahead producers in Alto Adige. When she took over running the two family estates, Castel Ringberg, above Lake Caldaro, and Kastelaz, above Termeno, she immediately set to

A basket of tools used in grape husbandry.

Almost bursting with sugar, black grapes hang from the vine.

A light mist delicately veils the vineyards at Cantine F. Oddero, in Piedmont.

work upgrading the vineyards. This, combined with a quality-orientated approach throughout, the result has been some impeccable wines, most notably the Gewürztraminer.

Trentino

MASO CANTANGHEL

Established 1983 *Owner* Piero Zabini *Production* 3,750 cases *Vineyard area* 16 acres (6.5 ha)

This well-run estate, typical of the smaller ones emerging in Trentino, concentrates on just half a dozen varieties and a similar number of wines. It is guided with quiet care and attention by Piero Zabini who, in common with many of his counterparts, remains restlessly dissatisfied with the quality he is producing (although there is more to be proud of than ashamed) and introduces numerous refinements year on year.

FERRARI

Established 1902 *Owners* Lunelli brothers *Production* 250,000–290,000 cases *Vineyard area* 190 acres (77 ha)

The company, which passed from the Ferrari family to the Lunelli family in 1952, has always concentrated on sparkling wine at the top end of the market. The Ferrari sparklers now rival the best in Italy. A separate estate, Lunelli, has been set up recently, producing a range of still wines in line with the enterprise's reputation.

FORADORI

Established 1880 *Owner* Elisabetta Foradori *Production* 11,000 cases *Vineyard area* 37 acres (15 ha)

If the fortunes of Teroldego Rotaliano have taken several strides forward in the past 15 years or so it is all down to Elisabetta Foradori who, convinced that the area could produce far better than the standard output suggested, has single-handedly pushed quality. The wines are stupendous, from the straight Teroldego Rotaliano through *crus* Sgarzon and Morei to Granato, the flagship. All have superb suppleness of fruit combined with firm structure and robust body.

TENUTA SAN LEONARDO

Established 1870 *Owners* the Marquises Guerrieri Gonzaga *Production* 8,000 cases *Vineyard area* 44 acres (18 ha)

Vines have been grown around this property in southern Trentino since at least the tenth century. The current owner, the Marquis Carlo Guerrieri Gonzaga, cultivates only merlot and cabernets sauvignon and franc and makes oaky, hugely powerful, slow-maturing wines which are a long way from Trentino norms.

POJER & SANDRI

Established 1975 *Owner* Fiorentino Sandri & C. *Production* 20,000 cases *Vineyard area* 57 acres (23 ha)

With high-sited vineyards at Faedo in northern Trentino, the steely, intensely perfumed delicacy of Pojer & Sandri's wines confound all those who claim there is a distinct difference between the styles of Alto Adige and Trentino.

DE TARCZAL

Established 1700 *Owner* Ruggeri dell'Adamo de Tarczal *Production* 10,000 cases *Vineyard area* 44 acres (18 ha)

Though initially famous for Pragiara, a cabernet/merlot blend, De Tarczal's forte is Marzemino, the most enjoyable, most dangerously drinkable of the area. He also produces a somewhat more serious Marzemino called Husar from selected grapes, and a small range of other varietals.

CANTINA LA VIS

Established 1948 *Owners* Cooperative, 800 members *Production* 250,000 cases *Vineyard area* 1,975 acres (800 ha)

This cooperative is responsible for about 10 percent of the entire production of Trentino yet the quality is unimpeachable, mainly because in 1985 a go-ahead management embarked on the "Quality Project" with the renowned viticultural/winemaking research institute of San Michele all' Adige. In 1990 followed the "Zoning Project," aimed at identifying which terrains best suited which varieties. Four ranges are produced, among which the La Vis line is reliably good and the Ritratti line remarkably good.

Friuli–Venezia Giulia

Friuli–Venezia Giulia (usually called simply Friuli) is to white wine what Piedmont and Tuscany are to red. The whites are, classically, restrained in tone, the epitome of refinement. Most are single-varietals, a large number of them. Recent years have seen considerable developments with Friuli's reds, however, with their quality beginning to approach that of the whites. Perhaps this should not be surprising, for the emphasis on white is relatively modern and post-Second World War.

Friuli's position east of Venice, straddling the top of the Adriatic sea and stretching around to Trieste and the Slovene border, east of all modern communications arteries, means few people pass through en route to elsewhere. Historically Friuli was a major crossroads, where north–south traffic from Austria to the Adriatic ports met east–west traffic to and from central Europe. A major cross-roads also tends to mean a major battleground and so it has been with Friuli. Critical battles have been played out there in numerous wars, which appears to have left the hard-working local people self-reliant, with a desire to make the most of the present. A significant proportion of Friuli's population is descended from refugees, especially from Istria, the peninsula south of Trieste that was once Italian but now Croatian. Despite all this, Friuli seems as intrinsically Italian as anywhere, certainly far more so than Alto Adige.

Landscape and climate

Friuli is a calm and quietly purposeful place, the balmy climate in its south moderated by the Adriatic sea and a more continental climate in its mountainous north. The main growing area is inland, where cool air currents from the north mix beneficially with the warm air from the south. The climate here tends to be gentler than in surrounding districts, its only stormy aspect the cold *bora* that occasionally blows fiercely from the northeast.

The wine-producing lands of Friuli divide into four. The coastal strip, an uplifted plain running southward to Trieste, with porous, limestone soil above a network of caverns and tunnels, includes the zones of Latisana, Annia, Aquileia and Carso, Aquileia being the best-known but Carso the most intriguing. The most prominent grapes are the white malvasia istriana and the red terrano, also

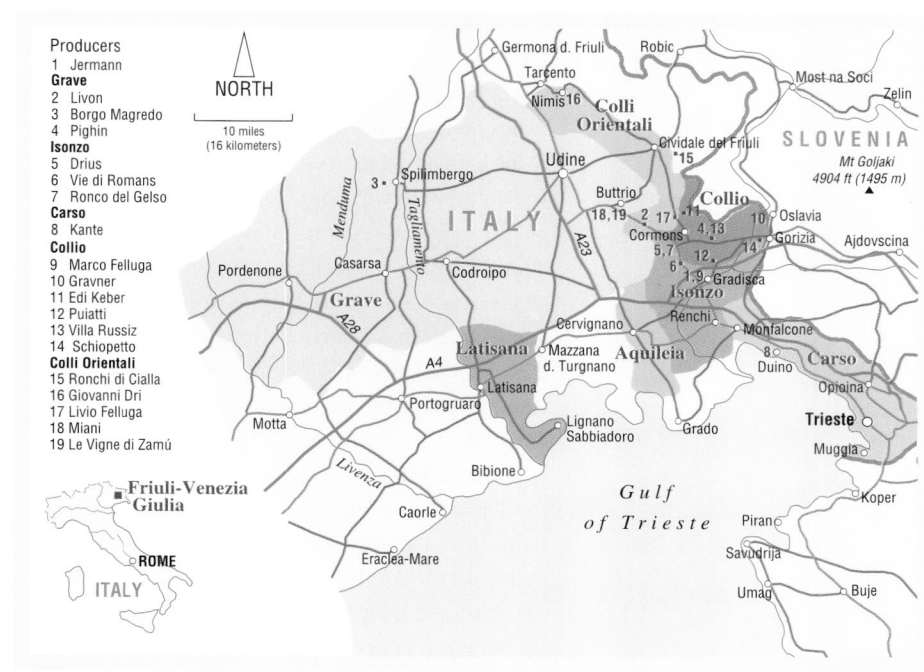

known as refosco d'istria. These make lean, some-what astringent, but softly fruited wines, which are perfect foils to the rich, central-European style food favored in Trieste.

The largest zone is the Grave, stretching across much of the region's southern half, an uplifted, fast-draining plain, rich in gravel, bisected by the Tagliamento river. The best quality wines come from the *magredi*, areas where the gravel is most concentrated and the topsoil sparse, most often seen near the Tagliamento and in the east of the

A cart loaded with old trellis poles, Colli Orientali del Friuli, Friuli–Venezia Giulia.

Coat of arms at the AZ. AG. Schiopetto winery, Collio, Friuli–Venezia Giulia.

zone. The Grave wines are the most representative of the region and good, but rarely exceptional.

The exceptional wines come from the twin zones of Collio and Colli Orientali, right on the Slovene border, where a range of hills, most of it in Slovenia, rises from the plain. Collio and Colli Orientali are produced solely on the hills. Collio is a crescent-shaped piece of land whose most intense wines come from the commune of Oslavia at its eastern edge. At its western extremity the river Judrio separates it from Colli Orientali. This completely artificial separation into two zones came about through squabbling between the provinces of Gorizia (Collio) and Udine (Colli Orientali). Colli Orientali initially continues the curve of the crescent then stretches northwest to the subzone of Ramandolo. The vast majority of the Colli Orientali wines come from that part of the zone lying closest to Collio.

The effects of slope, air currents and the reduced yields practiced by most growers in Collio and Colli Orientali give slow-maturing white wines of considerable depth and breadth and exhibiting classic Friuli restraint. They are in high demand and can be quite expensive.

It is in respect of price that Isonzo, the fourth part of Friuli, scores. Isonzo lies just south of Collio on flat land, most of it rich in iron which colors the soil with a tinge of red. Many producers in the zone are busy proving that Isonzo is capable of producing wines as good as those from the hills. Isonzo wines are today just a few notches below those of Collio and Colli Orientali in quality but considerably less expensive.

Vines and wines

The almost 30 varieties grown in Friuli (not all in each zone) comprise the expected internationals, a small group of Italian origin (pinot bianco, pinot grigio, riesling italico, moscato giallo, moscato rosa) and a fairly large group of local varieties. Among the reds the best-known is refosco dal peduncolo rosso (different from refosco d'istria) which makes chunky, brambly, herby wines. The most exciting is schioppettino (also called ribolla nera). Slow to come round, its wines are muscular, packed with ripe fruit, spicy and peppery, and enlivened by a good shot of acidity. Tazzelenghe ("tonguecutter") is strongly tannic when young but mellows if given sufficient aging. Other native varieties include pignolo and franconia.

The most important of the local white varieties is tocai friulano. Its wines are often drunk young, when they have a lively florality, but after a few years they develop a nuttiness with hints of fennel and overall are far more interesting.

In the past, ribolla gialla was almost always restricted to blends, being "too acidic." Increasing numbers of producers are realizing that, handled correctly, it can produce remarkable wines with an almost chardonnay-like butteriness but with a leaner, crisper edge and a fine lemony fruitiness. Verduzzo, also criticized for its acidity, comes into its own in Collio Orientali where it is fleshier, slightly nutty, with rich peach-like fruit. It can age for over a decade and matures to a deep, honeyed fruitiness, especially in the Cialla subzone. In the Ramandolo subzone it becomes a sweet wine from dried grapes, which enhances the honeyed softness.

For sweet wines picolot reigns supreme here. It is a troublesome variety, however, often flowering incompletely, prey to disease and yielding poorly. Handled properly, its wines can be superb— delicate, elegant, floral, dry-finishing, leaving the mouth perfectly clean, the antithesis of Sauternes-type sweetness. Other local whites include malvasia istriana and vitovska.

While there is nothing exceptional today in the winemaking techniques of Friuli, Collio was the pioneer of cool, controlled white wine vinification in Italy; this approach was once known nationally as the *metodo friulano*, the Friuli method.

Pinot grigio madness

Pinot grigio (pinot gris) is just one of the numerous varieties grown in Friuli and adjacent regions and not even one of the best; both pinot bianco

A weatherbeaten statue gazes down from the Abbey Rosazzo, Colli Orientali del Friuli.

and tocai friulano, for example, give wines that are more balanced, more attractive and longer-living. Yet Pinot Grigio has become famous worldwide and is perpetually in huge demand. Back in the 1960s, astute marketing by the large Santa Margherita company, based in the Lison–Pramaggiore zone (Veneto), made its Pinot Grigio the wine of the moment. Fairly rapidly, other wines from pinot grigio benefited from the spinoff until the variety itself practically became a brand, rather as Chardonnay is now. Inexplicably the fashion has never diminished. While the wines are enjoyable, there are better to be had. And, as always, fashion costs.

REPRESENTATIVE PRODUCERS

JERMANN

Established 1881 *Owner* Silvio Jermann *Production* 25,000 cases *Vineyard area* 110 acres (45 ha)

Jermann is one of the great names in Friuli wine, making slow-developing, beautifully honed wines of perfume, depth and varietal purity, also distinguished by bearing no DOC. Silvio Jermann studied enology in Italy and Canada, and maintains an outward-looking, innovative approach. Beside the varietal wines (including Rhine Riesling and Gewürztraminer), the estate is particularly renowned for Vintage Tunina, a white blend whose composition changes year by year, and the curiously named Where The Dreams Have No End, which has now mutated into Were Dreams, Now It's Just Wine, from oaked chardonnay.

Grave

LIVON

Established 1960 *Owners* Livon family *Production* 80,000 cases *Vineyard area* 370 acres (150 ha)

This large company, go-ahead and research-orientated, has holdings in Collio, Colli Orientali and Grave, and cellars each zone. The wines are of reliably good quality throughout the large range, particularly the *crus*, but the non-barriqued whites destined for long aging are the ones to watch.

BORGO MAGREDO

Established 1989 *Owner* Genagricola SpA *Production* 50,000 cases *Vineyard area* 545 acres (220 ha)

Borgo Magredo is Friuli's largest estate and one of the few not in family hands (Genagricola is an insurance company) but is modern and innovative. The high-density vineyards on one of Grave's *magredi* are very stony and drain swiftly. Eleven

varieties are produced, all of them reliable and well-typed.

PIGHIN

Established 1964 *Owners* Pighin family *Production* 95,000 cases *Vineyard area* 445 acres (180 ha)

Pighin is one of Friuli's largest winemaking concerns and makes wine exclusively from its own grapes. The vineyards were once situated solely in Grave, but the family bought a second estate in Collio with 74 acres (30 ha) of vineyard and now makes wine from both zones. The wines used to be well-made though mundane, and now have greater fleshiness and character. The range is large, with 25 or so wines being produced.

Isonzo

DRIUS

Established Late 1800s *Owners* Sergio & Mauro Drius *Production* 4,000 cases *Vineyard area* 25 acres (10 ha)

Despite producing wine for more than a century, this small, simply run estate is, relatively speaking, a newcomer on the scene, its wines only now reaching the high-quality standards of this competitive area. As in most estates in the region, the emphasis is strongly on the vineyard and there are leanings toward organic methods of vine cultivation. Seven varieties are grown at this estate, with only one red, cabernet sauvignon. The Tocai and Pinot Bianco lead the range.

VIE DI ROMANS

Established 1976 *Owners* Gallo family *Production* 5,850 cases *Vineyard area* 40 acres (16 ha)

Gianfranco Gallo is a perfectionist whose exceptional wines are exquisitely crafted at every stage from vineyard to bottling. The range is limited to varietal Chardonnay, Pinot Grigio, Sauvignon and Tocai along with a white blend, Flores di Uis and a red blend, Voos dai Ciamps. If ever there is an Isonzo estate capable of reaching Collio quality, Vie di Romans has to be the prime candidate.

RONCO DEL GELSO

Established 1972 *Owner* Giorgio Badin *Production* 8,000 cases *Vineyard area* 27 acres (15 ha)

Ronco del Gelso is distinguished by Giorgio Badin's great belief in the technique known as

There is a long-held belief that healthy soil has a beneficial effect on both the wine and its drinker. Winemaker Mario Gabriele smells a rock at Ronco del Gnemiz, Colli Orentiale del Friuli.

Silvio Jermann's curiously named chardon-nay "Were Dreams, Now It's Just Wine,"

hyper-oxygenation, that is blasting grape must with oxygen before vinification to "stabilize" it against post-vinification oxidation which he uses throughout. Badin is also a viticulture fanatic and much effort is spent on the densely planted vineyards. Just seven varieties are grown, sauvignon and tocai usually producing the best results.

Carso

KANTE

Established 1980 *Owner* Edi Kante *Production* 2,500 cases *Vineyard area* 18 acres (7 ha)

Although the Kante family has been producing wine for generations it was only in 1980 that they began bottling and ceased blending the varieties. The vines grow at 820 feet (250 m) on a sheltered site in topsoil, which had to be brought in; the cellars were excavated from the rocks. Kante works primarily with the classic malvasia istriana and terrano, and the rare indigenous grape, vitovska. He also has chardonnay and sauvignon growing in the vineyard.

Collio

MARCO FELLUGA/RUSSIZ SUPERIORE/ CASTELLO DI BUTTRIO

Established 1905/1964/1994 *Owners* Felluga family *Production* 58,000/20,850/2,100 cases *Vineyard area* 334/158/52 acres (135/64/21 ha)

The irrepressible Marco Felluga and his family have built up three fine estates by means of hard work and quality consciousness. The first, Marco

Felluga, owns no vineyards but buys in grapes from a consistent group of Collio growers. The second, Russiz Superiore, on well-sited, steep slopes within Collio, just over a mile (2 km) from the Slovene border, produces more intense wines in firmer mould. Castello di Buttrio is a newish acquisition, a hilltop site with 360° slopes which adds Colli Orientali to the portfolio. Early results here are distinctly promising.

GRAVNER

Established 1901 *Owner* Josko Gravner *Production* 3,300 cases *Vineyard area* 31 acres (12.5 ha)

Gravner's mind-blowing wines mark the peak of Collio achievement. Although he attributes their quality to his attention to the vineyards at Oslavia, straddling the Slovene border, outsiders look more at his winemaking methods. In contrast with traditional Friuli thinking, Gravner uses oak practically throughout for his whites and practices extended yeast contact and late bottling. These ideas have spawned a school of estates (Radikon, La Castellada, for instance) who follow Gravner closely, replicating his techniques. Gravner provides the final proof that Ribolla Gialla is anything but a second-rate wine.

EDI KEBER

Established 1957 *Owner* Edi Keber *Production* 4,200 cases *Vineyard area* 25 acres (10 ha)

Edi Keber is one of Collio's rising stars. The vineyards are practically sitting on the Slovene border and occupy a steep, well-ventilated, site. Keber was among the first in the area to cut his range to the bone, concentrating on the varieties that are best suited to his terrain. He now produces a fabulously refined Tocai and a richly fruited Merlot. There is also a white blend (tocai/ribolla gialla/ malvasia istriana/pinot bianco) and a red blend (merlot/cabernet franc) of similar quality.

PUIATTI

Established 1967 *Owners* Vittorio & Giovanni Puiatti *Production* 25,000 cases *Vineyard area* 27 acres (11 ha) + grapes brought in

Vittorio Puiatti (along with his son Giovanni) is the complete antithesis to Gravner in that he vehemently refuses to have anything to do with wood in his cellars. His Collio wines epitomize the classic Friuli style and are concentrated, intense, well-fruited and beautifully varietally typed. Vittorio Puiatti is the flagship range, while the Enofriulia range is simpler and offers fine value

Terracotta and white-washed winery buildings; a part of the landscape in Colli Orientali del Friuli.

for money; the Giovanni Puiatti line covers the wines from the Isonzo zone.

VILLA RUSSIZ

Established 1869 *Owner* Istituto A. Cerutti *Production* 15,000 cases *Vineyard area* 74 acres (30 ha)

The estate was founded under Austrian rule by the French nobleman Comte La Tour, who planted cuttings from French and German vines and is credited with initiating Friuli's wide range of international varieties. When the area again came under Italian rule after the First World War his widow moved to Austria and left the estate to the Italian state. The government used her gift to found a home for disadvantaged children, funded partially by the revenue from the wine business. Today the estate is run to very high standards and produces a good range of light, stylish wines, especially Tocai, Sauvignon, and Merlot.

SCHIOPETTO

Established 1964 *Owner* Mario Schiopetto *Production* 18,000 cases *Vineyard area* 57 acres (23 ha)

Although there could be one or two who might contest the point, most agree that Mario Schiopetto was the architect of the *metodo friulano*, bringing cool-temperature, controlled fermentation to the area and thence to the rest of Italy. Schiopetto traveled widely in Europe as a young man, learning all the latest vinification techniques. The vineyards sit on an exposed amphitheatre of land and the cellars are as hi-tech as one would expect. Schipetto wines are purely styled, long and very classy, and certainly live up to the almost awe-inspiring reputation of the estate.

Colli Orientali

RONCHI DI CIALLA

Established 1972 *Owners* Rapuzzi family *Production* 4,000–4,500 cases *Vineyard area* 36 acres (14.5 ha)

Ronchi di Cialla's wines are deep, concentrated, slow-developing, remarkably long-lived and of great individuality and personality. The estate straddles a hill on the eastern border of Colli Orientali in the subzone of Cialla, concentrating exclusively on indigenous grapes, most notably white verduzzo and picolit (which are both made into sweet wines), red schioppettino and refosco. Viticulture is carried on using partially organic techniques. Cialla Bianco, the estate's best-known white, is a highly successful dry blend of verduzzo/ribolla gialla/picolit.

GIOVANNI DRI

Established 1968 *Owner* Giovanni Dri *Production* 12,000 cases *Vineyard area* 20 acres (8 ha)

Giovanni Dri brought the wine Ramandolo, a dessert wine made from dried verduzzo grapes grown high on steep slopes, to public notice, then took up the fight to have Ramandolo recognized as a Colli Orientali subzone. The limelight has now passed to his neighbor and rival Dario Coos, who prefers late-harvesting for his Ramandolo and picks sequentially for optimum ripeness, but Dri retains his reputation as a pioneer and ground-breaker. As well as Ramandolo, he also produces Picolit, Refosco and others.

LIVIO FELLUGA

Established 1956 *Owners* Livio Felluga & family *Production* 54,000 cases *Vineyard area* 333 acres (135 ha)

Livio is the brother of Marco Felluga. They went their separate ways in the 1950s, with Livio gradually buying up plots of land, mainly in Colli Orientali and particularly in the Rosazzo subzone. The Felluga's wines, which are greatly admired in many circles, are slim-styled with the emphasis strongly on the side of elegance.

MIANI

Established 1985 *Owners* Pontoni family *Production* 850–1,000 cases *Vineyard area* 30 acres (12 ha)

Miani, though a newish estate, has already forged an enviable reputation for the supreme quality of its wines. This is achieved primarily by low yields, so low as to risk economic viability. The wines, made from a dozen varieties, regularly win awards and plaudits with their immense concentration, rich fruit and varietal fidelity.

LE VIGNE DI ZAMÒ

Established 1985/NA/1981 *Owners* Pontoni family *Production* 4,200/NA/8,500 cases *Vineyard area* 25/NA/37 acres (10/NA/15 ha)

The name Le Vigne di Zamò refers to a grouping of three estates owned by Colli Orientali's influential Zamò family: Vigne dal Leon, Ronco dei Roseti and Zamò & Zamò, each one situated in a different commune of the zone. Each estate has a fairly limited range of varieties that have been chosen to maximize the potential of its site, although Schioppettino shines at all three. This aside, at Vigne dal Leon Pinot Bianco stands out; Merlot marks out Zamò & Zamò (and the white blends here are notable too); and at Ronco del Gnemiz there is glorious Müller-Thurgau.

Rows of vines follow the foot of a hill in Colli Orientale del Friuli.

REGIONAL DOZEN

Carso Malvasia (Kante)
Colli Orientali del Friuli Chardonnay "Vigneto Ronc di Juri" (Girolamo Dorigo)
Colli Orientali del Friuli Merlot "Baolar" (Pierpaolo Pecorari)
Colli Orientali del Friuli Rosazzo Bianco Terre Alte (Livio Felluga)
Colli Orientali del Friuli Rosso Sacrisassi (Le Due Terre)
Colli Orientali del Friuli Sauvignon (Miani)
Collio Pinot Bianco "Amrita" (Mario Schiopetto)
Collio Pinot Grigio (Puiatti)
Collio Tocai Friulano (Villa Russiz)
Friuli Isonzo Pinot Bianco (Mauro Drius)
Friuli Isonzo Sauvignon "Vieris" (Vie di Romans)
Vintage Tunina (Vinnaioli Jermann)

Emilia–Romagna

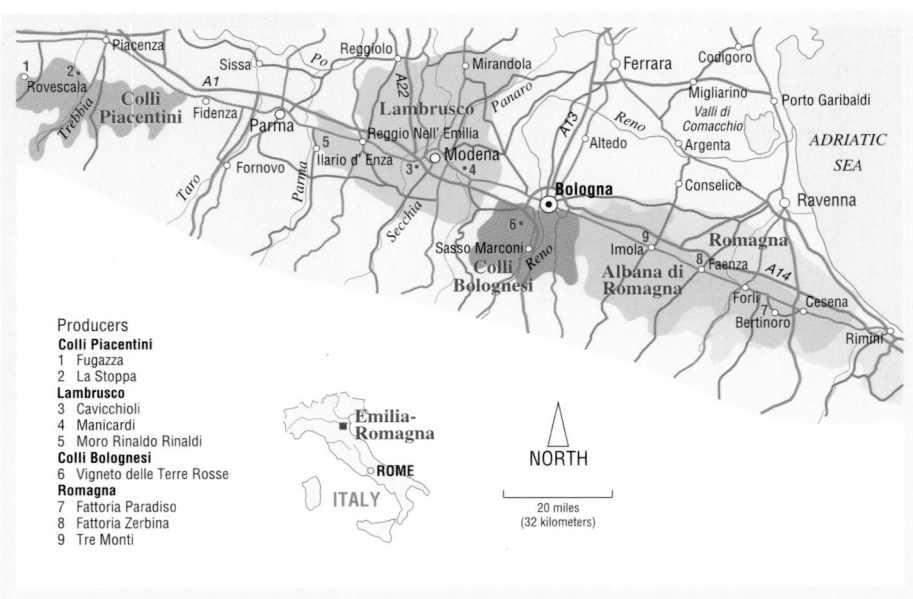

Producers

Colli Piacentini
1 Fugazza
2 La Stoppa
Lambrusco
3 Cavicchioli
4 Manicardi
5 Moro Rinaldo Rinaldi
Colli Bolognesi
6 Vigneto delle Terre Rosse
Romagna
7 Fattoria Paradiso
8 Fattoria Zerbina
9 Tre Monti

NORTH

20 miles
(32 kilometers)

Whatever system one might use to classify Italy, the region of Emilia–Romagna doesn't fit. It is a long, straggly region, almost bisecting the country and stretching for more than 150 miles (250 km) from Piedmont in the northwest to the Adriatic Sea and the Marche in the east. It is largely bordered to the north by the broad, rambling Po River and its flat, fertile valley, while the more southerly parts cover some of the more impenetrable reaches of the Apennines.

A villa in a vineyard, Emilia–Romagna.

Landscape and climate

Emilia–Romagna's topography and climate vary so much that to talk in broad terms about growing conditions there is meaningless. Even splitting it into its natural divisions—Emilia to the west of Bologna, its hub, and Romagna, east of Bologna—does not help a great deal.

The image of Emilia–Romagna, however, is of highly fertile, perfectly flat, hazy countryside, through the Po Valley, with pin-straight roads and dotted with occasional plane trees. This terrain, fine for fruit tree cultivation and livestock rearing, is famous for Parmesan cheese (Parmigiano reggiano) and Parma ham (prosciutto di Parma) but not, in general, for vines. The vineyard areas are sparsely clustered on the poorer soils of the hilly outcrops (but not on the cold Apennine slopes).

Vines and wines

In the far west lies the zone of Colli Piacentini, in effect an extension of the Oltrepò Pavese zone of Lombardy, with similar grape varieties and wine styles, except for gutturnio, a barbera/bonarda blend unique to the Colli Piacentini.

In the center is the Colli Bolognesi, a smallish area of low hills just outside Bologna, split into seven subzones, more or less one for each hilly outcrop. The core of this area is the quality subzone of Zola Predosa. The wines, mainly single-varietals, come principally from the indigenous variety, pignoletto; there is a Classico heartland denomination solely for pignoletto wines. A fair amount of barbera is grown, while the international varieties, cabernet sauvignon, merlot, chardonnay, sauvignon and riesling, produce excellent, well-fruited wines here.

Stretching across Romagna in the east are the extensive, overlapping areas of trebbiano di Romagna, albana di Romagna, sangiovese di Romagna, cagnina di Romagna and pagadebit di Romagna.

The strain of trebbiano grown here is similar to the somewhat neutral trebbiano toscano and it is rare to find a trebbiano di Romagna worthy of much more than easy drinking. Neither is the albana much more than a middle-ranking white variety that requires considerable dedication and tenacity to produce wines of more than passing interest; when Albana di Romagna was promoted to DOCG status in 1987, cries of dismay echoed around the wine world for months. Its raised status at least provided stimulus for improvement and albana is rarely the also-ran it once was. The wine comes in dry, semi-sweet, fully sweet, *passito* and sparkling styles, the *passito* version providing some of the best examples.

Most of Romagna's sangiovese is a different strain from Tuscany's and can have a lively rusticity to it that is distinctly unfashionable. The more forward-looking estates are gradually changing over to the Tuscan sangiovese. Cagnina is the same variety as the terrano (refosco d'istria) of Friuli's Carso zone, while the white pagadebit is the same as Puglia's bombino bianco.

Any outcrop of hills will see clusters of vineyards but the only other Emilia–Romagnan area of any importance lies on flat land near the city of Modena: the lambrusco zone.

Specialty wines

Several strains of lambrusco are grown over a fair swathe of central–eastern and northeastern Italy but concentrated near Modena. Its wine has become famous, or infamous, as something akin to sweetish, fizzy pop, a style that developed as a result of a natural tendency in the past: lambrusco frequently did not finish its fermentation before cold weather halted it. When spring arrived, the wine, by then bottled, was often sweet or became fizzy from a restarted fermentation or both; or bottles exploded. Yet these "errors" seemed to make the wine, inherently a little on the sharp side, more palatable, and gradually technology and marketing took over.

Not all lambrusco is like this, though. There are some dry versions around and some where the sweetness doesn't mask the wine's intrinsic fresh acidity and cherry-like natural character. It is the perfect foil for rich Emilian fare (salami, sausages and heavy cheesy sauces) and still one of the best picnic wines to be found.

There are three main strains: Sorbara is often made dryer than most and has good perfume and good character; Grasaparossa di Castelvetro is more fully flavored and often used for the sweeter wines; Salamino di Santa Croce has both richness and acidity.

White and pink are, in theory, still made from the red lambrusco grape but quite a bit of cheating goes on. These are pure marketing inventions with very little to offer and are best ignored.

REPRESENTATIVE PRODUCERS

Colli Piacentini

FUGAZZA

Established 1920 *Owners* Fugazza sisters *Production* 12,500 bottles *Vineyard area* 210 acres (85 ha)

Maria Giulia and Giovannella Fugazza's land straddles the border between Emilia's Colli Piacentini and Lombardy's Oltrepò Pavese so they have formed two estates, Romito in the former and Castello di Luzzano in Oltrepò. Maria Giulia looks after the vineyards and Giovannella the cellars. Their best wines are from bonarda and barbera, leading naturally to good gutturnio. They also work well with malvasia and moscato.

LA STOPPA

Established 1973 *Owners* Pantaleoni family *Production* 15,000 cases *Vineyard area* 64 acres (26 ha)

La Stoppa is professional in attitude and forward-thinking. The wines have a distinct style, partly from the estate's position in a valley at 820 feet (250 m), and partly from the direction taken by enologist Giulio Armani. Practically all the La Stoppa wines are aged at least partly in *barrique* but the use of new *barriques* remains moderate and carefully controlled. The wine called simply Stoppa (mainly cabernet sauvignon) and the pinot nero Alfeo rival the more traditional Macchiona (barbera/bonarda) for plaudits; a further half-dozen or so wines complete the range.

Lambrusco

CAVICCHIOLI

Established 1928 *Owners* Cavicchioli family *Production* 850,000 cases *Vineyard area* 86 acres (35 ha)

Although a large commercial undertaking, Cavicchioli has more of an eye to quality than most of the lambrusco merchants. Even their simplest wines, made from bought-in grapes, are always reliably well-made and well-typed. Their vineyards are mostly in the leading Sorbara sub-area and the excellent single-vineyard Lambrusco di Sorbara, Vigna del Cristo, is the clearest possible example that lambrusco is not always a wine to be discounted or dismissed. The Lambrusco di Modena, from a blend of four lambrusco strains, is also well above expectations.

Italy's great classic cheese, Parmigiano reggiano, is prized worldwide.

Vines staked individually, Emilia–Romagna.

chardonnay, a surprisingly complex malvasia, intriguing pinot grigio and a wonderful, multi-layered, minerally, balanced late-harvest riesling, Giovanni Vallania is proudest of his viognier, from one of Italy's first plantings.

Romagna

FATTORIA PARADISO
Established 1940 *Owner* Mario Pezzi *Production* 29,000 cases *Vineyard area* 100 acres (40 ha)

Mario Pezzi and his family are primarily responsible for overturning public cynicism about the quality of Romagna wines. The *cru* Sangiovese di Romagna, Vigna delle Lepri, was for a long time well above all competition, primarily because it was made from the Tuscan rather than Romagnan strain of sangiovese. It was Pezzi who wisely made the effort to repropagate the disparaged pagadebit. He also discovered a deep, richly fruited variety he dubbed barbarossa, from what appeared to be a natural mutation of a single plant in his vineyards, and has propagated this to excellent effect.

FATTORIA ZERBINA
Established 1966 *Owner* Maria Cristina Geminiani *Production* 15,000 cases *Vineyard area* 62 acres (25 ha) plus 49 acres (19 ha) leased

For its first 20 years Zerbina worked solely with indigenous grapes and sold its production locally. After studying in Bordeaux, Cristina Geminiani joined the estate and extended its horizons to both new varieties (and much denser vineyard plantings) and new markets. The range now confidently straddles local and international grapes, with marzieno, from a sangiovese/cabernet sauvignon blend, taking the helm. Albana (notably the *passito* scacco matto) and sangiovese also do very well.

TRE MONTI
Established 1972 *Owners* Davide & Vittorio Navicella *Production* 25,000 cases *Vineyard area* 114 acres (46 ha)

The estate is split into two plots, one on the first rises behind Imola, the other on the hills behind Forlì, about 18 miles (29 km) away, with good, south-facing exposures and altitudes around 650 feet (200 m). The largish range combines well-made wines from indigenous varieties such as albana and sangiovese; intense, barriqued international varietals such as chardonnay and cabernet sauvignon; and, most successfully, blends of the two, notably salcerella (albana/chardonnay) and boldo (sangiovese/cabernet).

MANICARDI
Established 1980 *Owners* Manicardi family *Production* 6,500 cases *Vineyard area* 42 acres (17 ha)

This is a very small estate in lambrusco terms but is well-known for its good quality *aceto balsamico* (balsamic vinegar). A recent move in its management from Enzo Manicardi to his daughters Livia and Raffaella has provoked a change of emphasis and a major upturn in the quality of the wines. All are from the Castelvetro sub-area and Lambrusco di Castelvetro strain. There is a dry version as well as the more common *amabile* and a dry, lightly sparkling version from lateish-picked grapes.

MORO RINALDO RINALDINI
Established 1972 *Owner* Rinaldi Rinaldini *Production* 12,500 cases *Vineyard area* 37 acres (15 ha)

This is one of the few estates still making "serious" sparkling lambrusco (dry), with its second fermentation being in bottle rather than in tank. Rinaldini also produces sparkling chardonnay, dry sparkling malvasia and a lightly sparkling pinot, all with bottle fermentation.

Colli Bolognesi

VIGNETO DELLE TERRE ROSSE
Established 1961 *Owners* Vallania family *Production* 5,800 cases *Vineyard area* 49 acres (20 ha)

Brother and sister Giovanni and Elisabetta Vallania practise vine cultivation as nearly organic as possible, use only the varieties that suit their terrain (in the prime subzone of Zola Predosa) and give those varieties full expression by avoiding any oak in their aging. While this approach gives rise to beautifully fruited, cleanly structured and long-lived cabernet sauvignon, notably in the Cuvée Enrico Vallania (named after their father), refined

Tuscany

The image of Italy for many people is that of central Tuscany: rolling hills, stately cypress trees, majestic olive groves and endless vistas of vineyards. Appealing as this vision is, it doesn't represent the whole of Tuscany, which runs east from the Mediterranean coast to the Apennines and south from the Ligurian gulf to the warm plains and soft hills of the Maremma. The heart of Tuscany is its central hills, the zone of Chianti. In wine terms, the southerly massifs of Montalcino and Montepulciano are also part of the heart.

The current wine scene was largely shaped by the break-up of the *mezzadria* (crop-sharing system) after 1945. The countryside had been marked by large estates with an impressive central villa or castle, grain store, oil mill and wine cellars, often a private chapel and the *case coloniche* (sharecroppers' cottages). Some owners bought out their *mezzadri* (sharecroppers) and moved towards specialized viticulture. Other estates fell into decay, leaving the way open for an influx of foreign buyers. Numerous ex-*mezzadri* stayed on, the land they acquired forming the small estates that spearheaded the revival of Tuscany's fortunes.

Vines and wines

The soul of Tuscany is the sangiovese grape. Although its clones vary—the sangioveto of Chianti Classico differs from Montalcino's brunello, which differs again from the prugnolo of Montepulciano—the underlying style is always distinct. Some liken its aromas to fresh tea with an overlay of prunes and sometimes fresh plums and/or cherries. It is often notably spicy, with cinnamon, clove and nutmeg the three most commonly sensed, with a good swathe of acidity that should be balanced by ripe tannins. Sangiovese makes lively wines without too much effort on the part of the producer. With more work it makes good-quality, mid-range wines of moderate character. From that point on, every extra ounce of quality requires exponentially greater viticultural care and winemaking skills, so that although it is possible to make absolutely stunning Sangiovese, it remains a major challenge. It is small wonder that some producers take the easier route, rounding out and powering up the troublesome grape with a proportion of friendly cabernet sauvignon.

Other traditional red grapes grown in the area include canaiolo, despised by many for its stalky, unfruity character but admired by the few who harvest it late from low yields; mammolo, strongly perfumed; ciliegiolo and colorino, deeply colored but now rarely seen. Among the international varieties, syrah is grabbing the spotlight.

Florence and the River Arno viewed from Piazzale Michelangelo.

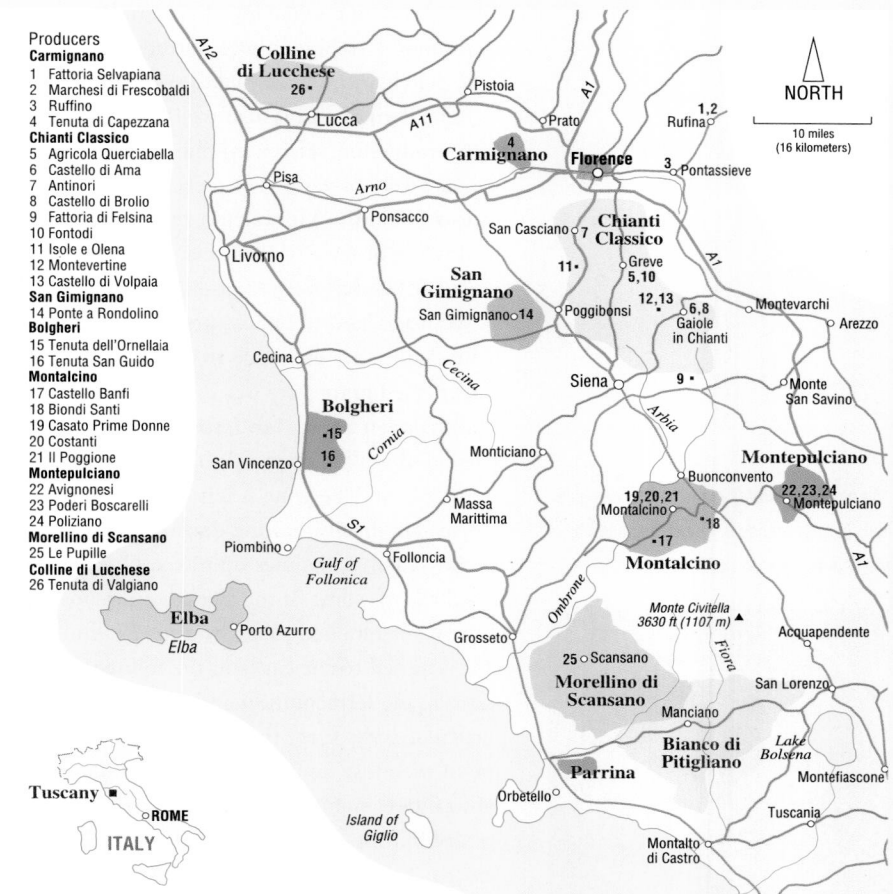

Producers
Carmignano
1 Fattoria Selvapiana
2 Marchesi di Frescobaldi
3 Ruffino
4 Tenuta di Capezzana
Chianti Classico
5 Agricola Querciabella
6 Castello di Ama
7 Antinori
8 Castello di Brolio
9 Fattoria di Felsina
10 Fontodi
11 Isole e Olena
12 Montevertine
13 Castello di Volpaia
San Gimignano
14 Ponte a Rondolino
Bolgheri
15 Tenuta dell'Ornellaia
16 Tenuta San Guido
Montalcino
17 Castello Banfi
18 Biondi Santi
19 Casato Prime Donne
20 Costanti
21 Il Poggione
Montepulciano
22 Avignonesi
23 Poderi Boscarelli
24 Poliziano
Morellino di Scansano
25 Le Pupille
Colline di Lucchese
26 Tenuta di Valgiano

A hilltop town in Chianti, surrounded by vineyards and the cypresses that are emblematic of Tuscany.

The black cockerel is known in Italy as gallo nero *but not abroad as the Gallo company of the USA blocked use of the name.*

Chianti and Chianti Classico

Any discussion of the wines of Tuscany has to begin with Chianti and especially Chianti Classico, the region's linchpin. The Chianti district is the land between Florence and Siena, Chianti Classico. Non-Classico Chianti covers a far wider and more variable area, about 75 miles (120 km) west to east from the coast to Arezzo, and a similar distance north to south, from Pistoia to south of Montalcino. Most of it falls into one of eight subzones including Chianti Colli Senesi, Chianti Montabano, Chianti Colli Aretini and Chianti Rufina. "Chianti" is a misnomer for much of the territory and its use irritates the Chianti folk, the "Chiantigiani." As the name became devalued in the 1970s and 1980s, many producers preferred not to use the denomination. Rufina apart, the wines are usually somewhat lighter than the Classico Chiantis and tend to be easy drinking, without great structure or weight. When Chianti was upgraded to DOCG in 1984, the whole area, Classico and non, was promoted. This caused innumerable protests at the time and is now recognized as a bad mistake, although amendments since have seen the criteria for Chianti Classico tightened. Chianti is made from sangiovese but not exclusively. Small quantities of canaiolo, trebbiano and malvasia are typically included. The inclusion of white grapes is a throwback to the nineteenth century, when the wine was preferred light, fresh and youthful. Only in the Classico zone is 100 percent sangiovese permitted. The DOCG also allows for a small percentage of "other" varieties, usually cabernet sauvignon.

Within the geological structure of Chianti Classico two soil types mark out the best sites: *galestro*, a clay-schist, and the limestone *alberese*. The communes of Radda, Gaiole and Castellina form "the golden triangle," the heart of the heart of Chianti. They are surrounded by Castelnuovo Berardenga, Barberino Val d'Elsa, Greve and Panzano, with San Casciano further north.

While not all wines display the black cockerel symbol (known in Italy as *gallo nero*), those that do belong to the Classico's marketing consortium, an influential and remarkably competent body. The symbol derives from historical Florence–Siena animosities: one day horsemen were to depart from both cities at dawn (announced by cockcrow) and the place where they met defined the border between the two territories. The Florentines trained their black cockerel to crow early and so gained the lion's share of the land.

The primary white variety is trebbiano toscano, usually called just trebbiano (ugni blanc in France). It is a rather unrewarding grape, fine as a neutral base blended with something more characterful, or for crisp, light, innocuous wines, but requiring great care to obtain something of interest. Most producers prefer to work with chardonnay, often turning out forceful, chunky, overtly oaky wines lacking charm and balance. Traditionally trebbiano was partnered with malvasia del chianti, which makes soft, round, gently perfumed wines and is also well suited to sweet wine production. Also used mainly for sweet wines is moscadello, a variant of moscato grown almost exclusively in the Montalcino zone. The only other local white of note is vernaccia, which produces the steely but full Vernaccia di San Gimignano.

Malvasia and trebbiano are used to good effect in Vin Santo, a wine made from *passito* grapes. The crushed grapes are put into *caratelli* (very small wooden barrels) to ferment. The barrels are sealed and are left exposed to winter cold and summer heat. The wine is left to ferment slowly and spasmodically, halting during winter, over several years, sometimes up to six. Once the wine is racked off, some of the sludge at the bottom of the casks is retained to act as a *madre* (mother). This is added to the casks in the following year, assisting the fermentation and helping to impose a particular style. Over the years the *madre* becomes one of the most fundamental aspects and each Vin Santo differs significantly from its neighbors. Some are dry but the more traditional styles are sweet. Another version of Vin Santo, called Occhio di Pernice, is made from red grapes.

Super-tuscans

Many quality Italian wines are not made in accordance with DOC(G) rules and so take on IGT status, a path pioneered in Tuscany (mainly in Chianti) in the 1970s and early 1980s. As the category IGT did not exist then, the wines were *vini da tavola*. For years producers focused on these wines, dubbed "Super-tuscans" ("*super-vini da tavola*") outside Tuscany—mostly 100 percent sangiovese or sangiovese/cabernet blends. Chianti has been rehabilitated and some of these wines could be DOCG, but most remain outside the net.

Montalcino

Brunello di Montalcino is one of Italy's most distinguished wines. It is made from the brunello clone of sangiovese and aged for four years before release, at least two in oak. It is rich, ripe, mouth-filling, powerful and intense, an important-occasion wine sold at important-occasion prices. The "younger brother" wine, Rosso di Montalcino, aged only one year, is zippier, fruitier and cheaper.

The village of Montalcino sits on an imposing 2000 feet (600 m) hill. Generally, wines from the northern slopes are more elegant, those from the east firmer and more structured, and those from the south bigger and broader.

Montepulciano

The wines of Montepulciano sit somewhere between those of Montalcino and those of Chianti. Geographically there are close links with Montalcino: Montepulciano is at similar height and latitude. The wine blends other grapes into the dominant sangiovese, here its prugnolo clone.

The vineyards stretch east from the village in two growing zones split by the Chiana valley. The wine's full name is Vino Nobile di Montepulciano and the rules specify a minimum aging period of two years. Some favor a more refined, elegant product, a "Wine for the Nobles," and others prefer blockbusters, "Noble Wines."

Bolgheri and Carmignano

The only area of Tuscany not dominated by sangiovese is Bolgheri. It is near the coast, practically flat, with heavy clay soils, and released no good wine until the 1960s. The Marquese Incisa della Rochetta, recognizing in the 1940s that conditions were not dissimilar from Bordeaux, planted vines bought from Château Lafite. The estate's cabernet-based Sassicaia was born in 1968 and quickly became touted as "Italy's best wine."

After 15 years Bolgheri became DOC; now Sassicaia is a recognized subzone. The wines can contain up to 80 percent cabernet sauvignon or 70 percent merlot or 70 percent sangiovese. White Bolgheri is similar—trebbiano, vermentino and sauvignon may be used, each up to 70 percent. There are also Rosé and Vin Santo versions.

Carmignano's boundaries were fixed in 1716. A small proportion of cabernet complements the base of sangiovese. Carmignano was once notable for its finesse, but its style is now moving toward greater attack and presence. Barco Reale di Carmignano fulfills the need for a lighter style.

The Maremma

Morellino di Scansano, a sangiovese-based wine from the morellino clone, made in the far south (the Maremma), is an interesting red. It is comparatively soft, round, open, and cherry-like. Other Tuscan producers, many of them important names, have been buying land in Scansano and creating Morellino estates. This will doubtless improve quality, but may also result in a change in style. Just south of the Morellino zone is the Parrina zone, producing sangiovese-based reds of mid weight and some good whites—trebbiano teamed with chardonnay and/or ansonica, a Sicilian grape (there called inzolia) found nowhere else on the Italian mainland. The Maremma also includes the Bianco di Pitigliano zone. This white is now showing signs of major improvement.

Winery and vineyards near Greve, Chianti. Traditional Tuscan farms are made of stone, with beamed ceilings, and often also have attic granaries.

The most important area for white wine production is the zone of San Gimignano. Vernaccia di San Gimignano can be pale-hued, light, clean and fresh or deep, ripe, round and fat, although it is probably best somewhere in between. Many producers make three versions of the wine, one from 100 percent vernaccia, one with a small proportion of chardonnay and one oaked.

REPRESENTATIVE PRODUCERS

Carmignano

FATTORIA SELVAPIANA

Established 1829 *Owner* Francesco Giuntini *Production* 10,000 cases *Vineyard area* 75 acres (30 ha)

Francesco Giuntini built up his estate to one of the classiest of all Chianti, receiving but not always taking advice from consultant Franco Bernabei. He has now passed the running of the estate to his late-adopted son Federico Masetti, who works in closer affinity with Bernabei. The Chianti Rufina is slow-developing, piercing, complex and refined, always a wine of great individuality and style; *cru* Berciachiale is broader and more powerful. There is also white Borro Lastricato from pinot bianco. Selvapiana additionally makes the Pomino of Fattoria di Petrognano.

MARCHESI DI FRESCOBALDI

Established 1300s *Owners* Marchesi di Frescobaldi *Production* 460,000 cases *Vineyard area* 2000 acres (800 ha)

The Frescobaldi family owns eight estates, Castello di Nipozzano (Rufina), Tenuta di Pomino and Tenuta di Castelgiocondo (Montalcino) being the most important. Their main holdings are in Chianti Rufina and Chianti Rufina *cru* Montesodi is their leading wine, punchy, spicy, full and well-oaked. The company is involved in a joint venture with California's Mondavi to make Luce and Lucente, both sangiovese and merlot blends.

RUFFINO

Established 1877 *Owners* Folonari family *Production* 350,000 cases *Vineyard area* 1730 acres (700 ha)

The company was founded by the Ruffino cousins and sold to the Folonari family in 1913. The name is very well known and adorned thousands of flasks in the days when much Chianti was sold in this eccentric packaging. The lower-priced Ruffino wines are still unexceptional but recent years have seen great effects from investment in the products of their more prestigious properties.

TENUTA DI CAPEZZANA

Established at least 12 centuries ago; under current ownership since 1926 *Owners* Conti Contini Bonacossi *Production* 42,000 cases *Vineyard area* c.220 acres (90 ha)

Conte Ugo Contini Bonacossi expended great efforts to ensure that the Carmignano DOC (and later DOCG) respected the area's traditions and reflected its wines' quality. He is also the zone's principal producer and has been untiring in advancing the wine's style: supremely elegant but with good grip and fine aging potential. Of the many other wines the estate produces the lively Barco Reale di Carmignano and the all-too-drinkable deep rosé, Vin Ruspo, stand out.

Chianti Classico

AGRICOLA QUERCIABELLA

Established 1974 *Owner* Giuseppe Castiglioni *Production* 15,000 cases *Vineyard area* 70 acres (28 ha)

The estate started with 2 acres (1 ha) and grew gradually to its present size, with cellar investment to match. The Chianti Classico is rich, full and stylish while the barriqued Super-tuscan Camartina (sangiovese/cabernet sauvignon) has plentiful attack with good mouth-feel and complexity.

CASTELLO DI AMA

Established 1970s *Owners* Castello di Ama SpA *Production* 33,000 cases *Vineyard area* 235 acres (96 ha)

Ama wines differ from most Chianti, stalkier, leaner and with a more restrained fruitiness that can give them noticeable refinement. The estate's principal fame lies in the vast amount of research

Cypresses line the road to the vineyard Castello di Volpaia in Chianti.

it undertakes into the microzones of its varying terrain and the grape varieties best suited to each. As well as three Chianti Classico *crus* with distinct characteristics, there are several varietals, including Merlot, Pinot Nero, Sauvignon and Chardonnay.

ANTINORI

Established 1300s *Owners* Marchesi Antinori *Production* 1.1–1.15 million cases *Vineyard area* c.850 acres (350 ha) plus grapes bought-in (c.60%)

This colossus of Tuscany produces immensely drinkable wines with broad appeal. The estate has been in the hands of the Marchesi Antinori for over 600 years and is currently run by Piero Antinori with Renzo Cotarella in charge of the winemaking. Santa Cristina and Chianti Classico Peppoli are popular; Solaia (cabernet/sangiovese) and Tignanello (sangiovese/cabernet) have proved the estate's worth at the higher end of the market.

CASTELLO DI BROLIO

Established 1141 *Owners* Barone Ricasoli SpA *Production* 92,000 cases *Vineyard area* 550 acres (220 ha)

The Ricasoli family have owned Brolio castle since the twelfth century. In 1874 Barone Bettino Ricasoli laid down the original "recipe" for Chianti (including significant quantities of white grapes). Now, back in family hands with Carlo Ferrini as consultant enologist, the wines have an up-front, confident style superior to any previous offerings. Casalferro (sangiovese) is the benchmark example.

FATTORIA DI FELSINA

Established 1966 *Owners* Felsina SpA–Poggiali family *Production* 20,500 cases *Vineyard area* 128 acres (52 ha)

The high regard in which Felsina and its wines are held reflect the intelligent, careful approach of Giuseppe Mazzocolin, son-in-law of the owner, who runs the estate, and consultant enologist Franco Bernabei. The Chianti Classico Riserva Rancia is full but refined and highly complex, and the Super-tuscan Fontalloro (sangiovese) develops slowly to yield amazing intensity and depth.

FONTODI

Established 1968 *Owners* Manetti family *Production* 16,500 cases *Vineyard area* 125 acres (50 ha)

The Manetti family produced terracotta for over three centuries. On turning to wine, Giovanni Manetti went for quality, and succeede—his wines have long been held up as archetypes. The benchmark wine is the Super-tuscan Flaccianello della Pieve, from 100 percent sangiovese, which sells at

very high prices; the Chianti Classico Riserva Vigna del Sorbo and the Syrah are receiving similar plaudits.

ISOLE E OLENA

Established 1971 *Owner* Paolo de Marchi *Production* 16,500 cases *Vineyard area* 110 acres (45 ha)

Paolo de Marchi is a winemaker of talent and individuality. Self-taught, he has a particularly lively, fruit-forward style, allied with great depth and complexity. The estate's top wine, Super-tuscan Cepparello (100 percent sangiovese) is extremely concentrated and slow-developing, and usually sells on allocation; the rich Vin Santo is one of the region's best. His Syrah is one of the most intriguing expressions of the grape in Italy.

MONTEVERTINE

Established 1967 *Owner* Sergio Manetti *Production* 5,000 cases *Vineyard area* 21 acres (8.5 ha)

Manetti left industry for "rural bliss" and never looked back. While producing small amounts for friends and family, his wine had such success at Italy's major wine fair that he decided to turn winemaker full-time. His son-in-law Klaus Reimitz is now in charge of running the estate. Manetti has eschewed the Chianti Classico denomination. A fine range is led by Le Pergole Torte (100 percent sangiovese), Il Sodaccio (sangiovese/canaiolo) and the surprisingly good M (trebbiano/malvasia).

CASTELLO DI VOLPAIA

Established for many centuries; under current ownership since 1967 *Owner* Giovannella Stianti *Production* 21,000 cases *Vineyard area* 100 acres (40 ha)

Volpaia's vineyards are set particularly high on a well-exposed site with a good sand content, which gives a special elegance to the wines. Giovannella Stianti took particular care over her choice of clones of sangiovese, which give the classy, assertive, long-lived wines a further edge. Apart from impeccable Chianti Classico there are two well-honed Super-tuscans, Coltassala (sangiovese) and Balifico (sangiovese/cabernet).

The centuries-old winery Castello di Volpaia reflected in a Chianti bottle.

A winery complex on a vantage point above vineyards near Greve, Chianti.

Part of Tuscany's charm are the picturesque medieval towns and villages dotting the countryside.

REGIONAL DOZEN

Brunello di Montalcino
    (Costanti)
Chianti Classico Riserva
    "Castello di Fonterutoli"
    (Mazzei)
Chianti Classico Riserva
    "Rancia" (Fattoria di
    Felsina)
Giallo dei Muri (Tenuta di
    Valgiano)
Morellino di Scansano (Le
    Pupille)
Nipozzano Chianti Rufina
    Riserva (Frescobaldi)
Poggio alla Gazze (Ornellaia)
Sassicaia (Tenuta San Guido)
Tignanello (Antinori)
Vernaccia di San Gimignano
    (Teruzzi e Puthod)
Vin Santo (Isole e Olena)
Vino Nobile di Montepulciano
    "Vigna del Nocio"
    (Boscarelli)

San Gimignano

PONTE A RONDOLINO (ALSO KNOWN AS TERUZZI E PUTHOD)

Established 1974 *Owners* Enrico Teruzzi and Carmen Puthod *Production* 25,000 cases *Vineyard area* 85 + 8.5 acres leased (35 + 3.5 ha)

After a serious accident that ended Carmen Puthod's career as a ballerina, she and her husband Enrico Teruzzi moved to an estate in Tuscany to overcome the trauma. There were vines on the estate and Enrico Teruzzi started making wine almost for fun, though he soom became immersed in its production. The round, rich style of Teruzzi's Vernaccia brought the estate to prominence but now it is the overtly oaked Terre di Tufi version that has achieved the greater critical acclaim.

Bolgheri

TENUTA DELL'ORNELLAIA

Established late 1970s *Owner* Marchese Ludovico Antinori *Production* 32,500 cases *Vineyard area* 170 acres (70 ha)

The Marchese Ludovico Antinori was drawn to Bolgheri after the success of the Marchese Incisa della Rochetta and the estate was founded just as Sassicaia was gaining fame. Originally with the assistance of André Tchelistcheff from California, the aim was "California style." Ornellaia (85 percent cabernet sauvignon/merlot/cabernet franc) is fatter, riper and punchier than Sassicaia but slightly less complex. The estate also stands out for a more approachable cabernet sauvignon/merlot red, Le Volte, for the intense Masseto (merlot) and the racy Poggio alle Gazze (sauvignon).

TENUTA SAN GUIDO (ALSO REFERRED TO AS SASSICAIA)

Established 1964 *Owner* Nicolò Incisa della Rochetta *Production* 12,500 cases *Vineyard area* 133 acres (54 ha)

As discussed on page 309, the Marquese Incisa della Rochetta was drawn to Bolgheri on noticing the region's similarites to Bordeaux. There is no doubt that Sassicaia is of supreme quality. It is highly concentrated and long-lived with fine oak integration, great complexity, a beautiful fruit/tannin interweave and very long on the palate. The only doubt is whether its personality can match its technical prowess.

Montalcino

CASTELLO BANFI

Established 1978 *Owners* Banfi Vintners USA (Mariani brothers) *Production* 650,000 cases *Vineyard area* 2,000 acres (800 ha)

The arrival of Banfi caused a huge shake-up in Montalcino. Where vineyards were generally small and scattered, Banfi bought up about 7,000 acres (2,800 ha) of land and planted extensively, with about 370 acres (150 ha) dedicated exclusively to Brunello di Montalcino. The cellar, one of Italy's largest, houses over 3,000 *barriques* and hundreds of larger barrels. Banfi also spearheaded the revival of the Moscadello di Montalcino. The range of wines produced is large. All are well-made and unimpeachable in type.

BIONDI SANTI

Established 1700s *Owners* Biondi Santi SpA *Production* 28,500 cases *Vineyard area* 110 acres (45 ha)

The estate is split into three separate holdings, Il Greppo (the hub), Villa Poggio Salvi and Jacopo Biondi Santi. As the "father" of Brunello di Montalcino, Biondi Santi is held almost in awe by many, a regard enhanced by the legendary longevity of the wines (stories abound of fabulous experiences from turn-of-the-century examples). The range (previously just Brunello and Rosso) has been enhanced by half-a-dozen other wines, especially Sassoalloro (sangiovese).

CASATO PRIME DONNE

Established 1998 *Owner* Fausto Cinelli *Production* 1,650 cases *Vineyard area* 32 acres (13 ha)

This new estate, run by Donatella Cinelli-Colombini, is swiftly creating a name for itself with an unusual Brunello, Prime Donne, whose style is formed by a team of four expert tasters, all women, who are directed to place more emphasis on intuition than technical evaluation when selecting samples. Unusually, Casato Prime Donne is run by a mainly female team.

COSTANTI

Established 1964 in current form *Owner* Andrea Costanti *Production* 4,200 cases *Vineyard area* 25 acres (10 ha)

The lands have been in the ownership of the Costanti family since 1550 and wine became a commercial activity at the end of the 1950s. The estate concentrates on the basics, Brunello and Rosso, with most effort being lavished on the vineyards. The wines are remarkably classy—firm, elegant and finely honed.

IL POGGIONE

Established early 1900s *Owners* NA *Production* 30,000 cases *Vineyard area* 155 acres (63 ha)

Il Poggione makes some of the most enthralling wines of Montalcino. The estate's direction was set by its winemaker, Pierluigi Talenti, who was a stickler for quality ("There are no bad vintages, there are only vintages in which you make more or you make less," referring to the rigorous grape selection applied) and had an intuitive feel for viticulture. It was his detailed work in the vineyards while other estates were thinking mainly of their cellars that brought Il Poggione to the fore. Talenti's place is now taken by Fabrizio Bindocci, who once worked beside him.

Montepulciano

AVIGNONESI

Established 1978 *Owners* Avignonesi SpA.–Falvo brothers *Production* 50,000 cases *Vineyard area* 250 acres (100 ha)

The Avignonesi cellars were established in the 1500s but the current regime dates from when the Falvo brothers took ownership. Avignonesi is the example par excellence of the big and powerful school of Vino Nobile di Montepulciano; their blockbuster wines are saved from unapproachability by plentiful supple fruit. There are about a dozen wines other wines in the range, of which the Vin Santo Occhio di Pernice is legendary.

PODERI BOSCARELLI

Established 1969 *Owners* De Ferrari Corradi family *Production* 5,800 cases *Vineyard area* 32 acres (13 ha)

Boscarelli is the finest representative of the elegant side of Vino Nobile di Montepulciano production. The estate places most of its attention on its immaculate vineyards and produces concentrated but refined wines of personality and supreme style. There are just four wines, all excellent. The highlight is Vino Nobile *cru* Vigna del Nocio, which has greater complexity and polish than the 100 percent sangiovese Boscarelli, also highly rated.

POLIZIANO

Established 1961 *Owner* Federico Carletti *Production* 50,000 cases *Vineyard area* 300 acres (120 ha)

The estate, originally run by Carletti's father, started bottling in 1980. Vineyards stretch over three sites and are densely planted. Carletti has the broadest technical knowledge of any in the zone, making wines that many regard as easily Montepulciano's best: full, rich and vigorous. Unusually, Carletti uses certain plots for Rosso di Montepulciano and others for Vino Nobile, and cultivates the grapes accordingly.

Morellino di Scansano

LE PUPILLE

Established 1972 *Owners* Gentili family *Production* 6,000–6,500 cases *Vineyard area* 40 acres (16 ha)

Le Pupille sets the tone in Scansano. The estate is always refining its approach, with incisive, quality-led ideas, and has a good feel for marketing. The wines are big and punchy yet they still have style and character, with Morellino made in three versions. There is also the highly regarded Saffredi (cabernet/merlot/alicante) and Solalto, which is a sweet wine (sauvignon/traminer/sémillon).

Colline Lucchesi

TENUTA DI VALGIANO

Established NA *Owners* NA *Production* 3,500 cases *Vineyard area* 25 acres (10 ha)

A rather rainy climate and a general air of complacency once held back the wines from the hills around Lucca, but the recently established Tenuta di Valgiano defies the norms. The young enologist, Saverio Petrilli, spent time in Australia and has put his experience there to good use, carefully honing the three Valgiano wines to high levels of refinement and individuality. The racy, savory white, Giallo dei Muri, comes from trebbiano, malvasia and vermentino with just a touch of chardonnay; of the reds, Rosso di Palistorti (mainly sangiovese/syrah/merlot) is vibrant and spicy, and Scasso dei Casari (sangiovese) is firmer and deeper; both of these wines are fruit-forward.

A cobbled street in the walled hilltop town of Monteriggioni, Tuscany.

The famous Duomo in Florence has a commanding view over its surroundings.

Central Italy

A woman buys grapes at Caprile, Castelli Romani, Lazio.

The central part of the Italian peninsula includes the regions of Marche, Umbria and Lazio (sometimes called Latium). Widespread plantings of sangiovese and trebbiano form the base for much of the wine seen, but each region has at least one variety indigenous to one or more zones which put their stamp on the wines.

MARCHE

The Marche stretches along the Adriatic coast for about 95 miles (150 km) and inland about one-third of the way across the peninsula. The coastal strip is primarily populated by sun-worshippers, the exception being the major port of Ancona; the hinterland is rural, tranquil and remarkably pretty.

The region is dominated by verdicchio, and Verdicchio. Once no more than a light, crisp but innocuous white wine, an easy accompaniment to the fish-based diet of the coast, Verdicchio has grown up. The notorious amphora-shaped bottle persists, at least for the Fazi Battaglia company, but the wine has far more to offer than such a gimmicky container might suggest.

The main shifts in Verdicchio came through lighter cropping, picking a little less early and not vinifying so cool that the life was squashed out of it. These developments gave the wine greater fruit, without compromising its essential acidity, and greater longevity (although most is still drunk within a year of harvest). Verdicchio is a fairly versatile variety and also responds well to lateish harvesting (a couple of weeks or so), which gives the wine an almost buttery richness, and to both pre-fermentation skin contact and oak aging, in *barriques* or larger barrels. The variety also seems remarkably suited to a sparkling variant. Throughout, the wine's intrinsic style remains: crisply acidic, softly fruited with flavors of various green and yellow fruits and gently creamy but with good power behind.

The main growing area, Verdicchio dei Castelli di Jesi, is fairly extensive, the vineyards mostly lying west of Jesi along two roughly parallel ranges 820–1,600 feet (250–500 m) high. Verdicchio di Matelica is smaller, lying further inland near the border with Umbria, and produces less than 10 percent of the quantity of the Castelli di Jesi. Its wines are generally agreed to be superior: more muscular, more intense and deeper.

Reds take second place in the Marche, yet there are two of note. Rosso Conero is produced on the dip slope of the Mount Conero massif below Ancona. It is made almost exclusively from montepulciano (the DOC allows up to 15 percent sangiovese but the best producers don't use any), a grape producing a deeply colored, deeply flavored, richly fruited but well-structured, brambly red. The best examples of Rosso Conero show good aroma and considerable grace.

The Rosso Piceno zone covers much of the southern Marche with scattered vineyards and extremely variable quality. The best wines come from its far south, a small area called, confusingly,

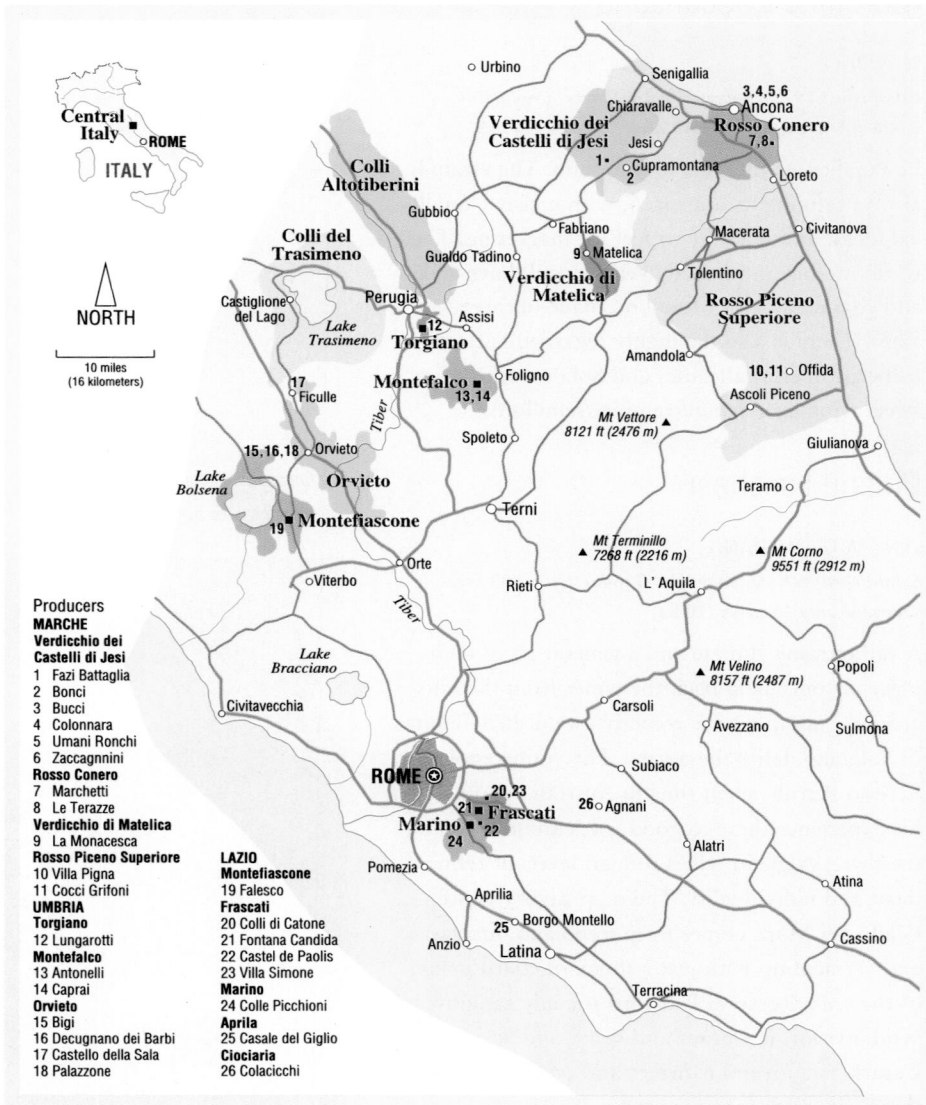

Central Italy

ITALY

NORTH

10 miles
(16 kilometers)

Producers
MARCHE
Verdicchio dei Castelli di Jesi
1 Fazi Battaglia
2 Bonci
3 Bucci
4 Colonnara
5 Umani Ronchi
6 Zaccagnini
Rosso Conero
7 Marchetti
8 Le Terazze
Verdicchio di Matelica
9 La Monacesca
Rosso Piceno Superiore
10 Villa Pigna
11 Cocci Grifoni
UMBRIA
Torgiano
12 Lungarotti
Montefalco
13 Antonelli
14 Caprai
Orvieto
15 Bigi
16 Decugnano dei Barbi
17 Castello della Sala
18 Palazzone

LAZIO
Montefiascone
19 Falesco
Frascati
20 Colli di Catone
21 Fontana Candida
22 Castel de Paolis
23 Villa Simone
Marino
24 Colle Picchioni
Aprila
25 Casale del Giglio
Ciociaria
26 Colacicchi

Rosso Piceno Superiore (not Classico). The better producers again work mainly with montepulciano (currently limited by the DOC to 70 percent, with at least 30 percent sangiovese).

The Marche also has a couple of oddities: Vernaccia di Serrapetrona, a sparkling red, which is made both sweet and dry, from the vernaccia nera grape (and nothing to do with Tuscany's white vernaccia); and Lacrima di Morro d'Alba, a strongly perfumed but somewhat evanescent red from the local lacrima grape.

Verdicchio dei Castelli di Jesi

FAZI BATTAGLIA

Established 1949 *Owners* Fazi Battaglia SpA *Production* 300,000 cases *Vineyard area* 840 acres (340 ha) + small proportion grapes bought in

Fazi Battaglia, one of the largest Verdicchio producers, and the best known by a long chalk, dreamed up the amphora bottle, which is still in use, in the 1950s. Several years ago the company took on the services of Franco Bernabei, one of Italy's most highly respected consultant enologists, to improve its rather indifferent wines. Even the base wine, Titulus, is now soundly drinkable and both the *cru* Le Moie and the oaked San Sisto versions are well-typed, as is the Rosso Conero.

BONCI

Established 1962 *Owners* Bonci family *Production* 25,000 cases *Vineyard area* 86 acres (35 ha)

This is one of Jesi's rising stars. The vineyards are at 1,500 feet (450 m) in some of the zone's best sites, two of the sites given over to research under the guidance of Milan University. The standard Verdicchio is clean and well-styled but the estate's flair is shown by their Verdicchio *crus*, Le Case and the perfumed, full, structured, warm, softly balanced San Michele. An attractive, sweet, *passito* Verdicchio and a finely tuned brut sparkling Verdicchio complete the range.

BUCCI

Established late 1700s *Owners* Bucci family *Production* 8,000 cases *Vineyard area* 50 acres (20 ha)

Ampelio Bucci, with consultant Giorgio Grai, has no interest in light, early-drinking wines, thus the estate's grapes are picked later than most, fermentation is slow, allowing plentiful yeast contact, and aging is initially in largeish oak barrels. The Villa Bucci selections best show the class of the estate and the Rosso Piceno is also of good character.

The small town of Poggio Lavarino straddles a terraced hill in Umbria.

COLONNARA

Established 1959 *Owners* Cooperative with about 200 members *Production* 125,000 cases *Vineyard area* 670 acres (270 ha)

Of the several cooperatives in the Jesi zone, Colonnara is in the vanguard for reliability and overall quality. The members' vineyards are overseen by an associated company, Cupravit, to ensure good viticultural standards. The flagship wine is Verdicchio dei Castelli di Jesi Cuprese, from selected grapes, with intriguing vegetal tones, slow development and good longevity. There is also an impressive sparkling Verdicchio.

UMANI RONCHI

Established 1955 *Owners* Bernetti family *Production* 350,000 cases *Vineyard area* 370 + 100 acres leased (150 + 40 ha) + grapes bought in

This colossus of the Marche scene has an equally high reputation for its Verdicchio and its Rosso Conero. It is the latter that is currently attracting greater attention in its three variants: the well-typed base version, the richer *cru* San Lorenzo and the oaked Cumaro. Under the guidance of consultant enologist Giacomo Tachis their new wine, Pèlago (cabernet sauvignon/montepulciano/merlot), is achieving acclaim. Among the Verdicchios, *cru* Casal di Serra stands out, but the entire range is excellent value for money.

Striking geometry in the vineyards of Torgiano, Umbria.

ZACCAGNINI

Established 1974 *Owners* Zaccagnini brothers *Production* 18,000 cases *Vineyard area* 70 acres (28 ha)

Silvio and Mario Zaccagnini were among the first to work with single-vineyard, high-quality Verdicchio wines. Their oak-free *cru* Salmagina, intense, characterful, finely balanced and of depth, is still one of the best. In addition there are two finely honed sparkling Verdicchios, Brut and Metodo Tradizionale.

Rosso Conero

MARCHETTI

Established c.1900 *Owners* Marchetti family *Production* 4,000 cases *Vineyard area* 30 acres (12 ha)

Since the first bottlings in the 1960s, the Marchetti wines have set the standard for Rosso Conero. Once they were full, soft and deep, but as son Maurizio progressively took over from father Mario the style became somewhat fresher and punchier while the intrinsic quality and longevity remained. Maurizio introduced the Rosso Conero selection, Villa Bonomi, now the estate's leading wine. A small amount of Verdicchio dei Castelli di Jesi is made from bought-in grapes.

LE TERAZZE

Established 1982 *Owners* Antonio and Georgina Terni *Production* 6,500 cases *Vineyard area* 30 acres (12 ha)

While Antonio Terni trained as an engineer, he and his English wife Georgina have an instinctive feel for wine, which has enabled their estate to rapidly take a leading place in the Rosso Conero zone. Their leading wine is the *barrique*-aged Rosso Conero Sassi Neri; the more youthful "standard" Rosso Conero ages in *botti* instead. There is also good Chardonnay and an excellent sparkler, Donna Giulia.

Verdicchio di Matelica

LA MONACESCA

Established 1966 *Owner* Casimiro Cifola *Production* 9,000 cases *Vineyard area* 55 acres (22 ha)

This estate began as a hobby for Casimiro Cifola but soon became his main occupation. It is now competently managed by his son Aldo. La Monacesca has long been the example par excellence of Verdicchio di Matelica in the zone. Until recently the estate has concentrated almost exclusively on the verdicchio grape, but is now beginning to work with red grapes.

Rosso Piceno Superiore

COCCI GRIFONI

Established 1969 *Owner* Guido Cocci Grifoni *Production* 25,000 cases *Vineyard area* 100 acres (40 ha)

Cocci Grifoni is one of the longest standing estates in the Piceno Superiore area. The wines have improved steadily over the years and now set the standards in the zone with their perfumed, full-bodied, ripely fruited style. The estate also works to good effect with the white wines of the area.

VILLA PIGNA

Established 1979 *Owners* Rozzi brothers *Production* 165,000 cases *Vineyard area* 420 acres (170 ha)

Villa Pigna is the best known name in Rosso Piceno Superiore and the zone's largest producer. Despite a large range of wines, including some from the adjacent region of Abruzzo, the Rosso Piceno Superiore is concentrated, rich and spicy.

UMBRIA

Umbria is the only land-locked region of peninsular Italy, a fact capitalized on by its publicists, who call it "Italy's green heart." Visitors know it more as the heart of ancient Etruria and the home of remarkable hilltop villages such as Assisi and Spello. Much of the region is formed of tightly packed, rounded hills, although it is cut through by the upper reaches of the River Tiber and is punctuated by the large Lake Trasimeno to the northwest. Both the lake and the northern part of the river have adjacent vineyards, Colli del Trasimeno and Colli Altotiberini respectively, where concerted efforts are being made to lift the wines from mundane to interesting, but the focus of Umbria lies south of Perugia, its main town.

The wines of Torgiano are better known than the size of the area would warrant from the efforts of the Lungarotti family. The Torgiano DOC more or less follows Lungarotti production norms, with varietal versions from chardonnay, pinot grigio, riesling italico, cabernet sauvignon and pinot nero, plus standard red Torgiano from a sangiovese-based blend, and white Torgiano from trebbiano (mostly) and grechetto.

Grechetto is Umbria's only native white variety of any importance. While it makes punchy but rounded and rather nutty wines of good character, it is rarely seen on its own, being used far more often to lift otherwise unexceptional, trebbiano-based wines. Its red counterpart is sagrantino, a magnificent variety that is able to make big, ripe, black-fruited, mouth-filling wines of tremendous depth, length and vigor.

Sagrantino is the powerhouse behind the red wines of the small but influential zone of Montefalco. Montefalco Rosso contains just a small proportion (10–15 percent), which is enough to give the sangiovese-based wine verve and individuality. The real impact of the grape is revealed in Montefalco Sagrantino, where it is used exclusively; there is also a super-concentrated *passito* version from semi-dried grapes, sweet, strong and massive. Such reds put the rather timid Montefalco Bianco (grechetto/trebbiano) into the shade.

There's good value to be had from the simple but up-and-coming Colli Amerini (white, mainly trebbiano; red, mainly sangiovese) in the south, adjacent to the border with Lazio, but the most important wine of southern Umbria is Orvieto. Orvieto, like most of the infamous names of old Italy, has shrugged off its poor reputation and now turns out trebbiano-based wines that are respectable, at the very least, and frequently well-made, with good character deriving from the increasing role of grechetto in the blend. A small component of verdello contributes freshness and weight. The old-style Orvieto was frequently a little sweet. Although most Orvieto is now completely dry, occasionally lightly sweet (*abboccato*) and semi-sweet (*amabile*) versions are still produced. Occasionally the vineyards are affected by noble rot, prompting fully sweet, botrytized styles of Orvieto, so impressive, richly but not cloyingly sweet and beautifully floral, that a few estates now produce botrytized styles in most years, whether noble rot appears naturally or not.

Torgiano

LUNGAROTTI

Established 1950 *Owners* Lungarotti family *Production* 200,000 cases *Vineyard area* 750 acres (300 ha)

Lungarotti is quite simply synonymous with Torgiano, the village and the wine. Within the village the family owns a famed hotel and restaurant, Le Tre Vaselle, and one of Italy's best equipped wine museums. The wine names,

Torre di Giano (white) and Rubesco (red), may even be better known than the denomination itself; the *riserva*-level wines, most notably *cru* Vigna Monticchio, have starry reputations, and the entire range is held in high consideration, although recent vintages have not quite hit the mark.

An avenue of trees lines the entrance to vineyards at Torgiano, Umbria.

Montefalco

ANTONELLI

Established Nineteenth century *Owners* Antonelli family *Production* 9,000 cases *Vineyard area* 50 acres (20 ha)

Although in the hands of the Antonelli family and producing wine for over 100 years, the estate's wines did not begin to gain their high-quality reputation until the 1990s. The wines are well-made, with the Rosso di Montefalco, the Sagrantino di Montefalco and the Sagrantino Passito all models of their type. There are also two good white wines from grechetto.

CAPRAI

Established 1971 *Owners* Caprai family *Production* 62,500 cases *Vineyard area* 200 acres (80 ha)

Arnaldo Caprai, a fabrics industrialist, bought this estate in 1971, and gradually added adjacent land. He concentrated on sagrantino to become one of Montefalco's leading producers, especially with Sagrantino di Montefalco Passito. When his son Marco took

Upright oak barrels in the famous Torgiano winery, Lungarotti.

Vineyards around the beautiful town of Assisi in Umbria.

REGIONAL DOZEN

Cervara della Sala (Castello della Sala)

Frascati Superiore (Colli di Catone)

Frascati Superiore "Vigna Adriana" (Castel de Paolis)

Orvieto Classico "Campo del Guardiano" (Palazzone)

Orvieto Classico "Pourriture Noble" (Decugnano dei Barbi)

Quattro Mori (Castel de Paolis)

Rubino (La Palazzola)

Sagrantino di Montefalcone (Arnaldo Caprai)

Torgiano Rosso Riserva "Vigna Monticchio" (Lungarotti)

Verdicchio dei Castelli di Jesi Classico (Bucci)

Verdicchio dei Castelli di Jesi Classico Superiore "Casal di Serra" (Umani Ronchi)

Verdicchio di Matelica (La Monacesca)

over the styles of the wines changed, bringing even greater success. The Sagrantino di Montefalco is now barriqued, huge in power and intensity and made for the long haul, especially the Sagrantino di Montefalco 25 Anni.

Orvieto

BIGI

Established 1880 *Owner* Gruppo Italiano Vini *Production* 400,000 cases *Vineyard area* 475 acres (193 ha) + grapes bought in

With a large proportion of the production exported, many people's ideas of Orvieto have been formed by this colossus. The wines are well-made and well-typed, especially the single-vineyard Orvieto Classico Torricella. There are also two varietal wines from grechetto, one, Marrano, *barrique*-fermented. All are good value.

DECUGNANO DEI BARBI

Established 1973 *Owners* Barbi family *Production* 11,500 cases *Vineyard area* 80 acres (32 ha)

The Barbi family had been grapegrowers for three generations before buying this estate in some of the best lands of Orvieto Classico. In the vanguard of quality production in the zone and intent on staying that way, they cultivate organically and continuously research clones of their varieties. The top wine of their range of Orvietos is the *barrique*-fermented IL (meaning "THE"), although purists prefer the non-oaked Orvieto Classico Decugnano dei Barbi. The simpler Orvieto Classico Barbi, a botrytized Orvieto, a sparkling wine and three reds complete the range.

PALAZZONE

Established 1969 *Owners* Dubini family *Production* 10,000 cases *Vineyard area* 62 acres (25 ha)

Palazzone produces some of the zone's best Orvieto, both straight and late-harvest (botrytized), and is one of the few to produce a varietal Grechetto. It has also gained importance for its wines made from international varieties, for example Armaleo (cabernet), L'Ultima Spiaggia (viognier) and Muffa Nobile (botrytized sauvignon).

CASTELLO DELLA SALA

Established 1977 *Owner* Marchese Piero Antinori *Production* 50,000 cases *Vineyard area* 350 acres (140 ha)

Castello della Sala is indeed a castle, medieval, fortressed and built around 1350. It was bought by Tuscany's famous Antinori family in 1940 and turned over to wine production in 1977. Although part of Piero Antinori's aim was to add Orvieto Classico to his range of Tuscan wines, most of the grapes planted on the clayey soils were chardonnay and sauvignon. The resultant wines, perfectly constructed, have won endless awards, especially Cervaro della Sala, from chardonnay (with a little grechetto). Muffato della Sala is from sauvignon, grechetto and others, botrytized. A Pinot Nero has also gained renown.

LAZIO

Part of the Orvieto zone strays into neighboring Lazio but is of little consequence. The important wines of Lazio, the region of Rome, are produced near the capital on the cool slopes of the hills rising close to its southeastern suburbs. In prime position is Frascati, whose fame did not arise solely from intrinsic superiority—its proximity to Rome was just as significant.

Frascati and its neighboring wines are made principally from trebbiano and the local malvasia di candia, blended in varying proportions. In theory the trebbiano gives freshness and the malvasia perfume and flavor, but the malvasia tends also to oxidize rapidly. Historically these wines were often deeply colored, flat and dull, with malvasia in the ascendant and no knowledge of reductive winemaking. Today the situation is very different but Frascati is the name that has stuck. Far more "frascati" is drunk around the world than could ever be produced in the 6,400 acres (2,600 ha) of vineyards in the zone. Its neighboring zones, Montecompatri–Colonna and Zagarolo to the east, Marino to the southwest, Colli Albani, Colli Lanuvini and Velletri, are still poorly known by comparison. Romans often refer to these wines disparagingly as "Castelli wines," Castelli Romani being a catch-all denomination for the simplest wines made anywhere on the Roman hills.

Much Frascati remains a commodity wine but an increasing proportion is of considerably finer quality. Malvasia di candia is a weakling member of the malvasia family, thus some more quality-conscious producers are opting for malvasia del lazio (also known as malvasia puntinata, also local) instead. One or two excellent wines are made exclusively from malvasia del lazio, but are not entitled to the Frascati denomination.

There are restricted plantings of southern Italy's greco in the region and outcrops of the local bellone and bonvino (bombino bianco), all used in minor roles in blends. There is more variety in the reds with considerable use being made of sangiovese and montepulciano, increasing plantings of merlot, and canaiolo and ciliegiolo taking supporting roles, especially in the north of the region. Lazio's indigenous red is cesanese, a wild, rustic variety of assured potential, if only someone could tame it. It grows primarily in the Ciociaria, east of Rome, the Castelli Romani hills, and in the coastal zone of Cerveteri.

The curious red aleatico, grown only around Gradoli on the northwest shores of Lake Bolsena, produces a deep, richly fruity, lively but soft dessert wine which is sometimes *liquoroso* (fortified). The remainder of the land around the lake is reserved for Italy's most strangely named wine, Est! Est!! Est!!! di Montefiascone. The story goes back to the twelfth century, when it is said a traveling bishop sent his scout ahead to find the best drinking holes. So excited was the scout on reaching a certain inn in Montefiascone that he chalked "Here it is" three times on the door, with exclamation marks. This tale now tends to cause embarrassment because, despite being made mainly from the uninspiring trebbiano toscano, with malvasia toscana and trebbiano

giallo, several producers are now turning out highly attractive, stylish wines under the name.

Montefiascone

FALESCO
Established 1979 *Owner* Riccardo Cotarella *Production* 20,000 cases *Vineyard area* All grapes bought in

Riccardo Cotarella is one of Italy's most esteemed consultant enologists and he imposes strict controls on his grapegrowers. His Est! Est!! Est!!! first brought the wine out of disrepute and there is now a *cru* version, Poggio dei Gelsi, nuanced and ripely fruity. Cotarella also produces a varietal Grechetto and Vitiano (merlot/cabernet sauvignon/sangiovese) from grapes grown in Umbria, but the flagship is Montiano (100 percent merlot), which is a punchy giant of a wine.

Frascati

COLLI DI CATONE
Established NA *Owners* Pulcini family *Production* NA *Vineyard area* NA

The wines of Colli di Catone are very much appreciated on export markets but they are often

A winery building flanked by poplars and vines at Torgiano, Umbria.

Poplar trees stand among rows of grape vines at Torgiano, Umbria.

The wine museum owned and run by Cantine Lungarotti in Torgiano, Umbria.

cold-shouldered in Italy. There is a broad range of Frascati from the simple but reliable to the top-notch. Antonio Pulcini was one of the first to recognize the superiority of malvasia del lazio and his top-flight Frascatis contain significant proportions. The deep, intense, complex Colle Gaio, made exclusively from malvasia del lazio, is one of the few wines of the zone to repay aging. There are also some experimental red wines.

FONTANA CANDIDA

Established 1958 *Owner* Gruppo Italiano Vini *Production* 625,000 cases *Vineyard area* 225 acres (91 ha) + grapes bought in

Fontana Candida is responsible for almost half of all Frascati produced, and exports about two-thirds of its production. The company's winemaker, Francesco Bardi, ensures good quality, well-styled wines throughout. The *cru* Santa Teresa, with 30 percent malvasia del lazio, is regularly one of the best Frascatis on the market. The Frascati Terre dei Grifi, lighter and fresher, has a higher proportion of trebbiano; also from the Terre dei Grifi range is a broad but nuanced wine from 100 percent malvasia del lazio.

CASTEL DE PAOLIS

Established 1985 *Owners* Santarelli family *Production* 6,500 cases *Vineyard area* 30 acres (12 ha)

When Frascati is discussed in Italy the name on everyone's lips is Castel de Paolis, the estate garnering the most interest and, often, the greatest admiration, even if there are a few detractors. Most rate highly the owners' intelligent approach and dedication, the quality of the fruit, and the continued emphasis on the zone's minor grapes as much as the estate's work with international varieties. Frascati Vigna Adriana tops the range.

VILLA SIMONE

Established 1980 *Owners* Costantini family *Production* 10,000 cases *Vineyard area* 50 acres (20 ha)

Piero Costantini bought the Villa Simone estate in 1980 with the express intent of making Frascati superior to anything else available. He replanted the vineyards with a goodly proportion of malvasia del lazio and modernized the cellar. The resul-

tant wines are elegant, individually styled and cleanly aromatic, especially the *crus* Vigneto Filonardi and Vigna dei Preti.

Marino

COLLE PICCHIONI

Established 1976 *Owners* Paola & Armando di Mauro *Production* 7,500 cases *Vineyard area* 22 acres (9 ha)

Paola di Mauro's wines, intense, complex, long-lived and fascinating, are the result not just of attentive vineyard management, intelligent vinification and careful aging but of reliance on the "minor" grapes of the zone. Marino Etichetta Verde, the estate's base wine, is far superior to the competition. Marino Etichetta Oro is several notches richer and deeper; Le Vignole is slow-developing and quite exceptional. Its red partner, Vigna del Vassallo, is from merlot, cabernet sauvignon and cabernet franc. The same grapes form the base of the fine Colle Picchioni Rosso.

Aprilia

CASALE DEL GIGLIO

Established 1968 *Owners* Santarelli family *Production* 37,500–50,000 cases *Vineyard area* 300 acres (120 ha)

The year 1984 marked the beginning of this estate in its current form when it embarked on a major research project to establish the varieties best suited to its lands, near the coast in Aprilia, about 30 miles (50 km) southeast of Rome. Now working with a range of international varieties, its best known wine is Satrico (chardonnay/trebbiano).

Ciociaria

COLACICCHI

Established 1950 *Owners* Trimani family *Production* 1,600 cases *Vineyard area* 12 acres (5 ha)

The Trimani family's main occupation is running one of Rome's largest, best stocked and longest established wine shops, plus an adjacent wine bar. The tiny but highly prestigious Colacicchi estate is a recent acquisition and the aim is to ensure that its wines, especially the flagship Torre Ercolana (cabernet sauvignon/merlot/cesanese), always match their lofty reputations. The wines are not released until they are ready for drinking; for Torre Ercolana, this means after about eight years. A younger red, Romagnano Rosso, is made from the same varieties, and a white, Romagnano Bianco, from a blend of local grapes.

Southern Italy

The south has long been regarded as the sleeping giant of Italy. Despite an abundance of grape varieties of indisputable quality, it has taken an unconscionably long time for a critical mass of good wine to be produced. Certainly the cautious approach of southern Italy is among the reasons behind this, but the lack of suitable schools of enology and research departments, poor infrastructure, the distance from main markets and lack of competition have all contributed. One or two of the regions are still metaphorically rubbing their eyes and stretching their legs, but others—Puglia leading the way—are now fully awake. The dynamism pervading the wine scene of southern Italy is very exciting.

The southern Italian regions comprise Abruzzo, Molise and Puglia, heading south from the Marche along the Adriatic coast; Campania and Calabria, south from Lazio along the western coast; Basilicata, the instep, joining the heel of Puglia to the toe of Calabria; and the island of Sardinia. Sicily, the other main island, is treated separately.

ABRUZZO

Abruzzo is one of Italy's most beautiful regions with breathtaking scenery, vivid colors and wonderful contrasts between the soft lines of its sandy beaches and the stark plunges of the Apennine peaks. It is also the region where montepulciano finds its greatest expression. The grape grows widely, with the resultant wines denominated as Montepulciano d'Abruzzo throughout even though they vary in style. The wines are most structured and probably at their most typical around Pescara, roughly in the middle of the region's 90 mile (140 km) eastern coastline. In the province of L'Aquila, in the cooler conditions of the Apennine slopes, they are lighter and more elegant. It is here that the version Montepulciano d'Abruzzo Cerasuolo, somewhere halfway between a red and a rosé, is usually at its best. In the hotter southern province of Chieti, the Montepulciano is fatter, weightier and can tend to coarseness if not handled with care. In the north, in the province of Teramo, the wine is stylish, succulently fruity and balanced.

A decorated facade in the town of Martina Franca in Puglia.

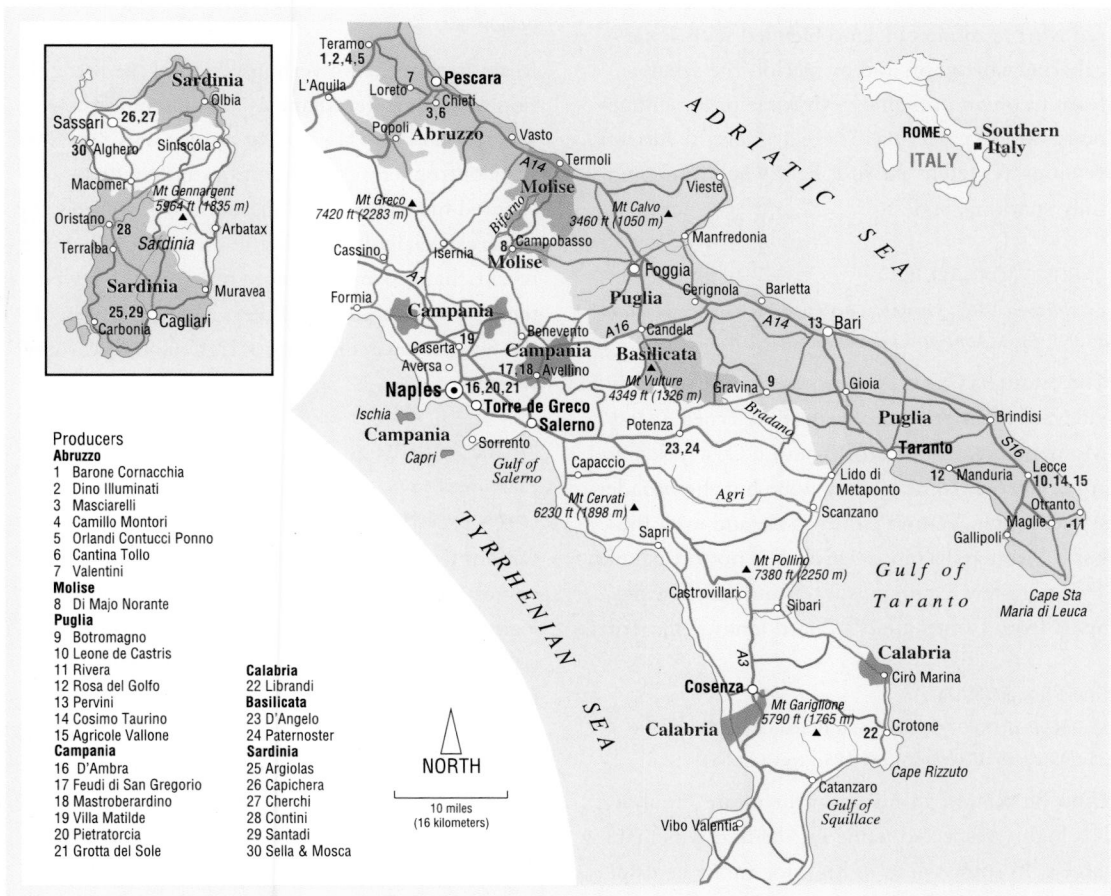

Producers

Abruzzo
1 Barone Cornacchia
2 Dino Illuminati
3 Masciarelli
4 Camillo Montori
5 Orlandi Contucci Ponno
6 Cantina Tollo
7 Valentini
Molise
8 Di Majo Norante
Puglia
9 Botromagno
10 Leone de Castris
11 Rivera
12 Rosa del Golfo
13 Pervini
14 Cosimo Taurino
15 Agricole Vallone
Campania
16 D'Ambra
17 Feudi di San Gregorio
18 Mastroberardino
19 Villa Matilde
20 Pietratorcia
21 Grotta del Sole

Calabria
22 Librandi
Basilicata
23 D'Angelo
24 Paternoster
Sardinia
25 Argiolas
26 Capichera
27 Cherchi
28 Contini
29 Santadi
30 Sella & Mosca

The white buildings of the town of Locorotondo, Puglia.

The sole Montepulciano d'Abruzzo subzone, Colline Teramane, covers the Teramo uplands. White wine in Abruzzo is similarly straight-forward in classification: practically the only denomination is Trebbiano d'Abruzzo. This can mean either that the wine is made from trebbiano toscano (*d'Abruzzo* meaning "from Abruzzo") or from trebbiano d'abruzzo (the local name for bombino bianco). Where the Tuscan trebbiano is used the wine can be boring; where trebbiano d'abruzzo is used the potential is far higher.

The extreme northeast corner sees a batch of top producers and the region's finest terrain. The wine Controguerra is produced solely here. The red is from montepulciano blended with some cabernet sauvignon and/or merlot; the white is from trebbiano toscano with some of the indigenous variety passerina. There are several varietal versions as well as *passito*, lightly sparkling and fully sparkling styles.

BARONE CORNACCHIA

Established 1960 *Owners* Cornacchia family *Production* 25,000 cases *Vineyard area* 80 acres (32 ha)

The estate has high, well-exposed, excellently sited vineyards and produces beautifully typed, classy Montepulciano. The *cru* Vigna Le Coste, rich and concentrated, is the leading wine but the broader-styled Poggio Varano comes close and even the basic Montepulciano d'Abruzzo is not far behind. There are few excursions into non-classic wines, apart from Controguerra Chardonnay, Villa Torri.

DINO ILLUMINATI

Established 1890 *Owner* Dino Illuminati *Production* 75,000 cases *Vineyard area* 195 acres (80 ha)

Dino Illuminati, grandson of the estate's founder, is a highly respected name in Abruzzo winemaking circles. In some wines of his wide range he displays

A trullo storehouse with its conical stone roof, Alberobello, Puglia.

the modernist's attraction to *barrique* aging and in others he looks for the light touch. The past few years have seen an increasing self-confidence in style, most notably with the three Montepulciano d'Abruzzos, Lumen (which contains 10 percent cabernet sauvignon and 5 percent merlot), Zanna and Riparosso. Nicò is made from late-harvested montepulciano grapes.

MASCIARELLI

Established 1981 *Owner* Gianni Masciarelli *Production* 50,000 cases *Vineyard area* 85 + 37 acres leased (35 + 15 ha)

Gianni Masciarelli's grandfather first planted vines in the 1930s but the estate took shape in 1981 when wines were first bottled. Masciarelli pays meticulous attention to vine cultivation, with the result that the wines have great structure and complexity. He is often cited for a celebrated Chardonnay, Marina Cvetic, named after his wife who works with him. The leading wine is Monte-pulciano d'Abruzzo Villa Gemma, a remarkable mix of elegance and power. Several other wines are produced and all are consistently well-made.

CAMILLO MONTORI

Established 1879 *Owner* Camillo Montori *Production* 40,000 cases *Vineyard area* 100 acres (40 ha) + grapes bought in

Montori was the powerhouse behind the recognition of Colline Teramane as a Montepulciano subzone and also the setting-up of a separate DOC for Controguerra. His attention to detail has ensured his wines have long been in Abruzzo's top rank, especially his leading Fonte Cupa line, but a recent changeover to a more overtly oaky style has tended to knock them off-key. Montori is one of the few producers making a Trebbiano d'Abruzzo worthy of note.

ORLANDI CONTUCCI PONNO

Established 1805 *Owner* Marina Orlandi Contucci *Production* 5,000 cases *Vineyard area* 67 acres (27 ha)

Orandi Contucci Ponno has been working with one of Italy's top enologists, Donato Lanati from Piedmont, and is Abruzzo's sole estate to make its reputation on wines other than Montepulciano. Its foremost wines are Liburnio (cabernet/merlot/-malbec/sangiovese) and Colle Funaro (made exclusively from cabernet). Chardonnay and sauvignon also feature significantly in the estates's range. The Montepulciano d'Abruzzo is nevertheless well-made and well-typed.

CANTINA TOLLO

Established 1960 *Owners* Cooperative *Production*
1 million cases *Vineyard area* 7,500 acres (3,000 ha)

Of Abruzzo's numerous cooperatives, Tollo has
long been the most attentive to quality. Wines are
produced in several quality ranges, led by Colle
Secco, the line that has given Tollo a strong
foothold in export markets. The full, *barrique*-
aged Montepulciano d'Abruzzo Cagiolo is the
cooperative's flagship wine. The wines are very
good value throughout.

VALENTINI

Established 1650 *Owner* Edoardo Valentini *Production*
0–4,000 cases *Vineyard area* 155 acres (63 ha)

Valentini handcrafts his wines into some of the
most exquisite bottles to be found anywhere. With
his main income from other sources, he can afford
to be as fussy as he likes and handles only the
peak of his grapes, sending the rest to a local
cooperative. He releases his wines only when he
considers them ready for drinking. The Montepulciano d'Abruzzo is legendary: slow-developing,
with great longevity and outstanding complexity;
while the Trebbiano d'Abruzzo is an astonishingly
rich, structured, deeply perfumed and multi-
layered wine.

MOLISE

Molise is Italy's ugly-duckling region, with the jury
still out on its swan potential. Formerly part of
Abruzzo, it was hived off in 1963 but has made
practically no impact since. In theory it has two
DOCs, Biferno, within the province of Campobasso to the east and including all Molise's coast-
land, and Pentro, further west, in Isernia province
—where not a single bottle is made.

In the entire region there is just one producer
of note, Di Majo Norante, whose vineyards are a
mere stone's throw from the coast. Di Majo's style
is therefore by default Biferno's style. Even so,
many of his wines fall outside the DOC, which is
based on montepulciano with some aglianico
(grown widely in Basilicata and Campania) and
trebbiano toscano (sic) for the red; and trebbiano
toscano, bombino bianco and malvasia bianca
for the white.

DI MAJO NORANTE

Established 1960s *Owner* Alessio di Majo *Production*
50,000 cases *Vineyard area* 150 acres (60 ha)

Molise's sole producer of any standing cultivates
organically and, apart from a couple of wines that

fit into the Biferno DOC, has concentrated on
varietals from the south's most prized grape varieties: falanghina, fiano, greco, aglianico and
moscato. The wines have always been individual
and characterful but quality has often been variable. The recent arrival of Riccardo Cotarella as
consultant enologist has given the wines a nudge
towards greater fruit and depth.

A basket of olives; local produce of Puglia.

PUGLIA

There could be no greater contrast than that
between Molise and its neighbor Puglia, stretching
over 220 miles (360 km) to Italy's heel-tip. With a
string of native grape varieties (which originated in
Greece or Asia Minor), Puglia is currently the
south's most go-ahead wine region. The center of
attention is the narrow Salento peninsula in the far
south whose torrid summer heat is mitigated by
the effects of both the Adriatic and the Ionian seas.
The other great plus for the area is the indigenous
red variety, negroamaro, the "bitterblack," long
renowned for deeply colored, impenetrably
intense, bitter-finishing and long-lived wines that
needed a touch of the aromatic red malvasia to
make them approachable. Salento's real fortune
was to find Severino Garofano, an enologist
capable of shaping negroamaro into a riper,
fruitier, far more drinkable wine without losing its
muscle and its intrinsic warm, minerally character,
and producers willing to accept the changes. With
low prices still prevailing in the area, the emergence of the Salento wines becomes inevitable.

Puglia has embraced the concept of DOC with
enthusiasm. There are ten DOCs, all rather similar,
for negroamaro-based wines in the Salento alone:

Streetscape in the Puglian town of Putignano.

Distinctive trulli storehouses outside the town of Locorotondo, Puglia.

Tasting a bottle of Vino Primitivo in Cantine Di Marco Martina Franca Martina, Puglia.

Alezio, Galatina, Lizzano, Matino, Nardò, Squinzano, Leverano, Brindisi, Copertino and Salice Salentino, the latter three encompassing most of the best producers.

The Salento's traditional wines from primitivo are also returning to prominence. Primitivo is still grown on *alberello* (low, individual, bush-like training) systems on the hot plains. It makes robust, mouth-filling, richly fruity and strongly spicy red wines that are either dry (or off-dry) and strongly alcoholic, or sweet and fairly strongly alcoholic. There are also even heftier sweet and dry fortified versions. Primitivo is almost certainly the same as California's zinfandel.

North of the Salento there is little of interest, apart from the light white Locorotondo, from the local verdeca and bianco d'alessano varieties, until one reaches the central vineyards northwest of Bari. Here uva di troia is the prime red grape, making rather firmer, more stylish wines than negroamaro, with an attractive mineral tang. Pampanuto is its white partner (possibly the same as verdeca). They are at their best in the wines of Castel del Monte, although the rather liberal DOC allows the red Castel del Monte to be made from any or all of uva di troia, aglianico and montepulciano, in any proportions, and the white from pampanuto, chardonnay and bombino bianco, with a similar freedom of proportions. There is a string of varietal versions too. The adjacent zone of Gravina is also attracting interest. The sweet red wine Aleatico di Puglia may be grown throughout the region, but most of its vineyards are in the center, close to Bari.

There is then a further gap in notable production until reaching the zone of San Severo in the region's north. Here, close to Molise, the montepulciano and bombino bianco varieties regain prominence. Despite the vigor of many of its reds, Puglia also produces some of Italy's most attractive and well balanced rosés.

BOTROMAGNO

Established 1991 *Owners* D'Agostini family and 100-odd suppliers of grapes *Production* 25,000 cases *Vineyard area* 300 acres (120 ha) + grapes bought in

This producer is an unusual arrangement formed from a fusion between the Gravina commune's cooperative and the estate of the D'Agostini family. It is the only producer of DOC Gravina which, with Severino Garofano, Puglia's leading enologist, as consultant, is reliably good. The company's trademark wine is Pier delle Vigne, a refined but warm and rounded wine from a *barrique*-aged blend of aglianico and montepulciano.

LEONE DE CASTRIS

Established 1665 *Owner* Salvatore Leone de Castris *Production* 250,000 cases *Vineyard area* 1,100 acres (450 ha)

The estate took on its current form in 1925 and gained fame half a century ago when it created Five Roses, a soft but fully flavored rosé that established Puglia's reputation for pink wines. Leone de Castris is also credited with shaping Salice Salentino. It is now renowned for the *barrique*-aged red Donna Lisa Salice Salentino Riserva, intense, structured, spicy and deep.

PERVINI

Established 1948 *Owners* Perrucci brothers *Production* 650,000 cases *Vineyard area* Grapes bought-in

The company began purely as a source of blending wine for northern producers, but in the 1990s the grandchildren of the founder switched to wine production in their own right. Although there is a good range of Salento wines, the Primitivo is Pervini's best-known offering, with plenty of fruit to balance its weighty structure.

RIVERA

Established 1959 in current form *Owners* De Corato family *Production* 130,000 cases *Vineyard area* 300 acres (120 ha); half this area owned outright

The estate has been in the hands of the Rivera family since the early twentieth century and is the leading producer of Castel del Monte with the Riserva Il Falcone a classic embodiment of the wine. For the last ten years the estate has been producing two lines. The traditional line includes Castel del Monte red, white and rosé, and the more modern Terre al Monte includes a range of varietals from aglianico, pinot bianco, sauvignon and chardonnay.

ROSA DEL GOLFO

Established 1939 *Owners* Lina and Damiano Calò
Production 8,500 cases *Vineyard area* Grapes bought-in

Rosa del Golfo is the name of both the company and its leading wine, showing a conviction in the potential and marketability of pink wine that is hard to match. Rosa del Golfo (the wine) is one of Italy's top rosés. From negroamaro and malvasia nera, it is comparatively deeply colored, ripely perfumed, mid-weight and pure-toned with abundant, strawberry-like fruit. Considerable work is being done on negroamaro-based reds and a verdeca-based white.

COSIMO TAURINO

Established late 1800s *Owners* Taurino family *Production* 75,000 cases *Vineyard area* 270 acres (110 ha)

The estate took on its present form in the 1970s when the cellars were constructed. Cosimo Taurino was the architect of the wines. Against all received wisdom in the area at the time he invested heavily in equipment and vineyards, turning his wines into some of Puglia's best. The estate's emblem is Patriglione, a big, overtly rich, chocolatey, spicy wine, while the leaner, firmer Notarpanaro is more typical of modern handling of negroamaro. A handful of other wines, all well-made, complete the range.

AGRICOLE VALLONE

Established 1979 *Owners* Vallone family *Production* 12,500 cases *Vineyard area* Grapes bought in

Vallone is known particularly for Graticciaia, from late-harvested negroamaro and malvasia nera grapes left to dry further after picking on *graticci* (straw mats). It is strong, powerful, richly fruited and long. Like most of the Salento's best estates, the wines are made by Severino Garofano, probably Puglia's most talented enologist.

CAMPANIA

If there is one wine name from Roman times that continues to resonate it is Falernum (Falernian). It would have been so easy for producers in northern Campania, the *Campania Felix* where Falernum was originally produced, to have simply capitalized on the name but today's Falerno was extensively

researched to ensure it matched its ancient forebear as closely as possible, while aiming for the highest modern standards in both vineyards and cellars. White Falerno del Massico comes exclusively from the characterful indigenous variety falanghina: floral, with elegant but pervasive fruit, notable depth and good longevity. The refined, well-structured red is predominantly from aglianico (described under Basilicata below) with a small amount of the punchy but somewhat rough-hewn piedirosso, also native.

Three of the Campania's most important wines, Taurasi (from aglianico), Greco di Tufo (greco) and Fiano di Avellino (fiano) come from the hill territory inland near Avellino. The climate is surprisingly cool with plentiful rainfall slowing ripening, and pronounced daytime–nighttime temperature changes, accentuating aroma. Taurasi, sometimes aggressive and tannic when young, is credited with tremendous longevity although recent years have seen an increase in more supple, more forward examples. Greco, crisply fruity when young, is often better after a few years' development, as is fiano. Fiano can develop considerable grace, refinement and complexity, and is one of the south's most intriguing varieties.

There is intermittent vine growth along the central part of the coast, near the focal point of Naples. The islands of Capri and Ischia both produce wine and although much is drunk *in situ* Ischia has a couple of producers of high standing whose wines have gained far wider attention. It is also the homeland of two local white varieties, biancolella and forastera. The volcanic slopes of Mount Vesuvius form another production area. Red and white Vesuvio are decent wines but rarely much more. Those with a little extra strength and concentration are called Lacryma Christi del Vesuvio. Aversa is home of the lemony fresh variety asprinio. The vines were once looped over trees, the resultant wines were rather sharp and lean but very refreshing. At least one producer has returned to this eccentric form of cultivation, mainly from a desire to maintain the area's traditions, but to surprisingly good effect. There are also sparkling versions.

Viticulture in Campania's south, mainly in the coastal area of Cilento, remains sporadic.

Fellini Alberello 1998; Puglia's traditional-style wines are returning to prominence.

Puglia stretches 220 miles (360 km) to Italy's heel tip.

Imposing steel tanks and a truck at Cantina del Barbera, Puglia.

D'AMBRA

Established 1888 *Owners* Andrea d'Ambra *Production* 45,000 cases *Vineyard area* 17 acres (7 ha) + grapes bought in

For a long time the leading producer on Ischia and the only one selling further afield, D'Ambra has been making attractive, freshly fruited wines, mainly from biancolella. Tenuta Frassitelli, from a single 10 acre (4 ha) holding, is generally regarded as the biancolella archetype. The company started bottling in 1955 and in 1976 entered a period of expansion, which was halted in 1999 in favor of improving the vineyard holdings and increasing the personality of the wines.

FEUDI DI SAN GREGORIO

Established 1986 *Owners* Capaldo and Ercolino families *Production* 85,000 cases *Vineyard area* 200 acres (80 ha)

Within a few years this company has moved from being an also-ran to being one of the best known Campanian names. The wines from this estate are reliable, carefully made, well-typed and well-priced. They are led by Campanaro and Pietracalda, both Fiano di Avellino, Serpico (aglianico/piedirosso/sangiovese) and Taurasi.

MASTROBERARDINO

Established 1878 *Owners* Antonio, Carlo and Pietro Mastroberardino *Production* 150,000 cases *Vineyard area* 150 acres (60 ha) + grapes bought in

Mastroberardino, historically one of the major names on the Italian wine scene, for years was practically the only representative of the south to have a reputation beyond local boundaries. It was also Mastroberardino that introduced Avellino's three leading wines: Taurasi, Fiano di Avellino and Greco di Tufo. The company now has considerable competition, with several of its former grape suppliers now making their own wine. The wines are reliably good if not exceptional quality, although older vintages of Taurasi show great longevity.

Vines planted in rows along the contours of the hills maximize the growing space.

VILLA MATILDE

Established 1963 *Owners* Salvatore & Maria Ida Avallone *Production* 30,000 cases *Vineyard area* 155 acres (63 ha)

This leading estate, the sole representative of Falerno and the one responsible for its revival, produces impeccable wines throughout its range. Vigna Camarato, made exclusively from aglianico, successfully straddles modern thinking on what an "important" wine should be like, with the variety's characteristic broad, minerally warmth. Both red and white Falerno are stylish, with the white *cru* Vigna Caracci having notable depth and substance. There is in addition an elegant, well-balanced rosé, Terre Cerase.

PIETRATORCIA

Established 1993 *Owners* Terra Mia Srl *Production* NA *Vineyard area* 17 acres (7 ha)

Pietratorcia was created by the young members of three long-standing Ischian families with the aim of putting Ischia's wines back on the map. Their initial results have been remarkably successful: the wines have depth, complexity and refinement, and oak, where used, is not allowed to dominate the fruit. The whites, notably Vigne del Cuotto and Vigne di Chignole, both Ischia Bianco Superiore, also have excellent integration.

GROTTA DEL SOLE

Established 1989 *Owners* Martusciello family *Production* 50,000 cases *Vineyard area* 17 acres (7 ha)

Grotta del Sole produces a large range of wines from throughout Campania but its interest lies in reinforcing the image of the area's traditional wines and restoring those fallen from favor—thus it has been the force behind the revival of traditional, tree-trained Asprinio (sparkling as well as still) and has also put much effort into the much-maligned Lacryma Christi del Vesuvio. Unusually, a Piedirosso *passito* is also produced.

CALABRIA

Calabria is one of Italy's most remote regions and one of the slower ones to fulfill its winemaking potential. A coastal plain fringes the mountains, with some good vineyard territory, yet many of its wines remain obscure or are produced in tiny amounts. Practically the only one with an international reputation is Cirò, both red and white Cirò being prime examples of Calabria's indigenous varieties, the red gaglioppo and white greco.

Greco is grown fairly widely and as well as dry wines sometimes makes sweet wines from dried grapes, notably in the southeast tip of Calabria, around the village of Bianco. A local variety, mantonico, is used for similarly styled wines in the same area but Mantonico di Bianco is more overtly sweet and less refined than the tightly knit and well-structured Greco di Bianco.

LIBRANDI

Established 1950 *Owners* Librandi family *Production* 125,000 cases *Vineyard area* 160 acres (65 ha)

In this introspective region the outward-looking attitude of the Librandi family has brought them to prominence. Opinion is divided on whether their top wine is the half-modernist Gravello, from a blend of gaglioppo with 40 percent cabernet sauvignon, or the strictly traditional Duca Sanfelice, exclusively from gaglioppo. Similarly, there are as many fans of their Critone (chardonnay/sauvignon) and the softly attractive rosé Terre Lontane (gaglioppo/cabernet franc) as there are of the classic white, rosé and red Cirò. Le Pasulle is a finely honeyed, rich but not cloying sweet wine made from mantonico.

BASILICATA

Basilicata is a one-grape, one-wine region. Its fortunes depend entirely on aglianico, almost certainly the south's finest variety, and one that already produces excellent wines. However, it almost certainly has the potential for wines of considerably greater distinction once the necessary research into the best clones and so on has been done. The name is believed to derive from *hellenico*, indicating the grape's Greek origins. The wines are initially tannic with firm balancing acidity, full and powerful, minerally and darkly fruity. They are also reputed to have astounding longevity although, since most examples are drunk within ten years, it is hard to confirm this claim.

Vines for Basilicata's one major wine, Aglianico del Vulture, are grown on the cool, east-facing slopes of the volcanic Mount Vulture. Most vineyards are planted high, averaging 1,600–2,000 feet (500–600 m), in much cooler and sometimes wetter conditions than might be expected at a latitude of 41°N.

D'ANGELO

Established 1944 (wines sold in bulk prior) *Owners* D'Angelo family *Production* 16,500 cases *Vineyard area* 60 acres (24 ha) + grapes bought in

The D'Angelo grapes come from some of Mount Vulture's best sites and the estate sets the pace in Basilicata. The *barrique*-aged Canneto is often the talking point but the straight Aglianico del Vulture (aged in large *botti*) can be better balanced and more characterful. There is also a more concentrated, more complex *cru* version, Vigna Caselle. D'Angelo additionally produces a rich white, Vigna dei Pini, from a chardonnay-based blend.

Green shutters keep out the sun in the town of Martina Franca, Puglia.

PATERNOSTER

Established 1925 *Owners* Paternoster family *Production* 10,000–12,500 cases *Vineyard area* 16 acres (6.5 ha)

The Paternoster wines, when on form (which these days happens ever more regularly), excel for attack, structure, density and deep, ripe fruitiness. The selection Aglianico del Vulture Don Anselmo is produced only when the vintage warrants it but the standard Aglianico, made every year, is more classically styled. There is a white wine, Bianco di Corte, from fiano, and a sparkling Moscato.

SARDINIA

For a long time Sardinia's wine fell into two categories: light, fresh, innocuous whites turned out by numerous cooperatives for the tourist masses that flocked to the Costa Smeralda and the other coastal resorts each summer; and heavy reds, usually from the cannonau variety, sometimes oxidized but much appreciated by the population of the island's interior. There are still innocuous whites aplenty but fewer oxidized reds and numerous wines to fill the space between.

Sardinia spent much of its past under Spanish rule and the influence remains in language and many other aspects of life, including wine. Cannonau, its best known red grape, producing warm, broad, often alcoholic reds, most typically in the highlands of the east, is the same as Spain's garnacha (also France's grenache). Carignano, planted only in the southwest of the island, in the area of Sulcis, is Spain's cariñena/mazuelo, and nièddera (also called bovale) is bobal/monastrell. Monica, also red and making lively drinkable wines throughout the island but grown mostly in

Green bottles with red wax caps in the laboratory at Cantine Di Marco, Martina Franca, Puglia.

REGIONAL DOZEN

Aglianico del Vulture
  (D'Angelo)
Amano Primitivo (Mark
  Shannon)
Carignano del Sulcis "Tre
  Torri" (Cantina Sociale di
  Santadi)
Greco del Tufo
  (Mastroberadino)
Montepulciano d'Abruzzo
  "Riparossa" (Dino
  Illuminati)
Primitivo di Manduria
  "Archidamo" (Pervini)
Salice Salentino Rosso Riserva
  "Donna Lisa" (Leone de
  Castris)
Taurasi (Feudi di San
  Gregorio)
Torbato di Alghero "Terre
  Bianche" (Sella & Mosca)
Turriga IGT (Antonio
  Argiolas)
Vermentino di Gallura
  (Capichera)
Vigna del Feudo (Felline)

the broad rolling plains of the south, is of Spanish origin too. Among the white grapes, nuragus grows prolifically, especially in the south, and produces plentiful soft, floral but unexceptional wine. Far more important is vermentino (again of Spanish origin), seen throughout the island but best expressing its lively, peach-like, almost buttery character in the cool hills of the Gallura in the northeast. Torbato, giving firm, creamy, lightly spicy wines, is grown sporadically near Alghero in the northwest and may compete with vermentino for quality but is a difficult grape to handle.

There is a strong local demand for sweet and fortified wines, some of the most interesting being made from malvasia and moscato, while the indigenous white nasco of southern Sardinia is often used this way as well. Vernaccia (another indigene, unrelated to Italy's other vernaccias) produces the island's leading strong wine. Vernaccia di Oristano comes from limestone soil; the casks develop flor and a sort of adapted *solera* system, which is used in its aging. It is no wonder that this strong wine is often compared with sherry, to which it can bear some resemblance.

ARGIOLAS

Established 1938 *Owners* Argiolas & C. SaS *Production* 75,000 cases *Vineyard area* 540 acres (220 ha)

Originally providing bulk wine to other estates, Argiolas started bottling in 1990 and took on the services of Giacomo Tachis, one of the top Italian consultant enologists. The wines are made predominantly from vermentino, nuragus, monica and cannonau and are of fine quality throughout, the top of the range being the *barrique*-aged red Turriga, from cannonau, carignano and others, and the partially *barrique*-aged white Angialis, from nasco and malvasia.

CAPICHERA

Established 1980 *Owners* Ragnedda family *Production* 18,500 cases *Vineyard area* 62 acres + 49 leased (25 + 20 ha)

By concentrating on super-low yields and meticulous care at every stage of production, the Ragnedda brothers have made Capichera far and away the Gallura's best estate. The Vermentina di Gallura is tightly knit, complex and concentrated with clean fruit, a touch of spiciness and good aging potential. A late-harvest, partially barriqued, semi-sweet version is greatly admired but probably not quite as successful. There is also a red wine made from carignano grapes grown in Sulcis.

CHERCHI

Established 1980 *Owner* Giovanni Maria Cherchi *Production* 11,000 cases *Vineyard area* 50 acres (20 ha)

The estate has been in family hands for generations and sold wine in bulk until 1980, after which it rapidly rose to become one of Sardinia's most sought-after names. Cherchi concentrates on Vermentino, which is produced in a restrained, elegant style, especially in the Vermentino di Sardegna Tuvaoes. There is also an unusual red made from cagnulari, a variety apparently found only on this estate.

CONTINI

Established 1898 *Owners* Contini family *Production* c.30,000 cases *Vineyard area* NA

Despite the unfashionability of the style and the poor offerings from much of the competition, Contini has managed to keep the sherry-like Vernaccia di Oristano a live force. The wines, especially the Riservas, have an intense nuttiness with great individuality and complexity. The company has a half-a-dozen or so other wines, mainly from vermentino, cannonau and nièddera.

SANTADI

Established 1960 *Owners* Cooperative (c.300 growers) *Production* 850,000 cases *Vineyard area* 1,235 acres (500 ha)

This cooperative uses Giacomo Tachis as consultant and has created an international reputation for Carignano del Sulcis. The wine comes in several versions including the partially barriqued, well-balanced, juicy Rocca Rubia and the fully barriqued Terre Brune. There are one or two other reds and an interesting group of whites.

SELLA & MOSCA

Established 1899 *Owners* Sella & Mosca SpA *Production* 500,000 cases *Vineyard area* 1,235 acres (500 ha)

Sella & Mosca was founded by two Piedmontese on lands behind Alghero which they reclaimed from marshland. It has been the leading estate of Sardinia, both in size and image, for generations, and has an extensive and ever-growing range of wines, all carefully made and of good style. This is practically the only producer to work consistently with torbato, most notably in the wine Terre Bianche. Anghelu Ruju, sweet, strong and port-like, from partially dried cannonau, is practically the estate's symbol but the more international Marchese di Villamarina (cabernet sauvignon) is also gaining respect.

Sicily

The island of Sicily, at the heart of the Mediterranean, furnished the ancients with the vital triumvirate of life, grain, grape and olive. It has been invaded by practically every power from the Phoenicians on, leaving its inhabitants with very mixed feelings toward authority. Even Garibaldi, in his successful campaign to unify Italy, made his first landing in Sicily.

Landscape and climate

Sicily is separated from the peninsula by a mere slit of water, but is markedly different from southern Italy. It is more savvy, more commercially aware, more forward-thinking, characteristics most probably deriving from the long-standing Marsala trade, which brought dealings with the sophisticated northern European markets.

Certainly Sicily was way ahead of the rest of the south in seeing the need to turn its wine production around. Strangely, after the first heady phase of development there was a lull—with almost a sense of complacency falling on the island—and only in the past few years has there been another rush of improvement.

Temperatures can soar in summer on the low ground, but there are plentiful cool sites in the hills that form the greater part of the island and the source of many of the serious wines. The grape varieties grown, mostly indigenous or quasi-indigenous, are well adapted to the varying conditions and ripen evenly.

Vines and wines

Sicily's master grape is nero d'avola. Although long recognized as the best on the island, only recently have people begun to appreciate just how good it really is. It yields deep color and intensely ripe, blackberry-like fruit with an undernote of brown sugar, and can give high alcohol, too (which makes it a first-class blending wine).

Sicily's other main red grapes are frappato (mainly found in the southeast and often used there to counterbalance nero d'avola), the light-hued nerello mascalese (responsible for the wines from Mount Etna) and perricone, also called pignatello (mainly used in blends).

Sicily produces considerably more white wine than red, however, and the grape seen most widely

A streetside stall in northern Sicily.

is catarratto. It is sometimes disparaged as an uninteresting variety and while it can make wines lacking grace it can also turn out well-structured, well-rounded wines with a good fruit core. More generally appreciated, particularly for its elegant, floral perfumes, is inzolia (sometimes called ansonica). It has a notable presence in most of the eminent Sicilian whites, apart from those based on chardonnay and the wines from Etna, which are made with the extremely localized carricante. Light wines are also made from damaschino and grecanico but neither is seen widely.

Grillo, grown mainly in western Sicily, can develop prodigious amounts of alcohol without

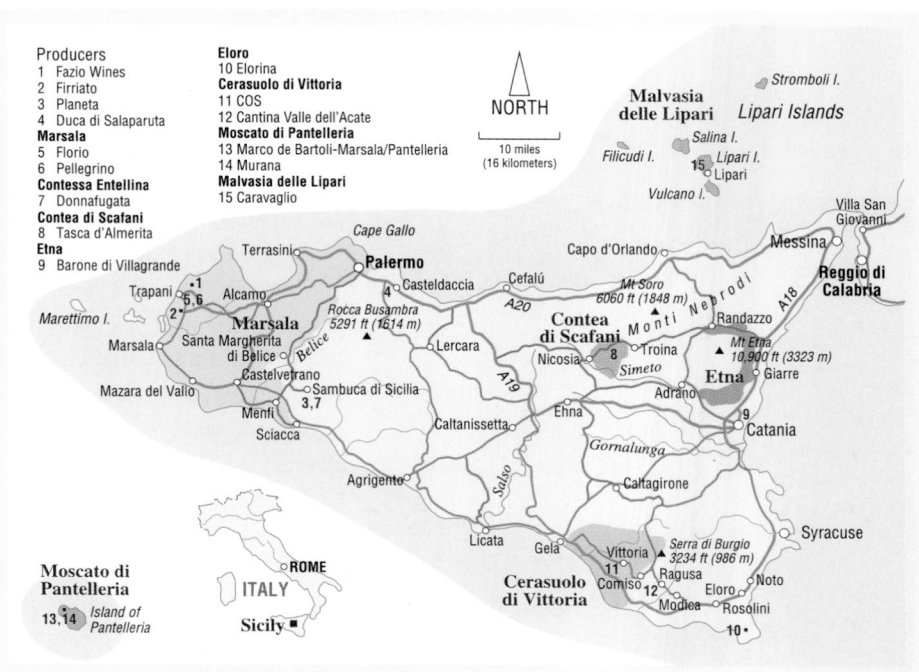

Cleanliness in the cellar is paramount.

losing any of its firm style or broad, nutty flavor and is easily the best grape for Marsala production. Yet plantings remain restricted and most Marsala houses primarily use catarratto. The sweet wines of the Aeolian archipelago to the northeast are made from malvasia and those of the island of Pantelleria to the southwest from zibibbo, the local name for muscat d'alexandria.

Apart from its sweet and heavy wines, Sicily did not worry too much about DOC in the past, producers tending to leave their names to speak for themselves. In the past few years, however, new DOCs have been springing up like mushrooms, mostly around the vineyards of the major producers. There has even been an attempt to create a broad-based regional DOC.

One of the few long-standing delimited areas is that of Alcamo in the northwest, one of the most extensive tracts of vineyard planting, mainly catarratto, anywhere. Few of the wines, if bottled at all, end up as more than innocuous summer quaffing. Things are more positive in the cool slopes of the steep, exposed hills behind Palermo in the north, where several notable producers make wines of character.

In eastern Sicily the most prominent area is around Etna. Vines grow mainly on the volcano's eastern flank, overlooking the sea, at altitudes of 1,300 to 3,300 feet (400–1000 m), with some of the best around 2,000 feet (600 m). Etna's wines once had great pedigree, according to local literature, and legendary longevity, before the area fell into decline. This state of affairs is being reversed but the wines are still patchy.

The southeast corner of the island, the zone of Eloro, was traditionally the hub of blended wine production, mainly from nero d'avola, which still gives some of its richest, fullest fruit here. Eloro

Tending the vines on a chilly morning.

reaches its peak in the subzone of Pachino. A few miles farther west is the zone of Cerasuolo di Vittoria. This wine is made from a convincing blend of nero d'avola and frappato and, although there are several fine examples being made, a definitive style has yet to emerge.

The central south has few vineyards of any worth, most being clustered at the western end in the zones of Menfi, Sambuca di Sicilia and Santa Margherita di Belice.

The cool central hills form additional good vine-growing territory. The zone of Contea di Scafani has been delimited, allowing as many as 15 varietal wines, as well as red, white and rosé blends, a sweet wine and a late-harvest sweet wine, not to mention a "novello"—all clearly planned by the one estate that dominates the area, Tasca d'Almerita, to give the maximum freedom in the development of its wine portfolio.

Marsala

Marsala has been both Sicily's fortune and its downfall. It brought prosperity and renown in the nineteenth century after the British formulated the basic model of the wine and created a market for it; it became a mark of shame in the later twentieth century when it was relegated to the kitchen, its quality far too low for actual drinking, with numerous flavored versions further diminishing its credentials. Now the quality has returned to the point where it can once more sit alongside its erstwhile partners, sherry, port and madeira.

Marsala comes in a broad array of styles. The grapes are grown in western Sicily, predominantly on the plains and lower hills near the coast. Although catarratto is the most widely used grape and grillo the ideal, up to seven varieties (three of them red) may be employed, in any proportions. The classic wine is a light nut-brown but the categories Oro, Ambra and Rubino exist for light golden, amber and ruby-red respectively.

The basic wine is fortified and often sweetened. The sweetening may be done with concentrated must or *cotto* (boiled must), but preferably with *mistella*, fresh must muted with wine alcohol (which both sweetens and fortifies). It is then aged in oak (although some cherrywood barrels are still around), the best wines going through a *solera* system similar to that used for sherry.

The wines are classified according to alcohol, aging and sweetness. Marsala Fine has 17 percent minimum alcohol and at least one year's aging; Marsala Superiore has 18 percent alcohol and two years' aging. With four years' aging it can become Superiore Riserva. Another year brings it to Marsala Vergine (also known as Marsala Soleras) as long as the wine is dry; Marsala Vergine/Soleras Riserva (or Stravecchio) must also be dry and rests for ten years in wood. Fine and Superiore categories may be further classified as Secco, Semisecco and Dolce, depending on level of sweetness.

Some bottles still sport initials such as IP (meaning Italia Particolare), SOM (Superior Old

Marsala), GD (Garibaldi Dolce) and LP (London Particular), a throwback to the old days of the Marsala trade. IP is now used on Marsala Fine only, the others on Marsala Superiore.

The satellite islands

Far off the southwest coast of Sicily, two-thirds of the way to Tunisia, lies the volcanic island of Pantelleria. Fierce winds rip through it, the sun beats down mercilessly on the black soil, and little can grow except capers, which cling spreadeagled to the rock faces, and low-planted vines whose roots can go deep enough to reach moisture. Stone walls form windbreaks and the vines, bush-trained, are often planted in small hollows to give them additional wind protection. Grapes grown are practically all zibibbo and make some of Italy's most delectable sweet wine.

The classic style is *passito*, with the early-ripening, sugar-rich grapes quick-dried on mats in the open air in late August and early September. Some producers use plastic tunnels to protect the grapes from rainfall and damp night air, others trust to luck. Moscato Passito di Pantelleria is redolent of dried fruits and cassata ice-cream; it is mouth-filling and luscious, but never cloying. Moscato di Pantelleria Naturale, lighter and fresher, is made from non-*passito* grapes (although some producers add a small quantity to give it a boost). Both types may be fortified, though this is not common, and the Naturale may be sparkling, which is even less common.

To the northeast of Sicily lie the Aeolian (Lipari) islands, an archipelago of volcanic outcrops. While theoretically wines can be produced throughout, in practice vines are cultivated only on the island of Salina. Trained low, as on Pantelleria, the vines here grow on narrow terraces. The styles produced are similar to those of Pantelleria: Passito and Naturale, both sweet and aromatic, the main difference being that the grape used is the Greek-originating malvasia, which gives broader, peachier characteristics.

Production on both Pantelleria and Salina is low, reflecting a lack of suitable vineyard territory, low yields and the small number of producers prepared to struggle with the labor-intensive conditions. Encouragingly, though, there are signs of an increase, especially on Pantelleria.

Sweet Moscato wines are also theoretically produced near Siracusa (Syracuse) and Noto in southeast Sicily but the quantities made are even more minute than on Pantelleria and Salina.

Grapes thrive on Sicily's cool slopes.

REPRESENTATIVE PRODUCERS

FAZIO WINES

Established 1990s (first vintage 1998) *Owners* Fazio family *Production* 3,000 cases and increasing *Vineyard area* 1,500 acres (600 ha)

This brand-new enterprise, created on an estate that has been in family hands for many generations, is being run with great enthusiasm, clear thinking and attention to detail. It has started strongly, with cleanly varietal müller-thurgau and sauvignon. Other varietals include cabernet sauvignon and merlot. The more traditional wines are grouped under the Torre dei Venti label. The red is exclusively nero d'avola, mid-weight, well-structured and well-woven; the soft, fleshy white is made entirely from inzolia.

FIRRIATO

Established 1982 *Owners* Di Gaetano brothers *Production* 350,000 cases *Vineyard area* 175 acres (70 ha); grapes bought-in from a further 980 acres (400 ha)

Firriato's wines are receiving rapturous reviews yet are still excellent value for money. A primarily Antipodean winemaking team led by Kym Milne gives the wines an international sheen that enables the estate to export almost 75 percent of its production, a range covering 30 labels. The emphasis at the quality end is on indigenous/international blends. The Santagostino red is from nero d'avola and syrah, the white from catarratto and chardonnay; Altavilla della Corte red also uses nero d'avola, this time with cabernet sauvignon, while the white blends grillo with chardonnay.

Vine rows are sited for maximum exposure to sunlight and protection from wind.

PLANETA

Established 1990s (first vintage 1995) *Owners* Planeta family *Production* 62,500 cases *Vineyard area* 500 acres (200 ha) plus 150 acres (60 ha) currently not in use

Founded by three youngsters, Planeta is an Italian phenomenon. In just a few years it has become one of the country's most esteemed estates, with impeccable wines throughout. There are excellent, purely toned, international varietals (cabernet sauvignon, merlot and, especially, chardonnay) but Planeta's skills show more in the blends of (mainly) native with non-native grapes: La Segreta Bianco (grecanico/cataratto/chardonnay), La Segreta Rosso (nero d'avola/merlot), Santa Cecilia (nero d'avola/syrah) and Alastro (grecanico/cataratto).

DUCA DI SALAPARUTA

Established 1824 *Owners* The Region of Sicily *Production* 700,000 cases *Vineyard area* All grapes bought-in

This company is often known by the name of its brand, Corvo, a trademark once synonymous with Sicilian wine. Much of the production is enjoyable, and of reliable if unexceptional quality, with a couple of wines aimed more squarely at the upper levels of the market: Duca d'Enrico, from nero d'avola, and Bianca di Valguarnera, from inzolia. Both are heavily oaked.

Marsala

FLORIO

Established 1833 *Owners* Illva di Saronno *Production* 250,000 cases *Vineyard area* NA

Florio is a long-standing, professionally run Marsala house, making distinguished wines. It lies right on the seafront in the old part of Marsala town and extends over 540,000 square feet (50,000 m^2) of which 40 percent is cellarage. Top of the range is Marsala Vergine Terre Arse, a concentrated dry Marsala with good nuttiness, followed by the lighter-styled Marsala Vergine Baglio Florio. Morsi di Luce is the result of Florio's interests in Pantelleria.

PELLEGRINO

Established 1880 *Owners* Pellegrino family *Production* NA *Vineyard area* 990 acres (400 ha)

Family-run and modern in its thinking, this well-known Marsala house is now concentrating as much on non-fortified wines as on its backbone fortifieds, leading to an extensive range. The most startling wine in the range of this winery is Ruby, a sweet *rubino* (red) Marsala Fine that provokes very mixed reactions.

Contessa Entellina

DONNAFUGATA

Established 1851 *Owners* Rallo family *Production* 62,500 cases *Vineyard area* 260 acres (105 ha)

The Rallo family's roots are in the production of Marsala but with this fourth generation the emphasis has changed to non-fortified wines. The range is broad, led by Tancredi (made from nero d'avola/cabernet sauvignon) and Chiaranda del Merlo (inzolia/ chardonnay) with Contessa Entelina Chardonnay La Fuga and Contessa Entelina Vigna di Gabri (inzolia) top of the support team. There is also attractive Moscato di Pantelleria and a powerful barriqued nero d'avola called Mille e Una Notte.

Contea di Scafani

TASCA D'ALMERITA

Established 1830 *Owners* Tasca family *Production* 210,000 cases *Vineyard area* 545 acres (220 ha)

Tasca d'Almerita is often called by the name of its best-known wine, Regaleali (also the name of the hamlet where it is situated). After the Second World War the estate became Sicily's leader. The wines remain excellently conceived and made, especially the flagship Rosso del Conte (nero d'avola/perricone), full, punchy and spicy, and Nozze d'Oro from tasca (probably sauvignonasse) and inzolia, rich, buttery and herbal. The varietals cabernet sauvignon and chardonnay are both big, concentrated and of impeccable varietal character.

REGIONAL DOZEN

Cerasuolo di Vittoria (COS)
Chardonnay (Planeta)
Frappato (Cantina Valle dell'Acate)
Litra (Abbazia di Sant'Anastasia)
Marsala Superiore Riserva "Vecchioflora" (Vinicola Italiana Florio)
Mille e Una Notte (Tenuta di Donnafugata)
Moscato Passito di Pantelleria "Bukkuram" (Marco de Bartoli)
Nero d'Avola (Settesoli)
Nozze d'Oro (Tasca d'Almerita)
Passito de Pantelleria "Solidea" (D'Ancona)
Santagostino Rosso (Firriato)
Torre dei Venti Rosso (Fazio Wines)

Etna

BARONE DI VILLAGRANDE

Established 1727 *Owners* Nicolosi family *Production* 6,700 cases *Vineyard area* 42 acres (17 ha)

Of all the estates struggling to produce lustrous wines from Etna, that coming closest is Barone di Villagrande with its steep vineyards at 2,000 feet (600 m). So far the firm, slow-developing white, Etna Bianco Superiore, is more successful than the troublesome red from nerello mascalese—troublesome because depth of color is given considerable importance in Italy and this grape naturally gives light-toned wines. From a holding on Salina comes an elegant, balanced Malvasia delle Lipari.

Eloro

ELORINA

Established 1978 *Owners* Cooperative *Production* 16,500 cases *Vineyard area* 620 acres (250 ha)

Originally producing strong and powerful wines for blending, an enlightened directorship has moved the emphasis within the past decade toward quality and bottled output. The wines are improving steadily, with a fresh and clean inzolia-based white and a well-structured red Eloro. The leading wine is Pachino, a massive wine that amply demonstrates the positive attributes of nero d'avola grown so far south (and some of its problems).

Cerasuolo di Vittoria

COS

Established 1980 *Owner* Giusto Occhipinti *Production* 20,000 cases *Vineyard area* 50 acres (20 ha)

In the 1980s Giusto Occhipinti aspired to make Cerasuolo di Vittoria the way he remembered it at his grandparents' table, rather than the dull, often oxidized wine he saw all around him. He gradually built Cos into by far the best Vittoria estate, the model others now try to emulate. Demand now regularly outstrips supply and the range has broadened with varietal inzolia, chardonnay and cabernet and some stunning nero d'avola.

CANTINA VALLE DELL'ACATE

Established 1981 *Owners* Jacono family *Production* 16,500 cases in 1999 (increasing to 50,000 in the next few years) *Vineyard area* 300 acres (120 ha)

In the past few years Valle dell'Acate has turned into one of the most go-ahead estates in Italy, primarily due to the frenetically active Gaetana,

daughter of the owner. The Cerasuolo di Vittoria aims more at fruit than weight compared with its counterparts but is always well balanced, well-integrated and attractive. There is also a very successful varietal Frappato, light and lively. The estate makes a good inzolia and a couple of other wines.

Moscato di Pantelleria

MARCO DE BARTOLI—MARSALA/PANTELLERIA

Established 1978 *Owner* Marco de Bartoli *Production* 5,000 cases *Vineyard area* 60 acres (25 ha)

That Marsala has been restored to a wine of quality is largely due to Marco de Bartoli. Starting with Vecchio Samperi, a "pre-British" (non-fortified) Marsala-type wine based on the grillo grape, and tub-thumping indefatigably for the ultimate in quality, de Bartoli put himself and his area's wines on the world map. He did the same for Pantelleria. Vecchio Samperi 20 Anni (20 years old, from *solera*) is still as fine as ever, as is the Moscato Passito di Pantelleria Bukkuram. Other wines in the range have seen changes over the years but retain their inimitable personality and individuality.

MURANA

Established 1984 *Owner* Salvatore Murana *Production* 3,750 cases *Vineyard area* 18.5 acres (7.5 ha)

Prior to 1984, Salvatore Murana sent all of his grapes, grown on some of Pantelleria's best sites, to the cooperative. When he started to produce his own wines they immediately provoked interest and now his range, made exclusively from zibibbo, gains the highest plaudits. The range is led by the *cru* Moscato Passito di Pantelleria, Martingana, lusciously rich and amazingly intense; followed closely by the *cru* Khamma and the lighter, more aromatic Mueggen. The delicate Turbè is non-*passito*, as is the dryish Gadì.

Malvasia delle Lipari

CARAVAGLIO

Established NA *Owner* Antonino Caravaglio *Production* NA *Vineyard area* NA

A local hero on the island of Salina and an emerging winemaker of note in Sicily, Caravaglio is hardly known beyond. Yet he makes archetypal Malvasia delle Lipari, both Naturale and Passito, and a respectable dry white, Salina Bianco.

Colorful bell peppers gleam on market stalls.

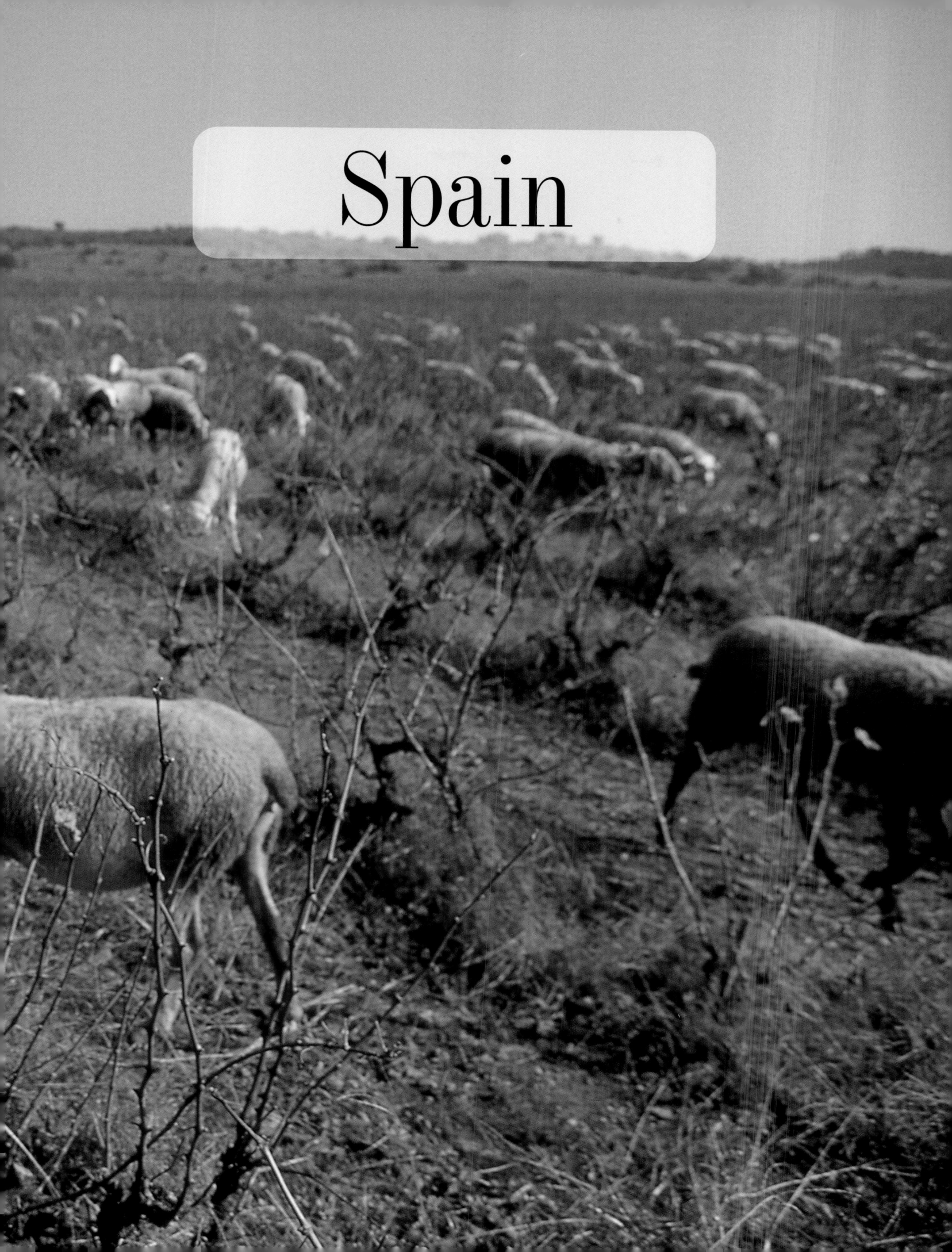

Spain

Spain

John Radford

In Spain at the turn of the twentieth century, wine was an agricultural product, produced alongside potatoes, tomatoes and peppers, and vines were grown to achieve quantity rather than quality. In those days, wine wasn't even regarded as an alcoholic drink—it was just another condiment in the gastronomic "mix" which included other essentials of the Spanish diet and formed the foundation of the *comida*—the midday meal which was the main food and drink event of the day. There were few famous names and only a couple of well-known regions—Jeréz and Rioja. Production often took place in local cooperative bodegas, and this is where the vast majority of the population went, usually on Sunday after church, to pick up their week's supply of wine.

A hundred years on, there are still sleepy neighborhood co-operatives which sell in bulk, and rural areas where food and wine come together with happy anonymity, but these are now in the minority as Spanish wine regions have rediscovered and, in some cases, reinvented themselves to meet something which no-one even knew existed a century ago: the market.

Spanish wine in the year 2001 is a microcosm of the whole vinous world, with frost-cool, fruit-up-front reds from mountain vineyards; classic dry whites with mouthwateringly ripe, citrus-fruit flavors; cava from Catalonia—the world's best-selling sparkling wine after champagne; and the old favorites too: gently oaky, rich and cigar-box-scented rioja and magnificently ancient *oloroso*.

Best of all, much of this success has been and is still being built on Spain's own native grape varieties. Although many of Spain's finest wines are made from such "international" varieties as cabernet sauvignon, merlot and chardonnay, many winemakers have, in the most literal sense, returned to their roots and are producing results which continue to astonish and delight. These include magnificent tempranillo (under its myriad regional nicknames), crisp verdejo in Rueda, peachy albariño and spicy godello in Galicia, the almost-forgotten graciano in Rioja and the formerly disregarded monastrell in the Levant. There are other varieties too, just waiting to be discovered.

Wine in the western world

The history of wine in Spain is the history of wine in western Europe. Long before the foundation of Rome in the eighth century BC, Phoenician traders were shipping wine from the river-ports of Asia Minor (Anatolia) across the Mediterranean in clay amphorae, bartering it along the north coast of Africa and the south coast of Europe for commodities like wheat, olives, sandalwood, perfumes, carpets and whatever else could profitably be traded. The Pillars of Hercules (the ancient name for the promontories flanking the Strait of Gibraltar) were then at the very edge of the world they knew, but that was soon to change when these early traders began to travel further afield, venturing south to do business with the scattered tribes of the west African coast.

Before long it became expedient for them to have a permanent base at the western end of the Mediterranean, and they established the city of Gadier (modern-day Cádiz) around the year 1100 BC. The city grew in importance and wealth at what was then the crossroads of world trade, and migrants from Greece began to arrive. It is not known whether the founders of Gadier or the new inhabitants planted vines in the area around the city (now the area where sherry is produced) but by about 500 BC wine was being made there, based on the wines of the Middle East and the eastern Mediterranean—sweet and naturally strong, as it needed to be to survive rolling sea journeys, a hot climate and inadequately sealed clay jars.

As trade and early civilization spread inland, other areas of what was to become Spain developed their own agriculture, including vineyards and ways of making wine. The basic method of making wine was very simple and still survives today in some country areas: a stone trough was excavated from a hillside as a receptacle for the harvested grapes; these were trodden in it by foot. The cloud of carbon dioxide gas released by the fermentation process blanketed the juice and prevented oxidation and, once the process was complete, a plug was removed from the side of the trough to allow the wine to run off into suitable vessels which would typically have been clay or earthenware jars. These were then left so that fermentation could complete in its own good time and, when the cloud of gas had dissipated, the jars would be topped up to brim-full to provide an airtight seal. This, and the small surface area of the mouth, reduced oxidation and was a reasonably efficient way of keeping the wine drinkable. Moving it about was a different matter, but as most wine was made, sold and drunk locally, this was not a problem. So it was to continue until the arrival of the Romans.

Rome annexed Spain after a long and bloody war with Carthage but was in full control by the end of the third century BC, and it was the Romans who turned winemaking from a cottage industry into a major business. This was because it was becoming prohibitively expensive to transport wine for the occupying legions from Italy. The obvious solution was to make it locally, and this is what the Romans did, even doing some early

Riddling—inverting the bottle and gently shaking it—is a process which dislodges the deposit of sediment in cava, Spain's most famous sparkling wine.

work in researching which vine varieties were best suited to which soil. In this way the primitive local winemaking methods were "industrialized" on a relatively large scale.

The next major influence on the viticulture of Spain was the invasion of the Moors from North Africa in AD 711. Their occupation peaked in the year 929 and then receded southeastwards until they were finally expelled from their last stronghold in Granada in 1492. The intervening years had seen variously prohibition, vineyards turned over to the production of table grapes and even occasional business ventures in which Moorish governors permitted the making of wine for export to Christian-ruled areas of Spain. However, the Moors' major contribution to Spanish viticulture was the introduction of distilling, which happened some time after the year 900 (no-one is quite sure precisely when).

The Moors used the process to obtain the dry extract residue for use in art, design and cosmetics, and the spirit for antiseptic and medicinal purposes, but the winemakers found quite a different use for it. They discovered that the problem of oxidation of wine could be solved by the simple expedient of fortifying it with grape spirit. This preserved the wine's traditional sweetness, increased its alcoholic strength and made it more easily transportable, which was an important consideration with the gradual opening up of export markets.

By the time the Moors left, the fortified wines of southwestern Spain were reckoned the world's finest and were finding their way far across the seas as the age of exploration got under way.

History

ANDALUSIA AND THE CANARY ISLANDS (1492–1790)
In 1587, Sir Martin Frobisher, one of Sir Francis Drake's captains, attacked the Spanish fleet at anchor in the harbor in Cádiz, leaving most of it in flames and allegedly carrying away 2,900 pipes of wine—nearly 2 million bottles in today's measures. Queen Elizabeth's government seized the moment and slapped an excise tax on every bottle before it hit a very thirsty market. Although sack—a sweet fortified wine from the Canary Islands, Madeira, Málaga and elsewhere—had been known in England for many years, the newly arrived bounty of so-called "Sherris-sack" (the Moorish name for the town of Scheris) or Xerez (the old Spanish spelling) was propelled into the lead by its sudden appearance on the English market.

The word "sack" is believed to come from the Spanish *saca*, meaning a withdrawal of wine from the barrel: merchants in Andalusia generally (and Jeréz in particular) issued invoices listing the *sacas* made by their customers and, since the major export market was England, this may have been anglicized as "sack."

Grand architecture and an expanding wine industry were two of the legacies of the Roman occupation in Spain.

Earthenware containers are still used for fermenting the grapes in some parts of Spain.

The other winemaking regions of Andalusia tended to follow the style; indeed, the Condado de Huelva and Montilla-Moriles willingly supplied the Jeréz region with their wines when it fell short during the boom years. Málaga weighed in with its own style of wine, fortified during fermentation to give a rich, sweet style which carved its own niche in export markets.

Further south, the Canary Islands were an important staging-post for ships travelling southeast to the expanding colonies of the East Indies and southwest to South America. Canary-sack was a lightly fortified sweet wine second only in popularity to "sherris" for much of the fifteenth and sixteenth centuries.

THE INDUSTRIALISTS (1790–1900)

Rioja, already the best-developed region producing non-fortified wines in Spain, led the way to a more organized approach to winemaking. In 1790, the Real Sociedad Económica de Cosecheros de la Rioja Castellana was formed—a successor to the mediæval guilds and protection societies and a forerunner of today's Consejos Reguladores. The society sought to protect the status and integrity of Spanish wines as well as looking after the growers' interests in markets at home and abroad.

In those days Bordeaux was every (non-fortified) winemaker's rôle-model in terms of technology, quality control and export success and forward-thinking landowners and wine-makers from Spain were regular visitors to France, anxious to learn its secrets. One early pioneer was Manuel Quintano who, around 1800, experimented with Bordeaux methods and 60-gallon (227-l) *barricas* (barrels) at his family vineyard in Labastida. His wines were successful and an export consignment to Cuba showed how much improved the wine could become in well-made, watertight, new-oak barrels. However, this proved to be a false start. *Barricas* were deemed to be too expensive and the winemaking methods too "foreign" for the traditionalists of the region, who gave Quintano the cold shoulder and decided to stick to their artesanal methods.

The great leap forward in winemaking came later. Political turmoil in Spain around the turn of the nineteenth century sent more radical thinkers abroad, and they continued the tradition of visiting Bordeaux to develop their knowledge of wine before returning home to Spain. Two of these were Camilo Hurtado de Améxaga (later Marqués de Riscal) and Luciano de Murrieta (later Marqués de Murrieta), pioneers who brought Bordeaux methods to Rioja, with Murrieta making the first of what we might recognize as "modern" rioja in Logroño in 1850 and Riscal founding a new vineyard in Elciego in 1856. Riscal established the first new Bordeaux-style bodega in 1859 and Murrieta bought the estate which now bears his name in 1870.

Old methods die hard, however. The thing that eventually changed the public mind was, of course, cash. *Viñeros* who refused to invest in the new oak casks and *bodegueros* who wouldn't sell the new wines changed their minds when they saw how profitable the new-style bodegas were once they had become established. So at the beginning of the nineteenth century the wine industry was well developed, with a good export trade to Spanish colonies in the Americas.

Then, in the 1860s, French vineyards were devastated by the insect pest phylloxera, and the steady trickle of export wine to France became a flood. But the French, naturally enough, wanted wines in the French style and of a similar standard, and those bodegas which could supply wines made in the Bordelais manner and aged in good, sound casks, got the best prices. Some few refused to change and, indeed, there are still growers in Rioja today who ferment in the old way and make *joven* wines for immediate sale, but the game was, effectively, up for the old guard and "modern" rioja became a fact of life. The wine business had become an industry in the fullest sense of the word and rioja has never since lost its lead in the world market for Spanish wine.

The other major development in Spanish wine in the nineteenth century was cava (Spanish for an underground cellar, as opposed to bodega, an above-ground cellar), the sparkling wine which was born in the shadow of champagne and now challenges it for world market share. Many winemakers, especially in northern and highland regions of Spain, had made fizzy wine by design or accident (sometimes with disastrous results) for years, but Madame Clicquot in Reims had shown by 1810 that you could take this unstable, volatile stuff and turn it into a consistent, world-class wine. That was the challenge, and seven major winemakers (nicknamed the "Seven Greek Sages")

met every Sunday after church in St Sadurní d'Anoya to discuss their experiments. Most ended in failure. Finally, Josep Raventós, head of a company called Codorníu, realized that somebody had to bite the bullet and get into massive new investment in winery equipment and technology. New vats, new fermentation techniques and what seemed to be fabulously expensive maturation and bottling régimes would be needed to produce commercial quantities of what was cheerfully nicknamed *xampán*. His gamble paid off, and the first bottle of cava went into production in 1872. Codorníu is now one of the biggest and most successful companies in the wine world.

THE MODERNIZERS (1900–1950)

Despite the devastation wrought by phylloxera, which continued well into the twentieth century, political turmoil at home and disastrous campaigns abroad, the Spanish wine industry flourished. In Catalonia, the success of cava raised the profile of the region generally and the prospect of radical change and republican sentiments made one of its cities, Barcelona, one of Europe's great cultural capitals. New bodegas were built, often in the flamboyant style of the eccentric architect Gaudí, and growers and winemakers felt strongly that they were now at the forefront of a new technology and a new interest.

As well, laws to ensure quality control and common standards were starting to be organized. Although the classification of DO (Denominación de Origen) was still some years away, the first Consejos Reguladores (Regulating Councils) were established. These consisted of a representative from each wine-producing company within a region as well as technical staff (chemists and œnologists), civil servants and representatives from local government. Their rôle was to oversee regulations according to planting, grafting, levels of production, methods of winemaking and aging of wines, and to take a lead in promotion. Rioja was the first region to establish a Consejo, in 1926, and Alella, Cariñena and Tarragona then followed. In addition, Consejos were established for some of the old-stagers: Montilla-Moriles and Jeréz in 1933 and Málaga in 1937.

Sadly, the flair and enthusiasm of the first quarter of the twentieth century were immolated in the bloodshed of the Spanish Civil War from 1936–38, and those companies which survived at all found that the rest of the world was involved in a war of its own and had little interest in wine.

THE "NEW-WAVERS" OF CATALONIA (1950–70)

By 1950, after a period of getting the cold shoulder from post-war Europe over General Franco's relationship with the defeated Axis powers, Spain's strategic importance brought it back into the western fold by 1950 and the wine trade was back in business once again.

By the end of the 1950s, however, it had become apparent that with a few exceptions most Spanish wine was regarded as cheap and cheerful plonk with few, if any, pretensions to quality. Rioja, sherry and valdepeñas had something of a following but the names of almost all other wine-producing regions were virtually unknown. It became apparent that Spain wasn't going to achieve anything until it improved its winemaking methods. The barrels and concrete vats which had revolutionized production 90 years previously were now hopelessly out of date but, to replace them, yet another round of massive change and enormous investment was going to be necessary.

Pioneers, as ever, came to the forefront. In Penedès it was the Torres family, the first to install stainless-steel fermentation technology; in Rioja it was Enrique Forner at Marqués de Cáceres; in Rueda it was "Paco" Hurtado de Amézaga, descendant of the legendary Marqués de Riscal. And there were others. No less than 15 DO regions were formally established in the two decades to

Below: *Wine (particularly sherry), is a favorite accompaniment to cured* jamón *(ham).*

Bottom: *Casks are sometimes used to age traditional wines after fermentation.*

Stainless steel fermentation tanks such as these are widely used although some wine producers still prefer traditional oak barrels.

1970, and exports boomed, especially with Spain's development as a tourist destination. By 1970, quite a few new names had emerged to lead the way in a "new wave" of Spanish winemaking, but much of the work was being done in one region: Catalonia. Here, a new region-wide Denominacion de Origen (DO Catalunya) was introduced in 1999 to allow wines from all the Catalan DOs to blend their wines together where necessary and simply carry the regional name, but this is unlikely to make a difference until well into the new century.

THE CHANGING FACE OF SPAIN (1980–2000)

In almost every century, most of Spain's best wines are the result of the unpredictable activities of a few people. One of the earliest mavericks was Eloy Lecanda who, in the mid 1870s, established a Bordeaux-style vineyard at the Pago de St Cecilia y Carrascal, an estate which is known today by the shorter name of Vega Sicilia. He planted cabernet sauvignon and merlot and discovered that they mixed well with the local grape, the tinto fino or tinto del país (tempranillo). However, it was to be more than a century before the estate's wines were gathered into the DO Ribera del Duero, in 1982. Since then, sales from the Duero district—and Castilla-León generally—have gone ballistic.

White wines—an area of wine-producing for which Spain was not widely known—came to the fore in the last 20 years of the twentieth century. Riscal had shown the maverick tendency with new technology in Rueda (Castilla-Léon) and it was followed by the Marqués de Griñón, the Sanz family and others. This was also the time when Galicia started to achieve its potential: European cash was made available to help build co-operative

wineries and the low-yielding but fabulously fresh, peachy and delicious albariño grape began to make its presence felt as growers and winemakers dared to make wines which, to be commercially viable, would have to sell at previously unthinkable prices. It worked. These were years of great development for Spanish wines and set the pattern for what has become Galicia's wine renaissance.

Landscape and climate

Spain is the third most mountainous country in Europe, after Albania and Switzerland, and this highland characteristic brings with it a wealth of microclimates and individual parcels of *terreño* (what the French call *terroir*) which make for wines of particular individuality.

In the north, the climate is dictated by the Cordillera Cantábrica, a series of mountain ranges which divide the vast upland plateau of central Spain from the north and northwest. This region is subject to the winds and rain coming from the Bay of Biscay and is known as "green Spain" because of its verdant pastures and woodlands. By Spanish standards, this is a cool, wet area which favors the growing of grapes for white wines. The great rivers which drain this area are the Ebro, which flows into the sea just south of Tarragona in Catalonia, and the Duero, which flows westwards into Portugal and out into the Atlantic at Oporto. These two rivers water more than, perhaps, half of Spain's finest vineyards.

Immediately south of the Cordillera Cantábrica are the areas which have achieved most in the export market for Spain over the last century and more. Rioja and Navarra straddle the Ebro on the south side of the mountains, where the clay soil is rich in chalk and iron in the highlands and the climate is continental, with long, hot summers and short, very cold winters with most rainfall concentrated in the spring and autumn. Lowland areas here tend to be alluvial with sandy soil. On the west side, the vineyards of Ribera del Duero are further south but higher in altitude, mitigating the effects of the sun on the vines with cooler night-time temperatures.

South to Madrid and beyond lies the mostly flat plateau of central Spain, averaging 2,000 feet (600 m) above sea level, surrounded by a ring of mountain ranges and with a climate which is extreme continental—over 100°F (38°C) in the summer and as low as –4°F (–20°C) in the winter. The wind slices across the great plain of La Mancha with a vengeance in season, hence the

famous windmills of the region, so ineffectually attacked by the legendary Don Quixote.

The eastern seaboard climate is warm and humid, with frequent rains along the coast and the lowland vineyards in Catalonia, hotter and drier in the Levant. Higher altitudes inland from the coast provide benefits for growing finer grapes, even this far south—as the land rises, temperature falls, and although highland vineyards get all the ripening heat of of the sun, they have a wider temperature range between day and night. This "rests" the vines so that the nutrients are still in the soil the next morning, when they can feed the grapes rather than the vine. Soils here are limestone-based, providing the basic carbonate which under-pins the world's greatest vineyards. The highlands of Catalonia provide one of the best hot-climate bedrocks for vines—schistose comes to the surface in Priorato, Alella and parts of the high Penedès—and its fragmented structure holds water and provides a refuge and a drink for the vine roots in the arid heat of summer.

Andalusia is the most consistently hot of all the regions, with a semi-arid climate and rivers which habitually dry up in the summer. It includes Jeréz (sherry country) and thus some of the oldest vineyards in Europe. Its saving grace (in wine-making terms) is the astonishingly chalk-rich soil of the province of Cádiz. This has provided the unique conditions for the production of a wine which has, at a conservative estimate, been made continuously for some 2,500 years. The grape is the palomino, grown in the "golden triangle" between Jeréz de La Frontera and the coastal towns of Puerto de St María and Sanlúcar de Barrameda. Other grapes grown in the Jeréz region include the pedro ximénez (PX) and the moscatel, which are used in sweetening wines but also may be found on their own. Typically, moscatel will have been fortified during fermentation to provide a naturally rich, sweet wine, and PX will have been dried in the sun before fermentation, providing a wine of intense color, richness and sweetness. Elsewhere, clay, chalk and limestone dominate the soils while traditional super-ripe grapes and high-strength wines denote the viticultural style.

The Canaries, 60 miles (100 km) off the coast of northwest Africa, have been under the control of Spain since the fifteenth century. There are seven islands in the archipelago. Of these,

The countryside around Catalonia is an important source of cork production.

Roses planted at the end of a row of vines
act as a biological control against mildew.

Lanzarote has the most dramatic landscape of any vineyard area in the world. The soil is made up of black volcanic ash and the vines are planted in hollows scooped out of it and surrounded with low walls to protect them from the wind. Red and white wines are made here, including sweet malvasía and moscatel from sun-dried grapes in the old Canary-sack style.

Wines: sherry, rioja and cava

SHERRY

Sherry owes its early prominence as an export wine to the *solera* system, in which wines from the new vintage are introduced into a *criadera*, or "nursery," which is already partly filled with wine from the previous vintage. The new wine takes on the characteristics of the old and this mixture is, in turn, passed to another, older *criadera* in the same way. Eventually, the wine passes into the *solera*—the final row of barrels—from which the *saca* will be withdrawn. The end result is a wine of impressive consistency, with a maturity out of all proportion to its actual age—the result of this careful fractional blending process. The ancient winemakers of the eastern Mediterranean used a similar system which they called *nama*—the process of leaving some of the last year's wine in the jar when adding the new vintage. The *solera* system replaced it when good-quality wooden barrels started to become readily available.

Jeréz/Xérès/Sherry y Manzanilla de Sanlúcar de Barrameda is the long-winded official name for the sherry denomination of origin, "copyrighting" the wine's name in Spanish, French and English as well as encompassing the *manzanilla* wines. Sherry has been through a very difficult time in the closing years of the twentieth century, partly thanks to changing fashions and partly, it has to be said, as a result of complacency in the industry, but its innate quality and the *solera* system now make it one of the world's best-value fine wines. There are several different styles of sherry:

Fino is one of the palest and driest of wines, lightly fortified (after complete natural fermentation) to 16–17 percent abv (alcohol by volume).

The grapes will have grown a thin film of yeast called *flor* during their time in the bodega which gives the wine a fresh, yeasty edge, most prominent in the *manzanillas* from Sanlúcar, where it is drunk as a table wine with seafood.

Amontillados are wines which started out as *finos* but which have been allowed to age for up to ten or fifteen years or longer. These may achieve anything up to 18 percent abv or even more, and have a long, dry, powerful style which never ventures into richness. Sadly, it's also a term used by mass-market blenders to denote a style of "medium" sherry—a term which is unlikely to appeal to many.

Olorosos are wines which have not been allowed to grow a yeasty *flor* coating and will have been fortified to 18 percent abv. They have a rich (though not sweet), nutty character and can age for many decades.

Palo cortado is an unusual type of wine which starts out growing *flor*, like a *fino*, but then loses it and develops in the *oloroso* style. These are some of the finest wines of Jeréz—rich, complex and long-lived.

Cream and *Pale cream* are blended wines for the mass market, usually with an *oloroso* base (pale creams are likely to have a *fino* base), mixed with sweetening wines and tailored to the needs of the export customer. The best of them may be very good. The rest tend to be very dull.

RIOJA

The winemaking district of Rioja is Spain's only DOC (Denominación de Origen Calificada), an august upper-level quality category. The wine of the same name is made mainly in Rioja but also in Alava (in the Basque Country) to the north—known as Rioja Alavesa—and in Navarra to the east. The highlands of La Rioja form the Rioja Alta and the lowlands and the vineyards in Navarra are known as Rioja Baja. Of these three subregions, the best grapes—mainly tempranillo and graciano—tend to come from the cooler Alta and Alavesa areas, with mazuelo and garnacha varieties coming from the warmer, drier Rioja Baja. However, most famous-name wines will consist of a mixture of most or all of these varieties.

The wine became famous by being aged in oak—typically new American oak, although smaller-pored French oak is now widely used—and its greatest examples are the old *reservas* which, at their best, have a wonderful mellow softness and age with consummate grace. In the

Alavesa region, particularly, however, they often make red wines from pure tempranillo and drink them young and fresh, in the old-fashioned style. These are delicious wines and only the ever-rising price of grapes prohibits their availability.

White and pink rioja is also made, of which the white, made usually from viura (macabeo) and malvasíá riojana grapes, is the most prominent. Traditional old whites are given a similar aging process to the reds and result in very rich, spicy, oaky and aromatic wines which have a small but very enthusiastic market. More modern styles may have just a touch of oak or none at all to maintain the full freshness of the grape.

CAVA

Cava's birthplace was Catalonia and today most of it still comes from the area around St Sadurní d'Anoia in the province of Barcelona, although there are also licensed cava areas in Rioja, Navarra and Valencia. When the denomination of origin (DO) laws began to be formalized in 1986 many production areas were excluded, and by 1991 when the process was completed more than 90 percent of all cava vineyards were to be found in Catalonia. This caused a certain amount of anger in regions which had made sparkling wines and called them cava until this point. However, these problems were largely solved by the local Consejos Reguladores formulating their own DO regulations for what they now called "*vino espumoso*" according to their own requirements.

Traditional cava continues to be made from any or all of the major three Catalan grape varieties: parellada, macabeo (viura) and xarel-lo. Although chardonnay has been planted in the area for more than a century, debate still continues as to whether it is an appropriate grape for cava. Of the "big two" cava producers, Codorníu thinks it is, whilst Freixenet thinks it isn't. Although chardonnay is widely used, the majority of producers stick to the main three local varieties.

The wine must be made by the *método tradicional* and must spend nine months on its lees before it can be released. Wines with at least 30 months' maturity can call themselves *gran reserva* although most don't, perhaps because it invites confusion with red wines.

What cava producers do particularly well is to make wines which are low enough in acid but sufficiently balanced to drink splendidly whilst young and fresh, at a modest price, and these are what dominate the market. There is, however, a small but increasing trend towards older, richer, more complex wines and, having conquered the supermarket trade in the twentieth century, this may be cava's goal for the twenty-first.

Wine law

Spain's wine laws fall into the standard European pattern, although a great deal of work is done outside the system and new, regional wines and maverick winemakers are threatening the whole edifice of wine regulation, not just in Spain but throughout Europe.

QUALITY WINES

The letters VCPRD stand for Vinos de Calidad Producido en Regiones Determinades as defined by the European Commission. (QWPSR, the English equivalent, stands for "Quality Wine Produced in Specific Regions.") Each region has a Consejo Regulador (Regulating Council) which includes members from the producing bodegas, local government and technicians. This council decides on what type of grapes can be planted, where they can be planted and aging methods. Spain had 57 accredited VCPRD wines at the beginning of the year 2000. Within this group, there are two further identifying categories:

The clay and limestone of Rioja's vineyards combine to form good growing conditions for the popular tempranillo grape.

Above: *The making of cava involves inverting and then freezing the neck of the bottle to remove the deposit.*

Top: *Widely spaced vineyards cut down on the amount of maintenance time needed.*

Denominación de Origen (DO) This term means "Denomination of Origin" and identifies the wine as a genuine product of its area under the control of the Consejo Regulador. It is equivalent to the AOC (Appellation d'Origine Contrôlée) in France and the DOC (Denominazione de Origine Controllata) in Italy. There are 56 of these in Spain.

Denominación de Origen Calificada (DOCa) There is still disagreement over exactly what this term means. Literally, it translates as "Qualified Denomination of Origin," and is theoretically equivalent to the Italian DOCG (Denominazione de Origine Controllata e Garantita). It is an upper-level grade, supposedly offering an additional guarantee of quality to the customer. Rioja was elevated to this grade in 1991 but, so far, no other wine has followed in its footsteps, probably because no-one could agree what the DOCa actually meant. Although arguments still rage, there has been a palpable improvement in the general quality of the wines since then.

TABLE WINES
This category divides into four:

Vino de la Tierra (VdlT), or "country wines," are equivalent to the French Vins de Pays de Zone and in Spain the term applies to wines with sufficient local style and character to make them individual. Controls are much less stringent than for DO wines and they are administered by the local office of the Ministry of Agriculture. There are about two dozen such areas and many are actively seeking promotion to DO status.

Vino Comarcal (VC), or "local wines," are made in areas larger than a VdlT zone (equivalent to the French Vins de Pays de Région and Vins de Pays de Département) and subject to more relaxed administration. There are about two dozen of these, the most prominent of which are seeking promotion to DO status.

Vino de Mesa de... (VdM de), or "table wine from ..." is a legal nicety to allow the mavericks to put a vintage date on their wines. For example, the Yllera family call their wine (a red wine made in a white-wine area) VdM de Castilla-León.

Vino de Mesa (VdM) is simply "table wine." It may only specify what color it is and that it is made in Spain. No regional grape variety or vintage qualifications are permitted.

Table-wine areas tipped for promotion in the early years of this century include:

VdlT Manchuela, a large area in eastern Castilla-La Mancha, contiguous with the DO Utiel Requena; it has had a provisional DO for many years. The main wines are reds made from bobal with some cencibel (the local word for tempranillo) and monastrell.

VdlT Valdejalón, in the west of Zaragoza (Aragón) has always been bulk-wine country but, as ever, there are those maverick bodegas trying to do something better, mainly around the north-western town of Moncayo.

VC Ribera de Arlanza is a region in Burgos (Castilla-León) which formerly shipped large quantities of wine to neighboring DO zones in the days when it was legal to do so. In the search for a new rôle, ambitious bodegas are planting tinto del país and lobbying for promotion.

VdM Medina del Campo is the name currently being used by red wine producers in the Rueda area, where the DO is for white wines only. It is expected to be admitted to DO status in due course. The production area is the same as that for Rueda, and the wines are mainly made from tinto fino (tempranillo).

AGING REGULATIONS

Spain has national regulations about the names which describe how wines are aged, particularly in oak casks. Some winemakers use American oak, some French, some new, some old, so the epithets are a bit of a movable feast for a creative winemaker. The vintage in Spain normally takes place in September/October.

Joven ("young") means the wine has had less than six months in oak casks, or none at all. These wines may be sold immediately after the vintage.

Crianza is one of those Spanish words thatis not easily translated. It comes from *criadera,* meaning "nursery," and it means that the wine has been to "nursery school" in terms of aging. In other words, it's had the minimum—usually six months in oak casks—"education" or "breeding."

White and pink *crianza* wines must spend one year in the bodega and may be sold on the first day of the following year (about 15 months after the vintage). Red *crianza* wines must spend two years in the bodega and may be sold on January 1 of their third year (about two years and three months after the vintage). Certain regions (including Rioja and Ribera del Duero) insist on a minimum 12 months in oak within this aging period.

White and pink *reserva* wines must spend six months in oak and may be sold on January 1 of their third year (i.e., about two years and three months after the vintage). These are quite rare. Red *reserva* wines must spend three years in the bodega, of which at least one must be in oak and at least one must be in bottle. They may be released on January 1 of their fourth year (i.e., about three years and three months after the vintage). Many more traditional houses exceed this minimum.

Gran reserva wines must spend six months in oak and may be sold on January 1 of their fourth year (i.e., about three years and three months after the vintage). These are very rare. Red *gran reserva* wines must spend a minimum of two years in oak and three years in bottle and may be released in their sixth year (i.e., about five years and three months after the vintage). Most of the greatest wines far exceed this minimum.

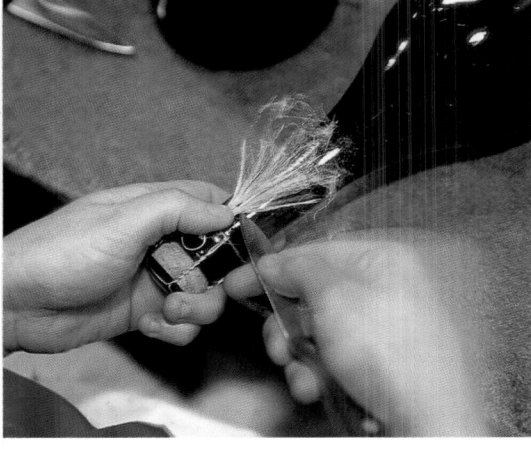

Below: *Some processes are still done by hand: a decorative tassel is added to a cava bottle.*

Bottom: *Once the deposit is removed, cava bottles are topped up before being corked.*

GALICIA AND THE BASQUE COUNTRY

Rías Baixas

Specialized hand tools are still needed for a variety of tasks in the wine trade.

Grapes for making still red wines are picked later in the year than white varieties.

Galicia is close to Portugal and separated from its nearest Spanish neighbor, Castilla-León, by mountains. Although in the past its wines have shared an affinity with vinho verde, nowadays new winemaking techniques and an enthusiasm for older native grape varieties have resulted in its own distinctive wine styles.

There are five DO zones—Rías Baixas, Ribeiro, Ribiera Sacra, Valdeorras and Monterrei (the most recent)—and the best wines in all of them are the whites, made from the albariño and the godello. At the eastern end of the region, the northern Basque provinces of Vizcaya (Bizkaia in Basque) and Guetaria (Getaria) on the coast of the Bay of Biscay produce a very small amount of a unique wine called chacolí (txakoli). There are two DOs—Chacolí de Vizcaya and Chacolí de Guetaria.

The peachy, fresh, crisp albariño grape put Rías Baixas on the vinous map, after growers and winemakers bit the bullet of lower production in return for better wines. There are suggestions that this is indeed the riesling of Germany, brought by monks establishing monasteries along the pilgrim route of the Camino de Santiago, but these have never been proved, although there are strong similarities. The wines from here vie with those of Rueda for the title of the best whites of Spain.

MARTÍN CÓDAX

Established 1986 *Owners* Local shareholders *Production* 11,000 cases *Vineyard area* 395 acres (160 ha)

Named after the man who first wrote music on paper, this is a smart new winery making a wine which is arguably the most popular on its home patch, as well being one of the best of its kind. Made only from the albariño grape, the wines are of excellent quality. The range includes the basic Martín Códax—a single-vineyard wine called Burgáns, Gallaecia, a late-harvest version, and Organistrum, a barrel-fermented wine with three months on the lees. Best wines: the entire range.

FILLABOA

Established 1988 *Owners* Private shareholders *Production* 28,000 cases *Vineyard area* 69 acres (28 ha)

This is a very attractive vineyard on a small private *granja* (estate) with the vines trained on the *silvo* system—a semi-pergola style with wires strung between small monoliths of the lovely pink, quartz-flecked granite which underpins most of the best vineyards in the Condado del Tea district of Rías Baixas. Kiwi-fruit was initially planted to provide an early income while waiting for the vines to mature. The wine is pure albariño and is one of the few wines of its type which ages well in the bottle. Best wine: albariño.

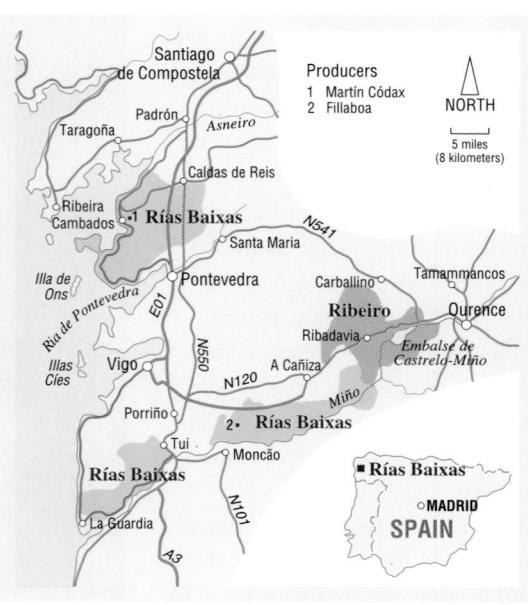

Other Galician Regions

Ribeiro

Wines have been made here since antiquity and exported for at least two centuries, although little of note happened in recent history until the 1990s when the giant local co-op led the way in new-style wines and the private sector followed suit. The best wines are whites made from godello—second only to the albariño in quality—and treixadura. New investment has made this a region to watch.

A. PORTELA

Established 1987 *Owners* Antonio González Pousa and Agustín Formigó Raña *Production* 25,000 cases *Vineyard area* 20 acres (8 ha)

The bulk of this bodega's production is a wine called Señorío de Beade, made from 40 percent jeréz (palomino), a grape which harks back to the days when the Franco régime would buy surplus wine from the growers for distillation, encouraging them to plant the highest-yielding varieties regardless of quality. However, the other 60 percent is made up of equal parts treixadura, torrontés and godello, all of which (especially the last) have considerable claims to quality. There's also a red under the same label made from caíño, ferrón and sousón. Best wines: Primacia de Beade (treixadura).

Ribeira Sacra

Possibly the most stunningly beautiful area in Spain, Ribeira Sacra sits around the gorge of the Rivers Sil and Miño and features incredibly steep slate-based vineyard slopes as well as historic monastic ruins—hence its name of "sacred valley." The best wines are very good but few, with great albariño whites and promising mencía reds.

MOURE

Established 1980 *Owners* Private shareholders *Production* 22,000 cases *Vineyard area* 15 acres (6 ha)

This is surely the most attractive part of Spain, and Adegas Moure, with its immaculately terraced vineyards, is situated in arguably its loveliest spot, high on the steep banks of the River Miño. In the summer José-Manuel Moure takes his guests to the top of the hill (there is a very convenient road) and serves a light lunch with his own albariño overlooking the bend in the river. He makes three wines under the Abadia da Cova label: the white albariño and two reds from the mencía, one *joven* and one *crianza*. Best wines: all are excellent.

Valdeorras

It's been around for a long time but is still waiting to achieve its full potential. One or two bodegas are working hard to establish the region as a center for quality white wines made from the godello and reds from the mencía, but much of the rest is unexciting.

A. TAPADA

Established 1989 *Owners* Local shareholders *Production* 7,500 cases *Vineyard area* 25 acres (10 ha)

This is a very sharp, state-of-the-art winery which is surrounded by its own small estate of vineyards. There are two wines, both called Guitian, one *joven* and one barrel-fermented with six months on the lees. This is probably the most expensive wine from Valdeorras. It is also most probably the best. Best wines: both Guitians.

Monterrei

This is a tiny area with a handful of producers making mainly unexceptional, bland wines from the palomino grape. However, there are some few quality white wines, made from the doña blanca and verdello. Red wines are made mainly from mencía and have yet to make their mark.

GARGALO

Established 1998 *Owners* Private shareholders *Production* 17,500 cases *Vineyard area* 49 acres (20 ha)

This is a new enterprise in this slowly emerging region. Winemaker Mónica Carballo Coede makes a white wine from treixadura, godello and doña blanca and a red from tempranillo, mencía and a little bastardo. It's too soon yet to say what is achievable here, but early results are promising. Best wine: Terra de Gargalo white.

The tempranillo grape, grown widely, is used in many of Spain's most famous wines.

REGIONAL DOZEN

Abadia da Cova Albariño, Moure
Albariño, Martín Códax
Fillaboa Albariño, Fillaboa
Guitian, A. Tapada
Lagar de Cervera Albariño, Lagar de Fornelos
Señorío de Otxaran, Virgen de l'Orea
Terra do Gargalo, Gargalo
Txomin Etxaniz
Valdamor Albariño, Valdamor
Vilerma
Viña Godeval, Godeval
Viña Mein

After riddling, the sediment in méthode champenoise *wines is frozen in the neck of the bottle in order to disgorge it.*

Ribera del Duero

The DO Ribera del Duero was awarded in 1982, 118 years after Vega Sicilia, its most famous bodega, was founded, but most of the modern bodegas were established in the twentieth century and it was only after a prolonged campaign that the classification followed. Progress was very swift after that and there has been massive development. Only red and pink wines are made within the DO. The major grape is the tinto fino (tinto del país/tempranillo) and some villages (mostly those who've been doing it for 100 years or more) are permitted to grow cabernet sauvignon. The wines are characterized by a soft, "summer-fruit" character and crisp, green tannins. They are splendid (if expensive) when made *joven* but some of the best wines of the region are the *crianzas*. *Reservas* tend to be a little heavy on the oak except in good years and only a few bodegas (such as Vega Sicilia) can make a really good *gran reserva*.

BODEGAS AALTO

Established 1999 *Owners* Mariano García, Javier Zaccagnini, private investors *Production* NA *Vineyard area* 91 acres (37 ha)

This is where Mariano García went after leaving Vega Sicilia, teaming up with Javier Zaccagnini, who used to be the director of the Consejo Regulador, and backed by a business group. Although they have no permanent bodega yet, they have ambitions to make wine up to the standards formerly associated with García. The company has

bought 90 acres (37 ha) of prime vineyard land in Quintanilla de Arriba and on the outskirts of Pesquera, and they plan to extend this to 150 acres (60 ha), although no wine will be made under the Aalto name until the vines are ten years old. In the meantime, they plan to buy grapes from old vines, establish the name and find a permanent home.

DEHESA DE LOS CANÓNIGOS

Established 1989 *Owners* Sanz family *Production* 15,000 cases *Vineyard area* 153 acres (62 ha)

This bodega (formerly the property of the Church), with its half-timbers and white paint, has a slightly Tyrolean look to it and is very different from the surrounding buildings in this, one of Ribera del Duero's finest villages. It grows tinto fino (tempranillo), cabernet sauvignon and a little albillo—a throwback to the old days of this area when a little white grape was always blended into the red to lift the color. The wine is simply called Dehesa de los Canónigos and made *crianza* or *reserva* according to the quality of the year and the development of the wine. It is one of the best of the region. Best wine: Dehesa de los Canónigos.

ALEJÁNDRO FERNÁNDEZ TINTO PESQUERA

Established 1972 *Owners* Fernández family *Production* 50,000 cases *Vineyard area* 494 acres (200 ha)

The great American wine pundit, Robert Parker, gave Pesquera a great review and there's no doubt that Pesquera has consistently achieved top quality even through some fairly patchy vintages. The company only makes one wine—Pesquera—which may be *crianza* or *reserva* according to the quality of the year, and is 100 percent tempranillo. In average years it's very good; in great years it's fantastic. Best wines: Pesquera; Condado de Haza; Alenza (Condado de Haza).

HACIENDA MONASTERIO

Established 1991 *Owner* Peter Sisseck *Production* 9,000 cases *Vineyard area* 153 acres (62 ha)

Not, as one might expect from its name, an ancient ecclesiastical fortress, this bodega is more like a giant pink flying-saucer parked on a hillside above the town. Appropriately enough, the wine-

Producers
1 Bodegas Aalto
2 Dehesa de los Canónigos
3 Alejándro Fernández Tinto Pesquera
4 Hacienda Monasterio
5 Pago de Carraovejas
6 Rodero
7 Vega Sicilia

making kit is of the space-age variety, but tradition is served by the winemaker, Peter Sisseck, who buys one-year-old bordeaux casks to age the wine. The plantation is of tinto fino, cabernet sauvignon, merlot and a little malbec, and just one wine—Hacienda Monasterio. There's also a small parcel of 60-year-old vines from which Peter makes Dominio de Pingus, a wine of rare artifice and concentration. Few people have seen it, fewer have tasted it, and fewer still can afford to buy it. Both wines are amongst the best of their kind. Best wines: everything, especially Dominio de Pingus.

PAGO DE CARRAOVEJAS

Established 1988 *Owners* José-María Ruiz Benito, Tomás Postigo, Hermanos Holgueras, Emilio Arranz *Production* 33,000 cases *Vineyard area* 173 acres (70 ha)

Carraovejas means "sheepfold" and it seems that this stretch of land in the shadow of the castle rock was used for that purpose before it was planted with vines. The winery, designed by wine-maker Tomás Postigo, is tiny and built into a hillside so that all the grape transfer can take place by gravity. Fermentation is in *autoevacuaciones*—self-emptying tanks which ensure that the must can be moved without using pumps—to minimize stress on the grapes. The resulting wine has soared in reputation (and price) and the company recently stopped making the *joven* version, sticking to *crianzas* and *reservas*. There is only one wine—Pago de Carraovejas—typically made of 75 percent tinto fino and 25 percent cabernet sauvignon, and it is excellent.

RODERO

Established 1991 *Owners* Rodero family *Production* 29,000 cases *Vineyard area* 183 acres (74 ha)

Carmelo Rodero and his wife, María Oña, both come from families which have grown grapes here for generations. Indeed, until recently the grapes were sold to Vega Sicilia, which is why they decided that if the grapes were good enough for Vega, they should be making wine for themselves. They sank every last peseta into a tiny winery and the two of them started work on their own. The wine won an award for its second vintage and they stuck to their quality guns by continuing to go for low-yield, high-quality grapes. The wine used to be sold under the Ribeño name but is now labeled Carmelo Rodero, a *joven* made from 100 percent tinto fino and *crianza* and *reserva* wines with, typically, 7 percent cabernet sauvignon. They are splendid. Best wines: everything.

VEGA SICILIA

Established 1864 *Owners* Alvarez family *Production* 31,000 cases *Vineyard area* 618 acres (250 ha)

This is the one which started off the quest for world-class wine in the Ribiera del Duero under Eloy Lecanda in 1864. Today, the bodega still has plantations of cabernet sauvignon, merlot, malbec and even a little albillo which date back to his early days, but the wines are mainly tinto fino and the wines as legendary as ever. The house, winery, and former church of St Cecilia from which the estate is believed to take its name are immaculately landscaped and kept, and this is the only winery in the region to have its own cooperage. The Alvarez family has owned it since 1982 and it was under their inspired winemaker, Mariano García Fernández, that the wine regained its status. He left in 1999 to start a new project and the current winemaker is the no less talented Javier Ausás López de Castro. Vega Sicilia Unico is the master-piece, spending from seven to twenty years in wood and bottle before release. Experts argue over whether the single vintage Unico is better than the Reserva Especial, which is blended from several years' vintages, but few outside the moneyed classes will ever get the opportunity to find out. There is a five-year-old *reserva* called Valbuena which is only released if the winemaker is happy with it. It is made only from wine produced in good to great years. Wine made in average and poor years is sold off for distillation, not into the wine market where the bodega might expect a much higher price for it. The company also owns Bodegas Alión at Padilla, a spanking-new bodega where the same winemaker turns out exemplary new-wave wines. Best wines: everything.

The cultivation of olive groves and the growing of grapes are two of the oldest forms of agriculture in Europe.

Other Castilla-León Regions

Rueda

This is the land of the verdejo, a grape which was simply waiting for technology to catch up with it. In the old days it oxidized so fast that the wine-makers gave up, and made a sherry-type wine, supplementing it with the high-cropping palomino grape and making rueda pálido (light and dry) and rueda dorada (softer and darker), semi-fortified wines which still have a niche market. However, Riscal revolutionized the area with inert gas and cold fermentation technology, as well as introducing the sauvignon. The best rueda today is likely to have been made from grapes picked in the early hours of the morning, before sunrise, blanketed with nitrogen or some other inert gas in the trailer in the vineyard, and chilled to about 60°F (15°C) before going for a very gentle pressing in a pneumatic press. Some wines are given a six-month dressing in oak, others are delivered fresh and crisp to the market in the spring after the vintage. This is arguably the best white wine of modern Spain (but see also Rías Baixas). Only white wines are made with the DO, although (often very good) red wines are made under the new (1999) VdlT Medina del Campo. This classification is shortly tipped to become a DO in its own right for red and pink wines, made from tempranillo, garnacha, cabernet sauvignon and merlot.

BELONDRADE Y LURTON

Established 1984 *Owners* Didier Belondrade and Brigitte Lurton-Belondrade *Production* 2,500 cases *Vineyard area* 30 acres (12 ha)

Why should a young French couple want to make wine in Rueda? They say it's because it was something different, more of a challenge than setting up in their native Bordeaux, and they both love the area. Brigitte Lurton-Belondrade is the wine-maker, along with her brother, Jacques, who is consultant winemaker at a number of bodegas in Ribera del Duero and Rueda. The wine is 100 percent verdejo in the modern style, and simply called Belondrade y Lurton. It's barrel-fermented and then left for a year on the lees, and is very good indeed. Best wine: Belondrade y Lurton.

CASTILLA LA VIEJA

Established 1976 *Owners* Sanz family *Production* 225,000 cases *Vineyard area* 247 acres (100 ha)

Sanz family wines have had considerable success internationally thanks to careful innovation and inspired winemaking. Today, the company turns out some of the region's very best wines under the Bornos label. Best wines: Bornos Sauvignon Blanc; Palacio de Bornos Rueda Superior.

MARQUÉS DE RISCAL–VINOS BLANCOS DE CASTILLA

Established 1972 *Owners* Vinos de los Herederos del Marqués de Riscal *Production* 180,000 cases *Vineyard area* 420 acres (170 ha)

Francisco "Paco" Hurtado de Amezaga, current head of the Riscal family, wanted to make a white wine worthy of his family name but he didn't like the traditional oaked or modern squeaky-clean whites being made in Rioja, so he looked all over northern Spain, and finally settled on Rueda, attracted by the verdejo grape, which he thought showed tremendous potential. Today, Riscal wines are amongst the best in the region, and feature a sauvignon, a verdejo (with some viura, or macabeo) and an oak-aged Reserva Limousin Verdejo with 11 months in the cask. All are sold under the Marqués de Riscal label. Best wines: Reserva Limousin, sauvignon.

The twisted shapes and thick trunks of these vines indicate that they are old plants.

Toro

Big and beefy, as you'd expect from a region named "Bull," there are white and pink wines here but the major interest is in the reds, made from the tinta de toro. This is the tempranillo but grown here in hotter, lower-altitude vineyards which give a thicker skin to the grape and more extract to the wine. The cabernet sauvignon and garnacha (mainly for pink wines) are also grown, and cabernet/tempranillo blends (although denied the DO) can be excellent.

FARIÑA

Established 1942 *Owners* Fariña family *Production* 30,000+ cases *Vineyard area* 988 acres (400 ha)

Manuel Farina, the best-known winemaker in the region, was one of the first in Toro to espouse new technology. Colegiata is the name for *jovenes* in white, pink and red; Gran Colegiata is for *reservas* and *gran reservas* and a "*semi-crianza*" (a red wine which has had oak age but less than the regulation six months). There's also a premium *joven*, Primero, made from the best selected grapes. Best wines: Primero; Gran Colegiata.

Cigales

Famous for its (excellent) pink wines, Cigales' best wines are, nevertheless, its reds, made from the ubiquitous tinto del país (tempranillo) with, here and there, an admixture of garnacha and cabernet sauvignon, which is classified as "experimental."

Bierzo

In the far northwest of the region, Bierzo owes more to the style of Valdeorras in neighboring Galicia than to the hefty wines of lower Castilla-León. Fresh whites from godello and doña blanca and (mainly) light reds made from mencía do most of the business here.

PEREZ CARAMES

Established 1986 *Owner* Antonia Barredo Lence *Production* 13,500 cases *Vineyard area* 79 acres (32 ha)

The "maverick" tendency is on show here: most of this bodega's wines don't carry the DO Bierzo because they're made from "forbidden" grapes such as cabernet sauvignon, merlot and pinot noir, although there's also the local mencía and a *maceración carbonica* wine called Consules de Roma. However, the best tend to be the non-DO wines, under the label Casar de Santa Inés. Best wines: Casar de Santa Inés Pinot Noir, Merlot.

The following wines are currently only allowed to be classified as Vino de Mesa de Castilla-León.

MAURO

Established 1980 *Owners* García Fernández family *Production* 13,000 cases *Vineyard area* 86 acres (35 ha)

This is another bodega which has built a reputation for excellence since its foundation, not least because the winemaker is the ubiquitous Mariano García, late of Vega Sicilia. Unlike its "neighbor" in Sardón, however, Mauro grows only tempranillo and garnacha, and the wines are made more in the traditional way of Ribera del Duero, even though the bodega is well outside the region. Winemaking is immaculate and the vines are now at their peak of maturity for producing good grapes. There are three wines: Mauro is a *crianza* with 13 months in the cask; Mauro Vendimia Seleccionada, although it's still labelled *crianza*, is made from best-selected grapes, with 24 months in the cask. The latest departure, San Roman, has 12 months in oak and is made from 90 percent tinta de toro.

ABADIA RETUERTA

Established 1996 *Owner* Sandoz *Production* 70,000 cases *Vineyard area* 504 acres (204 ha)

This is the old vineyard estate of the twelfth-century Abbey (Abadia) of St María. It was taken over as part of a wider business deal in the late 1980s by the pharmaceutical products group Sandoz who decided to re-establish the vineyard and build a new winery with the very latest high-quality installations. In a very short time they have succeeded brilliantly. The vineyard has tempranillo, cabernet sauvignon and a little merlot and, unfettered by the regulations appertaining to the DO Ribera del Duero (the western boundary of which is a mere 6 miles (10 km) away, winemaker Angel Anocibar Beloqui does as he pleases, and what he does pleases a lot of people. The wines are all called Abadia Retuerta. Best wines: the entire range but especially El Campanario; El Palomar; Pago Negralada and Pago Valdebellón.

Above: *Few wineries now use the traditional skills of a cooper on the premises.*

Top: *Collecting wine from the local co-operative is still part of the Sunday routine.*

Rioja

A much patched stone wall protects vines from the wind, as it has done for centuries.

Modern rioja was classified under the new system in 1926 and is now going through radical changes.

MARQUÉS DE CÁCERES–UNION VITIVINÍCOLA
Established 1970 *Owners* Forner family *Production* 65,000 cases *Vineyard area* NA

This bodega changed the face of Rioja when Enrique Forner moved back to Spain from Bordeaux and decided to make a "village wine," buying in grapes from growers in the locality and using minimal oak in the aging process. The bodega was the first to feature full-scale stainless steel technology. Enrique's original ambitions have mellowed a little with maturity and Cáceres now turns out some exemplary lightly oaked white wines, including the barrel-fermented Antea, as well as an impressive *gran reserva*. However, the wines still tend not to spend much more time than the statutory minimum in the cask. Best wines: Gran Reserva; Gaudium Reserva.

CAMPILLO
Established 1990 *Owners* Martínez Zabala family *Production* 'Limited' *Vineyard area* 124 acres (50 ha)

These are the Martínez of Faustino Martínez (and also owners of Bodegas Marqués de Vitoria) but Campillo is the flagship wine. For red wines, only the tempranillo grape is grown (a characteristic of many Basque riojas) but the company does buy in a certain amount of other grapes, notably graciano.

The winemaking kit is the latest, and the company mixes its *barricas* (barrels) 50/50 between French and American oak, with no wood more than four years old and most of it new or one to two years old. *Reserva* reds spend 18–24 months in the cask. There is also a barrel-fermented white made from 90 percent viura (or macabeo) and 10 percent "others." Best wines: Campillo, Reserva, Reserva Especial, Gran Reserva.

CVNE (COMPAÑÍA VINÍCOLA DEL NORTE DE ESPAÑA)
Established 1879 *Owners* Real de Asúa family *Production* 667,000 cases *Vineyard area* 1,364 acres (552 ha)

This is one of Rioja's most respected companies. In 1989, when CVNE installed a fully automated new winery with the stainless-steel technology, gravity-feed transfer systems and multiple-batch fermentation, it was probably the most modern installation in the world. CVNE also has a major share in Contino, one of the few single estates in Rioja. Until recently, this was run by José Madrazo Real de Asúa, and his retirement project is to re-examine the vineyards of Contino to see whether there is still greater quality to be had by dividing them up into individual parcels and vinifying the grapes separately. The wines are classic rioja, using the full mix of grapes, with the Viña Real range (Burgundy bottle) sourcing most of its tempranillo from the Rioja Alavesa and Imperial (Bordeaux bottle) from the Rioja Alta. Everything is first-class from this exceptional bodega, but some are more first-class than others. Best wines: *reservas* and *gran reservas* in the Imperial and Viña Real ranges; Real de Asúa Reserva; Contino.

MARTÍNEZ-BUJANDA
Established 1889 *Owners* Martínez Bujanda family *Production* 250,000 cases *Vineyard area* 988 acres (400 ha)

This is an old firm with a spanking new bodega with the very latest equipment. The wines range from a solid everyday range to some excellent new-wave stuff, including a barrel-fermented viura (macabeo), a varietal garnacha *reserva* with 20 months in oak and a new *gran reserva* which is openly 50/50 tempranillo/cabernet sauvignon.

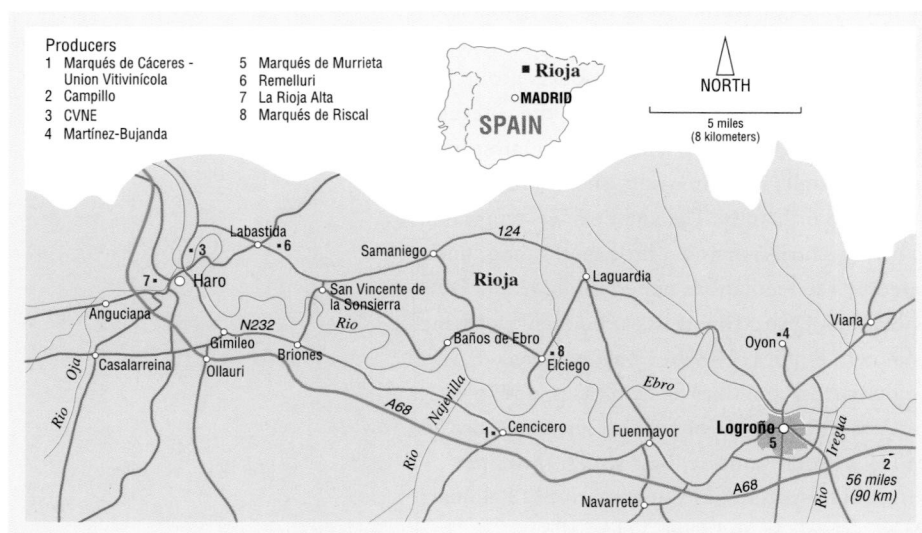

Producers
1 Marqués de Cáceres -
   Union Vitivinícola
2 Campillo
3 CVNE
4 Martínez-Bujanda
5 Marqués de Murrieta
6 Remelluri
7 La Rioja Alta
8 Marqués de Riscal

Rioja
MADRID
SPAIN

NORTH

5 miles
(8 kilometers)

Labastida
Samaniego
Haro
Anguciana
San Vincente de la Sonsierra
Casalarreina
Gimileo
Ollauri
Briones
Cenicero
Fuenmayor
Navarrete
Laguardia
Rioja
Baños de Ebro
Elciego
Ebro
Oyon
Viana
Logroño
2
56 miles
(90 km)

The latest development has been the first harvests from a single estate, Finca de Valpiedra, in Fuenmayor. Best wines: Vendimia Seleccionada Gran Reserva; Finca de Valpiedra; Valdemar.

MARQUÉS DE MURRIETA

Established 1872 *Owner* Dominios Creixell *Production* 400,000 cases *Vineyard area* 445 acres (180 ha)

This elegant bodega has been extended, new vineyards planted and the wines revamped to appeal to the modern market without sacrificing quality. The company also owns Pazo de Barrantes in the DO Rías Baixas, in Galicia. Best wines: Reservas; Castillo Ygay Gran Reservas.

REMELLURI

Established 1968 *Owner* J. Rodríguez Salis *Production* 33,000 cases *Vineyard area* 260 acres (105 ha)

Remelluri's bodega, tucked into the foot of the mountains, makes only *reservas*. It supplies 80 percent of its own grapes, mostly tempranillo. The winemaking is a mix of traditional and modern, using refurbished oak vats and stainless steel; the wine typically spends around two years in *barricas* (80 percent are made from French oak, the rest from American). The style and character of the wines are "textbook" for the Basque Country rioja. Best wines: everything.

LA RIOJA ALTA

Established 1890 *Owners* Aranzábal family *Production* 250,000 cases *Vineyard area* 740 acres (300 ha)

A member of the rioja "aristocracy," whose wine serves as a benchmark for many others. The very best wines are still fined with egg-whites and racked by hand; in the cellar next door automatic systems perform the same tasks. The wines are a mix of tempranillo, mazuelo, graciano and garnacha in varying proportions; aging is in a mixture of new and old oak (with an average age of six years). *Crianza*s normally have two years, *reserva*s three and *gran reserva*s four in oak. Best wines: everything, but especially Viña Ardanza; Grandes Reservas 890 and 904.

MARQUÉS DE RISCAL

Established 1860 *Owners* Hurtado de Amezaga family *Production* 300,000 cases *Vineyard area* 519 acres (210 ha)

This was the first bodega built to make rioja wine by the "Bordeaux method." The earliest plantations were cabernet sauvignon and tempranillo. The wines went through a difficult patch in the late 1970s—some of the old oak had become tainted with a fungal growth—but were back on form by the mid-1980s. Best wines: Barón de Chirel Reserva (60 percent tempranillo, 40 percent "other" grapes); Marqués de Riscal Reserva.

Rows of vines follow the curves of the landscape in northern Spain.

REGIONAL DOZEN

Barón de Chirel Reserva, Marqués de Riscal
Campillo Gran Reserva, Campillo
Castillo Irache, Irache
Chardonnay, Castillo de Monjardín
Contino, CVNE
Garnacha, Martínez-Bujanda
Lautus, Guelbenzu
Marqués de Cáceres Gaudium, Union Vitivinícola
Reserva 125 Aniversario, Chivite
Reserva, Remelluri
Reserva Tempranillo, Ochoa
Viña Ardanza Reserva, La Rioja Alta

Navarra

Once under the shadow of neighboring Rioja, Navarra has reinvented itself with a vengeance as a source of some of Spain's most interesting new wines. Thanks to support for the regional government through the enological research station in Olite, the range of wines has never been more exciting.

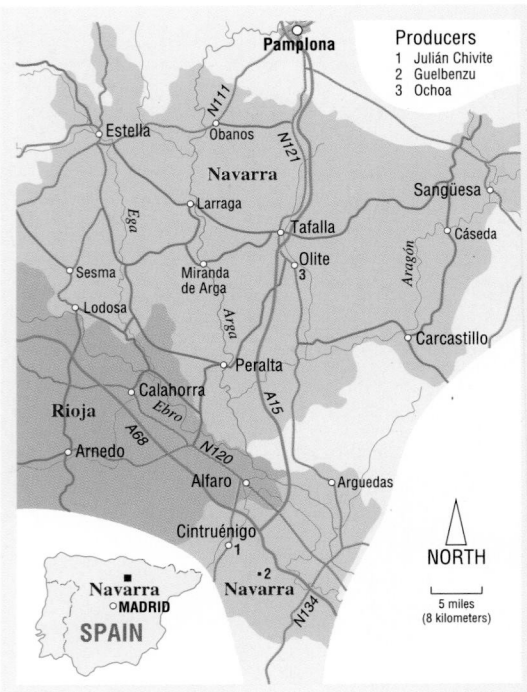

JULIÁN CHIVITE

Established 1647 *Owners* Chivite family *Production* 175,000 cases *Vineyard area* 865 acres (350 ha)

As recently as the early 1980s this company was the only serious exporter from Navarra and even today, given the massive explosion in new ideas and experimentation from this DO zone, the company holds a commanding lead in international recognition as well as size. The present company actually dates from 1860 and released a special edition—"Colección 125"—to mark the firm's 125th birthday in 1985. A barrel-fermented chardonnay with 11 months on the lees, and a tempranillo/merlot/cabernet *reserva* with, typically, 14 months have been made in every good year since then. Indeed, there's also a special *gran reserva* made from pure tempranillo with two years in oak and a splendid rich *vendímia tardía* (late vintage) moscatel with ten months in the barrel. The basic range is called Gran Feudo and features a particularly good pink wine made from 100 percent garnacha. Best wines: Colección 125 (the whole range—red, white, moscatel); Gran Feudo Rosado and moscatel.

The soft greens of a vineyard near Maneru contrast with the drier landscape around it.

GUELBENZU

Established 1851 *Owners* Guelbenzu family *Production* 25,000 cases *Vineyard area* 104 acres (40 ha)

This boutique winery can be found beside a lovely old house opposite the bullring in the small town of Cascante in the south of the region. The house wine is a *crianza*, mainly tempranillo; Guelbenzu EVO is a *crianza* dominated by cabernet sauvignon; Guelbenzu Jardín is a garnacha wine made from vines over 30 years old; and newcomer Guelbenzu Lautus, a tempranillo/merlot/cabernet/garnacha *reserva*. Best wines: Lautus; EVO.

OCHOA

Established 1845 *Owners* Javier and Mariví Ochoa *Production* 89,000 cases *Vineyard area* 299 acres (121 ha)

The Ochoa family has been in the wine business for several centuries but the modern-day company dates from 1986. Javier Ochoa has been one of the most tireless campaigners for quality both in Navarra and abroad. He was instrumental in setting up the research establishment EVENA (Estación de Viticultura y enologia de Navarra) which has done so much to improve quality and bring in new ideas to the district, and he's applied these in his own family vineyards too. He grows viura (the name Riojanos have for macabeo) and chardonnay for whites; tempranillo, garnacha, cabernet sauvignon and merlot for reds. He also pioneered the sweet moscatel wines which have been winning prizes all over the world. Best wines: Reserva; Gran Reserva; moscatel.

CATALONIA

Penedès

Penedès has an unquestioned lead in volume, reliability, innovation and quality-control throughout Catalonia. Every Catalan grape, almost every Spanish grape and many north European grapes are grown here in the myriad microclimates of the Baix-Penedès, Mitja-Penedès and Alt-Penedès, up to heights of 2,600 feet (800 m). The range of soils and altitudes provides perfect growing conditions for everything from the lightweight white wines for the beachfront market to impressive cabernet and chardonnay wines which can hold their vinous heads up anywhere in the world.

JANÉ VENTURA

Established 1914 *Owners* Jané Ventura family *Production* 24,000 cases *Vineyard area* 27 acres (11 ha)

This family firm turns out some excellent wines, especially cabernet sauvignon made in the new-wave style of Penedès, a barrel-fermented white made mainly from macabeo and an exemplary young white in the classic Catalan style. The company is small enough to have hands-on control of production under Benjamín Jané Ventura. Best wines: all the range, especially cabernet sauvignon and Finca els Camps barrel-fermented white.

CAVAS NAVERAN (SADEVE)

Established 1986 *Owner* Mitchell Guillerán, shareholders *Production* 5,000 cases *Vineyard area* 210 acres (85 ha)

As with many companies based in this area, Naveran is mainly a cava company, but makes some still wines under the DO Penedès: these may

be small in number but they are big in quality. The winemaking is strictly new-wave and focused on "international" grape varieties including viognier as well as chardonnay, cabernet and merlot. Best wines: Don Pablo Reserva; Naveran Crianza.

MIGUEL TORRES

Established 1870 *Owners* Torres family *Production* 2,5000,000 cases *Vineyard area* 3,212 acres (1,300 ha)

This is the company which did more than most to bring Spanish wine to the world after the Spanish Civil War, and its wines are now sold in more than 85 countries as a result. The present head of the family, Miguel A. Torres, has built on the solid foundation left by his father and extended the company's operations to Chile and the USA, where his sister, Marimar Torres, runs a brilliantly successful operation in California. Miguel was amongst the first to plant cabernet sauvignon and chardonnay in Catalonia but he also has a plantation of over 100 native Catalan varieties with which he experiments on a regular basis. The winery at Pacs del Penedès is an object-lesson in the marriage of new technology with traditional style and quality, and Torres wines are regular prizewinners in international competitions. Best wines: Fransola (sauvignon); Gran Viña Sol (chardonnay); Viña Esmeralda (moscatel/gewürztraminer); Waltraud (riesling); Atrium (merlot); Gran Coronas, Mas la Plana (both cabernet sauvignon); Milmanda (chardonnay from Conca de Barberà).

Workers clear the ground of weeds at the vineyards of Miguel Torres, Spain's largest family-owned wine company.

REGIONAL BEST

Aria, Segura Viudas, Freixenet
Cartoixa Scala Dei, Scala Dei
Dolc de l'Obac, Costers del Siurana
Flor de Maig Cabernet Sauvignon, Celler de Capcanes
Marfíl, Alella Vinicola Can Jonc
Mas Borras, Miguel Torres
Mil.lennium, Vinyes i Cellers Clua
Milmanda Chardonnay, Torres
Non Plus Ultra, Codorníu
Reserva de la Familia, Juvé y Camps
Tempranillo d'Anyada, Albet i Noya

Other Catalan Regions

Modern stainless steel vats hold the wine in Freixenet's extensive cellars at St Sadurní.

Cava

Cava's birthplace was Catalonia and today most of it still comes from the area around St Sadurní d'Anoia in the province of Barcelona, although there are "licensed" cava areas in Rioja, Navarra, Valencia, etc. When the DO began to be formalized in 1986 many production areas were excluded, and by 1991 when the process was completed more than 90 percent of all cava vineyards were to be found in Catalonia. This caused a certain amount of anger in regions which had made sparkling wine (*vino espumoso*) and called it cava until this point. However, these problems were largely solved by the local Consejos Reguladores formulating their own DO regulations.

CODORNÍU

Established 1551 *Owners* Raventós family *Production* 3,750,000 cases *Vineyard area* 2,965 acres (1,200 ha)

This is now the biggest of the cava companies, challenged only by Freixenet. The company's estate in St Sadurní is in idyllic landscape, housed in art nouveau buildings, and possesses the biggest cellars in the world, totaling 15 miles (25 km) on five underground levels. But this old-world charm hides a cutting-edge approach to the wine, with constant experiment and innovation. Codorníu introduced the first chardonnay to cava and is

Freixenet is one of the largest sparkling wine producers in the world.

experimenting with pinot noir as well as selecting its own clones of the classic "big three" grapes (parellada, xarel-lo and macabeo). Best wines: Cuvée Raventós; Non Plus Ultra; Raïmat Gran Brut.

FREIXENET

Established 1889 *Owners* Ferrer family *Production* 11,000,000 cases *Vineyard area* 642 acres (260 ha)

This is the other "big name" cava house (along with Codorníu) and the biggest sparkling wine producer in the world, with companies in the USA, Mexico and France. The bodega building is a magnificent art deco affair. Its most famous wine is Cordon Negro, in a distinctive black frosted bottle with a black-and-gold label. The Freixenet group includes Segura Viudas and Castellblanch which are run as separate operations. In general, Freixenet is against the use of chardonnay in cava, although its top-of-the-range *reserva real* contains about 20 percent of the grape. The latest development is a red-grape/white-grape monastrell/xarel-lo which promises well. Best wines: Reserva Real; Cuvée DS; Segura Viudas Reserva Heredad.

GRAMONA

Established 1921 *Owners* Gramona family *Production* 28,000 cases *Vineyard area* 72 acres (29 ha)

This is a small family-owned concern turning out relatively small quantities of impeccable wine in the best *artesanal* style. The grapes are the classic three and even the basic wine is aged for 18 months—double the legal minimum for cava. The top-of-the-range Celler Batlle, unusually, is made without any parellada—just 70 percent xarel-lo and 30 percent macabeo. Best wines: Tres Lustros; Celler Batlle.

JOSEP MARÍA RAVENTÓS I BLANC,

Established 1986 *Owner* Manuel Raventós i Negra *Production* 24,000 cases *Vineyard area* 217 acres (88 ha)

Scion of the Raventós family of Codorníu fame, Josep-María decided to make his own way in the world and set up in business hardly a stone's throw from the family estate. His taste in architecture is more modern but no less inspiring than that of his forbears, and his wines, similarly, show great style and panache. He grows chardonnay as well as the native grapes and established a name for the company very early on. Best wines: Reserva; Gran Reserva; Reserva Personal Manuel Raventós.

JUVÉ Y CAMPS

Established 1921 *Owners* Juvé y Camps family *Production* 200,000 cases *Vineyard area* 1,235 acres (500 ha)

This vineyard supports both cava and still wines made under the DO Penedès, but it is best known for its cava. The style is classic in the most formal sense of the word: a proper regard for tradition but with modern winemaking skills and long, slow, careful maturation for anything up to five years. A Juvé y Camps wine is likely to be the top cava on many a restaurant wine list. Best wines: Reserva de la Familia; Gran Juvé y Camps.

ROVELLATS

Established 1940 *Owners* Cardona Vallés family *Production* 25,000 cases *Vineyard area* 519 acres (210 ha)

This is a beguiling old bodega set in a fifteenth-century farmhouse with its own tiny chapel and ornamental gardens in the *bella epoca* style. The company grows some chardonnay (largely for varietal wines) as well as the native grapes and its wines are characterized by a tremendous freshness and balanced, crisp acidity. Best wines: Brut Nature; Grand Cru Masia Siglo XV.

AGUSTÍ TORELLÓ

Established 1955 *Owners* Torelló Llopart family *Production* 60,000 cases *Vineyard area* 272 acres (110 ha)

This is a company which makes an "estate" cava from its own vineyards at Can Marti de Baix just outside St Sadurní. Don Agustí himself is still in charge and the family provides most of the impetus for some of the Anoia valley's best wines. Only the native "big three" Catalan varieties are grown. The company's international fame was enhanced by the fabulously expensive Kripta (presented in a bottle in the shape of an amphora), proving that a relatively small producer can compete in quality terms with the big names of the cava industry. Some say that Kripta and Torelló's other masterpiece, Mata, are the finest cavas currently in production. Best wines: Kripta, Mata.

Alella

This area had a promising early start, although it is much reduced in size these days owing to urban sprawl from the city of Barcelona—its biggest market—immediately to the south. Alella wines are mainly white and made from pansá blanca (xarel-lo) and garnacha blanca grapes. There is also a substantial amount of chardonnay. The wines are fresh and light: new-wave examples may be barrel-fermented. There is some small amount of red, mainly made from ull de llebre (tempranillo).

Empordà-Costa Brava

Empordà-Costa Brava is on the border between Catalonia and France, an area which has reinvented itself as a dynamic and experimental zone. Formerly known mainly for unexceptional (although very pleasant) pink wines, the best wines now tend to be the reds, made from tempranillo, cabernet sauvignon, merlot, etc. The local classic is a sweet red made from sun-dried garnacha grapes called garnatxa del empordà, very much in the style of the *vins doux naturelles* made across the border in France.

CAVAS DEL CASTILLO DE PERELADA

Established 1923 *Owners* Suqué-Matue family *Production* 110,000 cases *Vineyard area* 247 acres (100 ha)

There's a magnificent castle in the village of Perelada which houses a glamorous casino and restaurant, and this is the head office of the Perelada wine company. In practice, only the company's cava is made here, in the cellars, with most of the vinous work being carried out across the road in a more prosaic winery, complete with a large-scale clubhouse which serves food. The winery equipment is totally modern and the company has built itself a reputation for quality in all its wines. The vineyards grow tempranillo, garnacha, cariñena and macabeo as well as cabernet sauvignon, merlot, chardonnay and sauvignon blanc. Best wines: Castillo Perelada Reserva; cabernet sauvignon.

Conca de Barberà

This highland area in the province of Girona produces mainly *joven* wines in all three colors although there is the odd exception: Miguel Torres' barrel-fermented Milmanda Chardonnay comes from here, and there are continuing experiments with oak-aged reds made from tempranillo and garnacha, often with an admixture of cabernet sauvignon and merlot.

The best wines in the Empordá-Costa Brava region are the reds.

CONCAVINS

Established 1988 *Owner* Luis Carbonell Figueras
Production 280,000 cases *Vineyard area* NA

This is a smart, modern bodega with a businesslike approach. Concavins was set up to take advantage of the unique growing conditions in this high-altitude area, and buys in grapes every year to suit its needs. Two separate ranges of wine are made here. First come the early-harvest (late August/early September) supermarket blends of macabeo, parellada and chardonnay which are put through the system in double-quick time, squeaky-clean and ready to roll (Hugh Ryman used to make wines here for most of the supermarkets in the UK). Then the vessels are washed out to be ready for the main harvest, which is likely to be cabernet sauvignon, merlot and tempranillo. These are given the full malolactic treatment followed by extended cask-age, typically 12–18 months for *crianzas* (the legal minimum is six months here) and anything up to two years for *reservas*. The wines are very good and quality control is excellent. Best wines: Castillo de Montblanc Cabernet Merlot; Via Aurelia Masia les Comes.

Costers del Segre

Cynics have suggested that the only reason this area was awarded the DO (in 1988) was because it was the home of Raïmat, the giant estate with Californian-inspired techniques and some admittedly excellent wines. Costers del Segre is fragmented into four subzones around the city of Lleida (Lérida): Raïmat, Artesa (both in the province of Lleida), Vall du Riu Corb and Las Garrigas (in Tarragona province). Some smaller firms are, however, beginning to appear. The wines come in all three colors; the best reds are generally made from tempranillo, cabernet sauvignon and merlot and the best whites from chardonnay and the "big three" Catalan grapes.

Filling bladders for the restaurant trade, a significant customer for many wineries.

RAÏMAT

Established 1918 *Owners* Codorníu family
Production 300,000 cases *Vineyard area* 3,706 acres (1,500 ha)

In Catalan *raïm* is a grape and *mà* (old Catalan *mat*) is the word for "hand." The estate (and the whole subregion of the DO) is named after the discovery of a terracotta plaque showing a picture of a bunch of grapes and a hand which was dug up in the early days of this company. The land, which had been destroyed by old salt lagoons, had to be ploughed up and replanted for several years with other crops to revitalize the soils. In the process the plaque turned up and the name was adopted, and it now forms part of the company logo. The wines are Californian-style, in a winery which looks as if it might have come from another planet: mirrored walls, vines on the roof, neo-classical portals and indoor water features all contribute to the effect. The wines aren't bad either: international varieties are to the fore although arguably the best wine (Abadia) is a tempranillo/cabernet mix. The company also makes cava (see Codorníu, above). Best wines: Mas Castell Reserva (cabernet sauvignon); Abadia Crianza (tempranillo/cabernet).

CASTELL DEL REMEI

Established 1780 *Owners* Cusiné family *Production* 89,000 cases *Vineyard area* 173 acres (70 ha)

Established in 1780, the company in modern form didn't emerge until 1870 and, from an outsider's point of view, not much happened here until the Cusiné family moved in, in 1982. Since then, the bodega has been quietly building its reputation on the international market. Winemaking is modern and cabernet, merlot, chardonnay and sauvignon blanc are represented alongside macabeo, parellada and tempranillo, which is here known under its old Catalan name of *gotim bru* ("brown bunch"—presumably descriptive of its color during ripening). Best wines: Castell del Remei 1780 Crianza; Castell del Remei Merlot Crianza; Castell del Remei Gotim Bru Crianza.

Pla de Bages

This is a relatively small zone in the province of Barcelona with a reputation for making sound if unexceptional wines in the past. However, excellent work has been done with the picapoll (the Spanish name for the French picpoul or piquepoul) grape for white wines and the cabernet sauvignon for reds, so perhaps we shall hear more.

MASIES DE AVINYÓ

Established 1983 *Owners* Roqueta family *Production* 8,000 cases *Vineyard area* 99 acres (40 ha)

This is a small but very promising company which was making export wines under the Ramon Roqueta label for many years before re-forming under the present name. The family has made wine

![vineyard and hilltop town]

for centuries at the Masia Roqueta (the family farmhouse) and opened a retail shop in Manresa in 1898 to sell it. They also installed the first automatic bottling plant, in 1964, and became a company formally in 1983. Wines today are sold under the company name and made from macabeo, picapoll (the French picpoul) and chardonnay for whites, garnacha, tempranillo, merlot and cabernet sauvignon for reds. Best wines: picapoll; cabernet sauvignon/tempranillo *crianza*.

Priorato

This is an ancient and beautiful region with eight centuries of wine-making tradition, high in the hills of the province of Tarragona and home to one of the toughest, blackest and longest-lived wines of Spain. In the same region, in the hilltop town of Gratallops, century-old garnacha vines and high-technology plantations of cabernet, merlot and syrah are producing some of the best new-wave wines of Spain—and some of the most expensive.

MAS MARTINET VITICULTORES

Established 1989 *Owners* Pérez Ovejero family *Production* 4,600 cases *Vineyard area* 25 acres (10 ha)

Another of the pioneering bodegas in Priorato, this small family firm turns out exemplary wines made

from garnacha, cabernet sauvignon, syrah and merlot from their small plantation near Falset. In 1996 they formed another company, Vall-Llach Mas Martinet at Porrera, about 6 miles (10 km) from Falset. Here, José Luís Perez and his daughter, Sara, (who make the wine between them) have established a vineyard of 135 acres (55 ha) where they make

a wine from cariñena and garnacha grapes with 5 percent cabernet sauvignon called Cims ("Peaks") de Porrera. The quality is outstanding. Best wines: Clos Martinet; Cims de Porrera.

ALVARO PALACIOS

Established 1989 *Owner* Alvaro Palacios *Production* 12,000 cases *Vineyard area* 99 acres (40 ha)

Alvaro, the scion of the family which owns Palacios-Remondo in Rioja, set up on his own along with a few like-minded entrepreneurs in the valley of the River Siurana in this remote, mountainous area of Priorato. Since then his wines have taken the world by storm. L'Ermita, for example, is now possibly the most expensive red wine in

Above: *An exuberant chalk drawing on a barrel, a reminder that in some places wine-making is still small-scale and individual.*

Top: *Vines near Poboleda, in Catalonia, show the first signs of fall.*

Cristal bota, a distinctively Spanish fashion in wine vessels, are used for drinking from, as well as storing the wine.

Spain, beating even the fabled Vega Sicilia. It is made from 100-year-old garnacha vines in a steep natural amphitheatre on ancient schistose bedrock. The finished wine has 15 percent cabernet sauvignon for aroma and 5 percent cariñena (the Rioja name for mazuelo) for color and spends 15 months in oak. Finca Dofi, his "estate" wine, is made with syrah and merlot as well as cabernet and cariñena. Las Terrasses is the mainstream wine, made from garnacha, cariñena and cabernet sauvignon. They are all magnificent. Best wines: everything.

Tarragona

This region has been associated with wine for centuries, as far back as Roman times when "terraconensis," as the local wine was then known, was exported to the capital in Italy. Its later fame rested on a single wine, now known as Tarragona Clásico. This is a fortified red wine made from garnacha grapes and stored in oak vats for a minimum of 12 years and used to be known in England, rather disparagingly, as "the poor man's port." Elsewhere, the DO produces all types of wine in all three colors, though 70 percent of Tarragona's wine production is white. Grapes grown include tempranillo, garnacha, cariñena and also cabernet and merlot. White wines tend to be made from the "big three" Catalan grapes (parellada, xarel-lo and macabeo) and/or chardonnay. Sweet whites are made from moscatel. Tarragona achieved DO status in 1976.

CELLER CO-OPERATIU DEL MASROIG
Established 1917 *Owners* Co-op members *Production* 225,000 cases *Vineyard area* 1,235 acres (500 ha)

There's been a good deal of change in the co-ops in Tarragona and this is an example of how new thinking in the winery and the vineyards is allowing these formerly bureaucratic and hidebound organizations to compete on the world stage. The grapes are the local specialties—garnacha blanca for whites and tempranillo (here called ull de llebre) and cariñena for reds—but the wines speak for themselves. Best wine: Les Sorts.

Terra Alta

This is a remote area of sleepy local co-ops (although the main co-op in Gandesa is doing impressive work and is housed in a splendid Gaudí-esque building). However, there are stirrings in the undergrowth and one or two "boutique" wineries are starting to make their names. The wines are generally reds made from hefty local grapes—cariñena and garnacha—along with tempranillo and, in the more forward-looking wineries, cabernet and merlot. Most white wine is made from garnacha blanca and parellada, although there is some very good macabeo and some experimental chardonnay.

PIÑOL
Established 1940 *Owner* Josefina Piñol *Production* 22,000 cases *Vineyard area* 62 acres (25 ha)

The first vines were planted by Arrufi Piñol and the third generation of his family is now involved in running the business. The winery has been progressively modernized and now has the full stainless steel kit. Grapes are bought in to top up the company's needs, and they grow or buy garnacha (blanca and tinta), macabeo, moscatel, tempranillo and cabernet sauvignon. Among a number of innovations are an interesting light, sweet wine called Josefina Piñol made from over-ripe garnacha blanca and Viñ Orosina, a dry-fermented moscatel. The top red wines are named L'Avi Arrufi ("Grandfather Arrufi") in memory of the founder. Best wines: L'Avi Arrufi Crianza; Nuestra Señora del Portal.

Vineyards in Terra Alta, one of the eight DOs in Catalonia.

CASTILLA-LA MANCHA

La Mancha & Valdepeñas

In the 1980s, La Mancha was still regarded as little more than a bulk-wine producer for the cafés and bars of Madrid, but it reinvented itself in the 1990s and, although there's still a lot of fairly basic wine being turned out, some of the best-value everyday wines in Spain are now being made here.

Famous for its fabulously warm, ripe and modestly priced *reservas* and *gran reservas*, Valdepeñas has resisted the temptation to diversify, though there are signs, especially among the smaller companies, that new ideas are on the way. In the meantime, the traditional wines of this area must be among the best value-for-money in the world.

VINÍCOLA DE CASTILLA, LA MANCHA

Established 1976 *Owners* Private shareholders *Production* 900,000 cases *Vineyard area* 494 acres (200 ha)

Living proof that big can be beautiful, this bodega was founded by the old RuMaSA group which was taken over by the government in 1983 to avoid its imminent collapse, and its holdings sold off. Vinícola de Castilla was bought by financiers, who could see which way the wind was blowing. Even though some of the technology is now old-fash-

ioned, it was so ahead of its time in those days that it still looks like a space-age installation. Today's spotless modern atrium and offices sit beside gleaming stainless steel equipment and complex computer controls. The wines have achieved a good deal in international competition. The company buys in most of its grapes and makes wine from viura, airén, chardonnay and sauvignon blanc (whites); and garnacha, cencibel (the local word for tempranillo), cabernet and merlot (reds). Best wines: Señorío de Guadianeja Reserve, Gran Reserva; Castilla de Alhambra Rosado, Tinto.

FELIX SOLIS, VALDEPEÑAS

Established 1952 *Owners* Solis family *Production* 11,000,000 cases *Vineyard area* 1,730 acres (700 ha)

As you drive along the N-IV between Madrid and Córdoba a mighty steel city rears up against the open sky on the outskirts of Valdepeñas. This is Bodegas Felix Solis, undergoing yet another expansion as a further 200 acres (80 ha) of land disappear under new buildings and storage warehouses, including the first fully automated, robot-staffed dispatch warehouse in Spain which will be able to handle 20,000 pallets of wine. Solis is the second-biggest wine company in Spain, after Bodegas y Bedbidas but B & B owns half a dozen wineries, whereas Solis has just the one ... for now. There are a number of ranges of wines, including Peñasol (everyday-quality table wines), Diego de Almagro, Los Molinos and the most famous brand—and some of the best-value red wine to come out of Spain—Viña Albali. Best wines: Viña Albali Crianza; cabernet sauvignon; tempranillo (*joven*); Diego de Almagro Crianza.

Above: *Corks are used to hold sulphur pellets, burned in the barrel to preserve the wine and to prevent bacteria.*

Top: *A wine press crushes the grapes to release the sugar, the first stage in wine-making.*

Producers
1 Vinícola de Castilla
2 Felix Solis

SPAIN
MADRID

La Mancha & Valdepenas

Guadiana
N420
Daimiel
Embalse de El Vicario
Ciudad Real
N IV
Manzanares
Embalse de Peñarroya
Membrilla
La Solana
La Mancha
Alhambra
Almagro
Moral de Calatrava
Azuer
Jabalón
N 412
Alcubillas
Valdepeñas
Jabalón
Valdepeñas
Embalse de la Cabezuela
Santa Cruz de Mudela
Torrenueva

NORTH
5 miles
(8 kilometers)

Despite difficult and often windy conditions, Castilla-La Mancha is one of Spain's largest producers of wine.

Other Castilla-La Mancha Regions

Almansa

There are other bodegas in Almansa but only one has any profile outside the area. Using only local grapes and making wine in the traditional way, Piqueras has shown that it can be done.

PIQUERAS

Established 1915 **Owners** Piqueras family **Production** 167,000 cases **Vineyard area** 248 acres (100 ha)

Almansa is often seen as a bit of "one-horse" DO as, year after year, the only bodega which makes itself felt in a wider market is this one. Winemaker Juan Pablo Bonete Piqueras has made it his business to succeed even if his peers are lagging behind. He grows (and buys) airén and macabeo for white wine and cencibel (the local word for tempranillo) and monastrell for red. The quality is excellent and there seems to be no good reason why other bodegas have not emerged to challenge for the leadership but, in the meantime, Piqueras reigns in this part of Spain. Best wines: Castillo de Almansa Crianza, Reserva.

VdlT Sierra de Alcaraz

MANUEL MANZANEQUE

Established 1992 **Owner** Manuel Manzaneque **Production** 12,000 cases **Vineyard area** 84 acres (34 ha)

At El Bonillo, these vineyards flourish at altitudes of 3,000–3,280 feet (900–1,000 m). The results have been widely admired: Manzaneque grows chardonnay as well as cabernet sauvignon, merlot, tempranillo and syrah and his wines are exemplary. Best wines: Chardonnay; Finca Elez Crianza (mainly cabernet); Gran Reserva.

VdlT de Castilla

After much lobbying by several prominent producers, the new Vino de la Tierra zone of Castilla was approved by the provisional government in 1999. The idea is that, rather in the manner of the Vin de Pays d'Oc in France, individual producers will now be able to experiment more, with less supervision, than they would be able to under DO regulation.

DEHESA DEL CARRIZAL

Established 1987 **Owner** Marcial Gómez Sequeira **Production** 4,200 cases **Vineyard area** 32 acres (13 ha)

Ignacio de Miguel Poch, who makes the wine here, does only one thing but does it very well—that is, to make a world-class cabernet sauvignon in these unclassified lands, some 30 miles (50 km) northwest of the city of Ciudad Real. The reputation of Dehesa del Carrizal has steadily advanced, to the point where it consistently challenges the finest wines of Spain in international tastings. The wine is 100 percent cabernet and spends, typically, 18 months in oak. Best wines: all of them.

VdM de Toledo

MARQUÉS DE GRIÑÓN

Established 1972 **Owners** Falcó family **Production** 12,500 cases **Vineyard area** 104 acres (42 ha)

Carlos Falcó de Fernández y Córdova, Marqués de Griñón and a grandee of Spain, has confounded the critics ever since his first commercial vintage in 1982. Feeling that the DO laws were a little too constricting, he decided to make wine the way he wanted it. The results have been outstanding, and his example set the tone for a whole generation of "maverick" winemakers who were to change the face of Spanish wine before the end of the century. Today, the marqués grows cabernet, merlot, syrah and petit verdot and makes varietals as well as a new wine made from cabernet, syrah and petit verdot. Indeed, this last venture was so successful that in 2000 he began regrafting his chardonnay vines to petit verdot.

Another project begun in 2000 was the planting of a new clone of graciano, so the future for the wines of the Dominio de Valdepusa is entirely red. Carlos Falcó is also involved with the Arco Bodegas group, making similarly unclassified wines in Castilla-León as well as mainstream DOCa wines in Rueda and Rioja. Anything which carries the Griñón name may be relied upon without question. Best wines: everything, but especially Dominio de Valdepusa Cabernet Sauvignon, Syrah; Emeritus.

REGIONAL DOZEN

Allozo Gran Reserva, Bodegas Centro-Españolas
Castillo de Alhambra Cencibel, Vinícola de Castilla
Castillo de Almansa Reserva, Piqueras
Corcovo Cencibel Joven, J.A. Megía e Hijos
Eméritus, Marqués de Griñón
Estola Gran Reserva, Bodegas Ayuso
Señorío de Mariscal Crianza, Bodegas Mariscal
Vega Moragona Crianza, Co-op La Magdalena
Vegaval Plata Reserva, Miguel Calatayud
Viña Albali Reserva, Bodegas Felix Solis
Viña Lastra, Co-op La Invencible
Yuntero Reserva, Co-op N.P. Jesús del Perdón

Andalusia

Jeréz

Jeréz/Xérès/Sherry y Manzanilla de Sanlúcar de Barrameda

About 20 companies now control the sherry business, under about 75 brand names. The wines themselves are as good as, or better than, they have ever been, even if nowadays the choice is not so wide as it once was.

PEDRO DOMECQ

Established 1730 *Owner* Allied-Domecq *Production* 600,000 cases *Vineyard area* 988 acres (400 ha)

In spite of its membership of the multinational Allied-Domecq group, this bodega has managed to maintain its individuality, albeit with a reduced range of wines to accommodate the other members of the group (which includes the British company John Harvey, of Bristol Cream fame). In common with many another major company the recent upturn in interest for "premium" sherry has encouraged Domecq to expand its quality range beyond the best-selling Fino La Ina. Best wines: Fino La Ina; Amontillado 51-1°; Sibarita Oloroso; Palo Cortado Capuchino; Venerable PX.

GONZÁLEZ-BYASS

Established 1835 *Owners* González family *Production* 890,000 cases *Vineyard area* 2,523 acres (1,021 ha)

This company, with its large-scale and beautiful bodega in the middle of Jeréz, went through a

difficult financial patch in the 1980s when outside investors were involved. However, the stock is now all back in the hands of the family and sound leadership has restored the company to its former pre-eminence. González-Byass claims to have produced the first *fino* in the modern style (Tio Pepe) in the 1850s, and has an impressive collection of ancient *soleras*. Their latest development is the "Añadas" collection of vintage sherries. Best wines: Tio Pepe; Amontillado del Duque; Apóstoles Dry Oloroso; Matúsalem Rich Old Oloroso.

Wineries in Jeréz are struggling to regain market share after a decline in the 1990s.

VINÍCOLA HIDALGO

Established 1792 *Owners* Hidalgo family *Production* 150,000 cases *Vineyard area* 494 acres (200 ha)

This company has been a leading producer of *manzanilla* for many years. The current head of the family, Javier Hidalgo, has an independent streak which has kept the company in the forefront of traditional winemaking while others have gone for the mass-market. His young wines have a freshness and lightness which make them very drinkable with food, especially with fish in one of the seafront restaurants in Sanlúcar. He also produces the very rare *manzanilla*, *amontillado* and *oloroso* styles. The family vineyards are in the district of Torrebreva and some of the vines are 80 years old. Best wines: La Gitana Manzanilla; Amontillado Viejo; Napoleon Oloroso; Palo Cortado Viejo.

EMILIO LUSTAU

Established 1896 *Owners* Luís Caballero group *Production* 200,000 cases *Vineyard area* 420 acres (170 ha)

This house has an excellent reputation for quality wines. Under the late Rafael Balao it established the "Almacenista" range of wines, bought from small producers and brokers and bottled in short

[Map of the Jeréz region]

Guadalquivir
Trebujena
La Algaida
MADRID
SPAIN
Bonanza
Cjo. de Mesas de Asta
Jeréz
Sanlúcar de Barrameda • 3
Chipiona
Alijar
La Parra
Peña del Aguila
Cjo. de laAtalaya
Jeréz
Guadalcacin del Caudillo
Estella del Marqués
1.2.4.6
Jeréz de la Frontera
Golfo de Cádiz
Rota
La Mata
5 •
El Portal
El Puerto de Santa María
Producers
Bahía de Cádiz
1 Pedro Domecq
2 González-Byass
3 Vinícola Hidalgo
4 Emilio Lustau
5 Osborne
6 Marqués del Real Tesoro
Cádiz
Puerto Real
Barrio de Jarana
NORTH
San Fernando
5 miles (8 kilometers)

*The cellars of Pedro Domecq, a company
famous for its sherry for over two centuries.*

runs for the "premium" sherry market, which has
been a brilliant success. When the Caballero group
bought Lustau in 1990, there were worries that it
might be subsumed into the core business (which
is "own label") but in the event this has not
happened. The bodega remains a law unto itself
and, with Caballero's backing, has gone from
strength to strength. Best wines: all wines are
amongst the best in the Jeréz region, but
particularly Manzanilla Pasada Manuel Cuevas
Jurado; Papirusa Manzanilla; Amontillado
Escuadrilla; Moscatel Superior Emilín; Pedro
Ximénez San Emilio.

OSBORNE
Established 1772 *Owners* Osborne family *Production*
750,000 cases *Vineyard area* 494 acres (200 ha)

An old firm in a magnificently restored bodega
building, Osborne still possesses some splendid
old *soleras* and makes some excellent wine, as well
as being famous for its brandies. Its brand identity
is well known by its silhouette bulls (which used
to carry a slogan until roadside advertising was
banned) which dot the countryside all over Spain.

The company owns the brand-name Duff-Gordon,
better known in some export markets than the
main company name, and took over Bobadilla
in the mid-1990s. Best wines: Fino Quinta; AOS
Solera Amontillado; Alonso El Sabio Oloroso;
P. Triangulo, P. Oloroso.

MARQUÉS DEL REAL TESORO
Established 1897 *Owner* José Estévez de los Reyes
Production 700,000 cases *Vineyard area* 1,003 acres (406 ha)

José Estévez bought the residuals of this dormant
company in the 1980s and went on to buy the
soleras of Tio Mateo (an excellent fino from the
ancient house of Palomino & Vergara) from John
Harvey, which was undergoing yet another metamorphosis within what was to become Allied-
Domecq. These were rehoused in a smart new
bodega on the Cádiz road. His latest acquisition is
the house of Valdespino in its entirety, including
the classic Inocente Fino, and it seems likely that
Valdespino will continue to be a separate entity.
Best wines: Tio Mateo Fino; Amontillado del
Principe; Inocente Fino (Valdespino); Solera 1842
Oloroso (Valdespino).

Other Andalusian Regions

Montilla-Moriles

The grape here is the PX (pedro ximénez), normally dried in the sun and turned into wine in a number of different styles. Much *montilla* is unfortified but achieves up to 15 percent alcohol by volume (abv) by natural fermentation. These wines are the mainstay of the region—modestly priced and sold in dry, medium and sweet styles. A new departure in style is *vinos jovenes afrutados* (young fruity wines) made from early-picked grapes, cool-fermented and sold immediately after the vintage. They are pleasant enough although rather neutral and lacking in character. The best wines of Montilla are fortified styles and possibly the only reason they aren't more prominent on world markets is because their names—*fino, amontillado, oloroso* and cream—cause them to be confused with sherry. At their very best, they are in the same league as sherry. One thing Montilla does with exemplary grace, however, is to produce the ancient PX wines: thick, black and fantastic poured into a little of the local ice-cream.

ALVEAR

Established 1729 *Owners* Alvear family *Production* 333,000 cases *Vineyard area* 618 acres (250 ha)

Alvear and business rivals Perez Barquero (see next column) teamed up in the 1990s to present a united "generic" front for *montilla* wines in a difficult market-place. The company is housed in a stately old bodega in the middle of the town, recently refurbished to provide a visitor center and areas for parties, weddings, barbecues and business meetings (a growth industry in these parts). However, winemaking is the key to its success and the approach is meticulous, with the result that Alvear produces some of the region's finest wines. Alvear is also a pioneer of the *joven afrutado* style. Its best-seller in Spain is CB Fino, named after a long-gone cellar-master called Carlos Bilanueva. Best wines: Capataz Fino; Solera Fundación Amontillado; Pelayo Oloroso.

PEREZ BARQUERO

Established 1905 *Owners* Compañia Vinícola del Sur *Production* 275,000 cases *Vineyard area* 309 acres (125 ha)

This bodega's faith in the future of *montilla* can be assessed by the fact that in early 2000 it spent half a billion pesetas extending the bodega to accommodate new tanks, a new fermentation hall and new bottling lines as well as redesigning its handling and dispatch routines. Along with Alvear (above), Perez Barquero provides a "generic" promotional stance for the region, and it obviously believes that it's working. Best wines: *fino, amontillado, oloroso* and PX (all under the Gran Barquero label).

Málaga

After its peak during the nineteenth century, the wines of this region have been in almost continuous decline. The present DO boasts only a handful of bodegas, most of them very small. The grape is the PX but here sunned and then fortified during fermentation to produce a wine of almost toffee-like richness. The best wines are aged in a *solera* and are incomparable, although, unfortunately, they are becoming harder and harder to find as the DO fades into oblivion.

Stakes stored for use in a vineyard.

Bullfighting, as well as wine drinking, is an integral part of Spanish culture.

LÓPEZ HERMANOS

Established 1885 *Owners* Burgos López family *Production* 110,000 cases *Vineyard area* 618 acres (250 ha)

This is a family firm doing its best to rekindle interest in the wonderful old wines of Málaga. In addition to the classic styles it produces a "pale cream" *oloroso* and a "dry" (more medium-dry) style as well. However, its biggest recent investment has been in a new state-of-the-art winery at Fuentepiedra, where the company plans to develop a new moscatel wine under the brand Pico Plata, a name López Hermanos purchased from Pedro Domecq in Jeréz. Best wines: Trajinero Oloroso; Cartojal Pale Cream; Málaga Virgen.

Condado de Huelva

Only old oak barrels are considered good enough to mature vintage sherries.

This region, between Jeréz country and Portugal, once shipped copious amounts of wine into the *soleras* of Jeréz but was left high and dry when the rules were more strictly enforced in the mid-twentieth century and only grapes from the Jeréz district were permitted to be used in sherry wines. As in Montilla, producers have turned to light, fruity *jovenes afrutados* and unfortified wines for the supermarket trade, although there is still a modest export bulk market in South America for the fortified wines. However, the main business hereabouts seems to be seasoning oak casks for the Scotch whisky industry: two years of *oloroso* wine in a new cask provides what a good malt needs for healthy development.

VC Aljarafe

There are only a few independent bodegas working outside the mainstream wine-producing areas of Andalusia. Most have a long way to go before they achieve international recognition.

JOSÉ GALLEGO-GÓNGORA

Established 1682 *Owners* Gallego-Góngora family *Production* 200,000 cases *Vineyard area* 296 acres (120 ha)

This company is run by the seventh generation of the family which founded it, in a small village to the west of Seville. Although the grape is the garrido fino, the wines are made very much in the Andaluz *generoso* style, and the wines are named "*fino*," "*amontillado*," etc., in the manner of sherry and *montilla*. In spite of the obscurity of this little corner of Andalusia the wines are quite astonishingly good: there are *jovenes afrutados* in the new fresh'n'crisp style, but the best work is still done with the fortified wines. Best wines: Amontillado Muy Viejo Selección Imperial; PX Dulce Añejo Selección Imperial.

Other Spanish Regions

VALENCIA

The autonomous Mediterranean region of Valencia is part of the Levante, a large area consisting of four provinces. There are five wine denominations within Valencia, including DO Valencia (see next page), and the wineries are among the most technologically advanced in Europe.

Alicante

This coastal region was best known in the 1950s for high-strength, sweet white wines, made from moscatel, and a legendary but expensive dessert red called fondillón, made from sun-dried monastrell grapes and aged for at least eight years. Both of these are still made and are justly popular, but modern Alicante also tuns out fresh, crisp whites from merseguera, airén and macabeo. The best wines are probably reds made from monastrell, garnacha, bobal and sometimes cabernet sauvignon. These may be aged to *reserva* level.

GUTIÉRREZ DE LA VEGA

Established 1978 *Owner* Pilar Sapena Sanchez *Production* 8,000 cases *Vineyard area* 25 acres (10 ha)

This is a small-scale bodega (tiny by Valencia standards) but it has an excellent reputation for elevating the sometimes mundane moscatel de Valencia into a high art, under the Casta Diva label. Winemaker Felipe Gutiérrez de la Vega puts the moscatel through its paces in various ways: as an *aguja* (slightly sparkling), barrel-fermented with five months on its lees, and tank-fermented fully dry. There's also a very good red wine called Viña Ulises Crianza made from cabernet sauvignon, girò, merlot, tempranillo and monastrell. Best wine: Casta Diva Cosecha Miel Dulce.

Utiel-Requena

Inland from Alicante, this is an area famed for beefy reds made from the bobal, often by the *doble-pasta* method of fermenting two lots of grapes in the same tank, with the second lot fermented over the lees

of the first, as well as its own lees. The resulting wine is hefty stuff and exported widely for blending with lightweight reds from elsewhere. Indeed, some of it goes to the DO Valencia where it's used to "fortify" the local reds—by special permission of the wine authorities. Young whites are made from the macabeo and merseguera and decent reds up to *reserva* level are made from tempranillo, garnacha and sometimes a little merlot or cabernet sauvignon.

VICENTE GANDIA PLA

Established 1885 *Owners* Gandía family *Production* 20,000 cases *Vineyard area* 247 acres (100 ha)

This big company was once based in the city of Valencia and makes wines under both DO names; the best-known from Valencia is probably Castillo de Liria. The main business is large-scale exports, and the company has a brand-new bodega with all the latest equipment, and the kind of "can-do" approach which has made Valencia a byword for export business for several hundred years. However, the bodega does also produce a range of its own wines, including a white macabeo and reds from tempranillo, cabernet sauvignon and monastrell. Best wine: Ceremonia Crianza.

Tempranillo grapes, used in many blends, make richly colored, long-lived wines.

Seville, at the heart of Andalusia, has a heritage of flamenco and bullfighting.

Vineyards have been part of the agricultural landscape of Spain for centuries.

prices are whatever you want to pay. Wines are tailor-made here to suit every importer. There's even a new sparkler and, with proposals afoot to combine all three Valenciano DOs into one, the range may increase even further.

SCHENK

Established 1927 *Owner* Schenk group *Production* 2,000,000 cases *Vineyard area* NA

This is a Swiss-owned company and part of a group which has wine interests all over the world. In common with most big Valenciano wine houses it produces large quantities of bulk wines for export as well as for selling all over Spain, but it also has its own range of wines, under the Cavas de Murviedro label. There are whites made from moscatel and merseguera and reds from monastrell, tempranillo and bobal. Best wines: Estrella (moscatel dulce); Los Monteros Crianza.

MURCIA

Inland from Valencia, the only real difference is that in Murcia they speak Spanish (Castellano) rather then Valenciano (a dialect of Catalan), and the food is, perhaps, more meat-oriented than the piscatorial gastronomy of the coast.

Jumilla

Jumilla used to be a place where large amounts of anonymous red wine were made and shipped around the country for blending in other regions, but almost nobody ever marketed the wine under its own name. As recently as 1990, you'd have laughed at anybody who suggested that you could make good—even great—wine from the humble monastrell grape but the truth was simply that nobody had really tried. When they did, the grape (known as the mourvèdre in France) showed reserves of spiciness and sheer rich fruit that no-one had suspected. Flushed with success, the winemakers of the region went on to make wines from garnacha and tempranillo of exemplary quality at silly prices. There is some decent wine, mainly made from airén, but the monastrell is king in these parts.

AGAPITO RICO

Established 1989 *Owners* Juan Sierva, Agapito Rico Martínez Production *Production* 45,000 cases *Vineyard area* 247 acres (100 ha)

Under careful husbandry and vinification the monastrell grape has shown itself to be capable of great things, and this is one of the bodegas which

Valencia

This DO, which shares the same name as the region it's in, really is the supermarket wine capital of Spain. There's an age-old export culture here (Valencia is Spain's second-biggest seaport after Barcelona) and a philosophy that the customer has always been right. You can buy a light, fresh, crisp, dry white made from the merseguera, a rich, sweet, fortified moscatel, a *crianza* red from tempranillo and cabernet, or anything in between. The bodegas are spotless, automated and brand-new; the winemakers trained in California, Montpellier, Barcelona or Melbourne; and the made that change happen. The vineyards are at an altitude of 2,300 feet (700 m), which helps to provide a good temperature range during the ripening season, and the winery is very much state of the art. The wines are called Carchelo and there is a *joven* made from monastrell and tempranillo, a *crianza* with some added cabernet sauvignon and varietal merlots with and without *crianza*, as well as a varietal syrah without oak. Best wines: the whole range, but especially merlot, syrah.

HUERTAS

Established 1996 *Owner* Antolin Huertas Manzaneque
Production 1,000,000 cases *Vineyard area* 1,920 acres (777 ha)

Although this is a large-scale bodega selling its wine all over Spain, its own vineyards provide only 4 percent of its needs in terms of grapes. Big though it is, it can still turn out some startlingly good wines. The best are the reds, all made entirely from monastrell. This is another bodega which has shown that with the correct handling, monastrell can be made into a truly excellent *joven* wine for (almost) immediate drinking. Best wines: Aranzo Crianza; Rodrejo (red *joven*).

Yecla

This is widely seen as another "one-horse" DO—indeed, it is the only DO which is applied to a single town. Yecla is sandwiched between Jumilla to the west and Alicante to the east and owes its current modest prominence to just one leading bodega. However, this is proof, if it were needed, that the traditional blockbusting high-strength wines that the area has always produced are not the only fruit. The monastrell here, as in Jumilla, has been teased out to give softness, fruit and a ripe, spicy fragrance as well as aging well in oak. There is some pleasant white, the best of which tends to be made from macabeo.

CASTAÑO

Established 1985 *Owners* Castaño family *Production* 333,000 cases *Vineyard area* 791 acres (320 ha)

Ramón Castaño has been doing his bit to put Yecla on the map and has been exporting his wines for the better part of 20 years. Although the company as presently constituted was only set up in 1985, the Castaños have been in the wine business since at least 1950. Innovation, as always, has been the key to success: the company grows monastrell, cabernet sauvignon, tempranillo and merlot and makes a white *joven* from macabeo as well as an unusual semi-sweet pink from monastrell. Its great strength, however, is the reds with *crianza*s and *reserva*s under the Pozuelo label. Best wines: Castaño Monastrell (*joven*); Hecula (monastrell/tempranillo/merlot).

Bullas

This is a large area south of Jumilla and almost as big as all the other Levantine vineyards put together. It struggled as a VdlT area for 12 years and kept just missing promotion to DO, but finally won through in 1994. The monastrell grape has done the trick here too, although there's also tempranillo and garnacha and a few forward-looking bodegas are experimenting with cabernet, merlot and syrah. White wines are mainly made from macabeo.

MADRID AND EXTREMADURA
Vinos de Madrid

There was amusement when these vineyards were awarded the DO in 1990 and, at that time, it was probably justified. It must have seemed then that an area dominated by a few old-fashioned co-ops was never going to achieve anything. Since then, however, some of the leading bodegas have pulled their act together and started to show wines with a bit of style, at moderate prices, and ideally suited to the unquenchable thirst for house-wine in the tapas bars of the city of Madrid. The best wines tend to be *joven* or occasionally *crianza* reds, made from tempranillo/tinto fino, but there's a lot of investment going on.

The ruins of ancient fortresses, built to repel Moslem invaders from the south, are a familiar sight in many parts of Spain.

Lush valleys and ancient villages are typical features of southwest Spain.

Ribera del Guadiana

An interesting exercise, this, in Extremadura, in the southwest of Spain. There had been six VdlT areas called Cañamero, Montánchez, Ribera Alta, Ribera Baja, Tierra de Barros and Matanegra, some of which (most notably Tierra de Barros) had achieved success in export markets and others which had not. The DO was created simply by drawing a line around all six of them but, owing to the obscurely democratic way in which the DO system works (see Wine Law), this was not as simple as it seemed. Bodegas in Tierra de Barros (right in the center of the DO zone, around the town of Almendralejo) cheerfully signed up for the new DO but others in the more outlying areas became increasingly less enthusiastic and several still bottle and sell their wines under the old VdlT names. However, it remains a fact that most of the best wines come from Tierra de Barros and economic pressure will probably bring everyone into the fold eventually.

INVIOSA
Established 1931 *Owners* Díaz family *Production* 85,000 cases *Vineyard area* 1,112 acres (450 ha)

This was the first bodega to recognize that the old VdlT Tierra de Barros wasn't going to get anywhere turning out the same old bulk wines it had made for generations. Marcelino Díaz, the current head of the family, took the decision in the early 1980s to branch out and explore the opportunities offered by "international" grape varieties and new technology. He planted chardonnay and sauvignon blanc alongside the native cayetana and pardina,

cabernet sauvignon, merlot and tempranillo and even graciano alongside the garnacha, and invested in stainless steel kit and new oak barrels. The results astonished everyone: the export market took the wines to its heart and today Bodegas InViOSA (Industrias Vinícolas del Oeste, SA) is the leading producer in the region. Best wines: Lar de Barros (white); Lar de Oro (range).

BALEARIC ISLANDS

Binissalem

This DO on Majorca—Spain's first offshore DO—got its ticket in 1991, but it wasn't until much later that the major bodegas of the region finished renewing their equipment and looking to markets beyond the peninsula. Interestingly, it was a Mallorquí by the name of Junipero Serra who, according to legend, took the first vines to California in the late 1700s, so presumably these were island vines. Today, however, most of the land is planted in mantonegro, a grape not found elsewhere in Spain. The wines it produces—with a little help from tempranillo and monastrell—are good to very good in quality and, with judicious use of oak, age well. There is some white wine made from moll (prensal), parellada and macabeo but this is, essentially, red-wine country.

MACIA BATLE
Established 1998 *Owners* Batle family *Production* 27,000 cases *Vineyard area* 124 acres (50 ha)

This small new family bodega is making great strides, especially when you consider that winemaker Agnau Calmés is working with the native Mallorquí grapes: prensal (or moll) for white wines, mantonegro and callet for pinks and reds. All the wines are under the Macia Batle name, and the company is already doing some export business in northern Europe. Best wines: Macia Batle red (two months in oak), white (*joven*).

Pla i Llevant de Mallorca

Promoted from VdlT at the turn of the century, this is an area of low-lying land, still growing a bewildering variety of grapes as the DO regulations are gradually applied. Much production goes to service the voracious tourist industry on the island, but there are those making something a little better from the ubiquitous mantonegro as well as the local callet and a bit of cabernet and tempranillo. White wines are largely *joven*, fresh, light and made from macabeo and parellada although there is a bit of chardonnay.

VINYES I BODEGUES MIQUEL OLIVER

Established 1912 *Owners* Oliver family *Production* 8,500 cases *Vineyard area* 25 acres (10 ha)

This is another small family concern: Miquel and Pilar Oliver share the winemaking duties and turn out some refreshingly different wines from this newly promoted area where much else of the production is singularly underwhelming. The Olivers grow moscatel (both alejandría and frontignan) for their white wine and callet, fogoneu, tempranillo, mantonegro and cabernet sauvignon for reds. Best wines: Mont Ferrutx Crianza; Ses Ferritges Reserva.

ARAGÓN

Somontano

Halfway up the south side of the Pyrenees, this region's unique microclimates, rich soils and traditional export market into southern France make it unique in northern Spain. Investment flooded in, in the late 1980s, and traditional wineries were traded in for the state-of-the-art kit in the mid-1990s when it became apparent that a cooler, wetter climate on the steep slopes of the River Vero could produce outstanding wine from almost any grape. The local candidates were the red moristel and the white alcañón, and these were joined by tempranillo, cabernet sauvignon, merlot, pinot noir, macabeo, chardonnay, chenin blanc, gewürztraminer and quite a few others. As the new vineyards matured towards the end of the 1990s, the smart, modern wineries began to turn out some spectacular wines, and this must be regarded as one of the most exciting new regions of Spain.

BODEGA PIRINEOS

Established 1993 *Owners* Co-op Somontano de Sobrabre, Instituto Aragonés de Fomento, Vinedos y Crianza de Alto Aragón (main shareholders) *Production* 450,000 cases *Vineyard area* 124 acres (50 ha)

This was once the local Co-operativa Sobrarbe-Somontano, privatized in 1993 and subsequently revolutionized in its winemaking (old concrete vats have been replaced with stainless steel). Today, the former members of the co-op are shareholders, but they deliver their grapes at vintage time just the same: macabeo and chardonnay for whites,

moristel, tempranillo, garnacha, merlot and cabernet sauvignon for reds. Best wines: Bodega Pirineos Merlot/Cabernet; Montesierra Crianza.

VIÑAS DEL VERO

Established 1986 *Owners* Private and institutional shareholders *Production* 125,000 cases *Vineyard area* 1,359 acres (550 ha)

This was a new start-up company funded by institutional finance to take advantage of the liberal regulations governing what could and could not be done in the then new DO of Somontano. An initial experimental plantation and bodega produced excellent results, giving way to the massive installation of today. The company grows chardonnay, gewürztraminer and local varieties for white wines, cabernet sauvignon, tempranillo, moristel, merlot and pinot noir for reds, and the winemaking, by Pedro Aibar, is innovative and pin-sharp. The wines are sold under the Viñas del Vero label. Best wines: the whole range, but especially chardonnay, gewürztraminer, Clarión (*joven* white), Gran Vos Reserva.

Cariñena

Meanwhile, back in the lowlands, this DO had been plugging away for 60 years and achieved some modest success for its red wines, made mainly from the garnacha. There's also tempranillo, a bit of cabernet sauvignon and a promising local called juan ibáñez which has yet to prove itself. Most of the wines are *joven*es, including whites, which are made mainly from macabeo.

SOLAR DE URBEZO

Established 1995 *Owners* Private shareholders *Production* 89,000 cases *Vineyard area* 247 acres (100 ha)

This is a mainly family affair, with Santiago Gracia in charge of the business and María-Asunción Gracia in charge of the winemaking. The company has taken a different approach to the traditional one favored by producers

Vineyards near the village of Alarban in Aragón form a patchwork of color.

The village of Maluenda in Aragón is in the heart of wine country.

in this DO zone in the past, and planted chardonnay, merlot, cabernet sauvignon and tempranillo as well as the ubiquitous garnacha. Going with the trend for younger, fresher wines there's an excellent *joven* made, rather surprisingly, from cabernet, tempranillo and garnacha, as well as a chardonnay with just one month in oak and a merlot/cabernet/tempranillo crianza. Best wines: Solar de Urbezo Crianza; Viña Urbezo (*joven*).

Campo de Borja

An ancient region famous for hefty reds, it is named after the family which owned the main town and estates, members of which, having changed their name to Borgia, went on to become popes and poisoners in the late fifteenth century. The wines have improved greatly since the award of the DO. There are some decent reds, made mainly from garnacha.

CRIANZAS Y VIÑEDOS ST CRISTO SOCIEDAD CO-OP

Established 1956　*Owners* Co-op members　*Production* 280,000 cases　*Vineyard area* 2,928 acres (1,185 ha)

Co-ops are traditionally slow to change their ways, but this one has moved with the times and installed new kit and new thinking. Its members grow macabeo, moscatel, garnacha and tempranillo and turn out some good wines under the hands of winemaker Modesto Francés Bernabeu. Best wine: Moscatel Ainzón Dulce.

Calatayud

Named after a Moorish chieftain who called his fortress Qalat ("Castle") Ayub, this fairly recent DO was known for little more than overheated red wines for many years. However, miracles take a little longer and one or two bodegas including, miraculously, a major local co-op, are turning out very good-quality wines at very modest prices. The best tend to be reds made from tempranillo and/or garnacha and monastrell.

VdlT Bajo Aragón

VENTA D'AUBERT

Established 1987　*Owner* Mühlemann family　*Production* 6,000 cases　*Vineyard area* 69 acres (28 ha)

This is a small bodega working away in a location which hasn't shown much promise for a while; the only other producer is a co-op, itself on the small side. But winemaker Stefan Dorst has worked hard with his small plantation of chardonnay, viognier, garnacha blanca, cabernet sauvignon, merlot, garnacha tinta and syrah and produced wines of a quality that would shame many a more famously situated bodega. Venta d'Aubert El Serrats is a white *crianza*, mainly chardonnay and viognier; Venta d'Aubert red is a cabernet/garnacha/syrah mix. Best wine: Domus Reserva (cabernet/merlot/garnacha/syrah).

CANARY ISLANDS

All but one of the seven islands in the archipelago (Fuerteventura) now make wine under the DO Regulations and Tenerife, the largest, has five DOs. Local wines are subsidized by the regional government, and many of them are excellent. The only reason they're not more widely known in export markets is the prohibitive cost of transporting them to mainland Europe.

Tacoronte-Acentejo, Tenerife

This is the largest and most well-established DO, encompassing the region around the town of Tacoronte in the northwest of the island. Producers here make mainly red wines from the listán negro grape. At their best these are excellent and age well.

INSULARES TENERIFE

Established 1992　*Owners* 500 local shareholder/growers　*Production* 56,000 cases　*Vineyard area* 1,235 acres (500 ha)

This is the modern face of the co-operative: Insulares Tenerife is not a bureaucratic dinosaur burdened with endless committees but a limited company running its own affairs, and very well too. The bodega is smart, new and fitted with the latest equipment with plenty of room for extra capacity when the need arises. The wines are amongst the best on the island and the bodega has serious ambitions to export, although the distance (and therefore cost) from the Canaries to the peninsula is the most daunting aspect. Best wines: Viña Norte (red and pink).

Valle de la Orotava

DO Valle de la Orotava is an area on the north-west slopes of Mount Teide, Tenerife's volcanic centerpiece. The wines of this region are mainly light, fresh whites and enjoyed by the vast holiday trade on the island.

VALLEORO

Established 1988 *Owners* 52 co-operative shareholders *Production* 67,000 cases *Vineyard area* 297 acres (120 ha)

This is a Sociedad Agraria de Transformación (SAT)—a kind of halfway house between an old-fashioned co-op and a limited company. The wines tend to be *jovenes* made in all three colors for the ever-thirsty holiday market, They are made from the listán blanco and listán negro, but there is some experimentation here, including barrel-fermentation for some of the white wines and *maceración carbonica* for some of the reds. The brand-name is Gran Tehyda, called after the towering crater of the volcano, Mount Teide. Best wines: Gran Tehyda Rosado, red.

Ycoden-Daute-Isora

Bodegas in the southwest region of Tenerife, around the town of Icod de los Vinos, are small and production is of mainly fruity, dry white wines made from the listán blanco grape. There is a small amount of sweet white malvasía in the old Canary-sack style.

CUEVA DEL REY

Established 1990 *Owner* Antonio Fernándo González *Production* 2,500 cases *Vineyard area* 35 acres (14 ha)

This is the size of operation which makes "boutique" wineries look as if they're on an industrial scale. Antonio González has built his own installation using small fiberglass tanks, and tempera-ture control is effected by a compressor made from an old freezer. His wines, however, are an excellent example of modern-style hands-on wine-making—light, fresh and fruity and ideally suited to the subtropical climate of the island. He makes just two wines: Cueva del Rey white (listán blanco) and red (listán negro).

TAJINASTE SAT

Established 1993 *Owners* Local shareholders *Production* 13,000 cases *Vineyard area* 198 acres (80 ha)

This is a small company, though building a reputa-tion for well-made fresh whites from the listán blanco grape and fruity reds from listán negro. Although the bodega has some new-oak casks (American) these tend to be used for fermentation. The rest of the winemaking is completely modern, with stainless steel installations, and freshness and fruit are what the winemaker is looking for. Indeed, the best wine is made by the process of *maceración carbónica*. Best wine: Viña Donia Tinto.

Lanzarote

Lanzarote, one of the most inhospitable wine-growing landscapes in the world, has an island-wide DO. Red and white wines are made, including sweet malvasía and moscatel from sun-dried grapes in the old Canary-sack style.

EL GRIFO

Established 1775 *Owners* Rodríguez-Bethencourt family *Production* 50,000 cases *Vineyard area* 99 acres (40 ha)

This is Lanzarote's leading bodega and carries on a tradition started by the same family some five generations ago. The bodega, which also has a small museum, is smart and full of new technology and the winemaking style is innovative. El Grifo is at the forefront in new-wave red and white wines, but its finest work is reserved for good old-fashioned Canary-sack made from the mal-vasía grape. Best wines: El Grifo Dulce; El Grifo Moscatel de Ana.

A cellar built into the side of a hillside creates a cool storage room for wine.

Portugal

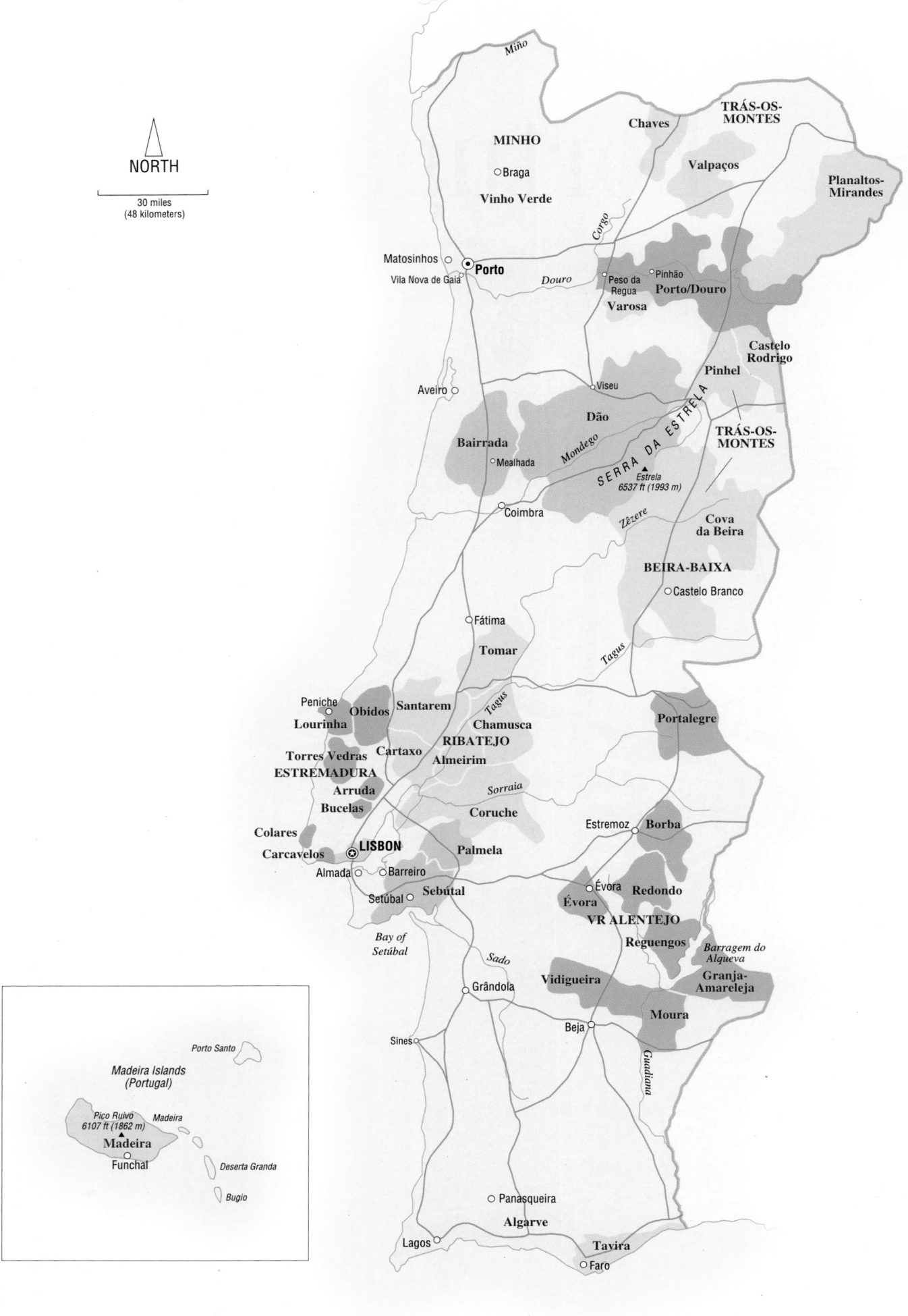

NORTH

30 miles
(48 kilometers)

MINHO

TRÁS-OS-
MONTES

Chaves

Braga ○

Valpaços

Planaltos-
Mirandes

Vinho Verde

Corgo

Matosinhos ○

Vila Nova de Gaia ◉ **Porto**

Douro

Peso da
Regua ○

○ Pinhão

Porto/Douro

Varosa

Castelo
Rodrigo

Pinhel

Aveiro ○

Viseu ○

Dão

Mondego

TRÁS-OS-
MONTES

Bairrada

Mealhada ○

▲ *Estrela*
6537 ft (1993 m)

Cova
da Beira

Coimbra ○

Zêzere

BEIRA-BAIXA

○ Castelo Branco

Fátima ○

Tomar

Tagus

Peniche ○

Obidos
○

Santarem

Lourinha

Cartaxo

Chamusca

Tagus

Portalegre

Torres Vedras

RIBATEJO

ESTREMADURA

Almeirim

Arruda

Bucelas

Sorraia

Coruche

Estremoz ○

Borba

Colares

Carcavelos

◎ **LISBON**

Palmela

Almada ○

○ Barreiro

○ Évora

Redondo

Setúbal ○

Sebútal

Évora

*Bay of
Setúbal*

VR ALENTEJO

Reguengos

*Barragem do
Alqueva*

Sado

Vidigueira

Granja-
Amareleja

Grândola ○

Moura

Beja ○

Sines ○

Guadiana

Porto Santo

*Madeira Islands
(Portugal)*

Pico Ruivo
6107 ft (1862 m) *Madeira*

Madeira ▲

Funchal ○

Deserta Granda

Bugio

○ Panasqueira

Algarve

Lagos ○

Tavira

Faro ○

Portugal

John Radford

If a country can be said to have reinvented itself almost from scratch in the last quarter of the twentieth century, then Portugal is that country. In the 1960s Portuguese wine was represented in the outside world by one rather underwhelming rosé in a pretty bottle—Mateus—and an assortment of half-forgotten names from the 1930s such as bucelas and setúbal. Madeira was considered only suitable for cooking or for elderly tastes and even port was in a decline regarded by many industry commentators as terminal. Even in the 1970s—the decade when a new generation woke up to wine—Portugal lagged. Enthusiasts leapt upon dão and vinho verde, a few hardy souls rediscovered colares and the red wines of the Douro, but interest was minimal and the wines were, all too often, inconsistent. Then came the 1980s… and something started stirring in the adegas (wineries) and vineyards. Portuguese

winemakers began to rediscover their native grape varieties and to use new technology to find out what they could really achieve. The consequences have been spectacular.

Portugal's centuries' old tradition of winemaking is celebrated in many of its ubiquitous blue and white tile-scapes.

History

Modern Portuguese wine history probably begins with the Treaty of Windsor (signed with England in 1386 and still in force today) which opened the way for international trade throughout northern Europe. In 1418, Portuguese settlement of the island of Madeira, off the coast of North Africa, provided another source for the heavy, heady wines of the day.

Port was born from a series of conflicts between the English and the French in the seventeenth century. Trade wars and high tariffs on French wine prompted English merchants to travel to Portugal, where they settled and began to export wine, to which they added brandy to fortify it for the journey. The port trade was helped by the Methuen Treaty of 1703 which admitted Portuguese wines to England at preferential duty rates.

Much of the modern shape of Portuguese wine production can be laid to the credit of Sebastião José de Carvalho e Mello, later Marqués de Pombal, who became prime minister after the accession of King José in 1750. He tightened up the regulations on port production after years of abuse and laid out much of the foundation for Portugal's wine regulation and quality control right up to the present day.

In 1910, when Portugal became a republic, only six wine regions were demarcated. These were Carcavelos, Colares, Dão, Moscatel de Setúbal, Port and Vinho Verde. The government, which added Bucelas in 1911 and Madeira in 1913, was swallowed up by a military coup leading to a dictatorship which lasted until 1975, and very little of significance—apart from the

creation of Mateus Rosé in 1942—happened in the wine world during that time.

Since the return to democracy, Portuguese wine has changed beyond recognition, now offering a splendid mix of ancient and modern, rustic and high-tech, new-wave and traditional that is, perhaps, unmatched anywhere else in the world.

There are two leading wine producers in Portugal, with interests in more than one region:

Sogrape was established in 1942 in Vila Real. The company came into being purely to make a new commercial rosé aimed squarely at the export trade. At the time, one of the founding shareholders was Fernando van Zeller Guedes who made vinho verde at the Quinta de Aveleda in Penafiel and he eventually became the major shareholder in 1981. Two years earlier, however, a family split had seen Quinta de Aveleda and Sogrape go their separate ways and it was to remain that way until 1997 when Sogrape took over Aveleda and united the two branches of the Guedes family once more. In the meantime, Sogrape had taken over or established wineries in the Vinho Verde region, the Douro (Casa Ferreira), port country (Offley-Forester, Ferreira), Dão (Quinta dos Carvalhais), Bairrada and the Alentejo. It is currently the biggest wine company in Portugal.

The *Symington group* might be described as the "royal family" of fortified wines in Portugal. Andrew Symington was a Scotsman who moved to Porto in 1882 to work for Warre's, a company whose main concern was in the textile industry, with port wine a small subsidiary business. Andrew much preferred the wine side of things, became a partner in the business in 1905, and was offered control of the Portuguese end of the company in 1912 when the head of the firm, George Warre, decided to return to London. By this time, Warre's owned the merged company which had once been Silva & Cosens and Dow's. Andrew bought Quarles Harris (to whose owners he was related by marriage) in 1920, and his heirs and the Warres shared control until 1961, when the Symington family bought out the remainder of the business. The Symington empire was now made up of Silva & Cosens, Dow and Warre, and incorporated Quinta do Bomfim, Quinta do Zimbro and Senhora da Ribeira. Further acquisitions since then include Graham's in 1970 (including its subsidiary, Smith Woodhouse) and Gould Campbell, also in 1970. It is currently the biggest producer of port in the country. As if this were not enough, the Symingtons moved into Madeira

A vineyard in the Douro valley, the area where the grapes for port are grown.

in 1988, taking over the Madeira Wine Company which by this time dominated production on the island, having absorbed most of the "famous name" brands since its first stirrings in 1913: Blandy's, Cossart Gordon, Leacock, Rutherford & Miles and no less than 23 other companies have now been assimilated into the Symington Madeira empire, accounting for some 40 percent of the island's production.

Landscape and climate

The country divides roughly in half, north and south of the Tagus River. The north is mountainous and a bedrock composed of schist, granite and slate rises steeply from the west coast to between 2,300 and 2,625 feet (700 and 800 m). The south is lower—mainly under 1,300 feet (400 m)—and based on sandstone, although as the land climbs towards the central plain of the peninsula limestone becomes more prominent on the outcrops.

The climate divides on similar lines. North of the Tagus there is more temperate influence, with higher rainfall in coastal areas, reducing as the land climbs towards the center of the peninsula. Here, summers are long and very hot and winters very cold: snow may lie on the mountain peaks for three months or even longer. In the south, the climate is more Mediterranean, with milder winters (although cold weather from the *meseta* (tableland) may bring occasional frosts) and hot, sometimes humid summers. There may be no rainfall at all in July and August.

In wine terms, Portugal can be split roughly into five mainland regions—the north, the area from the Douro to the Tagus Rivers, the center (Lisbon and the Tagus valley), Setúbal and the south, and the Algarve—and the islands of Madeira and the Azores.

THE NORTH

Here, the land climbs from the west coast towards the Spanish border into granite mountains with outcrops of schist in the highlands of the port country. The great contrast here in winemaking is between the light, fresh, usually fizzy wines of Vinho Verde and the heavyweights of the Douro, including port.

The northwest corner of Portugal is where vinho verde ("green wine") is grown. Country wines from the northeast are made in the area between the Spanish border to the north and east and four mountain ranges to the west. The northern part is high and inhospitable, and

known as the *terra fria* ("cold land") because, in spite of its baking-hot summers, it suffers bitterly cold winters and farming the land is very difficult. The southern part includes the Douro valley and is called *terra quente* ("hot land").

Port country is some of the most beautiful and spectacular in the world. The River Corgo flows into the Douro near where the town of Régua splits the main production area of DOC Porto into two: Baixo Corgo, the area around the town and the confluence, is the westernmost area for port production and also the coolest and wettest. Cima Corgo, upstream from Régua, is the heartland of top-quality port production, centered around the

The number of single-estate wineries has increased with the relaxation of government bureacracy and entry to the European Union.

Above: *The warehouse at the Cálem Port Lodge in the Douro Valley.*

Top: *New port wine at Cálem is matured in barrels and then shipped.*

town of Pinhão. It occupies three-quarters of the delimited port zone but has only 40 percent of the vineyards, although these are usually in the best geographical locations.

The unfortified wine classification for the wines of the Douro—DOC Douro—occupies the same boundaries as the DOC Porto. Although port grapes tend to occupy the best sites on the schistose soils, on the fringes of the region—especially in the highlands where the climate is a little cooler—grapes which are grown on granite-based soils make excellent reds.

FROM THE DOURO TO THE TAGUS

This is one of the oldest-established fine-wine areas of Portugal, covering the land which stretches between the points at which the Rivers Douro and Tagus cross the Spanish border. Dão and Bairrada are the most prominent wine areas in a landscape which is the most mountainous in the country, rising from sea level to some 6,500 feet (2,000 m) in the east.

THE CENTER: LISBON AND THE TAGUS VALLEY

The region of Estremadura stretches more than 95 miles (150 km) north of Lisbon along the coast and is home to a bewildering array of grapes and a reputation for decent if unexciting, everyday wines.

There are seven DOC regions within the Tagus valley which is broad and fertile, with alluvial soils and abundant agriculture and plenty of experimentation going on in the winemaking world.

SETÚBAL AND THE SOUTH

This region—which covers almost a third of Portugal—is mainly undulating plain, fertile and heavily farmed for every known agricultural or horticultural product. Setúbal has seen some of the most innovative and forward-thinking new ideas in recent years, with the creation of some splendid wines, as well as maintaining its reputation for the classic moscatel.

THE ALGARVE

This is Portugal's hottest region with a beautiful landscape including craggy inlets and subtropical inland areas. It also has a tradition of winemaking going back to the days when fortified sherry-type wines were made here and often shipped over the River Guidiana to Spain. The biggest threat to quality winemaking, however, has been the undemanding, high-volume tourist market along the coast which has produced a large amount of unexciting wine.

MADEIRA

This spectacularly beautiful volcanic island is 620 miles (1,000 km) from the Portuguese coast and 435 miles (700 km) from the coast of Morocco. The land rises steeply on all sides and the lower reaches are planted with everything from bananas to avocados as well as subtropical horticulture of every kind. Wine grapes are grown in terraced slopes, often high up towards the center of the island and in apparently inaccessible places. All in all, it's just about the last place on Earth you'd expect to find one of the world's greatest wines. There are no rivers on Madeira, but the vineyards are irrigated by a system of *levadas*—narrow aqueducts which channel the rainwater collected at the summit (about 6,000 feet, or 1,800 m) down to the vineyards below, where the rainfall is much lower. The climate is temperate, though often humid, with an average midwinter low of 64°F (18°C) and an average midsummer high of 72°F (22°C).

THE AZORES

This archipelago lies in the Atlantic 870 miles (1,400 km) west of Portugal, and consists of nine main islands, of which three make wines. In common with Madeira and the Spanish-owned Canary Islands, the Azores are volcanic in origin. The climate is subtropical with high humidity and the islanders grow cereals, vegetables and fruit (including, it is claimed, the world's finest pineapples), as well as grapes for wine.

Wines

PORT

It is popularly believed that port was invented early in the eighteenth century by English merchants who were searching for something to replace French wines, no longer available in England at the time because of the War of the

Spanish Succession, in which England and France were on opposite sides. One theory has it that port was the result of wine being doctored with alcohol to try to cover up the wine's harsh, tannic flavors; another, that at some time someone must have mixed brandy with the wine during fermentation, thus retaining the sweetness of the natural grape sugar. The invention is also accredited to the abbot of Lamego in the Douro valley in 1678, but it could have been discovered by several different people over a number of years.

Whatever the truth of the matter, methods of making port today remain largely traditional, though there is fierce argument over whether the grapes are better pressed and fermented in steel tanks or pressed by foot in *lagares* (stone troughs) as they have been for centuries. One method tries to satisfy both sides of the argument by combining technology and tradition in the form of stainless steel tanks with machinery the same size and shape as a human footprint—it even has toes!—to press the grapes. Another high-tech version has robot "feet" on hydraulic legs which are put to work in the *lagares* without needing to pause for rest.

Whichever method is used to press the grapes, the must is fermented to about 6–8 percent abv (alcohol by volume) and run off into holding tanks which are already a quarter full of a neutral grape spirit called *aguardiente*. This stops the fermentation without adding flavors or aromas to the wine. Then, after a suitable period of rest, the wine is passed to casks or tanks for maturation. A bewildering variety of grapes may be used to make port, but only half a dozen are generally accepted to be in the front rank: touriga francesa, tinta roriz, mourisco, bastardo and tinta cão and everyone's favorite, touriga nacional. Other top-class varieties are tinta francisca, tinta barroca, tinta amarela, periquita (also known as castelão frances) and sousão. There are nearly 30 varieties permitted for red wines and 20 for white. Most white port is made from a mixture which is likely to include gouveio, malvasia and rabigato (also known as rabo de ovelha).

All vineyards in port country are classified and graded according to the quality they normally produce. Points are awarded (or taken away) for altitude, yields, soil types, age and nature of vines

Barcos rabelos, the old flat-bottomed port boats, add color to the quay at Vila Nova de Gaia, across the river from Porto.

Sandeman's famous cloaked figure gives the brand an instantly recognizable identity.

Above: *A very old vintage boal, one of the four "noble" grape varieties grown in Madeira.*

Top: *Tinta negra mole grapes, the most widely grown variety in Madeira, arrive for vinification.*

and other factors which are deemed to affect the final quality of the grapes. The final scores are then banded into Grades A to F, and growers paid on a sliding scale according to the quality of what they produce.

Port is aged and classified according to its quality:

Vintage port is a single-vintage wine from the very best years, and spends two years in cask and the rest in bottle. Vintage ports are the region's greatest wines.

Single-quinta is made from the grapes of an individual *quinta* ("farm"). It has become popular in recent years to make a single-*quinta* in the years which are not quite great enough to make a full vintage. (An exception is Quinta do Noval which is the name of the estate as well as that of its finest wines.)

Colheita means "harvest"—that is, wine made from the harvest of a single vintage. (It can't be called "vintage" because that would confuse it with vintage port.) *Colheita* ports are single-vintage wines which are aged in wood until just before bottling. These may be very old, tawny-colored and delicately nutty in flavor.

Tawny, as its name implies, is a lighter style of port, blended from different vintages and aged in wood for six to seven years before bottling and sale. There are some very fine old tawnies of 20, 30 and 40 years old.

Late-bottled vintage is a vintage port, typically from a second-string year and aged in wood for four to six years or so before release.

Vintage character describes a port made "in the vintage style" but blended from a number of years.

Ruby is a basic everyday port wine which may be any age at all, and it can be very variable in quality. The best rubies will have been aged for around four years.

MADEIRA

The four noble varieties used to make madeira are malvasia (known by the English as malmsey), boal, verdelho and sercial. As well, there have always been plantations of terrantez, bastardo and moscatel on Madeira, as well as listrão on the neighboring island of Porto Santo. However, the number of all these grape varieties added together is insignificant when compared to the area planted with the most common grape in Madeira—the tinta negra mole.

As with many fortified wines, the heating and cooling effects of the trip across the equator in the age of exploration seemed to improve the quality of the wine, and this led to the unique methods of maturation used on the island ever since. Grapes are bought in from small farmers and the price paid reflects the quality of the grape. The noble varieties are fermented separately, often in oak casks or vats. Tinta negra mole is now typically fermented in concrete vats or stainless steel. The wines are fortified to 17–18% abv (alcohol by volume) during fermentation, as with port, although the moment of fortification varies according to the dryness required in the finished wine.

Estufa (meaning "stove") is the name of the unique method which Madeira producers use to reproduce the gentle heating and cooling effects of an equatorial voyage. Carried out incorrectly, it can seriously damage the wine, and there are those violently opposed to it in any form. Done gently, using the latest equipment, however, it can speed up the wine's development. A good modern installation will hold the wine in stainless steel tanks with a water-jacket containing hot water. The tank is heated gently to about 113°F (45°C) and then returned to the ambient temperature over a period of, perhaps, six months. This allows the wine to develop without bringing out unwanted flavors. Noble wines are usually aged by the *canteiro* system, in which casks of the wine are racked into heated warehouses and allowed to adjust to the changing ambient temperature. In either case the wines must be aged for three years before sale.

Colheitas (see port, above, for a definition) are single-vintage wines made from the noble varieties. Those from the very best years have been known to survive for up to 200 years. By law, they must be stored in cask for a minimum of 20 years and in bottle for a further two years before release. Madeira made from terrantez and moscatel grapes is governed by the same regulations; it is rare and usually found only as *colheita* wine.

Some *solera* wines are the result of a system of winemaking which comes from Jeréz country. Wines from a series of "scales," or rows, of increasingly old barrels are blended with younger wines of the same type. In effect, new wine goes in at one end and old wine comes out of the other after a period of many years. In this way the new wine takes on the characteristics of the old and matures much more quickly and with better quality control. Some *solera* wines may carry the date of foundation of the *solera*. These are now rare but some of the older wines are still available.

Malmsey, *boal*, *verdelho* and *sercial* must be made from 85 percent of the named grape. They are usually sold as 5-year-old, 10-year-old, 15-year-old and *colheita*.

Sweet, *medium-sweet*, *medium-dry* and *dry* madeiras are wines made from tinta negra mole—the financial foundation of the industry—and the four levels of sweetness are supposed to represent the styles of the four noble grapes.

Wine law

Several administrations over the past century have tried to organize the wine industry, with only limited success—until 1999, when all the anomalies were sorted out (for now). The new administrative body is the Instituto da Vinha e do Vinho (IVV) and the current terminology is as follows:

QUALITY WINE

The letters VQPRD stand for Vinho de Qualidade Produzidos em Regiões Determinadas (QWPSR in English—"Quality Wines Produced in Specific Regions"). This embraces two categories:

Denominação de Origem Controlada (DOC): This means "denomination of controlled origin" and is the equivalent of Spain's DO or France's AOC. The 22 regions so classified include the old traditional areas of winegrowing as well as some emergent new ones. They are each policed by a Regional Commission which makes decisions about planting, yield and wine styles. The two largest DOC regions (Ribatejo and Alentejo) are further subdivided (into six and eight subregions respectively), making a total of 36 DOC areas.

Indicação de Provenencia Regulamentada (IPR): This category was created for emergent wine areas which might wish to seek promotion at a later stage. Some are administered by their own Regional Commission, others directly by the IVV. There are currently nine regions in this classification. Regulations are slightly more relaxed than those for the DOC although IPRs still have quality-wine status (like the French VDQS).

TABLE WINE

This category divides into two:

Vinho Regional (VR) are country wines from fairly large areas. The regulations in this category are particularly important in that they allow growers and winemakers much more flexibility in the wines that they make as well as allowing a vintage date, some kind of regional name and the mention of grape variety/ies to appear on the label. Some of Portugal's most exciting new wines come under this apparently humble classification. Nine of them cover virtually the whole country, and they are administered directly by the IVV.

Vinho de Mesa (VdM) is, as its name suggests, a simple table wine. It may be made in and blended from grapes from any part of Portugal. There are few controls on the way it is made (except restrictions on gross yield) although, under European law, these wines may not carry any regional name (except the name of the country) or vintage date or grape variety. Vinho de Mesa Espumante (VdME) is classified simply as "sparkling table wine," with the same regulations as VdM, because there is no quality wine classification for sparkling wine in Portugal.

Peso da Régua, a vineyard-growing area at the confluence of the Douro and Corgo Rivers, is a major port town.

The North

Technology has replaced traditional winemaking methods in many co-ops.

VR MINHO

This is a country-wine area in the northwest. Its borders coincide, more or less, with those of the DOC Vinho Verde but regulation here is much less stringent and winemakers are experimenting with a whole range of grape varieties which go beyond those permitted in DOC wines. Wines may be vinho verde in style or off-the-wall with independent winemakers experimenting with new ideas.

Vinho Verde

This area is best known for its slightly under-ripe ("green") wines with a bit of slightly sparkling *spritzig* character, although locally these are likely to be red and drunk very young and very fresh. For export, the wines are mainly white and the best of them are made from the alvarinho grape in the subregion of Monçao, on the Spanish border. Other grapes include azal, loureiro, rabigato (rabo de ovelha) and trajadura. At their best, these are fresh, crisp, invigorating wines with a hint of a sparkle and a delicious dryness.

QUINTA DE ALDERIZ

Established NA *Owner* S.A. de Casa Pinheiro *Production* 6,000 cases *Vineyard area* 25 acres (10 ha)

From Monçao, along the Minho to the west of Melgaço, this is where much of the best alvarinho grows. The Sociedade Agrícola da Casa Pinheiro, which is based at the quinta, makes this excellent example. Best wine: Quinta de Alderiz Alvarinho.

ANTÓNIO ESTEVES FERREIRA

Established 1982 *Owner* António Esteves Ferreira *Production* 2,917 cases *Vineyard area* 25 acres (10 ha)

Situated at the Quinta de Soalheiro in Melgaço, in the Minho valley, just across the border from Galicia, in Spain. Best wine: Soalheiro Alvarinho.

SOGRAPE

Established 1947 *Owners* Sogrape *Production* 3,719,812 cases *Vineyard area* 988 acres (400 ha)

After the family split in 1979, Sogrape went on to develop its own vinho verde—Morgadio da Torre, made from 100 percent alvarinho—at its winery in Barcelos. Aveleda is still made at the quinta in Penafiel and the company now sells both brands. Best wine: Morgadio da Torre.

VR TRÁS-OS-MONTES

In the northeast of Portugal, country wines are light whites in the vinho verde style as well as heavyweight whites and reds largely unseen outside their home region. The southern part includes the Douro valley. Wine from here may be labeled "Vinho Regional Trás-os-Montes/Terras Durienses"—a legal nicety for winemakers who are geographically in the Douro valley but make wines which, for one reason or another, don't qualify for the DOC Douro (perhaps because they're planting unauthorized grapes).

The area includes Chaves, Valpaços and Planalto-Mirandes IPRs.

Produce from the vineyards around the town of Amarante in the Douro region has easy access to Porto via the Tâmega River.

Chaves IPR is in the northwest, by the River Tamega. Here, a grape called boal is grown, although there's some doubt as to whether it's the same boal that is grown in Madeira. Along with malvasia and gouveio it makes light whites in the vinho verde style. Chaves also makes some red from the Douro varieties, but quality is at an everyday level.

Valpaços IPR is on the upper reaches of the River Tua, roughly in the center of the *terra fria*. Producers in this area make light reds and pinks from a mix of Douro grapes, as well as a red sweet *mistelle* (fortified unfermented grape juice) called *jeropiga*.

Planalto-Mirandes IPR is on the border, where the River Douro comes in from Spain. This is a region of fairly heavyweight, bucolic reds and whites, again from mainly Douro varieties.

Douro

Such has been the interest and investment here— often by outsiders from other parts of Europe and from Australia—that the best wines of the region are now being made and sold by single-*quinta* producers, and Douro wines are beginning to be accepted as some of Portugal's finest. Although there is some very good white wine produced here, this seems to be destined to become one of Europe's great red-wine areas.

QUINTA DO CRASTO

Established 1615 *Owners* Jorge and Leonor Roquette
Production 19,000 cases *Vineyard area* 114 acres (46 ha)

This is a lovely old estate with a beautifully restored country house attached, which includes a small but elegantly decorated chapel. The wines are first-rate and there is some port. Since 1995, the Australian winemaker Donald Baverstock has commandeered most of the best of the grapes for the eponymous wine. The grapes are old-vine (up to 70 years)—touriga nacional, tinta roriz, touriga francesa and tinta cão—aged in oak (some American and some French). There are oak-aged and varietal wines made in a combination of traditional *lagares* and modern stainless steel. Best wine: Quinta do Crasto Reserva.

A. A. FERREIRA S. A.

Established 1751 *Owners* Sogrape *Production* 60,000 cases
Vineyard area 370 acres (150 ha)

This is an offshoot of the port house Ferreira which has been making what is perhaps Portugal's finest red wine—Barca Velha—since it was first

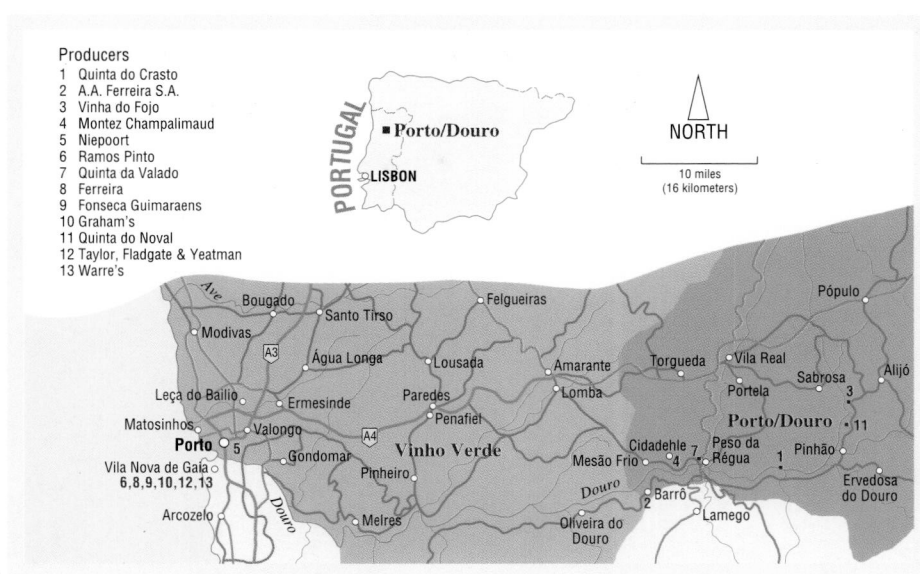

Producers
1 Quinta do Crasto
2 A.A. Ferreira S.A.
3 Vinha do Fojo
4 Montez Champalimaud
5 Niepoort
6 Ramos Pinto
7 Quinta da Valado
8 Ferreira
9 Fonseca Guimaraens
10 Graham's
11 Quinta do Noval
12 Taylor, Fladgate & Yeatman
13 Warre's

conceived in 1952. Sometimes described as Portugal's Vega Sicilia (after the famous Spanish wine), it is made from a combination of the finest port grapes and quality grapes from the higher, cooler vineyards and only made at all in the finest years. To balance acidity, 60 percent tinta roriz grapes are complemented with 40 percent touriga francesa, tinta barroca and tinta amarela. It spends 18 months in French oak and a further seven or eight years in bottle. Great vintages have lasted as long as 30 years. Wine which doesn't quite make the grade (although still amongst the Douro's finest) is called Reserva Ferreirinha and, since the take-over by Sogrape in 1987, there have been two more early-release wines: Callabriga and Vinha Grande. Best wine: Barca Velha.

VINHA DO FOJO

Established 1992 *Owners* Serōdio Borges family
Production 4,000 cases *Vineyard area* 17 acres (7 ha)

This family firm also owns the Quinta do Fojo and Quinta da Manuela in Pinhão, where they make port and sell it to the major shippers. The brother-and-sister team of Jorge and Margarida Serōdio Borges took over in the early 1990s and set about establishing a Douro red wine, made from the same grapes as they use for their port—tinta roriz, touriga francesa, tinta barroca, tinta cão, tinta amarela and touriga nacional—all from very old, low-yielding wines. The first vintage was the 1996 and, whilst it's too young to say definitively, opinion has it that this is one of the emerging greats of the Douro valley. Best wine: Fojo.

The winter task of pruning over-long shoots encourages vines to grow in straight rows.

The River Douro has been an aquatic highway for the wine trade for centuries.

MONTEZ CHAMPALIMAUD

Established 1922 *Owner* Montez Champalimaud *Production* 16,667 cases *Vineyard area* 123 acres (50 ha)

Miguel Champalimaud is a maverick winemaker who has shaken the Douro "establishment" on a number of occasions. When he bought the Quinta do Côtto in 1976 he unceremoniously dumped the estate's established wines (made from bastardo and sousão) and started to make something different which he called Quinta do Côtto. By 1982, he was producing a top-of-the-range version called Grande Escolha ("Great Choice"), made from touriga nacional, touriga francesa and tinta roriz. Grande Escolha is made in the best years from grapes from the oldest vines, and aged for 18 months in new Portuguese oak. The company also makes an interesting if unexceptional white from malvasia, avesso and sémillon and it makes port as well. Best wines: Quinta do Côtto, especially Grande Escolha.

NIEPOORT

Established 1842 *Owners* Niepoort family *Production* 5,000 cases *Vineyard area* 62 acres (25 ha)

An old-established port company which went into the Douro wine business relatively late, this firm has built quite a reputation since the early 1990s. Winemaker Dirk Niepoort makes a hefty red called Redoma at the Quinta do Carril (between Pinhão and Régua). Unusually, he also makes a white counterpart which shows great promise, made from gouveio and rabigato (rabo de ovelha) from highland vineyards to maximize available acidity, at the Quinta de Napolés. There's also a red made in the traditional way (in *lagares*) at the Quinta do Passadouro from tinta roriz and touriga francesa. Many of the vines here are more than 50 years old, and yield is very low. Best wine: Redoma (red).

RAMOS PINTO

Established 1880 *Owner* Champagne Louis Roederer *Production* 108,330 cases *Vineyard area* 494 acres (200 ha)

Part of the Ramos Pinto Port company and run by João Nicolau de Almeida, this company has been making Douro wines since the beginning of the 1980s. They make wine under the VR Trás-os-Montes/Terras Durienses at Quinta dos Bons Aires and under the DOC Douro from a mixture of grapes drawn from Quinta da Ervamoira in the Côa valley (douro superior) and Quinta de Bom Retiro in the Torto valley (cima corgo). The former provides grapes with freshness and acidity, the latter with weight, ripeness and structure, and the result is called Duas Quintas. Best wine: Duas Quintas Reserva.

QUINTA DO VALADO
Established 1995 *Owners* Ferreira family *Production* 15,000 cases *Vineyard area* 158 acres (64 ha)

This estate makes port wines for the parent company (Ferreira) as well as a range of reds and whites but, since 1995, winemaker Francisco Olazabal has switched half of production to produce two non-port wines under the DOC Douro, both called Vallado (spelled confusingly with two Ls). The white is made from fernão pires, malvasia, viosinho and rabigato (rabo de ovelha) and is very good, but the red is better. Red Vallado is made from tinta roriz, tinta barroca and tinta amarela and is sold as a young wine, without oak aging. Best wine: Vallado (red).

Porto

DOC Porto shares the same boundaries as DOC Douro in the subregion of VR Tras-os-Montes and these two areas dominate wine production, as very little wine is made under the VR regulations.

FERREIRA
Established 1751 *Owner* Sogrape *Production* NA *Vineyard area* NA

Antónia Adelaide Ferreira, great grand-daughter of the founder, José Ferreira, consolidated the foundations of this company in the early nineteenth century. She was known colloquially as Ferreirinha (which means "Little Ferreira" in Portuguese), a name which still appears on the labels today. Her great-great grandson, Vito Olazabal, steered the company to its present pre-eminence before his retirement in 1999, and Vito's son, Francisco, is the winemaker at Quinta do Valado (see Douro, above). The company was sold to Sogrape in 1987. Grapes for Ferreira port come from four quintas—do Porto (bought in 1863); do Seixo (1979); de Leida and do Caedo (1990). Best wines: LBV; Duque de Bragança 20-year-old tawny; vintages.

FONSECA GUIMARAENS
Established 1822 *Owner* Taylor, Fladgate & Yeatman *Production* NA *Vineyard area* NA

The founder of this company, Manuel Guimaraens, took over a company called Fonseca & Monteiro. Part of the deal was that whoever bought the company should keep the Fonseca name, no matter who owned it and indeed his word has been kept, even after having been taken over by Taylor's in 1948. The current head of the family is Bruce Guimaraens and the winemaker is his son, David, who trained at Roseworthy in Australia. Although Alastair Robertson of Taylor's is the majority shareholder, Fonseca has its own house style and its own sources of grapes—most notably the Quinta do Cruzeiro and the Quinta do Santo Antônio in the Pinhão valley. At the fighting end, Premium Ruby Bin 27 is the most famous name, but its aged tawnies are legendary in the trade, as is the late-bottled vintage (after four years in wood rather than two) which is branded Fonseca-Guimaraens. Best wines: 10-year old and 20-year-old tawny; Fonseca-Guimaraens LBV; vintages.

GRAHAM'S
Established 1820 *Owners* Symington family *Production* 180,000 cases *Vineyard area* 242 acres (98 ha)

This is one of the classic port houses, run by the Graham family until it was sold to the Symingtons in 1970. The purchase of the Quinta dos Malvedos in 1890 (sold in the 1940s and bought back in 1982) provided the company with excellent single-*quinta* wines in the boom years between the wars. When times got tough in the 1950s and 1960s, Graham's sourced most of its grapes from the Quinta das Lages. Today, grapes are harvested at the main Symington sites: Quinta do Bomfim, Quinta da Cavadinha and Quinta do Vesúvio. Best wines: LBV; old tawnies; single-*quinta* vintages (Malvedos, Vesúvio); but especially the great vintages.

QUINTA DO NOVAL
Established 1715 *Owners* AXA Millésimes *Production* 20,000 cases *Vineyard area* 200 acres (80 ha)

This wonderful estate has passed through many hands, but the defining moment in its history was in 1981 when a fire at the company's lodges in Vila Nova de Gaia resulted in disastrous losses of wine, archives and property, leaving the firm open to a take-over by AXA, the French-based insurance group which has built a portfolio of desirable wine

The traditional craft of a cooper is essential in building and maintaining the oak barrels still preferred by many winemakers.

In making red port, a process called auto-vinification extracts the maximum amount of color from the grapes.

Terraced vineyards contour the steep valleys of the Douro region.

properties from Bordeaux to Budapest. AXA demolished the crumbling farmhouse (except for the facing walls) and rebuilt an exact replica with modern methods, stocking it with choice antiques from the Paris market. Englishman Christian Seely was brought in to run it. Winemaking is a mix of traditional (*lagares*) and modern (stainless steel) and the wines are uniformly excellent. Best of all is the "nacional" vineyard—a small plantation of touriga nacional vines on natural, ungrafted roots, originated in the early days. Yield is low and the vines are old, but the vintage port made from this patch fetches prices beyond the dreams of King Midas. Best wines: the entire range, but especially old tawnies; vintages; and (for those in the money) nacional vintages.

TAYLOR, FLADGATE & YEATMAN
Established 1692 *Owner* Alistair Robertson *Production* NA *Vineyard area* NA

Originally a wool business, Taylor's moved into wine in a big way in the early 1700s and was the first English company to buy a property in the Douro, near Régua. The Taylor family made its first appearance in 1816, taking control by 1826. Joseph Taylor was joined by John Fladgate in 1836. Morgan Yeatman, a West Country wine merchant, came on board in 1838 and the company name has not changed since then.

Taylor's is now generally recognized to be the number one company in the port trade. Its major brands are LBV and some splendid old tawnies, but the jewels in the crown are wines produced by the two *quintas* Quinta da Terra Faita and Quinta de Vargellas. This last is a magnificent property turning out some of the finest wines in the region. It is also declared as a single-*quinta* in "off" years. Best wines: old tawnies; Quinta de Vargellas; vintages.

WARRE'S
Established 1670 *Owners* Symington family *Production* 170,000 cases *Vineyard area* 109 acres (44 ha)

This was the firm from which Andrew Symington began his conquest of the Portuguese fortified wine industry in 1882: the last Warre family investment was bought out in the 1960s and the last member of the family, Bill Warre, retired in 1991. The firm is one of the most reliable producers in the business and still turns out some peerless wines. The modern-day wines come from the main Symington *quintas*: da Cavadinha, do Bomfim and do Sol. Quinta da Cavadinha is sometimes declared as a single-*quinta* vintage in "off" years. At the popular end of the market, Warre's Warrior is a splendid premium ruby, and Nimrod an excellent tawny. Best wines: Quinta da Cavadinha; vintages.

The Douro to the Tagus

VR BEIRAS

This region covers the whole of the north-central part of Portugal, and wines made under the Vinho Regional epithet come in a huge array of styles, from sleepy local co-ops to some new-wave, experimental wineries. There are also some exciting new wines being made in the DOC regions within Beiras which are classified as VR because they don't fit in with current DOC regulations.

QUINTA DE FOZ DE AROUCE

Established 19th century *Owners* Foz de Arouce family
Production 2,000 cases *Vineyard area* 20 acres (8 ha)

Wines are made in a mixture of traditional and modern styles and aged for a year in Portuguese oak. Best wine: Quinta de Foz de Arouce.

SOCIEDADE AGRICOLA DE SANTAR

Established 1790 *Owner* Soc. Agrícola de Santar
Production 77,780 cases *Vineyard area* 247 acres (100 ha)

This is a single-estate winery, completely redesigned in the 1990s and concentrating on varietal wines under the hands of winemaker Pedro de Vasconcellos e Souza. Best wines: Castas de Santar Alfrocheiro Preto, Touriga Nacional.

The VR Beiras area includes within it (from north to south): Távora/Varosa, Beira Interior, Dão and Bairrada DOCs; and Lafões IPR.

Távora/Varosa

This area, which incorporates the former IPR areas of Varosa and Encostas da Nave, is mainly known for Douro-style reds and whites made from similar selections of grapes. However, the region is emerging, astonishingly enough, as a producer of some of Portugal's best sparkling wines, made from malvasia, chardonnay, sercial, pinot noir, etc., by the traditional method. This may be a future area of development.

CAVES DE MURGANHEIRA, VDME

Established 1974 *Owners* Partinvest, O. da Costa Lourenco
Production 83,000 cases *Vineyard area* 59 acres (24 ha)

This company, in the district of Varosa, has made its name in new-wave "classic method" sparkling wines (what used to be called, in more enlightened times, *méthode champenoise*), none of which are entitled to any kind of official quality classification but must be labeled VdME. The company produces one of Portugal's best wines, made from malvasia, chardonnay, sercial and pinto, with several months in oak after the first fermentation and a year on the lees after the second. Best wine: Murganheira Varosa.

Beira Interior

Incorporating the former IPR zones of Pinhel, Castelo Rodrigo and Cova da Beira, this is a very large area, covering much of the eastern part of the region along the Spanish border from the Coa in the north to the Tagus in the south. Wines made here range from some decent, full reds in the north (Castelo Rodrigo) through from co-op whites and reds and some rather uninspiring sparklers (Pinhel) to a wide selection in the large Cova da Beira zone. The landscape here varies so much that it is hard to put a general style on the wines, although the local taste seems to favor early-drinking reds, often made from rufete and castelão frances (joão de santarém/periquita).

Dão

One of Portugal's longest-serving wine areas fell into disrepute over years of official bureaucracy when only the co-ops could buy grapes from independent growers. This meant that independent winemakers had only their own resources to support their needs. This changed in the mid-1990s

Below: *Wines from Dão are enjoying a renaissance with the change of wine laws.*

Bottom: *Dão vineyards benefit from long hot summers and wet winters.*

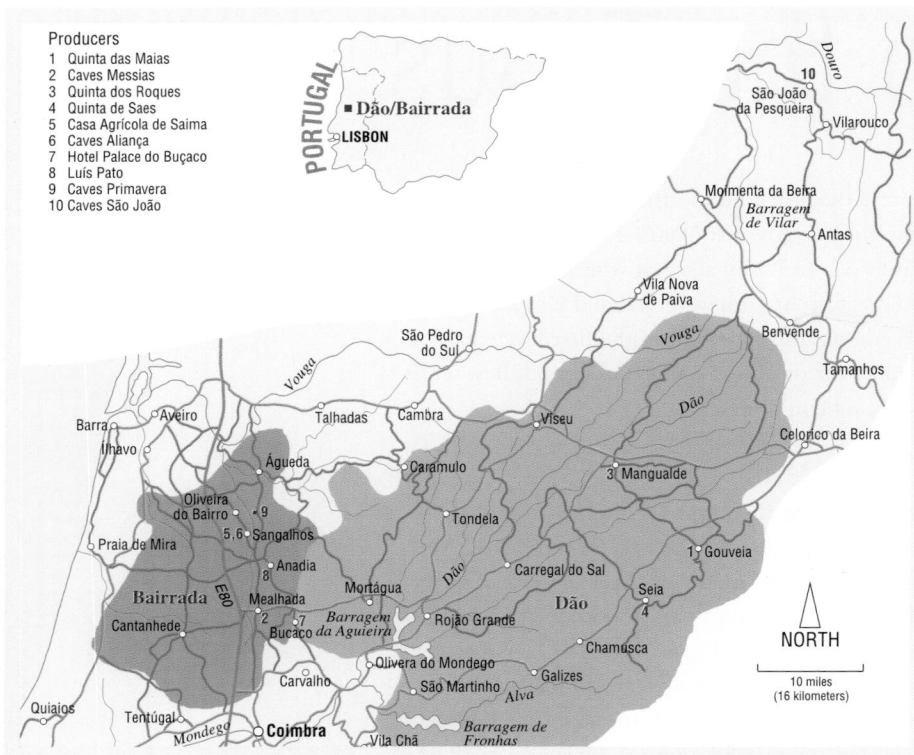

Producers
1 Quinta das Maias
2 Caves Messias
3 Quinta dos Roques
4 Quinta de Saes
5 Casa Agrícola de Saima
6 Caves Aliança
7 Hotel Palace do Buçaco
8 Luís Pato
9 Caves Primavera
10 Caves São João

*Wine tourism in Portugal is increasing,
along with the popularity of its wines.*

and some interesting new wines began to appear, although the co-ops still make most of the wine. Some new single-*quinta* wines are showing particularly well and Dão may be on its way back. The best wines are solid reds made from touriga nacional and any one of a number of other grapes, including bastardo, jaen and tinta roriz.

The best whites are made from cold-fermented encruzado. The new-wave wines have good fruit and a decent structure, the whites showing some fresh, crisp acidity and the reds drinking early but aging well.

QUINTA DAS MAIAS

Established 1990 *Owners* Soc. Agrícola Faldas da Serra Lda *Production* 20,000 cases *Vineyard area* 99 acres (40 ha)

Top class wines are made here, mainly from jaen, and vinified at the Quinta dos Roques. This is a high-altitude vineyard and the wines are aged, typically, in new French oak. Best wine: Quinta das Maias (jaen).

CAVES MESSIAS

Established 1926 *Owners* Messias family *Production* 83,330 cases *Vineyard area* 519 acres (210 ha)

This is a widespread family concern with vineyards in the Douro (for port), Vinho Verde and Bairrada as well as Dão. Best wine: Messias Reserva Touriga Nacional.

QUINTA DOS ROQUES

Established 1989 *Owners* Oliveira and Lorenço families *Production* 4,500 cases *Vineyard area* 99 acres (40 ha)

Manuel de Oliveira runs this vineyard. A new winery was built in 1990 and the wines show tremendous promise. Winemaking concentrates on quality reds made from touriga nacional, tinta roriz, tinta cão and others, although there are good whites made from bical, malvasia and sercial. Best wines: Touriga Nacional; Tinta Roriz.

QUINTA DE SAES

Established NA *Owners* Figueirido e Castro family *Production* NA *Vineyard area* NA

Also incorporating the Quinta da Pellada, this family-owned operation majors on touriga nacional, jaen and alfrocheiro, aged in oak, for red wines. There is also a good white, made from encruzado and bical. Best wines: Quinta da Pellada Touriga Nacional, Tinta Roriz.

Lafões IPR lies between Dão and the Vinho Verde region and its winemaking shows hints of both styles, with some light, fizzy whites and middle-weight reds. There is little wine made here that is of export interest.

Bairrada

This ancient wine-producing region in northern Portugal, close to the Atlantic coast, suffered from delimitation in the eighteenth century, but has reinvented itself at the beginning of the twentieth century and is now one of the country's most important and innovative areas. Most of its production is red wines, and most of these are made mainly from the local baga grape which, at its best, provides a wine of good color with a ripe fruit and considerable aging potential. Some of Portugal's most forward-thinking winemakers are working in this area and its combination of cooling temperate influences and varied micro-climates makes it an area of great opportunity for the enthusiast. White bairrada, which can also be very good, is produced here, and is generally made from the fernão pires (also known as the Maria Gomes) grape.

CASA AGRÍCOLA DE SAIMA

Established 1980 *Owner* Carlos de Almeida e Silva *Production* 7,780 cases *Vineyard area* 30 acres (12 ha)

Carlos de Almeida is a local doctor with a passion for wine and he shares his winemaker (Rui Moura Alves) with Caves São João. Wines are pressed and fermented in stone *lagares*; the whites made from bical and the reds from baga, castelão frances (joão de santarém/periquita) and tinta pinheira. Best wines: Casa de Saima Garrafeira (red).

CAVES ALIANÇA

Established 1927 *Owners* Neves family *Production* 833 cases *Vineyard area* 25 acres (10 ha)

This is a family-run company making wine here in Bairrada and also in Dão and the Alentejo. The winemaker is Francisco Antunes and he makes crisp dry whites from bical and chardonnay, as well as reds from baga and (under the VR Beiras) cabernet sauvignon. Best wines: Aliança Garrafeira (Bairrada); Galeria Cabernet Sauvignon (Beiras).

HOTEL PALACE DO BUÇACO (VDM)

Established 1917 *Owners* Almeida group *Production* 6,000 cases *Vineyard area* 37 acres (15 ha)

This is a mind-boggling, post-baroque, forest-fantasy palace built deep in the woodlands of the Serra de Buçaco as a country retreat for Carlos I. It was leased to Alexandre d'Almeida in 1917 and he turned it into a hotel and vineyard. The wines remain more or less as Almeida first created them. The red is made from baga, tinta pinheira and bastardo, pressed and fermented in stone *lagares* and aged for three years in enormous vats made from oak harvested from the surrounding forest. The hotel lists vintages from 1945 onwards, and there are those who say that to eat the roast suckling pig and to drink the red wines of the Palace do Buçaco is to experience the best gastronomy that Portugal has to offer. Best wines: all of them.

LUÍS PATO

Established 1980 *Owner* Luís Pato *Production* 25,000 cases *Vineyard area* 173 acres (70 ha)

Luís Pato has emerged as one of Portugal's most innovative and inventive winemakers. He has a passion for *terreno* (*terroir* in French) and has been able to experiment widely with the sandy and chalky soils in his vineyards. One small area (2 acres/1 ha) of ungrafted baga vines at the Quinta do Ribeirinho, planted in 1988, produces a low-yield 1,000 bottles under the Pé Franco (meaning "free," or "ungrafted" root) label, even in the best vintages. The concentration and quality are outstanding. Pato also makes some of Portugal's best new-wave sparkling wines. Best wines: Quinta do Ribeirinho (all variants but especially Pé Franco); Vinhas Velhas; Vinha Barossa.

The famous wines of the Hotel Palace do Buçaco are only available to guests.

CAVES PRIMAVERA

Established 1944 *Owners* Vital and Lucénio Rodrigues de Almeida *Production* 222,200 cases *Vineyard area* NA

This is a biggish winery making wines under the DOC Bairrada and the VR Beiras. The company is strong on new-wave sparkling wines and whites from bairrada and dão. However, the reds tend to be the best, mainly made from baga. Best wine: Primavera Bairrada Garrafeira.

CAVES SÃO JOÃO

Established 1960 *Owners* Alberto and Luís Costa *Production* 30,000 cases *Vineyard area* 86 acres (35 ha)

Much of the wine is bought in, ready-made, from local producers to supplement the production of the Quinta do Poço do Lobo. Red wines tend to be the best, sold under the Frei João label, with the *reserva* achieving the highest quality. In addition, there's a non-DOC cabernet sauvignon, and the company also makes wines in the DOC Dão. Best wines: Quinta de Poço de Lobo (baga, moreto, castelão nacional).

REGIONAL DOZEN

Arinto, Quinta de Dom Carlos
Buçaco Reserva, Hotel Palace do Buçaco
Cartuxa, Fundação Eugénio de Almeida
Encruzado, Quinta dos Roques
Garrafeira, Casa de Saima
Marquês de Borba, João Portugal Ramos
Quinta de Cabriz
Quinta da Pellada Touriga Nacional, Quinta de Saes
Quinta de Murta
Quinta dos Roques
Tinto Bruto, Caves Aliança
Vinha Barossa, Luís Pato

Lisbon & Tagus Valley

A shepherd looks after his flock, keeping the grass down in a vineyard.

VR ESTREMADURA

Estremadura is home to a huge range of grapes and decent, everyday wines. It has two IPR zones —Encostas d'Aire and Alcobaça—and eight DOC areas—Obidos, Lourinhã, Torres Vedras, Alenquer, Arruda, Bucelas, Colares and Carcavelos.

Encostas d'Aire IPR is a sizeable limestone-based area with wines which may have potential but, if this is so, it has yet to be realized. Whites are made from fernão pires, arinto, malvasia and others; reds include baga and trincadeira.

Alcobaça IPR has high-yielding vineyards and antiquated regulations—this area's wines are doomed before they're made. The wines (red and white) tend to be on the thin side and over-aged, although white-wine producers make the best of this by selling theirs off for distillation.

QUINTA DE PANCAS

Established 1973 *Owners* Soc. Agrícola Porto da Luz
Production 20,000 cases *Vineyard area* 111 acres (45 ha)

This lovely old estate produces outstanding wines in two styles: classic, made from arinto and jampal (white) and tinta roriz and touriga nacional (red), and "new-wave," made from chardonnay and cabernet sauvignon. Best wines: Quinta de Pancas Cabernet Sauvignon, Touriga Nacional, Tinta Roriz.

Obidos

Obidos has a well-developed co-op winemaking structure and turns out a large amount of (mainly undistinguished) wine. There is some decent red, made from joão de santarém (castelão frances /periquita), bastardo, etc.; most of the white is sold for distilling.

Lourinhã

Lourinhã is one of the few regions in Portugal which produces brandy (*aguardente*) and this is all it makes. It is considered to be Portugal's best brandy area and is one of only three other brandies in Europe to have a DOC or equivalent (the others are cognac and armagnac). The wine is made from alicante branco, alvarelhão, boal espinho, mariquinhas, malvasia rei and talia (white) and cabinda, periquita (castelão frances/joão de santarém) and tinta miúda (red). The spirit is distilled at 38 percent abv (alcohol by volume) and must be aged for a minimum of two years before bottling.

Torres Vedras

This high-production area has little to recommend it to DOC status. Whites are made mainly from vital, the light, uninteresting reds from mortágua and periquita (castelão frances/joão de santarém).

Alenquer

Alenquer is much more promising. Decent wines made mainly from arinto, fernão pires, vital (white) and joão de santarém (red) show promise, and there are experimental plantations of cabernet sauvignon and chardonnay.

Arruda

This small town is quite close to Lisbon. Producers there, such as Camarate and João de Santarém, make quite a lot of mainly red wine which has a certain youthful charm. There are also white wines made from fernão pires, arinto and vital.

Bucelas

This area produces a white wine known since Shakespeare's time. Bucelas must legally be a dry white wine made mainly from the arinto grape; it is capable of producing something fresh, crisp and delicious. So far, few have proved themselves, but there is still hope that this could become an important area for quality white wines. Some red is made but may only be sold as VR Estremadura.

QUINTA DA MURTA

Established 1995 *Owner* Cockburn Smithes *Production* 7,000 cases *Vineyard area* 37 acres (15 ha)

Winemaker Francisco Castelo Branco makes serious white wines here from arinto and a bit of esgana cão (sercial) and rabo de ovelha (rabigato). The wine is sold under the *quinta* name. Best wines: the whole range is very reliable.

These Portuguese wine bottles have woven 'gloves' and handles, making them considerably easier to pour from.

Colares

Colares wine at its best used to, and could again, command a high price. The best is red and comes from the sandy soils; it is 80 percent ramisco (the rest made up, typically, with joão de santarém and/or periquita/joão de santarém/castelão frances) and is dark, hard and tannic when young, only maturing after a decade or more. There's a second-string red made inland from the dunes which is usually sold locally, and there is some small amount of white colares made from malvasia, but this is of no great interest outside the locality.

Carcavelos

Tight on the edge of the city of Lisbon, Carcavelos has all but disappeared. Founded by the Marqués de Pombal (allegedly to provide a market for the grapes from his own estate in Oeiras), it turned out a sweetish fortified wine which enjoyed a certain amount of export business. Indeed, by the 1930s the area was a major producer and exporter, in spite of having been devastated by phylloxera. Today, however, few vineyards remain and the wine is not easy to buy. If you succeed, you'll find something made from arinto, boal, tinta negra mole, trincadeira and others. It's fermented dry and then fortified to 18–10 percent abv (alcohol by volume), often sweetened with a little *vinho abafado* (a *mistelle* of unfermented grape juice and spirit) and then aged for at least five years. The result is somewhere between dry *oloroso* sherry and tawny port.

QUINTA DA BARÃO

Established 1973 *Owners* Guimarães family *Production* NA *Vineyard area* NA

If you're quick, you may find one or two of the semi-fortified wines of this fabled *quinta* still on sale as the encroaching concrete of Lisbon moves ever outward. As recently as 1989 there was a vintage, under the hands of Manuel Vieira, but since then little has been heard. If you find it, drink it. Best wines: anything.

VR RIBATEJANO

Note the adjectival form, "Ribatejano," which distinguishes this country wine area from the DOC Ribatejo (see below). There are seven DOC regions within the Tagus valley and the VR classification is, as always, both for wine made outside the demarcated regions and wines made in unauthorized ways within them. The valley itself is broad and fertile, with alluvial soils and abundant agri-

Flowers growing between vine rows add a healthy diversity to the ecosystem.

culture and there's plenty of experimentation going on in the winemaking world.

CASA CADAVAL

Established NA *Owners* Local shareholders *Production* 30,000 cases *Vineyard area* 173 acres (70 ha)

This is the Ribatejano double-act of João Portugal Ramos and Rui Reguinga, making wines of international quality from pinot noir, cabernet sauvignon and trincadeira. Best wines: the entire range.

QUINTA GRANDE

Established NA *Owners* Local shareholders *Production* 1,400 cases *Vineyard area* NA

This is a small producer specializing in one major wine (also called Quinta Grande). It's made in the traditional way in stone *lagares* from trincadeira, periquita (joão de santarém/castelão frances) and grand noir, before spending some time in small (42-gallon/160-litre) casks of Portuguese oak. It ages with consummate grace. Best wine: Quinta Grande.

QUINTA DA LAGOALVA DE CIMA

Established Before 1900 *Owner* Soc. Agrícola Faldas da Quinta da Lagoalva de Cima *Production* 2,500 cases *Vineyard area* 124 acres (50 ha)

This is a vast agricultural estate in which wine plays only a very small part. However, the ubiquitous João Portugal Ramos makes the wine, along with Rui Reguinga, and the style is new-wave, with syrah, cabernet sauvignon and pinot noir alongside the traditional joão de santarém (castelão frances/periquita), and chardonnay beside the arinto and fernão pires. Best wine: Quinta da Logoalva de Cima (syrah).

The fertile soils of the Tagus valley provide ideal growing conditions for grapes.

The VR Ribatejano area includes within it (north to south): Ribatejo, Ribatejo/Tomar, Ribatejo/Santarém, Ribatejo/Almeirim, Ribatejo/Chamusca, Ribatejo/Cartaxo and Ribatejo/Coruche DOCs.

Ribatejo

This has become a kind of "portmanteau" DOC, rather in the manner of the French Côtes-du Rhône Villages some years ago, in which the name of the village could be appended to the name of the general appellation. In Ribatejo, several former IPR districts have been attached to its classification so that all the classified wines of the region now share its DOC status.

Ribatejo/Tomar

Site of a great convent–castle which once housed the Knights Templar, this small area used to be famous for its fairly hefty red wines but is now (in wine terms) but a shadow of its former self. The area grows joão de santarém (castelão frances/periquita) and castelão nacional for reds, and fernão pires, malvasia and others for whites.

Ribatejo/Santarém

Large-scale production takes place here in Ribatejo's regional capital, on the northwest bank of the Tagus. Most of the popular grapes are grown. Currently, the vast majority of the wines are sold for local consumption.

Ribatejo/Almeirim

Opposite Santarém, on the southeast bank of the Tagus, this is an area of encouraging quality with a good deal of work being done, especially on value-for-money everyday wines. Vines are planted onthe alluvial floodplain of the river and the valley slopes, and grapes from the latter tend to be better. The fernão pires grape is mainly grown for white wines and the joão de santarém (castelão frances/periquita) for reds, with some experimentation with "international" varieties.

Ribatejo/Chamusca

Immediately north of, and attached to Almeirim, this is a very similar area but dominated by co-op wines—mainly whites made from fernão pires.

Ribatejo/Cartaxo

Almost half the DOC Ribatejo's wine comes from this area in the fertile valley of the Tagus. It has great potential as a source of good, everyday, value-for-money wines, both red and white, made from the usual suspects.

Ribatejo/Coruche

This is a large area in the southeast of Ribatejo growing vines on the sandy, alluvial plains of the River Sorraia. The wines are red and white and of everyday quality, although one of the more forward-looking producers has been experimenting with a botrytized white made from fernão pires.

Setúbal & the South

VR TERRAS DO SADO

The Tagus flows into the Atlantic north of the Setúbal peninsula and the Sado flows into it south of the peninsula, hence the name of this new region.

JP VINHOS

Established 1922 *Owners* M. and A. Avillez *Production* 1,111,000 cases *Vineyard area* 1,235 acres (500 ha)

The present company dates from 1969 when its main *raison d'être* was to provide base-wine for the international fizzy rosé brand Lancers. Its prominence in world markets dates from as recently as 1987 when António Avillez hired the expertise of Australian winemaker Peter Bright to start building the company's own range of brands. João Pires Dry Muscat, a fully fermented moscatel wine, took the wine trade by storm and set the tone for the future. Since then, as well as more "mainstream" styles of wine, the company makes Cova de Ursa, a barrel-fermented chardonnay, Quinta de Bacalhoa, a cabernet/merlot, and Má Partilha, a pure merlot. It also makes fortified moscatel de setúbal but, as most of the wines break many of the rules governing the DOC Setúbal, they tend to be labeled with the regional name of Terras do Sado. Best wines: JP Moscatel de Setúbal; JP Tinta Miúda; Má Partilha.

The VR Terras do Sado area includes within it (north to south): Palmela and Setúbal DOCs.

Palmela

A range of new-wave wines is being made here. Excellent reds from periquita (joão de santarém/castelão frances) and fresh, crisp whites from fernão pires along with other styles and varieties are becoming the norm hereabouts. If they don't fit in with the regulations for the DOC, they're labeled with the VR name instead.

CO-OP AGRÍCOLA DE SANTO ISIDRO DE PEGÕES

Established 1958 *Owners* Co-op members *Production* 300,000 cases *Vineyard area* 2,298 acres (930 ha)

This co-op produced generic wines for decades and sold them to other wineries and merchants, but an improvement in confidence and the willingness of the market to try something new led it to produce its first ever "named" wine, made from 100 percent periquita (joão de santarém/castelão frances) and aged in big old vats of Portuguese oak. Best wine: Fontanário de Pegões Garrafeira.

PEGOS CLAROS

Established NA *Owners* Local shareholders *Production* 36,000 cases *Vineyard area* 198 acres (80 ha)

The company's best wine is 100 percent periquita, aged for a year in oak and sold under the Pegos Claros label. Best wine: Pegos Claros Periquita.

Setúbal

The great classic sweet wine is still made in the traditional way, fortified during fermentation (like port) and then allowed to macerate on its skins to give the classic muscat flavor. The grape is the moscatel de setúbal and the wine must consist of 85 percent of that grape to use the name. Other grapes include the arinto (to add fresh acidity) and other varieties of muscat, including the rare, pink-skinned moscato roxo.

JOSÉ MARIA DA FONSECA

Established 1834 *Owner* Diageo/Soares *Production* 1,300,000 cases *Vineyard area* 1,236 acres (500 ha)

A full range of wines is made here, from the everyday dry white Branco Seco Especial (BSE) to an impressive red made from (and called) periquita (joão de santarém/castelão frances), aged in new Limousin oak. There are excellent *garrafeira* wines—TE and RA—as well as Primum, which is made from touriga nacional, touriga francesa, tinta barroca and tinta cão, aged in new French oak. The company is best known for one thing: it has probably saved the moscatel de setúbal from extinction for the nation. José Maria da Fonseca himself started the business making fortified wines from the muscat grape, and ancient casks going back to the 1880s are still used judiciously by his descendants (the present owners) for blending. Best wines: all the range is good, but the jewels in the crown are the old vintages of moscatel de setúbal.

VR ALENTEJANO

The wines made in this vast area of east-central Portugal may be humble country wines or declassified (or unclassifiable) wines from the eight DOC regions within it.

REGIONAL DOZEN

Blandy's (any 10-year-old), Madeira Wine Company
Carcavelos, Quinta do Barão
Catarina, JP Vinhos
Colheitas, Oliveira
Lancers, JP Vinhos
Madeira, Artur Barros & Sousa
Malmsey (10 or 15-year-old), Henriques & Henriques
Moscatel de Setúbal, José Maria de Fonseca
Moscatel de Setúbal, JP Vinhos
Pêra Manca, Fundação Eugénio Almeida
Silva Vinhos Old Vintage wines, Barbeito
Vale de Judia, Co-op Agrícola de Santa Isidro de Pegões

Some producers carry out their own research to improve their winemaking.

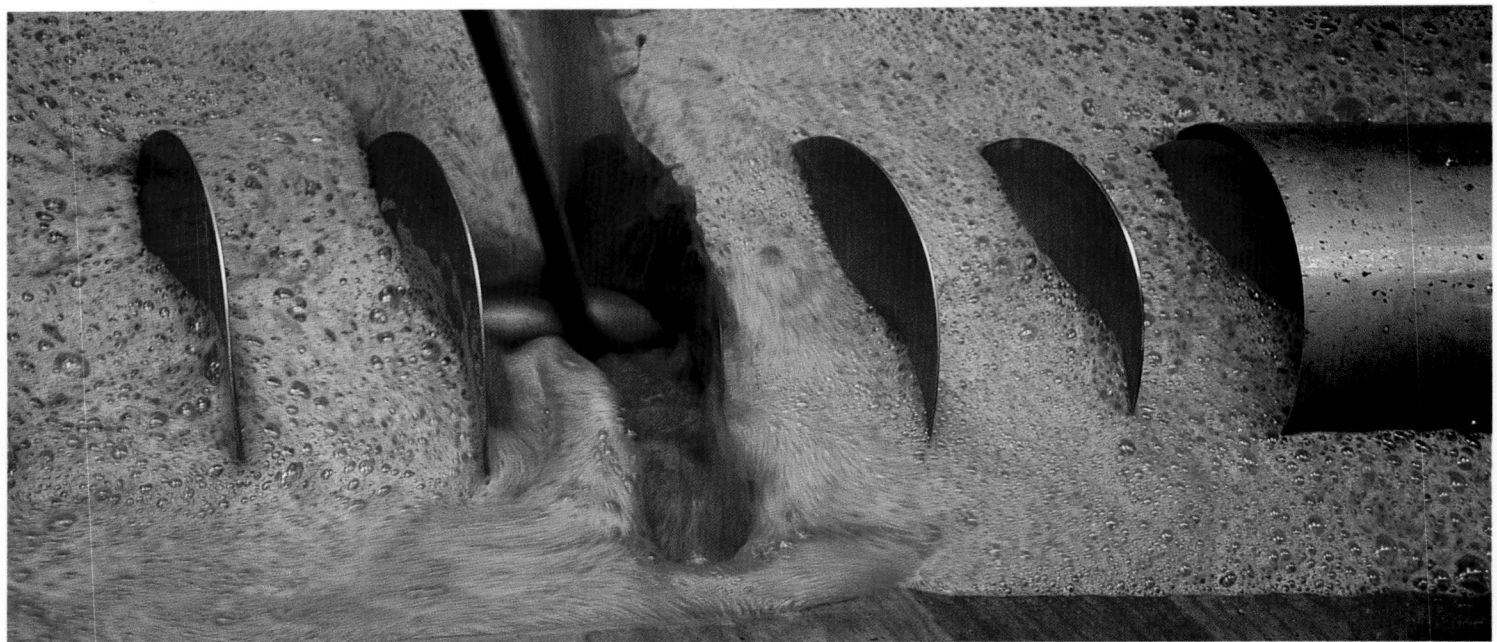

An Archimedes screw draws newly fermented wine to be barreled.

QUINTA DO CARMO

Established 1986 *Owners* Bastos family 50 percent, Domaines Baron de Rothschild 50 percent *Production* 35,000 cases *Vineyard area* 232 acres (94 ha)

The Rothschilds bought a half share in this family estate in 1992 and installed new stainless steel technology and French winemakers. The company grows alicante bouschet, aragonês (tempranillo), trincadeira and periquita (joão de santarém/castelão frances) and ages the wine in oak for varying periods. Best wine: Quinta do Carmo.

CORTES DE CIMA

Established 1994 *Owners* Jørgensen family *Production* 13,000 cases *Vineyard area* 74 acres (30 ha)

Hans Jørgensen makes the wine at this innovative vineyard near Vidiguera. He has planted aragonês (tempranillo), trincadeira, periquita (joão de santarém/castelão frances), syrah and cabernet sauvignon, and early vintages show extremely well. Best wines: Cortes de Cima Syrah, Reserva.

ESPORÃO

Established 1974 *Owner* Jose Roquette *Production* 200,000 cases *Vineyard area* 988acres (400 ha)

Luis Duarte and Australian Donald Baverstock make the wine here. The main wine, Monte Velho, and the second wine, Alandra, are both made in red and white. Most interesting is the Esporão label, used for a barrel-fermented white and a red made from trincadeira, aragonês (tempranillo) and cabernet sauvignon either all together (in the *reserva*) or in single varietal bottlings. Best wines: Esporão Reserva, Aragonês.

SOC. AGRICOLA DA HERDADE DOS COELHEIROS

Established NA *Owners* Local shareholders *Production* NA *Vineyard area* 59 acres (24 ha)

This winery, under the hands of winemaker Antonio Saramago, relies on cabernet sauvignon as its "backbone". Tapada de Coelheiros is made from cabernet, trincadeira and aragonês (tempranillo); Tapada de Coelheiros Garrafeira is cabernet and aragonês. Best wine: Garrafeira.

The VR Alentejano area includes: Alentejo/Portalegre, Borba, Redondo, Evora, Reguengos, Granja-Amareleja, Vidigueira and Moura DOCs.

Alentejo/Portalegre

Highest and coolest of the DOCs of the Alentejo, this area has schistose and granite soils and some good grapes—aragonês (tempranillo) and trincadeira—and wines from here are beginning to show well in terms of fruit and cleanliness. There is some white wine made mainly from fernão pires.

Alentejo/Borba

This is the best-known region of Alentejo outside Portugal. Two-thirds of the area is planted with red, made from periquita (castelão frances/ joão de santarém), mostly by the local co-op; the wines have fruit, freshness and a balanced acidity. There is also some decent white, mainly made from roupeiro and rabo de ovelha (rabigato).

Alentejo/Redondo

A higher altitude (1,970 feet/600 m) means slightly cooler vineyards, planted here on granite bedrock.

The reds (periquita, trincadeira) have a pleasantly ripe, fruity freshness. Whites (roupeiro, rabo de ovelha/rabigato) lag behind but show promise.

Alentejo/Evora

This area is making tremendous strides. Periquita (joão de santarém/castelão frances) and trincadeira are the varieties making it happen for reds. Whites —made mainly from arinto—are showing almost as well; Evora would seem to be very much an area to watch for real quality wines in the future.

FUNDAÇÃO EUGÉNIO ALMEIDA
Established 1950   *Owner* Fundação Eugénio Almeida *Production* 83,330 cases   *Vineyard area* 642 acres (260 ha)

This charitable trust makes wines under the supervision of the University of Evora. The vineyard is planted in trincadeira, periquita (joão de santarém/castelão frances), moreto, aragonês (tempranillo) and alfrocheiro. Cartuxa and wines under the Monte de Pinheiros and Eugénio Almeida labels are made. Best wine: Pêra Manca (trincadeira).

Alentejo/Reguengos

Another area starting to show well, this DOC also has an independent movement pushing for higher quality. There's good schistose soil here as well as granite, and aragonês (tempranillo) and trincadeira are grown, so the potential is tremendous.

Alentejo/Granja-Amareleja

Wines from here have a niche market locally. The area has granite and schistose bedrock, but poor soils, low yields, a semi-arid climate and old vines combine to produce small quantities of quite good wine from the moreto grape.

Alentejo/Vidigueira

Quite a large area and, unusually for so far south, mainly planted with second-rate white varieties such as perrum and diagalves (a table grape), there is also some rabo de ovelha (rabigato).

Alentejo/Moura

Alluvial clay soils beside the River Guadiana are the basis for this area's success. At least one independent producer, JP Vinhos, is now turning out wines of excellent quality.

VR ALGARVE

This holiday region produces its share of generic everyday wines, most of which go directly to the holiday trade along the coast.

VR MADEIRA

Why Madeira needs a VR when it has an island-wide DOC is not clear—perhaps it makes it easier for maverick winemakers to do their own thing outside the DOC. Such winemakers are, for the moment, however, conspicuous by their absence.

Madeira

ARTUR BARROS & SOUSA
Established 1881   *Owners* Sousa family   *Production* 500 cases   *Vineyard area* 11 acres (4.5 ha)

This very small producer is turning out excellent wines, made in the *lagar* and aged by the *canteiro* method. The company has *reservas* aged for ten years or more and some wonderful *colheitas* dating back to the 1930s. Best wines: *colheitas*.

BARBEITO
Established 1946   *Owners* Shareholders, Barbeito family *Production* NA   *Vineyard area* NA

Now Japanese-owned and mostly serving the Japanese market, Barbeito still has several venerable wines in its cellars, including one claimed to be from the 1795 vintage. More approachable (and affordable) is the splendid 1957, but all are good. Best wines: *colheitas*, 100-year-old malmsey.

HENRIQUES & HENRIQUES
Established 1850   Owners Cossart family and others Production 3,500 cases   Vineyard area 35 acres (14 ha)

John Cossart makes the wine here. The company moved into a new winery complex in 1994, and planted 25 acres (10 ha) of new vines. Ten-year-old noble grapes are excellent, and there's a panoply of ancient colheitas. Best wines: *colheitas*, Reservas Velhissimas.

MADEIRA WINE COMPANY
Established 1914   *Owners* Symington and Blandy families *Production* 130,000 cases *Vineyard area* NA

This group incorporates 27 companies. The main brand name is Blandy's, but older (now legally nonexistent) names still appear on labels. The noble wines (malmsey, boal, verdelho and sercial) are marketed in five, ten and fifteen-year-old versions. Best wines: *colheitas*.

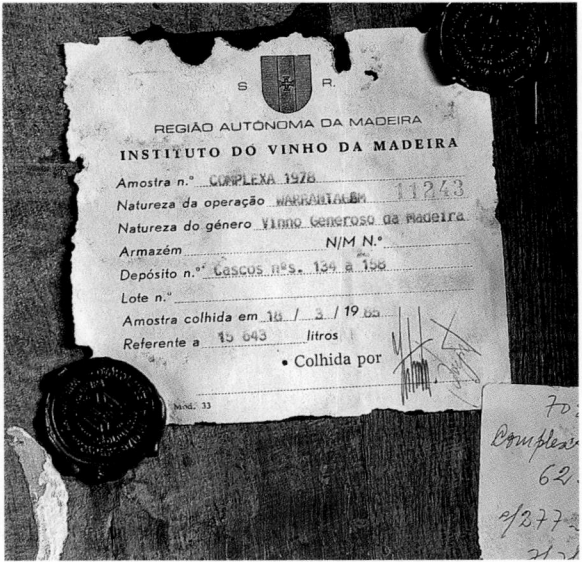

The official seal of approval on wine made by the Estufa method in Madeira.

England & Wales

Wink Lorch

The phrase "mad dogs and Englishmen" frequently comes to mind when discussing English wines. Being an island, England's weather is extremely fickle and even southern England is north of 50° latitude. Considering that Britain imports a wide range of wines at all price

levels from around the world, why would any-one contemplate planting a vineyard and making wine in such conditions? On the other hand, there is palatable wine produced from vineyards close to Alice Springs in the hot, arid, Australian interior; down the road from Niagara Falls in bitterly cold Ontario, Canada; and precari-ously close to the equator in the hills of India, so why not? The mad dogs are at least supported by Her Majesty the Queen, who often serves English wine to visiting foreign dignitaries.

Above: *Peter Hall among the vines at Breaky Bottom, Northtease, Sussex.*

Top: *Although Her Majesty the Queen often serves English wines to visiting dignitaries, neither her government nor her subjects are as supportive.*

Most of her subjects are not so supportive, nor is her government. Until the mid-1980s "British Wine" was subject to a lower level of excise duty than "English Wine." British Wine is the legal term for "made wine," that is, made in Britain from imported grape concentrate. Still sold in the UK it is a source of confusion on labels. A wine labeled English Wine must be made from fresh grapes grown in English vineyards. Both English and British wines are now taxed in the UK at the same level as all European Union wines, but unlike other UK farmers and vine-growers in Europe, English vineyard owners enjoy virtually no government subsidies. Despite this, vineyard area in England and Wales has grown from virtually zero 50 years ago, to about 494 acres (200 ha) in 1975 and 2,170 acres (878 ha) in 1999, down from more than 2,470 acres (1000 ha) in the early '90s.

There are about 400 active vineyards. and of these, just 14 are larger than 25 acres (10 ha), representing 38 percent of plantings. Production is erratic due to the variability of the weather, in recent years ranging from 712,800 gallons (2,700,000 l) in 1996 down to 171,600 gallons (650,000 l) in 1997. The average over 10 years has been about 166,667 cases per year. There has also been a consolidation in wineries, down from 150 in the early 1990s to 114 in 1998. More vine-growers are either selling their grapes or using the services of contract winemakers.

The English wine industry has been described as being full of "great British eccentrics," yet over the past 20 years or so, several wineries have proved that good-quality wine can be made from grapes grown in well-sited vineyards. Initially, all the efforts were with light, fresh, dry and medium-dry fruity white wines, and this style remains definitive. However, specialties such as late-harvest or lightly oaked white wines, unusual reds and traditional-method sparkling wines have enjoyed many accolades in the 1990s.

History

Vines have been grown in England and Wales since at least the Roman invasion, yet there is little evidence of wine production. By the time of the "Domesday Book," at the end of the eleventh century, 38 vineyards were cited, a third of them owned by monasteries. Viticulture continued in the Middle Ages, but cheaper imports were already becoming available.

The decline probably began in the fourteenth century, hastened by the end of a warm climatic period and, later, by the dissolution of the monasteries. In the eighteenth and nineteenth centuries, vineyards were planted and wine made, but on a small scale. Generally decorative vines or table grapes were grown under glass during this period. The Great Vine at Hampton Court, which was planted in 1768, still produces about 500 pounds (230 kg) of black hamburg grapes every year.

Following experiments carried out by pioneers such as Barrington Brock, who reported on vines growing in his garden, the first modern commercial vineyard, Hambledon Vineyard, was planted by Major-General Sir Guy Salisbury-Jones in 1951. Others followed and a fledgling industry was born. The vintage of 1976 was significant because an unusually hot summer allowed the production of reasonable quantities of good wine.

Landscape and climate

The climate in England and Wales, notoriously cool and damp, can be described as marginal for successful viticulture. To make the most of available heat and sunshine and to protect against the climatic hazards of wind, frost and damp, choice of vineyard site is crucial. Only in areas with a maritime climate and the warming effects of the Gulf Stream do grapes ripen at all this far north. In some summers, there is a distinct lack of sunshine and warmth during the growing season and this can lead to over-acidic, unripe grapes. Conversely, the long growing season is ideal for flavor development in certain varieties.

Total rainfall is no higher than in many northern European wine regions but it rains haphazardly throughout the year, often at harvest time. The results may be poor fruit set, an attack of mildew or rot hard to control, and dilution of the grapes. On this island, where one is never more than 60 miles (97 km) from the coast, wind is a major hazard and windbreaks must often be provided. Late frosts are also common.

With vineyards scattered across southern England and Wales, there is a wide variation in soil types. However, the north and south Downs in southeast England are favored for their limestone and chalk. Sharing some of the characteristics found in France's Champagne and Loire Valleys. This has proved ideal for the production of white wines and base wines for fine sparkling wines. On the negative side, soils in southern England often contain quite significant amounts of heavy clay. Many of the first modern English vineyards failed due to poor drainage.

Wine laws and labeling

English producers have been subject to European wine laws since 1973, when the UK joined the EU. However, until 1,235 acres (500 ha) of plantings were made, the country's vineyards were regarded officially as experimental and with average annual production remaining below about 2,800 cases, planting restrictions are not enforced.

The biggest point of debate remains the designation for "Quality Wine." A quality wine scheme involving analytical and tasting tests has been in place in England for some years. However, in the EU, officially designated "Quality Wines," such as Appellation Controlée wines in France, must not be made from "inter-specific crosses" or hybrid grape varieties. In England, one of the most successful varieties is the hybrid seyval blanc and other hybrids are also grown. Many producers are unhappy that some of their best wines cannot be given the official designation "English (or Welsh) Vineyards Quality Wine." A regional wine category has been introduced in which hybrids can be used (labeled "English Counties Regional Wine"), but the debate continues among members of the United Kingdom Vineyards Association as to how to both appease the EU officials and satisfy their own marketing demands. Today, although many wines qualify for quality or regional wine status, the vast majority are labeled "Table Wine."

Sparkling wine may be labeled as "English Quality Sparkling Wine" irrespective of variety, but only if made by traditional methods.

Regions

Vineyards are dispersed mainly south of a line from East Anglia, south of Birmingham, to south Wales. Many are sited not because they are in a particularly good place for growing vines, but because they are close to a tourist attraction, or simply on land owned by someone passionate about growing vines. The world's most northerly "commercial" vineyard is in Durham in northeast England, close to latitude 55°N.

About 60 percent of England's vineyards and most of the larger wineries are in the populous southeast, once called "The Garden of England." The counties of Kent, East Sussex and Surrey have been the most successful and each has more than 250 acres (100 ha). The Thames Valley including Berkshire, Buckinghamshire, Oxfordshire and the northern part of Hampshire, is the warmest vineyard region in England. The counties of West Sussex and Hampshire are also important.

Vines growing in county Surrey.

East Anglia including the counties of Essex, Cambridgeshire, Norfolk and Suffolk, has more than 250 acres (100 ha). The land is flat and fertile giving good yields but the region experiences strong winds. The Wessex region including Somerset, Wiltshire, Dorset and Avon, and the far southwestern counties of Devon and Cornwall have more than 250 acres (100 ha) among them. There are wide variations in climate with fierce westerly winds, so sites must be carefully chosen.

Moving north, the only significant counties are Gloucestershire, home to Three Choirs Vineyards, one of England's largest wineries, and Worcestershire. Wales has only 57 acres (23 ha), mostly in the south, split among 16 owners. The climate is similar to southwest England. There are four wineries in Wales and some vineyards take their crop to England for winemaking.

Vines and wines

Most of the white grape varieties grown are of German origin, many of them crossings developed to ripen in cool climates. These include müller-thurgau with 334 acres (135 ha) with 13 percent of total plantings, reichensteiner, (12 percent), bacchus (10 percent) and schönburger (8 percent), with huxelrebe, ortega, ehrenfelser, faberrebe and siegerrebe among the others planted. The main non-Germanic white grape, originating in France, is the hybrid seyval, the third-most important variety with 11 percent of plantings. Madeleine angevine, a table grape, has 7 percent of plantings, while the only classic variety with plantings of any

Late spring frosts are common. These pots are used to protect vines against frosts at Denbies Wine Estate, Dorking, in Surrey.

Vines and a view of winery buildings at Denbies Wine Estate, Surrey.

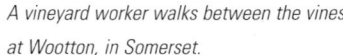

A vineyard worker walks between the vines at Wootton, in Somerset.

size is chardonnay (86 acres, 35 ha or 4 percent), mainly for use in sparkling wines.

Critics of English wines question whether the chosen grape varieties are the right ones, suggesting that more effort should be made with classic varieties. However, it was the climatic difficulties that early on dictated the choice, and with very few exceptions, the choice of plantings remains the same. Most of the German crossings give floral or fruit flavors, some quite leafy in character. White wines are light both in alcohol and flavor, and residual sugar has sometimes been used to disguise faults and high acidity. Today, however, the delicate dry and off-dry whites do better than medium styles. High acidity enables these wines to age well, and they often develop a better balance after a year, sometimes three or four years of bottle age.

Greater flavor intensity has been sought from oak vinification or aging, and seyval blanc seems to suit it well, but many wines lack the weight of fruit to cope with oak. A few wineries have achieved success with excellent dessert wines from botrytis-affected grapes. Several of the German varieties achieve high natural sugar levels and in certain vineyard sites, and when kept free of grey rot, they develop noble botrytis in most years. These dessert wines tend to be low in alcohol with vibrant honey and fruit flavors and high acidity balancing the sweetness.

Pinot noir is England's most planted red grape variety with 111 acres (45 ha) or 5 percent of total plantings. The only other classics are tiny amounts of cabernet sauvignon and merlot grown under plastic tunnels. Various obscure crossings and hybrids are planted with some success, among them dornfelder and dunkelfelder, developed in Germany, and among hybrids, rondo.

There are many dry and medium-dry rosés made and the best are light and fresh with delicate strawberry fruit. Reds have been much more of a struggle but there have been successes.

Good-quality traditional-method sparkling wines are made from base wine blends of German crossings, some also with seyval. However, certain producers have persevered with chardonnay and pinot noir and the resulting sparkling wines show tremendous quality. Other varieties are also proving good, such as auxerrois and pinot blanc in whites and pinot meunier and gamay among the reds. Some vineyards are being planted specifically for sparkling-wine production.

Skillful winemaking is essential for English wines as grapes are often harvested in very poor condition. England has several highly trained winemakers with worldwide experience and investment in winemaking equipment by the larger wineries has helped quality.

With most grape varieties, chaptalization is essential, but even then many wines end up with only 11 percent alcohol. De-acidification was widely practiced, but growers are working hard at achieving a better balance in the vineyard to avoid this. Back-blending with concentrated grape juice (sometimes obtained from outside England, usually Germany) used to be very common, even for so-called dry styles, and it is still used by some to make medium styles. Many wineries have a few oak barrels that are used for special lots, and some have experimented with oak chips and staves to add more mouth feel and character.

Grapes for making red wine (as opposed to the widely made rosés) need even more careful treatment to preserve what fruit and flavor they have. For sparkling wines, most wineries use the traditional method, the only really practical method for relatively small lots. Length of bottle aging post second fermentation depends partly on the grape varieties used in the base wine, as the aromatic varieties do not suit an autolytic, yeasty character.

Producers

Most producers sell only locally; from the farm gate and through local shops, pubs and restaurants. There is a steadily growing trend to extend facilities offered at vineyards to include other tourist-oriented attractions. This not only assists wine sales, but also provides much-needed extra revenue. A few producers have developed trade nationally and some export their product, but most UK retailers still do not stock English wines.

Some producers restrict themselves to estate wines; others include purchased grapes in their blends. As elsewhere, this is not always clear on labels. The producers below have all had an impact on the industry in England and Wales, and their wines are available beyond the cellar door.

CHAPEL DOWN WINES, TENTERDEN VINEYARDS, KENT
Established 1993 *Owner* Chapel Down Wines *Production* 30,000 cases *Vineyard area* 20 acres (8 ha)

Chapel Down is the largest producer of English wines, using grapes from their own vineyards, planted in 1977, and grapes from a further 250 acres (100 ha). One of the directors is experienced winemaker Stephen Skelton, the original owner of Tenterden. Until the 1999 vintage, the chief wine-maker was David Cowderoy, who had long experience in the English wine industry and internationally. Production is split 66 percent white, 26 percent sparkling and 8 percent red. The range of 16 wines includes a superb, herbaceous bacchus and a softer, more perfumed schönburger. Oak-aged whites are led by Epoch V, a creamy blend of varieties usually with müller-thurgau and reichensteiner. An attractive pinot noir is made as well as a spicy red blend, Epoch I, from rondo, dornfelder, pinot noir and gamay. Sparkling wines, too, have been consistently good. Chapel Down is also one of the largest contract winemakers.

DENBIES WINE ESTATE, SURREY
Established 1986 *Owner* Denbies Wine Estate *Production* 29,200 cases *Vineyard area* 265 acres (108 ha)

Situated only 30 miles from central London, Denbies Wine Estate is the showcase for English wines and claims to be the largest privately owned vineyard in Europe. Set amid a large bowl of vineyards, the winery and visitors center would not look out of place in California or Australia. The winery, built with no expense spared, has suffered from a lack of continuity of winemakers, but the arrival of John Worontschak (see Valley Vineyards below) as consultant since the 1999 vintage should change this. The Estate's biggest successes have been with the large-production and good-value Surrey Gold, a medium-dry blend, and a Special Late-Harvested white from a blend of Germanic varieties including the late-ripening optima and ortega. Pinot noir does well in Denbies

vineyard and has been pro-duced on its own and as a blend with dornfelder. Denbies' wines are from estate-grown grapes only.

NYETIMBER VINEYARD, SUSSEX
Established 1990 *Owners* Stuart and Sandy Moss *Production* 4,200 cases *Vineyard area* 40 acres (16 ha)

It took a couple from Chicago in the USA to prove that England could produce world-class wine. Nyetimber was England's first, and remains its largest, dedicated sparkling wine producer. The Mosses, who live on site in a house dating from Norman times, have invested money, energy and dedication in this venture. Chardonnay, pinot noir and pinot meunier vines, winemaking equipment and winemaking advice all came from Champagne. The wines have at least three years on yeast in bottle and are further aged before release. The complex Première Cuvée Blanc de Blancs is creamy and spicy, beautifully balanced and able to age. The Classic Cuvée, with 30 percent of the pinots in the blend, is equally stylish, but richer.

VALLEY VINEYARDS, BERKSHIRE
Established 1979 *Owners* Jon Leighton and partners *Production* 4,200 cases *Vineyard area* 25 acres (10 ha) plus 5 acres (2 ha) leased in Surrey

Born in England, Jon Leighton lived for 20 years in Australia, where he studied viticulture. Situated in a relatively warm Thames Valley site, the vineyard has always been his first priority. Long-term experiments with a range of training and pruning systems, as well as different varieties, have provided good crops. In 1988 he recruited a young Australian, John Worontschak, as winemaker. His skills and no-compromise attitude made a big difference to quality and set an example for other English wineries. John now has a winemaking consultancy based at Valley Vineyards and makes wine for many other vineyards. Valley Vineyards' range includes a fresh, aromatic dry white, Regatta, and an oaked Fumé. The Heritage range (made from purchased grapes) includes one of England's best oaked whites, Heritage Fumé, and a good-quality sparkling wine. The limited-edition Clocktower wines include a fine sparkling white gamay, one of the country's top pinot noirs and a luscious dessert wine, labeled Botrytis.

Carved barrel with crest, made in Austria in 1992. Denbies Wine Estate.

REGIONAL BEST

Bearsted Vineyard Brut NV, Kent
Beenleigh Red (Sharpham Partnership), Devon
Breaky Bottom Seyval Brut, Sussex
Camel Valley Vineyard Seyval Dry, Cornwall
Davenport Vineyard "Horsmonden" Dry, Sussex
Hidden Springs Dark Fields Red, Sussex

Central Europe

Most
Liberec
Bohemia
Roudnice
Melník
PRAGUE
CZECH
REPUBLIC
Pradёd
4893 ft (1492 m)
Ostrava
Pilsen
Vltava
Morava
Olomouc
Carpathian Mtns
Ceske
Budejovice
Brno
Southern
Moravia
Váh
Gerlachovský
8692 ft (2650 m)
Eastern
Slovakia
SLOVAKIA
Ondava
Nitra
Central
Slovakia
Kosice
Tokaj
Lesser
Carpathia
Nitra
Nitra
Tokaj-
Hegyalja
BRATISLAVA
Nové Zámky
Southern
Slovakia
Danube
Miskolc
Kékes
3312 ft (1010 m)
Northeast
Hungary
Tokaj
Nyíregyháza
Sopron
Györ
Tatabánya
BUDAPEST
Gyöngyös
Tisza
Debrecen
Northwest
Hungary
HUNGARY
Székesfehérvár
Szolnok
Körös
Lake Balaton
Kecskemét
Drava
Drava
Valley
Lake
Balaton
Lake
Balaton
Central South
Hungary
Maribor
Tolna
Triglav
9380 ft (2860 m)
SLOVENIA
Celje
Southwest
Hungary
Danube
Szeged
Sava
LJUBLJANA
Sava
Valley
Danube
Pécs
Subotica
Littoral
Sneznik
5890 ft (1796 m)
Novo
Mesto
ZAGREB
Vojvodina
Tisza
Rijeka
Karlovac
CROATIA
Osijek
Novi Sad
Pula
Srem
BELGRADE
Zadar
Banja Luka
Sava
Morava
River
Troglav
6274 ft (1913 m)
BOSNIA-
HERZEGOVINA
Drina
YUGOSLAVIA
Timok
Valley
ADRIATIC
SARAJEVO
Cacak
Cuprija
Split
Brac
Neretva
Mostar
Durmitor
8272 ft (2522 m)
Morava
River
Morava
Nis
Hvar
Leskovac
SEA
Dubrovnik
8432 ft
(2570 m)
Kosovo
Pristina
Vranje
Podgorica
Titov Vrh
9010 ft (2747 m)
Kumanovo
Lake
Skadar
Shkodёr
SKOPJE
Veles
Shёngjin
Laç
Korab
9052 ft (2760 m)
MACEDONIA
NORTH
TIRANA
50 miles
(80 kilometers)
Lushnja
Elbasan
Ohrid
Vlorё
Lake
Ohrid
Bitola
Devoll
Lake Prespa
ALBANIA

Central Europe

This is a story of winemakers picking up the pieces after decades of communism had left them with collectivized vineyards, a dearth of up-to-date equipment and neither the hard currency nor the know-how required for modern wine production. But, winemakers being the resourceful people they are, it is also a story of old identities being rediscovered and old traditions of quality being dusted off and re-examined.

None of these countries, with the exception of Hungary, has a great reputation for wine, although Slovenia deserves a better reputation than it has. Hungary's renown is based upon Tokaji, one of the world's greatest dessert wines; none of its dry wines, red or white, can yet approach Tokaji's quality. Entry to the European Community should give Hungarian wine the boost, and the international outlook, that it needs. The countries of the former Yugoslavia (again excepting Slovenia) have a recent history that can only hold back progress towards quality and modernity.

Slovakia is in decline as a wine producer, and while in the Czech Republic the vineyard area has also fallen, this country should, in theory, have a brighter future. There are bright spots of quality and enterprise here. The same, alas, is not true of Albania.

Moving a pallet of wine bottles, Vinselekt Michlovsky, Moravia (Czech Republic).

CZECH REPUBLIC

Helena Baker

The Czech Republic lies at the very heart of Europe, and the history of vine growing in this area dates from Roman times, with tools discovered that date back to AD 280. It shares a border with Germany and Austria to the southwest, but it has more in common with its southeastern neighbors, Slovakia and Hungary, and Poland to the north, thanks to their 40 years under communist control. During this time wine was treated as just another agricultural product, much like sugar beet or potatoes, and was produced to lowest common denominator level, generally in the form of a headache-inducing plonk drunk when the masses needed a change from the excellent beer.

Despite a new Wine Act, based largely on its German counterpart, which came into force on September 1, 1995, and the privatisation of most wineries, the rate of change has been sluggish, and the wines of the Czech Republic remain much of a mystery abroad—and at home, as any visitor will attest. This slowness is partly because the outlook

Vertically trained vines, Znovín Znojmo, Moravia (Czech Republic).

for many of the former agricultural cooperatives is uncertain: with the republic's eventual entry into the European Union, there will clearly be increased competition for Czech winemakers. However, some foreign capital has recently found its way into the country, principally through the takeover of the largest winemaking firm—Bohemia Sekt—by German multinational Henkell & Söhnlein.

Though the vineyard land is mostly rolling plains, the Danube basin or slightly higher slopes, and the climate continental, though a little dry, the Czech Republic does not yet produce sufficient wine for its own needs, and imports vast amounts from Slovakia and Spain. Vineyard planting has fallen from 37,000 acres (15,000 ha) in the 1980s to around 27,200 acres (11,000 ha) in 1999. Fraud and nefarious practices are rife, and there are blanket plantings of every available grape variety, when in the past only those deemed suitable to the climate and soil were planted.

Wines and producers

The main growing regions are in Southern Moravia, where Australian flying winemakers Nick Butler and John Worontschak recently produced a pleasing Moravia Hills for a British supermarket chain, until economic considerations put an end to the project. Nor should the much smaller Bohemian region, about 30 miles (48 km) to the north of Prague, be underestimated. Lying on an extension of the Alsace to Rheingau subsoil structure, it produces a distinctive type of wine: a very Germanic type of riesling with a hint of petrol, quite unlike the perfumed, flowery Moravian version of this grape variety.

Traditional white grape varieties (Czech synonyms or domestically used names appear in brackets) are riesling, pinot gris, pinot blanc, gewürztraminer, sauvignon blanc, grüner veltliner, welschriesling (laski or olasz rizlink, riesling italico), müller-thurgau, neuburger, sylvaner and moravian muscat (a cross between muscat ottonel and prachtraube), along with a number of locally produced crosses, such as aurelius (riesling X neuburger) or palava (gewürztraminer X müller-thurgau). Chardonnay is also making deep inroads.

Reds include regional favourites such as modrý portugal (blauer portugieser, portugais bleu, portugaljka), a variety that has nothing to do with Portugal whatsoever, frankovka (lemberger, blaufränkisch), svatovavřinecké (St Laurent, Sankt-Laurenttraube) and the crosses of the latter two cultivars (andré and zweigeltrebe), not to mention cabernet sauvignon, which does not really give of its best in these northern climes. Another internationally known grape variety, however—pinot noir—expresses itself surprisingly well, especially in the Bohemian region, its ideal *terroir*. The Holy Roman Emperor Charles IV brought it from Burgundy in the nineteenth century.

Despite a preponderance of poor product, it would be a mistake to imagine that no originality or specialization exists in the Czech Republic. Firstly, there is Miloš Michlovský, who has developed and cloned several new varieties which are more resistant to frost, fungi and diseases—he wins almost every contest in the country. Then there is Znovín Znojmo, whose Moravenka label has been available in the UK for some time through the Sunday Times Wine Club. Or take Mikros-Vin, whose Welschriesling ice wine was voted champion in 1999 at an annual Central European wine competition, beating its Slovenian, Croatian and even Austrian counterparts. As well, the two branches of the Lobkowicz family, from their respective restituted castles in Mělník and Roudnice, near Prague, are producing a range of fine wines. If there is a future for quality winemaking in this country, it will probably rest with these people and with the young generation of small winemakers, such as Olin Drápal of Kolby, who specialises in straw wine, Fano Mádl, an organic wine producer, and Radek Baloun.

SLOVAKIA

Helena Baker

Slovakia "divorced" Czechoslovakia in 1993, having been an integral part of it since 1918 (apart from a spell during the Second World War). It has much in common with its former other half: it has the same recent history, similar grape varieties have been planted, both speak similar languages and by and large the same economic conditions prevail in the two countries today.

Before the "velvet revolution" in 1989, Slovakia had 74,000 acres (30,000 ha) under vine, while today it has only 24,380 acres (9,687 ha) of registered vineyard planting—the country has ceased to be self-sufficient in the production of wine. In 1997, 6 million gallons (22.9 million l) of wine or grape must were imported, while approximately 2.64 million gallons (10 million l) is exported, mainly to the Czech Republic.

The cultivation of vines in Slovakia dates back to pre-Roman times, as attested to by archaeologists, who have discovered vineyard tools and clay vessels from around the seventh and sixth centuries BC.

Slovakia, though small, has quite varied soil composition, with subsoils ranging from those of volcanic origin (tufa, basalt) to limestone and slate with sandy, alluvial and gravel topsoil, and is prone to frost.

Workers in a cellar, Vibo Nitra, Nitra, southern Slovakia.

Wines and producers

The six growing regions of Slovakia are located around the central mountainous plateau, along the southern and eastern borders: Lesser Carpathia, Southern Slovakia, Central Slovakia, Nitra, Eastern Slovakia and Tokaj. This last is a small district, adjoining its illustrious Hungarian neighbor—the prices are much lower in Slovakia, and the careful investor can pick up many a bargain.

New wine laws which came into force at the end of 1996 classify wines into the following categories: table wines, quality varietal wines, quality brand wines, quality blends, wines with special attributes (equivalent to the Prädikat wines of Germany and Austria), sparkling wines, aromatised wines and Tokaj wines.

Grape varieties planted are very similar to those in the Czech Republic, with the addition of those of Hungarian or Austrian origin, such as irsai oliver, leányka, lipovina (hárslevelű), furmint, bouviertraube and locally developed crossings, such as devín, dunaj and alibernet. Best producers of quality light wines include Milan Pavelka of Pezinok, Vinárstvo Vinanza in Vráble, Víno Nitra, Vladimír Sodoma of Modra, Movino of Veľký Krtíš and Vladimír Mrva of Zeleneč.

Sparkling wine production, the first *méthode champenoise* production in Europe outside Champagne, was started by Jean Hubert, a wounded Napoleonic soldier who was returning from the battlefields of Russia but only made it as far as the arms of his nurse in Pressburg (today's Bratislava). There he set up Hubert J. E., in 1825. Today, sparkling wine is also produced by Víno Nitra. The company's Pálffy Sekt Brut was recently awarded the title of champion in a prestigious contest in the Czech Republic, where it beat the Bohemia Sekt brand on several counts.

HUNGARY

Alex Liddell

Located close to the very center of Europe, Hungary has been subjected to a diversity of influences that have long shaped its wine production. Currently, it is making a transition from over 40 years of centralized communist control to a democratic government and free-enterprise economy, with the prospect of joining the European Union in 2002. An awareness of this situation is the key to understanding recent developments in the Hungarian wine industry.

History

In the third century AD, when Hungary was part of the Roman Empire, vine cultivation in the province of Pannonia (part of the Danube Basin) was extensive. By the time the Magyars migrated to the region from Turkish Caucasia in the late ninth century, they found viticulture well established there and in other parts of the country.

Under the Magyars, Hungary became an independent kingdom on Christmas Day, 1000. In the thirteenth century, the arrival of settlers from wine-producing countries such as Italy strengthened existing viticultural traditions, and by the fifteenth century Hungarian wines were being exported. Wine production suffered a major setback when the Turks seized parts of eastern and central Hungary in 1541 and incorporated them into the Ottoman Empire. However, viticulture

(and export to the west) continued to thrive in the northern and western parts of the country, which came under Austrian Hapsburg rule.

After the expulsion of the Turks in 1699, the whole of Hungary remained under Hapsburg domination until 1867, despite sporadic bids for independence. During this period, German and Austrian immigrants profoundly influenced the development of Hungarian viticulture, and Tokaji (see below) became one of Europe's most prestigious wines. In 1867, a federated Austro-Hungarian Empire was formed; this lasted until 1918, when Hungary became an independent republic. In 1920, following a plebiscite, the republic became a kingdom, presided over by a regent.

Wine production slumped in the 1930s as a result of global depression, inefficient production methods, and the onset of World War II. Following the declaration of a communist republic in 1947, a program of redistribution and collectivization was introduced. This involved setting up cooperatives and state farms to produce grapes, and winery farms to make wine—all under the control of a state body, Hungarovin. A centralized exporting agency, Monimpex, was also established. Broadly, the objective was to supply Soviet-bloc countries with mass-produced ordinary wine. It says something for the system that, despite the run-down state of the winemaking industry postwar, the next

Near the Szabadzag Bridge in Budapest.

The Szabadzag Bridge, spanning the Danube amidst the beauties of Budapest.

quarter-century saw production grow by almost two-thirds, albeit at the expense of quality.

Much-needed reorganization and modernization took place in the 1960s, but early reforms ran out of steam and vinification methods lagged behind those of the noncommunist world. Gorbachev's 1986 antialcohol campaign in the USSR lost Hungary 33 percent of its wine exports, and the collapse of the Soviet system in 1991 brought that figure closer to 75 percent.

Widespread bankruptcy followed; some estimates put total vineyard losses at up to 25 percent, with wine production falling by about 50 percent. But the introduction of privatization laws and the sale of vineyards and wineries, enabled a much slimmed-down industry to survive, and production is recovering. Most significantly, with the industry free from the shackles of state control, spurred by the necessity of exporting in order to survive, and increasingly funded by overseas companies, the search for quality is now the driving force behind production. Moreover, entry into the European Union in 2002 will attract the sort of funding (in the form of subsidies to pay for up-to-the-minute technology) that has already transformed the wine scene in, for example, Portugal, and should have the same results in Hungary.

Landscape and climate

Hungary is a landlocked country located to the east of Austria and to the west of Romania, with a surface area of approximately 36,000 square miles (93,000 sq km). It is quite flat, with 65 percent of the land surface less than 650 feet (200 m) above sea level. Only the west and north have hilly areas, although the Tokaj-Hegyalja district in the northeast is gently undulating. The central Great Plain, which stretches east and southeast, constitutes approximately half of the country.

Two principal rivers cross Hungary: the Danube enters from the northwest, flows south through the capital, Budapest, and leaves the country in the south; the Tisza, a tributary of the Danube, enters from the northeast and flows southeast across the southern border. Hungary has many lakes, and Balaton, in the west of the country, at 48 miles (77 km) long and 230 square miles (600 sq km), is Europe's largest.

Hungary has a broadly temperate climate that varies from wet temperate in the west to continental in the east and Mediterranean in the south. Spring comes early, summers tend to be long and winters short. The Great Plain experiences the

Vineyards in the foothills near Tocal-Tokaj, Hungary's most well-known wine region.

most extreme conditions, ranging from very cold to hot and arid. The mean average temperature is 52°F (11°C), with a summer average high of 86°F (30°C) and about 10 hours of daily sunshine during the grape-ripening season. Rainfall averages 27–31 inches (700–800 mm) a year in the west, and 11.7–13.7 inches (300–350 mm) in the east. In Tokaj-Hegyalja, autumnal sunshine and mists favor the formation of botrytis.

The wine areas are evenly distributed throughout the country, except to the east of the Tisza River, and show considerable geological variation. Hilly areas, such as Eger, Tokaj-Hegyalja and the slopes north of Lake Balaton, have volcanic origins. Topsoils are generally mixtures of loess, sand and clay, with limestone and slate at Balatonfüred and degraded lava at Tokaj-Hegyalja. The Great Plain, on the other hand, is predominantly sandy.

Vines and wines

Hungary has a vineyard area of about 320,000 acres (130,000 ha), yielding a total annual production of 99 million gallons (375 million l), of which about 21 million gallons (80 million l) are exported. All methods of vine training can be found, from the most primitive to the most modern.

In common with other central European countries, Hungary used to be mainly a producer of white wines. In 1950, whites accounted for about 75 percent of total production, rosé wines (known locally as siller) for almost 20 percent, and red wines (most notably Egri Bikavér, or Bull's Blood) only about 5 percent. Red wine production began to increase in the 1960s, with new cabernet

REGIONAL DOZEN

Balatonboglári Borgazdasági Rt, Chapel Hill Barrique Fermented Chardonnay

Balatonboglári Borgazdasági Rt, Chapel Hill Sauvignon Blanc

Bock Pince, Villányi Cabernet Sauvignon

Gere Attila, Villányi Cabernet Sauvignon Barrique

GIA Kft, Egri Barrique Chardonnay

GIA Kft, Egri Cabernet Sauvignon

Hilltop Neszmély Rt, Bin AK28 Sauvignon Blanc

Hilltop Neszmély Rt, Riverview Kékfrankos

Royal Tokaji Wine Company Kft, Nyulászó Vineyard, 5 puttonyos Aszú

Szent Donatus Pincészet Kft, Balatonlellei Cabernet Sauvignon Reserve

Szent Donatus Pincészet Kft, Lellei Oak Aged Chardonnay

Tiffan's Bt, Cabernet Sauvignon/Cabernet Franc Grand Selection

Selecting and marking the best vines—just one of the vineyard worker's many tasks.

sauvignon and cabernet franc plantings, and in the late 1980s it increased rapidly in regions such as Szekszárd and Villány-Siklós. It is now over 30 percent of total production, and is expected to overtake white wine production within the coming decade. Rosé wine production has declined to a very small percentage of the total.

Of the grape varieties recognized in Hungary, 35 are white and 15 red. They include the following internationally known names (Hungarian names appear in brackets):

White Rhine riesling (rajnairizling), Italian riesling (olaszrizling), sylvaner (zöld szilváni), müller-thurgau (rizlingszilváni), gewürztraminer (tramini), pinot gris (szürkebarát), pinot blanc (weissburgunder), chardonnay, sauvignon blanc, sémillon, chasselas, muscat ottonel (ottonel muskotály), yellow muscat (sárga muskotály) and grüner muscateller (zöld veltelini).

Red cabernet sauvignon, cabernet franc, merlot (médoc noir), pinot noir (nágyburgundi or blauburgunder), lemberger (kékfrankos or blaufränkisch), blauportugieser (kékoportó) and zweigelt.

The following are either considered to be native Hungarian varieties, or are found almost exclusively in Transylvanian countries:

White furmint, ezerjó, hárslevelű, juhfark, kéknyelű, oremus, irsai olivér, leányka, királyleányka, csaba gyöngye, cserszegi fűszeres, cirfadli, kövidinka, kunleány and zefír.

Red kadarka.

Apart from Tokaji and Bikavér, which are traditional blends, Hungarian table wines are generally sold under their varietal names or, occasionally, as blends bearing a proprietary name.

Appellations and producers

There are currently 23 appellations, the newest being Bortermohelyk, granted in mid-2000. State laws prescribe types and quality categories, compositional standards, production methods, yields, labeling conventions and levels of quality control. A register of vineyards and wineries exists.

Hungary's 23 appellations fall rather conveniently into six groups.

LAKE BALATON

Balatonfeldvidek, Badacsony and Balatonfüred-Csopak extend from west to east along the north shore of Lake Balaton, for a long time the principal source of Hungarian white wines. Dél-Balaton lies south of the lake, with Balatonmelléke at its west end. All benefit from mesoclimates created by the large expanse of water.

Badacsony (5,000 acres [2,000 ha]) produces full-bodied, rather minerally wines which Hungarians are proud of, and like to describe as "fiery." The most common varieties are olaszrizling and rajnairizling (hereafter "the two rieslings"), szürkebarát and ottonel muskotály.

Balatonfüred-Csopak (4,500 acres [1,800 ha]) produces similar but often more elegant wines. Olaszrizling predominates, alongside some tramini, rizlingszilváni and relative newcomers chardonnay and sauvignon blanc. Winemaker Mihály Figula, bottling under his Fine Wine (Borászati Vállalkozás) label, is beginning to be noticed.

Balatonfeldvidek (4,000 acres [1,600 ha]), which is set farther back from the lake, produces slightly inferior wines, mainly from olaszrizling, szürkebarát and rizlingszilváni.

Dél-Balaton (7,500 acres [3,000 ha]) has a perhaps less glamorous history than its neighbors, but offers more interesting products. Balatonboglári Borgazdasági Rt is the region's largest winery—it is 96 percent-owned by German-based Henkell-Söhnlein. It exports dependable wines made by Kym Milne under the Chapel Hill label. German-owned Szent Donatus Pincészet Kft, established in 1993, is making rapid progress, and Ottó Légli. an independent winemaker, is clearly a rising star. Common varieties grown are olaszrizling, chardonnay, sauvignon blanc, kékfrankos, cabernet sauvignon and merlot.

Balatonmelléke (2,500 acres [1,000 ha]) became an appellation in 1997, and as yet has no track record, apart from László Bussay's promising Csörnyeföldi wines. Typical varieties include cserszegi fűszeres, zöld veltelini and rizlingszilváni.

Harvesting grapes, a vital part of the long winemaking process.

THE NORTHWEST

Six appellations are found here.

Sopron (4,500 acres [1,800 ha]) lies in the north of the region near the Austrian border, and about 50 percent of its production is of somewhat hard and acidic red wines, whose characteristics may be the result of the area's cooler-than-average summers and higher-than-average rainfall. The newly opened wineries have yet to show their mettle. Kékfrankos, zöld veltelini and leányka are the most common varieties.

Pannonhalma Sokoróalja (2,500 acres [1,000 ha]), situated south of Györ, produces low-quality white wines from the two rieslings, tramini, rizlingszilváni and chardonnay.

Aszá-Neszmély (3,700 acres [1,500 ha]), another white wine area, lies farther east and just south of the Danube. Hilltop Neszmély Rt, founded in 1993, has modern winemaking facilities here, but also operates in Sopron and Szekszárd. Headed by Akos Kamocsay, who was Hungarian Winemaker of the Year in both 1997 and 2000, the company exports under several labels (including Dry Leap, Badger Hill, Neszmély Estate and Kamocsay Borok) and provides 45 percent of all Hungarian exports to the United Kingdom. The most common varieties are the two rieslings, plus rizlingszilváni, leányka, sauvignon blanc and chardonnay.

Mór (2,200 acres [900 ha]) lies in a sheltered, hilly region south of Aszá-Neszmély, and is home to ezerjó, a white variety that has some aging potential. Wines are typically hot and acidic, and are softened by residual sugar. Other local varieties are leányka, irsai olivér, chardonnay, zöld veltelini and tramini.

Eytek-Buda (4,000 acres [1,600 ha]) is located east of Mór and southwest of Budapest and has been an appellation only since 1990. It mainly provides materials for sparkling wines, most notably for Hungarovin Borgazdaság's high-quality Törley and François President ranges (Hungarovin owns 70 percent of the vineyards here). Chardonnay predominates alongside olaszrizling, zöld veltelini and a little pinot noir.

Somló (1,250 acres [500 ha]), the smallest designated region, is a single hill midway between Pannonhalma-Sokoróalja and Balatonfeldvidek. Its traditionally acidic and oxidized white wines (olaszrizling, juhfark, furmint and hárslevelü) seem to be currently out of fashion, and at present only Imre Györgykovács appears able to make clean, character-laden wines.

THE SOUTHWEST

There are four appellations in this interesting and up-and-coming region. Although plagued by mildew and botrytis in the mid-1990s, it is more climatically suited to producing red grapes than any other part of Hungary is.

Szekszárd (5,000 acres [2,000 ha]) extends across low hills west and south of the town of the same name. White wines, which constitute 45 percent of production and are made mainly with olaszrizling and chardonnay, tend to be flabby. Reds include a Szekszárdi Bikavér, of which kadarka is a component, cabernet sauvignon and cabernet franc (hereafter "the two cabernets"), and kékfrankos, which is often elegant but on occasions can lack the depth of the Villány wines

Above: *Also in the Balascony region, rows of vines seem to lead towards the winery buildings.*

Top: *Barrels in underground cellars at a winery in the Balascony region, north of Lake Balaton.*

Harvesting grapes below trellised vines, which provide some welcome shade.

Villány-Siklós (5,200 acres [2,100 ha]) is Hungary's most important appellation after Tokaj-Hegyalja. Good white wines (olaszrizling, chardonnay, tramini and hárslevelű) abound in Siklós, but the reds of Villány—the kékfrankos, kékoportó, the two cabernets, pinot noir and zweigelt—arouse most interest. They have fullness of color, body and flavor, allied to soft tannins and an intense, spicy bouquet. Happily, there is plenty of talent to exploit these qualities. Attila Gere, Ede Tiffán and József Bock have all been Hungarian Winemaker of the Year in the 1990s, and they all make excellent quality wines. Bock's Jammertal vineyard and Gere's Kopar vineyard, in particular, yield wines of enormous structure and personality.

CENTRAL SOUTH

In the late nineteenth century, the area of vineyard on the Great Plain expanded rapidly, and by 1914 the region, with its phylloxera-resistant sandy soil, accounted for 45 percent of Hungary's entire vineyard area. Later, in the 1980s, it was the site of more than 50 percent of the nation's vineyards; however, following the collapse of communism it lost 80 percent of its trade.

Hajós-Baja (10,000 acres [4,000 ha]) stretches north on the opposite (east) side of the Danube from Mohács. The topsoil is loess, and white wines (olaszrizling and chardonnay) tend to lack acidity. Red wines (kadarka, kékfrankos and cabernet sauvignon) do better, but this remains a struggling, mass-production area.

Csongrád (14,000 acres [5,700 ha]), which lies east of the Tisza river and north of Szeged, and *Kiskunság* (74,000 acres [30,000 ha]), are remote and generally arid. Between 1988 and 1994, following the collapse of communism, their vineyard areas halved, and they remain in deep trouble. Local light commercial wines are made from much the same varieties as those in Hajós-Baja.

THE NORTHEAST

Mátraalja (17,300 acres [7,000 ha]) is a white wine area located in the foothills of the northern Mátra mountain range, near the town of Gyöngyös. Although olaszrizling, rizlingszilváni, leányka, hárslevelű, tramini, chardonnay and others are all grown here, the region is notable mainly for its ottonel muskotály. Danubiana Bt, under Swiss-German-Hungarian control, owns the old state farm and exports actively, as does the Szőlőskert Borászati cooperative, which bottles wine under the Nagyréde label.

found farther south (see below). Excellent wines come from Aliscavin Borászati Rt, and winemakers to watch include Támas Dúzsi, Ferenc Takler and Péter Vida, all of whom are now bottling wine under their own names.

Tolna (1,500 acres [600 ha]),which lies north of the town of Szekszárd, was first designated in 1997. It is almost entirely a white wine region, with olaszrizling, rizlingszilváni and some kadarka its main varieties. Európai Bortermelők Kft (European Wine Producers Ltd) makes excellent wines at Bátaapáti, which was formerly part of the Szekszárd appellation.

Mecsekalja (3,200 acres [1,300 ha]) stretches from Pécs to Mohács and produces mainly white wine. Most of the produce that isn't used to make sparkling wine is consumed locally. The region's specialty is Pécsi Cirfandli, another "fiery" wine.

Bükkalja (4,700 acres [1,900 ha]), which lies farther east, largely supplies wineries in Eger with olaszrizling, leányka and rizlingszilváni for sparkling wine production.

Eger (8,650 acres [3,500 ha]) is known worldwide for its Bull's Blood, or Egri Bikavér, a blend of at least three varieties drawn from kékfrankos, kékoportó, kadarka, blauburger, the two cabernets, merlot and pinot noir. After many years of indifferent produce, a serious effort is being made to transform the image of this popular wine. Results have been variable. Red varietals are also produced here, as well as some whites from leányka, olaszrizling and chardonnay. Vilmos Thummerer and Béla Vincze bottle consistently good wines under their own labels, but the area's leading winemaker is Tibor Gál, who works for a joint-venture company, GIA Kft, which he co-owns with Nicolò Incisa (of Sassicaia in Italy) and the German-owned Alpina company.

TOKAJ-HEGYALJA

This region produces Hungary's most famous wine, Tokaji, named for the northeastern town of Tokaj. Tokaji was allegedly described by Louis XIV—some say by Voltaire—as "the king of wines and the wine of kings," and was a favorite of Frederick the Great of Prussia (1740–86). Peter the Great (1682–1725) and Catherine the Great (1762–96) of Russia kept an agent in Tokaj to select their wines, as well as a troop of cossacks to escort them to St Petersburg. Tokaj's keeping capacity—the Tokaj Kereskedőház Rt possesses a bottle of the 1670 vintage, and a bottle of 1646 was auctioned by Sotheby's in 1984—is almost as remarkable as is its history.

The area around Tokaj was first delimited between 1660 and 1670, and its vineyards were assessed as first, second and third class by Count Rákóczi in 1700. This was the first vineyard classification in the world, predating the Pombaline demarcation of the Douro area in Portugal by over 50 years. It was overlooked until the 1980s and finally updated in March, 1995.

Today, Tokaj-Hegyalja includes 12,350 planted acres (5,000 planted ha) between the Bodrog and Szerencs rivers. About 83 percent is owned by independent grape-growers, while Tokaj Kereskedőház Rt (formerly the state-run Borkombinát) retains 1.6 percent. Out of more than a score of producers, ten foreign-owned joint-venture companies share about 10 percent of the appellation area. Hungarian producers hold the remaining

5 percent of the vineyards, but apart from Tokaj Kereskedőház, the owner of the former imperial vineyard of Szarvas Szölö, only Szepsy-Királyo Pincészet has so far demonstrated any great ability.

Tokaji is made from furmint, hárslevelű, sarga muskotály and, occasionally, oremus. The first two make rather uninteresting table wines; however, they are the base for the sweet Aszú, on which the reputation of Tokaji rests. Traditionally, this was made by picking botrytized grapes which, under the pressure of their own weight, slowly provided small quantities of a barely alcoholic syrup called Eszencia. The grapes were then mashed to a paste and added in hodfuls (*puttonyos*) of approximately 55 pounds (25 kg) to 36-gallon (136-l) casks of the one-year-old base wine to macerate. After racking, the resulting wine was matured in cask for three years or longer, stored, then as now, in rock-hewn galleried cellars up to 600 years old. The sweetness of the resulting Aszú wines was measured by the number of *puttonyos* added, Aszú Eszencia (about 8 *puttonyos*) being the highest quality, followed by Tokaji Aszú (5 and 6 *puttonyos*). Tokaji Szamorodni, generally produced when there is a shortage of botrytized berries, is made from bunches of grapes less than 50 percent affected by botrytis, and can be moderately sweet or dry. Two other types of less sweet wine, Forditás and Máslás, are only occasionally encountered.

The new companies have, however, modified the traditional method into an industrial process. Whole botrytized berries are added to base wine must, fermentation is stopped by cooling, and the *puttonyos* classification of the resulting wine is determined by an official scale based on sugar content. The new companies aim to produce a reductive, Sauterne-like wine, which some say is closer to the earlier Tokaji tradition. Traditionalists, led by Tokaj Kereskedőház, counterclaim that Tokaji has always been a mildly oxidative wine. The issue, highly politicized in Tokaj, will doubtless be resolved by the export markets, which have taken to the new-style wines in a big way.

Recently, a reduction in production of the hard-to-sell table wine in favor of easily exportable Aszú has ruined many grape growers. This problem is being tackled by the Tokaj Renaissance Association, a group of producers led by the energetic István Szepsy.

A striking blue cellar door—with lock and warning—in the Tokaj region.

Grand, ornate architecture in a restaurant in historic Budapest.

SLOVENIA

Margaret Rand

This almost landlocked country, with around 58,000 acres (23,000 ha) of vineyard (in 1998), has been making wine for millennia. However, the current face of its wine industry has been shaped by two more recent major forces: the Austro-Hungarian Empire and communism.

During the era of the Austro-Hungarian Empire, grape varieties tended to spread freely, so modern Slovenia shares grape varieties and wine styles with neighboring Austria, Croatia and northern Italy. Decades of communism followed the fall of the Austro-Hungarian Empire, but even under communism some small-scale private ownership was allowed. There was also a loophole in the law, which permitted growers to sell their wine over the border for hard currency. This money was then invested in modernizing the wineries, which meant that winemaking standards in the regions bordering Italy and Austria were higher than those in the rest of Slovenia, and those in other neighboring communist-controlled countries.

Slovenia emerged as an independent state in 1991; it was the first republic to break away from what had been Yugoslavia. That it did so peacefully meant that it has been safe from the destruction that has since marked much of the rest of the former Yugoslavia. Slovenia had long been one of the most prosperous parts of the region, and still is.

A winemaker closes a fermentation tank in Ankharanski, Slovenia.

The amount of privately held vineyard has increased rapidly since 1991; by 1998 only around a quarter of the total vineyard area remained under state ownership. The Slovenian wine industry is continuing to modernize—stainless steel and new barriques are tending to replace older oak casks and vats—and expand, with winemakers also seeking new export markets. Quality assurance in the industry is also being managed well: under Slovenian wine law only the best wines may be bottled in 75 cl bottles. These generally bear the seal of the PSVVS (Business Association for Viticulture and Wine Production), an organisation that polices itself quite effectively.

With Slovenia's amenable climate and landscape, plus the enthusiasm and energy of its winemakers, and a little help from a thriving tourism industry, the future for wine in this small country looks extremely healthy.

Vines and wines

There are three wine areas in Slovenia, all of which press against the country's borders: the centre of Slovenia produces no wine. The Littoral, or Primorska, region makes predominantly red wines; its climate is Mediterranean, though tempered by the nearness of the Alps. It has four subregions: the Brda hills in the north, which are a continuation of Friuli in Italy; Karst, tucked in behind Trieste; Vipava, further inland from Karst; and Koper, which occupies Slovenia's only stretch of coast. Barbera, refosco, cabernet sauvignon and merlot are responsible for most of the reds in this region, reds for which high acidity and high tannin are favored, in true Italian style. Pinot blanc and rebula (a local name for ribolla), picolit, malvaziji (malvasia), yellow muscat, chardonnay, pinot gris, furlaner tokaj (tocai friuliano) and others make the often very stylish whites.

The Drava Valley, or Podravje, is the other major region, and has a more continental climate: between them, these two regions produce some 85 percent of Slovenia's wine. Subregions here are Maribor, Sredjne (Central) Slovenske, Radgona-Kapela, Prekmurske, Ljutomer and Haloze. Wine styles vary according to whether regions border Styria in Austria, or Hungary: where the hills are an extension of Styria, light, clean, acidic wines are the norm; elsewhere, the wines are fatter and more flowery, and often sweeter. Ljutomer's best known wine is its Laski Rizling, which gave the region a bad name for decades. When made properly, however, it can be fresh, weighty and tasty. Other grapes grown in this region include gewürztraminer, pinot blanc, sauvignon blanc, riesling and šipon (probably an alias for Hungary's furmint), which makes a fiery, lively wine which deserves a wider audience.

The smallest region, the Sava Valley or Posavje, is divided into the subregions of Dolenjsko, Bela Krajina, Smarje and Bizeljsko. Summers are hot and autumns warm and sunny here; grapes include laski rizling, pinot blanc, sauvignon blanc and chardonnay for whites, and blaufränkisch, pinot noir, portugieser, gamay, kerner and zweigelt, as well as less familiar varieties such as rumeni plavec, seatlovrenka and zametovka.

CROATIA

Brian Jordan

Before civil war erupted in 1991, both Croatia and Slovenia were significant producers of wine, and had large and valuable export markets in Germany and Britain. This trade was decimated by the conflict, but since the cessation of hostilities there has been a rapid rise in wine production, from an average of 49 million gallons (187 million l) from 1991 to 1995 to 52 million gallons (196 million l) in 1996 and 60 million gallons (226 million l) in 1997.

During the time of the Austro-Hungarian Empire (1868–1918), the region, especially its picturesque coastline, was hugely popular with the imperial nobility, who built many palaces in the area and encouraged local wine production.

Of the two distinct growing regions, the main one is Kontinentalna Hrvatska (Inland Croatia), which covers much of the eastern half of the country and incorporates seven districts. The other, Primorska Hrvatska (Coastal Croatia), has four districts, extends along the entire seaboard and includes all the country's islands.

Wines and producers

The cooler and more fertile inland area produces mainly white wine (95 percent), especially from the dull but productive and undemanding laski rizling, or welschriesling, whereas 70 percent of coastal production is red wine. The inland region also produces fruity, straw-colored Kutjevacka graševina from Kutjevo, some quite respectable gewürztraminer, pinot blanc, sauvignon blanc, Johannisberg or Rhine riesling, and even muscat ottonel, especially from the slopes of Baranja.

Interesting reds from the coast include wines from the plavac mali vine. Dingač and postup from the Peljesac Peninsula are highly regarded—the full international potential of these two wines, as well as of wine from the Dalmatian sémillon grape, is yet to be fully explored. Other promising wines include those made on the Istrian peninsula from Italian refosco, as well as cabernet sauvignon, merlot, malvazija (red malvasia), gamay and pinot noir. The island wines also have potential, especially the whites, once oxidation problems are recognized and overcome. Bolski Plavac from

Brac and faros from Hvar seem, at the moment, the most likely to repay development.

More than half of Croatia's wines are allowed a geographical appellation. Additional and more valuable quality control is applied in the form of a Buxbaum system, based on tastings and administered by a wine-grading subcommission. Most wine production involves a combination of relatively modern methods and antiquated, but often ingeniously modified, equipment.

Hvar Island, pictured on the labels of local winery Plenkovic Wines Sv. Nedjela, in Croatia.

BOSNIA AND HERZEGOVINA

Brian Jordan

It is difficult to write with any authority about this war-torn state. In better days, the vineyards in the south of the country covered 12,350 acres (5,000 ha) around coastal Mostar and Dubrovnik and farther inland. By 1997, declared production figures had halved to 1.4 million gallons (5.4 million l). Red wines were always less than persuasive, mainly due to the popularity of the unimpressive blatina grape, but white wines made from zilavka—one of no less than nine internationally recognized wine grapes starting with "z"—displayed its typical and welcome acidity. Both varieties were mainly used for popular Samotok rosé wines. At the time of writing, it is impossible to predict future developments, and one can only hope that the situation improves dramatically.

Enologist Niksa Zglav, tasting wines from Hvar's Plenkovic Wines Sv. Nedjela, off the Dalmatian coast of Croatia.

SERBIA AND MONTENEGRO

Brian Jordan

As with so many East European countries, the effects of religious and political turmoil are impossible to ignore, or to measure. In Serbia this is particularly poignant, as before recent wars involving this dual state—and Montenegro is currently showing signs of a desire to split from Serbia—wine production was considerable, and growing at a healthy rate. Production figures in 1997, for example, were 40 percent behind Romania and 10 percent behind Hungary, respectively the first and second producers (by volume) of the 25 East European and near-Orient producer countries. Until 1997 no battles had been fought on Serbian ground, so the vineyards remained unaffected; sadly, this is no longer the case.

Serbia is the central state in the Balkans, and has in recent years constituted one of the two major states of Yugoslavia. Serbia has politically and culturally leaned toward the Slav nations, headed by Russia, while the south of Yugoslavia has leaned toward Islam and the north toward central European customs—Serbia has always been a political and religious front line. In line with the area's cultural leanings, most of Serbia's 106 million gallons (400 million l) of wine was in the past flavor-designed to suit Russian tastes. Only the three northern regions of Serbia, influ-

enced by neighboring Hungary and Romania, enjoyed wider acceptance, mainly as contributors to medium-sweet Yugo-brand blended wines.

The majority of vineyards follow the northerly course of the river Morava, from its source near Pristina in Kosovo to its confluence with the Danube, east of Belgrade, across relatively flat land with low rolling hills. As one would expect, the southern regions concentrate on red wines, while the more northerly regions are planted primarily with white grapes. Viticultural practices are not modern, and are still mainly carried out through huge underfunded cooperatives.

Wines and producers

Of Serbia's indigenous grapes, probably the finest is red prokupac, found everywhere south of the Danube valley, with its best expression around the tiny town of Cacak in the administrative district of Zupa, which is usually included in the Zahodnom-ravski or Zapadna Morava growing region. It is often, possibly unfairly, used to lend a fruity taste to a blend with pinot noir or gamay. When used as a single variety, it is usually only lightly fermented, to produce Zupska Ruzica Rosé. The most highly regarded white grape of this region, smederevka, originated close to where the Morava and the Danube meet, around the town of Smederevo. It produces medium-sweet fruity wines and is grown in over 90 percent of the vineyards in the area.

The Vojvodina region, bordering Hungary, grows quite a number of mainly white grapes, and achieves some success with both traminers and merlots. The majority of the remainder of Serbia's vineyards are planted with "European" varieties such as cabernet sauvignon, cabernet franc, merlot, pinot noir, sauvignon blanc, traminac (gewürz-traminer), sémillon, and italijanski rizling (welsch-riesling)—some of these display extremely unusual taste and bouquet signatures.

In Montenegro, wine production is small, though three regions are defined. The traditional Crmnicko Crno wine, from terraced slopes overlooking Lake Skadar, which used to be made from vranac and kratosija, is of greatest significance. It is now called Crnogorski Vranac, and is made using only the vranac grape.

Kosovo had, until its recent problems, a substantial export trade in basic wines with Germany—the Amsel-felder Kosovo Vino range of mainly red wines, in both dry and semi-sweet versions, from cabernet franc to burgundac (pinot noir), plus a little dry white and rosé.

Southern Central Europe, where land is flatter, and weather is drier and warmer.

ALBANIA

Brian Jordan

Albania is the least developed country in Europe, and its wine industry has failed to attract foreign investment or expertise. The government created a body charged with upgrading local varieties, growing conditions and production methods in 1990, but continuing political instability makes it unlikely that the nation will become a significant wine producer in the foreseeable future.

Parts of Albania are considered by some to be the last refuges of *Vitis vinifera* vines in Europe, yet little wine of international significance has ever been produced here. From the fifteenth century until the early twentieth century, Albania was part of the Ottoman Empire, and its Islamic rulers imposed restrictions on wine production in accordance with their religious beliefs. After the country gained independence in 1912, viticulture increased significantly. When phylloxera struck the vineyards in the 1930s, the area under plantation dropped to a mere 6,750 acres (2,730 ha), but it rose again under communism (1945–95) to 34,500 acres (14,000 ha). Current annual production is officially reported as 4.5 million gallons (17 million l), but this figure is based largely on hopeful government estimates.

Four wine regions rise successively from the coast: the coastal plain, which includes the capital Tirana plus the towns of Durrërski, Shkodra, Lezha, Lushnja, Fier, Vlora and Delvina; the hills, which includes Elbasan, Krujë, Gramsh, Berat, Prmet, Librazhd and Mirdita; the lower mountains around Pogradec, Korça, Leskovic and Peshkopi; and the largely uninhabited highland region, with vineyards as high as 3,300 feet (1,000 m). Good conditions for winemaking do exist here, but this potential is of academic interest until people's survival is more secure.

A third of the national crop is from white shesh i bardhë and red shesh i zi, both of which originated around the town of Shesh, near Tirana. The Hungarian red kadarka, known here as as kallmet, has probably the greatest potential. The village of Narta produced vlosh, a high-strength wine similar to the rancio wines of Catalunia and Roussillon, until the market for such wines declined. The country's most notable producers include the Durres Red Star cooperative, whose mavrud and cabernet franc are among the best of an otherwise uninspiring national output.

MACEDONIA

Brian Jordan

Macedonia is firstly famous as the homeland of Alexander the Great. Today, though, this once Yugoslav state—independence was gained in 1993—rests in delicate political balance with neighboring Greece: part of the old Macedonian kingdom is in Greece (and part is in southwestern Bulgaria). Greece appears to have some territorial interest in Macedonia, making this another far from stable period in the history of this often unstable region.

Worker in the vineyard in Macedonia.

"Close to ideal" would accurately describe Macedonia's grape-growing potential, in terms of landscape and climate, especially for red wines (80 percent of Macedonian output). Whites also have potential, particularly on the higher slopes of the eastern hills (the Pcinja-Osogovo region), and in the Pelagonija-Polog region around lakes Ohrid and and Prespa. Most vineyards are planted at quite high altitude. Vineyard plantings leave space between rows for tractors, but almost all the work is done by hand. As one might expect, winemaking practices here are generally not yet modernized. Unfortunately, the country's potential is likely to remain unrealized until there is sufficient political stability to make outside investment in Macedonia's wine industry attractive.

As Macedonia was until recently part of Yugoslavia, with no independent identity, some statistics are unavailable. However, the 75,000 acres (30,000 ha) of vineyards are said to produce more than 27 million gallons (100 million litres) of wine—double the output of New Zealand. Few outside the country have ever tasted these. The vast majority (90 percent) of red wine is produced from indigenous vranac and kratosija varieties—the two, blended, produce Kratosija, the country's most popular wine. Some cabernet sauvignon, merlot and grenache are also available.

The most common white varieties are laski riesling and local smederevka, often blended; small quantities of chardonnay and sauvignon blanc are also planted. Belan, from white grenache, is also popular—the zilavka variety, however, probably has greater potential.

Before the recent warfare, serious attempts at developing export trade—primarily red wines to Slovenia and German, which produce little red wine of their own—were being made: by Povardarie Co-operative, south of Skopje, for one.

John Boutari Rosé and Naoussa made from Macedonian xinomavro grapes; and Samos Vin Doux Rosé, made from moschato grapes by the Samos Co-op in Greece.

Eastern Europe

Eastern Europe

The countries in this chapter have all emerged from dominance by the USSR—in the cases of Moldova, Ukraine and Russia, they were part of the USSR itself, and in the cases of Bulgaria and Romania, they were client states. At the moment, the necessities of everyday life take priority over the making of fine wine in all these countries, and the local market has no particular regard for quality. The money needed to improve wine quality must come either from joint ventures or direct from export sales—and export markets aren't interested unless the wines are of decent quality in the first place.

Bulgaria has the longest history of producing export-friendly wines, and Moldova has at least as much potential. Romania's great problem is lack of consistency; the Ukraine and Russia focus on local markets but might—who knows?—yet prove to be sleeping giants.

Murmansk

Archangel

Lake Onega

Lake Ladoga

St Petersburg

Cherepovets   Vologda

Rybinsk
Yaroslavl   Kostroma
Tver   Ivanovo
Vladimir   Nizhniy No
Kaza

MOSCOW
Vitebsk   Smolensk
Kaluga   Ryazan'   Saransk   Sim
Tula
MINSK   Penza   Tol'ya
BELARUS   Bryansk   Lipetsk   Tambov
Gomel
Brest   Chernigov   Kursk   Voronezh   Saratov
UKRAINE   Sumy   Belgorod
Zhytomyr   KIEV   Kharkov
Lvov   Cherkasy   Poltava   Don
Dnepropetrovsk   Lugansk   Volgogra
Donetsk   Don Valley
ROMANIA   Balti   Odessa   Mariupol'   Rostov-on-Don
Cluj-Napoca   CHISINAU   Kherson   Astrakhan
6   Odessa   Sea of   Krasnodar   Stavropol
Timisoara   Ploesti   Azov
BUCHAREST   Crimea   Anapa
Constanta   Sevastopol   Sochi   Caucasus Mtns Mak
BULGARIA   Black Sea   Shkhara
SOPHIA   Suhindol   17,060 ft (5200 m)
Damianitza

Romania
1 Muntenia-Dealul Mare
2 Dobrudja
3 Transylvania
4 Moldavia
5 Oltenia
6 Banat

Bulgaria
1 Northern region
2 Eastern region
3 Southern region
4 Sub-Balkan region
5 Southwest region

425

A nursery vineyard in Bulgaria, where young vines are trained.

BULGARIA

James Aufenast

Bulgarian wine tastes different these days. Where once the country produced dark, rich oaked cabernets, now they are fresher, younger and more fruity. Which you prefer depends on your personal inclination, but the reasons for the change matter.

The nation emerged from communism in 1990, but it has taken weak post-communist governments a decade to implement reforms that will sort out land ownership, which will in turn allow wineries to start to control the grapes which they make into wine. Many wineries are still simply factories which buy in grapes from nearby growers. Traditionally, all the investment has been in the winery. Once land ownership is clarified and resolved, the vineyards, half of which have gone to rack and ruin, can be bought, and improved.

The last decade has also had an effect on the quality of Bulgarian wine. Increased emphasis on the winery rather than the grape has resulted in the production of too many identikit wines. In the early 1980s Bulgaria had a stock of aged reds, mostly cabernet sauvignon, which had significant depth of flavor, but most were sold off as the popularity of Bulgarian wine rocketed. This meant wineries started making more fruit-driven wines which relied on young oak rather than old age for their flavor. Nowadays the best wineries, particularly in the north of the country, retain some character in their wines, but a lot don't.

History

Unlike its Eastern European and Middle Eastern neighbors, Bulgaria has little claim to a great wine history. Wine flourished under the Greeks, but Turkish rule, with the Moslem religion that accompanied it, put an end to that. The story in the twentieth century, however, is more complex. Communism began to take hold in the 1930s, when Vinprom, a state monopoly, took over responsibility for the import and export of grapes. In 1947 the first fully fledged communist government nationalized wine production, and large cooperatives took over the vineyards.

In the 1960s the US soft drink company, Pepsico, looking for influence in Eastern Europe, sought to trade its cola for Bulgarian wine, and engineered contacts with Davis University, in California, to improve the quality of Bulgarian wine. Then Soviet President Gorbachev arrived.

His insistence in the 1980s on less alcohol in the USSR was disastrous for the Bulgarian wine industry—vast areas of vineyards were uprooted. Production fell drastically, from 119 million gallons (450 million l) in 1985 to 47.5 million gallons (180 million l) in 1990.

Production increased again during the 1990s, to 158 million gallons (600 million l), with 270,000 acres (110,000 ha) under vine. Vinprom was demonopolized in 1991, and investment in wineries subsequently has been immense, particularly by the biggest Bulgarian export company, Domaine Boyar. It received US$30.5 million from the European Bank for Reconstruction and Development in 1999. Wine companies throughout Bulgaria now intend to invest in the vineyards.

Initiated in 1978, the regulations are sometimes avoided by producers, in the manner of Super-Tuscans or some French *vin de pays*, but more often than not they are used. At the lowest level are Quality Wines, followed by Country Wines (the equivalent of *vin de pays*), then Reserve and Special Reserve (the last are varietal wines, aged for at least two years in the case of white wines, and three years for red). At the quality peak is Controliran (the equivalent of the French *Appellation Contrôlée*), with specified varieties taken from specific vineyards.

Landscape and climate

Bulgaria, though a tiny country, experiences huge temperature ranges from summer to winter—from 104°F (40°C) down to –13°F (–25°C). The Black Sea has an ameliorating effect on the climate of the land near it. The country includes one mountain range—the Balkan range—where wine is not grown; almost all other areas have some wine, but most wineries in Bulgaria are on the extensive plains—they were set up during the Soviet era, and were designed for mechanized harvesting. The northern Transdanubian plain and the southern Thracian plain, with their lush flatter areas, are home to the majority of the current wine industry.

Wine regions

NORTHERN REGION

Some of Bulgaria's most well-established—and best—wineries are in this region, which produces 11.6 million gallons (44 million l) from a vineyard area of 92,700 acres (37,500 ha). Seven of the 28 Controliran regions are here. The average northern temperature is slightly cooler than in the

REGIONAL DOZEN

Damianitza Melnik
Iambol Cabernet Sauvignon Royal Reserve
Perushtitza Pulden Cabernet Sauvignon Mavrud
Pomorie Barrel Fermented Chardonnay
Russe Cabernet Sauvignon, Yantra Valley
Russe Reserve Chardonnay
Schumen Chardonnay & Aliogoté
Slaviantzi Barrel Fermented Chardonnay
Sliven Young Vatted Cabernet Sauvignon
Stara Zagora Boyar Cabernet Sauvignon Special Reserve, Oriochovitza
Suhindol Cabernet Sauvignon
Svishtov Cabernet Sauvignon Special Reserve, Gorchivka

Taimyr
Peninsula

Olenek

Yenisei

CENTRAL

Lower
Tunguska

SIBERIAN

Yenisei

PLATEAU

Lena

Ob

RUSSIAN FEDERATION

Ob

Angara

Lena

URAL MOUNTAINS

Nizhniy Tagil

Tyumen

Irtysh

Tomsk

Krasnoyarsk

Lake
Baikal

Yekaterinburg

nyye Chelny
Chelyabinsk⊙

Kurgan

Omsk   Lake Chany   Novosibirsk

EASTERN SAYANS

YABLONOVYY RANGE

Magnitogorsk

Barnaul

Irkutsk
Ulan-Ude   Chita

amak

Ob

Orenburg
Orsk

NORTH

200 miles
(320 kilometers)

A nursery vineyard in Bulgaria, where young vines are trained.

BULGARIA

James Aufenast

Bulgarian wine tastes different these days. Where once the country produced dark, rich oaked cabernets, now they are fresher, younger and more fruity. Which you prefer depends on your personal inclination, but the reasons for the change matter.

The nation emerged from communism in 1990, but it has taken weak post-communist governments a decade to implement reforms that will sort out land ownership, which will in turn allow wineries to start to control the grapes which they make into wine. Many wineries are still simply factories which buy in grapes from nearby growers. Traditionally, all the investment has been in the winery. Once land ownership is clarified and resolved, the vineyards, half of which have gone to rack and ruin, can be bought, and improved.

The last decade has also had an effect on the quality of Bulgarian wine. Increased emphasis on the winery rather than the grape has resulted in the production of too many identikit wines. In the early 1980s Bulgaria had a stock of aged reds, mostly cabernet sauvignon, which had significant depth of flavor, but most were sold off as the popularity of Bulgarian wine rocketed. This meant wineries started making more fruit-driven wines which relied on young oak rather than old age for their flavor. Nowadays the best wineries, particularly in the north of the country, retain some character in their wines, but a lot don't.

History

Unlike its Eastern European and Middle Eastern neighbors, Bulgaria has little claim to a great wine history. Wine flourished under the Greeks, but Turkish rule, with the Moslem religion that accompanied it, put an end to that. The story in the twentieth century, however, is more complex. Communism began to take hold in the 1930s, when Vinprom, a state monopoly, took over responsibility for the import and export of grapes. In 1947 the first fully fledged communist government nationalized wine production, and large cooperatives took over the vineyards.

In the 1960s the US soft drink company, Pepsico, looking for influence in Eastern Europe, sought to trade its cola for Bulgarian wine, and engineered contacts with Davis University, in California, to improve the quality of Bulgarian wine. Then Soviet President Gorbachev arrived.

His insistence in the 1980s on less alcohol in the USSR was disastrous for the Bulgarian wine industry—vast areas of vineyards were uprooted. Production fell drastically, from 119 million gallons (450 million l) in 1985 to 47.5 million gallons (180 million l) in 1990.

Production increased again during the 1990s, to 158 million gallons (600 million l), with 270,000 acres (110,000 ha) under vine. Vinprom was demonopolized in 1991, and investment in wineries subsequently has been immense, particularly by the biggest Bulgarian export company, Domaine Boyar. It received US$30.5 million from the European Bank for Reconstruction and Development in 1999. Wine companies throughout Bulgaria now intend to invest in the vineyards.

Initiated in 1978, the regulations are sometimes avoided by producers, in the manner of Super-Tuscans or some French *vin de pays*, but more often than not they are used. At the lowest level are Quality Wines, followed by Country Wines (the equivalent of *vin de pays*), then Reserve and Special Reserve (the last are varietal wines, aged for at least two years in the case of white wines, and three years for red). At the quality peak is Controliran (the equivalent of the French *Appellation Contrôlée*), with specified varieties taken from specific vineyards.

Landscape and climate

Bulgaria, though a tiny country, experiences huge temperature ranges from summer to winter—from 104°F (40°C) down to –13°F (–25°C). The Black Sea has an ameliorating effect on the climate of the land near it. The country includes one mountain range—the Balkan range—where wine is not grown; almost all other areas have some wine, but most wineries in Bulgaria are on the extensive plains—they were set up during the Soviet era, and were designed for mechanized harvesting. The northern Transdanubian plain and the southern Thracian plain, with their lush flatter areas, are home to the majority of the current wine industry.

Wine regions

NORTHERN REGION

Some of Bulgaria's most well-established—and best—wineries are in this region, which produces 11.6 million gallons (44 million l) from a vineyard area of 92,700 acres (37,500 ha). Seven of the 28 Controliran regions are here. The average northern temperature is slightly cooler than in the south, because of the Balkan mountains. This helps the area produce well-balanced, structured reds, particularly at the Russe winery. This winery, by the Danube, is one of the few to have vineyards on hillsides, in this case in the Yantra valley. Its elegant cabernet-based reds and clean chardonnays are helped by the microclimate of the Danube. Nearby Svishtov, also on the Danube, produces red wines only, from the excellent Gorchivka vineyard. Further south is Suhindol, which specialises in cabernet sauvignon and produces one of the best wines in Bulgaria—Czar Simeon.

EASTERN REGION

This is a major white wine area— there are 81,500 acres (33,000 ha) under vine, producing 11.6 million gallons (44 million l). The continental climate is tempered by the presence of the Black Sea: summers are cooler, winters are warmer. The pick of the wineries is Pomorie, on the Black Sea, making floral, viscous chardonnays on a level with the sub-Balkan winery, Slaviantzi. Schumen has plain varietals that are much better than the branded Premium Oak wines, and Targovischte makes promising sauvignon blanc.

SOUTHERN REGION

Too many of the vineyards here (68,000 acres [27,500 ha] are under vine) are on flat land. That other blight of the Bulgarian wine industry, neglected vineyards, is also evident here. However, excellent soil—well-drained sand and clay—and the hilly southeastern section mean the region has plenty of potential. By the turn of the century it was producing 9.1 million gallons (34.5 million l). Perushtitza, in the west, is excellent for local varieties such as the rich mulberry-like mavrud, and the lively, appley misket. At Iambol, in the middle of the country, and at the neighboring sub-Balkan Sliven winery, high-tech winery equipment produces fruity, clean cabernet sauvignons. But both need to own vineyards. To the west the high altitude Oriachovitza vineyards produce some of the best cabernet sauvignon and merlot in Bulgaria, for the Stara Zagora winery.

SUB-BALKAN REGION

This is the most mountainous region in Bulgaria, though the wine industry has not taken advantage of this yet—it has a mere 15,900 acres (6,600 ha) under vine, and produces only 9.2 million gallons (35 million l). Most vineyards are in the foothills of the Balkans. Sliven is one of the biggest wineries

Vineyards on the outskirts of a town in southern Bulgaria.

in Bulgaria, producing about 5.3 million gallons (20 million l). It mostly turns out clean, well-made red wine (cabernet sauvignon and merlot), thanks to the input of Australian consultants Stephen Black and David Wollan. Slaviantzi produces some of Bulgaria's best chardonnays.

SOUTHWESTERN REGION

This is a hot region, and is bordered by Greece and Macedonia. It has 13,600 acres (5,500 ha) under vine, but as yet only 790,000 gallons (3 million l) is produced. The tasty, spicy melnik grape is a local variety that has potential, particularly at Damianitza. This winery is deep in the south of the country. The quality sometimes varies due to the heat, but some vineyards in the region are planted high, up to 3,300 feet (1,000 m), which gives them potential for greater longevity and improved concentration.

ROMANIA

James Aufenast

"The next Chile" or "the new Burgundy"? During the 1990s, these and other epithets were attached to the Romanian wine industry. However, storage and aging are low grade, and consistency is a problem—pinot noir can be full and savory and merlot can be grassy and herbaceous. Of the six main wine regions, only three export regularly and are of a quality that can be monitored. Exact production and land figures are unknown.

The potential is there, however, as 75 percent of the vineyards are planted on sloping sites. As French exporter Guy de Poix said when he visited Romania, "I thought I was in the Côte de Nuits." It's crazy to talk about Romanian pinot noir at the level of top burgundy, but the Dealul Mare region is producing some pinot noir to Bourgogne Grand Ordinaire standard. Another positive factor is that 1999, like 1997, was a good vintage. However, if Romania, by far the biggest wine grower in Eastern Europe, with around 568,000 acres (230,000 ha) under vine, is to gain a place on the world wine stage, it needs to match another comparison: Bulgaria's spending in the wine industry.

History

The Greeks settled the area now known as Romania in the seventh century BC, and may have brought winegrowing to the region. Certainly from the first century AD vines were being cultivated. Despite successive invasions by Turks, Russians and Austrians, growing continued uninterrupted, at least until phylloxera hit the vines in 1884. Romania became a socialist republic in 1947, but it wasn't until the 1950s and 1960s that new vines were planted to replace lost vineyards. The state owned 30 percent of vineyards, leaving 60 percent in the hands of cooperatives and 10 percent privately owned. This hasn't changed dramatically since independence, but the involvement of Halewood, a British company, has brought Western winemaking techniques, particularly to Dealul Mare. In 1999 it invested £2 million in the Romanian winemaking company Vinalcool Prahova, now renamed Prahova Winecellars.

The wine regulations are changing, but are at present still based on must weight and defined geographical areas. Vin de masa is the most basic wine. The next grade up is VS, which must have a potential alcohol content of 10.5 percent. DOC wines (similar to France's AC [previously VSO] wines) have a denomination of regional origin. Top of the range are DOCC wines (previously known as VSOC): CMD refers to late harvest, CMI to late harvest with noble rot, and CIB is similar to Sélection de Grains Nobles.

Landscape and climate

Romania is a mountainous country, but it also has plains—flowing south from the Transylvanian alps to the Danube, the country's border with Bulgaria, and west from the Carpathians to the border with Hungary. There is also a lower coastal plain, on the coast of the Black Sea. There are wine regions in all these areas. While the latitude of Romania and Bordeaux are the same, Romania's climate ranges between considerably greater extremes. However, the Black Sea does have a moderating effect on winter temperatures near the coast. Summer heat is not so much as to affect vines during their growing season, and rain is unlikely to impede grape harvests.

Wine regions

MUNTENIA

By far the major area is Dealul Mare, which translates as "big hill". It is also large in terms of red wine production. The wines of the region are the most Western palate-friendly, and the Research Institute of Valea **Călugrească** has been at the forefront of pioneering work on pinot noir in the

The warm, humid Murfatlar area produces rich white wines and late harvest wines.

region. Better Burgundy clones of the variety are being substituted for current clones from the Champagne region. At Tohani winery, grapes are macerated below 82°F (28°C) to ensure clean fruit flavors. Main varieties are cabernet sauvignon, merlot, pinot noir and feteãscã neãgrã, with some impressive experiments in sangiovese. Tohani is closely linked to the excellent Ceptura winery. The Urlati winery specializes in well-extracted merlot and cabernet sauvignon. In a subdistrict, Petroade, a golden, honeyed sweet wine from the tamîosa grape is produced.

DOBRUDJA

The humid, balmy vineyards of the Murfatlar region produce rich, luscious white and late harvest wines. There are some chardonnays cellared from 40 years ago. The Murfatlar winery majors in a range of floral versions of pinot gris and riesling italico (not Rhine riesling).

TRANSYLVANIA

This area is almost solely a producer of white wines, with the best wines coming from the Tarnave Valley. Styles tend toward the Germanic, with a flinty acidity in the better examples, such as Jidvei's Gewürztraminer. Temperatures are lower in the south, where Apold de Sus produces a lively méthode traditionnelle sparkling wine.

MOLDAVIA

With over a third of all Romania's vineyards, this is the largest area under vine. Northern Moldavia is predominantly white wine country, with the area producing the most famous Romanian wine, Cotnari. Further south, the Odobesti region makes good examples of the grapefruity, spicy feteãscã albã variety. Cotesti, south of Odobesti produces a minty-flavored merlot.

OLTENIA

West of Bucharest, the Drãgãsãni vineyards stretch into the Transylvanian foothills to heights of 2,300 feet (700 m). Sauvignon blanc and some late harvest wines are grown here. The Drincea region is warmer, and produces adequate examples of merlot and pinot noir.

BANAT

This region includes flat areas where table wines—Teremia and Recãs—are produced and hillier sites such as Buzias-Silãgiu, where white wines are made from the flourishing local creãtã grape.

Many vineyards in Eastern Europe still use traditional tools and methods.

MOLDOVA
Brian Jordan

Many ex-communist countries around southeastern Europe and the Black Sea warrant the description "have potential," but none more so than this land, ancient Bessarabia. A significant producer and exporter of wine since the Middle Ages, Moldova was later swept under Moslem influence, and like all countries similarly influenced, lost production. It was not until annexation by Russia in 1812 that production again began to increase.

History

Tsar Alexander chose Moldova's finest growing region, Chisinau, to develop Château Romanesti, a 1,500 acre (600 ha) wine estate planted—by invited French vignerons—with cabernet sauvignon, merlot, malbec and pinot noir for reds and rkatsiteli and aligoté for whites. The Romanovs also created a significant wine college, at nearby Stauceni. Nineteenth century Moldova was famed not only for superb table wines but also for "sherry" produced at Ialoveni, near the capital Chisinau, for sparkling wine from Cricova and brandy around Balti.

Then in the mid-nineteenth century, together with Walachia, it formed independent Romania. Before phylloxera decimated vineyards at the end of the century there were almost 110,00 acres (45,000 ha) under vine, a figure which, after replanting, rose continually, reaching a final figure of 470,000 acres (190,000 ha) in the late 1950s.

During the Second World War the major part of the Moldavian area was again annexed by Russia, finally achieving independence only in 1991. Although one of the smallest states in the former USSR, Moldova at that time had 10 percent of its landmass under vine, and was the source of Russia's finest red wines.

A series of bitter winters, coupled with the Gorbachev prohibitionist movement, reduced the area under vine to 445,000 acres (180,000 ha) by the mid-1980s—this figure has now risen to 457,000 acres (185,000 ha). Since independence, the population has been regaining its European—rather than Asian—heritage, and is forming ever closer ties with its natural cultural neighbor, Romania. Today Moldova is in sixteenth place in the world wine production tables, with 95 million gallons (360 million l).

These merlot vines have been extensively hand pruned and thinned.

Landscape and climate

Although Moldova has no coastline, the Black Sea moderates the climate of the southern wine region; the northern regions are cloudier and damper, and have more severe winters. The country is surprisingly flat, rarely rising above 1,150 feet (350 m). Temperature summation figures of 4,890°F (2,700°C) in the north and 6,150°F (3,400°C) in the south, coupled with annual rainfall of around 20 inches (500 mm), provide almost ideal (by European standards at least) growing conditions, and some of the problems experienced by other ex-USSR countries—winter vine protection, the use of primitive irrigation systems and a lack of mechanization—are unknown here.

Vines and wines

Of all ex-USSR countries, Moldova is most similar to Hungary, Romania and (especially) Bulgaria, in that is has quantities of "European" varieties already established—cabernet sauvignon, merlot and pinot noir for reds, and chardonnay, aligoté, sauvignon blanc, pinot gris, muscat ottonel, riesling and gewürztraminer for whites.

Additionally, Moldova has probably the best selection of quality grapes indigenous to Black Sea countries—saperavi, black sereskia and the teinturier variety gamay fréaux, plus the ubiquitous rkatsiteli and feteăscă. Six winemaking districts are delineated: Pucar, Balti, Ialoveni, Stauceni, Cricova, Romanesti and Hincesti.

The interest of Western winemakers is the surest endorsement of the potential of Moldovan wine. In the mid-1990s Penfolds, Ryman and Lurton were all variously involved at Hincesti winery (30 miles [50 km] south of Romanesti), and a Dutch/French consortium formed a joint venture with a group of Moldovan wineries. However, problems with consistency of quality, plus transportation difficulties, have persuaded these visitors, at least temporarily, toward regions with fewer immediate problems.

More recently, the European Bank for Regional Development has invested in the Acorex company. The company hopes to overcome these problems, and has built a state-of-the-art finishing and bottling complex near Chisinau, plus a totally modernized winery in the southwest of the country. However, despite technical input from Italy, plus Australian winemaking expertise, results so far are far from persuasive.

Pucar is in the southeast, midway between Chisinau and Odessa (the Ukrainian capital) and close to the southern border, and is a historic source of reds with aging potential. Old vintages of Negru de Purkar, from cabernet sauvignon and saperavi, Purpuruiu de Purkar, an unusual pinot noir and merlot blend, and Roshu de Purkar, a deep rosé from cabernet sauvignon, merlot and malbec, have all been well received in Britain recently. For whites from old vines, the best area may well be Tarakliya, which borders the Ukrainian coastal strip in the southwest, and produces respectable cabernet sauvignon.

At Cricova, 15 miles (25 km) north of the capital, Moldova's sparkling wine is produced in a bizarre city 260 feet (80 m) underground. The size of 25 villages, it has steel entrance doors large enough to admit articulated lorries and is networked by 40 miles (65 km) of roads and 75 miles (120 km) of galleries to mature the wines—this is virtually the same amount of underground storage as there is in Champagne. There are also luxurious dining and reception facilities, which used to hold quantities of the finest French wines. The theory has been advanced that this is where communism's elite—from Moscow as well as from Moldova—would have fled in the event of nuclear war.

UKRAINE

Brian Jordan

Like most countries around the Black Sea, wine production in this area actually stretches back into pre-history. After early tribes created settlements and developed viticulture, continued warfare and tribal movement conspired against systematic growth, and it was not until modern times that wine and the vine became significant in the agricultural life of the region.

History

When the near-island of Crimea, which has traditionally regarded itself as a separate country, became part of Russia under Catherine the Great at the end of the eighteenth century, wine production was again seriously investigated. Three individuals were responsible for the Ukraine's subsequent wine success. In the 1820s Count Mikhail Woronzov built first a winery and then a palace at Alupka, southwest of Yalta, followed by the now-famous Magaratch wine institute nearby. In the middle of the century, Prince Leo Golitsyn started sparkling wine production at Novy Svet,

with considerable success. Of greater significance was the Tsar's construction of Massandra, just inland from Yalta, at the end of the nineteenth century. Golitsyn was in charge of Massandra, which was not so much a winery as a centralised maturing facility, fed by 25 outlying wineries in the hills of Krymskiye Gory. It was primarily designed to produce sweet and fortified wines, for which this coastal strip is now famed.

By the early part of the twentieth century the Ukraine had 133,000 acres (54,000 ha) planted with vines, but the effects of both the First World War and the subsequent phylloxera scourge reduced this to 32,000 acres (13,000 ha) by 1920. At the start of the Second World War vineyards were up to an all-time high of 255,000 acres (103,000 ha). Again affected by war, though, this dropped to 168,000 acres (68,000 ha) by war's end. By the arrival of independence in 1991, more than 430,000 acres (175,000 ha), or 25 percent of all agricultural land, was under vine. In 1990 the Ukraine was producing 47 million gallons (180 million l), a considerable fall from a decade earlier, when 153 millon gallons (580 million l) was being produced. Unfortunately, this figure has since fallen even further.

Landscape and climate

It is important to differentiate between mainland Ukraine and the Crimea. The mainland has vineyards on the rather flat lands south of the Dnepr basin, and both northwest and southwest of Odessa, devoted to indigenous grapes, and vineyards to the north for bulk production wines. Crimean vineyards, on the other hand, concentrated on the surprisingly mountainous southern coastline of the peninsula, have significantly higher potential—albeit perhaps not frequently realised. Mainland temperatures range from 17°F (–8°C) to 66°F (19°C), and the southern coast of Crimea enjoys a milder 35°F (2°C) to 77°F (25°C).

Vines and wines

The major growing areas of Crimea, Odessa, Kherson, Nikolayev, Transcarpathia, and Zaporozh'ye account for 90 percent of the vineyard area. Around 60 viticultural regions have been specified, each with a selection of approved varieties for table use, distillation and wine production. With over 50 wine varieties approved, the Ukraine is not short of choice. Traditional central European and near-Asian varieties such as rkatsiteli and saperavi, and European varieties such as cabernet

Muscat varieties are grown in much of Eastern Europe—Moldova, the Ukraine and Russia.

Winter harvest awaiting processing.

RUSSIA

Brian Jordan

"Russia" is a surprisingly unspecific name, sometimes being used to refer to the USSR or the Soviet Union, the previous association of communist states, and even now inaccurately applied to its successor, the CIS or Confederation of Independent States (12 states out of the previous 16). All states and regions within the CIS produce wine, and have varying degrees of self-determination, but Moscow's influence can still be quickly felt if political aspirations become too pronounced. Russia includes Belorussia (also called Belarus or White Russia), which is sometimes quoted separately in wine statistics—the OIV, for example, lists Belorussia with 5 million gallons (19 million l) in 1997—but in fact is merely a processor of transported grapes, having no vineyards of its own.

sauvignon, gewürztraminer and aligoté are grown, as well as bastardo and sercial for fortified production, and a raft of indigenous and Magaratch-developed varieties. Products are often varietally named—Cabernet Kolchuginskoie, Aligoté Zolotaia Balka, Rkatsiteli Inkermanskoie, for example. One of the best blends is Alushta, named after a Crimean town. It uses cabernet sauvignon, morrastel and saperavi. Sparkling wine production is still important. The most commonly used varieties are pinot noir, riesling, fetiaska and aligoté, in varying combinations. Around 50 million bottles a year of Soviet sparkling wine (previously known as Champan-skoje or Soviet champagne) are produced, originating from Kiev, Odessa, Kharkov, Sevastopol, Artemovska and Sudak.

As with virtually all the vast Euro-Asian sector of the winemaking world, winemaking operations are generally still quite primitive, but around 60 percent of vineyards in the Ukraine are now mechanized. Because of the dryness of the climate, around 10 percent are irrigated. Ukraine is the most advanced among CIS nations in working toward wine laws, though more pressing commercial constraints are affecting this development.

The Massandra collection

The appearance of the Massandra collection, brought to London by David Molyneux-Berry MW in 1990, was a revelation to all who attended the pre-auction tasting (a few wines appeared later at post-auction functions as well). The collection was created by Golitsyn and dates back to 1880. Names such as "port", "madeira" and "sherry" were certainly pushed to their limits, perhaps beyond, but the wines were generally stunning. Wines such as 60-year old "white port", a 70-year old fortified muscat, and the 1922 and 1937 "madeira" simply redefined generally accepted views on aging, and on the potential of the Ukraine as a winemaking region.

History

In the early seventeenth century the Tsars established vineyards near Astrakhan, on the Volga estuary into the Caspian Sea, and viticulture was encouraged throughout the ancient kingdom. However, not surprisingly, consistently satisfactory results could only be relied on in the southern provinces—Russia has comparatively little land bordering the Black and Caspian Seas, and the remainder, away from the southern fringe and the moderating influences of its large areas of water, is, in general, far too cold. The five significant vineyard areas in Russia (in descending order of importance) are: Dagestan, along the Caspian Sea coast from Derbent to Makhachkala; the Krasnodar region, which embraces the Kuban valley from inland Maykop and Krasnodar itself to Novorossiysk on the Black Sea; Stavropol, an inland area northwest of Pyatigorsk, from the valley of the Kuban to the valley of the Terek; the Don valley, around Rostov to the Ukraine border; and Chechnya-Ingushetia, where there are likely to be few remaining vineyards, due to constant recent warfare. These regions represent 95 percent of Russian production, the balance split between Kabardino-Balkaria and Ossetia, further north.

Before its collapse, the USSR was at one time third largest world wine producer, with volumes even by the late 1980s still averaging around 525 million gallons (2000 million l). Of this, Russia contributed nearly 200 million gallons (750 million l), considerably reduced from

440 million gallons (1700 million l) in the early 1980s, before Gorbachev's anti-alcohol program.

Landscape and climate

The most suitable regions are unquestionably southern Dagestan and Krasnodar, and even here the continental effect produces severe winters, which necessitate soil covering for winter vine protection. Most areas have this constant problem: Rostov regularly reaches −13°F (−25°C), Krasnodar −4°F (−20°C) and even Dagestan regularly goes down to 14°F (−10°C), the temperature regarded as minimum for eiswein (ice wine) production in Germany and Austria (and which is only reached, at least in Germany, about twice a decade). Recent plantings of frost-resistant varieties developed at the All-Russia Potapenko Research Institute now account for 25,000 acres (10,000 ha) of relatively successful production.

Vines and wines

In the Krasnodar region, the Abrau district is known for dry riesling, "cabernet" and Soviet sparkling wine (*champanskoje*). Up the coast at Anapa, riesling is the specialty, while down the coast at Gelendzhik, aligoté features. Inland, the Stavropol region offers both dry riesling and silvaner alongside muscatel sweet wines. The Rostov region also offers sweet wines, the best known being Ruby of the Don, while the Caspian coast around Makhach-kala is almost exclusively sweet wine country, offering all shades of wine—brown and/or fortified, red and white—the best from Derbent, near the Azerbaijan border.

Early in the twentieth century vineyards were planted densely, with up to 4,050 vines per acre (10,000 vines per hectare). Later plantings reduced these figures and favored trellis systems with space for mechanization, not least for winter protection, using mechanized soil covering for the vines.

As with most countries in this region, physical survival has become the daily priority, but even before this, the most basic elements of businesslike wine production were generally missing, a lack of bottles being the most frequent problem. A sporadic supply to the undemanding Russian domestic market can be maintained, but export potential remains negligible.

Sparkling wines

Russia has long had a thirst for sparkling wines—so-called Shampanskoye (Champanskoje), also known as Shampooza, Shapashka, Shipoochka and Shampanoza. The area of greatest production is Moscow (20 million bottles a year), followed by Rostov (16 million), St Petersburg (10 million) and both Tsimlyansk and Nizhniy-Novgorod (9 million each). The USSR-developed continuous method, now also adopted in Germany and in Portugal for their US export Lancers, is used.

This method sees wine, sugar and yeast introduced into the first of five tanks. The increasing CO_2 pressure kills off yeast activity, so more yeast has to be continually added until fermentation is complete, when the wine passes into the second and third tanks. These contain, most popularly, wood shavings—or any material offering a large surface area in relation to volume. A certain amount of autolysis (reaction between the wine and the dead yeast cells) takes place before the liquid is pumped into the fourth and fifth tanks as relatively clear wine. The process takes three to four weeks, an efficiency which parallels continuous stills used for spirits production.

A sizeable Eastern European vineyard with new spring growth.

Southern Europe

Southern Europe

The country that towers head and shoulders above the others in this chapter is Greece. And yet it has only recently begun to show what it can do: for years its long and distinguished winemaking history seemed to be just that: history. But it has grape varieties found nowhere else in the world, and good ones, too: recent developments have shown that as soon as good, modern

BLACK SEA

Körklareli
Edirne
Mahya 3378 ft (1030 m)
Lüleburgaz
Zonguldak
Ereïli
Bla

Epanomi-
Thessalonika
Serrai Drama Xanthi Komotini
Thrace-
Marmara
Istanbul
Kartal Izmit
Düzce
Gourmenissa
Drama Kavala
Kesan Tekirdaü
Gebze Yalova Gölcük
Adapazarõ
Alexandropolis
Thassos
Central
Anatolia
Amyndeo Naoussa
Veria
Thessalonika
Agion Oros
Bandõrma
Bursa
Inegöl
Kozani
Katerini
Thermaïkos
Kolpos
Lemnos
Çanakkale
Ulundaï 8341 ft (2543 m)
Eskisehir
Mt Olympus 9567 ft (2917 m)
Lemnos
GREECE
Krania
Zitsa Ioannina
Larissa
Balökesir
AN
Corfu
Trikala
Karditsa Volos
AEGEAN
SEA
Edremit
Kütahya
Arta
Lesbos
Ayvalök
Po
IONIAN
SEA
Preveza
Sporades
Mítilini
Bergama
Akhisar
Afyon Bolvadin
Skopelos
Skiros
Aegean Coast
Manisa
Usak
Aksehir
Lamia
Mt Parnassos 8058 ft (2457 m)
Agrinio
Attica
Levadia Halkida Euboea
Chios
Chios
Çesme
Izmir
Bayõndõr
Aegean Coast
Beysehir Gölü
Kony
Cephalonia
Pátras
Patras
Aharnes Elefsina
Piraeus ATHENS
Andros
Aydõn
Denizli
Burdur Isparta
Amaliada
Corinth
Nemea
Mantinia
Tinos
Mykonos
Nikaria
Samos
Muüla
Mediterranean
Coast
Zakinthos
Peloponnese
Islands
Kalamata
Cyclades
Naxos
Kalimnos Bodrum
Amorgos
Astipalea
Antalya
Alan
Milos
Rhodes
Cape Matapan
Kithira
Santorini
Santorini
Rhodes
Sea of Crete
Stampalia
Hania Crete
Rethimnon Iraklion
MEDITERRANEAN SEA
Troodos
Idi 8055 ft (2456 m) Crete
Marathasa
Troodos V
MALTA
Dingli 820 ft (250 m) VALLETTA
Malta
Troodos So

winemaking is added to the Greek equation, the wines begin to look very attractive indeed to consumers elsewhere. That might be true of Turkey as well; nobody knows, because only 3 percent of its grape production gets turned into wine, and not very good wine at that. Wine counts for little in this country, and Turks prefer their alcohol in the form of brandy. Cyprus appears to be one big missed opportunity, as far as wine goes. It has a captive tourist market, and tourists would no doubt seek out Cypriot wines on their return home, if they were good enough. But they're not, and they don't. Will Cypriot wines ever change? The omens are not good. And Malta? Wine production here is small scale, but there are signs that more interesting wines are being made.

Sinop

Kastamonu

Bafra

Samsun

BLACK SEA

Merzifon

Fatsa

Ordu

Giresun

Trabzon

Rize

Black Sea Coast

Amasya

Kars

Kızılırmak

Sungurlu

Tokat

Kelkit

Bayburt

Aras

TURKEY

Sivas

Kara Dü. 9938 ft (3030 m)

Askale

Erzurum

kkale

Erzincan

Aürö

Yerköy

Central Anatolia

Körsehir

Kızılırmak

Akbaba Tepe 11,378 ft (3469 m)

Süphan Dü. 13,310 ft (4058 m)

Keban Baraji

Lake Van

Kayseri

Erciyas Dü. 12,844 ft (3916 m)

Elazöü

Bitlis

Aksaray

Malatya

Eastern Anatolia

Ergani

Niüde

Aladaü 12,319 ft (3756 m)

Nurhak Dü. 10,135 ft (3090 m)

Adöyaman

Euphrates

Diyarbakör

Batman

Kurtalan

Herakol Dü. 9308 ft (2838 m)

Baskale

li

Mediterranean Coast

Kahraman Maras

Siverek

Tigris

Hakkârö

Kadirli

Adana

Ceyhan

Gaziantep

Birecik

Sanlö Urfa

Mardin

Tarsus

Mersin

Osmaniye

Nizip

Sürüç

Kilis

Iskenderun

Hatay

Reyhanlö

Samandaüö

NORTH

100 miles (160 kilometers)

a CYPRUS

andaria

GREECE

Nico Manessis

Wine has been an integral part of Greek culture for over 3,000 years, partly because Greece's geographic location has made it a natural crossroads for many different cultures. Throughout the ages, the fortunes of Greek wine have followed the country's tumultuous history, closely mirroring its rises and falls, its successes and failures.

History

The Greeks are a seafaring people, taught by the Phoenicians, whose maritime trading routes and colonies in the Mediterranean area were vital for Greeks selling or bartering goods against their two agrarian surpluses, olive oil and wine. By the third century BC, an early form of appellation was established by the Northern Aegean island of Thassos, as attested to by a tablet outlining appellation rules. Wine was traded in amphorae carrying the seal of origin—Thassos, the name of the authority granting its *cru* status, and the potter's name—on the handle. Such wines would fetch a higher price than the other wines traded.

When Greece became a province of the Roman Empire, it was Greek wine that graced the empire's finest tables—Italian wine was not good enough.

During the Byzantine empire (330–1453 AD), Constantinople became the center of wine trading. The Venetians traded in Greek wine, carrying it to such diverse destinations as the Black Sea, Venice, Genova and England. It was also traded by Greek merchants, as far away as Poland.

During the Ottoman rule (1453–1821), Greek wine, with few exceptions, fell into total oblivion. However, by as early as 1860, three sweet wines had risen to unprecedented heights of success. Samos' Muscat was exported (until 1914) to Sweden, Switzerland and France. Santorini's Vinsanto, traded by the Venetians in the fourteenth century, found a huge market in Tsarist Russia until the Bolshevik revolution in 1917, which led to a decline to the island's wine fortunes. Mavrodaphne, a port-type wine, brought posperity and fame to the town of Pátras.

In the early 1950s, in the wake of two world wars and a brutal civil war, Greece was bankrupt, and suffering massive immigration to Athens, Australia, Germany and the United States. Thousands of acres of quality hillside vineyards were abandoned. The wine industry was ruined, leaving only a handful of large *négociants* (dating back to the mid- and late-1800s) churning out uninspiring branded table wines.

The Greek islands became the tourist destination of the 1960s, and since then, tourism has evolved into the nation's single largest industry. The standard of living has risen, and with it the demand for bottled wine. Exports to Greek expatriate communities commenced during this period as well, and retsina, a pine resin-flavored wine, became synonymous with Greek wine. By the mid-1970s, vintners had started to map out appellations and introduce higher standard labels.

Quality wine production moved into a higher gear again in the early 1980s. Greek enologists with postgraduate degrees from Australia, France and California founded small- and medium-sized wineries producing appellations. Local capital and European Union funding co-financed steady, considered investment in technology and vineyard management. However, this funding came at a great cost, as the EU wine surplus, commonly known as Europe's "wine lake," meant that Greek farmers had to uproot thousands of vineyards. Notwithstanding this, the end of the millennium found Greek wine gaining both commercial status and recognition from demanding export markets.

Landscape and climate

Greece is a mountainous country—most quality vineyards are found between sea level and an altitude of 2,800 feet (850 m). At the same time, there is a tremendous diversity in the types of soil, from sand, loam, clay, and schist (pink and gray-blue), to limestone, granitic and volcanic ashes.

The generally maritime climate undergoes continental influences at higher elevations, but Greece is mostly blessed with a near ideal climate for grape farming, as hail, fog and snow are rare (though rain-induced rot is not unknown).

Annual rainfall varies from region to region: while Crete and Santorini receive a rather paltry 10–14 inches (250–350 mm), the vineyards of Pátras receive 27 inches (680 mm) and those of Náoussa 35 inches (900 mm). On the Chalkidiki peninsula, rainfall is around 18 inches (450 mm).

Vintages do vary, with three weather factors playing a vital part in their shaping: rainfall, its quantity and the summer maximum temperatures.

This fragment of a wine press is from the fourteenth century, during the Ottoman rule.

For example, in 1997, a top vintage, temperatures never exceeded 91°F (33°C), whereas in 1998, a less good vintage, Greece suffered prolonged heat waves, with temperatures up to 100°F (38°C).

Island vineyards benefit from sea breezes and afternoon winds, and altitude and the shape of the mountain passes influence the rhythm of grape farming in those areas. Slow-maturing hillside vineyards, often with northern exposure, foster lower yields, high flavor and natural acidity.

Harvesting starts with white wines on the island vineyards (such as Cephalonia, Crete and Santorini) in mid-August, and moves to the mainland in mid-September. For red wine, and on the cooler plateaux such as Mantinia (with an altitude of 2,100 feet [650m]), harvesting takes place in early October. The age-old custom of sun-drying grapes on terraces for sweet wines is still practiced.

Vines and wines

In 1999, vineyard acreage stood at 173,000 acres (70,000 ha), with annual wine production at close to 10.6 million gallons (400 million l), making Greece the sixth-largest European wine producer and the fourteenth largest in the world. A wide spectrum of wine, encompassing all known classes and styles, is produced: it breaks down to roughly 70 percent white, 5 percent rosé, 3 percent sweet and 22 percent red. Sparkling wines remain the most underdeveloped category.

Phylloxera was first identified in northern Greece, in the mountainous region of Zitsa, in 1970, but thanks to a poor road network, its spreading was slow. Today, most Greek vineyards have been replanted with phylloxera-resistant rootstock, but a few pockets of ungrafted quality vineyards still exist, such as on the volcanic island of Santorini, where the vines' estimated average age is 80 years: the sand and volcanic topsoils are low in organic matter, and inhospitable to this destructive louse. Greek vineyards' other urgent problem is the grapefarmers' average age, which stands at over 60. Only in dynamic appellations or estates can one find young vintners.

Greece's great heritage of native grapes provides the raw material for some fascinating wines. Approximately 200 indigenous *Vitis vinifera* varieties have been identified, but currently only 30 of these are used to a commercial end.

The most important white grapes are assyrtiko, athiri, roditis, savatiano, vilana, robola, debina and muscat. Saved from the brink of extinction are the elegant lagorthi and the semi-aromatic

malagousia, while the blanc de gris moscofilero, with its grapey fruit and natural high acidity, is exclusive to Mantinia, in the middle of the Peloponnese. More recently a small amount of varieties such as chardonnay, sauvignon blanc, viognier and sémillon have been introduced—they are used either as blends or for varietal wines.

The undisputed finest red grapes are aghiorghitiko and xynomavro, which are principally found in the two top red wine appellations, Neméa and Náoussa. Others include kotsifali and mandelaria. The first cabernet sauvignon plantings date from 1963 at Averoff in Métsovo and Domaine Carras in Sithoniá, on the Chalkdiki peninsula. More recently, cabernet franc and merlot were added; the most sighted new plantings now are syrah.

Based on the French appellation model, Greece enacted its own legislation in 1971, and has since harmonized its vineyard and wine production legislation, after joining the European Union (then the EEC) in 1981. Thus there are 28 Appellations of Origin, two Appellations by Tradition and more than 70 *vin de pays*.

Vineyards in the Peloponnese, where almost a third of Greece's wines are produced.

The front doors of a winery in Crete, an island whose wine is improving.

MAINLAND GREECE

Drama

Drama was resurrected as a wine region in the 1980s, largely due to two leading estates: those of Nikos Lazaridis and his brother, Kosta Lazaridis.

Nikos Lazaridis has a post-modernist winery that would not look out of place in Napa: it has a spacious cellar, a large art gallery, plus several tasting rooms and halls for lectures and seminars.

Bakis Tsalkos crafts the finest Trebbiano-sourced wine in Greece. The early wine is tank fermented, and the later is a richer cask-fermented rendition. Magiko Vouno is the standout wine: the white is a low-yield barrique-fermented sauvignon blanc, the red a cabernet sauvignon-based blend.

Ktima Kosta Lazaridis produces wines, with the help of gifted winemaker Vassilis Tsaktsarlis, that are soft, with a fruit-driven style. The hugely successful, fruity Amethystos white is their mainstay. The Amethystos rosé, with its strawberry fruit, is a top cabernet sauvingon rosé, and the juicy Amethystos red combines limnio and cabernet sauvignon. The best red is Cava Amethystos.

Sithoniá is a pioneering estate established in 1965 by the late shipping magnate John Carras. The soil here is a combination of sandy and schist, and grows a mixture of indigenous and foreign grape varieties. It has a dry microclimate, better suited to red wines. The Syrah is a huge, brooding blockbuster oozing with (schistous) *terroir*.

Epanomi-Thessaloniki

Ktima Gerovassiliou has an estate of 75 acres (30 ha), with Bordeaux graduate Evangelos Gerovassiliou producing an impressive range of fruit-driven whites. Ktima Gerovassiliou, a cult status wine, is a blend of steely assyrtiko and the white peach and mint taste of malagousia. There is also a stunning 1997 Viognier—broad-shouldered, and with lively acidity. A red that is an off-beat blend of petite syrah and merlot is improving.

Goumenissa

J. Boutari Wineries S. A. has planted xynomavro and negoska varieties on the slopes of Mount Paikos. They make a crisp, light- to medium-weight red wine. The best vintages here are 1990, 1994 and 1997, the best wine Ktima Filiria.

Aidarinis Winery is a small artisan producer (which has recently moved to a larger winery), and produces Goumenissa Aidarini, and a new merlot/xynomavro blend.

Náoussa

The wines of Náoussa have a long history, having been exported in the nineteenth century to the prosperous Greek merchant classes of Alexandria, Egypt and the Austro-Hungarian empire. This was the first region to be granted an appellation in 1971. The climate has continental influences, but vintages vary enormously in quality: 1983 and 1991 were poor, but 1985, 1990, 1994 and 1997 were good. Vineyards here are home to the finest long-lasting xynomavro wines.

Ktima Kyr-Yanni, at Yannakochori, is the most forward-thinking and finest estate in Náoussa. It is 50 acres (123 ha), and is owned and managed by the charismatic Yannis Boutaris. It produces all-red cask-aged wines under four labels: Ktima Yanna-cochori, a blend of xynomavro and merlot; Ramnista, an all-xynomavro single vineyard wine; a thunderous Syrah; and a rich Merlot. New wines are in the works from even lower-yield old vines.

J. Boutari & Son was founded in 1879. A *négociant* with wineries in Goumenissa, Náoussa, Santorini and Crete, the company offers a full range of numerous appellations and produces pioneered single vineyard wines from Náoussa, Neméa and Crete. The varietal range includes assyrtico, roditis, moscofilero and xynomavro.

Vaeni-Náoussa, in Episkopi, is the appellation's growers' cooperative, and is managed by the dynamic Niki Katarahia. It offers white wines from blanc de noir. The best wine, Damaskinos, is the finest of Náoussa's old-style hard tannins.

Markovitis Bros, in Polla Nera, has been among the first to embrace organic farming. The vineyards have traces of magnesium, which contributes to wines' longevity, and produce Pegasos, a top red displaying cranberry fruit, as well as minute quantities of Riesling and Chardonnay.

Dalamaras is a historic artisan winery. Its top vineyards, which are in Koutiha, are planted with xynomavro which is over 55 years old, and produce wine of the deeply extracted style.

Ktima Karydas is an up and coming but tiny—5 acres (2 ha)—vineyard in Gastra which produces a deeply colored wine with lots of berry spicy fruit. This wine is improving with each vintage.

Foundis is a small-scale winery, with vineyards in Ramnista and Stranzta producing earthy and spicy wines that are suitable for short-term aging.

Melitzanis is another single vineyard in Gastra, with southern exposure and a unique *terroir*. It produces fruity wines with tomato vine and black olive flavors, characterized by "sweetness."

Amyndeo

This is a very cool region, and it produces wine high in malic acid. Aromatic whites are made from roditis, chardonnay, sauvignon blanc, gewürztraminer and blanc de noir; excellent rosé and red are produced from xynomavro. White wines are more consistent; rosé and red are good only in the top vintages: 1990, 1994 and 1997. Sparkling wines, both *cuve close* and *méthode classique*, are improving. onsulting winemaker Angelos Iatrides and partners have a new venture going here.

Amyndeo Co-Op now has the latest technology, and a new team of winemakers—a very good red was produced in 1999. A pot still is used to hand-craft tsipouro (a grappa-like, clear distillate).

Grippa Wines is a recent venture by Yannis Boutaris, and makes fine aromatic whites, good rosés and (vintage permitting) silky smooth reds. The Reserve (1997) is the best wine produced here.

Velvendos

This is bit of a no man's land, cultivated according to Macedonian grape-growing tradition. It is xynomavro country for reds and rosés. Obscure local red varieties, such as moscomavro, are also grown.

Ktima Voyatzis is home to local Yannis Voyatzis. He made a stunning red in 1997; the whites, including a blend of steely roditis, chardonnay and the perfumed malvasia aromatica, are improving.

Krania

Ktima Katsaros is home to Stella Katsaros, a child psychiatrist, cook and food author, and her husband Dimitri, a Larissa-based doctor. This couple have practiced organic farming for years in their vineyards, at 2,130 feet (650 m) on the foothills of Mount Olympus. A blend of cabernet sauvignon and merlot, a velvety smooth cask-aged smokey red, has been the only Ktima Katsaros wine, but 1999 was the maiden vintage of a barrique Chardonnay.

Zitsa

This cool plateau (1,640 feet [500 m]) is almost all given over to debina, producing still and fizzy light-bodied crisp wines, full of white pepper on the nose and green apple freshness on the palate.

Zitsa Co-Op was founded in 1972. Epirus was hard hit by the 1950s and 1960s rural exodus, but enologist-manager Vassilis Vaimakis has helped steer the region toward prosperity. Orion, sourced only from older vines, is the best product.

Métsovo is a picturesque mountainous pass, where empty terraces stand abandoned after vineyards were wiped out by phylloxera.

Katogi Averoff is where the late Evangelos Averoff, former defense minister and national benefactor, introduced cabernet sauvignon in 1963. Katogi Averoff was the first wine made here, and quality was patchy early on. The wine was later blended with Neméa-sourced aghiorghitiko. The estate has moved into higher gear under the founder's son-in-law, Sotiris Ioannou. French oak has been introduced, and a traminer planted at 2,790 feet (850 m) altitude is ripe and vibrant. Ktima Averoff is a new Cabernet Sauvignon, and other new wines are also being planned.

Attica

Attica is home to large *négociants* and a few quality estates, and was, until the 1950s, the nation's single largest vineyard, planted solely with savatiano. Following the growth of Athens, vine-planted land has shrunk to half its original 30,000 acres (12,000 ha).

Chateau Matsa, in Kantza, is one of the top estates. Owner and viticulturist Roxane Matsa is one of the few women in Greek wine—she is an

The private cellar storing the estate owners' selection.

Traditional skills and tools are still the best for tasks such as repairing oak barrels.

accomplished vineyardist, and now also a winemaker. Three white wines are produced: Chateau Matsa Vieilles Vignes, from savatiano; Laoutari, a vibrant assyrtiko, roditis and savatiano blend; and the fragrant and rare peachy Malagousia. A new red wine is also being produced.

Ktima G. Kokotos, is in Stamata, high above the bustle of Athens at 1,475 feet (450 m). Here civil engineer George Kokotos laid out a model vineyard and winery, which now produces a wide range of wines from brought-in grapes and estate cabernet sauvignon. The 1997 Chateau Semeli is the best wine to date, but for best value, try the Semeli red, a cask-aged neméa, aghiorghitiko and cabernet sauvignon blend.

D. Kourtakis is a large merchant offering honest, value for money wines. Third-generation enologist Vassilis Kourtakis produces a popular and consistent Apelia. The upmarket Kouros white is a Patrás-sourced roditis, and the red Kouros is a cask-aged vintage neméa. This winemaker also produces good retsina and is a major exporter.

THE PELOPONNESE

This region produces almost 29 percent of Greek wine, and is home to three quality appellations: Neméa, Pátras, and Mantinia.

Neméa

Neméa, with 5,200 acres (2,100 ha) under vine, is the region of the largest quality red wine appellation. It is planted exclusively with the richly colored smooth tannin aghiorghitiko. Neméa has a varied terrain, with two distinct vineyards: Neméa valley floor and high Neméa. A separate appellation is the next step, as is a long overdue *cru* system for high Neméa.

Gaia Wines, in Koutsi, is a promising new venture, and has a state-of-the-art winery. Partners are agronomist Leon Karatsalos and Bordeaux II graduate Yannis Paraskevopoulos, and they have set high standards. The affable Notios range is their mainstay. The red is a fruity, light aghiorghitiko. Gaia Wines has some of the lowest yields in quality Greek winemaking, with 2.86 tons per acre (7.14 t per ha) for the maiden 1997 vintage and 2.17 tons per acre (5.43 t per ha) for the 1998 (bottled, unfiltered). Gaia Estate is a dark, very fine wine, full of black cherries and smokey, cask-derived aromas, and has aging potential of perhaps 7–10 years. The going-places partners have also been brave enough to give a facelift to that much-maligned Greek specialty, retsina.

Their hand-crafted Ritinitis Nobilis is perhaps the most refined of its kind.

Papaioannou is home to veteran grape grower Thanassis and son George—these are perhaps the hardest working vineyardists in Greece. The best wine produced by these self-taught winemakers is the Palea Klimata (old vines), and they are also now producing a generously wooded Pinot Noir, plus a reliable white Roditis.

Octana, in the cool valley of Asprokambos (at 2,130 feet [650 m] altitude), is a new joint venture for Antonopoulos, Averoff and Strofilia. Only the southern-facing slopes fully mature, and then not for every vintage. Fruitiness and acidity come in abundance. This area is a great source of some serious, mouth-watering rosés.

Pátras

This major port connects Greece with Italy, and is home to light, crisp, dry wines and to Mavrodaphne dessert wines.

Antonopoulos, in Vassilikos, is a quality producer, managed by wine merchant Yannis Halikias. Winemakers Tassos Drossiadis and Mihalis Probonas are making a great range of delicate whites, including Mantinia and the refined Adoli Ghis, a high-quality cask-fermented chardonnay. The best red wine is Cabernet-Nea Dris (new oak), made from both estate-grown and brought-in grapes. Achaia vineyards, at 2,790 feet (850 m) altitude, have been planted with lagorthi.

Oenoforos is the territory of Angelos Rouvalis, blessed with intellect and modesty, and often referred to as "the silent force." His Asprolithi label is the undisputed leader in high Roditis—delicate, fresh, full of pear drops and minerality on the finish, it sets the standard. There is also a new and promising Cabernet Sauvignon. This producer's wines are full of *terroir*. Riesling and syrah have been planted in the north-facing cool-climate terraces overlooking the Corinthian gulf.

Ktima Mercouri, at Korakohori Helias, a 15-minute drive from ancient Olympia, is perhaps the prettiest estate in Greece. Here refosco and mavrodaphne are blended. There is an adequate Foloe Roditis, and a new wine, from mourvèdre and the rare avgoustiatis grape, is being prepared.

Mantinia

This 2,130 feet (650 m) plateau in the centre of the Peloponnese is home to the grapey blanc de gris variety moscofilero, whose aroma has the spice of a light gewürztraminer and a (dry) muscat.

Natural acidity is high. De-acidifying is necessary in poor vintages such as 1995 and 1996. The rose petal muscat aroma is more apparent in ripe vintages. This area is a very fashionable appellation.

Tselepos Vineyards & Winery is a fine estate, producing a more concentrated Mantinia than any other on the market, with a fruit-derived "smokeyness" on the nose. A fleshy and sappy wooded Chardonnay, a fresh-tasting Cabernet Sauvignon/Merlot blend, a playful Gewürztraminer and an improving *méthode classique* sparkler named Villa Amalia are also produced.

THE AEGEAN ISLANDS

Limnos

Limnos is a volcanic island producing sweet, sun-dried and fortified Muscat of Alexandria wines. It features two growers: the Co-Op, which specializes in the sweeter versions, and Honas-Kyathos, near Kaminia, which concentrates on bone-dry wines. **Samos** is home to the finest Muscat from the muscat blanc, a petit grain. The fortified Grand Cru label and the Vin Doux wines are exported in bulk to France. Top label Nectar, made with sun-dried grapes, is not fortified, and has peachy muscat flavors, followed by a very long finish.

Santorini

Santorini is a freakish volcanic island, has top quality vineyards planted with assyrtiko, the finest Greek white grape. There are two appellations here: the dry Santorini and the luscious, sweet, cask-aged Vinsanto. **Gaia Wines'** Santorini winery is located in a magnificent stone building, a former tomato paste canning factory, and produces the trendsetting, bone-dry Thalassitis. **Sigalas** is the newly constructed winery, in Kampos, near Oia, of mathematics teacher Paris Sigalas. His cask-fermented Vareli Oia is one the finest wooded Greek white wines. He is also producing very good Mezzo, a less sweet wine than Vinsanto.

Crete

There is a new momentum in this wine-producing island these days. **Ktima Lyrarakis**, inland from Heraklio at Alagni, focuses on near-extinct white varieties such as daphni and plyto, and produces the wonderful Syrah-Kotsifali. **Creta Olympias** produces quality Vilana-sourced dry whites. At Ziros, in Sitia, organic producer **Ekonomou** makes perhaps the finest Vilana in Crete, plus the quirky, pale-colored Liatiko "red."

Some winemaking in today's Greece looks much as it would have a hundred years ago.

THE IONIAN SEA ISLANDS

Cephalonia

Cephalonia is a verdant island whose best vineyards are to be found on limestone soils. Ungrafted high robola, with its trademark lemon and flint *terroir*, is unique in the Greek vineyard. **Gentilini**, in Minies, is a pioneer boutique winery. Vineyards and winemaking duties are overseen by Gabrielle Beamish, from Britain, who is producing a fruity and delicate Gentilini Classico and a new Syrah. **Metaxa**, in Mavrata, is another forward-thinking producer, and offers the rare white Zakynthino. The best wine here is Robola, with a modernist peachy aroma and a flinty aftertaste.

MALTA

Catherine Fallis MS

This trio of tiny islands—62 miles (100 km) south of Sicily and 180 miles (290 km) north of Tripoli, in Libya—was host to one of the oldest civilizations in the Mediterranean, dating back to around 5,000 BC. Great Phoenician temples (which predate the pyramids) and historic palazzos, plus sunbathing, scuba diving, sailing, yachting and golf, have attracted winter-weary travelers for decades. And with abundant local produce, as well as the bountiful delicacies of the sea, the occasional garlic-fried rabbit, and inexpensive local wine and beer, tourists and locals alike are well provided for.

Local consumption of wine, until recently, has allowed very little product into the export market. This may have been just as well, as most of the wine was nothing extraordinary. Today, though, a host of small families, plus outside investors such as Antinori, are producing some world-class, high-quality, individual, unique wines.

The Maltese islands consist of Malta, the largest island, at 150 square miles (390 sq km), plus the much smaller islands of Gozo and Comino. The total population is approximately 350,000. The airport and the capital, Valleta, are on Malta, as is the medieval town and former capital, Mdina, which used to be known as the "Silent City." Small fishing villages dot the coastline. The official languages are Maltese, a dialect of North Arabic with elements of Italian, and English. Most residents are also fluent in Italian.

Landscape and climate

The climate is temperate, with warm, dry summers averaging 90°F (32°C) and mild winters averaging 57°F (14°C). The average rainfall is

23 inches (580 mm); 90 percent of this falls in winter. Malta has 300 days of sunshine per year, with an average of 6.5 hours/day in winter and 10.1 hours/day in summer, making for a shorter than average growing season. Approximately 3,000 acres (1,220 ha) are under vine, planted on low hills and slopes. Harvest begins in August and is usually completed in September.

Vines and wines

Locally grown white table grapes ghirghentina and gennarua and red gellewza were in the past blended with grapes imported from Italy, with no indication of this on the label. Local authorities are cracking down on this, and there is an increased focus on new plantings of chardonnay, cabernet sauvignon, pinot bianco, trebbiano, and syrah.

Table grapes grown on bush vines without irrigation are slowly being replaced with *vitis vinifera* varieties, and the local agricultural board is experimenting with and promising to support the installation of irrigation systems. Winemaking practices are also improving, as French and Italian wine producers—including, most recently, the Antinori family, backers of the Meridiana wine estate in the ancient capital of Mdina—arrive, bringing knowledge and expertise with them.

Local consumption, once the only market, is continuing to grow, reflecting the healthy growth of tourism. Improved quality controls in the vineyards and the wineries and an expanded product range, geared to an international market have paid off: domestic beverage exports, including wine, were up to more than Lm (lira) 1 million (US$ 2.6 million) in 1997, and local winemakers are beginning to gain recognition on the international wine scene. Importers are visiting the islands more than ever before, and Malta's wines are beginning to appear in some mainstream markets.

For the local market, among the best-known wines are Emmanuel Delicata's Paradise Bay Red Wine and Gellewza Frizzante, clearly aimed at thirsty tourists. Delicata and Marsovin (whose Cheval Franc attracts attention at least for its play on Cheval Blanc of St-Émilion) together control about 90 percent of the local wine market.

Meridiana, an enterprise created by visionary Maltese wine expert Mark Miceli-Farrugia, is producing international-style wines, including barrel-fermented chardonnays, cabernet sauvignons and merlots. Successful smaller producers include Dacoutros Group, Farmers Wine Co-Op, Hal-Caprat, Master Wine, and Three Barrels.

White grape varieties are popular in southwestern Europe.

TURKEY

Brian Jordan

If Noah did indeed plant a vineyard on the slopes of Mount Ararat, then Turkey could reasonably claim to be the cradle of viticulture. Certainly, clear evidence of the domestic consumption of wine as early as 4,000 BC exists in the form of Hittite art. The advent of Moslem rule in the eleventh century slowed wine production, naturally, and the industry developed little until 1925, when, as part of his national modernization program, Kemal Ataturk constructed the first new winery in Turkey for 700 years.

Today, Turkey has the fifth-largest area of vines in the world, but its predominantly Moslem lifestyle dictates that most of these grapes—approximately 97 percent —are used for nonalcoholic products such as table grapes, currants and sultanas, grape juices and grape concentrates. Of the 3 percent fermented into wine, at least a quarter is distilled into local brandy or the aniseed-flavored spirit raki. White wines consumed domestically tend to be heavily oxidized and over-aged, while reds are relatively alcoholic and oversulfured. Export-quality wines are produced only fitfully, and find most favor in Turkish restaurants overseas. They are seldom more widely available, except in Germany, where there is a large Turkish expatriate population.

Appellations and producers

Turkey's seven official wine districts are Thrace-Marmara, the Aegean Coast, the Mediterranean Coast, the Black Sea Coast, Ankara, Central Anatolia and Eastern Anatolia. Thrace-Marmara, which borders Greece and Bulgaria, produces 40 percent of Turkey's wines. It has a typically Mediterranean climate, but unusually, and some may say unsuitably, it focuses on clairette, sémillon, riesling, gamay and pinot noir. The searingly hot Aegean Coast yields European varieties such as sémillon, grenache and carignan; given the chance, it would be suitable for naturally sweet dessert wines such as those found on the nearby Greek island of Samos. On the Mediterranean Coast, where the main industry is tourism, winemaking is less significant. However, both the Black Sea Coast and the Ankara region have considerable potential for wine growing. Vineyards in Central Anatolia are located at up to 4,000 feet (1,250 m), and suffer temperature extremes of −13°F (−25°C) in

winter and more than 100°F (40°C) in summer. Eastern Anatolia, bordering Georgia and Armenia, yields a lowly 374 gallons per acre (3500 l per ha).

The nationalized wine industry is administered by Tekel. Private producers are few, the best known and most reputable being Kavaklidere, Doluca, and Diren in Anatolia. Charmingly named hosbag (Thrace gamay) and buzbag (local varieties from Eastern Anatolia) are valued domestically, but the most consistent wines are those produced by Doluca. A quality wine scheme has been introduced with more than half an eye on association with the EU, but it seems to be limited to state-owned products. Production methods are relatively primitive, and stainless steel equipment and refrigeration are still something of a novelty, even in areas of high fall temperatures.

Several parts of Turkey show strong potential for quality wine production. However, continuing religious restrictions and political volatility mean that the country is unlikely to attract the kind of investment it requires to fully realize this promise.

These vines are in Marmara, where two-fifths of Turkey's wine is produced.

CYPRUS

Brian Jordan

Cypriot winemakers have produced few outstanding wines, despite the fact that they have been making wine for around 4,000 years. The earliest archeological evidence of viticulture here dates to the second millennium BC and includes decorations on pottery and wall hangings, as well as references in texts. By the time the Greeks occupied Cyprus around 300 BC, interisland trade was common, with wine being transported in amphorae. The Romans used amphorae and wooden barrels and animal skins. References to wine became increasingly prominent in Roman artworks; mosaics on Cyprus show trade, everyday wine consumption and festivals in which wine played a role.

Trade continued to thrive under Byzantine, Frankish and then Venetian rule. But t he Turks' 300-year domination of the island, which began in 1571, did little for the wine industry, with heavy taxation and religious restrictions compounding the effects of a series of vine blights. When the British took control in 1878, the situation began to improve. The phylloxera that devastated European vineyards in the late nineteenth and early twentieth centuries bypassed Cyprus, leading to an explosive expansion of the industry. However, by the interwar years, as Europe was resuming full-scale production, Cypriot winemaking had entered a decline that continues to this day.

In the postwar years, production has focused on grape concentrate and so-called "sherry." The

These young vines in Cyprus are staked, and will soon be wired as well.

former was produced primarily for the United Kingdom, where it was used to make "sherries" and "medicinal" wines; Sanatogen was the most widely known of these. Following the decline of this trade over the past 20 years, Cypriot producers discovered a new market for concentrates and cheap bulk wines in pre-Gorbachev Russia, but demand dwindled during the country's neoprohibition period, which began in 1986. New opportunities later emerged in Europe for "aromatic wines" such as premixed gluhwein and sangria, but Cyprus has recently lost much of this market, mainly to Spain. The industry now faces a bleak future.

Vines and wines

The principal winegrowing areas lie on the southeastern plain and the lower slopes of the Troodos Mountains, up to 4,265 feet (1,300 m) or, exceptionally, 5,250 feet (1,600 m) at Madhari. Table grapes cover a total of 5,000 acres (2,000 ha); wine grapes occupy approximately ten times that area. The irrigated plains are capable of awe-inspiring tonnages. These are normally sold as table grapes, though they have been used for concentrates and sherries. There is potential for quality wine production at higher altitudes. Generally, rainfall is low and confined to winter months, with an average of 19.5 inches (500 mm) a year at low altitudes and 35 inches (900 mm) on upper slopes. Irrigation is officially banned, largely as a result of overproduction problems.

Nearly three-quarters of Cypriot vineyards contain mavro (the Greek word for "black"), a less than impressive grape variety. Despite its name, it lacks color, which leads to the technique of bleeding off up to 40 percent of the juice to improve the juice-to-pulp ratio. Carefully grown at altitude, and with the crop restricted to 1.5 tons per acre (3.75 t per ha), it can develop a vegetal cherry character. High yields, often surpassing 10 tons per acre (25 t per ha), can easily be achieved, but there is a significant loss of flavor.

White xinisteri is the next most widely planted variety. Undistinguished and sensitive to overripeness, early picking and antioxidation procedures can give a lightly fragrant, rustic-flavored wine. Palomino and the ancient malvasia are frequently used to improve xinisteri's performance.

In 1958, the Department of Agriculture transported a batch of experimental varieties to its Model Winery for trials, which were supplemented in 1964 by microclimate examinations. By 1990, some limited stocks of these grapes, including carignan and grenache, were released. Unfortunately, 30-year gestation periods can hardly be considered competitive in the international market.

Appellations and producers

Six viticultural regions have been created: Pitsilia (the highest), with its subregion, Madhari; Troodos North; Marathasa; Commandaria; Troodos South, with its subregions, Afames and Laona; and Troodos West, with its subregions, Ambelitis, Vounitis Panayias and Laona Kathhikas. Production methods are generally primitive, resembling those of pre-1990 Eastern Europe. Transportation methods in particular leave a lot to be desired.

Virtually all the island's produce is vinified by KEO, ETKO, SODAP or LOEL—all cooperatives or quasi-cooperatives. With 4,500 growers as shareholders and a staff of over 600, KEO is the largest industrial employer on the island. ETKO is the island's oldest winemaker, producing around 33,000 tons (30,000 t) of grape per harvest. SODAP serves 10,000 grower families; similarly sized LOEL has an intake of around 35,000 tons (31,500 t). There are also a few boutique-style wineries. KEO has now shifted its focus toward trellised international varieties.

Island treasure

Commandaria, one of the world's oldest sundried or raisined wines, is a Cypriot specialty. The Greek poet Hesiod (around 800 BC) recommended this procedure for drying the grapes: "Show them to the sun ten days and nights, then cover them over for five, and on the sixth day draw off into vessels the gifts of joyful Dionysus."

The word Commandaria derives from the Castle of Kolossi, built as the Grande Commanderie, or headquarters, of the Knights of St John of Jerusalem in the twelfth century. The lands surrounding the castle were the primary source of Nama, which gradually became known as Vin de la Commanderie, or Commandaria. In the following centuries, many travelers visiting Cyprus referred to this wine. In 1804, the British Consul recor-ded annual production of the equivalent of 475,500 gallons (1.8 million l). But output dwindled, and today, despite legislation defining the permitted growing area and production method, the quality of Commandaria has also declined.

Yields are set at a maximum of 182 gallons per acre (1,700 l per ha) with a minimum of 28 ounces per gallon (212 g per l) sugar for the white variety, xinisteri, and 34 ounces per gallon (258 g per l) for black mavro, which must rise to 52–60 ounces per gallon (390–450 g per l) after at least a week's exposure to the sun. Fermentation must occur in the production area; it usually takes two to three months. After that, the wine must be examined and analyzed by the Ministry of Agriculture. It is then transported to cellars, where it may be fortified to a maximum of 20 percent alcohol.

By law, Commandaria must spend a minimum of two years in wood; in practice it may undergo a three-tier solera aging procedure. Before bottling, it is again examined and approved, whereupon it will be sold in wine shops for perhaps $US4.00; hardly the price of a quality product! Sadly,

Bush vineyards on the white soils of Cyprus.

today's Commandaria tarnishes its remarkable heritage, as a taste of one of the few surviving bottles of 100-year-old wine would show.

Trade restrictions

Cypriot agricultural authorities retain a legislative stranglehold on wine production, partly through vine importation controls. Because the island has never suffered from phylloxera, they argue, local plants must be protected. Severe quarantine restrictions have been placed on imported vines. This approach may no longer work, though: the northern third of Cyprus, under Turkish control since 1974, has vineyards but no importation controls. The losses to Cyprus's competitive potential by making vines unobtainable is more significant than any supposed benefits in phylloxera prevention.

It is unlikely that the government can continue to support the winemakers as it has. If the industry is to retain any international commercial potential it needs complete reorganization—there seems little willingness, at a political level, to do this.

Africa

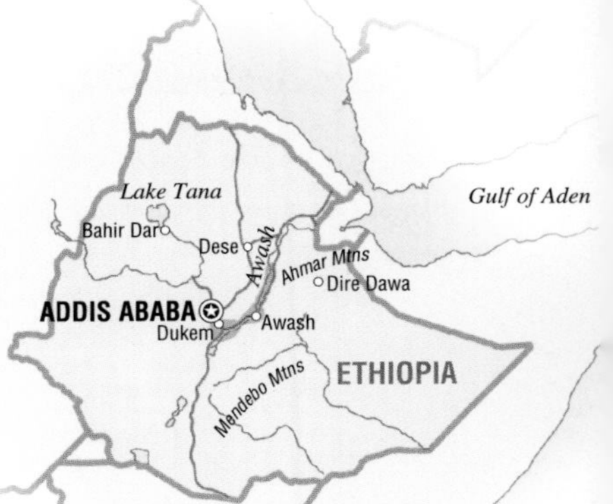

Zerhoun
Tangier
Rharb
Chellah **RABAT**
Casablanca
Safi
Zenata
Essaouira
Agadir
Marrakesh
Meknès
Beni Sadden
Beni M'Tir
Guerrouane
Saiss
Angad
Oujda
Berkane
Zaccar
Alger
Mostagenem
Oran
Medea
Mascara
Oran
Aïn-Bessem-
Bouria
Ghardaïa
ALGIERS
Annaba
Constantine
Bizerte-Mateur-
Tebourba
TUNIS
Kelibia-Cape Bon
Grombalia
Sousse
Thibar
Sfax
Gulf of Gabès
Rass Ajdir
El Goléa

Mediterranean Sea

MOROCCO
Atlas Mountains
ALGERIA
TUNISIA
Hoggar Mtns
Tamanrasset

Abu
Hummus
Alexandria
Port Said
CAIRO
Suez
El Minya
Nile
Asyût
Sohâg
EGYPT
Lake
Nasser
Aswân
Red Sea

NORTH

300 miles
(480 kilometers)

Lake Tana
Bahir Dar
Dese
Awash
Ahmar Mtns
Dire Dawa
ADDIS ABABA
Dukem
Awash
Mendebo Mtns
ETHIOPIA
Gulf of Aden

Having spent the twentieth century until the post-war years as part of the French Empire, the Maghreb countries, Al-Maghrebia (Morocco), Al-Jazairiya (Algeria) and Attunisia (Tunisia), have a similar background. They have all been exploited to produce huge quantities of wine for "cutting"—shipping in bulk for blending with some of the weaker French wines. Although the general impression of the landscape of "Arab" countries is of sand dunes with a nomadic population using camels for transportation and goats for food, there is a comparatively narrow strip of land along the Mediterranean and Atlantic coast north of the Atlas mountains that is very different. The vine-growing areas of the Maghreb countries are all contained within this frequently lush band. Egypt's wine production has been creeping up for the past 40 years or so and in Ethiopia, where the history of viticulture dates from the early Middle Ages, commercial production is also increasing. In Zimbabwe grape-growing was not undertaken commercially until about 1960.

Lake
Kariba
HARARE
Odzi
Mutare
ZIMBABWE
Gweru
Bulawayo
Esigodoni
Shashe

Guardian of the entrance to the tomb of Moulay I Smail, eighteenth century Sultan of Morocco.

MOROCCO

Brian Jordan

Morocco achieved independence from France in 1956. The Moroccan government nationalized the wine industry in 1973, then set about acquiring all the vineyards. By establishing price controls for grapes it gained total control by 1984. Twelve French-style appellations were introduced (Appellation d'Origine Garantie) which have been recognized by the European Union. The appellations are, from east to west, Angad, Berkane, Beni Sadden, Saiss, Zerhoun, Beni M'Tir, Guerrouane, Rharb, Zemmour, Zaer, Chellah and Zenata. However, vines continue down the often windswept Atlantic coast all the way to Essaouira.

Production in Morocco peaked at 80 million gallons (300 million l) from 136,000 acres (55,000 ha), but this had fallen to 10 million gallons (37.5 million l) from just 32,000 acres (13,000 ha) by 1997. The remainder had been converted to table-grape production or were too old or diseased. The state monopoly still exists but is now responsible for only 85 percent of output. Most of the balance comes from the relatively forward-thinking Les Celliers de Mèknes, producing AOGs Guerrouane and Beni M'Tir. As in Tunisia, the tourist explosion is providing an ever-increasing sales outlet. This means greater exposure of European palates to Moroccan wines, which, provided sources of foreign investment can be found, can point the way to realizing Morocco's acknowledged potential.

One bizarre product that enjoyed a brief notoriety in Europe during the 1980s and 1990s was a fully Kosher wine called Rabbi Jacob, marketed by *négociants* Sincomar and carrying a portrait of the Rabbi on the label. The wine was palatable, but buyers were probably attracted by the unlikely combination of a Kosher wine from a Moslem country. Another unusual wine is Gris de Boulaouane, produced from the only plantings of criolla (paìs in Chile, mission in California) east of the Atlantic. Although interesting, it is hardly exciting, except perhaps in the academic sense.

ALGERIA

Brian Jordan

At its height, Algerian wine production was 550 million gallons (2,000 million l) from almost 1 million acres (400,000 ha), equivalent to the USA's wine output today, and making the country the sixth-largest world producer at that time. And all this in a sparsely populated country with an annual consumption of less than a bottle per head. Wines were being made for export in bulk to France to "improve" France's otherwise anemic low-quality red wines. Together with neighboring Tunisia and Morocco, these Mahgreb countries were responsible for two-thirds of the world's international wine trade in the 1950s. However, demand for this torrent of wine—equivalent to 40.8 million bottles or almost a bottle per head for every French citizen at that time—dried up when, after a protracted and bloody campaign, Algeria gained independence in 1962. Moreover, most of the naturally francophile vineyard owners fled with the one million inhabitants who migrated across the Mediterranean. Numerous descendants of these "pieds noirs" are still found producing grapes in Corsica and across the sweep of lands bordering the Golfe du Lion.

Algeria is currently 35th in world wine production, hovering at around 13 million gallons (50 million l), a sixth of previous levels. The country's wine producers are torn between intermittent government desire to attract hard currency by fostering an active wine export market and the fluctuating pressures of extreme Moslem religious fundamentalism. Although wine exports are still the country's fifth-greatest export earner, an estimated 50 percent of the huge area of vineyards has now been converted to table grape production as aging vines become due for replacement.

Two Algerian *départements* have officially demarcated wine districts. From west to east these

Carignan vines at Morocco's Domaine de Sahari.

are Oran (which includes Coteaux de Tlemcen, Monts du Tessalah, Oued-Imbert, Coteaux de Mascara, Mostaganem-Kenenda and Mostaganem) and Alger (containing Haut-Dahra, Coteaux du Zaccar, Médéa and Aïn-Bessem-Bouïra). Much of this growing area has a climate similar to southern Italy or the Peloponnese, with annual rainfall averaging about 19 inches (500 mm), and growing conditions naturally tending to favor red wines.

The most recent spurt of export enthusiasm saw an association between the Office National de Commercialization des Produits Viti-Vinicoles (ONCV) and a British-based consultancy that created the Atlas Mountain Wine Company. Initial impressions were positive, vineyards full of mature carignan, cinsault and grenache in near-perfect disease-free growing conditions, plus an apparent government-backed interest in planting other internationally attractive vines. However, reality has shown that dire production facilities coupled with wavering government support in the face of continued religious pressures makes the wine potential of other underdeveloped countries more attractive.

TUNISIA

Brian Jordan

Because of a shortage of suitable areas, Tunisia has the lowest apparent potential for production of

modern wines of the three northern African countries. Yet its more benign political atmosphere and westernized approach to life and commerce makes it currently the most attractive for European importers. Tunisia's wine history dates from Punic times to the power of Carthage on the north coast, but production was forbidden throughout 1,000 years of Moslem rule until French colonization in 1881. By the time of national independence in 1955 the foundations were in place for a thriving wine industry. Despite being considerably smaller than either Algeria or Morocco, Tunisia's production rivaled theirs. However, work was still needed to repair the ravages of phylloxera, which struck in 1936 and continued to affect vineyards until the 1950s, and to meet the increasing demands for bulk wine from their sole export market, France. At the time, two appellations existed—Vin Supérieur de Tunisie and Appellation Controlée Vin Muscat de Tunisie for their liqueur muscats.

Loss of the French supply contract after independence produced extreme difficulties—production was 47 million gallons (180 million l) and the volume of wine became impossible to finance or to store, so vineyards were abandoned. In 1957 the government effectively nationalized the whole industry by helping cooperatives form larger associations and introducing a four-tier classification system: Vins de Consommation Courante, Vins Superieurs, Vins de Qualité Supérieure and Vins de Qualité Appellation d'Origine Controlée. Vineyards

Muscat vines at the Muscat de Kélibia Co-op, Tunisia.

Woman collecting prunings in the Khanguet region, Tunisia.

currently total 61,000 acres (25,000 ha) of which 37,000 acres (15,000 ha) grow wine grapes. Wine production is 9.8 million gallons (37.2 million l) according to the Office Internationale du Vin (OIV) and 12.6 million gallons (48 million l) according to the Tunisian Office National de la Vigne. These are generally rustic wines mainly consumed by undemanding tourists. Clean white wines and simple well-fruited reds are the best the country aspires to.

The four major growing regions are Grombalia (south of Tunis), Thibar (west of Tunis in semi-mountainous country close to the Algerian border), Bizerte-Mateur-Tébourba (on the north coast, encompassing the old vineyards of Carthage), and Kélibia-Cape Bon (on the headland east of Tunis). The association of cooperatives, Union Centrale des Coopératives Viticoles (UCCV), controls the entire industry, except for a few private companies, the four most important of which are Lavau, Tardi, Lamblot and Château Feriani all in Tébourba and the hills north of Tunis. In world terms, sweet muscats still command respect and dry versions are as good as anyones. Meaty red brands of acceptable quality (made mainly from carignan, grenache and cinsault) include Royal Tardi, Domaine Karim and Château Feriani.

Since 1966, German Blue Nun producers, W. Langguth Erben, have invested in Tunisia, importing Sidi Saad VdQAOC "Grand Cru Mornag" from alicante bouschet, grenache, carignan, mourvèdre and merlot in quantities of up to 1.25 million cases a year. Even more important, they are continuing their support with a 34 percent investment in a new 657-acre (266-ha) vineyard complex at Iktissad Estate. In addition, the Italian Calatrasi company, who use Australian and European winemakers throughout their operations, have also invested in Tunisian wine, with 500 acres (200 ha) up to 800 feet (250 m) above sea level in Grombalia, 40 miles (25 km) southeast of Tunis. Their new range is being launched at VinItaly 2000.

EGYPT

Brian Jordan

Although a tiny wine-producer, Egypt has an entry in the Office Internationale du Vin (OIV) figures, and is creeping up from an average of 530,000 gallons (2 million l) from 1986 to 1990, to 690,000 gallons (2.6 million l) in 1997. This comes from about 123,500 acres (50,000 ha) of vines mainly used for the production of table grapes. The wine produced is largely from the Gianaclis vineyards at Abu Hummus, about 50 miles (75 km) east of Alexandria in the Nile delta. Among local varieties, such as ezazi, kleopatra and taloni whites and rumi red, are plantings of chasselas, cabernet sauvignon and carignan. Three-quarters of the white wines are distilled and most reference books pour scorn on them. However, when the alternatives are vastly over-taxed imports, these wines are perfectly serviceable, especially the innocuous-sounding, non-specific but inoffensive blanc de blancs.

ETHIOPIA

Jeffrey Benson

Vines were grown and wines made here for use in the Holy Communion service of the Ethiopian Orthodox Church since the Middle Ages. Wine-making developed further with the arrival of Portuguese Catholic missionaries, who introduced grape varieties that were being cultivated in the Mediterranean regions of southern France at that time. As a result, grape wine came to replace the traditional wine made from honey as a common beverage. Extensive commercial wine production, however, did not get underway until about 1900 when Italian and Greek industrialists stepped in.

The best vineyards are about 8,300 feet (2,500 m) above sea level on the central plateau at Gouder, Dukem and Hollots. There are also vineyards along the Awash River valley. The main varieties grown are known locally as tikur weyn, dibulbulb atter, nech dibulbul and key dubbe, all of which probably originated in Mediterranean countries and the Middle East.

Awash Winery was the first commercial winery in Ethiopia, established in 1943. It employs experienced enologists trained in Italy. In collaboration with the Ethiopian Institute for Agricultural Research and the Debere Zeit Agricultural Research Center of Alemmaya University, Awash is conducting extensive research on more than 140 grape varieties to test their suitability for Ethiopian soil and climate. So far, about 20 are proving successful, including grenache, nebbiolo, petit syrah, canno nano, dodoma altico, sylvaner, ugni blanc, chenin blanc, zeirfandeler, awash negest, shitto woyne and moskoko gialo.

The winery produces a range of well-made wines, including Gouder Red, Dukem Red, Abadir Rosé, Awash Crystal, Axumite and Amba, as well as an aperitif wine, Kilik.

ZIMBABWE

Jeffrey Benson

The pioneers brought vines to Rhodesia, as Zimbabwe was then called, in about 1890, but grape growing was not undertaken commercially until about 1960. Rene Paynter, among other determined men, tested a variety of vines at Arlington in Umwinsdale, New Salisbury. Paynter eventually produced and marketed a white wine (St Christopher) and a light red (Rosa Maria) from isabella grapes in 1963.

Trade sanctions imposed by Britain after the Rhodesian government declared its independence in 1965 forced farmers to diversify and some, encouraged by Paynter's success, planted vines. David Hughes, distiller and wine production manager of African Distillers, imported 6,000 vines: clairette blanche, white french, pinotage (a pinot/hermitage cross), steen (chenin blanc) and red muscadel. These were distributed to the Eastern Districts, Hippo Valley, Marandellas and the Mazoe Valley. A group of farmers in Essexvale, Matabeleland, found the area promising. With ideal soil and low summer rainfall, there would be few problems from rain during ripening and harvesting, and irrigation would make up for the lack of winter rain. In Bulawayo, Monis Wineries established a winery that has since become one of the country's leaders. Both Monis and African Distillers, with vineyards near Odzi, helped local farmers by acquiring the best vines for them and guaranteeing to buy their crops at realistic prices.

When Zimbabwe gained independence in 1980, the wine industry was integrated under the control of three wineries: African Distillers (AFDIS), Cairns Wineries and Meadows Estate.

When it started in 1944, African Distillers (Rhodesia) Ltd was known as P. J. Joubert (Bulawayo) Ltd. Initially, it was a distributor of imported spirits, liquors and wine, but after acquiring its own distillery in Mutare and changing its name in 1946, it produced a range of spirits. In 1974 the company moved to its 100-acre (40-ha) headquarters at Stapleford with distribution centers at Bulawayo, Harare, Kweke, Masuingo, Mutare and Victoria Falls. High-quality wines are produced here under the supervision of New Zealand wine consultant Clive Hartnell for the Stapleford labels. AFDIS now owns three wine estates (Worringham Vineyard, Green Valley Vineyards and Bertrams Vineyards) producing 350,000 cases annually.

Worringham Vineyards was purchased in 1970, in the hills of Esigodoni, New Bulawayo, with 110 acres (45 ha) under vines on shale, slate and granite soil: chenin blanc, sauvignon, sémillon, merlot, pinotage and cabernet sauvignon. Green Valley Vineyards was purchased in 1975, in the foothills of the Eastern Highlands about 15 miles (25 km) from Mutare. This 620-acre (250-ha) estate has 135 acres (55 ha) under vines on sandy loam soil: chardonnay, cabernet sauvignon, merlot, clairette blanche, colombard and ruby cabernet. Bertrams Vineyards was purchased in 1980, just outside Gweru with 100 acres (40 ha) under vines on deep red loam soil: sauvignon, colombard, chenin blanc, pinotage, merlot, cabernet sauvignon, crouchen, muscat d'alexandrie.

In 1977 Cairns Holdings acquired full control of the Baoceas family's Monis Wineries. As production increased, a new winery, Mikuyu, was built in Marondera and placed under the direction of Australian winemaker Stuart Blackwell. In 1980 Cairns acquired Mateppe Estate and Ian Sieg took over as winemaker. Within a decade, new warehouses had been built and new bottling lines were installed at Mikuyu winery. Today, under the supervision of talented winemaker Sam Pfidayi, Cairns grows chardonnay, chenin blanc, sémillon, sauvignon, merlot, pinot noir, shiraz, gamay, cabernet sauvignon, colombard and pinot blanc. Wines from Mikuyu vineyards are of excellent quality. The vineyard area is about 143 acres (58 ha) with an annual production of 140,000 cases.

The original Meadows Estate vineyard was originally hacked out of virgin bush in 1899 by Englishman, Harold Christian. The Simleit family then acquired and owned Meadows Estate for three generations, but it was not until 1986 that it began producing very fine chardonnay, buckentraube, chenin blanc, gewürztraminer and colombard in beautiful surroundings about 22 miles (36 km) north of Harare. In 1955, David Simleit sold Meadows Estate vineyards to Rosanna Rose Farms and the brand name was acquired by Cairns, who produce specially selected wines under this label. A vineyard area of 120 acres (50 ha) produces about 4,000 cases per year.

Above: *A woman working in a vineyard near Kélibia-Cape Bon, east of Tunis.*

Top: *Sculpture celebrating the grape, Grombalia, Cape Bon, Tunisia.*

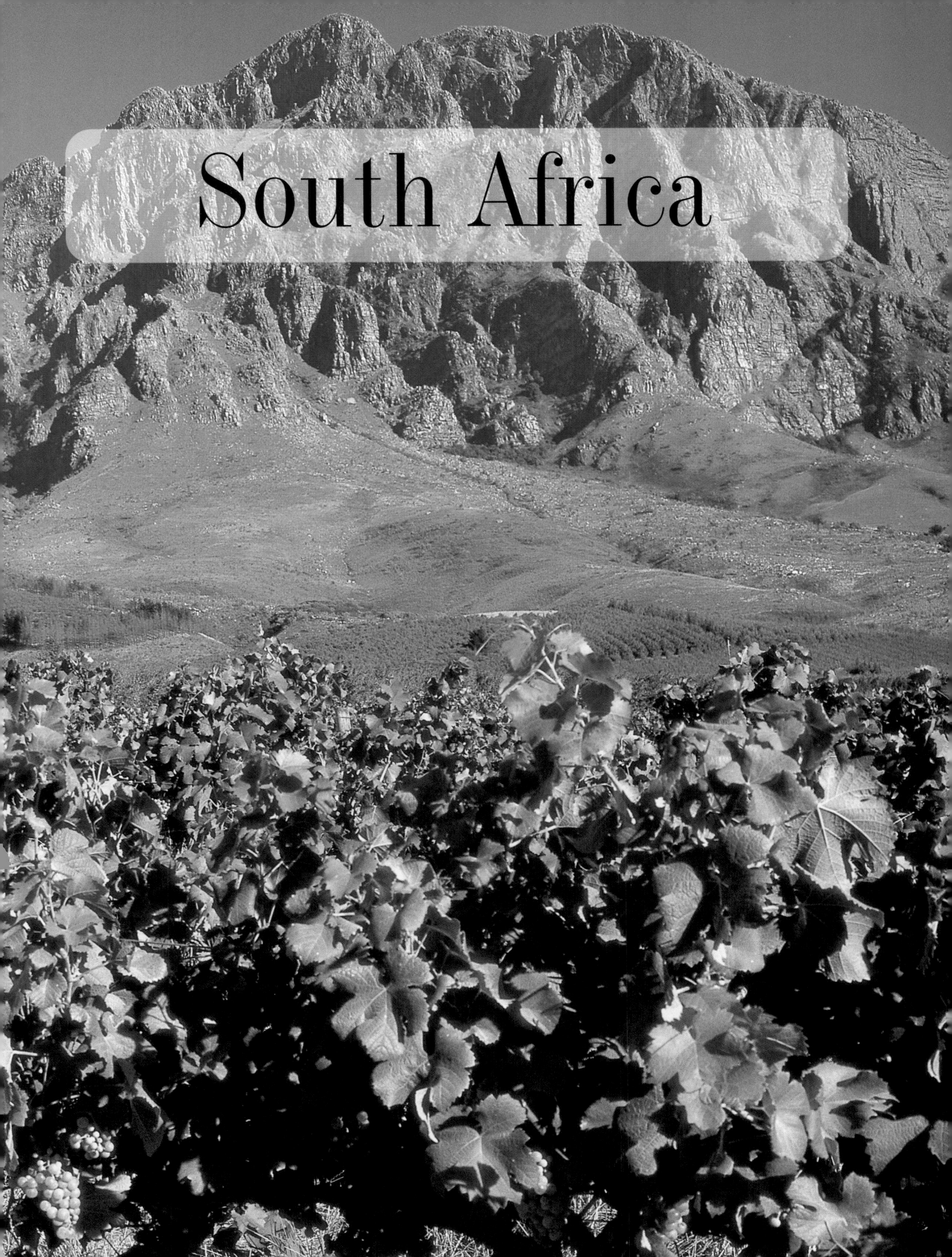

South Africa

NORTH

50 miles
(80 kilometers)

Limpopo

▲ *Blouberg*
6711 ft (2046 m)

Pietersburg

Mmabatho

Mafikeng

Rustenburg

PRETORIA

Marico

Krokodil

Midde

Lichtenburg

Roodepoort

Johannesburg

Carletonville

Soweto

Boksburg

Springs

Witbank

Bethal

Vanderbijlpark

Vereeniging

Stand

Potchefstroom

Vaal

Nosop

Kuruman

Vryburg

Klerksdorp

Orkney

Parys

Vaal Dam

Vo

Molopo

Sishen

Odendaalsrus

Kroonstad

Welkom

Virginia

Bethlehem

Ne

Harrism

Upington

**Orange River
Valley**

Ladys

Orange

Kimberley

Bloemfontein

Champagne Castle
11,073 ft (3376 m)

Orange

Vaal

Douglas

**Greenwater
Valley**

Orange

LESOTHO

S O U T H   A F R I C A

De Aar

Aliwal North

Carnarvon

Williston

Olifantsrivier

Vredendal

Roggeveld Mountains

Middelburg

Groot-Winterberg
7777 ft (2371 m)

Umtata

Queenstown

Cradock

Stutterheim

Olifants River

Saint Helena Bay

Cape Columbine

Picketberg

Nuweveldberge

Beaufort West

Graaff Reinet

King Williams Town

Fort Beaufort

Mdantsane

East London

**Swartland &
Tulbagh**

Franschhoek

Malmesbury

Worcester
Worcester

Klein Karoo

Ladismith

Calitzdorp

Oudtshoorn

Groot

Klipplaat

Grahamstown

Durbanville

Paarl

Langeberg

Kougaberge

Cape Town

■ **Stellenbosch**

Strand

Constantia

Simon's Town

Hermanus

Swellendam

Mossel Bay

Cape Seal

Uitenhage

Algoa Bay

Port Elizabeth

Cape of Good Hope

Overberg

**Robertson &
Bonnievale**

False Bay

Cape Agulhas

Cape Saint Francis

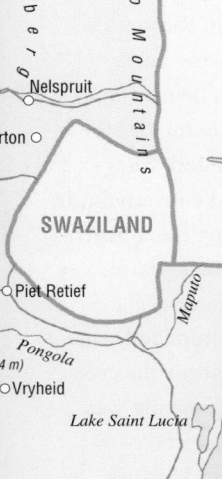

South Africa

Michael Fridjhon

The Cape wine industry originated with the start of formal white settlement in the middle of the seventeenth century. The Dutch East India Company identified Table Bay as a suitable site for the establishment of a colony to supply ships plying the long sea route between Europe and the East and appointed a former ship's doctor, Johan van Riebeeck, as its Commander. In April 1652 his expedition anchored at the foot of Table Mountain.

It is possible that Van Riebeeck brought grape seeds or even cuttings with him. Certainly, from the moment of his arrival he wrote with some enthusiasm about the agricultural potential of the Cape and urged the Company's Directors, the Lords Seventeen, to procure young trees and vine cuttings for him. The motivation for this request was pragmatic, fitting in with the original purpose of the settlement. Wine was a common enough beverage in the maritime world: it improved the ship's drinking water, stale after being transported in casks for several months; it had known antiseptic properties, useful in cases of gastro-intestinal illness; and it was held to be valuable in the treatment of scurvy.

Wines were customarily loaded in Amsterdam. The minimum amount, as stipulated by Company regulations, was sufficient to provide each crew member with a weekly ration. Much of what was available in the Dutch market at the time, at least that within the Company's procurement budget, turned to vinegar before it reached the equator. Van Riebeeck's halfway station was always destined to have a viticultural dimension, even though no one in his original party had any direct experience of grape-growing or winemaking.

The first successful consignment of cuttings reached the Cape in July 1655. Source material is believed to have been supplied from France, Germany, Bohemia and Spain. Muscat and muscadel types were probably included in the parcel. By the middle of 1656, Van Riebeeck was able to inform his masters that the cuttings were doing well. As a result more vines were sent out and these also appear to have rooted satisfactorily.

The first vineyards were obviously part of the Company's garden, so must have been close to where the city center is today. It was from these vines that Cape wine was first produced—on February 2, 1659. Van Riebeeck's logbook records both the quantity 4 gallons (15 l) and the varietal (muscadel). Despite a resounding silence as to its quality, the Commander seems to have been sufficiently inspired to seek out—for himself (and therefore in direct breach of Company policy)—additional land for vineyards. He obtained a

freehold grant of about 200 acres (80 ha) on what is now Green Point Common. This turned out to be a bad choice—cold, wet and flooded with brackish water in winter—so somehow Van Riebeeck successfully importuned Commissioner Cuneus to exchange it for a parcel near the source of the Liesbeek River. This area came to be known as Wynberg (Wine Mountain), a name that was later applied to the region farther south and around a promontory (where the present day suburb of Wynberg is situated). Van Riebeeck's Liesbeek farm—known as Bosheuwel—subsequently changed hands many times before its acquisition in the mid-nineteenth century by the trustees of the Colonial Bishopric Fund. They renamed the land Bishopscourt and converted it to premium residential use, thus ending the independent existence of the Cape's oldest wine farm.

Van Riebeeck's successor, Zacharias Wagenaar, was far less well-disposed to viticulture and wine production. His concern about food for the ever-increasing slave population—the Company was compelled to import rice for its labor force—far exceeded any interest in grapes. This situation prevailed for nearly two decades and might have continued indefinitely but for the arrival in the Cape of Simon van der Stel. The new Commander seems to have had a deep personal interest in wine and agriculture. The entourage he brought with him from his previous posting in Mauritius included Jean Marieau, of whom little is known except that he had lived in the south of France and knew something about winemaking. Whatever the level of his knowledge, it was more than in the resident population at the time. Both Marieau and Van der Stel contributed to the marked improvement in Cape wine recorded during the last two decades of the seventeenth century.

Van der Stel wasted no time in stamping his personality—and his name—on his dominions. He extended the settlement to include the Stellenbosch, some 25 miles (40 km) from Cape Town. Simon's Bay, Simon's Town and even the Simonsberg, separating Stellenbosch from Paarl, all reflect his enthusiasm for perpetuating his name. Stellenbosch itself was a necessary development: the free burgher population was growing and the families needed land to farm and space for expansion. Many of the great estates of today, mainly, but not exclusively in Stellenbosch, trace their land grants to Van der Stel.

It was during Van der Stel's tenure of office that France revoked the Edict of Nantes, effec-

Rugged mountains form a backdrop to the Delaire vineyards in Klein Karoo.

tively ending the religious tolerance enjoyed by Huguenots in that country since 1598. The Protestant countries in Europe—most notably Holland—offered shelter and asylum to their co-religionists. Some of the Huguenots who took up the Dutch offer were given the opportunity of migrating to the Cape and by 1689 some 200 had arrived. Van der Stel chose to settle them slightly farther away from Table Bay, in an area that came to be known as Franschhoek (French corner).

Most of the newcomers could claim little knowledge of vineyards or winemaking but, in the manner of most of the free burghers of the colony, they planted vines, along with fruit trees and vegetables. The Cape seems to have enjoyed a booming wine trade with ships that docked in Table Bay. Given contemporary comments about the quality of the wines, it is safe to assume that the alcohol—and possibly mineral and vitamin value—meant more to the purchasers than drinking pleasure.

Van der Stel's injunctions and regulations influenced the average quality of what was on offer. For example, he noted that much of what was produced showed all the signs of having been made from underripe grapes. In 1686 the council passed a resolution prohibiting any pressing of wine "before the vineyards have been visited by a committee and pronounced by the commander to be of the requisite maturity." Other regulations governing wine production related to cellar hygiene. For the rest, Van der Stel's decisions were generally more pragmatic measures designed to ensure that the Company's food requirements were not compromised by the farmers' enthusiasm for producing wine and selling it privately.

If the development of new agricultural areas and the promulgation of production guidelines are Van der Stel's major legacy to the wine industry, the farm he established became, in time, the country's export flagship. He gained ownership of a 1,850-acre (750-ha) tract of land less than 12 miles (20 km) from the Company's settlement. The grant was originally recommended by Rijkloof van Goens, Councillor of India and former Governor of Ceylon, but it was subsequently confirmed by High Commissioner Hendrik Adriaan van Rheede, Lord of Mydracht. Van Rheede arrived in the Cape in April 1685, armed with the full authority of the Lords Seventeen. Van der Stel's foresight in ensuring that his title to the land could not subsequently be disputed by the Company spared him the loss later suffered by Van Riebeeck at the end of his tenure of office.

The land he acquired for himself was a fertile valley south of Wynberg and east of Steenberg. He named it not, as was originally supposed, in honor of his wife (who had not accompanied him to the Cape) but probably as a mark of gratitude to Van Goens, whose daughter had been christened "Constantia." Van der Stel developed the property using Company slaves—at least until he could afford a permanent work force of his own. He sourced equipment and planting material from the Company's workshops and gardens and within ten years had planted 8,400 trees and nearly 100,000 vines. Promoted from Commander to Governor, the old man prospered. His estate became a model property, revealing in practice the farming virtues he actively encouraged among free burghers. Even before his retirement in 1699, his wines had acquired an international reputation—not only in Batavia (the normal market for Cape exports) but also in Amsterdam.

Van der Stel was succeeded as Governor by his son, Wilhem Adriaen, who attempted to establish at Vergelegen (across False Bay from Constantia) a property to rival his father's. Instead he managed to alienate the free burghers so much that they complained to the Company in Amsterdam and he was recalled in disgrace. A few years later, in 1712, the old man died, and his property was subdivided into three portions and sold off. Two of the sections became known as Bergvliet and Klein Constantia, while the remainder, which included the house and about 450 acres (180 ha) of land, was sold as Groot Constantia.

There are two separate threads to the story of Cape wine in the eighteenth century: the first traces the establishment of great farming estates, engaged in mixed agriculture but usually with a portion of vineyard and a passing interest in winemaking; the second follows the destiny of Constantia. There, within a few years of Van der Stel's death, the appellation enjoyed so substantial a reputation that its entire production was exported and visitors to the Cape made the trip to the property to observe and record its rhythms in their day-books and diaries.

Along the Stellenbosch Wine Route, visitors enjoy varied scenery as they visit the participating wineries for tastings.

Stellenbosch, now a cooperative, is one of about 80 wineries in the Stellenbosch area.

Neil Ellis produces an impressive range of quality red wines from these vineyards in the Jonkershoek Valley, Stellenbosch.

Bottles containing sparkling wines are rotated at regular intervals.

Great farming estates

The movement of the population from the original settlement at Table Bay into the interior was driven by the ever-increasing number of free burghers and settlers, and their penchant for producing large families. The Company granted properties in and around Stellenbosch and Paarl, then added to the allocations in Franschhoek, Klein Drakenstein and across False Bay, along the slopes of the Helderberg and also northwest toward the Piketberg. Few, however, can provide a detailed record of their winemaking activities and much of what is known relates to inventories filed at the time of a proprietor's death: vineyards, barrels, pot stills and winemaking equipment confirm that wine was very much part of the life of these Cape farms. However, with the exception of Constantia, most of these properties were unable to satisfy the more discriminating tastes of the export markets and criticism abounded.

At the former estate of Simon van der Stel, however, a process was taking place that would launch the property's wines into the very front rank of international brands. For more than a century they fetched prices that exceeded even those of the French first growths. The marketing genius behind the launch of Constantia was Johannes Colijn, who purchased a portion of Klein Constantia a few years after Van der Stel's death.

The 94 acres (38 ha) of Klein Constantia included some of the former Governor's white wine vineyards. Colijn's care in the winemaking, his commitment to developing an export trade (at prices substantially lower than the domestic market was prepared to pay) and his prudent purchase of other Constantia land as it came on the market all contributed to the growing value of the appellation.

By the 1740s the wines of Groot and Klein Constantia—both vinified under Colijn's direction—were firmly established. To keep its highly profitable allocation of Constantia, the Company exempted the properties from the payment of certain imposts. After Colijn's death his family continued to manage the winemaking and the brand in accordance with the precepts he had laid down and by 1776 Klein Constantia was valued at transfer at 61,680 guilders. Groot Constantia—five times its size—had, at the time of Van der Stel's death, fetched only 8,000 guilders.

But even this growing market for the wine was nothing compared with the boom that followed the acquisition of Groot Constantia by Hendrik Cloete in 1778. Although he spent a considerable sum on the vineyards and cellar, he also renovated the manor house and gave the estate the gracious charm that contributed to its image and prestige abroad. A great deal is known of Cloete's farming and winemaking practices. He made a fertilizer from manure and compost and insisted on rigorous (for the time) cellar practices and generous applications of sulfur.

With a contract to sell his crop to the Company (and a bonus calculated on the subsequent auction price in Amsterdam), Cloete enjoyed a high profile in international trade. His customers included several of Europe's crowned heads. Clearly the wine was not a price-sensitive commodity and when Cloete began negotiations with the Company for an increase in the upfront payment, he found them willing to act as his agent and to auction his wines in Amsterdam.

Surprisingly, Cloete never accepted this offer but instead negotiated an improved one-off selling price, payable in the Cape on delivery. To this the Company agreed gladly, but added two further conditions: the first was that the price should be fixed in perpetuity; the second was that this obligation should be registered against the title deeds of the property. This turned out to be a fatally short-sighted contract for the family and for the brand. When the British occupied the Cape in 1795 during the Napoleonic Wars, they took over and enforced the contractual rights the Company enjoyed. While these arrangements certainly helped to spread the fame of Constantia, the family was denied much of the benefit, since the price at which the wine was sold was fixed at about 25 percent of the true market value.

Changing times

Britain's policy of Imperial Preference initially saw a vastly increased demand for Cape wines, pretty much irrespective of quality. Then, as the punitive duties against European wines were lifted, prices and export volumes fell dramatically. With the emancipation of slaves, labor costs increased. Given the hand-crafted nature of Constantia's viticulture, this led to a decline in the quality of what was produced.

The next generation of Cloetes could not afford to invest the viticulture and grape selection with the same rigor. Preparing the compost, clearing the insects and pruning the vines had required a labor force of 52 slaves. A generation later the work was done by children. When Britain entered into a trade treaty with France in 1861, Cape wines lost their last vestige of tariff protection. By then odium was decimating the vineyards and there was no money left to face the catastrophe of phylloxera. When Jacob Pieter Cloete died in 1875, his estate was insolvent.

Ten years later, in 1885, the Groot Constantia estate had a new owner: the Government of the Cape Colony. The farm was to be converted, at the suggestion of Baron von Babo (an Austrian with limited winemaking experience) into a model farm for training purposes. Its history over the next decade was as depressing as the affairs of many wine properties of the Western Cape. Those charged with running it had little real viticultural expertise, the vineyards of American rootstock (established to provide a nursery for other grape farms in the Cape) had been hampered by poor cuttings, and the market was badly depressed.

By the mid-1890s there was a discernible turnaround. Recognizing the shift from fortified sweet wines to lighter table wines, the farm's managers established cabernet sauvignon vineyards. By the time phylloxera had wiped out the Cloetes' vines, Constantia was ready to plant for the new fashion. But while losses at Constantia had been halted, the same could not be said for the rest of the industry. Exports had remained weak since Gladstone's treaty with the French in 1860. The reputation of Cape wine, marred as much

by poor viticulture as it was by the activities of unscrupulous wine merchants, served to undermine selling prices. Attempts by growers to form their own export syndicate foundered on a tide of negative sentiment. The project obtained enough working capital and its samples were judged of adequate quality, but demand was so small and prospects of expansion so limited that, in the end, the enterprise went into voluntary liquidation.

Still, there were glimmerings of hope: the Anglo–Boer War (1899–1902) produced a temporary increase in demand, but this collapsed almost as soon as the Treaty of Vereeniging was signed. Over-production followed inexorably, and while the Cape government assisted producers with free expert advice, it was disinclined to take on the expense and effort of an export office. The success of the Groot Constantia farm—by 1903 it was showing a healthy profit—encouraged the authorities to increase the scope of this facility and to appoint a Government Viticulturist. The first incumbent was Raymond Dubois, who had been principal at the Rutherglen Viticultural College in Victoria, Australia. The Victorian Government objected to his departure and sent a strong protest to the Cape Department of Agriculture.

Dubois encountered a less-than-cooperative environment on his arrival, but he soon impressed a parliamentary select committee, obtained an increase in government assistance for training, and

The potential of cooler-climate vineyards, such as these in Franschhoek, was largely unappreciated until fairly recent times.

White grapes growing on solid supports.

Spectacular proteas, a species indigenous to the African continent, growing in the Swartberg Mountains, Klein Karoo.

ensured that there were funds for scientific research. His comments on the state of Cape wine at the time reveal that many of the problems experienced by the industry related to lack of dedication, insufficient capital and an almost indecent desire to dispose of the crop before it was in a saleable condition. Yet again there is evidence that the Cape was responsible for its own sales problems and that there was no geographical or viticultural impediment to quality wine production.

In 1905 the government initiated an arrangement by which cooperative wineries could obtain Treasury grants. Although not particularly successful, it was the forerunner of a format that in time became the key commercial structure on the Cape's viticultural landscape. As post-phylloxera production increased, wine prices dropped: cooperatives were able to assist in the processing and holding costs, but ultimately they were unable to insulate growers from the reality of the marketplace. The government, partly beholden to a strongly puritanical prohibitionist clique, could not accede to overt statutory price protection. For some time it managed to avoid imposing an excise tax but finally had to give in. This provoked widespread protest from farmers and the trade and contributed to the uniting of producer interests. By December 1916 the Paarl Farmers' Association had called a public meeting which, in turn, formed the "Co-operative

Viticultural Union of South Africa." In a very short time this name was changed to the "Co-operative Wine Growers' Association of South Africa" and the ultimately powerful organization came to be known by its Afrikaans initials, KWV.

The KWV

From the outset the KWV set about establishing a growers' cartel. Its stated purpose was to regulate the sale of wine and brandy so as to ensure an adequate return for its members, who, in turn, pledged that they would not sell their produce below the price determined by their directors. Within a year the organization was converted to a company. Its success, from a grower's perspective, was immediate and gratifying—the floor price for wine almost doubled.

In its first few years the KWV gained considerable ground, but it also encountered opposition from independent wine farmers and from the wholesale trade. Immediately after the First World War the economy flourished. Wine prices reached levels four times higher than in the pre-KWV era. Relations with producing wholesalers improved; the cartel became more efficient, arranging that whatever was surplus to the wine and brandy requirements of the industry would be destroyed. When the post-war boom ended and demand and wine prices both dropped, some of the members opposed the regulations and others operated where possible beyond their ambit. By 1922 the company was converted back to a cooperative but found itself without the power to discipline its members.

Clearly, statutory powers were needed, so in 1924 Parliament passed a Bill "to provide for the control and management of the wine and spirit industry." This was the first of the laws and amendments (others followed in 1928, 1940, 1946, 1957 and 1970) that entrenched the KWV and eventually enabled it to control every element of South Africa's wine and spirit industry.

Over time the KWV came to determine the minimum prices for all grape products—first distilling wine, then so-called "good wine" and, finally, even grapes destined for juice concentrate. Since it was a buyer of last resort it obtained the right to fix the total tonnage of a particular property. (This regulation was never applied to enhance quality, since these production quotas permitted yields that were sometimes as high as 20 tons per acre/50 tonnes per ha). The quota system also allowed the KWV to determine where, and by whom, vines could be planted. The result was that vineyards could be established only in traditional wine-producing areas. The occasional exception, such as the Orange River irrigation scheme, was driven by political considerations and in turn imbued the land with value because there was a guaranteed purchase—and purchase price—for the crop, irrespective of quality. Only when the law was changed in the 1980s (to authorize the transfer of quota from one farm to another in the same area) and when the system was finally scrapped a few years later did producers look farther afield, usually to cool-climate sites, to develop the quality potential of the Cape wine industry.

The KWV may have protected the country's growers from the full impact of market forces, but it did so at a vast cost to the country's fine-wine business. Minimum-price guarantees and a system that focused on yield, in potential alcohol, permitted the survival of the least efficient and undermined the initiative of the more adventurous. The imposition of trade sanctions against South Africa, mainly in the 1980s, postponed full recognition of how costly the KWV's regime had been. As the rest of the wine world came to understand—and meet—the quality expectations of the international market, South Africa languished in a vacuum.

The KWV's wealth grew as it used price-fixing mechanisms to provide cash flow for its expansion. Distilling wine, in other words product surplus to the natural wine industry, was paid for in two parts: the first payment comprised the non-surplus portion of the crop and was set at the percentage of non-surplus to total, applied to the distilling wine price. The second amount was paid only when the entire crop had been disposed of, and once all the costs associated with marketing the surplus had been deducted. If the distilling wine price was set at 100 units, and the surplus, as estimated by KWV, was 50 percent, farmers would receive an upfront payment of 50 units and deliver their entire distilling wine crop to the KWV. The company could market the non-surplus amount immediately so it had no exposure on its first payment. It would then trade the surplus portion, but pay farmers their bonus only when the remainder had been sold.

This basis of surplus determination created a substantial positive cash flow for the organization. In 1996, when KWV announced its intention of converting from a cooperative to a company (with a view to distributing wealth acquired over nearly eight decades to its members) the Minister of Agriculture opposed the scheme of arrangement in

the Cape High Court. He argued that KWV's assets were public in character and in part had been acquired as a result of its statutory authority. The KWV denied this, but a year later reached a settlement from which was born the South African Wine Industry Trust (largely funded by contributions from KWV). By agreement, KWV was then relieved of its statutory role. Notwithstanding the organization's vociferous denial that it had enjoyed an enormous advantage through its former status, the extent of its historic privilege became clear when its statutory powers lapsed. In 1998 and 1999 its profits tumbled dramatically.

While the real modernization of the Cape wine industry more or less coincided with the political transformation of South Africa, some of the regulations necessary to ensure a focus on wine quality had been established in the previous decades. The wine-of-origin legislation, for example, dates from 1972, becoming law in 1973. It was one of the first attempts by a country outside the EU to meet the product certification criteria of the European market. It defined and demarcated the major areas of origin (and later the sub-regions and wards). It distinguished between estate and branded wine and provided a policing and certification system to verify label claims relating to varietal, vintage and appellation. Launched at a time when producers were free to describe a wine without any regard to the contents, it provoked a chronic red wine shortage, accompanied by massive increases in the price of grapes such as cabernet sauvignon. This in turn suggests how little truth there had previously been to the varietal claims on the labels of major

Agricultural land in West Cape Province.

Secateurs, ready for vineyard chores.

red wine brands. It is probable that in the late 1960s most of these products contained less than 25 percent of the specified varietal.

The 1973 legislation contained a schedule that detailed an ever-increasing minimum percentage of the so-called noble cultivars required for certification in single-varietal wines. By the 1980s this had been parlayed up to 75 percent, the limit still applied for the domestic market. All exports comply with the international 85 percent minimum requirement for varietal and for vintage.

With the 1973 legislation came an arcane code covering broad areas of origin and highly specific sites, of which the estate was—and still remains—the smallest demarcated area permitted by law. Wines of origin can be produced only from grapes grown entirely in a specified area (unless a grower outside that area had been supplying grapes prior to 1973, on a contractual basis, to a cellar in another area of origin). An estate wine can be made only from grapes grown and crushed on a designated wine estate (though maturation and bottling can take place elsewhere). Site-specific production that does not comply with these regulations cannot be certified as such. The authorities (whose prior permission is required for the release of any wine that lays claim to vintage, varietal or origin) would certainly prohibit the sale of a Cape brand made and labeled like Heitz's Martha's Vineyard. Some wineries frequently circumvent these regulations with cuvée names, such as Hamilton Russell's Ashbourne Pinot Noir, but there is no guarantee—other than the producer's integrity and sense of

Picking commences in the Bouchard Finlayson vineyards in Overberg.

reputation—that the wine derives, year after year, from the same block of vines.

Given the great lack of product certainty in the era preceding the 1973 legislation and its many amendments, there can be no doubt that the wine-of-origin regulations have contributed substantially to the overall improvement of the Cape wine industry. It is true that certification panels, required by law to taste all wines purporting to come from a particular varietal, region or vintage (with a view to confirming the quality and veracity of its claims) have often lacked the expertise necessary to perform these statutory tasks. Vineyard and winery records enable the authorities to substantiate whether the cellar in question had access to the designated varietals within the specified appellation. However, the Wine and Spirit Board is also obliged to confirm that the wine is "typical" of the varietal or the vintage to which it lays claim. Critics of the regulations maintain that these certification panels may actually have retarded the progress of the Cape wine industry by imposing their own sometimes quite narrow aesthetic on the wines appearing before them. (A recent winner of the annual Chenin Blanc Challenge commented that he knew he had made a good wine because it had twice been refused certification.)

Notwithstanding these isolated examples, there is clear evidence of the progress achieved by the wine industry as a result of the more rigorous regulatory environment. Varietal consciousness and the beginnings of an understanding of *terroir* followed the wine-of-origin legislation. The next decade saw extensive plantings of a wide range of internationally accepted varietals. In 1973 the combined vineyard area of premium cultivars was less than 4 percent. By 1998 cabernet sauvignon, cabernet franc, merlot, pinot noir, shiraz, rhine riesling, gewürztraminer, sauvignon blanc and chardonnay constituted some 20 percent.

However, the country's grapegrowers discovered how far they had fallen behind only when political and trade isolation ended. The shortcomings of the wine-certification scheme were revealed once it became clear that the tasting standards of the bureaucrats administering it were not based on international benchmarks. At best they had provided assurance that wines bearing a regional denomination—Stellenbosch, Paarl or Constantia, for example—did indeed derive from those areas of origin. The much greater challenge—how to meet the quality and price expectations of an increasingly discerning market—has yet to be met.

Constantia

The Constantia region, indisputably the cradle of wine culture in South Africa, was only recently on the brink of extinction. By the 1970s there was just one surviving winery, Groot Constantia, and it depended on generous handouts from government to make ends meet. Adjacent properties still offered the semblance of an agricultural environment—some had vineyards and pastures, but were generally rundown and waiting for urban sprawl to make economic sense of real-estate development. Their logic seemed unassailable: Constantia was a mere 15 minutes' drive from the center of Cape Town; some of the city's finest residential properties lay within a 3-mile (5-km) radius of Van der Stel's original farm. The climate was substantially cooler than Stellenbosch and Paarl. With vineyard virus endemic to the Cape, grapes ripened unevenly and irregularly. Evidence of Groot Constantia's financial travails discouraged any of the neighboring landowners from seeking redemption through grapegrowing. By the early 1980s they seemed reconciled to waiting for land hunger to

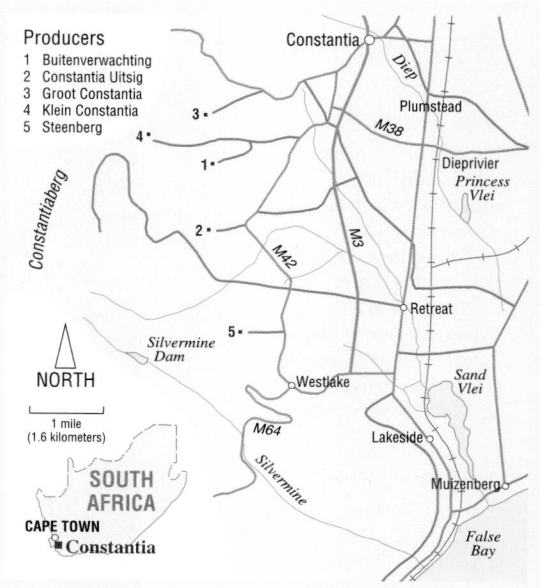

bump up their property prices, so they could leave. The turnaround, when it came, was swift, and the results have been so gratifying that even 15 years after the first vintages from Klein Constantia and Buitenverwachting, it seems impossible to visualize the depressed conditions from which the Constantia phoenix arose.

BUITENVERWACHTING

Established 1796 *Owners* C. and R. Müller, Trustees, Buitenverwachting Farm Trust
Production 60,000 cases *Vineyard area* 250 acres (100 ha)

Richard Müller chose a path similar to Klein Constantia for Buitenverwachting, adding a premium restaurant to his development. His sojourn there was briefer, but no less dramatic. When the US government expressed an interest in the connection between his wealth and his role in the sale of restricted technology to Russia before the fall of

Vines at Groot Constantia. The winery is a great tourist attraction and has a museum with centuries-old winemaking memorabilia.

REGIONAL DOZEN

QUALITY WINES

Buitenverwachting
   Chardonnay
Buitenverwachting Christine
Constantia Uitsig
   Chardonnay Reserve
Klein Constantia
   Sauvignon Blanc
Klein Constantia Shiraz
   (1997 and younger)
Steenberg Sauvignon
   Blanc Reserve

BEST VALUE WINES

Groot Constantia Chardonnay
   Reserve
Groot Constantia
   Gewurztraminer
Groot Constantia Rhine
   Riesling
Klein Constantia Rhine
   Riesling
Steenberg Sauvignon Blanc
Steenberg Semillon

Sauvignon blanc grapes at the Steenberg winery, where a consistently outstanding Sauvignon Blanc Reserve is produced.

the Berlin Wall, he chose to leave South Africa. Like Klein Constantia, Buitenverwachting has played a key role in the restoration of the region and the renewed reputation of Cape wines as a whole. The property has been immaculately laid out and focuses, where possible, on organic farming methods. Some of its white wines are consistent front rankers, notably the sauvignon blanc, rhine riesling and chardonnay. Several vintages of the proprietory red, a blend of cabernet franc and cabernet sauvignon sold under the brand name Christine, have come to enjoy almost cult status; an earlier merlot vintage won the Diners Club winemaker of the year award for the previous cellarmaster Jean Daneel.

CONSTANTIA UITSIG

Established 1881 *Owners* D. and M. McCay *Production* 15,600 cases *Vineyard area* 99 acres (40 ha)

This has been built up by Dave McCay, assisted by Andre Badenhorst, who helped establish Buitenverwachting some years earlier. The fame of its restaurants has somewhat overshadowed the wines. The current vintages, however, vinified at Steenberg, show that the property has the potential to produce complex and sophisticated whites. Sémillons from 1997 on are rich and textured with an underlying structure that suggests they are more than mere show wines.

GROOT CONSTANTIA ESTATE

Established **1685** *Owner* **Groot Constantia Trust**
Production **40,000 cases** *Vineyard area* **250 acres (100 ha)**

It was inevitable that the successes at Buitenverwachting and Klein Constantia would force a serious reappraisal of the plight of this estate. One of the top-three tourist attractions in the Cape—if not the country—its recent winemaking history has been less than glorious. While the rest of Constantia was enjoying a revival, the state farm was managed by a control board dominated by cronies drawn from the KWV. With the apparently unlimited resources the apartheid government seemed willing to throw at it, vineyards were uprooted, then replanted, then uprooted again. Contractors were enriched but the wines remained largely two-dimensional. There have been some successes: a few vintages of reserve chardonnays well worth tracking down; some fine rhine rieslings, a delicately fragrant gewürztraminer. In the run-up to the 1994 election, the Nationalist government passed legislation transferring the property to a Trust, appointing a majority of the trustees from among the KWV's ranks. The more recent vintages have not been markedly better, though the improved export environment has led to stronger sales and an end to the financial losses.

KLEIN CONSTANTIA ESTATE

Established **1823** *Owners* **Duggie and Lowell Jooste**
Production **45,000 cases** *Vineyard area* **184 acres (74.5 ha)**

Duggie Jooste purchased a rundown and derelict Klein Constantia and immediately began planting vineyards and planning a winery. His vision was to make quality wine, so he invested extensively in the most modern viticultural and cellar technology. His were among the first vineyards in the Cape to profit from detailed soil testing and a scientifically devised planting program. His close relationship with Stellenbosch Farmers Winery gave him access to cleaned-up and new cloned material and staff who knew what to do with it. For a time the farm was managed by Ernst Le Roux, who subsequently became managing director of Nederburg. The winemaker, Ross Gower, had served his appren-

ticeship at Nederburg before working a stint in New Zealand. The first vintage, the 1986, reminded the Cape of the extraordinary potential of Constantia: the sauvignon blanc won the trophy for the best white wine on the national young wine show; a year later the 1986 cabernet sauvignon carried off the trophy for the best wine on show.

Klein Constantia has subsequently acquired a special reputation for its Vin de Constance, a muscat de frontignan dessert wine bottled in a quaint eighteenth-century-lookalike flask. Vinified in the way that research suggests Cloete made the legendary wines of two centuries ago, it is sweet, but not cloying, a beautifully structured botrytis-free late-harvested beverage. It has been on the market for about 10 years, gaining a following across the globe. It has done more than any single wine to bring prominence to the Constantia area.

STEENBERG VINEYARDS

Established **1682** *Owner* **Johnnies Industrial Corporation (Johnnic)** *Production* **38,800 cases** *Vineyard area* **173 acres (70 ha)**

Steenberg had belonged to the Louw family for more than a century before it was sold for housing development in the late 1980s. It was the logical site for a golf estate linked to the vineyards and winery. The result has been a commercial and oenological success. A rigorously managed vineyard replanting program is starting to show gratifying results, with very good wines emerging from the newly constructed cellar. Once again, whites rather than reds have garnered most of the attention: sauvignon blanc has consistently been the most successful varietal on the farm, though sémillon seems also to have performed well lately. The best red remains the merlot.

Outbuildings at Steenberg Winery, one of the Cape's oldest farms.

Paarl

There has been long-standing rivalry between Paarl and Stellenbosch for supremacy in the South African wine industry. The boom that transformed Stellenbosch in the past decade has yet to make its mark on Paarl. The region is still characterized by medium-size cellars producing good, rather than extraordinary, wine. Still, the appearance of Glen Carlou and Veenwouden, and the revolution wrought by Charles Back at Fairview in the past decade, all suggest that an era of boutique wines of the highest quality is imminent.

Although the two towns are roughly the same age, each has developed along quite different lines. Separated by less than a half-hour drive, they feel worlds apart. Paarl is easily the larger in terms of area and population. It is also more industrialized and lacks the focus and charm that makes Stellenbosch more popular with tourists. Situated farther inland and shielded from the cool southeasterly breezes by the mountain range that forms an amphitheater around Stellenbosch, it is warmer and its wines more robust. Interspersed with the wine farms are table-grape vineyards, olive groves and orchards. Looming over the town is the great hill of granite, its vast gray-black boulders glistening in the rain, that gave the settlement its name—

Paarl literally means "pearl" in Dutch. Bounded by Wellington (north), Franschhoek (east) and Stellenbosch (south), Paarl is too spread out to offer the same homogeneity of style that characterizes Constantia. The Agter-Paarl vineyards near Wellington, for example, are substantially warmer than the sites adjacent to Stellenbosch.

BACKSBERG ESTATE

Established 1916   *Owner* Michael Back   *Production* 95,000 cases   *Vineyard area* 408 acres (165 ha)

The late Sydney Back, another innovator of the modern industry, grew up on a wine farm in the shadow of the Klein Babylonstoren mountain and embraced the estate-wine concept launched in 1973 with unparalleled enthusiasm. He established his winery not far from town, though closer to Stellenbosch and Franschhoek. A shrewd and unflamboyant visionary, he worked to establish the integrity of site-specific viticulture in South Africa. In his own viticultural and cellar practices he was meticulous and economical.

For more than two decades his wines were widely regarded as the best-value premium products on the market. He led the replanting revolution that followed the importation of quality chardonnay, sauvignon blanc and merlot material in the 1980s. Back grubbed up virus-infected clonal material, modernized fruit-handling methods and established commercial volumes of wood maturation long before most of his competitors. He also took the lead in setting up social responsibility programs—long before they were fashionable. Back's son Michael has maintained this policy: Backsberg's vineyard workers produce and manage their own separate brand, sold under the Freedom Road label.

FAIRVIEW

Established 1937   *Owner* Charles Back   *Production* NA   *Vineyard area* 800 acres (320 ha)

Undoubtedly the most innovative and international of present-day Paarl wineries, Fairview, southeast of the town, offers a range of intensely flavored opulent wines under a series of labels that now includes the West Coast Spice Route brand. The reds are generally more interesting that the whites, though the Fairview Viognier is a noteworthy

Newly picked grapes on their way to the crushers.

exception. From the competitively priced Goats do Roam (a Rhône-style red that trades off the goat's milk cheese business attached to the farm) to the complex and concentrated Spice Route Chenin, Pinotage and Shiraz, Charles Back's wines are strong and unequivocal expressions of the Cape.

GLEN CARLOU VINEYARDS

Established 1985 *Owners* W. M. Finlayson/Hess Holdings Switzerland *Production* 20,000 cases *Vineyard area* 111 acres (45 ha)

This deluxe boutique operation has come from nowhere to one of the country's top slots in less than two decades. Walter Finlayson has now handed over the cellar to son David, freeing up time to dedicate himself to his Ayrshire herd and his French-style farmhouse cheeses. Still, he can reflect with some satisfaction on the meteoric rise in the cellar's reputation. A succession of superb chardonnays, a very good cabernet-based blend, a chenin-chardonnay of unusual complexity and a fine vintage Port are the main wines in the range.

KWV INTERNATIONAL

Established 1918 (as a Cooperative) *Owners* Public Company *Production* 1–1.5 million cases *Vineyard area* Buys in grapes from members

The presence of KWV's headquarters in Paarl certainly adds weight to the town's claims to importance. The building itself dominates the main approach road and the organization is a substantial employer. Its erstwhile political clout ensures a disproportionately high standing in the corridors of power. Its purchase criteria also tend—perhaps by coincidence—to favor farmers in the region, rather than those owning cooler vineyards farther south. KWV's minimum wine price payments are based on the potential yield at 10 percent alcohol by volume, thus encouraging production in the warmer zones at the expense of the slower-ripening, less-alcoholic, cooler sites.

Notwithstanding a business philosophy that was originally based on surplus disposal, KWV has developed some of South Africa's best-known international wine brands. While much of the organization's activities over the years involved bulk alcohol trading, it was also the export arm of the Cape wine industry. Brands such as Roodeberg, a blended red (whose composition over the years has changed from being cinsaut- to cabernet-dominated) were very much the international face of South African wine until the 1980s. Among white wines, KWV's Chenin Blanc once occupied

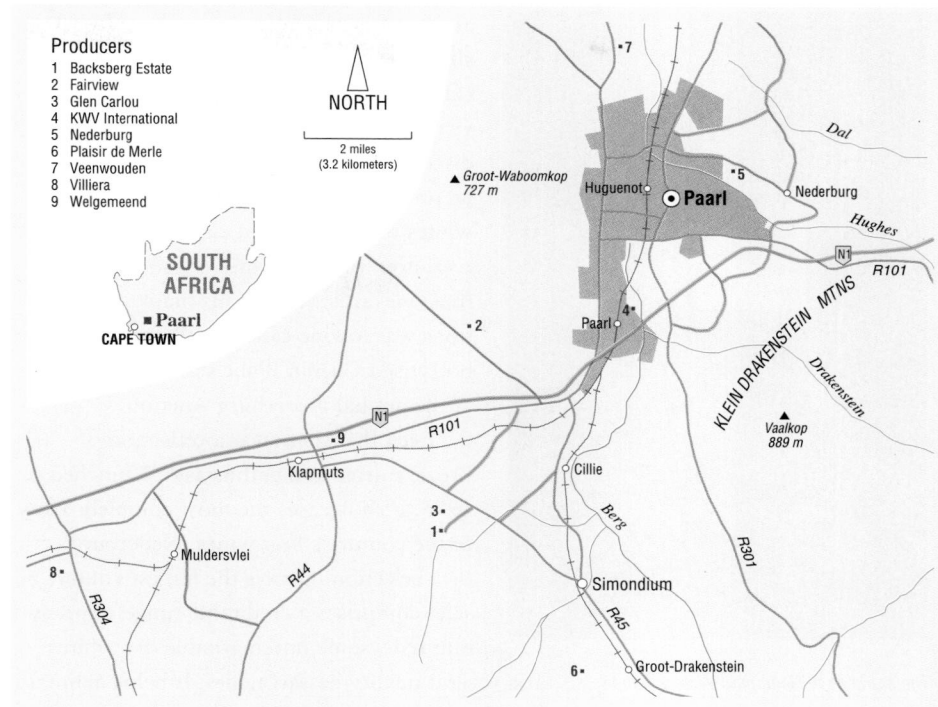

pride of place at the competitive—rather than cheap—end of the UK supermarket trade. Sanctions and boycotts in the 1980s changed all this.

When Cape wine re-entered world markets in the 1990s, KWV was ahead of many of its local competitors in designing wines to meet the expectations of European consumers. The Roodebergs and Chenin Blancs are still there, but so are the more sophisticated offerings in the Cathedral Cellars range. Under winemaker Kosie Möller this premium red wine selection was won a host of awards—locally and internationally—with one of the country's top Cabernet Francs, superb Shiraz, fine Pinotage and a consistently good blend sold under the proprietory name of Triptych. There are also some wonderful fortified wines dating back to the 1930s, mostly made from muscat varietals. Some are sold as Jerepigos—the generic term used to describe this style of wine—while others are still marketed as Port.

NEDERBURG WINES

Established 1791 *Owner* Stellenbosch Farmers Winery *Production* 800,000 cases *Vineyard area* 1,730 acres (700 ha)

While most of the better cellars are, unsurprisingly, south of the town, Nederburg, South Africa's largest premium winery, is slightly north. The first of the modern high-volume deluxe brands, this commercial leviathan came to dominate the fine-wine industry in the 1960s and 1970s. The German-born and Weinsburg-trained cellarmaster of that era, Gunther Brözel, played a role in the

Grapes pass through a mechanical destalker.

The entrance to Nederburg Winery, famed for its annual Auction, the most important event on the yearly wine calendar.

South African wine industry in many ways similar to that of Max Schubert in Australia. He arrived in the 1950s, just as the virtues of cold fermentation were being discovered in the Cape. For three decades he produced everything from German-style whites to cabernet and cabernet blends that rival even the best wines of modern, virus-free vineyards. Among his many innovations was a wine called Edelkeur, a botrytised Chenin Blanc still traded only at the annual Nederburg Auction.

Even the Auction is a reflection of Brözel's drive and enthusiasm. Launched in 1975, it showcases the most complete array of the country's best wines. Nederburg's own selection (always the largest volume on sale) comprises a creditable range of premium reds, some unremarkable dry whites and several quality dessert wines. It helps maintain the image of the brand in the presence of an increasingly ordinary high-volume everyday range.

PLAISIR DE MERLE, SIMONSBERG
Established 1964 *Owners* Stellenbosch Farmers Winery *Production* 35,000 cases *Vineyard area* 988 acres (400 ha)

Three centuries of history belies this property's oenological modernity. Close to Backsberg on the Franschhoek side of Paarl, it functions mainly as a supply farm to Nederburg. Successive replanting programs revealed specific vineyard blocks capable of producing super-premium wines. SFW accordingly established a small winery near the homestead to process this fruit. Paul Pontallier, Director of Château Margaux and consultant to the group,

Rows of vines in a valley sheltered by a rugged mountain range.

took a more hands-on role for the first few vintages and these reds show great concentration, with a richness and texture typical of the best Paarl wines.

VEENWOUDEN
Established 1990 *Owner* Deon van der Walt *Production* 5,500 cases *Vineyard area* 36 acres (14.5 ha)

Keeping it in the family, this northern Paarl property is owned by a Swiss-based tenor, whose brother, erstwhile golf pro Marcel, runs the cellar while his father Charles takes charge of the vineyards. This is one of the new stars in the Paarl constellation, producing a small quantity of hand-crafted wines of striking quality under the guidance of oenologist Michel Rolland, a Frenchman with an international reputation. Densely textured, with sweet ripe fruit and plenty of palate weight, these wines vindicate the views of those who have argued that the austere herbal qualities on Cape merlot and cabernet are merely evidence of poor viticulture. Both the Classic, a Bordeaux-style blend, and the Merlot are the cellar's flagships.

VILLIERA WINE
Established 1928 *Owners* the Grier family *Production* 100,000 cases *Vineyard area* 741 acres (300 ha)

Villiera also warrants special mention as one of the country's most popular good-value, high-quality operations. Cellarmaster Jeff Grier won the Diners Club Winemaker of the Year award and the annual Chenin Challenge in successive years. Notwithstanding show successes, pricing is surprisingly modest. The *méthode champenoise* bubbly, frequently the country's top-rated Cap Classique, sells for little more than the big-brand charmat wines produced in industrial cellars.

WELGEMEEND ESTATE
Established NA *Owner* W.A. Hofmeyr *Production* 3,500 cases *Vineyard area* 31 acres (12.6 ha)

Welgemeend, started by Billy and Ursula Hofmeyr and now run by their daughter Louise, warrants special mention. Billy played a seminal role in the creation of the modern Cape wine industry. A land surveyor with a passion for wine (and opera), he bought a small, unexceptional-looking property between Stellenbosch and Paarl in the 1970s. There he established the first classic Médoc-blend plantings, applying traditional French strategies in the vineyards and cellar. These were the first commercial plantings of merlot, malbec, cabernet franc and petit verdot and the Estate Reserve was the country's first Bordeaux blend.

Franschhoek

Settled by French Huguenots before the end of the seventeenth century, this region has only recently become a meaningful player on the Cape wine scene. The most obvious reason for this is that its cooler climate placed it at a disadvantage for most of the twentieth century when the industry was driven by the KWV's minimum wine price arrangements. Since payments were made on the basis of litres of wine at 10 percent alcohol, the areas that flourished were those with enough water and sunshine to stretch the crop and pump up the sugars. As viticulture became less lucrative, farmers turned to orchards for an income. The town itself was also relatively inaccessible. While Paarl lies on the national road between Cape Town and Johannesburg, Franschhoek is literally tucked away in a valley nearly 15 miles (25 km) to the east. Even tourists seemed to find Franschhoek a town too far.

The 1980s saw vast changes, many brought about by exactly those elements that had retarded its development. The discovery that quality wine production was not dependent on the KWV's purchase criteria focused attention on cooler regions. Franschhoek's unspoilt charm attracted wealthy investors for whom the extra distance from Cape Town was a positive advantage. The growers banded together under the banner of the Vignerons of Franschhoek. The village soon developed a more overt Huguenot/Cape Dutch/French feel as the old farm names were revived.

The success of the marketing efforts of small growers in this area led to an enormous increase in land prices and a proliferation of regional wines. Some of the producers who initially delivered their grapes to the cooperative for vinification have now built their own cellars; other long-established properties have replaced orchards with vineyards and today Franschhoek boasts some of the country's best-known wines.

BELLINGHAM

Established 1693 *Owner* Kangra Holdings (Graham Beck)
Production 350,000 cases *Vineyard area* 321 acres (130 ha)

Bellingham's name has become synonymous with two of South Africa's top-selling bottled wines. The property was owned by Bernard Podlashuk from the 1940s through to the 1960s and his

interest in wine led to the development of several products that came to dominate the more sophisticated wine trade. His Premier Grand Cru was a blended dry white that was, for much of the 1960s and 1970s, the only wine drunk at business luncheons. His other, called Johannisberger, was a fragrant semi-sweet late-harvest style. He created a trademark gable-shaped bottle for it and its sales grew to such an extent that the fruit had to be sourced from vineyards across the whole of the Western Cape.

The Bellingham brand name was acquired by Union Wine, one of the smaller national wholesalers, which was bought by Graham Beck. (Beck already owned a wine farm near Robertson and subsequently took over another wholesaler, Douglas Green of Paarl.) In due course Beck rationalized his various business arrangements: the Bellingham name now belongs to new shareholders, who own the merged Union Wine/Douglas Green wholesale operations and trade as DGB. Beck still owns the original Bellingham farm, where he has built a superb red wine cellar. The wines produced there are sold as Graham Beck Coastal (to distinguish them from the Robertson wines, which trade as Graham Beck Robertson). Though few, if any, of the Graham

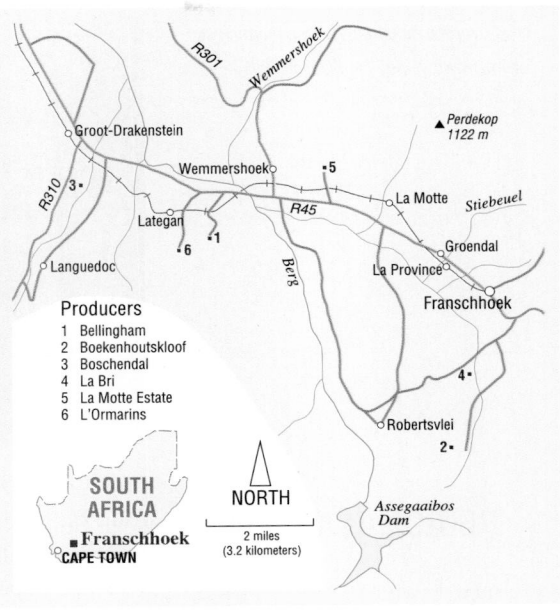

The grand Manor House, Boschendal Estate, near Franschhoek's boundaries with Paarl and Stellenbosch.

Mist over the mountains as the morning sun warms rows of vines in Franschhoek.

REGIONAL DOZEN

QUALITY WINES

Agusta Wines Chardonnay
Boekenhoutskloof Syrah
Boschendal Shiraz
Eikenhof Cabernet Sauvignon
La Motte Estate Millennium
L'Ormarins Cabernet
  Sauvignon

BEST VALUE WINES

Dieu Donne Chardonnay
Eikenhof Bush Vine Sémillon
Franschhoek Vineyards
  Pinotage
Mont Rochelle Blanc de Blanc
L'Ormarins Rhine Riesling
Von Ortloff Chardonnay

Flags wave in welcome at prestigious L'Ormarins Estate, Franschhoek.

Beck Coastal wines comprise pure Franschhoek fruit, the cellar supplies the largest volume of premium-quality wine produced in the region: very fine Cabernet Franc, Pinotage, Shiraz and Cabernet Sauvignon (mainly sold under a Reserve label) are the winery's flagship varietals, though the whites—made in an adjacent cellar—include a most creditable Sauvignon Blanc.

BOEKENHOUTSKLOOF

Established 1996 *Owner* Newcom Investments (Pty) Ltd
Production 18,000 cases *Vineyard area* 37 acres (15 ha)

This newcomer, one of the smaller producers who enjoy a reputation, has acquired something like cult status. Superripe fruit and dense rich tannins are the hallmarks of Marc Kent's Syrah and Cabernet, while his Sémillon serves to remind South African wine drinkers that traditionally this was the valley's most successful varietal.

BOSCHENDAL, GROOT DRAKENSTEIN

Established 1976 *Owner* Anglo American Corporation (Amfarms) *Production* 205,000 cases *Vineyard area* 1,235 acres (500 ha)

Located near the boundaries of Paarl and Stellenbosch, Boschendal came to prominence in the early 1980s through the sale of South Africa's first blanc de noir, which had immediate appeal for a wide segment of the market. The cellar is now better known for its white wines, most of which are respectable, rather than exceptional examples of a standard range of varietal and blended wines. Initially classified as an estate, its commercial success made the purchase of non-estate grapes almost inevitable. While most of its vineyards are situated within the area, it now buys fruit from growers throughout the Coastal Region.

LA BRI

Established 1694 *Owner* R. Hamilton *Production* 12,000 cases *Vineyard area* 50 acres (20 ha)

The late Michael Trull, who acquired La Bri Vineyards after a career in advertising, played a leading role in their transformation. He persuaded the local cooperative to vinify his grapes separately, marketing the wine initially under the name of La Bri Vineyards. This provoked the wrath of the estate-wine producers. They argued that since there was no verification that the wine in the bottle emanated from his farm, he was pretending to a site-specific appellation in contravention of the estate-wine regulations.

The authorities insisted that he remove the word "vineyards" from his label but could not prohibit him from selling wine under the La Bri trademark. Other growers profited from the same arrangement and within a few years there were at least ten Franschhoek farm names in the trade, all branded products vinified on behalf of the growers by the cooperative.

LA MOTTE ESTATE

Established 1695 *Owner* Hanneli Koegelenberg (née Rupert)
Production 15,000 cases *Vineyard area* 257 acres (104 ha)

The estate makes some very good reds, of which the Shiraz and the Médoc blend (sold as Millennium) are consistently the best examples. Both of the old Rupert family properties have been beautifully restored, and both vinify and bottle their wines on the estate.

L'ORMARINS ESTATE

Established 1694 *Owner* Anthonij Rupert *Production* NA
Vineyard area 494 acres (200 ha)

One of two Rupert family-owned properties, this producer offers a range of quality red and white wines in a reasonable volume. The other property is La Motte Estate.

Stellenbosch

Some 30 miles (50 km) northeast of Cape Town, Stellenbosch boasts several properties identified in land grants made in the last two decades of the seventeenth century. While few pretend to three centuries of viticulture, several have been associated with quality winemaking for much of this time. The early years of these farms were undoubtedly primitive: notwithstanding their proximity to the small settlement, the countryside was savage. Lions, elephants and hippos abounded and it took more than a century to hunt them out. There are still leopards in the Helderberg mountains, the backdrop to some of the region's most prestigious estates. The depredations of baboons in the high-lying vineyards are a real cost to many producers.

The area is divided into several sub-regions, each of which experiences a distinctly different climate. Nearest to False Bay, from Faure to Somerset West and running toward Stellenbosch itself, maritime influences prevail. The Helderberg is the boundary along the eastern flank, with vineyards reaching up 1,000–1,300 feet (300–400 m) above sea level. Sites at the higher altitudes lie in decomposed granitic soils, while those closest to the sea along the plain are sandy/alluvial and sometimes become waterlogged.

Stretching southwest from Stellenbosch toward Cape Town are several ridges. Those closest to the sea offer the coolest sites; those in more protected valleys running west and north, are home mainly to red wines. Devon Valley and the Bottelary Hills are the major sub-regions to the west of the town lying along these axes. The soils are often richer, redder and deeper, with oakleaf, hutton and estcourt grapes predominating.

To the east of the town a similar pattern of ridges, cliffs and valleys emerges. The sites to the south of the Simonsberg include Ida's Valley, Jonkershoek and the steep climb up the Helshoogte Pass; to the east of the Simonsberg, and running north toward Paarl, is the Muldersvlei bowl and Klapmutskop. The more protected locations tend also to be farther from False Bay; they are noticeably warmer, but still cooler than the Paarl vineyards a mere 10 miles (15 km) away.

Stellenbosch soils vary considerably. Almost all are acidic and it is now standard vineyard practice to add a great deal of lime at the time of replant-

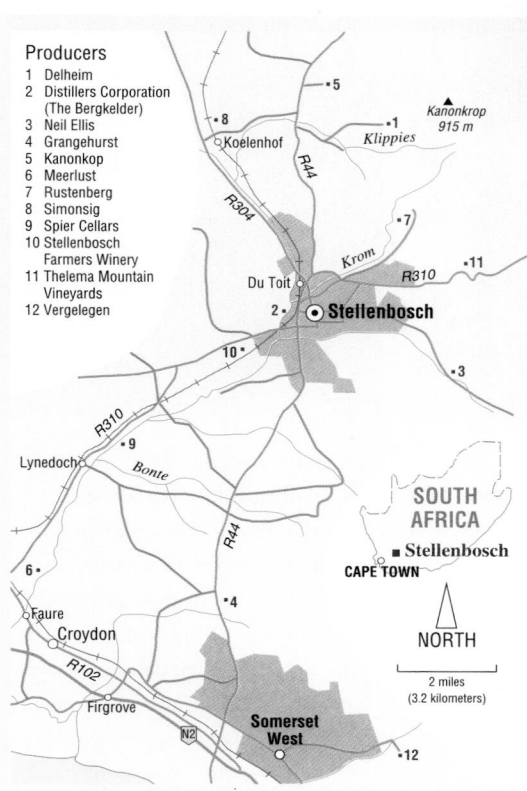

The cellar at Uitkyk Estate, one of the region's oldest and best-known estates, now owned by the Bergkelder's shareholders.

ing. Within a very small area there can be several different soil types, each with different water-retention properties. Uneven ripening of the grapes has its origins as much in geology as in canopy management and viticultural practices.

Newly planted vineyard at Kanonkop Estate.

*Wrought-iron detail on Oom Samie General
Store in Dorp Street, Stellenbosch.*

There are now some 80 wineries in the Stellenbosch region. Ten years ago the number was
roughly half. Given the flux and excitement, it is
easy to understand why the area is regarded as the
showcase of Cape wine. Some of the big brands of
yesteryear, although falling behind, still produce
creditable wine; the newcomers must work twice
as hard simply to get noticed. Long-established
contract growers suddenly decide to build their
own cellars and make new wines from old plantings. Investors from other industries acquire run-
down properties and breathe new life into them.
In this sense Stellenbosch lies at the real heart of
new-era South African wine.

DELHEIM WINES, SIMONSBERG
Established 1930 *Owners* H.O. Hoheisen and M.H. Sperling
Production 66,000 cases *Vineyard area* 371 acres (150 ha)

On the northern side of the town, Delheim is still
owned and managed by the people who developed
its bottled wine business through the Stellenbosch
Wine Route a quarter of a century ago. Like
Simonsig, its survival can be attributed to hard
work, good management, a strong retail presence
to build cellar-door sales and a shamelessly high
profile in the trade. Spatz Sperling—who is only
now relinquishing control of the day-to-day management of the business (his partner is active,
though retired, aged over 90)—was as happy to
win an award for the worst-taste wine label in the
industry as he was to take home a gold medal at
the national wine show. Recent improvements,
mainly in red-wine production, have encouraged
Sperling to draw a more marked distinction
between the popular and prestige side of his
business. Using separate vineyards across the valley

at Klapmutskop, he aims to establish the Vera
Cruz estate for his premium wines, retaining the
Delheim name for the tourist trade.

DISTILLERS CORPORATION (THE BERGKELDER)
One Stellenbosch wholesaler to emerge as a key
player in the wine market is Distillers Corporation.
It played an important role in transforming the
industry from branded to more *terroir*-based
products by entering into joint ventures with
individual farmers. Critics have rightly observed
that this approach involved a very liberal interpretation of the estate-wine concept: while the property's name appears on the bottle (in compliance
with the regulations of the 1973 legislation) most
of the elevage is performed not in the farm's cellar,
but at the Bergkelder's premises. From the wine
producer's point of view, this partnership arrangement has not always proved successful. The Bergkelder's effective control of all the arrangements,
marketing, sales and even disposal of surplus, cost
many of them their independence. Crippled by a
disappointingly slow flow of funds, several have
been forced to sell. Many of the region's oldest
and best-known properties, including Alto, Le
Bonheur and Uitkyk, are now owned—directly or
indirectly—by the Bergkelder's shareholders.

The company has also been an active player
in the non-estate wine market. Among its more
premium brands are several *méthode champenoise*
sparkling wines, all now produced at a special
facility in Devon Valley known as the House of
J. C. Le Roux. Its still wines include Fleur du Cap,
Stelleryck, Drostyhof and Cellar Cask—the last-
mentioned the pioneering bag-in-the-box brand
that revolutionized medium-priced and middle-
class wine consumption in South Africa in 1979.

Stellenbosch has long been associated with the
major wholesale producing merchants; their showcase wineries, head offices and business-support
organizations are all located in and around the
town. However, the change in the structure of the
wine trade in the past two decades has reduced
their importance in the community. Many farms
that, in the past, sold all their grapes in bulk to the
wholesale trade have now built their own cellars
and consumer interest has shifted from big brands
to these more boutique products.

The producing wholesalers did not give up
without a fight: they treated all attempts by small
producers to reduce their dependence on the
wholesale merchants as an act of betrayal. Crude
bullying tactics were widely employed, usually

involving threats never to make another bulk purchase—of grapes or wine—if the grower in question sold even one bottle of wine under the farm's label. This same strategy was also extended to the cooperatives—source of much of the blending material used for the wholesalers' brands. These strategies undoubtedly retarded the growth of South Africa's boutique and estate wine business. In the 1960s only a handful of producers were willing to risk the cost and cash-flow implications of shifting immediately from bulk to cellar-door sales. Three of them (Simonsig, Delheim and Spier) founded the Stellenbosch Wine Route, correctly identifying wine tourism as a key element in ensuring their own survival. Moving mainly into uncharted territory, they developed tasting rooms, trade distribution and retail selling networks.

NEIL ELLIS WINES, JONKERSHOEK VALLEY

Established 1990 *Owners* Neil Ellis Trust, Oude Nektar, London Stone (Pty) Ltd *Production* 35,000 cases *Vineyard area* 237 acres (96 ha), plus 74 acres (30 ha) elsewhere

A relative newcomer, Neil Ellis is a site-specific *négociant*-winemaker operation. Ellis worked as a cellarmaster and contract winemaker on several properties in the 1970s and 1980s before branching into his own business. Sourcing grapes from growers whose sites and practices satisfied his criteria, Ellis ran something of an itinerant winemaking set-up until he met up with Hans Peter Schröder. The latter had recently acquired the Oude Nektar Estate with its somewhat rundown vineyards and cellar.

There turned out to be more than a synergy of mutual needs and a partnership has been established that has changed the rankings of Cape producers. Ellis's wines now dominate the awards. His Reserve reds (mostly from the Oude Nektar vineyards) represent pretty much the acme of current Stellenbosch achievement while his regular range is almost as impressive. Most of the reds are made from Stellenbosch fruit, but there are white wines from Elgin and a sauvignon blanc from Groenekloof on the West Coast, near Darling.

GRANGEHURST, HELDERBERG-STELLENBOSCH

Established 1992 *Owner* Jeremy Walker *Production* 5,500 cases *Vineyard area* Buys in grapes from selected contractors

Not far from Vergelegen, but with far less investment, is the minuscule Grangehurst cellar. Perhaps more than anyone else in the region Walker has come to epitomize boutique wine production. In less than a decade, Grangehurst has won more

five-star ratings from South Africa's *WINE* magazine than any other producer. The focus is one red wine, partly from the farm's own vineyard blocks, partly from contracted growers in whose viticulture Walker naturally takes considerable interest. While Grangehurst's first few vintages were produced in an old squash court—a new permutation in the French fashion of *vin de garage*—commercial success now funds an expansion program. This may not produce a vast increase in the available quantities of the cabernet sauvignon, cabernet-merlot and pinotage that make up the basic range but it will at least ease the bottlenecks that threatened wine production in the early days.

KANONKOP ESTATE

Established 1910 *Owners* J. and P. Krige *Production* 30,000 cases *Vineyard area* 346 acres (140 ha)

Almost alone Kanonkop estate established pinotage as a varietal worthy of international repute; it is also very much one of the country's putative 'first growths.' The property was originally part of Uitkyk, so can lay claim to several centuries of wine production along the northeastern slopes of the Simonsberg. In the mid-twentieth century the Sauer family (father and son were both Cabinet ministers with a special interest in the wine industry) established bushvine vineyards with planting material from the original pinot noir–cinsaut crossing. From its first commercial bottlings, the 1973 vintage, Kanonkop was clearly a leading red-wine site with a particular potential for dense, almost Rhône-like pinotage. However, it was only in the late 1980s that winemaker Beyers Truter invested the varietal with the kind of vinification and wood aging that it needed to bring out the fruit, concentration and complexity of which the grape is clearly capable. Successive vintages of show-stopping quality—especially among the cuvées reserved for the Cape Winemakers Guild annual auction—have produced an international market for this wine and for the varietal. Truter is also the force behind the industry's Pinotage Producers' Association, which holds an annual competition to determine which are the best wines of the season.

Kanonkop's reputation does not rest solely on the quality of its Guild Pinotage. The regular cuvée is often as impressive (though

Stellenbosch cabernet sauvignon: Jordan 1993 and the limited release boutique Grangehurst 1993.

Vineyards on the slopes of the Simonsberg.

The sandy soil at Laibach Vineyards is no impediment to the forward-thinking Laibach family with their high-tech emphasis.

never as expensive) and its other reds, notably the Cabernet and the Paul Sauer Fleur (a cabernet blend), sell well in the super-premium segment of the market. The latter, incidentally, collected the Pichon Longueville Comtesse de Lalande Trophy at the 1999 International Wine and Spirit Competition for the best blended red on show.

MEERLUST ESTATE, FAURE-STELLENBOSCH
Established 1692 *Owner* Hannes Myburgh *Production* 45,000 cases *Vineyard area* 371 acres (150 ha)

Owned by the Myburgh family since the eighteenth century, Meerlust is both part of the ancient history of the Cape winelands and a child of the modern era. It enjoys an enviable reputation and commands consistently high prices for its cabernet-based reds, largely the fulfillment of the vision of the late Nico Myburgh. In the early 1970s he grasped two essential concepts that he rightly believed would dominate the industry as it moved toward the new millennium. The first was that farms selling grapes, rather than wine, could never hope to escape the tyranny of the middleman; the second was that wines of the future would have to meet international expectations and keep pace with world trends.

Myburgh decided to market wines under the Meerlust label (which he did through the Bergkelder from 1975). He also determined that the logical blending partner for his cabernet sauvignon was merlot and set about sourcing the appropriate planting material. He is credited with producing the country's first Bordeaux blend (though Billy Hofmeyr at Welgemeend beat him by a vintage). However, with a bigger marketing infrastructure, greater financial resources and more vineyards, he swiftly came to dominate the category. The launch of his first cabernet–merlot blend, the 1980 Rubicon, was hailed as a great leap forward for Cape wine: massive demand, limited supplies and the inevitable price squeeze that followed all enhanced its reputation. Nearly two decades later, Meerlust's right to command super-premium prices is never questioned. Each release of Rubicon (or Cabernet Sauvignon or Merlot

On the road to Delheim Wines, one of the three founder members of the Stellenbosch Wine Route, which has done so much to develop the wine industry in South Africa.

for that matter) is sold on allocation. Retailers and restaurateurs market Meerlust accordingly. The fact that the wines hardly ever perform well in shows or blind tastings has no measurable impact on the brand's position. Laid back, unflashy, lean by new-world standards, not obviously dense or concentrated, they are the heirs to Nico Myburgh's vision and cellarmaster Giorgio Dalla Cia's unwavering consistency.

RUSTENBERG WINES
Established 1682 *Owner* S. Barlow *Production* 40,000 cases *Vineyard area* 272 acres (110 ha)

One of the leading players under the Stellenbosch appellation, Rustenberg enjoys a long-established reputation, with records showing wine production spanning more than three centuries. Since the 1940s the property has been owned by the Barlow family. By the mid-1980s the farm (which in those days traded its white wines under the Schoongezicht label) was widely regarded as one of the Cape's "first growths." Then followed a decline, with a succession of poor vintages in the early 1990s. A change of winemaker and a spectacularly revamped cellar has resulted in a series of international awards. New Zealander Rod Easthope, who worked the 1996–99 vintages, cleaned up the production while Simon Barlow is now in active control of management. Given the speed and intensity of the turnaround, there is no doubt that Rustenberg deserves its current front ranking.

SIMONSIG ESTATE
Established 1953 *Owners* Malan family *Production* 160,000 cases *Vineyard area* 667 acres (270 ha)

The Simonsig estate was more than a wine-route pioneer, it was the first South African cellar to make a bottle-fermented sparkling wine and it has been in the avante-garde of most of the country's vineyard and cellar developments. The business grew because the Malans combined winemaking competence, innovative marketing and strong financial skills. When times were tough they offered house brands and second labels. They elected to operate as a wine estate, using the certification system—with its promise of site-specific viticulture—as an additional marketing tool. They participated in every high-profile selling opportunity, from the annual Nederburg Auction to the Cape Winemakers Guild sale. The breadth of their range (at one stage they offered about 20 different wines) has enabled them to fill every niche in the spectrum.

SPIER CELLARS

Established 1692 *Owners* Hydro Holdings *Production*
17,000 cases *Vineyard area* 138 acres (56 ha)

Spier, the third member of the founding Wine
Route triumvirate, never matched the commercial
success of Simonsig and Delheim. Even before Niel
Joubert's death, the farm's finances necessitated the
sale of tracts of vineyard. The core property was
sold to a syndicate led by Dick Enthoven. It has
now become a tourism feature on the Stellenbosch
landscape, with conference facilities, restaurants
and an open-air theatre. A small winery continues
to process grapes. The Jouberts, however, sold the
Spier name with another of their properties, so the
wines produced at Enthoven's winery are sold
under a variety of names, including the slightly
misleading IV Spears brand.

STELLENBOSCH FARMERS WINERY

Established 1925 *Owners* 30 percent each Rembrandt,
KWV, SAB; 10 percent public domain *Production* 31.6
million gallons (120 million l) *Vineyard area* 2,500 acres
(1,000 ha), plus bought-in grapes

For much of the twentieth century the reputation
of the region rested on the wholesale producing
merchants, the most important undoubtedly the
Stellenbosch Farmers Winery. Formed by William
Charles Winshaw, an American, the company's
early fortunes were somewhat erratic. It pioneered
many of the brands that comprised the unfortified
wine market in South Africa until the 1970s.
Names such as Grand Mousseux (still one of the
largest-selling sparkling wines), Château Libertas
(a popular dry red table wine first produced in the
1930s), Zonnebloem, Tassenberg, Lanzerac and
Lieberstein are all part of the more recent history
of the Cape wine industry. Much of the bulk wine
that went into these brands was sourced outside
the Stellenbosch region, particularly when the wine
market took off in the 1960s. In the minds of
consumers, however, especially until the 1973
wine-of-origin legislation disabused them of these
illusions, there was a direct correlation between
their favorite brands and the town of Stellenbosch.

THELEMA MOUNTAIN VINEYARDS

Established 1983 *Owners* McLean Family Trust and G. Webb
Production 25,000 cases *Vineyard area* 124 acres (50 ha)

A comparative newcomer, Thelema was founded
by Gyles and Barbara Webb and swiftly eclipsed
most of its competitors. Situated at the top of the
Helshoogte Pass, which separates Stellenbosch
from Paarl, Thelema was all fruit trees when the

Webbs discovered it. Modern
vineyard preparation, proper and
consistent viticultural practices
and inspired winemaking have all
combined to produce this cutting-
edge brand. A decade after the
release of its first vintage Thelema
had won every award of significance in the country. Webb's
disarming modesty belies one of
the most thoughtful and insightful
minds in the Cape wine industry.

VERGELEGEN, HELDERBERG

Established 1700 *Owners* Anglo
American Farms Ltd *Production* 65,000
cases *Vineyard area* 255 acres (103 ha)

The estate is not far from Meerlust, close to the coast and with a
history at least as ancient, although there is no real
record of production for most of the twentieth
century. It was founded by Willem Adriaan van
der Stel soon after he succeeded his father as
governor. He quickly turned it into a showcase
property, alienating the free burghers with whom
he competed shamelessly for the right to supply
ships rounding the Cape. After an extensive legal
battle during which the Dutch East India Company sided with the citizens of the colony, he was
sent back to Holland, his career in ruins. The
property itself was divided (some of those who had
been most vocal in opposing him were direct
beneficiaries) and the estate became a mere farming operation at the foot of the Helderberg.

Since the present owners took over in 1987,
vast amounts have been spent on restoring the area
around the homestead: a modern, multi-level
winery has been sunk into the crest of a nearby hill
and new vineyards have been established on sites
where the best *terroir* is not compromised by
undue exposure to the often gale-force winds
blowing off False Bay. These investments are now
paying handsome dividends: in recent years the
winery has collected an enviable number of
awards. Under current winemaker André van
Rensburg the wines have come into their own:
sauvignon blancs of great intensity, a chardonnay
with real palate weight, and some very promising
young reds. It is obviously too soon to say that
Vergelegen is assured a place among the Cape's top
wineries but it is clear that cynics who claimed
that the site was too exposed and windswept have
been proved wrong.

*Stainless-steel fermentation tanks at
Vergelegen, Stellenbosch.*

REGIONAL DOZEN

QUALITY WINES

Neil Ellis Shiraz Reserve
Grangehurst Cabernet Merlot
Kanonkop Pinotage Reserve
Rustenberg Peter Barlow
Thelema Chardonnay Reserve
De Trafford Shiraz

BEST VALUE WINES

L'Avenir L'Ami Simon
    Red Blend
Bouwland Cabernet Merlot
Brampton Sauvignon Blanc
Delheim Shiraz
Jordan Chardonnay
Morgenhof Chenin Blanc

Robertson–Bonnievale

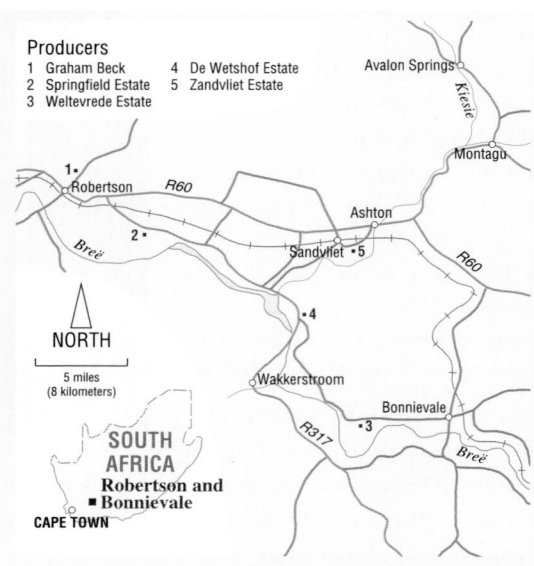

The Robertson–Bonnievale region, less than two hours' drive from Cape Town, is an area in transition. The commercial success of the appellation's front-runners is encouraging many of the bulk-grape farmers to look to their own vinification, and to take on their own marketing. Given the extensive replanting programs undertaken by the leading producers in the past five years, it is fair to assume that both product profile and brand leaders will change dramatically in the next decade.

The region was traditionally a brandy and fortified wine zone, a result both of its climate and the economics of the wine industry. The semi-desert inland areas lie beyond a cordon of mountains that shields them from much of the rainfall of the coastal region. Irrigation water from the

Many of the older wineries have artifacts, such as these beautifully carved barrels, dating from earlier times.

Breede and Hex rivers has turned the region into a market garden: much of the country's best fruit is produced in these fertile valleys.

Until the construction of the du Toitskloof tunnel, the mountain ranges were as much a psychological as a physical barrier. The apparent inaccessibility of the inland areas to residents of the Cape Peninsula limited the prospects of a retail wine trade, forcing producers to deal with regional and national wholesalers. The result was a bulk wine and spirits trade in which even the best growers could not imagine themselves independent producers of bottled wine.

The increased demand for table wine in the 1970s, enabled producers in Robertson and Bonnievale to prove that the region enjoyed prospects that wholesalers, mostly based in Stellenbosch and Paarl, had failed to recognize. Despite the warm daytime temperatures during the harvest season, the diurnal range was substantial, allowing the vines ample recovery time. Properly managed water supplies could produce appropriate controlled-stress conditions. Cold winters ensured a real period of dormancy. Soil properties were also potentially better than in more fashionable areas.

GRAHAM BECK WINES, ROBERTSON
Established 1983 *Owner* Graham Beck *Production* 150,000 cases *Vineyard area* 432 acres (175 ha)

Graham Beck's Robertson operation showcases the best of the new-generation wines in the region. Initially dedicated to Cap Classique (*méthode champenoise*) production, it slowly widened its range to offer red and white wines in several categories. Branded blends, such as Railroad Red and Waterside White have now been superseded by premium varietal wines. A shiraz—marketed as The Ridge Shiraz (partly to distinguish it from the generic wine from the Coastal Winery)—has already collected several awards.

But for all its recent successes with reds, the Graham Beck Robertson operation is still strongly identified with its bubblies. There are several cuvées, including an experimental sparkling pinotage, inspired by the sparkling shiraz of Australian producers such as Seppelts. The more standard fizz is still oak-fermented, with even the bottom-of-the-range assured of two years on lees. The winery at Robertson also produces one of the Cape's best and most popular muscadels.

SPRINGFIELD ESTATE, ROBERTSON

Established 1995 *Owner* Abrie Bruwer *Production* 40,000 cases *Vineyard area* 395 acres (160 ha)

A relative newcomer to the bottled-wine trade, the farm until recently sold its wines in bulk. But a succession of intense sauvignons followed by a wild yeast fermented Chardonnay have brought custom to the growing estate-wine business. Abrie Bruwer is something of a maverick, perfectly willing to stake a great deal on his intuition for anticipating market trends. He is now replanting vast tracts of the property. The first vintages of his cabernet sauvignon have been elegant, rather than concentrated, and suggest that, with older vineyards he will be in a position to match the best reds from the area.

WELTEVREDE ESTATE, ROBERTSON–BONNIEVALE

Established 1926 *Owner* Lourens Jonker *Production* 33,000 cases *Vineyard area* 250 acres (100 ha)

Like most other properties in the region, Weltevrede once focused solely on white and fortified wines. Recent plantings of cabernet sauvignon and merlot indicate a change in direction. KWV chairman Jonker has always been regarded as one of the area's innovators—he launched a wood-aged white wine as far back as the 1970s when most of his colleagues were seeking to capture only primary fruit. Good chardonnay, concentrated rieslings and an array of fortified muscats comprise the better wines in the range.

DE WETSHOF ESTATE, ROBERTSON

Established 1947 *Owner* Danie De Wet *Production* 35,000 cases *Vineyard area* 371 acres (150 ha)

Dedication, a regional spirit of togetherness and perhaps an innate sense of competition has produced a determination to outperform the better-established appellations. In the past 25 years several wineries have emerged, some with a stronger presence on the export rather than the domestic market. Chief among these has been De Wetshof, energetically driven by Danie and Lesca De Wet. When Danie returned from studying in Germany in the early 1970s, most of the cellar's wines were sold in bulk, with a token range sold under the estate label through the Bergkelder's partnership scheme. Public perception of the brand shifted after a replanting program, focused on

Walls of wine in a 300-year-old cellar.

internationally recognized premium varietals (and where these were not available, Danie joined the rest of the industry in a widespread illicit import program). By the second half of the 1980s he had a significant percentage of the total industry plantings of chardonnay. Success in the Diners Club Winemaker of the Year award, a well-managed separation from the Bergkelder partnership, and extensive international marketing have all played their role. Today the cellar is the undisputed success story of the region. Its best wines are generally held to be chardonnays, offered in a range of styles from unoaked to wood-fermented and barrel-aged. Surprisingly, the estate also produces a couple of very fine rieslings, one marketed as Mine d'Or, with mosel-like acidity masking the sugar, the other a botrytised noble late-harvest.

ZANDVLIET ESTATE, ASHTON

Established 1867 *Owners* Paul and Dan de Wet *Production* 75,000 cases *Vineyard area* 363 acres (147 ha)

Distant cousins Paul and Dan de Wet at nearby Zandvliet are widely regarded as the region's red wine pioneers. In the 1970s they planted shiraz along the banks of Cogman's River and made a light easy-drinking red which at least served to remind wine drinkers that the region could produce more than simple whites. More recently the red wine vineyards have been upgraded and replanted; the best are now on the limestone-rich Kalkveld slopes. The result of these efforts is impressive: dense, full-flavored shiraz wines, some vinified with French oak, others with American oak, all sold under a premium Zandvliet Kalkveld label. There is also a creditable chardonnay and a great-value second brand sold as Astonvale.

REGIONAL DOZEN

QUALITY WINES

Graham Beck Blanc de Blancs
    Méthode Champenoise
Graham Beck The Ridge
    Shiraz
Springfield Chardonnay
    Methode Ancien
Weltevrede Oude Weltevreden
    Chardonnay
Weltevrede Cape Muscat
Zandvliet Kalkveld Shiraz

BEST VALUE WINES

Astonvale Chardonnay
    (Zandvliet Estate)
Bon Courage Red Muscadel
Long Mountain Gecko Ridge
    Chardonnay
Long Mountain Merlot Shiraz
Nuy Muscadel
De Wetshof Estate Mine
    d'Or Riesling

Other South African Regions

DURBANVILLE

Among the scattered appellations outside the established premium wine areas are several of the Cape's best, and best-known, producers. Durbanville, just northwest of Cape Town, used to be home to many growers before urban sprawl and rising land prices brought in real estate developers. Amazingly, in the past five years, there has been a resurgence of interest in wine production, although on a boutique scale. Some of the cellars, such as Altydgedacht and Meerendal, are long-standing survivors; others, such as Bloemendal and Durbanville Hills are relatively new.

Proximity to the West Coast ensures cooler-than-expected daytime temperatures, while the deep soils of the Durbanville Hills, a mere 20 minutes from Cape Town, have great water-retention

Rocky ground makes cultivation difficult at Twee Jonge Gezellen Estate, Tulbagh.

properties. Meerendal has long been associated with one of the country's best-known shiraz wines, and as early as the 1970s produced good pinotage. Altydgedacht, owned by the Parker family for several generation, is another of the region's long-established estates. For years the only cellar in the Cape to offer a barbera, it also enjoyed a reputation for its gewürztraminer. Cabernet sauvignon and chardonnay have done well more recently.

DURBANVILLE HILLS
Established 1998 *Owners* Distillers Corp (7 farms) *Production* Not yet available *Vineyard area* Grapes from the 7 owner farms

Probably the most important development in the area has been the Durbanville Hills cellar, which crushes grapes from several growers as well as many of the established producers. The winery will breathe life into the region and will help to ensure that Durbanville fruit retains its appellation, instead of vanishing into an amorphous "coastal region" blend. Early releases show fine chardonnay and sauvignon blanc, with equally impressive reds waiting in the wings.

SWARTLAND AND TULBAGH

This traditional West Coast region is also seeing something of a boom: five years ago a few cooperatives and one estate represented all the productive capacity. Land prices are rising as winemakers from elsewhere discover the virtues of this area's relatively cool-climate fruit. A few new wineries have sprung up, and replanting programs are replacing non-premium varietals with sauvignon blanc, merlot and shiraz.

ALLESVERLOREN ESTATE, RIEBEEK WEST
Established 1872 *Owners* D. and F. Malan *Production* NA *Vineyard area* 395 acres (160 ha)

The name of this, the region's longest-established estate, literally means "all is lost." Located between Malmesbury and Riebeek Kasteel, it has enjoyed an enviable reputation for shiraz and port for most of the past two decades. The 1982 shiraz won a trophy at Vinexpo and the 1996 won the Diners Club Winemaker of the Year award. Until the rise of drier Portuguese-style ports, Allesverloren's version was the industry benchmark.

SPICE ROUTE WINE COMPANY, SWARTLAND
Established 1997 *Owners* Charles Back, Jabulani Ntshangase, John Platter and Gyles Webb *Production* 25,000 cases *Vineyard area* 450 acres (182 ha)

Originally established as a joint venture by four of South Africa's best-known names in wine, Spice Route has its own vineyards, but also sources fruit from neighboring farms. Early releases reveal great concentration, with a depth and complexity that has eluded many of the best wines from longer-established appellations.

TWEE JONGE GEZELLEN ESTATE, TULBAGH
Established 1710 *Owners* Krone family *Production* 40,000 cases *Vineyard area* 677 acres (274 ha)

Tulbagh is one of the country's most beautiful and least spoilt Cape Dutch villages. In the 1960s and 1970s the appellation was considered one of the best sources of white grapes in the country. This estate, one of the oldest, has been in the Krone family for generations. Current owner/winemaker Nicky Krone anticipated the growing market for sophisticated fizz and constructed a special Cap Classique cellar. His premium brand, a 50/50 blend of chardonnay and pinot noir made with no added preservatives, sells under the Krone Borealis label.

KLEIN KAROO

The town of Calitzdorp has come to be known as the port capital of South Africa. Scene of the country's annual port festival, it is home to several of the Cape's best port cellars, including Axe Hill, Boplaas and Die Krans.

BEAUMONT WINES, WALKER BAY
Established 1994 *Owners* Raoul and Jayne Beaumont *Production* 9,000 cases *Vineyard area* 119 acres (48 ha)

The Beaumonts of Beaumont Wines have somehow managed to extend the cool-climate message to a host of non-Burgundian varietals. Their pinotage is highly regarded, so are a couple of their chenin cuvées. Cutting-edge or rustic however, the Beaumonts and others in the region all have in common a dedication to produce wines of great personality at the limit of commercial viticulture in the Cape.

PAUL CLUVER ESTATE, ELGIN
Established 1996 *Owner* Paul Cluver *Production* 8,000 cases *Vineyard area* 133 acres (54 ha)

No review of the Cape's vineyards would be complete without an assessment of the vineyards and cellars around Elgin and Hermanus. One of the undisputed cool-climate zones, its history of premium viticulture is fairly recent. Elgin, for example, was famous for its apple orchards, though now Paul Cluver's cellar produces fine, elegant whites and has some promising young pinots still in cask. Together with the workers of the nearby forestry village, Cluver, Trevor Steyn and the forestry company have also developed another winery selling chardonnay and pinot noir under the Thandi label.

Perhaps the best-known cool-climate vineyards in South Africa are those adjacent to Walker Bay.

The region was really developed and promoted by Tim Hamilton Russell in the 1980s. His own cellar, as well as the breakaway Bouchard Finlayson, are widely regarded as the best exponents of pinot in the Cape.

GOEDVERTROUW ESTATE, WALKER BAY–BOT RIVER
Established 1984 *Owners* Arthur and Elreda Pillmann *Production* 1,000 cases *Vineyard area* 20 acres (8 ha)

Of several boutique wineries in the area, some, like Goedvertrouw estate, have a gently eccentric air about them. This is partly a result of their warm and friendly informality, partly a reflection of their dedication to natural and organic farming methods. The smallish production of these boutiques is no impediment to a strong export trade.

HAMILTON RUSSELL VINEYARDS, HERMANUS
Established 1976 *Owner* Anthony Hamilton Russell *Production* 15,000 cases *Vineyard area* 158 acres (64 ha)

Hamilton Russell, longtime head of the J. Walter Thompson advertising agency in South Africa, recognized—well before anyone else in the Cape—the importance of a slow and prolonged ripening season on fruit quality. He settled upon the Hemel-en-Aarde (literally Heaven and Earth) Valley near Hermanus and established vineyards on sites that did not even enjoy KWV production quotas. For years he battled with authorities for permission to farm grapes and make wine and was one of the first chardonnay and pinot producers in the Cape. Now, nearly 20 years later, while other cellars are often seen outperforming the Hamilton Russell wines, those who seek unflamboyance and restraint still regard them as industry classics.

Peter Finlayson (whose brother Walter founded Glen Carlou in Paarl) worked with Hamilton Russell in establishing the original vineyards and cellar of the Hemel-en-Aarde Valley. He subsequently set out to develop his own winery, funded by a consortium that included Burgundian Paul Bouchard—hence the Bouchard Finlayson name—and this is the second of the region's Pinot and Chardonnay specialists. Fruit for the cellar comes from Hemel-en-Aarde vineyards, as well as from Elgin and Villiersdorp. A spirit of friendly rivalry characterizes the two operations, though there is also a willingness to work together at events such as the annual Pinot Noir symposium.

The Red Hills area, near Calitzdorp, in Klein Karoo, is home to several of the Cape's best port cellars.

REGIONAL DOZEN

QUALITY WINES

Bouchard Finlayson Gaplin Peak Pinot Noir
Die Krans Vintage Reserve Port
Neil Ellis Elgin Chardonnay
Hamilton Russell Pinot Noir
KWV Cathedral Cellars Cabernet Franc
Spice Route Reserve Pinotage

BEST VALUE WINES

Darling Cellars Pinot Noir
Neil Ellis Groenekloof Sauvignon Blanc
Spice Route Andrew's Hope Red Blend
Spice Route Chenin Blanc
Swartland Wine Cellar Cabernet-Merlot Reserve
Swartland Wine Cellar Chardonnay

The Middle East

Brian Jordan

In all the countries of the Levant, including Syria and Jordan, wine production throughout the centuries has been affected to varying degrees by the rules of religious observance. Lebanon incorporates the biblical land of Canaan, famed for excellent wines. Throughout the Middle Ages wines from the Venetian ports of Sidon and the Tyre region were traded extensively, shipped alongside the legendary wines of Damascus. Production reached its peak period in Israel during the first four centuries AD when wine was exported all over the Roman world, even to the British Isles. Indeed, there was sometimes more wine than water and it had many uses: as medicine, for washing out houses, for dyeing clothes and for drinking. Estimates of consumption in Israel in ancient times are as high as 5–7 pints (3–4 l) a day for each person.

An Israeli flag marks the entrance to the vineyard at Mount Hermon.

ISRAEL

About four centuries of Moslem conquests (until 1000 AD) destroyed almost all of Israel's old vineyards, but the Crusaders found a few still operating and between 1100 and 1300 wine production actually increased again. In 1280 it was reported that "near Bethlehem there are still magnificent vines. The Moslems do not tend them, but the Christians make very good wine."

History

Commercial wine-production dates from Jewish re-population in the second half of the nineteenth century. Small household winepresses were in use to crush grapes bought from Arab vineyards in the surrounding hills. The first European varieties were planted in 1870 at the Mikveh Agricultural School, and Baron Edmund de Rothschild (at that time co-owner of Château Lafite and a sponsor of early Jewish pioneer settlement) had high hopes that viticulture would develop.

After the first harvest, Rothschild financed construction of two wineries at Richon le Zion (1889) for Judea and Zikhron Ya'akov (1892) for Samaria. Both were equipped with refrigeration, and both are still fully operational (owned by the giant Carmel Cooperative).

By the end of the century about half of Jewish land under cultivation was vineyard. The subsequent grape glut and wine surplus forced Rothschild to render further financial aid to compensate vineyard owners, who now uprooted vines and planted almonds, olives and citrus groves. In 1906 management of the two wine cellars was handed to farmers as the Carmel Cooperative.

Between the two World Wars Israel lost many export markets—USA to Prohibition, Russia through revolution, Egypt and the Middle East to Arab nationalism. When the state of Israel was founded in 1948 there were just 2,500 acres (1,000 ha) of vines and 14 wine cellars in the new nation. But despite success in major competition around the world, the wines were often categorized as "unusual," and Israel was thought a difficult country for wine production. However, in the past decade the Golan Heights Winery alone has won more than 30 Gold Medals and six international trophies at VinExpo, IWC, IWSC and Chicago. Gold Medals have also been collected by other producers such as Barkan, Segal, Tishbi and Carmel.

Landscape and climate

For a small country, Israel manages to encompass a variety of climate profiles. Volcanic-soil vineyards grow at up to 4,000 feet (1,200 m) in northern mountain regions, where snow is not unusual in winter. Here it is cool enough for sauvignon blanc and the serious production of sparkling wine. A Mediterranean climate gives a long, hot, dry spell from April to October and a short wet winter, ideal for serious quality production of European classic varieties. Much of Galilee is limestone soil, while coastal areas have well-drained sandy red soils with higher temperatures well suited to hot-climate vines.

Vines and wines

The unremarkable dabuki is Israel's only (alleged) surviving grape from biblical times. The most widely planted grape is emerald riesling, a riesling/muscadelle crossing by Professor Harold Olmo's University of California, Davis Campus (UCD). This is hugely popular on the domestic market, while UCD's other "hot-climate" variety, ruby cabernet, also exists in small quantities.

Other grapes planted mainly for volume wines include carignan and colombard plus one or two grapes developed locally at the Volcani Institute of Agricultural Research at Rehovot. One is argaman, from carignan crossed with Portuguese souzao; the other, roy, is a muscat of frontignan patriotically crossed with dabuki and named after Professor Roy Spiegel, who did the botanical work, but this variety is less popular.

Pruning the vines at one of Israel's outstanding vineyards, Golan Heights.

For quality wines Israel offers the world's best-known varieties: apart from the ubiquitous cabernet sauvignon, chardonnay and merlot, there's pinot noir for *méthode champenoise* sparkling wine, muscats (both sweet and dry), sauvignon blanc, gewürztraminer and riesling, cabernet franc, gamay, syrah, zinfandel, petite syrah. Experiments with barbera, nebbiolo, sangiovese and tempranillo are currently underway.

Wine laws

Israel's viticulture is divided into five regions:

Galilee (Galil in Israeli), embracing Lake Galilee, the Golan Heights and the southern slopes of Mount Hermon.

Shomron (Samaria), which includes upper central Israel plus Haifa and Mount Carmel.

Samson (Shimshon), covering the coastal area between the Judean Hills and the coastal plain.

Judean Hills (Harey Yuhuda), encompassing Jerusalem's hillside vineyards and the West Bank.

Negev, southern desert Israel.

On the face of it, Kosher Law applies to all wine production. For wine, kosher ("right" or "correct") means the winemaking process has been supervised to ensure that nothing non-kosher has been introduced and that only religiously observant Jews have come into contact with the product. Among other things, this means that the wines must be flash-pasteurized so as to remain kosher no matter who comes in contact with them.

Pasteurization makes little difference to inexpensive wines, but for serious wines it removes complexity and maturation potential. If wine isn't pasteurized, there's nothing that makes kosher wines different from other wine. However, interpretation and compromise are key. Larger companies comply generally with the law as locally interpreted, but several new, high-quality, boutique wineries are less constrained and use methods identical to wine producers in any other country.

Viticulture and winemaking

For years Carmel processed huge quantities of grapes with little quality incentive, but since 1984 Golan's quest for quality has been forcing Carmel to modernize. The developing boutique wineries have been a further spur. Irrigation is essential throughout Israel, and growing techniques from the Dr Richard Smart textbook are widespread.

Land and border disputes are common. Golan Heights, captured from Syria in the 1967 war, undoubtedly has the finest wine potential, but a land-for-peace initiative set up several years ago will see the area gradually returned to Syria, and long-term prospects are not clear. Some think Syria is unlikely to remove such a proven export earner, but a Moslem country is unlikely to see Golan's vineyards as a permanent fixture. Vineyards in the disputed West Bank of the Jordan could be affected in a similar way.

International influences

Bearing in mind Israel's geographical location, the most unusual aspect of production there may be the overwhelming influence of California. This came about through Israel's strong political affinity with the USA at a time when California's UCD was on the cutting edge of world vinous thought. In 1972, UCD's Dr Cornelius Ough toured Israel to select an ideal site for an advanced winery (he chose Golan Heights). Since those early days Golan and now other major export producers such as Barkan and Tishbi have used American UCD-trained winemakers to head operations.

In 1989 Israel caused a stir at the world's largest wine fair, Vinexpo, held every two years in Bordeaux. Wines awarded Gold Medals in this competition are further appraised for Grand Prix d'Honneur awards. An Israeli wine—Golan Heights Yarden Cabernet Sauvignon 1984 (one of their earliest vintages from relatively young vines)—won a Grand Prix d'Honneur. It was perhaps less of a surprise when Golan Heights won another Grand Prix d'Honneur in 1991 with a merlot, and again for cabernet sauvignon in 1993.

Producers

CARMEL

For many years this cooperative *was* Israeli wine. It was slow to change and its staff remained for years. The vaunted Carmel Rothschild Selection, suffering from pasteurization, was once famously overlooked by an American wine magazine selecting Israel's top ten wines.

Painting a vineyard scene on one of the huge barrels at the Carmel Cooperative.

Fermentation tanks in rows at the Golan Heights winery.

Attending to the brandy still at the Tishbi Wines plant.

GOLAN HEIGHTS WINERY

Established 1983 Co-operative/collective ownership
Production 300,000 cases *Vineyard area* 1210 acres
(490 ha)

The team here is dynamic, young and internationally aware. Previous CEO Segev Yerovan steered progress from the early days until handing over in 1998 to Shalom Blayer, ex-CEO of the Israeli Fruit Board. In 1999 Blayer started a three-year US$8.5 million expansion program.

TISHBI WINES AND BARON CELLARS

Both these concerns are vastly improved and both have an international marketing agreement headed by the dynamic Adam Montefiore, Export Manger for the Golan Heights Winery.

TSORA KIBBUTZ AND LATROUN MONASTERY BOUTIQUE WINERIES

Since the late 1980s when Margalit and Meron were created, a vibrant extra production layer has appeared to supply Israel's better-class restaurants and discerning home consumers. Ahead of others are Margalit, Meron and Castel. The largest and most likely to develop into a full commercial operation is Dalton in Upper Galilee with capacity to increase to 30,000 cases a year.

LEBANON

If Lebanon seems to accept warfare with equanimity, it's probably because the country has been fought over almost without respite for about 3,000 years and, for the foreseeable future this situation is likely to continue. Israel holds part of southern Lebanon and Syria influences the rest as a form of protectorate, with scruffy and dangerously inconsistent soldiers manning road blocs and causing either delays or detours.

Emerging from war-torn Lebanon, Château Musar startled Britain's wine trade in 1980 and proved that this ancient land could produce wine of international quality. Since then two other producers of note have emerged and now the ultimate accolade—Australasian flying winemakers are about to appear on the scene.

The underdeveloped Bekaa Valley ranks as one of the finest potential vineyard areas of the world. At an altitude of 3,300 feet (1,000 m) soils are predominantly gravel over limestone and there are virtually 300 days of unbroken sunshine with negligible risk of rain at vintage time. Conditions are so ideal that continuing stability in this region is certain to lead to more emphasis on wine production. Some grapes are also grown on the slopes of Lebanese mountains. Vineyards in the Bekaa are almost invariably bush vines with only Ksara and some Kefraya vineyards implementing modern training styles. The three major producers are exporters so they comply with overseas laws.

Producers

CHÂTEAU KEFRAYA

Owned by the descendant of a sort of feudal lord and with the winery in the castle grounds in the Bekaa itself, Kefraya is as idiosyncratic as Musar. Michel de Boustros is Francophile to an extreme and his winemaking methods are those of France two decades ago. Vine planting initiated by a past winemaker from southern France gives a legacy of uninspiring bourboulenc, clairette and ugni blanc for white wines and somewhat more rewarding reds from classic southern French red varieties. Michel is convinced of the excellence of his wines and heeds no alternative views.

CHÂTEAU KSARA

Established 1857 *Owners* Kassar, Chaoui, Sara & Sayegh
Production 100,000 cases *Vineyard area* 618 acres (250 ha)

In comparison with the two other main producers, Ksara is a breath of fresh air. Originally a Franciscan wine estate, it is now a vibrant young company headed by Charles Ghostine, Mr Lebanese Wine himself. Here vine-growing systems are modern, equipment is up to date and wines are in tune with competitively priced international market flavors. With the Bekaa potential at their disposal, a young marketing team at work and a currently stable political situation, Ksara is one to watch. Ex-lawyer Ghostine has somehow convinced the other two rich and individualistic Lebanese château-owners, that there is benefit to be gained by cooperating in a Lebanese promotional activity, and they regularly meet to advance the cause of Lebanese wine.

And perhaps most significant of all for Lebanon's long-term vinous future in the Bekaa is a new cooperative with modern equipment that will surely serve as an ideal base for outside winemakers to plunder the Bekaa potential. Total Lebanese production, which had sunk to 2.1 million gallons (82 million l) during the civil war has now risen to 8.2 million gallons (315 million l).

REGIONAL DOZEN

Barkan Classic Cabernet Sauvignon, Barkan
Castel Grand Vin, Ramat Raziel, Domaine du Castel
Emerald Riesling Reserve, Barkan Wine Cellars
Gamla Cabernet Sauvignon, Golan Heights Winery
Chateau Kefraya Les Tresors de Kefraya
Chateau Ksara Chardonnay
Margalit Cabernet Sauvignon, Margalit
Chateau Musar
Tishbi Brut NV, Baron Cellars
Tishbi Estate Sauvignon Blanc, Baron Cellars
Yarden Chardonnay, Northern Golan, Golan Heights Winery
Yarden Muscat, Lower Golan, Golan Heights Winery

CHÂTEAU MUSAR

As well as the widely known Château Musar, owner Serge Hochar has long produced an oaked white wine of singularly little appeal from obaideh (which Serge is convinced is chardonnay), meroué (which others suggest may also be chardonnay) and merweh (which may be sémillon) alongside his award-winning reds. He was voted a *Decanter* Man of the Year for his amazing exploits through 20 years of civil war, during which, despite vineyards and winery being separated by the war buffer zone or front line for much of the time, saw only the 1984 vintage lost. More recently, the influence of Serge's son Gaston and daughter Karine in the company is evidenced with production of Hochar Père et Fils, a red wine released without over-long maturation.

As a company, Château Musar is as quirky as its master. Musar's vineyards are mainly on the eastern slope of Mount Barouk, but other grapes are bought from growers in the Bekaa, all a significant distance across the mountains from the winery at Ghazir near the coast north of Beirut. A variety of grapes is used in the mainly cabernet sauvignon-based but cinsault- and carignan-influenced blend, but for each vintage Serge uses more of whichever variety he feels has been most successful that year. This makes vintage comparisons inappropriate as one is seldom comparing like with like. Winemaking at Musar is fairly primitive and maturation for the Château Musar brand is usually—and ideally in Serge Hochar's book—three years in barrique and four years in bottle. Tasting barrel samples of the new season's blending components before the cépage was decided, leaves no doubt that more is lost than gained by this over-long stay underground.

Critics suggest that Musar's wines have lost some of their magic and rumors regarding grape sourcing echo around the Bekaa. But despite antique equipment and systems, any loss in quality is more likely to be due to Serge's necessary concern for his multi-million capital-building projects than a loss in Lebanese quality potential. Younger family members point the way ahead at Musar.

SYRIA & JORDAN

Since the rise of strong fundamentalist religious attitudes in the 1970s, neither Syria nor Jordan is officially credited with wine production. Syria's comparatively large vineyards, 245,000 acres (100,000 ha) in the Aleppo, Homs and Damascus growing districts, produce mainly table grapes and dried fruit. Consequently, wine production has reduced, from over 1.5 million gallons (60,000 hl) to just over 200,000 gallons (8,000 hl) in the mid-1980s and is still declining.

Production from Jordan's Amman-Zarqua area, is consumed by a similar market. Around 7,500 acres (3,000 ha) now produces 26,400 gallons (1,000 hl) of wine; down from around 300,000 gallons (11,000 hl) in the early 1980s. It will be interesting to see what happens when Syria regains control of the Golan Heights.

Above: *Vineyards near the Beirut to Damascus Road, close to the Syrian border.*

Top: *A stone ruin at Baalbek in the lush Bekaa Valley, Lebanon.*

Asia

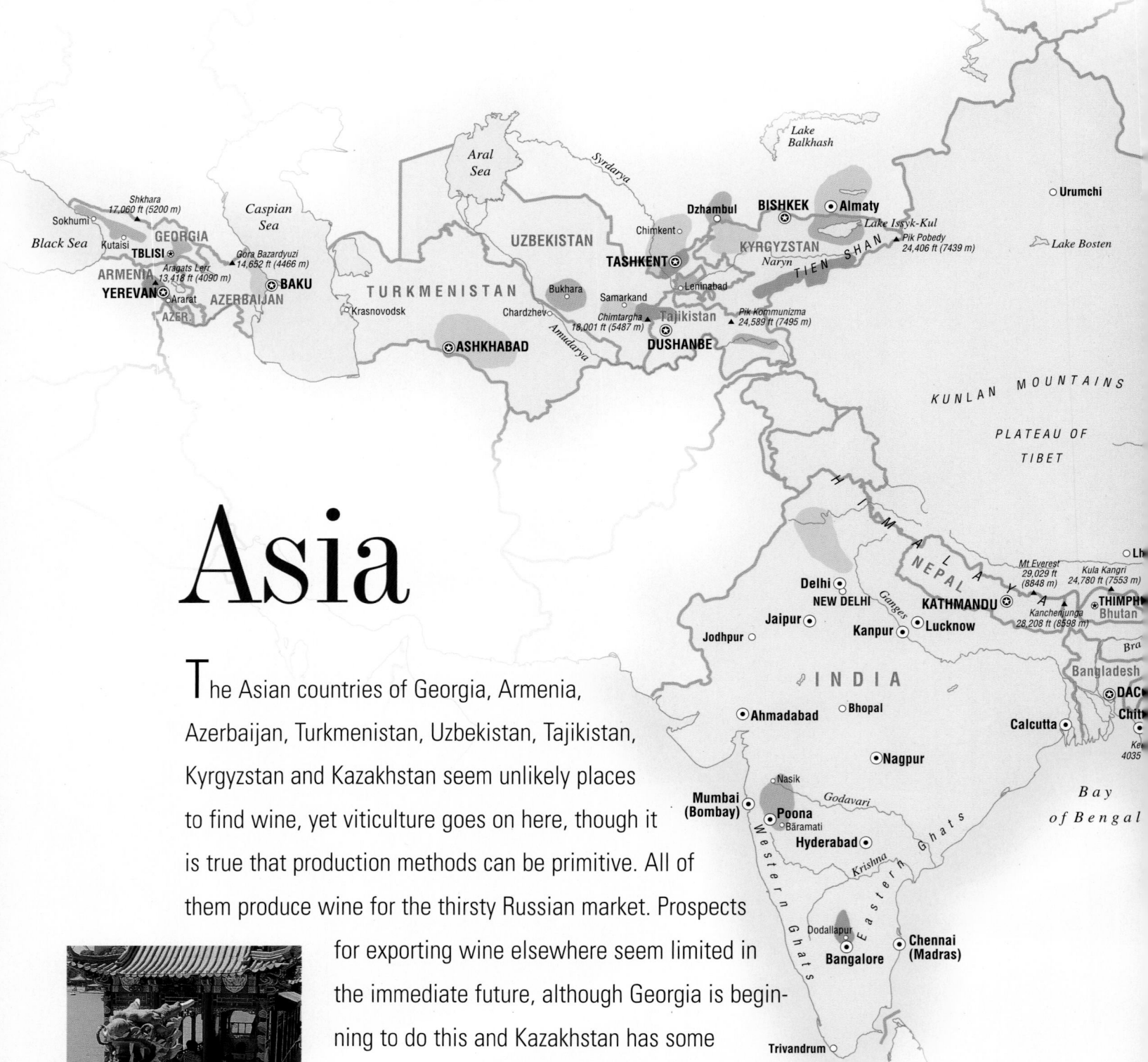

Asia

The Asian countries of Georgia, Armenia, Azerbaijan, Turkmenistan, Uzbekistan, Tajikistan, Kyrgyzstan and Kazakhstan seem unlikely places to find wine, yet viticulture goes on here, though it is true that production methods can be primitive. All of them produce wine for the thirsty Russian market. Prospects for exporting wine elsewhere seem limited in the immediate future, although Georgia is beginning to do this and Kazakhstan has some potential to do so. While India and China

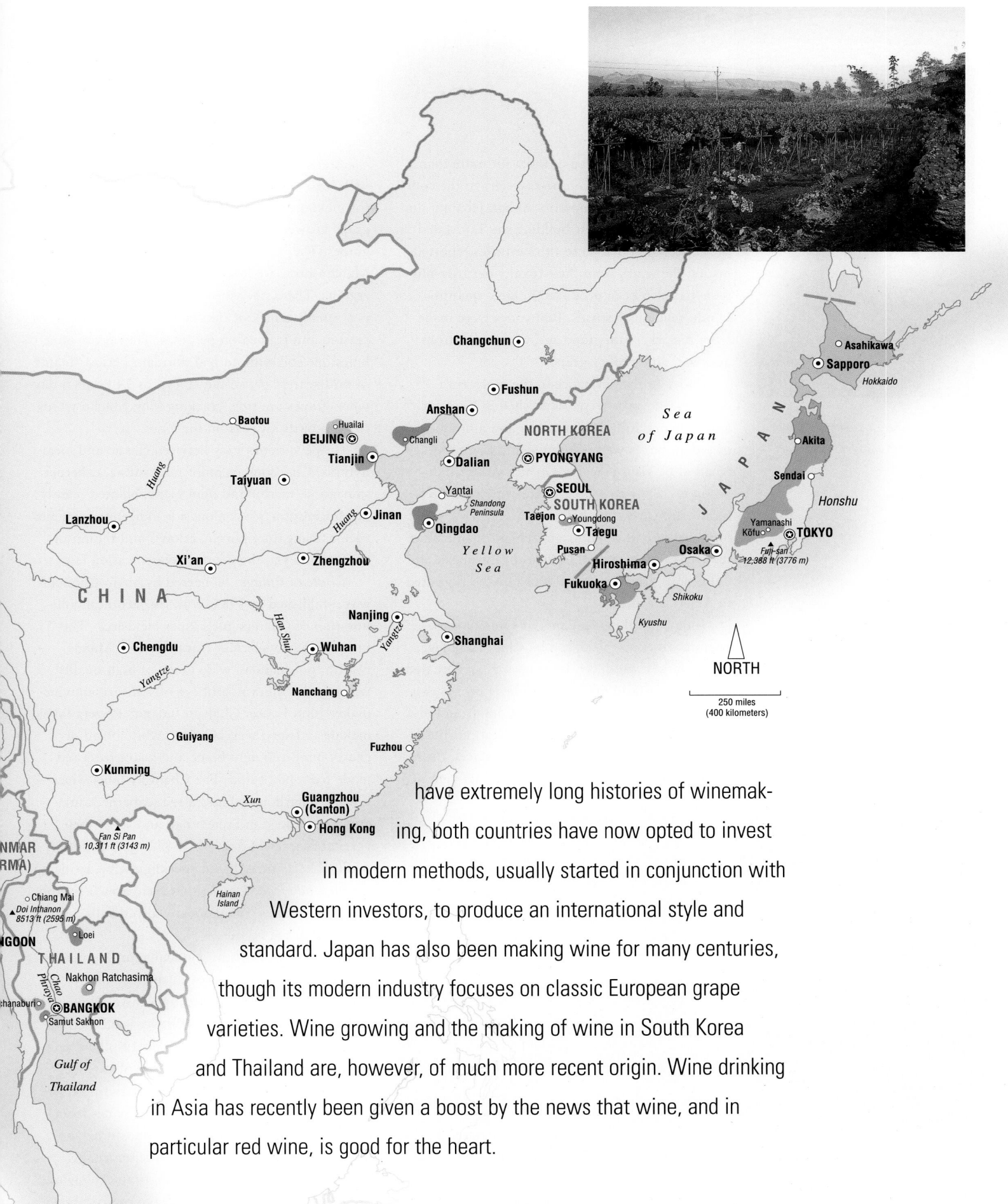

Changchun ⊙

⊙ Fushun

Anshan ⊙

○ Huailai
BEIJING ⊙
○ Changli
Tianjin ⊙

○ Baotou

Taiyuan ⊙

NORTH KOREA

⊙ Dalian

⊙ PYONGYANG

Sea
of Japan

⊙ Asahikawa
⊙ Sapporo
Hokkaido

Lanzhou ⊙

Huang

⊙ Yantai
*Shandong
Peninsula*

⊙ Jinan
⊙ Qingdao

⊙ SEOUL
SOUTH KOREA
Taejon ○ ○ Youngdong
⊙ Taegu

⊙ Akita

Sendai ⊙

Honshu

Xi'an ⊙

○ Zhengzhou

*Yellow
Sea*

Pusan ⊙
⊙ Hiroshima

Osaka ⊙
Yamanashi
Kōfu ○ ⊙ TOKYO
Fuji-san ▲
12,388 ft (3776 m)

C H I N A

Han Shui

Nanjing ⊙

Yangtze

Fukuoka ⊙

Shikoku

⊙ Chengdu

Wuhan ⊙

⊙ Shanghai

Kyushu

Nanchang ○

Yangtze

NORTH

○ Guiyang

250 miles
(400 kilometers)

⊙ Kunming

Fuzhou ○

Xun

Guangzhou
(Canton) ⊙
⊙ Hong Kong

▲ Fan Si Pan
10,311 ft (3143 m)

MNMAR
RMA)

*Hainan
Island*

○ Chiang Mai
▲ Doi Inthanon
8513 ft (2595 m)

○ Loei

GOON

THAILAND

○ Nakhon Ratchasima

anaburi ○ ⊙ BANGKOK
○ Samut Sakhon

*Gulf of
Thailand*

have extremely long histories of winemaking, both countries have now opted to invest
in modern methods, usually started in conjunction with
Western investors, to produce an international style and
standard. Japan has also been making wine for many centuries,
though its modern industry focuses on classic European grape
varieties. Wine growing and the making of wine in South Korea
and Thailand are, however, of much more recent origin. Wine drinking
in Asia has recently been given a boost by the news that wine, and in
particular red wine, is good for the heart.

INDIA

Jeffrey Benson

Distilling machinery in the tropical south-central state of Mahārāshtra in India.

In some areas of India where rainfall is scarce, vines are irrigated by flooding.

Wine has been produced in India for more than 4,000 years. Early European travelers to the courts of the grand mogul emperors Akbar, Jehangir and Shah Jehan (famous for building the Taj Mahal) in the sixteenth and seventeenth centuries reported tasting the wines from their royal vineyards and wine has also been produced in large quantities for Hindu religious festivals. Red wines were made from the arkesham grape and white wine from arkawati and bhokry grapes.

Under British influence in the nineteenth century, vineyards were established in Kashmir and at Bārāmati in Mahārāshtra and a number of Indian wines were exhibited and favorably received by visitors to the Great Calcutta Exhibition of 1884. However, Indian vineyards were totally destroyed by phylloxera in the 1890s. It took nearly half a century to replant them. More than 124,000 acres (50,000 ha) of European and indigenous grape varieties have now been grafted to American rootstock.

Today, lineal descendants of some of these historic wines are produced by Chateau Indage, India's largest producer. Its vineyards are situated at 2,600 feet (800 m) above sea level on the east-facing slopes of the Sahyadri Mountains and in west Mahārāshtra, 110 miles (180 km) north of Bombay. Currently the company produces 100,000 cases a year but with plans to expand its vineyard

area, a forecast of 830,000 cases annually is predicted. Of this, 70 percent will be sold on the domestic market and 30 percent will be exported around the world.

Areas with high temperatures produce grapes with high sugar and low acidity that are not ideal for making fine wine and in fact the majority of grape growers produce thompson seedless table grapes. The better vineyards, such as those at Mahārāshtra, are located in the cooler mountain regions. There, the vines are drip-irrigated, as there is normally a lack of rain during the growing season, and trained on pergolas. They grow on a limestone soil with no real dormant period. Teams of bird-scarers patrol the vineyards 24 hours a day when grapes are ripe, cracking long gaucho whips to keep birds away from the vines.

Grape varieties vary between classic and local hybrids. Chardonnay, pinot noir, shiraz, cabernet sauvignon, merlot and ugni blanc, planted mainly in Mahārāshtra, grow alongside indigenous varieties such as bangalore purple, arkavti and thompson seedless. As yet, there are no classification laws.

Chateau Indage, pioneered by Sham Chougule was established in 1984, with the technical collaboration of Champagne's Piper Heidsieck. The ultra-modern winery in Narayangaon, Mahārāshtra, produces an wide range of high-quality wines under the watchful eye of Californian winemaker John Locke. Chateau Indage's Riviera label includes a fruity, well-balanced white blend of chardonnay and ugni blanc and a soft fresh red made from pinot noir. The Chantilly label wines—a white (chardonnay) and a red (cabernet sauvignon)—are aged in French oak and show their varietal characteristics. Omar Khayyam is a top-quality chardonnay-based sparkling wine, made by the *méthode traditionelle*, that compares favorably with champagne. The company also distills a fine oak-aged grape brandy.

Grover Vineyards, in Dodballapur, 25 miles (40 km) north of Bangalore at the foot of the Nandi hills, is jointly owned by Kanwal Grover and Veuve Cliquot. Kanwal Grover is advised by two top French winemakers, Michel Rolland and Georges Vesselle. The vineyards are planted at 2,000 feet (6,500 m) above sea level and produce two crops a year. Still white and red wines from bangalore purple, clairette, cabernet, shiraz and thompson seedless grapes are made under the supervision of winemaker Bruno Yvon. The white is medium-dry and fairly bland; the red is cabernet-style with good depth of fruit.

CHINA

Jeffrey Benson

Historic records refer to the growing of grapes for winemaking near Beijing in 100 BC. During the next century, vineyards were developed in China along commercial routes, particularly the Silk Route, to make wine for the foreign traders. Under the Han dynasty, around 200 BC, grape varieties which had been developed in the northwest Xinjiang region (an area which lies on the same latitude as the south of France and northern Italy) were spread to other parts of China as demand increased. Before that, vines outside the Xinjiang region were grown without a professional knowledge of pruning, the end result being the production of poor-quality wines.

China experienced its first real development of a wine industry in 1892 with the creation of Zhang Yu Winery in Yantai (Shandong province) north of Shanghai, by Zhang Bishi, who had lived overseas and studied vine cultivation. Having traveled in Europe, Zhang brought back more than ten varieties of grape cuttings, mainly rieslings. He then employed experts from France and Italy to assist him with planting and winemaking. He also imported more than 600 oak barrels.

In 1910, a French religious community opened a winery called Shangyi in Beijing to produce wine to be used during mass. That was the beginning of what is now the Beijing Friendship Winery. In 1914, a large German colony in Qingdao (Shandong province) opened a winery and also introduced further grape varieties—riesling, sylvaner and muscat. Their wine was initially for sale within the German community, but they developed their market to other communities as planting increased.

In 1980, the wine market further evolved with the creation of the first joint venture between France and China, called Dynasty, to produce European-style wines. These wines proved to be very popular with Chinese restaurants, not only in China, but also abroad. In 1987, Groupe Pernod-Ricard created the Dragon Seal Wine Company in association with the Beijing Friendship Winery to produce and distribute European-style wines as well as other Chinese products such as Kuei Hua Chen Chiew, a sweet osmanthus-flavored wine with a 15 percent alcohol content.

The market for European-style wines has only really developed since 1992 due to an increased general awareness of wine and a growing export market. This has been mainly through the efforts of the major companies: Dynasty, Great Wall, Dragon Seal and Huadong (which is under the supervision of the Australian winemaker Charles Whish). With more than 200 wineries in China, fewer than ten have production capacities exceeding 11,020 tons (10,000 t) and they control more than 35 percent of the total market share. Smaller wineries include Yatai, Wei Fang and Jinan.

China's main wine-producing regions are situated north of Shanghai and southeast of Beijing on the Shandong Peninsula, in Hebei, Liaoning, Shanxi and Xinjiang provinces. The vineyards are planted with a multitude of grape varieties such as saperavi, welschriesling, gewürztraminer, pinot noir, merlot, cabernet sauvignon, cabernet franc, caringnan, muscat hamburg and beichun (a successful hybrid and prolific yielder), as well as the exotically named dragon's eye, cow's nipple and cock's heart. Nearly 500,000 acres (200,000 ha) of land is under vine, 30 percent of which is on rich, high-yielding alluvial soil. Recent vine plantings have been on well-drained south-facing slopes. Earlier plantings on flatter land suffered from the associated problems of high water tables, low winter temperatures in the northern vineyards, and fungal diseases in the humid southern vineyards.

Although beer and spirits continue to dominate the Chinese alcoholic beverage market, wine sales have experienced sustained growth since the early 1990s. The market was initially geared toward whites, but these wines were not popular (the consensus being that they were not dry enough) and tastes generally have moved toward red. Red wines now account for 80 percent of overall wine consumption in China.

The Great Wall of China lends its name to many products, including one of China's largest wine companies.

Winemaking has played only a small part in China's rich cultural history.

JAPAN

Jeffrey Benson

Vines are now grown all over Japan, though most produce grapes for the table.

It is believed that grape cultivation in Japan started in AD 718 when a high-ranking monk named Gyoki planted the koshu grape (a *Vitis vinifera*, not a native grape) in the Yamanshi district west of Tokyo and produced wine that was served at the Court of Nara. In the ninth century, Buddhist missionaries planted vines across the country, producing table grapes and experimenting with winemaking, and a monk named Kageyu Amemiya is known to have made wine in the Yamanshi district.

In the fifteenth and sixteenth centuries, Portuguese traders introduced red wines to the wealthy merchants and, in 1569, the great warlord Oda Nobunaga held a wine tasting of Portuguese-style wines for his Samurai generals. From that time until the Meiji restoration in 1868, Japan remained closed to the outside world and there are no records of grape growing or winemaking. Then, in 1870, two young men from Yamanshi prefecture went to France to study winemaking techniques. The rebirth of winemaking in Japan began when they returned and began making wine in Yamanshi. In addition to the koshu, other grape varieties were introduced such as delaware, campbell's early, isabella and catawba. Wine became popular and vine planting increased during the seventeenth century, when 8 foot (2.5 m) vines were trained on the "tanajitate system," spread out on wire supports like giant pergolas to counteract rot during the summer rains. This system is still used widely, together with the more conventional Guyot system of training two spurs from the vine onto low wire fences.

Because Japan's 125,000 acres (50,000 ha) of vineyards are subjected to climatic extremes from freezing winters to spring and autumn monsoons and summer typhoons, grape varietal selection is crucial. Recent experiments with classic European vines have proved most successful. Many vineyards are located on Honshū Island, on good south-facing slopes on the same latitude as the Mediterranean and the eastern United States. There, areas enjoy warm summers and cool winters, with the Sea of Japan moderating the summer heat and the central mountains absorbing some of the high rainfall. The Kōfu valley, in the Yamanashi prefecture, is the main wine-producing area. Other vineyards are located on the islands of Hokkaidō and Kyūshū.

Japanese wines have traditionally been sweet, with up to 33 ounces of sugar added per gallon (250 g per l). In 1970, the major wineries responded to demand and started producing drier wines using classic grape varieties such as chardonnay and cabernet sauvignon.

To protect farmers, the Agricultural Land Act allows wineries to own vineyards only for experimental cultivation, so wineries have to purchase their grapes from agricultural cooperatives or contracted grape growers. Although the 53,000 acres (21,400 ha) under vine produce 275,500 tons (250,000 t) of grapes, less than 10 percent are made into wine. Established varietals, kyoho, campbell's early and delaware, which represent more than 50 percent of Japan's plantings, are popular for making sparkling wines. Koshu, which is the oldest varietal (dating back to 1186) and produces a good medium-dry white wine, muscat bailey and neo-muscat represent another 40 percent. The remaining 10 percent are made up of sémillon, riesling, chardonnay, cabernet sauvignon, cabernet franc and merlot planted on soil with a high gravel content.

There are about 200 active wineries in Japan, with the greatest concentration in Yamanshi prefecture, which has 86. *Mercian*, with 27 percent of the domestic market, produces 3,500,000 cases annually. *Suntory* is a close second, with 25 percent of the market and producing 3,100,000 cases. *Sapporo* (1,200,000 cases), *Manns* (1,100,000 cases), *Saint Neige* (580,000 cases), *Hokkaidō* (280,000 cases) and *Hakodate* (240,000 cases) follow. Japan imports slightly more than half of its annual consumption of 20,000,000 cases.

Chateau Lumiere, a boutique winery owned by the Toshihiko Tsukamoto family, produces a fine cabernet sauvignon/cabernet franc/merlot blend from vines imported from Chateau Margaux in Bordeaux and a highly successful botrytised sémillon/sauvignon blanc. However, most of the bottled wine marketed as domestically produced is mainly constituted from imported concentrated grape juice and bulk wine. The amount of wine actually produced from domestically grown grapes is relatively low at just under 1,500,000 cases. Very little Japanese wine is exported because of the high cost and local demand.

SOUTH-EAST ASIA

Jeffrey Benson

THAILAND

Viticulture in Thailand started in 1960 with the production of table grapes for the local market. Small growers experimented with local and international grape varieties from pok dum to malaga blanc and thompson seedless, planting vineyards on alluvial, clay and sandy soil in the drier areas of the country.

In 1992, wine-loving Prime Minister Anand Panyarachua granted licenses to the kingdom's wine producers to encourage plantings and to improve the quality of local wine. To qualify, an individual or corporation had to own at least 370 acres (150 ha) and to have five years' grape-growing experience. Eight producers initially qualified for this license. In 1999, the law was relaxed, enabling any grape-grower to produce wine and today, 25,000 acres (10,000 ha) are under vine, mostly located south of Bangkok. They are planted mainly with pok dum, also known as "Black Queen," which produces light red and rosé wines with a grassy asparagus smell (similar to cabernet sauvignon), grenache, malaga blanc, muscat hamburg, colombard, ugni blanc, syrah, chenin blanc, nebbiolo and tempranillo.

Wine is still seen as a luxury item in Thailand and local taxes are high. Additionally, the Thai government did not sign the World Trade Organization agreement on viticulture and winemaking, so wine is imported without control of appellation or origin. The result of this is the presence of American chablis and Australian burgundy on the shelves in Thai shops.

KOREA

According to Ministry of Agriculture records, wine production in South Korea began in the mid-1960s, when a company called Jinro began producing a cheap table wine for the domestic market. Although Koreans are mainly drinkers of spirits, the wine sold steadily for many years. The big change came in 1995, when local grape farmers who could no longer cope financially with erratic table grape prices formed the Youngdong Wine Processing Farming Association (YPFA). This group of 67 farmers sent trainees to France and Italy to study winemaking and, in particular, the technique of freezing must as a clarification method.

In 1996, Chateau Mani made its debut. This red wine was produced by farmers south of Seoul from a local grape variety called camberbelly that is grown in the Mani Mountains at Jooksan-li. The new brand quickly became popular in fashionable restaurants, and the YPFA began exporting the wine to China. It is currently developing a superior blend using longer fermentation. The YPFA's success prompted some of South Korea's spirits and liqueur producers to begin producing wines. The Doosan Corporation is now a leader in this market, producing Special White and Cabernet from camberbelly grapes under the Majuang brand, as well as wines made from must imported from France and Germany.

By 1997, domestic sales of locally produced wines had grown to more than 600,000 cases. Some sources attribute the increase to the fact that Korean housewives were beginning to use western recipes that require wine and that bakeries are using red wine in breadmaking. In addition, as in other countries, growing health awareness is accompanied by a subsequent decrease in the consumption of spirits. In 1998, demand for locally produced wines dropped by 50 percent, due mainly to an increased demand for higher quality imported wine. The exception to this was Majuang, which continued to increase its sales against the trend.

South Korea has more than 40,000 acres (16,000 ha) under vine, with 75 percent of the grapes used for raisins and 25 percent for making wine for the domestic market. There are reports of a cooperative effort between North Korea and Oregon State in the USA to develop grape-growing interests.

A painted mask from Korea; wine production here is usually a blend of domestic and imported wine.

Although much of Thailand's population is Buddhist, wine drinking is slowly gaining a foothold in Thai culture.

TRANSCAUCASIA

Brian Jordan

AZERBAIJAN

The least developed of the three Transcaucausian nations, Azerbaijan also has the largest proportion of Moslem inhabitants. Yet its wine production level is high—currently 10.5 million gallons (40 million l)—and is exceeded only by Georgia, Ukraine, Uzbekistan, Russia and Moldova.

Archeological studies reveal that wine production here dates back at least 4,000 years. The volume of wine produced has varied, with the religious beliefs of successive rulers being the major determinant, yet even during periods of Moslem domination vineyards continued to flourish. At the end of the nineteenth century, the construction of a railroad linking Azerbaijan to the heart of Russia led to a boom in exports. Immediately before the First World War, 15 defined wine-producing districts were providing 10.5 million gallons (40 million l) per year. By 1930, state-controlled collective farms were responsible for almost the entire crop. The vineyard area increased to 81,500 acres (33,000 ha) at the outbreak of the Second World War, but had shrunk to 52,000 acres (21,000 ha) by war's end.

Production is concentrated in the republics of Nakhichevan and Nagorno–Karabakh. Climatic conditions in grape-growing areas vary from warm with dry winters to cool with significant precipitation, depending on exposure, altitude and latitude.

Traditional entertainment at a state-controlled collective farm.

The north is cold, though only about 10 percent of vineyards require winter protection (covering the vines with soil). Southern vineyards are much warmer and many (almost half the country's total) require irrigation.

Although rkatsiteli and pinot noir are the most commonly planted grapes, nearly all of the 17 officially recognized varieties are indigenous. Azerbaijan's most significant producers are two wineries in Baku, *Khanlar* and *Baku Sparkling Wines*, which between them offer more than 90 different brands. The country's best-known wines are the dry white Sadilly and the slightly spicy red Matrassa, which are made by a range of producers. Numerous sweet and fortified styles are also popular.

ARMENIA

The original grape vine *Vitis vinifera silvestris* was growing in Transcaucasia—the region that includes Armenia, Georgia, Azerbaijan and eastern Turkey —more than one million years ago, and archeological excavations have shown that vines have been cultivated here throughout history. However, development of the Armenian wine industry has been impeded by factors such as frequent wars and the religious restrictions imposed by Moslem rulers.

By the end of the First World War, only around 12,000 acres (5,000 ha) were under plantation. Following the absorption of the country into the USSR in 1922, viticulture was stimulated by the centralized Soviet control system. By 1991 and the fall of the communist regime, there were over 70,000 acres (28,000 ha) under cultivation, although there has been slight reduction since then. Table grapes now account for 10 percent of vineyard area. A major earthquake in 1988 had a serious impact on both industry and agriculture, and ethnic strife throughout the Transcaucasian region continues to limit economic development.

Most vineyards and the majority of wineries are located on the Ararat Plain, at an altitude of 1,300 feet (400 m). All vines need irrigation and spring frost is a major problem; some experimentation with cold-resistant varieties is currently taking place. Winemaking methods are relatively primitive, being based on the industrial, continuous-press systems typical of many former communist countries. About 1.7 million gallons (6.5 million l) are produced annually.

As one of the most southerly Soviet and CIS states, Armenia traditionally focused its wine production on strong, heavy wines and brandy for export to the north, with local consumption being restricted to bulk table wines. The more than 30 approved varieties include indigenous grapes such as rkatsiteli, khaket and voskeat, and internationally recognized names such as muscadine, muscatel, vardeljo (verdelho) and sersial (sercial). Generally, Armenian wines are unsophisticated, with the accent on strength. Arguably the best white and red wines are those from Echmiadzin and Norashen respectively.

GEORGIA

Georgia is situated south of the Caucasus Mountains, near Armenia, Azerbaijan and northeastern Turkey, in the region where *Vitis vinifera* survived the last great Ice Age. This Transcaucasian region is where people's relationship with the cultivated vine first began, some 5,000 years ago. For centuries viticulture has played an important part in Georgian agricultural and economic life. This influence has been helped by the fact that Georgia has been a Christian country since the fourth century BC, and not subject to the alcohol restrictions of Moslem lands.

By the late nineteenth century vineyard area exceeded 175,000 acres (71,000 ha), but the early arrival of phylloxera, coupled with the prevalence of fungal diseases, reduced this to 92,600 acres (37,500 ha) early in the twentieth century. Supported by the USSR's market demands, this vineyard area remained fairly constant at around 100,000 acres (40,500 ha) until the fall of communism, after which lack of funding has seen vineyards gradually and progressively decline. Official estimates presently suggest that there are 85,000 acres (34,400 ha) currently under vine, producing 18,000 gallons (68 million l) of wine a year.

In the north, the landscape is dominated by the Caucasus slopes—peaks along the northern boundary rise to over 16,500 feet (5,000 m). Growing conditions in Georgia are variable, affected by the considerable diversity of soil types and rainfall patterns—the east is dry, averaging 24 inches (615 mm) a year, while the Black Sea coastal area can reach 155 inches (4,000 mm).

A wide variety of training systems is required because of the range of growing conditions, with trellis and pergola being especially popular. Areas most prone to hail (all Georgia has hail problems) even use reticular shelters for protection.

Regions and districts are defined, and of the significant vines (there are said to be over 1,000 different varieties growing in Georgia), 38 are officially approved for commercial wine production.

Grapes are mainly indigenous varieties, but rkatsiteli and saperavi (the latter a teinturier grape with extraordinary aging potential) are also found elsewhere in Eastern Europe. White wines mainly use tsinandali or ghurdaani grapes, although small quantities of pinot noir, chardonnay and cabernet sauvignon, often of doubtful parentage, are also grown in Georgia.

As with all USSR satellite countries, the accent during the communist period was on sweet wine production—grapes in the south often achieve 30 percent sugar content at harvest. Some of the wines of Kakheti, the region responsible for 70 percent of Georgian output, prove an exception to this general rule, however. They are fermented in *kvevri*, earthenware pots not dissimilar to the *tinajas* of Valdepere, and have grape skins added during fermentation, not unlike Italy's *governo* system.

Georgian Wine and Spirits Company (GWS) is the only Georgian producer that has international significance, and French giant Pernod Ricard has recently acquired 51 percent of the company. Pernod Ricard chairman Levan Gachechiladze is now shipping export quality wine to Holland, and 1998 GWS Pinot Noir and 1998 GWS Matrasa were both commended in recent major European tastings, which is a significant achievement, considering the practical difficulties faced by export-oriented producers in Georgia. Gachechiladze claims a potential for "100 million bottles a year and we're only producing 3–4 million." It will be interesting to see how Pernod Ricard, whose investments normally support more recognisable brands (such as Australia's Jacob's Creek), succeeds in this country.

Vines in Georgia do not need protection from the cold, unlike many other Transcaucasian countries.

CENTRAL ASIA

Brian Jordan

KYRGYZSTAN

Kyrgyzstan, a small nation touching Uzbekistan in the west and China in the south and east, may seem an unlikely region for wine production, but its industry was developed, encouraged and financially supported during the latter part of the twentieth century by the thirst of the USSR for alcoholic drinks of all types.

From a token 12 acres (5 ha) of vineyards 100 years ago, commercial pressures saw a leap in planted area to 22,230 acres (9,000 ha) in 1996, alongside increased vineyards for dried fruits and table grapes, which now account for 15 percent of grape production.

This landlocked country has just three regions where vineyards are developed: the Chuia and Talas valleys, the Lake Issyl-Kul (or Ala-Kul) basin, and the southern strip of the country. The climate can fairly be described as "continental," with freezing winters, which necessitate earth protection for all vines excepting those in the Issyk-Kul basin, respectable summer average temperatures of around 77°F (25°C) and rainfall averaging 10 to 20 inches (250 to 600 mm). Irrigation is in widespread use. The slopes of the mountain chain that forms the natural border with China are home to some high-altitude vineyards, even up to 6,500 feet (2,000 m) in the Osh and Dzhalal-Abad table grape regions.

Grapes are an extensive mix of European, Russo-Chinese and indigenous, with 45 recognized varieties. Most popular are the unexceptional but heavy cropping bayan shirey, rkatsiteli and saperavi, with pinot noir, cabernet sauvignon and mourvèdre also planted. Paradoxically, cinsault is used for table grapes, but not for wine.

TAJIKISTAN

Tajikistan is a tiny Central Asian republic on the northern slopes of the Pamir and the Hindu Kush mountain ranges, where only the foothills, valleys and plateaux offer reasonable growing conditions. Unlike most neighboring states, where winemaking was developed by commercial pressures from the USSR, Tajikistan is on the ancient Silk Route, and has a long history of wine production—back to days preceding Alexander the Great. In the north, Moslem influence restricted vine cultivation for

wine quite severely, but Islam had a less potent influence in the south, and wine production continued to thrive there.

In the early period of the twentieth century, collectivization amalgamated private vineyards into cooperatives, and by 1940, 737,000 gallons (2.8 million l) were being produced from a total of 20,000 acres (8,000 ha). At the peak of its wine-producing arc in the mid-1980s, Tajikistan was producing 8.5 million gallons (33 million l). However, since the breakup of the USSR, the state of the industry has deteriorated

Grapes are grown at 2,950 feet (900 m) in the lowlands and up to 4,900 feet (1,500 m) on the foothills, in a continental climate—temperatures range from 23°F (–5°C) in winter up to 86°F (30°C) in summer, and rainfall is between 14 inches (350 mm) and 33 inches (850 mm). There are three areas of Tajikistan where grapes are grown—around Leninabad (Khujand) in the north, in the Ghissar valley, in central Tajikistan, and in the Vakhsh valley and Kuliab area, towards the southwest. The varietes found in Tajikistan are the normal mix for this part of the world—rkatsiteli, saperavi, bayan shirey and tagobi, plus alleged cabernet sauvignon and varieties of muscat—and there is the usual preponderance of sweet wines.

TURKMENISTAN

Turkmenistan has a history and tradition of grape production going back to the days of the Silk Route although formalized agriculture did not develop until after Turkmenistan's annexation by Russia at the end of the nineteenth century, and the subsequent development of the Ashkhabad Railway and the Karakumy canal.

The area under vine at the end of the nineteenth century was a mere 760 acres (308 ha). This has since grown considerably, and there were 66,700 acres (27,000 ha) under vine in 1990. However, with the breakup of the USSR, the area of vineyard has declined.

The country, much of which is desert, is hot—winter temperatures average 25°F (–4°C), summer temperatures average 82°F (28°C)—and very dry, with rainfall ranging from 3 inches (80 mm) in the northeast to 12 inches (800 mm) in the southern mountains. This means that most vineyards need irrigation, but few need winter protection.

Most vines—70 percent—grow in the Ashkhabad region, near the southern border. The eight wine varieties grown include bayan shirey, saperavi, kizil sapak, tara uzüm ashkhabadzi and

Cabernet franc grapes (top) and riesling grapes, along with other European and indigenous varieties, are grown in the high country of Central Asia.

terbash, plus (alleged) riesling. OIV statistics show
an average of 422,000 gallons (1.6 million l)
throughout the early 1990s, but then claim a
surprising and sudden upward leap to a 1997
production of 4.4 million gallons (16.8 million l):
a tenfold increase. (Perhaps a decimal point in
official statistics became misplaced.)

UZBEKISTAN

Officially the third largest wine producer of the
CIS states, statistics from Uzbekistan are generally
viewed with suspicion. It is claimed that the country is in the top half of the world producer league,
alongside Austria, but both the 1996 and 1997
crops appear to have matched each other to the
nearest gallon or liter, and both years show an
increase over Uzbekistan's 1991 to 1995 average,
at a time when surrounding states have shown
decreases in production as their previously profitable markets in the USSR dried up. It is by no
means clear where the vast quantities of Uzbekistan's alleged production go, but it certainly hasn't
been absorbed by the local market; with the
exception of Russian citizens now marooned in
Uzbekistan, the locals are largely indifferent to
the delights of wine.

The Pamir, Tian-Shan and Alkai mountain
ranges dominate the east of Uzbekistan, and 30
percent of the whole country is defined as "mountainous." The climate is continental—temperatures
can be as low as 27°F (–3°C) in winter and as high
as 90°F (32°C) in summer, and rainfall is moderate, from 40 inches (1,000 mm) in the mountains
to a tenth of that on the lowlands—and thus
conducive to grape production.

A melting pot of vine sources, some indigenous
vines are believed to have evolved as a result of
natural selection from the wild subspecies *Vitis
vinifera silvestris* Gmel. Some also came from Iran,
around the fifth century BC, some came from
Greek and Arab traders in the seventh century AD,
and some are believed to have come from China.

What had been a flourishing wine industry
withered under a millennium of Moslem domination beginning in the eighth century AD. Annexation by Russia in the second half of the nineteenth century undid the traditions of 1,000 years,
and started modern Uzbekistan's wine industry:
there was increased demand for high quality table
grapes for export, and European varieties were
added to those already being grown.

About 15 grape varieties are in common use
for wine production now, and they are those one
would expect in the Central Asian zone: rkatsiteli,
saperavi, bayan shirey and morrastel, plus riesling,
muscat rosé, hungarian muscat and aleatico.

There are ten defined zones, of which the most
important are Samarkand, Tashkent and Bukhara.
Viticulture in the Fergana valley, which began with
table grapes being grown in irrigated vineyards
from the sixth to the second century BC—these
were highly prized in China—still flourishes as
well. Irrigation is standard except in mountain
areas where rainfall exceeds 18 inches (450 mm),
and the standard USSR/CIS practice of covering
vines throughout the winter is usual. As is also
usual in ex-USSR countries, winemaking practices
are primitive in the extreme.

KAZAKHSTAN

Grape vine cultivation in this large and mostly
climatically harsh republic, a member of the CIS,
dates back to the seventh century AD, when vine
cuttings were brought by traders along the Silk
Route; some vine culture is also believed to have
traveled westwards from China.

Wine production only became organized
during the communist regime, but by the outbreak
of the Second World War this had only resulted in
a modest 1,250 acres (500 ha) of productive vines.
The area of vineyard escalated to 55,550 acres
(22,500 ha) by 1976, the majority of land area
largely in the hands of 26 specialized state fruit
and vine farms.

The country is so huge, stretching from the
shores of the Caspian Sea to the Chinese border,
that no generalizations can be made about it. The
majority of wine is produced in the
southeast, near Almaty, and the south,
in both the Dzambul and the Chimkent
regions. Winters are severe, down to
–67°F (–55°C) in the Chimkent region,
and vines in the southern and southeastern regions generally need winter protection. To this end, earth is banked
over them.

"European" grapes are grown:
rkatsiteli and saperavi plus alleged pinot
noir, cabernet franc, cabernet sauvignon, muscat ottonel and even aligoté.
However, winemaking practices are still
primitive, and still geared to exporting
to Russia. This emphasis also means
that sweet wines and sweet sparkling
wines are the norm. Production is steady
at 2.9 million gallons (11 million l).

*Local produce in Kyrgyzstan, the least
urbanized of all the ex-Soviet republics.*

Australia

Australia

Wine has been made in Australia for almost 200 years, but the large-scale growth of wine production is a recent development because a widespread culture of table wine drinking has only developed over the last 35 years. This recent development is characterized in the industry structure in which most wine is made by just a few large companies, in its willingness to ignore European tradition to produce interregional blends, and in the emphasis it places on technological development. The last 15 years has seen the emergence of very large companies, the largest of which, Southcorp, is responsible for almost 30 percent of wine production and incorporates such historic brand names as Penfolds, Lindemans, Wynns and Seaview. Also important are BRL Hardy, Orlando Wyndham (itself owned by the French company Pernod Ricard), Mildara Blass and Simeon Wines (most of whose production is sold in bulk). Between them, they control more than 70 percent of all production.

A number of renowned middle-ranking producers, such as McWilliams and Rosemount, are still family owned, however, while there are now over 1,100 wine companies in Australia, 98 percent of them produce less than 5 percent of all wine.

Darwin
Palmerston

Arnhem Land

Joseph Bonaparte Gulf

KIMBERLEY

King Leopold Ranges

Mt Broome
3 ft (935 m) ▲

Daly

Katherine

Roper

Ord

Victoria

Lake Argyle

Fitzroy

Gulf of Carpentaria

Mitchell

Cairns

Karumba

Mt Bartle Frere
5299 ft (1615 m) ▲

Leichhardt

Flinders

Townsville

Northern Territory

Barkly Tableland

Tanami Desert

Tennant Creek

Mount Isa

Georgina

Queensland

Lake Dalrymple

Mt Dalrymple
4190 ft (1277 m) ▲

Mackay

T SANDY

DESERT

Lake Mackay

ake sappointment

Gibson Desert

MacDonnell Ranges

Alice Springs

Lake Amadeus

Longreach

Rockhampton

Gladstone

egie

Katatjuta (Mt Olga)
3497 ft (1066 m) ▲
▲ Uluru (Ayers Rock)
2831 ft (863 m)

Finke

Simpson Desert

Diamantina

Cooper

Bundaberg

Maryborough

GREAT VICTORIA

▲ Mt Woodroffe
4708 ft (1435 m)

Musgrave Ranges

Marla

Alberga

Warburton

Strzelecki Desert

Bulloo

Charleville

South Burnett

Kingaroy

Gympie

Nambour

alia

Caboolture

Peroo

Warrego

Balonne

Toowoomba

Brisbane

DESERT

Lake Eyre

Coober Pedy

South Australia

Warrego

Warwick

Nerang

Granite Belt

e Carey

Lake Rebecca

Darling

Namoi

Round Mtn
5203 ft
(1586 m)

Ballina

lie

ke Lefroy

Nullarbor Plain

Lake Torrens

Flinders Ranges

Lake Frome

New South Wales

Grafton

Sawtell

Armidale

Northern Rivers

erance

Eucla

Great

Australian Bight

Ceduna

St Mary Peak
3832 ft (1168 m) ▲

Broken Hill

Macquarie

Tamworth

Port Macquarie

Port Augusta

Whyalla

Port Pirie

Dubbo

Mudgee

Muswellbrook

Hunter Valley

Maitland

Port Lincoln

Clare Valley

The Barossa
Riverland

Mildura

Northwest Victoria

Lachlan

Central Ranges

Orange

Bathurst

Cowra

Cessnock

Newcastle

Gawler

Adelaide

Adelaide Hills

Murray Bridge

Big Rivers

Griffith

Cootamundra

DIVIDING

Katoomba

SYDNEY

McLaren Vale

Langhorne Creek

Victoria

Murray

Wagga Wagga

Goulburn

Wollongong

CANBERRA
Australian Capital Territory

Coonawarra & the Limestone Coast

Horsham

Central Victoria

Echuca

Wangaratta

Rutherglen & NE Victoria

Albury

Wodonga

Southern NSW

Penola

Grampians & Pyrenees

Bendigo

Ballarat

Mt Hotham
6125 ft (1867 m) ▲

South Coast

Mt Kosciuszko
7312 ft (2229 m) ▲

Mount Gambier

Portland

Yarra Valley

Bairnsdale

Geelong

Melbourne

Moe

Sale

Gippsland

GREAT

Warrnambool

Port Phillip

Mornington Peninsula

Bass Strait

NORTH

200 miles
(320 kilometers)

Burnie

Devonport

Launceston

Mt Ossa
5305 ft (1617 m) ▲

Tasmania

Hobart

This concentration of production is also mirrored geographically. At one extreme, the state of South Australia makes more then half of all Australian wine and is home to the largest producers. At the other, Tasmania, with 8 percent of the companies, makes less than 0.5 percent of the nation's wine.

What is often forgotten in the pursuit of top wines like Penfold's Grange and Henschke's Hill of Grace is that half of all wine consumed in Australia is bulk wine, usually purchased in 1 gallon (4 l) casks. The basis of this wine—and many of the cheaper bottles of Australian wine sold in supermarkets around the world—is the multiregional blend. "Wine of southeastern Australia" on a label means that the wine could come from anywhere except Western Australia, that is, from any of 98 percent of the nation's vineyard area. Such wine may well be sold as varietal blends and will be distinctively Australian, but will fly in the face of the traditional European concept of terroir. However, this does not mean the wines are of poorer quality—these fruity, accessible wines have revolutionized the international wine market in the last two decades—and even Australia's greatest wine, Grange, is traditionally a blend from a

number of regions. These mass-produced wines could not exist without the viticultural development of Australia's vast irrigated areas. Most people could not name Australia's largest wine region, but Riverland, watered from the Murray River, produces more

than a quarter of the country's wine. Other areas such as Riverina are equally important.

While the all-purpose denomination of "southeastern Australia" covers many wines, the developing system of Geographic Indications to mark out the boundaries of the wine regions is based firmly on the states. Within the states is a hierarchy of zones, regions and subregions of varying sizes. And size rarely relates to volume—the largest region, Great Southern in Western Australia—produces less than 0.2 percent of the country's wine. Yet for all the reliance on large-scale production, there is a growing awareness of the importance of a regional, or even single-vineyard, imprint, especially on premium wines. While distinctive regional styles, such as Hunter Valley sémillon and Barossa shiraz (syrah), have been recognized for decades, many other regions (Clare, Coonawarra, Margaret River and Yarra Valley, for instance) are becoming known for making specific varietials in particular styles. Although not widely known now, Mount Barker riesling or Tasmanian sparkling wines may one day be considered world class.

Two things can be singled out to explain Australia's rapid rise to world-quality wine production. The first is the emphasis on technology. Australian wines are often criticized for being too clean, made with a focus on hygiene and minimum oxygen contact, however, the crisp and fresh value-for-money chardonnay that actually tastes of melon and peaches and seems run-of-the-mill today barely existed 20 years ago. Australia came to large-scale wine production without winemaking traditions and with the capital to invest in state-of-the-art equipment and a determination for technological perfection that is also emphasized in Australia's excellent university courses in viticulture and winemaking.

The second factor is the willingness, even keenness, of Australian winemakers to share their own ideas and to learn from their colleagues. An extension of this is the show system of wine competitions spawned by the regional agricultural shows, and it has been of inestimable value in raising the quality of Australian wine. Notwithstanding the obvious marketing benefits of winning medals, many winemakers use the

Below: *Tourism is encouraged through facilities such as this tasting room at the Mt Pleasant Winery, Hunter Valley.*

Bottom: *The Charles Melton vineyard in the world-renowned Barossa Valley.*

shows to learn from the judges about the strengths
and weaknesses of their wines.

The growing domestic popularity of Australian
wine has been mirrored by export growth. It has
risen in volume from 10.3 million gallons (39 million l) in 1987 to 57 million gallons (216 million l)
in 1998–99. Most of the exports are focused on
the UK market (45 percent), but the USA, Canada,
Japan and Scandinavia are also important. At the
same time, the rise in interest in the wines has
provoked the new phenomenon of wine tourism.
People have been visiting wine regions for years,
but deliberately encouraging tourists with tours,
accommodation, good food and a host of other
related attractions has become a major industry
in Australia today.

AUSTRALIAN WINE REGIONS

Australia is a large country—Margaret River is
further from the Hunter Valley than Jerez in Spain
is from Tokaji in Hungary—so, despite the distinctive national approach to wine, Australian wines
are not all the same. The wines of Margaret River
and of the Hunter Valley differ as much as sherry
and tokay do. The three most important wine-
producing states are South Australia, Victoria and
New South Wales. As well as bulk production,
they each have specific premium wine regions.

In South Australia, the Clare Valley is renowned for its riesling, and the warmer Barossa
Valley and McLaren Vale make big wines, especially from shiraz. Increasing attention is being
focused on the cool Adelaide Hills, with chardonnay, pinot noir and sparkling showing high
quality. The cooler Coonawarra and surrounding
Limestone Coast have developed an affinity for
cabernet and cabernet blends. Riverland is the
workhorse of South Australian regions. As befits
the most intensively planted state, a wide range
of styles is made.

In Victoria, the Western Victoria zone includes
the regions of the Grampians—once know as Great
Western, well known for its sparkling wines—and
the Pyrenees. Fortified wines are the specialty in
the hot region of Rutherglen. The state is now best
known for its fairly disparate cool-climate wine
regions, like the Yarra Valley and Mornington
Peninsula. The cool-climate regions of Gippsland,
Macedon and Geelong concentrate on pinot noir
and chardonnay, while the warm Central Victoria
region produces powerful and fruity reds.

Historically, the Hunter Valley, first planted
with vines in the 1820s, was the only renowned

area in New South Wales—for its
classic aged sémillons and distinctive
shiraz. More recently, geographically
diverse zones have been developed
ranging from the subtropical Northern
Rivers to the South Coast. In between,
the Central Ranges are producing some
notable wines, particularly chardonnay,
the Big Rivers region has gained a
following for its botrytized wines, and
the diverse Southern New South Wales
region is making typically cool-climate varieties.

In Western Australia, the cooler southern
regions, such as Margaret River and Great
Southern, are making high-quality table wines.
The longer established Margaret River region has
gained international recognition for its chardonnay and cabernet-based wines. The more newly
developed and isolated Great Southern is becoming known for its shiraz and riesling. The Swan
Valley, close to Perth, is one of the country's
oldest and hottest regions, and Geographe's
landscape and climate are similar to those of
its southern neighbor, Margaret River.

Queensland's most prominent wine-producing
region, the Granite Belt, takes advantage of its
high altitude to make a range of cool-climate
wines. Other regions, some of which are near
the coast, rely on grape varieties that can thrive
in hot and humid conditions.

Tiny Tasmania is the home of the small-scale
enthusiast, with only a couple of even moderate-
sized companies on the island. Although there is
no containing their determination with chardonnay and pinot noir, in the long term, aromatic
whites like riesling and sparkling wine may turn
out to be their most important wines.

Steve Charters **MW**

Above: *A cellar at Seppelt Great Western in Victoria.*

Top: *Winter vines at Tolpuddle Vineyard Estate in the small but beautiful Tasmania.*

Major Companies

Jeremy Oliver

SOUTHCORP WINES

Australia's largest wine company Southcorp Wines claims to be the seventh largest in the world. With sales of A$660 million (US$400 million) last year, A$313 million (US$190 million) of which were exports, it produces around 30 percent by value of all Australian wine. Spectacular international growth of its key brands, Lindemans and Penfolds, has been responsible for its 20 percent annual growth in earnings over the last six years.

Australia is probably the only nation whose largest company is attempting to make its best wine. Southcorp's commitment to quality can be seen in wines like Penfolds Grange and Bin 707 Cabernet Sauvignon, Wynns John Riddoch Cabernet Sauvignon and Michael Shiraz, Leo Buring Leonay Riesling, Seppelt Salinger, Coldstream Hills Reserve Pinot Noir and Reserve Chardonnay, the Devil's Lair Cabernet, plus the new white Penfolds Yattarna. Southcorp also produces many lower-priced brands like Queen Adelaide Chardonnay, Lindemans Bin 65 Chardonnay, Queen Adelaide Regency Red, Penfolds Koonunga Hill and Penfolds Rawson's Retreat. Southcorp's myriad brands cover virtually the entire spectrum of possible combinations of region, variety and price.

An old wooden church has been restored for the Hungerford Hill cellar door.

Penfolds produces the country's dominant range of red wines. Leo Buring is Australia's most prestigious maker of dry riesling. Wynns Coonawarra Estate is Coonawarra's most historic vineyard and makes some of its best reds. Seppelt is Australia's most substantial and seasoned maker of sparkling wines, and Devil's Lair is a leading maker of Margaret River cabernet and chardonnay. Coldstream Hills is one of the Yarra Valley's most important labels, and at Seppeltsfield in the Barossa Valley Southcorp has a unique resource of fortified wines, principally port and sherry.

Southcorp's 15,000 acres (6,000 ha) under vine makes it Australia's dominant vineyard owner and possibly the world's largest. Three-quarters of its 25 different vineyards are in South Australia, where the company is the largest owner of Terra Rossa soils in Coonawarra, has substantial plantings of mature vines in the Barossa Valley, and is a major owner of vineyards at Clare, Padthaway, McLaren Vale, Eden Valley and the Riverlands. It also owns vineyards in the Hunter Valley and Barooga in New South Wales; in the Yarra Valley, Elmhurst and the Murray Basin in Victoria, and Margaret River in Western Australia.

Its principal wineries are at Nuriootpa and Seppeltsfield in the Barossa Valley, and at Karodoc and Great Western, its specialist sparkling facility, in Victoria. It owns other wineries at Coonawarra and Riverland in South Australia, the Hunter Valley and Yenda (Griffith) in New South Wales, Margaret River in Western Australia and the Yarra Valley in Victoria. In 1999, these wineries crushed 247,000 tons (224,000 tonnes).

Outside Australia, Southcorp produces La Perouse wines in the Languedoc-Roussillon region of France and, in the same region, acquired the James Herrick brand in 1999. In the USA, it produces Seven Peaks wines in partnership with Paragon Vineyards in the Edna Valley, and in 1997 it purchased a site for a new vineyard development near Paso Robles, California.

History

Unlike its key brands, Southcorp is a recent addition to the annals of Australian winemaking. Southcorp's image is largely structured around Penfolds, Seppelt, Wynns and Lindemans, each of which were very significant and substantial individual enterprises and owners of major national labels until relatively recently. In 1994 the Penfolds Wine Group became Southcorp Wines after its parent company changed its name in 1993 from SA Brewing Holdings to Southcorp Holdings. SA Brewing already owned Seppelt, Queen Adelaide and Hungerford Hill when it purchased Penfolds in 1991. That transaction brought with it Kaiser Stuhl, Wynns Coonawarra Estate, Seaview, Killawarra, Tulloch, Tollana, Lindemans, Leo Buring, Rouge Homme and Matthew Lang.

Despite an enormous number of distinctive brands, Southcorp has successfully managed to

maintain the integrity and identity of each. Where Southcorp owns several distinct brands in a single region, it has steadfastly retained the individual stamp and style of each. However, with the exception of a small number of Seppelt wines, plus a few premier Lindemans Coonawarra and Penfolds Clare Estate and Magill labels, Southcorp tends to shun the single vineyard concept. The remarkable consistency in quality, style and character of Southcorp wines has contributed greatly to its success in Australian and international markets.

Key wines

Except for the excellent Devil's Lair and Coldstream Hills chardonnays and the Leo Buring rieslings, Southcorp's best wines are reds. However, the "White Grange" project, which culminated in the release of Yattarna after just four years of experimentation, has substantially closed the gap between Southcorp and other leading Australian makers of wood-matured white wines.

There is no doubt about the deservedly high status of Penfolds reds, culminating with Bin 707 Cabernet Sauvignon and Grange. Penfolds takes pride in having resisted fluctuations in wine fashion, even though today's wines are clearly more polished and better balanced while young than ever before. At the other end of the scale, new

Southcorp brands like Soho and Thirsty Fish have more contemporary looks and lighter tastes to provide a fashionable entry point for young new wine drinkers. Southcorp's collection of key Coonawarra labels is headed by Wynns, whose Black Label Cabernet Sauvignon perpetuates a rich tradition of longevity and value, while the Shiraz and Riesling represent fine value. Rouge Homme's reds occasionally flirt with more herbaceous expressions of sweet berry Coonawarra fruit, while Lindemans premier Coonawarra reds pack together sweet fruit and toasty oak.

The Hunter Valley provides Southcorp with a steadily improving collection under the Lindemans brand, plus the idiosyncratic Tulloch range, whose best wine by far is Hector Shiraz. Southcorp's McLaren Vale label has just undergone a revamp and renaming to Edwards & Chaffey, while the Tollana label is carried by a very affordable range of fine Eden Valley table wines.

The Seppelt, Penfolds, Killawarra and Seaview brands dominate the cheaper sparkling sector in Australia, while Seppelt's Great Western releases excellent premium-quality sparkling wines under the Salinger label. There's little doubt, however, that Seppelt has ceded its traditional place as the maker of Australia's best sparkling wines to Domaine Chandon and other recent arrivals into

Triple gables appear on the Wynns Coonawarra Estate label.

These black grapes are ready to be crushed.

Giant steel vats house Orlando Wines' huge production.

Patterned rows of Barossa Valley vines are backed by distant hills.

the sparkling market such as Yarrabank and Pirie.

Devil's Lair and Coldstream Hills fill some important niches for Southcorp. These cooler climate vineyards represent the cutting edge for Southcorp's winemakers, since they've been established in relatively youthful wine regions where experimentation with variety, clone and wine expression is still actively encouraged.

Even before its current program to double its red wine processing ability, Southcorp claimed to be the world's largest maker of premium red wine. Announced in late 1997, the $A405 million (US$245 million) investment over five years involves spending $A145 million (US$88 million) directly on vineyard and winery expansion, the most significant investment ever in Australian wine history. Another $45 to 50 million (US$27–30 million) is earmarked for additional oak cooperage.

With sales to North America and Europe up by 17 and 12 percent in the 1999 financial year, every red brand in its portfolio is presently in short supply. While nobody at Southcorp could expect to double the quantity of its premier labels within a mere five years, much of its investment in vineyards has taken place in the Limestone Coast region, adjacent to Coonawarra and Padthaway in South Australia's southeast corner, where red soils and consistently cool ripening seasons should produce excellent red wine.

ORLANDO WYNDHAM

One of Australia's giant wine companies, Orlando Wyndham is a fully owned subsidiary of Groupe Pernod Ricard. Its greatest asset is Jacob's Creek, Australia's principal export brand, which achieved sales of more than 3.5 million cases in 1999. The brand accounts for more than 20 percent of Australian table wine exports and is the single largest selling Australian bottled wine in the UK, Ireland, Norway, Japan, Singapore and New Zealand.

Orlando Wyndham's approach to growth contrasts dramatically with that of Mildara Blass, Southcorp and BRL Hardy. Its best-known wines tend to be its less expensive ones, and it is focused on growth of its existing brands rather than on acquiring other brands or establishing new labels. Its relatively small number of brands and their scale reflects a distinctive and long-term philosophy, no doubt encouraged by its French parent.

Orlando Wyndham's main production facility, at its original birthplace, Rowland Flat, in the Barossa Valley, is the company's center for white and sparkling wine production and final blending and packaging. Its second Barossa winery, Richmond Grove, has been converted into a large but specialist red wine cellar, although very fine rieslings are still produced there under the guidance of legendary winemaker John Vickery.

At Mudgee in New South Wales, the former Montrose winery has been refurbished as Orlando Wyndham Mudgee, while the Craigmoor winery has become the cellar door of the revamped Poet's Corner brand. Wyndham Estate remains the company's base in the Hunter Valley, and its other major New South Wales winery is Wickham Hill in the Riverlands.

The enduring exception in the company's collection of large production facilities is the historic Morris winery in Rutherglen, in northeast Victoria, where David Morris has been wisely left to practice his trade in much the same way that others in his family did before him.

Current vineyard holdings are around 4,800 acres (1,940 ha), mostly in South Australia, with the majority at Langhorne Creek, Padthaway and Coonawarra. Like most other large owners at Padthaway, Orlando Wyndham has reworked its plantings there, converting them from bag-in-the-box standard to a level consistent with its Saints range. With only 500 acres (200 ha) evenly divided between the Barossa floor and the Eden Valley, Orlando is not a substantial land owner at its winemaking headquarters.

History

Orlando Wyndham dates back to the small vineyard planted at Jacob's Creek in 1847 by Johann Gramp, a Bavarian immigrant who sent to Germany for the cuttings. The first vintage of 50 gallons (180 l) from this, the Barossa Valley's first vineyard, was in 1850. The company became G. Gramp and Sons Ltd in 1912, and the Orlando trademark was introduced that year. Growth was strong and steady until the onset of the 1930s depression.

In the early 1950s, managing director Colin Gramp introduced the German technique of using pressure tanks for fermentation to control the escape of carbon dioxide, slowing the rate of fermentation, to produce livelier, fresher and more aromatic white wines. Gramp's 1953 vintage was a remarkable wine that revolutionised white winemaking in Australia and initiated the now famous Orlando Special Vintage Barossa Riesling series. Orlando's second success story of the 1950s was Barossa Pearl, Australia's first naturally sweetened and effervescent wine, which was released in late 1956. It was as affordable as it was approachable and, although it would be viewed in a rather different light today, it introduced multitudes of Australians to wine.

In late 1970, the Gramp family sold out to Reckitt and Coleman, which had also purchased Morris Wines in Rutherglen and the Wickham Hill winery at Griffith in same year. Eighteen years later, Orlando was sold to a group of its directors, and Pernod Ricard obtained majority ownership in May 1989. By January 1990, Pernod Ricard had added the publicly listed Wyndham Group to its stable, and Orlando Wyndham was established.

Wyndham Estate dates back to the 1830s, when Hunter Valley pioneer George Wyndham founded the Dalwood vineyard which, after a period of ownership by Penfolds, was sold to its cellarmaster Perc McGuigan in the early 1960s. The McGuigans expanded rapidly in the 1970s and, by the time Pernod Ricard bought the company, Wyndham owned a number of successful brands and wineries, including Richmond Grove, Morris, Montrose and Craigmoor.

The very export-orientated Orlando Wyndham offers exceptional consistency and value in most of its labels, especially Orlando, Richmond Grove, Craigmoor and Montrose. The company is strongly entrenched in the UK, the USA and in several

Hunter Valley vineyards cover gently rolling hills.

Asian and European markets. A valid criticism of Orlando Wyndham is that it has largely ignored its Barossa heritage and has only recently reintroduced a small number of exclusively Barossa wines. Similarly, the company's portfolio hasn't exactly been strong on Hunter Valley wine.

Key wines

Synonymous with Orlando Wyndham, the Jacob's Creek label was introduced in 1976 with a 1973 blend of shiraz, cabernet sauvignon and malbec from Padthaway, Coonawarra and McLaren Vale. Its quality has remained consistent and its value unquestioned, especially the red blend and the Riesling. The excellent Saints range of Orlando wines was introduced in 1983 with the first-rate 1980 St Hugo Coonawarra Cabernet Sauvignon. It has been joined by the St Helga Riesling and St Hilary Chardonnay, which have always offered fine varietal expression and value.

Montrose has been making true-to-style expressions of red Italian varieties from its mature vineyard at Mudgee, and creating some excellent wines. Richmond Grove, originally developed as an Upper Hunter Valley label by the entrepreneurial Mark Cashmore, has relocated to the Barossa Valley, becoming a national brand in the process, and even encompassing a New Zealand sauvignon blanc. Its Barossa and Watervale rieslings, made in the traditional John Vickery style, are exceptional wines.

Orlando Wyndham's style reflects the long-term European approach of its parent, but that's not to suggest that it isn't moving quickly. Its ambition is

Montrose Wines specializes in red Italian varieties.

Vines were first planted on the Houghton Wines Swan Valley property in the 1830s.

Houghton Wines' swan logo welcomes visitors to the cellar door.

to export more than five million cases around the world each year by 2003.

BRL HARDY LTD

BRL Hardy is the largest of Australia's wine companies remaining as a single publicly traded entity. For years, it appeared to grow despite an apparent lack of strong brands, but recently has re-invented itself by focusing on its historic regional strengths, especially in McLaren Vale and Western Australia, and more recently in Clare, Padthaway and Coonawarra. The outstanding winemaking team has created a collection of red wines second only to Penfolds and developed a fine smorgasbord from Houghton to Nottage Hill to the Leasingham Bin wines and to its now established classics like Eileen Hardy Shiraz and the Tintara reds. An emergent class of fine sparkling wines under the Arras label has joined the excellent value Sir James brand and the popular Omni.

BRL's sales have increased from A$238.3 million (US$144.6 million) in 1993 to A$463.6 million (US$281.3 million) in 1998. Exports now represent around 40 percent of revenue, major markets being the UK, Canada, the USA, Japan and New Zealand. Export sales are based on the Nottage Hill, Stamps and Banrock Station labels, with some early promise shown by the Stonehaven label from Padthaway. The company crushed 242,400 tons (220,000 t) in 1999, up from 180,200 tons (163,500 t) in 1998.

The traditional Hardy vineyard base in McLaren Vale remains the focal point of its excellent red wines, headed by the Tintara and the new Reynell reds. It contributes to the flagship Eileen Hardy Shiraz, which also contains a strong Padthaway

component. Although BRL wineries are equipped with all the latest gadgetry, it takes a traditional approach for its best fruit. Around 7,200 tons (6,500 t) are processed at its Tintara winery; 2,200 tons of this (2,000 t) being put through open fermenters, all hand pressed in old basket presses, then hand-shoveled.

Outside McLaren Vale, BRL Hardy owns two major wineries in the Riverlands, others at Clare in South Australia, Buronga in New South Wales, and the Houghton winery in the Swan Valley in Western Australia. Its A$18 million (US$11 million) Stonehaven development at Padthaway in South Australia has an 11,000 ton (10,000 t) capacity, and a 4,400 ton (4,000 t) winery is pending in the Canberra region in the Australian Capital Territory. BRL also owns and operates the small Yarra Burn winery in Victoria's Yarra Valley and has a 50 percent stake in Margaret River's Brookland Valley in Western Australia and in Barossa Valley Estates in South Australia.

BRL Hardy's major vineyard assets its winery locations, but it also has substantial plantings at Coonawarra, Wrattonbully and Langhorne Creek in South Australia, at Frankland River, Mount Barker, Pemberton and Gingin in Western Australia and at Lake Cullulleraine at Sunraysia and Hoddle's Creek in the Yarra Valley, Victoria. Owner of 4730 acres (1915 ha) of vineyard, it is a joint venture partner in 940 acres (380 ha) and leases another 295 acres (120 ha) to complete its a total area under vine of 5965 acres (2415 ha).

The company also owns half a joint venture interest in a new Chilean wine brand, Mapocho, whose wines are made by Jose Canepa and distributed internationally through the BRL Hardy network. Overseas interests also include majority ownership of the Domaine de la Baume winery in Languedoc Roussillon, the D'instinto joint venture brand in Europe, a joint venture in New Zealand with Nobilo and National Liquor Distributors Ltd, and operating subsidiaries in Europe, USA and Canada.

History

The first job in Australia of Hardy's founder, English immigrant Thomas Hardy, was that of laborer for John Reynell of Reynella Farm. He later purchased the Bankside property on the River Torrens in 1853 and made his first wine in 1857. He bought the Tintara winery in 1876 and, by 1895, Hardy had become Australia's largest wine producer. Hardy's 1976 purchase of the Emu Wine

Company, which owned a winery at Morphett Vale, also delivered one of its greatest long-term assets, the Houghton brand in Western Australia. With the wheel turning full circle, Thomas Hardy & Sons Ltd bought Walter Reynell & Sons Ltd in 1982, shortly thereafter moving its base to the superbly restored and refurbished Reynella complex. Ten years later in 1992, Thomas Hardy was itself bought by Berri-Renmano, creating the entity BRL Hardy Ltd.

Despite the large proportion of cask wine in its total output, BRL's renewed confidence and performance has been driven by wine quality. Its viticulturists and winemakers have been permitted to set and achieve high standards across its entire bottled range, which sets it apart from the other four large Australian producers.

Key wines

BRL Hardy's top-end reds include those bottled under the Reynell, Tintara and Eileen Hardy labels, Leasingham Classic Clare Cabernet Sauvignon and Shiraz, Thomas Hardy Cabernet Sauvignon, Yarra Burn Cabernet Sauvignon and Pinot Noir and the Houghton flagship Jack Mann Red. Its selection of premier white wines, effectively Eileen Hardy Chardonnay and Leasingham Classic Clare Riesling, looks thin by comparison.

BRL's mid-market white table wines offer good value and consistency. The fine and flavorsome Hardy Siegersdorf Riesling and Houghton White Burgundy, the clean and refreshing Moondah Brook whites, the sumptuous and classically proportioned Crofters reds, and the Leasingham Bin series red wines are some of the best value wines under A$20 (US$12). At the cheaper end of the market are the environmentally friendly Nottage Hill and Banrock Station brands.

BRL Hardy has the quality wines and resources that would complement those of another large Australian wine producer, with the possible exception of Orlando Wyndham, that really wanted to take a dominant position in the marketplace. The only things preventing this from happening is its share price and the return it provides its current investors.

MILDARA BLASS

Unquestionably the most aggressive and profit-driven Australian wine company of any significance, Mildara Blass is a fully owned subsidiary of Australia's largest brewer, Fosters Ltd. It claims around 40 percent of the Australian sparkling wine market and 25 percent of Australia's premium table wine market. Its 1999 vintage was 10.2 million gallons (38.8 million l), sourced from its own 8,155 acres (3,300 ha) under vine plus its contracted grape suppliers.

Mildara Blass' annual sales of 5 million cases are worth A$562.7 million (US$341.4 million). Nearly half are exported, key overseas markets being the USA, UK and other European countries. More than half of its wine exports are to the USA, where sales rose by 25 percent in 1999. Wolf Blass, its most successful export brand, is the largest selling Australian wine in Canada and Mildara Blass' dominant brand in the UK, achieving an extraordinary 77 percent growth by volume in 1998. Mildara Blass also claims that its export-only Black Opal label is the largest selling "premium" Australian wine in the US.

Owner of more than 30 brands, Mildara Blass has assembled a major direct-selling business headed by the Australian company Cellarmaster, one of the world's largest wine clubs. It also owns wine clubs in Holland and Germany. Mildara Blass is working feverishly to meet pent-up global demand for red wine and, helped by its recent purchase of McLaren Vale producer Maglieri,

Hardy's Chateau Reynella is the head-quarters for BRL Hardy.

The tasting room at Maglieri wines in McLaren Vale.

increased its volume of red wine sales by 28 percent in 1999.

Mildara Blass owes much of its profitability to its focus on the top-priced 25 percent of the wine market and the top-priced 5 percent outside Australia. Its before-tax earnings for 1999 were up by a remarkable 46 percent to $120 million (US$79 million). Mildara Blass' expansionary style has paid great dividends with some subsidiaries, such as Yellowglen and Wolf Blass, but others like Krondorf, Tisdall and Balgownie, have lost their original direction and focus.

The Maglieri, Yellowglen, Black Opal, Andrew Garrett, Wolf Blass, Rothbury Estate, Saltram (Barossa), Baileys, Yarra Ridge and St Huberts and Ingoldby brands have now joined the company's home-grown collection of Jamieson's Run, Mildara Coonawarra, Annie's Lane, Robertson's Well, Half Mile Creek and Flanagan's Ridge. Mildara Blass also owns the wine club brands Pallhuber, Cellarmaster and Pelican Point. Its overseas acquisitions comprise 310 acres (125 ha) of developing vineyard in California, where the company owns the Bayliss & Fortune brand, plus a winery in Chile producing the Dallas-Conte range of wines "made in the Australian style." Mildara Blass also owns bottling, packaging and wine delivery services that contribute about A$100 million (US$61 million) per year to its revenue.

History

Although its history dates back to 1888, the Mildara trademark wasn't registered by the then Mildura-based company until 1937. After the Second World War, remained largely a sherry producer well into the 1960s. The first Mildara red table wine was made in 1951. After acquiring a controlling interest in Walter Reynell & Sons in 1952, Mildara enjoyed more than 20 years of successful with its multi-regional "yellow label" series. A desire to make finer and more elegant reds led winemaker Ron Haselgrove and son Richard to Coonawarra in 1953, where he bought Mildara's first vineyard site in 1955 and steadily increased Mildara's vineyard ownership. The company built its Coonawarra winery in time for the 1973 vintage, and its Coonawarra wines gradually supplanted the yellow label series as Mildara's premier reds. Mildara acquired the historic Eden Valley wine producer Hamiltons in 1979, then bought Yellowglen in 1984 and Balgownie in 1985, heralding a decade of acquisitions whose highlight was the purchase of Wolf Blass Wines Ltd in 1991.

Wolf Blass fashioned the first wines destined for release under the Wolf Blass label in 1966 while working as winemaker for Tolley, Scott and Tolley. He left that company in 1973 to pursue his own brand, at the Bilyara site outside Nuriootpa, in South Australia, in 1969. His first wine was a Yellow Label red. Five years later he began his remarkable run of three straight Jimmy Watson Trophies. Chief winemaker John Glaetzer, who joined the company in 1975, has more than maintained the company's brilliant record in Australian wine shows. Wolf Blass issued the prospectus for Wolf Blass Wines Ltd in 1984. Six years after Mildara purchased Wolf Blass, Mildara Blass was itself bought by Fosters Brewing, which then added the Rothbury Group to its stable in 1998.

As a business, it is hard to pin weaknesses on Mildara Blass. Its performance has been exceptional for more than a decade, and it has shown larger and more established Australian makers that wine can indeed generate returns on investment comparable with other industries. It is clearly less interested in what are now called "super premium" wines, but focuses almost exclusively on the purchase or development of solid mid-market brands where a return can be made. It's not the most prestigious of Australian wine companies, nor is it likely to be, but it is the most profitable.

Mildara Blass now owns several brands based in or adjacent to Coonawarra. However, in its efforts to create a strong market presence for the Jamiesons Run, Robertson's Well and other labels, it has virtually left its famous Mildara Coonawarra brand to wither on the vine.

The straw mulch and blue sky contrast with the Maglieri Vineyard's vines.

Key wines

The small number of outstanding Mildara Blass wines includes the excellent reds of Nigel Dolan at Saltram in the Barossa Valley, which are released under the Saltram and Mamre Brook labels. His Metala reds, the Original Vines Shiraz especially, are also excellent value. Wolf Blass reds have changed very little over the years, so its new regionally labelled table wines of considerable character have been greeted with some interest. Wolf Blass rieslings, especially the Gold Label, are justifiably rated highly for quality and value.

The three new Clare Essentials rieslings support the claim by Mildara Blass to be taken seriously as a maker of top-shelf table wines. Annie's Lane is another standout brand for its apparently under-priced delivery of excellent Clare Valley table wines, atop of which sits the Contour Shiraz.

Mildara Blass sees its future as one of the world's great premium wine companies. Its continued expansion will be based on increasing exports, making more wine in other countries and in developing a global net of direct-selling wine clubs, which already account for 10 percent of the world's wine club market.

ROSEMOUNT ESTATE

Rosemount Estate could be judged by its premier wines, the Roxburgh Chardonnay, Balmoral Syrah, Mountain Blue Shiraz Cabernet, or its Show Reserve series, but the Oatley family, who owns the company, and its head winemaker Philip Shaw prefer as a yardstick the Diamond Series wines, especially the Chardonnay and Shiraz, and its very affordable early-drinking reds like the Shiraz/Cabernet and Shiraz/Grenache.

Rosemount Estate remains a family company, headed by founder Bob's son Sandy and son-in-law Keith Lambert. The Oatleys have invested more than A$100 million (US$61 million) in recent years and have rejected offers to sell out for around A$200 million (US$122 million). The company has more than doubled production in the last three years to around three million cases. Sales in the USA and Europe account for more than 60 percent of production, while domestic Australian sales are climbing at a rate of more than 20 percent per year. Annual sales are close to A$200 million (US$122 million).

A rose garden welcomes visitors to Rosemount Estate in the Hunter Valley.

A new state-of-the-art winery has been constructed adjacent to the original one in Denman, New South Wales. The company's vineyard assets of more than 4,000 acres (1,600 ha) reflect a mature approach to the matching of variety with region. Around 50 to 60 percent of Rosemount's production is still supplied by contracted growers. Instead of developing a range of regional brands encompassing all of the major red and white varieties, Rosemount has concentrated on making a large number of possible regional and varietal combinations in New South Wales, South Australia and Victoria.

The Upper Hunter remains a major source of Rosemount's premier chardonnay and sémillon, while the cooler volcanic slopes of Mount Canobolas near Orange are yielding flinty, refined chardonnay, some rather leafy cabernet sauvignon and very promising cabernet franc. In South Australia, Rosemount has a new red wine vineyard at Coonawarra, but has most closely linked its fate with shiraz from McLaren Vale. Sourced from a number of old vine vineyards, Balmoral is one of Australia's leading shiraz. Much of the material for the Diamond Label reds comes from Langhorne Creek, while Adelaide Hills is an important source of Rosemount's cool-climate sauvignon blanc and chardonnay. At Mudgee in New South Wales, shiraz, cabernet sauvignon and merlot are grown for the Mountain Blue and Hill of Gold wines, and the red Italian varieties could play a significant future role. Rosemount also has a largely red wine vineyard at Langhorne Creek and purchases as fruit a small amount of Clare Valley riesling and Yarra Valley chardonnay.

This statue of McWilliam's founder, John J. McWilliam, is at the company's Hanwood winery.

History

Bob Oatley planted 50 acres (20 ha) of shiraz and gewürztraminer at Denman in 1968. The company's first vintage, in 1974, yielded limited quantities of hermitage (shiraz) and rhine riesling. The next year, Rosemount added cabernet sauvignon, cabernet shiraz and traminer. By combining wise vineyard purchases with development of its own vineyards, Rosemount quickly acquired substantial holdings in the Upper Hunter Valley.

Although its first multiple award-winning wines were rhine rieslings and traminers, made from Hunter Valley fruit, Rosemount was only just behind Tyrrell's in pioneering chardonnay, making its first in 1979. The 1980 Show Chardonnay took a double gold medal at Bristol. Winemaker Philip Shaw made Rosemount's first Roxburgh Chardonnay in 1983, creating a lineage of flagship wines. The purchase of Ryecroft Vineyards in 1991 firmed up Rosemount's fruit supply in McLaren Vale. In 1999 a new and technically advanced winery was completed adjacent to the old.

Rosemount's greatest strength lies in the character and commitment of its owners and their employees. It's well and profitably managed, well resourced and directed, and has a clear plan for ongoing expansion without the need to raise public capital. Its other great strength is the quality of wine across its portfolio.

Key wines

Rosemount's flagship wines are Balmoral Syrah, Mountain Blue Shiraz Cabernet and Roxburgh Chardonnay. The Show Shiraz is a sumptuously wooded McLaren Vale. From the same region, the GSM and Traditional present modern Australian expressions of red rhône varieties and older-styled cabernet blends, respectively. The Show Cabernet Sauvignon, is one of the region's most underrated.

Its Show Sémillion is barrel fermented and matured like a chardonnay, while the Orange Vineyard Chardonnay presents a reserved expression of clear, bright fruit flavors with lingering mineral acids. Other chardonnays are the reserved, peachy and minerally Giant's Creek Chardonnay and the savory and long-living Show Reserve Chardonnay, both from Upper Hunter fruit. The popular and affordable Diamond Label Chardonnay still offers more interest and complexity than most of its competitors. Its Diamond Label reds have proven immensely popular in overseas markets like the USA.

Rosemount's owners don't see any reason to sell out and can't see the point in going public.

One can expect Rosemount to continue to grow and gradually add more combinations of region and variety to its top end, especially with cool-climate pinot noir from Victoria and shiraz from Victoria's new Heathcote region.

McWILLIAM'S

McWilliam's vies with Rosemount Estate for the title of Australia's largest family-owned wine company, and also its fifth-largest winemaker, crushing around 33,000 tons (30,000 t) annually. The sixth-generation company grows about a third of its total crush itself, a figure kept relatively low by the large volume of fruit it purchases in the Sunraysia area near its Robinvale winery in Victoria. Its largest export markets are the UK, the USA and New Zealand, with encouraging growth in Germany, Singapore and Japan.

Until recently McWilliam's focused on huge volumes of fortified and relatively uninteresting table wines from its traditional home of Griffith in the Riverina, plus some less-than-outstanding, but very affordable old-fashioned red and white table wines from Mount Pleasant in the Hunter Valley. Through a series of mergers, most of which ultimately became acquisitions, McWilliam's now boasts regional bases in Coonawarra, the Yarra Valley and Hilltops (New South Wales) and is sourcing fruit from Margaret River in Western Australia. The McWilliam's winemaking team headed by Jim Brayne has developed fine and very affordable wines from these new areas, and has refocused on its traditional strengths in the Hunter and Riverina, greatly improving the quality and of its entire range.

McWilliam's 2,050 acres (830 ha) of vineyards are in the Riverina, Hilltops, the Hunter Valley, Coonawarra and the Yarra Valley. Its largest holdings are 800 acres (325 ha) in the Riverina, mostly planted with shiraz and chardonnay. Shiraz, sémillon and some chardonnay make up most of its 257 acres (104 ha) of Hunter plantings, while cabernet sauvignon and shiraz are the main grapes at Coonawarra with 690 acres (280 ha) and Barwang's 252 acres (102 ha) in the Hilltops region.

McWilliam's small number of prestige labels are relatively recent introductions to its range. The company is instead staking a strong claim in the middle of the premium bottled market with clean, lively and approachable wines that don't require long cellaring periods. The jewel in its crown is the classic old Mount Pleasant property in the Lower Hunter Valley. These vineyards, some of which date back to 1880, are the backbone of the Mount Pleasant range, providing the grapes for some limited-release runs like OP & OH (Old Paddock and Old Hill) Shiraz, Rosehill Shiraz and the Maurice O'Shea Shiraz. The Lovedale Vineyard is the basis for the Elizabeth Sémillon and the Lovedale Sémillon. Its purchase of Brand's and its subsequent expansion has made McWilliam's the third largest vineyard owner in Coonawarra, while the company has reworked its relatively small plantings at Lillydale Vineyards in the Yarra Valley, where it still purchases most of its fruit.

History

Northern Irish immigrant Samuel McWilliam planted his first vines at Corowa, New South Wales, in 1877. His son John James McWilliam planted the first grapes at Hanwood in the Riverina in 1913 and built a winery there in 1917. Another followed at Yenda in 1920. The family acquired the Beelbangera winery in 1944 and built another at Robinvale in 1961 to handle its ever-increasing production, which peaked in the late 1970s. The Hanwood winery became the company's center for white wines and fortifieds, where McWilliam's really made its name.

Mount Pleasant was originally developed by Charles King in 1880 on the area's excellent red volcanic soils. It was bought by the O'Shea family in the early 1900s, and son Maurice, having studied viticulture and enology in France, assumed winemaking responsibilities in 1925. In 1932 he sold half the company to McWilliam's, which bought the entire company in 1941. As Mount Pleasant's winemaker for four decades, O'Shea was one of Australia's greatest. Brian Walsh took up the reins after O'Shea's death in 1956, and the present incumbent Phil Ryan arrived in 1978.

McWilliams began to move into new wine regions in 1989 with its involvement with Barwang, first established in 1969. A year later it purchased half the Brand family's Laira operation in Coonawarra, which it bought entirely in 1994, the same year it bought Lillydale Vineyards in the Yarra Valley.

In the mid-1990s, McWilliam's chief executive Kevin McLintock brought renewed energy to the company, and the family put many millions of dollars into infrastructure. It has greatly improved packaging and marketing, creating a new and contemporary feel to its steadily increasing range. Its wines are better than ever, and most are exceptionally affordable for their quality.

Key wines

The best known of McWilliam's quality wines is Mount Pleasant Elizabeth, a rich and deliciously flavorsome version of the classic Hunter Valley sémillon. At its price there is no finer white wine in Australia. The Lovedale Sémillon is a much creamier, more concentrated version of this wine, with extraordinary palate length and tingling fresh acids. The complex and gamey OP & OH Shiraz with suggestions of chocolate and spice. The more modern the Rosehill Hermitage, enunciates the raspberry and red currant expressions of shiraz. The very best of Mount Pleasant's shiraz crop is kept for a label dedicated to O'Shea himself, an oakier, but polished and fine regional wine.

Some of McWilliam's very best wines are the Barwangs, which are full of character, long-living and very distinctive. The Yarra wines of Lillydale, the Margaret River wines under the Samphire label and the Brand's Coonawarra wines are good, honest and reliable and around half the price of many of their competitors. The McWilliams Limited Release Botrytis Sémillon from Griffith fruit is shaping up exceptionally well. The Hanwood range of table wines delivers good value for money, and the old McWilliam's fortifieds, led by the classic Show Reserve label, are habitually brilliant.

The McWilliam family is keen to pursue further expansion plans, especially in Clare and McLaren Vale. Meanwhile, it continues to increase and improve its own plantings, notably with petit verdot, pinot noir, shiraz and the new hybrid tyrian, in the Riverina. It plans to release a new premium range featuring shiraz and grenache from the Barossa Valley and an Eden Valley riesling.

Chardonnay vines are labeled at the Cowra Estate vineyards.

The tasting room at Brand's of Coonawarra was the first in the district.

WESTERN AUSTRALIA

Margaret River

Peter Forrestal

In a little over 30 years, the small quiet farming community of Margaret River (which previously had depended on the dairy industry, some beef production, potato farming and forestry) has become a flourishing center for an internationally recognized wine industry. A key factor in this development has been the ability of the region's wineries to produce top-quality wines. Although the area is responsible for only about 1 percent of Australia's production, its wines make up as much as 20 percent of the premium market. The cost of production is high, partly because yields throughout the region are low and partly because the majority of wineries are small in size with a consequent impact on economies of scale.

The 1990s have seen an exponential increase in quality, especially from the most well established wineries. Margaret River chardonnay and cabernet sauvignon are particularly highly regarded, with the region producing many of Australia's best examples of these varietals. Its delicious sémillon/sauvignon blanc blends are popular on restaurant wine lists throughout Australia and overseas.

Although winemaking in Western Australia stretches almost as far back as European settlement, the first vineyards in the Margaret River area were small plots planted for family use by European immigrants in the early twentieth century. Later, in 1955, the distinguished American viticulturist, Professor Harold Olmo from the University of California at Davis, spent eight months at the University of Western Australia working on the viticultural problems facing the wine industry in the Swan Valley. He suggested in an aside that Margaret River might also prove to be suitable for growing premium grape varieties. That spawned a research paper by University of Western Australia agronomist Dr John Gladstones, published in the *Journal of the Australian Institute of Agricultural Science* in December 1965, that looked at the potential of Margaret River for viticulture. Gladstones' paper served as a catalyst for the establishment of wineries in the Margaret River region.

Margaret River has the most maritime-influenced climate of any Australian wine region. It has the lowest mean annual temperature range—13.7°F (7.6°C)—and a long, dry period from October to April with only 7.8 inches (200 mm) of rain. Its major problems come with the strong salty winds in spring, which affect budburst and keep yields low. Chardonnay is particularly affected by this. The dominant soil type is gravelly or gritty sandy loam formed from granite and gneissic rock. As sloping sites tend to lose moisture quickly, there is often a need for irrigation.

Large vineyards have been established in the former potato growing area in the north of the region. These have level surfaces, very fertile sandy loam soils, a plentiful supply of water and less severe growing conditions than in the settled viticultural areas of the

Margaret River's Amberley Estate vineyard bordered by a dam.

region. Two groups have emerged. One believes that overcropping is inevitable at Jindong and the resulting poor-quality wines will damage the reputation of Margaret River. The other, with a stake at Jindong, believes that high-quality fruit can be produced at commercially acceptable yields with careful watering, pruning and canopy management. They also believe this will lead to affordable wines of good quality.

A major development of the past few years has been the entry into the region of the major Australian wine companies. Southcorp has purchased the high-profile Devil's Lair and BRL Hardy has bought 50 percent of Brookland Valley. McWilliam's has entered into an agreement with Abbey Vale to become involved in the winemaking and release some of their production under the Samphire label. In all these cases the large companies have vowed to maintain quality while growing the brands. Meanwhile, because of its world-class wines, the professionalism of its wine industry, wonderful surfing beaches, picturesque bushland and thriving cottage industries, Margaret River has become an internationally significant tourist destination.

AMBERLEY ESTATE

Established 1986 *Owners* a syndicate *Production* 60,000 cases *Vineyard area* 78 acres (32 ha)

This large-scale producer relies on other growers as well as its own vineyards to produce wine from within the Margaret River appellation. While Amberley has always declared that commercial success was its primary goal, the winery has been able to achieve that as well as produce wines of exemplary quality at reasonable prices. Their Sémillon Sauvignon Blanc is one of the region's better examples of that blend. The Shiraz and Cabernet Merlot consistently have good varietal definition, smooth texture and abundant flavor.

BROOKLAND VALLEY VINEYARD

Established 1984 *Owners* BRL Hardy and the Jones and Poynton families *Production* 7,500 cases *Vineyard area* 50 acres (20 ha)

Outstanding show results have encouraged public interest in Brookland Valley wines, firstly with the tropically fruited Sauvignon Blanc and then the powerful, full-flavored Chardonnay. Expansion

has been inevitable since BRL Hardy acquired a half share in 1997. Two regional wines (a white and red under the Verse 1 label) have been introduced and a winery will be built for the 2001 vintage. A state-of-the-art vineyard edging a dam on the Willyabrup Brook forms a backdrop for the idyllic Flutes Cafe.

CAPE MENTELLE

Established 1970 *Owners* Veuve Clicquot and David Hohnen *Production* 65,000 cases *Vineyard area* 297 acres (120 ha)

The Cape Mentelle vineyard was one of the region's first and its fine wines have ensured its continuous place at the forefront of Margaret River's wine producers. The winery hit the national spotlight by winning Australia's most prestigious award, the Jimmy Watson Trophy, in consecutive years with their 1982 and 1983 Cabernet Sauvignon. Hohnen and winemaker John Durham have steadily refined the reds and produced some impressive whites, especially its powerful and complex Chardonnay and a classy Sémillon Sauvignon Blanc.

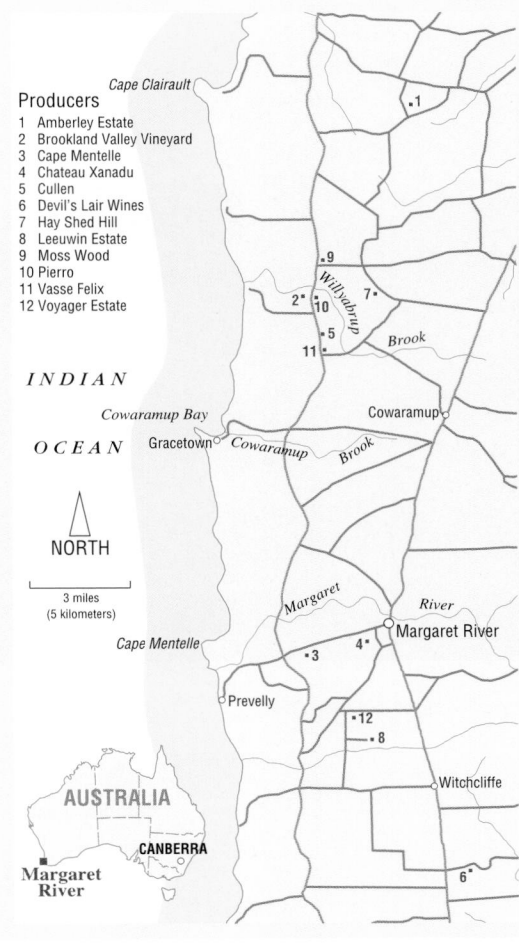

Producers
1 Amberley Estate
2 Brookland Valley Vineyard
3 Cape Mentelle
4 Chateau Xanadu
5 Cullen
6 Devil's Lair Wines
7 Hay Shed Hill
8 Leeuwin Estate
9 Moss Wood
10 Pierro
11 Vasse Felix
12 Voyager Estate

Vines at Cape Mentelle, Margaret River.

Vineyard at Cullen, Margaret River.

The entrance to the Hay Shed Hill Vineyard, Margaret River.

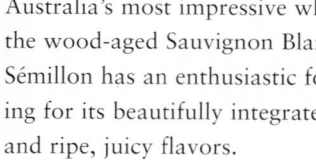

entity. While the Pinot Noir has gone, the Cabernet and especially the Chardonnay continue to go from strength to strength. The Fifth Leg wines (one white and one red) are very good quality regional blends.

HAY SHED HILL VINEYARD
Established 1973 *Owners* Liz and Barry Morrison *Production* 17,000 cases *Vineyard area* 45 acres (18 ha)

When the Morrisons bought the former Sussex Vale in 1989, they sold off the fruit for four years until they believed that the vineyard was performing well enough to supply their own label. They have established a smallish state-of-the-art winery and stylish cellar door outlet and have marketed their wines with flair. The Sauvignon Blanc, Sémillon and Chardonnay all show good varietal definition and are clean, fresh and flavorsome, while the Pinot Noir and Cabernet are the most appealing of the reds.

CULLEN
Established 1971 *Owners* the Cullen family *Production* 16,000 cases *Vineyard area* 70 acres (28 ha)

Cullen was the third winery established in Margaret River and has since been among the industry's leaders. First Dr Kevin Cullen and then his wife, Diana, guided the fortunes of the winery, but their youngest daughter, Vanya, has been winemaker since 1989. Highly regarded as a show judge, Vanya has transformed Cullen into one of Australia's finest boutique wineries. Their complex, classically structured, velvety Cabernet Merlot is the country's best, the Chardonnay is among Australia's most impressive while the wood-aged Sauvignon Blanc Sémillon has an enthusiastic following for its beautifully integrated oak and ripe, juicy flavors.

DEVIL'S LAIR WINES
Established 1981 *Owners* Southcorp *Production* 25,000 cases *Vineyard area* 86 acres (35 ha)

Devil's Lair was the first Margaret River winery to be taken over by one of the major Australian wine companies and, consequently, it has been watched closely. Although senior winemaking executives are involved with management, it appears that winemaker Janice McDonald is able to develop Devil's Lair as a separate

LEEUWIN ESTATE
Established 1969 *Owners* the Horgan family *Production* 35,000 cases *Vineyard area* 230 acres (95 ha)

This showcase winery, venue for a biennial international wine tourism conference, acts as a magnet for tourists. While the entrepreneurial energy of Denis and Tricia Horgan has done much to promote Leeuwin, its reputation rests on the quality of its Art Series Chardonnay, regarded by most commentators as the best produced in Australia. Since the first release in 1980, these opulent, full-flavored and complex whites age more gracefully than any other Australian chardonnay. The Prelude Chardonnay and the Art Series Cabernet Sauvignon are also highly regarded.

MOSS WOOD
Established 1969 *Owners* Keith and Clare Mugford *Production* 5,500 cases *Vineyard area* 21 acres (8.5 ha)

Moss Wood is one of Australia's best boutique wineries and its vineyard one of the country's most distinguished viticultural sites. Credit for its success must be shared by Margaret River pioneer, Dr Bill Pannell, and his winemaker, Keith Mugford, to whom he sold the property in 1985. The Cabernet is recognized as one of the best produced in Australia, while the Chardonnay and Sémillon are highly sought after. Nearby Ribbon Vale has been purchased recently and will be marketed as a separate vineyard.

PIERRO

Established 1980 *Owner* Mike Peterkin *Production* 9,000 cases *Vineyard area* 21 acres (8.5 ha)

Mike Peterkin is one of a rare breed—a medical practitioner who is also a qualified winemaker and viticulturist. Peterkin thinks of himself as a vigneron and his primary focus is on the vineyard. Attention was first focused on Pierro because of the intense, pristine flavors of its Chardonnay, one of Australia's best. The Sémillon Sauvignon Blanc is excellent, while the Pinot Noir and Cabernets seem to improve with each vintage. A new winery and the purchase of the Fire Gully Vineyard mark two steps forward for Pierro.

VASSE FELIX

Established 1967 *Owners* Heytesbury Holdings *Production* 55,000 cases *Vineyard area* 84 acres (34 ha)

Vasse Felix is a multiregional winery that owns the first vineyards established in both Margaret River and Great Southern. It has also been one of the state's outstanding wineries over the past decade. Both the Shiraz and the Noble Riesling are the best produced in the west, and their Sémillon and Cabernet are among the Margaret River region's finest. Their top wines each year appear under the multiregional Heytesbury label, and the red blend is outstanding. A superb new winery has been built in Willyabrup and the company has undertaken massive viticultural expansion at Jindong.

VOYAGER ESTATE

Established 1978 *Owner* Michael Wright *Production* 27,000 cases *Vineyard area* 183 acres (74 ha)

Since Voyager took over the mature vineyards of Freycinet Estate in 1992, winemaker Stuart Pym has produced increasingly complex and interesting wines. The Chardonnay is outstanding and ranks with the region's best. Of the others, the Sémillon and the reserve wines under the Tom Price label are most impressive, but all are worthy of close attention. Mining magnate, Michael Wright, has spared nothing in his quest to be noticed, and the manicured lawns, lavish rose gardens and stunning Cape Dutch architecture ensure a memorable visit to Voyager Estate.

CHATEAU XANADU

Established 1977 *Owners* Chateau Xanadu Wines Ltd *Production* 47,000 cases *Vineyard area* 334 acres (135 ha)

Expansion is the key word at Xanadu since the public company takeover from the Lagan family who started the winery. A cash injection has seen significant growth in the area under vines and a major winery expansion. In the 1980s, Xanadu had a reputation for its whites, but improved vineyard management under Conor Lagan and winemaker, Jürg Muggli, dramatically improved the quality of the reds in the 1990s. The cabernets (especially the Reserve) are among the region's best, while the oak-matured Sémillon, the Chardonnay and the Sémillon Sauvignon Blanc are highly recommended.

Below: Gardens at Leeuwin Estate, a showcase winery attracting many tourists.

Bottom: The vineyard at Pierro, Margaret River.

Great Southern

Peter Forrestal

Vineyard at Alkoomi, Great Southern.

While Professor Harold Olmo was investigating the wine industry in the Swan Valley, he visited Great Southern and wrote a report suggesting that the areas between Mount Barker and Rocky Gully had many similarities to western Europe and would be suitable for producing premium wines. The influence of this report was enormous, although not immediate. Almost ten years later, the Western Australian Department of Agriculture responded by planting experimental vines on the Pearse property at Forest Hill, near Mount Barker. This, in turn, sparked other vineyard developments in the area.

Great Southern is Australia's largest, and Western Australia's coolest, viticultural region. It consists of five subregions centered around Mount Barker, with Denmark, Frankland, Albany and the Porongurups all at least a half-hour drive away. While the climate of both Denmark and Albany are moderated by the sea, Frankland and Mount Barker experience more continental

conditions. In particular, the greater temperature variability inland means that although the average mean temperatures are lower, there are more extreme high temperatures. Fortunately, this tends to occur before ripening, so fruit quality is not affected adversely. Rainfall, too, tends to be more variable further inland, where much of the region contains towering hardwood forests of karri, marri and jarrah. Soils tend to be either loams derived from granite and gneissic rocks or lateritic gravelly sandy loams.

Not surprisingly, given the size of the region, different subregions appear more suitable to some varieties than others. Mt Barker has been particularly successful as a producer of riesling, cabernet sauvignon, pinot noir and shiraz; Denmark with chardonnay and pinot noir; Frankland with riesling, cabernets and shiraz; Albany with chardonnay and pinot noir; and the Porongurups with riesling.

The last decade has seen significant change. Many of the growers have become more involved in the wine industry and are seeking greater control over wine production by having their own wineries. From mature vineyards such as Forest Hill at Mt Barker, Westfield (leased to Houghton) and Alkoomi at Frankland, Bouverie and Wyjup (Plantagenet) and Windy Hill (Goundrey), the quality of fruit is so impressive that there has been widespread development in recent years. Great Southern is becoming an increasingly important producer of premium wines, and its best wines are stunningly good. However, its relative isolation, lack of world-class tourist infrastructure and the part-time nature of much of the wine industry has meant that its growth and international exposure has been comparatively less impressive than that of Margaret River.

ALKOOMI

Established 1971 *Owners* the Lange Family *Production* 45,000 cases *Vineyard area* 140 acres (57 ha)

Merv and Judy Lange, who were among the region's pioneers in the 1970s, have been in expansion mode in the 1990s. Production has doubled in the past five years and looks to increase dramatically as investment vineyards in which they have interests come on stream. The quality of their

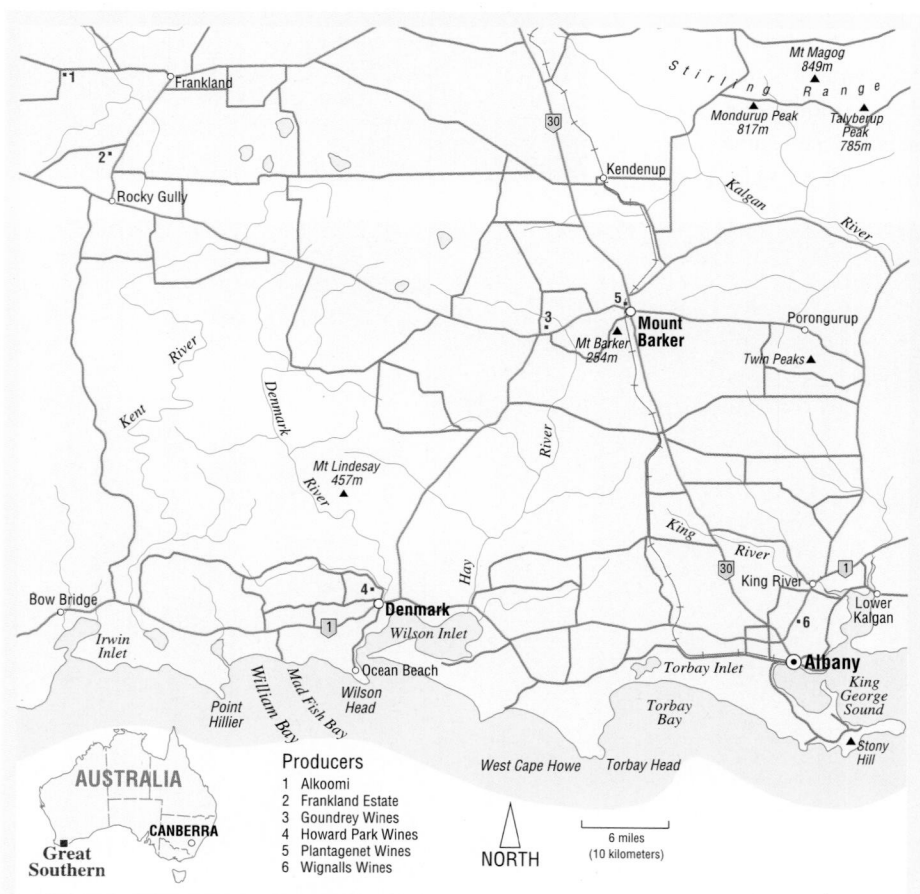

Producers
1 Alkoomi
2 Frankland Estate
3 Goundrey Wines
4 Howard Park Wines
5 Plantagenet Wines
6 Wignalls Wines

NORTH

6 miles
(10 kilometers)

AUSTRALIA

CANBERRA

Great Southern

wines is constant and their best wines continue to delight serious wine lovers. The Riesling is one of the region's best and the Sauvignon Blanc is crisp, refreshing and flavorsome.

FRANKLAND ESTATE

Established 1988 *Owners* Barrie Smith and Judi Cullam *Production* 10,000 cases *Vineyard area* 69 acres (28 ha)

This energetic and passionate producer has made an important contribution to the promotion of the riesling grape by offering an annual Riesling Scholarship and, in 1999, ran an international Riesling Seminar in Sydney. Its own carefully managed vineyards are close to maturity and are producing wines of great flavor and complexity. The zesty, limey Riesling and spicy, peppery Shiraz are very good, while the flagship Olmo's Reward (a predominantly merlot/cabernet franc blend) is outstanding.

GOUNDREY WINES

Established 1978 *Owner* Jack Bendat *Production* 200,000 cases *Vineyard area* 432 acres (175 ha)

Nowhere in Great Southern has there been expansion such as that seen at Goundrey since its acquisition by American, Jack Bendat. The winery's capacity has been increased threefold and vineyard plantings have proceeded apace. In three years, production has risen from 33,000 to more than 200,000 cases. While it has not been possible to expand this rapidly using only Western Australian fruit, it is the intention at Goundrey to satisfy demand from local grapes as soon as this is possible. Wines are available at all prices, with the Reserve Shiraz being the standout red.

HOWARD PARK WINES

Established 1986 *Owners* Jeff and Amy Burch *Production* 30,000 cases *Vineyard area* 62 acres (25 ha)

Howard Park is one of the West's most significant producers, with major wineries in both Denmark and Margaret River. The Howard Park Riesling is one of Australia's best half dozen—a tight dry style, full of flavor but fashioned for the long haul. The Cabernet Merlot is also highly regarded—a full-bodied, opulent and powerful red that demands cellaring. The Madfish label

is particularly popular in the restaurant trade, with an unwooded and wooded Chardonnay, Pinot Noir and Shiraz made for the export market only. The White and Red blends, made for the Australian market, are well made, fruity, medium-priced wines.

PLANTAGENET WINES

Established 1974 *Owners* Lionel Samson Pty Ltd *Production* 40,000 cases *Vineyard area* 200 acres (81 ha)

Although he has just sold his share in the business, Plantagenet owes a major debt to its founder, Tony Smith. More than 25 years of pioneering endeavor has established Plantagenet as one of the state's preeminent wineries. As a contract winemaker for up to 20 vineyards, Plantagenet has been a major force for quality winemaking in the region. The winery produces several very good to outstanding wines, notably its Cabernet Sauvignon, Shiraz and Riesling. All the Plantagenet wines offer consistent high quality and good value.

WIGNALLS WINES

Established 1982 *Owners* Bill, Patricia and Robert Wignall *Production* 5,000 cases *Vineyard area* 54 acres (22 ha)

Wignalls has gained a reputation for the quality of its Pinot Noir as a result of outstanding show results in the late 1980s and early 1990s. Now, after some production difficulties, the Pinot is back to its best. Although the vineyard remains the key to their operation, a new winery has given the Wignalls and winemaker Ben Kagi greater control over production.

The winery at Goundrey Wines provides a backdrop for the vineyards.

REGIONAL DOZEN

QUALITY WINES

Frankland Estate Olmo's
 Reward
Goundrey Reserve Shiraz
Harewood Chardonnay
Howard Park Riesling
Plantagenet Shiraz
Wignalls Reserve Pinot Noir

BEST VALUE WINES

Alkoomi Sauvignon Blanc
Castle Rock Riesling
Gilberts Shiraz
Karriview Pinot Noir
Pattersons Pinot Noir
Springviews Riesling

Other Western Australian Regions

Peter Forrestal

SWAN VALLEY

Olive Farm (1830), thought to be Australia's oldest continuous winery still in use, was established within a year of the founding of the Swan River Colony at Perth. Sandalford (1840) and Houghton (1859) were planted in the Swan Valley soon after. Until the 1960s, most Western Australian vineyards were concentrated in this region, although inland plantings were attempted without long-term success. On a more substantial scale, Slavic migrants developed family vineyards in Swan Valley and the surrounding Swan District during the 1920s and 1930s, where they produced fortified and table wines for local consumption.

The importing of vine materials was banned until the late 1950s to keep Western Australia free from phylloxera, so many of the classic varieties were not available to grapegrowers. While still enforcing strict quarantine measures, the Department of Agriculture released varieties such as chardonnay, sémillon, sauvignon blanc, cabernet franc, merlot and pinot noir for the first time during the 1970s. This was both a result of pressure from adventurous new vignerons and an impetus to further develop viticulture in the west.

Before the 1970s, 80 percent of the warm Swan Valley's produce was fortifieds and 20 percent table wines, but this has now been completely reversed. Growers have replanted much of the vineyard land with varieties more suited to table wine production. This, together with modern technological developments—the more widespread use of stainless steel, better refrigeration and the use of more expensive oak—have led to substantial improvements in quality.

Swan Valley has a hot Mediterranean climate. Compared with other Australian wine regions, it has the highest mean January temperature [75.7°F (24.3°C)], lowest summer rainfall [4.2 inches (107 mm)], lowest relative humidity (47%) and the most sunshine hours (9.7). The valley is a flat, alluvial plain that has deep loamy soils with very good moisture retention. Its warm climate is best suited to chenin blanc, verdelho and fortifieds, although chardonnay and shiraz can also be impressive.

For historical reasons and because of its proximity to Perth, two of the state's largest companies, Houghton (owned by BRL Hardy) and the independent Sandalford, have their headquarters in Swan Valley. Otherwise, the wineries of the area are quite small, family-owned businesses that offer modestly priced wines of very good to reasonable quality at the cellar door.

HOUGHTON WINE COMPANY

Established 1836 *Owners* BRL Hardy *Production* 500,000 cases *Vineyard area* 1,186 acres (480 ha)

Houghton is by far the largest and most influential wine company in the west, as it owns, leases or buys

Vines at Lamont Winery which also boasts a stylish cellar door, art gallery and restaurant.

fruit from vineyards in virtually all regions in the state. The Houghton's White Burgundy is still one of Australia's best selling white wines and represents remarkable value for money. Significant investment in winemaking equipment and vineyard development over the past 15 years and exemplary winemaking and viticulture have meant that Houghton makes outstanding wines at every price. The super-premium Jack Mann red blend is as good as it gets, while the Crofters and Moondah Brook range include many excellent wines.

LAMONT WINERY

Established 1974 *Owners* Corin and Kate Lamont and Fiona Warren *Production* 7,000 cases *Vineyard area* 12 acres (4.8 ha)

Increased investment in equipment and skillful winemaking by Mark Warren has produced outstanding show results in the last five years and dramatically improved the Lamont profile. The winery is best represented by the Chenin Blanc, Verdelho and Vintage Port, while the Barrel Fermented Chardonnay, Family Reserve Cabernet and Frankland Riesling are impressive. The family-run winery complex features a stylish cellar door, art gallery and restaurant.

SANDALFORD WINES

Established 1840 *Owners* Peter and Debra Prendiville *Production* 70,000 cases *Vineyard area* 358 acres (145 ha)

Sandalford, one of the state's oldest wineries, is currently undergoing a revival of fortunes. Since the Prendivilles have taken over, there has been substantial investment in the vineyards (especially in Margaret River), a major upgrading of the winery and development of tourist facilities. The quality of Sandalford wines, which are sourced from most of the state's viticultural regions, has risen dramatically under senior winemaker Bill Crapsley. His sound, well-made wines represent good value.

TALIJANCICH WINES

Established 1932 *Owners* James and Hilda Talijancich *Production* 8,000 cases *Vineyard area* 40 acres (16 ha)

The Talijancich fortifieds have long been among the best produced in Swan Valley. Currently available are red and white liqueurs under the Julian James label and a special

release of the thick, lush and opulent 1969 Liqueur Tokay, with its deep, lingering treacle and molasses flavors. The most interesting of winemaker James Talijancich's table wines are his Sémillon and Verdelho, which gain complexity from solids contact and bottle development.

WESTFIELD

Established 1922 *Owners* the Kosovich family *Production* 4,500 cases *Vineyard area* 30 acres (12 ha)

John Kosovich has continued to defy expectation by regularly producing outstanding wines in the unfashionable Swan Valley. Few would pick the Westfield Chardonnay as a warm-climate wine; fewer would expect it to age as gracefully as it does. The Liqueur Muscat is one of Australia's best, a rarity for a wine that does not come from Rutherglen. Kosovich has recently been joined by his son, Anthony, and together they operate the Swan Valley property and the new Bronze-wing vineyard at Manjimup.

GEOGRAPHE

Newly formed Geographe covers a wide and diverse region from Capel to the Ferguson Valley in the Bunbury hinterland, the farming lands of Donnybrook and the dairy country around Harvey. Vineyards are being planted at an

Westfield winery produces a Liqueur Muscat that rivals those of Rutherglen in Victoria.

The Darling Range in the background of the Talijancich Wines vineyard, Swan Valley.

An old flat-topped wagon with barrels at Peel Estate, near the Geographe region.

Emerald Park vineyard since 1976, believes that the area is ideally suited to the production of medium-price dry reds and particularly likes its shiraz, cabernet, zinfandel and grenache.

CAPEL VALE

Established 1974 *Owners* Dr Peter and Elizabeth Pratten *Production* 85,000 cases *Vineyard area* 400 acres (160 ha)

Capel Vale, one of the west's largest producers, now sources 85 percent of its production from its own vineyards in Geographe, Pemberton, Mount Barker and Margaret River. The pick of their reserve range is the Whispering Hill Riesling, which is one of the best sourced from Great Southern. The Capel Vale wines represent good value, especially the tropical-fruited Sauvignon Blanc Sémillon, the smooth rich Merlot, and the earthy, spicy Shiraz.

PEEL ESTATE

Established 1974 *Owners* Will Nairn, Mal Nairn and Anne Miller *Production* 8,000 cases *Vineyard area* 40 acres (16 ha)

Peel Estate is not actually in any of the Western Australian Geographical Indications since the South West Coastal region no longer exists, but it's not far outside Geographe. Will Nairn has been making good quality wines in an unfashionable area for more than 25 years. The best of the range are the wood-aged Chenin Blanc, which becomes mellow and honeyed with about five years in the bottle and ages for much longer, and the spicy, black-fruited Shiraz.

PEMBERTON

The viticultural potential of the area around the timber towns of Pemberton and Manjimup was first mooted by Dr John Gladstones in a 1977 research paper which drew attention to its similarities with Burgundy. The Manjimup area has moderately fertile, lateritic gravelly sands and gravelly loams. It is ideal for grape growing, having a comparable climate to Bordeaux. It has similar mean temperatures and almost identical sunshine hours, although with heavier rainfall, more temperature variability and less relative humidity.

The transition from marri forests to karri about half way between Manjimup and Pemberton marks a climatic change as well as a shift in soil

astonishing rate by farmers seeking to diversify, by large companies looking for cheaper vineyard land, and by major investment groups keen to take advantage of tax losses and of Western Australia's potential for export.

There are fertile, brown loamy soils on the coastal strip from Capel to Harvey. Temperatures in the warm, sunny growing season are moderated by the sea and by the early sea breezes during summer. The area is best suited to merlot, chardonnay and verdelho. Its major winery is the long established Capel Vale, which draws grapes from many parts of the state.

In the Ferguson Valley and the hills behind Harvey, vineyards have been planted between 250 and 300 metres above sea level. These receive about 10 percent more rainfall and have a more moderate climate than on the flat. The soil is granitic gravel over clay loam which retains water better than the alluvial sands nearer the coast. The most suited grape varieties appear to be shiraz, chardonnay, sémillon and sauvignon blanc. Largest winery in the Ferguson Valley is the newly established Willow Bridge, which has Rob Bowen as its winemaker and 65 hectares under vine.

Donnybrook is on a continuation of the Darling Scarp, with fruit trees occupying the valley flats and vineyards on its undulating slopes. The fertile soils there contain decomposed granite and ironstone gravel. This is a warm area for growing grapes, with hotter peaks and colder troughs than areas closer to the coast. David Hohnen of Cape Mentelle, who has sourced grapes from the 50 acre type. The climate of Pemberton is cooler, with lower temperatures, fewer sunshine hours, more rainfall and greater relative humidity. Although the gravelly loams are found in some of the higher slopes of Pemberton, the soil generally changes to the more fertile loams formed from gneissic rock that is associated with vigorous growth.

There is still debate about which grape varieties are most suitable for the region, with John Gladstones recommending the cabernet varieties, shiraz and chardonnay for Manjimup and pinot noir and the cabernet varieties (especially cabernet franc and merlot) for Pemberton. In each case, he warns that cabernet sauvignon will only succeed in the warmest sites. Chardonnay and pinot noir have proved extremely successful as a sparkling wine base, with the Maiden Wood bubblies being most impressive.

The establishment of the Smithbrook vineyard (now owned by Petaluma) and Salitage in the late 1980s stimulated interest in the region. In the 1990s, Houghton bought and revitalized the Maiden Wood vineyard, while Capel Vale, Domaine Chandon, Evans and Tate, Howard Park and Sandalford have all sourced a significant volume of grapes from the area.

The stars of the region to date have been winemakers who have established their reputations elsewhere. Moss Wood founder Bill Pannell and his son Dan have established Picardy, convinced that the area will produce outstanding pinot and chardonnay. Their best wine so far is a stunning velvety Merlot Cabernet, while the Picardy Shiraz pushes the boundaries for the variety. Both John Kosovich (Westfield) and John Brocksopp (Leeuwin Estate) have planted retirement vineyards in the region. Kosovich's Bronzewing Chardonnay has been outstanding, while Brocksopp has produced tiny quantities of a fruity roussane and a fine, medium-bodied shiraz with clear varietal definition. Keith Mugford makes a fine, taut chardonnay and a spicy, savory pinot from the Lefroy Brook vineyard that is sold under the Moss Wood label.

Below: *A sign detailing the winemaking calendar at Alkoomi Wines.*

Bottom: *Vines disappearing into the horizon at Cape Mentelle.*

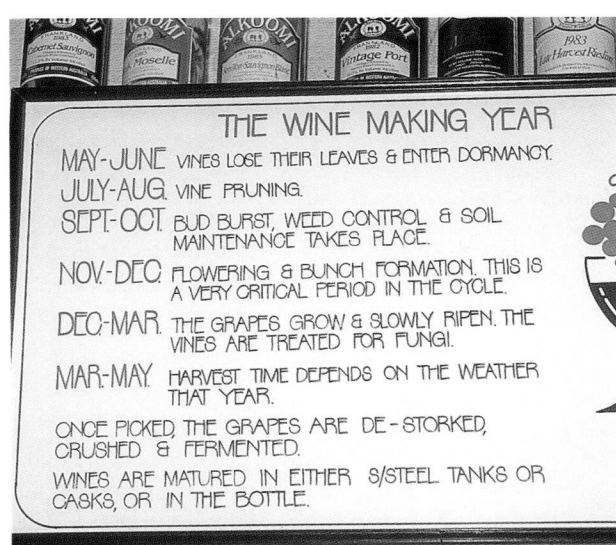

THE WINE MAKING YEAR

MAY-JUNE VINES LOSE THEIR LEAVES & ENTER DORMANCY.
JULY-AUG. VINE PRUNING.
SEPT-OCT. BUD BURST, WEED CONTROL & SOIL MAINTENANCE TAKES PLACE.
NOV.-DEC. FLOWERING & BUNCH FORMATION. THIS IS A VERY CRITICAL PERIOD IN THE CYCLE.
DEC-MAR. THE GRAPES GROW & SLOWLY RIPEN. THE VINES ARE TREATED FOR FUNGI.
MAR-MAY. HARVEST TIME DEPENDS ON THE WEATHER THAT YEAR.

ONCE PICKED, THE GRAPES ARE DE-STORKED, CRUSHED & FERMENTED.
WINES ARE MATURED IN EITHER S/STEEL TANKS OR CASKS, OR IN THE BOTTLE.

SOUTH AUSTRALIA

Clare Valley

Sally Marden

The Clare Valley is a pretty, winding, wooded region two hours' drive north of Adelaide, with a history of winemaking that dates back to the time of first European settlement, when English settler John Horrocks first planted vines at Hope Farm in 1840. His pioneering efforts were followed by plantings at Sevenhill in 1852 and Spring Vale (subsequently Quelltaler) in 1853. Expansion was steady rather than swift until the changes that occurred with turn of the century.

At the same time as these early viticultural experiments, the Clare area was being populated by a diverse range of settlers, many of whom were heading north to stake a claim on land or minerals. They included English miners from Cornwall coming to exploit local sources of tin and copper, German-speaking Silesians venturing a little further north than the majority of their contemporaries who had settled in the Barossa, and English and Irish entrepreneurs spreading north from Adelaide.

The beginning of the twentieth century saw rapid expansion of Clare's fledgling wine industry. In 1890, there were about 250 acres (100 ha) of vineyards; ten years later there were more like 1500 acres (600 ha). Two producers, Stanley Wine Co. and Quelltaler, were the main forces at the time, making wines that were largely for export to England. Development slowed after that period to the point where the area of land under vine actually decreased, but the industry had established itself and continued to advance steadily.

It is a curious region climatically and stylistically. Set in the middle of the hot, dry mid-north wheat belt of South Australia, with hot summers and little ground water, Clare somehow manages to produce wines that would appear to come from a considerably cooler, wetter climate. This is perfectly illustrated by Clare's best-performing and best known wine, riesling, the finest examples of which are found in the Mosel in Germany, and in Alsace. Those northern European classics are born out of a very different climate to Clare, and yet this South Australian pocket produces similar wines. This apparently odd characteristic is generally attributed to cool afternoon breezes that blow

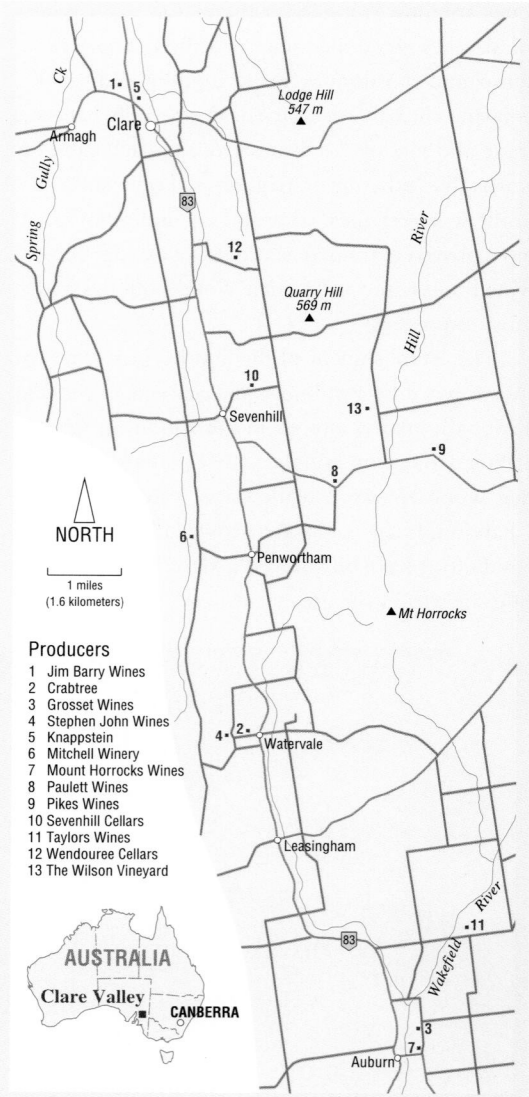

Producers
1 Jim Barry Wines
2 Crabtree
3 Grosset Wines
4 Stephen John Wines
5 Knappstein
6 Mitchell Winery
7 Mount Horrocks Wines
8 Paulett Wines
9 Pikes Wines
10 Sevenhill Cellars
11 Taylors Wines
12 Wendouree Cellars
13 The Wilson Vineyard

through the Clare Valley in the warmer months, slowing and prolonging the ripening of the grapes. (Alsace is not actually as cool and wet as its position would suggest. It is second only to the southern area around Perpignan in terms of sunny and dry weather, and probably experiences similar summer conditions to Clare.)

Clare's main competitor in the riesling stakes is actually much closer, though, lying just an hour away in the Eden Valley. Examples from both regions are regarded as Australian classics, but they differ somewhat in style: Eden Valley's are all

restrained lime juice and steely in character, whereas Clare's add floral, perfumed and spicy characters to the citrus aspects. Riesling is not the only star in Clare, however. The region also produces big, firm peppery shiraz and elegant minty cabernets, both with plenty of backbone.

The quality of the wines being made in the region has inevitably attracted the attention of the region's major companies, and there has been much corporate waltzing and investment from the 1980s onwards. The Clare Valley is now a mix of the large and small, as well as the old and new, but the most renowned producers—like Grosset, Wendouree and Mitchells—have maintained their independence and remain small.

JIM BARRY WINES

Established 1959 *Owners* the Barry family *Production* 85,000 cases *Vineyard area* 494 acres (200 ha)

The Barry family's association with Clare began as far back as 1946, when Jim Barry worked the vintage at the Clarevale Co-operative as an enology student. He returned after graduating as winemaker, then established his own label in 1959 (while also overseeing the birth of Taylors Winery). Today, four of his six children are involved in the winemaking and operation of the business. Originally gaining a reputation for its Watervale riesling, Jim Barry Wines is now best known for its big, high-quality, full-bodied reds, the most highly sought after of which is The Armagh.

CRABTREE

Established 1982 *Owners* Robert and Elizabeth Crabtree *Production* 4,000 cases *Vineyard area* 32 acres (13 ha)

UK-born Robert Crabtree read law at Oxford and was a successful barrister in England, but always pursued his interest in winemaking. He decided to follow his heart and came via Bergerac in France and Gisborne in New Zealand to Watervale, where he began to produce wines in the early 1980s. By 1998, he and wife Elizabeth, a part time midwife, had built their own winery and were producing tight, elegant, delicate rieslings. The reds, too, are on the delicate side for Clare, showing a refreshing elegance and refinement. The Cabernet sauvignon and a shiraz/cabernet blend are particularly good.

GROSSET WINES

Established 1981 *Owners* Jeffrey Grosset *Production* 8,000 cases *Vineyard area* 20 acres (8 ha)

When it comes to Australian riesling, Jeffrey Grosset is the undisputed king. His superb wines have brought him numerous awards, including Riesling Winemaker of the Year at the 1998 Riesling Summit in the grape's German heartland. He makes two styles, one from Watervale, one from Polish Hill, but both have in common

Rows of vines at Pikes Polish Hill vineyard stretch away toward the surrounding hills.

The tasting room at Jim Barry wines is a source for the Barrys' gutsy red wines.

The tasting room at Knappstein is housed in an historic stone building.

the elegance and complexity of great riesling. Grosset's other wines should not be forgotten, however. His highly acclaimed cabernet blend, Gaia, and the fragrant Adelaide Hills pinot noir are also testament to the intelligence and dedication of Grosset's winemaking, and show that they are no less effective when applied to his reds.

STEPHEN JOHN WINES

Established 1994 *Owners* Stephen and Rita John *Production* 4,000 cases *Vineyard area* 15 acres (6 ha)

Stephen John is a respected veteran of the Australian wine industry. Formerly chief red winemaker with Seppelt in the Barossa and chief white winemaker with Wolf Blass, he set up on his own in Clare in 1994. Here, he makes an increasingly popular range of wines, with his Watervale Riesling and Chardonnay attracting particular acclaim. Stephen John also makes a very good lightly oaked dry white pedro ximenez, with lifted herbal characters and a clean, crisp palate.

KNAPPSTEIN

Established 1976 *Owners* Petaluma Pty Ltd *Production* 40,000–45,000 cases *Vineyard area* 220 acres (89 ha)

Knappstein is housed in an historic old stone ex-brewery and cordial factory in the town of Clare. Its links with fine wines began in 1976, when Tim Knappstein bought the building and began making an excellent range of classic Clare wines. Knappstein sold the business to Petaluma in 1992, but little has changed in terms of quality. Its riesling is still the epitome of the region—fresh, floral and spicy—while cabernet sauvignon, shiraz and cabernet/merlot are all big blockbuster examples that need time to settle down.

MITCHELL WINERY

Established 1975 *Owners* Andrew and Jane Mitchell *Production* 80,000 cases *Vineyard area* 150 acres (61 ha)

Jane and Andrew Mitchell established their winery in the wooded western hills of the Clare on an old family property in 1975. They built their reputation on producing fine riesling, and theirs is consistently one of the country's best. Of their elegant reds, the Peppertree Shiraz, has captured most attention, with its stylish berry and spice characteristics, fine tannins and smooth finish. They also produce rich, oily lemon-scented sémillon.

MOUNT HORROCKS WINES

Established 1982 *Owners* Stephanie Toole *Production* 5,500 cases *Vineyard area* N/A

Originally established by brothers Lyall, Trevor and Rodger Ackland, Mount Horrocks was bought by Stephanie Toole in 1993. A recent arrival in the Clare Valley, she has been a passionate and effective advocate for the local vigneron association while reviving this label through committed and dedicated winemaking. As well as a classic Watervale riesling, which has impressive fruit purity, Toole also makes a complex chardonnay, an outstanding fruit-driven shiraz and one of the country's best dessert wines—the Cordon Cut Riesling. Her flair for innovative marketing can be seen in the conversion of the old Auburn railway station into the Mount Horrocks cellar door.

PAULETT WINES

Established 1983 *Owners* Neil and Alison Paulett *Production* 14,000 cases *Vineyard area* 25 acres (10 ha)

Paulett Wines is in the picturesque Polish Hill River area in Clare, where the quality of the hilltop views almost matches the quality of the wines. The Paulett's gravity-fed winery uses an eclectic mix of modern technology and traditional winemaking techniques. Red wines are made with the help of basket presses and 100-year-old slate open fermenters. As one would expect, Neil Paulett produces riesling in a classic Clare style—elegant, restrained and amenable to aging—but it's his reds that really stay in the mind. The Andreas Shiraz is particularly good, with terrific body, structure and oak balance, but the Cabernet/ Merlot and Shiraz are also great drops.

Because of high demand, Grosset Wines' cellar door is open for only about six weeks in the year.

PIKES WINES

Established 1984 *Owners* the Pike family *Production*
29,000 cases *Vineyard area* 94 acres (38 ha)

The Pikes have been producing a label since 1878,
but the early bottles were for soft drinks and ales,
not wines. It was third-generation brothers Neil
and Andrew Pike who started putting the family
name onto wine bottles when they established
Pikes Wines in 1984. Their property is in one of
the cooler parts of Clare, resulting in a longer
ripening season for the grapes and a later harvest
than most. This produces intense flavors, complexity and fine acidity, resulting in elegant, long-lived
wines. Highlights are their riesling and a good
herb-scented sangiovese.

SEVENHILL CELLARS

Established 1851 *Owners* Society of Jesus (Jesuits)
Production 20,000 cases *Vineyard area* 124 acres (50 ha)

The Sevenhill property was bought by father
Aloysius Kranewitter in 1851 for the Jesuits, and
the following year the brothers planted vines for
making altar wine. They must have taken to it
rather well, because today their wines are eagerly
sought after by a much wider audience. Their reds
in particular are full of rich, spicy flavors and deep
berry characters. The winery itself is a popular
spot with visitors, with old underground cellars
and the Jesuits' St Aloysius Church nearby.

TAYLORS WINES

Established 1969 *Owners* the Taylor family *Production*
230,000 cases *Vineyard area* 1,360 acres (550 ha)

The biggest winery in the region, Taylors dominates the local industry and the southern end of
the Clare Valley. When ex-Sydney wine merchants
Bill Taylor and his sons, John and Bill, bought
their first vineyards by the Wakefield River near
Auburn, a fascination with Bordeaux wines led to
them planting 178 ha of cabernet sauvignon. The
first wine released under the Taylors label, a 1973
cabernet, won gold medals at every national
Australian wine show. Since then, the company's
reputation for producing high quality reds has
grown, though today, the emphasis is as much on
whites. A new premium range under the St
Andrews label was launched in late 1999.

WENDOUREE CELLARS

Established 1895 *Owners* Tony and Lita Brady *Production*
2,500 cases *Vineyard area* 30 acres (12 ha)

Tony Brady makes small quantities of huge, powerful red wines that are generally regarded as

*St Aloysius Church is the backdrop for the
vines at the Jesuit-owned Sevenhill Cellars.*

among Australia's best. They sell out as soon as
they are released on the mailing list and are nigh
on impossible to obtain. The range includes cabernet, malbec, mataro (mourvedre) and shiraz, plus
varying blends of the four. There is also a redoubtable vintage port style made with muscat of
alexandria. All the wines age beautifully.

THE WILSON VINEYARD

Established 1974 *Owners* the Wilson family *Production*
5,000 cases *Vineyard area* 37 acres (15 ha)

Zinfandel is not often seen in Clare (or Australia
as a whole, come to that), but John Wilson and his
winemaker son Daniel have long been doing
interesting things with it at their Polish Hill River
winery near Sevenhill. They have all the usual
suspects—riesling, chardonnay, cabernet sauvignon, shiraz—but also produce outstanding wines
from grapes that are lesser known locally, including gewürztraminer, nebbiolo, petit verdot and
malbec. These are classically good wines, not least
of which is a top-notch sparkling red.

The Barossa

Sally Marden

Mountadam Vineyard offers spectacular views of the Eden Valley from the High Eden Ridge.

The Barossa can justifiably claim to be Australia's best known wine region, and is arguably its most important. Here, among the patchwork spread of neat vineyards and rolling hills an hour northeast of Adelaide, are more than 50 wineries, including the home bases and headquarters of most of Australia's leading wine companies. Southcorp (in the form of Penfolds, Tollana and Seppelt), Orlando and Wolf Blass are based here, as are Yalumba, Peter Lehmann and Grant Burge. It has the greatest concentration of bottling plants and industry service providers of any Australian wine region. The country's finest and best known wines also come from here—Penfolds Grange is born, bred and made in the Barossa, (and contains mostly local fruit), as is Henschke Hill of Grace and a raft of Parker 99-pointers from lesser known niche producers. It has also produced some of Australia's best-known brands, from Barossa Pearl in the 1950s to Jacobs Creek today. But it is not simply big business or well known labels that make the Barossa stand out in wine terms—its distinct and complex heritage and culture make this wine region quite unlike any other.

At first glance, the Barossa seems dichotomous. There are two regions within it, each producing distinctive styles of wine. The Eden Valley is high-altitude hill country, producing elegant, structured wines, the finest and best known of which are rieslings. The Barossa Valley is on the valley floor, where classic, full-bodied old-vine shiraz and grenache are the order of the day. Each area was settled in the late 1830s by two very different groups of migrants, with their own particular cultures, lifestyles and religions. Up in the hills it was English farmers and gentry, while down in the valley it was mainly German-speaking peasant farmers from Silesia (now part of Poland and eastern Germany) who established European-style villages and settlements.

But cultural differences didn't seem to stand in the way too much here. Mixed hamlets, villages and townships sprang up, farms were established and the settlers developed a strong sense of community. Equally importantly, they quickly realized that grapevines were one of the most suitable and flourishing crops, whether in the hills or the valley. For the English, bottles and casks from Bordeaux

and Burgundy suffered badly on their passage through the tropics. And for the Silesians, viticulture and winemaking were as much a part of their tradition as making sausages or pickling vegetables. So, via this unexpectedly successful intertwining and establishment of lifestyle and cultures, the first Barossa wines were made in the 1840s, and many of the same vineyards planted then are still being worked today. Some of the oldest vines in the world can be found here, and many of the 500-plus growers producing grapes in the Barossa today are fifth- and sixth-generation descendants of the original settlers.

The Barossa's winemaking industry grew rapidly during the late nineteenth century, and by the turn of the century it was the most important wine region in Australia. Inevitable cycles of boom and bust followed through the twentieth century, as did changes in taste. An early dependency on fortified wines was gradually exchanged for table wines (although some of the country's finest fortifieds are still made at Seppeltsfield and elsewhere in the region).

The Barossa faced its own unique pressures, too. The sense of community spirit that had been built up since settlement was severely tested by tensions between English descendants and those with German heritage during the Second World War. But the desire to maintain the community was strong, and organizations and events were started to rekindle a sense of unity, including the biennial Barossa Vintage Festival that still thrives today. The Silesian influence has given the area a unique food culture, and Australia's most distinctive regional cuisine. It has shaped the landscape with its mix of vineyards, historic cottages and churches, and provided the force behind some of Australia's most successful wine companies.

Max Schubert, who first made Penfolds Grange, was a Barossa winemaker, as was Colin Gramp, who revolutionized winemaking in the region in the 1950s by introducing cold-pressure fermentation for white wines and secondary fermentation for sparkling wine at Orlando. At the same time, similar groundbreaking work was being undertaken by John Vickery at Leo Buring and Peter Lehmann at Saltram. Until these pioneers came along, fortified wines had been the mainstay of the Barossa, but from the 1950s these winemakers and others started to produce the table wines that were to become the region's benchmarks—robust, full-bodied shiraz and steely dry riesling. These two wine styles remain the Barossa classics,

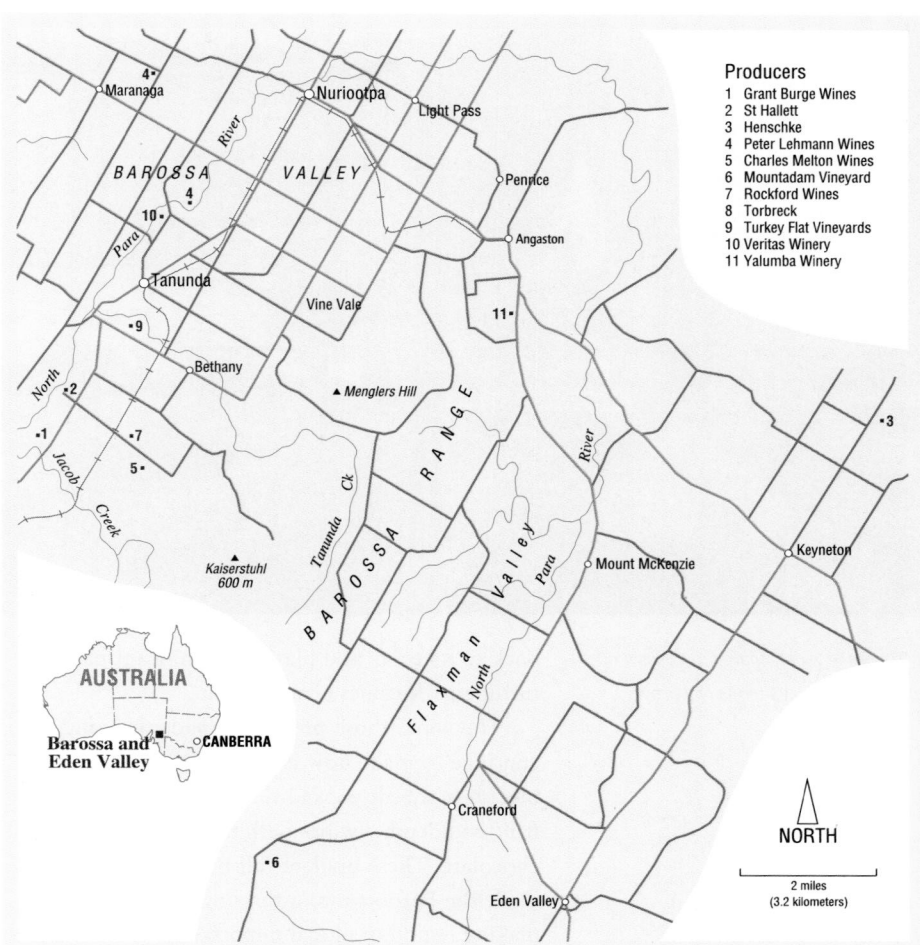

Producers
1 Grant Burge Wines
2 St Hallett
3 Henschke
4 Peter Lehmann Wines
5 Charles Melton Wines
6 Mountadam Vineyard
7 Rockford Wines
8 Torbreck
9 Turkey Flat Vineyards
10 Veritas Winery
11 Yalumba Winery

and are known throughout the world, but it wasn't too long ago that both fortune and fashion threatened to decimate the region.

During the late 1970s and the early 1980s, the Barossa's big sturdy reds found few fans. Demand dwindled as the world's drinkers discovered chardonnay and sought dry white wines. The South Australian Government instigated a subsidized vine-pull scheme, and substantial amounts of Barossa old shiraz, grenache and mourvedre vines —the backbones of the old fortified industry— were ripped out. Thankfully, not everyone followed suit. Peter Lehmann, disillusioned when his bosses refused to buy growers' red grapes, left Saltram and set up on his own with a formal commitment to buy local fruit from independent growers. And Lehmann certainly wasn't alone in recognizing the value of dry-grown old-vine Barossa grapes. A number of winemakers and growers also bit the bullet and either set up their own small independent wineries, or started producing wines that highlighted their Barossa heritage. These producers, including such notables as Rockford, Charles Melton, Grant Burge, St Hallett, Elderton and Bethany, brought the region

Tidy vines in widely spaced rows show off the Barossa Valley's fertile brown soil.

Respected Barossa reds: Rusden Grenache 1998, and Rockford 1998 Black Shiraz.

year on average—giving ideal conditions for top riesling. But it also seems to suit the shiraz, cabernet and chardonnay grown there, resulting in wines that tend to be tighter and more elegant than their valley brethren. A lesser-known Rhône classic, viognier, is also thriving in the hills, producing some interesting new wines for Yalumba.

In 1996, in response to European pressures, the Barossa winemakers and grape growers decided to define just what and where the Barossa is and where the Barossa and Eden Valleys start and end. The Geographic Indications provide security against misuse of the names by other regions or wineries, and the delineation of vineyard land guards against rampant growth. The names can only be used on labels for wines with at least 85 percent fruit from the regions, and wineries can use the zone name Barossa to reflect a blend of fruit from the two regions.

back to its roots and played a significant part in turning its fortunes around again.

The wines those producers made then and continue to make now exemplify the Barossa. Big blockbuster reds packed full of spice, tannin, rich fruit and depth—wines with tar and leather and chocolate. These opulent full-bodied beauties have made the Barossa into a thriving premium wine-making region of global importance. Eden Valley is enjoying similar success with its classically crisp rieslings. Names like Leo Buring, John Vickery, Pewsey Vale and Steingarten have long been known to wine lovers, but a "riesling revival" is leading to wider distribution and acceptance, with the Australian charge being led by Eden Valley and its northern neighbor Clare.

There's more to the Barossa than shiraz and riesling. On the valley floor, with its Mediterranean climate of cool wet winters and hot dry summers, the brown fertile soils will grow just about anything that's planted. Apart from shiraz, the grapes that do best, though, are fellow Rhône varieties grenache and mourvèdre, and plenty of interesting blends are now appearing. Grenache, which is notoriously difficult to ripen, responds particularly well here. Cabernet sauvignon can be ripe and full-bodied. The most prevalent white grape is sémillon, which traditionally has received a large dose of oak. These days, both oaked and unoaked are produced, and the best provide a luscious, lemony mouthful.

Up in the Eden Valley, cooler temperatures result in a longer growing season. Soils are rockier and more acidic, and rainfall in winter is much more significant—an extra 10 inches (255 mm) per

GRANT BURGE WINES, BAROSSA VALLEY

Established 1985 *Owners* Grant Burge Wines Pty Ltd
Production 100,000 cases *Vineyard area* 815 acres (330 ha)

A fifth-generation Barossa Valley winemaker, Grant Burge is Barossan to his bootstraps. His family heritage of winemaking started with his great-great grandfather, John Burge, who settled in the Barossa in 1854 on one of the first vineyards established in the area. Today, Grant and his wife Helen operate the largest privately owned vineyard network in the Barossa. His winemaking history has recently come full circle. In 1972, he teamed up with Ian Wilson and purchased the fledgling Krondorf winery. After 14 years, they had built it into a national brand and sold it to the Mildara Group. In 1988, Burge started his own premium wine business, Grant Burge Wines, which has been such a success that, in late 1999, he was able to buy back Krondorf.

HENSCHKE, EDEN VALLEY

Established 1868 *Owners* C. A. Henschke & Co.
Production 40,000 cases *Vineyard area* 285 acres (115 ha)

Cyril Henschke, a fourth-generation descendant of Silesian grape growers, was one of the Australian wine industry's true pioneers in the 1950s, developing and marketing, among others, quality single-vineyard table wines from two of his best sites—Mount Edelstone and Hill of Grace.

A generation on, Stephen and Prue Henschke have built on those foundations in stellar fashion, nurturing the old vines, refining their techniques and running both vineyards and winery with intelligence and insight. The Henschke's vines are now as much as 130 years old, and their wines are among the best produced anywhere.

PETER LEHMANN WINES, BAROSSA VALLEY
Established 1979 *Owners* Peter Lehmann Wines Ltd
Production 230,000—250,000 cases *Vineyard area* 90 acres (36 ha)

Peter Lehmann is regarded by many as the godfather of Barossa winemaking. Without his unfailing espousal of and commitment to the region, it is safe to say the Barossa wouldn't enjoy quite the exalted position it does today. A fifth-generation Barossan and son of a Lutheran pastor, he founded his eponymous winery in 1979, after his employers—Saltram—refused to buy local growers' grapes during a wine glut. His long-standing commitment to those growers and their Barossa fruit has become legendary, and provides the backbone for the winery's consistently outstanding shiraz, cabernet and riesling wines.

CHARLES MELTON WINES, BAROSSA VALLEY
Established 1984 *Owners* Charles Melton Wines *Production* 7,000—8,000 cases *Vineyard area* 42 acres (17 ha)

The eponymous winemaker here is not called Charles at all (he's Graeme), but is still known to mates in the Barossa and the industry as Charlie. The reasons really don't matter, but the intense spicy refined red wines produced at his compact winery at the foot of the Barossa Ranges certainly matter a great deal. When he set up the business in 1984 after a 10-year apprenticeship under Peter Lehmann, Melton wanted to take a new approach with grapes and wine styles that were being neglected elsewhere in the Australian industry. Using and cherishing old dry-grown grenache and shiraz grapes, he's become the Barossa's very own Rhône Ranger, his grenache/shiraz/mourvedre blend Nine Popes reaching cult status.

MOUNTADAM VINEYARD, EDEN VALLEY
Established 1972 *Owners* David & Adam Wynn Pty Ltd
Production 50,000 cases *Vineyard area* 125 acres (50 ha)

David Wynn developed Mountadam on the beautiful High Eden Ridge after an exhaustive search throughout Australia for the best vineyard site to grow chardonnay. His son Adam became winemaker in 1984 after successfully completing his winemaking studies in Bordeaux. After nearly three decades, Mountadam is firmly established as one of Australia's super-premium wine companies, producing a range of elegant and refined wines. Mountadam Chardonnay sits happily with the greats (and with considerably less fuss and price hype than some newer super-premiums).

ROCKFORD WINES, BAROSSA VALLEY
Established 1984 *Owners* Tanunda Vintners Pty Ltd
Production 20,000 cases *Vineyard area* NA

Robert O'Callaghan, one of the Barossa's most passionate and respected winemakers, moved from St Hallett to start his own winery in 1984. From the start, he played a critical role in preserving the old plantings of Barossa shiraz that are vital to his full-bodied, richly flavored wines. The winery itself is a superb collection of stone and galvanized iron buildings containing restored nineteenth century equipment—old stationary engine-driven crushers, slate open fermenters and century-old wooden basket presses—which is used to make Basket Press Shiraz, the dark and dangerous sparkling Black Shiraz, Dry Country Grenache and others.

ST HALLETT, BAROSSA VALLEY
Established 1944 *Owners* Lindner McLean Vineyard & Cellars Pty Ltd *Production* 90,000 cases *Vineyard area* 125 acres (50 ha)

Big Bob McLean, St Hallett's chief executive, could be the man for whom the phrase "larger than life" was coined. Renowned for his love of long lunches, his river boat and life in general, he's full-bodied, generous and brimming with character—much like the premium table wines made at St Hallett. McLean and his talented winemaking director Stuart Blackwell were part of the group that recognized the value of the glorious old vine fruit available in the Barossa. A raft of gutsy shiraz, including the sought-after Old Block, are notable, but should not eclipse the Eden Valley Riesling and some lovely and easy-drinking blends.

TORBRECK, BAROSSA VALLEY
Established 1994 *Owners* Torbreck Vineyards Pty Ltd *Production* 2,500 cases *Vineyard area* 50 acres (20 ha)

David Powell learned his winemaking skills at the knee of Barossa legend

Grapes for many of the Barossa Valley's best wines are hand picked.

Steel vats and oak barrels fill Charles Melton Wines' outdoor processing center.

Robert O'Callaghan, and he's been using them well since he went out on his own and built his tiny new winery near Marananga. Traditional in style, and very much in the classic Barossa big red mold, Torbreck wines have swiftly won acclaim and attention, to the point where finding them at all is no small achievement.

TURKEY FLAT VINEYARDS, BAROSSA VALLEY

Established 1992 *Owners* Peter and Christie Schulz
Production 10,000 cases *Vineyard area* 42 acres (17 ha)

Fourth-generation Barossa viticulturist Peter Schulz and his wife Christie opened the Turkey Flat winery in 1993, but the birth of Turkey Flat really took place 145 years earlier when a far-sighted Silesian refugee first planted shiraz vines there on the banks of Tanunda Creek. Peter's family bought the land in the late 1800s, named it Turkey Flat after the bush turkeys that wandered there, maintained the vines, and developed a thriving butchering business. The 145-year-old shiraz vines and the 120-year-old bluestone former butcher's shop and cellar are now producing classic Barossa varietals and a spicy mourvedre-based blend.

VERITAS WINERY, BAROSSA VALLEY

Established 1955 *Owners* Rolf Binder *Production* 15,000 cases *Vineyard area* 95 acres (38 ha)

After years of using traditional equipment and methods in a cramped setting to produce his huge

complex red wines of great character and often brooding intensity, Rolf Binder is spreading his wings in a cavernous new cathedral of a winery just outside Tanunda. Plenty of people have lined up to pay homage to Binder's wines over the years and, in 1998, the faithful were joined by US wine guru Robert Parker, who awarded his Magpie Estate label a celestial 99 points out of 100.

YALUMBA WINERY, BAROSSA VALLEY

Established 1849 *Owners* S. Smith & Son *Production* 980,000 cases *Vineyard area* 1,260 acres (510 ha)

Australia's oldest family-owned winery, as the heart of S. Smith & Son invariably labels itself, celebrated its 150th birthday in 1999—a deeply satisfying moment for CEO Robert Hill-Smith to be sure. It was Hill-Smith, with his brother Sam, who took the deep financial plunge in 1989 to bring the company back solely into family control. Another plunge was taken shortly thereafter— away from a traditional reliance on ports and sherries into table wines. Talented winemakers and marketing savvy have since taken Yalumba to a comfortable position. The company produces successful wines at all levels, from consistent and reliable basics like Angas Brut and Oxford Landing, through the Antipodean, Growers, Pewsey Vale and Heggies ranges, to the big benchmark reds, for example, The Menzies, The Signature and Octavius.

Adelaide Hills

Sally Marden

The Adelaide Hills region lies less than half an hour's drive from Adelaide's flat suburban sprawl, up in the steep, wooded ranges that border the city's eastern edge. It stretches from Mount Pleasant in the neighboring northerly wine region of Eden Valley, down to Mount Compass and the hills behind McLaren Vale in the south. It is cool, and not just in meteorological terms—its restrained, lifted whites and elegant reds are fashionable and attracting increasing international acclaim. Some of Australia's most respected wine-makers—people like Brian Croser, Stephen and Prue Henschke, Tim Knappstein and Geoff Weaver—have major interests in the area.

But the Adelaide Hills is not simply a trendy new wine region. From 1840 to 1900, there were as many as 195 grape growers and winemakers in the area. Legend has it that the Adelaide Hills was even the source of Australia's first exported wine, a hock from Echunga that was sent to Queen Victoria in 1845. The fact that wine production in the region had all but died out by 1910 is probably due to the preference of the day for rich, ripe, high-alcohol warm-climate reds, such as those that come from the Barossa.

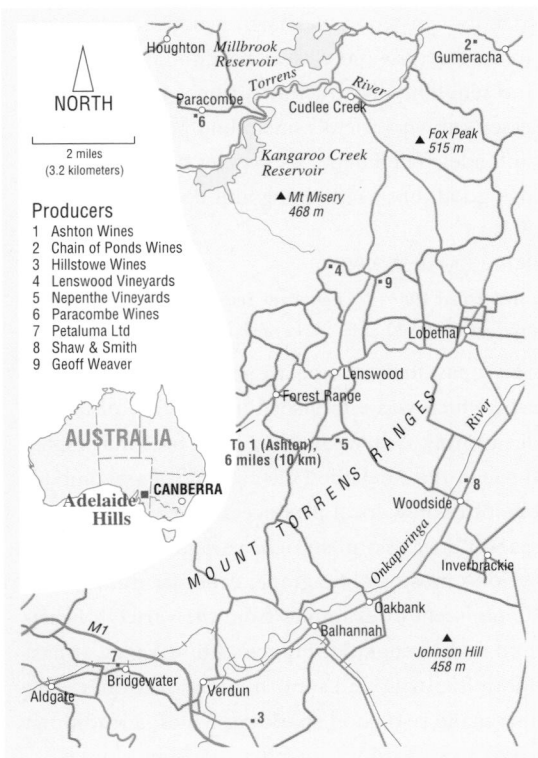

Producers
1 Ashton Wines
2 Chain of Ponds Wines
3 Hillstowe Wines
4 Lenswood Vineyards
5 Nepenthe Vineyards
6 Paracombe Wines
7 Petaluma Ltd
8 Shaw & Smith
9 Geoff Weaver

The mixed pastoral landscape of steep little valleys, winding roads, orchards and switchback vine rows provides Australia with one of its most picturesque wine regions. English oaks, green pasture and a fair bit of mist and rain give a European feel to the area, and there are numerous microclimates and subregions. This makes any generalization about conditions and suitable varieties hazardous, but the region's cool, moist climate provides excellent results from the most widely planted white grape, chardonnay, including two of Australia's most prestigious and expensive—Petaluma Tiers and Penfolds Yattarna. Riesling is successful here also, showing lime-blossom characters when young and aging well, and nowhere else in Australia can match this region for sauvignon blanc. Not surprisingly, it also produces fruit and base wines for some of Australia's better sparkling wines.

As for the most widely planted red, indeed the most widely-planted grape, this would perhaps make a good trivia question. Although the Adelaide Hills is fast gaining a reputation for quality pinot noir, it is cabernet franc that dominates in terms of quantity.

A timber mill once stood on the site of Hillstowe Wines' Adelaide Hills vineyards.

A small gallery adjacent to the tasting room at Ashton Hills Vineyard.

Grapes for Nepenthe Vineyards' popular wines are picked by hand.

REGIONAL DOZEN

QUALITY WINES

Ashton Hills Reserve Pinot
  Noir
Chain of Ponds Ledge Shiraz
Lenswood Vineyards
  Chardonnay
Petaluma Tiers Chardonnay
Nepenthe Lenswood Semillon
Geoff Weaver Chardonnay

BEST VALUE WINES

Bridgewater Mill Chardonnay
Chain of Ponds Riesling
Henschke Greens Hill Riesling
Pibbin Rosé
Shaw and Smith Sauvignon
  Blanc
Talunga Shiraz

ASHTON HILLS VINEYARD

Established 1982 *Owners* Stephen George
and Peta van Rood *Production* 1,750 cases
Vineyard area 7.4 acres (3 ha)

With a winemaking pedigree that
includes assisting with the legendary
long-living reds of Wendouree in
Clare, Stephen George was destined to
do something special at his Ashton
Hills property, where the cool-climate
growing conditions are similar to those
of Champagne and Burgundy in
France. And that he has. His constant
experimentation in different varieties,
clonal selection, trellis designs and
management systems has resulted in a
range of elegant, clean, finely flavored
wines. Chardonnay and riesling are
complex, harmonious and redolent of
the best from Europe. His pinot noir is impressive,
whether in a luscious, strawberry-fresh deep rosé
style, or the richer, gamier, spicier reserve version.
Obliqua, a cabernet/merlot blend, is also excellent.

CHAIN OF PONDS WINES

Established 1993 *Owners* Caj and Jenny Amadio
Production 8,000 cases *Vineyard area* 57 acres (23 ha)

The Amadios were highly regarded growers of
Adelaide Hills fruit for several years before they
began saving some of their finest grapes for their
own premium-quality wines in 1993. Since then,
they have become equally well respected as winemakers. Their wines, both red and white, tend
towards tight restraint in their youth and definitely
benefit from a few years aging. Their riesling
shows intense lemon and spice characters, and
their cabernet sauvignon is in the classic blackcurrant, herbaceous and cedar wood mold.

HILLSTOWE WINES

Established 1991 *Owners* the Laurie family *Production*
13,000 cases *Vineyard area* 74 acres (30 ha)

Chris Laurie is the fourth generation of the Laurie
family to make wine in South Australia, and now
has his son Hamish working alongside him. The
family business was based further south in
McLaren Vale, where they still have vineyards, but
they also bought land in the Hills where a timber
mill had once stood 40 years ago. Today, their hills
property near the tourist mecca of Hahndorf—
known as Udy's Mill Vineyards—produces delicate, smoky chardonnays and light, fragrant pinot
noirs with vegetal complexity.

LENSWOOD VINEYARDS

Established 1981 *Owners* Tim and Annie Knappstein
Production 8,000 cases *Vineyard area* 66 acres (26.7 ha)

Tim Knappstein has been quietly making his
presence felt in the Australian wine industry for
nearly 40 years. Single-handedly revolutionizing
the wines of his family's company, Stanley Wines
of Clare, he took the Australian wine show circuit
by storm during the late 1960s and early 1970s
with his Leasingham bin label wines. In 1976, he
set up on his own in Clare and established his own
eponymous label. In 1981, he expanded into the
cooler climes of the Adelaide Hills, establishing the
vineyards at Lenswood where he could indulge his
passion for making top-quality chardonnay and
pinot noir. He sold his Clare base to Petaluma in
1992, and moved full-time to Lenswood. The
resulting wines are consistently good and classic in
style, particularly the chardonnay, riesling, cabernet sauvignon and pinot noir.

NEPENTHE VINEYARDS

Established 1994 *Owners* James Tweddell *Production*
6,500 cases *Vineyard area* 62 acres (25 ha)

One of the brightest new stars in the South
Australian firmament, Nepenthe, named after an
ancient Egyptian herbal drink with legendary
powers, has swiftly gained cult status, and their
wines sometimes sell out within hours of release.
Peter Leske is the man behind them, working at
Nepenthe's state-of-the-art, environmentally
friendly Lenswood winery to produce wines with
great structure and class. Chardonnay, pinot noir
and sémillon all attract attention, but so do the
lesser known varietals, including pinot gris and
zinfandel. The Fugue, a cabernet merlot/blend, is
also good, but needs aging and decanting.

PARACOMBE WINES

Established 1983 *Owners* Paul and Kathy Drogemuller
Production 1,500 cases *Vineyard area* 30 acres (12 ha)

Tiny quantities of wine are produced at this property, which was established in the wake of the
devastating Ash Wednesday bush fires that raged
through the Adelaide Hills in 1983. Paracombe is
one of the few local producers to make and
market a successful straight varietal wine from the
region's most prolific grape, cabernet franc.
Reminiscent of examples from the variety's heartland and stronghold, France's Loire Valley, it has
light plum fruit and some mineral overtones. They
also make two good sparkling wines, a traditional
pinot noir/chardonnay and a sparkling shiraz.

PETALUMA LTD

Established 1976 *Owners* Petaluma Ltd *Production* 30,000 cases *Vineyard area* 309 acres (125 ha)

One of Australia's most well known and respected wine producers, Brian Croser established Petaluma in Adelaide Hills' Piccadilly Valley subregion in 1976. Two years later, Petaluma became a joint venture with Australian wine legend Len Evans. In 1985, Champagne producer Bollinger became a major shareholder and the company went public in 1993. It has since acquired a number of well known labels, including Mitchelton, Tim Knappstein, Stonier and Smithbrook. Brian Croser has been the driving force throughout. Fruit is sourced from several regions, with the Adelaide Hills vineyards yielding premium grapes for stellar chardonnay (including the rare and expensive Tiers), riesling and the Croser pinot noir/chardonnay sparkler. There is also has a second label, Petaluma's Bridgewater Mill.

SHAW & SMITH

Established 1989 *Owners* Martin Shaw and Michael Hill-Smith *Production* 24,000 cases *Vineyard area* 60 acres (24 ha)

These two Australian wine legends specialize in white wine production and they make some of the finest examples in the region. Shaw, formerly a winemaker at Petaluma, and Hill-Smith, a writer, judge, producer, consultant and master of wine,

started the business determined to concentrate on sauvignon blanc and chardonnay. They quickly gained a reputation for producing modern, clean classics of both. Their chardonnay is balanced; creamy and smooth, with multiple layers of subtle flavors, while their sauvignon blanc is a match for some of New Zealand's finest.

A vintage truck signs the way to the tasting room at Hillstowe Wines.

GEOFF WEAVER

Established 1982 *Owners* Geoff and Judith Weaver *Production* 5,000 cases *Vineyard area* 27 acres (11 ha)

Geoff Weaver is a firm adherent to the old maxim that good wine is made in the vineyard, and the quality of the fruit from his Stafford Ridge property certainly reinforces that belief. He aims to make sure that each grape variety is allowed to express its classic characteristics through fresh, complex wines. The theory works well, with chardonnay showing rich, buttery characters and white peach fruit, sauvignon blanc that's tight, green, peppery and pungent, and riesling with balanced fruit and citrus flavors. Grape growing and winemaking are not the only arts at which Weaver excels—his lovely painting of Stafford Ridge is used on his labels.

Petaluma's Piccadilly Valley vineyards produce grapes for Brian Croser's elegant chardonnays.

McLaren Vale

Sally Marden

Most Australian wine regions take their influence from the migrants who settled there. In the Barossa it was German-speaking Silesians, in the Riverland Italians, but in McLaren Vale it was a group of Englishmen who started the ball rolling. Two in particular laid the foundations for the region and really left their mark—John Reynell, who first planted vines in the area in 1838, and Thomas Hardy, whose influence has been integral to the region since he bought and developed the Tintara vineyards and winery in 1876.

Wheat dominated in the early days, but the pioneers recognized that this region 64 miles (40 km) south of the center of Adelaide was perfect for vines, so it was not many years before grapes became the most important crop. By the start of the twentieth century, there were 19 wineries in the district, mostly producing dark, high-alcohol, tannic dry reds (with a reputation for medicinal qualities) or fortifieds, which were predominantly snapped up by the English market. The conviction and vision of Reynell, Hardy and others has been validated by the vital role the region plays in premium wine production today.

Things didn't always go swimmingly, however. There were serious interruptions to supply and development during the two world wars. Then in the 1970s, taste and fashion switched from big robust red wines to dry light white wines. This caused serious problems for a number of years in McLaren Vale, where the red vines outnumbered white by about three to one, and many vines were grubbed out and replanted, or regrafted. But this seems to have ended up doing far more good than harm, since the introduction of new varieties like chardonnay, sauvignon blanc, merlot and cabernet franc allowed wine producers to expand their repertoires with considerable success.

Bordered to the east by the southern ranges of the Adelaide Hills and to the west the Gulf of St Vincent, the diverse landscape of McLaren Vale varies from steep ranges and gorges to wide open plains, with beaches and cliffs, rivers, hills, olive groves, orchards and ocean views in between. The terrain is undulating and soil types vary widely, but red-brown or gray-brown loamy sands are dominant. There is also significant climatic variation, due to differing degrees of exposure to or protection from the nearby sea and its cooling influence. Summer rainfall is low, so irrigation of the vineyards is generally necessary; however the presence of the Onkaparinga River and its tributaries ensure that water is always close at hand.

Because of this geographical and climatic diversity, nearly all grape varieties flourish here, and especially those suited to premium styles. The resulting wines tend to be intense, full-flavored reds and powerful, fruit-driven whites. Shiraz is a mainstay, producing deep-colored, richly flavored wines with distinctive velvety characters (as opposed to the spicy/peppery characters found, say, in Barossa shiraz). Cabernet sauvignon tends to smoothness, with a ripe richness and hints of chocolate, and merlot also does well. Among the whites, chardonnay excels here, producing classic examples at many levels, from big rich, buttery, toasty wines to elegant, peach-flavored fruit-driven examples. Sauvignon blanc thrives here too, giving herby, asparagus-flavored wines with a prickly intensity. The region also produces some good fortifieds and is home to a wide range of sparkling wines. As in so many regions in Australia and

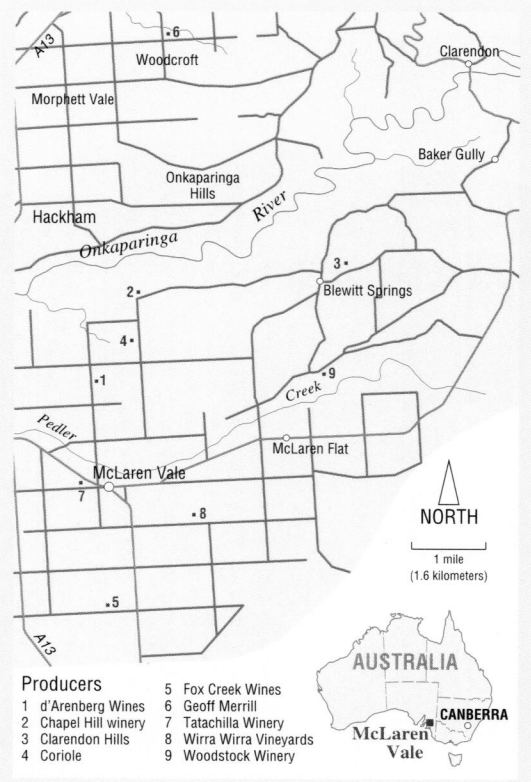

Producers
1 d'Arenberg Wines
2 Chapel Hill winery
3 Clarendon Hills
4 Coriole
5 Fox Creek Wines
6 Geoff Merrill
7 Tatachilla Winery
8 Wirra Wirra Vineyards
9 Woodstock Winery

worldwide, pinot noir here struggles to graduate from being a sparkling wine component to a fully-fledged varietal red wine. McLaren Vale's 50 wineries are a mixed bunch in size, style and stature, with everything from one-man cellar-door operations to corporate behemoths. But the biggest of all of them is no new-comer—it's BRL Hardy, the current incarnation of the company started by Thomas Hardy in the mid-1800s. Having bought Chateau Reynella, now Hardy headquarters, from his contemporary, John Reynell, Hardys kept expanding, acquiring new businesses at home and abroad, but the heart has always stayed in McLaren Vale. In addition, Southcorp has a significant stake in the region with its Seaview winery (given an upmarket re-branding as Edwards & Chaffey in 1999), as have Mildara Blass and Rosemount. But most of the wineries are considerably smaller, resulting in a range and variety of wines that reflects the diversity of the region and its producers.

sensible (all machinery either glides or slides), yet graceful, wineries in the area, and tucked it unobtrusively into the side of the hill. Her wines are always robust, balanced and fine, whether the traditionally styled shiraz, cabernet sauvignon and blends, or chardonnay (with and without wood). She also makes a very good verdelho.

A traditional-style wooden veranda adorns the winery building at d'Arenberg Wines.

Wine being tested at Chapel Hill Winery.

D'ARENBERG WINES

Established 1912 *Owners* d'Arenberg Wines Pty Ltd
Production 120,000 cases *Vineyard area* 270 acres (110 ha)

A McLaren Vale stalwart since 1912, d'Arenberg has managed to move gracefully and intelligently with the times. It was d'Arry Osborn who built up the business from the 1950s onwards, making big earthy reds and fortifieds, but his son Chester has held sway since the mid-1980s. Chester rejuvenated the old cellars and vineyards, brought in small stainless steel tanks and gave the winemaking a bit of a revamp. Both the whites and reds have since attracted increasing acclaim, as has the recently added d'Arry's Verandah restaurant.

CHAPEL HILL WINERY

Established 1977 *Owners* Gerard Industries Pty Ltd
Production 60,000 cases *Vineyard area* 108 acres (44 ha)

The redoubtably down-to-earth Pam Dunsford is probably heartily sick of reading this, but she will always be the first woman in Australia to have graduated as an enologist. In 1987, she moved to Chapel Hill, where she designed one of the most

CLARENDON HILLS

Established 1970 *Owners* Clarendon Hills Nominees Pty Ltd *Production* 18,000 cases *Vineyard area* NA

Always in the sought-after category, the reds from Clarendon Hills have become even more scarce in recent years, thanks largely to a string of recommendations from influential commentators (especially in the USA). Situated on the northern fringes of McLaren Vale, the winery takes fruit from small plots of old vines in the hilly slopes bordering the Adelaide Hills region. The resulting wines are huge, intense, complex, multi-layered beasts which often owe more in style to France than Australia. Not for the faint-hearted or the financially challenged.

The tasting room at Tatachilla Winery, which was named Australian Winery of the Year for 1996–97.

CORIOLE

Established 1968 *Owners* the Lloyd family *Production* 34,000 cases *Vineyard area* 75 acres (30 ha)

An interesting variety of grapes and styles come out of this winery, often with a slight Italian accent. The winery underwent extensive upgrading and expansion when it was purchased by the Lloyd family in 1967. Mark Lloyd introduced sangiovese under his label in the mid-1980s and has since also developed the respected Diva, a sangiovese/cabernet blend aged in new French oak. His classic earthy regional blends are also good.

FOX CREEK WINES

Established 1995 *Owners* the Watts and Roberts families *Production* 16,000 cases *Vineyard area* 150 acres (60 ha)

One of the most exciting recent additions to the McLaren Vale scene, Fox Creek has made a substantial impact, with its Reserve Cabernet, Reserve Shiraz and JSM Shiraz/Cabernets blend all attracting plaudits. The turn of the new century has been a time of change, with Dan Hills and Tony Walker taking over as resident winemakers from Sparky and Sarah Marquis (who retain a consultancy role), and a new winery complex has been commissioned, complete with traditional-style open fermenters recreated in stainless steel.

GEOFF MERRILL

Established 1980 *Owners* Stratmer Vineyards Pty Ltd *Production* 100,000 cases *Vineyard area* 55 acres (22 ha)

Complete with remarkable handlebar moustache, Geoff Merrill, formerly chief winemaker at Chateau Reynella wines, has at times gained almost as much attention for his hard playing

outside the winery as the hard working within. But this shouldn't detract from the quality of the wines he and winemaker Goe DiFabio produce. Real food wines, the reds are ripe and generous, but with supporting structure and elegance, while the whites are full-bodied and matured. He also makes a cracking good rosé.

TATACHILLA WINERY

Established 1901 *Owners* Consortium headed by Vic Zerella and Keith Smith *Production* 100,000 cases *Vineyard area* 37 acres (15 ha)

It is only in recent years that Tatachilla has really found its level. Owned for many years by a local growers cooperative, it was bought in 1993 by a consortium, then re-vamped and re-opened in 1995. Since then, with winemaker Michael Fragos at the helm, the wines have steadily improved and regularly do extremely well on the Australian wine show circuit. The winery was named Australian Winery of the Year for 1996–97 by Vogue Entertaining magazine. Cabernet sauvignon and merlot are particularly good.

WIRRA WIRRA VINEYARDS

Established 1894 *Owners* Greg and Roger Trott *Production* 60,000 cases *Vineyard area* 200 acres (80 ha)

Noted cricketer Robert Strangways Wigley (whose initials are used on the winery's flagship shiraz today) established Wirra Wirra, but the place fell into ruin after he died in 1924. It was revived and restored by cousins Greg and Roger Trott in 1969. They, with winemaker Ben Riggs, have been responsible for increasingly good wines, both white and red, including the popular Church Block cabernet blend and the rich and creamy Cousins sparkling pinot noir/chardonnay. Respected winemaker and consultant Tony Jordan took over as chief executive in the late 1990s.

WOODSTOCK WINERY

Established 1974 *Owners* Collett Wines Pty Ltd *Production* 35,000 cases *Vineyard area* 50 acres (20 ha)

Woodstock was bought by Doug Collett with his sons Scott, Ian and Stephen in 1973. After a long stint abroad, Scott settled there as winemaker. He has since become known for producing consistently good wines in a range of styles, from dry white to dessert, but it's his reds that attract the largest following. Being a strong believer in living life to the full, with good food and great wine, Collett and his wife have opened a restaurant and entertainment complex next to the winery.

REGIONAL DOZEN

QUALITY WINES

Chapel Hill The Vicar
  Cabernet Sauvignon Shiraz
Clarendon Hills Piggott Range
  Vineyard Shiraz
Fox Creek JSM Shiraz
  Cabernets
Rosemount GSM Grenache
  Shiraz Mourvedre
Tatachilla Clarendon Vineyard
  Merlot
Wirra Wirra RSW Shiraz

BEST VALUE WINES

Chapel Hill Verdelho
d'Arenberg d'Arry's Original
  Shiraz Grenache
Maglieri Chardonnay
Scarpantoni Block 3 Shiraz
Shottesbrooke Chardonnay
Tatachilla Growers Chenin
  Semillon Sauvignon Blanc

Coonawarra and the Limestone Coast

Alex Mitchell

Coonawarra is known throughout Australia and the world for its elegant yet richly flavored cabernet sauvignon. Its fame rests on a narrow strip of paprika-colored soil: terra rossa. This loam overlays well draining limestone and a high water table, and produces exceptional grape development and characters. It is only about 12.5 miles (20 km) long and 1 mile (1.5 km) wide, narrowing at each end, and varying in depth from a few inches to 3 feet (a few centimeters to a meter). Many of the great names in Australian wine history are still found in the area.

Although Coonawarra is more well known, the Padthaway region 53 miles (85 km) north now produces more grapes. Seppelt was the first to plant vines there, in 1963, when land was readily available and affordable. The suitability of the soil and climate for grape growing were soon evident, though ironically for white (notably chardonnay) rather than red varieties. Hardys and Lindemans have invested here also, and the area continues to be characterized by large companies growing fruit for use in a variety of products.

Less than 18.5 miles (30 km) from the coast, Mount Gambier is South Australia's southern-most viticultural region and awaits assessment of its full potential. There are five small producers, chardonnay and cabernet sauvignon being the dominant varieties. The Mount Benson region, on the coast, is one of Australia's newest. Lindemans planted experimental vines there in 1978, and Southcorp remains a significant investor, along with Cellarmaster Wines and, more recently, M. Chapoutier & Co, one of France's Rhône Valley producers.

John Riddoch discovered the region's viticultural potential, planting vines, largely shiraz and cabernet sauvignon, in 1890. He built the substantial limestone winery that remains at Wynns Coonawarra Estate today. But Coonawarra was a minor player compared to other South Australian vineyard regions. Despite the quality of its production, a vine-pull scheme was introduced in the 1930s because table wine sales were low, and two-thirds of Coonawarra vines were sacrificed to dairy, orchards and livestock. In 1951, David Wynn and his father Samuel purchased the remains of the original Riddoch property, and believing in the quality of Coonawarra when others had dismissed it. It is a testament to the calibre of the area's grapes that many of the names responsible for Coonawarra's development since the 1950s—Brand, Lindeman, Redman and Wynn—are still found on the wine labels.

Nearly a million years ago, the ocean extended as far inland as the Naracoorte Ranges, and over a series of ice ages it gradually withdrew to its present position, leaving Coonawarra 93 miles (150 km) from the current coastline. The famous terra

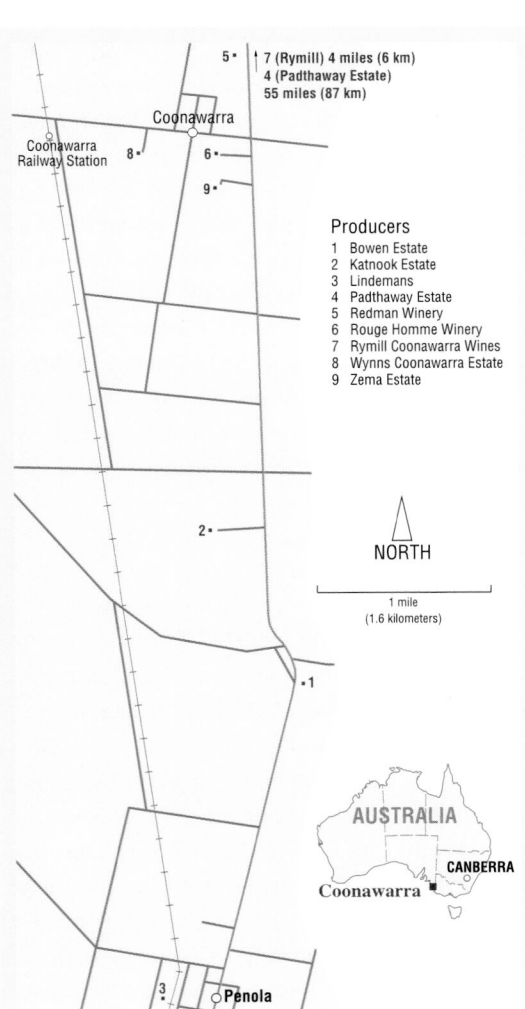

7 (Rymill) 4 miles (6 km)
4 (Padthaway Estate)
55 miles (87 km)

Coonawarra

Coonawarra Railway Station

Producers
1 Bowen Estate
2 Katnook Estate
3 Lindemans
4 Padthaway Estate
5 Redman Winery
6 Rouge Homme Winery
7 Rymill Coonawarra Wines
8 Wynns Coonawarra Estate
9 Zema Estate

NORTH

1 mile
(1.6 kilometers)

AUSTRALIA

CANBERRA
Coonawarra

Penola

REGIONAL DOZEN

QUALITY WINES

Bowen Estate Cabernet Sauvignon

Hollick Ravenswood Cabernet Sauvignon

Katnook Estate Odyssey Cabernet Sauvignon

Majella Cabernet Sauvignon

Parker First Growth Cabernet Sauvignon

Wynns John Riddoch Cabernet Sauvignon

BEST VALUE WINES

Lindemans St George Cabernet Sauvignon

Penley Estate Hyland Shiraz

Redman Cabernet Sauvignon

Rymill Merlot Cabernet

Wynns Coonawarra Estate Shiraz

Zema Estate Cluny Cabernets

The carefully tended vineyard at Bowen Estate is hand pruned.

rossa is the result of clay, organic material and minerals being deposited on top of the limestone, and exposed iron-rich particles being oxidized to a rich russet red. Patches of this exceptional soil are found throughout the region, though nowhere in such concentration as in Coonawarra. The Limestone Coast lacks significant mountains, so the climate is maritime, although areas further north and inland experience less rainfall and more sunshine than their coastal neighbors. Spring frosts and rain during vintage are well known, but generous cloud cover and mild temperatures are common throughout the region, allowing grapes to ripen slowly and gradually develop sweet, full fruit flavors without loss of acidity.

When shiraz became the dominant red grape in Australia and fortified the dominant wine style, Coonawarra retained small plantings of cabernet sauvignon, the variety which has become its forte. The cool climate and terra rossa combine to give distinctive perfume and complexity to the wines. Coonawarra cabernet displays the expected blackcurrants, plums, cassis and chocolatey richness of the variety, but is frequently tinged with hints of mint and eucalyptus.

Though somewhat of a bridesmaid now to cabernet, shiraz from the Limestone Coast has a fine history and remains a powerfully spicy form of the variety. Riesling from this area is surprisingly good, in a fruity and fragrant style made by only a few producers, most notably Wynns and Hollick. Rymill and Katnook Estate both envisage a great future for sauvignon blanc in the region. Chardonnay has seen mixed fortunes in Coonawarra, but has become the forte of Padthaway, where it

makes elegant but fruity still wines and complex sparkling wines. Mount Benson and Robe are still experimenting, but some recently released shiraz has been surprisingly lush, especially when treated with French oak.

BOWEN ESTATE, COONAWARRA

Established 1972 *Owners* Doug and Joy Bowen *Production* 15,000 cases *Vineyard area* 60 acres (25 ha)

The family-owned and managed Bowen Estate has a well earned reputation for wines that reflect the premium nature of Coonawarra fruit when it is carefully tended, hand pruned and sensitively handled. Doug Bowen was a young Roseworthy graduate when he purchased and planted his plot of terra rossa in 1972. Bowen's wines have layers of intense flavor, a lush mouthfeel and remarkable length, and will further reward those who have the patience to cellar them carefully.

KATNOOK ESTATE, COONAWARRA

Established 1890s *Owner* Wingara Wine Group *Production* 60,000 cases *Vineyard area* 595 acres (240 ha)

The Katnook Estate name is derived from the original property established by John Riddoch in Coonawarra in the 1860s, although the Katnook brand wasn't established until 1979. The second vintage of Riddoch's wines was made in the woolshed at Katnook, a building that still constitutes part of the winery complex, as does John Riddoch's homestead. The estate produces some of Coonawarra's most intensely flavored and painstakingly crafted wines. A recent Jimmy Watson trophy for the 1997 Shiraz highlights the calibre of the wines, even unfinished. Odyssey, a wine of huge flavor and structure yet fine balance and complexity, is made from the top 1 percent of hand-selected cabernet fruit.

LINDEMANS, COONAWARRA

Established 1908 *Owner* Southcorp Wines *Production* 9,000 cases *Vineyard area* 250 acres (100 ha)

British immigrant and Australian viticultural pioneer, Dr Henry John Lindeman planted his Cawarra vineyards in the Hunter Valley of NSW in 1843. His name is now one of Southcorp's most successful brands. The Lindemans Coonawarra trio of Pyrus, Limestone Ridge and St George, the brand's flagship wines, are crafted from premium Coonawarra fruit and made only in great vintages. St George is one of Australia's classic single vineyard cabernets and shows rich plums, chocolate and smoky wood on the palate.

PADTHAWAY ESTATE, PADTHAWAY

Established 1979 *Owners* Dale Baker and Ian Gray
Production 6,000 cases *Vineyard area* 125 acres (50 ha)

The site of settler Robert Lawson's sheep property, this vineyard was the area's sole attraction until recently. The gracious Padthaway Estate Homestead built in 1882 remained the Lawson family residence until 1980, when it was sold for use as luxury accommodation. Padthaway Estate's sparkling wine demonstrates the potential of the area for cool-climate white grapes.

REDMAN WINERY, COONAWARRA

Established 1966 *Owners* the Redman family *Production* 20,000 cases *Vineyard area* 80 acres (30 ha)

Bill Redman went to work in the Riddoch vineyards in 1901—the year of John Riddoch's death. In 1908, he purchased 40 acres (16.2 ha) of Riddoch vines and establish a winery. He sold much of his "burgundy" to the British market in a commercial contract with Tolleys until they cancelled his contract in the early 1920s because the quality of his Coonawarra reds made it difficult for them to sell their other wines. In 1954, the Redman's family company became Rouge Homme and their wines were marketed under that label. After Lindemans bought Rouge Homme in 1965, Owen Redman purchased 16 acres of aged shiraz vines from a colleague and Redman Winery made a shiraz from the 1966 vintage. Redman's red wines, which are all they have ever made, have a characteristic leafy edge to the flavors and are gutsy and tannic.

ROUGE HOMME WINERY, COONAWARRA

Established 1954 *Owner* Southcorp Wines *Production* 73,000 cases *Vineyard area* 500 acres (200 ha)

The winery begun by the Redman family was acquired by Lindeman's in 1965. The wines are always of Coonawarra origin and of consistently good quality, offering value for money and something for all tastes. The Richardsons Red Block, a blend of classic bordeaux varieties, boasts a Jimmy Watson Trophy. It has all the fruit intensity and tannic strength expected of wine from established Coonawarra vines, tinged with an intriguing spiciness and green vegetal notes.

RYMILL COONAWARRA WINES, COONAWARRA

Established 1974 *Owner* Peter Rymill *Production* 50,000 cases *Vineyard area* 395 acres (160 ha)

Perhaps the closest thing Coonawarra has to a château, the Rymill winery, opened in 1990, is a masterpiece of modern grandeur and design. Picturesque vine plantings and distant red gums can be seen from its upper level balconies, and the ultra modern stainless steel winery can be viewed from an internal platform. Rymill wines are made to express unique regional characters and to complement food. Their sauvignon blanc hints at the potential of this variety in the region.

WYNNS COONAWARRA ESTATE, COONAWARRA

Established 1891 *Owners* Southcorp Wines *Production* 380,000 cases *Vineyard area* 1,975 acres (800 ha)

No visit to Coonawarra is complete without a pilgrimage to the historic limestone building, the first winery in the area, completed by John Riddoch in 1896. It was a facility much admired in its day, boasting cool basement storage rooms, a steam powered crusher, and even cooling coils for the stone fermenting tanks. After the death of its visionary founder in 1901, the property suffered gradual decline until Samuel Wynn and his son David purchased it for £22,000 (US$35,000 today) in 1951. Their success in the following years was the impetus for investment in Coonawarra by many other companies. The classic shiraz beloved by many as Wynns Hermitage remains a benchmark, and the black label Cabernet Sauvignon is collected every year by aficionados. The premium John Riddoch Cabernet Sauvignon and Michael Shiraz are made only in exceptional years.

ZEMA ESTATE, COONAWARRA

Established 1982 *Owners* Demetrio and Francesca Zema *Production* 10,000 cases *Vineyard area* 125 acres (50 ha)

In the 1960s, when he was a painter at nearby Penola, Demetrio Zema made small batches of wine at home and dreamed of owning a vineyard and winery on terra rossa. His dream came true in 1982, and now the entire Zema family contributes to the winemaking process. They retain traditional vineyard practices, favoring dry-land viticulture, hand pruning, and part barrel fermentation. The results are superb—rich, plump fruit flavors with earthy aromas and robust tannins which suggest that careful cellaring will reward the wine lover well. The family hand selects their premium fruit to produce small quantities of the Family Selection Cabernet Sauvignon, which like their other wines, is exceptional value for money.

The working winery can be viewed from a platform inside Rymill Coonawarra Wines.

Grapes are shoveled into a crusher at Padthaway Estate.

Other South Australian Regions

RIVERLAND

Sally Marden

With so much attention and emphasis placed on the fashionable premium-wine producing regions, it would be easy to forget that the driving force in Australia's wine industry is the far less glamorous, vast open space of the Riverland. These endless acres of vines, watered by the mighty Murray River, pump out more than half of South Australia's grapes and a third of the country's total crush. They provide the fruit for the Australian wine that most people, at home and abroad, drink most of—the big name brands, the bags-in-boxes, the everyday quaffers. They are honest, enjoyable, good-value wines that are full of flavor.

Without the Riverland, nowhere near the number of people who currently enjoy a glass or two of Oxford Landing, Jacob's Creek, Lindemans Bin 65, or brands with other household names would ever have tasted Australian wine, or perhaps even have known that it existed. Nor would the Australian wine industry be enjoying the enormous global success that it does. Much of the credit for the apparently inexorable rise in wine exports should go to the growers and winemakers of the Riverland (even though it very rarely does). Without them, Australia simply couldn't meet the demand for its wines or invest in its future.

When you see the endless rows of vines, posts and wires, with computer-controlled irrigation systems stretching to the horizon, or the seas of stainless steel tanks and sheds that resemble chemical refineries more than wineries, it can seem a bit like battery farming for grapes. The wines produced are generally simple, straightforward, fruit-driven styles that are made in huge quantities for instant fulfilment rather than for careful cellaring. But, as in the rest of the industry, fruit quality, technical know-how and the wines themselves are improving all the time, and some enthusiastic producers are now taking the Riverland to a much higher plane.

It's hot and dry there, but the brown sandy loam soils, just an hour from the Barossa, are reasonably fertile. Rainfall is low and the rate of evaporation is high, so there is little risk of disease The main concern for the future of the Riverland is the health of the Murray River, where water levels are dropping and salinity levels are rising fast. It is hoped that new, more sensitive irrigation systems will help to alleviate the pressures on this invaluable water resource.

ANGOVE'S

Established 1886 *Owners* the Angove family *Production* 750,000 cases *Vineyard area* 1,185 acres (480 ha)

Established by migrant Cornishman Dr William Angove, this is now one of Australia's largest privately owned wine companies. The business moved to Renmark in 1910, where it has since built up a successful range of good-value varietals, fortified wines and spirits, including Australia's best known brandy, St Agnes. Labels include the Classic Reserve, Stonegate, Sarnia Farm, Butterfly Ridge and Misty Vineyards ranges.

BANROCK STATION

Established 1994 *Owners* BRL Hardy Wine Ltd *Production* 1.5 million cases *Vineyard area* 615 acres (250 ha)

The showpiece of the Riverland and an example of what can be achieved in this environmentally sensitive and stretched region, Banrock Station is a groundbreaking vineyard property, wetland reserve and visitor center near Kingston-on-Murray. Everything has been done with the environment and conservation in mind, from the solar-powered, recycled-water-using visitor center with stunning views over the wetland lagoons and river, to the computer-controlled vineyard irrigation. Even the Banrock Station wines use recycled and recyclable packaging, and a contribution from the sale of every bottle goes to Landcare Australia. The wines

Stacks of wooden barrels.

themselves show what the region can achieve with the right handling, with a delightful sparkling chardonnay, and fresh, modern examples of unwooded chardonnay, shiraz, cabernet/merlot and sémillon/chardonnay. These are good wines made with environmental common sense and marketing genius—the perfect wine brand for the turn of the century, and one which has already positioned itself as world leader.

BERRI ESTATES

Established 1922 *Owners* BRL Hardy Wine Ltd *Production* 7,920,000 cases *Vineyard area* NA

Originally a growers cooperative formed by soldiers returning from the First World War, Berri Estates focused on spirits until the mid-1930s, but moved into fortifieds and table wines in a big way in subsequent years. The company merged with fellow Riverland giant Renmano in 1982. Berri Estates is Australia's largest single winery and distillery and can process 77,000 tons (70,000 t) of grapes every year. There is storage room for 18.5 million gallons (70 million l). Berri's size and history are more notable than its range of wines.

BONNEYVIEW WINES

Established 1976 *Owners* Robert Minns *Production* 5,000 cases *Vineyard area* 6 acres (2.5 ha)

Not your average Riverland winery, this. The boutique Bonneyview was established by English cricketer Robert Minns on the shores of Lake Bonney. Not only is its size and style incongruous, so is its range of wines, which rely on the comparatively rare petit verdot. As well as a straight varietals, the winery also produces blends with merlot and cabernet sauvignon. With a popular cellar door and restaurant, Bonneyview makes an interesting contrast to the industrial-scale enterprises of its nearest neighbors.

KINGSTON ESTATE WINES

Established 1979 *Owners* Kingston Estate Wines Pty Ltd *Production* NA *Vineyard area* 370 acres (150 ha)

Another one of the Riverland producers doing exciting things and seriously committed to raising its own and the region's profile. The combination of improved-quality fruit with innovative, contemporary winemaking results in a range of good-value, fruit-driven varietal wines that are attracting much attention. CEO Bill Moularadellis is one of the industry's great marketers (and a good self-publicist), doing much to increase awareness of his wines, with a recent emphasis on merlot.

NORMANS LONE GUM WINERY

Established 1853 *Owners* Normans Wines Ltd *Production* 220,000 cases *Vineyard area* 235 acres (95 ha)

Normans' Lone Gum operation started life as Wein Valley Estates and was one of the many major processing sites for the thousands of tons of grapes that are produced in the Riverland every year. Now, with Normans at the helm, a wide range of commercial wines continues to be produced in casks and bottles, but these have been joined by several more upmarket ranges using fruit from the Riverland and beyond. These include the Normans Lone Gum Vineyard range of chardonnay (unwooded and wooded), plus cabernet/merlot, cabernet sauvignon and shiraz/cabernet.

This tasting room offers a geometric display of resting bottles.

Plump grapes destined for the crusher.

RENMANO WINERY

Established 1914 *Owners* BRL Hardy Wine Ltd *Production* 1.5 million cases *Vineyard area* 348 acres (141 ha)

This is yet another arm of the BRL Hardy empire that so dominates the Riverland region. The winery was built in 1914 and became Australia's first cooperative two years later, when it was bought by a group of 130 local grape growers. It remained as a cooperative until the merger with Berri Estates in 1982. The wines produced are limited to the Chairman's Selection Reserve Chardonnay, the River Breeze range and a large selection of casks. The cellar door sells the entire BRL Hardy range.

VICTORIA

Grampians and Pyrenees

Alex Mitchell

The discovery of gold in the craggy granite outcrops of western Victoria in the 1850s attracted thousands of immigrants who brought with them the trappings of "civilization"—including the vine. The cool climate led to the area becoming well known for its sparkling wines, especially from such producers as Seppelt in the Grampians.

The 1960s Remy Australie development in the Pyrenees saw large-scale plantings of trebbiano for the production of brandy, a market that was to dwindle and be replaced with table wines. The 1970s brought enthusiastic newcomers, and vineyard areas that had been devastated by phylloxera at the turn of the century are again bearing fruit. Cool-climate red wines are emerging as the stars.

The landscape varies from flat, golden pasture (reflecting another major product of the area—wool) to rugged granite escarpment. The winters are cold and wet, the summers cool and dry. Annual average rainfall is around 21.5 inches (550 mm) and vines struggle without supplementary irrigation. Soils are mostly underlain by heavy clay which restricts root development and water storage and can also precipitate temporary waterlogging. Spring frosts are not uncommon and vineyards are purposefully sited on slopes to avoid them.

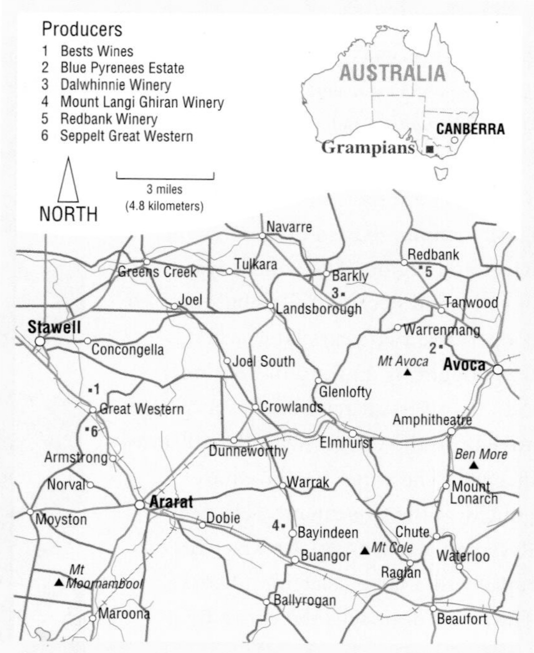

Premium shiraz from such producers as Mount Langi Ghiran, Dalwhinnie and Seppelt Great Western has earned both domestic and international praise. Flavors vary from region to region but are always of juicy berry fruits. Fans of the peppery, spicy spectrum of shiraz may be surprised by the dominance of chewy fruit flavors like black cherries, plum jam and raspberries.

Most winemakers employ the subtlety of French oak to complement the fragrant, earthy fruit. The tannins are elegant but sound. Cabernet sauvignon, demonstrating its chameleon-like nature in this difficult climate, is frequently minty and tinged with eucalyptus. It is generally riddled with purple fruit flavors and at times austere and closed.

Sauvignon blanc from the Pyrenees is distinctive. The wines are increasingly flavorsome and complex as vignerons learn to manage the fruit and winemakers enjoy the minimal handling it requires. A flinty dryness enriched by soft tropical fruit flavors suggests that this area may become a source of great varietal interest.

Ballarat frequently suffers the coldest temperatures in the state, but the winemakers of the region are turning this to their advantage to produce pinot noirs of superb complexity. More recent plantings of sangiovese, pinot grigio and viognier are adding interest and suggest that the area is yet to show its breadth. The remote far southwest of Victoria, where the climate is maritime, is sparsely planted so far, and the Seppelt vineyards at Drumborg are the most significant vineyard development.

Producers
1 Bests Wines
2 Blue Pyrenees Estate
3 Dalwhinnie Winery
4 Mount Langi Ghiran Winery
5 Redbank Winery
6 Seppelt Great Western

BESTS WINES, GRAMPIANS

Established 1866 *Owners* the Thomson family
Production 10,000 cases *Vineyard area* 62 acres (25 ha)

This historic vineyard in the Great Western subregion contains some of the world's oldest shiraz vines, and winemakers Viv Thomson and Michael Unwin make a superbly concentrated wine, The Thomson Family Shiraz, from those grapes. The fourth generation of the family to preside over the vineyard combines their care-taker role with canny business growth.

BLUE PYRENEES ESTATE, PYRENEES

Established 1963 *Owners* Remy Australie
Production 100,000 cases *Vineyard area* 555 acres (225 ha)

Established by Remy Australie as a source of white wine for brandy, this estate has moved with the market to become a distinguished producer of sparkling and still red table wine. Winemakers Kim Hart and Greg Dedman focus upon produc-ing wines with flavors representative of the region, and their red blend combines cool-climate caber-net mintiness with warmer berry flavors of shiraz, merlot and cabernet franc.

DALWHINNIE WINERY, PYRENEES

Established 1976 *Owners* David and Jenny Jones
Production 4,500 cases *Vineyard area* 44 acres (18 ha)

Winemaker David Jones produces outstanding cabernet sauvignon, chardonnay and shiraz that show regional definition and intensity of fruit flavor, reflecting low-yield viticultur-al practice. The Eagle Series Shiraz is released in only exceptional years.

MOUNT LANGI GHIRAN WINERY, GRAMPIANS

Established 1970 *Owners* Trevor Mast and Riquet Hess *Production* 25,000 cases *Vineyard area* 173 acres (70 ha)

This is a breathtakingly beautiful vineyard stretching into the base of the eponymous mountain. Wine-maker Trevor Mast's premium shiraz is one of Australia's finest cool-climate reds, and it can be difficult to obtain. The cabernet merlot, riesling and chardonnay are regional benchmarks. Recent releases of pinot grigio and san-giovese show a keen eye for devel-opment of the area's potential for these varieties.

REDBANK WINERY, PYRENEES

Established 1973
Owners Neill and Sally Robb
Production 62,000 cases
Vineyard area 54 acres (22 ha)

Sally's Paddock Red Blend has become a collectible in Australia. Winemaker Neill Robb's rich and deeply flavored flagship wine recog-nizes that regional cabernet sometimes shows best when blended with other varieties, in this case shiraz and malbec.

A scarecrow guards a vineyard in the Pyrenees.

SEPPELT GREAT WESTERN, GRAMPIANS

Established 1865 *Owners* Southcorp Wines Pty Ltd
Production 2 million cases *Vineyard area* 790 acres (320 ha)

This is the old man of the region and the big company investment pioneer. During the late 1860s, vigneron Joseph Best contracted unem-ployed gold-miners to dig nearly 2 miles (3 km) of tunnels into the soft granite for the purpose of storing and maturing wine in the variable Australian climate. The heritage-listed "drives" hold more than 8,000 gallons (30,000 l) of maturing sparkling wines. The large Seppelt production plant processes fruit from many regions, but estate-grown fruit stars in both the still and sparkling shiraz.

The Dalwhinnie vineyard in the Pyrenees.

Rutherglen & North East Victoria

Alex Mitchell

The history of North East Victorian viticulture is littered with names that to this day evoke the region—Brown, Morris, Sutherland Smith, Campbell. As with much of Victoria, the 1850s gold rush brought a market for wine to the North East and the prosperity to allow the construction of a railway between Rutherglen and Melbourne, which was so vital to export success. The first records of vines in the area are from 1851 and, as the gold veins were exhausted, miners and entrepreneurs turned to the vine and its bountiful response to the northern sunshine. By 1870 Rutherglen was the largest vineyard area in the colony.

North East Victoria also benefited from the change in public tastes in the late 1890s to stronger red and fortified wines. The government, recognizing the apparent economic viability of Rutherglen, responded to the spreading scourge of phylloxera by forcing vineyard eradication in other Victorian areas in a futile attempt to save the North East. The 1970s return to favor of big, lush table wines has seen North East Victoria shine again with its generously flavored reds and whites. However, consumer interest in its opulent fortifieds appears to be waning.

Rutherglen and Glenrowan are the epitome of a hot, continental climate, with blisteringly hot days and chilly nights. Spring frosts can be a problem and rainfall is low at 23 inches (590 mm) per annum. The Ovens Valley, overlooked by Mount Buffalo, has the high rainfall and cooler temperatures of an elevated region. The beautiful King Valley reflects its mountainous landscape, varying from sparse to abundant rainfall and from sterile to exceptionally fertile soils.

Brown Brothers plantings at Milawa in the King Valley serve as a mini-nursery for Italian grape varieties in Victoria. When Italian immigrants populated the region after the Second World War to grow tobacco, they also grew, made and consumed table wine. The Brown family was able to sell table wine to them at a time when Australians had turned away from it, and they repaid the favor by encouraging local growers to develop their vineyards and contracting their grapes. Hence, nebbiolo, dolcetto, aleatico, moscato, barbera and the Spanish variety graciano are still among the Brown Brothers range.

Rutherglen has also specialized in durif and shiraz to make its superb vintage ports, and transforms the brown muscat grape into rich, dark barrel-aged liqueur muscats that are unique to North East Victoria. The local version of "tokay," also a liqueur, is a product of the muscadelle grape; nowhere else in the world is it put to this use.

Viticultural techniques vary throughout North East Victoria in response to microclimates. In the alpine regions of the King and Ovens Valleys, frost protection in both spring and autumn is of great concern. On the hot, flat plains of Rutherglen, vine canopies are generous to prevent overripening and burning of fruit.

ALL SAINTS ESTATE, RUTHERGLEN

Established 1864 *Owner* Peter Brown
Production 22,000 cases *Vineyard area* 143 acres (58 ha)

All Saints Estate won Australia's first international wine medal at the Vienna Exhibition in 1873 and

Large barrels and an old iron water cart at Baileys of Glenrowan.

has continued to produce high-quality table wines and fortifieds since then. Their Reserve Label Muscat and Tokay are some of the region's finest.

BAILEYS OF GLENROWAN, GLENROWAN

Established 1870 *Owners* Mildara Blass Ltd *Production* 28,000 cases *Vineyard area* 124 acres (50 ha)

The wines from this producer remain high-quality beacons despite its acquisition in 1996 by the Fosters Brewing Group's wine arm. Standouts in the range include the 1920s Block Shiraz and the Founders Muscat and Tokay.

BROWN BROTHERS MILAWA VINEYARD, KING VALLEY

Established 1889 *Owners* the Brown family *Production* 900,000 cases *Vineyard area* 717 acres (290 ha)

One of Australia's most successful family operations, Brown Brothers sources fruit from many of the surrounding regions, always acknowledging special vineyards on the labels. Consistency of quality and a kaleidoscope of varietals and styles have made them firm favorites with wine lovers.

R. L. BULLER AND SON, RUTHERGLEN

Established 1921 *Owners* R. L. Buller and Son Pty Ltd *Production* 5,000 cases *Vineyard area* 67 acres (27 ha)

The Calliope vineyards, named for a naval ship on which the founding Buller served, remain unirrigated and so produce small parcels of intensely flavored fruit, particularly shiraz. Museum releases of liqueur muscat and tokay have been outstanding.

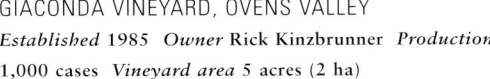

CAMPBELLS WINES, RUTHERGLEN

Established 1870 *Owners* Colin and Malcolm Campbell *Production* 40,000 cases *Vineyard area* 173 acres (70 ha)

The current owners are the fourth generation of the Campbell family to operate the winery and maintain a nostalgic link to Scotland with their Bobbie Burns label. Their Barkly Durif is an extraordinarily beefy wine made from a variety almost unique to this region.

CHAMBERS ROSEWOOD WINERY, RUTHERGLEN

Established 1858 *Owner* William B. Chambers *Production* 10,000 cases *Vineyard area* 118 acres (48 ha)

Winemaker Bill Chambers, a chairman of judges in Melbourne, is a fiercely opinionated exponent of his region. His luscious Rare Tokay and Rare Muscat, only released in small quantities, are among the world's top sweet fortifieds.

GIACONDA VINEYARD, OVENS VALLEY

Established 1985 *Owner* Rick Kinzbrunner *Production* 1,000 cases *Vineyard area* 5 acres (2 ha)

A relatively new development in the region, this winery is producing outstanding wines that are rationed out to a mailing list and restaurants. One of Australia's most opulently flavored, although elegantly structured, chardonnays is complemented by a surprisingly burgundian pinot noir.

MORRIS WINES, RUTHERGLEN

Established 1859 *Owners* Orlando Wyndham Group *Production* 60,000 cases *Vineyard area* 250 acres (100 ha)

Veteran winemaker David Morris is an ebullient character who produces fortifieds that are benchmarks of the region. His table wines, especially the rich, full-bodied durif, boast a loyal following.

PFIEFFER WINES, RUTHERGLEN

Established 1880 *Owners* Christopher and Robyn Pfieffer *Production* 10,000 cases *Vineyard area* 64 acres (26 ha)

This historic 1880 winery was taken over and revamped by the Pfieffers in 1984. Chris Pfieffer is one of the main forces behind the 1998 introduction of a four-tiered classification system for quality muscat and tokay. His Old Distillery Tawny Port is made from 26 Portuguese grape varieties using solera-style blending.

Above: *All saints Winery at Wahgunyah.*

Top: *Entry to the Rutherglen region.*

Yarra Valley

Kate McIntyre

In 1838 William Ryrie established Victoria's first commercial vineyard at the Yering cattle station in the Yarra Valley. By 1850 Ryrie had sold his property to an aristocratic young Swiss settler, Paul de Castella, who thought little of the wine-producing potential of the area until his guests had finished his last bottle of Pommard one drunken night. In desperation, he dragged a bottle of Ryrie's previously untouched "home brew" from the cellar. It was immediately judged as "better than Pommard" and de Castella's interest in wine making in the Yarra Valley was piqued.

Along with Yering Station, St Hubert's and Yeringberg were also established at this time. The Yarra Valley went on to enjoy international success in the late 1800s winning gold medals at European wine shows. In 1889 Yeringberg was awarded a Grand Prix at the Paris Exhibition—one of only 14 given and the only one in the southern hemisphere.

However, a combination of economic depression, the threat of phylloxera and the temperance movement brought an end to the valley's wine history. The cows moved in and wine production was all but forgotten.

Reg Egan was the first to replant vines in the area in 1963 at Wantirna Estate, but it was two doctors, John Middleton (Mount Mary) and Peter McMahon (Seville Estate), who led the push in the early 1960s to re-establish the Yarra Valley as a premium wine-producing area. Others soon followed and, in the 1970s, the valley became a wine region again.

Today the Yarra Valley is one of Australia's most successful and diverse wine-producing regions. Its undulating hills contain small boutique wineries and larger more commercial enterprises. Close to Melbourne, it has become an attractive tourist destination with a well-developed bed and breakfast trade and numerous restaurants. The Yarra Valley Vignerons Association ensure the success of festivals such as Grape Grazing (in early March).

The combination of good soil—light-gray topsoil on heavy clay on the valley floor and red soil on the southern slopes—and a cool temperate climate makes the Yarra ideal for growing grapes and making premium wine. The warmest vineyards can ripen shiraz and cabernet sauvignon admirably, while the cooler sites produce leaner wines and are better for pinot noir and chardonnay. Along with merlot, these are the predominant grape varieties grown in the valley. Sauvignon blanc, pinot gris, marsanne and roussanne have been planted recently, but have not generally taken off yet.

As in Burgundy and the Rhône, the best vineyard sites are midway up a slope facing the sun. Although the Yarra Valley suffers more frosts and temperature fluctuations than the Geelong and Mornington regions, it is generally warmer, so more successful with cabernet sauvignon and merlot.

Winemaking and viticultural techniques are varied. Some fruit is harvested by hand and some by machine, which determines the style of trellising used. Variations of cane and spur pruning seem to be the most popular.

Some of Australia's first sparkling wine was produced from base wine from the Yarra Valley in the 1880s by Frenchman Auguste d'Argent. A *Crème de Boosie* won a gold medal in Amsterdam in 1883. With this background, it's no surprise that the Yarra Valley is one of Australia's premium sites for sparkling wines and was selected by Champagne houses Moët and Chandon and Devaux as the site for their Australian sparkling wine ventures—Domaine Chandon and Yarrabank.

Producers
1 Coldstream Hills
2 De Bortoli Wines
3 Diamond Valley Vineyards
4 Domaine Chandon
5 Gembrook Hill Vineyard
6 Metier
7 Mount Mary Vineyard
8 Oakridge Estate
9 Seville Estate
10 TarraWarra Estate
11 Yering Station Vineyard
12 Yeringberg

DE BORTOLI WINES

Established 1987 *Owners* the De Bortoli family *Production* 150,000 cases *Vineyard area* more than 320 acres (130 ha)

De Bortoli, one of the biggest players in the Valley, does not sacrifice quality for quantity and produces excellent wines across its range. Its professionally run cellar door facility carries five labels of varying style and price and houses a great restaurant. The winemaking team—Steven Webber, David Bicknell and David Slingsby-Smith—are formidable in their expertise and their wines are well made. The top of the range shows a lot of new oak, which falls into balance with age, and the cheaper Windy Peak range relies exclusively on fruit. Their Reserve Shiraz won the 1997 Jimmy Watson award.

COLDSTREAM HILLS

Established 1985 *Owners* Southcorp Wines Pty Ltd *Production* 50,000 cases *Vineyard area* 114 acres (46 ha)

Founded by James Halliday, one of Australia's wine industry greats, Coldstream Hills is one of the Yarra's best-known wineries. Halliday established the winery and vineyard to specialize in limited-production, premium-quality pinot noir, chardonnay and cabernet sauvignon/merlot. In 1996, Southcorp acquired the vineyard and the brand, while retaining Halliday as head winemaker. Coldstream Hills has recently included a merlot, a sauvignon blanc and a pinot gris in its portfolio, but it is the old stalwarts—chardonnay and pinot noir—that continue to excel. Current winemaker Paul Lapsley is ensuring the quality of the wines remains high.

DIAMOND VALLEY VINEYARDS

Established 1976 *Owners* David and Catherine Lance *Production* 6,000 cases *Vineyard area* 8.6 acres (3.5 ha)

David Lance is producing some of Australia's best pinot noir. Unfortunately for long time supporters, the word has got out and it is increasingly hard to get. The Close Planted Pinot Noir is the best, but the Diamond Valley Estate Pinot Noir comes a close second. Bright garnet in color, with sappy, red berry fruit, the wine shows delicate yet intense purity of fruit that is instantly alluring and improves with four to six years aging. Diamond Valley wines are available by mail order.

DOMAINE CHANDON

Established 1987 *Owners* Moet et Chandon *Production* 120,000 cases *Vineyard area* 225 acres (90 ha)

Moet et Chandon purchased the Green Point vineyard in the Yarra Valley in 1987 and planted

125 acres (50 ha) with the traditional champagne varieties—pinot noir, chardonnay and pinot meunier. In 1994 they established another 100 acres (40 ha) in the Strathbogie Ranges. Chandon has always asserted they are not attempting to make a clone of champagne in the Yarra Valley, but to produce the best Australian sparkling wines using traditional methods. Reserves of older wines are being built up and the wines are becoming world class. The elegant 1993 Millenium Reserve, a very limited wine released for the year 2000 festivities, bears testimony to this.

Domaine Chandon's production and visitor facilities are a striking juxtaposition of old and new. The restored historical homestead is used for private functions and administration while the awe-inspiring Riddling Hall and Green Point Reception are used as the cellar door facilities.

GEMBROOK HILL VINEYARD

Established 1983 *Owners* Ian and June Marks *Production* 3,000 cases *Vineyard area* 15 acres (6 ha)

Gembrook Hill doesn't have the high profile of so many producers in the area, but passionate weekend vigneron Ian Marks keeps a meticulous vineyard and its fruit makes lovely wine. He produces a fresh fruity sauvignon blanc, a complex toasty chardonnay, and a deceptively light-appearing pinot noir that has sweet fruit, complexity, length and elegance. All three are great food wines and improve with four to five years bottle aging. A new winery was established in 2000 with Ian the winemaker and Martin Williams as consultant.

The cellar door facilities at Domain Chandon Winery have spectacular views of manicured vineyards and gardens with the rest of the Yarra Valley in the distance.

Above: *The harvest.*

Top: *Vines heavy with fruit at the Harcourt Valley Vineyard.*

METIER

Established 1996　*Owner* Martin Williams
Production 600 cases　*Vineyard area* 20 acres (8 ha)

Martin Williams, Victoria's first Master of Wine, spends most of his time as a consultant winemaker for many Valley producers. But at Metier, where he can do whatever he likes, he produces a chardonnay and a pinot noir with complex flavors and aromas that would excite any burgundy lover. The wines rely more on secondary flavors and aromas and elegant structure than on primary fruit to keep the taster interested. Produced in tiny quantities, these wines are definitely worth seeking out.

MOUNT MARY VINEYARD

Established 1971　*Owners* John and Marli Middleton
Production 3,500 cases　*Vineyard area* 37 acres (15 ha)

Dr John Middleton, a founder of the modern Yarra Valley wine industry, holds firm views on just about everything. This conviction has helped establish his wines as some of the greatest in Australia. His intense Cabernets Quintet (cabernet sauvignon/cabernet franc/merlot/malbec/petit verdot) always lives up to its reputation, as does his long-living Pinot Noir. The wines are available by mail order, at exclusive restaurants or sometimes at auctions.

OAKRIDGE ESTATE

Established 1978　*Owners* Oakridge Vineyards Ltd
Production 30,000 cases　*Vineyard area* 25 acres (10 ha)

Michael Zitslaff and his team at Oakridge specialize in top-quality cabernet sauvignon, the Reserve Cabernet Sauvignon being one of the best from the area. Despite its hefty A$99 price tag (US$60), the impressive Reserve Merlot usually sells out. Jim and Irene Zitslaff started out with a small vineyard and one cabernet-based wine. Son Michael returned to the family property in 1990 with plans to expand and the company went public in 1997 to finance a new winery and vineyard. The quality of the wine has been maintained and, as the company has grown, so has its reputation.

SEVILLE ESTATE

Established 1972　*Owners* Brokenwood Wines Pty Ltd and Peter McMahon　*Production* 2,500 cases　*Vineyard area* 20 acres (8 ha)

Dr Peter McMahon shared a medical practice with John Middleton (Mount Mary) in the 1950s and also shared Middleton's aspirations to create great wine. The vineyard was planted in 1972 and McMahon retired in 1982 to be a full-time winemaker. In 1997 the McMahons sold a controlling share of the estate to Brokenwood Wines, but continue to be involved in a consulting role. With input from Iain Riggs of Brokenwood, long-time winemaker Alistair Butt maintains the wines' traditional high quality. The Seville Estate Shiraz is everything you could want from a shiraz—rich, with spicy black pepper and ripe savory fruit, wonderful depth, length and complexity.

TARRAWARRA ESTATE

Established 1983　*Owner* Marc Besen　*Production* 6,000 cases　*Vineyard area* 72 acres (29 ha)

TarraWarra, under the expert supervision of winemaker Clare Halloran, is regarded as one of the top producers of pinot noir in the Yarra Valley and in Australia. The Tarrawarra Pinot Noir is powerful yet complex, with excellent structure supporting intense red and black berry fruit and brambly characters. The wines are made to last and are at their best with a little age.

YERING STATION VINEYARD

Established 1838, re-established 1987　*Owners* the Rathbone family　*Production* 15,000 cases　*Vineyard area* 290 acres (117 ha)

The historical site of Victoria's first winery, Yering Station is not resting on its laurels. Winemaker Tom Carson produces a range of wines, some of which, the Yering Station Reserve Pinot Noir in particular, are superb. The pinot and chardonnay in the relatively new Reserve range are complex and lovely. Yering Station's new winery and restaurant facility rivals the grandeur of Domaine Chandon, a rivalry also manifested in Yering Station's joint venture with Devaux Champagne to produce the elegantly delicious Yarrabank Cuvee.

YERINGBERG

Established 1863　*Owner* Guill de Pury　*Production* 550 cases　*Vineyard area* 32 acres (13 ha)

Guill de Pury is a direct descendant of the Guillaume de Pury who first established Yeringberg in 1863. The original winery building lay untouched from 1921 until 1969, when de Pury replanted a few acres of vines and made a bit of wine in the old cellar. The wines are in short supply and have been little known until recently. The Yeringberg White reflects the wines of old, with the richness and depth of flavor that come from marsanne and roussanne. The chardonnay is rich and cheesy and ages gracefully. The savory pinot noir has red cherry and dusty musty forest-floor characters and elegant structure.

Mornington Peninsula

Kate McIntyre

Compared with the Yarra Valley and Geelong, the Mornington Peninsula has a fairly patchy history as a wine region. By the mid-nineteenth century, the Yarra and Geelong had well-established vineyards producing good-quality wines, but the Peninsula had only a handful of amateur vineyards. The depression of the 1890s and the average quality of the wine, not phylloxera, which has never come to the Peninsula, spelled the end of these few early enterprises.

The wine industry really got started on the Mornington Peninsula when Ballieu Myer planted his first vineyard in 1974 at Elgee Park. A couple of others followed his lead—including the Whites at Main Ridge in 1975, the Keffords at Merricks Estate in 1977 and the Stoniers in 1978. The second wave took place in the early 1980s: Dromana Estate, Moorooduc Estate (the author's family's estate), Kings Creek, Karina Vineyard, and Tanglewood Downs, which put in small plantings of around 5 acres (2 ha), considered to be huge at the time.

Still very much a boutique winery region, the Mornington Peninsula, now boasts more than 100 vineyards, all less than two hours drive from Melbourne. The region thrives on the tourism

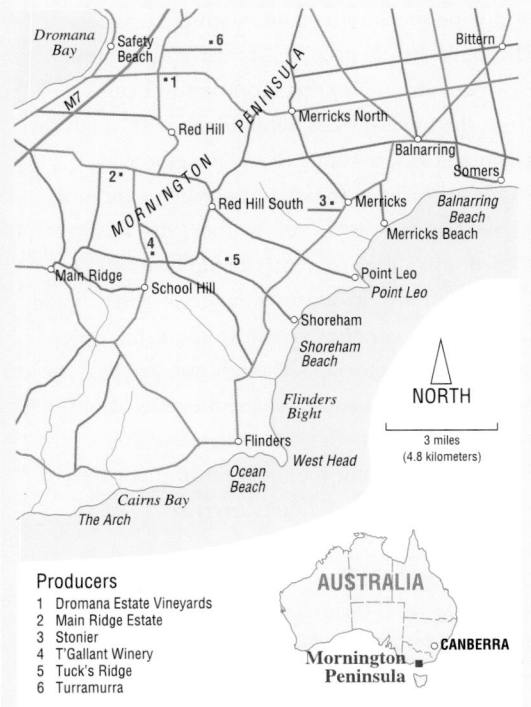

Producers
1 Dromana Estate Vineyards
2 Main Ridge Estate
3 Stonier
4 T'Gallant Winery
5 Tuck's Ridge
6 Turramurra

Merricks vineyard with garden to the fore and bush in the background.

industry. Winery visits are an attractive adjunct to the beautiful beaches and picturesque landscapes that have earned the Peninsula the title of Melbourne's holiday playground. It continues to evolve as a serious wine region, with many producers crafting elegant and complex wines. Quality improves with every vintage as vines become more and more established. The promise of true greatness for the region beckons.

The Peninsula has a hilly landscape where aspect and orientation are all-important. The often marginal climate is cool to cold, with a maritime influence that helps prevent frost and mitigates temperature fluctuation. Soil type varies from sandy loam on clay to red volcanic soil. A small region itself, the Peninsula can be broken into at least five not yet classified subregions: Moorooduc Downs, Red Hill, Dromana, Merricks and Main Ridge. The subregions show very diverse soil types and microclimates, and the wines reflect these differences.

A young region that is still developing its style, the Mornington Peninsula specializes in medium-bodied dry table wines and is beginning to have some success with sparkling wines. The predominant and most successful grape varieties are

Main Ridge Winery produces elegant complex wines from a marginal site.

chardonnay and pinot noir. The Mornington Peninsula promises great things from pinot noir, the best already showing good complexity and structure, ranging in style from elegant and ethereal to huge, rich and impressive.

Chardonnay ranges from crisp, fruit-driven unoaked wines with a fruit spectrum ranging from citrus and melon through to tropical pineapple aromas and flavors, to complex wines exhibiting varying degrees of traditional burgundian wine-making techniques. These include battonage, fermentation in French oak barrels, extended maturation on lees, malolactic fermentation and, in some cases, use of indigenous yeasts.

Cabernet sauvignon was planted originally due to incorrect weather data suggesting the Peninsula was a much warmer region than it is. It came to light that the data had been collected from a courtyard in Frankston—a city more than 6 miles (10 km) north of the northernmost vineyard area. This courtyard was walled-in, sheltered from the brisk winds that are such a feature of the Peninsula's climate and paved in concrete that sucks up a lot more heat than grass and vines. Cabernet is difficult to ripen, even on the warmer sites, and often shows vegetal, capsicum aromas. The occasional fully ripened cabernet is elegant, with cassis and cigar-box aromas, suggestive of the bordeaux style. These wines enjoy more popularity overseas than in Australia because of their restrained style. Shiraz and sauvignon blanc are enjoying recent success in the warmer sites and pinot gris, which does very well in the climate, is being touted as the "next big thing."

Viticultural and winemaking practices vary on the Peninsula. Canopies are generally trained to 5 to 6.5 feet (1.5 m to 2 m) in height, and the Scott Henry trellising system is very popular as it opens the canopy to the sun—an important feature in this cool-to-cold climate. Tuck's Ridge is experimenting with "big vine viticulture" with encouraging results (see vineyard entry). Wine-making is generally very controlled, but the influence of Burgundy can be seen here in barrel ferment, lees stirring and malolactic fermentation, as winemakers experiment with their chardonnay and pinot noir.

The Mornington Peninsula does best with the burgundian varieties—pinot noir and chardonnay—due to the marginal maritime climate. "Wild yeast" ferments and unfiltered wines (what the burgundians have done for centuries) are now all the rage for special reserve releases, with fabulous results. This loosening of the winemaker's control over the fermentation can be nerve-wracking at first, but generally has some exciting results in terms of complexity and added texture in the wines.

DROMANA ESTATE VINEYARDS

Established 1982 *Owners* Gary and Margaret Crittenden *Production* 10,300 cases *Vineyard area* 12 acres (4.9 ha)

A former proprietor of wholesale nurseries, Gary Crittenden chose a promising looking bit of land in Dromana and turned his natural green thumb and impressive business acumen to the viticulture and wine-production game with great success. Dromana Estate now boasts the largest range of wines on sale on the Mornington Peninsula— from the lower-priced Schinus range through the Dromana Estate range to the Reserve wines. Made exclusively from estate-grown fruit and fermented by natural yeasts, the 1997 Reserve Chardonnay is particularly complex and rich. Crittenden also produces a range of wines made from Italian varieties grown in the King Valley, in northern Victoria. Although not strictly Mornington Peninsula wines, they are of out-standing quality—the "i" Sangiovese and Nebbiolo represent the most faithful Australian renditions of these Italian varieties.

MAIN RIDGE ESTATE

Established 1975 *Owners* Nat and Rosalie White *Production* 1,100 cases *Vineyard area* 6 acres (2.4 ha)

Pioneers of fine wine production on the Mornington Peninsula, Nat and Rosalie White's vineyard is possibly the most marginal of sites in the region—the now-extinct gewürztraminer was superb, but only produced a crop every second year. Nat, with skilled viticulture and sensitive winemaking, thumbs his nose at the difficult conditions by producing wines of elegance and complexity in all but the most difficult years. The Half Acre Pinot is the finest and most complex of all—never a blockbuster, but at its best, something more subtle, mysterious and alluring.

STONIER

Established 1978 *Owners* Petaluma Ltd
Production 22,000 cases *Vineyard area* 150 acres (61 ha)

Brian and Noel Stonier bought the property in 1977 and cannot remember what possessed them to plant vines. It must have been providence, as the winery has continued from strength to strength over the years, culminating in being the first Mornington Peninsula vineyard to receive outside investment from "one of the big boys." Petaluma bought the controlling share in Stonier's, and the name changed to Stonier in 1998. Tod Dexter has been making the wine here since 1987 and has developed the fruit-driven, easy-drinking pinot noir and chardonnay styles in the Stonier range. The richly complex Reserve Chardonnay and Pinot Noir also illustrate Dexter's desire to maintain maximum fruit integrity with the added complexity of extended oak treatment.

T'GALLANT WINERY

Established 1990 *Owners* Kevin McCarthy and Kathleen Quealy *Production* 10,000 cases *Vineyard area* 25 acres (10 ha)

Kevin McCarthy and Kathleen Quealy are movers and shakers of the Mornington Peninsula—most renowned for their outspoken support of pinot grigio/gris and unoaked chardonnay. A young innovative couple of professional winemakers who are never short of an opinion on where the Peninsula should be headed, McCarthy and Quealy produce fresh, fruit-driven unoaked chardonnay and two versions of pinot gris—the Tribute Pinot Gris in homage to the alsace wines made from this variety and a pinot grigio in a crisper, more flinty Italian style. Their Lyncroft Pinot gets better each year, with rich, soft dark berry fruit and velvety tannins. The distinctive labels were designed by fashionable Melbourne graphic designer Ken Cato. The image and style of wines are young, attractive and original—a breath of fresh air, but certainly not lightweight.

TUCK'S RIDGE AT RED HILL

Established 1986 *Owner* Peter Hollick
Production 12,000 cases *Vineyard area* 280 acres (113 ha)

Roseworthy graduate and Tuck's Ridge winemaker Daniel Greene aspires to making Australia's best pinot noir, and the jump in quality from the 1996 to the 1997 vintage is testimony to the coming of age of this vineyard and winemaker. But credit also must go to vineyard manager Shane Strange who has radical theories about how to get the best from pinot noir vines. His "big vine" theory allows the vines' natural vigor to prevail in the belief that a larger vine will ripen larger crops more efficiently. So far, it has proved very effective, producing pinot noir of wonderful complexity and character.

TURRAMURRA

Established 1989 *Owners* David and Paula Leslie
Production 7,000 cases *Vineyard area* 25 acres (10 ha)

Although a relative newcomer, David Leslie has established a very good reputation for his wines. Since completing the wine science degree at Charles Sturt University and retiring from medicine in 1995, he has been producing pinot noir, chardonnay and sauvignon blanc that fully deserve the accolades they are receiving. The 1997 Pinot Noir won the trophy for best Mornington Peninsula Red Wine from the Australian Sommeliers Association in 1998. It shows ripe dark berry fruit and brambly aromas, hints of truffle and a firm intense structure on the palate.

Picked grapes below a vine at Moorooduc Estate.

Dromana Estate has the largest range of wines on the Mornington Peninsula.

Other Victorian Regions

Alex Mitchell

GIPPSLAND

Gippsland, spreading over a large area of Victoria's southeastern corner, is the state's most recent area of viticultural rebirth, with current plantings beginning in the 1970s. Like many of its counterparts, it had a significant table wine industry in the late nineteenth century that suffered decline for a multitude of economic and agricultural reasons. More recently, isolation and the scattered nature of the wineries has kept it from achieving wider recognition.

Cool-climate viticulture is aided by good rainfall, and cool-climate classics chardonnay and pinot noir dominate production. Spiciness and complexity characterize the fruit flavors. However, rainfall, soils, temperature and terrain vary considerably, reflecting the size of the zone and proximity to the coast. Likewise, styles vary with *terroir*, but production of sparkling wine is negligible.

BASS PHILLIP WINES

Established 1979 *Owners* Phillip and Sairung Jones
Production 1,400 cases *Vineyard area* 44 acres (18 ha)

Some declare Bass Phillip Pinot Noir to be without equal in Australia. It is certainly a labor of love for winemaker Phillip Jones, whose closely planted vines require traditional hand-pruning and harvesting. His chardonnay is also made with distinction.

LYRE BIRD HILL WINES

Established 1987 *Owners* Robyn and Owen Schmidt
Production 1,000 cases *Vineyard area* 6 acres (2.4 ha)

Lyre Bird Hill is close to the coast and the resulting wines are spicy and subtly layered. Winemaker Owen Schmidt's spicy Shiraz and Pinot Noir are of particular note.

NICHOLSON RIVER WINERY

Established 1978 *Owners* Ken and Juliet Eckersley
Production 1,800 cases *Vineyard area* 15 acres (6 ha)

This regional pioneer produces one of Australia's richest and most opulent chardonnays, which is available only at the cellar door. Winemaker Ken Eckersley makes minimal use of preservatives, and fastidious grape handling is central to the winemaking approach and the resultant quality.

PHILLIP ISLAND VINEYARD & WINERY

Established 1994 *Owners* David and Catherine Lance *Production* 3,000 cases *Vineyard area* 5 acres (2 ha)

With first vintage in 1997, this pioneering vineyard is yet to realize its potential. The Lance family has a distinguished cool-climate winemaking history at their Diamond Valley Vineyards in the Yarra Valley. The winery's first releases, chardonnay, sauvignon blanc, merlot and cabernet from the 1997 vintage, were well received.

Nicholson River Winery uses minimal preservatives in its opulent chardonnays.

Nicholson River Winery

MACEDON

Traditionally a cool summer haven for the well-heeled of early twentieth-century Melbourne, this region is dominated by the 3,300 feet (1,000 m) high Mount Macedon. It owes its 1850s wine-producing beginnings to the gold rush but was then devastated by phylloxera. A 1970s resurgence consisted mainly of family concerns. The elevation of the Macedon Ranges makes it one of Australia's coldest regions. Wind chill, autumn frosts and unforgiving granite soils add to the challenge and lack appeal for larger companies.

The region's forte is sparkling wine made from the traditional combination of chardonnay and pinot noir. The climate requires fastidious canopy management and faultless varietal and site selection, but the wines are crisp and intensely flavored. An acid backbone gives elegance to whites. Pinot noir can be earthy and complex. Shiraz from the region has developed a cult following, showing spice, surprising fruit weight and soft tannins.

COPE-WILLIAMS, MACEDON

Established 1977 *Owners* Romsey Vineyards Pty Ltd *Production* 5,000 cases *Vineyard area* 20 acres (8 ha)

Winemaker Michael Cope-Williams makes fine wines made from the region's best varieties. The r.o.m.s.e.y. Brut is soft, rich and toasty.

CRAIGLEE, SUNBURY

Established 1976 *Owners* Tarra Vale Pastoral Co Pty Ltd *Production* 2,200 cases *Vineyard area* 25 acres (10 ha)

Previously considered to be in Macedon, Craiglea is in the newly identified neighboring Sunbury region. Despite the vintage variations, winemaker Pat Carmody makes superb multi-layered Shiraz and Chardonnay in frustratingly small quantities.

HANGING ROCK WINERY, MACEDON

Established 1982 *Owners* John and Anne Ellis *Production* 15,000 cases *Vineyard area* 30 acres (12 ha)

The large production here reflects sourcing of fruit from other Victorian wine regions. Winemaker John Ellis' wines are of consistently good quality, the locally grown Macedon Cuvee is a standout.

KNIGHT GRANITE HILLS WINES, MACEDON

Established 1979 *Owners* Llew, Gordon and Heather Knight *Production* NA *Vineyard area* 25 acres (10 ha)

Winemaker Llew Knight's wines have a distinctive cool-climate elegance, particularly the Riesling and the Shiraz. One of the first vineyards planted here, it is now a benchmark for the region.

The Hanging Rock vineyard with view to the surrounding hills.

VIRGIN HILLS, MACEDON

Established 1968 *Owners* Vincorp Wineries Ltd *Production* 4,000 cases *Vineyard area* NA

This esoteric winery produces only one wine—an elegant shiraz/cabernet sauvignon/malbec/merlot blend with spice and soft fruit. The winemaking here is preservative-free.

GEELONG

Geelong had a thriving wine industry in the late 1800s, a ready market in Melbourne only 62 miles (100 km) away, and an influx of European settlers. But by the turn of the century a nervous government had reacted to the discovery of phylloxera in the region by eradicating the vineyards, and it was the late 1960s before vines grew again. However, there are now about 50 vineyards producing wine for the local and export markets.

As one of Australia's most southerly regions, Geelong enjoys a long ripening period extending into May, allowing grapes to develop complexity and depth of flavor. Strongly maritime influenced, the *terroir* offers scant summer rainfall, chill winds and poor clay soils. When Geelong wine is good, it is very good. Predictably, pinot noir and chardonnay are grown with distinction in the southerly climate. All the cool-climate viticultural tricks are required to protect slow-ripening fruit. Ironically, low rainfall neccessitates irrigation during vine growth.

BANNOCKBURN VINEYARDS

Established 1974 *Owners* the Hooper Family *Production* 7,000 cases *Vineyard area* 62 acres (25 ha)

Winemaker Gary Farr frequently works vintage in Burgundy when his work at Bannockburn is done.

REGIONAL BEST

Cleveland Winery Macedon
   Brut
Cleveland Winery Pinot Noir
Craiglea Shiraz
Cobaw Ridge Chardonnay
Cobaw Ridge Shiraz
Cope-Williams r.o.m.s.e.y Brut
Hanging Rock Winery
   Macedon Cuvee
Knight Granite Hills Riesling
Knight Granite Hills Shiraz
Rochford Pinot Noir
Virgin Hills Red Blend

The exceptional quality and complexity of his Pinot Noir, Chardonnay and Shiraz demonstrate his skill in realizing the potential of grapes from Geelong. These are cult wines from a producer who avoids the trappings of the marketplace.

IDYLL VINEYARD

Established 1966 *Owners* Daryl and Nini Sefton
Production 4,500 cases *Vineyard area* 37 acres (15 ha)

The Seftons are credited with the resuscitation of the Geelong wine industry in the 1960s. Their plantings are the oldest vines in the region and their pungent wines, especially the Gewürztraminer, are regarded with admiration and affection both domestically and internationally.

PRINCE ALBERT VINEYARD

Established 1975 *Owners* B. A. and S. J. Hyett
Production 500 cases *Vineyard area* 5 acres (2 ha)

Pinot noir is the sole product of this vineyard and it is carefully tended and sensitively handled in the making. The vineyard and winery are certified organic and winemaker Bruce Hyett's wine receives minimal filtering to retain its fragrant characters.

SCOTCHMANS HILL VINEYARD & WINERY

Established 1982 *Owners* David and Vivienne Brown
Production 30,000 cases *Vineyard area* 160 acres (65 ha)

This is the largest producer of the region, enjoying a strong following for its consistently good value. Scotchmans does well with pinot noir and chardonnay but the surprise is winemaker Robin Brockett's softly tropical, yet refreshing, sauvignon blanc.

Rows of vines at Scotchmans Hill Vineyard & Winery.

CENTRAL VICTORIA

The warm climate of Central Victoria's lower regions makes it highly suitable for red wines with powerful fruit flavors, particularly shiraz and cabernet. This was recognized as early as 1873, when a Bendigo wine was reportedly expelled from the Vienna Exhibition because the judges felt it was too good to justify its claim of origin.

The Bendigo region, with its undulating hills and dense eucalyptus forest, has a modest annual rainfall of 21.5 inches (550 mm) making irrigation a necessity. Established in the 1850s, wine production declined at the end of that century. Since the 1960s, it has become home to many small wineries that produce small quantities of high-quality wine.

The flat, fertile land of the Goulburn Valley was settled in the 1850s by farmers and graziers. Despite the low annual rainfall of 24 inches (600 mm), sheep and grain thrived in the warm climate. In 1860 the Tahbilk Vineyard Proprietary was formed to produce quality wine from extensive plantings, chiefly of red grapes. Phylloxera only partly destroyed the area and some of the original 1860s vines still produce fruit today. Marsanne grown in commercial quantities is exclusive to the Goulburn Valley. Chateau Tahbilk and Mitchelton produce some of Victoria's best value and most interesting white wines from it. Aged marsanne is a rare treat for the patient collector.

The Central Victorian Mountain Country is completely different climatically. At 1,000 to 6,000 feet (300 to 1800 m) above sea level, it is influenced by altitude throughout. Rainfall is double that of its counterparts in the zone. Yields are lower and frosts are a concern (most vineyards experience snow in winter). The Mountain Country specializes in cooler climate varieties—chardonnay is its forte for both still and sparkling wines. Riesling and gewürztraminer are developing a following for their crisp and fresh fruit flavors and balanced acid.

The red wines of Central Victoria often show distinctive minty, herbaceous characters. The wines tend to be strongly colored and have powerful fruit flavors. Shiraz occupies the most acreage, closely followed by cabernet sauvignon. The warmer areas produce generous yields, but strong sunshine and low rainfall require canopy management.

CHATEAU TAHBILK WINES, GOULBURN VALLEY

Established 1860 *Owners* the Purbrick Family *Production* 100,000 cases *Vineyard area* 310 acres (125 ha)

This is Victoria's oldest winery and it still occupies some of the original buildings. Some of the oldest vines in the country still produce an intensely flavored shiraz. The marsanne is a collectors' favorite, aging to honeyed richness.

DELATITE WINERY, CENTRAL VICTORIAN MOUNTAIN COUNTRY

Established 1982 *Owners* Rosalind and David Ritchie *Production* 12,000 cases *Vineyard area* 62 acres (25 ha)

Picturesque vineyards produce superb cool-climate wines. The ethereal fragrance of winemaker Rosalind Ritchie's riesling and gewürztraminer demonstrates the potential for these varieties here.

JASPER HILL VINEYARD, BENDIGO

Established 1976 *Owners* Ron and Elva Laughton *Production* 3,000 cases *Vineyard area* 57 acres (23 ha)

Two separate shiraz vineyards named after the Laughtons' daughters produce the much lauded and deliciously different Emily's Paddock and Georgia's Paddock wines. The vines are not irrigated and so produce only small quantities of grapes, which are carefully pressed and softly oaked—they are benchmark reds of the region.

MITCHELTON WINERY, GOULBURN VALLEY

Established 1969 *Owners* Petaluma Ltd *Production* 200,000 cases *Vineyard area* 350 acres (142 ha)

Mitchelton is the largest producer of the area, with a reputation for quality and distinctive regional flavor profiles. Winemaker Don Lewis produces a huge range. The Valley's specialty is white marsanne, but the riesling, shiraz and cabernet (particularly the Print Label range) are all outstanding.

PASSING CLOUDS, BENDIGO

Established 1974 *Owners* Graeme Leith and Sue Mackinnon *Production* 3,000 cases *Vineyard area* 15 acres (6 ha)

The reds of Passing Clouds have a devoted following. Graeme's Blend (shiraz and cabernet) exploits the chocolatey richness of both varieties; Ondine, a sparkling wine made from the same two varieties, shows rich cassis flavors and spice.

PAUL OSICKA WINES, BENDIGO

Established 1955 *Owner* Paul Osicka *Production* NA *Vineyard area* 30 acres (12 ha)

This vineyard helped revitalize the region's wine industry in the 1950s. It remains family owned

and run and maintains a low profile, much to the relief of aficionados of the Shiraz and Cabernet.

PLUNKETT'S WINERY, CENTRAL VICTORIA

Established 1991 *Owners* Alan Plunkett *Production* 16,000 cases *Vineyard area* 198 acres (80 ha)

The Plunkett family have grown grapes in the high country here since the 1960s. They now produce a range of tightly structured and flavored wines. The whites are clean and bracing. The reds have a fruit intensity and fine tannic backbone that cellaring should reward.

WATER WHEEL VINEYARDS, BENDIGO

Established 1972 *Owners* Cumming Murphy Nominees *Production* 20,000 cases *Vineyard area* 198 acres (80 ha)

This is the largest of the Bendigo region's producers. Winemakers Bill Trevaskis and Peter Cumming consistently produce excellent value wines. The whites are refreshing and lightly fruited; the reds are generously flavored.

WILD DUCK CREEK ESTATE, BENDIGO

Established 1980 *Owners* Diana and David Anderson *Production* 500 cases *Vineyard area* 10 acres (4 ha)

This small producer eschews commercial attention but receives it anyway. The intense concentration and huge structure of the Duck Muck make it a collectors' item. Made only in exceptional years and with alcohol levels approaching that of fortified wine, it demonstrates the varied expressions of shiraz that are possible in the Bendigo region.

A tractor brings in a load of black grapes at Chateau Tahbilk.

REGIONAL DOZEN

QUALITY WINES

Jasper Hill Emily's Paddock Shiraz
Jasper Hill Georgia's Paddock Shiraz
Mitchelton Print Label Shiraz
Passing Clouds Angel Blend Red
Passing Clouds Graeme's Blend Red
Wild Duck Creek Estate Duck Muck

BEST VALUE WINES

Chateau Tahbilk Marsanne
Delatite Dead Man's Hill Gewürztraminer
Mitchelton Blackwood Park Riesling
Paul Osicka Shiraz
Plunkett's Unwooded Chardonnay
Water Wheel Shiraz

Tasmania

Michele Round

Tasmania is a small island with a sublime landscape off the southeast corner of Australia. Add pure air to the long growing season of a cool, temperate climate and you get a perfect home for some of the world's finest culinary produce, with some elegant wine styles to match.

In the colony's early days, hard liquor held sway. Wine production began with optimistic but ill-fated plantings in the mid-nineteenth century; however it then lapsed into a century of neglect. The story of a vigneron pinning bunches of grapes to unyielding vines to impress investors is one example of several quaint follies.

Claudio Alcorso, who founded Moorilla Estate in 1958, and Andrew Pirie (of Pipers Brook Vineyard) stand tall in the rebirth of Tasmania's wine industry. Both "new islanders" with a vision (and not just in wine—Alcorso also founded a major textile company), they followed in the footsteps of another immigrant, Jean Miguet, who established the first modern vineyard at Lalla in 1956. Miguet's influence was significant on the pinot noir aspirations of the young Pirie, who was searching for a southern hemisphere equivalent of the great wine growing regions of France.

Geographic Indications denote Tasmania as one region, but this simplistic notion does not stand up to close examination. Tasmania can be divided into six subregions: the Northwest, Tamar Valley, Pipers Brook/River, East Coast, Derwent/ Coal River Valleys and Huon Valley. The Northwest's fertile red soils and 400 inches (1000 mm) of rain make it the most marginal of the subregions. The dry southeast's rocky soils and blonde plains, and its capacity to ripen cabernet sauvignon in good vintages put it at the other end of the spectrum.

Experience and a willingness to experiment have pared down the grape selections in Tasmania's varied regions. Savvy cabernet producers now limit plantings to the warmer slopes of the Tamar Valley, Coal River Valley and East Coast. Pinot noir growers have found that a combination of microclimate and careful clonal selection for their area plus immaculate winemaking is producing wines with layered bouquets

A rainbow crowns a typical Tasmanian winter vineyard scene, complete with cows and horses.

and subtle, lingering flavors. Riesling is emerging as a star variety, and it is proving its vinous versatility with excellent examples from both the warmer and drier Derwent/Coal River Valleys and the cooler, muggier Pipers Brook area.

A benchmark style of chardonnay is yet to emerge. Tasmanian winemakers, like many of their mainland counterparts, are making very peachy-fruity, buttery styles. At present, chardonnay is finding its perfect expression alongside pinot noir in Tasmania's sparkling wine industry. A list of 20 of Australia's best must include five from Tasmania: Pipers Brook Vineyard's Pirie, Hardy's Arras, Taltarni's Clover Hill, Yalumba Jansz and Stefano Lubiana Vintage Brut. For a region that produces less than 1 percent of Australia's sparkling wines, this is an impressive achievement.

FREYCINET VINEYARD

Established 1980 *Owners* Geoff and Sue Bull *Production* 8,000 cases *Vineyard area* 22 acres (9 ha)

Consistently making one of the best pinot noirs in the country, Freycinet Vineyard's national reputation is enhanced by its chardonnay, riesling, and the full-flavored sparkling Radenti. Winemaker Claudio Radenti is married to the Bull family's winemaker daughter Lindy and he has continued to ensure the success of this small vineyard. The East Coast region is naturally warm and this, coupled with the vineyard's sun-embracing amphitheater, gives the team ample opportunity to work with ripe fruit—something of a luxury in Tasmania's mostly marginal climate.

STEFANO LUBIANA

Established 1990 *Owner* Stefano Lubiana *Production* 7,000 cases *Vineyard area* 18.5 acres (7.5 ha)

Stefano Lubiana and his family came to Tasmania to make cool-climate wines, and the state is in-debted to his considerable talents. Not only does he make an increasingly interesting range of wines under the Lubiana label, Stefano has been vital to the development of the state's sparkling wine industry. Providing contract winemaking and con-sultancy services to small and large makers like Elsewhere, Lake Barrington Estate and the mighty Pipers Brook Vineyard is just part of the picture: the Stefano Lubiana NV Brut and Vintage Brut are regarded nationally as very fine wines.

MOORILLA ESTATE

Established 1958 *Owner* Moorilla Estate Unit Trust *Production* 9,000 cases *Vineyard area* 31 acres (12.5 ha)

Once the flagship of the Alcorso family, business difficulties and a family rift saw the sale of the vineyard to a consortium of business interests. A new management team, vineyard acquisitions in the Tamar Valley (incorporating the St Matthias label) and the considerable talents of wine maker Alain Rousseau combine to produce consistently high-quality wines. The riesling is always a delight, pinot noir varies from excellent to outstanding, the chardonnay has been well showered with wine show medals and merlot from the better vintages shows the potential that this grape variety has in Tasmania. Moorilla Estate is significantly commit-ted to wine tourism: tasting facilities at Claremont are immaculate, Claudio Alcorso's fabulous 1960s home on the Derwent River has been converted to an antiquities museum and sophisticated function area, and summer concerts are held on the lawns.

PIPERS BROOK VINEYARD

Established 1974 *Owner* Pipers Brook Vineyard Ltd *Production* 60,000 cases *Vineyard area* 435 acres (176 ha)

Now a publicly listed company with the authorita-tive figure of Andrew Pirie as principal, Pipers

Brook Vineyard boasts a range of wines from several labels and seven vineyards scattered throughout the subregions of Pipers Brook and the Tamar Valley. An ongoing search for great pinot noir is complemented by the refined package of pinot gris, gewürztraminer and a well-pedigreed riesling which are marketed as an Alsatian trio. Several tiers of quality are available, from the budget Wave Crest range through to the single-vineyard Summit Chardonnay, luxurious bubbly Pirie, and a super-premium pinot noir first released in mid-2000. The Ninth Island label, with its distinct market presence, now has its own cellar door, in addition to those at Pipers Brook Vineyard and Strathlynn. The company's major focus on export has been rewarded by a national export award and a market presence in Europe and North America.

STONEY VINEYARD

Established 1973 *Owners* Peter and Ruth Althaus *Production* 5,000 cases *Vineyard area* 25 acres (10 ha)

Former Swiss IBM executive Peter Althaus and his wife Ruth came to Tasmania as a result of his experiences at a southern hemisphere Cool Climate Winemakers Conference. His expressed love for the wines of Bordeaux led him to one of Tas-mania's better sites for growing cabernet sauvig-non—the almost continental climate of the dry Coal River Valley. Their premium Domaine A Cabernet Sauvignon and Pinot Noir are mostly sold interstate and overseas and command an influential list of devotees. The more immediate-drinking Stoney Vineyard label includes Aurora, a white wine made from classic red varieties.

Above: *A lush planting of* Convolvulus cneorum *adds to the scenic views at Stoney Vineyard.*

Top: *Vineyards of the Derwent/Coal River Valleys.*

Hunter Valley

Ken Gargett

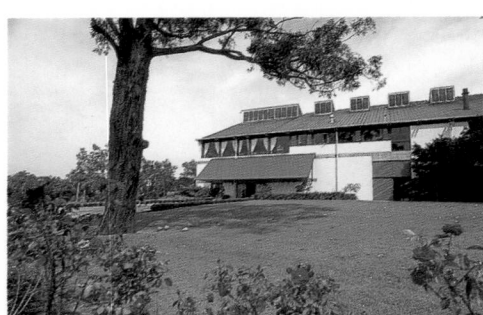

Although grape growing in New South Wales began soon after the arrival of the First Fleet in 1788, with vines planted near what is now Circular Quay in Sydney Harbour, the NSW wine industry first grew to prominence in the Hunter Valley. It is possibly Australia's best known wine area internationally and its proximity to Sydney ensures its position as Australia's most visited wine region. Its unique sémillons ensure its place in the hearts of wine lovers everywhere.

The Hunter Valley was settled soon after it was named in 1797, but focus then was coal, not wine. It wasn't until the 1830s that James Busby, considered to be the father of Australian viticulture, and several others planted vines. The Pokolbin and Rothbury subregions, now the center of the Lower Hunter vineyard area, weren't planted until the 1860s. The early vineyards proved encouraging and the Hunter Valley Viticultural Association was formed in 1847. George Wyndham founded the Dalwood vineyards, which later belonged for a period to Penfolds, and Dan Tyrrell made his first vintage in 1883—at the age of 14—beginning an amazing run of 76 consecutive vintages. At that time, the Hunter Valley was seen as ideal for grapes—it was hot, disease free and the rainfall is believed to have been more appropriate than that of today. The Lower Hunter has endured its ups and downs, but it has never suffered total failure like so many early Australian wine regions in Victoria and South Australia.

In 1921, one of Australia's greatest winemakers made his appearance. After studying in France, Maurice O'Shea returned to the Hunter to run the Mt Pleasant vineyards and winery his family had purchased. The vineyards had been established in 1880 by another legendary Hunter figure, Charles King. O'Shea joined with McWilliams in 1932, which was a difficult time in the Hunter as the market had changed considerably and 85 percent of production was devoted to fortifieds. The area under vines decreased from almost 2,600 acres (1,050 ha) in the mid-1920s to just over half that a decade later. Although consumers were not seeking the wines O'Shea and others were producing, the wines he made in the 1940s and 1950s are still eagerly sought at auction today and many still drink superbly.

Until 1963, all Hunter Valley wineries were large commercial enterprises. In that year, however, Dr Max Lake launched Lake's Folly, Australia's first "boutique" winery, an event that would change the face of the country's winemaking. With Max's son Stephen as consultant winemaker, Lake's Folly

The McWilliams Mt Pleasant vineyards at Pokolbin, Hunter Valley.

REGIONAL DOZEN

QUALITY WINES

Brokenwood Graveyard Shiraz
McWilliams Mount Pleasant
   Lovedale Sémillon
Rosemount Roxburgh
   Chardonnay
Scarborough Chardonnay
Tyrrell's Vat 1 Sémillon
Tyrrell's Vat 47 Chardonnay

BEST VALUE WINES

Drayton's Family Shiraz
Lindemans Hunter River
   Sémillon
McWilliams Mount Pleasant
   Elizabeth Sémillon
Pepper Tree Shiraz
Rothbury Estate Hunter Valley
   Sémillon
Tyrrell's Old Winery
   Chardonnay

still enjoys cult status. Another of the great figures of Australian wine, Len Evans, also made his mark in the Hunter when he began Rothbury Estate.

Despite the Hunter's extensive plantings, dozens of wineries and a host of cellar door operations, many people today think the Hunter is unsuitable for viticulture. They believe that much of the soil is too acidic and too much is heavy clay; that the Hunter is too warm and humid, even though it is uniquely positioned to take advantage of cloud cover and sea breezes; and that the probability of rain during harvest is too high. There is no doubt that site selection is critical and, notwithstanding the current proliferation of new plantings, the area under vine today is smaller than it was 25 years ago after the region boomed in the early 1970s.

If there is one grape upon which the Lower Hunter has built its reputation, it is sémillon. Chardonnay is now more extensively planted, but aged Hunter sémillon is justifiably world famous. In time, these wines pick up toast, honey, butter and lemon characters that are utterly entrancing. Over the years, Tyrrell's, McWilliams, Lindemans, Rothbury, Brokenwood and others have excelled at the style. The district's chardonnay is popular, but its richness is not to the taste of every palate. Verdelho is likely to prove the pick of the other whites.

Hunter shiraz is as distinctive as the region's sémillon. Indeed, the Hunter's earthy, leathery flavors envelop all of its reds but work best with shiraz. It seems improbable that pinot noir could work in the Hunter, and most agree that it doesn't and that it loses varietal character. But many

wineries—notably Tyrrell's—persist in planting it. Many of the great O'Shea wines and some of Lindemans finest "Hunter River Burgundies" contained a small percentage of pinot.

Grapes were successfully grown in the Upper Hunter in the second half of the nineteenth

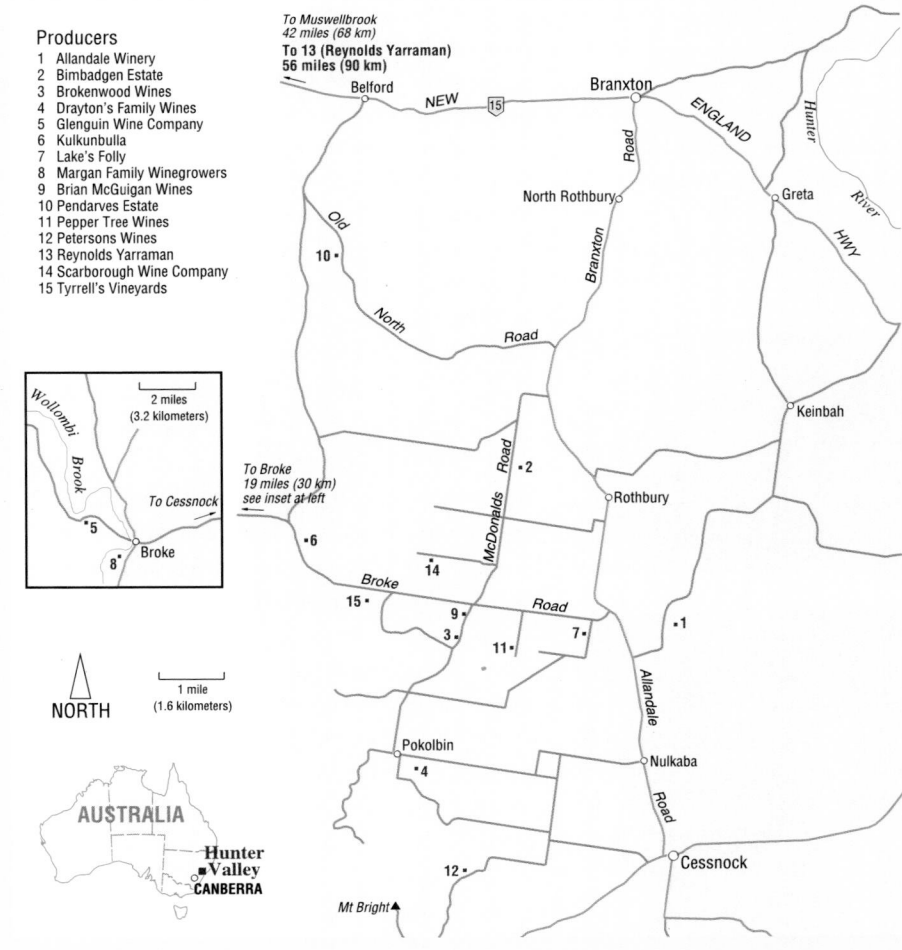

Producers

1 Allandale Winery
2 Bimbadgen Estate
3 Brokenwood Wines
4 Drayton's Family Wines
5 Glenguin Wine Company
6 Kulkunbulla
7 Lake's Folly
8 Margan Family Winegrowers
9 Brian McGuigan Wines
10 Pendarves Estate
11 Pepper Tree Wines
12 Petersons Wines
13 Reynolds Yarraman
14 Scarborough Wine Company
15 Tyrrell's Vineyards

Vineyards and rose gardens at Tyrrell's, Hunter Valley.

Below: *An old wine barrel used as a sign at the Allandale Winery, Hunter Valley.*

Bottom: *Drayton's Family Wines in the Hunter Valley.*

century, but production had ceased by 1910, probably because of the slow transport of the day and its greater distance from Sydney. The shift in tastes from table to fortified wine was also significant. Penfolds moved there from the Lower Hunter in 1960 but struggled. Their focus was on red wines but subsequent experience has shown that the region is best suited to whites. They also learned the hard way that irrigation is imperative. In 1996 Penfolds sold to Rosemount and the other major winery of the district, Arrowfield, commenced operations. They have since been joined by surprisingly few small operations. As with the Lower Hunter, there is a potential problem with rain during vintage in the Upper, but the overall rainfall is lower. The Upper Hunter has proved itself to be particularly well suited to both chardonnay and sémillon, but less so for reds.

ALLANDALE WINERY, LOWER HUNTER
Established 1978 *Owners* Wally and Julie Atallah
Production 15,000 cases *Vineyard area* 17 acres (7 ha)

Allandale was a famous vineyard in the 1800s, winning much acclaim around the world and operating, much as today's winery does, by working with selected growers. Now revived, this highly regarded winery has developed a solid following during winemaker Bill Sneddon's decade-long

tenure. The Chardonnay is popular, and there is also a range of wines made from fruit from the Hilltops district. The mailing list occasionally provides access to back vintages.

BIMBADGEN ESTATE, LOWER HUNTER
Established 1972 *Owner* Mulpha Australia Pty Ltd
Production 50,000 cases *Vineyard area* 110 acres (45 ha)

A traditional range of wines is made by a modern winery at Bimbadgen Estate. There have been a series of name changes to this winery with the latest meaning, rather appropriately, "lovely views." Winemaker van de Scheur has considerable experience in the district and is one of the industry's lateral thinkers. He has set up several innovative schemes to involve consumers ranging from invitations to planting days (which save time and money) to special clubs (which engender loyalty and save on marketing costs).

BROKENWOOD WINES, LOWER HUNTER
Established 1970 *Owners* private syndicate *Production* 60,000 cases *Vineyard area* 140 acres (57 ha)

A flagship winery for the Hunter region, Brokenwood owns the highly regarded Yarra winery, Seville Estate and also has significant interests in Cowra. Although Brokenwood has long sourced fruit from around the nation for its wines, the single-vineyard Graveyard Shiraz, from land that was once intended to be a cemetery, stands out. In extreme demand, this wine has established itself as the region's top shiraz. The Sémillon, one of the region's most enjoyable young sémillons, is also well received.

DRAYTON'S FAMILY WINES, LOWER HUNTER
Established 1853 *Owners* Max Drayton and family *Production* 100,000 cases *Vineyard area* 200 acres (80 ha)

The Drayton family has been making wines in the Hunter Valley for 150 years. Although perhaps not as prominent as they once were, the size of their production is testimony to the support their wines have in the market. A number of ranges are available, the best being the Premium—especially the Verdelho and Bin 5555 Shiraz—and the Individual Vineyard wines.

GLENGUIN WINE COMPANY, LOWER HUNTER
Established mid-1980s *Owner* Robin Tedder *Production* 15,000 cases *Vineyard area* 37 acres (15 ha)

Winemaker Robin Tedder, Master of Wine and merchant banker, teams well with his viticulturist brother Andrew to make this one of the most exciting emerging wineries in the region. The wines are all from individual vineyards, even with fruit that is sourced from Mudgee and Orange. The Mudgee Shiraz is confirmation of just how good an area that is, but long-term fame is likely to come from the Hunter Sémillon. The early releases suggest that they will rate with the best.

KULKUNBULLA, LOWER HUNTER
Established 1996 *Owners* Kulkunbulla Pty Ltd *Production* 2,400 cases *Vineyard area* 15 acres (6 ha)

Originally part of the Brokenback Estate, formerly owned by Rothbury, this small company has made a significant impression in its first few years. Winemaker Gavin Lennard is the driving force behind it, with both financial and physical support from the other shareholders. Early releases suggest that their future lies with chardonnay, though the sémillons will no doubt take a higher profile in time.

LAKE'S FOLLY, LOWER HUNTER
Established 1963 *Owner* Peter Fogarty *Production* 4,000 cases *Vineyard area* 30 acres (12 ha)

Australia's first boutique winery, and the forerunner of so many more, was sold in May 2000 to Perth businessman Peter Fogarty. Founder Dr Max Lake (a surgeon, prolific author and respected show judge) changed the face of the wine industry in Australia and quickly established a cult following for Lake's Folly. The range consists of a Cabernets—a blend of cabernet sauvignon, petit verdot, shiraz and merlot—and a Chardonnay, both of which benefit from extended cellaring. Max's son Stephen, who had been winemaker in recent years, now plays a consulting role.

Below: *Vineyard at the boutique Lake's Folly, Lower Hunter.*

Bottom: *The entrance to the tourist stop at Brian McGuigan's Wines, Lower Hunter.*

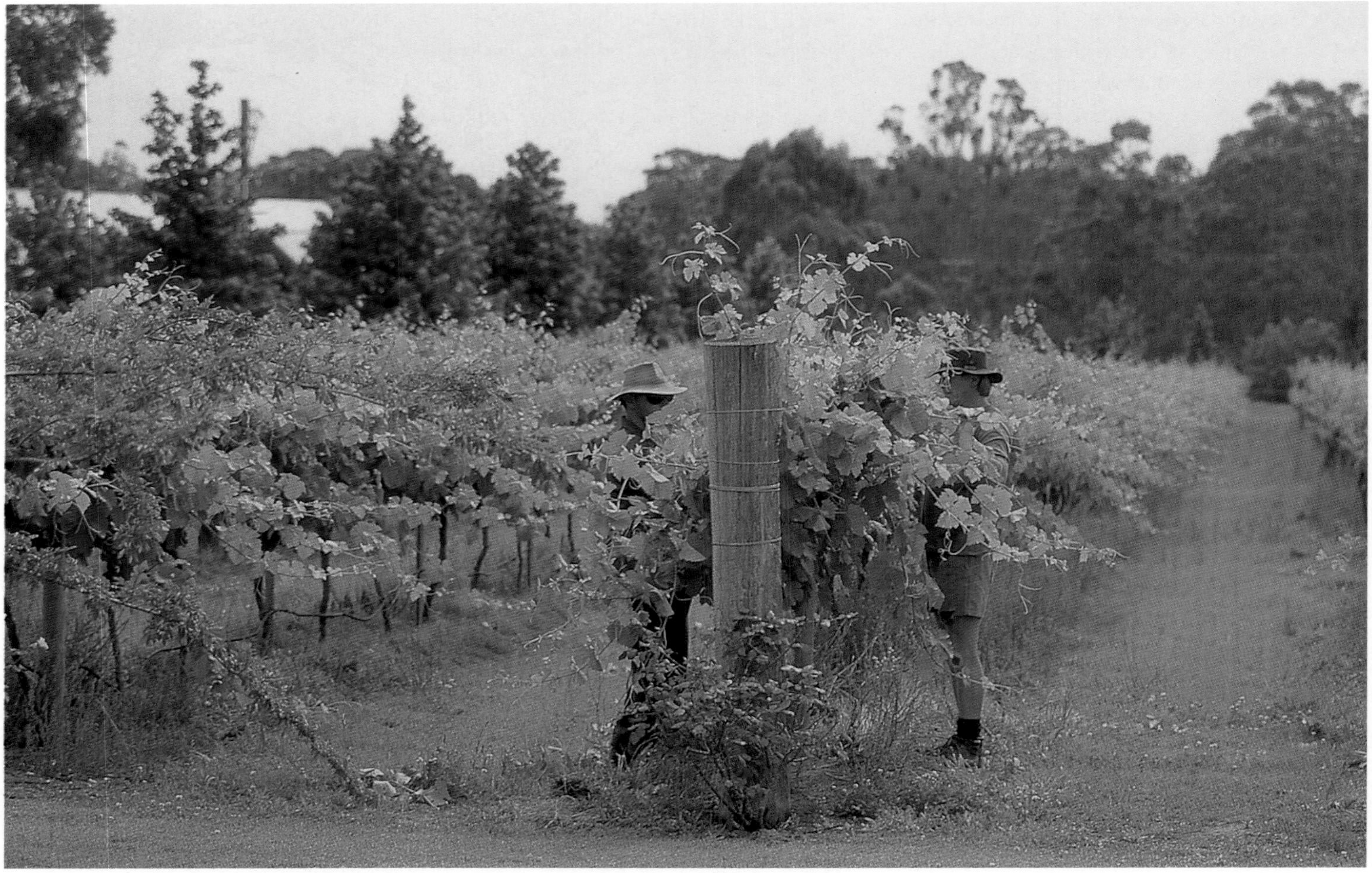

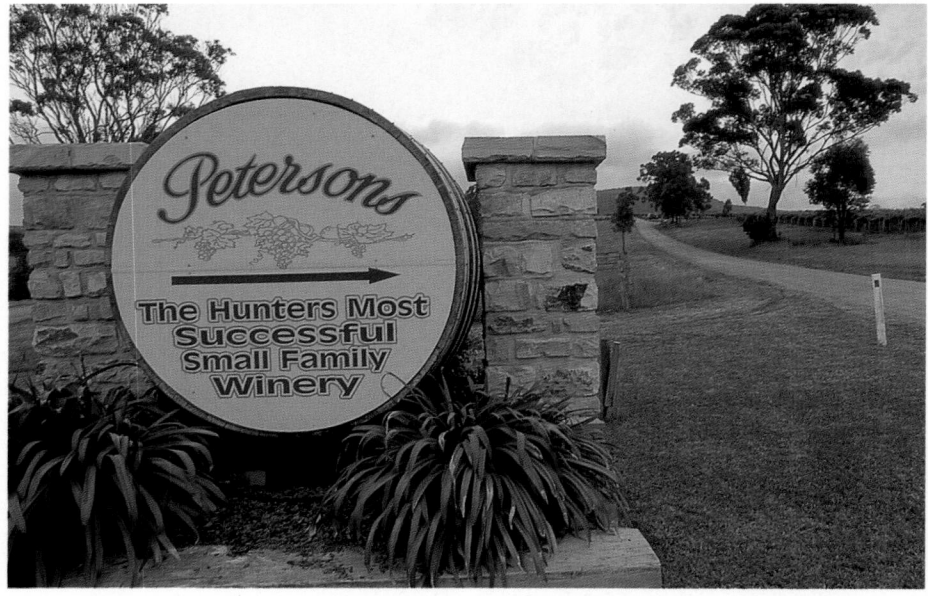

Above: *Many of the super-premium wines at Petersons Wines are only available at the cellar door.*

Top: *Workers in the vineyard at Pepper Tree Wines, Lower Hunter.*

MARGAN FAMILY WINEGROWERS, LOWER HUNTER

Established **1997** ***Owners*** **Andrew and Lisa Margan**
Production **20,000 cases** ***Vineyard area*** **85 acres (35 ha)**

Son of the famous Australian wine writer, Frank Margan, winemaker Andrew learned his craft at Tyrrell's before venturing forth on his own with this winery in the Broke Fordwich subregion. An advocate of careful selection of varieties for particular sites and of restricting yields, his first releases have been well received, especially the Sémillon and Shiraz.

BRIAN MCGUIGAN WINES, LOWER HUNTER

Established **1967** ***Owners*** **Brian McGuigan Wines Ltd**
Production **620,000 cases** ***Vineyard area*** **3,170 acres (1,280 ha)**

Brian McGuigan is a significant producer of competent wines and has built a devoted following over the years. One of the Australian wine industry's great marketers, he did much to pave the way for Australian producers in the tough American market during his time at Wyndham Estate. More recently he has turned the old Hungerford Hill Wine Village into a tourist stop that includes a cheese company, restaurant, cafe and bakery in addition to the winery and tasting facilities.

PENDARVES ESTATE, LOWER HUNTER

Established **1986** ***Owners*** **Philip and Belinda Norrie**
Production **5,500 cases** ***Vineyard area*** **50 acres (20 ha)**

Philip Norrie has managed to combine several careers—medical practitioner, winemaker,

historian and author—while also founding the Australian Medical Friends of Wine. His vineyards are situated on an outcrop of limestone that is unique in the Hunter. The range of wines reflects his eclectic interests. As well as the standards, he has joined a number of other Hunter wineries in championing verdelho and other more rarely encountered varieties such as chambourcin.

PEPPER TREE WINES, LOWER HUNTER

Established 1983 *Owners* Pepper Tree Wines Pty Ltd
Production 75,000 cases *Vineyard area* 150 acres (60 ha)

The Pepper Tree winery forms part of an attractive complex incorporating Roberts Restaurant and The Convent Guesthouse. They have a significant interest in Coonawarra's Parker Estate and multi-regional blends are a specialty. Winemaker Chris Cameron intends to create his biggest splash with merlot, aiming to make Australia's best.

PETERSONS WINES, LOWER HUNTER

Established 1981 *Owner* Colin Peterson *Production* 15,000 cases *Vineyard area* 40 acres (16 ha)

Originally founded by Colin Peterson's father, Ian, this small winery has attracted a serious following, particularly for its Chardonnay. The Back Block reds are also valued, but many of the super-premium wines are only available to cellar door visitors. The associated Peterson House, opened in 1993, specializes in premium sparkling wine.

REYNOLDS YARRAMAN, UPPER HUNTER

Established 1968 *Owners* Jon and Jane Reynolds
Production 15,000 cases *Vineyard area* 150 acres (60 ha)

Winemaker Jon Reynolds had a successful career with Houghtons and Wyndham before taking over the old Horderns Wybong Estate, which dated back to 1837. Since then, he has made some wonderful wines, especially the Sémillon. His wines from fruit sourced from the Orange district are also highly recommended.

SCARBOROUGH WINE COMPANY, LOWER HUNTER

Established 1987 *Owners* Ian and Merrelea Scarborough
Production 10,000 cases *Vineyard area* 30 acres (12 ha)

This winery, with a sensational view, is planted on one of the few patches of terra rossa in the Hunter Valley. Former contract winemaker Ian Scarborough produces one of the region's very best chardonnays, and also makes very small amounts of pinot noir in some years. A second chardonnay is produced for export markets.

TYRRELL'S VINEYARDS, LOWER HUNTER

Established 1858 *Owners* Murray and Bruce Tyrrell
Production 750,000 cases *Vineyard area* 205 acres (510 ha)

Edward Tyrrell planted the first vines on this estate in 1858. In 1883, at age 14, Dan Tyrrell took over the winemaking and worked 76 consecutive vintages before nephew Murray took over the reins. Shiraz and sémillon (especially their Vat 1 Sémillon) star, but the pioneering Vat 47 Chardonnay is one of Australia's finest. Tyrrell's commercial lines, particularly the Long Flat wines, are also popular.

Below: *Barrels of 1998 cabernet sauvignon at Reynolds Yarraman, Upper Hunter.*

Bottom: *Tyrrell's Vineyards in the Lower Hunter.*

Other New South Wales Regions

Ken Gargett

The Cassegrain Vineyards are in an unlikely location in the lush subtropics of northern New South Wales.

NORTHERN RIVERS

Most people would consider the lush subtropics of northern New South Wales an unlikely place to find grapes, but grapes there are, and several wineries to go with them. Some of New South Wales' earliest vineyards were in the Northern Rivers zone. Colonial surveyor Henry Fancourt White planted the first in 1837, and there were more than 30 within three decades. After a period of decline, winegrowing was revived at Hastings River by the Cassegrain family in the 1980s.

Irrigation is unnecessary but the significant rainfall and high humidity can be a problem. This is one reason why the Cassegrains turned to chambourcin, a grape that is highly resistant to mildew and produces a wine of intense color and flavor. A French hybrid developed in the nineteenth century, chambourcin is no longer found in its original home and, as a hybrid, it is not allowed to be re-imported there. Both chardonnay and sémillon have been successful in some vintages.

CASSEGRAIN VINEYARDS, HASTINGS RIVER

Established 1980 *Owners* the Cassegrain family *Production* 55,000 cases *Vineyard area* 260 acres (105 ha)

This impressive establishment in an unlikely location led the winemaking revival in the region. While early vintages were variable, winemaker David Barker's wines have been much more consistent in recent years. He makes a range of wines, including Sparkling, Rosé and Chardonnay, but it is his Chambourcin that has gained prominence.

CENTRAL RANGES

The Central Ranges regions all lie about 185 miles (300 km) inland in an area west to north-west of Sydney. One of them, Mudgee, is among Australia's oldest viticultural regions. The other two, Cowra and Orange, are relative newcomers.

German settlers planted the first vines in Mudgee in 1858. The story from then on is depressingly familiar. Others followed and soon there were more than 50 vineyards supporting a thriving wine industry. The 1872 gold rush drew more people but the depression of 1893 virtually destroyed viticulture in the region. A few hardy souls persisted, notably one of the original families, the Roths, at their Craigmoor winery.

There was little else until the late 1960s revival, led by Bob Roberts, whose Huntington Estate soon established a reputation for excellent wines and has since become known for hosting an exceptional annual music festival.

Huntington Estate was followed a year later by Botobolar, where Gil Wahlquist established one of the first vineyards in Australia to use organic methods, a practice continued by subsequent owners. Montrose commenced in 1974 with winemaker Carlo Corino, a native of Italy's Piedmont. Not surprisingly, Montrose led the way in Australia with plantings of barbera, sangiovese and even nebbiolo.

Few of the several small wineries that followed built a reputation to match that of Huntington Estate and they suffered the indignity of seeing much of their production head east to produce some of the Hunter's more celebrated wines. This trend stopped when larger producers moved into the region. Orlando-Wyndham relocated wine-making from the Hunter to Mudgee and now owns Montrose and Craigmoor, and Mildara Blass followed with Half Mile Creek. But the winery most likely to bring Mudgee to the attention of the world is Rosemount Estate with its superb Mountain Blue Shiraz Cabernet and the new Hill of Gold range, represented by a chardonnay, a cabernet sauvignon and an excellent shiraz. These wines have shown that Mudgee fruit can make first class wines.

Although close to the Hunter as the crow flies, the two districts are separated by the Great Dividing Range, giving Mudgee a cooler, drier climate. Most vineyards rely on irrigation. Cabernet sauvignon has been particularly successful in the region and shiraz has done well. There are also significant plantings of chardonnay.

In Cowra, vines were first planted in 1973 with chardonnay by far the predominant grape. The region quickly made a name for itself with some exciting releases by Rothbury Estate in the Hunter Valley and by providing part of Adelaide Hills producer, Petaluma's, early Chardonnay. Other outside producers such as Brokenwood and Hungerford Hill in the Hunter Valley and Richmond Grove from the Barossa all make wines from Cowra fruit. Cowra Estate is the highest profile local winery, though as with the others, wines are made outside the district. The increase in interest in the district has allowed the establishment of crushing facilities and it probably will not be long before the first winery is established. Cowra is considerably warmer than most people

Above: *Outdoor tasting area at the Craigmoor Winery, Mudgee district.*

Top: *The entrance to the Highland Heritage Estate and Mt Canobolas Vineyard in the Orange district.*

BLOODWOOD, ORANGE

Established 1983 *Owners* Stephen and Rhonda Doyle *Production* 3,000 cases *Vineyard area* 21 acres (8.5 ha)

Pioneers of the Orange region, the Doyles have built a devoted following. Still one of the district's smaller producers, they sell an eccentrically named range of wines through the cellar door, a popular newsletter and a few specialist outlets. Chirac is their sparkling, so named for the French gentleman's contribution to nuclear testing. Their best chardonnay is called Schubert, in honor of the creator of Grange, notwithstanding their wine is a white.

Above: *Hay in a field in front of the vineyards and winery at Steins Wines, Mudgee district.*

Top: *Miramar Vineyards in the Mudgee district.*

imagine, warmer than both the Hunter and Mudgee districts, although humidity is low. It has proved to be a good source of dependable, excellent value commercial whites.

The region of Orange, with an altitude between 2,000 and 3,000 feet (600 and 900 m) above sea level, is centered around Mount Canobolas and has proved very successful for grape growing. The climate varies from the cool slopes of Mount Canobolas to the much warmer, neighboring lower districts. Night temperatures during the growing season can be very cool and, because most of the rain falls in winter and spring, irrigation is needed. Wind makes careful site selection imperative but reduces the risk of spring frosts. Bloodwood Estate planted the first vines in the early 1980s. Much of the production of the district goes to large outside producers such as Rosemount Estate and Rothbury in the Hunter Valley. Chardonnay plantings far exceed all others and have produced some memorable wines, especially from producers such as Rosemount and Reynolds Yarraman. Cabernet sauvignon is also now established and shiraz looks very promising.

COWRA ESTATE, COWRA

Established 1973 *Owners* John and Evelyne Geber *Production* 30,000 cases *Vineyard area* NA

Cowra Estate was purchased in 1995 by John Geber, a successful South African businessman and cricket fanatic (his premium wines are the Classic Bat range). Fruit from these vineyards went to the early Petaluma chardonnays. Geber is not afraid to back rosé, but has had more success with it in the export market. Cowra Estate wines are excellent value.

ANDREW HARRIS VINEYARDS, MUDGEE

Established 1991 *Owners* Andrew and Deb Harris *Production* 130,000 cases *Vineyard area* 250 acres (100 ha)

Andrew Harris Vineyards is one of the major reasons for the increasing national recognition of Mudgee as a premium wine district. Although only a decade since Andrew and his wife Debbie purchased a large sheep farm in the southern part of the region, there have already been a number of highly successful releases made under contract by Frank Newman. There are three tiers of wines: Premium, Reserve and the super-premium shiraz/ cabernet blend dubbed The Vision.

HUNTINGTON ESTATE, MUDGEE

Established 1969 *Owners* Bob and Wendy Roberts *Production* 15,000 cases *Vineyard area* 106 acres (43 ha)

Bob Roberts revived quality winemaking in Mudgee several decades ago and has been the torchbearer for the region ever since. His wines, particularly his underpriced reds, have been very successful and age extremely well. Huntington is also famous for its annual music festival. Richard Tognetti, Artistic Director of the Australian Chamber Orchestra and the Huntington Music Festival, is married to winemaker Susan Roberts, daughter of Bob and Wendy.

LOWE FAMILY WINE CO, MUDGEE

Established 1987 *Owners* David Lowe and Jane Wilson
Production 4,000 cases *Vineyard area* 37 acres (15 ha)

David Lowe began his career at Rothbury Estate in the Hunter Valley and rose to chief winemaker before turning to consultant winemaking for numerous small producers, something he still does today. He and his wife and co-winemaker, Jane Wilson, have been making wine from their Mudgee fruit, supplemented with fruit from the Hunter and Orange since 1987. They established a winery in late 1999.

BIG RIVERS

Big Rivers is one of the heros of the Australian wine industry. A lot of its wine ends up in the ubiquitous casks, but it also produces much "sunshine in a bottle"—the flavorful, great-value wines that sell so well both in Australia and as exports. Most Big Rivers producers make huge quantities of wine but sprinkled among these mega-establishments are a number of smaller, rarely-encountered wineries. Sémillon is the most widely planted grape but chardonnay plantings are increasing. Shiraz is by far the dominant red variety.

Many of the original Big Rivers growers were returned servicemen from the First World War or Italian immigrants who moved to the area after both world wars. But it was the McWilliam family who pioneered viticulture in the area in 1912. The prevalent style produced was fortifieds to match the national taste at the time. The McWilliam clan also pioneered the move to premium table wines, but the climate ensures that Big Rivers will remain an important source of fortified material.

Big Rivers is a hot dry region in southwest New South Wales centered in the Riverina area. It could not have become a top wine-producing area without irrigation. Ironically, irrigation is also the source of Big Rivers' poor reputation domestically—that of a soulless mass producer of bulk wines. It is now producing some surprisingly good wines. Where growers are prepared to restrict yields through canopy management, pruning and

minimizing irrigation, the quality of the wine has improved greatly, but its old reputation is hard to shed.

Where Big Rivers has stunned critics and the public alike, has been with its botrytis sémillons. Pioneered in 1982 by the de Bortoli family, these luscious and concentrated dessert-style wines are world class and have propelled the district into another dimension, drawing it to the attention of wine lovers around the world.

A sign for cellar door sales at de Bortoli in the Riverina.

DE BORTOLI

Established 1928 *Owners* de Bortoli family *Production* 3 million+ cases *Vineyard area* 527 acres (213 ha)

If ever a wine company has made the leap from a producer of nondescript bulk wine to the top shelf, this is it. Much of de Bortoli's production is intended for the volume market, but its astonishing botrytis sémillons—Noble One (in particular the incredibly successful first vintage from 1982) and Black Noble—changed public perception of both de Bortoli and the Riverina forever.

CHARLES STURT UNIVERSITY WINERY

Established 1978 *Owners* Charles Sturt University
Production 17,500 cases *Vineyard area* 52 acres (21 ha)

The Riverina College of Advanced Education, now known as Charles Sturt University, offered Australia's first degree course in winemaking in 1975 under the direction of Brian Croser,

Vats at Charles Sturt University where students learn to make (and sell) wine.

A mural at Miranda Wines in the Riverina.

SOUTHERN NEW SOUTH WALES

The three regions that comprise Southern New South Wales—Hilltops, Canberra and Tumbarumba—each show distinctive characteristics and are grouped together for geographical rather than viticultural reasons. Yugoslavian immigrants planted vineyards at Hilltops at the end of the 1800s, but apart from that, all three regions have been producing wine for no more than a couple of decades.

In 1975, grapegrowing was reintroduced to Hilltops in a small way at the Barwang vineyard as part of an overall farm diversification. There were only 32 acres (13 ha) under vine when McWilliams purchased the property in 1989. They have increased plantings tenfold and been joined by a couple of tiny wineries and several growers. The altitude of Hilltops—more than 1,500 feet (460 m) above sea level—is a major factor in wine quality. The dry summer makes irrigation necessary and frost is a concern. Chardonnay, cabernet sauvignon and especially shiraz have proved most successful to date. The McWilliams Barwang wines have established the potential of the region.

The Canberra District is the most established and nationally recognized wine region in Southern New South Wales. Irrigation is essential here, and there is considerable variation between summer and winter temperatures, more so than in most other Australian districts. The first plantings in 1971 by Dr Edgar Rick at Lake George were followed by the development of almost 20 more small vineyards. The face of the Canberra District is changing however. What was once little more than an area of hobby farms and amateur winemakers is now home to a 625 acre (253 ha) vineyard and a 2,200 ton (2,000 t) winery established by BRL Hardy, one of Australia's biggest wine producers. Chardonnay, shiraz, cabernet sauvignon and riesling have done well here and there is some support for pinot noir and sauvignon blanc.

Tumbarumba, the youngest of the Southern New South Wales regions, is high and remote. Previously the preserve of fly fishermen, grapes were first planted here in the early 1980s. There are still only about 1,000 acres (405 ha) under vine. BRL Hardy has an interest in Tumbarumba but Southcorp, Australia's largest wine company, is the major presence. There are a couple of tiny wineries also. Tumbarumba is one of the cooler regions in Australia and most of its grapes go into sparkling wines. Sauvignon blanc is the

founder of Petaluma. It has a fully operational commercial winery and the cellar door on the campus stocks a wide range of wines. The school has not only produced many of Australia's finest young winemakers, but has also enjoyed critical success for its wines.

CRANSWICK ESTATE

Established 1976 *Owners* Cranswick Estate Wines Ltd
Production 800,000 cases *Vineyard area* 670 acres (270 ha)

General manager Graham Cranswick Smith organized a management buyout of Cranswick Estate in 1991 when it was producing the base for Cinzano's vermouth. He then devoted his attention to the export market and Cranswick Estate soon became one of Australia's most successful wine producers. It was floated on the Stock Exchange in 1997. There has been a series of good value releases, especially the sémillon. The botrytis sémillon, Autumn Gold, is one of the region's best.

MIRANDA WINES

Established 1939 *Owners* Sam, Jim & Lou Miranda
Production 2.5 million cases *Vineyard area* NA

Like de Bortoli, Miranda started out as a bulk wine producer in the Riverina region and has since branched into the quality arena. Miranda has done so by venturing into the Barossa and Clare Valleys in South Australia and King Valley in Victoria. The company has several labels of varying quality, including Miranda, Somerton, Mirrool Creek and Wyangan Estate, as well as the Show Reserve Range and the Golden Botrytis Sémillon.

predominant table wine to date but chardonnay could eventually become the most prominent white, and pinot noir has a lot of potential.

CLONAKILLA, CANBERRA DISTRICT

Established 1971 *Owner* John Kirk *Production* 1,200 cases
Vineyard area 33 acres (13.5 ha)

This is one of the very earliest wineries in the region and Tim, the son of founder Dr John Kirk, is the current winemaker. He makes a range of wines but is most interested in the Rhône varieties. Tiny quantities of a straight viognier are made and a very small amount of that grape is added to the Shiraz in true Rhône fashion, resulting in a delicious, spicy and very highly rated wine.

LARK HILL, CANBERRA DISTRICT

Established 1978 *Owners* David and Sue Carpenter
Production 6,000 cases *Vineyard area* 10 acres (4 ha)

The Carpenters are typical of many of the region's small producers—former academics seeking a life among the vines. One of Australia's higher wineries at a lofty 2,820 feet (860 m), they operate through a cellar door and have built a solid following. Their Chardonnay has been the star, but their Pinot Noir has its devotees and is one of the best from the district.

SOUTH COAST

Although its climate is not subtropical like the Northern Rivers, the South Coast zone has similar problems—summer rainfall, humidity, rot and mildew. Consequently the area's winemakers have been attracted to chambourcin, but chardonnay, shiraz and cabernet sauvignon have all done well in good vintages as well. Most winemaking is done by contract.

Wineries are a late addition to the South Coast, most dating back no further than the 1970s. Few are household names and fewer aspire to be so, but some—notably Coolangatta Estate and Cambewarra Estate—are producing quality wines. The heart of the area, the beautiful Shoalhaven region, is tourist territory and its wineries would not exist without them. The South Coast also contains the outlying Sydney region, where Vicarys Winery has been operating continuously since 1923.

Below: *The entrance to one of the highest wineries in Australia, Lark Hill, Canberra District.*

Bottom: *The Brindabella Hills Winery vineyard in the Canberra District.*

Queensland

Ken Gargett

Mount Tambourine's lush vineyards produce only a portion of the grapes used in its wine production.

New plantings across Queensland—in established regions such as the Granite Belt, districts like Toowoomba and the Burnett that haven't seen vineyards for decades, and completely new viticultural locales like Mt Tamborine and Mt Cotton—will soon lead to its wine production exceeding that of Tasmania. Queensland's enological history began around 1850 with German settlers in the Toowoomba district, though the vineyards soon declined. In 1862, Ernest Seidel planted grapes at St George. The State's oldest continually operating winery, Romavilla, followed a year later, and the Granite Belt's first grapes were planted soon after. In the late 1960s, the Puglisi family started selling wine made from a blend of the table grapes muscat and waltham cross. Others soon followed, but it was only after vine quarantine laws were relaxed in 1973 that things started to roll.

Conditions in this huge state are extremely varied. The Granite Belt, at 2,300 to 3,300 feet (700 to 1,000 m) above sea level, is one of the highest wine regions in Australia. It is normally 9 to 18°F (5 to 10°C) cooler than coastal districts and snow is not unknown. In the Burnett, fertility, rain during harvest and the possibility of hail are potential problems. Western Queensland is hot and dry. Even in the established Granite Belt, it is too early to identify the most successful varieties. Cabernet sauvignon and shiraz dominate, and merlot is showing much potential, but pinot noir is less successful. There is some interest in red Italian varieties. Chambourcin's ability to withstand rain and humidity has given it a following outside the Belt. Sémillon and chardonnay are by far the most successful whites.

GRANITE BELT PRODUCERS

BALLANDEAN ESTATE WINERY
Established 1968 *Owners* Angelo & Mary Puglisi
Production 9,000 cases *Vineyard area* 80 acres (32 ha)

Angelo Puglisi pioneered table wines in the Granite Belt, and his efforts with different grapes have helped establish which varieties are most suited to the area. Ballandean's best wines are its Black Label Cabernet and Chardonnay, while the idiosyncratic Late Harvest Sylvaner has its supporters.

KOMINOS WINES
Established 1976 *Owner* Tony Comino *Production* 4,000 cases *Vineyard area* 35 acres (14 ha)

Tony Comino's reds, particularly the Shiraz, impress more than the whites. The winery exports half of its production, mostly to Asia. Tony has a serious interest in Greek varieties and makes his Vin Doux in the style of the dessert wine from the island of Samos.

PRESTON PEAK WINES
Established 1994 *Owners* Ashley Smith and Kym Thumpkin
Production 3,000 cases *Vineyard area* 24 acres (10 ha)

Preston Peak now has a winery in Toowoomba in addition to its Wyerba facility. The owners are also involved with the Stanthorpe Wine Centre and new vineyards at Canungra. Their whites show a delicate touch, while the reds are among Queensland's most elegant. They have been especially successful with their flagship Chardonnay.

ROBINSONS FAMILY VINEYARDS
Established 1974 *Owners* the Robinson family *Production* 2,000 cases *Vineyard area* 30 acres (12 ha)

Robinsons was one of the first producers of quality wine in the Granite Belt. Its cabernet, shiraz and

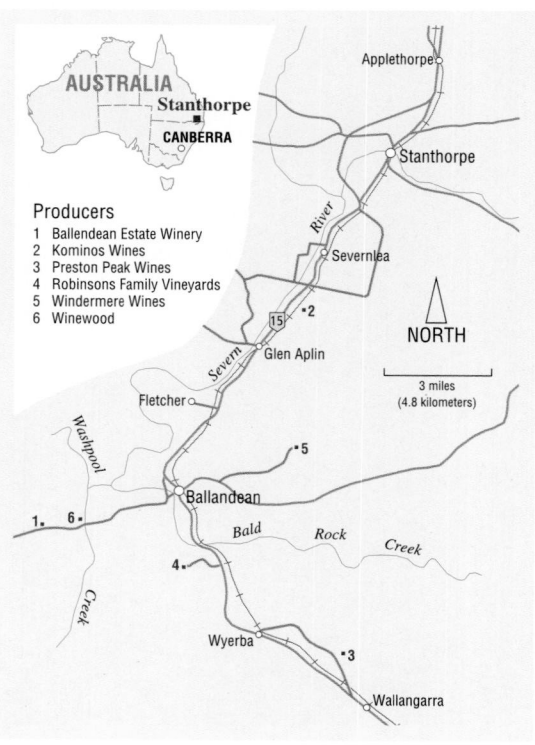

AUSTRALIA
Stanthorpe
CANBERRA

Producers
1 Ballandean Estate Winery
2 Kominos Wines
3 Preston Peak Wines
4 Robinsons Family Vineyards
5 Windermere Wines
6 Winewood

Applethorpe
Stanthorpe
Severnlea
NORTH
15 2
Glen Aplin
3 miles
(4.8 kilometers)
Fletcher
5
Ballandean
Bald Rock Creek
1. 6
4.
Wyerba
3
Wallangarra

robust vintage ports have good track records, but the vintage sparkling wine is its best.

WINDERMERE WINES

Established 1995 *Owner* Wayne Beecham *Production* 600 cases *Vineyard area* 10 acres (4 ha)

Housed in a converted 1930s fruit-packing shed 3,180 feet (970 m) above sea level, Windermere Wines is one of the highest and most isolated wineries in Australia. Its shiraz is among the region's best and its sangiovese/cabernet sauvignon blend shows promise as well.

WINEWOOD

Established 1985 *Owners* Ian and Jeanette Davis *Production* 1,000 cases *Vineyard area* 10 acres (4 ha)

Ian Davis's love of the Rhône is evident in his new plantings of viognier, rousanne, grenache, mataro and shiraz and his nuturing of a varietal marsanne in a big, full style with considerable oak. His shiraz includes 5 to 10 percent marsanne.

OTHER QUEENSLAND PRODUCERS

BARAMBAH RIDGE WINERY AND VINEYARDS, SOUTH BURNETT

Established 1995 *Owner* South Burnett Wines Ltd *Production* 7,000 cases *Vineyard area* 17 acres (7 ha)

Barambah Ridge has an imposing state-of-the-art winery. Grapes are purchased to supplement needs and contract winemaking is carried out for many clients throughout Queensland and beyond. First indications are that the Barambah Ridge whites are more successful than the reds.

CLOVELY ESTATE, BURNETT

Established 1997 *Owner* Clovely Estate Ltd *Production* 200,000 cases *Vineyard area* 450 acres (180 ha)

The size of this new Burnett operation is not insignificant by any standards, but it is massive for Queensland. Its three labels, in ascending order of quality, are Fifth Row, Left Field and Clovely Estate. Much of the production will be exported.

MOUNT COTTON WINERY, BRISBANE

Established 2000 *Owner* Sirromet Wines Pty Ltd *Production* 21,600 cases, increasing to 144,000 cases *Vineyard area* 12 acres (5 ha) at Mt Cotton; 200 acres (80 ha) at Ballandean

This new state-of-the-art winery on the outskirts of Brisbane was developed as part of a tourist complex where visitors can observe all stages of

the production of sparkling wine. Chambourcin has been planted in the hot and humid surrounding vineyards, and 20 different varieties have been planted at Ballandean.

MOUNT TAMBORINE VINEYARD & WINERY, SOUTHEAST QUEENSLAND

Established 1991 *Owner* Queensland Vineyard & Winery Pty Ltd *Production* 12,500 cases *Vineyard area* 63 acres (26 ha)

Mount Tamborine's vineyards provide only a small percentage of the grapes for its winery, the rest being sourced from vineyards throughout Australia. Its sparkling wines are popular, but spend little time on lees. Its fortifieds have been well received. Its best red is a Padthaway shiraz.

ROMAVILLA WINERY, SOUTHEAST QUEENSLAND

Established 1863 *Owners* David and Joy Wall *Production* 2,500 cases *Vineyard area* 20 acres (8 ha)

In this 120-year-old winery, ancient oak barrels stand alongside the latest stainless steel equipment. Romavilla's wide range encompasses some delicate whites (including one of Australia's better chenin blancs), mid-weight reds that are striving for elegance, and heavenly fortifieds.

STONE RIDGE VINEYARDS, THE GRANITE BELT

Established 1981 *Owners* Jim Lawrie and Anne Kennedy *Production* 1,450 cases *Vineyard area* 2.5 acres (1 ha)

Jim Lawrie's Stone Ridge wines reflect regionality and age well, although his Mt Sterling wines are designed for early drinking. He produces some of the area's finest shiraz, good malbec and mataro, a tiny quantity of warm-climate pinot noir and a range of idiosyncratic whites.

REGIONAL DOZEN

Ballandean Late Harvest
  Sylvaner
Granite Ridge Cabernet
  Sauvignon
Kominos Shiraz
Preston Peak Chardonnay
Robinsons Family Sparkling
Romavilla Very Old Tawny
  Port
Rumbalara Semillon
Severn Brae Shiraz
Stone Ridge Shiraz
Violet Cane Vineyard Merlot
Windermere Sangiovese
  Cabernet
Winewood Shiraz Marsanne

One of many panoranic vineyard views in Queensland's Granite Belt.

New Zealand

North Cape

Kaitaia

Kerikeri

Whangarei

Auckland

Great Barrier
Island

Kaipara Harbour

*Hauraki
Gulf*

Takapuna

Waiheke Island

Waitakere

◉ **Auckland**

Manukau

Thames

Papakura

NORTH ISLAND

**Waikato/
Bay of Plenty**

Waikato

Tauranga

*Bay
of Plenty*

East Cape

Hamilton

Matamata

Whakatane

*Lake
Rotorua*

Rotorua

Tokoroa

Raukumara Range

Gisborne

Gisborne

*North
Taranaki
Bight*

*Lake
Taupo*

Taupo

Turangi

Wairoa

New Plymouth

▲ Mt Egmont (Mt Taranaki)
8259 ft (2518 m)

▲ Mt Ruapehu
9174 ft (2797 m)

*Hawke
Bay*

*Mahia
Peninsula*

Cape Egmont

Hawkes Bay

Napier

*South
Taranaki Bight*

Hastings

Cape Kidnappers

Wanganui

TASMAN

Feilding

Palmerston North

SEA

NEW ZEALAND

Golden Bay

Takaka

Levin

Cook

Te Horo

Wairarapa/Wellington

*Tasman
Bay*

Strait

Upper Hutt

Masterton

Nelson

Porirua

Gladstone

Nelson

Blenheim

◉ **WELLINGTON**

Martinborough

Wairau

Wairau Valley

Cape Foulwind

Marlborough

SOUTH

Buller

▲ Mt Travers
7668 ft (2338 m)

PACIFIC OCEAN

Kaikoura

Greymouth

SOUTH ISLAND

Waipara

SOUTHERN ALPS

**Canterbury/
Waipara**

Waipara

Pegasus Bay

▲ Mt Cook (Mt Aoraki)
12,313 ft (3754 m)

Rakaia

Christchurch

Lyttelton

*Canterbury
Plains*

Banks Peninsula

*Lake
Pukaki*

Ashburton

*Lake
Wanaka*

*Canterbury
Bight*

▲ Mt Aspiring
9938 ft (3030 m)

Wanaka

Omarama

Timaru

Waitaki

Queenstown

**Central
Otago**

*Lake
Wakatipu*

Oamaru

Lake Te Anau

Te Anau

Clutha

*Otago
Peninsula*

Dunedin

Waiau

Mataura

Invercargill

Foveaux Strait

Stewart Island

▲
NORTH

75 miles
(120 kilometers)

New Zealand

Joelle Thomson & Paul White

New Zealand's wine production pales in significance compared with its profile as a wine-producing nation. The country currently makes around 15.8 million gallons (60 million l) of wine annually, which equates to just 0.2 percent of the global total, yet all over the world its wines are both well known and highly sought-after. They first shot to fame in the mid- to late

1980s when the country's inimitable Marlborough Sauvignon Blanc attracted attention in Europe. Since then, New Zealand has proved it has similar potential for making small quantities of other high-quality wines, particularly Martinborough Pinot Noir and Gisborne Chardonnay.

New Zealand is situated in the southern hemisphere between the 32nd and 47th parallels. If it were in the northern hemisphere, it would extend, approximately, from the Champagne region of France to the south of Spain. But the country's isolation—the nearest sizeable landmass is Australia, 1,000 miles (1,600 km) away—and its maritime climate make the viticultural conditions, and the wines, unique. New Zealand's cool climate is its greatest asset for wine production, but the associated problems of high rainfall and humidity constitute a major challenge for winemakers.

Oak barrels line the cellars of the Esk Valley Estate in Hawkes Bay on the North Island.

Grapes are grown all over New Zealand, with the exception of the west coasts of the North and South Islands and Stewart Island in the far south. There are nine official wine-producing regions: Auckland, Waikato/Bay of Plenty, Gisborne, Hawkes Bay and Wairarapa/Wellington in the North Island; and Marlborough, Nelson, Canterbury/Waipara and Central Otago in the South Island.

History

Vines were first planted in New Zealand by the Reverend Samuel Marsden in 1819, at Kerikeri in what is now the Northland area of the North Island. The first wine was made at nearby Waitangi in 1836 by James Busby. In the 1890s, Dalmatian immigrants began to plant vines in Northland and near Auckland, where many of the wineries they founded still operate today. Historically, the Hawkes Bay region is almost as significant as Northland and Auckland, being home to both the country's oldest winery, Mission Estate, founded in 1851, and the country's oldest winery building still in operation, Te Mata Estate Winery, which was originally established in 1886.

The first viticulturist employed by the New Zealand government was Dalmatian-born Romeo Bragato, whose tenure ran from 1895 to 1909. His work included the identification of phylloxera and pinpointing suitable regions for grape growing. Bragato is remembered as a man of foresight; unfortunately, when he left the country, growers came up with the spectacularly unsuccessful idea of replacing diseased *Vitis vinifera* grapes with disease-resistant hybrid varieties. The quality of wine suffered as a result, and it was not until the second half of the twentieth century that *Vitis vinifera* varieties were taken seriously again.

Another setback in the development of the wine industry was the emergence of the New Zealand Temperance Society. Formed in 1836, it was particularly influential between 1881 and 1918, when restrictive liquor legislation was in place. However, soldiers returning from the First World War bolstered opposition to the society and it began to lose power before a ban on all alcohol took effect; its influence continued to dwindle during the 1920s and 1930s.

The wine industry was also inhibited by the country's conservative licensing laws. Until 1881, winery sales were illegal and the only outlets for alcohol were hotels. It was only in 1955 that shops specializing in wine were permitted to sell wine and in 1960 that restaurants were finally granted licenses to do the same.

New Zealand's modern wine industry really began with the planting of vines in Marlborough in 1973 by Montana Wines. This was followed in the 1980s by small plantings in other areas such as Wairarapa/Wellington, Canterbury/Waipara, Central Otago and Northland. Since then, the industry has grown quickly, with the number of wineries rising from 97 in 1984 to 334 in 1999. The four largest—Montana, Corbans, Villa Maria and Nobilo Vintners—dominate the industry.

The growth of the New Zealand wine industry during the latter part of the twentieth century was accompanied by an increase in the consumption of quality, bottled wine at the expense of beer, the traditional national tipple, and the advent of more tolerant licensing laws. In the 1960s, 90 percent of all wine sales consisted of fortified wines; by the mid-1990s this figure had dropped to just 8 percent. Fully licensed restaurants are now the norm in New Zealand and since 1990 supermarkets have been permitted to sell wine.

Between 1989 and 1999, New Zealand's wine exports rose from 686,000 gallons (2.6 million l) to 4.4 million gallons (16.6 million l). Three-quarters went to the United Kingdom, but the United States is also becoming an important market.

Climatic variations

Generally, wine-producing regions in the North Island are warmer and wetter than those in the South. The exception to this is the Wairarapa/ Wellington region, which is located at a similar latitude to Nelson and Marlborough at the top of the South Island. Marlborough, Martinborough in the Wairarapa, and Gisborne have the country's most consistent conditions for grape growing, with high levels of sunshine, low rainfall and little risk of frost around vintage time.

Canterbury and Central Otago in the southern half of the South Island have long been considered marginal for grape growing due to the relatively high risk of frost, low heat summation and the consequent lack of consistent annual grape quality and production. But as growers succeed in matching grape varieties with specific sites, some consistency is starting to show. Central Otago is New Zealand's

The choice of grape is crucial for successful winegrowing in the central South Island.

only wine-producing region with a continental climate. This means that frost is a constant threat around vintage time, which can be as late as June. Throughout the rest of the country, the vintage takes place between February and May, depending on the grape variety and region.

Drip irrigation is not only permitted but is essential on many of the country's stonier vineyards, particularly in the drier areas of Marlborough, Canterbury/Waipara, Wairarapa/Wellington, Hawkes Bay and Central Otago.

Vines and viticulture

New Zealand now has a total vineyard area of 20,163 acres (8,160 ha). Three-quarters of the vines are planted in the country's three largest and fastest-growing wine regions, Marlborough, Hawkes Bay and Gisborne.

White grape varieties currently account for around 70 percent of the national vineyard. Chardonnay is the most planted variety followed by sauvignon blanc and müller-thurgau. Over the next few years, plantings of müller-thurgau are expected to decrease while those of pinot gris, riesling, gewürztraminer and sémillon are likely to increase significantly. Red-grape plantings are currently dominated by pinot noir, followed by cabernet sauvignon and merlot; however, plantings of merlot are soon likely to overtake those of cabernet sauvignon. Other grapes grown in relatively small quantities throughout the country include breidecker (a hybrid of seibel and müller-thurgau), chasselas, chenin blanc, flora, palomino, pinot gris, reichensteiner, sylvaner, blauburger, cabernet franc, malbec, pinotage and syrah.

New Zealand soils are naturally highly fertile. As a result, many of the country's vines suffer from high vigor and overcropping, which tend to produce some overtly herbaceous wines. In the late 1980s and throughout the 1990s, close attention was paid to site selection and the country's newest vineyards are planted on less fertile sites, including stony soils that would previously have been considered inappropriate for grape growing.

Vine vigor can still be a problem, but many growers now use it to their advantage to produce high yields and make large quantities of wine. Others have developed techniques to combat associated problems, including judicious pruning, careful choice of trellising systems and the growth of various grass species such as chicory (whose long tap roots draw water away from the grape vines) between vine rows. Some of the country's

Planted mainly on alluvial soils, the vineyards of Hawkes Bay enjoy abundant sunshine.

top-quality chardonnays now come from high-vigor sites. Low-vigor soils needing fertilization can be ministered to with organic fertilizers.

The biggest problems faced by growers are botrytis, powdery mildew and downy mildew, all of which are exacerbated by the generally high humidity. Although powdery and downy mildew can be controlled adequately with environmentally benign elements such as copper and sulfur, to date botrytis is a problem without an organic solution.

The principal challenge facing the wine industry is to develop more environmentally friendly vineyard practices. In working toward this, the Winegrowers of New Zealand society set up the Integrated Wine Production (IWP) scheme in 1995, which provides grape growers with guidelines for managing their vineyards in a sustainable manner, including recommendations for minimizing the use of fungicides and pesticides.

Auckland

Vineyard workers prune the vines at Waiheke Vineyards on Waiheke Island.

Auckland is the name of New Zealand's largest city and its most diverse wine-producing region. The latter incorporates the subregions of Northland and Matakana in the north; the far-flung Great Barrier Island; and Greater Auckland, Kumeu/ Huapai, Henderson and Waiheke Island near the city of Auckland. Currently, Auckland has 793 acres (321 ha) of grape vines—a figure that is likely to increase by about 20 percent in the next few years—and constitutes around 4 percent of the national vineyard. There are about 80 wineries here—the highest number for a single region.

With significantly warmer mesoclimates than many other New Zealand wine regions, some of Auckland's subregions have proven to be extremely well suited to the late-ripening cabernet sauvignon grape. However, the country's most widely planted grape variety is chardonnay, with 24 percent of the total vineyard area, followed by cabernet sauvignon on 18 percent and merlot on 15 percent. Plantings of chardonnay, merlot, pinot noir, sauvignon blanc and pinot gris are all expected to increase in the next few years.

Northland is a sparsely populated, narrow, string-bean-shaped landmass that extends 162 miles (260 km) north of Auckland city. The subregion's wineries are generally small, and most concentrate on red wine production, mainly cabernet-sauvignon- and merlot-dominated blends plus a little pinotage

and shiraz. Chardonnay, gewürztraminer, müller-thurgau and sémillon are among the whites made in small quantities. There is a vast array of soil types, ranging from porous volcanic soils to friable clay, with varying degrees of permeability: in some areas, the clay is free-draining with an alluvial base; in others, underlying rock strata inhibit drainage. Site selection is therefore critical. The grape ripening season is long and hot, with high sunshine hours and little risk of frost or hail. The high humidity and annual rainfall—about 46.8 inches (1,200 mm)—are combated with carefully chosen vine trellising systems and judicious spraying.

Vines are planted as far north as Ninety Mile Beach, where the country's most northerly winery, Okahu Estate, produces high-quality reds, including shiraz- and cabernet-sauvignon-dominated blends, as well as a range of others made from pinotage, chambourcin and merlot. Farther south, there are several vineyards and wineries around Kerikeri, a popular holiday destination, and near Whangarei, the country's most northerly city.

In the rolling green countryside to the south, a group of wineries clustered around the coastal town of Matakana produces small amounts of top-quality red wine. Matakana has a cool maritime climate with the associated trappings of high humidity and annual rainfall—about 46.8 inches (1,200 mm). Fortunately for growers, most of the rain tends to fall during the winter months of July to September. In summer, the prevailing wind is a warm, wet northeasterly, which creates difficulties for thin-skinned grape varieties. Soils vary, but are generally clay loams with a limestone or sandy base.

Matakana's first wines were high-priced reds made in the late 1980s at the Antipodean winery by Jim and Petar Vuletic. Today, the Antipodean is owned and operated by Michelle Chignell-Vuletic, Petar's wife, who continues to make small quantities of quality cabernet-based wines. Shortly after the establishment of the Antipodean, the Heron's Flight winery was founded by David Hoskins and Mary Evans, whose Cabernet Sauvignon, which hit the shelves in 1991, confirmed the region's ability to ripen this grape consistently. Several new wineries opened here in the late 1990s, most of them small and concentrating on chardonnay, pinot gris, riesling and cabernet-based reds.

Stainless-steel fermentation tanks tower over the vines at the House of Nobilo in Kumeu.

From the coast at Matakana, one can look out across the Hauraki Gulf to the Coromandel Peninsula and several islands, including, on a clear day, Great Barrier Island, nearly 44 miles (70 km) away. With high rainfall and humidity, it is home to just one operational vineyard, John Mellars of Great Barrier Island, which yields only small quantities of cabernet sauvignon. However, there are several small vineyards under development here and many of their owners believe that Great Barrier has similar viticultural potential to acclaimed Waiheke Island. Unlike Waiheke, however, Great Barrier is not protected by the Coromandel Peninsula and rainfall is higher.

The subregions around the city of Auckland—Greater Auckland, Kumeu/Huapai and Henderson—are not renowned for good viticultural conditions. Rainfall is high—51 inches (1,300 mm) at Kumeu and 54.6 inches (1,400 mm) at Henderson. Soils vary from clay to loam, overlying deep sandstone-based subsoils; poor drainage in some of the clay soils can compound the high rainfall and humidity. Partly as a result of these conditions, large quantities of fruit have to be sourced from Hawkes Bay, Gisborne, Marlborough and Canterbury. Yet this is the capital of winemaking in New Zealand, and the four largest producers—Montana, Corbans, Villa Maria and House of Nobilo—all have their head offices in Auckland city.

Dalmatian immigrants were among the first to plant vines here and a roll call of winery owners still turns up a proliferation of Dalmatian names such as Babich, Brajkovich, Fredatovich, Jelich and Yelas. The Yelas family owns Pleasant Valley Wines in Henderson, the Auckland area's oldest winery and the oldest in the country that still belongs to the family that founded it.

The Greater Auckland subregion includes the recently developed Clevedon area, to the south of the city. Winemaking here was pioneered by the likes of Ken and Diane Mason, who, in 1991, planted their 5-acre (2-ha) Arahura vineyard with cabernet grapes. There are now 12 vineyards, most of which are around 5 acres (2 ha) in size. The soil consists of fertile topsoil on heavy clay loam. Weather conditions can be trying late in the ripening season with high humidity and rainfall, and a lack of sunshine immediately prior to the vintage. Stringent pruning and planting on north-facing slopes are necessary. Clevedon is planted mainly with red grape varieties such as cabernet sauvignon, malbec, merlot and a handful of Italian grape varieties including sangiovese and nebbiolo.

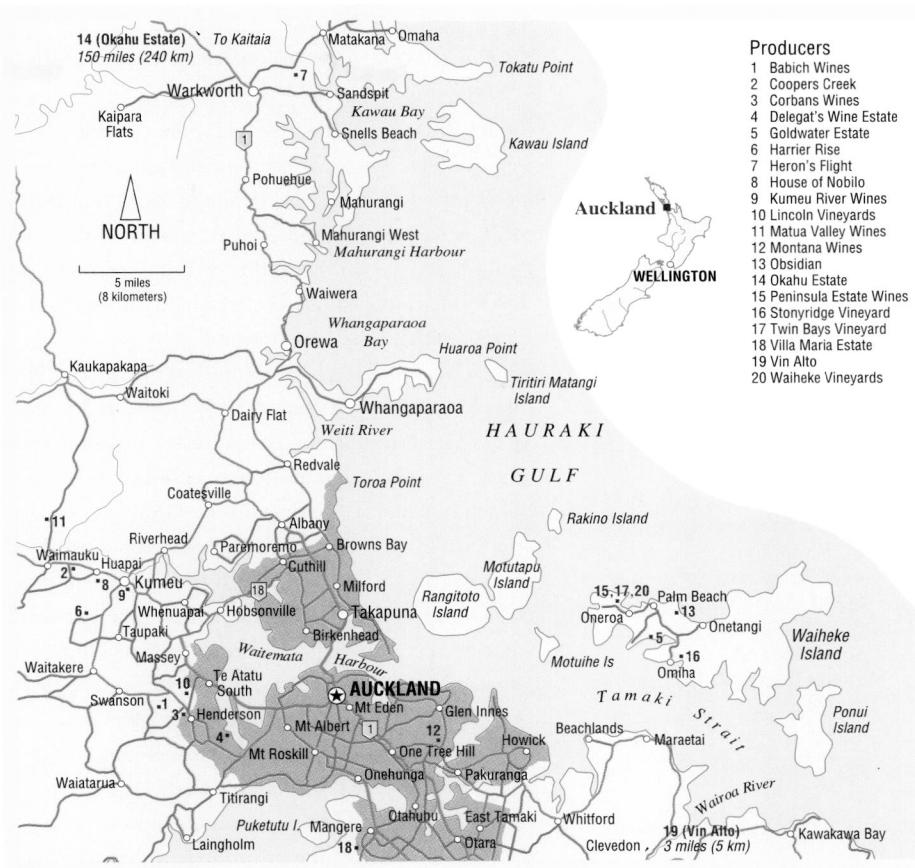

Producers
1 Babich Wines
2 Coopers Creek
3 Corbans Wines
4 Delegat's Wine Estate
5 Goldwater Estate
6 Harrier Rise
7 Heron's Flight
8 House of Nobilo
9 Kumeu River Wines
10 Lincoln Vineyards
11 Matua Valley Wines
12 Montana Wines
13 Obsidian
14 Okahu Estate
15 Peninsula Estate Wines
16 Stonyridge Vineyard
17 Twin Bays Vineyard
18 Villa Maria Estate
19 Vin Alto
20 Waiheke Vineyards

Waiheke Island is situated in the Hauraki Gulf, about half-an-hour's boat journey from Auckland city. This was once an alternative-lifestyler's paradise, and its population rose significantly in the late twentieth century. Winemaking began in the late 1970s when Kim and Jeanette Goldwater of Goldwater Estate planted their first vines at Putiki Bay. After the Goldwaters came winemaker Stephen White, who started Stonyridge Vineyard at Onetangi. There are now about 15 wineries on the island, with several more under development.

Most of Waiheke's winemakers concentrate on cabernet sauvignon, cabernet franc, malbec, merlot and chardonnay. Some are trialing pinot noir, sangiovese and other Italian varieties. Waiheke's strength is its hot, dry climate. Although the island's position in the Hauraki Gulf means that it is exposed, the nearby Coromandel Peninsula shields it from the worst of the weather. It has 30 percent less rainfall than Auckland, less humidity and more sunshine, and its grapes ripen about a week earlier. The biggest problem is occasional severe storms, which have been known to wipe out much of the crop. The quantities of wine made are tiny, even on a New Zealand scale, but the cabernet sauvignon and merlot are among the country's best and most reliable in terms of consistent ripeness.

Matakana Estate is one of several wineries set up recently in the Matakana subregion.

REGIONAL DOZEN

QUALITY WINES

Goldwater Esslin Merlot
Goldwater Estate Cabernet
 Sauvignon/Merlot
Kumeu River Maté's
 Chardonnay
Stonyridge Larose Cabernet
Villa Maria Reserve Barrique
 Fermented Chardonnay
Vina Alta Retico Amarone-
 style Cabernet Franc,
 Merlot UC
Waiheke Vineyards Te Motu

BEST VALUE WINES

Collards Chenin Blanc
Kumeu Brajkovich Cabernet
 Franc
Kumeu Brajkovich Signature
 Series Chardonnay
Kumeu Brajkovich Signature
 Series Merlot
Nobilo Huapai Valley
 Pinotage

The Babich vineyard in Greater Auckland.

BABICH WINES

Established 1916 *Owners* Babich family *Production* NA
Vineyard area 297 acres (120 ha)

Babich was established by Croatian gumdigger
Josip Babich, who has been memorialized by the
company's Patriarch series. The modern reputation
of Babich rests on good-quality, sharply priced
domestic wines. In the 1990s, it began to focus on
developing increasingly higher-quality wines with a
more sophisticated international style for export.
Since then, all Babich wines have tended steadily
toward more subtle characters better suited to consuming with food than as a stand-alone beverages.

Beyond the original 49-acre (20-ha) vineyard,
Babich has major holdings in the Gimblett Road
and Fernhill areas of Hawkes Bay, with substantial
new plantings in Marlborough to supplement contract supplies there. The top-of-the-range Patriarch
Chardonnay and Cabernet Sauvignon are big,
powerful wines produced only in exceptional years.
Irongate Chardonnay and Cabernet Merlot are
consistently full flavored, but more elegantly styled
and structured for bottle aging. The Mara Estate
range, developed for restaurants, produces some of
the country's best value in subtle fruit, underplayed
winemaking and finesse, and has an outstanding
Syrah to its credit. A "Winemakers" series pitched
between this and Irongate is stylish and well made.
Babich's main-line Marlborough Sauvignon Blanc
and Pinot Gris, Gisborne Unwooded Chardonnay
and Hawkes Bay Chenin Blanc provide some of
New Zealand's best-value varietals.

COOPERS CREEK

Established 1980 *Owners* Andrew and Cindy Hendry,
and shareholders *Production* 50,400 cases
Vineyard area 42 acres (17 ha)

Founded by Andrew Hendry
and Oregon winemaker Randy
Weaver, Coopers took off in
the late 1980s with the arrival
of winemaker Kim Crawford.
Before departing for his own
label in the late 1990s, Crawford
had gathered medals, trophies
and accolades throughout the
English-speaking world for the
string of brilliantly executed,
consumer friendly, fruit-driven
wines made during his tenure.
Coopers' savvy range of brands
has covered virtually every niche
market available with well-priced,

full-flavored, stylishly made wines from Auckland,
Gisborne, Hawkes Bay and Marlborough fruit.
Main-line strength lies in a range of regionally
specific chardonnays, Marlborough sauvignon
blancs and a couple of Hawkes Bay's best rieslings
(basic and reserve) grown on Jim Scotland's exceptionally cool, coastal vineyard. Top wines include
the ripe, toasty, sappy Swamp Reserve Chardonnay
as well as the Reserve Merlot, Huapai Cabernet
Merlot, Merlot/Cabernet Franc and the rich, sappy
100 percent Cabernet Franc. Recently, the use of
clever marketing and frivolous labeling on the
Fat Cat Chardonnay (14 percent alcohol, obvious
oak, low acid) and Sourpuss Sémillon (ripe, crisply
tart, varietally correct) have spun silk out of sows'
ears by tapping into an unsophisticated youth
market adrift in alcoholic sodas. In 1998, the
winery was rocked by a mislabeling scandal
which brought current winemaker Simon Nunns
onto the scene and resulted in one of New
Zealand's tightest auditing systems.

CORBANS WINES

Established 1902 *Owners* Publicly listed shareholders
Production 1,570,000 cases *Vineyard area* 1,483 acres
(600 ha)

In 1902, Lebanese immigrant Assid Corban planted
4 acres (1.5 ha) with syrah, cabernet sauvignon
and chasselas. His company has since grown into
New Zealand's second-largest winery, and has a
strong history of innovation and leadership. Early
achievements included several New Zealand firsts:
cultured yeasts (1949), stainless steel tanks (1958),
temperature-controlled fermentation (1962), and
charmat-processed sparkling wine (1962).

Corbans is a brand-driven company with a
broad range of still and sparking wines at virtually
every price and quality level. In 1968, it established a second winery at Gisborne, followed by
wineries in Hawkes Bay (1987) and Marlborough
(1993). Regionally specific brands were developed
in association with these wineries (respectively,
Huntaway and Longridge, and Stoneleigh—see
below), broadening Corbans' multitiered, cross-
regional parent brand. Above the bulk level,
Corbans' wines start with the inexpensive, competent White Label varietals, followed by a more
regionally distinct Estate Range, and, when vintage
quality merits, the premium Private Bin and ultra-
premium Cottage Block ranges. Strengths in
méthode traditionnelle wines include the mid-
priced Verdi and the pricier Amadeus, both pinot
noir and chardonnay based.

The future will see Corbans shift away from cheap bulk wine and a focus on the domestic market toward greatly expanded exports driven by higher quality wines and an increasing emphasis on single-vineyard and regional characteristics.

DELEGAT'S WINE ESTATE
Established 1947 *Owners* Jim and Rosemari Delegat
Production NA *Vineyard area* NA

Delegat's has focused primarily on chardonnay, sauvignon blanc, merlot and cabernet sauvignon, drawing on Hawkes Bay and Marlborough fruit for their basic and reserve range of wines. A separate company was developed for their highly successful Marlborough brand, Oyster Bay (see p. 615). In hot years, the Hawkes Bay Reserve range—Cabernet/Merlot, Merlot and Cabernet Sauvignon—can be varietally correct, full of big black-fruit and licorice flavors, and richly textured, and displays tight structures. The Hawkes Bay Chardonnay Reserve tends to be big and oaky, with strong malo-influenced buttery characters. All are relatively good value.

GOLDWATER ESTATE
Established 1978 *Owners* Kim and Jeanette Goldwater
Production 22,320 cases *Vineyard area* 35 acres (14 ha)

Visionaries, the Goldwaters opened up Waiheke to winemaking more than 20 years ago, proving that the region could produce top-quality bordeaux blends. On the advice of viticulturist Richard Smart, the original home vineyard now contains equal parts cabernet sauvignon and merlot, with some cabernet franc. Vine maturity has helped produce increasingly spectacular results in the 1990s. The Esslin Merlot is packed with spicy oak and meaty, savory varietal characters, and shows tremendous length and well-integrated tannins for long-term aging. The Cabernet/Merlot blend is seamless, with grippy tannins, coffee, chocolate and tobacco characters needing five to seven years to mellow. The Zell Vineyard Chardonnay, Waiheke's first white, is creamy textured, finely balanced and suave compared to their fruitier, more powerful Marlborough Roseland. Both wines are French-oak fermented and lees aged. Goldwater Dog Point Sauvignon Blanc (a marriage of herbs, gooseberries, passionfruit, dense textures and taught structure) is classic Marlborough.

HARRIER RISE
Established 1986 *Owner* Tim Harris *Production* 3,960 cases *Vineyard area* 12.3 acres (5 ha)

Harrier Rise's closely planted cabernet sauvignon, cabernet franc and merlot are vinified using traditional bordeaux practices (that's to say, extended post-fermentation maceration), resulting in lighter, finer, generally more subtle and savory blends designed for long-term cellaring. Regular output includes pure cabernet franc and merlot bottlings under the Harrier Rise label, with the Uppercase brand kept for less serious, fruit-forward, easy drinking styles. In exceptional years, Reserve Bigney Coigne Merlot is produced.

The Goldwater Estate was the first vineyard to be planted on Waiheke Island, in 1970.

Most producers use large stainless-steel fermentation tanks for whites and rosés.

Vines and grapes depicted in stained glass at the House of Nobilo winery, Huapai.

HERON'S FLIGHT

Established 1988 *Owners* David Hoskins and Mary Evans
Production 2,160 cases *Vineyard area* 11.1 acres (4.5 ha)

This quirky winery makes distinctive wines and is honest enough to reduce prices on wines from weaker vintages. The home vineyard was planted mostly with cabernet and merlot, with smaller portions of chardonnay, sangiovese and montepulciano (later identified as brunello). The sangiovese was later pulled up. The La Cerise Merlot/Cabernet blend is a bright, easy-drinking, café quaffer; the Montepulciano is richer and meatier. Both show impressive Italianate style colored by bitter red-cherry characters.

HOUSE OF NOBILO

Established 1943 *Owners* Nobilo family, BRL Hardy and other shareholders *Production* 350,000 cases
Vineyard area 79 acres (32 ha)

One of several Dalmatian pioneers, Nobilo gained a reputation for quality reds in the 1960s and 1970s, later shifting to bulk whites, then refocusing on a wide range of varietals from the mid-1980s. An alliance with Australia's Hardys and the recent purchase of quality-defined Selak's (see p. 616) have further strengthened Nobilo's position as New Zealand's fourth-largest winery.

Innovation and risk-taking are the hallmark of this company—witness its transformation of müller-thurgau-based White Cloud into an international brand, the stylishly packaged, mid-priced Icon series, and the bargain varietals Fernleaf series. The Huapai winery uses fruit from Hawkes Bay (Smith Dartmoor), Gisborne (Dixons, Tietjen), and Marlborough (Matador, Drylands) for its best vineyard-designated bottlings. Its strongest suits include the Grand Reserve Chardonnay, a cross-regional blend (made only when merited), and the Icon range's Gewürztraminer and Riesling. The everyday varietal range—especially the Pinotage—are always well made and often excellent value.

KUMEU RIVER WINES

Established 1944 *Owners* Melba Brajkovich and family
Production 30,240 cases *Vineyard area* 62 acres (25 ha)

Kumeu River is one of New Zealand's finest small wineries. Winemaker Michael Brajkovich remains committed to Kumeu soil long after most other Auckland wineries have shifted to other regions: his Maté's Vineyard is a state-of-the-art replant of the original estate, his Merlot is from a nearby 25-year-old vineyard, and his Kumeu Chardonnay draws from five Kumeu sites. In 1986, he adopted indigenous yeast fermentation to amplify *terroir* and because he "didn't want his wine identified by other winemakers' yeast strains."

All Kumeu River chardonnays are 100 percent whole bunch pressed, wild yeast, barrel and malolactic fermented, then lees and oak aged. They share seamless textures, fine balance and buttery flavors. Listed four times in *Wine Spectator*'s Top 100, Kumeu Chardonnay pioneered this style; it is now widely emulated. The basic "lightly wooded" Brajkovich signature series is aged in four-year-old French oak; the Kumeu River (mendoza clone) shows a stronger new-oak influence than the subdued, nutty, long-lived Dijon clone 95 Maté's Vineyard. A stint at Bordeaux's Château Magdelaine resulted in Brajkovich's early commitment to merlot and cabernet franc—these grapes, plus malbec, make up the winery's top red, Melba. Recent pinot noir and pinot gris releases suggest a promising future with these varietals.

The main Huapai vineyard of the country's fourth-largest winery, House of Nobilo.

LINCOLN VINEYARDS LTD

Established 1937 *Owners* Fredatovich family
Production 18,000 cases *Vineyard area* 2.5 acres (1 ha)

This old Auckland winery has plodded along
with sound and reasonably priced, but generally
uninspiring varietals made with fruit from
Gisborne and Hawkes Bay as well as the home
estate. A recent rebranding and repositioning
suggests the potential to lift the company out of
the doldrums. Lincoln's strength lies in the mid-
priced Heritage range, which includes a zingy,
herbaceous Marlborough Sauvignon Blanc and
a butterscotch-and-toast Gisborne Chardonnay.
Neither is subtle, but both give the mouth a good
ride for the money. The misnamed, low-priced
Winemaker's Reserve Merlot represented
outstanding value in its first two vintages.

MATUA VALLEY WINES

Established 1973 *Owners* Ross and Bill Spence, Margan
family and Mark Roberston *Production* 155,000 cases
Vineyard area 494 acres (200 ha)

In 1971, fresh from wine studies at California's
Fresno State University, Ross Spence chased down
New Zealand's two existing sauvignon blanc vines
in Corbans' trial block vineyard at Kumeu. Using
these, he and brother Bill planted the country's first
sauvignon vineyard. By 1974, the seeds of a revolution had been bottled, and New Zealand sauvignon
blanc was born. Matua hasn't stopped innovating
since. Other firsts to their credit include commercial
quantities of pinot gris and unwooded chardonnay,
with more recent forays into grenache and malbec.
All are well made, varietally true and good value.

Beyond the 54-acre (22-ha) estate vineyard,
the company draws heavily on fruit from Gisborne
(Judd Estate) and Hawkes Bay (Smith Dartmoor,
Matheson). Matua's stand-alone Marlborough
operation, Shingle Peak (see p. 616), is made at the
Rapaura Vintners contract winemaking facility, of
which it is part owner. Both the top-label Ararimu
Chardonnay and Cabernet Merlot are produced
only in exceptional years and are stylish, flavor-
filled, concentrated and smooth. The Judd Estate
Chardonnay is a classic, big-fruited Gisborne-style
wine and the Smith Dartmour red range can be
excellent value in ripe years. The new Innovator
series provides an outlet for ongoing experiments
with small-batch production, and the new Settlers
Series covers the cheap, easy-drinking end of the
market. Matua's Unwooded Chardonnay pioneered
this style in New Zealand and remains one of the
best, vibrantly pure, mid-priced examples available.

MONTANA WINES

Established 1944 *Owners*
Corporate Investments Limited
Production 2.25 million cases
Vineyard area 3,460-plus acres
(1,400-plus ha)

Founded by Croatian Ivan
Yukich, Montana is New
Zealand's largest winery
and its most sophisticated
international brand. After
its Marlborough Sauvignon
Blanc won London's
International Wine Challenge White Wine of the
Year award in 1989, Marlborough, sauvignon and
Montana became synonymous. No other single
event or winery has done as much to establish
New Zealand wine internationally.

The company takes its name from the Croatian
word for mountain. In the US, however, it has been
forced to rebrand as Brancott Estate (see p. 609)
to avoid confusion with the state of the same name
and San Francisco's famous football star, Joe.

Montana first expanded to Mangatangi in
Waikato, then Gisborne in 1972; it subsequently
planted the first vines in Marlborough in 1973
and absorbed New Zealand Penfold's in 1985. Key
influences have been associations with Bordeaux
negoçiants Cordier and Champagne house Duetz.
Both traded traditional stylistic refinement for experience with sun-filled, high-acid New Zealand fruit.

Montana's branding strength lies above its bulk
wines, starting with the Montana range, which is
regionally and varietally typical, and moving up
through the stylish Saints, Montana Reserve and
Church Road ranges, and the "letter-designated"
single-vineyard Estate wines. All deliver focused
fruit flavors, well-balanced and refined textures, and
crisp acids, using each region's varietal strengths—
Marlborough's chardonnay, riesling, pinot noir and
sauvignon blanc; Gisborne's chardonnay, gewürztraminer and sémillon; and Hawkes Bay's cabernet
sauvignon, chardonnay, merlot and pinotage.

The Duetz influence has led to a shift away from
fruit-driven *méthode traditionnelle* toward savory
complexity and elegance. The sparkling wines are
now made primarily from traditional champagne
grapes, with the bargain-priced Lindauer, which includes chenin blanc, and the rich, biscuity, Lindauer
Reserve (pinot noir and chardonnay) among the
country's best-value bubblies. Farther up the scale,
the Duetz Marlborough Cuvée and Blanc de Blancs
are among New Zealand's most elegant sparklers.

*Oak barrels stand by fermentation tanks,
ready for filling, at Kumeu River Wines.*

*Kumeu River has gained international
renown for its Kumeu Chardonnay.*

An elegant terrace overlooks the estate at Stonyridge Vineyard on Waiheke Island.

OBSIDIAN

Established 1993 *Owners* Andrew Hendry, Lindsay Spilman and Kim Crawford *Production* 1,584 cases *Vineyard area* 22 acres (9 ha)

This Waiheke venture was born out of Coopers Creek and set up by owner Andrew Hendry and former winemaker Kim Crawford in order to tap into the Waiheke "goldrush." Wine is sold *en primeur* with unsold residue released later at a higher price. The Cabernet/Merlot blend has yet to prove itself, but expectations are high.

OKAHU ESTATE

Established 1988 *Owner* Monty Knight *Production* 2,880 cases *Vineyard area* 5.4 acres (2.2 ha)

New Zealand's most northerly winery has earned its stripes for daring. Flagship wine Kaz Shiraz, a big, concentrated, peppery syrah, has performed consistently since the mid-1990s, and the Kaz Sémillon is full of mealy, earthy, aromatic complexity with typical waxy textures. Both are consistently among the country's best examples of these varietals. In lesser years, they are declassified as Okahu and usually represent excellent value. The Okahu portfolio also includes a dozen interesting, good-quality varietals, most notably an outstanding Reserve Pinotage packed full of burgundian aromas and textures.

PENINSULA ESTATE WINES

Established 1986 *Owner* Doug Hamilton *Production* 1,512 cases *Vineyard area* 11 acres (4.5 ha)

This stunning Waiheke vineyard (70 percent cabernet sauvignon, 20 percent merlot, 6 percent cabernet franc and 4 percent malbec) is situated on the harbor. Somewhat in the shadows of Goldwater and Stonyridge, its main cabernet blend tends to have less ripe and leafier, more aromatic qualities and a coarser tannic structure than its stellar neighbors. Consequently, the wines take a few more years to integrate. Declassified wine is used for the secondary Oneroa Bay label.

STONYRIDGE VINEYARD

Established 1982 *Owner* Stephen White *Production* 1,296 cases *Vineyard area* 34 acres (13.6 ha)

Stephen White's rapier-witted newsletter is as smart as the wine he makes. His Waiheke flagship, Larose

Stonyridge is the source of New Zealand's most expensive red wine, Larose Cabernet.

Cabernet, is New Zealand's most expensive wine and, arguably, its best bordeaux-style red. A blend of cabernet sauvignon, merlot, cabernet franc, malbec and petite syrah, it consistently sells out *en primeur*, leaving a long list of customers waiting for a sniff of the next vintage. For those lucky enough to purchase, White insists (tongue half in cheek) that his wine is only for drinking and has threatened to put out a Mafia contract on anyone caught selling bottles at auction—a reasonable concession given White's claim that his wines "will cure most illnesses and make the drinker more attractive to the opposite sex."

The key to Stonyridge Larose is intensive vineyard management following organic principles, low cropping (under 1.3 tons per acre [23 hl per ha]) and traditional winemaking practices stemming from White's time at Château Palmer in Bordeaux. Intense and savory, Larose is defined by condensed textures and multileveled flavors and is stacked full of fine-grained tannins. It ages superbly: the legendary 1987, tasted a decade later, was still relatively young, and had years of life ahead. Declassified Larose combined with fruit from Fenton Vineyard (now Twin Bays) makes up a secondary range, the Airfield label, a more forward style that is usually very good in its own right. New estate plantings will replace Fenton content in time. The home vineyard also produces a limited-quantity Syrah, and a malbec-dominated blend is in the works.

TWIN BAYS VINEYARD

Established 1989 *Owners* Barry and Meg Fenton *Production* 468 cases *Vineyard area* 5 acres (2 ha)

Twin Bays Vineyard's cabernet sauvignon, merlot, and cabernet franc were formerly used in both Stonyridge's Airfield label and early versions of Twin Bays' own wine. Both were made by Stephen White and were stylistically similar. In the mid-1990s, Kim Crawford introduced a softer, fruitier style of winemaking, but recently John Hancock from Trinity Hill has returned to a bigger, gruntier, grippier approach. In difficult Waiheke vintages, Twin Bays is completely declassified and sold locally as The Red.

VILLA MARIA ESTATE

Established 1961 *Owner* George Fistonich *Production* 298,800 cases *Vineyard area* 185 acres (75 ha)

Andrew Fistonich, a Dalmatian immigrant, established Mountain Vineyards outside Auckland in the late 1940s. From that seed, his son George grew Villa Maria into the country's third-largest wine producer, which now includes a new winery in Marlborough and two separate wineries in Hawkes Bay: Esk Valley and Vidal's (see pp. 597 and 602). More recently, Villa Maria transformed itself into an exclusive producer of premium wines, which dominated the New Zealand wine show circuit during the late 1990s. The key to their success lies in close attention to viticulture under Steve Smith's inspired direction. The estate's near-perfect fruit has made the work of a string of top-flight winemakers (Elise Montgomery, Rod McDonald, Gordon Russell and, currently, Michelle Richardson) relatively easy.

Villa remains pragmatic about region-specific wines, opting to blend across regions to maintain brand- or range-style consistency. The solid Private Bin varietal ranges (strong in riesling and sauvignon blanc) have steadily backed away from an obvious fruit-driven style as viticulture has improved, opting for an uncluttered, more elegant, nervier style under Richardson's care. The mid-range Cellar Selection Sauvignon Blanc, Chardonnay and Riesling are generally excellent, with very pure varietal expressions and often a distinctive regional flair. The top-flight Reserve range, made only in good years, consistently produces two of New Zealand's best sauvignon blancs: the zesty, unwooded, leafy, passionfruit-laden Clifford Bay, and the deeper, darker, sweatier, more savory Wairau Valley, which is lightly kissed with oak. Both the Riesling and Gewürztraminer in this range combine power and intensity with elegant restraint; so too the blend of cabernet, merlot, malbec and franc, with its savory, cigar-box

overtones and fine-grained tannins. Finally, the Noble Riesling's varietal character is never overshadowed by botrytis, and consistently shows a multilayered, well-structured palate.

VIN ALTO

Established 1996 *Owners* Margaret and Enzo Bettio
Production 1,440 cases *Vineyard area* 49 acres (20 ha)

This quirky, against-all-odds winery was established recently by Italian goods importer Enzo Bettio to make Amarone and *ripasso*-style wines. The Italian producer Masi has offered assistance in adapting dried-grape techniques to a region that is considerably more humid than most of Italy. Grapes used so far include syrah, cabernet franc and a number of Italian varieties. Early results have been promising.

WAIHEKE VINEYARDS

Established 1988 *Owners* Paul Dunleavy and
Terry Dunleavy MBE *Production* 1,584 cases
Vineyard area 12.3 acres (5 ha)

Situated on a rise overlooking the Stonyridge, Miro and Obsidian vineyards, Waiheke Vineyards is the brainchild of retired New Zealand Wine Institute CEO Terry Dunleavy. Its top wine, Te Motu (Maori for "the island"), is a long-lived Cabernet/Merlot full of black-fruit, licorice and olive aromas, and with smooth textures and good length. A second, more sharply priced wine, Dunleavy, incorporates declassified Te Motu and can be a bargain in hot, large-production years. Currently, winemaking is supervised by Mark Robertson at Matua Valley, but a winery is planned.

*Visitors to Matakana Estate in Northland
are welcomed with open arms.*

*Waiheke Vineyards, on Waiheke Island
produces fine cabernet blends.*

Waikato/Bay of Plenty

Situated a short distance south of the city of Auckland, the neighboring districts of Waikato and Bay of Plenty make up New Zealand's smallest wine region. It includes just 13 widely scattered wineries and only 247 acres (100 ha) of vineyards—barely 1 percent of the national total. The majority of the wineries are very small, even by New Zealand standards, although there are some larger establishments which source their grapes from farther afield. The region is divided into four subregions: Te Kauwhata, Hamilton, the Bay of Plenty and the Mangatawhiri Valley.

Wine was first made in Waikato around the turn of the twentieth century at the Te Kauwhata

Research Station by visiting viticulturist Romeo Bragato. He left in 1909, but, following a hiatus in the station's winemaking, J. C. Woodfin expanded Te Kauwhata's vineyards in the late 1920s. In the 1930s and 1940s, the station was used to make wine for American troops based in New Zealand, after which it was upgraded and used has a government research station. In the 1980s, it was bought by two of the station's officers, Tom van Dam and Dr Rainer Eschenbach, who incorporated it in their winery, Rongopai.

Another Waikato winemaking pioneer was the Chinese immigrant Joe Ah-Chan who started Totara Vineyards at Thames on the Coromandel Peninsula in the 1920s. Totara was originally named Goldleaf Vineyards, but the name was changed in the 1950s by a later owner, Stanley Chan (no relation to Joe Ah-Chan).

The Te Kauwhata area has relatively high levels of sunshine and few frosts, but is very humid and wet—47–51 inches (1,200–1,300 mm) of rain fall each year. Many of the wineries use canopy management and vineyard spraying programs to counter the damp conditions; others turn the climate to their advantage to produce some of New Zealand's finest botrytized dessert wines. Te Kauwhata is renowned for its heavy clay loams, which appear to favor chardonnay more than any other grape variety.

The city of Hamilton serves a farming community and a fast-growing urban population. There are only a few vineyards around the city; all are small and situated on heavy clay-loam soils best suited to chardonnay and, some say, pinot noir. Although there is plenty of sunshine, rainfall levels are similar to those in Te Kauwhata and high humidity results in regular fogs.

The aptly named Bay of Plenty region has rich, fertile soils and is best known for its kiwi-fruit production. It experiences high levels of sunshine but also high levels of rainfall (33 inches [850 mm] annually) and humidity, particularly during the all-important ripening cycle in February and March. As a result of these less-than-ideal viticultural conditions, wine production has not been pursued vigorously here. Those who have tried believe that the conditions are at least better than those in the Auckland region, but nowhere near

Bottom: *Mills Reef has a vineyard, but most of its fruit comes from Hawkes Bay growers.*

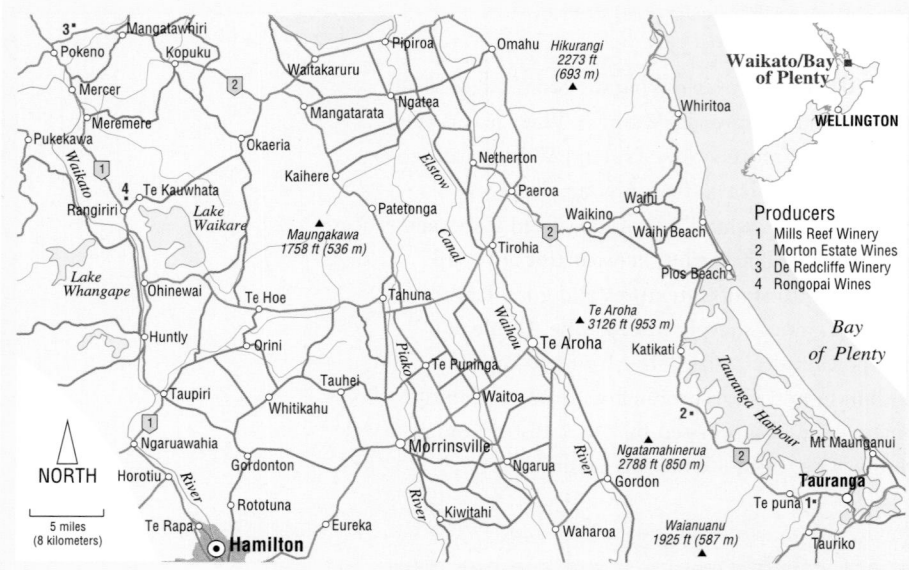

Producers
1 Mills Reef Winery
2 Morton Estate Wines
3 De Redcliffe Winery
4 Rongopai Wines

as ideal as those in Gisborne, Hawkes Bay and Marlborough—from where the Bay of Plenty's wineries source most of their grapes.

The most northerly subregion in the Bay of Plenty is the Mangatawhiri Valley, about one hour's drive south of Auckland. This secluded, fertile valley is home to just one winery, De Redcliffe. It obtains most of its grapes from Hawkes Bay and Marlborough, but is growing increasing quantities of good-quality pinot noir.

The most planted grape variety in the Waikato/ Bay of Plenty region is chardonnay (15 percent), followed by cabernet sauvignon (13 percent) and sauvignon blanc (11 percent). Other varieties include, in significantly smaller amounts, breidecker, chenin blanc, gewürztraminer, various muscats, palamino, riesling, sylvaner, blauberger, merlot and pinot noir. Steady growth is expected over the next few years, most of which will be the result of increased plantings of cabernet sauvignon, chardonnay, sauvignon blanc and malbec.

MILLS REEF WINERY
Established 1989 *Owners* Preston family *Production* 30,960 cases *Vineyard area* 40 acres (16 ha)

Former kiwi-fruit winemaker Paddy Preston switched to grapes and has built a credible range

of wines. Most of the fruit now comes from the family's own vineyards located on Mere Road in Hawkes Bay. The Moffatt Road range started out as a selection of cheap and cheerful, relatively simple, commercial varietals and has steadily improved in quality. The Reserve range shows strength in its Chardonnay, Cabernet Sauvignon, Merlot and Cabernet/Merlot, while the flagship Elspeth series, which has the same varietal mix but is produced only in top years, shows more intensity and greater longevity. The vintaged Méthode Traditionnelle (a chardonnay-dominated pinot noir blend) has steadily refined a more austere, complex style over the years and is among the best from Hawkes Bay vineyards.

MORTON ESTATE WINES
Established 1982 *Owner* John Coney *Production* 76,320 cases *Vineyard area* 835 acres (338 ha)

A medium-sized establishment, Morton Estate is renowned for consistent quality across a broad range of distinctive Marlborough and Hawkes Bay varietals, and the recent arrival of winemaker Evan Ward (former Corbans chief, Hawkes Bay winemaker, and sparkling-wine specialist) has enhanced its already solid reputation for sparkling wines. New vineyard plantings and a new

Morton Estate has gained a reputation as an outstanding producer of sparkling wines.

REGIONAL BEST
Rongopai Winemakers Reserve Botrytised Chardonnay
Rongopai Winemakers Reserve Botrytised Riesling

Plantings in the De Redcliffe vineyards have shifted away from red varieties to whites.

Rongopai Wines occupies the buildings of the historic Te Kauwhata research center.

winemaking facility in Hawkes Bay have set the stage for massive export expansion.

At the bottom of the three-tier output, the Mill Road range offers generally good quality and value, the Unwooded Chardonnay being its star. The mainstay White Label has a Marlborough range including a crisply herbaceous Sauvignon Blanc, sharply priced Pinot Noir (smooth, with hints of smoky bacon and red fruits) and a classy, tightly structured Chardonnay. The Hawkes Bay range includes a Syrah (all blackberries, vanilla and pepper, with fine-grained tannins) and a rich, flowery, vanilla-and-oak-filled Chardonnay. In the top-end Black Label range, a creamy, deeply viscous, meltaway Chardonnay is consistently among the country's finest, and the Merlot is the pick of the reds.

Morton's fine *méthode champenoise* range consists of a chardonnay-dominated Recently Disgorged; a classy, complex Black Label (dominated by meunier but also incorporating chardonnay and pinot noir) released five years after vintage; as well as a good-value, finely balanced NV Brut.

DE REDCLIFFE WINERY
Established 1976 *Owner* Otaka Holdings *Production* 43,200 cases *Vineyard area* 62 acres (25 ha)

Originally established as red wine specialist, De Redcliffe has gone through a number of owners and directional changes over time. Currently, its strengths lie in white wines, particularly sémillon, although the home vineyard also produces a stylish, fruity Mangatawhiri Chardonnay. Both the Marlborough Riesling and Sauvignon Blanc are fruit focused, crisply structured and relatively underpriced. The 20-year-old Millennium Reserve Tawny Port is New Zealand's best, and much more Australian in style than Portuguese.

RONGOPAI WINES
Established 1982 *Owner* Tom van Dam *Production* 10,450 cases *Vineyard area* 10 acres (4 ha)

Originally the site of the historic viticultural research center Te Kauwhata, Rongopai's building and trial vineyards date to before the First World War. Former employee van Dam earned his reputation in the 1980s producing late-harvested, often botrytis-infected dessert wines made from a wide range of grape varieties, including chardonnay, riesling, pinot noir, scheurebe and müller-thurgau. This style remains the winery's main strength.

Gisborne & Hawkes Bay

The east-coast wine regions of Gisborne and Hawkes Bay in New Zealand's North Island are close to each other geographically but distant relations when it comes to the wines they produce.

Gisborne township's biggest claim to fame is that as the country's most easterly center, it is the first place to see the light of each new day. And at the dawn of its winemaking development, it is the vibrant glow of its whites that have made the area's reputation. Traditionally a bulk grape-growing area where müller-thurgau and muscat ruled the viticultural roost, Gisborne is now known, to those who live there and to many New Zealanders, as the country's chardonnay capital. Industry giants Montana and Corbans dominate plantings and production. The other local wineries are all small in size, yet are known for producing individualistic styles of high-quality wine: the Millton Vineyard, for instance, was the country's first fully certified organic winery.

Viticulture got off to a false start here in the 1850s when Marist missionaries, thinking they had reached their original destination of Hawkes Bay, began to plant vines. Once they realized their mistake, they swiftly moved on to their original destination. Later, however, the German-born Friedrich Wohnsiedler planted a small vineyard in Gisborne and began to make wine in the early 1920s. After his death in 1956, Wohnsiedler's family gradually lost control of the vineyard, but his name lives on in one of the country's biggest mass-market wines, Montana Wohnsiedler Müller-Thurgau. Both Montana and Corbans spent large sums upgrading their Gisborne wineries and replanting vineyards in the late 1990s, but otherwise recent expansion has been slow.

Most of the region's 3,575 acres (1,447 ha) of vineyards lie in valleys close to Gisborne township, known collectively as the Poverty Bay Flats. The soils here are generally volcanic, overlying mixtures of sandstone and clay, but vary widely. Soils in the Patutahi area, for instance, are lighter and have better drainage than many of the others, which accounts for this area's high-quality

gewürztraminer and chardonnay. As old vines are replanted in different areas and on different slopes, more information will become available.

Sunshine levels in Gisborne are high, but so is the humidity. The region also has relatively high rainfall, with an annual average of 36.5 inches (936 mm), much of which falls immediately prior to the harvest. Although the generally fine weather attracts many vacationers, the success of white-grape varieties reflects Gisborne's status as a cool-climate grape-growing area.

Chardonnay is Gisborne's most planted variety, with 41 percent of the vineyard area. This figure is expected to rise in the next few years alongside increased plantings of pinot noir, sémillon, gewürz-traminer and merlot. Concurrently, chenin blanc, müller-thurgau, muscat and sauvignon are expected to decrease and flora to disappear entirely. The gewürztraminer produced here vies with Marlborough's as New Zealand's best. Similarly, the chardonnay rivals the best offerings from Hawkes Bay and Marlborough, and, with its

Top: *Millton Vineyard in Gisborne is one of the world's leading organic wineries.*

Above: *The cellars at Church Road Winery.*

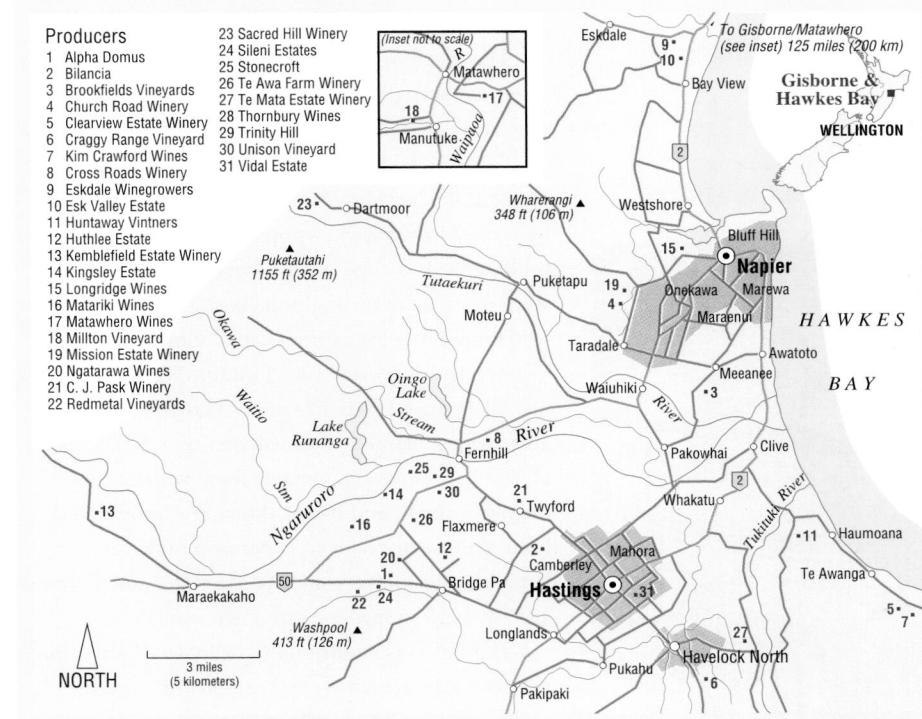

Producers
1. Alpha Domus
2. Bilancia
3. Brookfields Vineyards
4. Church Road Winery
5. Clearview Estate Winery
6. Craggy Range Vineyard
7. Kim Crawford Wines
8. Cross Roads Winery
9. Eskdale Winegrowers
10. Esk Valley Estate
11. Huntaway Vintners
12. Huthlee Estate
13. Kemblefield Estate Winery
14. Kingsley Estate
15. Longridge Wines
16. Matariki Wines
17. Matawhero Wines
18. Millton Vineyard
19. Mission Estate Winery
20. Ngatarawa Wines
21. C. J. Pask Winery
22. Redmetal Vineyards
23. Sacred Hill Winery
24. Sileni Estates
25. Stonecroft
26. Te Awa Farm Winery
27. Te Mata Estate Winery
28. Thornbury Wines
29. Trinity Hill
30. Unison Vineyard
31. Vidal Estate

Stained glass makes an elegant sign at the Brookfields Winery in Hawkes Bay.

intense melon and tropical fruit flavors, is certainly the most distinctive of those made in New Zealand. Of the red wines, merlot has so far shown the most promise. Plantings of pinot noir are predicted to increase faster than merlot, but mainly to provide a base for sparkling wines rather than to create single-variety products.

Although Gisborne is the country's third-largest grape-growing region, it makes up only 16 per cent of the total New Zealand vineyard area, and this figure is likely to decline as other areas grow more rapidly.

Hawkes Bay currently accounts for a hefty 27 percent of the total New Zealand vineyard area; it also produces the country's most diverse range of wines, from tropical sauvignon blanc and elegant chardonnay to gutsy merlot and cabernet-based reds. The region was named for Admiral Sir Edward Hawke by Captain James Cook, when Cook first mapped New Zealand in the late 1770s. The wine industry centers on the twin cities of Napier and Hastings and the smaller township of Havelock North.

Vines were first planted in Hawkes Bay in the 1850s by Marist priests, whose vision lives on at the country's oldest winemaking company, Mission Estate Winery, which is still run by the order. Hawkes Bay is also the site of New Zealand's oldest winery, Te Mata Estate in Havelock North, which was established by Bernard Chambers in 1896 and has recently produced some of the Bay's premium cabernet-sauvignon-based reds as well as some fine chardonnays.

The most significant figure in the recent history of winemaking in Hawkes Bay is Tom McDonald, who took over a vineyard and winery in the late 1920s from a Marist brother. Widely acclaimed as the father of Hawkes Bay reds, McDonald believed in the region's potential for quality table wine at a time when sweet port and sherry were *de rigueur* throughout New Zealand. The McDonald Winery is now called Church Road Winery and is owned by Montana Wines.

There are 41 wineries in the Hawkes Bay area, with a planted vineyard area of 5,772 acres (2,337 ha). However, most of these wineries are relatively small, and recent short-term growth has been mainly the result of expansion undertaken by large industry players such as Montana and Corbans and by small to medium-sized new wineries.

The Bay has traditionally been seen as the most promising region in New Zealand for cabernet- and merlot-based red wines, but the quality

depends on where the grapes are grown. The soils here are all alluvial and vary vastly. The range includes fertile soils (mainly on and around the region's many rivers and old riverbeds), arid soils (many of which have a significant volcanic component, known in the region as "red metal"), and clay-based and silt-and-sand based soils. A smattering of well-drained limestone soils provides some of the country's most impressive chardonnay, merlot, cabernet and syrah.

The stony soils of the Gimblett Road area have been developed relatively recently and are now home to a growing number of wineries whose focus is firmly on the red varietals: cabernet franc, cabernet sauvignon, malbec and merlot. Along with its soils, this area's high level of sunshine and intense heat are thought to provide the best conditions in the region for these grapes.

Generally, Hawkes Bay has a cool maritime climate. The average annual rainfall is 32.2 inches (825 mm), and the bay regularly records the highest average hours of sunshine in New Zealand. Relatively light spring frosts and year-round sea breezes affect certain vineyard sites.

Chardonnay is the most widely planted grape variety, with 1,569 acres (635 ha) or 27 percent of the area's current vineyard plantings, and is predicted to increase over the next few years. Although cabernet sauvignon is the next most planted grape variety, covering 971 acres (393 ha), it is likely to be overtaken soon by merlot. Currently on level pegging with merlot at 778 acres (315 ha) is sauvignon blanc, which produces wines that are more tropical in flavor and softer in texture than the more intense Marlborough style. Proportions of cabernet sauvignon, cabernet franc, pinot noir and syrah are also likely to increase in the near future. Other varieties include chenin blanc and müller-thurgau, which are predicted to decline rapidly, and palamino and sylvaner, which are expected to disappear altogether. There are also small quantities of breidecker, chasselas, gewürztraminer, malbec, pinotage, pinot gris, riesling, sémillon, sylvaner, viognier and a handful of Italian reds that are in experimental phases.

Many producers feel that cabernet franc, malbec and merlot hold the key to consistently high-quality red blends, rather than cabernet sauvignon, the traditional mainstay of Hawkes Bay reds. Those focusing on these varietals include Esk Valley, Sileni Estates, Te Awa Farm and Unison Vineyard. Pinot noir has not yet thrived here, but it is felt that the grape has potential if

grown in an appropriate soil and mesoclimate. Sileni, for example, has planted the variety in a vineyard located 330 feet (100 m) higher than most others in the district, in soil said to resemble that of Martinborough. The company believes that this will eventually allow it to produce commercial quantities of very good pinot.

ALPHA DOMUS

Established 1991 *Owners* Ham family *Production* 9,360 cases *Vineyard area* 49 acres (20 ha)

This stylish producer has wonderfully arcane branding: "Alpha" is made up of the initial letters of the family members' first names, and the Latin *domus* means "family" or "house"—hence "Ham family"; furthermore, the label's airplane crest alludes to nearby Bridge Pa Airfield. The basic Alpha Domus range sits on the stylish side of commercial, and stars a crystal-clear, unwooded Chardonnay as well as a big, ripe Merlot/Cabernet. The reserve AD series Cabernet/Merlot/ Malbec is inky, expansive and smooth in most years; the AD Chardonnay consistently nutty, creamy and pineapple-fruited; and the barrel-fermented Sémillon/Sauvignon complex and leesy.

BILANCIA

Established 1997 *Owners* Lorraine Leheny and Warren Gibson *Production* 850 cases *Vineyard area* 2 acres (0.8 ha)

This winery's gifted young winemaker–owners have been strongly influenced by the time they spent at Trinity Hill (see p. 602), and early results have raised high expectations for this new label. The unfined, French-oaked Merlot is a complex mix of coffee, plums and vanilla, with a long, smooth finish. The tank-fermented, spicy, earthy Pinot Grigio, with its pure, explosive flavors, differs stylistically from the barrel-fermented (old oak), lees-aged Reserve Pinot Grigio, which is delicately perfumed, grapey, and has elegance, tremendous length and complexity. Both are among New Zealand's better warm-climate styles. The French barrel-fermented Chardonnay is rounded, nutty and creamy, and a syrah is earmarked for the future. One to watch.

BROOKFIELDS VINEYARDS

Established 1937 *Owner* Peter Robertson *Production* 9,360 cases *Vineyard area* 15 acres (6 ha)

Although established in 1937 as a sherry specialist, this winery's modern history began in 1977 when

Mist drifts across the plains behind the Te Mata Estate Winery in Hawkes Bay.

Lavender blooms near the winery buildings and fermentation tanks of Church Road.

it was purchased by Peter Robertson. A former chemist who worked under the legendary Tom McDonald, Robertson has more recently collaborated over several vintages with Albert Mann from Alsace, France; this has led to a dramatic stylistic evolution of his Gewürztraminer, Riesling and Pinot Gris. All have taken on a more subtle, elegant Alsatian character, focused on clean, less tropically colored fruit, condensed textures, and firm acid support—and all are excellent. Traditional Brookefields strengths include the Gold Label Reserve Cabernet, Cabernet/Merlot, and Marshall Bank Chardonnay. These show focused fruit, with French oak influence and smooth textures, and are designed for fine dining.

CHURCH ROAD WINERY
(FORMERLY THE MCDONALD WINERY)

Established 1897 *Owners* Corporate Investments Ltd
Production 213,840 cases *Vineyard area* 848 acres (343 ha)

Historically one of New Zealand's most important wineries, Church Road was founded by a former Mission lay brother, Bartholomew Steinmetz, in 1897 as Taradale Vineyards. Steinmetz eventually sold out to apprentice Tom McDonald in 1926. McDonald's winery proved that cabernet sauvignon had a future in New Zealand with an outstanding 1949 vintage; this was followed by a string of successful 100 percent cabernets in the 1960s and early 1970s. In 1988, after a merger with Australia's McWilliams and McDonald's death, the winery (and its 588 acres [238 hectares] of old vineyards) was purchased by Montana as a base for its Hawkes Bay operations.

Montana turned to Bordeaux *negociant* Cordier for technical advice in the development of Church Road's benchmark cabernet/merlot style, which displays ripe berry-fruit characters, a kiss of French oak, smooth-grained but firmly structured tannins and a general air of restrained elegance. The barrel-fermented Chardonnay and Sauvignon Blanc display a similar balance of fruit intensity and more subtle complexity.

A slow-developing Reserve Chardonnay, Cabernet/Merlot and occasional Merlot are produced from outstanding fruit in exceptional years and show greater intensity, complexity and tighter structures. Two Grand-Cru-class limited releases were added to the range recently: an expensive, long-lived, bordeaux blend named Tom in memory of McDonald, and a multilayered, plush-textured, botrytis-infected sémillon called Virtue.

CLEARVIEW ESTATE WINERY

Established 1988 *Owners* Tim Turvey, Helma van den Berg and Ward family *Production* 4,000 cases *Vineyard area* 25 acres (10 ha)

Clearview Estate has a liking for blockbuster chardonnay styles with enough alcohol (frequently more than 14 percent) to stun an ox. The top-of-the-line, super-concentrated, 100 percent new oak fermented Reserve Chardonnay consistently ranks among the country's more powerful examples; so too their Reserve Merlot, Reserve Cabernet Franc and Basket Press Cabernet Merlot, all made only in the best years. Rarer still, the cabernet-dominated merlot/franc/malbec blend, Old Olive Block, is produced from only the best fruit in exceptional years. A high-brix, botrytized Chardonnay is also produced when merited.

CRAGGY RANGE VINEYARDS

Established 1998 *Owners* Terry Peabody and Steve Smith MW
Production 4,000 cases *Vineyard area* 272 acres (110 ha)

A promising venture, uniting American business acumen and New Zealand's top viticulturist, Steve Smith, this winery is intent on producing nothing but high-quality, single-vineyard wine. Until the newly planted 99-acre (40-ha) Gimblet Vineyard and 173-acre (70-ha) Martinborough sites come on line, fruit will continue to be supplied by strictly supervised contract growers using carefully selected, site-specific vineyards. Marlborough-sourced first releases include the condensed, minerally Rapaura Road Riesling from 20-year-old fruit; a classic, pungent-with-sweat-and-passionfruit Sauvignon; and a well-focused, beautifully balanced Strugglers Flat Pinot Noir. The Hawkes Bay Chardonnay is beautifully integrated with underplayed oak. Winemaking here never obscures *terroir*.

KIM CRAWFORD WINES

Established 1996 *Owners* Kim and Erica Crawford
Production 49,000 cases *Vineyard area* None

Kim Crawford, who has been dubbed "Winemaker of the Year" several times in several places, established his reputation at Coopers Creek and Saint Clair, and as a consultant to many other wineries. Striking out on his own on this label, he had early success with a vibrant Marlborough Sauvignon Blanc and a pure, well-focused, unoaked Chardonnay. More recently a higher-quality range (Hawkes Bay Reserve Chardonnay, Merlot and Cabernet Franc) has shown sharply etched varietal characters, richness and style. A super-reserve range (produced only in exceptional years) was recently released, including the Pia Chardonnay, Tane Merlot/Cabernet Franc, Reka Botrytised Riesling as well as a Méthode Traditionnelle. All are excellent and distinctive.

CROSS ROADS WINERY

Established 1990 *Owners* Lester O'Brien and Malcolm Reeves *Production* 9,000 cases *Vineyard area* 12.4 acres (5 ha)

O'Brien and Reeves were old friends who taught at university together in New Zealand back in the 1970s, and years later bumped into each other again in Paris. This chance encounter inspired the name of the resulting winemaking partnership. Cross Roads' reputation rests on a high-quality, mid-priced range with strength and consistency in all varietals. Of these, the focused, fleshy Gewürztraminer, well-balanced Chardonnay and peppery Syrah are especially good, and the varietally focused, fleshy Pinot Noir is consistently one of the best in Hawkes Bay. The top-end, concentrated Talisman, a bordeaux blend with unknown additions, and a toasty, buttery Reserve Chardonnay should both cost more.

ESKDALE WINEGROWERS

Established 1973 *Owner* Kim Salonius *Production* 1,584 cases *Vineyard area* 10 acres (4 ha)

This winery is known for extremely long oak aging. The Cabernet/Merlot is left on new French oak for three years and the Chardonnay for two. The saving grace comes from the ripeness and concentration of Hawkes Bay fruit and a willingness on the part of the maker not to release the bottled wine until it is ready to drink. Current releases can be five to six years old.

ESK VALLEY ESTATE

Established 1933 *Owner* George Fistonich *Production* 43,200 cases *Vineyard area* 7.4 acres (3 ha)

Formerly the Glenvale Winery, this estate was purchased by Villa Maria and renamed Esk Valley in 1987. As part of the Villa Maria group, Esk has benefited greatly from viticulturist Steve Smith's input; as a result, its vineyard-driven quality increased markedly in the late 1990s.

Reds are the Esk Valley's main strength, but the creamy, oaky, complex Reserve Chardonnay and seriously made, highly underrated, oak-aged Chenin Blanc are outstanding in their own right. Produced only in exceptional years, The Terraces is a blend of merlot, malbec and cabernet franc which ranks among New Zealand's two or three best bordeaux blends. The Reserve Merlot/Malbec/Cabernet Sauvignon is often close in quality. Esk Valley has clearly demonstrated how fundamental malbec can be in taking fruit-driven style into more complex, savory realms.

HUNTAWAY VINTNERS

Established 1968 *Owners* Corbans *Production* 780,000 cases *Vineyard area* 284 acres (115 ha)

Providing a branded label and base for Corbans Gisborne operations, Huntaway Vintners is one of the county's largest wineries. Its mid-priced range focuses on the varietals that Gisborne does best: chardonnay, gewürztraminer, merlot, sémillon, pinot gris and, to a lesser extent, cabernet sauvignon. All Huntaway wines are good value, flavor filled and well made. The ripe, lychee-driven, fleshy Gewürztraminer and grapy Pinot Gris are often excellent value, high-quality wines, and the outstanding, consistently ripe, fleshy Sémillon is one of the few in New Zealand worth cellaring. Corbans' new emphasis on site-specific, viticulturally improved varietals should see these wines enhanced further in future.

Clearview Estate's restaurant allows visitors to sample the winery's produce with food.

At Huntaway Vintners, the wine is transferred to oak barrels following fermentation.

The distinctive calligraphy of the Millton label welcomes visitors to the winery.

HUTHLEE ESTATE

Established 1984 *Owners* Devon and Estelle Lee *Production* 1,800 cases *Vineyard area* 16 acres (6.5 ha)

Huthlee began by resurrecting a fallow vineyard in 1984 and then selling fruit to other wineries until 1991. Since then it has built up an impressive range of well-made, good-quality reds from bordeaux grapes. Their fleshy, stylish 100 per cent Cabernet Franc and meaty Merlot are always underpriced for their quality, and the Cabernet Sauvignon and blends are consistently complex, concentrated and well-structured for age. A recently introduced Pinot Gris displays remarkable spice, earthiness and steely acids.

KEMBLEFIELD ESTATE WINERY

Established 1993 *Owners* Kaar Field and John Kemble *Production* 14,400 cases *Vineyard area* 146 acres (59 ha)

John Kemble, former assistant winemaker at Ravenswood in Sonoma, and partner Kaar Field established their inland vineyard on elevated rolling hills. It has taken the locals some time to understand Kemble's tighter, finer, Californian-influenced, suave approach to New Zealand fruit. Strengths lie in an aromatically restrained, condensed, bone-dry Gewürztraminer; an elegant, earthy, seamless Chardonnay; and a fine-grained, plummy Merlot. The wines in the second range, Terrace View, are extremely well made, clean and varietally focused for a sharp price. Quality has steadily improved since Kemblefield's own vineyards started coming on line after 1996.

New Zealand's oldest winery, Mission Vineyards, was founded in 1851.

KINGSLEY ESTATE

Established 1991 *Owner* Kingsley Tobin *Production* 720 cases *Vineyard area* 15 acres (6 ha)

Kingsley Estate are certified organic winemakers specializing in cabernet sauvignon and merlot varietals and blends. Intense viticultural practice, low yields and healthy vines have recently paid dividends in the form of stylish, concentrated, supple reds, considered by many to be among the best produced in Hawkes Bay.

LONGRIDGE WINES

Established 1981 *Owners* Corbans *Production* 450,000 cases *Vineyard area* 741 acres (300 ha)

Formerly a Hawkes Bay label under Cooks but now owned by Corbans, Longridge produces very reliable, commercially styled wines at sharp prices. The range's strong points are one of the country's better inexpensive gewürztraminers, which is consistently ripe and fleshy, and an oak-driven, tropical-fruit Sauvignon Blanc. Longridge's red wines previously showed unripe, herbaceous qualities, but have improved lately as a result of Corbans' recent focus on viticulture.

MATARIKI WINES

Established 1981 *Owner* John O'Connor *Production* 8,640 cases *Vineyard area* 89 acres (36 ha)

Matariki are relatively new players with serious intentions to make quality wine. Two vineyards at Gimblett Road and Te Mata Peak service a purpose-built winery with the capacity to crush over 1,100 tons (1,000 t). Grapes planted include syrah, sangiovese, chardonnay, pinot noir, sauvignon blanc and bordeaux varieties. The first limited-release chardonnays and red blends are promising.

MATAWHERO WINES

Established 1975 *Owner* Dennis Irwin *Production* NA *Vineyard area* 79 acres (32 ha)

Matawhero made its name in the mid-1980s with a series of concentrated, edgy gewürztraminers more structurally akin to Alsace than anything in the South Pacific. Subsequent vintages have been irregular: sometimes brilliant, sometimes noble failures. Other wines in the range are generally made in austere styles that need considerable bottle age to develop their full potential. Sometimes they also (intentionally?) reflect volatile, oxidative, low-tech winemaking styles. A good example of this, the recently released, fully mature 1989 Matawhero Bridge (a blend of malbec, merlot, cabernet sauvignon and cabernet franc) has wonderfully

complex, gamey nuances. Matawhero deserve bonus points for pushing the boundaries of winemaking.

MILLTON VINEYARD

Established 1984 *Owners* Millton family *Production* 12,000 cases *Vineyard area* 49 acres (20 ha)

One of the world's greatest organic wineries, Millton follows the biodynamic philosophies of Rudolph Steiner. It produces two of New Zealand's best whites: the barrel-fermented Te Arai Chenin Blanc, which is seamless, concentrated and long lived, and the Opou Riesling, which is fleshy, seamless and clear as a bell. Almost as good are the top-of-the-range, barrel-fermented, selected-fruit Clos Ste Anne Chardonnay and the second-level Barrel-Fermented Chardonnay. The recently introduced Malbec is a fine-grained, flavor-filled, elegant red. A lively, sharply priced, off-dry, summer-quaffing Muskats@Dawn is clever marketing at its best, and the Late Harvested Chenin Blanc shows a feel for this varietal rarely seen outside of the Loire.

MISSION ESTATE WINERY

Established 1851 *Owner* Society of Mary *Production* 62,000 cases *Vineyard area* 87 acres (35 ha)

Established in 1851 by the Marist Brothers, Mission is New Zealand's oldest winery. The early vineyards were moved several times as a result of floods and the Maori Wars, settling in their present location in 1910. Not only can Mission Estate claim the first plantings of pinot gris in the southern hemisphere, but it was also a primary source of vines for many of New Zealand's vineyards. More recently, improved viticulture, a shift toward organic practices, careful deselection and brand repositioning have led to improved quality across its three ranges: Estate, Reserve and Jewelstone. At the lower level, the Estate's Pinot Gris, Riesling, Gewürztraminer and Merlot can offer outstanding value and personality. The strengths of the middle-level Reserve range are the Chardonnay, Sémillon, Cabernet/Merlot and Merlot. Jewelstone is only produced in the best years and its leading wines are the Pinot Grigio, Noble Riesling and Chardonnay.

NGATARAWA WINES

Established 1981 *Owners* Alwyn and Brian Corban *Production* 25,000 cases *Vineyard area* 49 acres (20 ha)

Alwyn Corban pioneered a subregion called the "Ngatarawa triangle," which has subsequently become hot Hawkes Bay property. A scion of the Corban clan, he struck out on his own with Ngatarawa in the early 1980s, and has quietly improved his wines little by little over the years. Output is divided into the good-value Stables range and the top-line Glazebrook, both of which err on the understated, slightly austere side of fruit-forward, but are longer lived and more elegant for it. The Stables Noble Harvest Riesling and superpremium Alwyn are among Hawkes Bay's best. Both the Glazebrook Chardonnay, which displays underplayed oak, and the rich, supple Merlot/Cabernet Sauvignon improve with age and are complex, interesting wines. Ngatarawa are quietly experimenting with viognier.

C. J. PASK WINERY

Established 1982 *Owners* Pask family *Production* 35,000 cases *Vineyard area* 148 acres (60 ha)

Chris Pask planted Gimblett Road's first grapes in 1982, and took on winemaker Kate Radburnd (formerly of Vidals) in 1990. Pask's strength lies in standard-range and reserve-quality Merlot and Cabernet Sauvignon and in a 70 percent Cabernet/Merlot blend. Remarkably consistent, the base range can closely match the reserve's quality level in hot years. All show vibrant varietal characters with generous, but not overpowering, well-integrated sweet oak, with the Reserve range more concentrated and structured to age.

Pask Chardonnay is a fruit-driven, very lightly oaked style, whereas the more powerful French-oak-fermented Reserve Chardonnay is buttery, and displays a deep, multilayered complexity. Pask also produces an inexpensive but good-quality, ageworthy Chenin Blanc.

REDMETAL VINEYARDS

Established 1992 *Owner* Grant Edmonds *Production* 1,296 cases *Vineyard area* 10 acres (4 ha)

Named after his vineyard's red-metal soils, and planted exclusively with bordeaux varieties—cabernet sauvignon, merlot, malbec and cabernet franc—Grant Edmond's winery has produced a string of richly flavored and supple wines. The top-line, unfined Basket Press Merlot/Cabernet Franc bursts with fruitcake aromas and flavors, and has a long, smooth finish. In the best years, a super-premium, highly concentrated Merlot is produced for long-term cellaring. The Redmetal Merlot/Cabernet Franc echoes its Basket Press counterpart but is cheaper and has a more forward style.

SACRED HILL WINERY

Established 1982 *Owners* Mason family *Production* 42,264 cases *Vineyard area* 49 acres (20 ha)

Under the leadership of Tony Bish (formerly of Rippon) and consultant Jenny Dobson (now at Te Awa Farm), Sacred Hill's reputation soared in the late 1990s, primarily on the strength of Rifleman's Chardonnay and the Basket Press reds. Rifleman's

Sileni's stylish modernist winery houses restaurants and conference facilities.

Reserve Chardonnay shows condensed textures, with complex, nutty aromas and flavors, while the Sauvage Reserve Sauvignon Blanc is barrel and wild yeast fermented on new French oak—big, bold stuff. Basket Press Cabernet Sauvignon, Merlot and Cabernet Sauvignon/Merlot are all concentrated, savory, grippy reds for long-term cellaring. The inexpensive Whitecliff range is solid, showing uncluttered fruit and balanced acids.

SILENI ESTATES
Established 1997 *Owners* **Avery, Cowper and Edmonds families** *Production* **5,040 cases** *Vineyard area* **247 acres (100 ha)**

Sileni is one of Hawkes Bay's newest and most visually striking wineries, and has extensive plantings waiting to come on line. The plan is to present a full range of culinary and wine tourism activities on site including restaurants, a wine and food education center and conference facilities. The smart team of winemaking specialists has produced excellent early results, with notable offerings including the plummy, toasty Merlot and long, impeccably balanced Chardonnay.

STONECROFT
Established 1982 *Owner* **Alan Limmer** *Production* **2,500 cases** *Vineyard area* **15 acres (6 ha)**

Stonecroft's considerable reputation rests on two varietals, syrah and gewürztraminer, an odd couple that tends to overshadow a portfolio that is strong on all counts. Stonecroft were syrah pioneers and have proved that Hawkes Bay can produce ripe, seamless, elegant examples of this varietal. The Gewürztraminer is one of New Zealand's most thrilling: delicately spiced, earthy, minerally, creamy and steely. Concealed in the shadows of these two are an outstanding, dense, atmospheric, smoky Chardonnay as well as the Crofter/Ruhanui blends of syrah, cabernet and merlot. A zinfandel is currently being developed.

TE AWA FARM WINERY
Established 1992 *Owners* **Lawson family** *Production* **20,000 cases** *Vineyard area* **94 acres (38 ha)**

Drawing on chardonnay and bordeaux varietals from closely planted vineyards at Roys Hill and Gimblett Road, Te Awa blossomed under Jenny Dobson's winemaking in the late 1990s. Dobson was formerly at Sacred Hill and prior to her arrival at Te Awa had spent a dozen years at Château Senegac in Bordeaux. She brought a stylistic feel for making complete wines with

The vineyards and winery at Te Awa Farm.

nonintrusive oak, broad savory aromatic and flavor components, and fine-grained but firm structure. The cheaper Longlands range and reserve-level Boundary and Frontier ranges share similar qualities, with the last two more intense, complex and concentrated. All are excellent.

TE MATA ESTATE WINERY
Established 1896 *Owners* **Buck and Morris families** *Production* **28,000 cases** *Vineyard area* **185 acres (75 ha)**

Everything the Te Mata Estate team turn their hands to is tastefully done: marketing, architecture and, of course, wine. The winery's modern history begins with John Buck and Michael Morris's shared vision to resurrect the estate's fallow vineyards and delapidated buildings. From its first vintage in 1979, Te Mata's Cabernet/Merlot blend established a benchmark for all other New Zealand bordeaux blends, and eventually became the country's most famous red.

Steadily improved viticulture, careful blending and declassification are the keys to Te Mata's quality. A three-tiered red range begins with the bottom-end Cabernet Sauvignon/Merlot, often excellent value as a result of catching intentional spillage from the upper-tier Coleraine and Awatea. Both wines are blended cabernet sauvignon, merlot and franc, defined by seamless, smooth textures, complexity and concentration. The Coleraine is the more so

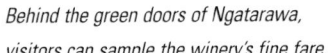

Behind the green doors of Ngatarawa, visitors can sample the winery's fine fare.

The Trinity Hill vineyards include a wide range of experimental grape varieties.

Trinity Hill's Syrah, Merlot, and Cabernet/Merlot all share similar mixtures of varietally associated aromas, nicely supported by sweetly spiced oak. Each displays tremendous complexity, very long flavors, an expansive (sometimes explosive) mid-palate, and fine tannins. All are among the region's best. The Cabernet Sauvignon is as alcoholic as they come in New Zealand (14 percent) and shows roasted, spirity characters—hot vintages could easily be mistaken for Australian Barossa Valley wines. Secondary-range Shepherds Croft Merlot/Cabernet Franc/Syrah and Shepherds Croft Chardonnay are distinctive, well made and good value. Trinity always make excellent wine, suggesting wonderful things to come when the principal vines reach full maturity—not forgetting, of course, all those wildcard experimental grape varieties left up their sleeve.

and built for longer-term aging, while the cheaper Awatea drinks at about two years. Another Kiwi icon, Elston Chardonnay, is fully French-oak and malolactic fermented, resulting in an earthy, buttery, mealy, minerally, long-lived wine. Declassified Elston often makes Te Mata Chardonnay excellent buying. The Bullnose Syrah is steadily reaching the highest levels of style and quality, and a viognier style is currently under development.

THORNBURY WINES

Established 1998 *Owners* **Steve Bird and McCutcheon family**
Production 3,600 cases *Vineyard area* 16 acres (6.5 ha)

Former Morton Estate winemaker Steve Bird has established his own label backed up with recent plantings. The first releases, made with bought-in grapes, have included a smart Merlot—all fruitcake, game, licorice and mint—and a subtle Chardonnay, with integrated honey, nut and apple aromas, which is both viscous and expansive. A big, classically styled, herbaceous Marlborough Sauvignon Blanc is also produced.

TRINITY HILL

Established 1993 *Owners* **Wilson, Janes and Hancock families**
Production 28,000 cases *Vineyard area* 62 acres (25 ha)

After a dozen years building Morton Estate's reputation for consistent quality, John Hancock went into partnership with friends to start Trinity Hill. The winery's focus is on distinctive, high-quality wines made from their own Gimblett-Road-grown fruit, supplemented with grapes from other supervised growers. Varietal emphasis is on classics, but there are also experimental plots of viognier, tempranillo, touriga nacional, roussanne, nebbiolo and montepulciano.

UNISON VINEYARD

Established 1993 *Owners* **Anna-Barbara and Bruce Helliwell**
Production 2,160 cases *Vineyard area* 15 acres (6 ha)

A classy operation that also produces balsamic vinegar and includes an olive grove, Unison employs close planting, low yields and intensive viticulture to produce rich, concentrated wine—effectively, wine made in the vineyard. Red-wine specialists, their flagship Unison Selection is a spicy, mouth-filling, beautifully balanced blend of cabernet sauvignon, merlot and syrah (the term "Selection" refers to a preselection of grapes carried out in the vineyard rather than barrel selection). An underground cellar was recently constructed for temperature control.

VIDAL ESTATE

Established 1905 *Owner* **George Fistonich** *Production* 54,000 cases *Vineyard area* 49 acres (20 ha)

Spanish immigrant Joseph Vidal established a vineyard and converted stables into a winery in 1905. In 1976, Vidal's became part of the Villa Maria group, which then developed the winery's reputation for producing solid, well-made varietals at more than reasonable prices. High points include a consistently full-flavored, long-lived Cabernet/Merlot and a viscous, beautifully structured Noble Sémillon. Recently, Vidal has re-branded, becoming the first New Zealand winery to develop styles and packaging based primarily on consumer response. The result is a range—including Sauvignon Blanc, Chardonnay, Riesling and Cabernet Sauvignon—of clean, varietally focused, fruit-driven, well-balanced wines.

Vidal Estate's publicity and marketing skills have helped broaden its customer base.

Wairarapa/Wellington

Like the country's own presence in the wine world, New Zealand's sixth-largest winemaking region has forged a reputation that far outweighs its level of production. Wairarapa/Wellington was formerly known as Martinborough, after the tiny town of the same name that produced the region's first wines in the early 1980s (the first vintage was produced in 1984) and, as a result of an unwavering commitment to quality, put that name on the global wine map. However, after grapes were planted in the northern Wairarapa areas of Masterton and Gladstone, and on the western side of the island at Te Horo, northwest of Wellington, the current, more all-encompassing name was adopted.

Vines were first planted in Wairarapa in the late nineteenth century, when Masterton farmer William Beetham is known to have grown pinot noir, pinot meunier, hermitage, black hamburgh, black muscat, gold chasselas and the white Spanish grape doradillo. Unfortunately, around the turn of the century Masterton became one of the first towns in New Zealand to be affected by prohibition, and in 1908 viticulture vanished from the region. It wasn't until the late 1970s that Dr Derek Milne, a soil physics and geology specialist, having noted favorable grape-growing conditions in Martinborough, cofounded Martinborough Vineyard, now a top-quality pinot noir and chardonnay producer. Others who helped pioneer grape growing and winemaking around this time include Dr Neil McCallum of Dry River Wines, Clive Paton of Ata Rangi and Stan Chifney of Chifney Wines (now owned by Margrain).

There are currently 33 wine producers in Wairarapa/Wellington. That constitutes 12 percent of the country's winemakers, but only 3 percent of the country's vines. Moreover, the region's average vineyard size of 12.1 acres (4.9 ha) is less than half the national average of 26.6 acres (10.8 ha). However, in recent years there has been a rapid increase in the area under production: between 1998 and 1999, Wairarapa/Wellington expanded by 33 percent, from 521 acres (211 ha) to 694 acres (281 ha)—and several more large wineries and vineyards are under development.

So far, most soil research has focused on the Martinborough area. Three distinctive types have been found there, of which two are alluvial and one is clay loam. The alluvial soils on the river terraces, home to most of the region's vineyards, are identified as either Martinborough loam or Tauheranikau stony silt loam, both of which are estimated to be between 3,000 and 7,000 years old. Few vineyards have yet been planted on other soils, such as the older clay loams on the undulating hills around the town of Martinborough.

Wairarapa/Wellington is the North Island's coolest and driest winemaking region, with an

The small town of Martinborough is the "capital" of the Wairarapa wine region.

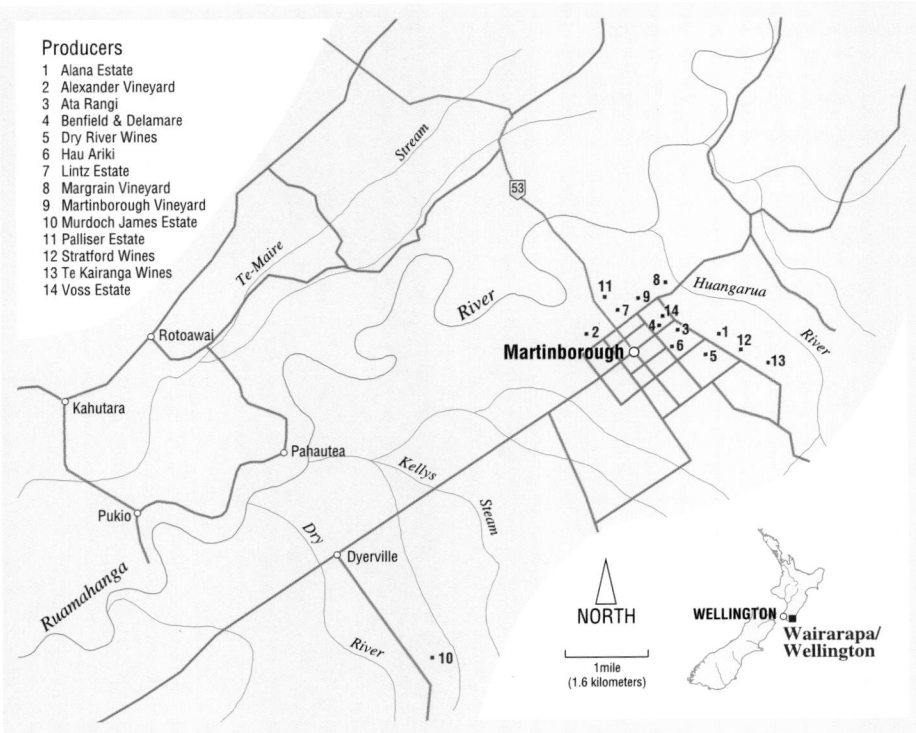

Producers
1 Alana Estate
2 Alexander Vineyard
3 Ata Rangi
4 Benfield & Delamare
5 Dry River Wines
6 Hau Ariki
7 Lintz Estate
8 Margrain Vineyard
9 Martinborough Vineyard
10 Murdoch James Estate
11 Palliser Estate
12 Stratford Wines
13 Te Kairanga Wines
14 Voss Estate

Above: *The facilities at Margrain Vineyards include a restaurant and accommodation.*

Top: *Dry River's impressive range of whites and reds is available only via mail order.*

average temperature of 57–59°F (14–15°C) and an average annual rainfall of approximately 29.3 inches (750 mm). The vineyards are often battered by onshore winds that blow north from the rough Cook Strait across the flat, exposed plains of southern Wairarapa.

Although some local winemakers believe in the potential of cabernet sauvignon and merlot, most have pinned their hopes on pinot noir and chardonnay. The former is the most planted grape variety, covering 224 acres (91 ha), or 32 percent of the vineyard area compared to cabernet's 64 acres (26 ha). Within the next few years, pinot noir is expected to account for almost 50 percent of the vineyard. There are two particular pinot noir styles here: one tends to be more intensely fruit-driven and have higher alcohol, whereas the other is generally earthier and lighter.

The region's best chardonnays are stylistically complex, with flavors ranging beyond the realm of more fruit-driven styles. Sauvignon blanc also thrives here, producing wines that are intense in flavor and do well in both domestic and overseas markets. Many growers are also committed to high-quality, low-cropped riesling, which performs extremely well. Wairarapa/Wellington's pinot gris is among the best in the country, and although plantings of it are small they are expected to increase. Also outstanding is the tiny quantity of gewürztraminer, which is unfortunately particularly susceptible to the region's strong winds.

Wellington, the nation's capital, lies just over one hour's drive from Martinborough and the southern Wairarapa. Aptly known as "the windy city," it has significantly higher rainfall than the Wairarapa, from which it is separated by the Rimutaka Range. Despite the presence of vineyards at nearby Te Horo, Wellington is not now, nor likely to become, home to any vines or wineries, mainly because the climate is not conducive to viticulture.

ALANA ESTATE

Established 1997 *Owners* Alana and Ian Smart *Production* 2,160 cases *Vineyard area* 30 acres (12 ha)

This relatively new enterprise follows an enlightened winemaking philosophy based on minimal intervention and gentle handling, and utilizes a purpose-built, gravity-fed winery. This traditional bordeaux technique ensures an undisturbed flow of wine all the way through crush to fermentation and racking, resulting in supple, flavorful wines. Generally, the Alana styles are reserved and designed to age: they include a lees-aged Sauvignon Blanc; a barrel-fermented Chardonnay; a floral, semidry, Riesling; and a savory, velvety Pinot Noir—all of which bode well for the future.

ALEXANDER VINEYARD

Established 1991 *Owners* Kingsley and Deborah Alexander *Production* 720 cases *Vineyard area* 10 acres (4 ha)

Former meteorologists Kingsley and Deborah Alexander have built their foundations on closely

The vineyard managers at Margrain go to great lengths to protect their valuable vines.

planted cabernet franc and cabernet sauvignon. They began by producing a serious, tightly knit, concentrated pure Cabernet Franc and a drink-early, beaujolais-style cabernet franc called Dusty Road. Subsequent vintages have seen the Cabernet Franc broadened and firmed up with cabernet sauvignon and merlot, and the portfolio expanded to include a savory, velvety Pinot Noir. The winery's small scale and French-inspired style have so far produced promising results.

ATA RANGI

Established 1980 *Owners* Clive Paton, Phyll Pattie, Alison Paton and Oliver Masters *Production* 5,000 cases *Vineyard area* 25 acres (10 ha)

Ata Rangi means "new beginning" in Maori. The winery's pinot noirs are always among the best in the southern hemisphere, and they have twice won the coveted Bouchard-Finlayson Pinot Noir trophy, placing Ata Rangi in the vanguard of early non-Burgundian winners alongside Mondavi Reserve and Domaine Drouhin. The pinot noir styles are consistently complex, multilayered and richly textured. Even in extremely hot vintages (1996 and 1998, for example), they have remained free of overcooked fruit and excessive alcohol, while in difficult, rainy vintages (1995, for instance) they have escaped the rot and dilution that has plagued other vineyards.

Ata Rangi also produces two barrel-fermented chardonnays: Craighall is designed for bottle maturation and marked by a savory complexity, while Petrie is for early drinking and has fruit to the fore. The savory Célèbre is cabernet/merlot based, untypically spiced with syrah, sangiovese, and nebbiolo, and contrasts with a charming rosé made from a similar blend. Recent additions to the range include a powerful Pinot Gris and a pure-fruit, young-vine Pinot Noir.

BENFIELD & DELAMARE

Established 1987 *Owners* Bill Benfield and Sue Delamare *Production* 187 cases *Vineyard area* 5 acres (2 ha)

Originally established as an alternative to the pinot-dominated Martinborough camp, this winery has focused on developing the intensive style of viticulture required to grow cabernet and merlot. Closely planted vines (cabernet franc, cabernet sauvignon, malbec and merlot), each carrying a single cane, are trained low to the ground to avoid wind and collect heat. Although production remains on a small scale, the winery's mainstay product, Benfield & Delamare, has gained a strong

reputation for quality, consistency and longevity. In substandard vintages, it is declassified and marketed as A Song for Osiris.

DRY RIVER WINES

Established 1979 *Owners* Dawn and Neil McCallum *Production* 3,900 cases *Vineyard area* 22 acres (9 ha)

From the very beginning, Dry River took an uncompromising approach to quality, resisting commercial pressures by selling directly, and at high prices, to the public via mail order. This strategy seems to pay off: the majority of Dry River wines sell out almost immediately. A biochemist with a doctorate from Oxford University, Neil McCallum established his reputation with Alsatian varietals (pinot gris, gewürztraminer and riesling vinified in both dry and sweet styles), at a time when these wines were ignored by most New Zealanders. More recently, his stiffly spined, dark and brooding Pinot Noir has achieved cult status. It undergoes a prefermentation maceration, followed by a combination of partially destemmed, whole-bunch and whole-berry fermentation, and is subsequently aged in French oak and bottled unfiltered.

Low cropping from bunch-thinning and leaf-plucking ensure Dry River wines are deep in extract, concentrated and complex, but never at the expense of structure. All are crafted for long bottle maturation, err on the side of austerity, and on the whole require between five and ten years to open up. Recent results with syrah and viognier also suggest tremendous potential.

HAU ARIKI

Established 1994 *Owner* Hau Ariki Marae *Production* NA *Vineyard area* 8.7 acres (3.5 ha)

Hau Ariki (meaning "god of wind") is one of two Maori-owned operations in New Zealand—a significant development in a wine industry that relies so heavily on the Maori language for its branding. Iwi elder George Hawkins manages the operation with former Mission viticulturist Mike Eden. Marae land has been planted with pinot noir, cabernet sauvignon and sauvignon blanc. The Cabernet Sauvignon has tended toward green, leafy unripe characters, but the other wines (Pinot Noir and Sauvignon Blanc) have been on a par with similarly styled Lintz wines (see below).

Ata Rangi's Célèbre blend includes unusual varieties such as sangiovese and nebbiolo.

REGIONAL DOZEN

QUALITY WINES

Ata Rangi Pinot Noir
Benfield & Delamare
   Cabernet Sauvignon
Dry River Pinot Gris
Dry River Gewürztraminer
Martinborough Vineyards
   Reserve Pinot Noir
Palliser Estate Sauvignon
   Blanc

BEST VALUE WINES

Alexander Dusty Road
   Cabernet Franc UC
Margrain Riesling UC
Palliser Estate Riesling
Pencarrow Chardonnay
Pencarrow Sauvignon Blanc
Stratford Riesling UC

The tasting room at Martinborough Vineyard is surrounded by flower-filled gardens.

LINTZ ESTATE

Established 1989 *Owners* Lintz family and 600 share-holders *Production* 5,040 cases *Vineyard area* 21 acres (8.5 ha)

Winemaker Chris Lintz studied viticulture and winemaking at the Geisenheim institute in Germany and has a German wife. Not surprisingly, riesling is one of his specialties: as well as semisweet and late harvest styles, he produces a bottle-fermented Brut. Other strengths include the consistently ripe Vitesse Cabernet Sauvignon; the savory, velvety Moy Hall Pinot Noir; and the crisp, dry, focused Pinot Meunier Rosé. The winery's holdings include auxerrois, cabernet sauvignon, chardonnay, gewürztraminer, merlot, optima, pinot gris, pinot meunier, pinot noir, riesling, sauvignon blanc and syrah, and it plans a significant expansion of pinot gris and pinot noir plantings. Frequently intriguing, Lintz's wines are all high-quality, well-made products.

MARGRAIN VINEYARD

Established 1992 *Owners* Daryl and Graham Margrain *Production* 864 cases *Vineyard area* 10 acres (4 ha)

Incorporating a conference center, accommodation and a restaurant, Margrain is a cleverly conceived establishment. Its unfiltered Pinot Noir is rich, complex and structured to age, its Pinot Gris massive and highly alcoholic. In 1998, it produced an outstanding, tightly structured Merlot, highly concentrated from purposely low-cropped vines. Care and low cropping have also created a perfumed, complex, tightly structured Riesling and a finely balanced Chardonnay. Margrain recently purchased the vineyards of local pioneers Chifney Wines.

MARTINBOROUGH VINEYARD

Established 1980 *Owners* Derek and Duncan Milne, Claire Campbell, and Russel and Sue Schultz *Production* 6,336 cases *Vineyard area* 67 acres (27 ha)

So far, Martinborough Vineyard's reputation rests on one man, winemaker Larry McKenna.

An Australian, McKenna is to New Zealand pinot noir what another pioneering godfather, Californian David Lett, has been to Oregon pinot noir. Much of the credit for the New Zealand pinot boom can be attributed to his role as the driving force behind the Southern Pinot Noir Workshop and as an advisor to many of New Zealand's young pinot makers.

Both the Martinborough Vineyard Pinot Noir and the Reserve Pinot Noir (which took out the Bouchard-Finlayson Trophy in 1997) are distinguished by a quest for greater complexity within the bounds of subtlety and multilayered textures—McKenna clearly understands that the search for the holy grail of perfect pinot noir is endless. These wines are never as ripe and powerful as they could be, but always more interesting for it. Among the other Martinborough varietals, the Chardonnay is consistently rich, and well structured for mature drinking, while the Pinot Gris, which is barrel-fermented in old oak, is one of New Zealand's finest. The Martinborough Vineyard Riesling and Late Harvest Riesling (and, when produced, the Gewürztraminer) are also regularly among the best in their categories nationally. At the time of writing, McKenna had just moved on to pastures new and handed over the Martinborough winemaking reins to Claire Mulholland.

MURDOCH JAMES ESTATE

Established 1986 *Owner* Roger Fraser *Production* 2,160 cases *Vineyard area* 27 acres (11 ha)

Originally, Murdoch James established itself as a consistent grower of shiraz and pinot noir for Ata Rangi; after 1986, Ata Rangi's Clive Paton began to vinify a separate lot for this label. Recently, Murdoch James purchased the old Blue Rock winery and vineyard, thereby doubling its capacity and gaining access to mature chardonnay, pinot noir, riesling, and sauvignon blanc vines. Former Te Kairanga winemaker Chris Buring now oversees the combined operations. The Murdoch Syrah is rich, peppery, supple and finely structured.

PALLISER ESTATE

Established 1989 *Owner* Richard Riddiford *Production* 20,000 cases *Vineyard area* 247 acres (100 ha)

Palliser Estate is currently focusing on pinot noir and sauvignon blanc, with a view to supplying a rapidly expanding export market. Its Pinot Noir is dense and highly alcoholic with extremely ripe fruit characters; the Sauvignon Blanc is big, richly textured and complex and has good length. Both wines have gathered a clutch of trophies. The winery also produces an understated, elegant Chardonnay and a consistently ripe, full-bodied, lime-infused Riesling. The sophisticated Méthode Traditionnelle consistently ranks among the country's top sparklers, while the modestly priced second label, Pencarrow, regularly represents extremely good value, echoing the estate range in a more fruit-led, drink-now style.

STRATFORD WINES

Established 1987 *Owner* Stratford Canning *Production* 468 cases *Vineyard area* 10 acres (4 ha)

Margrain winemaker Stratford Canning's own label is already matching Margrain's quality— no mean achievement. Stylistically, the Stratford wines are more austere, complex and uncompromising than Margrain's, suggesting that Canning could rise rapidly to the top of Martinborough's hierarchy. He has already demonstrated a gift for riesling and pinot noir: the former is intense and lime-infused, the latter spicy, complex, multilayered, focused and tightly structured. His Chardonnay is brilliantly balanced, fine-grained and flavorful, but also elegant and restrained. This is another vineyard with great potential.

TE KAIRANGA WINES

Established 1978 *Owners* 160 shareholders *Production* 10,080 cases *Vineyard area* 86.5 acres (35 ha)

Te Kairanga (meaning "land where soil is rich and food plentiful" in Maori) once seemed to be driven more by a desire for profit than a search for quality. Recently, however, lower yields, careful canopy management, more effective subsite identification and improved winemaking have all contributed to better products. Te Kairanga's Reserve Chardonnay and Pinot Noir, formerly both hugely fruited, alcoholic, oaky and a bit clumsy, have been transformed and now display greater complexity and tighter structures. Furthermore, the Castlepoint Cabernet/Merlot now ranks regularly among the better buys in New Zealand reds.

VOSS ESTATE

Established 1988 *Owners* Annette Atkins and Gary Voss *Production* 1,400 cases *Vineyard area* 12 acres (5 ha)

This small winery produces large-scale, often highly alcoholic chardonnays and pinot noirs with intensely ripe flavors. Its flagship is Waihenga, a blend of cabernet sauvignon, merlot and cabernet franc. It is a fruit-filled, rounded, dense, claret-style wine with fine but well-structured tannins.

The winery buildings at Palliser Estate.

Marlborough

Marlborough offers the best conditions in the country for growing white grapes.

Located on the southeastern tip of the South Island and centered on the Wairau Valley and the town of Blenheim, Marlborough is New Zealand's largest wine region and home to its most famous viticultural product, Marlborough sauvignon blanc. Wine was first produced here in the 1870s by a local farmer called David Herd, but the industry really began in 1973 when Montana planted vines at the Brancott vineyard. These were the first grapes to be grown on a commercial scale in the South Island, and at the time there was no shortage of doubters who felt that the region was too cool for viticulture. Yet, just two decades later, Marlborough sauvignon blanc had wowed the wine world.

Hot on the heels of Montana came major wineries such as Cloudy Bay and Hunter's, as well as the smaller Te Whare Ra and a host of others throughout the 1980s and 1990s. Today, there's a strong French connection in the region, with many of the local manufacturers of sparkling wines being inspired, advised and sometimes partly owned by French Champagne houses. For example, Champagne Deutz has links with Montana Wines; Veuve Clicquot Ponsardin with Cloudy Bay; and Domaine Chandon, Moet et Chandon's Australian arm, with Hunter's.

In terms of the number of wineries in the region, Marlborough is only the second-largest wine-producing area (it has 60 to Auckland's 80), but in terms of vineyard plantings and wine production it is by far the largest. There are 8,591 acres (3,477 ha) of grapes planted—39 percent of the national total—and this figure is likely to increase rapidly over the next few years. Marlborough's subregions are Renwick/Rapaura, Fairhall, Brancott Valley, Omaka, the newish Waihopai, Awatere Valley and the Kaikoura Ranges, a developing area that has yet to produce any wine.

One of Marlborough's greatest viticultural strengths is its free-draining alluvial soil, and variations in its makeup account for a stylistically diverse range of wines. The rich alluvial silt loams of Wairau Valley were traditionally home to intensive arable crops such as sweet corn, peas and beans, and now produce some of Marlborough's most intensive sauvignon blancs and rieslings. In Renwick/Rapaura, the alluvial soils contain a significant amount of sand and stone that gives the sauvignon blanc a distinctive pungency and intensity of flavor. The smooth, rounded stones are also exceptionally free-draining and provide a degree of heat retention.

The soils in Fairhall and Brancott Valley also have a significant amount of gravel, but more clay; home to the country's largest vineyard (Montana's Brancott Estate), they are the source of many of the region's best pinot noirs. The smaller subregions of Omaka and Waihopai both have gravelly silt loams with a strong clay influence. In the narrow, thriving Awatere Valley region, alluvial gravel sits on wind-borne loess, which tends to hold more water than the gravel soils found on the floor of the Wairau Valley; as a result, the Awatere Valley produces some of the region's most intensely flavored sauvignon blancs.

Marlborough has a relatively cool maritime climate with generally warm days and cool nights, and an annual rainfall of about 25 inches (650 mm), which tends to be spread evenly throughout the year. It receives abundant sunshine—about 2,500 hours a year—with Blenheim township regularly claiming New Zealand's highest annual average. Climatic threats to vines include infrequent spring frosts and the regular, dry, northwesterly winds

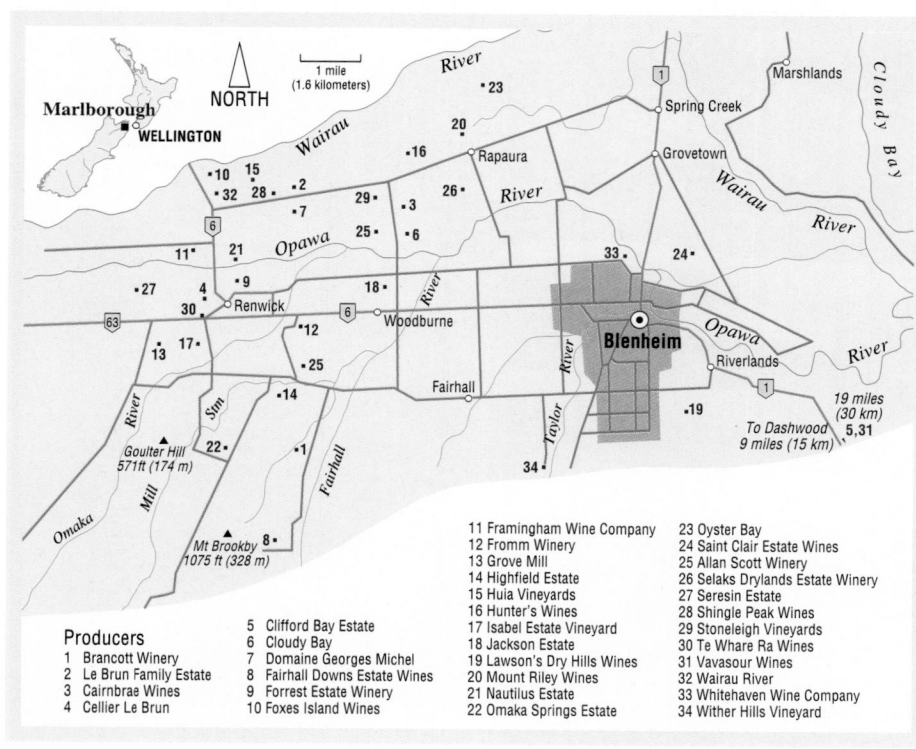

Producers
1. Brancott Winery
2. Le Brun Family Estate
3. Cairnbrae Wines
4. Cellier Le Brun
5. Clifford Bay Estate
6. Cloudy Bay
7. Domaine Georges Michel
8. Fairhall Downs Estate Wines
9. Forrest Estate Winery
10. Foxes Island Wines
11. Framingham Wine Company
12. Fromm Winery
13. Grove Mill
14. Highfield Estate
15. Huia Vineyards
16. Hunter's Wines
17. Isabel Estate Vineyard
18. Jackson Estate
19. Lawson's Dry Hills Wines
20. Mount Riley Wines
21. Nautilus Estate
22. Omaka Springs Estate
23. Oyster Bay
24. Saint Clair Estate Wines
25. Allan Scott Winery
26. Selaks Drylands Estate Winery
27. Seresin Estate
28. Shingle Peak Wines
29. Stoneleigh Vineyards
30. Te Whare Ra Wines
31. Vavasour Wines
32. Wairau River
33. Whitehaven Wine Company
34. Wither Hills Vineyard

The Wairau Valley offers rich alluvial soils, with high levels of gravel and clay in places.

which can not only increase the danger of drought but also significantly diminish crop levels.

Sauvignon blanc is Marlborough's most widely planted grape variety, covering around 3,600 acres (1,457 ha) and accounting for 42 percent of the total vineyard. The second most planted variety is chardonnay followed by pinot noir, riesling, cabernet sauvignon and much smaller quantities of breidecker, chenin blanc, gewürztraminer, müller-thurgau, pinot gris, sémillon, cabernet franc, malbec, merlot, pinotage and syrah.

With few exceptions, Marlborough sauvignon blanc tends to be more intense in flavor and have higher acid levels than sauvignon blanc produced in other parts of New Zealand. Although it is traditionally seen as a wine that is made in the vineyard and requires little input from the wine-maker, a new-style sauvignon is slowly emerging that has more oak and malolactic fermentation influences, and can be aged. Marlborough's chardonnay can be of a very high quality, as can the riesling, which many winemakers believe has great, and as yet untapped, potential.

When it comes to red wines, winemakers have traditionally pinned their hopes on cabernet sauvignon. About 326 acres (132 ha) are under production, making it the region's fifth-most planted grape variety; however, it accounts for only four percent of the vineyard area. Merlot was long thought to hold promise for reds in

Marlborough, but has failed to reach the planting levels of cabernet. Plantings of pinot noir, on the other hand, have risen steadily, and although significant quantities are used in the production of sparkling wine, the wines have now claimed a place among the country's best.

Over the next few years, it is likely that sauvignon blanc wines will become even more dominant, occupying close to 50 percent of the total vineyard area. Plantings of chardonnay, pinot noir and riesling are also likely to continue to increase; cabernet sauvignon, on the other hand, is expected to continue a steady decline to around half its current plantings.

BRANCOTT ESTATE

Established 1973 *Owner* Montana *Production* NA
Vineyard area 2,100 acres (850 ha)

Montana (see p. 587), who pioneered winemaking in Marlborough in the early 1970s with sauvignon blanc, now uses Brancott Estate for branding wines that it sells in America. Drawing on fruit grown at the Brancott vineyard, Fairhall Estate, Renwick Estate, Kaituna, and Squires Vineyards, the winery feeds regionally blended and single-vineyard varietals into Montana's commercial and higher-quality wines, including the highly regarded Reserve range. Brancott also has offers *méthode traditionnelle* range which includes its Deutz Marlborough Cuvée and Lindauer.

REGIONAL DOZEN

QUALITY WINES

Cloudy Bay Sauvignon Blanc
Corbans Cottage Block
　Noble Riesling
Framingham Classic
　Riesling UC
Fromm La Strada Reserve
　Pinot Noir
Villa Maria Reserve
　Marlborough Chardonnay
Villa Maria Wairau Reserve
　Sauvignon Blanc

BEST VALUE WINES

Babich Marlborough
　Sauvignon Blanc
Grove Mill Sanctuary Riesling
Matua Shingle Peak Pinot Gris
Montana Lindauer Reserve
　Méthode Champenoise
Mount Riley Sauvignon Blanc
Selaks Drylands Chardonnay

Montana uses the Brancott Estate to produce wines for the American market.

New graftings in a nursery at Brancott.

LE BRUN FAMILY ESTATE
Established 1996 *Owners* **Daniel and Adele le Brun**
Production **2,160 cases** *Vineyard area* **10 acres (4 ha)**

Champenois Daniel le Brun proved to the world that New Zealand had the potential to produce great sparkling wine. Establishing his vineyard in chardonnay, pinot meunier and noir, he carved subterranean storage caves deep into the Renwick Hills and built the Cellier Le Brun winery (see below)—all before 1983. In 1987, he lost control of that company and later withdrew as a partner, eventually setting up this establishment in 1996. His first new sparkling wine, Daniel No. 1—a fine-grained, elegant, *blancs de blancs* chardonnay—suggests a return to form.

CAIRNBRAE WINES
Established 1980 *Owners* **Murray and Daphne Brown**
Production **15,000 cases** *Vineyard area* **45 acres (18 ha)**

The Browns are former Corbans growers who established their own winery in 1992 and employed Kim Crawford to supervise the winemaking. Cairnbrae's stony-soiled vineyard sits on a hill overlooking neighbor Cloudy Bay, and is among the region's first to ripen. Stylistically, the wines carry Crawford's clean, fruit-focused touch. So far, strengths include the silky, citrusy semidry Riesling; nonherbaceous, tropical-fruit-driven Sauvignon; and buttery, mendoza-clone Chardonnay. Pinot gris and pinot noir will shortly be added to the portfolio.

CELLIER LE BRUN
Established 1980 *Owner* **Recene Paint** *Production* **21,600 cases** *Vineyard area* **79 acres (32 ha)**

Originally established by Frenchman Daniel le Brun, this winery was the first to prove New Zealand could make great sparkling wine. Daniel le Brun eventually lost control in 1996 and has moved on to the Le Brun Family Estate (see above). The new owners have maintained both style and quality, adding the reasonably priced, well-made Terrace Road range which includes a Sauvignon Blanc, Chardonnay, Méthode Traditionnelle and a Pinot Noir that is consistently among New Zealand's best buys. The sparkling range (which draws on chardonnay, pinot meunier and/or pinot noir) includes a medium-bodied, yeasty Brut NV; the Brut Tache, a pinot-dominated rosé; a full-bodied vintage; and the crisp, elegant Blanc de Blancs (chardonnay). A Millennium Cuveé was also made.

CLIFFORD BAY ESTATE
Established 1994 *Owners* **Eric and Beverley Bowers**
Production **11,500 cases** *Vineyard area* **49 acres (20 ha)**

Initially, the Bowers contracted out chardonnay and sauvignon from their vineyard in the Awatere

Valley. As show results reinforced the view that Clifford sauvignon fruit had something special, they quickly developed their own label made by Vavasour's Glenn Thomas. Their first release, the 1997 Sauvignon Blanc, won gold at all of New Zealand's annual wine competitions. The wines produced since (Chardonnay, Sauvignon Blanc and Riesling) have been marked by expansive, tropical-fruit flavors and full bodies.

CLOUDY BAY

Established 1985 *Owners* Cape Mentelle and Veuve Clicquot Ponsardin *Production* 100,800 cases *Vineyard area* 198 acres (80 ha)

No one can deny Cloudy Bay's status as *the* iconic white of the South Pacific. Dressed in one of wine's most elegant and recognizable labels, no other Australasian brand, excepting perhaps Penfold's Grange, is as famous worldwide. Cloudy Bay is to New Zealanders what Grange is to Australians: a source of national pride and a unique cultural product on a par with the best in the world. The Cloudy Bay story is well known in the wine world: suave boys from Cape Mentelle in Western Australia's Margaret River region fall in love with Marlborough's amazingly pure, vibrant sauvignon fruit; an intermarriage made in heaven follows; and worldwide success ensues.

All of the wines rank with the country's best. The Sauvignon Blanc, an explosion of mangoes, passion fruit and pungent sweat, is not far off MW Bob Campbell's well-coined phrase "like bungee jumping into a gooseberry bush," while the newly released, barrel-fermented Te Koko Sauvignon (preaged four years and on oak for 18 months) has a quieter voice. The long-lived Chardonnay is a flavor mix of low-yield fruit, French-oak fermentation, both wild and inoculated yeast, lees age and partial malo. The Pelorus Méthode Traditionnelle, a pinot/chardonnay blend made with full malo and barrel fermented, helped set a benchmark for top-end Kiwi bubblies. The Pinot Noir has steadily evolved a style that is multilayered, complex and elegant. Made in small quantities, both the Late Harvest Riesling and relatively new Gewürztraminer are overlooked jewels in their own right.

DOMAINE GEORGES MICHEL

Established 1998 *Owner* Georges Michel *Production* 792 cases *Vineyard area* 10 acres (4 ha)

Frenchman Georges Michel, owner of Château du Grandmont in Beaujolais, bought the old Merlen winery and now has Grandmont's wine-maker, Guy Brac De La Perrier, fly in on a regular basis to oversee winemaking here. The marriage of French style and ripe Kiwi grapes has produced a Sauvignon Blanc and Chardonnay marked by fine textures, great length and tropical-fruit characters, but kept in check by layers of savoriness. Stylistically wild by French standards, the result is restrained for a Kiwi wine. A Pinot Noir is planned and many wish Beaujoulais's gamay grape were given its day here.

FAIRHALL DOWNS ESTATE WINES

Established 1981 *Owners* Ken and Jill Small, Stuart and Julie Smith *Production* 6,840 cases *Vineyard area* 79 acres (32 ha)

Originally a contract grower, since 1994 this Brancott Valley vineyard has produced its own label at Forrest Estate Winery (see below). The first-vintage 1996 Sauvignon Blanc set the style for what was to come, with a punchy mix of passion fruit and nettles in a full, rich texture. The Chardonnay is large-scale with generous toasted butterscotch characters. Recently a Pinot Gris has been added to the range.

FORREST ESTATE WINERY

Established 1989 *Owner* John Forrest *Production* 28,000 cases *Vineyard area* 173 acres (70 ha)

Trained biochemist Dr John Forrest initially gained hands-on winemaking experience with Corbans and Grove Mill; thereafter he planted grapes for his own label in 1989 and established an onsite winery in 1996. Forrest is a proponent of low cropping and intensive viticulture, with a preference for transparently fruited, nonoaked wine, and his portfolio has consistently shown savory

Cellier Le Brun was the first New Zealand winery to make outstanding sparkling wines.

With its distinctive label design, Cloudy Bay is one of New Zealand's best known wineries.

complexities, suppleness and structure. Strengths include a densely textured, lees-aged Sauvignon Blanc that carries a touch of barrel-fermented sémillon (5–15 percent); a lees-influenced, lightly oaked, partially malo-fermented Chardonnay; and, in ripe years, a plummy, richly textured Merlot that is often among Marlborough's better examples of this varietal. Forrest is codeveloping a vineyard and label in Hawkes Bay with Australian viticulturist Bob Newton, producing a bordeaux blend branded Cornerstone.

A riesling specialist, Framingham also produces gewürztraminer and pinot gris.

FOXES ISLAND WINES

Established 1992 *Owner* John Belsham *Production* 2,520 cases *Vineyard area* 13.6 acres (5.5 ha)

John Belsham manages the contract winemaking facility Raupara Vintners and is an equal partner with Matua and Wairau River there. Foxes Island is his private label, which focuses only on chardonnay and pinot noir. The earthy, elegant, creamy, complex Chardonnay has been consistently better than the Pinot Noir, but recent vintages have seen a riper, more savory, style evolving in the latter, promising greater things in future.

FRAMINGHAM WINE COMPANY

Established 1981 *Owners* Rex and Paula Brooke-Taylor *Production* 17,000 cases *Vineyard area* 37 acres (15 ha)

Marlborough's premiere riesling producer, Framingham originally grew grapes for Corbans. In 1986, the company's owners helped establish Grove Mill, before developing their own label in 1990. Recently, it has developed a vintage-swapping relationship with Gruss of Equisheim in Alsace, whereby winemakers from the two wineries work the harvests in both regions. Framingham Riesling, Dry Riesling and Late Harvest Riesling

Grove Mill's mainly white output draws on its own vineyards and those of its shareholders.

are all marked by purity of varietal character, silky textures and great length. A new Pinot Gris and Gewürztraminer follow similar lines, erring on the side of restraint and subtlety. Additional plantings of syrah, merlot and montepulciano showed promise during Marlborough's run of hot vintages in the late 1990s.

FROMM WINERY

Established 1992 *Owners* Georg and Ruth Fromm *Production* 3,456 cases *Vineyard area* 15 acres (6 ha)

The Fromms, fourth-generation Swiss winemakers who specialize in pinot noir, established their Marlborough plantings in 1992 after visiting compatriot Hatsch Kalberer, then assistant winemaker at Matawhero. Bucking what was the norm in Marlborough, the Fromms' planned to make red wines, and at a time when Marlborough was firmly committed (incorrectly) to cabernet sauvignon, they planted pinot noir, malbec, syrah, sangiovese, merlot and cabernet franc. Understanding that success with these varieties required labor-intensive viticulture of a type not yet conceived of in the region, the Fromms' introduced close planting, shoot thinning, leaf plucking and bunch dropping. Since then, their output has demonstrated to all the importance of commanding the vineyard absolutely.

Fromm's La Strada and, in good years, La Strada Reserve labels are marked by velvety textures, well-integrated fine tannins, rich flavors and deep aromas. The consistency of La Strada Pinot Noir during the cool Marlborough 1995 and 1996 vintages had many local producers thinking they should pull out their cabernet and replace it with this grape. Fromm's radical approach has quietly begun a revolution that is only now yielding results.

GROVE MILL

Established 1986 *Owners* Public shareholders *Production* 55,000 cases *Vineyard area* 99 acres (40 ha)

David Pearce, formerly Corbans' Gisborne chief winemaker, has shaped wine styles here from day one, drawing primarily on Wairau Valley fruit grown under contract by many of Grove Mill's shareholders. The winery's reputation rests mainly on a spicy, semisweet Riesling marked by high levels of alcohol, extract, glycerol and 0.6–0.7 ounces (18–20 g) of residual sugar; and a Sauvignon Blanc, made with some barrel fermentation, malo and a small sémillon component, which is stylistically more variable but always a mix of Marlborough "sweatiness" and tropical fruits. All the estate wines are free run juice. The Sanctuary Unwooded

The distinctive Italianate buildings of Highfield Estate crown the home vineyard.

Chardonnay, Sauvignon Blanc and Riesling are consistently high quality and excellent value.

HIGHFIELD ESTATE

Established 1990 *Owners* Shin Yokoi and Thomas Tenuwera
Production 16,000 cases *Vineyard area* 10 acres (4 ha)

This modern Tuscan-style winery has so far produced a commercial range of wines marked by safety rather than excitement. Its premium label, Elstree, has rarely commanded the quality or flair expected within its price bracket. The one exception is the Elstree Cuveé Méthode Traditionnelle, a light, elegant, blend of equal parts chardonnay and pinot noir. The arrival of winemaker Alistair Soper may improve past performance.

HUIA VINEYARDS

Established 1996 *Owners* Claire and Mike Allan
Production 7,600 cases *Vineyard area* 20.5 acres (8.3 ha)

Winemaking partners Claire (ex-Corbans) and Mike (ex-Cloudy Bay) Allan previously established a reputation at Lawson's Dry Hills with consistently exciting, high-quality wines. Although it is early days, their own newly established winery should soon be among the best of Marlborough's smaller producers. The estate vineyards were chosen for their low vigor and planted in the newest French clones available, and are intensively managed. Winemaking follows low-tech traditions, using natural yeast, minimal intervention and no fining. The first-release wines show great promise: the Dijon Clone 95/96 Chardonnay is subtle, minerally, long and seamless with a fine viscosity; the Gewürztraminer displays delicate roselike aromas but is explosive and nervy on the palate; the spicy Pinot Gris has similar palate weight; and the fine-grained Pinot Noir has mushroom characters.

HUNTER'S WINES

Established 1980 *Owner* Jane Hunter OBE *Production* 40,680 cases *Vineyard area* 45 acres (18 ha)

After the premature death of her husband Ernie in 1987, Jane Hunter (a former Montana chief viticulturalist) took over stewardship of Hunters. She has since been awarded an OBE for her contributions to the international promotion of New Zealand wine. Historically, both Hunter's and Cloudy Bay's unoaked sauvignon blancs have provided barometers with which to guage each successive Marlborough vintage. Hunter's refreshingly herbaceous, passionfruit-filled version also has a riper, fuller, barrel-influenced, fumé-styled cousin, which is a classic in its own right. The pure mendoza-clone Chardonnay, incorporating purposely underplayed barrel fermentation, malo, and lees aging, was among the first New Zealand chardonnays to be recognized by British commentators in the mid-1980s for its high quality. More recently, a steady refinement in the style of Hunter's Pinot Noir suggests a tremendous future. The two bargains of the range are an off-dry, spicy Riesling and an intensely aromatic, creamy-textured Gewürztraminer, both displaying deep extract and excellent acid support. A relationship with Domaine Chandon has ensured Hunter's Brut consistently ranks in the country's top five bubblies.

The recently established Forrest Estate Winery focuses on nonoaked styles.

Trained vines at Hunter's Wines, which makes one of Marlborough's benchmark sauvignons.

ISABEL ESTATE VINEYARD

Established 1982 *Owners* Michael and Robyn Tiller
Production 15,000 cases *Vineyard area* 124 acres (50 ha)

Isabel Estate established its reputation as a top-quality contract grower for Cloudy Bay. The vineyard's calcium-rich soil contains a high quantity of fossilized shellfish that imparts strong mineral qualities to the fruit. Here, viticulture is paramount, intensive and heading toward organic certification. In 1994, Isabel began producing wine under its own label, turning to viticulturally trained winemaker Jeff Sinnott. Since then, the winemaking has been *terroir*-oriented and noninterventionist, employing natural yeasts and soft handling. The three wines—Chardonnay, Pinot Noir and Sauvignon Blanc—share a complex style, with transparent fruit underpinned by savory complexities, seamless textures and great length. An estate that shows great potential.

JACKSON ESTATE

Established 1988 *Owners* John Stichbury, Tony Nightingale, Colin Churchouse and Dave Williams
Production 50,000 cases *Vineyard area* 104 acres (42 ha)

Established originally as a grape grower, Jackson Estate has always focused on growing good fruit using carefully managed, unirrigated vineyards and strategies such as low yields, leaf plucking and bunch dropping. The wines use only grapes from their own estate and are made at Raupara Vintners by Australian flying winemaker Martin Shaw. Jackson's strengths include: a focused, herbaceous Sauvignon Blanc with crisp, unbusy textures; a powerful, buttery, oaky Chardonnay that ages well; a punchy, bone-dry Riesling; and a vintaged, lees-aged Méthode Traditionnelle Brut (60 percent pinot noir and 40 percent chardonnay) with pronounced toasty, autolytic characters and elegance.

LAWSON'S DRY HILLS WINES

Established 1982 *Owners* Ross and Barbara Lawson, and shareholders *Production* 21,000 cases
Vineyard area NA

Lawson's Dry Hills proved that small is good in Marlborough, and for most of the last ten years has produced interesting, high-quality wines. Originally a contract grower, the home vineyard is planted exclusively with gewürztraminer and considered one of the best sites in Marlborough for that variety. Recently, Lawson's has consistently produced one of the region's top gewürztraminers: intensely focused, stylish and long, with a nervy, acid spine. German-trained winemaker Mike Just's Wairau-Valley-sourced 1999 Sauvignon Blanc was also universally considered among the best produced that year.

MOUNT RILEY WINES

Established 1995 *Owners* John Buchanan and Steve Hotchin
Production 15,480 cases *Vineyard area* 131 acres (53 ha)

Mount Riley was originally a winemaking and grape-growing partnership between Buchanan, Hotchin and Alan Scott, which drove a highly regarded second-tier label for Scott. Eventually it became a stand-alone label holding significant acreage in four vineyards and producing wines made at Raupara Vintners by Bill Hennessy. The range is generally regarded as undervalued in re-lation to its quality. In particular, the Sauvignon Blanc and Riesling are seen as bargain-priced, classic expressions of typical Marlborough style. A winery is under development.

NAUTILUS ESTATE

Established 1986 *Owner* Yalumba *Production* 55,000 cases
Vineyard area 54.3 acres (22 ha)

The New Zealand arm of Yalumba's empire is a major shareholder in Raupara Vintners and owns vineyards in the Wairau and Awatere Valleys. Generally, its styles show restraint and balance, with an emphasis on clean, clear fruit characters. The best wines include a classic, herbaceous Sauvignon Blanc; a complex, refined Cuvée Marlborough Méthode Traditionnelle; and a fine-grained, nutty Chardonnay. The excellent-value second label, Twin Island, has successfully added a NV Pinot/Chardonnay Méthode Traditionnelle to the well-made, varietally defined Chardonnay, Sauvignon Blanc and Riesling.

OMAKA SPRINGS ESTATE

Established 1989 *Owners* Geoffrey and Robina Jensen
Production 20,160 cases *Vineyard area* 148 acres (60 ha)

Omaka owns substantial vineyards in the Omaka Valley, where it has also established a 20-acre (8-ha) olive grove. The wines are highly regarded in Europe for their emphasis on restrained fruit, subtlety and structure. The strongest suits are a lightly oaked Chardonnay and a consistently fine-grained Sauvignon Blanc blended with 10 percent sémillon. In ripe years, a pure, unwooded, plummy Merlot is a bargain. Generally, the wines are reasonably priced, good examples of food rather than bever-age wines. New vineyards of gamay, pinot gris and pinot noir will extend the portfolio.

OYSTER BAY

Established 1990 *Owners* Jim and Rosemari Delegat
Production NA *Vineyard area* NA

Oyster Bay vineyards is Auckland-based Delegat's (see p. 585) Marlborough operation. It is situated in Wairau Valley on shallow, stony soils above deep layers of free-draining river shingle. Both the Sauvignon Blanc and Chardonnay are fruit focused, clean, and consistently well made. The latter is 75 percent barrel fermented in new French oak and lees influenced, but purposefully avoids malolactic fermentation to preserve structure and fruit focus.

SAINT CLAIR ESTATE WINES

Established 1978 *Owners* Neal and Judy Ibbotson
Production 20,000 cases *Vineyard area* 99 acres (40 ha)

Saint Clair was established in 1994 by contract growers Neal and Judy Ibbotson as their own brand. Beyond the original estate, their holdings include vineyards in the Omaka, Awatere and Raupara subregions. Remarkably, every Saint Clair wine produced so far has won a medal somewhere in the world. Stylistically, they bear winemaker Kim Crawford's clean, focused, fruit-driven hallmark. The basic range is good value, with an excellent, supple, complex, single-vineyard Awatere Sauvignon Blanc and a plummy, richly textured Raupara Merlot often among Marlborough's best.

ALLAN SCOTT WINERY

Established 1990 *Owners* Allan and Catherine Scott
Production 44,000 cases *Vineyard area* 104 acres (42 ha)

A former Corbans chief viticulturist, Allan Scott also helped established Montana's first Marlborough vineyards in 1973. He struck out on his own in the 1990s and his winery, opposite Cloudy Bay

A former contract grower, Isabel Estate now produces its own range of wines.

The Lawson's Dry Hills estate southeast of Blenheim is planted only with gewürztraminer.

The mountains of the Southern Alps loom over the vineyards of the Wairau Valley.

on Jackson Road, is now among the country's top 20 producers. Scott's wines have consistently been among Marlborough's best each year, with his Riesling and Sauvignon tending stylistically toward understated fruit, austerity and a zesty acid structure. Recently, he has added a specially selected Prestige reserve range and a Méthode Traditionnelle without affecting the quality of his standard lines.

SELAKS DRYLANDS ESTATE WINERY
Established **1934** *Owners* **Nobilo** *Production* **90,000 cases**
Vineyard area **45 acres (18 ha)**

Drylands was originally established by Auckland-based winemakers Selaks to source and process Marlborough fruit for white varietals and a Méthode Champenoise. Since its takeover by Nobilo in 1998, the winery has also produced Nobilo's multitiered Marlborough range, including its top-end Icon Series. The Drylands' range quickly established itself in the mid-1990s with a run of bargain-priced, distinctive, single-vineyard wines including a herbaceous, passionfruit-laiden, lees-aged Sauvignon Blanc and a barrel-fermented (both French and American oak), lees-stirred Chardonnay. Both have consistently been among Marlborough's best buys.

SERESIN ESTATE
Established **1992** *Owner* **Michael Seresin** *Production*
15,840 cases *Vineyard area* **136 acres (55 ha)**

A film director and cinematographer, Seresin has invested heavily in a winery and estate that should become major stars in Marlborough. Intensive viticulture, clonal selection and wild yeast ferments ensure complex, subtle, understated wines across the range. The low-cropped, varietally pure Dry Riesling is among Marlborough's top five, the

Sauvignon Blanc (10 percent sémillon) is just as good, and the Chardonnay, Pinot Gris and Pinot Noir are distinguished by underplayed fruit, savoriness, finesse and balance.

SHINGLE PEAK WINES
Established **1990** *Owner* **Matua Valley**
Production **25,200 cases** *Vineyard area* **40 acres (16 ha)**

Auckland-based Matua Valley Wines (see p. 587) created medium-priced Shingle Peak as their Marlborough brand. Produced at Raupara Vintners (which is partly owned by Matua, Foxes Island and Wairau River), this label is renowned for its innovation, high quality and low prices. The Sauvignon Blanc, Riesling and Méthode Traditionnelle (made up of 80 percent pinot noir and 20 percent chardonnay) are normally among the best-value examples in the country, and the Pinot Gris was the first good-quality, New Zealand version available on a commercial scale. Similarly perceived as underpriced, the Shingle Peak Pinot Noir usually sells out quickly.

STONELEIGH VINEYARDS
Established **1989** *Owner* **Corbans** *Production* **340,000 cases**
Vineyard area **457 acres (185 ha)**

Stoneleigh Vineyards is Auckland-based Corbans' (see p. 584) Marlborough brand, and one of New Zealand's most internationally successful labels. Its strong reputation rests primarily on its zesty Sauvignon Blanc, which shows typical Marlborough "sweatiness," and the tightly knit, ripely fruited, honeysuckle-and-lime-scented Riesling. The impressive range also includes a sharply priced, well-made, fruit-forward Pinot Noir and a more commercially driven, obviously oaked Chardonnay. Stoneleigh also handles other Marlborough-designated Corbans brands.

TE WHARE RA WINES
Established **1979** *Owners* **Joyce and Allen Hogan**
Production **3,600 cases** *Vineyard area* **17.3 acres (7 ha)**

Difficult to find but worth the hunt, Te Whare Ra (meaning "house in the sun" in *Maori*) is a small winery that sells its produce only at the cellar door or via mail order. A variety of wines ranging from dry to sweet are produced from gewürztraminer, riesling, sémillon, and chardonnay, depending on the nature and variability of the vintage. Te Whare Ra's strength lies in dry, medium and late-harvested (bunch or berry selected) versions of gewürztraminer and riesling, all of which are quirky wines with complex personalities.

VAVASOUR WINES

Established 1986 *Owners* Tony Preston, Peter Vavasour and 25 shareholders *Production* 30,000 cases *Vineyard area* 72 acres (29 ha)

Vavasour was the first to open up the Awatere Valley, now acknowledged as having one of the region's prime mesoclimates. From the start, transplanted English winemaker Glenn Thomas has consistently produced top-quality, varietally focused wines, with a touch of European restrained elegance. The mid-priced Dashwood wines are excellent value: rich and sharply etched in ripe years, unexpectedly complex in difficult years when they incorporate declassified Vavasour. Both Vavasour Chardonnay and Sauvignon Blanc are barrel fermented, intense but supple, and finely balanced. Limited-quantity, single-vineyard versions are even more complex, concentrated and refined. A pinot noir style is still evolving, but showing tremendous potential.

WAIRAU RIVER

Established 1978 *Owners* Phil and Chris Rose *Production* 39,600 cases *Vineyard area* 247 acres (100 ha)

Originally contract growers for Montana, the Roses continue to sell grapes to other wineries. In 1991 they developed their own label and in 1995 they bought into the winemaking facilities at Raupara Vintners. Wairau's focus has been on a big, butter-and-oak Chardonnay, and a zingy, full-bodied, herbs-and-passionfruit-scented Sauvignon. Both are well made and reasonably priced.

WHITEHAVEN WINE COMPANY

Established 1993 *Owners* Greg and Sue White, Simon Waghorn, and three partners *Production* 13,000 cases *Vineyard area* 30 acres (12 ha)

Whitehaven occupies the 140-year-old building that once housed the Wairau Brewery. The company doesn't own vineyards, preferring to develop a close relationship with growers. Waghorn, a former Corbans Gisborne chief winemaker, works for a number of small wineries (including Bladen and Koura Bay), and has thus shaped styles across the region. Early Whitehaven wines were clean, focused examples of what Marlborough does best; recently, some have developed more distinctive personalities.

WITHER HILLS VINEYARD

Established 1987 *Owners* Brent and John Marris *Production* 20,000 cases *Vineyard area* 230 acres (93 ha)

The Marrises are Marlborough boys: John became the region's first contract grape grower in 1975 and son Brent the first qualified winemaker. The latter returned home in 1987 to set up a winery in the Wairau Valley with his father, intending to make top-flight wines. The ten trophies won since then suggest this was a smart move. From its first vintage, the Chardonnay has been a Marlborough classic: huge, with mouthfilling tropical-fruit flavors, and butterscotch and toasted oak. The Sauvignon Blanc has excelled for its opulent textures and intense tropical flavors, and the Pinot Noir has the potential to be one of the region's best.

Just a portion of the wines stored in the underground cellars at Cellier Le Brun.

A fine Riesling and Sauvignon Blanc are among the highlights of Allan Scott's range.

Nelson

An ingenious trompe l'œil mural depicts the characteristic landscape of the Nelson region.

The small, sunny and isolated region of Nelson held a strong appeal for potters, artists and other craftspeople during the late twentieth century, and since the early 1970s it has also attracted a small but dedicated band of winemakers. There are now 22 wineries in the region; however, most of them are small—they cover a total of only 432 acres (175 ha), or just 2 per cent of the total New Zealand vineyard area—and two long-established players, Seifried Estate and Neudorf Vineyards, dominate the region's production and profile. Moreover, development here is relatively slow compared to the country's other wine regions.

Vines were first planted in Nelson in the 1840s by German farmers, who were initially convinced of the region's potential but subsequently discouraged by the prospect of clearing large tracts of dense bushland. Most left not long after they arrived, moving on to Australia's Barossa Valley where they founded the local wine industry. Small vineyards were planted in the Nelson area in the 1860s and 1870s by F. H. M. Ellis in the Takaka area, where wine was made from grapes and other locally grown fruit, but production died out a short time afterward. In the middle of the twentieth century, an enthusiastic Frenchman, Viggo du Fresne, began to make wine at a small vineyard on Ruby Bay, but Nelson's modern industry only really got underway in the early 1970s when Austrian-born Hermann Seifried planted his

vineyard in the Moutere Hills. Today, Seifried Estate produces over half of Nelson's wine.

The region's hub is the city of Nelson, around which grapes are grown in two distinct areas, the Waimea Plains and the Moutere Hills. The wineries are divided evenly between the two areas, but most of the grapes are cultivated on the plains. The stony soils here produce grapes similar to those grown in Marlborough, and as Marlborough's plantable vineyard area runs out, its wineries are increasingly sourcing fruit from this part of Nelson. The Moutere Hills boast heavier soils with a clay-gravel mix. The gravel creates good drainage, while the clay provides a degree of water retention that is of particular benefit before the harvest, when rainfall is at its lightest. Wines produced from grapes grown in the Moutere Hills tend to be less upfront and fruity than their Waimea Plains counterparts. The chardonnay and pinot noir from this area are particularly good.

Located at the northwestern tip of the South Island, Nelson tends to be slightly cooler and wetter than Marlborough (where grapes are often picked a week earlier). The region has the highest rainfall of all the South Island grape-growing areas, with an average of 38.2 inches (979 mm) per annum. As most of this rain usually falls during the winter months, the growing season tends to be dry, with high levels of sunshine and relatively few dangerous spring frosts.

Chardonnay, occupying around 27 percent of the region's vineyards, is the most planted grape variety, followed by sauvignon blanc, pinot noir and riesling. Other varieties include cabernet franc, cabernet sauvignon, gewürztraminer, malbec, merlot, pinot gris and sémillon. It is thought that chardonnay will continue to dominate in the next few years, alongside sauvignon blanc, pinot noir and a little additional gewürztraminer and merlot. Plantings of riesling and cabernet sauvignon are not expected to increase greatly.

The white grapes have provided Nelson's most successful wines, with chardonnay and riesling being the star performers, followed by sauvignon blanc, the best of which rivals Marlborough. Although the pinot noir can also be of high quality, the cabernet sauvignon tends to display the herbaceous characters typical of a cool-climate region.

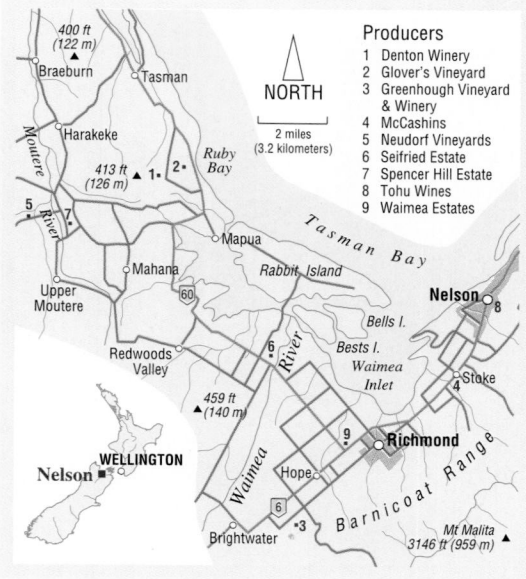

Producers
1 Denton Winery
2 Glover's Vineyard
3 Greenhough Vineyard & Winery
4 McCashins
5 Neudorf Vineyards
6 Seifried Estate
7 Spencer Hill Estate
8 Tohu Wines
9 Waimea Estates

DENTON WINERY

Established 1996 *Owners* Richard and Alexandra Denton
Production 2,052 cases *Vineyard area* 5 acres (2 ha)

This small winery shows great promise. First releases of its Reserve Chardonnays have been big, ripe and full of butterscotch characters, but also display a cutting acidity that provides balance. Its best wine so far is a spicy, floral, semidry Riesling with good length and extract.

GLOVER'S VINEYARD

Established 1984 *Owners* Dave and Penny Glover
Production 1,800 cases *Vineyard area* 17 acres (7 ha)

A mathematician who was exposed to full-bodied reds while researching in Australia, Dave Glover jumped ship, studied winemaking at Charles Sturt University and then headed home to New Zealand to make wines with spine. His pride and joy, produced only in ripe years, is a gutsy and seriously tannic Cabernet Sauvignon. More consistent are a minerally Riesling and a herbaceous Sauvignon Blanc, both of which have a knife-edge acidity that will support long-term development. The Pinot Noir is somewhat less convincing: all iron fist, no velvet; however, a recent Syrah showed good varietal character and balance.

GREENHOUGH VINEYARD & WINERY

Established 1980 *Owners* Andrew Greenhough
and Jennifer Wheeler *Production* 2,160 cases
Vineyard area 12.4 acres (5 ha)

A former art historian, Andrew Greenhough bought an existing vineyard and replanted it with the clones and density he determined would produce high-quality pinot noir, riesling, sauvignon blanc and chardonnay. Recent vintages suggest he is reaching his goal. The wines of the reserve Hope Vineyard range are ripe, focused expressions of their respective varietals, with seamless textures, complexity, balance and length; similar in style to Neudorf (see below) and not far off in quality. A star on the rise.

MCCASHINS

Established 1998 *Owner* Bryan Leslie
Production 14,400 cases *Vineyard area* 99 acres (40 ha)

McCashins was New Zealand's most successful microbrewer which, after selling distribution rights to a multinational, shifted attention to making hand-crafted wines. Although it is early days, the quality is good and expansion appears to be both well thought out and resourced. Production includes a Marlborough Sauvignon Blanc, Nelson Riesling, and vintaged Méthode Traditionnelle.

Nelson's vineyards enjoy high levels of sunshine during the growing season.

REGIONAL DOZEN

QUALITY WINES

Greenhough Chardonnay UC
Greenhough Hope Pinot
 Noir UC
Neudorf Moutere Chardonnay
Neudorf Moutere Reserve
 Pinot Noir
Neudorf Sauvignon Blanc
Spencer Hill Tasman Bay
 Chardonnay

BEST VALUE WINES

Seifried Dry Riesling
Seifried Gewürztraminer
Seifried Gewürztraminer
 Ice Wine
Seifried Riesling
Waimea Estate Riesling UC
Waimea Estate Sauvignon
 Blanc UC

The Seifried family were pioneers in Nelson and now have the region's largest vineyards.

NEUDORF VINEYARDS

Established 1978
Owners Tim and Judy Finn
Production 7,920 cases
Vineyard area 15 acres (6 ha)

Few people would argue that Neudorf makes New Zealand's finest Chardonnay. An animal scientist by background, Tim Finn brought scientific discipline to viticulture and winemaking early on in Nelson, locating a climate and soil that produce just enough fruit ripeness to allow aspects of *terroir* to shine through. Both of Neudorf's chardonnays share similar seamless textures and a meltaway finish, but Moutere is considerably more savory and slower to develop than the brighter-fruited, more forward Nelson.

The Brightwater Riesling and the Sauvignon Blanc are often among the country's top examples of these varietals. The floral Brightwater is especially dense and very long, whereas the Sauvignon has a finely etched structure and strong aromas. The Pinot Noir has been less successful, primarily due to early clonal selection, but the newer Dijon-clone replacements have shown more subtle aromatic qualities and multilayered complexity.

SEIFRIED ESTATE

Established 1973 *Owners* Hermann and Agnes Seifried
Production 80,000 cases *Vineyard area* 218 acres (88 ha)

The Seifrieds were among the vanguard who established Nelson as a viable wine region. Systematically, they have planted new vineyards in each of its subregions and are now its largest producer. Austrians by birth, they show a consistent gift for economically priced, classy rieslings and gewürztraminers, produced in a variety of dry, semidry, and late-harvested styles. The Old Coach Road range provides solid value for money, and a recently launched Winemaker's Collection has provided a successful forum for more serious varietal expression. Export success in Austria and Germany in the early 1980s was followed by a UK-specific label called Redwood Valley, which has produced a trophy-winning Sauvignon Blanc and a highly regarded, ageworthy, barrel-fermented Chardonnay.

SPENCER HILL ESTATE

Established 1990 *Owners* Philip and Sheryl Jones
Production 12,000 cases *Vineyard area* 57 acres (23 ha)

Winemaking viticulturist Philip Jones adds a bit of Californian flare to Nelson's portfolio: ever unpredictable and innovative (synthetic corks, wild yeast ferments), but also able to give people exactly what they want. His bread-and-butter Tasman Bay Chardonnay is a big, fruit driven, full-of-oak-and-butterscotch Kiwi classic. Every vintage has snatched gold or a trophy somewhere. The Tasman Bay Sauvignon Blanc and Pinot Noir consistently deliver a similar, fruit-forward message. Closer to Jones' heart, the single-vineyard Spencer Hill range is nervier, concentrated, complex, savory and seamless—the result of intense viticulture and complicated, sometimes dangerous, winemaking. Although batch produced, these are worth chasing down. Recent experiments with barrel-fermented pinot gris and pinotage are distinctive and promising. Jones also has plans to produce wines in California during the off-season.

TOHU WINES

Established 1998 *Owners* Wakatu Incorporation, Ngati Rarua Atiawa Iwi Trust and Wi Pere Trust *Production* NA
Vineyard area NA

This is a Maori partnership between tribal groups, or Iwi, represented by the Wakatu Incorporation of Nelson, Ngati Rarua Atiawa Iwi Trust of Motueka and Wi Pere Trust of Gisborne. The business, based in Nelson, has no plans yet for a winery, preferring to focus on producing varietals that are strongly associated with regions, principally for export. Those released so far include a Marlborough Sauvignon Blanc and chardonnays from Gisborne. The basic Chardonnay is unwooded, while the Reserve is barrel fermented and lees aged—quite a classy, understated drop. Both wines are made by Tony Bish of Sacred Hill in Hawkes Bay.

WAIMEA ESTATES

Established 1997 *Owner* Trevor Bolitho *Production* 4,824 cases *Vineyard area* 190 acres (77 ha)

Waimea Estates is being developed on land that was formerly a successful orchard on the Waimea Plains, and incorporates a café with a focus on local produce. The size of the operation and quality of the initial offerings (Sauvignon Blanc, Riesling and Chardonnay) suggest this is a winery to watch in future. The vineyard will also roll out merlot, cabernet/merlot, pinot noir and noble riesling wines as these vines reach maturity.

Canterbury/Waipara

The winegrowing areas of Canterbury and Waipara, on the east coast of New Zealand's South Island, are classified as a single entity, but in reality they are quite different. The soils, climates and styles of wine produced in each area have little in common; indeed, all they share is an ability to produce excellent chardonnay, pinot noir, riesling and, to a lesser extent, sauvignon blanc.

Together, Canterbury and Waipara form the country's fourth-largest wine-producing region. However, with just over 4 percent of the total national vineyard area, they are a long way behind the third-largest area, Gisborne. Currently, there are 39 wineries in Canterbury/Waipara, with a total of 896 acres (363 ha) under production. Canterbury has traditionally been the focus of grape growing and winemaking, but Waipara is increasingly being recognized as a producer of top-quality, and perhaps even more consistent, wines.

The Canterbury region surrounds the South Island's largest city, Christchurch. Despite the area's strong English heritage, it was French pioneers who first planted grapes here in the 1840s, on Banks Peninsula, to the east of the city. A small group of growers continues to work on the peninsula and a strong French influence still pervades the nearby township of Akaroa. Grapes were planted in the area again in the mid-twentieth century but failed to thrive. Canterbury's wine industry was finally kick-started by a group of wine enthusiasts at Lincoln University in Christchurch, who trialled a wide range of grape varieties in the early 1970s.

There are two main winegrowing areas in Canterbury: Banks Peninsula and the Canterbury Plains, to the west of the city. The soils in both areas are mainly alluvial, consisting of large river boulders intermingled with silty loam, and tend to be very free-draining. Soils in the Port Hills, located between Christchurch and the port of Lyttelton, have a higher clay content and more volcanic material. Generally, the soils are suited to chardonnay, pinot gris, pinot noir and riesling, but it's too early in the region's viticultural life to say which locations best suit individual varieties.

Canterbury's climate is cool maritime, with a low average annual rainfall of about 23.6 inches (606 mm). Frosts in both spring and fall, and regular, hot, northwesterly winds and cool, easterly sea breezes can create problems. As a result, vintages tend to vary significantly from year to year.

The most planted varieties are chardonnay (160 acres [65 ha]), pinot noir (150 acres [61 ha]) and riesling (106 acres [43 ha]), followed by pinot gris, sauvignon blanc, müller-thurgau and small plantings of merlot, breidecker, sémillon, gewürztraminer and syrah.

Waipara was traditionally a farming area, but severe droughts in the 1970s and various viticultural experiments have recently turned attention toward the potential of winegrowing. The first person to grow vines in the region was John McCaskey of Glenmark Wines, who planted hybrid varieties in the 1970s and *Vitis vinifera* vines in the 1980s. Although Waipara's vineyards

Along with chardonnay, pinot noir is a specialty at Waipara's Mountford Vineyard.

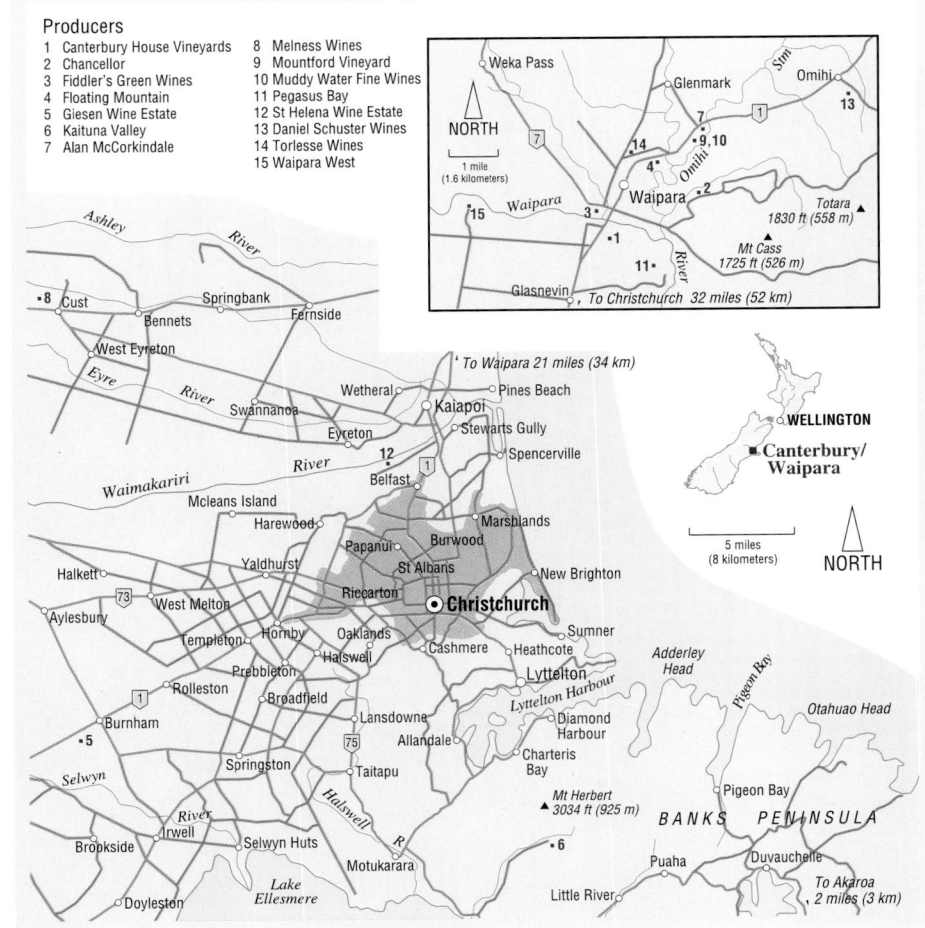

Producers

1. Canterbury House Vineyards
2. Chancellor
3. Fiddler's Green Wines
4. Floating Mountain
5. Giesen Wine Estate
6. Kaituna Valley
7. Alan McCorkindale
8. Melness Wines
9. Mountford Vineyard
10. Muddy Water Fine Wines
11. Pegasus Bay
12. St Helena Wine Estate
13. Daniel Schuster Wines
14. Torlesse Wines
15. Waipara West

REGIONAL DOZEN

QUALITY WINES

Giesen Botrytised Riesling
Giesen Reserve Pinot Noir
Pegasus Bay Aria Late Picked
    Riesling
Pegasus Bay Chardonnay
Pegasus Bay Pinot Noir
Pegasus Bay Riesling

BEST VALUE WINES

Corbans Private Bin Amberley
    Riesling
Giesen Canterbury Riesling
St Helena Pinot Blanc
St Helena Pinot Gris
St Helena Riesling
Torlese Gewürztraminer

The Mountford Vineyard winery offers fine views of the rolling Canterbury countryside.

are small, interest in the area is strong and recent growth has been rapid. However, expansion in Waipara (and Canterbury) is expected to slow during the next few years.

Waipara has lower rainfall and fewer frost problems than Canterbury, and is sheltered from the cool, easterly breezes by the Teviotdale Hills. The average annual rainfall is about 21.5 inches (550 mm), most of which falls in winter and early spring. Southerly winds are a double-edged sword for grape growers in spring, as they can interfere with fruit-set but also virtually eliminate overcropping, resulting in more intensely flavored wines.

There are two principal soil types in Waipara: silty alluvial soils beside the Waipara River and silty loams with patches of clay to the north of the river. The local consensus is that the former are best suited to cabernet sauvignon, which makes up 9 percent of the Waipara vineyard, and the latter are more appropriate for chardonnay and pinot noir. Most of the wines produced in Waipara are more full-bodied than their Cantabrian counterparts, probably as a result of the drier, less frost-prone climate.

The most planted grape variety in Waipara is sauvignon blanc (74 acres [30 ha]), followed by riesling (71 acres [29 ha]), chardonnay (69 acres [28 ha]) and pinot noir (66 acres [27 ha]). Cabernet

sauvignon is the next most-planted grape variety (22 acres [9 ha]), despite the fact that the resulting wines tend to be relatively herbaceous in flavor. It is followed at a long distance by cabernet franc, gewürztraminer, pinotage and sémillon.

CANTERBURY HOUSE VINEYARDS

Established 1997 *Owners* Michael Reid and Kathleen Corsbie
Production 20,000 cases *Vineyard area* 124 acres (50 ha)

Taking advantage of a major injection of funds from American backers, Canterbury House aims to triple production within the next three years and produce 150,000 cases of wine by the end of the next decade. Plantings currently underway will eventually produce chardonnay, merlot, pinot gris, pinot noir, sauvignon blanc, riesling and viognier. Initial offerings have been impressive, and although the long-term plan is to focus on pinot noir, the Sauvignon Blanc was awarded a trophy for best of vintage in New Zealand, and the Pinot Gris and Merlot are stylishly full-flavored.

CHANCELLOR

Established 1982 *Owners* Anthony and Helen Willy
Production 7,560 cases *Vineyard area* 41.5 acres (16.8 ha)

With plants nearing 20 years of age, Chancellor has some of North Canterbury's oldest grapevines.

The wines are currently made at Waipara Springs Winery by Kym Rayner, but an onsite winery is planned. So far, Chancellor's strengths have been in whites, with clean, well-focused sauvignon blancs and rieslings, and respectable chardonnays. The reds have been less consistent, with the Cabernet Sauvignon successful only in hot years.

FIDDLER'S GREEN WINES
Established 1997 *Owner* Barry Johns
Production 2,664 cases *Vineyard area* 37 acres (15 ha)

This small, relatively new winery was originally planted with sauvignon blanc and riesling; more recently, pinot noir, chardonnay and pinot meunier have been added. Made by Evans at Waipara West, the wines—a ripe, highly concentrated Sauvignon Blanc and a delicately floral, off-dry Riesling—suggest great potential, particularly when the other grapes come online.

FLOATING MOUNTAIN
Established 1992 *Owner* Mark Rattray *Production* 720 cases *Vineyard area* 10 acres (4 ha)

"Floating Mountain" is the translation of the Maori name for nearby Mount Maukatere. A graduate of the famous Geisenheim winemaking institute in Germany, Rattray consults for several wineries. His own venture (formerly known as Mark Rattray Vineyards) is planted densely with pinot noir and chardonnay, and will soon also include sauvignon blanc and scheurebe. Rattray's aim is to produce high-quality pinot noir and chardonnay, using yields restricted to less than 1.8 tons per acre (31.5 hl per ha). The 1998 Chardonnay was a whopping 15 percent alcohol, whereas the pinots produced so far are more tightly knit and marked by a tannic structure that will require time in bottle before it can be assessed accurately.

GIESEN WINE ESTATE
Established 1981 *Owners* Theo, Alex and Marcel Giesen
Production 54,000 cases *Vineyard area* 124 acres (50 ha)

Established by the Giesen brothers, immigrants from the Rheinpfalz, this is Canterbury's largest operation and is currently establishing a second winery in Marlborough. Giesen wines have always demonstrated a remarkable European sense of balance, finesse and restraint combined with clean, well-focused New Zealand fruit. The Marlborough Sauvignon Blanc is consistently one of the country's best buys; so too its low-yield, Pfalz-influenced, off-dry Riesling, which is floral and steely, and has mouthwatering acidity and high extract.

The free-draining vineyard consistently produces the dry botrytis that drives one of New Zealand's best late-harvested rieslings. During the mid-1990s, Giesen found repeated success with a complex pair of silky pinot noirs: one estate-grown, the second using fruit provided by Isabel Estate and other vineyards in Marlborough. Its restrained Chardonnay is typical of the best Canterbury reserves, retaining a crisply acidic inner structure even after full malo and barrel fermentation. Most Giesen wines need a few years in bottle to show their best.

KAITUNA VALLEY
Established 1993 *Owners* Grant and Helen Whelan
Production 576 cases *Vineyard area* 25 acres (10 ha)

Grant and Helen Whelan are pinot noir specialists with vineyards in both South Canterbury and Marlborough's Awatere Valley. The former was established in 1979, but replanted in 1999 with narrow rows of burgundian clones of pinot noir and chardonnay. The owners' attention to intensive vineyard management is a reflection of their other business, a vine nursery. The Pinot Noir from the 20-year-old plot has won several trophies—a testament to growing good fruit and letting it speak for itself.

ALAN MCCORKINDALE
Established 1996 *Owner* Alan McCorkindale *Production* 864 cases
Vineyard area 5 acres (2 ha)

Managing winemaker for many years at Corbans Marlborough, Alan McCorkindale has now established a small vineyard in

Canterbury House's winemakers have devised all sorts of strategies to protect their vines.

After years of service, decommissioned wine barrels are left to gather moss.

At the Pegasus Bay winery, the staff have found a novel use for empty wine bottles.

Muddy Water's vineyards include stocks of experimental varieties such as sangiovese.

Waipara to make *méthode traditionnelle* sparklers from selected clones of chardonnay, pinot noir and pinot meunier. His first release, Millennium Brut, has an elegant style, savory flavors and pronounced autolytic characters. McCorkindale also produces a Riesling, Chardonnay, Pinot Noir and Sauvignon Blanc from fruit provided by contract growers in Marlborough. One cannot underestimate his influence throughout Canterbury, where he currently makes wines for four other wineries.

MELNESS WINES
Established 1993   *Owners* Colin and Norma Marshall
Production 1,440 cases   *Vineyard area* 1.5 acres (0.6 ha)

Melness's wines are made at the Pegasus Bay winery (see below) using this organic estate's tiny output supplemented by contract fruit grown in Canterbury, Waipara and Marlborough. Generally, they have the generous textures and rich flavors of Pegasus products, the Chardonnay, Riesling and Sauvignon Blanc being the winery's best wines.

MOUNTFORD VINEYARD
Established 1990   *Owners* Michael and Buffy Eaton
Production 1,188 cases   *Vineyard area* 10 acres (4 ha)

This is a tiny, tightly focused operation, incorporating tastefully designed accommodation. The winery specializes in only two varietals: Chardonnay and Pinot Noir, both made by blind winemaker C. P. Lin (currently studying for the MW exam), who is well known for his sharp sense of smell and taste. Although it is early days, the first pinot noirs have shown ripe cherry flavors, richness and concentration, and the Chardonnay has tended toward a more obvious, full-on, buttery style. One to watch.

MUDDY WATER FINE WINES
Established 1996   *Owners* Michael and Jane East   *Production* 4,032 cases *Vineyard area* 30 acres (12 ha)

Muddy Water is a translation of the Maori word "Waipara." Estate plantings include pinot noir, chardonnay and riesling, with small experimental stocks of shiraz, sangiovese, cabernet sauvignon, cabernet franc, merlot and pinotage. Recently, the Pinot Noir has shown a savory complexity and firm structure. In contrast, the Sauvignon Blanc is opulent, tropical-fruit driven and highly alcoholic, and the fat, fleshy Riesling is full of honeysuckle and tart grapefruit characters, and the Chardonnay is fine-grained and nutty. A red called Laborare, which is blended from the experimental varieties, is a less convincing Waipara answer to Wairarapa's Ata Rangi's Célèbre (see p. 605).

PEGASUS BAY
Established 1992   *Owners* Ivan and Chris Donaldson
Production 19,440 cases   *Vineyard area* 100 acres (40 ha)

Under the leadership of neurologist Professor Ivan Donaldson, an international wine judge and wine writer, Pegasus Bay has established itself in a short period as one of New Zealand's top wineries. The vineyard commands a sheltered location, and subsequently experiences higher temperatures than other Waipara sites. The site and intentionally low yields have resulted in more consistent offerings than those produced by many of its neighbors. Generally, the wines are rich and ripe, but with added savory dimensions and multilayered complexities that lift them above the fruit-driven norm.

Pegasus rieslings have been outstanding: both the Arias, the off-dry and the late-harvest, are marked by silky, seamless textures; complex, varietally focused aromas; and rich, minerally flavors. The savory Chardonnay employs burgundian oxidative techniques, whole-bunch pressing and extended lees aging to construct complexity and drive length. In sharp contrast, the whopping great Sauvignon Blanc/Sémillon reeks of mango, guava and other tropical fruits. The unfiltered, voluptuous Pinot Noir is headed in the right direction, although it has tended toward excessive alcohol and overripe fruit flavors in hot vintages. In these same hot years, however, the Maestro and the Cabernet Sauvignon/Merlot both shine splendidly, possessing classic cigar-box and cedar aromas and dense textures. A second label, Main Divide, drawn from declassified Pegasus Bay and Marlborough fruit, can represent good value.

ST HELENA WINE ESTATE
Established 1978   *Owner* Robin Mundy   *Production* 16,200 cases   *Vineyard area* 74 acres (30 ha)

St Helena was the first Canterbury winery to focus on the pinot family, and by making the company's 1982 and 1984 "breakthrough" pinot noirs, winemaker Danny Schuster proved that the grape had a future in New Zealand. Owner Robin Mundy clearly has a knack for spotting star winemakers

early on in their careers: following Schuster, he employed Mark Rattray (now at Canterbury House and Floating Mountain) and then Petter Evans (now at Waipara West). Current winemaker Alan McCorkindale, formerly of Corbans Marlborough, has lifted quality throughout the good-value, but commercially styled, slightly pedestrian range. A recently introduced Reserve range (Pinot Noir, Chardonnay and Pinot Gris) has demonstrated sharper varietal definition as well as complexity, good length and a dash of excitement. The future looks bright for St Helena.

DANIEL SCHUSTER WINES

Established 1984 *Owners* Daniel and Mari Schuster
Production 4,536 cases *Vineyard area* 42 acres (17 ha)

Daniel Schuster is an internationally respected flying viticulturist and coauthor of the classic work *The Production of Grapes and Wine in Cool Climates.* An Austrian by birth but a longtime citizen of New Zealand, Schuster pioneered pinot noir at St Helena in the 1980s and has since established his own winery at Omihi Hills. As an early proponent of *terroir*-defined wine and food-friendly styles, his views are often at odds with an industry known for its bold fruit and emphasis on the winemaker as superstar. His Canterbury and high-priced Selection range (Chardonnay and Pinot Noir), made from Omihi Hills fruit, show restraint and subtlety.

TORLESSE WINES

Established 1990 *Owners* Kym Rayner and seven shareholders
Production 7,200 cases *Vineyard area* 45 acres (18 ha)

In the future, Torlesse hopes to double production; in the meantime, it will continue to supplement its modest output with fruit from contract growers in Marlborough. The estate wines are labelled Waipara Reserve; of these, the Chardonnay and Cabernet Sauvignon are of a high standard. The other varietals are, for the most part, well made, interesting and reasonably priced; they include a Pinot Gris, off-dry and dry rieslings, and a rich, edgy Gewürztraminer that is often an excellent buy.

WAIPARA WEST

Established 1989 *Owners* Paul and Vic Tutton and Lindsay Hill *Production* 5,472 cases *Vineyard area* 50 acres (20 ha)

Waipara West is pioneering a new subregion of Waipara, situated farther inland and high above the valley floor. Winemaker Petter Evans, formerly of St Helena Wine Estate, is a pinot noir specialist who evidently has a gift for that grape variety: recent vintages have shown deeply viscous textures, complex aromas and explosive flavors. The equally interesting Riesling is long, condensed and nervy, with an added mineral complexity. Other notable Waipara products include a savory, well balanced Chardonnay and a complex and herbaceous but fine-boned Sauvignon Blanc.

Pegasus Bay's winery has been designed in a style that suggests a French château.

Central Otago

Chard Farm's location takes full advantage of shelter and abundant sunshine.

Situated on the 45th parallel, Central Otago is New Zealand's and the world's most southerly winegrowing region. It is also one of the country's smallest wine-producing regions, with just 2.5 percent of the country's total vineyard area. Long-term this percentage is not expected to rise dramatically; however, growth has been rapid in recent years: between 1995 and 1999, plantings grew from 420 acres (170 ha) to 1,262 acres (511 ha). The main trigger for this was the success of pinot noir, which now accounts for 73 percent of the region's vines. It is followed by chardonnay, riesling, pinot gris and sauvignon blanc, and much smaller quantities of breidecker, gewürztraminer, sémillon, cabernet franc, cabernet sauvignon, merlot and syrah. Future increases in vineyard area are expected to come mainly from increased plantings of pinot noir, pinot gris and riesling.

Vines were first grown in Central Otago by a Frenchman named Jean Désire Feraud during the gold rush of the 1860s, and his unusually named "Burgundy red," "aniseed liquor" and "Constantia wine" won prizes at Sydney and Melbourne wine shows in the late 1870s. Feraud subsequently set his grape growing aside to become the mayor of Clyde township and concentrate on the region's general irrigation requirements, but some of his wines are still held by the Clyde museum.

Around the turn of the twentieth century, viticulturist Romeo Bragato declared Central Otago suitable for grape growing, with the proviso that growers were prudent in their choice of varieties and used irrigation. But no one took his words to heart until the 1970s, when Rolfe and Lois Mills of Rippon Vineyard at Lake Wanaka and Alan Brady, then of Gibbston Valley (and now at his own winery, Mount Edward), began to plant vines.

Central Otago was traditionally thought of as one grape-growing region, but it has recently been recognized as having four main subregions: Gibbston, Wanaka, Alexandra and Cromwell, which is further divided into the three distinct areas of Bannockburn, Lowburn and Bendigo. A fifth subregion, Lake Hayes, has few plantings, most of which are devoted to sparkling wine production.

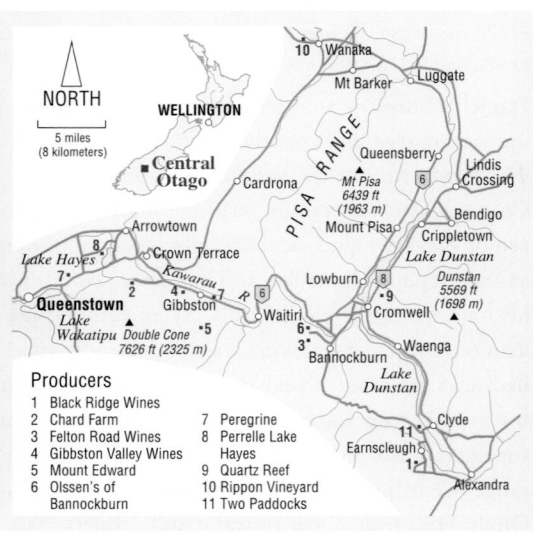

Producers

1 Black Ridge Wines
2 Chard Farm
3 Felton Road Wines
4 Gibbston Valley Wines
5 Mount Edward
6 Olssen's of
   Bannockburn
7 Peregrine
8 Perrelle Lake
   Hayes
9 Quartz Reef
10 Rippon Vineyard
11 Two Paddocks

The area's most planted subregion is Cromwell, with 60 percent of the total vineyard, followed by Gibbston with 27 percent, Alexandra with 8 percent and Wanaka with 4 percent.

Central Otago is New Zealand's only inland wine region, and the nearest city, Dunedin, is 171 miles (276 km) away. Viticulture is marginal here. The soils are all alluvial gravels, with some schist from glacial valleys, and because they are so free-draining, irrigation is usually required. Most vineyards lie 650–1,000 feet (200–300 m) above sea level and are planted on hillsides to take advantage of the region's high sunshine levels and avoid frost, which can affect the grape's growing cycle in spring at budburst and in autumn at ripening time. The dry summers, cold dry winters and low annual rainfall of 17.7 inches (454 mm) mean that humidity, and therefore the risk of vine disease, is low.

Differences in the style of wines arising from slight variations in climate and soil in each of the subregions are slowly being noticed. Gibbston and Wanaka, which are home to the oldest vines and have the coolest climates, tend to produce more earthy, delicate styles of pinot noir compared to the more fruit-driven, lush styles emanating from other subregions. The warmest areas, Bannockburn and Alexandra, are already showing that they could yield outstanding chardonnay and gewürztraminer.

Both the chardonnay and sauvignon blanc grown in Central Otago tend to be higher in acid than elsewhere in New Zealand, although both produce classic fruit-driven styles. The region now has more than twice as many plantings of pinot noir as Martinborough, and its winemakers clearly have every intention of challenging that region's dominance. Central Otago also has the potential to produce top-quality pinot gris, plantings of which are increasing. As tends to occur with pinot gris grown anywhere, the styles vary widely, from fresh and bracingly acidic to opulent and lush.

BLACK RIDGE WINES

Established 1981 *Owners* Verdun Burgess and Sue Edwards *Production* 2,664 cases *Vineyard area* 20 acres (8 ha)

No other New Zealand winery has as strong a claim to its *terroir* as Black Ridge: Verdun Burgess dynamited his entire vineyard out of micaceous schist. With their strong *terroir* influence and austerity, early Black Ridge vintages were difficult for fruit-loving New Zealanders to appreciate. Ultimately, however, the wines have won many converts and not a few hearts. The style remains relentlessly austere and bone dry, evidenced by

the Gewürztraminer and Riesling, both of which are infused with strong mineral characters and taught structures. Black Ridge wines age well: a vibrantly delicate, pure-fruit 1993 Pinot Noir, for example, had evolved into a magnificently complex, savory, finely structured wine when finally tasted in 1999.

The rocky soils of Black Ridge posed a major challenge to proprietor Verdun Burgess.

CHARD FARM

Established 1987 *Owners* Rob and Greg Hay *Production* 21,600 cases *Vineyard area* 37 acres (15 ha)

Chard Farm was replanted by the Hay brothers in 1987. Since then it has proved the advantages of cool-climate viticulture, while steadily overcoming the disadvantages. The leanness of cooler years has been fleshed out, ensuring a more consistently generous texture through which pure-fruit aromas and sharply focused flavors shine. The lees-stirred Pinot Gris, finely etched Sauvignon Blanc and Judge and Jury Chardonnay are brilliant food wines, while the Riesling and Gewürztraminer often show great aromatic depth and a steely spine. The top pinot noirs (Finla Mor and Bragato) generally need time to marry textures and evolve savory characters. New secondary labels have been introduced, covering single-vineyard wines from emerging hot spots such as Bannockburn, Lowburn and Lake Hayes.

FELTON ROAD WINES

Established 1991 *Owners* Stewart and Kate Elms *Production* 6,480 cases *Vineyard area* 30 acres (12 ha)

Felton Road arrived on the scene with a flourish

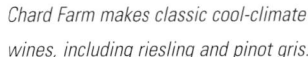

Chard Farm makes classic cool-climate wines, including riesling and pinot gris.

The oldest stone cottage in Central Otago is now the tasting room at the Peregrine winery.

Riesling; a nervy, well-focused Pinot Gris made from 20-year-old vines; and the excellent-value, unwooded Greenstone Chardonnay.

MOUNT EDWARD

Established 1988 *Owner* Alan Brady *Production* 14,400 cases *Vineyard area* 2.5 acres (1 ha)

Alan Brady, founder of Gibbston Valley, has given up management to get his hands dirty once again growing grapes and making wine. Although his operation is tiny, one should not overlook his 25 years' experience in the region. The focus is on pinot noir and getting viticulture, clones and hardware correct from the start, ensuring excellent wines follow. The first vintage showed complexity and a sophisticated understanding of the grape.

OLSSEN'S OF BANNOCKBURN

Established 1989 *Owners* Heather McPherson and John Olssen *Production* 4,680 cases *Vineyard area* 25 acres (10 ha)

Formerly a contract grower for Chard Farm, this new winery, located in the warm Bannockburn region, has struck out with its own label and a range shaped by one of Chard Farm's winemakers, Duncan Forsyth. Both the Riesling and Sauvignon Blanc are marked by finesse: the former is dry, full and minerally, the latter crisp, focused and herbaceous. So far the pinot noirs have shown respectable depth of flavor and broad aromatics, with sufficient balance and structure to age well.

of concentrated pinot noirs and a pair of richly textured, highly aromatic, steely rieslings (dry and semidry). Early success appears to owe much to the winery's warm Bannockburn location, devotion to low-yield viticulture and employment of traditional winemaking practices including the use of wild yeasts to stamp *terroir* on the wines from their inception. Blair Walter's input should not be discounted, however: he has previously worked pinot noir at Sokol Blosser in Oregon, USA; Tarrawarra in Australia's Yarra Valley; and Domaine de l'Arlot in Burgundy, France.

GIBBSTON VALLEY WINES

Established 1981 *Owner* Ross McKay *Production* 14,400 cases *Vineyard area* 74 acres (30 ha)

Founded by Alan Brady (now at Mount Edward), Gibbston Valley is one of the region's largest wineries. It draws fruit from many parts of Central Otago and Marlborough. When the local vintage is strong, the wines are site specific; in more difficult years, cross-blending helps fill in the gaps. Winemaker Grant Taylor stays on top of new

The temperature in Gibbston Valley's cellar is kept at a constant 56°F (13.5°C).

pinot noir developments by working vintages in Oregon and California, USA, and in Domaine Dujac , Burgundy. To date, his pinot noirs, which display the deep perfume, rich texture and firm structure that typify cool-climate pinot, have won seven international trophies. Other highlights include a finely balanced, complex

PEREGRINE

Established 1998 *Owners* Greg Hay and Adam Peren *Production* 6,480 cases *Vineyard area* 50 acres (20 ha)

This is a joint venture between Chard Farm's Greg Hay, Austrian winemaker Rudolf Bauer and Adam Peren. Its first-release Sauvignon Blanc won a national trophy for best of year, trouncing allcomers from Marlborough. Initial offerings have focused on cool-climate whites: pinot gris, riesling, sauvignon and chardonnay—all clean, crisp and well made.

PERRELLE LAKE HAYES

Established 1990 *Owners* Greg Hay and John Darby *Production* 7,200 cases *Vineyard area* Currently 12.4 acres (5 ha), but expanding progressively to 370 acres (150 ha)

Perrelle Lake Hayes is a new winery underpinned by a massive vineyard development backed by former Levi-Strauss president Tom Tusher. It aims to become Otago's largest sparkling-wine producer and, ultimately, the country's best. Taking champagne as its inspiration, the company focuses on traditionally, rather than technologically, driven methods. Its range includes a vintaged Perrelle Lake Hayes Blanc de Blancs Brut (100 percent chardonnay), Perrelle Lake Hayes Grande Cuvée Brut (65 percent pinot noir and 35 percent chardonnay, with two years on lees), a vintaged Perrelle Lake Hayes Cuvée J Cuvée de Prestige (75 percent chardonnay and 25 percent pinot noir, aged 3 years), and a vintaged Arcadia Lake Hayes Brut (40 percent pinot noir, 10 percent pinot meunier and 50 percent chardonnay). The serious intentions of this company cannot be ignored.

QUARTZ REEF

Established 1996 *Owner* **Bendingo Estate Partnership**
Production **NA** *Vineyard area* **7.4 acres (3 ha)**

Austrian Rudolf Bauer, formerly winemaker at Giesen and currently responsible for the Two Paddocks, Peregrine and Dry Gully vineyards, has formed a partnership with Clotilde Chauvet (of the Champagne house Marc Chauvet) and other financiers. Quartz Reef Chauvet NV Méthode Traditionnelle (80 percent pinot noir and 20 percent chardonnay) is made from Marlborough fruit and aged two years on lees. Its strawberry characters and creamy palate are clearly shaped by French and Austrian concepts of elegance and restraint. Other projects include a Pinot Noir and a Pinot Gris, both of which display multilayered complexity.

RIPPON VINEYARD

Established 1975 *Owners* **Rolfe and Lois Mills**
Production **6,984 cases** *Vineyard area* **31 acres (12.6 ha)**

For many years, this lakeside vineyard, located beneath a stunning mountain backdrop, was run on strict organic principles. It has since abandoned certification but retains its devotion to intensive, renewable viticulture. Stylistically, the wines are tightly knit, elegant and understated, although they need time to show their best. The range includes a durable Riesling; a fine-boned, seamless Chardonnay; an elegantly structured Sauvignon Blanc; a broadly perfumed, nervy Gewürztraminer; and an oddball, grapey osteiner. The Pinot Noir is often among New Zealand's best, displaying cherry and mushroom complexities, focused fruit, refined textures and juicy acids.

TWO PADDOCKS

Established 1997 *Owner* **Sam Neill** *Production* **NA**
Vineyard area **5 acres (2 ha)**

This winery's major claim to fame is its proprietor, movie star Sam Neill. Fortunately, Neill appears to understand just how much time, money and effort is required to set up a vineyard that will eventually produce great pinot noir. Initially, the wines were made by Rudi Bauer, but Dean Shaw subsequently took over the helm.

Perelle Lake Hayes vineyard, Central Otago. Winters here are cold but dry, meaning that the risk of vine disease is low.

Canada

632

Melville I.

Banks
Island

Prince
of Wales
Island

Baffin
Island

Admundsen
Gulf

Victoria
Island

Gulf of Boothia

Foxe
Basin

Fort McPherson

Koidern

Mt Logan
19,550 ft (5959 m)

Yukon Territory

Mackenzie

Mackenzie Mountains

Great
Bear Lake

North West Territories

Repulse Bay

Nunavut

Cape Dorset

Southampton
Island

Salluit

Haines Junction

Whitehorse

Baker Lake

Fort Simpson

Yellowknife

Great
Slave Lake

Dubawnt
Lake

Watson Lake

Yathkyed
Lake

Hay River

CANADA

Nueltin
Lake

HUDSON
BAY

ROCKY

British
Columbia

Peace

Alberta

Lake Athabasca

Wollaston
Lake

Athabasca

Cree Lake

Reindeer
Lake

Churchill

Churchill

Nelson

Belcher
Islands

Fort Severn

Queen
Charlotte
Islands

Peace River

Churchill
Lake

Manitoba

Severn

James
Bay

La Ronge

Ontario

Wask

Mt Waddington
13,176 ft (4016 m)

MOUNTAINS

Edmonton

Saskatchewan

Cedar
Lake

Grand
Rapids

Lake
Winnipeg

Albany

Moose
Factory

Vancouver
Island

Fraser

Kamloops

Calgary

Saskatoon

Lake
Winnipegosis

Lake
Seul

Lake
Nipigon

Cochra

Fraser
Valley

Lake Okanagan
Kelowna

Vancouver

Lake
Manitoba

Kenora

Vancouver Island

Victoria

Okanagan
Valley

Medicine Hat

Regina

Winnipeg

Lake of
the Woods

Thunder Bay

Lake
Superior

Sudbury

NORTH

Lake Hu

200 miles
(320 kilometers)

Lake Michigan

Lake Erie
North Shore &
Pelee Island

Lak

Canada

Tony Aspler

Canada was hardly recognized as a wine producing country until an Ontario dessert wine—the 1989 Inniskillin Vidal Icewine—won the Grand prix d'honneur at the 1991 Vinexpo in Bordeaux. This and subsequent prize-winning wines reflect the improvement in quality achieved since 1970 in the effort to counter Canada's legacy of inferior wines. Conscientious producers have worked together to develop an appellation system based on European models. The Vintners' Quality Alliance (VQA) governs the use of geographic or varietal designations, grape types and viticultural and winemaking practices. Now codified in the legislation of two producing provinces, Ontario and British Columbia, VQA requires passage into law at the federal level before international acceptance is complete. However, the sale of alcoholic beverages in Canada is controlled by provincial monopolies (apart from Alberta, where it is privatized) and, consequently, wine prices carry heavy markups. These monopoly markup systems are so inflexible that many Canadian wines are sold only in the province of origin.

Niagara Falls, with American Falls on the left and Horseshoe Falls on the right.

Wine is made in four distinct zones across Canada where microclimates provide respite from winter's icy blast. Ontario has the lion's share, with 80 percent of the country's wineries located in the Niagara Peninsula within a short distance of Niagara Falls. The remaining three areas are in the provinces of British Columbia, Québec and Nova Scotia. Because of the marginal climate, both hybrid and vinifera grape varieties are used, but with increasing emphasis on the latter. In the past the emphasis was on white grape varieties, although several red varieties, notably cabernet franc, pinot noir and gamay, have now been found to produce well.

Today, the industry is populated by serious winemakers who measure their success against internationally accepted standards. The development of the VQA appellation system has done much to advance quality and even lower priced, non-VQA wines benefit from the industry's overall attention to making better wines. One man stands out as a leader in this search for excellence: Donald Ziraldo, who founded Canada's first "boutique winery" in 1974, has been the driving force behind the establishment of the VQA. Awarded the Order of Canada in 1998 for his dedication to the industry, he was also involvedl in founding the Cool Climate Oenology and Viticultural Institute, Canada's first wine school, at Brock University in St Catharines, Ontario, in 1999. The scientific and educational contributions of this facility will help to keep Canada in the forefront of winemaking advancements.

History

Experience has shown that wine from indigenous North American grapes comes up short on palatability. If it is true that Lief Ericsson's crew made wine from the grapes they found in 1001, they could certainly be forgiven for a hearty endorsement of the wine's virtues after their undoubtedly harsh ocean crossing.

When the first stalwart European settlers arrived and settled in and around Québec and Montréal in the sixteenth century, wine was among their many deprivations. As in many areas of European settlement, the Catholic Church was instrumental in early wine production. In Canada, these early wines were based on local grapes and, according to the Jesuit missionaries, they were suitable only for mass. Since then, vineyardists have been searching for more desirable grape types that can survive the harsh northern climate and experimentation has identified zones where vinifera vines can thrive. Many excellent wines are now made from chardonnay, pinot blanc, riesling, cabernet franc, pinot noir and other desirable vines in suitable microclimates.

made by BC's Andrés Wines as the low-alcohol answer to Portugal's Mateus Rosé, became Canada's most recognized wine. Fortunately it was a temporary fad and consumers gradually started to demand a greater variety, which was fulfilled by an increase in imported European table wines. Many vineyards have now reached the levels of maturity that support the development of super-premium wines. The concomitant investment in technology has moved the Canadian wine industry into a position where it can compete with confidence at the international level.

Landscape and climate

Winter is the most critical climatic factor influencing the production of wine in Canada. Even the most vine-conducive regions are susceptible to the occasional spell of –4°F (–20°C) weather. Where wine is most successfully produced, large bodies of water provide some degree of protection against extreme cold and spring frost.

Canada's Niagara Peninsula is on the same latitude as the Midi in France and Italy's Tuscany, but lacks the benefit of a balmy Mediterranean climate. Fortunately, the certainty of freezing temperatures has benefitted the industry by assuring the production of icewine consistently every year. That vines can survive in Ontario at all is due to the mitigating influence of Lake Ontario and Lake Erie. In British Columbia, winemaking is dominated by tiny wineries, the majority of which sell their entire capacity at the farm gate. Most of the production occurs in the Okanagan Valley, which is located on the same latitude as France's Champagne, but the altitude and the semi-desert environment give Okanagan wines their unique character. Lively flavors and high acidity result from the marked fluctuation between hot daytime and very cool nighttime temperatures. Lake Okanagan is about 62 miles (100 km) long and provides a moderating influence on the climate.

The climates of Québec and Nova Scotia are less conducive to vine growing, particularly vinifera varieties. In Québec, the hybrids seyval, vidal and maréchal foch exhibit the required characteristics. However, even they must be hilled up with earth during the freezing winter and then uncovered for the growing season. In the maritime province Nova Scotia, the industry survives by blending local wines with imported wines, but homegrown specialties are produced. Two hardy Russian varieties, michurinetz and severny from the genus *Amurensis*, are cultivated locally.

Winemaking began in earnest in Ontario when Count Justin de Courtney purchased and expanded on some 1811 plantings near Toronto. He had some success in the 1860s producing wines from European varieties. Meanwhile, the regions that produce Ontario's wine today were being established on the Niagara Peninsula and Pelee Island. However, Ontario wine producers faced an uphill battle against the growing temperance movement. The ensuing struggle lasted more than 30 years, profoundly affecting the nature of the wines produced, and the results are still seen in the government monopoly on alcohol sales introduced in the early 1940s.

In British Columbia, winery development took a similar path if on a smaller scale. The first vineyard in BC's Okanagan Valley was planted in the nineteenth century by the Oblate fathers to make wine for sacramental purposes. Commercial ventures were established around Lake Okanagan, then other areas followed on Vancouver Island and on some smaller islands between Vancouver Island and the mainland. Much of the early wine industry centered on fruit other than grapes, and it wasn't until an oversupply of apples in the 1930s caused prices to drop that many farmers turned to grapes.

In the 1960s, light, sweet sparkling wines became the rage in North America, and a 7 percent alcohol sweet sparkler called Baby Duck,

Riesling icewine grapes on the Niagara Peninsula, Ontario.

Vines and wines

The first imported French vine cuttings were planted (unsuccessfully) in 1619 in the north of the United States; a few cross-pollinated with indigenous varieties, and these hybrids became vital to the emerging North American wine industry. Some very palatable wines are still made from such varieties as the white vidal and seyval blanc and the red maréchal foch and baco noir.

Many single varietal wines are made throughout Canada; blends of classic Bordeaux varieties, particularly reds, are increasing in Ontario and British Columbia. Proprietary blends are made for the lower price ranges, but they are not entitled to a VQA designation. Preferred vinifera grapes are mostly French and German varietals. Hybrids are grown in all provinces and are the mainstay of the industry in Québec and Nova Scotia. A few specified, high-quality hybrids are permitted by the VQA designation in Ontario and BC. Indigenous grape varieties are not suitable for wine.

Laws

To a varying degrees, the governments in Canadian provinces control the sale of alcoholic beverages, but winery owners have designed a set of standards regarding the production of wine. The Vintners' Quality Alliance (VQA) was established in Ontario in 1989 as a voluntary set of regulations. The VQA Act passed the Ontario provincial legislature in 1990, to become law in mid-2000. A similar system has been adopted in British Columbia, with some minor variance in criteria. Discussions aimed at harmonizing the Ontario and BC guidelines to form "VQA Canada" standards are progressing. Talks are also underway with Québec and Nova Scotia. The VQA rules cover a variety of quality issues, including:

- The boundaries of the designated viticultural areas (DVAs).
- The quantity of the wine that must be from grapes grown in the DVA specified on the label. If a vineyard is specified, 100 percent must be from that location.
- The quantity of the wine that must be from the specified vintage.
- The types of grapes—only vinifera or certain specified high-quality hybrid grapes may be used.
- The definitions of terms such as "select late harvest," "icewine" etc.

Meanwhile, it is difficult to obtain Canadian wine outside the producing province—the liquor monopolies treat wine made in another province as an import, forcing prices up. Also, competition for shelf space in shops is fierce. Outside Canada, protectionist policies in the European Union preclude Canadian wine's access to that market. In 1998, Canada sold less than $1 million of wine to Europe, but Europe sold about CAN$350 million (US$237.1 million) of wine in Canada.

Icewine

Icewine's phenomenal success has catapulted the Canadian wine industry into the international arena. Usually made from riesling and vidal grapes, icewine's concentrated bouquet and sweet taste is balanced by high acids, creating an elegant dessert wine. Producing icewine is always a gamble, though: the longer the grapes stay on the vine, the higher the risk of loss. Most producers wrap their vines in netting to protect them from birds and other fauna. The grapes can be lost to rot and mold if the autumn is overly wet.

In winter, the temperature must fall below 18°F (−8°C) and stay between 18°F and 3°F (−16°C) during picking and crushing. Then the water in the grapes freezes, and the thick, sweet juice can be pressed. If the temperature rises, the juice will be diluted and the wine will be ineligible as icewine; too cold, and the grapes are too hard to press. Picking is done by hand, and at night—even a few rays of sun can lift the temperature above the critical level. Pickers can be called out at the last moment—Christmas and New Year festivities are often disrupted by this time-sensitive operation.

British Columbia

Although much of BC's early wine was made from fruit other than grapes, a determined handful of purists persisted in seeking the appropriate varietals and the most suitable locations. Those locations have been largely confined to the Okanagan Valley, with a few vineyards established in the Fraser Valley, closer to Vancouver, in 1991 and on Vancouver Island in the mid-1990s.

In the 1920s, Hungarian enologist Dr Eugene Rittich and his brother planted 44 varieties of vinifera grapes to see if they would survive the winter. Since then, most of the varieties they determined to be suitable have been replaced by well-known French and German varieties. Grapes finally came into demand and farmers planted vineyards as quickly as they could in the 1930s when the price of apples dropped because of oversupply. However, despite vineyard expansion, wine production still did not assume a high profile until a law was passed in 1960 obliging wineries to use a minimum of locally grown grapes. In the four ensuing years, acreage quadrupled, mostly planted in hybrids.

In the late 1970s, British Columbia liberalized the liquor policy to support the wine industry and grape growers and contracted world-famous viticulturist Helmut Becker to test a number of European grape varieties. Of 27 European varietals tested, auxerrois, bacchus, ehrenfelser, pinot blanc, gewürztraminer, müller-thurgau, schönburger and scheurebe proved most suited to the BC climate. The federal and provincial governments then collaborated to sponsor a five-year grape growing program that resulted in German-style varietal wines dominating the industry for many years.

The Canada–US Free Trade Agreement signed in 1988 caused a major crisis in the BC wine industry, as it became apparent that the continued dependence on hybrid varieties would not provide a competitive edge in the new, liberalized market. Growers took advantage of government incentives and tore up about 65 percent of their acreage and replanted with vinifera vines. Many of these new vinifera plantings leaned more to French varietals, such as chardonnay, pinot blanc and pinot gris. Consequently, more wineries started producing drier, French-style wines. Growers were slower to embrace red varieties, but initial plantings in the warmer, southern end of the Okanagan Valley are promising. Pinot noir, cabernet franc, merlot and cabernet sauvignon are all in great demand.

Because of the high acidity resulting from the very hot days and very cool nights, sparkling wines, made from the traditional chardonnay and pinot noir grapes, have been very successful.

It took several years for the vineyards to produce, but wineries were then able to justify bottling premium wines and the market was eager to accept them. The 1993 International Wine and Spirits Competition in London confirmed the fact that the BC wine industry had come of age when it conferred the Avery Trophy for Best Chardonnay in the World on the 1992 Mission Hill Grand Reserve Chardonnay.

As in any cool-climate wine-producing region, care must be taken to locate vineyards where the risk of spring frost is minimal and to choose varieties, even clones, appropriate to the various microclimates. The Cool Climate Oenology and Viticulture Institute at Brock University is researching such specifics as canopy management, clone selection and even yeast selection in British Columbia to assist the wineries in making the right choices. Because the wine industry is still so young, viticulture and winemaking practices are continually evolving. In general, winemaking techniques follow the established criteria used in many European countries. For instance, most wineries have facilities for cold fermentation and oak aging. Small barriques, similar to those used by the famous Bordeaux châteaux, in either French or American oak, are preferred.

Freshly harvested gewürztraminer grapes.

Okanagan Valley

The majority of British Columbia wineries are found in the Okanagan Valley, parts of which experience near-desert conditions. Etched out by a retreating glacier, this long, steep valley runs north–south, nearly equidistant from the Rocky Mountains to the east and the Pacific coast to the west. The southernmost tip of the valley reaches almost to the US border. Lake Okanagan stretches about 62 miles (100 km) and is a mitigating influence on climatic extremes. Consistent and predictable summers provide a favorable environment for vines. A dramatic difference between the heat of the days and the cold of the nights contributes to high levels of acid in the wine, imparting structure and aging potential. Autumns are mild until the middle of October, when average temperatures drop significantly and any grapes not intended for icewine must be harvested.

In the warmest area, south of Lake Okanagan, average rainfall over the course of the year is a meagre 6 inches (15 cm), making irrigation a necessity. At the southernmost point of the valley, Osoyoos Lake is a mitigating influence in winter. Just north of this, part of the west side of the valley is called the "Golden Mile" for its row of contiguous wine properties. Further to the north, the area around Okanagan Falls and Vaseaux Lake also enjoys reliably hot daytime temperatures.

Continuing north, Naramata supports a wide range of grape types from hardy ehrenfelser to heat-loving syrah. Kelowna, in central Okanagan, is slightly cooler and from there north, crisp, flavorful German-style whites abound. Pinot noir and chardonnay are also cultivated successfully.

ANDRES WINES
Established 1961 *Owner* Andrés Wines (BC) Ltd
Production 500,000 cases *Vineyard area* 200 acres
(90.8 ha) contracted

Once known best for Baby Duck, the sweet sparkling success of the 1960s and 1970s, Andrés now has a diversified portfolio of blended and premium wines. When BC's quality revolution began in the 1970s, Andrés, which had 300 acres (122 ha) under contract with the Inkameep Indian Band, planted its vineyards to a variety of hybrid and vinifera vines. Currently, 95 percent of Andrés' contracted vineyards are planted to vinifera varieties for use in VQA wines under the Bighorn Vineyards and Peller Estates labels.

BLUE MOUNTAIN VINEYARD & CELLARS
Established 1991 *Owners* the Mavety family *Production* 12,000 cases *Vineyard area* 60 acres (24 ha)

A Burgundy-like climate, an established vineyard of pinot blanc, pinot gris, chardonnay and pinot

Vineyards at Naramata in the Okanagan Valley, British Columbia.

noir and a talented father-and-son team of wine-makers have made Blue Mountain one of the Okanagan's leading producers. When long-term grape growers Ian and Jane Mavety decided to make their own wine, they barrel-fermented their pinot blanc and their pinot gris and launched a stunning pinot noir. They also make some commendable sparkling wines. Winemaking duties fall to Ian and his son Mark, but they consult with California's Raphael Brisbois for the bubblies.

BURROWING OWL VINEYARDS

Established 1994 *Owners* the Wyse family and partners
Production 12,000 cases *Vineyard area* 290 acres (117 ha)

This vineyard has proven to the world that BC can produce great reds, in this case, merlot. The Wyse family's winery uses gravity flow to move the wine through the winemaking process. Winemaker Bill Dyer, who has a master's degree in enology from the University of California at Davis and worked for ten years at Sterling Vineyards in the Napa Valley, is enthusiastic about both the soil and the climate at Burrowing Owl Vineyards.

CALONA WINES

Established 1932 *Owner* Cascadia Brands *Production* 30,000 cases *Vineyard area* 360 acres (146 ha)

Wine from apples and other fruit formed the original basis of this company before the founding Capozzi family set out to emulate the prosperity of their fellow compatriots, the Gallos, in California. Proprietary blends have always contributed to the

financial success of this company but recently Calona has made a commitment to VQA wines. Varietal wines and two premium lines, Private Reserve and Artist Series, have won medals in recent competitions thanks to owner investment and the talents of winemaker Howard Soon.

CEDAR CREEK ESTATE WINERY

Established 1986 *Owner* David Ross Fitzpatrick *Production* 30,000 cases *Vineyard area* 40 acres (16 ha)

Formerly Uniake Winery, the name was changed with the new ownership in 1986. Under the direction of Kevin Willenborg, the emphasis is on pinot blanc, chardonnay, pinot noir and merlot, but German white vinifera grapes and Bordeaux reds round out the product line. French oak is used extensively both for fermentation of whites and for aging.

DOMAINE COMBRET

Established 1993 *Owner* Robert Combret *Production* 10,000 cases *Vineyard area* 30 acres (12 ha)

Originally from Provence, France, the Combret family has been in Canada since 1992. From their first Canadian vintage, 1993, they won a silver medal at the Challenge International du Vin at Blaye-Bourg in Bordeaux for a riesling made in the Alsatian style. Their chardonnay from the same vintage did well in an annual challenge held in Burgundy. Robert Combret's son Olivier, who trained at Montpellier, fulfils Domaine Combret's winemaking responsibilities.

GEHRINGER BROTHERS ESTATE WINERY

Established 1985 *Owners* Walter and Gordon Gehringer *Production* 15,000 cases *Vineyard area* 60 acres (24 ha)

The Gehringer brothers studied enology in Germany at Geisenheim and Weinsberg before they transformed their father's vineyard into a full-scale winery. They frequently use sussreserve, a technique of adding unfermented grape juice or grape concentrate to the wine before bottling, which is often used in Germany and elsewhere to counterbalance tartness in the wine. Their icewine can be depended upon to win medals.

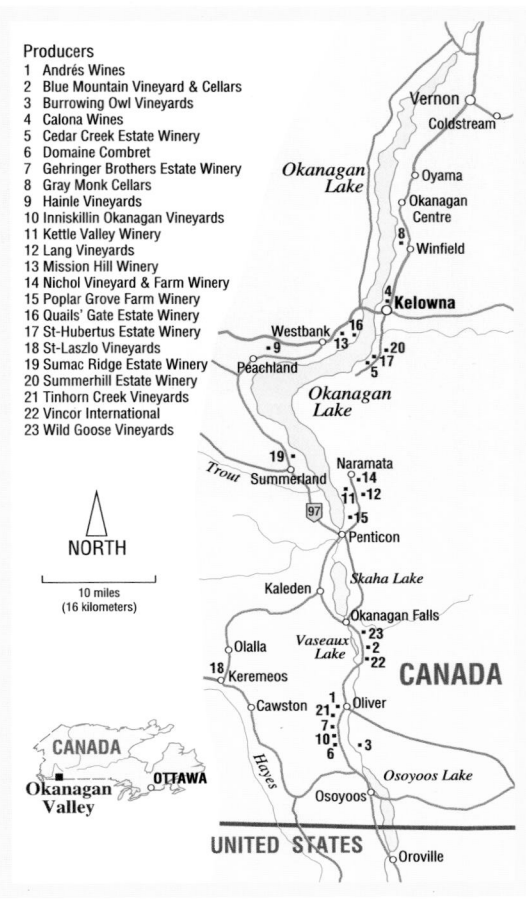

Producers
1 Andrés Wines
2 Blue Mountain Vineyard & Cellars
3 Burrowing Owl Vineyards
4 Calona Wines
5 Cedar Creek Estate Winery
6 Domaine Combret
7 Gehringer Brothers Estate Winery
8 Gray Monk Cellars
9 Hainle Vineyards
10 Inniskillin Okanagan Vineyards
11 Kettle Valley Winery
12 Lang Vineyards
13 Mission Hill Winery
14 Nichol Vineyard & Farm Winery
15 Poplar Grove Farm Winery
16 Quails' Gate Estate Winery
17 St-Hubertus Estate Winery
18 St-Laszlo Vineyards
19 Sumac Ridge Estate Winery
20 Summerhill Estate Winery
21 Tinhorn Creek Vineyards
22 Vincor International
23 Wild Goose Vineyards

Signs mark wine routes in various regions throughout Canada.

GRAY MONK CELLARS

Established 1982 *Owners* George and Trudy Heiss
Production 42,000 cases *Vineyard area* 49 acres (20 ha)

George Heiss' delicate German-style wines have made their mark in competitions both in Canada and abroad. The Heiss' son George Jr studied winemaking in Germany and another son, Steven, is involved in the business side. In 1990, they redesigned their packaging and introduced a premium line. They are currently upgrading equipment and replanting where necessary. They cultivate their own vines at a nursery near the winery.

HAINLE VINEYARDS

Established 1978 *Owners* the Hainle Family *Production* 5,500 cases *Vineyard area* 18.5 acres (7.5 ha)

Hainle Vineyards produced Canada's first icewine in 1977 and went into commercial production the following year. Walter Hainle died in a hiking accident in 1995, and his son Tilman is now at the helm. He trained at Weisberg and worked at Uniake Cellars (which later became Cedar Creek) until 1985, when he joined the family enterprise. In 1991, Tilman introduced champagne method sparklers from pinot blanc, chardonnay, pinot noir and pinot meunier. Hainle vineyards are certified organic and Tilman uses as little sulphur dioxide as possible in production.

INNISKILLIN OKANAGAN VINEYARDS

Established 1994 *Owner* Vincor International *Production* 25,000 cases *Vineyard area* 22 acres (9 ha)

In their merger with Cartier/Brights in 1992, Vincor International acquired a winery in the Okanagan. When they bought Inniskillin Ontario, they were able to launch the Inniskillin Okanagan label using grapes from the Inkameep vineyard leased from the Osoyoos Indian Band. They have also acquired Okanagan Vineyards. At first, Inniskillin Ontario founders Donald Ziraldo and Karl Kaiser managed the vineyard, but Australian winemaker Philip Dowell was hired as general manager and Sandor Mayer as winemaker in 1998. Inniskillin's primary focus is producing premium and ultra-premium VQA wines.

KETTLE VALLEY WINERY

Established mid-1980s *Owners* Tim Watts and Bob Ferguson *Production* 1,650 cases *Vineyard area* 11 acres (4.5 ha)

Founders Bob Ferguson and Tim Watts planted a vineyard in the mid-1980s featuring Burgundy's greats, chardonnay and pinot noir. They have since gradually added Bordeaux red varietals and some shiraz. They aim to limit the number of wines they produce and focus on oak-aged premium wines.

LANG VINEYARDS

Established 1993 *Owners* Guenther and Kristina Lang
Production 5,000 cases *Vineyard area* 15 acres (6.1 ha)

After coming to Canada from Germany in 1980, the Langs bought an Okanagan vineyard. They replaced existing vines with new grape varieties and made wine as a hobby. In the late 1980s, the Langs and their neighbors, the Klokockas of Hillside Estate Winery, campaigned for legal changes to allow grape growers to develop small wineries on their properties. After legislation was passed, they built a winery where they could showcase rieslings and other vinifera-based wines.

MISSION HILL WINERY

Established 1981 *Owner* Anthony von Mandl *Production* 205,000 cases *Vineyard area* 600 acres (243 ha) owned or controlled

Inspired by Robert Mondavi in the Napa Valley and the tradition of the French château, Anthony von Mandl's focus for Mission Hill is quality and innovation. The decision to hire New Zealand winemaker John Simes in 1992 was immediately rewarded when his first vintage, 1992 Mission Hill Grand Reserve Chardonnay won the Avery Trophy for Best Cchardonnay worldwide.

NICHOL VINEYARD & FARM WINERY

Established 1992 *Owners* Alex and Kathleen Nichol
Production 1,500 cases *Vineyard area* 4.9 acres (2 ha)

In 1989, Alex Nichol acquired an alfalfa field at the foot of a granite cliff. In the ensuing three years, he transformed it into an enviable vineyard. The sun reflects off the wall of stone, and the rock face retains enough heat to allow one of the rare BC plantings of syrah to flourish. Alex Nichol has built a considerable reputation for his intensely flavored and elegant wines.

POPLAR GROVE FARM WINERY

Established 1997 *Owners* Ian and Gitta Sutherland
Production 1,500 cases *Vineyard area* 7 acres (3 ha)

Ian Sutherland's grape mix is two-thirds red to one-third white, and his aim is to keep the winery small. The composition of the clay loam soil in his vineyard is much like that of St Emilion, so Ian planted merlot and cabernet franc. His white grapes are chardonnay and pinot gris. He launched his first chardonnay with resounding success.

QUAILS' GATE ESTATE WINERY

Established 1989 *Owner* Dick Stewart *Production* 60,000 cases *Vineyard area* 115 acres (47 ha)

Few winemakers believed in 1989 that there was a future for red varietals in BC, but the search for the perfect pinot noir inspired Quails' Gate founder Dick Stewart and his son Ben to research new varietal clones and experiment with canopy management and high-density planting. The winemaking at their new CAN$2 million (US$1.4 million) production facility has benefitted from the talents of two Australian winemakers, first Jeff Martin, then Peter Draper, a Roseworthy Agricultural College graduate who died suddenly during the 1999 harvest. The crush was completed by Simon Osika, on loan from BRL Hardy's Houghton Winery in Western Australia.

ST HUBERTUS ESTATE WINERY

Established 1920 *Owner* Leo Gerbert *Production* 10,000 cases *Vineyard area* 52 acres (21 ha)

The St Hubertus vineyard is one of the oldest in BC and a number of operable antique machines are displayed on the property. Leo Gebert acquired the property in 1984 and named it after the Gebert family lodge in Switzerland. A neighboring vineyard, Oak Bay, is owned by Leo's brother Andy. They grow mostly vinifera varieties including pinot noir, gamay noir, pinot meunier, merlot, riesling and pinot blanc. Their wines are single varietals, although wine styles differ for the St Hubertus and the Oak Bay labels—the former unoaked, the latter either fermented or aged in oak.

ST LASZLO VINEYARDS

Established 1970s *Owners* the Ritlop family *Production* 5,000 cases *Vineyard area* 10 acres (4 ha)

The first crush from this vineyard planted to both hybrid and vinifera graped was in 1978. Joe Ritlop does not use chemicals in the vineyard and avoids sulphides, sorbates and preservatives in the winery. He also prefers to allow the natural yeasts to produce fermentation in his full-bodied wines. He he makes some remarkable late-harvested wines, including a Tokay Aszu.

SUMAC RIDGE ESTATE WINERY

Established 1979 *Owner* Vincor International *Production* 50,000 cases *Vineyard area* 131 acres (53 ha)

Sumac Ridge, the first medium-size winery in BC, was sold in early 2000 to Vincor International, Canada's largest wine company. It was established by Harry McWatters, who is an important force in the Canadian wine industry. In 1991, Harry went into partnership with Bob Wareham to develop Black Sage Vineyards, 115 acres (47 ha) of some of the best vineyard land in Canada and the major source of grapes for Sumac Ridge. Black Sage is planted to premium varietals, mostly red, including cabernet sauvignon, cabernet franc, merlot, pinot noir and malbec. Its white varieties include chardonnay, pinot blanc and sauvignon blanc. In 1995, Harry bought Hawthorne Mountain Vineyards from Albert and Dixie LeComte, who had rejuvenated the 1961 vines and built a winery in 1986. Over the years, hybrid vines have been replaced with *vinifera*. Bruce Ewart has taken over winemaking responsibilities. Oak is an important element in the Sumac Ridge style.

SUMMERHILL ESTATE WINERY

Established 1987 *Owner* Stephen Cipes *Production* 20,000 cases *Vineyard area* 60 acres (24 ha)

Summerhill Winery has built a one-eighth size replica of the Cheops pyramid in Egypt in which to age wines. Results of taste tests over a period of three years have been unanimous, with tasters finding that wine aged for 30 to 90 days in the pyramid tastes richer and smoother than the same wine aged traditionally. Over the last five years, Summerhill's *méthode champenoise* sparklers have outsold French champagne in British Columbia. Pyramid or no, Summerhill red, white and sparkling wines, attractively packaged in Italian-designed bottles, have received many awards.

Still at Mission Hill Winery, Okanagan Valley, British Columbia.

TINHORN CREEK VINEYARDS

Established 1993 *Owners* Bob and Barbara Shaunessy and Kenn and Sandra Oldfield *Production* 40,000 cases *Vineyard area* 160 acres (65 ha)

Influenced by the success of the Napa Valley, winery founder Bob Shaunessy started buying up existing vineyards at a time when small growers were bearing the brunt of the pull-out program. The Shaunessys then went into partnership with Kenn and Sandra Oldfield, and now Sandra is winemaker and Kenn is viticulturalist and general manager. In a few short years, the partners have acquired many accolades for their wines. The California influence is evident in their use of American oak and in the concentrated flavor of the wines. Winery visitors are invited to take one of the two hiking trails leading to the ruins of the Tinhorn Creek gold mine after which the winery is named. The views from the trails on the way to the ruins are quite spectacular.

VINCOR INTERNATIONAL (JACKSON-TRIGGS)

Established 1982 *Owner* Vincor International Inc. *Production* 2 million cases *Vineyard area* 750 acres (304 ha) owned or leased

Vincor's winery in Oliver went into production in 1982, drawing on grapes from the Inkameep vineyard farmed by the Osoyoos Indian Band. In 1996, the company signed a lease agreement with the band to develop 2,000 acres (810 ha) on the Osoyoos Lake Bench. In the southernmost tip of the Okanagan Valley, this area benefits from long hours of sunlight, high daytime heat and cool nights. Vincor has planted 500 acres (203 ha) to date and is evaluating 56 combinations of varietal, clone and rootstock. When fully developed, this land has the potential to double the supply of high-quality grapes in British Columbia. These Vincor vineyards will be dedicated to super- and ultra-premium pinot noir, chardonnay, cabernet sauvignon, merlot and sauvignon blanc.

WILD GOOSE VINEYARDS

Established 1990 *Owner* Adolf Kruger *Production* 5,000 cases *Vineyard area* 10 acres (4 ha)

Adolf Kruger, a consulting electrical engineer, had planted his vineyard in 1984 and was an established winemaking hobbyist, but turned to winemaking during a recession when engineering contracts were hard to come by. He shares the winemaking with his son Hagen, while other family members look after different aspects of the winery. Their production is mostly riesling, gewürztraminer, pinot noir, pinot gris and merlot, produced with minimal filtration and maximum personal attention to detail.

Irrigation at the new Vincor plantings, Osoyoos, Okanagan Valley, British Columbia.

Other BC Regions

VANCOUVER ISLAND

The Cowichan Valley on Vancouver Island and the few wineries on nearby smaller islands enjoy a climate more like that of Ontario's Niagara Peninsula than that of the Okanagan, with mild overnight temperatures. The wines from this area show soft acids and rich fruit flavors. Wineries are a fairly new phenomenon for Vancouver Island, but their intitial results indicate that this region has considerable potential.

DIVINO ESTATE WINERY

Established 1982 *Owner* Joe Busnardo *Production* NA
Vineyard area 39.5 acres (16 ha)

Joe Busnardo grew grapes and experimented in the Okanagan for over 25 years before moving his license to Vancouver Island in 1996. His favored grape types reflect his Italian Veneto heritage and he has planted merlot, cabernet franc, cabernet sauvignon, pinot noir, trebbiano, tocai, pinot bianco, pinot grigio and malvasia. He uses no oak and encourages soft, fruity characteristics through whole-berry fermentation.

VENTURI-SCHULZE VINEYARDS

Established 1993 *Owners* Giordano Venturi and
Marilyn Schulze *Production* 500 cases *Vineyard area*
20 acres (8 ha)

Giordano Venturi, an electronics instructor from Italy, and his wife Marilyn Schulze, an Australian-born microbiologist, bought a picturesque 100-year-old farm at Cowichan Bay and planted 25 different grape varieties. From those, they chose the 11 best performers—pinot noir, auxerrois, pinot gris, schönberger, madeleine sylvaner, siegerrebe, ortega, kerner, chasselas, gewürztraminer and madeleine angevin—to remain in their organically farmed vineyard. Producing very small quantities of handcrafted wines, they destem manually to prevent bitter flavors, avoid prolonged skin contact and often leave the wine in contact with the lees. In a separate building, Giordano produces balsamic vinegar, in keeping with his origins near Modena.

FRASER VALLEY

The Fraser Valley is within half an hour's drive of Vancouver, and is a more temperate and humid area than the Okanagan, producing wines with a softer flavor profile than those from the Okanagan Valley. There are two wineries in this region—one of these grows vines and the other vinifies Okanagan fruit.

DOMAINE DE CHABERTON

Established 1991 *Owner* Claude Violet
Production 25,000 cases *Vineyard area* 55 acres
(22 ha)

When Claude Violet came to British Columbia from his native France, he transported 350 years of winemaking heritage to the Fraser Valley. Domaine de Chaberton is the only winery growing grapes in this British Columbia designation just north of the United States border. The wines, from bacchus, madeleine angevine, madeleine sylvaner, ortega, chardonnay and chasselas doré, are sold locally as well as being exported to places as diverse as France, Taiwan, China, Hong Kong and Japan.

REGIONAL DOZEN

QUALITY WINES

Blue Mountain Pinot Noir
Cedar Creek Platinum Reserve
  Chardonnay
Gehringer Riesling Icewine
Jackson Triggs Merlot
Mission Hill Chardonnay
  Reserve
Quails' Gate Pinot Noir
  Family Reserve
Sumac Ridge Meritage

BEST VALUE WINES

Calona Vineyards Artist
  Reserve Chardonnay
Gray Monk Unwooded
  Chardonnay
Hawthorne Mountain
  Chardonnay
Hester Creek Estate Pinot
  Blanc
St Hubertus Riesling
Sumac Ridge Gewürztraminer
  Private Reserve
Tinhorn Creek
  Gewürztraminer

ONTARIO

In 1811, a vineyard was planted by Johann Schiller with labrusca and hybrid varieties in Mississauga, just outside of Toronto, to make wine for personal use. Count Justin de Courtney purchased a parcel of the land from Schiller's descendants and added to it. He actively lobbied the government to support the development of wine production, and worked determinedly to prove that European varieties could not only thrive but produce better wines than Burgundy. His efforts were finally vindicated in 1867 when the judges at the French exposition in Paris recorded that the wine he submitted "resembled more the great French table wines than any other foreign wines" they had tasted. Unfortunately, de Courtney was never able to capitalize on his success as the government grants on which he depended ceased.

During the time de Courtney was courting favor in Europe, a handful of vineyardists had discovered the potential of the Niagara Peninsula across Lake Ontario from the burgeoning metropolis of Toronto and, at the turn of the century, there were 35 commercial wineries operating there. The grape variety most commonly used at that time was the concord, an indigenous labrusca variety first identified by a grower in the northern United States. The concord is virtually indestructible, being resistant to both cold and infestation but it is better suited to making juice and jelly than making wine.

The first larger size winery to attain commercial success in Canada was Vin Villa, founded by a partnership of three American gentlemen farmers in 1866. They established their cellars on Pelee Island, Canada's southernmost territory located just off the shore of Lake Erie. A rival winery broke ground a few months later. Although it was planted originally to the hybrid catawba, the Pelee Island Wine and Vineyard Company's modern incarnation now comprises the largest planting of vinifera vines in Canada. Both wineries owed much of their success to an ambitious grocer from Brantford, Ontario, Major J. S. Hamilton, who was responsible for marketing these wines in Canada and the United States. Hamilton's company eventually absorbed the Pelee Island Wine and Vineyard Co. At about the same time, George Barnes started up a winery in St Catharines, Niagara's largest town, and his company operated until 1988. In Toronto, Thomas Bright and a partner also opened a winery that later moved into Niagara. It became known as T. B. Bright's and Co. and exerted a considerable influence over the nascent wine industry.

Coincident with the growth of wineries, however, came an increasingly strong temperance movement, although its influence was redundant during the First World War, as alcohol was diverted to the war effort for making explosives. The Ontario Temperance Act of 1916 prohibited the sales of beverage alcohol, and the distilleries converted their facilities to produce industrial alcohol. In the normal course of events, this could have destroyed the wineries but, once peace was declared, the Ontario Grape Growers' Lobby convinced the government to exempt from the act products made from Ontario-grown grapes. Wineries were able to sell only from their winery stores and purchases were limited to 6 gallons (23 liters) per person. While alcohol was liberally dispensed for medicinal purposes, wine was the only alcoholic beverage permitted for sale. Many saw this as a license to print money. At the start of Prohibition, there were ten wineries in Ontario; when Prohibition ended in 1927, there were 67.

Again, concord was the grape of choice and the lack of interest in quality control did little to contain its less desirable characteristics. Sugar, water, color and sulfur were added and the results were, for the most part, red port-style wine or something akin to sherry. Canadian consumers,

Below: *Vines and picked grapes in Ontario.*

Bottom: *De Sousa winery, Ontario.*

unused to traditional European products, came to accept and expect this style of wine. Concerned about these high-alcohol wines, the government set an upper limit of 20 percent for alcohol content in 1932. The grape growers then lobbied the government to allow fortified wine, enabling them to pour any spoiled wine into the still to make grape spirit for their new fortified products. One of the favorite labels of the day was Bright's Sherry, which earned the nickname "Bright's Disease."

The solace these cheap strong wines provided during the Great Depression stirred the Temperance Union, which was finally placated when alcoholic beverages were legalized with sales restricted to government-run shops in a monopoly system closely resembling the one operating in Scandinavia at the time. It has been liberalized somewhat over the years, but tight control remains over selection and pricing. When customers started demanding reliable quality, the government imposed controls that were not much of an improvement by today's standards. However, a handful of dedicated winemakers pursued the uphill quest for quality. In the 1930s, Adhemar de Chaunac, a chemist and winemaker for Bright's, imported 40 varieties from France, including chardonnay and pinot noir. Both these *vinifera* vines and eight of the hybrids proved themselves up to the rigors of the Canadian climate and this success encouraged other wine industry leaders to develop vinifera-based vineyards.

Gradually consumers began to demand a greater variety, which was fulfilled by an increase in imported European table wines. In 1976, the Ontario wineries appealed to the government for assistance, which they received in the form of promotion and stocking changes in the government-run stores and, more importantly, grants to replace labrusca vines with vinifera varieties. During the 1980s, Ontario wine industry professionals developed the VQA system in an effort to accelerate acceptance of their wines in potential export markets. This spurred an increase in small wineries and a recognition among larger players that they could produce excellent wines at reasonable prices and meet specific criteria of excellence.

The wine-producing areas of Ontario benefit from the proximity of two of the Great Lakes, Ontario and Erie. In the summer, the two lakes absorb and hold enough heat to cushion winter's frigid attack. The exchange of warm and cool air over land and water creates a constant flow that benefits most of the areas where vines are grown,

although the cool lake breezes in spring and early summer may retard growth and cooler daytime temperatures can affect quality in the first mile or two (1.6–3.2 km) from the shoreline.

Many growers thought that only indigenous (labrusca) and hybrid grape varieties could survive, but a few daring people proved that hardy varieties of vinifera such as riesling and chardonnay could thrive. In the late 1970s, the provincial government's assistance program to the wine industry included five-year interest-free loans to replant vineyards with vinifera and superior hybrid vines. Most growers planted white grapes known to be cold resistant, but some planted a broad range of white varietals and a number of reds. Now it has been shown that the vines can thrive, the percentage of red grapes has increased significantly. Favored reds are cabernet franc, pinot noir, merlot, cabernet sauvignon, gamay noir, baco noir and maréchal foch. Recently, a few plantings of syrah have been put in. Favored white varieties are chardonnay, riesling, pinot blanc, pinot gris, gewürztraminer, chenin blanc, sémillon and vidal.

Vineyard sites with the appropriate microclimates minimize the risk of spring frost and appropriate varieties for those microclimates must be chosen. In high-risk areas, such as the Niagara plain, fans are sometimes used to circulate the air in cold spells. Ontario wineries are benefitting from research at the Cool Climate Oenology and Viticulture Institute at Brock University into canopy management, clone selection and yeast selection. Viticulture and winemaking techniques are continually evolving in this young industry, but generally follow European traditions.

Above: *Pinot noir grapes at Inniskillin vineyard, Ontario.*

Top: *Joseph's Estate Wines, Ontario.*

Niagara Peninsula

Lake Ontario's influence diminishes inland, on a level plain where cold air can settle. Spring frosts are a problem here—protective measures such as using fans to move the air are sometimes needed. In summer, temperatures rise quickly and fruit matures well—the heat contributes to ripeness, and translates into intense flavors. Chardonnay, for example, can show tropical nuances not found in the cooler Niagara Bench vineyards further inland. There the terrain slopes up the Niagara Escarpment—the area has good drainage and the incline causes constant air circulation, almost eliminating spring frost and humidity-related disease. The cooler environment there encourages the acid needed for balance and elegance; the warmer temperatures of the plain give more intensity and richness.

CAVE SPRING CELLARS

Established 1986 *Owners* Len Pennachetti and Angelo Pavan *Production* 60,000 cases *Vineyard area* 155 acres (63 ha)

Cave Spring Cellars' ultra-premium wines exhibit concentrated fruit, reflecting their Bench *terroir* and winemaker Angelo Pavan's signature elegance.

Cave Spring is one of the few medium size wineries in Niagara to use only vinifera varieties.

CHÂTEAU DES CHARMES

Established 1978 *Owners* Paul Bosc and Rodger Gordon *Production* 100,000 cases *Vineyard area* 250 acres (101 ha)

With 250 acres (101 ha) spread over four vineyards, Château des Charmes has the most winery-owned vineyard land in Niagara. Founder and winemaker Paul Bosc was the first to plant a 100 percent vinifera vineyard in the area, and was instrumental in promoting its use. Paul's first Canadian chardonnays, which clearly reflect the time he spent studying at Dijon, provided the inspiration for other local winemakers, and his champagne-style sparklers are much admired.

HENRY OF PELHAM

Established 1983 *Owners* the Speck family *Production* 70,000 cases *Vineyard area* 225 acres (91 ha)

Paul, Matthew and Daniel Speck took over the winery in 1993 on the death of their father. They are direct descendents of Nicholas Smith, who was

Picking riesling icewine grapes on the Niagara Peninsula, Ontario.

deeded land by the Crown for his loyalist stance in serving as a bugle boy in the war of 1776. The Specks and winemaker Ron Giesbrecht concentrate on chardonnay, riesling, cabernet sauvignon and baco noir. They are recognized as the region's best producer of baco noir.

HHERNDER ESTATE WINES

Established 1991 *Owner* Fred Hernder *Production* 10,000 cases *Vineyard area* 600 acres (243 ha)

Fred Hernder, a third-generation grape grower, had his eye on a particular property for years—he bought it in 1988, planning a juice business, but tourists kept asking to taste his wine. So Fred hired a part-time winemaker, and never looked back. Winemaker Ray Cornell, now full-time, coaxes intensity and fresh fruitiness out of vidal and baco noir and complexity and elegance out of merlot, cabernet sauvignon, cabernet franc, sauvignon blanc, chardonnay, pinot gris and riesling.

HILLEBRAND ESTATES

Established 1981 *Owners* Andrés Wines *Production* 340,000 cases *Vineyard area* 30 acres (12 ha)

Hillebrand Estates was founded in 1979, but was sold in the early 1980s to Underberg of Switzerland. Infusions of capital from the Swiss enabled the little winery to invest in technology and grow by leaps and bounds. Andrés Wines bought it from Underberg in 1994. Although now a large winery, Hillebrand nonetheless focuses on VQA wines and varietals, chardonnay in particular.

INNISKILLIN WINES INC.

Established 1975 *Owners* Vincor International Inc. *Production* 200,000 cases *Vineyard area* 120 acres (49 ha)

Inniskillin started the quality wine revolution in Canada when Donald Ziraldo and Karl Kaiser applied for a boutique winery license—the industry was then dominated by large companies. Donald and Karl introduced well-made varietal wines and, later, single-vineyard labels. When 1989 Inniskillin's Vidal Icewine won a gold medal at Vinexpo in 1991, Canada was finally recognized as a cool-climate wine-producing country.

KITTLING RIDGE ESTATE WINES & SPIRITS

Established 1993 *Owner* John K. Hall *Production* 60,000 cases *Vineyard area* N/A

Kittling Ridge is one of the few winery/distillery combinations in Ontario. Founded in 1970 as the Rieder Distillery, it obtained a winery licence in 1993. By 1995, it was Ontario's sixth largest winery. Kittling Ridge buys grapes from the Niagara Bench and from the town of Niagara-on-the-Lake. They also buy grapes from France, Italy, Chile and California. Winemaking is under the direction of owner John Hall; about 10 percent of the production is VQA.

Wine education at Hillebrand Estates, Ontario.

KONZELMANN WINERY

Established 1984 *Owner* Herbert Konzelmann *Production* 40,000 cases *Vineyard area* 83 acres (34 ha)

Enologist Herbert Konzelmann trained at Weinsberg and managed his family facility in Württemberg for nearly 30 years before buying a vineyard in Niagara-on-the-Lake. His winemaking background is obvious in his riesling, gewürztraminer, subtle pinot noir and stunning icewine. Herbert does uses French and Yugoslavian oak, but his true style emerges in the wines from stainless steel.

LAKEVIEW CELLARS ESTATE WINERY

Established 1991 *Owners* Eddy Gurinskas, Larry Hipple and Stuart Morgan *Production* 11,000 cases *Vineyard area* 13 acres (5 ha)

Eddy Gurinskas, a grower and award-winning amateur winemaker, with his wife Lorraine, moved to a commercial winery in 1991. In 1996 neighboring growers Larry and Debbie Hipple entered into partnership with them; Stu and Ginnie Morgan followed in 1997. Lakeview is known for intense cabernet sauvignon and merlot.

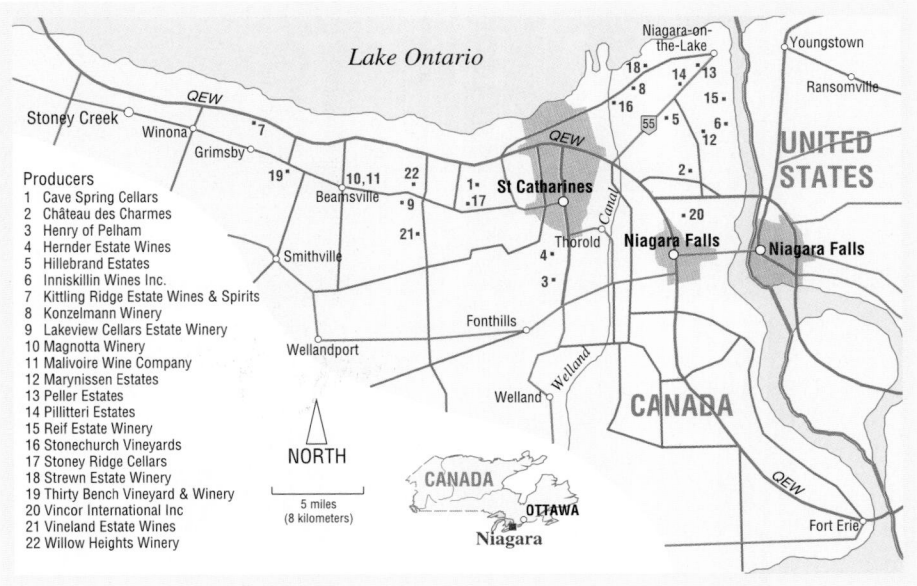

Producers
1 Cave Spring Cellars
2 Château des Charmes
3 Henry of Pelham
4 Hernder Estate Wines
5 Hillebrand Estates
6 Inniskillin Wines Inc.
7 Kittling Ridge Estate Wines & Spirits
8 Konzelmann Winery
9 Lakeview Cellars Estate Winery
10 Magnotta Winery
11 Malivoire Wine Company
12 Marynissen Estates
13 Peller Estates
14 Pillitteri Estates
15 Reif Estate Winery
16 Stonechurch Vineyards
17 Stoney Ridge Cellars
18 Strewn Estate Winery
19 Thirty Bench Vineyard & Winery
20 Vincor International Inc
21 Vineland Estate Wines
22 Willow Heights Winery

MAGNOTTA WINERY

Established 1990　*Owners* Gabriel and Rosanna Magnotta
Production 250,000 cases　*Vineyard area* 72 acres (29 ha)

Gabe Magnotta built his business up to production of 250,000 cases in only eight years, collecting a room full of awards along the way. He and his wife Rosanna operated a large juice business until 1990 when they purchased a defunct winery. They made a number of commercially successful international blends, then acquired 72 acres (29 ha) in the Niagara Peninsula to develop a line of VQA wines, including vidal icewine in still and sparkling styles and a novel cabernet franc icewine.

MALIVOIRE WINE COMPANY

Established 1998　*Owners* Martin Malivoire and Moira Saganski　*Production* 2,000 cases　*Vineyard area* 65 acres (26 ha)

Martin Malivoire erected a large Quonset hut on a slope of the escarpment, where he takes advantage of gravity to limit the need for pumps. The winery focuses on premium wines from gewürztraminer, chardonnay, pinot noir and pinot gris. Under the direction of the talented consultant winemaker, Ann Sperling, the wines reflect elegance and balance. Ann has bottled several wines using both natural and synthetic corks and will compare them over the course of their maturation.

MARYNISSEN ESTATES

Established 1990　*Owners* the Marynissen family and Tony Doyle　*Production* 10,000 cases　*Vineyard area* 70 acres (28 ha); 65 acres (26 ha) in production

John Marynissen was well known as a grape grower and award-winning amateur winemaker when he opened Ontario's first small winery in 1990. His chardonnay and cabernet, both planted during the 1970s, are some of the oldest in the region. Located on the Niagara Plain, about midway between the lakeshore and the escarpment, Marynissen is well positioned in the region's warmest zone. Far enough from the lake's cool spring breezes, the vineyards can usually benefit from a slightly earlier start to the growing season. John uses carbonic maceration for reds and uses oak, mostly French, for both fermenting and aging.

PELLER ESTATES

Established 1991　*Owner* Andrés Wines　*Production* 750,000 cases　*Vineyard area* 240 acres (97 ha)

Andrés Wines, founded by Andrew Peller in 1961, became famous for its success with Baby Duck, a low-alcohol sweet sparkler that enjoyed enormous success in the 1970s. To change their image, Andrés developed a line of VQA wines under the Peller Estates label. In 1994, Andrés expanded their line by buying Hillebrand Estates Winery. Branded labels and very competitively priced VQA wines are widely available across the province. Peller Estates has broken ground on a new winery facility in Niagara-on-the-Lake, slated to open in the spring of 2001.

PILLITTERI ESTATES WINERY

Established 1993　*Owner* Gary Pillitteri　*Production* 20,000 cases　*Vineyard area* 37 acres (15 ha)

Winery founder Gary Pillitteri came to Canada from Sicily after Second World War and started growing grapes in the Niagara. Already a reputed amateur winemaker, Gary inaugurated his winery in 1993. A second generation of Pillitteris and their spouses now manage the vineyards, farm market, bakery, greenhouse and tasting room. Winemaker Sue-Ann Staff, who trained at Roseworthy Agricultural College in Australia, produces a range of wines including barrel-aged chardonnay, riesling dry, pinot grigio, vidal sussreserve, gewürztraminer icewine and cabernet sauvignon.

REIF ESTATE WINERY

Established 1983　*Owner* Ewald Reif　*Production* 35,000 cases　*Vineyard area* 135 acres (55 ha)

Ewald Reif brought 13 generations of winemaking tradition with him when he emigrated to Canada from Germany. His scenic vineyard, along the gorge of the Niagara River where it spills into Lake Ontario, benefits from the effects of the massive lake. In 1987, Ewald's nephew Klaus,

Below: *Pillitteri Estates Winery, Ontario.*

Bottom: *Reif Estate Winery, Ontario.*

who had trained at Geisenheim, took up winemaking duties and immediately made a reputation for himself with a stunning vidal icewine that was subsequently included in Robert Parker's top ten of the year. He now shares winemaking responsibilities with Roberto de Domenico.

STONECHURCH VINEYARDS

Established 1990 *Owners* the Hunse family *Production* 30,000 *Vineyard area* 150 acres (61 ha)

Grape growers since 1972, the Hunse family now operates one of the largest estate wineries in Ontario and 85 percent of production is VQA. Winemaker Jens Gemmrich, from Germany, is trained in cooperage as well as in viticulture and enology. Their production of chardonnay, riesling, vidal late harvest, pinot noir, reserve cabernet sauvignon and other wines grew from 500 to 30,000 cases between 1990 and 1995.

STONEY RIDGE CELLARS

Established 1985 *Owners* Cuesta Corporation *Production* 70,000 cases *Vineyard area* 134 acres (54 ha)

When winemaker Jim Warren founded Stoney Ridge Cellars he produced 500 cases from a tin shed. In 1990, he went into partnership with grape grower Murray Puddicombe and they built a winery in Winona. They sold the winery to Ottawa investors in 1998, with Jim continuing as chief winemaker. They produce 52 different wines, mostly varietally-named from well-known French and German varieties, from three lines: Stoney Ridge Cellars, Cuesta Estates for premium wines and Woods End, a lower priced range.

STREWN ESTATE WINERY

Established 1994 *Owners* Joe Will and Jane Langdon *Production* 17,000 cases *Vineyard area* 26 acres (11 ha)

A vast, restored 1930s fruit cannery houses Strewn Winery. Winemaker/owner Joe Will, who trained at Australia's Roseworthy Agricultural College, cut his teeth in Canada working for Pillitteri and used Pillitteri's facility when he first struck out on his own. Strewn is committed to making premium wines from local grapes, including riesling, pinot blanc and the traditional Bordeaux red varieties.

THIRTY BENCH VINEYARD & WINERY

Established 1994 *Owners* Dr Tom Muckle, Yorgos Papageorgiou, Frank Zeritsch and Deborah Paskus *Production* 7,000 cases *Vineyard area* 40 acres (16 ha)

This tiny winery boasts the "driest vineyard on the (Niagara) bench." Riesling is the emphasis here and all styles are made. Increasing quantities of vidal, chardonnay and a range of red vinifera are also made. The winery's philosophy emphasizes extensive cropping and long barrel aging.

VINCOR INTERNATIONAL

Established 1993 *Owner* Vincor International Inc. *Production* 190,000 cases *Vineyard area* 300 acres (122 ha)

Canada's wine giant emerged from the union of T. G. Bright and Cartier, the two most influential wineries in Canadian history. Vincor's corporate diversification includes winery ownership in several provinces, an importing agency, home winemaking supplies distributors, bulk bottling and approximately 160 retail outlets. With about a dozen labels, the best bear the Jackson-Triggs name—they are among the few VQA wines generally available across Canada. Vincor is building a new winery under the Jackson-Triggs banner in Niagara-on-the-Lake to showcase their wines.

VINELAND ESTATE WINES

Established 1988 *Owner* John Howard *Production* 30,000 cases (potential 70,000) *Vineyard area* 300 acres (122 ha)

Perched high on the side of the Niagara Escarpment, this winery has an unimpaired view of Lake Ontario. The constant flow of air from the lake protects vineyards near the escarpment by minimizing the effects of extreme heat and cold. Riesling is the most planted grape on the estate, the legacy of previous owner, German grape grower Herman Weis. It thrives on the well-drained slope of clay and loam. Winemaker Brian Schmidt is expanding the repertoire of red and white varieties with notable success.

WILLOW HEIGHTS WINERY

Established 1994 *Owners* Ron and Avis Speranzini *Production* 6,000 cases *Vineyard area* 12 acres (5 ha)

Ron Speranzini's goal is to emulate the wines of Burgundy and, after practicing for many years as an amateur, he now makes very limited quantities of handcrafted pinot. In 1998, the yield was thinned to 2 tons per acre (35 hl/ha), and the resulting wine showed delicate red berry fruit with a very elegant, balanced structure. Besides pinot noir, Willow Heights' wines include chardonnay, riesling, vidal, gewürztraminer, merlot and cabernet franc.

The Stonechurch Trail at Stonechurch Vineyards, Ontario.

Other Ontario Regions

LAKE ERIE NORTH SHORE & PELEE ISLAND

In the Lake Erie North Shore and Pelee Island regions, summer temperatures are warmer than in Niagara. However, Lake Erie is considerably shallower than Lake Ontario and cools more quickly in winter. In colder years, the lake freezes over and ice packs often surround Pelee Island.

COLIO WINES OF CANADA

Established 1978 *Owners* Enzo DeLuca and Joe Berardo
Production 200,000 cases *Vineyard area* 180 acres (73 ha)

The Colio vineyards are located within the North Shore Lake Erie VQA appellation, but the winery buys grapes from all three of Ontario's delimited grape-growing areas. Many of Colio's wines are brand-named and sold within the lower price ranges, but they manage to escape the ordinary by reason of winemaker Carlo Negri's flair. A new line, established in 1999, under the Colio Estates Vineyard label, introduced premium and ultra-premium wines. It includes a line of red and white varietals and

a vidal icewine. The winery now has a considerable export market.

LEBLANC ESTATE WINERY

Established 1993 *Owners* Lyse and Pierre Leblanc
Production 3,500 cases *Vineyard area* 50 acres (20 ha)

Leblanc is a two-generation, family-run winery. Vineyardists Alphonse and Monique Leblanc first planted grapes in 1984. Their son Pierre and his wife Lyse took the initiative to turn the property into a winery in 1993. Their first major investment was the purchase of one American oak barrel. Since then, the young couple has purchased the winery and Lyse has taken on responsibility for the vineyard and the winemaking. By interfering as little as possible in the winemaking process, she aims to reveal the inherent qualities of the grapes. She works primarily with pinot blanc, riesling, seyval and vidal.

PELEE ISLAND WINERY

Established 1980 *Owner* Wolf von Teichman
Production 200,000 cases *Vineyard area* 500 acres (202 ha)

The Pelee Island vineyards, on about the same latitude as California's northern border and the island of Corsica, enjoy Canada's southernmost exposure. While not exactly Mediterranean in climate, Pelee Island does enjoy the longest growing season and some of the hottest daytime temperatures in Canada. Chardonnay and a number of German varietals were among the first varieties planted, but reds now form an important part of the portfolio. Pelee Island has the largest plantings of vinifera vines of any Ontario winery, and their VQA bottlings are very competitively priced. Winemaking has been under the direction of Walter Schmoranz, a German expatriate, since 1986.

Chardonnay grapes, Ontario.

Other Canadian Regions

QUÉBEC

Canada's first wine was made in Québec to fulfill early settlers' religious needs. Made from local grapes, these sixteenth-century wines left much to be desired. Growing grapes for wine was disappointing and efforts in the 1700s and 1800s were eventually abandoned. Québec has a difficult climate for vine growing, particularly of vinifera varieties. Winter is vine-splittingly cold, with many days of 5°F (–20°C). Summers are short. Sunny days are humid and thunderstorms are common. Snow storms are not uncommon into the middle of April and there is danger of frost through May. By October, there is too little warmth to encourage further ripening.

The region in which grapes are grown is situated on a vast glacial plain to the south and southeast of Montreal. The soil, comprised of black earth and heavy clay, is more suitable for dairy farming and market gardens. However, pockets of alluvial gravel scattered throughout the area provide suitable sites for vineyards. The western sector of this plain, called the Montérégie, is marginally warmer than the neighboring Eastern Townships, where vineyards are clustered in the Dunham area. Experience is showing that some varieties that grow well in the Montérégie are not so successful in the Townships.

Vinifera varieties are in the minority in this region, although some growers have microclimates where auxerrois, chardonnay and riesling can thrive. Preferred white hybrids are seyval blanc, vidal, cayuga, geisenheim, éona, cliche-vandal for whites, and de chaunac, maréchal foch, st croix, seyval noir, baco noir and chancellor for reds. One advantage of the cold is that in some of the lesser varieties, the least attractive characteristics are minimized, in particular a peculiar musky odor termed "foxy."

Because of the particularly harsh winters, grape selection is of paramount importance. "Hilling," the practice of cutting the vines back and covering them with earth during the winter is common. A few growers are experimenting with vine variety, trellising and microclimate as an alternative practice. Many of the wineries must supplement their wine sales with fruit wines and ciders as well as preserves, maple products and soft goods.

The colorful altar in the world-famous Notre Dame Basilica, Québec.

VIGNOBLE ANGELL

Established 1985 *Owner* Jean-Guy Angell *Production* 2,000 cases *Vineyard area* 18 acres (7 ha)

St-Bernard de Lacolle is about as far south in the Province of Québec as one can go, and this southern advantage gives Vignoble Angell a growing season about three weeks longer than most other Québec wineries. One of the first Québecois vineyardists, Jean-Guy Angell's estate is now the largest family-owned winery in the province, with over 40,000 vines in the ground, although only 9 acres (3.6 ha) are in production. The Angells have planted merlot and pinot noir for some experimental bottlings. They also make seyval blanc, vidal, chardonnay and de chaunac.

Château Frontenac, Québec City, Québec.

LE VIGNOBLE ANGILE

Established 1985 *Owners* Nick Raymond and Manon
Boulet *Production* 500 cases *Vineyard area* 5.5 acres (2 ha)

On the north shore of the St-Lawrence, near
Québec City, Nick Raymond and Manon Boulet
make wine from 5 acres (2 ha) of hardy hybrid
grapes and 20 acres (8 ha) of strawberries and
raspberries. They ferment and age in stainless
steel and make a méthode champenoise sparkling
wine. Still table wines are blended and produced
in dry white and rosé styles.

DOMAINE DES CÔTES D'ARDOISE

Established 1984 *Owner* Jacques Papillon *Production*
1,600 cases *Vineyard area* 20 acres (8 ha)

Planted in 1980 in the Dunham area by Christian
Barthomeuf, this vineyard was the first in the province. It enjoys a microclimates warm enough to
support vinifera varieties and has the advantage of
a protective horseshoe shape. Riesling and gamay
are grown, and a number of successful hybrids.
The name Côtes d'Ardoise refers to the slate that
is contained in the soil. Current owner Jacques Papillon has hired Vera Klokocka and John Fletcher,
former owners of Hillside Estate Winery in British
Columbia, to oversee production of one of the
broadest ranges produced by a Québec winery.

VIGNOBLE LES ARPENTS DE NEIGE

Established 1992 *Owner* Gilles Séguin *Production* 2,000
cases *Vineyard area* 12 acres (5 ha)

King Louis XIV's advisors, referring to Québec,
may not have thought that a few acres of snow
were worth fighting for, but Les Arpents de Neige

owner, Gilles Séguin, thinks his few acres of
snow are well worth the effort. Working with
French winemaker Jean-Paul Martin, Les Arpents
de Neiges makes an excellent seyval and some
blended wines from hybrids.

VIGNOBLE DIETRICH-JOOSS

Established 1986 *Owners* Victor Dietrich and Christiane
Jooss *Production* 2,700 cases *Vineyard area* 12 acres (5 ha)

With Alsatian roots and a generations-long
tradition in winemaking, husband and wife team,
Victor Dietrich and Christiane Jooss, established
their winery in the Richelieu Valley, south of
Montréal, and have experimented with many
different varieties to find the best for their microclimate. While currently emphasizing white varieties, they feel the reds chasselas, gamay and some
pinot varieties could do well. They are also trying
varieties from Australia, the United States and
South America. Victor's daughter, Stéphanie, is
studying enology in Montpellier, France.

VIGNOBLE MOROU

Established 1991 *Owners* Étienne Héroux and Monique
Morin *Production* 1,000 cases *Vineyard area* 4.5 acres (2 ha)

Originally planted in 1987 to 18 different grape
varieties, this vineyard now contains the ten that
are best suited to the climate and soil—seyval,
vidal, seibel, geisenheim clones, cayuga white, de
chaunac, maréchal foch, gamay and chancellor.
Owners and winemakers Étienne Héroux and Monique Morin emulate the growers in Meursault who
open the doors to their white wine cellars in cold
weather. Étienne rolls all the wine vats outside for
up to a week in 24°F (–5°C) weather to precipitate
tartaric acid, a procedure that avoids having to de-
acidify chemically. Grapes are harvested manually.
Wine is made from each variety, then carefully
blended to obtain the best balance and quality.

VIGNOBLE DE L'ORPAILLEUR

Established 1982 *Owners* Hervé Durand, Frank Furtado
and Pierre Rodrigue *Production* 6,500 cases *Vineyard area*
24 acres (10 ha)

This winery's name came from a statement by
Québecois folk singer, Gilles Vigneault, who once
said that, "Making wine in Québec is like panning
for gold." But founder Hervé Durand must be a
successful prospector, because l'Orpailleur has
become the leading winery in the province. Originally from the south of France, Durand studied
enology in Dijon, then went to Argentina to
teach it before coming to Québec to practice it.

Marc Grau, who hails from the south of France, has been winemaker since 1991. L'Orpailleur's Seyval is a standard-setter in Québec.

LA VITACÉE

Established 1979 *Owners* Réjean Gagnon and Alain Loiselle
Production 200 cases *Vineyard area* 10 acres (4 ha)

This winery in the Montérégie may be tiny, but it is important in terms of experimental planting. To discover which varieties can survive the winter without hilling, owners and winemakers Réjean and Alain Loiselle have trained hybrids to high trellises, then strung a line of 60-watt light bulbs along the top to ward off frost. From their experimentation, they have selected some hybrids such as de chaunac and st croix for increased plantings and plan to quadruple the vineyard size. They work with enologist Luc Rolland in the production of the wine and use Missouri oak to age the reds.

NOVA SCOTIA

Like Québec, the climate of Nova Scotia is less conducive to vine growing, particularly of vinifera varieties, than those of British Columbia and Ontario. The industry survives by blending local wines with imported ones, although homegrown specialties are produced. Two hardy Russian grape varieties, michurinetz and severny from the genus amurensis are cultivated locally. After almost 60 years of experimental planting, Agriculture Canada deemed Nova Scotia's climate only marginally suitable for table grapes in 1971. But Roger Dial, who founded the first winery in Nova Scotia in 1980, proved that hardy varieties such as the Russian michurinetz and severnyi could thrive. Later trials have shown that certain resistant vinifera vines could grow in protected microclimates. (Dial's winery went bankrupt, but may be revived under new ownership.)

The wineries are located in the Annapolis Valley, in the west of the province bordering the Bay of Fundy, and on the northeast shore overlooking the Northumberland Strait between Nova Scotia and Prince Edward Island. In both cases, the sheltered bodies of water provide the necessary mitigating forces. Nova Scotia is limited by a much shorter growing season than either Ontario or British Columbia, and average daily temperatures are considerably lower. The selection of grape types is limited by these conditions, but slow ripening over a cool summer benefits the flavor and structure of the wine.

Only about 200 acres (80ha) of vines are growing in the province. Plantings of early-ripening vinifera vines are increasing, but are often hilled up during winter as in Québec. Grapes of choice are seyval blanc, new york muscat, l'acadie blanc and geisenheim clone gm for whites. The most widely planted reds are michurinetz and maréchal foch. Vineyard location is the most important consideration, and the emphasis is on early ripening grape varieties. Here, as in Québec, wineries need to add fruit wines and accessories to their wine shop inventory. Nova Scotia wineries often supplement their limited volumes by bottling imported wines either blended with local produce or as 100 percent imports.

JOST VINEYARDS

Established 1984 *Owner* Hans Christian Jost *Production* 35,000 cases *Vineyard area* 65 acres (26 ha)

Hans Jost had owned a winery in the Rhine Valley before coming to Canada in 1970. Establishing himself as a grape farmer in Nova Scotia, he opened the second cottage winery in the province in 1984. When Hans died in 1988, his son Hans Christian, who had studied winemaking at Geisenheim, took over operations. The Jost vineyards are planted mostly to hybrids including maréchal foch, de chaunac, seyval, geisenheim clone 6493-4, baco noir and vidal, but they buy vinifera grapes—mostly chardonnay and riesling—from Ontario and the State of Washington to increase volume.

Riesling grapes.

SAINTE FAMILLE WINES

Established 1989 *Owners* Suzanne and Doug Corkum *Production* 4,500 cases *Vineyard area* 30 acres (12 ha)

This tiny winery is situated within the confines of an old Acadian village founded in 1680. The vineyard's protected site on a south-facing slope by the Avon River allows chardonnay, riesling and cabernet franc as well as a selection of hybrids to thrive. Winemaker Suzanne Corkum leans towards clean, crisp whites and barrel-aged reds. She uses Nevers, Limousin and Allier oak, and has plans to try some barrel fermentation for the whites.

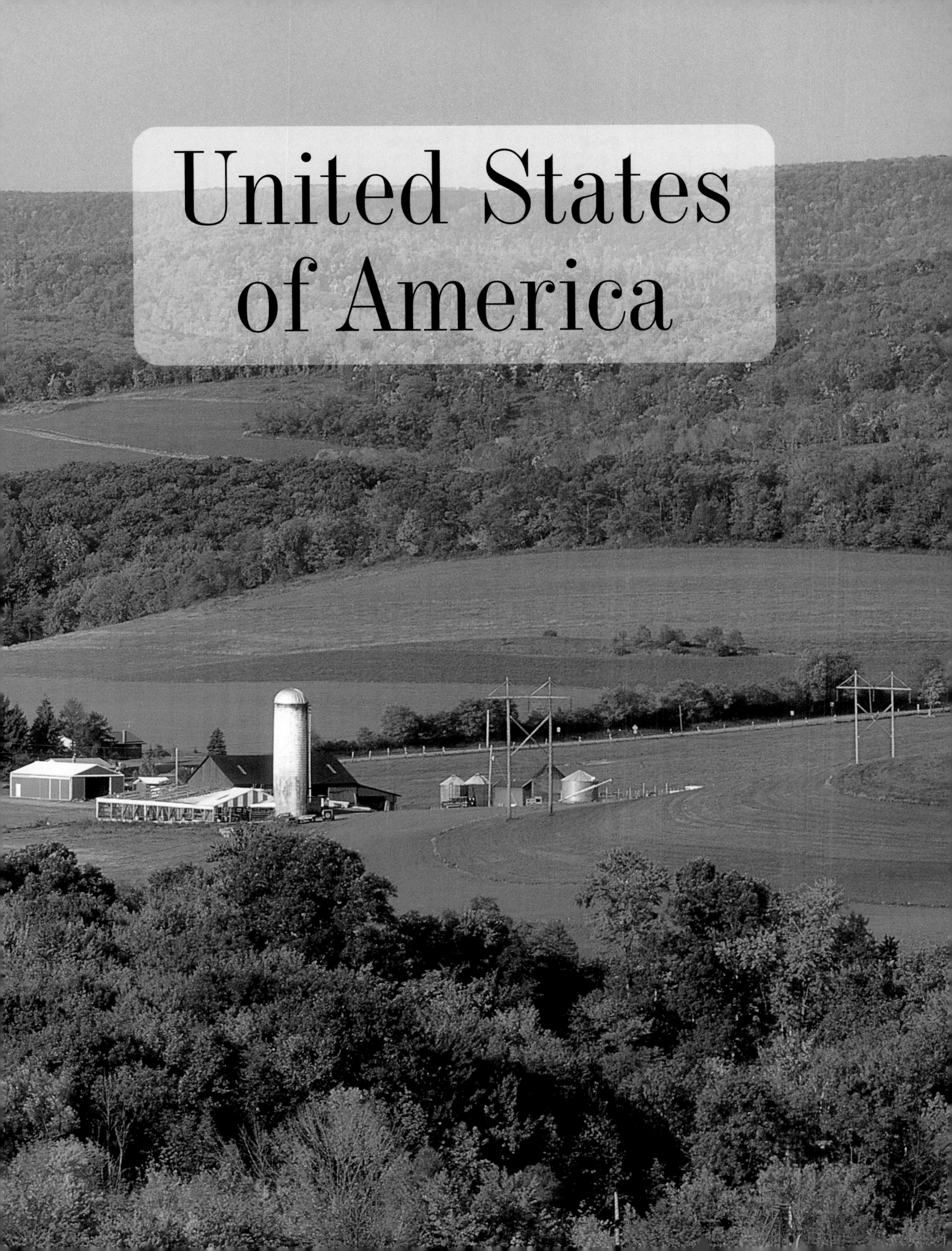

United States of America

656

United States of America

Now the fourth-largest wine producer worldwide, America's impact upon the vine has loomed large. Phylloxera, Prohibition, the University of California at Davis and American scientific and economic clout have shaped the American and the international wine industries.

Grapevines were so abundant in the wilds of North America that explorer Leif Ericson called it "Vineland." Early European settlers celebrated this abundance, though they were dismayed that the native varieties produced wine with an unpleasant "foxy" characteristic. Grapevines traveled back and forth across the Atlantic. In the late 1800s the great regions of Europe were decimated by the root louse phylloxera—a native of North American soils, taken to Europe via cuttings. Although native American vines are resistant to the louse, the pest infested European vineyards.

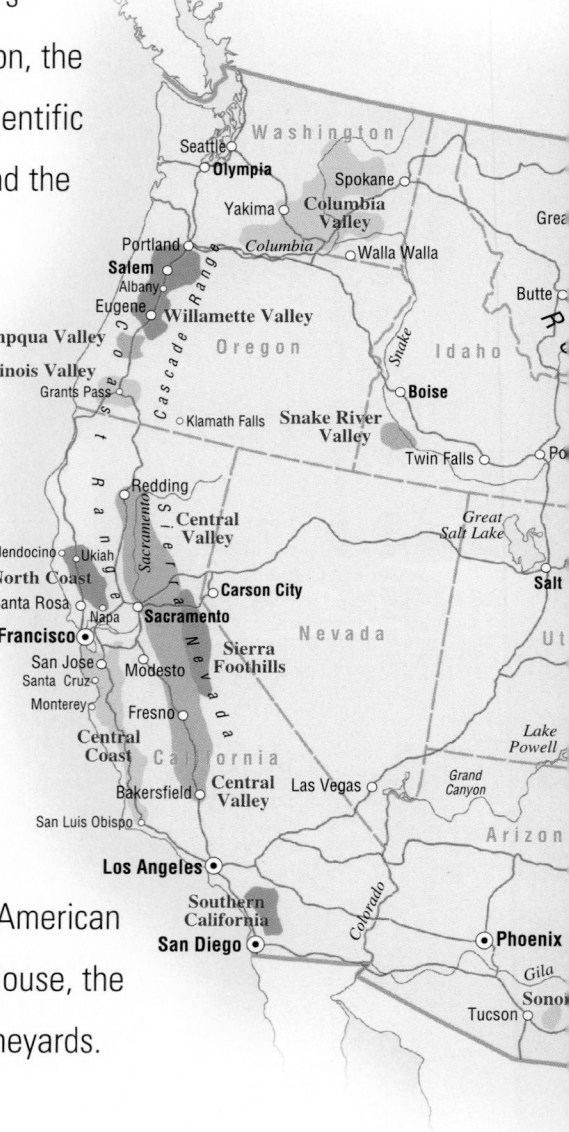

NORTH

200 miles
(320 kilometers)

America, though, while being the source of the devastation was also the source of the cure in the form of resistant root-stock for grafting. California dominates the American wine industry and the ascendancy of the vine in the United States is directly linked to California's history. Early colonists soon turned from native varieties to imported grape varieties and winemaking expertise from Europe for their wine needs. Repeated attempts to establish the European vine on the east coast failed, despite heroic attempts by the likes of Thomas Jefferson. Fungal diseases and phylloxera proved insurmountable until as recently as 40 years ago.

1 Hudson River Region
2 Western Connecticut Highlands
3 Southeastern New England
4 Central Delaware Valley
5 Lancaster Valley
6 Cumberland Valley
7 Catoctin
8 Shenandoah Valley
9 Northern Neck George Washington Birthplace
10 Monticello
11 North Fork of Roanoke
12 Rocky Knob

Chicago's skyscrapers in early sunshine.

Christianity was significant in establishing viticulture in California, New Mexico and Texas. In 1769, Father Juniperro Serra founded the first of 21 California missions (in San Diego) along the El Camino Real (Royal Highway) up the coast. By 1823 these had reached Sonoma County at Solano. The missions were secularized in 1833 by the Mexican government; the Solano vineyard fell into the hands of General Vallejo, who became a prominent grower. A small-scale industry evolved, particularly in the Los Angeles region, where vines were irrigated from the Los Angeles River.

Production in Ohio reached its peak in the 1850s. A challenging climate, industrial expansion and the rise of California combined to stem production in the east. In 1848 the California gold-rush began—the state's population grew thirty-fold and winemaking boomed. The mission grape dominated the state's viticulture, producing better sweet wine and brandy than table wine.

European varieties were imported as early as 1833, when Jean Louis Vignes, a French cooper, brought in non-mission vines. *Vitis vinifera* varieties were planted during the next two decades. Some believe that Sonoma producer Agoston Haraszthy—"father of California viticulture"—was the source of new varieties, but by 1861, when he searched Europe in for cuttings, new varieties had been in California for three decades.

During the 1880s, the University of California, with Professor Eugene W. Hilgard, was the guiding light. By 1880, zinfandel, which probably arrived between 1852–1855, was the first choice of quality-minded vineyard owners. The first *vinifera* plantings in Washington State took place in 1876.

In the early 1900s, Sonoma was the wine center of the United States. French, Swiss and Italian winemakers greatly improved wine quality—California wine was winning awards in Europe. With Prohibition in 1919 came darkness for the industry. Some wineries survived by producing sacramental and medicinal wines; some were saved by selling grapes for home winemaking. There was a shift to grapes with high yields and fruit that survived shipping—petite sirah, carignane and alicante bouchet. Curiously, alcohol consumption increased during Prohibition. Organized crime boomed, monopolizing alcohol distribution.

Prohibition ended in 1933, but the wine industry was slow to recover—the nation had developed a preference for spirits. Professor William V. Cruess's *Principles and Practices of Winemaking* helped producers move away from sweet and fortified wines. Over the ensuing decades, a core of the UC Davis faculty, including Winkler, Olmo, Amerine, Singleton, Ough, Kunkee and Webb, helped restore the California wine industry and influenced generations of winemakers worldwide.

In 1936, Winkler began to develop his heat summation theory, categorizing climatic regions. By 1944, Winkler and Amerine had published their data, which was used to decide which varieties should be planted where. Tchelistcheff arrived in the Napa Valley in 1937 and was hired by Beaulieu Vineyards. Winery problems then included excessive sulfuring of harvested grapes, hot fermentations controlled by ice additions to vats, little sharing of knowledge among producers, stuck fermentations, volatile acidity and a limited market. In 1938 Tchelistcheff introduced coil refrigeration. He was also the first to use in oak barriques —these changes took decades to gain acceptance.

In 1943 the Mondavi family acquired the Charles Krug Winery—a learning ground for the legendary Robert Mondavi. Other quality-minded producers included Mayacamas, Buena Vista, Martin Ray, Stony Hill, Inglenook and Louis Martini. Efforts by industry and academia led to the development of commercial yeast; clean, faultless, fruity varietal wines became the industry's goal.

In 1948 Zellerbach's Hanzell Winery (north of Sonoma) was planted with pinot noir and chardonnay. The cellar's temperature and humidity mimicked burgundy. Hanzell produced the first quality chardonnay, laying the groundwork for the later boom. The 1950s saw a revival of the industry. Quality improved as plantings increased, and better winery hygiene, use of stainless-steel equipment, temperature control and commercial yeast came into greater acceptance.

The 1960s heralded the modern era of wine production with Heitz and Mondavi opening wineries in the Napa Valley. Mondavi embarked on vineyard and winery trials in a successful quest for quality. Château Ste-Michelle and Columbia Winery first put Washington State on the map. Gallo greatly impacted the industry by introducing chablis blanc and hearty burgundy in 1964. While these wines did not have anything to do with Burgundy, they were clean, fruity, reasonably priced and an introduction to quality table wines for millions of Americans.

In 1973, an important year, Moët & Chandon began production of Chandon sparkling wine in Napa Valley and was the first champagne house in the United States. The 1973 vintage produced California wines that shook the wine world by winning the famed Paris tasting. This 1976 competition pitted California chardonnay and cabernet sauvignon against top wines from Burgundy and Bordeaux. The French judges ranked the 1973 Stag's Leap Cabernet Sauvignon the top red and the 1973 Château Montelena Chardonnay the top white—creating a marketing bonanza for the California wine industry, which could then claim wine as fine as any in the world.

Lett and other pinot noir specialists established vineyards and wineries in Oregon during the early 1970s. Further California expansion took place in 1979 with Opus One, a joint venture between Mondavi and Baron Philippe de Rothschild. Producers from other parts of the world have followed with ventures in California, including Torres, Moueix, Perrin, Antinori and Southcorp.

Prices stagnated in the late 1980s as supply exceeded demand. A new strain of phylloxera— biotype-B—appeared in Napa Valley and spread throughout California and into Oregon. As most of California's vines were planted on AXR-1 or *Vitis vinifera* stock, this created much damage. Luckily, the spread of phylloxera and the time to vine death takes years, allowing for the existing vineyards to be ripped out and replanted with resistant rootstock. Producers faced enormous debts that forced them into partnerships and restructured corporations. In 1993 there were initial public offerings in Robert Mondavi Winery, with Berringer Wine Estates in 1995. Replanting has afforded the opportunity to rethink—variety, clone, rootstock, spacing, trellising, aspect and irrigation, so quality should improve markedly.

Meanwhile, quality and quantity improved in Oregon, Washington, New York (Finger Lakes and Long Island) and Virginia, and impressive efforts have come from New Mexico and Texas.

Production in the early 1990s gained momentum when economic expansion brought increased demand. After a flurry of reports on the benefits of moderate wine consumption, red wines, such as cabernet sauvignon, pinot noir, zinfandel and, particularly, merlot, became especially popular with health-conscious consumers. With producers trying to hold onto export market gains and maintain dominance in domestic markets, some bought wine or vineyards in the Languedoc region, France, to help with production shortfalls. In spite of increased replanting costs, increased bordeaux prices and increased demand, record sales and record prices led to record profits.

Currently another threat looms, Pierce's disease, particularly because of a new vector, the glassy-winged sharpshooter. Previous epidemics of Pierce's disease occurred in 1892–1906 and the 1930s, wiping out thriving vineyards in Anaheim.

Despite some ideal climates for growing quality wine grapes, the American wine industry has had to grapple with many challenges. To date, the three "Ps," Prohibition, phylloxera and Pierce's disease, have been the most overpowering. California—the state and its wine industry— continues to be an innovative, dominant and resilient force. With a new wave of viticulture and a melding of the science and art of winemaking, the future of world-class wine from America appears to be a promising one.

Patrick Farrell MW

Vines are sometimes netted to protect the fruit from birds until harvest time.

Washington State

Paul White

At the beginning of the millennium Washington State's phenomenal growth saw one new winery opening every 13 days. During the past 20 years a base of 19 wineries has grown to 145, with an increase in vineyard area from 5,000 to 25,000 acres (2,023 to 10,117 ha). Currently ranked second in premium varietal production within the USA, Washington State now exports its wine to more than 40 countries.

History

The growing of *Vitis vinifera* here can be documented from 1876 when Italian immigrants brought cinsault to Walla Walla. Prohibition stopped early twentieth-century winery growth in its tracks, but after the Second World War business recovered and there were soon 38 wineries. Washington's modern history begins with associated vintners Nawico and Pommerelle, the precursors of Château Ste-Michelle and Columbia Winery, which demonstrated the viability of *vinifera* varietals progressively throughout the 1950s and 1960s. Thereafter, Washington's reputation for excellence in wines spread from its delicately perfumed riesling in the 1970s, to accolades in the 1980s for its elegant, well-focused merlots and chardonnays. The future looks just as bright for newcomers viognier and syrah.

Landscape and climate

Washington's geology has been much influenced over time by volcanic activity and flood erosion on a monumental scale. Lava flows provided basalt foundations for both the gentle slopes and sharply etched east–west ridges now covered in vines. As glaciers retreated 16,000 years ago, they left behind a free-draining gravel bed up to 250 feet (76 m) deep, with shallow, stone-studded, sandy topsoil—perfect for low-vigor grape-growing.

Washington State is divided climatically by the volcanoes of the Cascade Mountains. These effectively capture the clouds flowing off the Pacific Ocean, soaking western Washington with some 50 inches (127 cm) of rain annually, and leaving less than 8 inches (20 cm) to fall on eastern Washington's Columbia River basin.

The generously irrigated, ever-sunny Columbia River Valley contains 99.9 percent of Washington's vineyards. The Columbia's growing season is marked by an intense early ripening period followed by a long, gentle "Indian summer" finish. Cool nights and consistent conditions create the deep perfumes, crystal-clear fruit flavors and excellent natural acidity that define Washington's cool-climate wine styles.

Wines and vines

Eastern Washington's wine styles are defined by intense, vibrant fruit and juicy natural acids. They are seen as relatively inexpensive alternatives to California wines. The state's most-planted grapes, merlot and chardonnay, generally show elegant style, varietal purity, fine structure and balance. Both cabernet sauvignon and franc are bottled as straight varietals and/or combined with merlot in "Meritage" blends, among the most bordeaux-like in the country. Although difficult varietals to sell, Washington's sauvignon blanc, chenin blanc and sémillon are among the finest examples in the US.

Newcomers syrah, malbec and viognier show tremendous promise, but nebbiolo and sangiovese have, so far, been less consistent. Experimental plantings of carmenère, marsanne, rousanne and mourvèdre suggest that these have great potential. More serious treatment of grenache, cinsault and lemberger (blaufränkisch) has brought new life to these older, workhorse grapes. Relatively small quantities of other varieties are grown in western Washington's milder, wetter regions.

For premium wines, winemakers prefer that the grapes are picked by hand.

Yakima Valley

Washington's largest AVA (American Viticultural Area) is the Columbia Valley with 25,000 acres (10,125 ha) of vines planted inside a total area of 10.7 million acres (4,333,500 ha). It was conceived as a blanket appellation for virtually all of the state's vineyards. Within this large area are two smaller, more climatically distinctive AVAs: the semi-arid Yakima Valley and Walla Walla River Valley. Relatively cooler than the surrounding Columbia AVA, the Yakima Valley produces about 40 percent of the state's wine. The region is bounded by the evocatively named Rattlesnake Hills and Horse Heaven Hills.

CHINOOK

Established 1983 *Owners* **Kay Simon and Clay Mackey**
Production **3,500 cases** *Vineyard area* **7 acres (2.75 ha)**

Former Château Ste-Michelle winemaker Kay Simon established Chinook with partner Clay Mackey, intent on keeping the operation small enough to manage on their own. Stylistically, Chinook sauvignon blanc, chardonnay and sémillon support, rather than dominate food. All are fine-textured, subtle and crisp.

HOGUE CELLARS

Established 1982 *Owners* **Hogue family** *Production* **400,000 cases** *Vineyard area* **1,800 acres (729 ha)**

One of the leaders in the region, Hogue is a largish winery with the will and ability to do small-batch winemaking. All of the wines show crystal-clear varietal characters, understated elegance and are inexpensive for their quality. Highlights include riesling from 26-year-old vines; a spicy, fleshy fumé blanc; leesy, creamy, crisp chardonnay; a more intense, nutty, complex Vineyard Selections Chardonnay; a blackberry and vanilla syrah with fine tannins; minty, juicy merlot; and a meaty, mocca, tobacco-tinged Genesis Cabernet Franc that is soft and deeply juicy.

KESTREL VINTNERS

Established 1995 *Owners* **Walker family** *Production* **12,000 cases** *Vineyard area* **104 acres (42 ha)**

Drawing fruit from this Yakima estate's low-cropped 29-year-old vines, winemaker Ray Sandidge's aim is to be outlived by his wines. Kestrel reds have a powerfully intense elegance, and are

slow to unfold. The syrah is tarry, minty and explosive, and easily worth its relatively high price. Sandidge's merlots and cabernets are tightly structured and may just see him out as he hopes.

KIONA

Established 1979 *Owners* **Holmes and Williams families** *Production* **NA** *Vineyard area* **30 acres (12 ha)**

Kiona is sited in chalky, high-pH soil on one of Yakima's driest, hottest sites, Red Mountain. Its lemberger vines are the oldest in the state and its cabernet grapes are considered among the best produced. Known for solid, well-made, fruit-forward, excellent-value wines, with strengths especially in late-harvested riesling, chenin blanc and lemberger wines.

WASHINGTON HILLS

Established 1988 *Owners* **Harry Alhadeff and Brian Carter** *Production* **70,000 cases** *Vineyard area* **103 acres (42 ha)**

Smartly conceived, with three-tier branding, this winery produces a broad range of varietals, including gewürztraminer and viognier. Entry level Washington Hills offers excellent value chenin blanc, dry riesling, sémillon, chardonnay and merlot. Mid-range Bridgman chardonnay, merlot, syrah and cabernet show more varietal definition and reasonable complexity for the price. The Apex Reserve Range's Gewürztraminer Ice Wine and Late Harvest Riesling are outstanding.

Itinerant pickers from Mexico, here working at Hogue Cellars, follow the grape harvest up the west coast.

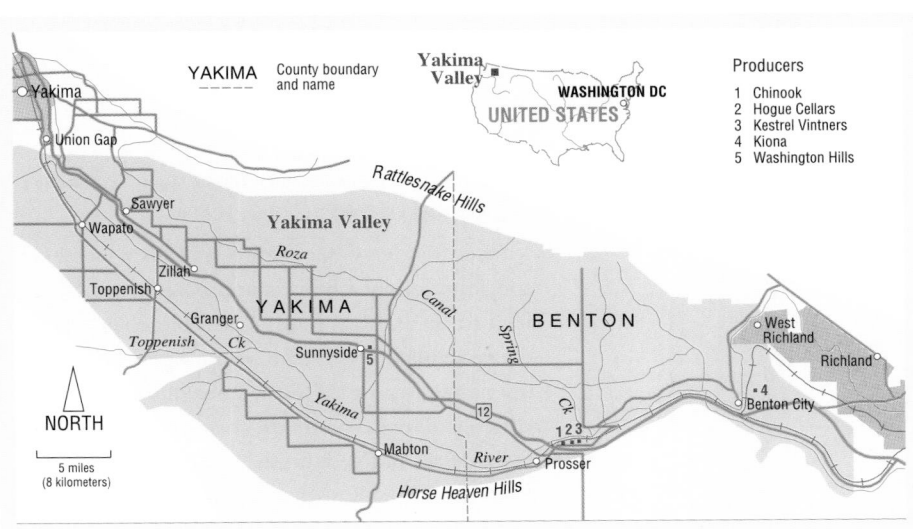

Ivy grows over a long-disused wine press.

OTHER WASHINGTON PRODUCERS

BOOKWALTER

Established 1983 *Owners* Bookwalter family *Production* 12,000 cases *Vineyard area* 5 acres (2 ha)

Viticulturist Jerry Bookwalter and his winemaker son John follow a holistic approach, leaving the fruit to ripen for as long as possible, then letting the wine make itself. The chenin blanc and chardonnay they produce show outstandingly pure varietal characters and are very good value, while the reds are unfined, unfiltered, richly and ripely fruited, and finely structured, with great length and balance—impressive, under-valued wines.

CANOE RIDGE

Established 1993 *Owner* Chalone Wine Group *Production* 32,000 cases *Vineyard area* 156 acres (63 ha)

Originally it was planned to grow only merlot, but Canoe Ridge has since also produced distinctive cabernet and chardonnay. The strong pinot noir experience of former Acacia Winery winemaker John Abbott now shapes deeply perfumed, velvety, elegant merlots. His chardonnays have a classic delicacy and purity, with crisp apple characters and fine-boned textures. Although underrated and underpriced, Canoe Ridge's cabernets show ripe blackcurrant characters, impressive mid-palates and fine structures.

CAYUSE

Established 1997 *Owner* Christoph Baron *Production* 2,000 cases *Vineyard area* 22 acres (9 ha)

Cayuse's grape-growing philosophy is completely organic and Baron's winemaking style is non-interventionist. Unfined and unfiltered, all of Baron's wines are stylistically generous without being obvious: Columbia Syrah is spicy and elegant, Walla Walla Syrah is a mixture of berry fruits and pepper, and Cobblestone Syrah hints at sage, thyme and violets with a soft and richly textured palate.

CORUS BRANDS

Established 1962 *Owner* Corus Brands *Production* 355,000 plus cases *Vineyard area* 1,168 acres (473 ha)

Washington's second-largest winery, Corus Brands was formed in 1962 as Associated Vintners. It was renamed Columbia Winery in 1984 and, as Corus Brands it now also includes bargain-priced Covey Run and mid-level Paul Thomas. Winemaker David Lake at Columbia Winery has crafted a smart range of carefully structured, age-worthy, single-vineyard Otis, Sagemoor and Red Willow cabernet sauvignons. Lake pioneered sangiovese and pinot gris in Washington and is in the process of proving the qualities of mourvèdre, tempranillo, malbec and viognier. Both Covey Run and David Thomas enjoy reputations for clean, pure varietal characters at sharp prices.

DeLILLE CELLARS/CHALEUR ESTATE

Established 1992 *Owners* Charles and Greg Lill, Jay Soloff, Christopher Upchurch *Production* 3,574 cases *Vineyard area* NA

Sharply focused, site-specific, unfiltered wines have brought DeLille to the fore of Washington's more serious producers. Best wines include a super-concentrated, deeply integrated savory Chaleur (cabernet sauvignon/merlot/cabernet franc), a counterpoint to the plummy merlot-dominant D2. Chaleur Doyenne Syrah shows classic blackberry and white pepper aromas and a typically firm dusty tannic palate. A classy, beautifully balanced sauvignon/sémillon white is also produced.

DUNHAM

Established 1995 *Owners* Dunham family *Production* 1,400 cases *Vineyard area* 60 acres (24 ha)

Winemaker Eric Dunham produces small batches of high-quality unfined, unfiltered reds. His Dunham III is a concentrated, meaty, spicy pure cabernet sauvignon with fine tannins. Also worth a try is a brambly, peppery, supple, fine-grained syrah.

L'ECOLE NO 41

Established 1983 *Owners* Clubb family *Production* 17,000 cases *Vineyard area* NA

Marty Clubb makes Washington's best sémillons— ripe and rich-textured Fries Sémillon and barrel-fermented L'Ecole No 41 Sémillon, with green walnut and citrus characters. Another steal is the beeswax, melon and citrusy chenin blanc. Reds show strength through a finely structured Seven Hills Merlot; expansive Apogee merlot/cabernet blend; and meaty, smooth, viscous Walla Walla Cabernet Sauvignon.

GLEN FIONA

Established 1995 *Owner* Ronald White, Tony Weeks, Berle "Rusty" Figgins *Production* 3,000 cases *Vineyard area* NA

Rusty Figgins studied winemaking at Wagga Wagga in Australia, and now mainly produces variant blends of syrah, spiced by grenache, cinsault or viognier. Vinification style takes its cue from the vintage, following an eclectic Franco-Australian mix of cold maceration, basket pressing, wild and rhône yeast fermentation in neutral old oak, resulting in personality-filled wines: a peppery, concentrated Columbia Valley syrah; and a fleshy, broadly perfumed Walla Walla syrah blend (5 percent viognier).

HEDGES

Established 1987 *Owners* Hedges family *Production* 6,500 cases *Vineyard area* 240 acres (97 ha)

Hedges prefers "complete" blended wines over straight varietals, offering interesting aromas, condensed flavors and supple textures. With new plantings of syrah, and Portuguese grape varieties touriga nacional, tinta and sousão, Hedges' future

looks intriguing. Best wines include an early-drinking Merlot/Cabernet Columbia Valley; a meaty, savory but elegant Three Vineyards and a French-oak-fermented, cassis-like Red Mountain Reserve structured for long life.

LEONETTI CELLAR

Established 1977 *Owners* Gary and Nancy Figgins *Production* 5,500 cases *Vineyard area* NA

Leonetti is Walla Walla's oldest winery and has its oldest merlot vines. The original vineyard, planted in 1974, is managed through intensive low-yield viticultural practices. Recent plantings have added cabernet franc, petit verdot, carmenère and syrah. Stylistically, Leonetti's cabernet sauvignon, cabernet sauvignon Reserve, merlot and sangiovese are big, powerful and oak-driven, with layers of opulent fruit. These are seriously sought-after wines.

MATHEWS

Established 1993 *Owner* Matt Loso *Production* 3,000 cases *Vineyard area* NA

Mathews draws in fruit from a number of top vineyards, including highly rated cabernet sauvignon from Elerding Vineyard. Its portfolio includes the explosive, dense, finely tannined Mathews Elerding Cabernet Sauvignon; unfiltered, subtly oaked Mathews cabernets blend and a weighty sémillon with one-third sauvignon.

Pickers work their way along rows of ripening fruit, harvesting with care.

Tightly bunched white grapes.

McCREA CELLARS

Established 1988 *Owners* McCrea family *Production* 2,800 cases *Vineyard area* NA

McCrea's best includes a big, juicy, jammy, fruit-forward Boushey Vineyard Syrah, a much more restrained, elegant Ciel du Cheval Syrah, Cuvée Orleans Syrah (with 6 percent viognier) and Tierra del Sol, a spicy, velvety grenache/syrah blend. A low-cropped viognier shows textbook spicy apricot aromas and a balanced, creamy texture.

QUILCEDA CREEK VINTNERS

Established 1979 *Owners* Golitzen family *Production* NA *Vineyard area* NA

Alex Golitzen and his son Paul make Washington's most famous cabernet sauvignons. French oaked, unfined, unfiltered, these complex, densely structured wines are consistently composed of fruit from the state's best sites: Kiona, Mercer, Klipsum and Ciel du Cheval.

SALISHAN VINEYARDS

Established 1976 *Owners* Joan and Linc Wolverton *Production* 5,000–6,000 cases *Vineyard area* 9 acres (4 ha)

Salishan pioneered this small vineyard, which was western Washington's first *vinifera* vineyard. It is now farmed as organically as the fickle, wet, climate allows. Joan Wolverton's focus is on silky, delicately perfumed, finely structured pinot noir.

SEVEN HILLS WINERY

Established 1980 *Owners* Hendricks and McClellan families *Production* NA *Vineyard area* NA

Sitting on Walla Walla AVA's Oregon side, this winery produces big, boldly fruited, chunky, long-lived, 100 percent cabernet sauvignon and merlot sourced from low-yield, deficit-irrigated Klipsun and Seven Hills Vineyards.

STIMSON LANE VINEYARDS & ESTATES

Established 1967 *Owner* Shareholders *Production* 2,500,000 cases *Vineyard area* 1,200 acres (486 ha)

Impeccably professional, brilliantly marketed and smartly branded, Stimson Lane is the cornerstone of Washington's industry and makes high-quality premium wines in ever-increasing volumes. Its two major brands—Château Ste-Michelle and Columbia Crest—account for 70 percent of Washington's wine production. Its single-vineyard chardonnays, merlots and cabernets now rank among America's best. Originally conceived in 1984 as a volume label to free CSM's upmarket expansion, Columbia Crest has steadily evolved into a high-quality producer in its own right, particularly with its Reserve Range. Recent wine-making collaborations with Antinori of Italy, Petaluma of Australia and Dr Loosen of Germany have ensured the company remains on the cutting edge of both American and international wine styles.

WATERBROOK WINERY

Established 1984 *Owners* Rendal family *Production* 27,000 cases *Vineyard area* 14 acres (6 ha)

This is one of Walla Walla's original boutique wineries and maintains top quality at sharp prices. Best values include a light, grassy, seamless sauvignon blanc (23 percent sémillon) and a nutty, melt-in-your-mouth chardonnay. The merlot, cabernet sauvignon and Red Mountain "Meritage" show focused varietal characters and nice tannins.

ANDREW WILL

Established 1989 *Owner* Chris Camarda *Production* 350 cases *Vineyard area* NA

This Vashon Island winery makes tiny quantities of vineyard-designated wines from Ciel du Cheval, Boushey, Klipsun and Pepper Bridge. Carmarda's supple, plummy, finely structured, age-worthy merlots, as well as Sorella, a cabernet sauvignon-dominated merlot/franc blend, and sangiovese and chenin blanc are all highly sought after.

WOODWARD CANYON

Established 1981 *Owner* Richard Small *Production* 11,000 cases *Vineyard area* NA

Richard Small, one of Washington's great boutique winemakers, helped put Washington cabernet, merlot and chardonnay on the premium map. Drawing low-yield fruit primarily from the lower Columbia and Walla Walla areas and a high-density planted home vineyard, wines are unfiltered, unfined and not acidified. Woodward Celilo Chardonnay shows complex savory characters and is finely structured, counterpointing a fat, fleshy, peachy Walla Walla Chardonnay. Woodward reds include a juicy, chocolatey merlot with explosive mid-palate; a dark, dense old-vine cabernet; and Charbonneau, a complex, silky, seamless merlot/cabernet sauvignon/franc blend.

OREGON

Paul White

Oregon has long held a unique reputation for progressivism and non-conformity in North America, so it should come as no surprise that its wine industry grows the world's most difficult grape—pinot noir—in a hostile environment. As well as embracing harsh growing conditions, Oregonians imposed some of the world's toughest labeling laws on themselves in the 1970s, with varietal content and stated region of origin set at 100 percent. Although varietal content was eventually relaxed to 90 percent, with cabernet sauvignon given dispensation down to 75 percent, these parameters remain high by world standards.

History

Although Oregon's first *Vitis vinifera* was planted in 1847, only a handful of early vineyards and wineries survived past Prohibition, and even some of these petered out later. The modern industry began in the 1960s and scored a breakthrough when Eyrie Vineyards' 1975 Pinot Noir achieved second place within a top flight of Cru-class burgundies at the Gault/Millau Wine Olympics in France in 1979. The late 1980s brought steady growth and the mid-1990s saw progress through improved viticulture in evening out previous difficulties with vintage variation. Now ranked fourth in US production with an annual output of nearly one million cases, Oregon has 136 wineries, with 383 vineyards and 10,000 acres (4,050 ha) planted in *vinifera* varieties.

Landscape and climate

Like Washington, Oregon is climatically divided into dry eastern and wet western halves by the volcanic Cascade Mountains, which block clouds generated by the Pacific Ocean and cast a rain shadow over the great western valley. This maritime influence is somewhat mitigated by Oregon's northern position at the 45th parallel, which contributes lengthened days, indirect sunlight and a broad diurnal temperature range within a long growing season. It is cooler and wetter than both Washington and California, although the growing season is relatively dry, peaking with 90°F (32°C) temperatures in July that gradually taper into the warm days and cool nights of fall.

Vines and wines

Winemaking in Oregon tends to follow traditional burgundian practices, primarily using barrels of French or Oregon oak. The wineries are small, labor-intensive operations and hand-picking remains the rule. Virtually all of the wineries produce perfumed pinot noirs in a style that echoes perfumes, structures and textures found in Burgundy. These wines often require up to seven years to open up, with many capable of evolving for a decade or more. Chaptalization is allowed, but rarely applied.

Pinot gris, Oregon's sexiest variety, is made in a style based on barrel and tank fermentation. Other Alsatian varieties, gewürztraminer, pinot blanc and riesling, have thrived in the cool climate, and show consistently ripe, well-focused varietal characters in well-executed dry styles. Both riesling and gewürztraminer are often good value in semi-sweet, late-harvest and ice wine styles. Recently introduced burgundian chardonnay clones have brought fuller, better balanced wines—clones from California failed to ripen fully under the gray skies. Both white and red wines show subdued European fruit characters with nicely balanced acidity.

Black grapes still increasing in sweetness late in the season.

Willamette Valley

New cuttings get off to a good start..

Some 60 miles (96 km) wide and 100 miles (160 km) deep, the wet Willamette Valley AVA (40 inches/102 cm precipitation per annum) is home to 104 wineries. Almost all focus primarily on pinot noir, with riesling, chardonnay, pinot gris, pinot blanc, sauvignon blanc and gewürztraminer fleshing out their portfolios. Vineyards are planted in relatively infertile soil on gentle slopes, primarily clustered around the Red Hills of Dundee, with the rest scattered throughout Yamhill County, Washington County and the Eola Hills.

AMITY VINEYARD

Established 1974 *Owner* Myron Redford *Production* 10,000 cases *Vineyard area* 12 acres (5 ha)

In addition to complex, ageworthy, old-vine pinot noir, Amity also makes creditable gamay noir, and spicy, full-bodied, dry-styled riesling, gewürztraminer and pinot blanc. Ever driven to innovate, Amity has developed a sulfur-free organic pinot noir labeled ECO Wine.

ARCHERY SUMMIT WINERY

Established 1995 *Owners* Andrus family *Production* 10,000 cases *Vineyard area* 100 acres (40 ha)

Echoing Domaine Drouhin (see below) with a monumental, gravity-fed winery driven by California style and capital, Archery Summit is the brainchild of Gary Andrus of Pine Ridge in the Napa Valley. Its strength lies in a range of single-vineyard pinot noirs, infused with spicy oak and jam-packed with fruit complexity and layers of texture. Expensive, but very smart wines.

ARGYLE WINERY

Established 1986 *Owners* Brian Croser and Cal Knudsen *Production* 33,000 cases *Vineyard area* 120 acres (49 ha)

Visionary Australian winemaker Brian Croser, of Petaluma, created Argyle intending to make *méthode champenoise* from chardonnay and pinot noir, but has subsequently attracted as much attention for his equally high-quality still wines, chardonnay and riesling.

BEAUX FRÈRES

Established 1988 *Owners* Mike Etzel, Robert M. Parker and Robert Roy *Production* 3,000 cases *Vineyard area* 30 acres (12 ha)

High-quality Beaux Frères established its close-planted, multi-clone, low-yield vineyard for optimum grape production. The pinot noir is unfined, unfiltered and dominated by new oak, in an opulent forward-fruit, high-alcohol style. Sulfur levels are deliberately kept low.

BETHEL HEIGHTS

Established 1977 *Owners* Caastel, Web and Dudley families *Production* 10,000 cases *Vineyard area* 50 acres (20 ha)

Pioneers of the important Eola Hills region, this winery produces multi-clone, low-cropping, estate-grown pinot noir. The best of the bunch includes the old-vine Southeast Block Reserve and Flat Block, both of which are full-flavored and structured to age brilliantly.

CAMERON

Established 1984 *Owner* John Paul *Production* 3,250 cases *Vineyard area* 4 acres (1.6 ha)

This is an important small producer of unfiltered single-vineyard and organic pinot noir, fleshy, complex chardonnay and pinot blanc (disguised as pinot bianco). Abby Ridge and Clos Electric pinot noirs are both excellent and improve with age.

DOMAINE DROUHIN

Established 1987 *Owner* Joseph Drouhin *Production* 12,200 cases *Vineyard area* 74 acres (30 ha)

Domaine Drouhin represents the greatest and most undisputed recognition by France of Oregon's potential. In 1987, burgundian *négociant* house Joseph Drouhin planted a vineyard in Dundee with double the normal US vine density, then built a monumental, state-of-the-art, gravity-fed winery. Drouhin's pinots, now considered Oregon benchmarks, show an elegantly underplayed, multi-layered complexity that consistently ranks among the best produced anywhere outside Burgundy. Cuvée Laurene, a wine of outstanding quality, is made only in top vintages.

POLK
County boundary and name

NORTH

10 miles (16 kilometers)

Columbia River
MULTNOMAH
Forest Grove · Hillsboro
Portland
WASHINGTON
Gaston
CLACKAMAS
West Linn
Yamhill
Oregon City
Carlton
Newberg
McMinnville
Canby
Willamette Valley
YAMHILL
Sheridan
Woodburn
Willamina
MARION
Salem

Producers
1 Amity Vineyard
2 Archery Summit Winery
3 Argyle Winery
4 Beaux Frères
5 Bethel Heights
6 Cameron
7 Domaine Drouhin
8 Elk Cove Vineyards
9 Evesham Wood
10 Eyrie Vineyards
11 Rex Hill Vineyards
12 King Estate Winery
13 Panther Creek Cellars
14 Ponzi Vineyard
15 St Innocent Winery
16 Willamette Valley Vineyards
17 Ken Wright Winery

Dallas
POLK
Monmouth
Willamette Valley
BENTON
Corvallis
LINN
Albany
Jefferson
Willamette Valley
WASHINGTON DC
UNITED STATES
12 · 35 miles (56 km)

ELK COVE VINEYARDS

Established 1977 *Owners* Campbell family *Production* 15,000 cases *Vineyard area* 100 acres (40 ha)

Among Oregon's early handful of premium producers, Elk Cove's *terroir*-influenced pinot noirs have consistently erred on the side of subtlety, balance and elegance with an impressive silky texture. The best will age well for two decades. All of the wines from this rather small winery are reliably good, with outstanding quality in the dry and late-harvested versions of riesling, pinot gris and gewürztraminer.

EVESHAM WOOD

Established 1986 *Owner* Russ Raney *Production* 3,000 cases *Vineyard area* NA

Unpretentious high-quality producer Evesham Wood makes complex, multi-layered, single-vineyard pinot noirs at fair and reasonable prices. The styles here lean toward black fruit characters, barnyardiness and silken textures. Unfiltered Cuvée J was named after legendary burgundian winemaker Henri Jayer, a fitting tribute to a great man. Both a fleshy pinot gris and complex, earthy chardonnay are superb.

EYRIE VINEYARDS

Established 1966 *Owners* Lett family *Production* 8,000–10,000 cases *Vineyard area* 50 acres (20 ha)

Visionary founding father of Oregon pinot noir, Lett deserves equal credit for similarly establishing the Alsatian varietals pinot gris, muscat and riesling. Lett follows traditional burgundian winemaking practices, opting for a lighter, more delicately perfumed style of pinot noir. Tight and austere while young, these wines often begin to blossom only at 5–10 years of age. Eyrie's pinot meunier ranks among the best produced anywhere and his ground-breaking pinot gris remains a benchmark for the area.

KING ESTATE WINERY

Established 1992 *Owners* King family *Production* 400,000 cases *Vineyard area* 785 acres (318 ha)

Oregon's largest winery, King Estate brings the large volumes, economy of scale and critical mass desperately needed to drive export growth and promote "brand" Oregon in new markets. Controlling North America's most clonally diverse pinot gris, chardonnay and pinot noir vineyard, King Estate has created a foundation of well-made, inexpensive varietals with tremendous potential for expansion into the upmarket arena.

Fall foliage, dazzling in the sunshine.

PANTHER CREEK CELLARS

Established 1986 *Owners* Kaplan family *Production* 7,300 cases *Vineyard area* Grapes are bought in

Produces high-quality, unfiltered, low-production, low-yield (less than 180 cases), single-vineyard ageworthy pinot noirs with generous fruit and balanced structures. Worth seeking out is *sur lee* Melon, made from the melon de bourgogne grape.

PONZI VINEYARD

Established 1974 *Owners* Ponzi family *Production* 7,200 cases *Vineyard area* NA

Ponzi has stuck with chardonnay, pinot gris, pinot noir and riesling planted in 1970. Its velvety, red fruit, smoky bacon, mushroomy pinot noir consistently ranks among Oregon's most complex. Other wines show rich textures and clean ripe fruit.

REX HILL VINEYARDS

Established 1982 *Owner* Paul Hart *Production* 40,000 cases *Vineyard area* 400 acres (162 ha)

All Rex Hill wines show excellent fruit purity and fine balance. Pinot noirs show distinct *terroir* characters through a single-vineyard range and multi-layered complexity at Reserve level. Whites include a crisp unoaked sauvignon, varietally focused pinot gris and pinot blanc, and a fine-boned chardonnay. Bargain label Kings Ridge wines are well made, easy drinking and sharply priced.

ST INNOCENT WINERY

Established 1988 *Owners* Mark Vlossak *Production* 7,000 cases *Vineyard area* NA

Sharing winemaker Mark Vlossak with Panther Creek, the quality and styles of this winery are based on a different fruit source and made into a

REGIONAL DOZEN

BEST WINES

Archery Summit Single
  Vineyard Pinot Noirs
Beaux Frères Pinot Noir
Domaine Drouhin Pinot Noir
  and Cuvée Laurene
Eyrie Pinot Meunier
Ponzi Reserve Pinot Noir
Ken Wright Single Vineyard
  Pinot Noirs

BEST VALUE WINES

Amity Pinot Blanc
Argyle Reserve Riesling
Bridgeview Dry
  Gewürztraminer
Firesteed Pinot Noir
Foris Chardonnay
Rex Hill Kings Ridge
  Pinot Gris

wide range of single-vineyard, concentrated, fine-grained pinot noirs, chardonnays and pinot gris.

WILLAMETTE VALLEY VINEYARDS
Established 1988 *Owners* Shareholders *Production* 85,000 cases *Vineyard area* 50 acres (20 ha)

This winery goes from strength to strength. Fruit is drawn from two vineyards and is intensively managed. From its beginning, WVV has shown steady improvement across a broad range of wines, with strengths in pinot noir, pinot gris, chardonnay and riesling.

KEN WRIGHT WINERY
Established 1994 *Owner* Ken Wright Cellars *Production* 7,000 cases *Vineyard area* 28 acres (11.5 ha

Ken Wright draws grapes from a wide range of microclimates and soil types, producing single-vineyard pinot noirs that clearly delineate *terroir* differences within the Willamette Valley. The wines are complex and condensed and the melony chardonnay and pinot blanc are excellent.

OTHER OREGON PRODUCERS
The Umpqua Valley AVA mainly produces pinot noir, cabernet sauvignon, chardonnay, riesling and sauvignon blanc. Farther south, in the hotter, drier and more elevated Rogue Valley, riesling, gewürztraminer, pinot gris, cabernet sauvignon, chardonnay, cabernet franc, merlot and sémillon are favored. The state's eastern vineyards, near Colombia Gorge and the Walla Walla AVA, generally sell their grapes to Washington wineries.

BRIDGEVIEW VINEYARDS
Established 1980 *Owners* Kerivan family and Ernie Brodie *Production* 64,000 cases *Vineyard area* 74 acres (30 ha)

This southern Illinois Valley winery consistently produces some of Oregon's best-value varietals from a closely planted vineyard. The riesling, pinot noir and chardonnay are well-made, ripely flavored and sharply priced. They are among Oregon's best-value wines.

HENRY ESTATE WINERY
Established 1972 *Owner* Scott C. Henry III *Production* 14,500 cases *Vineyard area* 31 acres (12.5 ha) plus

An early pioneer of the Umpqua Valley, Scott Henry is famous for having developed a trellis system for vines that is now widely used in vineyards throughout the USA. His pinot noir shows dominant new oak aromas with a lightish color and delicate perfumes.

The cool nights grapevines love also suit pumpkins, enhancing their storing qualities.

IDAHO

Catherine Fallis MS

Idaho is on a similar latitude to Bordeaux. Its wineries fall under the state classification of AO, or Appellation of Origin. Idaho is officially a subzone of tri-state Pacific Northwest with Oregon and Washington. Ste Chapelle Winery along with the Idaho Grape Growers and Wine Producers Commission (17 wineries and 20 growers) is currently determining boundaries in order to complete a multi-AVA application. Snake River Valley and two sub-AVAs of Sunny Slope and Arena Valley, a moon crater 20 minutes northwest of the Oregon border, are proposed.

The Pacific Northwest is the second-largest area in North America for *vinifera* grape production, with more than 45,000 acres (18,210 ha) under vine across the three states. Not unexpectedly, Idaho's contribution is the smallest. Reports to the commission suggest 653.5 acres (265 ha) are under vine, but a more accurate figure is 1,000 acres (405 ha). The commission charges dues (US$5 per acre) only on producing acres. Total case production is unknown as it is not reported to the commission, but wine production is the seventh-largest value-added cultural endeavor in the state, contributing an estimated US$10–$20 million annually to the state's coffers.

Growth is slow, as the industry is in a stranglehold by the local legislature. Several hundred thousand acres of affordable, plantable land with available water lie fallow. But interest from larger, outside businesses is increasing.

Varieties in production include cabernet franc, cabernet sauvignon, chardonnay, chenin blanc, lemberger (blaufrankisch), gewürztraminer, merlot, pinot gris, pinot noir, riesling, sauvignon blanc, sémillon and syrah. Experimental plantings of tempranillo, valdespino, viognier and zinfandel show great promise.

History

British fur traders established Fort Boise in 1834. In 1862, gold was discovered and vines were planted—French and German immigrants were credited with bringing cuttings from Europe. Their expertise paid off. At the 1898 Chicago World's Fair a Clearwater River Valley wine won a prize and at the 1904 International Exposition a local wine placed second behind Château Cheval Blanc. Prohibition delivered the first blow to the industry in the 1920s. In 1971 the industry began to recover from its second handicap by gaining freedom from the state-monopoly liquor stores. Wines could now be sold in food outlets, and grape growing was re-established. Ste Chapelle produced the first commercial wines in 1976 and several others began production in the 1980s.

There are still fewer than 20 commercial wineries in Idaho. With 57 percent of residents teetotal Mormons, producers must market their wines outside the state and look to sophisticated markets such as Santa Monica, New York, Seattle, Europe and parts of Asia. Competition comes mainly from the more widely accepted and recognized Oregon and Washington wines.

Landscape and climate

The wine industry is in two segments, with the growers in the southwest clustered around Boise—in Gooding, Twin Falls, Owyhee, Ada and Canyon counties. Canyon County, just south of Nampa, especially the Dry Lake Valley subzone, is slightly warmer than the Snake River vineyards. Ste Chapelle is a big customer in this area. The wineries, conversely, are set up in the central west.

The climate is inhospitable—conditions are arid with warm days and very cool nights. Differences of up to 35°F (19°C) between daily low and high temperatures mark the short growing season. Rainfall is low—less than 10 inches (25 cm) annually. Severe winters delay bud break. Sixteen hours a day of intense sunshine is common, offsetting the cold temperatures. The area is classified low Region II on the Winkler-Amerine scale. To the east, the Rocky Mountains protect the area from arctic storms but winters are long and challenging.

Vines and wines

High-stress climatic conditions (high altitude and abundant sunshine) produce unique wines with both high natural alcohol and high natural acidity. Fully ripe, high-acid, bone-dry, characterful riesling is a specialty, but it is not as popular as the chardonnays, which range from lean and tart to rich, viscous, oaky and buttery. Bordeaux varietals are coming into their own, though many are bolstered with Washington fruit. Similar to Australia's multi-district blends, Ste Chapelle produces Idaho/Washington labeled merlot and cabernet sauvignon. Camas and other wineries produce solely from Washington State fruit. Idaho is one of four places in the world where all the vineyards are planted on their own roots. The glass-laden, nutrient-deficient soil is inhospitable to the vine louse, phylloxera.

A healthy bloom on ripening black grapes.

Snake River Valley

Snake River Valley is currently the most important and certainly the most well-known of the wine-producing regions in Idaho, but it is worth noting that regions in the southwest are emerging and at present provide huge quantities of fruit for the Snake River Valley wineries.

Most of Idaho's wineries are clustered near the Washington and Oregon borders in the high mountain valleys of the Snake and Clearwater rivers and are concentrated in an area rather appropriately named Sunny Slope. These rivers, as they do in all premium wine-producing zones of the world, provide a climate-tempering influence in the region.

The most desirable vineyard sites can be found in the south-facing hillsides along the Snake River, where convection currents pull freezing air off the hillsides during winter and cool the vines during summer. The average vineyard elevation is about 2,500–3,100 feet (760–940 m), although a handful are as high as 4,500 feet (1,370 m).

KOENIG VINEYARDS AND DISTILLERY

Established 1995 *Owners* Greg and Kristen Koenig
Production 1,000 cases *Vineyard area* 4 acres (1.6 ha)

Small-lot barrel-fermented chardonnay as well as single-vineyard cabernet sauvignon, zinfandel and merlot are Greg Koenig's specialties. His brother Andrew operates the newly opened European-style eaux-de-vie brandy distillery. The Koenigs recently completed a winery and visitors' tasting room in Caldwell, just a short drive southeast from Boise.

SAWTOOTH WINERY

Established 1988 *Owners* Corus Brands Inc *Production* 10,000 cases *Vineyard area* 15 acres (6.1 ha)

Idaho's second-largest winery, the former Pintler Cellars is now part of Corus Brands Inc—the Pacific Northwest's second-largest group of wineries. Former owner Brad Pintler is now the general manager and winemaker, helping to retain the small family-owned winery's reputation while still taking advantage of the marketing resources of the new owner. The vines date back to 1982 and include chenin blanc, riesling, sémillon and cabernet sauvignon. More recent plantings include viognier, pinot gris, cabernet franc, merlot and syrah. The winery and vineyards are set on the rim of Hidden Valley near Nampa in the heart of the Snake River Valley, and they have a panoramic view right over the Owyhee Mountains.

STE CHAPELLE WINERY

Established 1976 *Owner* Corus Brands, Inc *Production* 135,000 cases *Vineyard area* 640 acres (259 ha) plus, 600 acres (242 ha) newly planted

Ste Chapelle Winery in Caldwell, named for La Sainte Chapelle, or Saint's Chapel, built by Louis IX in thirteenth-century Paris, was Idaho's first and is now its largest winery. Ste Chapelle is replanting or directing the redevelopment of more than 1,000 acres (404 ha) of the original vineyard sites first discovered in the nineteenth century. Winemaker Chuck Devlin joined Ste Chapelle Winery just before harvest in 2000. He sees syrah and riesling as the varietals with the most potential for the area, and there are plans afoot to increase production to 300,000 cases a year.

OTHER IDAHO PRODUCERS

CAMAS WINERY

Established 1983 *Owner* Stuart L. Scott *Production* 3,700 cases *Vineyard area* Grapes are bought in

The Scotts purchase grapes from independent growers and crush them in the field. They gather wild huckleberries, elderberries and plums in the nearby Clearwater, St Joe and Kaniksu National Forests. Their eclectic range of wines includes both *vinifera* varietals and fruit wines, handmade sparkling wines, honey meads and an Ethiopian hopped honey wine.

Camas is one of the oldest wineries in the state, taking its name from the local lily, which at one time was widespread on the Palouse Hills. The bulbs were used as food by the starving men in Thomas Jefferson's Corps of Discovery led by Lewis and Clark. Nowadays pigs become "wild hogs" for this delicacy.

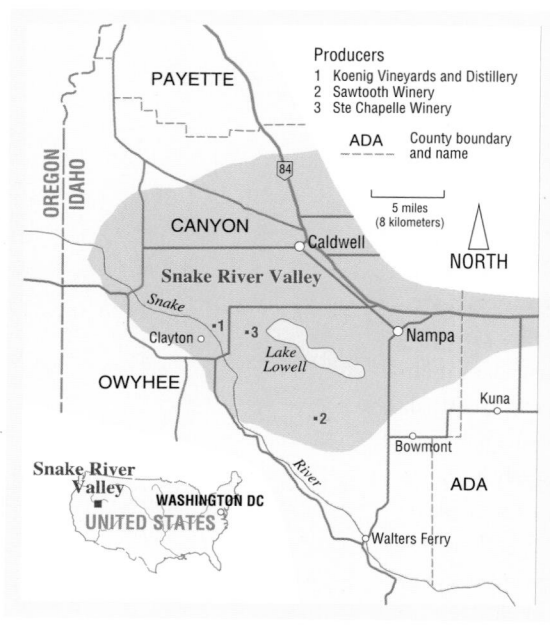

CARMELA VINEYARDS

Established 1988 *Owners* Roger and Nancy Jones
Production 12,000 cases *Vineyard area* 29 acres (11.7 ha)

This Glenns Ferry winery includes vineyards, golf course and restaurant. The vineyards are adjacent to the Three Mile Island State Park, where Oregon Trail wagon trains crossed 150 years ago. Winemaker Stephanie Martin, previously of Rose Creek Vineyards, produces 100 percent estate-grown and bottled blush, riesling, chardonnay, sémillon, merlot, lemberger, cabernet franc and cabernet sauvignon.

PEND D'OREILLE WINERY

Established 1995 *Owners* Stephen and Julie Meyer
Production 2,000 cases *Vineyard area* Grapes are bought in

Stephen and Julie's shared experiences in winemaking include the 1985 harvest in Meursault and seven years at Roudon-Smith Winery in the Santa Cruz Mountains. Chardonnay, pinot noir, merlot, cabernet franc, cabernet sauvignon, a bordeaux red blend and a "bistro" blend are all handcrafted using traditional French methods. The Meyers purchase local fruit for chardonnay and pinot noir, but their most notable wines to date are made with fruit from Columbia Valley, Washington.

SOUTH HILL/HEGY'S WINERY

Established 1989 *Owner* Frank Hegy *Production* 900 cases
Vineyard area 2 acres (0.8 ha)

One of Idaho's smallest wineries. Fruit is pressed with an antique Italian press and all wine, including wine for two Catholic churches, is bottled, labeled and corked by hand. Production includes chardonnay, chenin blanc, pinot noir and lemberger.

Widely spaced vine rows make it easy to harvest the grapes mechanically.

The seal of the state of California.

CALIFORNIA

The Golden State is a land of myths, movies and trends with worldwide influence. The state's vinous impact looms large, despite the checkered history of the wine industry over the past 100 years. The University of California (UC) at Davis has influenced several generations of winemakers from around the world. California was at the forefront of modern, hygienic winery practices that revolutionized warm climate wine production. California has been a trendsetter, for good or for bad, in the development of the clean, fruity and overtly oaked style of wine now produced in many parts of the world. Californian wine continues to be the model by which the world's largest economy sets its palate.

The journey from the Californian mission vineyards of the eighteenth century to the present day of heady prices and record profits has been difficult. Cycles of boom and bust have been created by markets, disease, politics, war, folly, insight and forward thinking. Prohibition from 1919–33 had effects upon the American wine industry which linger to this day. A modern wine industry arose during the 1950s and 1960s and grew in fits and starts, only to be hit with phylloxera biotype B during the 1990s. Resilient as ever, Californians view this as an expensive lesson and opportunity to improve upon the past's viticultural mistakes. Replanting and record profits have softened the phylloxera blow.

More than 554,000 acres (224,370 ha) of wine grapes are planted in California. California is the fourth largest wine producer in the world after France, Italy and Spain. Californian wine accounts for 91 percent of production and 72 percent of wine sales in the USA. Ninety-eight percent of USA wine exports hale from California and these have increased five-fold in value and three-fold in volume since 1990. Wine is big business—retail sales for 1999 totaled US$13 billion. It represents the number one finished agricultural product in the leading agricultural state.

In 2000, 55 percent of the California crush was red grapes and 45 percent was white grapes. Chardonnay was by far the leading white variety over colombard and chenin blanc. Cabernet sauvignon was the leading red, and was slightly ahead of zinfandel.

Landscape and climate

Understanding the Californian climate is not easy. Two myths need dispelling—first, that autumn is cooler than summer, second, that bathing beauties in skimpy bathing suits frolic in the ocean. The reality? Autumn is frequently warmer than summer, especially near the Pacific coast. Surface water temperatures are cold for most of the year along the California coast. Only in the south, and then only for a month or two during summer, does one venture into the Pacific Ocean without a wetsuit.

California's topography was created by the Pacific and North American tectonic plates. This sometimes unholy marriage has created two mountain ranges that impact upon the state's viticulture. The westernmost is aptly named the Coastal Range and the range further inland is the Sierra Nevada Range. Between these two is the famed Central Valley, one of the great agricultural regions on earth. The Coastal Range runs parallel to the Pacific Ocean along most of California's coastline. Up to 4,000 feet (1,221 m) in elevation, it can be a major obstacle to the cooling influence of the Pacific Ocean. The famous inversion layer of the Los Angeles basin and the resulting smog are testament to this effect.

Surface water temperatures along the coast are cooler than expected for mid-latitude Pacific Ocean. The combination of a Pacific high (present much of the year) and flow from the northwest yields winds that blow parallel to the coastline (Carioli's Force). This, in turn, causes the subsurface movement of ocean water termed the Ekman Spiral, which results in the net transport of surface water away from the shore and out to sea. Colder water from the depths then replaces the surface water resulting in water temperatures of 50–60°F (10–16°C) throughout the year. This

Schied Vineyards along Route 25, California.

upwelling is strongest in summer and weakest in winter.

The cool to cold coastal water temperatures influence climate in two ways. Air over the water is cooled and water vapor condenses to form a marine layer, which cools the morning to early afternoon and reduces sunshine in affected regions. The cool air also serves onshore breezes that are typically 20–30 miles per hour (32–48 km per hour) when maximal in late afternoon. The cooling effect is profound enough so that homes built along the coast, south of Los Angeles, do not require air conditioning.

As the inland is warmed by the day's sunshine two forces are created to promote this powerful onshore wind. A temperature gradient between the cool coastline and the warm to hot interior is formed. As the hot inland air rises, a pressure gradient combines with the temperature gradient to generate the cooling breeze from the Pacific Ocean.

The Coastal Range, which helps to create the cooling of the Pacific Ocean's surface, also helps to modulate the effect of these breezes on the interior of California. In those areas where the mountains run parallel to the coast, the onshore breeze is blocked and only the coastal plain is cooled, but at several locations the Coastal Range turns perpendicular and permits the cooling effect of the onshore wind to permeate inland. Similarly, gaps in the coastal range—the most famous being Golden Gate in San Francisco—also permit the cool afternoon and evening breezes to gain entry to the interior valleys of the state.

West to east orientation is thus more important in terms of temperature along coastal California, than north to south. While southern California is warmer than central and north, coastal regions of the south are cooler than inland regions of the north.

During the early autumn, the Pacific high usually weakens, lessening both the marine layer and the onshore winds. This results in net autumn warming. The regional weather pattern may further change when a strong inland high and a weakening Pacific high create a pattern of offshore winds. Both daily maximum and minimum temperatures increase during these periods.

Climate is of supreme importance to Californian viticulture. Areas with significant coastal effects—Carneros, Sonoma, Arroyo Grande and Santa Barbara—may indeed have cooler summer temperatures than such classic regions as Bordeaux and Burgundy. Cool evening temperatures cause grapes to retain good natural acidity levels.

Although summer temperatures may be lower in such coastal regions than classic regions, or even cool regions like Oregon, autumn climate patterns differ markedly. Whereas daily maximal temperatures decrease, sometimes markedly, during the autumn in the classic regions in Europe and in the Pacific Northwest, the reverse tends to take place during the early fall period in coastal California. This allows for continued ripening, usually with cool evening temperatures. Under such conditions, and depending upon how long the "hang time" is prolonged, it is possible to obtain grapes with a ripe flavor profile suggesting a warm climate, while retaining the acidity of a cooler climate.

Thus, climate and aspect play greater roles than soil type in influencing viticulture in California. The coastal mountains and valleys were under the Pacific Ocean 250 million years ago. Great earthquakes caused by the interaction of the Pacific and North American tectonic plates, moved what are now Napa and Sonoma Valleys, and much of the coast, eastward. Marked volcanic activity has further complicated the geological picture. Soils vary markedly and include shale, sandstone, limestone, sandy loams, clay loams, gravel, granite, sand and volcanic. Short distances may yield much variation among soil types.

New plantings at Chalone Vineyards, California, backed by the Pinnacles National Monument.

The beginning—newly planted vines at Eden Valley, California.

Vines and wines

Since the 1850s California has experienced a metamorphosis in varieties and styles of wine. Sweet and fortified wines from the mission grape gave way to the ever-versatile zinfandel. The fortunes of riesling, colombard and chenin blanc have risen and fallen. Zinfandel, chardonnay and cabernet sauvignon finished the twentieth century as dominant in the blush, white and red table wine categories. Sweet and fortified wines have gone out of fashion though some very good examples remain.

Generalizations regarding style miss wines on the vanguard, which may be the standard bearers 20 years hence. General styles do exist, especially since many winemakers were trained at either UC Davis or Fresno State. There is increasing cross-pollination with producers in France, Italy, Australia and South America; this has blurred some of the boundaries both geographically and stylistically. As new plantings mature and new opinion makers appear, these styles should evolve too.

Wine critics play a vital role in the development of style. Critics have immense power in setting wine styles—retailers and producers use critic-generated scores to sell wines. Producers then try to emulate the high scoring win;this is a situation not unique to the USA.

Varietal wines (those with at least 75 percent of the variety on the label) have long been dominant in California. But changing styles means that a cabernet sauvignon wine is now more likely to contain merlot, sometimes all five red Bordeaux standards. In homage to Cote Rotie, syrah producers are increasingly blending up to 10–15 percent viognier. Most varietal labeled chardonnay and pinot noir are not blended.

Meritage wines are blends of Bordeaux varieties, either red (cabernet sauvignon, cabernet franc, merlot, malbec, petite verdot) or white (sauvignon blanc, sémillon, muscadelle) which must meet legal criteria (*see* Wine laws).

Wine laws

California's wine is subject to both state and federal laws. The Bureau of Alcohol, Tobacco and Firearms (BATF) has a powerful regulatory role in both designation and distribution. American viticultural areas (AVAs) are awarded by BATF, and are based on geography and history. AVAs were established in 1978. There are now 137 in total, 81 in California.

Unlike France's system, there are no proscribed vineyard or winemaking techniques tied to an AVA. Neither are there limits on varieties grown. Certain AVA designations, such as "Napa Valley" are associated with quality by the consumer, and wines from such AVAs fetch higher prices.

BATF is a law enforcement organization within the Department of Treasury. It has three missions: revenue collection, enforcement and regulation. BATF collects federal taxes on tobacco and alcohol. It is also charged with fighting smuggling, investigating arson and the regulation and control of guns and explosives. This organization's forerunners were prominent during Prohibition.

Varietal and place of origin fall under state and federal laws, with the more stringent standard being that to which the industry is held. Wine labeled as California must be entirely made from grapes grown within the state.

The content standard for county of origin or varietal designation is 75 percent. A wine containing 75 percent cabernet sauvignon and 25 percent merlot may be labeled as varietal cabernet sauvignon. One with 70 percent cabernet sauvignon and 30 percent merlot may not carry a single varietal designation. Such a wine may be labeled with no varietal description or with the relevant percentages. An AVA origin labeled wine carries an 85 percent or more content requirement. A designated vineyard (such as Martha's Vineyard) is even more stringent: 95 percent of the grapes originate from the designated vineyard.

The term "meritage" stems from a movement begun in 1988 by the Meritage Association in response to changing definitions of varietal wine. It applies to blended, bordeaux-style wines. Such wines must meet standards of production figures and price.

Self-explanatory road sign.

There is no classification system of vineyards or producers based on quality. There is no legal definition of the term "reserve"—which usually refers to selected, higher quality grapes and special handling techniques such as barrique aging—currently, but there is a move to define this usage.

Wineries are not obliged to state what varieties, by percentage, went into making any wine, as long as at least 75 percent is from the varietal named on the label. Increasingly, though, wineries do detail the varietal breakdown.

The laws governing the distribution of wine are currently being hotly contested at state and federal levels, by those who seek to reduce regulation and open up markets and those trying to protect their tax revenue or distribution interests.

The three-tiered system—producer/importer, wholesaler and retailer—was set up to increase competition and counter organized crime. Distribution is controlled at federal, state and local levels—this is all a throwback to the repeal of Prohibition in 1933. During Prohibition organized crime had a monopoly on alcohol distribution; today, the "legitimate" involvement of organized crime in the distribution of alcohol is discussed in hushed tones within the industry.

Under the three-tiered system, a producer or importer may only sell to a wholesale distributor (except for cellar door sales by a producer), who may then sell to a retailer, who may then sell to the consumer. Protagonists in all levels of the system actively lobby government to protect their turf. Those who lobby well may gain exceptions to the system. Some states, such as Pennsylvania or Vermont, directly control retailing via a government-enforced monopoly. A confusing system it is!

Direct wine shipment is the contentious issue, particularly because of the growing popularity of sales via the Internet. Both state and federal laws apply to direct shipment. Twelve of the 50 states, so called "reciprocity" states, allow the shipment of wine by producers or retailers directly to the consumer. Such purchases may be made via telephone, mail order or the Internet.

Such a free market threatens the three-tiered system and the economic interests of wholesale distributors and many retailers. It is also a threat to government monopolies and revenues. Twelve states currently have limited direct shipping and may require permits from the shipper and/or the consumer. Five states make the direct shipment of wine a felony. Two others will use a felony charge, but only on a shipper who ships without a permit.

The twenty-three remaining states prohibit direct shipments by a common carrier such as the postal service, or any of several parcel delivery services.

Direct shippers keep testing the waters through a variety of ways and illegal shipments are not uncommon. They are also testing the limits of the law via legal action. Neo-prohibitionists, who are bound by religious and cultural beliefs, have also taken to this issue like bees to honey. Some religious groups believe the consumption of alcohol to be sinful. Others take this further and want to ban the sale of wine over the internet. Money, markets, politics, religion and alcohol do not mix well in the Unites States of America.

Viticulture

California is a prime location for viticulture, with its dry, warm climate. Dry weather keeps many diseases and pests at bay; sunshine and lack of rain

The vivid colors of fall at the Talley Vineyard, in California.

during the growing season allows long "hang time." Without imminent disease or weather pressures, Californian viticulturalists can wait to pick at the optimal time of ripeness for almost every vintage.

Although history has offered challenges to California's winegrowers, their flexibility and adaptation to their physical environment has yielded success. Since the experiences of the pioneers of California viticulture were diminished due to Prohibition, winegrowers were very open to research and innovation. As a result, the face of California viticulture has been forever changed. Additionally, the trend in the winery towards "wine is grown not made" has placed greater emphasis on vineyard practices.

Although Prohibition created a lapse in California's wine production, the greatest challenge to the industry both past and present has been phylloxera—a grape-root louse which begins as a mere nuisance reducing yields, but eventually bleeds and kills the vine. Once thought resistant to phylloxera, AxR1 rootstock began to fail in the mid-1980s falling prey to "biotype B," a new mutation.

Extensive replanting of vineyards began and continues, putting an economic strain on the industry. But this offered grape growers an opportunity to regroup. Much of the previous vine material had been planted according to guidelines intended for bulk wine or raisin production. With replanting, viticulturalists could determine the best match of site to vine and rootstock materials. Greater diversity of plant material is now available. Clones of varieties such as the Dijon series from Burgundy have recently been introduced and

may improve grape quality. More international varieties are being used as growers propagate their own vine and rootstock materials. Sharing of information is a vital and common occurrence.

As California's vineyards are replanted, training and pruning methods are also getting a facelift. California "sprawl" originated as the popular "anti-training" of vines—they grew wild with much less guidance from the viticulturalist. With technology and mechanization, the need for tractors, rippers and other machinery necessitated more orderly vine training. Many producers moved to a three-wire system to allow for canopy management. These training systems improve air circulation, decrease disease pressure and the need for spraying, and help let more light into the canopy. Quality has improved with less vegetal flavors, less vine vigor and greater ripeness. Innovative new forms of trellising and pruning are adopted from other regions. Although most vineyards are tractor-friendly and mechanization has increased, harvesting for premium production is mainly done by hand.

Traditionally, California has benefitted from a large labor force of migrant farm workers at harvest time, but lately, fewer are available. More vineyards are employing full-time workers or hiring vineyard management companies to provide a core group of expertly trained workers.

California's generally warm and dry climate keeps disease pressure from becoming a major threat. Despite this, in the early days chemicals were used in great quantities at the mere hint of danger. Overuse led to chemicals killing good insects as well as bad, and the creation of the "superbug" as insects became immune to stronger chemicals. In recent years, environmental, governmental and consumer pressures have forced vine growers to explore more natural means of disease and pest control. The big buzzword in California is now sustainable agriculture, agriculture with an eye towards the environment while allowing chemical intervention when necessary. Some growers have embraced the organic or biodynamic bandwagons, either using no pesticides or going so far as to perform rituals in the vineyards. At any rate, California viticulturalists have become more aware of the delicate balance of the ecosystem and, as a result, are more considerate in terms of vineyard practices.

Major vineyard problems still exist. Frost, sunburn, birds, mold and mildew are kept to a minimum via physical or chemical means. But the

Bottom: *Roses and vineyards at Wildhorse Vineyard San Luis Obispo, California.*

Below: *A barrel sign announcing the entrance to Paragon Vineyards in the Eden Valley, California.*

two major players are still phylloxera and Pierce's disease. Although not forgotten, the dread of phylloxera has been supplanted with a new fear—Pierce's disease. It is spread by a bacterium transported by the blue-green sharpshooter. Once it has taken hold there is no current treatment for it. Most prevalent in riparian areas, the bugs infect nearby vineyards and there is the fear that new vectors, like the glassy-winged sharpshooter, will travel up the highway system to ravage more vineyards.

Irrigation is commonly used in most of California with the exception of a few dry-farmed sites. Weather in California is distinct from most wine regions in that there is often little or no rain during the growing season, the majority falling during the winter. Without irrigation, vine growing would be near impossible and controlled drip irrigation allows careful control of watering. Strict legislation controls water rights and sufficient water may not always be available for the vineyard and winery.

Although many innovations of agricultural techniques have been offered to California's viticulturalists, in recent years the movement has been towards a balance of tradition and technology. Lacking a thorough and consistent history, California has been looking abroad for expertise. They have gleaned a wealth of information and have brought it home. The upcoming challenges will be met and conquered with this openness to new ideas. California's future looks bright.

Vinification

Vinification in California lacked Europe's centuries-old tradition of trial and error. Science, particularly through the leadership of Professor Hilgard at UC, usurped the role of traditional winemaking. Chemical analysis and the fledgling fields of microbiology and biochemistry were considered. The founding of the enology department at UC Davis was to have the most profound impact upon vinification in the state.

A few enlightened producers such as André Tchelistcheff introduced temperature control and improved hygiene. University researchers, funded by industry and government, focused on giving the winemaker more control in the process. Long before such quality improvement gurus as

Deming, the faculty at Davis were proponents of "no defects" in winemaking.

Vinification in California encouraged the production of clean, fruity wine free of the taint of volatile acidity, oxidation or Brettanomyces. Cultured yeast, hygiene, stainless steel, temperature control and the use of the chemistry and microbiology laboratory were central to this. A tradition of experimentation by variety, lot, yeast, temperature, maceration and elevage was carried out by UC Davis and by industry luminaries such as Robert Mondavi. Such innovation was to change winemaking, not only in California, but also worldwide.

AROMATIC & NON-BARREL FERMENTED WHITE WINES

As in much of the world, modern technique includes crushing and destemming followed by some period of cold settling. Of note is the fact that vineyards and wineries are usually in close proximity. Skin contact has usually been frowned upon although some producers opt for purposeful contact to improve aromatics.

Most fermentations are inoculated with one of the many strains of commercial yeast and a cool, temperature-controlled fermentation employed to yield a clean, fruity wine. Smaller producers are increasingly successful in spontaneous ferments. Malolactic fermentation may be inoculated or, less commonly, occur spontaneously. Many producers block the secondary fermentation in this style of wine, often with sterile filtration. Many are then bottled early.

Winery building and vineyards at Blossom Hill Winery, Paicines, California.

Above: *A sign at Clairborne & Churchill Winery, California.*

Top: *The Sunstone Vineyard, California, tasting room is reminiscent of those in the countryside around Provence, France.*

Less expensive styles of chardonnay and other varieties may then receive the kiss of oak. Oak chips at the lower end and several months of barrique maturation for somewhat more upscale wines. French and American oak are both used.

BARREL FERMENTED WHITES

At the upper end, chardonnay is barrel fermented, usually in new and newish French barriques. Cool rooms and cellars are increasingly used for temperature control. Most are still inoculated, though there is a trend towards more spontaneous fermentations. Lees stirring and contact are used to variable degrees. Increasing numbers of producers are opting not to filter their wines. It is not uncommon for other varieties such as sauvignon blanc, viognier, marsanne, pinot blanc, pinot gris and others to be so treated.

Technical skill varies between producers though the trend is for less overt diacetyl notes and for more judicious use of oak. When well made, California chardonnay is a world class wine.

BLUSH AND ROSÉ WINES

White zinfandel is the benchmark here. Most are treated as aromatic white wines, fewer are back blended with red wine. Fermentations are often stopped to leave the wines off dry. Sterile filtration and early bottling are the norm. Increasingly, dry versions are made from such varieties as pinot noir, sangiovese and cabernet sauvignon.

PINOT NOIR AND OTHER RED WINES

After either crush/destem or whole cluster pressing, temperature-controlled warm (80°F [30°C] or

more) fermentation is performed in open top, stainless steel vessels. Punching down is performed for extraction and a limited post-fermentation maceration may be employed. Increasing numbers of producers ferment spontaneously.

French oak maturation in new and used barrels for 9–12 months is common. American oak barrels are increasingly used. Oak chips are employed at the lower end. Increasing numbers of producers bottle their wines unfined and unfiltered, though finishing techniques are variable.

Other varieties (like zinfandel, syrah, grenache and mourvèdre) may be produced in a similar manner, often with an increased frequency of punching down, slightly lower fermentation temperatures and a longer post-fermentation maceration.

CABERNET SAUVIGNON AND OTHER REDS

Bordeaux is used as a model here, though most fermentations are inoculated. Closed top fermenters are employed. Fermentation temperatures are warm yet controlled. Pumping over is used for extraction. Post-fermentation maceration tends to be two to four weeks, or longer.

Oak barrels (French more than American, though both are widely used depending upon price and desired style), oak staves and oak chips are all employed with barrel maturation regimens at one year, though this varies. Clarification is via a combination of racking, fining and filtration, though increasing numbers of wines are unfiltered.

Other varieties, particularly merlot, cabernet franc, sangiovese, zinfandel and syrah are treated in a similar manner, though often with shorter macerations, more American oak and shorter periods of barrel maturation. Wines at the top end tend to be treated in a manner very similar to top cabernet sauvignon.

SPARKLING WINES

Inexpensive wines are cleanly produced using bulk methods. French champagne houses, transplanted cava producers and American concerns produce sparkling wines using traditional techniques.

SWEET AND FORTIFIED WINES

Modern techniques as applied in Oporto and Germany are employed. One innovation is the cryo-extraction, whereby an icewine is induced by placing harvested grapes into freezers and then continuing production as per an icewine. Bonny Doon has been particularly successful here.

Patrick Farrell MW and Rebecca Chapa

Mendocino & Lake County

Rebecca Chapa

Forty-one wineries have their home in Mendocino, north of Sonoma County and 90 miles (145 km) north of San Francisco. The region is possibly the most geographically diverse in California with mountain ranges, valleys and lakes producing a wide variety of terrains and climates. Most vineyards are located on hillsides, with only 15 percent of producers growing grapes on the valley floor. Of 2,248,000 acres (909,753 ha) of available agricultural land, only 14,263 acres (5,776 ha) are planted as vineyards. There are 300 of these, with a surprising 25 percent of acreage certified organic. No single producer in Mendocino farms more than 1,000 acres (405 ha). Varietal selection is diverse, with gewürztraminer, riesling, petite sirah, syrah and zinfandel appearing as often as chardonnay, pinot noir, sauvignon blanc and cabernet sauvignon. The vineyard area of Lake County, to the east of Mendocino, covers about 5,500 acres (2,225 ha).

History

First planted under vine in the 1850s following the gold rush, Mendocino's grape growers concentrated on cultivating the hillsides in order to leave room for other crops on the flatlands. Since the region was isolated, wines were sold locally, missing out on exposure to major markets gained by more easily accessible wineries in Napa and Sonoma. Prohibition shut down most wineries until the 1960s. At this time, better transport created a surge in Mendocino's wine industry. For the first time wineries began focusing on making their own wine rather than selling grapes to bulk producers. Recent years have seen a renewal of interest and investment in Mendocino wines, which is a hopeful sign of better things to come.

The first vineyards in Lake County were planted in the 1870s but were ripped out to provide room for other crops when Prohibition took hold. Although slow to recover—today Lake County still has only five wineries—investment in vineyard land by large companies is growing, as is the buying of fruit for labels such as Fetzer and Robert Mondavi.

Climate and landscape

Climate throughout the Mendocino region is diverse, ranging from cool to cold on the coast and at higher altitudes, to warmer temperatures on the valley floors. Cool nights retain acidity in the fruit, while warm days allow for ripeness. Rhône varieties such as viognier and grenache do well in warmer areas like the McDowell Valley, while cooler regions such as the northwest section of the Anderson Valley are planted with cool-climate varieties including pinot noir. Soils are similar to those of Sonoma County with light texture, sand, gravel and powdery consistencies and tend to be well drained. Rainfall is about 37 inches (94 cm) a year.

To the east of Mendocino, Lake County is well known for cool nights and hot days during the growing season. From the west the county is shielded from fog and moisture by the Mayacamas Mountains while Clear Lake moderates the climatic influence on the vineyards.

Postbox and sign for the Lazy Creek Vineyards, Mendocino.

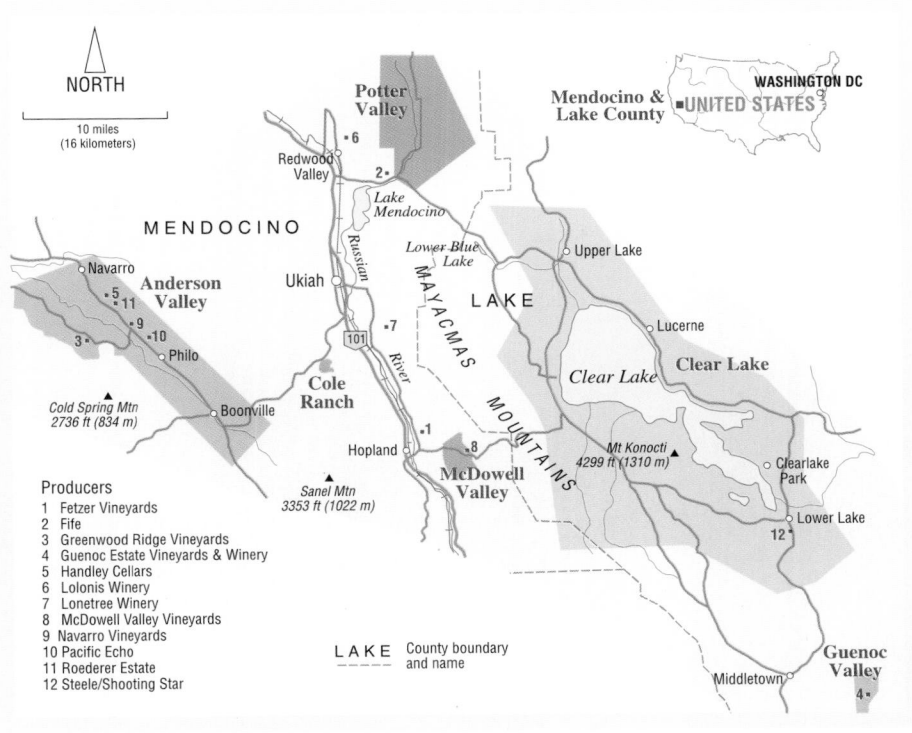

Producers
1 Fetzer Vineyards
2 Fife
3 Greenwood Ridge Vineyards
4 Guenoc Estate Vineyards & Winery
5 Handley Cellars
6 Lolonis Winery
7 Lonetree Winery
8 McDowell Valley Vineyards
9 Navarro Vineyards
10 Pacific Echo
11 Roederer Estate
12 Steele/Shooting Star

A tasting room for the environmentally aware Fetzer Vineyards, Mendocino.

Producers

FETZER VINEYARDS, MENDOCINO

Established 1968 *Owners* **Brown-Forman** *Production* 2,900,000 cases *Vineyard area* 750 acres (304 ha)

In 1968, the barn of Home Ranch in Redwood was converted into a winery and the flow of wine began. From these humble beginnings a small family business eventually became the giant that Fetzer is now. By 1985, the company took its slogan, "From the earth to the table," one step further by farming all its vineyards organically. Fetzer became known as a visionary in the organic realm, and other projects, such as natural filtration and solar power, further demonstrate its dedication to the environment. Fetzer owns its own barrel-making facility, Mendocino Cooperage, the only USA winery to do so. Sundial Chardonnay is great value.

FIFE, MENDOCINO

Established 1996 *Owner* **Dennis Fife** *Production* 10,000 cases *Vineyard area* 13 acres (5 ha)

Fife uses minimum handling and great fruit to make some fierce reds. The Redhead Zinfandel, named partly after the brick-red soil it grows in, is spicy and fiery without the coarse texture of some zinfandels. MAX is a blend of syrah, petite sirah, charbono and zinfandel.

Vines at the Navarro Vineyards, Mendocino.

GREENWOOD RIDGE VINEYARDS, MENDOCINO

Established 1980 *Owner* **Allan Green** *Production* 7,000 cases *Vineyard area* 16 acres (6 ha)

Allan Green is a great advocate of his region and every year since 1983 has held the large and very entertaining California Wine Tasting Championships at his winery. He makes fantastic wines too and Greenwood Ridge—which sits about 1,400 feet (427 m) above sea level, above the fog and frost—is well known for its pinot noir and zinfandel. It was the first winery to release wines under the new Mendocino Ridge appellation in 1998.

GUENOC ESTATE VINEYARDS & WINERY, LAKE COUNTY

Established 1982 *Owner* **Orville Magoon** *Production* 100,000 cases *Vineyard area* 340 acres (138 ha)

The Guenoc Estate, which covers the southern parts of Lake County, all of Guenoc Valley and the northwest portions of Napa Valley, includes some of California's oldest vineyards. Lillie Langtry, actress and winemaker, owned the property from 1888 to 1906. Elevations range from 800–1,500 feet (244–457 m) above sea level and soils are rocky and alluvial. The region's warm days and cool nights are great for growing bordeaux varieties and specific emphasis has been placed on carmenère. In 1981, Guenoc Valley was recognized as an AVA, the first in the USA owned by a single proprietorship.

HANDLEY CELLARS, MENDOCINO

Established 1982 *Owner* **Milla Handley** *Production* 15,000 cases *Vineyard area* 25 acres (10 ha)

Milla Handley makes prime chardonnay and pinot noir using traditional techniques to create soft, supple, drinkable wines. Pinot Mystère, made from pinot meunier, packed with jammy fruit, is a great example of what can be made of the variety on its own.

LITTORAI, MENDOCINO

Established 1993 *Owners* **Heidi and Ted Lemon** *Production* 1,000 cases *Vineyard area* NA

Littorai is best known for its Sonoma wines, though Ted and Heidi Lemon, two of California's best winemaking consultants, are sure to put Mendocino on the map. Indeed, Littorai wine is so popular that it is hard to find. Ted Lemon also makes pinot noir at One Acre Vineyard in the Anderson Valley, and it is possibly the best wine Mendocino has ever produced.

LOLONIS WINERY, MENDOCINO

Established 1920 *Owner* Petros
Lolonis *Production* 30,000 cases
Vineyard area 300 acres (121 ha)

Lolonis has been in the business of growing vines since before Prohibition. The winery itself was started in 1982. Lolonis is strongly opposed to using chemicals for most pest control, preferring to use natural methods such as ladybugs and praying mantis to control leaf hoppers and spiders.

LONETREE WINERY, MENDOCINO

Established 1994 *Owners* John
Scharffenberger and Casep Hartlip *Production* 1,800 cases
Vineyard area 74 acres (30 ha)

With the expertise of former maker of sparkling wines John Scharffenberger and viticulturist Casey Hartlip, Lonetree has been able to make interesting wines. Vineyards lie at 1,800 feet (550 m) elevation on relatively fertile decomposed sandstone with veins of red loams. Eaglepoint Ranch supplies fruit for the project, including prime zinfandel, syrah and sangiovese. Sangiovese is a favorite of the line, offering ripe cherry-fruit flavors.

McDOWELL VALLEY VINEYARDS, MENDOCINO

Established 1970 *Owners* Bill and Vicky Crawford
Production 18,400 cases *Vineyard area* 250 acres (101 ha)

This producer, which farms 90 of its acres (36 ha) organically, makes wines from traditional Rhône varieties like grenache, syrah and viognier. Especially popular is its grenache rosé, a tasty dry alternative to white zinfandel.

NAVARRO VINEYARDS, MENDOCINO

Established 1974 *Owners* Deborah Cahn and Ted Bennett
Production 32,000–35,000 cases *Vineyard area* 60 acres
(24 ha)

Navarro produces many styles from dry to *vendange tardive*, and even makes grape juice. Vineyard management includes natural methods of pest control so, when faced with the problem of a prolific insect, larvae of the pest's natural enemies are introduced. Pinot noir from Navarro is offered in both traditional and newer styles, and the gewürztraminer is excellent. All wines are consistently high quality.

PACIFIC ECHO, MENDOCINO

Established 1981 *Owners* Louis Vuitton Moet-Hennessy
Production 45,000 cases *Vineyard area* 97 acres (39 ha)

This *méthode champenoise* sparkling wine property in Mendocino's Anderson Valley was established by John Scharffenberger. In 1981, as Scharffenberger Cellars, it was the first winery to make sparkling wine from Anderson Valley fruit. The wines have bright berry flavors from the pinot noir portions and appley complexities from the chardonnay. Vivacious acidity makes them a perfect aperitif.

ROEDERER ESTATE, MENDOCINO

Established 1982 *Owners* Champagne Louis Roederer
Production 70,000 cases *Vineyard area* 350 acres (142 ha)

As the first investment by the Champenois in Mendocino, Jean-Claude Rouzaud believed firmly that Anderson Valley was an ideal place for his Californian *méthode champenoise* property. Great care is taken to produce optimal grapes and to vinify in the French style. The wines are perhaps California's most elegant, and often indistinguishable from French champagne.

STEELE/SHOOTING STAR, LAKE COUNTY

Established 1991 *Owner* Jedediah T. Steele *Production*
35,000–40,000 cases *Vineyard area* 28 acres (11 ha)

Jed Steele started as a cellar worker at Stony Hill in Napa and went on to become founding winemaker at Edmeades, where he produced the first icewine in the United States, before starting up his own Lake County property. The syrah is a very accessible style with soft, bright fruit and a reasonable price tag.

A vineyard in autumn at the Roederer Estate, Mendocino.

REGIONAL DOZEN

QUALITY WINES

Greenwood Ridge Pinot Noir
Fife Redhead Vineyard
   Zinfandel
Handley Pinot Noir
Littorai One Acre Vineyard
   Pinot Noir
Lonetree Sangiovese
Navarro Méthode Ancienne
   Pinot Noir
Roederer Estate Ermitage

BEST VALUE WINES

Fetzer Eagle Peak Merlot
McDowell Valley Vineyards
   Grenache Rosé
Navarro Dry Gewürztraminer
Pacific Echo Brut
Shooting Star Syrah

Sonoma County

Rebecca Chapa

Sonoma County is north of San Francisco and west of Napa Valley, adjacent to the Pacific coast. The region has 172 wineries on 43,314 acres (17,542 ha) and produces 104,162 tons (94,475 t) annually. Although on a grand scale geographically, Sonoma has more small wineries than Napa. And although it is quieter than the Napa Valley in the middle of the summer tourist season, Sonoma is *the* hot spot for grape-growing in California with the highest value of grapes in the county. Significant vineyard plantings are concentrating on producing prime grapes for the premium segment of the market.

History

Although Sonoma's wine history began before that of the Napa Valley, it was on a much smaller scale. Here, instead of wealthy investors concentrating only on wine, many of the area's pioneers were Italian farmers who grew grapes with a variety of other crops. In 1823, the last, most northerly Californian mission was built in Sonoma, creating more of a focus on the growing of grapes. Soon after, William Hill planted the first non-mission varieties in Sonoma.

In 1857, Count Agoston Haraszthy, a Hungarian who became known as the "father" of the Californian wine industry, arrived in Sonoma and started the Buena Vista winery. He was influential in bringing vine material back to California from Europe and the 100,000 cuttings he imported from France, Italy and Spain changed viticulture in Sonoma for ever. A surge in plantings followed, resulting in production levels of 132,000 tons (119,724 t) of grapes from a total of 180 wineries, and plantings by 750 vineyards of 49,000 acres (19,845 ha). These levels dwindled after Prohibition, never to regain their vast numbers. Today, however, the future in Sonoma looks promising with an increase in the number of big-name

wineries doing business here, including Gallo, the largest wine company in the world.

Climate and landscape

Slightly cooler than Napa, cool sites in Sonoma County are ideal for growing more delicate varieties. The climate varies dramatically according to individual appellation—fog and offshore breezes keeping temperatures low by the ocean, near gaps in the coastal range and to the south near Carneros.

Producers

BENZIGER FAMILY WINERY

Established 1981 *Owners* Benziger family *Production* 180,000 cases *Vineyard area* 65 acres (26 ha)

Originally, Mike Benziger bought wine in bulk to sell under the Glen Ellen label. It became a successful brand on its own and was sold to Heublein. Now the Benzigers can finally concentrate on their original intention—to create affordable premium wines. Merlot and chardonnay offer exceptional value.

DAVIS BYNUM WINERY

Established 1965 *Owners* Bynum family *Production* 15,000 cases *Vineyard area* 61 acres (25 ha)

Davis Bynum was originally working for the *San Francisco Chronicle* when he tried his hand at making a homemade petite sirah from Mondavi grapes. It was so successful that by 1965 he had decided to buy a winery in Albany. Today, his winery in the Russian River Valley makes premium wines, with pinot noir at the forefront.

CARMENET VINEYARDS

Established 1982 *Owners* Chalone Wine Group *Production* 75,000 cases *Vineyard area* 280 acres (113 ha)

Carmenet was the first winery since the repeal of Prohibition to use underground caves for all of its wine aging. Its name comes from an old French word for the grapes used in bordeaux blends, the specialty of the winery. Both the vineyards and the winery are carved into volcanic rock and the elevation at 1,700 feet (518 m) provides fruit of great intensity. Concentrated mountain wines are Carmenet's specialty and Dynamite and Moon Mountain bottlings are good examples.

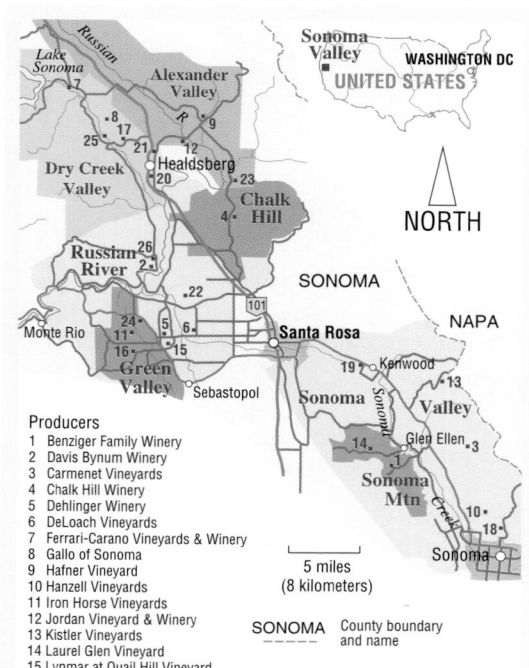

Producers
1 Benziger Family Winery
2 Davis Bynum Winery
3 Carmenet Vineyards
4 Chalk Hill Winery
5 Dehlinger Winery
6 DeLoach Vineyards
7 Ferrari-Carano Vineyards & Winery
8 Gallo of Sonoma
9 Hafner Vineyard
10 Hanzell Vineyards
11 Iron Horse Vineyards
12 Jordan Vineyard & Winery
13 Kistler Vineyards
14 Laurel Glen Vineyard
15 Lynmar at Quail Hill Vineyard
16 Marimar Torres Estate
17 Pezzi-King Vineyards
18 Ravenswood Winery
19 St Francis
20 Seghesio Family Vineyards
21 Simi Winery
22 Sonoma-Cutrer Vineyards
23 Stonestreet
24 Topolos at Russian River Vineyards
25 Unti Vineyards & Winery
26 Williams & Selyem Winery

SONOMA   County boundary
- - - - -   and name

CHALK HILL WINERY

Established 1972 *Owners* Frederick and Peggy Furth
Production 75,000 cases *Vineyard area* 300 acres (121 ha)

Chalk Hill was granted a viticultural appellation in 1984. Chalk Hill Winery produces the only 100 percent estate-bottled wines in this appellation. The site is also known for conducting one of the largest private clonal experiments in the USA in which 17 chardonnay clones are being studied. Vineyards sit at 200–600 feet (60–185 m) elevation and plantings run up and over the hillsides rather than on terraces, in order to protect the natural shape of the hills. Chalk Hill is most appreciated for its white wines—sauvignon blanc, chardonnay and pinot gris. It also produces a botrytized sémillon with exquisite peach and apricot flavors.

DEHLINGER WINERY

Established 1975 *Owner* Tom Dehlinger *Production* 7,000 cases *Vineyard area* 50 acres (20 ha)

Taking advantage of the cool and foggy weather of the Russian River Valley, the vines at Dehlinger produce outstanding chardonnay, pinot noir and syrah. Winemaking techniques aim to extract as much flavor as possible from the grapes and on this prime site, there are tons to be had.

DeLOACH VINEYARDS

Established 1975 *Owners* Cecil and Christine DeLoach *Production* 185,000 cases *Vineyard area* 800 acres (324 ha)

In 1969, San Francisco firefighter Cecil DeLoach was looking for land in Sonoma on which to grow grapes. He found it and by 1971 left San Francisco to live on the ranch. He finally left his day job in 1980. At first, DeLoach's concentrated on selling its grapes to other vintners, then it branched out into making its own wines. One of DeLoach's specialties is vineyard-designated zinfandels from old vines. The OFS (Our Finest Selection) line also offers a richer style of chardonnay.

FERRARI-CARANO VINEYARDS & WINERY

Established 1981 *Owners* Don and Rhonda Carano
Production 150,000 cases *Vineyard area* 1,200 acres (486 ha)

Don and Rhonda Carano from Reno, Nevada, have made their mark on the region by producing a number of great wines. Best known for its chardonnay, the winery also produces a Reserve fume blanc with 100 percent barrel fermentation

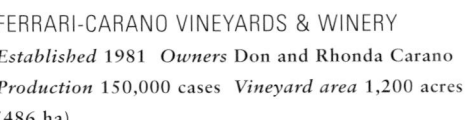

California's oldest premium winery, established in 1857, is the Buena Vista Winery in the Sonoma Valley.

Vineyard at the Benziger Family Winery, Sonoma Valley, which aims to create affordable premium wines.

and extended lees aging. Winemaker George Bursick has worked wonders with sangiovese for Siena, a proprietary wine. Memories of the Reno area inspired a rare sweet dessert wine called El Dorado Gold, almost impossible to find.

FLOWERS WINERY

Established 1990 *Owners* Joan and Walt Flowers *Production* 10,000 cases *Vineyard area* 23 acres (9 ha)

Flowers is the new hot ticket. One of the pioneers of the rugged Sonoma Coast near Jenner, where the Russian River flows into the Pacific Ocean, the winery enjoys an altitude just higher than the fog line and benefits from the best of both worlds—natural air conditioning and plenty of sunshine. Flowers will be sure to produce a long line of great chardonnays and pinot noirs if current trends continue. Top of the line is the Moon Select Pinot Noir. Also look out for Perennial, a blend that changes yearly but usually includes zinfandel, pinot noir and pinot meunier.

Bottom: *Stored wine casks at Ferrari-Carano Winery, Sonoma County.*

Below: *Gardens leading to the tasting room at Ferrari-Carano Winery.*

GALLO OF SONOMA

Established 1991 *Owners* E. and J. Gallo Winery *Production* 1,000,000 cases *Vineyard area* 2,800 acres (1,134 ha)

As the largest winery in the world, and with a reputation for producing mere table wines, E. and J. Gallo was not expected to hit it big with a premium line of Sonoma wines. Critics are eating their words now as Gallo of Sonoma reaps its rewards (and awards), proving that it can offer value at all price levels. An interest in environmental issues has resulted in every acre under vine being matched by preserving one in its natural habitat.

HAFNER VINEYARD

Established 1976 *Owners* Hafner family *Production* 11,700 cases *Vineyard area* 100 acres (40 ha)

Hafner is a small family operation in Alexander Valley and it plans to stay this way to maintain consistent quality. After converting a prune and pear ranch to vineyard in 1976, it concentrated on producing chardonnay and cabernet sauvignon. Wines are sold only through a mailing list and to restaurants.

HANZELL VINEYARDS

Established 1953 *Owners* Barbara and Alex deBrye *Production* 2,700 cases *Vineyard area* 26 acres (10 ha)

These vineyards were originally established by J. D. Zellerbach, whose passion for burgundy brought changes to Californian winemaking and continues to be a force in the winemaking at Hanzell. Small French barrels and stainless steel equipment were just a few of his early innovations. Pinot noir and chardonnay are recommended.

IRON HORSE VINEYARDS

Established 1978 *Owners* Sterling family and Forrest Tancer *Production* 36,000–45,000 cases *Vineyard area* 246 acres (100 ha)

Audrey and Barry Sterling and Forrest Tancer founded this winery in Sonoma's Green Valley in 1979 with the goal of making unique high-quality wines. Only estate-grown grapes and those from Forrest's mother's ranch, T-bar-T, in Alexander Valley, are used to ensure high-quality fruit. Iron Horse is particularly noted for its sparkling wine.

JORDAN VINEYARD & WINERY

Established 1972 *Owner* Tom Jordan *Production* 8,000 cases *Vineyard area* 275 acres (111 ha)

Located in the Alexander Valley, Jordan is a top producer of cabernet sauvignon and chardonnay

and strives to produce wines that go well with food. The region has a long growing season with sufficient warmth for ripeness and fog to retain acidity. The site was originally planted with prunes, but is now covered with rows of cabernet sauvignon, cabernet franc, merlot and chardonnay. Jordan's cabernet is very drinkable in its youth, but ages successfully as well. When the 1978 was made, skeptics believed it was too well integrated to age but a tasting of that vintage today proves that older wines don't need tannin and harshness to mature well.

KISTLER VINEYARDS

Established 1978 *Owner* Steve Kistler *Production* 23,000 cases *Vineyard area* 115 acres (47 ha)

If you're looking for some of the best Californian chardonnay, Kistler is the one. Each release, limited quantities of this coveted wine are allocated to certain restaurants nationwide. The chardonnay is barrel-fermented in a good percentage of new French oak and undergoes *sur lie* aging and malolactic fermentation. Gentle handling and no filtration or fining, unless vital, result in a rich tropical-fruit chardonnay with great persistence of flavor. Dry-farmed pinot noir is also a project in the works that looks incredibly promising due to low yields and dry farming.

LAUREL GLEN VINEYARD

Established 1981 *Owner* Patrick Campbell *Production* 4,000 cases *Vineyard area* 35 acres (14 ha)

Laurel Glen produces 100 percent estate-grown wines from 30-year-old vines and sells them under the Laurel Glen and Counterpoint labels. As well, it uses grapes from Chile and Argentina to make a red blend called Terra Rossa and REDS ("a wine for the people"), a bistro-style wine. Syrah and sangiovese are experimental varieties currently being used to add aromatics.

LYNMAR AT QUAIL HILL VINEYARD

Established 1990 *Owners* Lynn and Mara Fritz *Production* 5,000 cases *Vineyard area* 42 acres (17 ha)

Lynmar is a boutique winery specializing in burgundian varieties grown in the dry-farmed Quail Hill Vineyard in Russian River. The vineyard cherishes its famed Goldridge soil, a combination of well-drained sand, silt and clay. Gentle handling is the mantra in order to best express the *terroir* of this special vineyard. All wines are aged in French oak. The chardonnay is a great standout from the typical oaky, buttery style with mineral qualities

and acidity that make it taste French. The Five Sisters Pinot Noir is a limited release concentrating on the five best barrels of pinot noir. It is a knockout.

MARIMAR TORRES ESTATE

Established 1992 *Owner* Marimar Torres *Producer* 15,000 cases *Vineyard area* 81 acres (33 ha)

Marimar Torres came to California from Spain in 1975 to create a winery in the Green Valley, in the southwest corner of the Russian River Valley, one of its coolest regions. The Don Miguel Vineyard on the estate honors her father, Miguel Torres, who created the Torres wine dynasty in Spain. Dense spacing and low training are more traditional to Burgundy than California, which may be why the wines are so distinctive. Marimar uses an element of Spanish tradition as well by adding a small percentage of parellada, a white grape from Catalonia, to the chardonnay. Clonal selection of each variety is also carefully managed to give complexity. Chardonnay and pinot noir are the only wines produced.

MEREDITH VINEYARD ESTATE

Established 1997 *Owners* Merry Edwards and William C. Bourke *Production* 2,500 cases *Vineyard area* 22 acres (9 ha)

Merry Edwards has a Masters in Foodscience Enology and has done research on pinot noir clones. With only two pinot noir bottlings, Edwards is able to give the wine her full attention. The wines exhibit firm structure and long deep plummy finishes.

PETER MICHAEL

Established 1983 *Owner* Sir Peter Michael *Production* 7,000–9,000 cases *Vineyard area* 76 acres (31 ha)

Peter Michael is one of those producers whose wines sell out in seconds. Wines are made with traditional methods on mountain vineyards with limited production, thus the demand exceeds supply without fail. Vines grow on 45° slopes for the most part and elevations of 2,000 feet (610 m) allow for long slow ripening. Rocky volcanic soils further control vine vigor and productivity. Chardonnays include Mon Plaisir and Belle Côte, and if you see Point Rouge, buy it. A bordeaux-style blend, Les Pavots, and L'Après Midi, a sauvignon blanc, are also winners.

Wineries in every direction in the Sonoma Valley, California.

NAJIOLA-SPENCER VINTNERS

Established 1995 *Owners* Tony A. Najiola and Sam Spencer
Production 2,500 cases *Vineyard area* NA

Although a relative newcomer, Najiola-Spencer produces a line of ripe and fruity wines—Favorito—that has achieved great intensity. Its zinfandel has rich primary fruit flavors while its Rhône-style red blend is rounded with more complexity. The idea is to offer wines that go well with food—in other words, are not over-oaked or over-ripe. Since the company does not own any vineyards, it can concentrate on finding the best fruit possible and can exercise great flexibility with the ingredients it uses. The wines are great now and, with continued dedication, can only be expected to get better.

PEZZI-KING VINEYARDS

Established 1994 *Owners* Jim and Jane Rowe *Production* 20,000 cases *Vineyard area* 60 acres (24 ha)

Pezzi-King has recently reached cult status. The Zinfandel is especially popular due to its clean berry flavors with balanced tannins and alcohol. All vineyards on the estate are organically farmed if possible. The winery also purchases high-quality fruit, mostly from hillsides or old vines. Although the chardonnay and sauvignon blanc are often overlooked in favor of their red wines, they are some of the best in Sonoma.

RAVENSWOOD WINERY

Established 1976 *Owners* Joel Peterson, Reed Foster and public shareholders *Production* 250,000 cases *Vineyard area* 18 acres (7 ha)

Most of the fruit is purchased, often from dry-farmed sites with 70–100-year-old vines. The

Grape harvest at Ravenswood Winery, Sonoma Valley.

Ravenswood logo—"No wimpy wines"—is borne out in its powerful zinfandels, ranging from complex vineyard-designates to a great-value zinfandel from Lodi. Although about three-quarters of the production is zinfandel, Ravenswood also does wonders with bordeaux varieties, especially its Gregory Cabernet Sauvignon, which has a hint of mint, and its stalwart merlot from the famed Sangiacomo Vineyard in Carneros. Every wine this winery puts out tends to be at least good quality if not outstanding.

RUTZ CELLARS

Established 1993 *Owner* Keith Rutz *Production* 6,000 cases *Vineyard area* NA

Most of the fruit is sourced from the Russian River Valley and Martinelli and Dutton Ranch pinot noir are some of owner Keith Rutz's most prized ingredients. For Rutz Cellars, red Grand Cru burgundy is the model for pinots and chardonnays are sculpted with Grand Cru white burgundies in mind.

ST FRANCIS

Established 1979 *Owners* Joseph Martin, Lloyd Canton and Kobrand Corp. *Production* 200,000 cases *Vineyard area* 800 acres (324 ha)

Named after the patron saint of the last mission on the California trail, St Francis was built in 1979. While it is noted for producing characteristically fruity yet firm red wines, St Francis may be better known as the first premium winery to experiment with synthetic corks. It now uses them for its entire production. Old Vine Zinfandel is chocolatey and full in body.

SEGHESIO FAMILY VINEYARDS

Established 1902 *Owners* Seghesio family *Production* 100,000 cases *Vineyard area* 400 acres (162 ha)

The vines planted here in 1910 are the oldest surviving sangiovese vines in the USA. Originally a bulk wine producer, in 1983 the family began to bottle under its own name. Wine is still made from a "Chianti Station" field blend of 85 percent sangiovese, 10 percent canaiolo nero and 5 percent malvasia with trebbiano. The Omaggio ("homage") bottling is a tribute to founders Edoardo and Angela Seghesio, made from grapes planted for their centennial in 1995. The wine is succulent with bright barbera and sangiovese, tempered with the structure of merlot and cabernet sauvignon.

SIMI WINERY

Established 1876 *Owners* Canandaigua Brands *Production* 120,000 cases *Vineyard area* 300 acres (121 ha)

Simi was founded by two Tuscan brothers, Giuseppe and Pietro Simi. Cellars were built in 1890, but in the meantime, the first few vintages were made in San Francisco. Sendal is a tasty white bordeaux blend.

SONOMA-CUTRER VINEYARDS

Established 1973 *Owners* Brown-Forman *Production* 80,000 cases *Vineyard area* 400 acres (162 ha)

Sonoma-Cutrer has always been at the forefront of innovation, with cooling tunnels, sorting tables, membrane presses and the like, making its wines state-of-the-art. One of California's first wineries to concentrate on only one variety, it was also the first to vineyard-designate chardonnay. The Russian River Ranches bottling is the stand-by, while the Cutrer Vineyard label has more intensity and needs more time to come around. Wines from Les Pierres Vineyard have a mineral note reminiscent of white burgundy. The last two wines took so long to evolve that a new cellar was built specifically for their barrel aging. The mission was to maintain a constant 48°F (9°C) temperature. To achieve this, leader of the pack once again, Sonoma-Cutrer devised a cooling system in the ceiling and floor that consists of tubes filled with chilled water and glycol.

STONESTREET

Established 1989 *Owners* Jess S. Jackson and family *Production* 60,000 cases *Vineyard area* 1,300 acres (526 ha)

This property in the Alexander Valley is just one of Kendall-Jackson's many wineries. Stonestreet specializes in chardonnay, pinot noir, cabernet sauvignon and merlot with some sauvignon blanc. Another Kendall-Jackson winery, Hart-ford Court, is located in Sonoma's Green Valley sub-appellation of the Russian River Valley. It is a superb producer of single-vineyard pinot noir and zinfandel. The family-owned wine giant is best known for the Kendall-Jackson Vintner's Reserve Chardonnay, the top premium consumer brand in the USA.

TOPOLOS AT RUSSIAN RIVER VINEYARDS

Established 1978 *Owner* Michael Topolos *Production* 18,000 cases *Vineyard area* 27 acres (11 ha)

The Russian River Vineyards have existed since 1963. Owned by the Topolos family since 1978,

Statue of St Francis, after whom the St Francis Winery, Sonoma Valley, was named.

they are now the source for environmentally friendly wines with most of the production organic with some bio-dynamic plantings. Dry-farmed old vines produce deep purple berries that pack a punch in the Piner Heights Zinfandel. Other wines include sauvignon blanc, pinot noir and charbono.

UNTI VINEYARDS & WINERY

Established 1998 *Owners* Unti family *Production* 3,600 cases *Vineyard area* 26 acres (10 ha)

Newcomer Unti is making a name for itself with a line of powerful reds including zinfandel and syrah from Dry Creek Valley. The families planted these grapes along with sangiovese for the simple reason that it's what they enjoy drinking. Early reports suggest that consumers agree with them. Oak is restrained in order to keep the wines drinkable upon release.

WILLIAMS & SELYEM WINERY

Established 1981 *Owner* John Dyson *Production* 6,000 cases *Vineyard area* 38 acres (15 ha)

When lovers of pinot noir hear the two words Williams & Selyem they begin to salivate. So successful is the winery that it sells its entire production via mailing list—90 percent to the public, with the remaining 10 percent going to a few lucky restaurants. Burt Williams and Ed Selyem created the Hacienda Del Rio Winery, changing the name in 1983. At this time the operation was incredibly simple—a small garage housed the winery and case production was controlled by the amount of space available. In 1989 the winery moved to Healdsburg to better digs and was later bought in 1998 by John Dyson. All fruit is hand-sorted and moves by gravity without pumping.

Chardonnay grapes on the vine—the dry, warm, clear weather of Sonoma County suits this variety well.

Napa Valley

Rebecca Chapa

Known around the world as the top premium wine-growing region in North America, the Napa Valley's diversity of appellations and wine styles defies definition. Some believe that with time, Napa Valley's diversity will be further made evident by appellations as detailed as those of Burgundy. A favorable climate and the talent of its winemakers contribute to its fame, though the scourge of phylloxera has forced Napa's viticulturalists to review their choice of varieties and to concentrate on more strategic plantings.

Below: *The Napa region welcomes many visitors each year.*

Bottom: *Lush Napa Valley vineyards surrounding winery buildings.*

History

The Valley was originally settled by Wappo Indians who called it Napa, meaning "Land of Plenty," a name that was adopted by future settlers. Napa's first homestead and the first property to plant grapevines was established by George Yount, for whom the town of Yountville is named, in 1836. In 1861, the first commercial winery was built by Charles Krug in St Helena and by 1889 there were more than 140 wineries in Napa Valley. Phylloxera hit with devastating effect in the early 1890s and in 1920 Prohibition put many wineries out of business. These were hard setbacks to overcome— by 1960 wineries numbered a mere 25. However, by 1990 the wine industry had picked up and over 200 were operating. Today, the number has swelled to over 240, with 37,486 acres (15,182 ha) of a total of 297,000 acres (120,285 ha) under vine, yielding 102,354 tons (92,835 t) of fruit.

During Napa's evolution the Napa Valley Vintners Association, formed in 1943, and the Napa Valley Grape Growers Association (1975), were integral at marketing and improving the region's wines. They remain a driving force. A 1968 ordinance promoting agriculture as the prime use of land, protects 30,000 acres (12,150 ha) of land for grape-growing and further regulations thwart erosion. Currently, the latest battle is in trying to prevent certain producers from using the name "Napa" if their wines do not meet the requirements of the grape source.

Climate and landscape

Napa Valley includes part of the Carneros region at the mouth of the San Pablo Bay. It stretches about 30 miles (48 km) to the northwest and is a mere 5 miles (8 km) wide near the city of Napa, narrowing to 1 mile (1.6 km) near Calistoga. Covering 297,000 acres (120,285 ha) with 35,000-plus planted to grapes, to the west, the valley is bounded by the forests of the Mayacamas Mountains that separate it from Sonoma Valley; to the east, the much drier and rugged Vaca range.

Climate is primarily Mediterranean, with warm, dry summers and wet, cool winters. Rain is rare in the growing season and most occurs from October through early May. Fog, drawn up the valley as the air heats up inland during the day, is pulled in from the bay and can be seen in the more southerly areas. Its effect is to keep the vines cool, which retains the natural acidity in the fruit. Nights tend to be cool and the days warm, allowing for slow ripening. Traveling north from Carneros to Calistoga in the summer, the temperature increases dramatically by as much as 1 degree per mile.

Soils are diverse—32 different types last count —created by volcanics and earth movements. Many faults cross the area. Volcanic ash and lava have deposited significantly along the Mayacamas. Soils tend to be less deep and rockier on the mountainsides than in the valley, stressing the vines, a condition which some believe produces higher quality wines. Sub-appellations of the valley include Atlas Peak, Howell Mountain, Los Carneros, Mt Veeder, Oakville, Rutherford, St Helena, Spring Mountain District, Stags Leap District and Wild Horse Valley. New appellations are continually being proposed as understanding of microclimate and soil increases. The latest is Diamond Mountain District.

Producers

ANDERSON'S CONN VALLEY VINEYARDS

Established 1983 *Owners* Gus and Phyllis Anderson
Production 7,000 cases *Vineyard area* 26 acres (10 ha)

Anderson's vineyards are situated where Conn Creek flows from Howell Mountain, at 400 feet (122 m) above sea level. Wines from this property are incredibly concentrated—a result of dry farming as well as the high altitude. Red wines are made with whole berry fermentation in order to achieve rich round soft tannins and bright fruit. The wines gain elegance in French oak and are not fined or filtered. The newest wine to the line is a ripe and fruity pinot noir, but the winery is best known for its exquisite cabernet sauvignon.

ARAUJO ESTATE WINES/EISELE VINEYARD

Established 1990 *Owners* Bart and Daphne Araujo
Production 3,350 cases *Vineyard area* 36 acres (15 ha)

In 1991, Araujo made its first Eisele bottling and this boutique winery is now known for cabernet sauvignon, sauvignon blanc and syrah from Eisele Vineyard. The site, east of Calistoga and the Napa River, enjoys cool winds that flow in through the Chalk Hill gap. Sauvignon blanc has a hint of oak

and viognier blended for complexity. Eisele Vineyard cabernet sauvignon is deeply concentrated with an elegant yet firm texture and intense fruit character of black plums. Eisele cabernets have also been produced by Ridge, Conn Creek and Phelps.

BEAULIEU VINEYARD

Established 1900 *Owners* United Distillers & Vintners
Production 1.1 million cases *Vineyard area* 1,200 acres (486 ha)

Georges de Latour from Bordeaux established Beaulieu Vineyard in 1900 and was instrumental in importing grafted vines from France that were phylloxera-resistant. His business survived Prohibition by making high-grade altar wine for the Catholic Church. In 1938, André Tchelistcheff, an innovator who taught others techniques such as malolactic fermentation, cold fermentation and filtration, joined Beaulieu. The founder's vision lives on in the winery's prestigious Georges de Latour Private Reserve Cabernet Sauvignon.

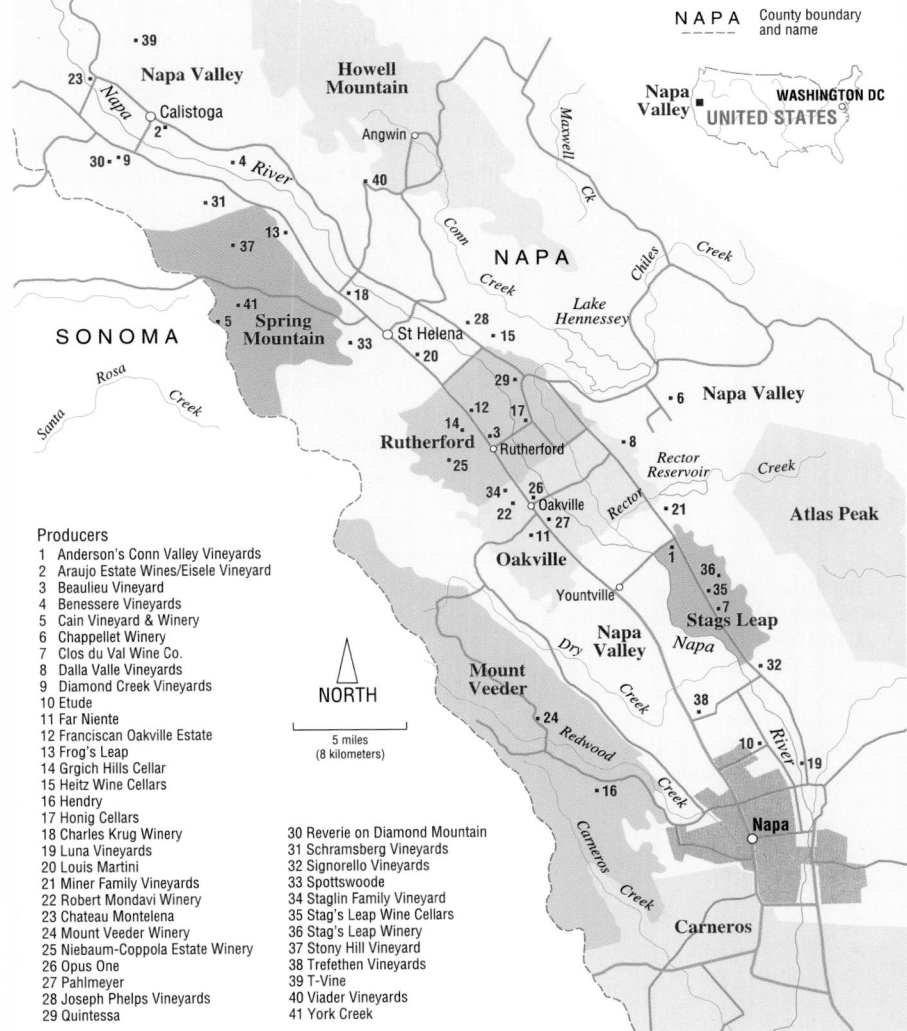

Producers
1 Anderson's Conn Valley Vineyards
2 Araujo Estate Wines/Eisele Vineyard
3 Beaulieu Vineyard
4 Benessere Vineyards
5 Cain Vineyard & Winery
6 Chappellet Winery
7 Clos du Val Wine Co.
8 Dalla Valle Vineyards
9 Diamond Creek Vineyards
10 Etude
11 Far Niente
12 Franciscan Oakville Estate
13 Frog's Leap
14 Grgich Hills Cellar
15 Heitz Wine Cellars
16 Hendry
17 Honig Cellars
18 Charles Krug Winery
19 Luna Vineyards
20 Louis Martini
21 Miner Family Vineyards
22 Robert Mondavi Winery
23 Chateau Montelena
24 Mount Veeder Winery
25 Niebaum-Coppola Estate Winery
26 Opus One
27 Pahlmeyer
28 Joseph Phelps Vineyards
29 Quintessa
30 Reverie on Diamond Mountain
31 Schramsberg Vineyards
32 Signorello Vineyards
33 Spottswoode
34 Staglin Family Vineyard
35 Stag's Leap Wine Cellars
36 Stag's Leap Winery
37 Stony Hill Vineyard
38 Trefethen Vineyards
39 T-Vine
40 Viader Vineyards
41 York Creek

The tasting room and vineyard of Domaine Carneros, Napa Valley.

BENESSERE VINEYARDS

Established 1995 *Owners* John and Ellen Benish
Production 2,500 cases *Vineyard area* 36 acres (15 ha)

Benessere is at the forefront of the Italian varietal craze. Winemaker Chris Dearden makes a killer sangiovese. He has a little help from some friends, though. His two consultants are both on Italy's DOCG tasting board and help Benessere adapt Italian viticultural practices to California's microclimates. The result is a sangiovese with cherry aromas reminiscent of Italy's best. Though still in its infancy, Benessere Vineyards can be expected to master the variety.

ROBERT BIALE VINEYARDS

Established 1991 *Owners* Aldo Biale, Robert Biale, Al Perry and Dave Pramuk *Production* 4,000–5,000 cases *Vineyard area* 11 acres (4 ha)

The Biale family has been making wine since Aldo's vineyard was planted in 1937. Its production is primarily vineyard-designated zinfandel with small amounts of sangiovese, old-vine barbera and petite sirah. Biale zinfandels have incredible depth of berry flavors, spice and complexity.

CAIN VINEYARD & WINERY

Established 1980 *Owners* Jim and Nancy Meadlock
Production 18,000 cases *Vineyard area* 84 acres (34 ha)

Cain Five—a meritage produced from the Spring Mountain District which is a blend of all five major Bordeaux varieties—is Cain Vineyard & Winery's most respected wine. Thin soils on the steep mountain slopes keep yields from these vineyards lower and elevations of up to 2,100 feet (640 m) help to keep the vines cool, resulting in concentrated and complex fruit. Cain Cuvée, a lighter style, is a great alternative to Cain Five and Cain Musqué is 100 percent sauvignon blanc from the floral musqué clone grown in Monterey.

CHAPPELLET WINERY

Established 1967 *Owners* Don and Molly Chappellet
Production 30,000 cases *Vineyard area* 110 acres (44 ha)

Chappellet was the second winery built in Napa Valley after Prohibition. This is a beautiful property on Pritchard Hill overlooking Lake Hennessey to the east of Napa Valley. Vineyards are at elevations from 800–1,800 feet (245–550 m) and 50 percent are dry-farmed. The Old Vine Cuvée Chenin Blanc, from vines planted in the 1960s, is proof that quality chenin blanc can be produced in Napa Valley. A *moelleux*-style chenin blanc is also outstanding.

CLOS DU VAL WINE CO.

Established 1972 *Owner* John Goelet *Production* 75,000 cases *Vineyard area* 300 acres (121 ha)

The Bordelais heritage of Clos du Val's general manager, Bernard Portet, has enabled the company to master bordeaux varieties, especially cabernet sauvignon. The winery produces an elegant cabernet sauvignon from Stag's Leap fruit, well balanced in structure with integrated oak influence. Its Carneros Pinot Noir is firm and rich in structure. The wine has great acidity, and is much better paired with a rack of lamb than salmon. Ariadne is a sémillon/sauvignon blanc blend with refreshing acidity and a rich mouth-feel. These wines are meant to be accessible, with restrained alcohol and wood aging that matches the wine rather than overpowering it.

CORISON WINES

Established 1987 *Owner* Cathy Corison *Production* 2,000–3,000 cases *Vineyard area* 10 acres (4 ha)

Cathy Corison's very limited production of cabernet sauvignon is fleeting once released, but if you can get it, is well worth the trouble. The blends, made mostly from vineyards between Rutherford and St Helena, emphasize the distinct character of cabernet sauvignon from the different sites. A vineyard-designate cabernet sauvignon called Kronos Vineyard is a recent release. The 25-year-old cabernet sauvignon vines here are grafted to St George rootstock, resistant to phylloxera. The yields are low, but as a result of this and vine age, the fruit is of exceptional quality.

DALLA VALLE VINEYARDS

Established 1986 *Owner* Naoko Dalla Valle *Production* 3,300 cases *Vineyard area* 25 acres (10 ha)

The winery specializes in cabernet sauvignon blended with some cabernet franc and merlot, but Dalla also makes Pietre Rosse, a spectacular sangiovese. Its cabernet sauvignon and a small proprietary bottling called Maya are collectors' items at auctions. Both wines are long-lived, lean and tannic in their youth, but will develop exceptional grace with some age.

DCUBED CELLARS

Established 1994 *Owner* Duane D. Dappen *Production* 1,000 cases *Vineyard area* 1.25 acres (.5 ha)

A hot new winery, DCubed Cellars stole the show at the Zinfandel Advocates & Producers (ZAP) tastings in San Francisco with its rich, ripe zinfandels. Duane D. Dappen, winemaker, expertly molds a zinfandel packed with flavor, yet without the harshness of excessive tannin and alcohol found in some. A Napa Valley bottling and a Howell Mountain bottling will both be available in June 2000. Since production is limited the wine is hard to find.

DIAMOND CREEK VINEYARDS

Established 1968 *Owners* Al and Boots Brounstein *Production* 3,000 cases *Vineyard area* 20 acres (8 ha)

Originally a pharmacist, Al decided to pursue his passion for wine and waterfalls and has accomplished both in a vineyard oasis with man-made waterfalls. He was one of the first to focus attention on *terroir* in California and his site contains three distinct soil types, after which he has named his wines—Gravelly Meadow, Red Rock Terrace and Volcanic Hill. They are some of the first of California's vineyard-designated wines and the winery is California's first cabernet-only estate.

ETUDE

Established 1982 *Owners* Tony and Michelle Soter *Production* 8,000 cases *Vineyard area* NA

Etude prides itself on being a proprietary label rather than an expression of place. The fruit that is used by Etude is purchased from Napa and Carneros sources. Tony Soter produces primarily pinot noir and cabernet sauvignon. Although Etude's pinot noir is famous for fueling the California pinot craze, the cabernet sauvignon should definitely not be missed. Its elegant yet forward fruit is balanced by a round texture and persistent finish.

FAR NIENTE

Established 1885 *Owners* Gil Nickel, Dirk Hampson and Larry Maguire *Production* 35,000–40,000 cases *Vineyard area* 200 acres (81 ha)

Far Niente was originally founded in 1885, but fell into disrepair after closing during Prohibition. In 1979, Gil Nickel purchased the estate and restored it. Now Far Niente produces cabernet sauvignon and a rich chardonnay with ripe tropical-fruit flavors. The winery uses gravity to move wine to ensure gentle handling. In 1989, Dolce, a botrytized dessert wine made from sémillon and sauvignon blanc, was created, proving that sauternes-style wines can be made in California.

FRANCISCAN OAKVILLE ESTATE

Established 1973 *Owner* Canandaigua Brands *Production* 130,000 cases *Vineyard area* 240 acres (97 ha)

Franciscan Oakville concentrates on wines from the valley floor near Rutherford grown primarily on loam soils. Agustin Huneeus, chairman, believes that "wine is a statement of place" and strives to make that evident in his wines. Cuvée Sauvage Chardonnay was Napa Valley's first chardonnay that was 100 percent wild-yeast fermented. Magnificat is an intensely concentrated bordeaux-style blend. Merlot and zinfandel have deep fruit and great varietal character.

FROG'S LEAP

Established 1981 *Owners* John and Julie Williams *Production* 50,000 cases *Vineyard area* 137 acres (55 ha)

The name of this winery comes from a property near Mill Creek which in the nineteenth century supplied frogs to San Francisco restaurants. The winery was established there but has since moved to an old barn site in Rutherford. The quality of wines is consistent and the merlot is especially popular. Rutherford, a new blend of bordeaux varieties, is full of ripe, blackberry fruit. Sustainable agriculture is important to the winery and followed closely in its growing practices.

GRGICH HILLS CELLAR

Established 1977 *Owners* Miljenko (Mike) Grgich and Austin Hills *Production* 60,000 cases *Vineyard area* 200 acres (81 ha)

This petite and feisty winemaker arrived in Napa in 1958 from his homeland in Croatia. Since 1977, Grgich has produced renowned chardonnays that are known to be exceptionally age-worthy. His zinfandel and cabernet sauvignon are also winners.

Below: *Winemakers in Napa Valley wax lyrical about their produce.*

Bottom: *Opening hours at this popular Napa Valley winery.*

Experience the Napa Valley region by riding the wine train.

Wine press from the Napa Wine Company, established in 1877.

maker Kristin Belair is incredibly adept at making reasonably priced savory wines from high-quality Rutherford fruit.

HOWELL MOUNTAIN VINEYARDS

Established 1988 *Owners* Jerre Sears, Joyce Black Sears and Mike Beatty *Production* 2,000 cases *Vineyard area* 63 acres (25 ha)

Pair consultant Ted Lemon with optimal fruit sources, and the result is some of the very best wines in the valley. The Beatty Ranch and Black Sears vineyards are celebrated for their amazing zinfandel. Not for the faint-hearted, these wines are packed with berry fruit and a firm kick as well as a rich chocolate character with spicy notes and a tremendous finish. Production is limited, so buy all you can find.

KONGSGAARD WINE

Established 1996 *Owners* John and Maggy Kongsgaard *Production* 800 cases *Vineyard area* 10 acres (4 ha)

Immediately upon release, most of the Kongsgaard Chardonnay was hoarded by collectors. The reason is simple—it is one of the finest chardonnays ever produced in California with a rich, smooth texture, full fruit, long finish and bright acidity. Syrah is also made by Kongsgaard.

CHARLES KRUG WINERY

Established 1861 *Owners* Peter Mondavi family *Production* 65,000 cases *Vineyard area* 803 acres (325 ha)

Cesare Mondavi bought the Charles Krug winery in 1943 and it was influential in the modernization of winemaking in the Napa Valley, instituting practices like sterile filtration, temperature control and oak-aging experiments. Charles Krug now produces a wide range of good-quality wines.

LANG & REED WINE CO.

Established 1996 *Owners* John and Tracey Skupny *Production* 2,000 cases *Vineyard area* NA

Tracey and John Skupny have created a demand for cabernet franc in California, even if it is only for their version. All grapes are contracted from optimal fruit sources and the ripe black fruit character of their wines is true to the variety, without any overly green or herbaceous character, demonstrating the delicacy cabernet franc can achieve when yields are limited.

HEITZ WINE CELLARS

Established 1961 *Owners* Heitz family *Production* 40,000 cases *Vineyard area* 335 acres (136 ha)

This company was originally in the business of finishing wines for others, but, in 1965, made the decision to make its first cabernet sauvignon. In 1968, it produced a stellar vintage from Martha's Vineyard grapes (and was the only winery to receive fruit from there) and the Martha's Vineyard bottling is now a well-known commodity on the auction scene. Heitz has also made wines from Stag's Leap Wine Cellar's Fay Vineyard, and Bella Oaks. Heitz wines typically have a very distinctive mint and eucalyptus character.

HENDRY

Established 1992 *Owners* George Hendry, Susan Ridley and Jeff Miller *Production* 6,000 cases *Vineyard area* 123 acres (50 ha)

This boutique winery is a favorite amongst lovers of cabernet sauvignon, zinfandel and pinot noir. Its location, between Mt Veeder and Carneros, results in wines with concentrated mountain fruit, yet with bright refreshing acidity. Due to contrasting *terroir*, Hendry split the vineyard into blocks and the wines are intended to show the different characters of these. Production is small but the recent addition of a winery should increase Hendry's output.

HONIG CELLARS

Established 1981 *Owners* Honig family *Production* 35,000 cases *Vineyard area* 58 acres (23 ha)

Honig started with sauvignon blanc, and then introduced cabernet sauvignon in 1989. Wine-

LUNA VINEYARDS

Established 1995 *Owners* E. Michael Moone, George Vare and John Kongsgaard *Production* 25,000 cases *Vineyard area* 66 acres (27 ha)

Luna is an up and coming winery specializing in sangiovese co-fermented with merlot and syrah for richness. Its pinot grigio comes from estate vineyards and is evolving as the vines age. Merlot is also produced from estate fruit and exhibits an approachable style in its youth, but has enough stuffing to age. The winemaking team here studied in Alsace, Friuli, Alto Adige and Tuscany to explore international techniques in order to apply them in California.

LOUIS MARTINI

Established 1922 *Owners* Martini family *Production* 150,000 cases *Vineyard area* 600 acres (243 ha)

Louis P. Martini began clonal trials on pinot noir and chardonnay in 1948, resulting in the UC Davis chardonnay clone 108 which is now widespread throughout California. Martini is also believed to have been the first to plant pinot noir. Martini's primary vineyard sites are in Sonoma Valley, Monte Rosso, Russian River Valley, Los Vinedos del Rio, Napa's Chiles Valley, Glen Oaks and in Napa's Pope Valley. Its line of classic varietals and Reserve wines are excellent value, especially the Reserve Cabernet Sauvignon.

MINER FAMILY VINEYARDS

Established 1998 *Owners* David and Emily Miner *Production* 7,000 cases *Vineyard area* NA

This company's aim is to concentrate on small batches of high-quality wines. Fruit comes mostly from Oakville Ranch Vineyards & Winery. Since its inception in 1989, Oakville Ranch has been highly praised for its merlot and chardonnays. Miner has specialized in cabernet sauvignon, merlot, sangiovese, pinot noir and viognier. Especially popular, its rosé of sangiovese sold quickly the first summer it was released, proving that it can be fashionable to drink pink wine.

MIURA

Established 1997 *Owner* Emmanuel Kemiji *Production* 2,500 cases *Vineyard area* NA

Miura, named after the breeder of the most famous fighting bulls in Spain, is a reminder of Master Sommelier Emmanuel Kemiji's European heritage. Once employed by the Ritz Carlton San Francisco, he now uses his expert palate to create distinctive wines from some of California's best vineyards. Currently, he produces merlot from Carneros, pinot noir from Pisoni Ranch and chardonnay fashioned after white burgundy. A bordeaux-style blend is the only departure from the single-vineyard/single-variety theme.

ROBERT MONDAVI WINERY

Established 1966 *Owners* Public shareholders *Production* 350,000 cases *Vineyard area* 1,500 acres (607 ha)

Robert Mondavi is one of the most influential people in California's winemaking history. In 1943, he joined the Charles Krug winery owned by his family and learned about California winemaking. A trip to Bordeaux in 1962 inspired him to pursue his own goals and in 1966 he opened his own winery. Robert Mondavi has never rested on his laurels and his experiments into almost every aspect of viticulture and vinification have contributed significant technological advances to the region. In 1979, he went into partnership with Baron Philippe de Rothschild of Chateau Mouton-Rothschild to create Opus One. Recently Mondavi expanded to Chile and Italy and now covers all levels of the market, from value wines such as Woodbridge to prestige cuvées like Opus. Special projects include a winery that specializes in Italian varieties and a collaboration with NASA to use aerial imagery to pinpoint phylloxera's spread through vineyards. Mondavi was the visionary behind the American Center for Food, Wine and the Arts, which is set to open in fall of 2001. Robert Mondavi Winery is currently the largest exporter of premium California wine, reaching more than 90 countries.

Entrance to the winery of one of California's most influential winemakers.

CHATEAU MONTELENA

Established 1882 *Owners* Barrett family *Production* 35,000 cases *Vineyard area* 120 acres (49 ha)

Chateau Montelena is renowned for the famous Paris Tasting of 1976, when its second vintage of modern chardonnay, the 1973, won as the top white wine. Although this spurred the growth of chardonnay as a premium California wine, Chateau Montelena is probably just as acclaimed for its red wines, and the cabernet sauvignon has been proven to age extraordinarily well in vertical

Below: *Wine as inspiration for movies? Francis Ford Coppola's tasting room.*

Bottom: *Futuristic Opus One vineyards and tasting rooms.*

tastings. As a result, this is one of the first California wineries to offer its cabernet *en primeur* and it has been quite successful.

MOUNT VEEDER WINERY

Established 1986 *Owner* Canandaigua Brands *Production* 10,000 cases *Vineyard area* 40 acres (16 ha)

Mount Veeder is known for wines with intense mountain fruit. Vineyards are located in the Mayacamas hills, where vines must struggle on rocky soil, steep slopes and contend with a shortage of water. As a result, yields are low and grapes are small and concentrated with black fruit character. Mount Veeder was the first Napa Valley property to plant all five bordeaux varieties. Its best wines are the reserve blend, cabernet sauvignon, merlot and zinfandel.

NIEBAUM-COPPOLA ESTATE WINERY

Established 1975 *Owners* Francis Ford Coppola and Eleanor Coppola *Production* 160,000 cases *Vineyard area* 294 acres (119 ha)

Film director Francis Ford Coppola purchased the home of Captain Gustave Niebaum, founder of the Inglenook Estate, in 1979 and acquired the remainder of the estate from Heublein in 1995. Most noted for Rubicon, a bordeaux blend, Coppola also has added three lines, Francis Coppola Diamond series, Francis Coppola Presents and Gustave Niebaum Collection.

OPUS ONE

Established 1979 *Owners* Baroness Philippine de Rothschild and Robert Mondavi *Production* 30,000 cases *Vineyard area* 104 acres (42 ha)

The scale of this winery is awesome, considering it is solely devoted to the production of one wine—a meritage or cabernet blend. The wine is made with the utmost care, from densely spaced vines, hand-picked and sorted fruit to careful vinification and 18 months aging in French oak. Opus is aged 18 months in bottle before release. Even though luscious upon release, Opus One has the capacity to age. The 1979 and 1980, the first releases, remain vibrant and alive today.

PAHLMEYER

Established 1986 *Owner* Jayson L. Pahlmeyer *Production* 5,000 cases *Vineyard area* 35 acres (14 ha)

When Jayson Pahlmeyer began his endeavor, he concentrated on obtaining the very best bordeaux clones and bringing them to California. Current production includes a red bordeaux-style blend, and a popular chardonnay. The chardonnay is usually unfined and unfiltered, often throwing a cloudy deposit in the glass, but true devotees of the brand don't mind, for it is packed with flavor.

PATZ & HALL WINE CO.

Established 1988 *Owners* Donald and Heather Patz, James Hall and Anne Moses *Production* 10,000 cases *Vineyard area* NA

Patz & Hall could be listed under almost any region, as their fruit hails from California's top sources, but they are based in Napa where their first wine, a 1988 Napa Valley Chardonnay made from the Caldwell Vineyard, was born. The Patz & Hall Wine Co. has formed close relationships with their growers in an effort to produce the best pinot noir and chardonnay possible. Their wines have gained a huge following.

JOSEPH PHELPS VINEYARDS

Established 1973 *Owners* Joseph Phelps family *Production* 85,000–100,000 cases *Vineyard area* 395 acres (160 ha)

In 1974, Phelps produced Insignia, the first proprietary bordeaux-style blend from California. In that same year, Phelps produced California's first syrah, and put rhône-style wines on the map with the Vin du Mistral line. Le Mistral, a rhône blend, is a great example, and the Phelps viognier shows exceptional richness and floral character. Phelps also makes high-quality cabernet sauvignon, sauvignon blanc and many others, including a line of late-harvest dessert wines. Insignia and Backus Cabernet Sauvignon are the top-of-the-line reds, suitable for long cellaring.

QUINTESSA

Established 1990 *Owner* Agustin Huneeus *Production* 1,500 cases *Vineyard area* 280 acres (113 ha)

Owned by Agustin Huneeus and marketed and distributed by Franciscan Estates, this special property is in the Rutherford appellation and has distinctively different soils, elevations and microclimates. Quintessa wines are elegant in style, improving each year as the vines age.

REVERIE ON DIAMOND MOUNTAIN

Established 1993 *Owners* Evelyn and Norman Kiken *Production* 2,100 cases *Vineyard area* 30 acres (12 ha)

Reverie is located in prime vinegrowing territory, right next to Diamond Creek Vineyards on Diamond Mountain. The Kikens produce predominantly red wines, with cabernet sauvignon making up 40 percent of the plantings. ASKiken (pronounced "ass kicken") is, as its name suggests, a powerful red table wine and there is a ripe and fruity cabernet franc. Experimental varieties such as barbera and tempranillo should yield interesting wines. Merlot, one clone of which is from Chateau Petrus in Bordeaux, is also stellar. All the wines are estate-grown and produced.

SCHRAMSBERG VINEYARDS

Established 1862 *Owner* Jamie Davies *Production* 48,000 cases *Vineyard area* 54 acres (22 ha)

In 1965, when the late Jack Davies and his wife, Jamie, purchased the property they realized that not many wineries were making *méthode*

champenoise wines in California. They decided to go for this corner of the market and to concentrate on exceptional fruit quality. By 1967, they released the first California sparkling wine produced with chardonnay that had a vintage date. In 1971, they were first to produce a California blanc de noirs. Their J. Schram bottling rivals the best French champagne.

SIGNORELLO VINEYARDS

Established 1985 *Owner* Ray Signorello Jr *Production* 8,000 cases *Vineyard area* 42 acres (17 ha)

Ray Signorello Sr began this vineyard project with the intention of growing grapes for other vintners but the company now produces its own line of distinctive wines. Signorello focuses on gentle treatment to create wines supple in their youth. This is particularly evident in its rare pinot noirs from Las Amigas and Martinelli vineyards. The Founder's Reserve Cabernet Sauvignon is incredibly concentrated, yet has polished tannins that enable it to be enjoyed young as well. Signorello has also been a leader in making a name for sémillon in California generally and their 600 cases are in high demand.

SPOTTSWOODE

Established 1882 *Owner* Mary Weber Novak *Production* 6,000 cases *Vineyard area* 40 acres (16 ha)

Located to the west of St Helena, Spottswoode was named after the Spotts family who purchased the estate in 1910. The vineyards were replanted by the current owner and this was followed by

Originally intended as a source for other vintners, Signorello now produces its own distinctive wines.

Napa Valley—home of California's oldest established and most productive wineries.

the first vintage of cabernet sauvignon in 1982. The vineyard is organically farmed.

STAGLIN FAMILY VINEYARD

Established 1985 *Owners* Shari and Garen Staglin
Production 9,000 cases *Vineyard area* 50 acres (20 ha)

Staglin is a family-owned vineyard on prime acreage which makes limited quantities of some exquisite wines. Its cabernet sauvignon has lush fruit flavors yet sufficient power to enable it to age, and its chardonnay is well balanced in oak with focussed fruit. The sangiovese, Stagliano, is a benchmark for the variety but is only available in small quantities. Minimal handling highlights the essence of this great fruit source.

STAG'S LEAP WINE CELLARS

Established 1972 *Owners* Warren and Barbara Winiarski
Production 65,000 cases *Vineyard area* 180 acres (73 ha)

Warren Winiarski is famous, not only for the victory of his 1973 Cabernet Sauvignon at the Paris Tasting in 1976, but because he has always been ahead of the pack in producing wines of optimal quality in Napa Valley. While well known

for the longevity of Stag's Leap Cask 23 Cabernet, SLV and Fay Vineyard wines are also beginning to gain ground. The latest venture is a new chardonnay from Arcadia Vineyard.

STAG'S LEAP WINERY

Established 1893 *Owner* Beringer Wine Estates *Production* 50,000 cases *Vineyard area* 240 acres (97 ha)

This winery was the first established in the Stag's Leap District, a prime location for growing cabernet sauvignon. Robert Brittan, winemaker, also works wonders with petite sirah.

STONY HILL VINEYARD

Established 1952 *Owners* Peter and Wilinda McCrea
Production 5,000 cases *Vineyard area* 40 acres (16 ha)

In 1943, Eleanor and Fred McCrea, parents of Peter, bought a ranch on Spring Mountain. They decided to concentrate on producing chardonnay, but also planted riesling, gewürztraminer, sémillon and pinot blanc to add interest. Stony Hill's chardonnays are possibly the most ageworthy white wines in California. Their distinctive Burgundian style, along with lean acid, subtle oak and lack of

malolactic fermentation, may be part of the reason. At any rate, the wines are amazing, especially the older chardonnays that are at their peak five to ten years after harvest.

TREFETHEN VINEYARDS

Established 1973 *Owners* John and Janet Trefethen *Production* 60,000 cases *Vineyard area* 650 acres (263 ha)

Trefethen has the largest contiguous vineyard in Napa under single, private ownership. The property is built on historic Eschol Estate and its winery is one of the few remaining wooden gravity flow structures built in 1886 by architect Hamden McIntyre. Chardonnays and cabernet sauvignons are just a few of the wines born here. Trefethen has a great program of releasing Library Reserve wines, both whites and reds, which are cellared for a good deal longer than normal.

T-VINE

Established 1992 *Owner* Greg Brown *Production* 3,500–4,000 cases *Vineyard area* NA

You have to love a winery whose winemaker delivers the wine in person. Not only is he the delivery guy, but Greg Brown is also the sales and marketing team, vineyard manager, accountant and winemaker. He seems to enjoy this situation, though, since all of his resources go into the end product rather than to a large staff. And the wine really is evidence of this. A grenache blended with some petite sirah for color and weight is a joy. Zinfandel is mouthwatering yet ultra-ripe.

VIADER VINEYARDS

Established 1989 *Owner* Delia Viader *Production* 2,200 cases *Vineyard area* 23 acres (9 ha)

Delia Viader was born in Argentina and she has created an estate that produces a St Émilion-style cabernet sauvignon/cabernet franc blend from Howell Mountain fruit. Fruit is grown on steep hillsides at 1,100 feet (335 m) above sea level. Contrary to most plantings in California, the rows run up and over hillsides, rather than across, for maximum sun exposure. Vines are closely spaced with 2,000 plants per acre (809 per ha) planted in primarily volcanic soils. The fruit is organically farmed "to maintain the fine balance between struggle and survival, which results in grapes and finally wines of character and distinction." The high proportion of cabernet franc in the blend (about 40 percent) makes Viader unique among other California proprietary reds.

YORK CREEK

Established 1991 *Owner* Fritz Maytag *Production* 600–700 cases *Vineyard area* 125 acres (51 ha)

Fritz Maytag started York Creek long after his Maytag blue cheese and Anchor Steam Brewery were popular. The winery specializes in a full-bodied red blend from grapes grown at the top of Spring Mountain—an ecologically diverse site that Maytag proudly notes has 24 tree species, commemorating them on his wine labels. One of the only wineries to produce a worthwhile Californian port, the York Creek version is made primarily of zinfandel and petite sirah fortified with brandy from the estate vineyard.

Trefethen Winery and the intoxicating sight of fruit on the vine.

Carneros

Rebecca Chapa

Carneros straddles Napa and Sonoma Counties at their southernmost points and huddles closely around the San Pablo Bay, a northern part of the San Francisco Bay. It encompasses 36,900 acres (14,944 ha), of which 15,147 acres (6,138 ha) are suitable for viticulture, although currently only 6,200 acres (2,511 ha) are planted. Of this, 48 percent is planted with chardonnay, 32 percent with pinot noir, 5 percent with cabernet sauvignon and 6 percent with merlot.

History

Bordered by the Napa River to the east and by the Southern Pacific rail tracks to the south, Carneros was well positioned to ship wine to San Francisco in the early days of winemaking in this region. Its first winery, the Winter Winery, was built in 1870. Between the late 1870s and 1880s, infestations of phylloxera stopped the industry in its tracks, ravaging almost all the vineyards. The advent of Prohibition also prevented further development of wineries. A resurgence in investment started in the 1960s and it was in full force by the 1980s, when development reached its current pace.

Carneros was defined as an AVA in 1983 and after that occurred, investment in the area took off with purchases of land by large companies such as Freixenet and Robert Mondavi. In 1985, the Carneros Quality Alliance, which is quite possibly California's most effective viticultural appellation marketing association, was born.

Climate and landscape

Unlike Napa Valley or Sonoma, the boundaries of Carneros were delineated by its distinctive climate, due to the effects of the bay and differences in elevation. Producers in Carneros thus used climatic rather than historical or political differences as a method for defining their borders.

As a result, the character of Carneros wines is special and recognizable. The area's rather interesting microclimate is influenced by the San Pablo Bay, which has a moderating effect on temperature in spring and winter, helping to lengthen the growing season. In the summer, fog rolls off the bay to cool the vineyards in the mornings and afternoons. However, proximity to the bay also creates wind in certain parts of Carneros where it stresses the vines. Elsewhere, it helps prevent rot on the vines by drying out dew from the morning fog.

The region consists of low-lying land at sea level near the bay and rolling hills to the north, which reach an altitude of 1,000 feet (305 m) in the westerly hills. Soils are mostly clay-based and usually shallow. Carneros is a Region I growing area, on the Winkler-Amerine heat summation scale, and is ideal for cooler climate grape varieties such as pinot noir and chardonnay which are able to ripen while still maintaining good acidity. Winemakers are also exploring other varieties, notably merlot. Carneros has a much lower annual rainfall than both Napa and Sonoma Counties (22 inches/56 cm), so irrigation is vital.

ACACIA

Established 1979 *Owner* Chalone Wine Group *Production* 60,000 cases *Vineyard area* 100 acres (40 ha)

Acacia is known for vineyard-designated pinot noir and for chardonnay. 1986 saw the launch of a refreshing brut sparkling wine, and in 1991 Acacia finally began sharing the zinfandel that they had made for 10 years on the side with the public. Although chardonnay is the money-maker, making up 60–65 percent of production, pinot noir is the soul of the winery. The Beckstoffer Vineyard vines, part of the original Martini Ranch, are some of Carneros' oldest pinot noir. As a result, its wines are intensely concentrated and complex.

ANCIEN WINERY

Established 1992 *Owners* Ken and Teresa Bernards *Production* 2,500 cases *Vineyard area* NA

The name of this winery is a tribute to the winemakers of old and their contribution to viticulture.

Growers note special features and attach these to the end of the vineyard rows.

Its pinot noir has an incredible silky texture with bright cherry fruit.

BUENA VISTA WINERY

Established 1857 *Owner* A. Racke Co. *Production* 135,000 cases *Vineyard area* 935 acres (379 ha)

Buena Vista is California's oldest premium winery. Its founder, Agoston Haraszthy, was one of the first to introduce *vitis vinifera* to the USA. Although Buena Vista is the largest estate winery in Carneros, it has not lost sight of quality. Its wines tend to have bright fruit with refreshing acidity due to their cool vineyard sites, and chardonnay is great value.

CARNEROS CREEK WINERY

Established 1972 *Owners* Francis and Kathleen Mahoney *Production* 34,000 cases *Vineyard area* 200 acres (81 ha)

This was the first winery that was built after Prohibition in Carneros. The winery has been involved in a 12 year research project into pinot noir clones and its own pinot noirs have intense fruit and a rich structure.

DOMAINE CARNEROS BY TAITTINGER

Established 1987 *Owner* Champagne Taittinger & Kobrand Corp. *Production* 45,000 cases *Vineyard area* 110 acres (44 ha)

Lightness and delicacy are the goals for Domaine Carneros wines. Most cuvées are primarily pinot noir with some chardonnay and pinot meunier. Production includes a premium *méthode champenoise* and a proprietary blanc de blancs, la Rève. The Domaine Carneros still pinot noir rivals other top California favorites.

DOMAINE CHANDON

Established 1973 *Owner* Louis Vuitton Moet-Hennessy *Production* 350,000 cases *Vineyard area* 1,100 acres (445 ha)

Domaine Chandon is probably the most recognized sparkling wine producer in California. Although its museum, restaurant and grounds are exquisite, the quality of the wine has been the driving force behind the winery. A leader in innovation, and with the resources of Moët et Chandon at its disposal, Domaine Chandon has been able to greatly enhance

méthode champenoise production throughout California. Its still pinot meunier, with its bright jammy fruit, is helping to create a following for that grape.

GLORIA FERRER

Established 1982 *Owner* Freixenet S.A. *Production* 82,000 cases *Vineyard area* 335 acres (136 ha)

The Ferrer family from Spain, owners of Freixenet, S.A., are the largest producers of *méthode champenoise* wine in the world. The wines tend to rely heavily on pinot noir in the blend and are exceptional value for this quality of wine, not only in California, but internationally. The Royal Cuvée is a particularly good aperitif.

HAVENS WINE CELLARS

Established 1984 *Owners* Michael and Kathryn Havens, Jon and Russell Scott *Production* 16,000 cases *Vineyard area* 5 acres (2 ha)

Although it only has 5 acres, Havens' merlot is a wonderful example of how the intense flavors of Carneros merlot can be tamed. In a sea of merlot that often tastes nothing like the grape, here is an example that is very true to the variety.

Producers
1 Acacia
2 Buena Vista Winery
3 Carneros Creek Winery
4 Domaine Carneros by Taittinger
5 Gloria Ferrer
6 MacRostie Winery
7 Kent Rasmussen Winery
8 Saintsbury
9 Schug Carneros Estate
10 Truchard Vineyards

NORTH

10 miles
(16 kilometers)

NAPA County boundary and name

Row upon row of well-spaced vineyards is a common sight in these regions.

Skilled workers hand picking for quality production of premium wines.

deeply concentrated wine capable of long-term aging.

SAINTSBURY

Established 1981 *Owners* Richard A. Ward and David W. Graves *Production* 48,000 cases *Vineyard area* 55 acres (22 ha)

Although Saintsbury makes chardonnay, it is best known for its pinot noir which makes up two-thirds of its output. Three styles are made—Garnet, for light, easy drinking; Carneros, rich and firm; and Reserve, the richest. Grapes come from 12 vineyards, and a gentle handling regimen is thought to be the key to its success. A special bottling of Brown Ranch Pinot Noir has been produced since 1996.

MACROSTIE WINERY

Established 1987 *Owner* Steve MacRostie *Production* 12,000 cases *Vineyard area* NA

Only French oak is used at this winery, and gentle fruit handling and *sur lie* aging are considered integral to creating superior texture in the wines. Fruit is all bought from Carneros' top growers, but recently MacRostie acquired a vineyard on Wildcat Mountain and production will begin there soon.

KENT RASMUSSEN WINERY

Established 1986 *Owner* Kent Rasmussen *Production* 25,000 cases *Vineyard area* 14 acres (6 ha)

Kent Rasmussen trained in South Africa and the Barossa Valley in Australia. This diversity has given him a wide frame of reference for winemaking. The winery is particularly noted for its premium pinot noir and chardonnay. A second label called Ramsay was created specifically for more eclectic varieties such as marsanne, nebbiolo, sangiovese, petite sirah, alicante bouchet and refosco. Ramsay also specializes in a great-value pinot noir with smooth black-cherry flavors.

ST CLEMENT VINEYARDS

Established 1878 *Owner* Beringer Wine Estates *Production* 25,000 cases *Vineyard area* 32 acres (13 ha)

St Clement was the eighth bonded Napa Valley winery established by Fritz Rosenbaum, a stained glass merchant from San Francisco. The winery is well known for its cabernet sauvignon, chardonnay, sauvignon blanc and merlot, but Oroppas, which is its blend of cabernet sauvignon, merlot and cabernet franc is king. This is a rich, spicy,

SCHUG CARNEROS ESTATE

Established 1980 *Owner* Walter Schug *Production* 20,000 cases *Vineyard area* 42 acres (17 ha)

Walter Schug has created pinot noir and chardonnay with great acid balance. Chardonnay is fermented in French oak and aged *sur lie* while pinot noir is fermented in a rotary fermenter (only five exist in the USA) under strict temperature control. All wines undergo extended bottle aging to ensure that they are ready to drink upon release.

ROBERT SINSKEY VINEYARDS

Established 1986 *Owners* Robert M. Sinskey and Robert M. Sinskey Jr *Production* 25,000 cases *Vineyard area* 150 acres (61 ha)

Robert Sinskey was originally an eye surgeon before the wine bug bit him. Now he produces incredibly silky textured pinot noir, as well as merlot which has become a standard for the variety. Most wines come from Carneros plantings, which provides the wines with vivacious acidity. This winery's chardonnay is very clean in flavor, one of the few from California to be made without malolactic fermentation.

TRUCHARD VINEYARDS

Established 1989 *Owners* Tony and Jo Ann Truchard *Production* 11,000 cases *Vineyard area* 250 acres (101 ha)

Truchard initially provided grapes to other well-known wineries, but by 1989 it was producing wine on its own. It is definitely on the right track, especially with pinot noir and spicy syrah. Truchard uses only estate fruit for its own wines and sells 80 percent of the grapes it produces.

Central Valley

Catherine Fallis MS

The Central Valley AVA runs 400 miles (645 km) north to south, or nearly three-quarters the length of the state of California. The spectacular Sierra Nevada range to the east protects this massive AVA from the desert climate of Nevada and the coastal ranges to the west soften the effects from marine influences. The demarcation begins just north of Redding at Shasta Lake, near the Oregon border and runs to Bakersfield in the south (just north of Los Angeles). This AVA is divided into two subzones—north, the smaller cool Sacramento River Valley; south, the hot multi-county San Joaquin Valley.

Fine wine production centers around Sacramento River Valley. With the exception of Yolo county, which borders the southern tip of Mendocino County, the prime growing zones here are approximately 70 to 100 miles (112 to 160 km) east to northeast of San Francisco Bay. Six of the eight AVAs are here—Clarksburg (which includes the sub-AVA Merritt Island), Dunnigan Hills, tiny and adjacent Suisin Valley and Solano County-Green Valley and Lodi. Grapes from Yolo and Sacramento Counties and the northern half of San Joaquin County are highly sought after by fine wine producers of the north and central coasts.

Clarksburg AVA fruit is prized by 30 major wineries including Gallo, Beringer, Sebastiani, Glen Ellen, Mondavi Woodbridge, Clos du Bois, Louis Martini and Baron Herzog. Sutter Home and Korbel Champagne Cellars have their own vineyards in the area.

Lodi AVA, which overlaps Sacramento and San Joaquin Counties, stands unsurpassed for premium varietals including chardonnay, sauvignon blanc, cabernet sauvignon, merlot and zinfandel. It produces more than Napa and Sonoma combined. Only recently producers such as Burgess, Clos du Val, M. Cosentino, J. Lohr, Ravenswood and Turley have credited Lodi as the fruit source on their wine labels.

The southern half of the AVA is the San Joaquin Valley. This flat, hot high volume area includes the southern tip of San Joaquin County (south of Lodi and Stockton), Stanislaus County with Modesto and the new, high-elevation two-winery Diablo Grande AVA, Merced County, Madera County and Fresno County with its namesake city of Fresno. The Madera AVA overlaps parts of Madera and Fresno Counties. The south-ern-most part comprises Kings, Tulare and Kern Counties and extends just south of Bakersfield.

Central Valley demarcated acreage is 900,000 (364,225 ha)—more than three times that of Bordeaux. Distribution is: Solano County–Green Valley AVA 2,560 (1036 ha); Suisin Valley 15,360 (6216 ha); Dunnigan Hills AVA 89,000 (36,020 ha); Clarksburg AVA 64,640 (26,160 ha) (including Merritt Island AVA 5000 (2023 ha)); Lodi AVA 458,000 (185,350 ha); Madera AVA 230,000 (93,080 ha); and Diablo Grande AVA 30,000 (12,140 ha).

The largest reported wine county is San Joaquin. It includes Lodi and is 57, 430 acres (23,240 ha), followed by Fresno at 45,529 acres (18,425 ha); Madera at 43,413 acres (17,570 ha); Kern at 31,930 acres (12,920 ha); and Merced at 15,494 acres (6,270 ha).

Stanislaus County, home to wine giants Gallo and Franzia, has no report of total acreage other than that of the demarcated Diablo Grande AVA at 30,000 (12,140 ha).

San Joaquin County's 1998 grape sales reached US$222,080,668, just slightly less than revenues from Sonoma County, and higher than Napa. Three-quarters of Cali-fornia's grape tonnage (including raisan and table) is generated in the Central Valley. Kern and Fresno Counties are first and second (Napa is third) in the top ten counties providing vineyard employment.

Colombard is the most widely planted varietal, followed by chenin blanc. Sauvignon blanc, sémillon, muscat, chardonnay, zinfandel, grenache, barbera, carignane, carnelian, cabernet sauvignon, merlot, mourvèdre, petite sirah and ruby cabernet are also widely planted. Planting of pinot

Wine grapes in full, delicious bloom.

Map labels:

Central Valley — WASHINGTON DC — UNITED STATES

8 · Sacramento · Davis · 80 · Lodi · Clarksburg · SACRAMENTO · SOLANO

7 · Lodi · 2,6,10 · SAN JOAQUIN · Stockton · 3 · Oakdale · Modesto · 5 · La Grange · Diablo Grande · STANISLAUS · Turlock · Patterson · 4 · Atwater · Merced · MERCED · Los Banos · MADERA · Madera · Biola · Mendota · Fresno · Chowchilla · 9 · Madera

MERCED — County boundary and name

NORTH — 25 miles (40 kilometers) — 20 miles (32 km)

Producers
1 Bogle Vineyards
2 Clayton Vineyards
3 Delicato Vineyards
4 Isom Ranch
5 Gallo
6 Jessie's Grove
7 Lucas Winery and Vineyard
8 Phillips Vineyards
9 Quady Winery
10 St Amant Winery

gris, sangiovese, viognier and syrah is on the rise. Thompson seedless, classified as "raisin-type grapes" by California's Agricultural Statistical Service, covers 267,000 acres (108,050 ha) and is included in production figures by the mass-producers in the south.

Total annual case production is hard to pinpoint, as the largest producer, Gallo, won't provide figures. The fortress at Modesto is virtually impenetrable. Jancis Robinson MW got in by helicopter

Irrigation lines are used extensively for the crops of California.

once. Her report in the autobiographical *Tasting Pleasures* (*Confessions of a Wine Lover* in some countries) is enlightening. Second largest producer Robert Mondavi's Woodbridge reports production of 1.5 million cases.

Lodi-Woodbridge is an area to watch. It is a community with immensely strong ties to agriculture, primarily that of grape growing, and the amount of visible wealth is astounding. Large new homes surrounded by acres of old vines has become a common sight.

History

If not for the dams built over a century ago to trap melting snow from the Sierra Foothills, and the network of irrigation canals feeding most of the valley's vineyards, this flat, arid land would not have thrived. Leon Adams in *The Wines of America* calls it "more fabulously productive than the delta of the Nile." The 1850s saw many wineries being established in Lodi and further south in the valley. Flame tokay put Lodi on the map and until the late 1970s was dominant in the area. Germans, Italians and Armenians began producing vast quantities of sweet, fortified and sparkling wine for mass consumption.

Unlike much of Napa and Sonoma Valleys, Central Valley growers have long histories in the wine industry, some going back two centuries. Central Valley producers survived Prohibition by shipping fruit to the east. Young Mondavi and Gallo family members bragged of how many cases they could pack in a day. After Prohibition, the rival families turned their attention to agribusiness and mass production of inexpensive, well-marketed wines. Thunderbird, Ripple, Boone's Farm, Tott's and Cook's filled the cups of the masses for decades. In the 1960s and 1970s premium north coast producers looked towards Lodi zinfandel for its extra power and depth. And today they are coming back in droves.

Landscape and climate

The Sacramento River Valley is a warm inland area, classified as Region IV, similar to the Mediterranean district Languedoc-Roussillon. Temperatures climb as high as 100°F (38°C) during the peak of summer. However, the nearby Golden Gate Gap sends its fog and marine breezes as far inland as Lodi. In the summer months cool westerly "carquinez" breezes moderate the climate in Lodi. Clarksburg AVA also has a long, dry growing season, warm summer days, rich alluvial soils and cooling Delta breezes on summer evenings. In January and February the multitude of waterways and rivers create fog conditions.

The San Joaquin Valley is classified as Region IV on the Winkler-Amerine scale, warming to Region V in the deep southern plains. The valley floor flatlands of fertile sandy loam are marked with a network of irrigation canals and levees harnessing water from inland rivers and Sierra Nevada snow melts.

Vines and wines

The Sacramento River Valley produces premium whites and reds. Regional style markers are balance, softer tannins in the reds, dry, restrained and rich fruit character and moderate oak usage. Clarksburg AVA produces good chenin blanc and the Clarksburg chardonnay is worth watching. Dunnigan Hills AVA is notable for the rhône-style and late-harvest wines of R. H. Phillips. Suisin Valley and Solano County–Green Valley AVAs each have one winery and are beginning to establish their identity—a task which is not easy in the shadow of the famous neighbor Napa.

Zinfandel and carignane grown in Lodi is some of the finest anywhere in the state, even at the current high tonnage levels. Most of the Lodi reds exhibit softer tannins, have a distinct varietal character and tend to be more judiciously oaked than their showy neighbors.

The latest techniques in trellising, irrigation and pest management are in full use in the Sacramento River Valley, where enthusiasm for such techniques is high. The Lodi Woodbridge Winegrape Commission has launched the industry's only district-wide Integrated Pest Management program to reduce pesticide and herbicide usage. Fertile alluvial soil, heat and irrigated vines yield large crops. Eight tons per acre (20 t per ha) is standard; quality conscious producers are at half that or less. Surprisingly even the oldest head trained, dry farmed vines are still capable of high yields. Industrial farming including flood irrigation, pesticide application by plane and machine harvesting dominate in the San Joaquin Valley.

Upscale winemaking—with an emphasis on experimentation, artistry and premium winemaking techniques—dominates in the north. Conversely, science and control are prevalent in the south, where continuous bulk production techniques yield consistent quality at low prices. California is far better at this large scale production than any region in the world.

Producers

BOGLE VINEYARDS

Established 1978 *Owners* Bogle family *Production* 125,000 cases *Vineyard area* 1,000 acres (405 ha)

Vineyard Manager Warren Bogle is the sixth generation to farm the fertile Delta soil—the family has been farming grapes since the 1800s. Winemaker Christopher Smith produces affordable chenin blanc, chardonnay, merlot, petite sirah and zinfandel from estate and sourced fruit. The California Delta is a natural habitat for the ringneck pheasant, still seen on the Bogle label.

CLAYTON VINEYARDS

Established 1988 *Owners* Clayton Russell *Production* 2,000 cases *Vineyard area* 40 acres (16.2 ha)

A former foundry worker who discovered wine while making presses for Louis Martini, the proprietor Clayton Russell, with winemaker Jim Yerkes, and wife Shirley, produces old vine dry farmed, head pruned Lodi zinfandel and, more recently planted petite sirah.

DELICATO VINEYARDS

Established 1924 *Owners* Indelicato family *Production* NA *Vineyard area* 120 acres (48.5 ha) Manteca, 1600 acres (648 ha) Lodi, 7,500 acres (3035 ha) Monterey

Gaspare Indelicato immigrated from a small village in Italy to Manteca, California and planted the first grapes for Delicato Vineyards in 1924. If not

Above: *Half pressed shiraz grapes.*

Top: *Picker's gloves.*

Dense vineyards in the Santa Lucia highlands.

for the Depression, this farmer would never have turned to winemaking. This winery's syrah is excellent value. Limited quantities of the first ultra premium wines—US$40 chardonnay, merlot and syrah—have been released under a new Delicato Monterey Vine Select label. Unrefined and unfiltered, these handcrafted estate wines are from the best vine rows of the San Bernabe vineyard in Monterey.

ISOM RANCH

Established 1997 *Owner* Donald Panoz *Production* 5,000 cases *Vineyard area* 50 acres (20.3 ha)

This and the planned Diablo Grande Vineyards are the only two wineries in the brand new Diablo Grande AVA. The nearest town, Patterson, is 20 miles (32 km) away. San Jose is only 25 miles (40 km) away as the crow flies, but seemingly much further—at 2,000 foot (655 m) the ranch is powered by generator and connected to the outside world by cell phone. Twelve varietals planted include the more modern rhône and italian choices.

GALLO

Established 1933 *Owners* Gallo family *Production* (est) 2,000,000 cases *Vineyard area* est 9,000 acres (3640 ha)

E. & J. Gallo had estimated sales in 1998 of US$1.5 billion and the family-owned firm employs approximately 5,000 people. Famous wines include Tott's, Andre, Ballatore and Eden Roc sparklers, Bartles and James and generics Hearty Burgundy and Golden Rhine. More Gallo wine is consumed than any other brand in the world.

JESSIE'S GROVE

Established 1998 *Owner* Greg Burns *Production* 2,500 cases *Vineyard area* 320 acres (130 ha)

A 32-acre (13 ha) live oak grove was the inspiration for the winery's name. The grove and vines planted in 1890 remain to this day. Part of one small patch of organically farmed estate zinfandel

goes to Turley each year for their "Spenker Vineyards Lodi Zinfandel"—Greg Burns calls his wine from this same patch "Royalty." Burns is crafting world class zinfandel, transforming the original 1830 barn into a winery and tasting room and putting in an equestrian trail.

LUCAS WINERY AND VINEYARD

Established 1978 *Owner* David Lucas *Production* NA *Vineyard area* 20 acres (8.1 ha) old vine, 10 acres (4.1 ha) new plantation

Lucas' old vine zinfandel was one of the first to gain special notice for the region. He is now building a winery that is specifically designed to nurture and coddle zinfandel. He also produces a most quaffable chardonnay.

PHILLIPS VINEYARDS

Established 1984 *Owners* Phillips family *Production* 2,700 cases *Vineyard area* 170 acres (68.8 ha)

Phillips uses outstanding directly varietal old vine carignane, newly planted syrah, along with the usual suspects of cabernet sauvignon, chardonnay, white zinfandel for their wines; also, the not so usual blends such as "Don's special blend/Lodi red," from carignane, syrah and symphony. All are straightforward, honest and ready to drink.

QUADY WINERY

Established 1977 *Owners* Quady family *Production* 15,000 cases *Vineyard area* NA

Electra, Elysium and Essensia are Quady's muscat line. Elysium is a fortified black muscat—rich, deep and syrupy. Essensia is a paler, more delicate and floral fortified orange muscat. Electra is light, fizzy and frothy, modeled after Moscato d'Asti. Quady Starboard port is made of tinta cao, tinta alvarelho and tinta rouriz from Amador, as are the vintage and non-vintage bottlings.

ST AMANT WINERY

Established 1980 *Owners* Richard and Barbara St Amant Spencer *Production* 4,500 cases *Vineyard area* 34 acres (13.8 ha)

This winery produces excellent old vine zinfandel, smoky, deep and low acid barbera, rich and decadent viognier, ripe and briny roussanne and a port-style wine from five port varietals in open top fermenters à la Portugal. In fact, St Amant uses these lagare-like low, wide vats to help integrate the tannins on all their reds. St Amant also bottles a Mohr-Fry Ranch zinfandel. Though low-profile, this is a winery to watch.

Sierra Foothills

Rebecca Chapa and Catherine Fallis MS

This region, off the beaten path and called the "Mother Lode" by some, was initially settled by those seeking gold in "them thar hills" during the the goldrush. When the supply dried up many decided to stay in the area and turned to grape growing. The wine industry of the Sierra Foothills was significantly larger than either Napa or Sonoma at that time, but today the region's industry (about 50 wineries) is small in comparison with other Californian regions.

The Sierra Foothills region covers almost 300 miles (480 km); its range covers 2,600,000 acres (1,522,000 ha). It spans the counties of Yuba, Nevada, El Dorado, Amador, Calaveras, Tuolumne and Mariposa. Rustic country roads wind through pastoral scenes recalling a past era. In 1900, the region had 200 bordellos; now converted, they house restaurants and bed & breakfasts across the region.

French, Spanish and German immigrants arrived in the region, too late for the gold rush and looking for something to do. With European ancestry, winemaking seemed a natural choice. A large percentage of family winemakers were of Italian heritage, with wine an essential ingredient at the dinner table.

Winemaking survived Prohibition largely due to the influence and authority of the archdiocese. The Sierra Foothills region protected bootleggers and supported a large market for sacramental wines. The Sierra Foothills fared better during Prohibition than other north coast regions. Today, a lot of wine producers are retirees. While entrepreneurs exist, their investments are not on the scale of Napa or Sonoma. A few newcomers, like Robert Smirling of Renwood, are stirring interest and providing education and inspiration to raise the bar for Sierra Foothills wine. His newfangled ideas and investments have a few old-timers riled up. Change comes slowly here.

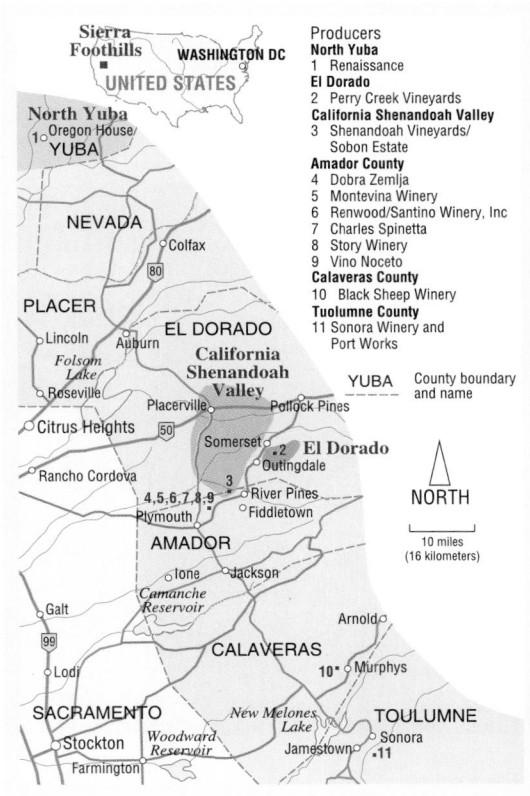

Producers
North Yuba
1 Renaissance
El Dorado
2 Perry Creek Vineyards
California Shenandoah Valley
3 Shenandoah Vineyards/ Sobon Estate
Amador County
4 Dobra Zemlja
5 Montevina Winery
6 Renwood/Santino Winery, Inc
7 Charles Spinetta
8 Story Winery
9 Vino Noceto
Calaveras County
10 Black Sheep Winery
Tuolumne County
11 Sonora Winery and Port Works

Climate

Climate ranges from Region III to Region IV on the Winkler-Amerine heat summation scale and varied exposures and elevations create significant fluctuations over the region. Nights are often cold, even in summertime, with cold air flowing from the peaks of the Sierra Nevada mountains into the vineyards at night. Spring frosts are a danger and make some sites inhospitable for grape growing. Most elevations range from 1000–3000 feet (305–915 m).

The magnificent Sierra Nevada mountains viewed from the eastern side.

The huge expanse of Donner Lake in the Sierra Nevada mountains.

Initially wines were the inexpensive, easy-drinking styles along with dessert wines, port and sherry. Today, investments and pressure from purchasers of fruit have pushed growers to produce more zinfandel, barbera, sangiovese, syrah and Bordelais varieties.

This region's wines tend to be less oaky than those from other regions, and have rich, dense, fruit character. Old vine wines have outstanding concentration and Italian and rhône styles are gaining popularity.

There are four AVAs in the region: North Yuba, El Dorado, California Shenandoah Valley and Fiddletown. In April 2001, the 250-acre (101 ha) Fair Play AVA was approved. Eleven wineries in the region focus on mountain-grown fruit. At elevations of 2,000 to 3,000 feet (610 to 915 m), Fair Play has the highest average elevation of any California appellation.

WINE REGIONS

North Yuba

North Yuba was established as an AVA in 1988. North Yuba is generally synonymous with the Renaissance winery. Renaissance has terraced hillsides planted between 1,700–2,300 feet (520–755 m). The entire region covers 22,400 acres (9065 ha), most unplanted. Annual rainfall is relatively high at 37 inches (14.5 cm) and with well-drained soils, sauvignon blanc and riesling do

very well. The region's vineyard area is now a great deal smaller than it was in the early 1900s. During Prohibition much was replanted to orchards.

RENAISSANCE
Established 1976 *Owners* The Fellowship of Friends *Production* 34,600 cases *Vineyard area* 365 acres (148 ha)

This is the largest mountain vineyard in America with 600 feet (196 m) of vertically contoured terracing and 27 distinct plots. Twelve plots are planted to cabernet sauvignon, which has become winemaker Ben Gideon's specialty. Late harvest sauvignon blanc and newly released viognier and syrah are less rustic and austere. This isolated religious campus, with the majestic snow-capped Sierra Nevadas in the background and the amphitheater of vineyards and winery, is one of the most beautiful settings in the world. Though isolated and hard to find, it is only 75 miles (120 km) from state capital Sacramento. Renaissance created the first circular fermentation room; three concentric rings of stainless steel tanks surround a central work area and the wine flows by gravity into naturally cooled cellars driven into the Sierra bedrock.

El Dorado

El Dorado was granted an AVA in 1983. Most of its 16 wineries are east and southeast of Placerville. All are more than 1,400 feet (460 m) above sea level. Prohibition left this AVA a shell with a mere 12 acres (5 ha) under cultivation, until the Boeger family built their estate. Currently about 416 acres (168 ha) are part of El Dorado County. Cool nights help the grapes retain high acidity, yet the grapes have no problems ripening; soils are mainly granitic, deep and well-drained. El Dorado is a prime site for Italian varieties.

EDMUNDS ST JOHN VINEYARDS
Established 1985 *Owners* Steve Edmunds and Cornelia St John *Production* 4,000 cases *Vineyard area* no estate acreage

Recent investment in El Dorado, in land called "The Higher Ground" will provide fruit to replace supplies from Napa and Sonoma. Only a few dozen cases have come off this site so far. The winery has a long-held reputation for rhône varietals, most notably a Sonoma Valley Durrell Vineyard syrah.

El Dorado production includes a Wylie-Fenaughty syrah: Wylie is near Georgetown and Fenaughty near Placerville; a Matagrano Vineyard sangiovese: Matagrano is near Lotus; and a St Johnson Vineyard pinot grigio. Another popular wine is a "Rocks and Gravel" Cotes-du-Rhône style blend of Sonoma syrah, Mendocino grenache and El Dorado mourvèdre.

PERRY CREEK VINEYARDS
Established 1989 *Owner* Michael Chazen *Production* 30,000 cases Vineyard area 155 acres (62.7 ha)

Zin Man, a Sierra Foothills zinfandel release, is one of the more notable wines produced here. Look for the Wenzell Vineyard mourvèdre, a cabernet franc and the mistelles which are made up of grape must fortified with local Alembic Brandy. Vintage and classic cars, a walk-in humidor and a bed & breakfast complete the offerings of this wine "resort."

California Shenandoah Valley
The Bureau of Alcohol, Tobacco and Firearms has ruled that the "Shenandoah Valley of the West" must be labeled as California Shenandoah Valley in order to prevent confusion with "Shenandoah Valley" on the east coast. The region has 1,300 acres (526 ha) that overlap El Dorado and Amador counties. The AVA was founded in 1983. Snowy winters give way to warm springs, which allow for growth, and cool night air flowing from the Sierra Nevadas preserves the grapes' high acidity. The region's total expanse stretches over 10,000 acres (4047 ha).

SHENANDOAH VINEYARDS/SOBON ESTATE
Established 1977 *Owners* Leon and Shirley Sobon *Production* 38,000 cases *Vineyard area* 167 acres (67.5 ha) plus 146 acres (59 ha) organically farmed

Sobon Estate is the oldest winery in America with continuous production since 1856 and today it is the prestige label for the house. The Sobon family moved here from Los Altos in 1977. Leon's love of zinfandel led him to Amador County, where the old vines, rocky soil and long growing season com-bine to produce some of the most complex zins anywhere in the world. The Sobon Estate's Rocky Top, Cougar Hill and Lubenko bottlings are each reflective of a particular old vine zinfandel site. Shenandoah sangiovese planted on an old lava flow is intensely varietal, with leather and mint rounding out the luscious dark cherry flavors.

Amador County
Amador County is home to Shenandoah Valley and Fiddletown AVAs and is a key source of old vine zinfandel. High annual rainfall enables dry farming. Spring frost is common, but zinfandel fares well because it buds late. Amador County's grape acreage increased during Prohibition by supplying grapes for home winemaking.

DOBRA ZEMLJA
Established 1995 *Owners* Milan and Victoria Matulich *Production* 1,600 cases *Vineyard area* 15 acres (6 ha)

Milan Matulich, from Croatia, says these richly extracted, powerful wines are "domestic wines made with imported people." He found this land with its granitic, sierra series soil to be what he sought. Dobra Zemlja means Good Earth—the winery produces zinfandel and sangiovese (deep, unctuous and smoky); syrah, viognier (rich, dry and elegant) and marsanne (used for blending).

MONTEVINA WINERY
Established 1973 *Owners* Trinchero family *Production* 90,000 cases *Vineyard area* 600 acres (243 ha)

The first post-Prohibition winery in Amador, in 1905, 100 acres (40.5 ha) of zinfandel was planted; cabernet sauvignon in the 1960s. Recent plantings include barbera, sangiovese and syrah. The vineyards were CCOF-certified (California Certified Organic Farmers) for ten years until a recent uncontrollable dust mite problem. Montevina is famous for its affordable barbera and zinfandel, and esoteric bottlings such as aglianico, freisa, refosco and aleatico. The premium Terra d'Oro line is well structured and dense.

RENWOOD/SANTINO WINERY, INC
Established 1979 *Owner* Privately-held corporation *Production* 35,000 cases Renwood; 30,000 cases Santino *Vineyard area* 417 acres (168 ha)

Renwood/Santino's outspoken CEO has elevated the reputation of Amador zinfandel. Quality is high and the grand-père and grandmère bottlings are sought after internationally. Popular Santino bottles of moscato del diavolo and white harvest zinfandel are still produced, but focus is now on the Renwood line of zinfandel, plus rhône and italian varietals. Barbera here gets ultra ripe and

Below: *The luscious beauty of the raw material.*

Bottom: *The grape leaf in fall.*

sheds its characteristic acidity; the d'Agostini bottling follows suit. An Australian basket press and cryoextraction are used to produce a zinfandel icewine that tastes of orange blossoms.

CHARLES SPINETTA

Established 1984 *Owner* Charles Spinetta *Production* 5,000 cases *Vineyard area* 80 acres (32 ha)

Charles is a fifth generation winemaker whose forebears worked with the Gallos and Mondavis, who also originated here in Amador. Old vine zinfandel and barbera are highlights, as is chenin blanc released in three styles.

STORY WINERY

Established 1971 *Owners* Bruce and Jan Tichenor *Production* 2,500 cases *Vineyard area* 42 acres (17 ha)

Some of these hilltop vineyards date back to the early 1900s and include the oldest Mission vines in the state. Vines as thick as trees stretch their thick, gnarly arms as high as five feet (1.6 m). Both a dry and a sweet mission are produced from this block, as well as a zinfandel/mission blend called "miss-zin" but straight zinfandel is of most interest, especially that from Picnic Hill vineyard. Sonora Winery has purchased fruit from this vineyard since 1995 for their old vine zinfandel release. Newer plantings include barbera and sangiovese.

VINO NOCETO

Established 1990 *Owners* Jim and Suzy Gullet *Production* 2,800 cases *Vineyard area* 21 acres (8.5 ha)

Indigenous nut trees on the property inspired the Italian "noce" in the winery's name. Jim Gullet has

A hand picker proudly displays the harvest.

quickly established a reputation for ripe, round, strawberry and cherry-laden sangiovese in an elegant, lightly oaked style, in contrast with most of the North Coast sangioveses whose overt oakiness masks varietal character and charm. Vino Noceto's version sells out within weeks each year. A new riserva sangiovese is made from selected lots with extended aging. In summer, they make frivolo, a sparkling moscato. The winery here custom crushes several batches of fruit for North Coast producer Folio a Deux each year.

Calaveras County

Just south of Amador, this region is about 500 acres (1012 ha) and has seven wineries. Cooler temperatures make this a Region II (Winkler-Amerine scale), which is particularly good for chardonnay and sauvignon blanc— both would thrive on the limestone and volcanic soils.

BLACK SHEEP WINERY

Established 1986 *Owners* Dave and Jan Olson *Production* 3,900 cases *Vineyard area* no estate acreage

Black Sheep is consistently producing small lots of very well-priced quality zinfandel here near the town of Murphys. The showy Amador County zin comes from the Clockspring Vineyard in the Shenandoah Valley; it's aged exclusively in American oak; the Calaveras County zin is aged half in American and half in French oak and has a hint of black pepper. A 100 percent French colombard called True Frogs Lily Pad White is a snob-buster— a slightly sweet white quaffer.

Tuolumne County

SONORA WINERY AND PORT WORKS

Established 1986 *Owners* Private Partnership *Production* 4,000 cases *Vineyard area* 3 acres (1.2 ha)

Originally named "Chateau Garaj," Sonora has established a sound reputation for vintage port produced with the same varietals and techniques as those in the famous Douro Valley in the north of Portugal. They are also known for old vine zinfandels. Newer projects include a vinho tinto, a dry red from three port varietals, which has met with much critical acclaim, and a soon-to-be-released tawny port. Sonora is located halfway between Stockton and the Yosemite National Park.

San Francisco Bay

Catherine Fallis MS

That the very mention of San Francisco conjures up images of the magnificent Golden Gate Bridge, rugged coastline and some of the best wining and dining in North America, was not lost on those who petitioned for this AVA. Awarded in 1999, the BATF's approval of this AVA has met with much controversy from the industry. The area overlaps five counties which border the San Francisco Bay—San Francisco, San Mateo, Santa Clara, Alameda, Contra Costa and parts of Santa Cruz and San Benito. Vineyards are planted on 5,800 of the 1,566,720 acres (634,043 ha) in the region and there are 39 wineries.

Export-minded Wente family of the Livermore Valley led the petition, convinced that buyers would recognize one of the world's favorite tourist attractions on labels, whereas the Livermore Valley appellation would mean little. But is there more substance than just the conviction that the tourist symbols would promote sales?

In fact, the Golden Gate Gap is the only break in North America's western coastal range. This unique opening to the cool Pacific Ocean has far-reaching effects, providing a source of cool air and fog which travels into the sometimes baking Central Valley as the hot air rises. Imagine a clockface, with the gap at the Golden Gate Bridge at the 9:00 position. At the 12:00 to 1:00 position, this marine influence heads up into San Pablo Bay and into Carneros and the Napa Valley. At 2:00 the cool air and fog funnels into Lodi. At 3:00, Contra Costa County is the beneficiary, followed

by the Livermore Valley at 4:00. So, with as much proximity to the cooling source as Napa and with similar daily temperatures, the case seemed assured for this AVA not to be lumped into the vast Central Coast AVA.

In addition to bringing more recognition to Livermore Valley itself, this new AVA is also home to several other appellation "orphans." Producers in the western Livermore Valley whose acreage falls outside of the current delineation previously deferred to the Central Coast AVA. Now they can use the San Francisco Bay appellation. Livermore Valley's Wente and Concannon vineyards are phasing in this use on their labels. The Livermore Valley Winegrowers Association would like to see "San Francisco Bay–Livermore Valley" as the origin noted.

Other appellation orphans include those from Contra Costa County—a lone producer in Martinez, the Conrad Viano Winery—and all of the wines produced from Oakley fruit including those from Bonny Doon, Cline Cellars, Jade Mountain and Rosenblum Cellars.

San Francisco's world famous icon—the Golden Gate Bridge.

CONTRA COSTA COUNTY

Lumped into the larger Central Coast AVA until 1999—and now included in the slightly smaller San Francisco Bay AVA—the century old vineyards that remain in this community are shrinking daily. Pre-Prohibition, more than 6,000 acres (2428 ha) were planted and the area was home to 27 wineries. Today some 1,500 acres (607 ha) are planted to zinfandel, mourvèdre, carignane—"kerrigan" in local dialect—alicante bouchet, chardonnay and palomino, but not a single winery remains.

ALAMEDA County boundary and name

NORTH

10 miles (16 kilometers)

Producers
1 Conrad Viano Winery
2 Cedar Mountain Winery
3 Concannon Vineyards
4 Chouinard Vineyards
5 Fenestra Winery
6 Ivan Tamas Winery
7 Retzlaff Vineyards
8 Wente Vineyards Estate Winery

San Francisco Bay WASHINGTON DC UNITED STATES

Clyde Nichols
Martinez
Concord
Pleasant Hill Clayton
Sparkle
Walnut Creek
Lafayette CONTRA COSTA
Alamo Contra Costa
Moraga
Danville
Tassajara
San Ramon
Altamont
Castro Valley Dublin Ulmar Cayley
Midway
San Francisco Bay 4 miles (6.5 km) Livermore
Pleasanton
ALAMEDA
Livermore Valley
Union City Scotts Corner

REGIONAL DOZEN

QUALITY WINES

Bonny Doon Vineyards Old
    Telegram Mourvèdre
Cline Cellars Live Oak
    Vineyard Zinfandel
Cline Cellars Small Berry
    Mourvèdre
Cline Cellars Bridgehead
    Vineyard Zinfandel
Jacuzzi Reserve Zinfandel
Jade Mountain Mourvèdre
Rosenblum Carla's Reserve
    Zinfandel
Turley Duarte Zinfandel

BEST VALUE WINES

Cotes d'Oakley Vin Blanc, Vin
    Gris and Vin Rouge
Cline Cellars Ancient Vines
    Zinfandel
Rosenblum Chateau La Paws
    Cote du Bone Mourvèdre
Viano Vineyards Zinfandel

Cable cars and Alcatraz prison in the
background.

Contra Costa County is an important source of old vine zinfandel and rhône varietals. Rhône Rangers Bonny Doon, Cline Cellars, Jade Mountain and zinfandel masters Rosenblum and Turley especially favor Oakley fruit. Even Ridge veteran Paul Draper leased a 10 acre (4 ha), century-old mourvèdre plot here for mataro.

Vineyard growth, however, has been threatened—strip malls and housing developments have left very little room for agriculture. Almond trees compete with grapes for the remaining patches of sandy soil. Still, there are many in the area who share an intense sense of loss about this and, thankfully, a revival may be imminent—500 acres (202 ha) of new vineyards have been planted in the last three years.

One of California's finest pre-Prohibition wine regions, Contra Costa County was first planted by Marsh in 1846. Strentzel from Poland, naturalist Muir and educator Swett followed over the next few decades. In the late 1890s Christian Brothers began making wine at their local novitiate. Many Italians settled in the area and with them came fine winemaking traditions. They planted the bulk of what remains today, especially zinfandel and mourvèdre. During Prohibition many survived by selling sacramental wine, but it's only in the last twenty years that the area has been recognized as a source of premium fruit. The Rhône Ranger movement started in Oakley— with old vine mourvèdre— still a highly sought after old vine fruit source.

Vineyards in Oakley are on flatlands at the confluence of the Sacramento and San Joaquin Rivers and have very deep sandy soil. A soft breeze comes through each afternoon and evenings are 10–35°F (2–12°C) cooler than afternoons. Fog sometimes comes up on the water, but it doesn't come out onto the vines. Winter rainfall is usually 10 inches (25 cm) providing ideal conditions.

Vines and wines

Mourvèdre is close to a century old here and finds particular success. It has to struggle to ripen and produces a small crop. Carignane too, maintains acidity, allowing its particular varietal character to come through.

Old vines of all types are common and give dense, richly fruited wines. Lower end blends are reminiscent of days when wine was made of field blends mixed with water. The premium "zins" and mourvèdre's represent the other extreme, fashioned into super extracted, lavishly oaked and expensive wines. Cline's Small Berry Mourvèdre has a distinctive chocolate mint note, which, with its almost port-like alcohol, makes it a wonderful wine to enjoy after dinner. All but the low end wines have marked longevity.

Most vines are gnarly, dry farmed and have taken 75–120 years of head-pruning. Light sandy soil allows for deep root penetration and facilitates drainage. Crops are small, with an average of 1.5 tons per acre (3.75 t per ha). Fruit is hand harvested, with alicante bouchet proving especially challenging. With its big leaves and small bunches these patches are the pickers' least favorite.

Producers

CLINE CELLARS

Established 1982 *Owners* Cline family *Production* 200,000 cases *Vineyard area* 170 acres (68.8 ha)

Following in the footsteps of his maternal grandfather Valeriano Jacuzzi (of pump and spa fame) Fred Cline founded Cline Cellars at the old Fripo Winery near Oakley. With long-term grower contracts going back three generations and a rich family history in the area, he was soon a leading force in the community. He even helped to establish the local Chamber of Commerce. For a variety of reasons Fred relocated the winery to Carneros, where, in 1986, his brother Matt joined as winemaker. Cline Cellars is renowned today for their Italian-inspired old vine Contra Costa zinfandels and mourvèdres, as well as for Carneros estate marsanne, roussanne and syrah.

ROSENBLUM CELLARS

Established 1973 *Owners* Kent and Kathy Rosenblum *Production* 60,000 cases *Vineyard area* no estate vineyards

The Rosenblums started making wine at home and now make wine out of a warehouse near Oakland, with fruit from Ukiah to Santa Barbara. Two of their four signature zins come from vineyards in

Oakley—Carla's and Continente; Henry's is from Napa Valley and Maggie's is from Sonoma. The wines have deliberately soft tannins and take full advantage of the 25 percent allowable blending, adding zin, cabernet sauvignon, or carignane.

CONRAD VIANO WINERY

Established 1888 *Owners* Viano family *Production* 3,500cases *Vineyard area* 125 acres (50.6 ha)

Located in Martinez, just at the mouth of San Pablo Bay where it narrows into the Carquinez Straits, this fourth generation family winery produces century old vine zinfandel and white and red blends reminiscent of their Italian ancestors. Their Hillside White is a blend of French colombard, muscat and chenin blanc and the Hillside Red is zinfandel and gamay. Show up at their rustic tasting bar and you are in for a treat; it's as entertaining as the tasting glass—a tumbler!

LIVERMORE VALLEY

The Livermore Valley AVA demarcates a 10 x 15 mile (16 x 24 km) transverse valley nestled into the base of San Francisco Bay's coastal ranges. This and the similar west to east openings at Santa Barbara are the only two transverse coastal valleys in the state. Fog and wind—the major climatic influences—funnels in daily across the valley from the Golden Gate Gap into Central Valley. Proximity to Silicon Valley, only 30 miles (48 km) away and San Francisco, only 40 miles (64 km) has provided a constant battleground between developers and growers.

Unlike San Jose, whose fate was loss of vineyards, housing developers here have actually stimulated the growth of vineyards. In a unique wine country model developers must contribute a percentage of land to permanent agriculture and make a donation to a land trust for each home that they want to build.

The valley is unique too in its unusual combination of Ph. D.s and cowboys. The Lawrence Livermore Lab employs hundreds of local science minded folk, many of whom moonlight as winemakers in a search of a creative outlet.

Current delineation of the AVA covers 96,000 acres (38,850 ha), of which 5,000 (2023 ha) are planted to vines today. In 1998 only 2,000 acres (809 ha) were planted to vines. Growth will cap at 8,000 acres (3238 ha) at the first phase of current plan build out. Varieties planted include the famous d'Yquem-cutting sauvignon blanc and

Victorian architecture features in these houses facing Alamo square, San Francisco.

sémillon, Wente clone chardonnay, cabernet sauvignon and the first varietally labeled petite sirah. Secondary varietals include malvasia bianca, pinot gris, merlot and zinfandel. New plantings are primarily syrah and sangiovese. More than 650,000 cases are produced using local fruit, with Concannon, Ivan Tamas and Wente leading in volume. Local grape supply cannot fulfil the demand from local wineries. Many producers source fruit from Monterey and Lodi and some of the smaller producers form cooperatives with larger local and non-local wineries for better buying power. The cost per acre is US$30,000–50,000 for unplanted vineyard land, which is a bargain in comparison with prices in the North Coast.

History

California's wine pioneers discovered the rocky, well-drained soil and ideal climate of the Livermore Valley in the 1800s just when Wells Fargo gold trains, horse-runners and bandits were running through the area.

Over 100 years ago the Wente's, Concannon's and others started making wine here. Today these families are still the leaders of the Livermore Valley. Wente selected a Montpellier clone originating in Burgundy's Corton-Charlemagne and the only clone in California at that time, from Gehr's vineyard in Pleasanton. This Wente clone produced over one third of all Californian chardonnay even in the 1960s. Wetmore of Cresta Blanca vineyard brought sémillon and sauvignon blanc cuttings back from Chateau d'Yquem in Bordeaux. His wines won gold medals in the Paris Exposition of 1889. This notoriety brought a second gold rush to California, especially to the Livermore Valley.

By 1900 more than 20 wineries and 20,000 acres (80,940 ha) were in production. The few that survived the first challenge of phylloxera faced a second blow—Prohibition. A few survived selling sacramental wine and shipping fruit to the east coast for home winemaking.

Landscape and climate

The Livermore Valley is a west to east valley that draws in the cool marine layer from the nearby Golden Gate Gap (mirroring the Napa and Sonoma Valleys with the map sideways). Morning fog gives way to warm and sometimes baking hot afternoon sun. The heat stays for about four to five hours, but from these five to ten days each year, the average moves upwards. Unlike the North Coast, however, cool marine breezes bring the temperature down dramatically. The evenings are cool to cold, especially in July. Cooler evening temperatures in summer allow grapes to retain high natural acidity. Most of the Livermore Valley is classified as Region III according to the Winkler-Amerine system, though locals quip that "we are region II-and-a-half."

With deep gravelly sedimentary soil the area has been historically compared to the Graves region of Bordeaux—primarily gravel with shale ridges in the western canyons. Pockets of heavy clay, red clay and loam and rock and loam are scattered throughout the valley floor.

Vines and wines

Cabernet sauvignon is the signature red wine, with petite sirah a close second. The bordeaux white varietals of sémillon and sauvignon blanc represent the leading whites. In the cooler, foggier zones growers plant chardonnay and merlot. Petite sirah has performed well here. New plantings of syrah and pinot gris show early promise.

Chardonnay is richer and of higher alcohol than those from Sonoma and less markedly oaked than those of Napa. Pear and melons are better descriptors than the guava and pineapple of Arroyo Seco in Monterey. The Wente clone gives characteristics of apples, peaches and bananas. Cabernet sauvignon is beautifully round with classic dark berry fruit and balanced acidity. Lavishly oaked examples are few and far between, even at the super premium level. Is it *terroir* or technique? Mirassou believes rocky soils and long hang time produce wines with earlier accessibility than those from the North Coast.

Gravelly soil provides excellent drainage and heat retention into the cooler evening. Many growers are transitioning from the Californian sprawl to a divided canopy. Permanent overhead irrigation systems were invented here and are common. Many vineyards are farmed organically, but few mention this on their labels. Growers are constantly on guard to prevent the return of phylloxera to the area.

Livermore Valley growers were the first in the nation to machine harvest and to field crush and press. Large scale night harvesting is common. Many winemakers draw on fruit sources outside of the AVA, especially from Monterey, Lodi and the Santa Cruz Mountains. There is intense competition for local fruit from all points, most notably from the North Coast.

Vinification styles vary dramatically. Overall, restraint is the word of the day. More sophisticated than ever before, this unusual mix of hobbyists and fifth generation wine growers are very confident. Experimentation with techniques, tanks, yeast strains, is ongoing and information is accessible to anyone who asks. The cooperative spirit is alive and well, especially from big brother Wente. Styles run the gamut from whites made in a squeaky clean mass production style to reds made in small lots with extended maceration, press fractions and bottled unfiltered. Little mention is made of native yeast fermentations. Oak use varies. The smaller producers on a shoestring budget use American barrels and French innerstaves.

Producers

CEDAR MOUNTAIN WINERY
Established 1990 *Owners* Earl and Linda Ault *Production* 4,000 cases *Vineyard area* 17 acres (6.8 ha)

Earl and Linda Ault represent two of the valley's Ph. D.s. Linda quips "It doesn't take a rocket scientist to make wine, but it helps." Cedar Mountain Winery's signature wine is cabernet sauvignon, which ages beautifully and has consistently been awarded gold medals. While Cabernet sauvignon may have put Cedar Mountain on the map, they have also garnered national accolades for port wines such as Cabernet Royale, made from their estate.

The valley's ripened offerings.

CONCANNON VINEYARDS

Established 1883 *Owners* Wente (50%), Jim Concannon
and other limited partners (50%) *Production* 85,000 cases
Vineyard area 220 acres (89 ha)

Irish immigrant James Concannon established
Concannon in the 1800s. If Concannon were
"frenchified" would they be as famous as the wines
of Haut Brion? Who knows, but in the meantime
look to this producer for world class sauvignon
blanc, chardonnay, petite sirah—they were the
first winery to produce it varietally—and cabernet
sauvignon. Winemaker Tom Lane, a former
botanist, is developing a line of rhône varietals.

CHOUINARD VINEYARDS (CURRENTLY OUTSIDE THE LV AVA)

Established 1985 *Owners* George and Caroline Chouinard
Production 5,500 cases *Vineyard area* 6.5 acres (2.6 ha)

During his career as an architect, George designed
several wineries. The Chouinards were drawn to
this area because of its similarities to the climate
of the Napa Valley without the price tag. Their
isolated 100 acre (40.4 ha) estate perched at the
top of the Walpert Ridge is far removed from
"civilization." Picnics and hiking are encouraged,
as is sampling the deeply flavored, elegant, estate
chardonnay and cabernet sauvignon.

FENESTRA WINERY

Established 1980 *Owners* Lanny and Fran Repogle
Production 7,500 cases *Vineyard area* 9.5 acres (3.8 ha)

The winery has roots in the 1800s, when it was
the famous Ruby Hill winery. In 1980, the property
housed the George True Winery. And a red blend,
"True Red" is so named in his memory. Fenestra
exports a sémillon/chardonnay blend and a smoky
Lodi syrah to England. The Lodi syrah is an
undiscovered bargain on these shores. Lanny likes
to experiment (after teaching chemistry for 30
years) and likes to think of each wine as an individual, or perhaps as a really good student.

IVAN TAMAS WINERY

Established 1984 *Owners* Ivan Tamas Fuezy, Steven
Mirassou Sr. & Jr. *Production* 60,000 cases *Vineyard area*
7 acres (2.8 ha)

Steven Mirassou Jr is sixth generation of one of
America's oldest winemaking family. He and partners Fuezy and Steve Sr produce a full line of
wines at everyday prices. They are one of the largest producers of pinot grigio in the state, with
fruit sourced from Arroyo Seco in Monterey. Their
Livermore terrain and sangiovese are notable, as is
their reserve line of Livermore chardonnay and

*Part of the processing—running off newly
pressed shiraz grapes.*

cabernet sauvignon. Steve Jr just launched a new
ultra premium cabernet sauvignon from estate fruit
under the name of Steven Kent. Despite its elegant,
reserved, softly oaked style, the first release of this
US$45 red has met with critical acclaim.

RETZLAFF VINEYARDS

Established 1979 *Owners* Robert and Gloria Retzlaff
Taylor *Production* 3,000 cases *Vineyard area* 14 acres
(5.6 ha)

After selling their crop to Wente for several years
the Taylors started their own winery. Though they
believe this is cab country, they also produce merlot,
zin, chardonnay and sauvignon blanc. Their unique
"lab sample" label perhaps was inspired by Robert's
background in chemistry—yes, he is a Ph. D. Their
motto: "Dinner is the best time of day" is especially
true if their wine is on the table.

WENTE VINEYARDS ESTATE WINERY

Established 1883 *Owners* Wente family *Production*
300,000 cases *Vineyard area* 2000 acres (809 ha)

Certainly the "Robert Mondavi" of Livermore
Valley, the Wente family is integrally part of the
region. Carolyn Wente petitioned for the AVA
status. The Wente's have an undying commitment
to their area and to quality, that started over 100
years ago. Today over 80 percent of California's
sauvignon blanc, sémillon and chardonnay originates from the Wente (and former Cresta Blanca)
clones. Concentrations are especially high in the
North Coast. The family sells 100,000 cases domestically; the remaining 200,000 are sold in 150
countries. Recently the family purchased the famous
Cresta Blanca Winery, a state historic landmark
and restored it and its original sandstone caves as a
sparkling wine facility.

REGIONAL BEST

Cedar Mountain Blanches
  Vineyard Cabernet Sauvignon
Chouinard Chardonnay
Concannon Petite Sirah
Elliston Pinot Gris
Fenestra Sémillon
Garre Grenache
Ivan Tamas Trebbiano
Retzlaff Cabernet Sauvignon
Stony Ridge Malvasia Bianca
Wente Crane Ridge Reserve
  Merlot

North Central Coast

Catherine Fallis MS

California's North Central Coast begins at San Francisco Bay and ends north of Paso Robles in Monterey. The section covers the Santa Cruz Mountains and the adjacent Santa Clara Valley wine regions, the land between the Pacific Ocean and the Diablo Ranges just south of San Francisco which includes San Mateo, Santa Cruz, Santa Clara and parts of San Benito counties.

Vineyards in the remote Santa Cruz Mountains, just as in the metropolis of San Jose, and Silicon Valley—are few and far between. Wineries, however, abound. Santa Cruz boasts 43 and Santa Clara 21. Winemakers use the abundant vineyards of Monterey as their primary source of fruit.

SANTA CLARA VALLEY

This is "the valley," the only valley to the locals, who live encapsulated in their unique environment. Santa Clara Valley is the Silicon Valley—no vineyards (except for a few patches to the south near "garlic capital" Gilroy in the San Ysidro AVA)—every square inch of land serves the techmasters.

The Santa Clara AVA covers 332,800 acres (134,680 ha), including San Ysidro sub-AVA at 2,340 acres (947 ha) and part of Pacheco Pass AVA, a small valley that overlaps Santa Clara and San Benito counties. Vine area is small—an estimated 200 acres (81 ha), most of this in San Ysidro clustered in the southeast near Gilroy and inland and north of the mouth of Monterey Bay.

The powerful marine influence, drawn in along the Pajaro River, cools the warm plains. This area is known as the Hecker Pass, after the 152 Highway and you will find traces of another era, much like a deserted Highway 29 in Napa Valley, with boarded-up houses and abandoned vineyards.

One notable exception is the inviting tourist-oriented Zanger Casa de Fruta, which farms more than grapes. Sarah's Vineyard, famous for chardonnay is here, and the grenache for Bonny Doon's Clos de Gilroy is farmed nearby. The largest wineries in the valley are Mirassou and

J. Lohr—showplaces housing offices rather than functioning wineries; grape growing and winemaking activities take place in Monterey or in the Livermore Valley.

History

The Santa Clara Wine Growers Association states proudly that Santa Clara Valley is "the oldest continuously producing region in the state," although the landscape has changed dramatically over time. Franciscan friars planted at the Mission Santa Clara de Asis in 1777 and provided vine cuttings to other locals, many of whom were French immigrants. By the 1830s the Santa Clara Valley, with its bustling village of San Jose, was the hub of the California wine industry. To the north, in San Mateo County, Emmet Rixford planted "La Questa Vineyards" at Woodside in the late 1800s. His cabernet sauvignons were a benchmark for the era and are still referred to. Three acres (1.2 ha) of the original vineyards are still farmed by the Mullen family.

A Frenchman, Antoine Delmas, brought over cuttings to replace the mission vines. Unfortunately this spread phylloxera and by the 1890s many of the vineyards were destroyed. The remaining vineyards were grafted over to resistant American rootstock brought back from France and by the early 1900s there were more than 100 wineries and 8,500 acres (3,440 ha) of vines.

After Prohibition, when many survived by selling sacramental wine or grapes to home winemakers, there were still 61 wineries in business. One of the most historic and beautiful is the Paul Masson Mountain Winery in the Santa Cruz Mountain foothills near Saratoga. This winery hosted a "Music in the Vineyards" concert series for several decades. Like fellow winemaking colleagues, they have now relocated to Monterey. Governor Leland Stanford's old cellar is now a bank in the Stanford shopping center and this beautiful rural environment has become a congested metropolis in just two decades.

Landscape and climate

Without a topographical map, the area looks like a mirror image, if slightly thinner, of the jagged demarcation of Santa Cruz Mountains AVA.

Producers
1 Cooper-Garrod Vineyards
2 J. Lohr Winery
3 Mirassou Vineyards and Champagne Cellars
4 Bonny Doon Vineyard
5 Clos Tita
6 David Bruce Winery
7 Kathryn Kennedy Winery
8 Mt Eden Vineyards
9 Ridge Vineyards
10 Savannah-Chanel Vineyards

A few boutique wineries are tucked into the east-facing inland foothills; these few fiercely independent souls petitioned for AVA status in the early 1990s. To the south, the San Ysidro AVA stands as another bastion of independence.

Vines and wines

These hardy and fiercely independent winemakers have very little production with which to make themselves known (which makes commenting on Santa Clara wine styles or wine growing and wine-making virtually impossible). Only a handful are distributed outside the borders but those tasted are a testament to their unique origin, and are truly reflective of distinct philosophies. These winemakers could well be saying "beancounters and marketers be off with you, we are making wines to please ourselves."

Producers

COOPER-GARROD VINEYARDS

Established 1994 *Owners* Cooper and Garrod families *Production* 3,000 cases *Vineyard area* 21 acres (8.5 ha)

The Garrod family purchased land from the Mount Eden Orchard and Vineyard Company in 1893. Following his great-grandfather's footsteps, Jan Garrod began replanting the estate vineyards in the 1980s. Today these unirrigated hillside vineyards are planted to chardonnay, cabernet sauvignon and cabernet franc, each of which are vinted and bottled separately.

J. LOHR WINERY

Established 1974 *Owner* Jerry Lohr *Production* 550,000 cases *Vineyard area* 1,735 acres (702 ha)

Once a research scientist at NASA, while developing land and building custom homes in Santa Clara, Santa Cruz and Monterey, Jerry Lohr was investigating the best grape-growing regions of California. He planted in Monterey, but established his winery in San Jose. Winemaker Jeff Meier crafts a single vineyard, estates, "Cypress," and a de-alcoholized line, Ariel. Bestsellers include a fairly dry "Bay Mist" riesling and a valdiguie, formerly known as gamay. Paso Robles syrah shows promise.

MIRASSOU VINEYARDS AND CHAMPAGNE CELLARS

Established 1854 *Owners* Jim, Daniel and Peter Mirassou *Production* 105,000 cases *Vineyard area* 15 acres (6.1 ha) in Santa Clara; 800 acres (324 ha) in Monterey

America's oldest winemaking family is based here in San Jose, with cellars for sparkling wine and still wine barrel aging at the historic novitiate in nearby Los Gatos. The Mirassous were one of the first to plant in Monterey in 1961—their major vineyard area today. Fifth-generation brothers Jim, Daniel and Peter, with sixth-generation Heather, David and Mark oversee the winery in Santa Clara as well as the Mission and San Vincente vineyards in Monterey. The family is credited with innovations such as controlled irrigation, mechanical harvesting and crushing, the mobile vineyard press and night harvesting. Their pinot blanc is consistently ranked as one of California's finest.

Grapes ripening in the sunshine.

SANTA CRUZ MOUNTAINS

Hippies and hitchhikers share granola and clove cigarettes with suddenly rich computer fiends. As if in a Berkeley that time forgot, spirituality, hemp and incense reign supreme in this isolated corner of the world, where the softer, gentler atmosphere suits the highly creative and fuels the fires of the iconoclastic. Getting here is an effort. This dizzying mountain terrain is not for the lazy. You will suffer badly in anything but a low-slung, sleek, growling sports car; your high-center-of-gravity 4WD will mark you as fair game as you try to maneuver it through these vertiginous and sometimes excruciatingly narrow passes.

The Santa Cruz Mountains play host, albeit unwillingly, to America's premier mountain vineyard area. In 1981, AVA status—the first based on geophysical and climatic factors—was granted. Elevation contour lines at 400 feet (122 m) in the west and 400–800 feet (122–244 m) along the eastern face mark the borders and surround the Santa Cruz Mountain range from Half Moon Bay in the north, to Mt Madonna near Watsonville in the south.

The 350,000 acre (141,640 ha) AVA covers parts of three counties, San Mateo, Santa Cruz and Santa Clara. Locals estimate that about 750 acres (304 ha) are under vine, mostly in terraces on the steep hillsides above the fog line at daybreak. Sub-AVA Ben Lomond Mountain covers 38,400 acres (15,540 ha) northwest of Santa Cruz, 70 acres (28 ha) of which are planted to vines. Vineyard

expansion is unlikely. Pierce's disease continues its devastation through the area and the struggle for urban development is ongoing. Total production is just under 500,000 cases per year. Grape tonnage in 1998 was reported to have a value of US $4,807,000.

History

The Santa Cruz Mountains were first recognized as a premium wine-producing region in the late 1800s. Many local wines won awards throughout the century at events such as the San Francisco and Paris exhibitions. Much later, in the famous 1976 Paris challenge of California vs. France, two of the 11 wines chosen to represent California's best were local. "Count" Haraszthy, prominent in California winemaking, planted his "San Mateo County" vineyard here at the southern tip of the San Andreas Lake in 1854, but 40 wineries and as many as 4,000 acres (1,418 ha) of vines barely survived Prohibition. Many original vineyards, which grew alongside grain, corn, potatoes, beans and sugarbeets, are now planted with Christmas trees. One of the oldest and largest Santa Cruz wineries, Martinelli, founded in 1868 in Watsonville, today produces only apple cider and apple juice. Luckily, visionary Martin Ray, who had grown up in the Mount Eden foothills, purchased the Paul Masson Champagne Company right after Prohibition and started producing 100 percent varietal table wines. His pinot noir was notable and made international news. Ray brought partners in during the 1960s in an effort to expand. They, in turn, began to take over his vineyards, renaming the estate Mount Eden Vineyards in 1972. Martin Ray is credited with creating the boutique winery model. Today's visionaries include Jeffrey and Eleanor Patterson, owners of Mount Eden Vineyards, Paul Draper of Ridge Vineyards, Kathryn Kennedy and Randall Grahm of Bonny Doon.

Landscape and climate

AVA borders are defined according to elevation contour lines. Many vineyards are as high as 2,000 feet (610 m) with spectacular views of San Francisco and San Jose. Steep-sloping vineyards face in all directions with the west always cooler

Fall paints the leaves in autumnal beauty.

than the low-lying inland eastern side. Constant ocean breezes and maritime fog has facilitated the spread of Pierce's disease, which has all but ravaged these coastal vineyards. Up into the ridges, especially to the east, the climate cools down substantially. Most of the AVA is classified I on the Winkler-Amerine heat summation scale. The soils vary from sandy to heavy clay to barren rocky shale. Shallow soil and the cool climate restrict yields to about 2 tons per acre (5 t per ha).

Vines and wines

One of America's cooler climate wine-growing regions, the area's reputation rests on its pinot noir and more recently its chardonnay. The long-lived intense, brooding and tarry cabernet sauvignons of Kathryn Kennedy, Ridge Vineyards and Mt Eden, however, are stealing the spotlight.

Randall Grahm resists what he calls the ever-monotonous and monochromatic chardonnay and cabernet sauvignon. He first planted pinot noir here at the coastal vineyards of Bonny Doon. Results were not impressive so the young idealist switched to rhône, italian types and some obscure varietals. His vineyards were one of the first to fall victim to Pierce's disease and he now sources fruit from Monterey (as do most producers), Washington State, Spain, France, Contra Costa, and Germany.

The average growing season is 300 days; some years, harvest continues well after Thanksgiving. The challenge is great in this cool, rugged terrain and individual styles vary greatly, but all agree that the fruit, not the winemaker, is responsible for greatness. In the 1960s, the industry learned about the winery; in the 1990s the vineyard was the focus. Most vinification is typical of California approaches, but a few small producers still release rustic reds with untamed mountain tannins.

Producers

BONNY DOON VINEYARD

Established 1983 *Owners* Grahm family *Production* 190,000 cases *Vineyard area* 70 acres (28.3 ha) bearing, 70 acres (28.3 ha) newly planted in Monterey

Iconoclast and self-proclaimed "tortured flower child" Randall Grahm has single-handedly brought more attention to the Santa Cruz Mountains than anyone else. His newsletter reaches far-flung corners of the world; there are doon-heads everywhere! Luckily, his production is vast enough to reach the legions of devoted fans. His determination comes in the face of great challenges: Pierce's

disease, which caused total devastation of vineyards at Bonny Doon, and an ill-fated winery plan for Pleasanton in the Livermore Valley. He jokes about his current "winery," a former granola factory in an outlying area of Santa Cruz on the "wrong" side of the tracks. The tasting room up at Bonny Doon remains and is well worth the drive. Look forward to the next chapter about life on Planet Doon, where, Grahm says, living is all about taking chances.

CLOS TITA

Established 1997 *Owner* Dr David Estrada *Production* 400 cases *Vineyard area* 1 acre (0.4 ha)

For David and his wife Brita winemaking is a relaxing hobby. Their tiny vineyard surrounds their mountain-top home above the Scott's Valley on the Kennedy Ridge. David's passion for French wines has led to his releases of a brambly estate pinot noir, an unusual, petrolly chardonnay/viognier blend—he has 50 vines of viognier—and a tarry, elegant cabernet sauvignon made with grapes from Peter Martin Ray. Though production is tiny, the wines have made their way into the Enoteca chain in Tokyo and to a handful of local restaurants and wine shops. The name comes from their passion for Burgundy "Clos" and Brita's nickname "Tita."

DAVID BRUCE WINERY

Established 1964 *Owner* David Bruce *Production* 40,000 cases *Vineyard area* 20 acres (8.1 ha)

Former dermatologist David Bruce was one of the first in his profession to support wine as a healthful beverage. His "Ten Little Known Medical Facts

Above: *Late-harvest grapes shrivel and sweeten on the vines.*

Top: *The russet tones of these vine leaves herald the impending fall harvest.*

REGIONAL BEST

Bonny Doon Vineyards Le
   Cigare Volante California
Clos Tita Estate Pinot Noir
Kathryn Kennedy Lateral
Kathryn Kennedy Maridon
   Vineyard Syrah
Kathryn Kennedy Meritage
Mt Eden Reserve Cabernet
   Sauvignon
Ridge Montebello Cabernet
   Sauvignon
Thunder Mountain Cabernet
   Sauvignon

about Wine that You Should Know," revised 1991, includes: "Bad old age can be reversed by a glass of wine," and "Liver disease is decreasing during a period of increasing wine consumption and decreasing spirits consumption." His inky colored, full-bodied, decadently oaked pinot noirs have had a following for years. His petite sirah is so densely colored it is almost black. His wines also manage to avoid the gripping rustic mountain tannins.

KATHRYN KENNEDY WINERY

Established 1973 *Owner* Kathryn Kennedy *Production* 3,800 cases *Vineyard area* 8 acres (3.2 ha)

After viticultural courses at UC Davis, Kathryn planted own-rooted cabernet sauvignon on inland rolling foothills near Saratoga, with its moderate marine influence. This small scale encourages intense involvement with all aspects of production—pruning by hand and bottling unfiltered. In 1981, Kathryn's youngest son, Marty Mathis, became winemaker. In addition to long-time cult-status cabernet sauvignon and Lateral, a blend of cabernet franc and merlot, recent releases include a richly structured Maridon Vineyard syrah and a crisp, dry chenin blanc/viognier blend, "Shhh."

MT EDEN VINEYARDS

Established 1972 *Owners* Jeffrey and Eleanor Patterson (major shareholders) *Production* 15,000 cases *Vineyard area* 42 acres (17 ha)

Martin Ray developed this former Paul Masson property into a dramatic ridgetop wine estate in

Hand-picked grapes in California.

the 1940s and 1950s. Partners came in to facilitate the planned expansion in the early 1960s and proceeded to take over; in 1972 they formed Mt Eden. Patterson, president in 1993, crafts two styles of chardonnay: a French-style estate version that fools burgundy fans with its nutty, erotic notes, and the much fruitier, more forward California style "MacGregor Vineyard" bottling. The estate cabernet is deeply colored, lusciously fruited and velvety. Mt Eden wines are notable for their longevity. The Pattersons promote the concept of wine enjoyment at the table through photo and poetry exhibitions.

RIDGE VINEYARDS

Established 1959 *Owner* A. Otsuka *Production* 55,000 cases *Vineyard area* 60 acres (24.3 ha)

Paul Draper, CEO, winemaker, famous internationally, was named *Decanter*'s Man of the Year 2000. His wines are very popular with the British trade, notably Hugh Johnson, Harry Waugh and Jancis Robinson, particularly his Montebello cabernet sauvignon—estate-grown, old-vine fruit that is very restrained early in its life. Americans, according to Draper, prefer the showier, more opulent, corporal zinfandels. Draper is a perfectionist; wine from each plot in this fractured limestone ridge is identified and tasted before blending. Aside from the estate Montebello Cabernet Sauvignon and a series of North and Central Coast zinfandels, releases include an alicante, chardonnay, grenache, mataro, petite sirah and syrah.

SAVANNAH-CHANEL VINEYARDS

Established 1996 *Owners* Michael and Kellie Ballard *Production* 4,800 cases *Vineyard area* 14 acres (5.7 ha), 50 acres (20.2 ha) in Carmel Valley

Frenchman Pierre Pourroy settled in the eastern foothills outside Saratoga in 1892 and named his estate Monmartre, misspelling his hometown near Paris. After Prohibition the winery became known as the Congress Springs Winery. When the Ballards purchased the estate and winery, with old-vine zinfandel and cabernet franc blocks dating from the early 1900s, they renamed it after their daughters Savannah and Chanel. The 3-acre (1.2-ha) cabernet franc block is believed to be the oldest in the state. The Mt Eden Clone chardonnay is richly textured, bright and most widely available. Tiny lots of zinfandel, carignane, cabernet franc are intensely spicy and flavorful; new Central Coast pinot blanc, pinot noir and zinfandels are promising.

Monterey County

Catherine Fallis MS

A world-class jazz festival, the Laguna Seca speedway and international golf tournaments draw visitors to the Monterey Peninsula as does the wild and untamed coastal beauty, but it won't be long before wine steals the spotlight. Only 100 miles (160 km) from San Francisco, and just one hour from the heart of Silicon Valley, this sophisticated yet cozy cluster of oceanfront villages is one of America's favorite vacation spots. Big Sur, Carmel, Pebble Beach, Spanish Bay, Pacific Grove and, in downtown Monterey, Cannery Row are the hot spots for tourists and locals alike. Venture inland, though, to an as yet undiscovered destination—Monterey's glorious wine country.

Franciscan friars planted the first vines here at Soledad Mission in the 1800s. In 1915 Francis Will Silvear planted muscat and thompson seedless, then, after Prohibition, chardonnay and pinot noir, with the idea of producing sparkling wine at what is now Chalone Vineyards. The full potential of the region was widely recognized in the 1950s and 1960s, after a 1944 UC Davis study conducted by Professor A. J. Winkler and Maynard A. Amerine. They reported a climatic range here from low Region I near Monterey Bay to low Region III at King City—comparable with Napa, Sonoma, Burgundy and Bordeaux. The report came at a time when demand for table wine was increasing as steadily as the demand for new housing developments, especially in the Livermore and Santa Clara valleys. Wente, Paul Masson, Mirassou, and J. Lohr initially sought land for vineyards here.

California coastal living is far different from what one might imagine. Fleece and fireplaces, hot cocoa and wool are more appropriate than hot little bikinis and ice-cold beer. The Monterey Peninsula coastline is cool, humid and foggy most of the year, especially in the morning. The sun is shining brightly, however, about 10 miles (16 km) inland. This is the pot of gold at the end of the rainbow; warm sun soaks the chill out of your bones. This is Steinbeck country. All you see for miles are rows of grape vines. You may encounter the occasional horseman on this former cattle-grazing land. And you certainly will have the chance to try some of the best Mexican food on the planet—Monterey is a former Mexican territory and many vineyard crews are second- and third-generation workers. English is a second language in the towns and villages. What you won't see quite yet are the bells and whistles of an established wine country. Apart from the sophisticated Carmel Valley, restaurants and accommodations are few and far between, as are tasting rooms and gift shops.

The wine industry here is concentrated in the Monterey and San Benito counties primarily where the vast Salinas Valley draws the marine influence into the warmer inland. A few scattered AVAs have found remote sites at cooler, high elevations where grapes struggle to ripen at all, but when they do, they have unique qualities and a distinct signature of their origin.

Well-tended vineyards in the Carmel Valley.

Producers
1 Bernardus Winery
2 Calera
3 Chalone
4 Cloninger
5 Galante Vineyards
6 Hahn Estates/Smith & Hook Winery
7 Heller Estate/Durney Vineyards
8 Joullian
9 Lockwood
10 Morgan
11 Paraiso Springs Vineyards
12 Robert Talbott Vineyards

Monterey and surrounding areas fall under the larger North Central Coast AVA. Monterey County ends just 30 miles (48 km) north of Paso Robles, the beginning of the South Central Coast.

The six AVAs of San Benito County are San Benito; Paicines; Cienega Valley and its sub-appellation, Lime Kiln Valley; Mount Harlan; and Pacheco Pass, a small valley overlapping with Santa Clara County. Mount Harlan is the county's most relevant AVA, home of Josh Jensens' world-famous Claera Winery, and Pietra Santa, Enz, De Rose, and Flint wineries. The seven AVAs of Monterey County are Monterey (which is geographically located in the Salinas Valley) and its four sub-AVAs of Arroyo Seco, Hames Valley, San Lucas, and the Santa Lucia Highlands, plus Chalone and Carmel Valley.

Monterey County was sixth of the top ten counties in California in 1998 with wine grape coverage at 134,699 acres (54,5112 ha). Demarcated acreage includes Monterey AVA 35,758 acres (14,470 ha), which confusingly does not include figures for Arroyo Seco 18,240 acres (7,380 ha); Hames Valley 10,240 acres (4,144 ha); San Lucas 33,920 acres (13,470 ha); and Santa Lucia High-

lands 22,000 acres (8,900 ha). Carmel Valley wine grape cultivation is a substantial 19,200 acres (7,770 ha); Chalone 8,540 acres (3,456 ha). San Benito County includes the San Benito AVA at 45,000 acres (18,211 ha) (which includes sub-AVAs Cienega Valley, its sub-AVA Lime Kiln Valley and Paicines); Pacheco Pass at 3,200 acres (1,295 ha) and Mount Harlan at 7,440 acres (3,010 ha).

Monterey County was fourth in the US top ten in 1998 for grape sales revenue, after Sonoma, San Joaquin and Napa at US$168,970,808. Monterey enjoys particular success with riesling, chardonnay, pinot blanc, cabernet sauvignon, pinot noir and syrah. Chardonnay is the most widely planted, at 14,555 acres (5,890 ha). Cabernet sauvignon is the second most widely planted, at 3,607 acres (1,460 ha) and merlot is third at 2,990 acres (1,210 ha). Secondary varietals include gewürztraminer, inzolia, muscat blanc/canelli, sémillon, viognier, white riesling, malvasia bianca, orange muscat, valdiguie, petite sirah, nebbiolo and petit verdot.

This vast area is poised to become a significant contributor to the California wine industry. Monterey walks proudly if still a bit awkwardly among her more stylish North Coast neighbors.

The undeniably beautiful seascape of the Big Sur coastline attracts numerous visitors but many remain unaware it is just a short journey inland into Monterey's wine country.

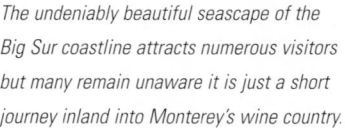

Landscape and climate

The Salinas Valley, or Monterey AVA, bears a striking resemblance to the Napa Valley. The wide mouth of the valley is too cool for grape growing. Like San Francisco, where you need a sweater especially in the summer, it bears the full brunt of strong marine influences. Heading due south along the 101 Freeway into the heart of the 12 mile (19 km) wide valley brings you to Soledad—the center and the outpost in the first round of expansion inland. At the base of the Santa Lucia mountain range to the west, or the coastal range, a handful of wineries have nestled into the foothills and have successfully petitioned for AVA status.

These Santa Lucia bench vineyards are planted on terraces facing southeast, giving extended exposure to the sun before afternoon breezes from the Pacific lower the temperature. Farther south, with Greenfield as the base, is Arroyo Seco, which begins with a narrow Santa Lucia canyon then flattens out over the valley floor. Bordeaux varietals thrive at the warmer terraced canyon mouth; "Greenfield Potatoes" or 3–4 inch (7–10 cm) cobblestones mark the soil in the plains. Their drainage and heat-retaining qualities give chardonnay and riesling their signature tropical character.

Wente is a major force in this area, producing 20,000 cases of Arroyo Seco Brut Reserve sparkling wine each year. Continuing south to King City, the San Lucas AVA straddles the freeway rather than tucking up into the coastal foothills. Its vineyards are set into alluvial fans and terraces ranging from 500–1,200 feet (152–366 m). The valley floor proper is just too windy here for fine wine production. Shale and sandstone soil, warm days and cool nights give deeply colored and flavored Bordeaux varietals, chardonnay and syrah.

Hames Valley marks the southern tip of the valley near Bradley. Once again nestled up into the foothills and thus protected from the Salinas Valley winds, Hames Valley is similar to southern neighbor Paso Robles in its shaly loam soil and warm climate. Cabernet sauvignon here is intense. The world's largest contiguous vineyard, San Bernabe, (8,300 planted acres—3,361 ha) between King City and San Lucas, is owned by Delicato Vineyards of the Central Valley and produces one third of the total output of Monterey. This vineyard is known as the "Hope Diamond" in the industry. San Bernabe's *terroir* is unique. Much of the vineyard is on ancient (now stabilized) Aeolian sand dune remnants (65 percent of San Bernabe soil is of this type). Nowhere else in the county is this soil type

found in such an uninterrupted expanse. It is the most diverse single vineyard in the world, a remarkable matrix of soils and 22 distinct microclimates. As such, an AVA application was filed in early 2001.

Chalone AVA is a one-winery appellation 1,800 feet (550 m) above Soledad in the Gavilan Mountain range near the eerie dormant volcano, the Pinnacles National Monument. Clay, decomposed granite, quartz crystals and limestone in the soil coupled with a long, cool growing season allow particular success with chardonnay, pinot noir and chenin blanc.

Carmel Valley has a long history of cabernet sauvignon going back to Father Juniperro Serra in the 1800s. Well-drained gravelly terraces, very warm days and very cool nights, especially in the Cachagua district (Esselen Indian word for Hidden Springs), produce intensely varietal cabernet sauvignons, merlots and sauvignon blancs. The Tularcitos Ridge to the northeast provides additional physical isolation and protection from the nearby Pacific Ocean.

San Benito County's most important AVA is Mt Harlan, a single winery appellation. Josh Jensen's Calera vineyards are planted in limestone outcrops some 2,200 feet (720 m) up into the Gavilan Range across the San Benito County line. At this elevation temperatures are low even in the peak of summer. Drop back down into nearby Hollister to the north and feel the baking heat.

A common factor throughout Monterey and San Benito counties is lack of rainfall. Average rainfall is 10 inches (4 cm), not enough to ripen grapes. Judicious use of irrigation from the massive underground river, the Salinas, provides balance between growth of vines and maturation of the grape.

Vines and wines

The long growing season with short daily bursts of heat gives intense varietal character if crops are restrained and the fruit reaches full maturity on the vine. Well-developed colors, excellent balance of sugar and acid, fruit true to the natural flavor of the varietal and the ability to age are becoming the descriptors for Monterey. Bordeaux varietals thrive in the warmer Carmel and southern Salinas Valley locations with their hot, dry days and cool nights. Burgundian varietals show restraint in the higher elevations, but give full throttle, showy, ripe, opulent expressions closer to the valley floor,

A bust of author John Steinbeck, Cannery Row, in downtown Monterey.

Petit verdot, a component in the bordeaux mix, is grown in Monterey County.

The old bell at Soledad Mission was cast in Mexico in the seventeenth century.

REGIONAL DOZEN

QUALITY WINES

Bernardus Marinus Cabernet
   Sauvignon/Merlot/Cabernet
   Franc
Calera Jensen Mount Harlan
   Pinot Noir
Chalone Vineyard The
   Pinnacles Chardonnay
Galante Red Rose Hill Carmel
   Valley Cabernet Sauvignon
Joullian Carmel Valley
   Cabernet Sauvignon
Morgan Reserve Pinot Noir

BEST VALUE WINES

Jekel FOS Reserve
   Chardonnay
Lockwood Cabernet
   Sauvignon
J. Lohr Bay Mist Monterey
   White Riesling
Monterra San Bernabe Ranch
   Syrah
Morgan Monterey/Sonoma
   Sauvignon Blanc
Paraiso Springs Riesling

where less day-to-night variation in temperature exists. Rhône and Italian varietals show early promise, especially syrah, which is vibrantly fruity, sometimes smoky and not nearly as heavily oaked as it is in the North Coast.

Anyone who has tasted through library collections of Chalone, Calera, or Durney will attest to their incredible longevity. The potential is strong across the board as Monterey struggles through adolescence and comes into adulthood.

Budbreak is two weeks earlier than other California regions; harvest is two weeks later. Grapes here have up until recently been farmed primarily for tonnage, not for fine wine. Unlimited water from the underground Salinas River fed overhead irrigation systems, allowing for plentiful production. However, the large-volume production caused imbalance in the vines; foliage grew out of control, too, and caused the Monterey "veggies" or the green bell pepper or even asparagus character prevalent in many early cabernet sauvignons and sauvignon blancs. Implementation of better farming techniques, including the use of new clonal material, tighter spacing, better trellising (better air and sun penetration into the grapes), controlled canopies and judicious irrigation has allowed for fully ripe, highly evolved fruit.

Vinification techniques reflect the golden era of California winemaking. Winemakers are taking less and less credit for their successes. Far from the ego-driven wine styles of the north coast, where a "signature style" is mandated by deep-pocket marketing types, here the attitude is more like "I have only to look to the vineyard to make good wine. With better fruit, we will have better wine."

The Robert Mondavi Winery is credited with the creation of the Central Coast Vineyard Team, or CCVT, which investigates ways to reduce pesticide use. Its Positive Points System measures integrated farm management and its positive environmental effects in Monterey as well as in San Luis Obispo and Santa Barbara County.

Producers

BERNARDUS WINERY

Established 1990   *Owner* Bernardus Marinus Pon
Production 50,000 cases   *Vineyard area* 52 acres (21 ha)

Pon owned the oldest "wynkoper" distribution house in his native Holland and visited Bordeaux regularly to buy stock. One of his dreams was to create a red wine of equal quality to the finest Bordeaux. He chose the Carmel Valley for its

strong track record of producing intense, complex and long-lived cabernet sauvignon and merlot. The newly released Marinus shows great promise. His respect for nature is reflected in his vineyard approaches and has also led to the preservation of more than 300 live oaks on this former Native American land in the Cachagua Valley.

CALERA

Established 1975   *Owner* Josh Jensen   *Production* 30,000
cases   *Vineyard area* 47 acres (19 ha); 28 acres (11.3 ha)
newly planted

Early viognier pioneer and burgundy fanatic Josh Jensen chose Mt Harlan high in the Gavilan Mountains for the site of his vineyard. He named this former limestone quarry and kiln Calera, (Spanish for lime kiln). Jensen's early success with vineyard-designated pinot noir and chardonnay as well as America's first world-class viognier helped focus attention on San Benito County as a fine wine producing region. Calera single-vineyard pinot noirs are some of the longest lived in America, certainly rivalling their peers in the Cote d'Or.

CHALONE

Established 1960   *Owners* Château Lafite-Rothschild 50
percent, 12,000 shareholders 50 percent   *Production* 35,000
cases   *Vineyard area* 326 acres (132 ha)

For a winery that boasts the fourth-largest number of stockholders in the world (Ben and Jerry is third) its wines are incredibly personal and hand-crafted. Winemaker Dan Karlsen modestly credits his well-drained limestone based soils, high altitudes and mature vines—not his talents—for the benchmark chenin blanc, chardonnay, pinot blanc and pinot noir. Despite his challenges—his remote vineyards are susceptible to gophers, birds, snakes and wild boar—he manages to turn out outstanding wines. Founder Dick Graff is credited with initiating the use of malolactic fermentation and fermenting and aging white wines in barrel. Chalone Vineyard is the oldest producing vineyard in Monterey County, has its own AVA, is located 1,800 feet (549 m) above the Salinas Valley floor in the Gavilan Mountains and is just north of the Pinnacles National Monument, a dormant volcano.

CLONINGER

Established 1988   *Owners* Loren Cloninger and the
Boskovich family   *Production* 3,200 cases   *Vineyard area*
50 acres (20.2 ha)

Loren Cloninger grew up here in the benchlands of the Santa Lucia mountains. He recalls when the area was dotted with dairy farms and when Swiss settlers made their own sausage and wine. He and Joe Boskovich used to farm lettuce and broccoli for the Boskovich family's produce-packing business. He observed the profitable transition to grapes on the valley floor, but felt the rocky benchland would also produce great wine. Today one of the area's remaining dairy farms houses the winery and the adjoining farmhouse, where his grandmother was born in 1896, houses the tasting room. Winemaker Dave Paige crafts an intense chardonnay, rich and smoky pinot noir and a complex, powerful Carmel Valley cabernet sauvignon.

GALANTE VINEYARDS

Established 1994 *Owners* Galante family *Production* 5,000 cases *Vineyard area* 70 acres (28 ha)

Jack Galante is a fifth-generation Californian. His grandfather, J. F. Devendorf, was the founder of Carmel. The family purchased this former cattle ranch in Carmel Valley in 1969 and in 1983, planted the vineyards, but Jack waited ten years before making his first release. He hired winemaker Greg Vita, a graduate of UC Davis, and vineyard manager Eliud Ortiz, a native of Guatemala, to complete the team. Estate wines include Blackjack Pasture, Red Rose Hill and Rancho Galante cabernet sauvignons. The Rancho Galante is drinkable right out of the gate; the others would benefit from a few years in the cellar, especially the more tannic Red Rose bottling. All three are intense, deeply fruited, rich, balanced wines that represent a benchmark for the region and for the state. Galante is also well known for its top-quality cut garden roses, grown beside the vines and shipped all over the country.

HAHN ESTATES/SMITH & HOOK WINERY

Established 1974 *Owners* Nicolaus Hahn family *Production* 105,000 cases *Vineyard area* 936 acres (379 ha)

Nicky Hahn, a Swiss citizen, started his professional career as a arbitrageur in Paris. During a stint in England, Hahn discovered California wines. This led him on a two-year search for a winery of his own. After discovering Monterey, he planted five vineyards in the western Santa Lucia Highlands and in Arroyo Seco. Winemaker Art Nathan credits the beneficial microclimate of these Santa Lucia benchland vineyards for the varietally intense quality of his wines. Hahn Estates is the budget line and cabernet franc is particularly noteworthy. The premium Smith & Hook line excels with a cabernet sauvignon aged in American

oak just like that of Silver Oak and Beaulieu Vineyards. The Smith & Hook Masterpiece line includes a rich, tropical, Arroyo Seco chardonnay.

HELLER ESTATE/DURNEY VINEYARDS

Established 1970 *Owner* Gilbert Heller *Production* 20,000 cases *Vineyard area* 120 acres (48.5 ha)

British Masters of Wine and Parisian sommeliers love these 100 percent organically farmed cabernet sauvignons, merlots and chenin blancs almost more than the locals. Heller has given the former Durney Vineyards an expensive overhaul—he renovated the winery, hired new winemaker Rex Smith from Napa Valley merlot star Cuvaison and has earned the high-maintenance "organically farmed" certification from the CCOF. This Carmel Valley winery is a benchmark producer.

JOULLIAN

Established 1982 *Owners* Ed Joullian and Dick Sias *Production* 12,000 cases *Vineyard area* 40 acres (16.2 ha)

A partnership of the Joullian and Sias families of Oklahoma City, this 655-acre (265-ha) estate in the heart of Carmel Valley is a dream come true. After extensive and expensive contouring and terracing, the families planted 40 acres (16.2 ha) to primarily Bordeaux varietals, with a small area going to chardonnay, zinfandel and petite sirah. Winemaker Ridge Watson, who was apprenticed at Château Carbonnieux in the Graves district of Bordeaux, is turning out truly world-class sauvignon blanc and cabernet sauvignon. He is tinkering with petite sirah because he likes what another "Ridge"— Paul Draper's Ridge Vineyards—does with it.

LOCKWOOD

Established 1989 *Owners* Paul Toppen, Phil Johnson, Butch Lindley *Production* 104,000 cases *Vineyard area* 1,850 acres (749 ha)

This is one of the largest single contiguous vineyards in the county and produces premium fruit that is keenly sought after by some of the

A statue commemorating Father Juniperro Serra, founder of some of the early missions.

Above: *A saint's niche at Carmel Mission.*

Top: *Winery sign and "château" buildings in Carmel Valley.*

the consumers lining up at the door. Morgan is Dan's mother's maiden name. The vineyards are in the Santa Lucia Highlands, also the site of the future winery and tasting room.

PARAISO SPRINGS VINEYARDS
Established 1987 *Owners* Rich and Claudia Smith *Production* 20,000 cases *Vineyard area* 400 acres (162 ha)

The family is very active in the wine grape growing community locally, nationally and internationally. Their estate vineyard in the Santa Lucia Highlands is just two miles (3.2 km) from historic Soledad Mission, site of Monterey's first vineyard. It is no surprise that wine-maker Zorn, born in West Berlin and trained in enology at Bad Kreuz-nach, makes the benchmark riesling of the county. In fact, the bone-dry, rich, petrolly riesling caught the attention of connoisseurs around the globe. Answering to consumer demand, however, the winery recently reverted to an off-dry style. Paraiso Springs is renowned for its elegant, deeply flavored pinot noir, syrah, chardonnay and pinot blanc. Zorn makes Cobblestone chardonnay, a joint venture with the Levine family, owners of the Arroyo Seco vineyard, as well as own-label Tria with fellow winemaker Bill Knuttel of Chalk Hill.

ROBERT TALBOTT VINEYARDS
Established 1983 *Owners* Talbott family *Production* 24,000 cases *Vineyard area* 700 acres (283 ha) Santa Lucia Highlands, 24 acres (9.7 ha) Carmel Valley

Classic rich, buttery, toasty and expensive chardonnay has built an international reputation for this small family winery. The Talbott Tie company may have provided the seed money, but award-winning wines such as Diamond T, the results of the first chardonnay vineyard planted, and Case, a pinot noir named after Talbott's eldest daughter Sarah Case, are earning their keep on their own. Winemaker Sam Baldares selects just a few barrels from the famous Sleepy Hollow Vineyard for Cuvèe Cynthia chardonnay, which is bottled unfined and unfiltered. The newest addition to the portfolio of wines is the Kali-Hart chardonnay, a lighter, less toasty chardonnay named after their daughter. Logan is a second label. All wines are 100 percent estate grown.

most elite wineries in the state. The founding partners chose this site at the base of the Santa Lucia range because of its unique shaley loam soil, a well-drained, calcareous "chalk rock." Wine-maker Stephen Passagnano prefers fruit-forward, well balanced and food-friendly wines. He adds a dash of Italian varietal refosco to his cabernet sauvi-gnon, which gives it an exotic orange peel note; and adds 10 percent to beef up his bold, peppery syrah. The last release for the time being of the popular barrel-fermented pinot blanc was in 1998. Phyl-loxera destroyed the block, but it has been replanted with identical budwood.

MORGAN
Established 1982 *Owners* Dan and Donna Lee *Production* 50,000 cases *Vineyard area* 65 acres (26.3 ha)

Morgan chardonnay and pinot noirs have earned accolades for many years. Dan Lee grew up in the Central Valley working odd jobs on farms, but winemaking fascinated him. It made use of the nuts and bolts of science, allowed a chance to be creative and felt right to his agricultural roots. Today winemaker Dean De Korth, a burgundy fanatic—he worked with Olivier LeFlaive, Pierre Morey and Dominique Lafon before settling in Monterey—is best known for his reserve pinot noir and chardonnay. His newly released syrah and pinot gris are sure to keep the press humming and

South Central Coast

Patrick Farrell MW

California's central coast runs from Santa Barbara in the south to Santa Cruz in the north. The south central coast is comprised of two counties: San Luis Obispo (SLO) in the north and Santa Barbara (SB) in the south. Proximity to the cooling effect of coastal waters and breezes is particularly marked in these regions. The transverse orientation of the coastal mountain range allows the channeling of cool marine-influenced air inland, resulting in cool climates in the westerly reaches of the Santa Ynez, Santa Maria, Los Alamos and Edna valleys. Long growing seasons (up to 190 days), sunshine and relative warmth in the fall ensure ripe grapes with good retained natural acidities. Paso Robles, on the coastal range's easterly side, is less influenced by the Pacific and has a much warmer climate. The region has expanded rapidly and has attracted investment from the Napa Valley, Europe and Australia. Recognized for their quality, grapes from the central coast are shipped throughout the state.

Map

Producers

Paso Robles
1 Adelaida Cellars
2 Eberle Winery
3 Hidden Mountain Ranch
4 Justin Vineyards & Winery
5 Martin & Weyrich Winery
6 Meridian Vineyards
7 Peachy Canyon Winery
8 Pesenti Winery & Vineyards
9 Tablas Creek Winery
10 Tobin James Cellars
11 Victor Hugo
12 Wild Horse Winery
13 York Mountain Winery

Edna Valley & Arroyo Grande
14 Alban Vineyards
15 Claiborne & Churchill
16 Corbett Canyon Vineyard
17 Edna Valley Vineyard
18 Laetitia Vineyard & Winery
19 Saucelito Canyon
20 Seven Peaks

Santa Barbara County (SBC)
21 Au Bon Climat (ABC)
22 Andrew Murray
23 Babcock
24 Brander/Domaine Santa Barbara
25 Byron
26 Cambria
27 Fess Parker
28 Fiddlehead
29 Foxen
30 Hitching Post
31 Lane Tanner
32 Longoria
33 Qupe
34 Rancho Sisquoc
35 Sanford
36 Whitcraft
37 Zaca Mesa

10 miles
(16 kilometers)

NORTH

UNITED STATES WASHINGTON DC

South Central Coast

SANTA BARBARA   County boundary and name

San Luis Obispo County is comprised of four AVAs: Edna Valley, Arroyo Grande, Paso Robles and York Mountain. Edna Valley and Arroyo Grande are adjacent and have many shared characteristics, including a joint vintners' and grape growers' association. York Mountain is a small, one-winery AVA in western Paso Robles.

EDNA VALLEY AND ARROYO GRANDE

Located next to the charming university town of San Luis Obispo, Edna Valley was granted AVA status in 1982. Arroyo Grande is located just to its south. Together they cover 2,000 acres (810 ha). With missions nearby, viticulture in these regions dates back to 1859, when French immigrant Pierre Dalladet planted vines in San Luis Obispo. Edna Valley's development as a wine-producing region really began in the late 1960s, with the Niven family being particularly prominent. The Nivens are owners of the 1,000-acre (405-ha) Paragon Vineyard and have formed two important strategic alliances, the first being a partnership with the publicly traded Chalone Wine Group in the formation of Edna Valley Winery in 1980. The most recent partnership occurred more than 10 years ago when Australia's giant South-corp bought into the Seven Peaks Winery.

Arroyo Grande has also been involved in international partnerships. Maison Deutz was a 1982 Franco-American joint venture involving the Deutz Champagne house. Currently owned by other Frenchmen and renamed Laetitia, this one-time sparkling-wine-only specialist now also produces table wines.

Edna Valley is region I–II on the Winkler-Amerine heat summation scale. The east-to-west valley opens up to the cooling effects of the Pacific Ocean at Morro Bay 15 miles (24 km) away. Arroyo Grande's climate varies significantly as one moves inland. Westerly Laetitia is only about 2 miles (3.2 km) from the Pacific and is region I for most vintages. Talley is 8 miles (12.9 km) from the coast and is region I–II. Saucelito Canyon is another 12 or so miles (about 19 km) inland and is a warm region III. Soils consist of sandy and clay loams over limestone that was once under the ocean and contains abundant marine deposits.

A Wine Trail guides visitors in the area.

REGIONAL BEST

QUALITY WINES

Edna Valley Winery Reserve Chardonnay
Laetitia Estate Pinot Noir Reserve
Laetitia Cuvee "M" Sparkling Wine
Saucelito Canyon Zinfandel
Talley Reserve Pinot Noir, Chardonnay

BEST VALUE WINES

Seven Peaks Chardonnay, Merlot, Shiraz
Corbett Canyon Chardonnay, White Zinfandel, Cabernet Sauvignon

US$10–13 a bottle, these wines emulate Alsace with either dryness or lowish levels of residual sugar. They part company from Alsace in their ripeness of fruit, lime and peach for the riesling and floral lychees for the gewürztraminer.

CORBETT CANYON VINEYARD

Established 1979 *Owner* **The Wine Group of San Franciso** *Production* **1 million plus cases** *Vineyard area* **70 acres (28.4 ha)**

Corbett Canyon Vineyard, the largest regional producer with very competitive prices (US$5–6 or less per bottle) and innovative marketing, produces successful commercial-quality wine that is particularly good for the low price. Varietal wine is cleanly made, true to variety and unadorned with oak.

Above: *White grapes in the Edna Valley.*

Top: *Laetitia vineyards.*

Vines and wines

Edna Valley and Arroyo Grande represent a continuum of viticulture from the 1970s to the present era. Saucelito Canyon is an exception with its 100-year-old zinfandel vines. More recent plantings have included newer clones and altered spacing as in the rest of the state. Modern techniques mirror much of California with some notable exceptions. Maison Deutz brought classic champagne-production techniques to the region. These, along with traditional techniques from Burgundy, continue to be practised at Laetitia by the French winemaker there. Seven Peaks has an Australian winemaker producing wines in the Roseworthy tradition.

Producers

ALBAN VINEYARDS

Established 1986 *Owner* **John Alban** *Production* **5,000 cases** *Vineyard area* **60 acres (24.3 ha)**

Rhône enthusiast John Alban reports having been "hooked" by his first Condrieu tasted during his studies at Fresno State University. A post-graduation stint in France's Rhône Valley further confirmed John's passion. Alban winery was the first all-rhone variety winery in California. Grenache, syrah, viognier and roussanne are produced. Wines are well made and good value.

CLAIBORNE & CHURCHILL

Established 1983 *Owners* **Clay Thompson and Fredricka Churchill** *Production* **4,800 cases** *Vineyard area* **NA**

This winery's riesling and gewürztraminer are some of California's finest examples. Retailing at

EDNA VALLEY VINEYARD

Established 1979 *Owners* **Chalone Wine Group and the Niven family** *Production* **100,000 cases** *Vineyard area* **1,000 acres (405 ha)**

The wines here are well made, well priced and reliable for chardonnay and pinot noir. A traditional-method sparkling wine available at the winery is also good.

LAETITIA VINEYARD & WINERY

Established 1981 *Owners* **Nebil "Bilo" Zarif and Selim Zilkha** *Production* **22,000 cases** *Vineyard area* **185 acres (75 ha)**

Previously known as Maison Deutz, this beautiful winery is located just off the 101 Freeway. Perched on a hilltop among rolling vines, the winery has a view out to the Pacific Ocean 2 miles (3.2 km) away. Sparkling and table wines here are made from chardonnay, pinot blanc and pinot noir. The sparklers are good to very good quality and are well priced. Commercial production of table wines began to soar during the 1990s at the same time as prices for sparkling wines were languishing.

SAUCELITO CANYON

Established 1974 *Owners* **Bill and Nancy Greenough** *Production* **2,000 cases** *Vineyard area* **8 acres (3.2 ha)**

Located in the upper and warmer reaches of Arroyo Grande, Saucelito Canyon boasts 100-year-old zinfandel vines. The zinfandel is rich and ripe, with characteristic brambly fruit that has tobacco and spice notes. It competes well with other examples statewide.

SEVEN PEAKS

Established 1996 *Owners* Niven family and Southcorp
Production 55,000 cases *Vineyard area* 1,737 acres
(703.5 ha)

A joint venture between the Niven family and
Australia's giant Southcorp (of Penfolds and Lindeman's fame), this is still a relatively new venture.
Varietals are well priced at under US$10 a bottle,
among the lowest price points of Niven ventures.

PASO ROBLES

Paso Robles, the largest of the San Luis Obispo
County AVAs, consists of 20,000 acres (8,100 ha)
planted. In 1999, 2 million cases were produced by
45 wineries. This represents remarkable growth,
up from 6,500 acres (2,633 ha) and 25 wineries in
1994. Grapes are processed locally as well as being
shipped throughout the state.

Here, the coastal range is oriented north to
south, with only a small opening to the cooling
effects of the Pacific Ocean at the Templeton Gap.
Paso Robles is thus a warm region, with a history
of producing better red wines, particularly full-
throttle zinfandels, than whites.

Unlike Santa Barbara County, where the rich
and famous from Hollywood may be found relaxing and riding horses in the latest fashions, Paso
Robles is real cowboy country with nary a starlet
in sight. Producers seem more blue collar as well,
although corporate giant Beringer has a major
stake in Paso Robles in Meridian. The hilly and
somewhat cooler west side is divided from the
flatter east side by Highway 46.

Paso Robles' vinous traditions date back to the
eighteenth and nineteenth centuries. Just 8 miles
(12.9 km) outside Paso Robles proper is the mission San Miguel, where the first grapes were
grown in 1797. Current traditions of dry-farmed
zinfandel grown on the west side's rolling hills
were begun in the 1880s by Andrew York. French
and Italian immigrants followed suit over the next
several decades. Despite Prohibition, some vineyards were planted, on their own roots, in the
1920s only to succumb to a phylloxera outbreak
during the 1940s. Vineyards were then replanted
onto resistant Rupestris St George rootstock. Such
vineyards are excellent sources of old-vine zinfandel and include Pesenti, Martinelli and the Dusi
Ranch. The west side hills were preferred for vineyards as they provided some frost protection.
Zinfandel was a favored variety partly because of
its large second crop, which provided additional
insurance against the first being hit by frost.

Growth occurred on the flatter, hotter and
drier east side in the 1970s. Under the guidance of
University of California at Davis' Professor Olmo,
vineyards were planted on their own roots, with
overhead sprinklers for irrigation and frost protection. Gary Eberle, then winemaker at Estrella
River, was one of the first to plant syrah and cabernet sauvignon. The 1980s saw continued growth
on both east and west sides. Justin was established
on the west side and drip irrigation and cabernet
franc were introduced. In the late 1980s, Martin
Brothers and Caparone introduced Italian varieties
such as nebbiolo, sangiovese and pinot grigio. In
1989, phylloxera biotype A (not the genetically
changed biotype B that had already struck Napa
and Sonoma) struck Paso Robles.

Planting and replanting occurred through the
1990s. The region did well as the nation turned to
red wine. Zinfandel, cabernet and merlot plantings
all increased. New rootstocks, new clones, new
varieties and higher-density plantings were all the
rage. Canopy management had become a common
catchword. The 1990s also saw the arrival of the
Perrin family from the famed Château Beaucastel
in southern France. The family teamed with
importer Robert Haas of Vineyard Brands. The
new venture, Tablas Creek, includes rhône varieties imported from Beaucastel and has shown
early promise.

Paso Robles is the warmest of California's
coastal valleys and stands at region III–IV on the
Winkler-Amerine scale, but this is just part of the
story. In summertime, daytime maximum temperatures may reach as high as 100°F (38°C) but the
minimum temperature on the same day may be as

Extensive vineyards near Paso Robles.

The crest of Martin & Weyrich Winery.

low as 45°F (7°C). Diurnal variation is marked, usually 40–50°F (4–10°C). Cool air makes its way through the Templeton Gap in the late afternoon to early evening. By mid-evening, a sweatshirt or sweater are needed for outdoors. The early morning is very cool and thus it takes a while for the land and vines to heat up.

The west side is hilly and somewhat cooler than the flat east side. Well-drained soils are of low-to-moderate vigor. Sandy or clay loam soils are based on the degradation of granite, serpentine, shale or sandstone. Those based upon shale are most common. Rainfall occurs mostly during the winter. Western vineyards average 30 inches (76 cm), while the east side receives a paltry 9 inches (23 cm) annually.

Vines and wines

Planted varieties include zinfandel, chardonnay and the classic varieties from Bordeaux, the Rhône Valley and central–northern Italy. Older, phylloxera-resistant plantings are on Rupestris St George rootstock. Own-rooted vines are either scheduled for replanting or doomed to repeat history. A host of resistant rootstocks is being utilized, including 110R, 140R, 1103P and 3309C. Nematodes can cause problems in this area and this may influence the choice of rootstock.

Overhead sprinklers are used for frost protection, particularly on the east side. New plantings tend to be at higher densities than the old 8 x 10 feet (2.4 x 3.1 m) plantings. Since the climate is warm and dry, there is little disease pressure and many growers are opting for an organic approach.

Cover crops and decreased spraying are popular measures. Netting is increasingly used to protect vines from bird damage.

Techniques vary little from other parts of California. Oak is commonly used as a seasoning. Better efforts are being made to use oak in a supporting role and to allow the underlying fruit to speak for the wine. Many smaller producers are making their wines with an eye to minimizing such interventions as fining and filtering. Many also try to keep sulfur dioxide at a minimum.

Producers

ADELAIDA CELLARS

Established 1981 *Owners* the Van Steenwyk family
Production 9,000 cases *Vineyard area* 75 acres (30 ha)

Named after a now-defunct village, Adelaida takes advantage of the warm dry climate to farm organically. Indigenous rather than commercial yeast ferments the wines. Despite the warm climate, Adelaida produces one of the better chardonnays in the region and its cabernet sauvignon is better still.

EBERLE WINERY

Established 1983 *Owner* Gary Eberle *Production* 25,000 cases *Vineyard area* 42 acres (17 ha)

Gary Eberle, once a lineman on Penn State's football team, was involved in the planting at the Estrella River Winery and was one of the first to introduce syrah to the region. His wines are good across the board and very reliable, and his ripe-styled cabernet ages very well. The syrah and viognier are regional standards.

HIDDEN MOUNTAIN RANCH

Established 1997 *Owners* the Changala, McHenry and Vignola families *Production* 3,000 cases *Vineyard area* NA

Hidden Mountain Ranch, better known as HMR, was first established some 30 years ago by a Beverly Hills cardiologist named Stanley Hoffman. California's notable consultant Andre Tchelistcheff brought immediate credibility to the project. Now owned by three families, HMR continues in that tradition. Most impressive was Dusi Ranch's old-vine zinfandel, which was voted the Best Red Wine at the 2000 San Diego Wine Competition.

New plantings in Paso Robles.

JUSTIN VINEYARDS AND WINERY

Established 1981 *Owners* Justin and Deborah Baldwin
Production 30,000 cases *Vineyard area* 72 acres (29 ha)

Investment banker turned wine proprietor Justin
Baldwin was one of the first to plant cabernet
sauvignon on the hilly west side of Paso Robles.
Other Bordeaux varieties, chardonnay and Italian
varieties complete the mix. The well-made chardonnay is a rich, warm-climate style. The red
wines are more successful. Isoceles is a Bordeaux
blend that has consistently scored well. Not inexpensive at US$38, it is one of the region's best
cabernet blends and ages well. Justinification, a
merlot and cabernet franc blend, is also very good.
Italian varieties show promise.

MARTIN & WEYRICH WINERY

Established 1981 *Owners* David and Mary Weyrich
Production 28,000 cases *Vineyard area* 190 acres (77 ha)

Among the first to specialize in Italian varieties,
Martin & Weyrich produces moscato, pinot grigio,
sangiovese and nebbiolo. The moscato is delight-
fully floral, fizzy, somewhat sweet and well priced.
Pinot grigio is cleanly made from Paso Robles and
Santa Barbara fruit, which lend natural acidity to
this nicely balanced wine. Reds have been rustic.

MERIDIAN VINEYARDS

Established 1988 *Owner* Beringer Wine Estates *Production*
500,000 cases *Vineyard area* 3,500 acres (1,418 ha)

Meridian wines are well priced and well made.
Chardonnay is sourced from Santa Barbara County
while zinfandel, merlot, cabernet sauvignon and
syrah are grown in Paso Robles. Meridian has
been a leader in vineyard and canopy management,
as demonstrated by its clean and varietally correct
style. These are wines for early enjoyment, though
the red wines can improve with several years in
bottle. Syrah is the most recent addition and is
commendable. Deeply colored, it has the smoked-
meat, leather and violet aroma and flavor profile
found in good examples from the northern Rhône.
Chuck Ortman is the senior winemaker.

PEACHY CANYON WINERY

Established 1988 *Owners* Doug and Nancy Beckett
Production 30,000 cases *Vineyard area* 88 acres (36 ha)

Although good Bordeaux varietal and blended
wines are made here, the real interest lies in zinfandel. Peachy Canyon has a well-deserved reputation for putting some wonderful zinfandel fruit in
the bottle. Expansion is in the works with the
recent purchase of Twin Hills Winery.

PESENTI WINERY AND VINEYARDS

Established 1934 *Owners* the
Nerelli–Pesenti family *Production*
10,000 cases *Vineyard area* 2 acres
(0.8 ha)

Pesenti is a long-established
traditional producer located on
the western hillsides. The best
wines are from 50-year-old, dry-
farmed zinfandel vines that yield
only 1–2 tons per acre (2.5–5
tonnes per ha). There's nothing
fancy here, sometimes to the
detriment of the white wines.
The zinfandel can be a spectacular bargain. A 1996 estate zinfandel cost only US$15 a bottle
and was a classic. Dark, bold
and full throttled, this "zin" had
expansive blackberry fruit that
went on and on.

TABLAS CREEK WINERY

Established 1992 *Owners* Robert
Haas and the Perrin family *Production* 3,000 cases
Vineyard area 57 acres (23 ha)

Tablas Creek unites the owners of Château Beaucastel in Châteauneuf du Pape and their importer,
Vineyard Brands. The Perrin–Haas venture is novel
in several ways. The site was chosen with Rhône
varieties in mind and a small vineyard was planted
with available planting materials, though at high
densities. Cuttings from the Perrins' French vineyards were then shipped over and cleared through
the US Department of Agriculture. A state-of-the-
art nursery was set up with facilities to green graft.
These plantings from the French vine cuttings are
only just getting into the bottle. Early efforts at red
and white blended wines have been reasonably
good, although the anticipation is that the wines
will improve.

TOBIN JAMES CELLARS

Established 1987 *Owners* Tobin James and the Silver family
Production 20,000 cases *Vineyard area* 16 acres (6.5 ha)

Tobin James was formerly the winemaker at
Peachy Canyon and continues to produce some of
the region's most exciting zinfandels. The wines
tend to be bold and firm with piercing fruit. Chardonnay and cabernet are less successful. Playing
off the legend of Jesse James and the shared sur-
name is the James Gang Reserve Zinfandel, which
at US$24 a bottle is not a steal.

A picnic at Meridian Vineyards, Paso Robles.

VICTOR HUGO

Established 1997 *Owners* Victor and Leslie Roberts
Production 2,500 cases *Vineyard area* 75 acres (30 ha)

Petite sirah is genetically identical to duriff, an undistinguished French variety. The densely colored version from Victor Hugo packs a load of berry fruit framed in oak and some powerful tannins. Such a wine argues the *terroir* concept well; indifferent in a cool climate, the variety does well here. Cabernet and meritage are less successful.

WILD HORSE WINERY

Established 1983 *Owners* Ken and Tricia Volks *Production* 85,000 case *Vineyard area* 50 acres (20 ha)

Wild Horse is a reliable source of well-made and well-priced merlot and cabernet sauvignon. Syrah and mourvèdre are relatively recent, and successful, additions. Both rhône-inspired wines are well structured with true varietal character and good intensity of ripe fruit.

YORK MOUNTAIN WINERY

Established 1882 *Owner* Max Goldman *Production* 4,000 cases *Vineyard area* 5 acres (2 ha)

Established by Andrew York as the Ascension Winery, York Mountain Winery is the region's oldest winery in continuous operation and was the first commercial winery in the region. Owing to the winery's location in far western and cooler Paso Robles, and its long history, York Mountain Winery was awarded its own AVA in 1983.

Byron Estate vineyards cling to the slopes.

SANTA BARBARA COUNTY (SBC)

The Santa Ynez, Santa Maria and Los Alamos valleys are Santa Barbara County's AVAs and comprise 4,000, 12,000 and 8,000 acres (1,620, 4,860 and 3,240 ha) respectively. Located 90 miles (145 km) north of Los Angeles, Santa Barbara's vineyards seem far removed from the hustle and bustle of "La-La Land." Half-an-hour's drive northeast of beautiful Santa Barbara, the region is unusual in that the coastal range is perpendicular to the coastline. Cool maritime air and morning fogs yield some of California's cooler vineyards.

This expanding region consists of 18,000 acres (7,290 ha) and 46 wineries producing more than 1 million cases of wine. Chardonnay and pinot noir are the primary varieties, though fine examples of both rhône and bordeaux varieties may also be found. Some 55 percent of the region's harvest is crushed elsewhere. Local wine volume increased 230 percent between 1992 and 1998.

Although there were vineyards for Santa Barbara's mission at the end of the eighteenth century, the region currently planted did not participate in the statewide wine boom of the mid-to-late nineteenth century. In 1892, nearby Carpenteria claimed the world's largest grapevine, a 50-year-old mission vine with a trunk 9 feet (2.7 m) in circumference, producing up to 10 tons (9 t) annually. Novelty aside, modern history dates back to the early 1960s with plantings in the Santa Maria and Santa Ynez valleys. Wineries followed in the 1970s. Vineyards were initially planted with a host of varieties, cabernet sauvignon being the most commonly planted. The cool climate, coupled with excessive canopies, made for unripe, vegetative cabernet, which damaged the region's reputation.

With the nationwide boom in chardonnay during the 1970s and 1980s, the regional reputation improved markedly, as chardonnay does very well in the cool climate. Pinot noir plantings increased with critical acclaim. Vineyards expanded throughout the remainder of the century. Large concerns from northern California were drawn to the region. Robert Mondavi purchased Byron and greatly expanded plantings. Kendall-Jackson established Cambria while Beringer planted chardonnay and pinot noir for the Meridian brand.

Santa Barbara is at the demarcation between central and southern California. The natural expectation is that vineyards here would be warmer than those north of San Francisco, but they are not. In fact, westerly vineyards in the Santa Maria and Santa Ynez valleys are among the coolest in California. Broccoli ripens in the very cool, far-western portions of these coastal valleys, but wine grapes do not.

The opening of the Santa Maria Valley is much larger than the Santa Ynez Valley, which accounts for cooler conditions at similar distances from the coast. Thus as one moves farther inland, conditions change from untenable for grape growing to region I on the Winkler heat summation scale to region II. As the coastal influence ultimately falls off inland, temperatures rise rapidly, yielding regions III and IV.

There are mesas and rolling hills with altitudes to 1,500 feet (457.5 m). Higher altitudes and northerly slopes will be cooler, although proximity to the coast is still the most important factor. Growers are increasingly planting on hillsides. Santa Barbara County is dry, receiving 8–10 inches (20–25 cm) of rain a year, mostly from November to March. Soils are variable, tending toward sandy loams. The growing season is long. In 1997, budbreak was a little early, occurring on February 1. The harvest of early varieties such as chardonnay began in early September, while syrah was harvested several weeks later. In 1999, the length of time from budbreak to harvest was between 170 and 192 days, depending on location and variety.

More so than in northern California, Santa Barbara is prone to some of the warmest temperatures during the fall. Maximum temperatures may be 85–90°F (29–32°C), cooling off to 50°F (10°C) at night. This gives an extended growing season that allows chardonnay, pinot noir and syrah to ripen. Vintage influences which varieties ripen to their optimum.

Vines and wines

Chardonnay here combines ripeness with good-to-very-good retained natural acidity. Most are barrel fermented with the better wines having a balance between apple, pear or tropical fruit notes and oak. Many other white varieties are treated like chardonnay with the better efforts letting the fruit show through the influence of new oak.

Pinot noir in Santa Barbara has had a spiced-tea note added to very good underlying berry fruit. This seems to have been a function of planting material. New clones do not have the herbal notes and are nicely perfumed. Overall, the style is fairly robust and occasionally somewhat rustic. Better producers, such as Au Bon Climat, Longoria or Lane Tanner, produce some of California's best efforts from this elusive variety.

Merlot, cabernet franc and cabernet sauvignon are certainly less ripe than their Napa counterparts. Herbaceousness has been problematic in the past but planting on warmer sites and better canopy management is yielding riper fruit. Syrah shows promise here, exemplified by Qupe's string of successes. Warmer vintages add smoked-meat aromas to clean-berry fruit. Cooler vintages tend toward peppery notes. The better wines have good acidity and balanced tannins. Some new to the variety, particularly with the 1997 and 1998 vintages, had problems with dominant green tannins. Styles will certainly evolve as newer clones and plantings mature.

Vineyards planted during the 1970s through to the early 1990s were not planted on rootstock. Phylloxera was discovered in 1994 but has spread slowly on the sandy soils. New plantings were at higher densities, involved a variety of rootstocks, new varieties and different clonal selections of such standards as chardonnay and pinot noir.

Producers

AU BON CLIMAT (ABC)

Established 1982 *Owners* Morgan and Jim Clendenen
Production 24,320 cases *Vineyard area* 43 acres (17 ha)

Jim Clendenen produces some of California's best pinot noir and chardonnay. His pinot noir brims with berry fruit and shows intense yet delicate flavors, balance and length. His chardonnay demonstrates both power and finesse, while retaining good acidity and balance. Additionally, Jim is part of the brains trust that combines the talents of ABC, Qupe, Makor, Il Podere de Olivos, Vita Nova and the Hitching Post. Other ventures include Vita Nova and Ici La Bas. Vita Nova has been successful with Italian varieties and Bordeaux blends. Its Acceomicus, a blend of petite verdot and cabernet sauvignon, shows nice cassis fruit and proves that fine efforts are possible from Santa Barbara County with these varieties.

Outside of Burgundy, pinot noir is making headway only in New Zealand and the USA.

REGIONAL BEST

QUALITY WINES

Au Bon Climat Bien Nacido
  Reserve Chardonnay, Pinot
  Noir
Brander Sauvignon Blanc
  Cuvee Natalie
Byron Estate Pinot Noir
Foxen Bordeaux Blends
Qupe Viognier, Syrah

BEST VALUE WINES

Brander Sauvignon Blanc
Sanford Vin Gris (Pinot Noir)
Rancho Sisquoc Sylvaner

ANDREW MURRAY

Established 1990 *Owners* the Murray family *Production* 6,500 cases *Vineyard area* 30 acres (12 ha)

Andrew Murray is a talented young rhône-variety specialist producing some exciting wines. Early efforts have been laudable, with very good syrah, viognier, roussanne and marsanne.

BABCOCK

Established 1984 *Owners* the Babcock family *Production* 12,000 cases *Vineyard area* 70 acres (28 ha)

Brian Babcock's chardonnay and pinot noir, especially the Grande Cuvée, are excellent wines. Brian also produced fine dry rieslings until phylloxera struck. The 11 Oaks sauvignon blanc is one of the state's best, and Italian varieties show promise.

BRANDER/DOMAINE SANTA BARBARA

Established 1975 *Owner* Fred Brander *Production* 5,400 cases *Vineyard area* 42 acres (17 ha)

Fred Brander produces some fine sauvignon blanc. The "natural" has lime, grassy and mineral notes suggestive of a ripe sancere. Bordeaux varieties produce interesting wines under the Brander label. Domaine Santa Barbara is a good source of both chardonnay and pinot noir.

BYRON

Established 1984 *Owner* Robert Mondavi Corporation *Production* 40,000 cases *Vineyard area* 1,300 acres (526.5 ha)

Ken Byron Brown (founder and winemaker) produces excellent chardonnay and good-to-very-good pinot noir. A recent tasting of pinot noir made from new Burgundian clones revealed perfumed aromatics and finesse suggestive of fine burgundy.

CAMBRIA

Established 1986 *Owners* Jess Jackson and Barbara Banke *Production* 120,000 cases *Vineyard area* 1,250 acres (506 ha)

Cambria, part of the Kendall-Jackson empire, is a good source of mid-to-high-end chardonnay and pinot noir. Consistency is a trademark here, so expect Cambria's syrah to be very good as well.

Consistency is built into the wines of the sweeping Cambria Estate.

FESS PARKER

Established 1989 *Owners* Fess and Eli Parker *Vineyard area* 311 acres (126 ha)

Texas-born Fess Parker is television's Daniel Boon and Davey Crockett. Wines here have improved over the past several years— the winery is a good source of pinot noir, chardonnay and viognier.

FIDDLEHEAD

Established 1989 *Owner* Kathy Joseph *Production* 2,450 cases *Vineyard area* 23 acres (9 ha)

Kahty Joseph produces a good sauvignon blanc, but her pinot noir brings her most acclaim. Her pinot noir comes from Santa Barbara and from Oregon, thanks to disparate harvest dates.

FOXEN

Established 1987 *Owners* Bill Wathen and Richard Dore *Production* 12,000 cases *Vineyard area* 15 acres (6 ha)

Foxen produces bold, well-crafted wines. Chardonnay is uniformly excellent; pinot noir is muscular and ages well. Foxen's Bordeaux blends prove that given the right site, these varieties can do well here. The barrel-fermented chenin blanc is one of the best examples in the state.

HITCHING POST

Established 1991 *Owners* Frank Ostini and Gray Hartley *Production* 2,600 cases *Vineyard area* NA

Frank Ostini is owner and chef of the two restaurants for which the wines are named. The smokiness from the grill matches game notes in the very well made pinot noir to a tee. The local pinots are a perfect match for barbecued steak or ostrich.

LANE TANNER

Established 1989 *Owner* Bob Lindquist *Production* 2,200 cases *Vineyard area* NA

Lane Tanner, the winemaker, is a pinot noir lover, advocate and specialist, and a most reliable source of pinot noir. Aromatics and texture are the focus here—oak and tannins are under control. The winery has begun to make a syrah as well.

LONGORIA

Established 1982 *Owners* Rick and Diana Longoria *Production* 3,500 cases *Vineyard area* 8 acres (3.2 ha)

Rick Longoria's pinot noir is one of the region's best, as are his merlot and cabernet franc. The 1997 Pinot Noir Reserve from the Bien Nacido vineyard combines expansive notes of smoky game, berry fruit and oak on the palate with good balance and length of finish.

QUPE

Established 1982 *Owner* Bob Lindquist *Production* 17,000 cases *Vineyard area* 12 acres (4.9 ha)

Qupe means golden poppy in the local Chumash Indian language. Bob Lindquist, the rock-solid counterpoint to Jim Clendenen's flamboyance, produces very good chardonnay, and is one of California's leading "rhône Rangers." He also makes fine viognier, marsanne, syrah and red rhône blends. His syrah is the region's benchmark, with berry aromatics and smoked-meat flavors framed in oak.

RANCHO SISQUOC

Established 1972 *Owner* Flood Ranch Company *Production* 10,000 cases *Vineyard area* 208 acres (84 ha)

Sylvaner from this property is one of the state's best inexpensive wines (US$6–8 a bottle). Chardonnay and sauvignon blanc are also well made and well priced. Rancho Sisquoc produces some of the region's best red Bordeaux-style wines, using cabernet franc, cabernet sauvignon and merlot.

SANFORD

Established 1981 *Owner* J. Richard Sanford *Production* 50,000 cases *Vineyard area* 137 acres (55.5 ha)

Richard Sanford helped found one of the region's most acclaimed vineyards, the Sanford & Benedict, in the western reaches of the Santa Ynez Valley. Sanford produces excellent chardonnay and pinot noir. The vin gris made from pinot noir is one of the state's best rosés.

WHITCRAFT

Established 1985 *Owner* Chris Whitcraft *Production* 3,000 cases *Vineyard area* NA

Chris Whitcraft produces 3,000 cases of chardonnay and pinot noir by hand, with minimal intervention. He has had a wealth of tasting experience and is most familiar with burgundian wines and techniques. His wines are rich, balanced, full of flavor, and elegant. Most are sold at the winery.

ZACA MESA

Established 1973 *Owners* the Cushman family *Production* 37,617 cases *Vineyard area* 247 acres (100 ha)

Winemaker Dan Gehrs, who arrived several years ago, is making good chardonnay, viognier and roussanne. Even better is the syrah, which is known for intensity of berry, smoky flavors reminiscent of the northern Rhône.

A winery sign invites visitors to sample the wares of this large estate.

Southern California

Patrick Farrell MW

Southern California, that land of surfin' dudes, glitz and celluloid, has a rich wine history. Production flourished in Los Angeles and Orange counties through the early part of the 1900s until Pierce's disease, then aptly named Anaheim disease, wiped out commercial grape growing in Orange County. Escalating real-estate prices and suburban sprawl led to the demise of commercial viticulture in Los Angeles County. Other than curiosities such as good cabernet sauvignon grown in Beverly Hills or Malibu, Temecula and Cucamonga are Southern California's AVAs of significance. Ever-growing metropolitan Los Angeles chips away at Cucamonga's old vines—first planted in 1838—offering them an uncertain future. Pierce's disease has ravaged Temecula and places this improving region in peril. Yet, both regions are important from historical and current viticultural perspectives.

Los Angeles has long been the population and commercial center of California. The state's first wine industry, which retained primacy until the latter nineteenth century, developed here. Cucamonga was known for strong, sweet wines; sandy soil discouraged phylloxera and encouraged expansion in the late nineteenth century, increasing fourfold from 1870–1890. As the greater Los Angeles area grew during the twentieth century, vineyard land gave way to homes, industry, roads and the Ontario airport. Vineyard area shrank from 20,000 acres (8,093 ha) in 1960 to 1,000 (405 ha) in 1997.

Temecula's experimentation with vineyards began in the 1960s. Industrialist Ely Callaway first planted vines in 1969 and by 1974 had a winery. However, Temecula languished in the shadow of Napa, Sonoma and Santa Barbara counties. Quality has been improving, but the discovery of Pierce's disease, and especially of a new vector, the glassy-winged sharpshooter, has cast a pall over the region.

The San Gabriel and San Bernardino Mountains—in the greater Los Angeles area—create a favorable climate and a smog-causing inversion layer even though they are 50 miles (80 km) from the coast. The cooling effects of the Pacific Ocean yields a temperature gradient from the cool coast to the very warm mountain foothills.

The Cucamonga Valley sits near the eastern edge of this plain and is very warm, though evenings are cooled by Pacific breezes. At the Temecula Valley, closer to San Diego than to Los Angeles, the coastal range approaches the coast and a gap in the mountains brings cooler air some 22 miles (35 km) inland. Temecula is a warm region; its altitude of 1,400–1,600 feet (427–488 m) also contributes to the moderate climate.

Vines and wines

The Cucamonga Valley still contains 1,000 acres (405 ha) of vines, though there has been a progressive loss of vineyard land to industry and housing. Old, dry-farmed vines maintain such rhône varieties as mourvedre, syrah, grenache and cinsault, which have become particularly fashionable in California. Old vine mission grapes are still found and provide a vital link to the past. Deep sandy soils have protected the vines from phylloxera and the absence of citrus and other hosts for the leafhopper have kept Pierce's disease away.

Viticulture in Temecula has seen quality improvement over the past decade, particularly with canopy management and new varieties. Although chardonnay has been successful, the shift to rhône and italian varieties better suited to the warm climate has yielded the best wines to date.

Tragedy struck in the form of Pierce's disease (PD). This bacterial disease disrupts the vine's ability to transport water from the roots to the leaves and has no known cure. There were some successful spraying programs, but a variation of the vector has created havoc statewide. Glassy-winged sharpshooters also feed on citrus trees—one reason southern California has had so many problems. Of greater concern is the insect's ability to infect oleander shrubs. How does this affect the production of wine? The glassy-winged sharpshooter could reach all the state's vines because the California freeways are lined with attractive, drought-resistant oleanders. Research into PD has increased markedly—spikes laden with the antibiotic tetracycline have proved somewhat successful in combating the problem.

5 miles
(8 kilometers)

To Los Angeles
55 miles (88 km) Quail
Valley Sun City

Lake Elsinore

Lake
Elsinore

15   215

RIVERSIDE

NORTH

RIVERSIDE

County boundary
and name   Murrieta

Lake
Skinner

Temecula
Valley

UNITED
STATES WASHINGTON DC

Temecula
Valley

Vail Lake

Temecula

Creek

To San Diego
50 miles (80 km) SAN DIEGO

Producers
1 Callaway Vineyard & Winery
2 Cilurzo Vineyard & Winery
3 Hart Winery
4 Maurice Carrie Vineyard & Winery
5 Mount Palomar Winery
6 Temecula Crest Winery
7 Thornton Winery

Cucamonga viticulture techniques provide a link to the past—Galleano still utilizes old redwood fermenting tanks that were standard issue in California before the stainless-steel, temperature-control revolution. Fortified wine production and solera systems remain integral to the production of old-vine, palomino-based "sherry" and angelica.

Still, sparkling, sweet and fortified wines are all represented in the two regions, with table wines having the greatest economic impact. Both are too warm to produce high-quality chardonnay, though Temecula chardonnay, specifically Callaway's has had good marketing and commercial success.

Some producers sourced better-quality, cool-climate chardonnay fruit from the central coast regions. Some 65 percent of Temecula's planted vines are chardonnay, much of it belonging to regional giant Callaway. Viognier here has been high quality, clean and fruity with variable amounts of oak. Chenin blanc produces a clean, floral fruity wine with good retained acidity. Cabernet sauvignon and merlot from Temecula—though not as successful as petite sirah or zinfandel—have improved and produce rich, alcoholic and tannic wines.

The real excitement comes from other varieties. Cucamonga produces alcoholic, full-throttle rhône-style wines from old-vine grenache, syrah, cinsault, carignane and mourvedre. Galleano has been the standard-bearer, producing interesting wines without California's penchant to season with new oak. Temecula has also produced good wines from the same Rhône varieties, as well as barbera, sangiovese and cortese. Hart and Thornton Wineries from Temecula have produced very good red rhône-style wines with grapes from Cucamonga. Traditional method sparkling wine is produced, particularly by Thornton, though chardonnay and pinot grapes are sourced from cooler portions of the Central Coast.

Old-vine palomino and several Portuguese varieties provide excellent material for fortified wines from Cucamonga. Sherry and port-style wines have richness and length of finish—some of the state's best.

CUCAMONGA VALLEY

The Cucamonga Valley's 1,000 acres (405 ha) has vines scattered amid freeways, the Ontario airport, industrial developments and new housing. The city of Rancho Cucamonga is its hub. This warm region sits 30–45 miles (48–72 km) east on the I-15 interstate from Temecula. Though in decline as a viticultural region, it remains an important

source of old-vine grenache, mourvedre, syrah, zinfandel and mission for the state. Cucamonga fruit is shipped to winemakers in Temecula, Napa, Sonoma and on the Central Coast.

GALLEANO WINERY
Established 1927 ***Owner*** Don Galleano ***Production*** 9,000 cases ***Vineyard area*** 100 acres (40.1 ha) owned; 500 acres (202 ha) leased

Galleano is a producer of note—it is a resource for dry-farmed, old-vine rhône varieties and zinfandel. The Galleano winery and housing buildings are historic landmarks under siege from industrial expansion. Wine prices are very reasonable. The grenache rosé has attracted many medals; it is dry, clean and packed with peppery, berry grenache. Zinfandel, grenache, carignane and mourvedre—barrel and vat—demonstrate purity of varietal fruit and great character.

J. FILIPPI WINERY
Established 1922 ***Owners*** Filippi family ***Production*** 40,000 cases ***Vineyard area*** 200 acres (80.2 ha)

Giovanni Filippi first planted his vineyard in 1922. The Filippis survived Prohibition by shipping grapes for home winemaking and selling sacramental wine. Son Joseph A. Filippi graduated from UC Davis and expanded the winery. During the 1960s production reached several hundred thousand gallons per year with a capacity of 1,000,000 gallons (4,550,000 l). Despite shrinking vineyards in the region, Filippi is expanding by planting new vineyards locally, including syrah, viognier and sangiovese. They are also sourcing grapes from Napa, Sonoma, Monterey, Temecula and the Central Coast.

TEMECULA VALLEY

Temecula in Luiseno Indian means "where the sun shines through the mist." Cool air from the Pacific 22 miles (35 km) away, moderates temperatures from late afternoon via the Rainbow and Santa Margarita gaps in the coastal mountain ranges. Well-drained granite soils and low rainfall necessitate irrigation. Phylloxera has not been a problem here, despite many own-rooted vines. Pierce's

Fall colors and the rich red soil.

REGIONAL BEST

QUALITY WINES

Hart Barbera, Mourvèdre, Syrah, Zinfandel
Thornton Vintage Blanc de Blanc
Mount Palomar Cortese
Orfila Syrah
Viognier

BEST VALUE WINES

Hart Grenache Rosé
Callaway Dolcetto
Galleano Zinfandel, Grenache Rosé

Mechanical harvesting in Santa Ynez Valley.

disease remains the primary challenge to the more than 3,000 acres (1,214 ha) of vines and 28 varieties. More than 200 acres (80 ha) were lost in 1999 to the glassy-winged sharpshooter with about 30 percent of vines affected.

CALLAWAY VINEYARD & WINERY

Established 1969 *Owner* Allied Domecq Wines *Production* 250,000 cases *Vineyard area* 740 acres (299 ha)

The largest and most commercially successful winery in Temecula, Callaway has staked its reputation on well-priced, lees-aged chardonnay. Viognier, pinot gris and chenin blanc are all well made. Once a white wine specialist, Callaway now produces several reds, the best an inexpensive dolcetto showing expansive cherry, earthy palate notes. Sweet Nancy is a botrytized chenin blanc that is simply one of California's best.

CILURZO VINEYARD & WINERY

Established 1968 (vineyard), 1978 (winery) *Owner* Vincenzo Cilurzo *Production* 10,000 cases *Vineyard area* 40 acres (16.1 ha)

The Cilurzo family runs a pleasant tasting room. Wine quality is much improved in recent years while prices remain reasonable. Priced less than US$10, the chardonnay, sauvignon blanc, chenin blanc and old-vine zinfandel all drink well. Red wines, including merlot, reserve merlot and petite sirah reserve, demonstrate ripe fruit, power and balance. The late-harvest petite sirah is a delight.

HART WINERY

Established 1974 (vineyard), 1980 (winery) *Owners* Hart family *Production* 4,000 cases *Vineyard area* 11 acres (4.5 ha)

Hart has a reputation for the best quality production in Temecula. Every wine has balance and delightful fruit that is allowed to take center stage, with judicious use of oak. The grenache rosé is one of California's best blush wines. Viognier demonstrates wonderful apricot aromatics with refreshing acidity and balance. Red rhône varieties are all well made, as is barbera. With rare exceptions, cellar-door prices represent very good value.

MAURICE CARRIE VINEYARD & WINERY

Established 1986 *Owners* G. Budd and M. C. Van Roekel *Production* 25,000 cases *Vineyard area* 120 acres (48.6 ha)

Carrie is one of the more visitor-friendly wineries in Temecula with a long wine bar and affable staff.

Cleanly made wines sell at good prices. This is a popular stop on limousine winery-hopping tours.

MOUNT PALOMAR WINERY

Established 1975 *Owners* Poole Properties Inc. *Production* 14,000 cases *Vineyard area* 75 acres (30.4 ha)

Mount Palomar makes quality wines and also supplies grapes to other growers. Most remarkable is an unoaked, cleanly made cortese with good intensity of fruit, lively acidity, good balance and a long finish. Varietal and blended white rhône varieties under the Rey Sol label, were also successful.

TEMECULA CREST WINERY

Established 1994 *Owners* Carol and Phil Bailey *Production* 3,500 cases *Vineyard area* 15 acres (6.1 ha)

The Bailey family also owns the Bailey winery, but Temecula Crest's wines are decidedly better than those of the "flagship." Value is found in the sauvignon blanc, riesling and cabernet blanc. Also notable, the Ranch Red—a blend of cabernet, merlot and sangiovese. Winemaker Steve Hagada's own small brand, Piedra, looks promising. Barrel samples of syrah, sangiovese, grenache and barbera all have a hand-crafted feel.

THORNTON WINERY

Established 1981 *Owners* Sally and John Thornton *Production* 30,000 cases *Vineyard area* 6 acres (2.4 ha)

Previously called "Culbertson," Thornton retains a good reputation for sparkling wines and, now, for some good, still wines. A good chardonnay is sourced from Santa Barbara. Most impressive is the range of rhône and italian varieties demonstrating good varietal character without excessive oak. Viognier, barbera, a southern rhône blend and old-vine zinfandel are all impressive. The excellent Café Champagne stands in the grounds and it is well worth having a meal there.

SAN PASQUAL VALLEY

Located 15 miles (24 km) from the Pacific Ocean, the San Pasqual Valley AVA is cooler than either Temecula or Cucamonga. This is also the newest area, and one that is up and coming.

ORFILA VINEYARDS & WINERY

Established 1994 *Owner* Alejandro Orfila *Production* 10,000 cases *Vineyard area* 40 areas (16 ha)

Orfila's wines have been turning heads over the past two years. Its syrah and viognier have received rave reviews and won handfuls of medals. The merlot and sangiovese are also well done.

EASTERN UNITED STATES

Marguerite Thomas

In the early 1990s the wine industry in the eastern United States was restricted to isolated vintners producing regional curiosities with a modest local following. Aggressively flavored and usually sweet, wines were almost always made from native American grapes (principally *Vitis labrusca*) and/ or French–American hybrids. Today the European *Vitis vinifera* dominates the east and its wines are attracting critical acclaim, both internationally and in upscale restaurants.

The whites showed the earliest promise, especially riesling, chardonnay and the hybrids seyval and vidal. More recently, however, red wines— cabernet sauvignon, cabernet franc and merlot— have also improved. The rise of the region's best is an inspiring tale that combines equal parts technology, foresight, good farming and good fortune.

History

Wine has been made in the United States since Europeans arrived. The colonists found grapes in the new land—there are more grape varieties in the region between the Atlantic coast and the Rocky Mountains than anywhere else on earth. Unfortunately, these grapes produced wine with unappealing aromas and flavors, described as "foxy"— current thinking suggests the culprit is o-amino acetophenone. European cuttings were brought to Virginia in 1619, and for 350 years America struggled to establish a viable commercial wine industry. Freezing winters and hot, humid summers took their toll, but the worst enemy was disease. While native grapes were resistant to Pierce's disease, black rot, phylloxera, mildews and other indigenous fungal problems, European imports were not.

Once phylloxera was brought under control in the late 1800s, California's wine industry soared. In the cooler, damper eastern states, *vinifera* vines remained an impossible dream and viticulturists turned to hybrids. With improved vineyard practices, the industry began to flourish, particularly around Lake Erie and the Finger Lakes.

Yet before the boom had begun, it was all over. In 1920 the 18th Amendment to the Constitution of the United States was enacted, prohibiting the manufacture, sale, transportation or importation of alcoholic beverages. Prohibition lasted until 1933, when the 21st Constitutional Amendment, repealing the 18th, was passed. During the 13 dry years, thousands of wineries across America were forced to shut; a hundred or so in California and New York survived by making sacramental wines for the clergy, medicinal wines for pharmacies, wine-based health "tonics" and fresh grape juice concentrate. Some wineries pressed grapes into "wine bricks" for sale to home winemakers— heads of households were allowed to make 200 gallons (757 l) of wine annually for personal use.

With Prohibition repealed, California began to rebuild its wine industry. In the east, progress was slow—vineyards had been ripped out, winemaking equipment broken, winemaking skills forgotten. Until farm winery Acts were passed (mostly in the 1970s), state winery licenses were prohibitively expensive for all but the largest wineries. State and local laws regulated a host of activities such as days and times wineries could open and they could not sell wine direct to consumers (see below).

Leon Adams, in *The Wines of America*, writes that the American wine industry was "reborn in ruins." Many eastern wineries replaced native grape varieties with hybrids. Philip Wagner, founder of Boordy Vineyards in Maryland, helped develop and promote hybrids as a more palate-pleasing alternative to the labrusca grapes. But they were still a long way from the flavor profile of wines from Europe or California.

Change in the east came via an émigré from the Ukraine. Dr Konstantin Frank had successfully grown *vinifera* grapes back home— freezing winters could not be the reason European vines died in eastern America, he said. Disease and pests were the problem, and these could be controlled by modern science.

One of the few to listen was Charles Fournier. Formerly chief winemaker at Veuve Clicquot, Fournier came to Gold Seal Vineyards in New York's Finger Lakes in 1934. Gold Seal, founded as the Urbana Wine Company in 1865, had prospered until Prohibition, and

Riesling were among the earliest varieties grown in the East.

The beautiful Art Deco Chrysler Building overlooks New York's urban maze.

Statue of first president George Washington in lower Manhattan.

Fournier's mission was to recapture its former greatness. Fournier hired Frank in 1953, and together they began grafting grapes onto cold-resistant rootstock found locally and in Canada; they also initiated new trellis-training methods.

In 1957, when temperatures around the Finger Lakes dropped to –25°F (–4°C) about a third of the buds on local native and hybrid vines perished, but the *vinifera* vines that Frank and Fournier had planted were relatively unscathed. Winemaking on the eastern coast suddenly shifted course.

It was almost 30 years before various states in the east began to cultivate vines in earnest. Virginia maintained a modest wine industry until Prohibition, but struggled to regain momentum after Repeal (early vintners were Thomas Jefferson and George Washington). Only in the past decade has growth surged: in 1976, for example, Virginia had six wineries; by 1999 it had 60.

Ninety percent of all American wine is produced in California. With the remaining 10 percent divided among the other 47 wine-producing states, the output from each is a comparative trickle. For example, Sakonnet, the largest winery in New England, produces 50,000 cases a year—the output for a medium-sized California winery. An average eastern winery turns out 6,000–8,000 cases annually. Yet production continues at an astonishing rate. In 1995, for example, Virginia produced 75,000 cases; by 1998 the figure was 214,340 cases. Other states may soon be producing wine commercially. Vermont, whose climate was considered too extreme for viticulture, has recently seen successful plantings of *vinifera*.

Factors driving the extraordinary recent boom include the strong economy of the late 1980s and 1990s, technological advances, improvements in winemaking techniques and vineyard practices, the lifting of some restrictive laws, and the increased education and interest of consumers. Support and assistance from state governments, notably New York and Virginia, and scientific and practical help from Cornell University and Virginia Institute of Technology, have also played critical roles.

Landscape and climate

There are three distinct viticultural areas: Benchlands, Atlantic Uplands and Mountains. The Benchlands are benches of sand, sediment and stone formed from debris left by drifting glaciers thousands of years ago. The Benchlands include southeastern Massachusetts and the coastal sections of Rhode Island, Connecticut, Long Island, New Jersey and Virginia. Weather here is usually temperate due to the moderating influence of the Atlantic Ocean and Long Island Sound. Farther inland, the viticultural region around Lake Erie resembles the Benchlands, with its gravel and loam glacial soils and a climate moderated by the deep waters of the lake. Benchland soils are generally well drained, and because the coast tends to be warmer than inland, grapes ripen more completely.

The Atlantic Uplands, also known as the Piedmont, is a vast plateau between the coastal zones of the Atlantic Ocean and the eastern mountain ranges. The Uplands has mineral-rich, well-drained soils and a relatively long growing season. Characterized by gently rolling hills, the viticultural Uplands include northern New Jersey, the Delaware River Valley, much of Pennsylvania, Maryland, northern and central Virginia, Connecticut, the Hudson River Valley and Finger Lakes regions of New York.

Grapes struggle in the high altitudes and harsh climate of the eastern mountainous regions, but in certain isolated microclimates in the mountains of Virginia and central Pennsylvania the right combination of soil and sunlight provides a hospitable environment for vines. Because the mountain air tends to be drier than in the humid Benchlands and Uplands, fungus and mildew are less virulent. Grapes ripening slowly during the long cool growing season develop intense colors and flavors.

Vines and wines

Until the 1950s, *Vitis vinifera* could not survive the pests and climate-induced diseases of the eastern United States. Before French–American hybrids were introduced, all wine in the east was made from native grapes or from either natural (chance pollination) or deliberate crosses. The most important grape in the east was concord, a dark grape cultivated from wild *V. labrusca* seeds. Norton, another domesticated native, gave a red wine without foxy flavors. (Norton is enjoying a mini-renaissance.) Other important native or naturally hybridized grapes include alexander, delaware, catawba, dutchess, isabella, ives and niagara.

Popular French–American hybrids include elvira, baco, cayuga, chambourcin, chancellor, marechal foch, seyval blanc, vidal blanc and vignoles. These varieties are rapidly being replaced by *vinifera*, although some vintners continue to work with them. Vintners consider hybrids more dependable, and believe the best examples are good enough to compete with any wine.

The best white grapes in the east include chardonnay with a wide stylistic range, but wines are more likely to show the restraint of French chardonnay than the fruitiness of California wine. Riesling (dry, semi-dry or sweet) is well-suited to the cooler regions around Lake Erie and the Finger Lakes. Gewürztraminer, especially from New England and the Finger Lakes, can yield fragrant and delicate wines. Seyval blanc, perhaps the finest French–American hybrid, can resemble a fragrant blend of chardonnay and pinot blanc. Vidal blanc promises most—especially grapes from the Finger Lakes or the mountains of Virginia—as a late-harvest or icewine with intense honeyed flavors and bracing acidity. Vignoles (also called ravat) also makes outstanding late-harvest and icewine.

The best red grapes in the east include merlot, arguably the dominant red in Virginia and on Long Island, where it can produce full-bodied lively single-varietal wines and is important, with cabernet sauvignon and cabernet franc, in red blends. Cabernet franc is often thin and herbaceous, but is getting better, with medium body and a balance of fruit and acidity. Sometimes good as a single varietal, cabernet sauvignon is at its best in bordeaux-style blends. Pinot noir is starting to show (in the Finger Lakes, for example) but is very dependent on a good weather, full ripeness and low yields—-as well as superior winemaking.

Laws

Laws regulating the marketing, sales and distribution of wine are extremely complex. One lasting effect of Prohibition is that the regulation of liquor laws remains under the jurisdiction of individual states, resulting in a frustrating tangle that varies from state to state, even community to community.

Nationally, wine is under the control of the Bureau of Alcohol, Tobacco and Firearms (BATF) which regulates the way it is taxed, classified, marketed, labeled, sold and consumed. Joining BATF regulations are state and local statutes, with the infamous three-tier marketing system that links manufacturers (producers, vintners, *négociants*), wholesalers/distributors and retailers. Encouraged by these last groups, most states forbid or partially restrict shipment of wine direct to consumers, which is most harmful to wineries in the east. With so many states, and so many different wineries, allowing sales direct from winery to consumer seems like the logical solution, but powerful lobby groups resist rationalization of the laws.

Green vistas and fertile farmland in Pennsylvania, part of the Atlantic Uplands.

New York State

New York state is arguably the most promising wine-producing state in the east. Along with Virginia, it has led the eastern states in wine production since the repeal of Prohibition. Locals even seem to have acquired a taste for the foxy wines produced in the early days. Although wine production goes back 170 years, two-thirds of the state's 139 wineries have been established since 1985. The industry is a work in progress; certain varietals—for example, riesling from the Finger Lakes—may be better suited to the east than to more temperate West Coast climes.

BEDELL CELLARS

Established 1980 *Owners* John and Susan Bedell
Production 8,500 cases *Vineyard area* 30 acres (12 ha)

John "Kip" Bedell began full-time winemaking in 1990 and has has a great influence on other Long Island vintners, particularly in overcoming the variability of eastern growing seasons. His merlot, chardonnay, cabernet and a riesling dessert wine ("Eis") are outstanding.

FOX RUN VINEYARDS

Established 1990 *Owners* Scott Osborne and Andy Hale
Production 14,000 cases *Vineyard area* 50 acres (20 ha)

One of Finger Lake's most exciting wineries, Fox Run was bought by Scott Osborne in 1994. Canadian-born winemaker Peter Bell was trained in Australia (at Charles Sturt University). Fox Run's aromatic and crisp riesling demonstrates its excellent potential in this region. The blanc de blancs is a refreshing sparkler and recent vintages of reserve pinot noir have been showing well.

DR FRANK'S VINIFERA WINE CELLARS/CHÂTEAU FRANK

Established 1963 *Owners* Frank family
Production 25,000 cases *Vineyard area* 76 acres (31 ha)

Founded by Dr Konstantin Frank and now run by his son Willy. The riesling and gewürztraminer are among the region's best. Recent chardonnays have been crisp and flavorful. Sister winery, Château Frank, makes sprightly sparklers.

MILLBROOK VINEYARDS & WINERY

Established 1985 *Owners* John and Kathe Dyson
Production 15,500 cases *Vineyard area* 52 acres (21 ha)

This winery was formerly an old dairy farm in the Hudson River region. Among Millbrook's productions are an oaky chardonnay, a fragrant, full-bodied tokay and a cabernet franc infused with sweet berry overtones.

PALMER VINEYARDS

Established 1986 *Owner* Robert Palmer *Production* 25,000 cases *Vineyard area* 120 acres (48.6 ha)

One of Long Island's largest wineries and one of the east's most recognized labels. The pinot blanc, barrel-fermented chardonnay, gewürztraminer and merlot all tend to be fuller-bodied and bolder-flavored than many of their counterparts.

HERMANN J. WIEMER VINEYARD, INC.

Established 1980 *Owner* Hermann J. Wiemer *Production* 12,000 cases *Vineyard area* 65 acres (26 ha)

A native of Germany's Moselle region, and arguably the most respected vintner in the east, Wiemer is at home with the cool climate and glacial soils of the Finger Lakes. Riesling and gewürztraminer reminiscent of Alsace, as well as trockenbeerenauslese-style late-harvest riesling are stunners. Recent chardonnay has also been impressive.

WOLFFER ESTATE

Established 1992 *Owner* Christian Wolffer *Production* 9,000 cases *Vineyard area* 50 acres (20 ha)

Formerly Sagpond Vineyards, this is the most important winery on Long Island's South Fork. Winemaker Roman Roth's production is admirably restricted to a few varietals, a flinty and refreshing chardonnay and a merlot with juicy cherry flavors. The sparkling has elegance and structure.

OTHER EASTERN PRODUCERS

BARBOURSVILLE VINEYARDS, VIRGINIA

Established 1976 *Owners* Zonin family *Production* 25,000 cases *Vineyard area* 120 acres (48.6 ha)

Founded by Zonin, Italian winemakers, Barboursville was the first producer to succeed with *vinifera* varieties in Virginia. Winemaker Luca Paschina produces Italian classics—pinot grigio, sangiovese

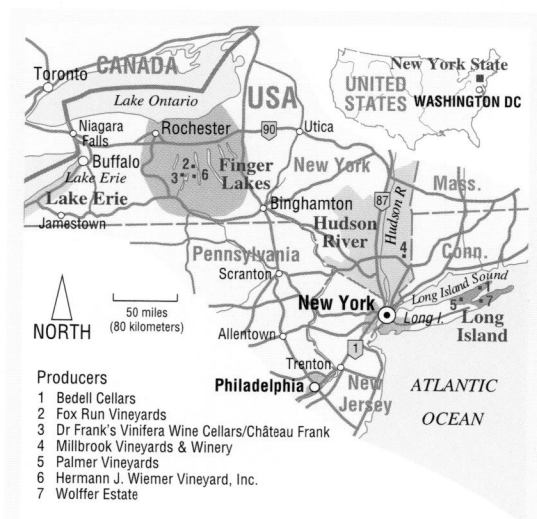

Producers
1 Bedell Cellars
2 Fox Run Vineyards
3 Dr Frank's Vinifera Wine Cellars/Château Frank
4 Millbrook Vineyards & Winery
5 Palmer Vineyards
6 Hermann J. Wiemer Vineyard, Inc.
7 Wolffer Estate

and barbera, as well as chardonnay, merlot, pinot noir, cabernet franc and cabernet sauvignon. Good vintages of lush dessert wines—philéo (muscat, riesling and malvasia) and malvasia reserve.

CHADDSFORD WINERY, PENNSYLVANIA

Established 1982 *Owners* Eric and Lee Miller *Production* 30,000 cases *Vineyard area* 30 acres (12 ha)

Like many eastern wineries Chaddsford produces an astonishing range of wines from hybrid and *vinifera* grapes. Good vintages produce fruity pinot grigio and high-end chardonnays, as well as some complex cabernet blends.

HORTON VINEYARDS, VIRGINIA

Established 1993 *Owners* Dennis and Sharon Horton *Production* 25,000 cases *Vineyard area* 100 acres (40.5 ha)

From a few vines planted in 1983, the winery is today one of Virginia's success stories. Dennis Horton concentrates on viognier, marsanne, syrah, mourvèdre, grenache and malbec. Another hot-climate success is touriga nacional. Horton's norton, a native grape that produces inky purple wine redolent of plums and cherries, is a favorite.

LINDEN VINEYARDS, VIRGINIA

Established 1988 *Owner* Jim Law *Production* 6,000 cases *Vineyard area* 16 acres (6.5 ha)

Linden's wines are among the best in Virginia. "[The grapes] ripen in October, when the fruit has great intensity," Law says, which helps explain the appeal of the powerful chardonnay, the aromatic seyval, the luscious sauvignon blanc (like a New Zealand wine) and the rich cabernet sauvignon.

SAKONNET VINEYARDS, NEW ENGLAND

Established 1985 *Owners* Susan and Earl Samson *Production* 50,000 cases *Vineyard area* 45 acres (18 ha)

The Samsons are dedicated to making and marketing eastern wine. Winemaker John Sotello, formerly with California's prestigious Iron Horse, has helped guide Sakonnet's evolution. Among its best wines are fragrant gewürztraminer, peachy vidal blanc, elegant fumé blanc and rich chardonnay.

WESTPORT VINEYARDS, MASSACHUSETTS

Established 1991 *Owners* Russell family *Production* 1,200 cases *Vineyard area* 80 acres (32 ha)

This Massachusetts winery is one of the premiere sparkling wine producers in the east. The blanc de blancs are fresh and delicate; blanc de noirs are fuller and creamier. Brut Cuvée RJR aims for Champagne-like complexity. Ninety percent of Westport's wine is made from estate-grown fruit.

WHITE HALL VINEYARDS, VIRGINIA

Established 1994 *Owners* Antony and Edith Champ *Production* 5,000 cases *Vineyard area* 25 acres (10 ha)

This Virginia winery won awards with its very first releases. It makes outstanding chardonnay, pinot gris, gewürztraminer, cabernet sauvignon, cabernet franc, merlot and soliterre, a vidal dessert wine.

A vineyard sign welcomes visitors to the winery of New England's largest producer.

Tending the vines at Brimstone Hill Winery, on the Shawangunk Wine Trail, New York.

Other US Regions

Marguerite Thomas

Building drystone walls is a skill taken from the Old World to the New by early settlers.

THE SOUTHWEST

The Southwest is the oldest wine-producing region in the United States. Spanish missionaries planted grapes in New Mexico in the 1500s, and in Texas in the 1600s. Scores of vineyards and wineries thrived until 1920 and Prohibition. Replanting did not begin in earnest until the 1970s. Today Texas is the fifth-largest wine-producing state in the US with more than 3,000 acres (1,214 ha) of mostly *vinifera* grapes and 32 commercial wineries (six more scheduled to open in 2000). New Mexico has 22 wineries and foreign investment (especially from France) has been strong. Colorado has 26 wineries, with virtually all its vineyards on the western slopes of the state.

The Southwest, where the sun shines intensely from cloudless skies, has the warmest summer weather of any grape-growing region in the US, yet winters can be bitterly cold. The lack of water in parched areas is a problem for vines. Best growing sites combine high altitude, dry air and relatively cool temperatures during the growing season.

As in most other states, restrictive laws make selling wine a challenge, although this is starting to change. In Arizona, for example, recent changes in state law will make it easier for vintners to sell their wine direct within the state itself.

Chardonnay, cabernet sauvignon and merlot all do well in most of the southwestern viticultural regions. Sauvignon blanc, chenin blanc and riesling are also favored. Zinfandel is gaining a foothold, particularly in western Texas, and syrah, sangiovese and tempranillo all show promise. Good dessert wines, especially fortified port-style wines, are quite successful in areas where the hot summers and cold winters resemble the climate in the Douro Valley in Portugal.

CALLAGHAN, ARIZONA

Established 1991 *Owner* Kent Callaghan *Production* 1500–2,000 cases *Vineyard area* 17 acres (7 ha)

Callaghan is by far the most visible of the handful of wineries in Arizona. The winery's specialty is well-structured tannic blends of cabernet sauvignon with merlot and cabernet franc. Syrah looks extremely promising and recent plantings of petit verdot, mourvèdre, tempranillo and touriga francesca also seem headed for success.

COLORADO CELLARS, COLORADO

Established 1978 *Owners* Richard and Padte Turley *Production* 10,000 cases *Vineyard area* 20 acres (8 ha)

The state's oldest winery and perhaps its largest, Colorado Cellars wines include dry riesling, chardonnay, merlot and port. A perennial best-seller is Road Kill Red, a semi-sweet lemberger.

FALL CREEK VINEYARDS, TEXAS

Established 1975 *Owners* Ed and Susan Auler *Production* 35,000 cases *Vineyard area* 65 acres (26 ha)

Fall Creek produces chardonnay, chenin blanc, riesling, cabernet sauvignon and merlot. Of particular note is the high-end and very limited Meritus, a blend of merlot, cabernet sauvignon and malbec.

TWO RIVERS WINERY, COLORADO

Established 1999 *Owners* Bob and Billie Witham *Production* 3,000 cases *Vineyard area* 17 acres (7 ha)

Colorado's youngest winery, Two Rivers has already been getting good press for its chardonnay and merlot, and especially for its earthy cabernet sauvignon. The attractive winery facility is in Grand Junction. Production is expected to double over the next few years.

THE MIDWEST

The weather is always a challenge in the Midwestern states, but recent viticultural research, advances in cool-climate production technology and a string of good vintages have all contributed to some outstanding progress.

The Midwest's strongest wine-producing states are Ohio, Michigan and Missouri. In the early 1800s, Ohio was an important producer of native and hybrid wine grapes, especially the catawba. By the 1850s, it was the leading wine-producing state in the United States, but by 75 years later, disease and Prohibition had destroyed most of the region's wine industry. Serious rebuilding did not begin until the 1970s, but Ohio is now booming—it boasts 70 wineries.

Michigan had only a few wineries before Prohibition, but boutique wineries are now thriving, particularly in the southwestern corner of Lake Michigan's shoreline.

In Missouri, the first wines were made in 1823 by French Jesuits. Stone Hill—the state's leading wine estate—was founded in 1847. It became a mushroom farm during Prohibition.

The stable temperatures of the Great Lakes' deep waters warm the air blowing across the lakes, reducing the threat of late spring and early fall frosts and prolonging the growing season. In winter, heavy snow packs insulate the dormant vines.

Because of the severe Midwest winters, cool-climate grapes do best. Hybrids dominate, but *vinifera* types are gaining a following. White wines are riesling, chardonnay, gewürztraminer, seyval and vignoles. Pinot noir (for sparkling wine) and cabernet franc lead red *vinifera* plantings.

The Midwest's prospects are bright, as Ohio has introduced initiatives and incentives that have effectively promoted viticulture and winemaking. Neighboring states are beginning to follow suit.

CHALET DÉBONNÉ VINEYARDS, OHIO
Established 1971 *Owner* Debevc family *Production* 25,000 cases *Vineyard area* 80 acres (32.4 ha)

This venerable Ohio producer makes creditable chardonnay, riesling, vidal and, more recently, much-acclaimed pinot gris.

FIRELANDS WINE COMPANY, OHIO
Established 1987 *Owner* Paramount Distillery *Production* NA *Vineyard area* 210 acres (85 ha)

This company grows most of its grapes on North Bass Island, on Lake Erie. The focus is almost entirely on *vinifera*—riesling, cabernet sauvignon, cabernet franc, chardonnay, gewürztraminer and Italian-style unoaked pinot grigio.

CHÂTEAU GRAND TRAVERSE, MICHIGAN
Established 1974 *Owners* O'Keefe family *Production* 50,000 cases *Vineyard area* 112 acres (45.5 ha)

This winery established Michigan's *vinifera* industry. The johannisberg, riesling, pinot gris, chardonnay, pinot blanc, icewine and cabernet franc are all noteworthy.

HARPERSFIELD VINEYARD, OHIO
Established 1986 *Owners* Logan family *Production* 2,500 cases *Vineyard area* 14 acres (5.7 ha)

Talented Ohio winemaker Wes Gerlofsky is producing inspired chardonnay, riesling and gewürz-traminer.

L. MAWBY VINEYARDS, MICHIGAN
Established 1978 *Owner* Larry Mawby *Production* 3,000 cases *Vineyard area* 12 acres (5 ha)

Mawby's sparkling brut wines include chardonnay/pinot noir/ pinot meunier cuvée, blanc de noirs, blanc de blancs, rosé and vignoles.

PENINSULA CELLARS, MICHIGAN
Established 1994 *Owner* David Kroupa *Production* 3,500 cases *Vineyard area* 10 acres (4 ha)

This is Michigan's youngest premium producer. Look especially for the chardonnay, pinot gris and (in good years) cabernet franc.

ST JULIAN WINE COMPANY, MICHIGAN
Established 1936 *Owner* David Braganini *Production* 200,000 cases *Vineyard area* 200 acres (81 ha)

Michigan's oldest and largest winery makes a vast assortment of wines from hybrid and *vinifera* grapes.

STONEHILL WINERY, MISSOURI
Established 1847 *Owners* Held family *Production* 7,000 cases *Vineyard area* 92 acres (37 ha)

Stonehill produces hybrid and a few labrusca wines. Especially noteworthy are a bold red norton, a deliciously dry seyval, and a good sparkler.

THE WALLERSHEIM WINE COMPANY, WISCONSIN
Established 1972 *Owners* Robert and JoAnn Wallersheim *Production* 40,000 cases *Vineyard area* 23 acres (9.3 ha)

Wisconsin's top winery produces mostly red hybrid maréchal foche, plus some *vinifera*.

Freshly harvested gewürztraminer grapes.

Expanses of well-spaced, trained vines—typical of a United States' vineyard.

Mexico & South America

It is well known that Chile and Argentina have the potential to unsettle the best traditional winemakers: but neighbouring Mexico, Peru, Brazil and Uruguay each have a significant industry and great history behind them. Mexico and Peru were the most important centers of Spain's colonial empire and each had a viceregal court. As a consequence, they transplanted many of Spain's habits including the cultivation of vines and winemaking. Both Mexico and Peru are a touch hot for the best

viticulture, yet important winemaking industries survive in each. Brazil was the jewel in Portugal's empire and has inherited an interest in wine. Its economy is currently the most important in Latin America and its domestic wine market is huge. The core of Brazil's wine industry nestles on the cooler southern border with Uruguay which has a most successful wine industry. Tannat is a grape variety that is as adaptable as any and in Uruguay's several wine regions it has achieved an expressive quality found nowhere else in the world.

NORTH

250 miles
(400 kilometers)

Pico da Neblina
9888 ft (3014 m)

Macapá

Negro

Amazon   *Amazon*   Belém

Iquitos   Manaus   Santarém   São Luís

Piura   Fortaleza

Chiclayo   Imperatriz   Teresina

Tapajós   Natal

Trujillo   Nevado de Huascarán   Pucallpa   Campina Grande
           22,204 ft (6768 m)   Juázeiro do Norte   João Pessoa
Chimbote   Caruarú   Recife

                        Ucayali   Rio Branco   Maceió

                                                                              *Represa de   Serra do Escorial
                                                                              Sobradinho*   4031 ft (1229 m)
                                                            BRAZIL   Aracaju

LIMA   Feira de
           PERÚ   Santana   **Salvador**

        Ica   Cuzco
                                                                                                                    Itabuna
    Nevado Coropuna ▲   *Lake
    21,074 ft (6425 m)*   Titicaca*   Cuiabá

                    Arequipa   Anápolis   ◎ **BRASÍLIA**
                                                              Goiânia   Montes Claros
        Tacna

                                                        Uberlândia
                                                                  Uberaba   **Belo Horizonte**

                                            Campo Grande   São José do   Vitória
                                                              do Río Prêto
                                                                      Ribeirão
                                                                      Prêto
                                            Presidente Prudente   Nova Iguaçu
                                                                                        ◉ **Rio de Janeiro**
                                            Londrina   São Paulo
                                            Rio Grande do Sul

                                    Foz do Iguaçou   Curitiba

                                                              Itajaí
                                            Passo Fundo   Lajes   Florianópolis

                                            Frontera
                                                    Santa María

                                                    Porto Alegre
                                Rivera   *Lagoa dos Patos*
                        Artigas   Pelotas
                        URUGUAY   Rio Grande
                                            Lagoa Mirim
                    Colonia
                    Montevideo
                    Canelones ◎ **MONTEVIDEO**
                        Rio de la Plata

MEXICO

Mexico benefits from its long links with Europe as well as having California as a nearby, accessible and influential winemaking example. This gives it a certain charm combined with some of the scientific approach so typical of its northern neighbor. Taken as a whole, these elements make for some pretty interesting vinicultural potential within a geographical and climatological setting that, in truth, is not ideally suited to *Vitis vinifera*.

History

When Hernán Cortés set out for Mexico in 1520 he was initially charged by the Crown of Spain with trying to establish worthy trade links with what was already recognized as a sophisticated and wealthy empire. It was the glint of precious metals and the promise of unimaginable wealth and power that corrupted this enterprise. The truth is that not all of the Aztec empire's peoples were happy with their rulers, and many welcomed the Spaniards as the lesser of two evils. In turn, the conquistadores found in Mexico a land in which they soon felt at home, if not entirely at ease. They set about building a large-scale facsimile of Spain, including vineyards.

Sampling the wares at a wine seller's in Parras, Baja California, Mexico.

Within four years of their arrival, Cortés was advocating that all Spanish settlers plant grape vines. The cooler northern region of the Viceroyalty of New Spain, as Mexico became known, was called la California, an area far better suited to viticulture than the warmer south. One of the priests charged with establishing vineyards around the missions of New Spain was Juan Ugarte and he most probably planted the first mission grapes in northern Mexico and California. In fact, the oldest surviving winery in Mexico, Bodega Marqués de Aguayo was founded in 1593. Today it produces a tiny amount of wine, most of it, as is often the case in Mexico, reserved for distilling into brandy.

Brandy production and edible grapes were the most important oulet for viticulture until early in the twentieth century. Mexico might have bumbled along happily in this fashion had it not been for welcome advice from California. The Concannon family, winemakers in Livermore Valley, persuaded the Mexican government to invest in viticulture and quality varietals, many of which were shipped from Europe and planted in new settings. This groundbreaking work was followed by the insightful drive of Antonio Perelli-Minetti, who planted a considerable expanse of quality varietals in the area around Torreón.

At this point Mexican viticulture was hit by a double-barrelled blow of massive proportions that virtually undid the previous good work. First came the disaster of phylloxera, followed rapidly by the anti-establishment Mexican Revolution of 1910. It wasn't until well into the 1940s that efforts were made to improve the quality of Mexican wines. Even now, edible grapes and those destined for brandy absorb most of the efforts of viticulture in Mexico. Major world-wide producers such as Domecq, González Byass, Hennessy and Martell all have significant investments in Mexico. Sparkling wine interests have also entered the market with not inconsiderable force, including Freixenet and Martini & Rossi. These firms pick early to ensure acidity in their grapes. Cinzano and Seagrams are equally well-established.

Wine regions

Baja California in the northwest and the high-altitude valleys of the Sierra Madre offer the best potential for winemaking. Their slightly cooler nights give enologists at least a chance of capturing something like the varietal aromas so sought after.

Baja California has a climate and topography as well suited to large-scale quality viticulture as Mexico can muster. More than 10,000 acres (4,000 ha) are planted here, mainly near Ensenada in the Guadalupe Valley. Bodegas Santo Tomás makes commendable chardonnay and some cabernet sauvignon that, although not aromatically spot-on, is passable. Bodegas Santo Tomás and Monte Zenic give Mexican winemaking a diversity that is evident in the varieties used. You can find wines from chardonnay to viognier, from barbera through cabernet sauvignon to pinot noir here. Bodega Santa Tomás alone grows 14 different varieties. L. A. Cetto makes Mexico's most memorable and recommendable range of wines. Their nebbiolo and petit syrah have met with some critical success, although not every harvest has yielded a wine you could express full confidence in, which gives some idea of the difficulties enologists have to work against. Stainless steel has brought significant improvements in Mexico, as wine storage used to be one of the prime causes for the wholesale oxidation of wines kept in tanks at relatively high temperatures. Earlier bottling is another factor that is influencing wines positively.

Laguna, Torreón, has seen recent investment at Bodega Vergel. New vinification equipment struggles admirably to coax aromatic life out of grapes that grow in a warm climate, even those that have been planted at some altitude.

Parras Valley, Saltillo, north of Mexico City, is almost certainly America's earliest viticultural enclave. An altitude of 1,500 feet (458 m) comes to the rescue here. Still, brandy remains king. Of historical note is Bodegas de San Lorenzo, founded in 1626. Viñedos San Marcos is quite a modern establishment, producing reasonable sparkling wine and some modest cabernet sauvignon.

San Juan del Río takes viticulture to 6,000 feet (1,830 m). This altitude allows for somewhat more aromatic potential in the grapes near harvest time. Cavas de San Juan makes some interesting cabernet sauvignon and tentative pinot noir under the Hidalgo label here. Its Carte Blanche sparkling wine is worthy of note.

Above: *Vineyards set among the muted tones of the Guadalupe Valley, Mexico.*

Vineyard workers grafting cabernet sauvignon onto phylloxera-resistant rootstock. Casa Madero, Pajas Valley, Mexico.

Corked bottles of chardonnay at Chateau Camou, Guadalupe Valley, Mexico.

Sonora is home to extensive plantations of the Thompson seedless variety. This is mostly edible grape and brandy territory.

Zacatecas and Aguascalientes plateaus grow grapes at up to 7,000 feet (2,135 m). Some vines are now reaching maturity at around 30 years old and Bodegas Altiplano has some reasonable wines. A new region called Querétaro may yet provide further potential for aromatic properties in varietals that have been carefully selected.

PERÚ

As the focal point of Spain's imperial presence in South America, Perú was the first country on the continent to benefit from viticulture. The elegance of the Viceroyalty of Perú required table grapes and wines to accompany South America's best and most diverse cuisine. This is not to say that there wasn't already a predisposition toward fermented beverages in Perú. The Incas considered alcohol as one of the Sun God's gifts, and deemed the drinking of *chicha* (fermented purple corn) an acceptable way of acknowledging the god's munificence.

Just-picked moscatel beneath the vines at Castillo Viejo, Uruguay.

History

The fabulous wealth of the Incas, whose gold represented the Sun God and silver the Moon God, initially attracted Spanish adventurers and ruffians who were, nevertheless, intent on retaining the habits of home. The first vineyards were planted in the 1540s under the instructions of Francisco Pizarro, the *conquistador*.

Lima, Perú's colonial capital, became a hub for culture, architecture, music and literature, a vice-regal capital of some splendor. By the 1560s up to 98,840 acres (40,000 ha) were planted. However, climatic conditions in Perú, part of which sits astride the equator, did not favor the production of quality wine. However, with the advent of distillation into grape brandy in the 1650s, courtesy of Franciscan missionaries, the prospects for viticulture changed considerably.

The Pisco River disgorges into the Pacific Ocean 100 miles (160 km) south of Lima. The Pisco Valley proved a suitable spot for cultivating moscatel, torontel, albillo and a host of lesser-known grape varieties, all destined to be distilled into a spirit also called Pisco.

Landscape

Perú is divided into three main geographical areas: coastal (bordering the Pacific to the west), central mountain (made up of two huge cordilleras of the Andes with an altiplano or high-altitude plain), and the Amazon Basin (to the east). All viticulture of note takes place on the coastal area, reaching up into the foothills of the Andes. This area is made up of a sandy-alluvial strip of varying width, punctuated by oases arising wherever rivers flow down with life-giving water from the Andes. Winter temperatures remain too high for vines to go into full dormancy, which makes it difficult to restrain vigor, although careful monitoring of anhydrous stress can yield reasonable results. Most Pisco producers can obtain two harvests per year.

Vines and wines

Quality wine production is concentrated mainly around the city of Ica, 209 miles (336 km) south of Lima. Surprisingly, there is a single producer in Lima itself, Santiago Queirolo, halfway between Lima and its port, Callao. These two towns were once distinct urban centers, with the Queirolo between them. Today Lima has engulfed its environs, including the hardy Queirolo. Where its grapes are grown today is open to question but all credit must go to it for tenacity.

The main force in Peruvian wine-making today is Tacama, based a short distance outside Ica. Tacama began life as an Augustinian convent but in 1889 it passed into private ownership. With 370 acres (150 ha) of vines on alluvial soils, it is as well suited to viticulture as is currently feasible. Vine dormancy is (just) possible between July and August, with flowering occurring in October. Stainless steel and temperature control have transformed production, which can total 3 million liters (792,000 gallons). Varietal malbec and blends such as Gran Vino Tinto Reserva Especial form the backbone of quality production.

Another important producer is Viña Ocucaje, also based in Ica. Owned by Jesuits in the sixteenth century, the vineyards were bought by the Rubini family, the present owners, in the 1930s. Other producers are Canepa in Tacna and Fábrica Nacional de Licores in Surco.

BRAZIL

If big is beautiful, Brazil has it all. Commercially, demographically and geographically, Brazil is a giant. Artistically and musically its contribution cannot be ignored. With 180 million people, all determined to make their mark on life, this is hardly surprising. The eighth-largest economy in the world (twice the size of Russia's) is certainly a place to sell wine. Although Brazilian interest in wine is still nascent, with annual consumption currently at less than half a gallon (2 l) per capita, the potential is plain to see.

What is also clear to those in charge of the Brazilian economy is that even this small amount multiplied by 180 million would mean a hemorrhage of hard-earned currency if all that wine had to be imported. Fortunately for the national exchequer, although perhaps not so for the winelover, Brazil is South America's third-largest wine producer after Argentina and Chile.

History

Brazil was settled by the Portuguese, who soon introduced *Vitis vinifera* into their new territory. Evidence suggests that grapes were growing near São Paulo as early as 1532. However, greater success was encountered farther south, where the Jesuits established their missions, which operated autonomously in the region of Rio Grande do Sul, and vineyards appear to have yielded reasonable harvests from about 1628. Political and religious squabbling in Europe eventually doomed these efforts and all trace of them was lost.

Serra Gaucha was settled by determined Italian immigrants who brought with them barbera, bonarda, moscato and trebbiano vines, but the most successful were hybrids, particularly isabella. Viticulture became something more of a commercial possibility once the nation was able to build a communications network, at the beginning of the twentieth century. This gave growers and winemakers access to the markets of cities such as Rio de Janeiro and São Paulo. By the late 1920s, cooperatives were forming to market the products.

Landscape and climate

Brazil is not ideal for viticulture. Straddling the equator and home to the world's largest rainforest, conditions are far too moist and hot for grapes, so viticulture is concentrated in the southernmost regions. There are two main clusters: Rio Grande do Sul, which includes the hilly Serra Gaucha region inland from Pôrto Alegre, and Frontera, close to the border with Uruguay and Argentina.

Vineyard at Pedro Domecq, Baja California, Mexico.

A touch of old Mexico. Flowers adorn the cellar entrance at Pedro Domecq.

as Moët & Chandon, Martini & Rossi and Remy Martin are all found here. Sparkling wine is made to reasonably high standards and Serra Gaucha may be better suited to this type of production than to still wine. Aurora cooperative is based in Bento Gonçalves and makes a commendable effort to market respectable still wines, but it must be heartbreaking to watch rain bucket down at harvest time as a normal occurrence.

Such hardships have not stopped enterprising concerns, such as Miolo, from investing in state-of-the-art vinification equipment. One of the Carrau brothers, better known for winemaking in Uruguay, is based in Frontera and these newer concerns are slowly moving Brazilian wine into a new age of viticulture. The *parrera*, or traditional overhead vine-training, is being discarded in favor of more advanced styles in an effort to improve fruit quality. Fruit is certainly the key to the future here, where there is so often a need to chaptalize.

It is very difficult to find varietal character in grapes grown in such warm conditions. When you add the problems inherent in humid climates, you begin to understand the task facing Brazilian winemakers. This is not an easy or forgiving country in which to make good wine.

URUGUAY

When wine buyers first started to trace wines from interesting places around the world, few would have considered this small cosmopolitan country. Despite this, Uruguayan wines have been a presence at international wine fairs for longer than those of Argentina. Its winemakers have succeeded in penetrating even the most demanding markets with products that are imaginative and well made. With an annual domestic wine consumption of some 8 gallons (30 l) per head, international wine-lovers are lucky to see any of it. The future holds great promise for this tiny producer nation.

History

Once part of the administrative region of La Plata (Argentina) under Spanish colonial rule, Uruguay was first settled in 1726 by 25 families from the Canary Isles sent out by Royal Decree to found Montevideo. With them came knowledge of how to make wine in difficult conditions. It is presumed that the earliest varieties grown, solely for domestic consumption, were all related to the moscatel.

Even here humidity, rainfall and heat can cause problems, particularly near harvest—anti-fungal warfare is a part of life here. While Serra Gaucha developed as a result of immigrant settlement, Frontera was chosen for its viticultural potential on slightly more scientific grounds and so holds most promise. There have also been some attempts at tropical viticulture near Recife in the north, but these have yet to attract serious attention.

Vines and wines

Only the bravest or those with most to gain pit themselves against the elements to make wine here. Many of them may be more attracted by the size of the potential market than by the prospect of making extraordinary wine. Market leaders, such

Uruguay became independent in 1828 and some form of nascent wine industry must have existed because in 1835 a banquet in honor of Manuel Oribe, second President of the republic, included Uruguayan wines.

A Tarragona-born Catalan, Francisco Vidiella arrived in Uruguay in 1837. Having made his fortune in a grocery store, he traveled to Europe in 1873 and became so fascinated by wine that he returned to Uruguay with bundles of vine stalks. Within seven years he had succeeded in producing substantial fruit from the folle noire variety that went on to take his name in Uruguay. The arrival, in 1838, of Pascual Harriague, a hardworking Basque, also had a profound effect on Uruguayan viticulture. After making his fortune, he set about making wine in the style of the Médoc. The grape he eventually chose was tannat and by 1883 he had 300 *barricas* maturing in his bodega.

Recognizing the potential for a wine industry the government offered, in 1885, a prize for the greatest production. Francisco Vidiella won 60,000 pesos for good-quality wine made from domestically harvested grapes (folle noire) in quantities exceeding 60 pipes; and Pascual Harriague picked up 20,000 pesos for 20 pipes of tannat wine.

Modern times

With its close ties to Britain, Uruguay prospered. Montevideo blossomed into an exceptionally smart and cosmopolitan city with one of the highest per capita incomes in the world, and the sea resort of Punta del Este became the Côte d'Azur of South America. Wine-drinking was part of life for this prosperous nation. The loss of trading links with Britain after the Second World War led to turbulent times in the Uruguayan economy. Investment slowed and the social cohesiveness of this once-thriving nation came under severe strain. Uruguay has had to look to export markets to sustain its industry and all the evidence promises success.

Vines and wines

Uruguay has eight wine regions encompassing 15 smaller sub-regions. The most important of these are Canelones (near Montevideo), Montevideo, Colonia (on the northeastern bank of the River Plate) and Artigas (near the Brazilian border to the north). There are a touch over 24,700 acres (10,000 ha) of vineyards planted, divided among 370 bodegas. Total annual production is in the region of 24 million gallons (91 million l) per year. Many bodegas harvest vines from different

regions, some local and some distant. This leads to quite a range of wines, from high-quality locally harvested wine to cheap, demijohn wine sold for downmarket domestic consumption.

While Uruguay may not have the ideal, dry and sunny conditions found in central Argentina or Chile, careful vineyard techniques allow for more than adequate viticultural conditions. Rainfall, especially toward the Brazilian border, causes some problems that must be controlled with fungicides. One solution adopted in 1984 was to train vines on the Lyre system, known here as the *Lira*. This system, invented in 1970 by Dr Alain Carbonneau, optimizes photosynthetic effect and foliage aeration. To date, about 865 acres (350 ha) have been planted and are growing under this system, the most significant area anywhere in the world. Another important fact is that the tannat planted by Harriague has adapted very well to its local environment and has gone on to make exceptionally smooth and velvety wine with depth and complexity. Today there is more tannat planted here than anywhere else.

Producers

CALVINOR, ARTIGAS

Established 1975 *Owners* Cooperative *Production* 177,780 cases *Vineyard area* 346 acres (140 ha)

An impressive bodega in a warm and humid area near the Brazilian border, this big modern winery takes full advantage of vineyards that must be carefully managed to produce fruit at the optimum moment. The results are surprisingly good, especially when you realize that Calvinor mainly aims for the value-for-money market. If they set their minds to it, Calvinor could aim even higher.

Montevideo, Uruguay's picturesque capital at the broad mouth of the Rio de la Plata.

Daniel Pisano corks a bottle in the cellars at the family-owned Pisano winery, Uruguay.

Reaping the rewards of the season at Castillo Viejo, Uruguay.

IRURTIA, COLONIA

Established 1913 *Owners* Irurtia family *Production* 500,000 cases *Vineyard area* 865 acres (350 ha)

This bodega harnesses cabernet franc (probably Uruguay's second-best grape) and tannat to good effect. Try the Posada del Virrey Tannat.

LOS CERROS DE SAN JUAN, COLONIA

Established 1854 *Owners* Terra family *Production* 111,110 cases *Vineyard area* 198 acres (80 ha)

This concern is deserving of inclusion in history books and maybe even the list of World Heritage sites. The ancient winery is near the beautiful town of Colonia, by the mouth of the River Plate. Deep below the old stone building lies a large cistern encircled by a complex of Edwardian copper piping. The remarkable thing is that in the early 1900s a German winemaker was trying to cool his fermentations by means of cold water. He collected the winter rainfall off the roof and stored it in the underground cistern at close to freezing point. During fermentation he would draw the water out through his specially designed pipes, driving the flow with steam pumps, and chill the fermenters. This is surely one of the earliest sophisticated temperature-controlled fermentation systems.

Vineyards and buildings at Establecimineto Juanicó, Canelones, Uruguay.

Today's winemaker, Estela de Frutos, makes deep and chewy tannat wines from grapes grown in what are among the most interesting and picturesque vineyards in Uruguay.

ESTABLECIMINETO JUANICÓ, CANELONES

Established 1979 *Owners* Deicas family *Production* 355,555 cases *Vineyard area* 544 acres (220 ha), plus 988 acres (400 ha) managed

With its impressive vineyards, this winery exudes an air of efficiency and enthusiasm. It made a name for itself by selling to Britain's ultra-demanding Marks & Spencer. Wines such as the exquisite Preludio demonstrate clear vision and attention to detail, down to using the tiniest percentage of petit verdot to complement a tannat, cabernet franc and cabernet sauvignon blend.

PISANO

Established 1924 *Owners* Pisano family *Production* 22,220 cases *Vineyard area* 42 acres (17 ha)

Cesare Pisano arrived in Montevideo in 1914 with $45 in his pocket. Today the family's artisan-made wines sell in distinctive bottles around the world. Wines, such as Tannat RPF, or Pinot Noir RPF, tend toward ripeness on the nose, but have good fruit extraction and well-rounded structure.

CASTEL PUJOL, MONTEVIDEO

Established 1976 *Owners* Carrau brothers *Production* 100,000 cases *Vineyard area* 222 acres (90 ha)

There is a sense of purpose in the way this bodega goes about the business of making its wines. The ancestors of the Carrau brothers include a Catalan winemaker as far back as 1752. In their old colonial-style winery near Montevideo they ferment and oak-age a wide range of well-made wines. The jewel in this bodega's crown, though, is a brand-spanking-new, purpose-built winery located further north, close to the Brazilian border. It is a gravity-fed winery, with the upper level reception area enclosing the grape-crushers and de-stalkers. Below that is the vinification chamber, where stainless-steel vinifiers form a large star shape, and below that again is the oak-aging cellar, itself surrounded by the bottle-aging space. Wines made at this facility are just beginning to make an appearance on the market.

STAGNARI, CANELONES

Established 1930 *Owners* Stagnari family *Production* 38,890 cases *Vineyard area* 99 acres (40 ha)

From vineyards in Canelones as well as from others as far as a whole day's truck-ride away, this bodega produces tannat wines that are among Uruguay's most memorable (Tannat Viejo) as well as some that are less so. Young Héctor Stagnari is a talented enologist. Operations at the bodega are managed by his sister Virginia.

CASTILLO VIEJO

Established 1927 *Owners* Echeverry family *Production* 266,666 cases *Vineyard area* 346 acres (140 ha)

Talented antipodean enologist Duncan Killiner works hard to bring out the best in these vineyards, producing Uruguay's best white wine. The Catamayor Sauvignon Blanc (also found under the 4 Corners label) is delicate and yet profound.

REGIONAL DOZEN

QUALITY WINES

Chardonnay del Museo 1999, Carrau
Preludio 1995, Juanico.
Sauvignon Blanc 1999, Castillo Viejo
1752—Tinto del Museo, Carrau.
Tannat 1998 RPF, Pisano
Tannat Viejo 1994, Stagnari

BEST VALUE WINES

Cabernet Franc 1999, Castillo Viejo
Cabernet Sauvignon 1999, Calvinor
Cabernet Sauvignon 1999, Stagnari
Merlot 1999, Abuelo Don Domingo, Falcone
Merlot 1998, De Lucca
Sauvignon Blanc 1999, Castillo Viejo

Chile

Harold Heckle

Chile's location on the south western extremity of Latin America lends it a certain air of splendid isolation. This sensation is reinforced by the presence of the Andes mountain range which acts as both border and barrier. Shifts in the Earth's crust, or plate tectonics, are moving the American continents relentlessly westwards. The monumental collision caused as the continental land mass hit the submerged Pacific plates threw up the Andes mountains in the southern hemisphere and the Rocky mountains in the northern hemisphere as evidence of this remorseless and violent impact. A smaller mountainous ridge rises up to 3,000 feet (900 m) above sea level on the forward edge of the continental landmass. Seen from outer space, the impression is of two parallel ridges, one far bigger than the other, with the smaller nearest the ocean. The outcome of this geological effect is to

create a longitudinal depression, called a "valley," along a significant stretch of Chile's landmass. But this great depression, which varies in width from 25 to 50 miles (40 to 80 km) is not, in fact, a valley at all.

NORTH

200 miles
(320 kilometers)

Vineyards at Cousiño Macul, in the Maipo Valley near Santiago.

With the Andes rising to almost unbelievable heights to the east, the valley extends southward from latitude 32° to 42°, where it begins to submerge and form stunning, fjord-like inlets.

The protected environment created between the two ranges provides a sheltered cradle for flora and fauna. The only problem is that low levels of rainfall limit life to a semi-arid existence on relatively newly exposed and poor soil in most of the valley. The violence of the geological forces that created the Andes means that much of the surface is not so much soil as the chaotic remnants of smashed and tortured rock.

Agriculture

It is difficult to be precise about the age of human settlement in the valley. Recent research, mainly from new archaeological digs nearby in Argentina, has uncovered much new evidence that will take time to decipher fully. It seems that human beings have existed in the area for longer than was previously thought. What is certain is that different human settlements clustered along the coast and the valley, all the way down to Tierra del Fuego, surviving by fishing and limited agriculture. Several tribes became dominant and grew in size and sophistication. Some of these tribes were very spirited and not only survived colonization, but in some cases, for example the dark-eyed Araucanos, were never completely subdued by the colonizers.

Several important tribes, such as the Araucanos and the Mapuche, are extant to this day, although fairly well assimilated into the population.

Agriculture moved to a totally different level of complexity after the arrival of the Incas, who seem to have been exceptionally talented agriculturists with a positive genius for irrigation. Whatever agriculture was already in existence was transformed dramatically under their administration and influence. The Incas harnessed the available water with an intricate array of canals, dams and storage tanks; they even devised a legal framework that ensured its equitable distribution and guaranteed that water was available to all.

Naturally enough, this development transformed agriculture and the underlying ecology of the valley. Silt from the rivers improved the fertility of the land and farming became an established way of life. By the time the Spanish conquistadores arrived in about 1536, comfortable subsistence was no longer an issue and the indigenous population would have stood at about 500,000.

The arrival of the vine

The agriculture the Spaniards found yielded a wealth of food items they had never before seen. Tomatoes, maize, chilies and a vast array of tubers and potatoes the likes of which no one could have imagined. The spot chosen for the new capital city, Santiago de Chile, was strategically placed at the northern edge of the valley, from then on to be known as el Valle Central, the central valley. Each of the smaller valleys criss-crossing the Valle Central retained the name of its river, some reflecting the pre-Columbian cultures that had flourished there. So to this day you will find, from north to south, rivers and valleys called Aconcagua, Casablanca, Maipo, Rapel, Curicó, Maule, and Bío-Bío.

To begin with viticulture was not an imperative. Although vines were imported into Mexico early on, the first Spaniards to arrive in South America were much more interested in the glint of gold. The political reality they faced was also pretty snarled. Some vines were inevitably imported with other foodstuffs and would have entered South America via Perú. It is generally assumed that vines arrived near Santiago de Chile in the mid-sixteenth century. To complicate matters even further, by the seventeenth century, in an effort to try and protect and even boost domestic wine production in the Iberian Peninsula, Spain dictated that no wine should be produced in the new lands of *las indias*, the Indies (the name is a throwback to the quest for the spices of India that had in the beginning prompted Iberian maritime quests). It is difficult to imagine how the instigators of this law ever imagined it could be enforced.

The first varieties grown appear to have been grapes for eating, throwing up the possibility that perhaps vineyards were not necessarily planted but that vines grew as a result of people spitting out pips from raisins originally imported from Spain. What is certain is that it was always going to be difficult to enforce the letter of the law in such a vast expanse of land. Research suggests that small vineyards, producing wine for personal consumption, were soon in full swing around the early settlements, which had sprung up within about a day's ride from one another.

Another factor in the early spread of viticulture involves the Church. As an integral part of the holy sacrament, wine simply had to be available for the communion service. Early missions would have ensured a supply of wine by one means or another, and we can be sure that law-enforcement agencies would have been reluctant to tell bishops and priests that their vineyards might be in contravention of existing regulations. In fact, the grape variety that proliferated in the Viceroyalty of New Spain (which later became Mexico) and its northernmost province of La California is to this day known as *mission*. This same variety is known by the name of *país* in Chile and *criolla chica* in Argentina. Cereza, still found in substantial quantities in Argentina, may have originated from a table grape subsequently used for winemaking.

As more settlers arrived from Europe, mainly migrants from the harsh, southwestern provinces of Spain, grape-growing became a well-established adjunct to farming. We can imagine that winemaking was equally prevalent. Evidence of this can be found in a recommendation sent by the Governor of Chile in 1678, exhorting Spain to lift the ban on vineyards so as to encourage the establishment of more homesteads or *estancias*. By this stage it must have been obvious that grapes were well-suited to the environment. A lack of humidity during the vegetative and fruit cycles led to healthy bunches come harvest time, the dry conditions reducing the risk of fungal infections to an absolute minimum. The absence of downy and powdery mildew would have meant bigger yields and healthier crops than were possible in Europe.

Advanced viticulture

When Napoleon intervened in Spain, placing his brother on the throne, Spain's American colonies felt a shiver of apprehension and a desire to break away. While turmoil built up in Latin America, Chile began its process of secession on September 18, 1810, and by February 12, 1818, it was at last free to determine its own destiny.

In the early 1830s, a forward-thinking Frenchman named Claude Gay obtained the backing of the Chilean government to establish a nursery for botanical species from around the world. Called

Central Valleys wines: Concha y Toro Don Melchor cabernet sauvignon 1995, and rosé 1999; and Santa Carolina sauvignon blanc 2000.

Chardonnay grapes rich with the promise of the harvest. Concha y Toro, Santiago.

Laborers in the vineyard. Women pruning vines near Santiago.

Magellan, the Drake Strait, the Bellingshausen Sea and Antarctica. To the west is the largest ocean in the world and to the east the immutable, magnificent Andes Mountains. Only the Himalaya is more daunting and massive. These natural barriers still keep Chile free of the dreaded mite. What is more, the landscape within this impressive framework just happens to be the type of geography that *Vitis vinifera* loves.

However, it was only toward the end of the 1970s that the term "viticultural paradise" first began to be applied seriously to the long, narrow slip of a country that is Chile. The Greeks once thought in similar terms of Italy, which they called Enotria, the land of wine. Yet there was something different about Chile. Those who really knew their stuff were showing increasing interest in Chilean viticulture. The rumors, it seemed, simply refused to go away.

A geographical aspect worth considering is the location of Chile's vineyards. At between 32°30' and 38° south latitude, they are a similar distance from the equator as some of their northern hemisphere equivalents, such as southern Spain and northern Africa. The cooling effect of the Pacific currents, and the significant barrier to continental heating supplied by the Andes (solid rock four miles high is impressive insulation by any standards), ensure a cooler environment than would seem possible. The Humboldt current in particular brings the cooling influence of the Antarctic to the door-step of Chile's coastal regions.

Much of the Valle Central would be stony desert were it not for some crucial factors. The great altitude of the Andes inevitably traps and precipitates clouds and atmospheric humidity as high-altitude rain and snow, there is even permafrost in places. As temperatures fluctuate, snow melt runs down the precipitous slopes and makes its way to the sea. The consequences flowing from this are in several ways important to life in the valley. First, the water creates oases and the erosion at higher altitudes fill the rivers with silt which they disgorge in the valley, providing a more attractive *milieu* for plant life. Significantly, the

the Quinta Normal, it was to play a decisive role in South American, and even world, viticulture. A wide range of botanical specimens was brought in, including a fairly complete compendium of grape varieties. This collection of plants, isolated from the infections that later ravaged vineyards across the world, proved invaluable in restocking nursery vineyards in Europe. This fine effort was helped by the work begun under the instigation of Silvestre Ochagavía Echazarreta, a wealthy Chilean landowner of Basque ancestry. Determined to make wines similar to those he had sampled while on a grand tour of Europe, Echazarreta imported a good supply of cuttings of the classic varietals, along with a French winemaker.

Looking back, it is difficult to imagine the disaster for European agriculture that was the phylloxera infestation of little more than a century ago. Whole rural populations were plunged into despair, even starvation, and never again would vines grow trouble-free in European soil. In the catastrophe's aftermath, Europe turned to Chile for virus-free vine cuttings.

Landscape and climate

Chile's geographical isolation had enabled it to survive without becoming infected, and it is hard to imagine a more impregnable fortress. To the north lies the Atacama Desert, almost certainly the driest place on earth. To the south, the Strait of rivers inevitably breach the second ridge on their way to the sea, opening the ecosystem of the valley to maritime influences.

This maritime influence helps to temper further the natural tendency toward desertification. First, it provides moisture, causing a welcome increase in localized precipitation. Once the sun has cleared the Andes range and daylight temperatures rise in the valley, rising hot air draws in cooling, humid air from the coast. At night the effect is reversed, with wind moving back down to the sea via the breaches in the ridge caused by the many rivers that drain the mountain range. Annual rainfall averages are generally below 32 inches (800 mm) in the wettest areas. The rainy season comes in winter and its effects are felt mostly in the south and to a lesser extent to the west, in the shadow of the coastal ridge. A further effect of the seaward flow of rivers from the Andes can be seen in the smaller valleys they carve across the main central valley, criss-crossing it at right angles. The visible effect is a constant undulation in the main valley and with it, an angular exposure of soil surfaces.

Spanish influence

Spain left its imprint on Chilean society in the deeply held concept that land and land ownership gives status to those involved. Generations of gentleman farmers, owners of vast estates, began to devote more time to viticulture and winemaking, cementing the country's viticultural future. But perhaps because of Chile's troubled history, it is more in a spirit of discovery rather than of rediscovery that people are once again taking notice of Chile, and there is a lot to take into account.

Chile's population grew rapidly throughout the eighteenth and nineteenth centuries principally through European migration. The eighteenth-century migration came chiefly from Spain and was composed to a great extent of Basque families moving to the Americas to make their fortunes *(hacer su América)*. Nineteenth-century immigrants tended to originate more from Germany, Italy and England. A 1952 census indicated that only about 127,151 Araucanian Indians survived in Chile. Fortunes made by exploiting Chile's vast natural wealth, be it by mining the large mineral deposits revealed by the Andes to extract gem stones, or by fishing, fruit-growing or other agriculture, gave rise to a land-owning class that felt it appropriate to include winemaking estates in its portfolios.

Wealthy families would own imposing mansions in Santiago and *estancias* within a day's drive of the capital. Eventually, about ten powerful families (principally Basque) controlled fruit and wine production in Chile, their *bodegas*, or wineries, sprinkled around the capital city. While a burgeoning middle class consumed wine, export markets were also sought to supplement sales. Chilean wine became popular throughout Latin America (with the exception of Argentina, which produced sizeable quantities itself) finding ready markets in countries whose climate was not as suited to the vine as Chile's.

Labor to operate the *estancias*, including the vineyards and bodegas, was provided by *inquilinos*, resident workers hired by the estate, and by *afuerinos*, migrant workers used during the harvest season to pick grapes and provide casual labor. To a certain extent, this system still survives. Among the major crops are wheat, barley, oats, rye, maize, potatoes, peas, lentils, rice and beans. Closer to the cities you find artichokes, radishes, lettuce, asparagus, tomatoes, onions and garlic.

A beef and dairy industry exists, and farther south sheep for wool and meat are also raised. Pre-eminent among the crops, though, fruit reigns. Great fortunes have been made by selling and exporting fruit. Within this sector, wine started to become an important contributor to the economy in about 1875, when Chilean wines first began to appear at international expositions.

By the turn of the century, winemaking represented a significant industry in Chile. In 1939 the government borrowed foreign funds to further promote Chile's agricultural sector. At this time winemaking would have followed the tradition

Harvest at Cousiño Macul and a worker carries riesling grapes along the row.

Vintage Cabernet Cosecha 1937. Cousiño Macul winery, Santiago.

One characteristic that helped Chilean red wines at this time was their inherently deep and stable color. Despite treatment, this did not precipitate out as dramatically as might have been expected, leaving an attractive-looking wine, as is often the case. When the phylloxera outbreak threw many talented winemakers into unemployment, a significant number found work in Chile. Interestingly, Chilean employers showed a preference for French winemaking skills.

European migration after the Second World War also played a role in swelling the numbers of domestic wine consumers. Many Germans arrived in Chile following the collapse of the Third Reich, and their predilection for riesling is reflected in changes within Chile's vineyards.

Per capita consumption of wine in Chile had increased to the point where it became attractive to the exchequer from a taxation point of view. That said, Chile, with its significant indigenous population and broad-based mixed-blood working class, would never match Argentina's huge per-capita consumption. Slowly, as taxes increased, the incentive to be bold and invest more receded from the Chilean wine industry. To some extent, complacency and fat-cat thinking set in. The wealthy, landed class saw no good reason to continue pampering the wine industry.

that had been imported into Rioja Alavesa in Spain from Bordeaux. The concept of *el Médoc Alavés* (Alava is the heart of winemaking in the Basque country) would have come with immigrant Basques. Grapes would be harvested and transported to the winery where de-stalking machines would begin the process leading to fermentation. Fermenting would take place either in large wooden vats, *tinos,* or in tiled tanks. Afterwards the wine would pass into large *toneles,* usually of Bosnian oak, sometimes made and assembled in France, disassembled then shipped in pieces and reassembled *in situ.* After this, the wine might pass into smaller barrels, or large blending tanks prior to bottling. Red and white wine would exhibit oxidative characteristics, with very little expected to reduce much further in bottle, although special wines would be made by bodegas with aging in mind. These more expensive wines were aimed at more select consumers who did not expect to have a "drinking" wine immediately available.

Toward the end of the 1960s, investment in the industry was very slow and quality was generally patchy. Still, Chile's reputation was already beginning to take shape and it was possible to find some respectable wine at very good prices. Wines such as Concha y Toro and Undurraga continued to find export markets in Latin America. Even as far away as England, adventurous wine buyers, such as Ted Hale, working for John Harvey & Sons of Bristol (established in 1796), were able to locate good wine. A red wine listed as "Valparaiso tinto" was on Harvey's wine list from 1961 to 1965 for the princely sum of seven shillings a bottle. This wine opened Harvey's eyes and alerted them to the potential. Greater success was to follow, as attested by this entry in their 1974 wine list: "Wine has been grown in Chile for nearly four centuries, and it now has the reputation of producing the best wines in South America. Nearly all the vines are of European origin and, unlike their European counterparts, they can be grown on their own roots, because the phylloxera parasite has never reached Chile. The wine listed is a good *ordinaire* made from the Cabernet grape, the great red wine grape of Bordeaux."

A display in the tasting room at Concha y Toro in Chile's Maipo Valley.

This wine had several merits that made it a talking point at the time and still remembered. The first was a great price relative to its quality and flavor. Although aromatically not particularly varietal in a way that the greater British public would have instantly recognized (having been brought up on the more focused character of claret), it still managed to present open and exciting fruit cushioned within hints of wood. On the palate this fruit was weighty and full, in short, a mature wine wearing a very humble price tag. At around 14 percent alcohol, the cabernet was an instant hit in the wine-bar trade that was beginning to sweep the country. Another point often mentioned was its deep and attractive cherry color.

Chile then descended into a period of political turmoil that led to little wine being exported and even less new money being directed to vineyards and wineries. Harvey's discontinued importing the line. Table grape exports to the USA for a time topped the popularity charts. This was perhaps just as well, for Chile has dedicated about 124,000 acres (50,000 ha) to their cultivation.

Technology and modernization

Nothing remains the same for long in regions as promising as Chile. In 1979 a youthful Miguel Agustín Torres, having graduated from college in Dijon, Burgundy, and visited Napa, found himself responding to two impulses. The first was a certain need to break out of the family's traditional base in Catalonia, Spain. His time in Dijon had opened his eyes to freedom of expression, something not encouraged under Franco. Napa had refined this concept further. Miguel Agustín needed to find his own means of expression, away from the influence of home. His father don Miguel agreed wholeheartedly and accompanied his son to Chile.

Miguel Agustín's second impulse was not dissimilar to those of the early conquistadores. The Torres family had heard of Chile's reputation as a paradise for wine and knew it was worth checking out. This is how Miguel Agustín puts it: "The privileged geographical situation, climate and the absence of phylloxera, as well as its ancient wine tradition, made my father, Miguel Torres, decide in 1979 to acquire vineyards in Chile ... we have bought around 300 hectares (740 acres), but plan to augment that significantly in coming years."

The land bought by Torres is in Curicó and when he began to build the winery things began to stir. Other bodegueros were perturbed by the new equipment being brought in. Some were driven to

A picker's knife set against sauvignon grapes. Carta Vieja, Loncomilla Valley.

ask, "Why do you need all this stainless steel?" Miguel responded with: "This is the way to make wine now." The bodegueros argued that they had been making and selling wine for a very long time and had no need for all of this technology.

All the bluster was just a natural response to change. It was clear to everyone that Chile needed investment. Slowly, other estates began the process of modernization. At the Torres winery an enthusiastic José Puig was put in charge of sorting things out. To this day Miguel takes personal charge of vinification in Chile. An early success was a *rosado* (rosé), made exclusively from cabernet sauvignon grapes. Another departure for Torres was the first appearance of a sparkling wine.

Torres in Spain has its base in Vilafranca del Penedès, Catalonia, right in the heart of Cava country. Yet Torres makes a point of not producing a Cava. In Spain it specializes in still wine. So it was with great interest that people first began to see a sparkling wine from the Torres stable. The first sparkling wines, in truth, were no match for Catalonia's best products, something that put a smile on the face of more than one competitor. With the passage of time, however, Miguel Torres' Chilean sparkling wines have won over many converts. Still wines such as Miguel Torres Santa Digna began a revolution in winemaking that was to alter, radically and permanently, winemaking in Chile and, indeed, in Latin America as a whole.

The concepts of hygiene and of stainless steel, of modern viticultural practices and of forward-thinking viniculture brought about by Miguel Torres cannot be overstated. Most people today know of the unique and enormous contribution

Cabernet sauvignon in the making at Viña Los Vascos, Santiago.

Chardonnay being harvested at Sta Isabella de Pirque/Concha y Toro, Santiago.

this engaging Catalan winemaker made to by bringing Chile into the twentieth century. It is typical of his modesty that he credits his late father as the catalyst for the Chilean wine revolution

Conditions in Chile were pretty basic in the early stages of the makeover. One of the pioneers of modernization was enologist Ed Flaherty. He arrived in Chile looking for a challenge. That is precisely what he found. Brought up to believe that hygiene is everything, he soon saw that things were not so simple in Chile. "When I first came here I was driven up to the winery. It was a pretty dusty little place. I asked where the water was and got a quizzical look. 'What do you need water for? We make wine here.' I told them I needed water to wash things down. They said, 'Oh, the well's over there.' Only recently have hot water and steam been an option for wineries in Chile."

Export drive

Commercially, the tables started to turn when wine writers became aware of Chile's great potential, as spotted by Miguel Torres. Jan Read, who had introduced many to Spanish wine and sherry, was commissioned to write a book about the wines of Chile. What he saw as he researched his book encouraged him to advise his son Carlos, who was working in the wine trade in London, to consider taking up where Harvey's had left off. Initial contacts confirmed that Chilean wineries were hungry for export orders. Foremost among these was Santa Rita, from the Maipo Valley.

It was Santa Rita that spearheaded the drive for international consumers, with the British market its principal target. The wines exhibited some of the characteristics that had made Chilean wine the toast of the wine-bar generation. The same deep and stable color was there. Good fruit concentration led onto velvety structures on the palate. But there was something more, something new. This "new generation" Chilean wine bore a much greater noseful of fresh and clean berry fruit aromas. The old oxidative characteristics had given way to reductive varietal wines. There was supple, ripe fruit in the mouth. All for a very modest price. Consumers loved the wines, especially the Santa Rita 120 range (named after Bernardo O'Higgins' 120 patriots, who once hid in Santa Rita's bodega during the liberation struggles).

There is some evidence that the demand took Santa Rita by surprise. Such was the strain placed on their facilities that some corners may have been cut and problems ensued. At one stage, following the discovery of Sorbitol in the wines, the Health and Safety Inspector of the Ministry of Agriculture, Fisheries and Food removed all Santa Rita wines from wine shops in the UK. Sorbic acid gives wine a jammy, fruity quality. Sorbitol is prohibited in wines sold within the European Union, which the winemakers at Santa Rita must have known. It was a chastening experience.

This episode had a salutary effect on the Chilean wine industry—if Chilean wine were to prosper, it must to do so on sound foundations. Santa Rita tightened up its act, broke off relations with its agent in the UK, and won the right to set up its own representative office and re-import. This was the first step toward a promotional office for the wines of Chile.

Other bodegas were also beginning to make inroads into the market. Cousiño Macul, from Maipo, offered smoky blackcurrant and capsicum-infused aromas in its cabernet sauvignons, making them irresistible to the restaurant trade. Concha y Toro, also from Maipo offered quality wine, with its Casillero del Diablo making an impact. The stage was set for Chile's new wine age.

Export successes

Worldwide interest in fine wine was reaching new peaks, particularly in the USA and the UK. The fresh-faced approach that California and Australia had pioneered and Miguel Torres had extolled was also taken up by Chilean bodegas. Investment in the wine sector grew, and included finance from overseas. Many Old World concerns opted for the Torres formula, forming partnership ventures with Chilean companies or trying to go it alone.

Playing its strongest hand, Chile began by improving and marketing its red wines. This was a sound ploy, as consumers were opting more for red wine than white at just about this time.

Chardonnay grapes undergo the first stages of the winemaking process.

Winemakers knew instinctively that they were on safe ground here—Chilean wines have never had a problem with color. Color is always stable, even when racked continually in wood. There is seldom (if ever) a need to add tannins. This fact was to have an unexpected bonus when it was revealed that Chilean wines contain the highest measurable levels of flavonols (a compound believed to be health-promoting) of all wines tested in a university-sponsored research program. So, as well as being varietal, fruity, deeply colorful and clean on the palate, Chilean wine is also good for you.

Naturally enough, it was cabernet sauvignon that appeared first. Along with its great color came aromas that were pure and beguiling. It wasn't hard work to enjoy Chilean reds—they were joyful and cheap. Initially, cabernet was harvested slightly early, leading to capsicum and tomato bush aromas, formerly considered faults in the wine but now, to some extent thanks to Chilean cabernets, quite enjoyed by winelovers around the world.

Next, Chile turned to white wines. By this time new money was being invested, including in new areas such as Casablanca. Research had shown that cooler areas would help produce aromatically charged white wines. Chile's winemakers, led by buyers who now insisted on buying wines "by nose," knew that the aromatic quality of their

wines was crucial to conquering new markets. Casablanca seemed a good choice for a new location. Although it was farther north and nearer the equator, it was cooled by maritime influences. The gamble paid off.

Sauvignon blanc was the variety of choice in many of the new plantations. The results were more than encouraging. Eye-witnesses tell of how a young Chilean winemaker turned up at New Zealand's Cloudy Bay's winery, eager to watch and learn as much as he could about this magical enterprise. Later on he was to acknowledge his debt, although they are not amused by his claim that he actually "worked there." The young man was Ignacio Recabarren, the enologist who was to lead Viña Casablanca to trophy-winning status several times in years to follow. By the late 1990s Chilean sauvignon blanc became the hit of the wine-bar and health-club circuit in Britain and the USA. This was a major breakthrough—unlike a chardonnay, a sauvignon blanc needs to stand out to be taken at all seriously.

Tackling the top end

Having now established a reputation for good-quality and good-value wines, both red and white, the Chilean wine industry set about tackling the next hurdle, top wines. While overseas markets

Gift of the seasons. Torres merlot beckon from the vine at Concha y Toro.

had been conquered and exports were rising exponentially, one criticism that stung was that Chile was underselling its wines. To right this situation winemakers knew that they had to convince serious wine buffs, as well as the wine press, that their wines were equal to any, at whatever level. Renewed efforts to improve vineyard techniques were combined with greater investment in wineries and a focused approach to maximizing potential. Joint ventures with some of the greatest stars in the firmament of enology cemented this process further. So a new generation of Chilean super-wines was born. Names like Château Lafite-Rothschild, Château Mouton-Rothschild, Lurton, Robert Mondavi, Marnier Lapostolle and others were folded into the fabric of Chilean wine not only to raise the profile of the products, but also to focus people's appreciation of what was going on. As the wines emerged, towering wines aimed at capturing exclusive markets, so too the price of Chilean wines generally began to rise.

Great names have been added to the nomenclature of serious winemaking. Caballo Loco, Montes Alpha "M", Almaviva, Domus Aurea, Finis Terrae, Seña all stand as testaments to the unimpeachable quality of Chilean wine. Towering quality and high prices were not going to be the last word, though. The concept was to alert consumers that Chile was no flash in the pan. To a certain extent, two pieces of good fortune intervened next to provide Chile with the following lines of attack.

Checking fermentation of chardonnay at the Cousiño Macul winery, Santiago.

When the first French vines were selected for export to the Quinta Normal, it was natural that Bordeaux should provide the backbone of the stock chosen. Apart from cabernet sauvignon, merlot proved easily adaptable to the Chilean soil, more so than malbec, which did better on the *mendocino* soils of neighboring Argentina. Chile was fortunate in this, for just as the international market developed a taste for merlot, Chile's blockbuster merlots hit the shelves. The ripe, seductive fruit, hints of chocolate and supple friendliness of these wines made for a winning combination that is set to reach new heights as winemakers further refine their techniques. Certainly, merlot has given Chile a powerful commercial product.

The next piece of good fortune came about when French ampelographers reclassified what had been thought to be merlot planted in Maipo and Panquehue as carmenère. It seems that, early on, the wrong clone might have been shipped out from France and propagated as merlot. Whatever the circumstances surrounding its introduction, carmenère has done very well, adapting splendidly to Chilean conditions. Today it offers a distinguishable alternative to the supple fruit of merlot, while still appealing to the same type of palate. So in the unlikely event of consumers tiring of merlot, there is a perfect alternative available.

In this way Chile was able to broaden the range of its offerings while retaining their unique characteristics. Good fortune and a sharply focused approach have ensured that these wines will continue to attract attention for the foreseeable future. Argentina might have its malbec, South Africa its pinotage and Uruguay its tannat, but Chile has great-value sauvignon blanc and very accessible merlot and carmenère. All of these wines come together under the umbrella of top wines of increasing sophistication.

It might be worth pointing out here that most Chilean wines are made from grapes bought in from numerous vineyards. What this means is that it is quite difficult to be specific about exactly where grapes were grown, unless there is a specific mention on the label, and then you have to take the winery's word for it. What you can be sure of, though, is that a region like Panquehue produces almost no white grapes, so the grapes used to make white wines are bought in. There may come a time when specific *terroir* may be explored in Chile, but for the moment I would advise caution when trying to apportion precise *terroir*-borne characteristics to wines.

Central Valleys

MAIPO VALLEY

This is perhaps the best-known name in Chilean wine, mainly because the valley is nearest to the capital, Santiago. As many of the original bodegas were built within a day's drive of the city, many are dotted around Maipo and its sub-regions, including Llano de Maipo and Buin. Today, those regions which are offering higher-quality fruit deserve greater recognition.

CONCHA Y TORO

Established 1883 *Owners* Public company *Production* 11,000,000 cases *Vineyard area* 8,154 acres (3,300 ha)

Another Maipo bodega with a great history, its Puente Alto vineyard provides grapes for the Marqués de Casa Concha cabernet sauvignon, for Don Melchor and Casillero del Diablo. These are wines that seldom disappoint. Cabernet sauvignon (and a great barrel-fermented sauvignon blanc) form the basis of these quality wines. A less-expensive line called Trio offers great value for money. When it comes to high-quality wine, Concha y Toro has linked up with none other than Château Mouton-Rothschild to produce Almaviva. The inside of this winery looks a bit like Opus One, in California. The vineyard forms part of Puente Alto. To ensure that quality control is kept up to its legendary standards, it is Mouton that calls the shots here. As a consequence, some very high prices are paid for Almaviva wines. By all accounts, the price is worth paying. Every vintage has seen notable improvement.

VIÑA AQUITANIA

Owners Paul Pontalier (of Château Margaux) and Bruno Prats (of Cos D'Estournel)

This bodega produces another interesting wine that is well worth keeping an eye on: Paul Bruno, named after the two joint owners. The grapes are from vines adjacent to those of Domus Aurea on the Quebrada Macul and the first vintage was in 1994. From all accounts, the first vintages have had some teething problems evident in blind tastings, where the wines haven't done terribly well. Rumor has it that both the 1997 and 1998 vintages have righted the problems, but only time will tell. The 1998 vintage is the first to be widely available on the international market.

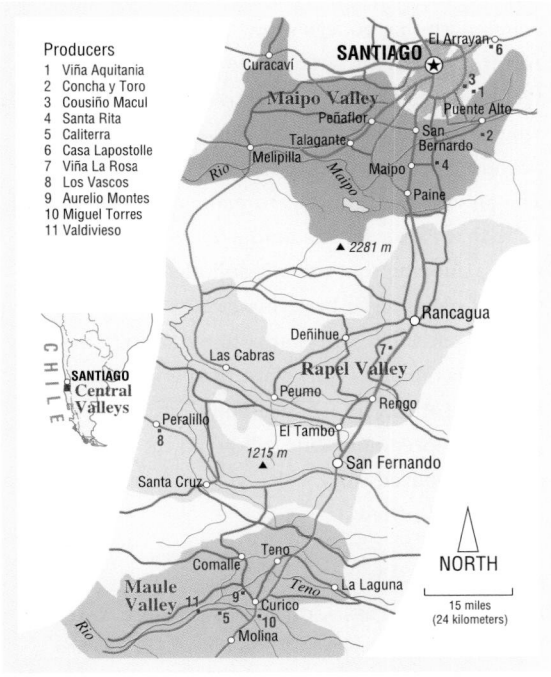

Producers
1 Viña Aquitania
2 Concha y Toro
3 Cousiño Macul
4 Santa Rita
5 Caliterra
6 Casa Lapostolle
7 Viña La Rosa
8 Los Vascos
9 Aurelio Montes
10 Miguel Torres
11 Valdivieso

COUSIÑO MACUL

Established 1856 *Owners* the Cousiño family *Production* 200,000 cases *Vineyard area* 1,359 acres (550 ha)

The grand old dame of the area is Cousiño Macul. A traditional bodega in the old sense of the word, there was a time when it was considered the greatest. Certainly it produced pungent and beguiling cabernet sauvignon that few others producers could match at the time.

Fermentation vessel containing 1986 cabernet. Concha y Toro.

REGIONAL DOZEN

QUALITY WINES

Almaviva, Baron Philippe
   de Rothschild and Viña
   Concha y Toro
Clos Apalta, Casa Lapostolle
Cordillera, Miguel Torres
Montes Alpha "M"
Robert Mondavi—Eduardo
   Chadwick, Seña
Triple C, Santa Rita

BEST VALUE WINES

Concha y Toro Explorer Pinot
   Noir
Errazuriz Wild Ferment
   Chardonnay
Miguel Torres Cordillera
Sauvignon Blanc from Casa
   Lapostolle, Viña Casablanca
   or Viña Carmen
Valdivieso Caballo Loco
Viña Gracia Merlot

Today, Cousiño Macul's Antiguas Reservas still sells well, but the sparkle has gone from the tiara. Compared to Chile's best, there is a tiredness beginning to creep into this wine. The company needs a shake-up. This is precisely what has happened with this bodega's new project: Domus Aurea. Produced from a single vineyard on the Quebrada de Macul slope above Cousiño Macul's vineyards in suburban Santiago, this wine is full of promise. The winemaker is Ignacio Recabarren. The aim of the venture is to make a single-vineyard wine that expresses the unique *terroir* of the Maipo valley, showing that there is still plenty of life in the old region. The first vintage was in 1996.

Not satisfied with that collaboration, Cousiño Macul has joined forces with the peripatetic Lurton brothers to produce Finis Terrae, an expensive super-premium wine following the Bordeaux blend. Produced since 1992, this wine has engendered good reviews.

SANTA RITA

Established 1880 *Owners* Cristalerías de Chile S. A. 56.1%, Bayona S. A. 23.5%, others 20.4% *Production* 6 million cases *Vineyard area* 4,940 acres (2,000 ha) not all producing

The range of wines here, from the value-for-money 120 selection (that includes a seductive Pinot Noir from Casablanca) to the recently released Triple C,

Grape harvesting boxes wait beneath the vines for the pickers.

are worthy ambassadors for Chilean enology. Medalla Real is a line that offers more quality and concentration than 120, as does Santa Rita Reserva. Note that Reserva in this case simply means "good wine" and is not subject to strictly defined standards imposed by a regulatory body. The winery brings fruit in from vineyards spread throughout the valley, notably from Casablanca, Rapel and Maule. Interestingly, the wines are now labeled as coming from specific, denominated areas. For example, according to the labels, Santa Rita Reserva Sauvignon Blanc comes from DO Valle del Maule, and Triple C (Premium Red Wine) from DO Valle del Maipo. This latter is quite a wine, by the way.

RAPEL VALLEY

Farther south, and slightly cooler than Maipo is Rapel. This vine-growing area is subdivided further, with Cachapoal to the north and Colchagua to the south. Most important wineries have major vineyard holdings here, including Santa Rita, Santa Emiliana and Undurraga. There is no doubt of the depth and concentration that wines from this valley can achieve. Cono Sur succeed in making interesting pinot noir at 13 percent by volume. Smaller, "boutique" wineries, such as Luis Felipe Edwards, are also worth keeping an eye on. Based in Colchagua, they make a good-value cabernet sauvignon called Pupilla. Greater concentration is to be found in Luis Felipe Edwards Cabernet Sauvignon, while toppping the list is the cabernet sauvignon Reserva. Luis Felipe Edwards' spectrum is broadened by carmenère and chardonnay.

CALITERRA

Established 1989 *Owners* Errazuriz Panquehue

A fusion between Chile and California, in 1996 Caliterra became a joint venture between the Chadwick and Mondavi families. Winemaker Miguel Rencoret oversees a sparkling new state-of-the-art winery in the Arboleda del Guique, Colchagua Valley and new plantations have enabled the establishment to supply 50 percent of its needs. The facilities are definitely space-age in appearance, and when illuminated at night they make for a breathtaking spectacle among the rows of vines. It takes nine people to operate this modern bodega, four in winter and a total of 25 at harvest time. For the moment sauvignon and chardonnay are complemented with merlot and cabernet. In the future syrah, malbec, sangiovese and carmenère will bolster the range. Grapes are

obtained from all of Chile's producing areas. The bodega has a capacity of 1,663,200 gallons (6.3 million l), but as yet there are no facilities for oak aging. An eyecatching array of gleaming stainless-steel tanks, ranging in capacity from 2,750 to 22,000 gallons (12,500–100,000 l), makes up the rows. All of these tanks can be heated to hasten malolactic fermentation. Reservas are sent away to barrels in Curicó and San Felipe, Panquehue.

CASA LAPOSTOLLE

Established 1994 *Owners* Marnier-Lapostolle (Grand Marnier), France and Rabat family, Chile *Production* 180,000 cases *Vineyard area* 741 acres (300 ha)

Some ventures succeed in capturing the imaginations of winelovers the world over. One such is Casa Lapostolle. This winery set off something of a chain reaction that generated headlines all over the world with the launching of its superb Cuvée Alexandre merlot. So seductive is this wine that some wine experts consider it a good alternative to Pétrus. Reactions are perhaps a little more subdued these days, but Casa Lapostolle continues to put forward great wines at what are very affordable prices. Casa Lapostolle's more recent Clos Apalta takes its carmenère/merlot to an unfiltered and highly concentrated level of quality. The first vintage of this very attractive wine was 1997.

VIÑA LA ROSA

Established 1824 *Owners* Ossa family and Señor Recaredo Ossa *Production* 480,000 cases *Vineyard area* 1,483 acres (600 ha), increasing

The winery lies 75 miles (120 km) south of the capital Santiago in the Rapel Valley. Palm trees native to Chile surround the vineyards, making of Viña la Rosa a memorable landmark. It is from these palms that the bodega gained its inspiration to name a new range of wines La Palmería.

Chardonnay, cabernet sauvignon and merlot have been developed with an eye to the export markets. La Rosa is still owned by the founding family, who planted vines for the first time in the 1830s. With a capacity of 3,432,000 gallons (13 million l), this bodega is certainly worth knowing about, especially as it has access to good-quality, recent plantings of syrah, merlot, carmenère and cabernet sauvignon varieties.

LOS VASCOS

Established 1982 *Owners* Domaines Barons de Rothschild (Lafite) & Viña Santa Rita *Production* 400,000 cases *Vineyard area* 1235 acres (500 ha), only 741 acres (300 ha) producing

Los Vascos is another headline-grabbing establishment, but if you consider the fact that Château Lafite-Rothschild has been a partner since 1988, this is hardly surprising.

Cabernet sauvignon vines growing at Viña Los Vascos near Santiago.

Reaping the harvest. Picking cabernet sauvignon, Viña Los Vascos.

wines is beyond doubt. His Montes Alpha cabernet sauvignon is vivid and concentrated. His super premium Montes Alpha "M" has one drawback, it seems to be made to age for ... well, no-one has tasted one nearing maturity. The whole range is closed tight. There will be some stunning wines when they open up. While waiting for this happy event, you might like to try his refined sauvignon blanc or malbec.

MIGUEL TORRES, CURICÓ

Establiahed 1979 *Owners* the Torres family *Vineyard area* 740 acres (300 ha)

Torres is pursuing some interesting projects. His Maquehua Chardonnay is fermented in small barriques of new Nevers oak and kept on lees for eight months. What makes this wine particularly attractive is the fact that it is made from a very careful clonal selection. After two decades of careful identification, isolation and propagation, Torres selected three clones to make this wine: clone RC32, from Rio Claro, the coldest mountainside vineyard; clone SFN64, from the San Francisco del Norte estate; and clone Ma18, from the Maquehua estate. The idea behind this wine is to express fully the unique characteristics of Chilean chardonnay. In terms of *tinto*, Cordillera is made from ancient cariñena vines from high up, nestled among the foothills of the Andes. The wine's *assemblage* combines the qualities of the old cariñena (60 percent) with syrah (30 percent) and merlot. Here Miguel Torres intends to bring out the depth and finesse that ancient vines can lend to a wine, not forgetting of course that pre-phylloxera cariñena provides a potent link with the Torres family's ancestral past in Catalonia.

VALDIVIESO, LONTUE

Established 1879 *Owners* Mitjans, Gil and Coderch families *Production* 600,000 cases *Vineyard area* 494 acres (200 ha)

Lontue is just to the south of Curicó, and here Jorge Coderch makes a fine selection of wines. The Barrel Selection malbec provides proof that you don't have to go to Argentina for supple, deep malbec. Valdivieso Single Vineyard Reserve Cabernet Franc or Merlot are very attractive wines. Top of the list is Caballo Loco. Vinified in a Bordeaux style, the wine is produced only in good years from Valdivieso's very best grapes. Fermented only in small quantities, it sells out very fast. Usually Caballo Loco sports a number on the label, depending on which release it is. The third release, for example, is Caballo Loco No 3.

MAULE VALLEY

With the arrival of Miguel Torres in this region, history began to change for Chilean winemaking. Torres chose Curicó, situated directly south of Colchagua, although his vineyards are slightly to the east and near the cooling influence of the Andes. Maule contains other regions that are equally interesting, such as Cauquenes, Linares, Lontue, Parral and Talca. More than 61,775 acres (25,000 ha) make up this viticultural region.

AURELIO MONTES, CURICÓ

Established 1988 *Owners* Douglas Murray, Alfredo Vidaurre, Aurelio Montes and Pedro Grand *Production* 280,000 cases *Vineyard area* 544 acres (220 ha)

The vineyards contain some immaculate rows of recently planted clones. The quality of Aurelio's

Other Chilean Regions

COQUIMBO

This is the most northerly region in Chile. Too hot to make viable quality wine, the grapes grown here are used to make another famous drink, Pisco. The history of Pisco is not exactly clear. One theory has it that the name comes from it having been exported from northern Chile to the Peruvian port of Pisco. This idea doesn't stand up though, as Pisco is a tiny port that services no major city, except Ica, which has been producing Pisco for even longer than any place in Chile. So it seems that Pisco is really a Peruvian drink that has been absorbed into Chilean culture to such an extent that it has almost (but not quite) obliterated its early roots. The commercial mind-set in Chile is such that it was Chile, rather than Perú, that made a success of this product.

Basically, Pisco is an *aguardiente*, literally a "firewater." It is distilled from muscat and pedro ximénez grapes. The process takes place in pot stills to give four categories of Pisco: Gran Pisco (43 percent by volume), Reservado (40 percent), Especial (35 percent) and Selección (30 percent). The better-quality Piscos all spend time in wood, although much of this wood is now so old that little color is imparted to the spirit. While Pisco can be, and is, taken as a post-prandial drink, it really shines in the inimitable and superb cocktail Pisco Sour. This aperitif is second to none.

Aconcagua Valley, farther south, straddles the Aconcagua River and is the most northerly of Chile's quality wine regions. Inland from the coast, at Viña Panquehue, lies the Don Maximiano vineyards of Errazuriz. This looks like hot, semi-desert country, until you feel the cooling winds that blow refreshingly in from the sea.

ERRAZURIZ PANQUEHUE, VIÑA PANQUEHUE
Established 1870 *Owners* Chadwick family *Production* 405,000 cases *Vineyard area* 927 acres (375 ha)

On west-facing slopes, Errazuriz has constructed some very impressive vineyards from which Ed Flaherty and his team obtain cabernet sauvignon, merlot and carmenère of great concentration and flavor. Fungal disease is virtually unknown in this climate. Ed Flaherty takes up the story: "All the top reds are here. The whites come from Casablanca. The proportion favors reds 70 percent, 30 percent and 75 percent of our grapes are self-supplied. We have a 5,500 barrel capacity. We bought 70 percent French oak, destined to chardonnay, pinot and our top reds. American oak is used in the cabernet reserva and syrah. Fortunately, here in Chile we pay standard US prices for oak. Nacional, a new Chilean cooper, has been making barrels for four years. We've bought some and I'm impressed with their standard."

Cabernet is Errazuriz's specialty. Pedro Izquierdo, the winery's viticulturist, cultivates 185 acres (75 ha) planted on hills in Panquehue where cabernet reigns supreme. The oldest vines were planted in 1976 and are still yielding. Most vines are trained on two- or three-wire vertical trellises with 40 percent transparency, although there are still some traditional, old-style overhead-trained vines left. This system is known as *parrón*. Pedro says he keeps the remaining *parrón* "for sentimental reasons." He has also started experimenting with nebbiolo and sangiovese grapes.

Vats being sulfured at the winery of Errazuriz Panquehe, Santiago.

A view of the barrel room at Santa Carolina.

chance to burn the mist away during the day due to cloud cover that develops in coastal oases such as this. The clouds reduce the amount of direct solar radiation falling on vine leaves, further slowing the vegetative cycle. It has been calculated that bright sunshine falls here for about 200 days a year as opposed to some 300 days farther inland.

Casablanca is a relatively new wine region. Planting began in the early 1980s, concentrating on white grapes. Initially, chardonnay was the grape of choice, but since then considerable plantations of sauvignon blanc have gone in as a result of its relative success in export markets. To begin with, Concha y Toro was responsible for some initial planting. Since then this company has been joined by Caliterra, Carmen, Cono Sur, Errazuriz, Santa Rita, Villard and Viña Casablanca, among others. Specialist growers supply white grapes to a good number of Chile's principal wineries as word has spread that this is good winemaking territory and that the wine is easily marketable. Some cabernet sauvignon and merlot complement the white varieties grown here.

Some wines are labeled as coming simply from the Valle Central. This is the safest and most honest way of describing wines made from fruit that might include grapes trucked in or bought from specialist growers in suitable vineyards up and down the valley. An example of this is the Vistasur merlot, made by Vistamar. This is not the case with more upmarket wines such as Casa Lapostolle's Chardonnay and Chardonnay Cuvée Alexandre, which clearly displays "Casablanca Valley" on the label. Here, Michel Rolland has used French oak barriques to draw out local expression from single-vineyard Casablanca fruit.

The real class of this bodega can be seen in the uniform quality of its array of wines, from delicate and quite special Wild Ferment Chardonnay (made with natural yeasts), to characterful Sauvignon Blanc and Chardonnay. The high spots are, as Ed says, in the reds. These now include pinot noir, syrah, a Curicó Merlot that would please anyone, Aconcagua Merlot Reserva to blow the cobwebs away, and some gloriously aromatic cabernet blends, culminating in the Seña that combines cabernet with 10 percent carmenère and a touch of merlot. "Watch out for our new fermentation techniques," adds Ed, someone worth listening to.

CASABLANCA VALLEY

While nearer the coast, this is still technically part of Aconcagua. West of Santiago and south of Valparaiso and Viña del Mar, the location is just south of 33° latitude. Despite its apparently northern location, this region's success centers on a river valley that opens directly onto the Pacific Ocean. As a result, it is exposed to maritime effects almost continually. It was Alexander von Humboldt who first made a detailed study of the cooling effects of Pacific currents and the ocean's main cooling current is named after him. Rising in the Antarctic regions as well as from melt from drifting icebergs, these currents make swimming on the Pacific coast, as far up as nearly equatorial Chiclayo, in Perú, a bracing experience. Goose pimples are the norm when swimming on much of this coast, even at the height of summer. The weather conditions that tend to affect the Casablanca Valley are dominated by the cool waters offshore. Fog and mist are commonplace morning phenomena here. What is more, the sun does not always get a

VIÑA CASABLANCA

Established 1992 *Owners* Viña Santa Carolina S. A. *Production* 80,000 cases *Vineyard area* 148 acres (60 ha), plus 544 acres (220 ha) under long-term lease

Viña Casablanca was set up by Santa Carolina to exploit the success the region has had with white varieties. Winemaker Ignacio Recabarren has guided this bodega to international acclaim, using fruit from the Santa Isabel Estate, but red grapes are bought in from other areas to enhance local bodegas' *tinto* vinification.

BÍO-BÍO VALLEY

This is the southernmost viticultural region of Chile. Once dedicated to the more humble varieties of grapes, such as moscatel de alejandria and país, recent times have witnessed a much keener interest in quality plantations. New wineries are continuing to spring up in Chile, despite the fact that there is a limit to the soils available for the planting of vines. There are test plantings of 20 different varieties in the Bío-Bío Valley, mourvèdre and viognier among them.

VIÑA GRACIA
Owners Cópora Wineries

Córpora Wineries is a division of Córpora (a conglomerate including some stunningly beautiful resort hotels). Córpora established Viña Gracia, an exceptionally stylish winery, to vinify fruit from vineyards in Aconcagua, Maipo, Cachapoal and, notably, Bío-Bío. The winery is run by Jacques Antoine Toublanc, a Frenchman. Fruit harvested in distant vineyards travels during the cool of night in 1,100-pound (500 kg) bins. All white grapes are tested for botrytis, leaves and potential sugar, then chilled to 50°F (10°C) and pressed. About 15 percent is macerated for between 6 and 8 hours.

The *tintos* go straight to tanks. For whites the harvest normally starts at the beginning of March, while the harvesting of *tintos* runs from March 15 to the end of April.

Jacques enjoys working in Chile. Chardonnay gains finesse when made from free-run juice and when pressed gently moves to somewhat more honeyed and vegetal nuances. Eventually, with greater pressing pressures, green aromas creep in.

The *tintos* are fermented in new stainless-steel tanks. One thing that is notable about vinification in Chile is that good color is easily obtained. There is no need to add tannins, nor is it necessary to aim for long maceration. The bodega has a total capacity of 1.25 million gallons (4.7 million l). Only French wood from French coopers is used in its 60-gallon (225 l) barriques, although Jacques would like to try larger barrels. Jacques likes to experiment with yeasts and has achieved some interesting results. One is a barrique-fermented chardonnay from Tatiwe made using yeast 1080, a culture native to Portugal's Vinho Verde.

The foreman oversees the harvest in the vineyards at Viña Los Vascos, Santiago.

Argentina

Harold Heckle

When Argentine wine began to appear in the international market few consumers realised the magnitude of the phenomenon involved, the size of the genie that had been released from the bottle. The truth is that never again would there be a discovery on such a scale. This was the last great undiscovered land, in wine terms, left on earth. Its size and its isolation are both subjects that merit special attention, but even more intriguing for the wine lover is the potential encompassed within such a vast viticultural landscape.

Argentina is of great importance to the wine world because of the amount of land dedicated to the vine, the quantity of the wine produced, the diversity of terroir involved, the specific varietals grown and, as a consequence, the styles of wine possible. It vies with the United States for the position of fourth largest wine producer, behind Italy, France and Spain which is surprising, as until recently almost no wine was exported from Argentina.

It ranks with the United States as fourth-largest wine producer, after Italy, France and Spain, so it is rather surprising to find that until very recently Argentina exported almost no wine. Things are changing fast. No one can be in any doubt that, despite a stumbling start, Argentine wine will soon form an important part in the broad spectrum of international wines available to consumers around the world. The quality now apparent reminds us that the slumbering giant has only recently awakened. How far it will choose to go, and how great it will become are questions to exercise the mind and stir the imagination.

History

Recent archeological investigations are uncovering an inhabited past far more ancient than had previously been thought possible for the lower end of South America. The great expanse of Argentina and the comparative isolation of important sites has made it relatively difficult to study and many areas are virtually new to scientific exploration. Estimates vary greatly, but by the time European settlement began in the 1500s, there were probably more than 300,000 people, speaking quite an array of languages that have now disappeared. No great cities, like those found in Aztec Mexico or Inca Perú, were built at this end of South America.

From Mendoza up through the northwest, the population was under the sway of the Inca Empire. Sophisticated pottery, weaving, music and farming techniques developed as a result.

The plains of Mendoza, from San Rafael through Luján de Cuyo, are arid scrubland, except on the banks of the rivers that crisscross the plain. This area is about 1,000 miles (1,600 km) inland and some rivers simply well up into lakes, never reaching the ocean. The Incas harnessed river water and turned the plains into a large oasis, capable of sustaining a hardworking agricultural population. Evidence of their sophisticated irrigation network, with clear-headed laws to govern its use, as well as a system of roads that linked the Argentine regions with the rest of the Inca Empire survive to this day.

European discovery is still a matter of dispute. Amerigo Vespucci formerly received much of the credit, but historians now doubt this claim. It is far more certain that Juan Díaz de Solís sailed around the River Plate in 1516, followed by Ferdinand Magellan (who sailed into the southern strait) in 1520. Sebastian Cabot discovered the Paraná River and established the fort of Sancti Spiritu, rescuing two survivors of the Solís expedition in the process. These men told of a wealthy people in the interior and of a mountain of silver.

Vineyards lining the road at Chandon, Mendoza.

Encouraged by the profitable conquests of Perú and Mexico, and desperate to counter Portugal's rising power in Brazil, Charles V of Spain sent one of his favorites, Pedro de Mendoza, one of Spain's wealthiest noblemen (who financed the expedition himself) to Argentina in 1535. This was the largest and most serious expedition to America so far, with 11 ships, 2,150 men, 100 horses and even a historian, Ulrico Schmidel. Mendoza founded Nuestra Señora Santa María del Buen Aire (later Buenos Aires) in 1536. Food was scarce and high-handed treatment soon antagonized the native inhabitants, who first withdrew their supplies and then began to attack. Seriously ill, Mendoza sailed for home in 1537, but died on the way.

Spain lost interest in the region and later settlement came via Argentina's neighboring Spanish colonies. The first permanent settlement, Santiago del Estero, was founded by Francisco de Aguirre, who arrived from Chile in 1553. San Juan and Mendoza were both founded in 1562 by groups migrating from Chile, while Peruvians founded Tucumán (1565), Córdoba (1573), Salta (1582) and La Rioja (1591). In terms of government, Argentina became a subordinate territory of the Viceroyalty of Perú. Contact with Spain, letters, laws, edicts as well as cultural influences all traveled down via the west coast and Lima, finally arriving in Argentina. This gave Argentines a sense of detachment from the mother country and from the world in general.

Later, in 1776, Spain attempted to shore up this colony of growing importance by creating the Viceroyalty of La Plata, with its capital in Buenos Aires. The main thrust was to recognize the growing trade potential of the region and to counter the threat posed by Portugal's colony in Brazil. Portugal's natural ally, Great Britain, was Spain's traditional *bête noir*. Buenos Aires did not necessarily regard Britain as an enemy but more as a possible partner in smuggling. An illegal trade with Britain began to take shape, giving the capital of the new Viceroyalty even greater wealth and cosmopolitan allure. The city grew rapidly from a population of 2,200 in 1726 to 45,000 in 1800, in the process attracting merchants, teachers, dancers, painters, musicians and rogues from countries such as France, Portugal and Italy.

With an expanding cosmopolitan population, drawn mainly from countries with a wine tradition, demand for wine inevitably increased. Attempts to cultivate vines near the capital proved disastrous. *Vitis vinifera* simply did not take to the

Weinert-sémillon arriving in boxes at the Bodega.

east coast of South America. Disease and rot proved major problems. Poor drainage of subsoils compounded this unhappy situation. What little wine was produced obviously met with little or no success, because attempts to grow vineyards in this region were soon abandoned. Wine had to be imported into the burgeoning capital from European, mainly Spanish, sources, at great expense. Compare this to the gastronomic plenty South America afforded its citizens. For the first time in their lives many immigrants were able to afford meat on a regular, if not daily, basis, something unknown to those they had left behind. But meals without wine must have seemed strange to them.

The American Revolution, followed by the French Revolution, Napoleon's intervention in Spain and the influence of the Enlightenment in Europe unsettled the colony deeply. When the British invaded La Plata, the Spanish Viceroy fled in panic and Buenos Aires buckled under the force of a British army heartened by successes in other parts of the globe. Alarmed by this new and far from welcome intervention, the inhabitants of the northern region of Montevideo (now Uruguay) gathered an army and rode to the rescue of their cousins in Buenos Aires. The well-organized counterattack succeeded in expelling the British and fomenting a feeling of nationalistic pride and independence. The eventual outcome was set.

Argentina declared its independence from Spain on July 9, 1816, by which time it had become a homogeneous European-based society. The native population had been driven to virtual extinction by assimilation, cruel repression and

Redeemable tokens given to grape pickers at Finca Flichman, Mendoza.

force of arms. Particularly self-reliant and bellicose tribes, such as the Quilmes, were forcibly banished from their homelands and marched to compounds more than 1,000 miles (1,600 km) away, where, demoralized, their independence and will to live was finally crushed. Agricultural prosperity based on cereal-farming and the export of cattle hides was transforming Argentina into an affluent nation. Increasingly, city dwellers of Buenos Aires looked to Europe, and particularly France and Italy, for inspiration. In their turn, migrants from many European nations swamped ships bound for Argentine ports, determined to make their fortunes. Italy, Spain, Poland and Russia, in that order, supplied significant numbers. Buenos Aires became a major focus for international culture and Argentina became the eighth-richest nation on earth. A greater national character, backed up by the beginnings of a distinguishing culture, began to emerge.

The arrival of the vine

In 1556 a Spanish priest called Juan Cedrón arrived in Santiago del Estero from La Serena, Chile, with cotton and grain seeds and vine stalks. It seems fair to suppose that he planted these and, almost certainly, became Argentina's first winemaker. It is likely that this early Spanish-American grape was the same variety as was introduced into Chile and California. In Argentina it is now known as *criolla*, or *criolla chica*, in Chile as *país* and in California as *mission*. Vines were well-established in Mendoza by the sixteenth century.

Although these early wines were intended mainly for local consumption, word began to spread that they were better than some made elsewhere. Although Spanish law maintained that wine should be imported from Spain, by the eighteenth century a trickle of trade with Buenos Aires, already a strong market for wine, can be detected from the sub-Andean region, particularly from San Rafael in Mendoza. The main problem was the distance between producing area and potential wine market, over harsh terrain where roads were constantly being cut by flash floods.

Things progressed slowly until 1880 when French botanist Aimé Pouget introduced the first French varieties. He had witnessed developments in Chile, especially the establishment of the Quinta Normal (*q.v.*). He chose Mendoza as the site for new plantations and discovered, much to his delight, that top-quality vines thrived. One variety that did particularly well in the western and north-western areas of Mendoza was *la uva francesa*, the French grape, or malbec (sometimes spelled malbeck). Such was the perceived quality of this adapted variety that much of the red-grape plantations were dedicated to it, especially around Mendoza city and in neighboring Luján de Cuyo. Grown at around 2,623 feet (800 m) above sea level, it produced a lusty red wine, full of color and vibrancy that survived well in barrel, bottle and the leather pouch.

Because of transport difficulties, production was limited to what Mendoza and its environs could consume. Then in 1885 a British company opened the first railroad linking Mendoza with Buenos Aires and *mendocino* winemakers had a quick and safe means of getting wine to the thirsty capital. A great explosion in wine-related activity began in Mendoza with rapid proliferation of vineyards and *bodegas*. Quality was not initially sacrificed to profit, but a book, *Las viñas y los vinos en Mendoza* (*Vines and Wines in Mendoza*), published in 1884 by Eusebio Blanco, indicates that certain circles in Buenos Aires were skeptical, despite an innate nationalistic pride in anything Argentinean. Blanco set out to prove that good viticulture could yield wines in Mendoza of high enough quality to satisfy even the palates of those who had tried fine European products. Determined to take things one step further, Blanco's son-in-law, Tiburcio Benegas, set about improving every element of winemaking in Mendoza. His bodega, El Trapiche, with 618 acres (250 ha) of European varietal vineyards, is one of the early monuments to enology in the Americas.

Demand for wine in Buenos Aires continued to outstrip supply. Recognizing a golden opportunity, Juan Giol, a hired hand at El Trapiche, worked hard and bought himself a small vineyard called Las Heras. He later rented a small bodega in Alto Godoy and began, through his wife's contacts, to deal with Bautista Gerónimo Gargantini and Pascual Toso, both also recent immigrants. Giol and Gargantini got on well and found themselves making and selling wine together with singular success. In 1896 they split with Toso and bought 119 acres (48 ha) in Maipú.

By 1897 they began building their first purpose-designed bodega. Sales in 1898 reached 1,056,000 gallons (4,000,000 l). By 1911 this figure had risen tenfold, with 400 men employed including 80 coopers, 1,112 acres (450 ha) of productive vines, 371 acres (150 ha) just planted and 18,533 acres (7,500 ha) of land awaiting plantation. Two other bodegas had been absorbed by this stage, one next to the railroad. To facilitate transportation to the railroad, Giol built a wine pipeline (the first in the world) linking all his bodegas. He also dissolved his association with Gargantini and established Bodegas y Viñedos Giol S. A. with a working capital of $10,000,000 and the powerful Banco Español del Río de la Plata as guarantor. From being a hired hand, Giol, at 44, was outright owner of the world's largest wine-making concern and known throughout the country as the King of Wine. Eventually, he returned to Italy and settled on 7,413 acres (3,000 ha) in San Polo di Piave, returning to Argentina only sporadically to oversee his remaining financial interests.

By this time, annual Argentine wine consumption had peaked at nearly 26.4 gallons (100 l) per capita. With little regard for quality the industry went head-on into mass production. Good-quality vineyards, including some prize malbec plots, were grubbed up and replaced with whatever yielded the most grapes. More often than not this was the vigorous cereza grande, a large pink grape, criolla and cereza, all high yielders. Vast amounts of pink wine were sold in demijohns, from which corner stores filled smaller bottles. Wine prices rose, despite poor quality, and greed made some owners reluctant to improve their plant and vineyards.

The collapse began in 1980, with the national economy struggling and Argentina's foreign policy taking several turns for the worse. The huge Grupo Greco, financed by its own bank, collapsed, bankrupting Bodega Arizu, which had until then been the world's largest vineyard. Another disaster followed in 1988 when the government-sponsored Giol group crashed. There was a last-ditch attempt by the establishment to stabilize the market by controlling large segments of it, and when that failed the Argentine wine industry sank into the doldrums. There are still vast untended, overgrown vineyards and abandoned workers' houses dotted around San Rafael in Mendoza. To make matters worse, the Falklands/Malvinas War put the brakes on Argentina's international trade possibilities. The hyper-inflation and poor fiscal control that followed made it impossible to fix costs and prices, driving yet another nail into the coffin.

From this low point Argentina has risen once again to merit inclusion in international markets.

Pickers with boxes filled to the brim, wait for the truck at Proviar Vineyards.

Among the first to recognize the potential was David Stevens, MW, who built alliances with the Pulenta family, owners of the huge Peñaflor winery. More widespread interest, however, was not shown until the early 1990s. Today, thanks to the wine boom in neighboring Chile, many buyers, importers and international winemaking concerns are investing in existing and new enterprises. One very encouraging sign is that Argentine consumers appear to be realizing that they don't have to take whatever is offered. They are demanding better quality, a fact reflected in plummeting sales of cheap wine and a dramatic increase in the domestic consumption of fine wine.

Broquel Reisling waits in the cellars at Peñáflor, Mendoza.

Landscape and climate

Argentina is sometimes referred to as six continents crammed into one immense country, so diverse and extensive is its geography. From almost-Amazonian rainforest in the north, to colossal Andean landscapes, to glimmering sandy beaches, to never-ending grassy plains, to semi-arid desert, to alpine splendor, to near-Antarctic Patagonian majesty, Argentina sweeps from north of the Tropic of Capricorn (21° 46') to Tierra del Fuego at latitude 55° 03' south. From sea level to 22,816 feet (6,959 m) higher (Mount Aconcagua), there is

Proviar malbec vines at Vistalba near Mendoza.

enough variety within this nation to include the widest imaginable spread of climatic conditions.

To the east lies the Atlantic Ocean, to the west, running north–south, the Andes, a colossal range pushed up by the massive telluric collision of tectonic plates as the Americas moved west toward the sub-Pacific plates. Interestingly, the resultant folds in the earth's crust do not form a single mountain range. In fact, different mountain ranges formed at different times. The Cordón de Plata, is noticeably older, darker in color, smaller and more eroded than the principal cordillera of the Andes, which rises to incredible heights. From some vantage points in Mendoza, between San Rafael and Mendoza city, the mountains seem to hang high in the sky, almost like a Chinese painting on an incredible scale. Farther west, in Chile, is a second mighty cordillera of the Andes.

The undulations and foothills east of the Andes are important because they offer diverse habitats for plants and wildlife as well as potential viticultural *terroir*. Another point worth noting is that pre-Andean valleys and hollows can trap and hold lower temperatures, which can have a bearing on the life-cycle and well-being of grapes. Cool air descending from the glacial peaks of the Andes is sometimes trapped by such formations, and under

some circumstances the mountains act as obstacles to the warming effect of the alluvial plain stretching away to the east.

This alluvial plain extends from where the foothills of the Andes get smaller, north from about latitude 38° south. The debris of erosion and fragmentation brought down by the rivers spreads out all over the plains, in some places to a considerable depth. Further east, where humidity from the ocean precipitates more readily, layers of wind-blown loess form a landscape that appears almost flat. This flatland is known as the Pampas.

Nearer the Andes, 1,000 miles (1,600 km) inland, rainfall is much less frequent. Snow-melt water and rainfall precipitated by the high Andes find their way onto the plains via rivers that grow and diminish with dramatic fluctuations only possible in such a large-scale landscape. The rivers and watertable are the principal sources of water in this otherwise harsh environment. Lack of rainfall is only part of the problem. When the rare precipitation does come, it can do so in torrents, or worse, in hailstones sometimes the size of tennis balls. Whole sections of the countryside can be washed away or flattened.

Although phylloxera does exist—you can occasionally see the mites clinging onto *vinifera* roots when you pull them up—they seem to be kept well in check by a number of factors. Perhaps most crucial is the flood irrigation used to water the vineyards. Being aerobic, phylloxera probably detests being flooded. Global warming is a worry, though, as water runoff from the Andes appears to be diminishing with warmer weather, an effect that is quite noticeable in Argentina. This has led to many growers opting for drip irrigation. In these cases most growers have taken the precaution of grafting vines onto resistant American rootstock.

Wine regions

Within Argentina are five main wine-producing regions spread over 15 geographically very different provinces.

Mendoza is responsible for about 95 percent of all exports because its 1,038 bodegas produce 75 percent of Argentina's wines, and it was the first region to adapt to higher-quality production. The region's suitability to viticulture is obvious. Not only are the waters of the Andes free of pollution, but brilliant sunshine and dry weather mean that fungicide spraying is almost unnecessary. Some vineyards use herbicides to keep weeds at bay, but by and large Mendoza vineyard care is natural and well-attuned to modern health and ecological considerations. In some regions conditions are conducive to developing wine styles of character.

San Juan, to the north of Mendoza, has yet to provide winelovers with a winery of note. This situation may change soon, as massive investment has gone into planting international varietals in new, irrigated vineyards. When El Niño brought bad weather to Mendoza, San Juan came to the rescue with fruit of reasonable quality. The future may hold a few surprises, despite relatively high temperatures during grape-maturation periods.

La Rioja is famous for its torrontés grape, locally called torrontés riojano. A conflict arising out of the name (vis-à-vis Rioja, Spain) has been resolved by referring to wines made here as coming from Famatina Valley, in the foothills of the Andes north of San Juan. Originally this area supplied cheap wines for mass consumption on the domestic market but has now begun to move upmarket. The Cooperativa La Riojana is the largest in America. With a sizeable research budget and the help of talented overseas enologists, it is now a major presence on export markets, providing good-value wines at the modest end of the scale. Their Santa Florentina torrontés has tamed the wildest excesses of the variety (using native

yeasts) and offers a charming aperitif wine. Red wines are benefiting from antipodean techniques.

Salta is composed of many valleys, including Valles Calchaquíes, surely one of the most beautiful wine-producing valleys on earth. Bodegas Etchart (also found in Mendoza) has its principal winery here, where winemaker José Luis Mounier controls production of some fine wines. Outstanding among them is the older, more mature style Arnaldo B. Etchart. This wine blends malbec with varying quantities of cabernet sauvignon and other French varietals to give quite an active nose and a well-rounded palate. Michel Rolland helped shape these wines. Etchart has made an art of torrontés wines and this variety is at its most subtle here. Varietal cabernet sauvignon has won positive comment and will continue to improve.

Another important local producer is Michel Torino, a winery owned by the Lavaque family. It is currently being remodeled, if not totally rebuilt, so the wines are in transition and of no great depth for the moment. New plantations have absorbed a huge amount of cash and there are other plans. Grenache was specially brought in and may provide quite interesting results.

Río Negro, in the south of Patagonia, contains a wine region of great promise. A deep rift valley protects the region around the General Roca, providing a macroclimate that appears to suit viticulture and soft fruits exceptionally well. The main producer here is Humberto Canale. From good-quality fruit come wines with some delicacy and a great deal of promise. With greater investment in the winery who knows what may be possible. Other ventures wothy of note here are the French-owned Fabre-Montmayou, makers of the well-received Infinitus wines. Bernardo Weinert also owns some vineyards down here.

Ripe cabernet sauvignon grapes on the vine, Finca Flichman, Mendoza.

Mendoza

Mendoza's wine-producing regions can be divided roughly into three areas, the main cluster in the north, more or less surrounding the sprawling city of Mendoza, one higher up and nearer the Andes to the west, and one to the south, toward the middle of the province.

The cluster around the city straddles the Mendoza and Tunuyán rivers and includes two of Mendoza's three DOs *(Denominación de Origen)*, Luján de Cuyo and Maipú. This area is itself subdivided into three regions.

La Zona Alta, properly known as Región de la Zona Alta del Río Mendoza, but also referred to as *Primera Zona*, the First Zone. It is blessed with some of the most picturesque vineyards in the world. The snow-capped Andes and smaller red Cordón de Plata act as a spectacular backdrop. The visual effect is made more striking by the fact that the area devoted to viticulture is flat, perfect cycling country. The soil is made up of the moraine and waterborne deposits eroded from the Andes. The surface is a very pale tan, fine, sandy, almost clay-like crust with negligible organic matter. It drains well and is ideal for high-quality wine. More than 300 bodegas cultivate almost 50,000 acres (20,235 ha) of vineyards in this area. *Región del Norte* and *Región del Este* are lower than the Zona Alta and together encompass 210,000 acres (84,985 ha) dedicated to viticulture. Soils of the Región del Norte tend to be less porous and permeable than the other regions, favoring young fruity wines, both white and red. The Región del Este has a more complex soil structure. Some areas have deep upper layers with good water retention; others have solid rock strata near the surface and poor water retention.

Región del Valle de Uco (the Uco Valley Region), nearest the Andes, to the east, is divided into Tupungato, Tunuyán and San Carlos. At 3,300 feet (1,006 m) above sea level, this is the highest of Mendoza's regions and is currently attracting the most attention. Its soils are stony, alluvial sediments that produce quality wines. There are now more than 3,500 acres (1,417 ha) of vineyards.

A blending vat holding almost 1,154,000 gallons (5.25 Ml), Pináflor, Mendoza.

Producers
1 La Agrícola
2 Bodegas y Viñedos Santa Ana
3 Bodegas Leoncio Arizu
4 Bodega Balbi
5 Bodegas Valentín Bianchi
6 Bodega Catena
7 Bodega Chandon
8 Navarro Correas
9 Dolium
10 Bodega Escorihuela
11 Bodega Esmeralda
12 Bodegas Etchart
13 Finca Flichman
14 Bodegas y Viñedos Goyenechea
15 Bodegas Lavaque
16 Bodega Norton
17 La Rural
18 Bodegas Suter
19 Trapiche
20 Domaine Vistalba
21 Bodegas & Cavas De Weinert

Región del Sur in the south is divided into General Alvear and San Rafael, Mendoza's third DO. At an altitude of 2,600 feet (793 m) above sea level and with sandy soils it can yield wines with delicate fragrance.

Vines and wines

It goes without saying that in any wine area as large as Mendoza there will be a bewildering array of grape varieties grown. The Zona Alta imparts special characteristics to many of the varieties grown there. Those that reach standards of world-class include bonarda, malbec, chardonnay and tempranillo (or tempranilla). Local torrontés grapes are somewhat more delicate than some found in other provinces.

The Región del Norte produces lively chenin blanc, ugni blanc and sangiovese. You will also see a great deal of pedro ximénez. The Región del Este specializes in cabernet sauvignon, syrah, sangiovese, chenin blanc, chardonnay and some less-than-typical sauvignon blanc. The cooler Valle de Uco yields chardonnay, merlot and malbec. The Región del Sur can claim some chardonnay, cabernet sauvignon and bonarda.

The powerhouse of Argentine winemaking, Mendoza is in a state of constant dynamic flux with new entities starting all the time and old ones folding or merging with others. Starting in San Rafael, many *mendocino* bodegas are making an impact with the quality of their wines.

Nicolás Catena's holding company now controls about 25 percent of Argentina's top-quality vineyards with international varietals as well as substantial vineyard holdings in San Juan. Catena has reached this dominant position by employing a mix of strategies including careful investment, stealth, corporate buy-outs and even hostile takeovers. His stable now includes some of the most remarkable wineries in Argentina: Bodega Catena, Bodega Escorihuela and Bodega Esmeralda (see producers below).

Producers

LA AGRÍCOLA, MAIPÚ

Established 1963 *Owners* the Zuccardi family *Production* 1,555,555 cases *Vineyard area* 1,063 acres (430 ha)

Initially established as a showpiece for an irrigation system devised by engineer owner Zuccardi, using pre-cast concrete sections, the winery later became an independent venture under the guidance of son, José Alberto Zuccardi. Land acquired in the Zona Este of Mendoza was converted to vineyards and irrigated by the Zuccardi system. Today La Agrícola is arguably Argentina's most successful exporter of wine. Hard-working and adaptable, José Alberto looks after the vineyards (with admirable anti-hail protection), the modern winery and international business. His recently launched "Q" (quality) range includes some notable wines, a winner being an American oak-aged tempranillo that is deep and full of non-Spanish character. Generally speaking, his whole range, from Santa Julia Chardonnay to supple Malbec Oak, is very good value.

BODEGAS Y VIÑEDOS SANTA ANA, GUAYMALLÉN

Established 1891 *Owners* Santa Carolina (Chile) and Luis Alfredo Pulenta *Vineyard area* NA

This large bodega in the grand Argentine style has its own railroad siding and still sends trainloads of wine to Buenos Aires. Bought with Chilean (Santa Carolina) money, it has been modernized to a high standard, with a keen eye to exporting. While its current wines are still in a transitional stage, the future looks promising. A 100 percent syrah is packed full of deep, attractive fruit.

BODEGAS LEONCIO ARIZU, LUJÁN DE CUYO

Established 1901 *Owners* the Arizu family *Vineyard area* 988 acres (400 ha)

With some of the best-tended vineyards in the Mendoza region, the white wines from here are improving dramatically, especially the sauvignon blanc, but unfortunately the quality of the vineyard isn't always reflected in the wines. Some reds have good fruit extraction, but also seem to fade far too rapidly. Improvements are afoot.

BODEGA BALBI, SAN RAFAEL

Established 1930 *Owner* Allied Domecq
Production bought-in grapes

Highly efficient and well thought out, this bodega's aim is to make good-value wines for everyday drinking. Balbi is singularly successful with a range of bright, well-made white wines. They also make a rosé that sells well in most markets, a rare thing. Their reds are approachable, clean and well-focused. Allied Domecq has helped transform this bodega.

BODEGAS VALENTÍN BIANCHI, SAN RAFAEL

Established 1928 *Owners* the Bianchi family *Vineyard area* 865 acres (350 ha)

This old bodega is something of a rabbit warren, cramped and labyrinthine, in the middle of town. A long list of wines show the definable house style of vinification here and it isn't to everyone's taste. That said, they manage to extract some good fruit, for example, from wine made from Elsa's Vineyard grapes (look for this on the label). Recent attempts to take the wines further upmarket include building a modern wine plant on the outskirts of the city, where they are beginning to produce some commendable traditional method sparkling wine. The range they call Famiglia Bianchi reflects their Italianate family roots.

BODEGA CATENA

Established 1999 *Owner* Nicolás Catena

The newest and without a doubt most innovative winery in Argentina, Susana Balbo (of Bodegas Martins) planned and built this bodega on budget in record time, the first woman to head such an important and ambitious project in the country. Its cavernous hall boasts the latest vinification equipment imaginable, including computer-controlled robots that crush grapes directly above the gravity-fed tanks and later sink the caps individually for each tank. The design brings to mind a Maya

Harvest time, and cabernet sauvignon grapes await the truck. Trapiche, Mendoza..

Fermentation tanks in pristine surroundings at San Telmo, Maipú.

Winemaker Raoul de la Mota in the cellars at Bodegas & Cavas de Weinert, Mendoza.

NAVARRO CORREAS, MAIPÚ

Established c.1798 *Owners* CINBA *Vineyard area* Small holdings in Luján de Cuyo, Maipú and Tupungato

This bodega's current vineyards include the land that was once Tiburcio Benegas' famous bodega El Trapiche. The drinks company CINBA has invested heavily to bring this once-struggling company back into the winemaking limelight. Its bottle-fermented 100 percent pinot noir (with a blush) is Argentina's best bubbly. Though successful on the domestic market, the reds and whites have still to overcome their fusty image.

DOLIUM, AGRELO

Established 1998 *Owner* Mario Giadorou

Financed and constructed by retired stainless-steel engineer Mario Giadorou, this impressive bodega was built largely underground, which, while adding to the expense, has obvious benefits. With a design allowing for adaptation to future technological improvements, this state-of-the-art bodega ran into teething problems with its first harvest because of the eccentricities of Giadorou's ex-partner. To repair the damage Giadorou turned to Susana Balbo, who heads Catena's latest winery project, to sort out the problems and the future for the venture is looking brighter.

BODEGA ESCORIHUELA, GODOU CRUZ, MENDOZA

Established 1884 *Owner* Nicolás Catena *Vineyard area* 106 acres (43 ha) Rivadavia, 22 acres (9 ha) Maipú

The wines made here are aimed at the humbler end of the market and include the own-label and supermarket brands that Catena deals with. The bodega has an excellent restaurant, competently run by acclaimed chef Francis Malman and his able assistant Connie Aldao, right in the winery, a top food spot in metropolitan Mendoza.

BODEGA ESMERALDA

Established 1970s *Owner* Nicolás Catena

Formerly Catena's flagship enterprise, where Pedro Marchevsky and José Galante, with assessment by Paul Hobbs, crafted Argentina's best wines. In the Catena Alta range, the chardonnay is right up there in world class, the malbec definitive and the cabernet sauvignon sets new standards. Below this category are Catena wines, providing extraordinary complexity for the price. Alamos Ridge wines fill the next medium-price bracket with some aplomb, and below these the bodega produces an interesting range of wines called Argento, which should not be missed.

pyramid. Without question, the wines emerging from here are bound to provide another quantum leap in terms of quality. The winery nestles beside Catena's Agrelo vineyards, not too far from the Tupungato plantations.

BODEGA CHANDON, AGRELO, LUJÁN DE CUYO

Established 1959 *Owners* Moët & Chandon *Production* Millions of cases *Vineyard area* ±1.235 acres (±500 ha)

This was Moët & Chandon's first venture outside France, causing outrage in their home country at the time (they don't use the traditional method to make sparkling wine). Today Bodega Chandon provides the domestic market with its top-selling charmat-style sparkler. The varietal chardonnay is very clean and is a great success in restaurants.

BODEGAS ETCHART, PERDRIEL, LUJÁN DE CUYO

Established 1938 (Salta), 1992 (Mendoza) *Owners* Pernord Ricard *Production* 666,667 cases *Vineyard area* 138 acres (56 ha)

This firm has two bodegas, one in Mendoza, the other in northern Salta. The firm's best work is done at the bodega in Salta.

FINCA FLICHMAN, MAIPÚ

Established 1873 *Owners* Sogrape, Portugal *Production* 1,000,000 cases *Vineyard area* 494 acres (200 ha)

The vineyards are an interesting patchwork. Some very poor, stony soil has recently been planted with selected clones and provided with drip irrigation. After transformation by its new owners, there will undoubtedly be some interesting wines made in the next few years, with more vineyard area being planted. Another vineyard is, to contrast, covered over with topsoil specially carted in early last century. Sogrape will no doubt sharpen the image of the wines.

BODEGAS Y VIÑEDOS GOYENECHEA, SAN RAFAEL

Established 1868 *Owners* the Goyenechea family *Vineyard area* 250 acres (100 ha)

Traditional Basque-influenced styles of winemaking are maintained here. The Goyenechea family has been here for generations and the old bodega shows its history. Some of the not inconsiderable stretches of vineyards are covered with anti-hail mesh. Investment has recently been directed toward vineyard care, leaving winery modernization for later, so the better wines tend to be the younger ones that go into bottle rapidly. A bright and lingering chardonnay is worth trying and the young reds are full of good fruit.

BODEGAS LAVAQUE, SAN RAFAEL

Established late 1980s *Owners* Rodolfo Lavaque and others *Vineyard area* 408 acres (165 ha), plus bought-in grapes

This small, family-run bodega is surrounded by vineyards which were planted relatively recently. Lavaque began his working life in the clothing industry where he and financial partner Freddy Mattei discovered a talent for marketing. Eager to follow in the footsteps of his winemaking grandfather, Lavaque made the move into the wine industry. Apart from the small bodega (producing fine merlot with eight months aging in new French oak) the firm operates a large blending and bottling facility that provides supermarkets with a range of medium-priced products. The partners also own Michel Torino in Salta.

BODEGA NORTON, LUJÁN DE CUYO

Established c.1890 *Owners* the Swarowski family *Vineyard area* 74 acres (30 ha) Agrelo, plus 395+ acres (160+ ha) Luján de Cuyo

Founded in the nineteenth century by an Englishman involved in the railroads, this bodega enjoyed an auspicious early period, but its fortunes slid downhill until it was bought by the Swarowski family, widely known for Austrian crystal. Michael Halstrick, Swarowski's stepson, is in charge of Norton and is aiming to make Bodega Norton a household name worldwide. The heavy investment made in new and replanted vineyards, as well as in a fantastic new vinification plant, seems certain to make his wish come true. Family links at one stage united Carlos Falcó, Marqués de Griñón, with the Norton name, and there may still be a collaboration, especially as Griñón appears to produce a line of wines in Argentina under the watchful eye of Norton's very talented and impressive staff. The truth being, of course, that Norton is not prepared to play second fiddle to anyone. Norton Privada is a Bordeaux-style wine that ages very well in bottle, serving to demonstrate very clearly the long-term potential of the winery. Chardonnay has also come a long way, with improvement showing in recent vintages. Lighter and less exalted wines, such as

Workers loading trucks with cabernet sauvignon, Finca Flichman, Mendoza.

A harvest worker takes a moment to reflect while waiting for the truck

A gleaming vat at Trapiche, Mendoza.

making passable but unremarkable sparkling wines and forgettable still wines to some pretty tight and muscular efforts.

TRAPICHE, MENDOZA (MAIPÚ)

Established c.1900 *Owners* Luis Alfredo Pulenta and others
Vineyard area 1,235 acres (500 ha)

Peñaflor is the largest bodega in Mendoza and Trapiche is an appendage to it. The family behind this landmark winery has seen turbulent times engulf their operations. A buyout headed by a branch of the family with links in the USA seems to have stabilized things a bit. While the family has business interests in other fields, wine was the basis of its fortune. Today family members are producing quite an array of wines, from basic mass-produced tetra bricks called Thermidor (with the local nickname of Terminator) to some fine products under the Trapiche label. The bodega appears to be in two minds about whether to leave Trapiche as its premium line or whether it should upgrade the Peñaflor line to a similar level. Certainly it has access to good-quality fruit from family-owned vineyards in Mendoza (such as the impressive El Chiche), including some plantations growing high in the Uco Valley.

DOMAINE VISTALBA, LUJÁN DE CUYO

Established c. 1990 *Owner* Fabré Montmayou
Vineyard area 124 acres (50 ha)

This charming little French-owned château-style winery in Vistalba is in prime malbec country (Vistalba also has some vineyards in Río Negro, in Patagonia). Balanced, well-extracted, complex wines are made here with typical Gallic flair. Chardonnay and malbec are worthy examples.

BODEGAS & CAVAS DE WEINERT, CARRODILLA, LUJÁN DE CUYO

Established 1976 *Owners* Bernardo Weinert
Vineyard area NA

When Michel Rolland helped make wines here, wine writers such as Robert Parker gave them a good write-up. Since then the winery has gone through an up-and-down period. Enologist Raul de la Mota has now left, making way for new blood. Some of the wines are deep and well extracted, but quality has been variable, mainly because, although the fruit is of good quality, the winery has yet to modernize. Old wood is still used to store wine, at times to very good effect, at others less than convincing. Carrascal is a traditional line and some premium malbec is also sold.

the vivacious torrontés, provide depth to a line that also includes a very acceptable sparkling wine.

LA RURAL, COQUIMBITO, MENDOZA

Established 1885 *Owners* Nicolás Catena and Rodolfo Reina Rutini

This bodega is controlled by Catena which has a 51 percent holding. Onlookers have seen how enologist Mariano Di Paola has consistently improved and fettled his wines to international standards. A line to look out for is Rutini, merlot and chardonnay. Some super-premium wines are also on the drawing-board, so expect great things.

BODEGAS SUTER, SAN RAFAEL

Established c.1900 *Owners* the Suter family *Vineyard area* 544 acres (220 ha)

The bodega was originally founded by a Swiss couple who subsequently became very successful in the Argentine market and today, winemaking is just one of the family's activities. Their firm also sells machinery and vehicles. For a time it seemed they had lost interest in wine then, spurred on by the potential of overseas sales, they went from

Wine Reference Table

While every effort has been made to provide an interesting selection of wines across many countries, tastes and price ranges, this list is by no means exhaustive. The table below is intended to be a guide only. The asterisks represent the approximate price of each wine in its country of origin. One asterisk represents easily affordable wines, two asterisks denote a moderate expense and three asterisks a more costly wine. Foods listed under compatible foods are intended only to be suggestions. Of course it is possible to drink any wine with any food; these suggestions are simply a guide.

FRANCE

Wine name	Region	Style	Flavor/Bouquet	Compatible Foods	Price Range
A. Zimmermann Fils Gewurztraminer Cuvée Alphonse	Alsace	White	Citrus, spicy	Asian	**
AE Dor Cognac	Cognac	Brandy	Spirity, fiery	After dinner	***
Aimery Sieur d'Arques Limoux Toques et Clochers Terroir Haute Vallée	Languedoc	Sparkling	Citrus, smoky, minerally	Aperitif	**
Alain Graillot Crozes Hermitage	Rhône Valley	Red	Berry, spicy, earthy, minerally	Pork, beef	**
Alfred Gratien Brut NV	Champagne	Sparkling	Toasty, berry, austere	Chicken	**
Alfred Gratien Cuveé Paridis	Champagne	Sparkling	Berry, toasty, yeasty	Veal	**
Alfred Gratien Vintage	Champagne	Sparkling	Berry, complex, nutty	Fish	**
Amiot-Bonfils Puligny Montrachet Les Demoiselles	Puligny-Montrachet/Burgundy	White	Mandarin, nutty	Fish	**
Ampeau Meursault Perrières	Meursault/Burgundy	White	Citrus, spicy, nutty	Cheese	**
Arbois Savagnin (Frédéric Lornet)	Jura	White	Zingy, citrus	Shellfish	**
Arbois Trousseau Vieilles Vignes (Jacques Puffeney)	Jura	Red	Berry, earthy	Lamb	**
Arbois Vin Jaune (André et Mireille Tissot)	Jura	White	Nutty, complex	Chicken	**
Auguste Clape Comas	Rhône Valley	Red	Berry, earthy, minerally, complex	Beef, lamb	**
Auguste Clape St Peray	Rhône Valley	White	Floral, fruity	Shellfish, fish	**
Ayala Vintage	Champagne	Sparkling	Berry, citrus	Shellfish	**
Bachelet Charmes Chambertin Vieilles Vignes	Gevrey-Chambertin/Burgundy	Red	Gamey, leathery	Duck	***
Baldes Cahors Château Triguedina	Southwest France	Red	Spicy, herbaceous, tannic	Lamb	**
Banyuls Dom La Tour Vieille Vin de Méditation (Vincent Cantie et Christine)	Languedoc	Fortified	Chocolatey, powerful, rich	Nuts	**
Barthod Chambolle Musigny	Chambolle Musigny/Burgundy	Red	Berry, spicy	Pasta	**
Baud Père et Fils Côtes du Jura Chardonnay	Jura	White	Melon, spicy	Fish	**
Baud Père et Fils Côtes du Jura Tradition Blanc	Jura	White	Melon, fruity	Fish	**
Bergerac Château Tour des Gendres (Luc de Conti)	Bordeaux/Southwest France	Red	Berry, spicy	Cold meats	**
Bergerac Château Tour des Gendres Cuvée la Gloire de Mon Père (Luc de Conti)	Bordeaux/Southwest France	Red	Berry, minerally	Stew	**
Bergerac Sec Moulin des Dames Anthologia (Luc de Conti)	Bordeaux/Southwest France	White	Herbaceous, zingy, citrus	Fish	**
Bernède et Fils Cahors Clos la Coutale	Southwest France	Red	Herbaceous, spicy, earthy	Sausages	**
Biesbrouck Cahors Dom des Savarines	Southwest France	Red	Berry, tannic	Lamb	**
Billecart-Salmon Blanc de Blancs	Champagne	Sparkling	Citrus, elegant	Aperitif	**
Billecart-Salmon Brut	Champagne	Sparkling	Citrus, floral, berry	Shellfish	**
Billecart-Salmon Cuvée N.F. Billecart	Champagne	Sparkling	Complex, citrus, berry, elegant	Fish	***
Billecart-Salmon Rosé	Champagne	Sparkling	Berry, floral	Lamb	**
Billecart-Salmon Rosé Cuvée Elizabeth	Champagne	Sparkling	Berry, complex, floral	Pork	**
Bisquit Cognac	Cognac	Brandy	Spirity, fiery, earthy	After dinner	***
Bize Savigny-Les-Beaune Les Vergelesses	Savigny-lès-Beaune/Burgundy	Red	Minerally, spicy	Cold meats, stew, offal	**
Blain-Gagnard Chassagne Morey	Chassagne Montrachet/Burgundy	White	Minerally, citrus	Fish	**
Blain-Gagnard Criots-Bâtard-Montrachet	Chassagne Montrachet/Burgundy	White	Minerally, complex, rich	Fish	***
Bollinger R.D.	Champagne	Sparkling	Complex, powerful, berry, yeasty	Chicken	***
Bollinger Special Cuvée	Champagne	Sparkling	Powerful, berry, apples, complex	Antipasto	**
Bollinger Vieilles Vignes Françaises	Champagne	Sparkling	Complex, berry, rich	Game	***
Bollinger Vintage	Champagne	Sparkling	Berry, complex, toasty, powerful	Fish	**
Bonhomme Macon Viré	Maconnais/Burgundy	White	Citrus, spicy	Pasta	**
Bonneau du Martray Corton Charlemagne	Aloxe Corton/Burgundy	White	Complex, nutty, smoky, spicy	Fish	***
Bonnezeaux Cuvée Prestige (Philippe Gilardeau)	Anjou-Saumur/Loire	Sweet	Sweet, mandarin	Dessert	***
Bouchard Père et Fils Beaune Vigne de l'Enfant Jésus	Beaune/Burgundy	Red	Berry, earthy	Lamb	**
Bouvet-Ladubay Saumur Brut Trésor	Anjou-Saumur/Loire	Sparkling	Crisp, fruity, citrus	Aperitif	**
Bouvet-Ladubay Saumur-Champigny Les Non Pareils	Anjou-Saumur/Loire	Red	Berry, spicy	Cold meats, stew, offal	**
Boyer Martenot Meursault	Meursault/Burgundy	White	Tropical fruit, citrus	Chicken	**
Bruno Paillard Vintage	Champagne	Sparkling	Crisp, citrus, berry	Shellfish	**
Burc et Fils Cahors Château Pineraie	Southwest France	Red	Spicy, herbaceous, berry	Sausages	**
Burguet Gevrey Chambertin Vieilles Vignes	Gevrey-Chambertin/Burgundy	Red	Berry, spicy, earthy	Lamb	**
C. H. Blanc des Millenaires	Champagne	Sparkling	Complex, citrus, berry	Veal	***
Cabardès Château Salitis (Alice Depaule-Marandon)	Languedoc	Red	Berry, spicy	Game	*
Cabardès Château Ventenac Cuvée les Pujols (Alain Maurel)	Languedoc	Red	Earthy, berry	Stew	**

FRANCE *(continued)*

Wine name	Region	Style	Flavor/Bouquet	Compatible Foods	Price Range
Cahors Château Haute-Serre (Georges Vigouroux)	Southwest France	Red	Earthy, minerally	Lamb	**
Cahors Château Lamartine (Alain Gayraud)	Southwest France	Red	Berry, herbaceous, tannic	Cold meats, stew, offal	**
Cahors Château Triguedina Prince Probus	Southwest France	Red	Berry, earthy	Cheese	**
Campadieu Banyuls Blanc Vial-Magnères (Monique Sapéras)	Roussillon	Fortified	Rich, sweet, spirity	Chocolate	**
Campadieu Banyuls Dom de la Rectorie Hors d'Age Cuvée du Docteur Camou (Marc and Thierry Parcé)	Roussillon	Fortified	Chocolatey, spirity, sweet	Dessert	**
Campadieu Banyuls Grand Cru Cellier des Templiers Cuvée Amiral (François Vilarem)	Roussillon	Fortified	Chocolatey, rich, powerful, sweet	Fruit	**
Campadieu Banyuls Grand Cru Cellier des Templiers Cuvée Amiral (Henry Vidal)	Roussillon	Fortified	Sweet, chocolatey	Chocolate	**
Campadieu Banyuls L'Etoile Grande Réserve	Roussillon	Fortified	Chocolatey, sweet, spirity	Dessert	**
Campadieu Collioure Dom de la Rectorie Cuvée Coume Pascole (Marc and Thierry Parcé)	Roussillon	Red	Earthy, gamey	Cold meats, stew, offal	*
Campadieu Collioure Dom La Tour Vieille (Vincent Cantie et Christine)	Roussillon	Red	Spicy, earthy	Lamb	**
Campadieu Côtes de Roussillon Cazenove	Roussillon	Red	Berry, spicy	Stew	*
Campadieu Côtes de Roussillon Dom Ferrer-Ribère Empreinte des Temps (Denis Ferrer et Bruno Ribière)	Roussillon	Red	Gamey, spicy	Cold meats, stew, offal	**
Campadieu Côtes de Roussillon Dom Joliette Cuvée (André Mercier)	Roussillon	Red	Gamey, berry	Pasta	*
Campadieu Côtes de Roussillon Domaine du Mas Cremat (Jeanin-Mongeard)	Roussillon	Red	Berry, spicy	Stew	**
Campadieu Côtes du Roussillon Villages Dom des Chenes Les Alzines Razungles	Roussillon	Red	Berry, smoky	Pork	**
Campadieu Côtes du Roussillon Villages Dom Força Real Les Hauts de Força Real (J-P Henriqués)	Roussillon	Red	Spicy, earthy	Pasta	**
Campadieu Côtes du Roussillon Villages Dom Gauby Vieilles Vignes (Gérard Gauby)	Roussillon	Red	Berry, earthy	Game	**
Campadieu Maury Dom la Pleidade Vintage	Roussillon	Fortified	Chocolatey, rich	Dessert	**
Campadieu Maury Mas Amiel Vintage Réserve (Charles Dupuy)	Roussillon	Fortified	Spirity, smoky, chocolatey	Nuts	**
Campadieu Muscat de St Jean de Minervois Dom de Barroubio (Marie-Thérèse Miquel)	Roussillon	Fortified	Chocolatey, spirity	Chocolate	**
Campadieu Rivesaltes Domaine Cazes Cuvée (Aimé Cazes)	Roussillon	Fortified	Spirity, powerful, chocolatey	Fruit	**
Camus Cognac	Cognac	Brandy	Spirity, complex, minerally	After dinner	***
Canard-Duchéne Vintage	Champagne	Sparkling	Berry, floral, yeasty	Fish	**
Carillon Bienvenues Bâtard Montrachet	Puligny-Montrachet/Burgundy	White	Citrus, spicy	Fish	***
Carillon Puligny Montrachet Les Perrières	Puligny-Montrachet/Burgundy	White	Smoky, citrus	Chicken	**
Cattier Brut	Champagne	Sparkling	Yeasty, berry, floral	Shellfish	**
Cattier Clos du Moulin	Champagne	Sparkling	Berry, complex, powerful	Chicken	***
Cave Co-op de la Lavinière Minervois La Cave des Coteaux du Haut-Minervois	Languedoc	Red	Spicy, berry	Sausages	*
Cave Coopérative de Taradeau Oppidum	Côtes de Provence/Provence	Red	Berry, gamey	Stew	**
Cave de Cairanne Côtes du Rhône Villages Cuvée Temptation	Rhône Valley	Red	Berry, peppery, powerful	Beef, lamb	**
Cave de Chautagne Vin de Savoie Chautagne Gamay	Savoie	Red	Berry, spicy	Cold meats, stew, offal	**
Cave des Vignerons de Saumur Saumur Blanc les Pouches	Anjou-Saumur/Loire	White	Zingy, citrus, minerally	Fish	**
Cave Kientzheim-Kaysersberg Muscat Réserve	Alsace	White	Grapey, citrus	Chicken	**
Cave Vincole de Pfaffenheim et Gueberschwihr Gewurztraminer Grand Cru Goldert	Alsace	White	Spicy, chalky	Asian	**
Cave Vincole de Pfaffenheim et Gueberschwihr Gewurztraminer Grand Cru Zinnkoepfle Westhalten	Alsace	White	Spicy, floral	Asian	**
Cave Vinicole de Pfaffenheim et Gueberschwihr Gewurztraminer Cuvée Bacchus	Alsace	White	Spicy, complex, smoky	Fish	**
Cave Vinicole de Turckheim Gewurztraminer Vieilles Vignes	Alsace	White	Spicy, floral	Chicken	**
Cave-Coop des Vins d'Irouléguy Irouléguy Dom de Mignaberry	Landes, Gascogne and Pyrenees/Southwest France	Red	Earthy, berry	Cold meats	*
Caves des Hauts de Seyr VDP Coteaux de Charitois Chardonnay Le Montaillant	Vin de Pays	White	Tropical fruit, citrus	Veal	**
Chablis (A. Boudin)	Chablis/Burgundy	White	Minerally, spicy	Shellfish	**
Chablis (L. Michel)	Chablis/Burgundy	White	Citrus, minerally	Shellfish	**
Chablis Les Clos (V. Dauvissat)	Chablis/Burgundy	White	Minerally, complex, citrus	Veal	***
Chablis Les Preuses (V. Dauvissat)	Chablis/Burgundy	White	Citrus, floral, minerally	Fish	***
Chainier Cognac	Cognac	Brandy	Spirity, earthy	After dinner	***
Chamayrac Coteaux du Languedoc La Clape Château Mire l'Etang Cuvée Tradition	Languedoc	Red	Peppery, berry	Pizza	*
Chambolle Musigny (P. Rion)	Chambolle Musigny/Burgundy	Red	Elegant, berry	Duck	**
Chandon de Briailles Corton Bressandes	Aloxe Corton/Burgundy	Red	Berry, earthy, complex	Duck	***

FRANCE (continued)

Wine name	Region	Style	Flavor/Bouquet	Compatible Foods	Price Range
Chandon de Briailles Pernand Vergelesses Ile de Vergelesses	Pernand-Vergelesses/Burgundy	Red	Minerally, floral	Veal	**
Chapoutier Châteauneuf-du-Pape La Bernadine	Rhône Valley	Red	Jam, peppery, rich	Beef, lamb	**
Chapoutier Côtes du Rhône Belleruche	Rhône Valley	Red	Berry, spicy, juicy	Pizza, chicken	*
Chapoutier Côtes du Rhône	Rhône Valley	White	Stone fruit, minerally	Fish, chicken	**
Charbaut Certificate	Champagne	Sparkling	Berry, citrus	Cheese	**
Charles Heidsieck Brut Mis en Cave NV	Champagne	Sparkling	Berry, floral, yeasty	Shellfish	**
Charles Heidsieck Champagne Charlie	Champagne	Sparkling	Berry, complex, powerful, rich	Chicken	***
Charles Heidsieck Vintage	Champagne	Sparkling	Berry, complex, toasty	Veal	**
Charmes Chambertin (C. Dugat)	Gevrey-Chambertin/Burgundy	Red	Spicy, earthy, gamey	Lamb	***
Chassagne Montrachet Girardin	Chassagne Montrachet/Burgundy	White	Spicy, citrus, smoky	Fish	**
Chassagne Montrachet Les Embrazées (Bernard Morey)	Chassagne Montrachet/Burgundy	White	Citrus, complex, spicy	Cheese	**
Château Angélus	St-Émilion/Bordeaux	Red	Minerally, plums	Lamb	**
Château Ausone	St-Émilion/Bordeaux	Red	Minerally, earthy, plums, herbaceous	Beef	***
Château Balestard-la-Tonnelle	St-Émilion/Bordeaux	Red	Herbaceous, minerally, spicy	Game	**
Château Barrabaque	Fronsac, Canon-Fronsac/Bordeaux	Red	Berry, earthy	Cold meats	**
Château Barreyre	Bordeaux Supérieur/Bordeaux	Red	Herbaceous, fruity	Stew	**
Château Bastor-Lamontagne	Sauternes, Barsac/Bordeaux	Sweet	Sweet, floral, mandarin	Dessert	***
Château Batailley	Pauillac/Bordeaux	Red	Berry, spicy, herbaceous	Stew	**
Château Beau-Séjour Bécot	St-Émilion/Bordeaux	Red	Minerally, tannic, herbaceous	Beef	**
Château Beaucastel Châteauneuf-du-Pape Hommage à Jacques Perrin	Rhône Valley	Red	Berry, jam, complex	Beef, lamb	**
Château Beaucastel Châteauneuf-du-Pape	Rhône Valley	Red	Powerful, tannic	Beef, lamb	**
Château Beaucastel Châteauneuf-du-Pape	Rhône Valley	White	Floral, citrus, intense	Fish, veal	**
Château Beaucastel Châteauneuf-du-Pape Roussanne Vieilles Vignes	Rhône Valley	White	Floral, citrus, stone fruit, rich	Fish, veal	**
Château Beaucastel Côtes du Rhône Coudoulet	Rhône Valley	Red	Berry, earthy, minerally, rich	Chicken, veal, pork	**
Château Beaucastel Côtes du Rhône Coudoulet	Rhône Valley	White	Stone fruit, floral, rich	Fish, veal	**
Château Beaucastel Côtes du Rhône Perrin Reserve	Rhône Valley	Red	Berry, herbaceous, spicy	Chicken, veal, pork	**
Château Beaucastel Côtes du Rhône Perrin Reserve	Rhône Valley	White	Stone fruit, floral, powerful	Fish, chicken, veal	**
Château Beaumont	Haut-Médoc/Bordeaux	Red	Berry, smoky	Cold meats, stew, offal	**
Château Beauregard	Pomerol/Bordeaux	Red	Spicy, minerally, plums	Lamb	**
Château Beauséjour	St-Émilion/Bordeaux	Red	Minerally, berry	Lamb	**
Château Bel Air	Entre-Deux-Mers/Bordeaux	Red	Herbaceous, berry	Stew	**
Château Bel-Air La Royère	Premières Côtes de Blaye/Bordeaux	Red	Berry, fruity	Stew	**
Château Bel-Air Marquis d'Aligre	Margaux/Bordeaux	Red	Smoky, berry	Lamb	**
Château Belair	St-Émilion/Bordeaux	Red	Berry, plums	Stew	***
Château Belgrave	Haut-Médoc/Bordeaux	Red	Berry, plums	Lamb	**
Château Bellerive Quarts de Chaume Quintessence	Anjou-Saumur/Loire	Sweet	Sweet, mandarin	Fruit	**
Château Beychevelle	St-Julien/Bordeaux	Red	Berry, herbaceous, tannic	Stew	**
Château Biston-Brillette	Moulis/Bordeaux	Red	Spicy, berry	Pasta	**
Château Bonnet (also Bordeaux)	Entre-Deux-Mers/Bordeaux	Red	Herbaceous, berry	Stew	**
Château Branaire	St-Julien/Bordeaux	Red	Berry, floral	Cheese	**
Château Brane-Cantenac	Margaux/Bordeaux	Red	Berry, herbaceous	Cold meats	**
Château Brillette	Moulis/Bordeaux	Red	Herbaceous, berry	Pork	**
Château Brondelle	Graves/Bordeaux	White	Citrus, herbaceous, vanillin	Fish, chicken	**
Château Brulésécaille	Côtes de Bourg/Bordeaux	Red	Berry, spicy	Cold meats, stew, offal	**
Château Cabrieres Châteauneuf-du-Pape	Rhône Valley	Red	Jam, spicy, leathery	Beef, lamb	**
Château Calissanne (Jean Bonnet)	Coteaux d'Aix/Provence	Red	Berry, spicy	Cold meats, stew, offal	**
Château Calon (Montagne)	St-Émilion/Bordeaux	Red	Herbaceous, plums	Lamb	**
Château Calon-Ségur	St-Estèphe/Bordeaux	Red	Berry, tannic	Lamb	**
Château Camensac	Haut-Médoc/Bordeaux	Red	Minerally, berry	Cheese	**
Château Canon de Brem	Fronsac, Canon-Fronsac/Bordeaux	Red	Spicy, berry	Pork	**
Château Canon	Fronsac, Canon-Fronsac/Bordeaux	Red	Herbaceous, tannic	Cold meats	**
Château Canon	St-Émilion/Bordeaux	Red	Smoky, berry	Cold meats	***
Château Canon-La Gaffelière	St-Émilion/Bordeaux	Red	Berry, herbaceous	Cold meats, stew, offal	**
Château Cantemerle	Haut-Médoc/Bordeaux	Red	Berry, spicy	Cold meats, stew, offal	**
Château Cantenac Brown	Margaux/Bordeaux	Red	Herbaceous, spicy, smoky	Lamb	**

FRANCE *(continued)*

Wine name	Region	Style	Flavor/Bouquet	Compatible Foods	Price Range
Château Cap de Faugères	Côtes de Castillon/Bordeaux	Red	Berry, licorice	Pork	**
Château Carbonnieux	Pessac-Léognan/Bordeaux	Red	Minerally, berry	Beef	**
Château Carsin (also Cadillac)	Premières Côtes de Bordeaux/Bordeaux	Red	Berry, minerally	Cold meats	**
Château Cassagne Haut-Canon	Fronsac, Canon-Fronsac/Bordeaux	Red	Minerally, herbaceous	Pasta	**
Château Castelneau	Entre-Deux-Mers/Bordeaux	Red	Berry, herbaceous	Pizza	*
Château Castenet-Greffier	Entre-Deux-Mers/Bordeaux	Red	Spicy, earthy	Stew	**
Château Cayla	Cadillac/Bordeaux	Red	Earthy, berry	Pizza	*
Château Certan de May	Pomerol/Bordeaux	Red	Berry, floral, complex	Game	***
Château Charmail	Haut-Médoc/Bordeaux	Red	Berry, herbaceous	Stew	**
Château Chasse-Spleen	Moulis/Bordeaux	Red	Berry, tannic	Stew	**
Château Cheval Blanc	St-Émilion/Bordeaux	Red	Minerally, berry, powerful, complex, herbaceous	Lamb	***
Château Cissac	Haut-Médoc/Bordeaux	Red	Berry, tannic	Sausages	**
Château Citran	Haut-Médoc/Bordeaux	Red	Spicy, minerally	Cheese	**
Château Clarke	Listrac-Médoc/Bordeaux	Red	Herbaceous, berry	Pasta	**
Château Clerc Milon	Pauillac/Bordeaux	Red	Berry, herbaceous	Lamb	**
Château Climens	Sauternes, Barsac/Bordeaux	Sweet	Sweet, complex, honey	Dessert	***
Château Clinet	Pomerol/Bordeaux	Red	Berry, tannic, minerally	Beef	***
Château Clos Haut-Peyraguey	Sauternes, Barsac/Bordeaux	Sweet	Sweet, honey, mandarin	Cheese	***
Château Cos d'Estournel	St-Estèphe/Bordeaux	Red	Minerally, tannic, herbaceous, berry	Beef	***
Château Cos Labory	St-Estèphe/Bordeaux	Red	Berry, tannic	Lamb	**
Château Côte Montpezat	Côtes de Castillon/Bordeaux	Red	Minerally, earthy	Cheese	**
Château Coufran	Haut-Médoc/Bordeaux	Red	Smoky, herbaceous	Lamb	**
Château Couhins-Lurton	Pessac-Léognan/Bordeaux	Red	Berry, minerally	Pasta	**
Château Coussin (Jean-Pierre Sumeire)	Côtes de Provence/Provence	Red	Earthy, gamey	Cold meats	**
Château Coutet	Sauternes, Barsac/Bordeaux	Sweet	Sweet, honey, mandarin	Dessert	***
Château d'Angludet	Margaux/Bordeaux	Red	Earthy, berry	Cheese	**
Château d'Archambeau	Graves/Bordeaux	White	Stone fruit, waxy, vanillin	Fish, chicken	**
Château d'Arlay Côtes du Jura Vin Jaune	Jura	White	Nutty, complex	Chicken	***
Château d'Armailhac	Pauillac/Bordeaux	Red	Berry, tannic	Lamb	**
Château d'Epiré Savennières	Anjou-Saumur/Loire	White	Minerally, spicy	Shellfish	**
Château d'Issan	Margaux/Bordeaux	Red	Tannic, berry	Cold meats, stew, offal	**
Château d'Yquem	Sauternes, Barsac/Bordeaux	Sweet	Sweet, complex, honey, mandarin, citrus	Foie gras	***
Château Dalem	Fronsac, Canon-Fronsac/Bordeaux	Red	Elegant, spicy	Pork	**
Château Dauzac	Margaux/Bordeaux	Red	Plums, floral	Stew	**
Château de Bachen Tursan Baron de Bachen (Michel Guérard)	Landes, Gascogne and Pyrenees/Southwest France	White	Melon, oaky, spicy	Fish	**
Château de Berne (Bruno Guillermier)	Côtes de Provence/Provence	Red	Minerally, herbaceous, spicy	Cold meats	**
Château de Cérons	Cérons/Bordeaux	Red	Spicy, herbaceous	Sausages	**
Château de Chamirey Mercurey	Côte Chalonnaise/Burgundy	Red	Berry, earthy	Cheese	**
Château de Chantegrive (also Cérons)	Graves/Bordeaux	White	Citrus, minerally	Fish	**
Château de Chasseloir Muscadet de Sèvre et Maine	Pays Nantais/Loire	White	Minerally, citrus, zingy	Shellfish	**
Château de Chelivette	Premières Côtes de Bordeaux/Bordeaux	Red	Minerally, herbaceous	Pork	**
Château de Cugat	Bordeaux Supérieur/Bordeaux	Red	Berry, spicy	Cold meats, stew, offal	**
Château de Fargues	Sauternes, Barsac/Bordeaux	Sweet	Sweet, citrus, mandarin	Dessert	***
Château de Fesles Bonnezeaux Château de Fesles	Anjou-Saumur/Loire	Sweet	Sweet, apples, honey	Dessert	***
Château de Fieuzal	Pessac-Léognan/Bordeaux	Red	Minerally, tannic, herbaceous	Beef	***
Château de Fontenille	Entre-Deux-Mers/Bordeaux	Red	Herbaceous, plums	Cold meats, stew, offal	*
Château de Francs	Bordeaux-Côtes de Francs/Bordeaux	Red	Smoky, herbaceous	Sausages	**
Château de Fuissé Pouilly Fuissé	Maconnais/Burgundy	White	Minerally, citrus	Fish	**
Château de Goulaine Muscadet de Sèvre et Maine Cuvée des Millénaires	Pays Nantais/Loire	White	Minerally, citrus, floral	Fish	**
Château de l'Abbaye de St-Ferme	Bordeaux Supérieur/Bordeaux	Red	Herbaceous, berry	Cold meats	**
Château de l'Escarelle (M. Lobier)	Coteaux Varois/Provence	Red	Spicy, earthy, herbaceous	Cold meats	**
Château de l'Etoile Crémant du Jura	Jura	Sparkling	Fruity, citrus	Aperitif	**
Château de l'Etoile L'Etoile Vin Jaune	Jura	White	Nutty, spicy	Chicken	**
Château de la Gardine Châteauneuf-du-Pape Cuvée des Generations	Rhône Valley	Red	Berry, jam, vanillin, intense	Beef, lamb	**

FRANCE (continued)

Wine name	Region	Style	Flavor/Bouquet	Compatible Foods	Price Range
Château de la Grille Chinon	Touraine/Loire	Red	Earthy, berry	Cold meats, stew, offal	*
Château de la Nerthe Châteauneuf-du-Pape Cuvée des Cadettes	Rhône Valley	Red	Berry, vanillin, powerful	Beef, lamb	**
Château de la Ragotière Muscadet de Sèvre et Maine	Pays Nantais/Loire	White	Citrus, minerally	Shellfish	**
Château de la Violette Vin de Savoie Abymes	Savoie	White	Citrus, apples	Salad	**
Château de Malle	Sauternes, Barsac/Bordeaux	Sweet	Sweet, citrus	Dessert	***
Château de Meursault Meursault	Meursault/Burgundy	White	Citrus, spicy	Chicken	**
Château de Myrat	Sauternes, Barsac/Bordeaux	Sweet	Sweet, fruity	Fruit	**
Château de Parenchère	Bordeaux Supérieur/Bordeaux	Red	Berry, plums	Stew	**
Château de Pibarnon (Eric de St Victor)	Bandol/Provence	Red	Earthy, berry	Stew	***
Château de Plaisance Coteaux du Layon Confidence	Anjou-Saumur/Loire	Sweet	Sweet, mandarin, honey	Dessert	**
Château de Pourcieux (Michel d'Espagnet)	Côtes de Provence/Provence	Red	Spicy, berry	Veal	**
Château de Reignac	Bordeaux Supérieur/Bordeaux	Red	Minerally, berry	Lamb	**
Château de Ripaille Vin de Savoie Ripaille	Savoie	White	Slight sparkle, crisp, citrus	Aperitif	**
Château de Roquefort (Raimond de Villeneuve Flayosc)	Côtes de Provence/Provence	Red	Herbaceous, berry	Lamb	**
Château de Saint Cosme Gigondas	Rhône Valley	Red	Berry, spicy, peppery	Chicken, veal, pork	***
Château de Sales	Pomerol/Bordeaux	Red	Earthy, plums	Lamb	**
Château de Targé Saumur-Champigny	Anjou-Saumur/Loire	Red	Berry, plums	Stew	**
Château de Tracy Pouilly-Fumé	Center/Loire	White	Zingy, herbaceous	Pork	**
Château de Valandraud	St-Émilion/Bordeaux	Red	Herbaceous, minerally, berry	Cold meats	***
Château de Villeneuve Saumur-Champigny Vieilles Vignes	Anjou-Saumur/Loire	Red	Berry, gamey	Game	**
Château des Noyers Coteaux du Layon Réserve Vieilles Vignes	Anjou-Saumur/Loire	Sweet	Sweet, mandarin, citrus	Dessert	***
Château des Roques Vacqueyras	Rhône Valley	Red	Jam, peppery, rich	Pork, veal, beef	**
Château des Tourtes	Premières Côtes de Blaye/Bordeaux	Red	Spicy, berry	Cold meats, stew, offal	**
Château Doisy-Daëne	Sauternes, Barsac/Bordeaux	Sweet	Sweet, mandarin, minerally	Dessert	***
Château Doisy-Védrines	Sauternes, Barsac/Bordeaux	Sweet	Sweet, citrus, mandarin	Dessert	***
Château du Breuil Coteaux du Layon Orantium	Anjou-Saumur/Loire	Sweet	Sweet, honey	Dessert	**
Château du Cléray Muscadet de Sèvre et Maine (Sauvion et Fils)	Pays Nantais/Loire	White	Minerally, melon, citrus	Shellfish	**
Château du Cros	Loupiac/Bordeaux	Sweet	Sweet, mandarin	Dessert	**
Château du Hureau Coteaux du Saumur	Anjou-Saumur/Loire	White	Medium-sweet, mandarin, minerally	Fruit	**
Château du Hureau Saumur-Champigny Cuvée Lisagathe	Anjou-Saumur/Loire	Red	Berry, fruity	Cold meats, stew, offal	**
Château du Mont	Ste-Croix-du-Mont/Bordeaux	Sweet	Sweet, honey	Dessert	**
Château du Nozet Pouilly-Fumé	Center/Loire	White	Complex, spicy, grassy	Fish	***
Château du Seuil (Philippe Carreau-Gaschereau)	Coteaux d'Aix/Provence	Red	Berry, earthy	Stew	**
Château du Tertre	Margaux/Bordeaux	Red	Berry, earthy	Cold meats	**
Château du Trignon Gigondas	Rhône Valley	Red	Berry, jam, tannic, complex	Pork, beef	**
Château Ducluzeau	Listrac-Médoc/Bordeaux	Red	Berry, smoky	Stew	**
Château Ducru-Beaucaillou	St-Julien/Bordeaux	Red	Berry, minerally, herbaceous, tannic	Beef	***
Château Duhart-Milon	Pauillac/Bordeaux	Red	Berry, tannic	Beef	**
Château Durfort-Vivens	Margaux/Bordeaux	Red	Berry, herbaceous, tannic	Cold meats, stew, offal	**
Château Falfas	Côtes de Bourg/Bordeaux	Red	Herbaceous, plums	Pasta	*
Château Ferrière	Margaux/Bordeaux	Red	Berry, plums	Stew	**
Château Ferry Lacombe (Frédérique Chossenot)	Côtes de Provence/Provence	Red	Minerally, spicy	Pasta	**
Château Figeac	St-Émilion/Bordeaux	Red	Herbaceous, berry, minerally, tannic	Cheese	***
Château Fleur Cardinale	St-Émilion/Bordeaux	Red	Berry, spicy	Lamb	**
Château Fonbadet	Pauillac/Bordeaux	Red	Berry, herbaceous, tannic	Pork	**
Château Fontenil	Fronsac, Canon-Fronsac/Bordeaux	Red	Minerally, floral	Cheese	**
Château Fougas	Côtes de Bourg/Bordeaux	Red	Smoky, herbaceous	Stew	**
Château Fourcas-Dupré	Listrac-Médoc/Bordeaux	Red	Plums, smoky	Cold meats, stew, offal	**
Château Galoupet (Jean-Pierre Marty)	Côtes de Provence/Provence	Red	Berry, spicy	Stew	**
Château Garraud	Lalande de Pomerol/Bordeaux	Red	Berry, herbaceous	Lamb	**
Château Gaudrelle Vouvray Réserve Personelle Moelleux	Touraine/Loire	Sweet	Sweet, citrus, honey	Dessert	***
Château Gazin	Pomerol/Bordeaux	Red	Berry, tannic, minerally	Stew	**
Château Gilette	Sauternes, Barsac/Bordeaux	Sweet	Sweet, complex, honey, mandarin	Cheese	***
Château Giscours	Margaux/Bordeaux	Red	Plums, spicy	Lamb	**
Château Gloria	St-Julien/Bordeaux	Red	Plums, herbaceous, tannic	Lamb	**
Château Grand Mayne	St-Émilion/Bordeaux	Red	Berry, tannic	Stew	**
Château Grand Ormeau	Lalande de Pomerol/Bordeaux	Red	Spicy, earthy	Pork	**
Château Grand Renouil	Fronsac, Canon-Fronsac/Bordeaux	Red	Berry, plums	Stew	**

FRANCE *(continued)*

Wine name	Region	Style	Flavor/Bouquet	Compatible Foods	Price Range
Château Grand-Mouëys	Premières Côtes de Bordeaux/ Bordeaux	Red	Minerally, plums	Cheese	**
Château Grand-Puy-Ducasse	Pauillac/Bordeaux	Red	Berry, smoky	Beef	**
Château Grand-Puy-Lacoste	Pauillac/Bordeaux	Red	Plums, herbaceous, spicy	Lamb	**
Château Gressier-Grand-Poujeaux	Moulis/Bordeaux	Red	Spicy, herbaceous, berry	Sausages	**
Château Greysac	Médoc/Bordeaux	Red	Herbaceous, floral	Pork	**
Château Grillet Condrieu	Rhône Valley	White	Floral, fruity, minerally, elegant	Fish, fruits	***
Château Gruaud-Larose	St-Julien/Bordeaux	Red	Minerally, earthy, herbaceous, complex, tannic	Beef	***
Château Guerry	Côtes de Bourg/Bordeaux	Red	Plums, herbaceous	Lamb	**
Château Guiraud	Sauternes, Barsac/Bordeaux	Sweet	Sweet, complex, citrus	Dessert	***
Château Haut Bertinerie	Premières Côtes de Blaye/ Bordeaux	Red	Plums, herbaceous	Sausages	**
Château Haut Carles	Fronsac, Canon-Fronsac/ Bordeaux	Red	Plums, spicy	Stew	**
Château Haut-Bages-Libéral	Pauillac/Bordeaux	Red	Herbaceous, berry	Cold meats, stew, offal	**
Château Haut-Bailly	Pessac-Léognan/Bordeaux	Red	Herbaceous, spicy, tannic	Cheese	**
Château Haut-Batailley	Pauillac/Bordeaux	Red	Berry, tannic	Cold meats, stew, offal	**
Château Haut-Beauséjour	St-Estèphe/Bordeaux	Red	Berry, spicy, herbaceous	Stew	**
Château Haut-Brion	Pessac-Léognan/Bordeaux	Red	Complex, tannic, minerally, berry	Lamb	***
Château Haut-Chaigneau	Lalande de Pomerol/Bordeaux	Red	Earthy, herbaceous	Stew	**
Château Haut-Grelot	Premières Côtes de Blaye/ Bordeaux	Red	Plums, herbaceous	Cheese	**
Château Haut-Marbuzet	St-Estèphe/Bordeaux	Red	Berry, tannic	Beef	**
Château Jonqueyres	Bordeaux Supérieur/Bordeaux	Red	Berry, floral	Pork	*
Château Kirwan	Margaux/Bordeaux	Red	Tannic, herbaceous, berry	Lamb	**
Château l'Arnaude (H. & A. Knapp)	Côtes de Provence/Provence	Red	Berry, herbaceous, spicy	Pasta	**
Château l'Arrosée	St-Émilion/Bordeaux	Red	Berry, spicy, tannic	Cold meats, stew, offal	**
Château L'Eglise-Clinet	Pomerol/Bordeaux	Red	Spicy, berry, minerally	Cold meats, stew, offal	***
Château L'Evangile	Pomerol/Bordeaux	Red	Minerally, berry, tannic	Cheese	***
Château La Cardonne	Médoc/Bordeaux	Red	Berry, herbaceous	Lamb	**
Château La Conseillante	Pomerol/Bordeaux	Red	Plums, floral, spicy	Lamb	***
Château La Dominique	St-Émilion/Bordeaux	Red	Berry, spicy, complex	Lamb	***
Château La Fleur Cailleau	Fronsac, Canon-Fronsac/ Bordeaux	Red	Earthy, herbaceous	Cold meats, stew, offal	**
Château La Fleur Milon	Pauillac/Bordeaux	Red	Berry, herbaceous	Stew	**
Château La Fleur Pétrus	Pomerol/Bordeaux	Red	Complex, berry, plums, herbaceous	Stew	***
Château La Gaffelière	St-Émilion/Bordeaux	Red	Minerally, berry, herbaceous	Lamb	**
Château La Lagune	Haut-Médoc/Bordeaux	Red	Berry, herbaceous, tannic	Game	**
Château La Louvière	Pessac-Léognan/Bordeaux	Red	Spicy, minerally, tannic	Pasta	**
Château La Mission Haut-Brion	Pessac-Léognan/Bordeaux	Red	Complex, tannic, herbaceous, minerally	Lamb	***
Château La Mondotte	St-Émilion/Bordeaux	Red	Herbaceous, berry, smoky, tannic	Beef	***
Château La Rame	Ste-Croix-du-Mont/Bordeaux	Sweet	Sweet, honey	Dessert	**
Château La Raz Caman	Premières Côtes de Blaye/ Bordeaux	Red	Berry, spicy	Pasta	**
Château La Rivière	Fronsac, Canon-Fronsac/ Bordeaux	Red	Berry, tannic	Game	**
Château La Tour Blanche	Sauternes, Barsac/Bordeaux	Sweet	Sweet, honey, citrus	Dessert	***
Château La Tour Carnet	Haut-Médoc/Bordeaux	Red	Smoky, berry	Cold meats, stew, offal	**
Château La Tour de By	Médoc/Bordeaux	Red	Berry, plums	Stew	**
Château La Tour Figeac	St-Émilion/Bordeaux	Red	Minerally, herbaceous, berry	Stew	***
Château La Tour Haut-Brion	Pessac-Léognan/Bordeaux	Red	Minerally, herbaceous, tannic	Lamb	**
Château La Vieille Cure	Fronsac, Canon-Fronsac/ Bordeaux	Red	Herbaceous, spicy	Pork	**
Château la Canorgue Côtes du Lubéron	Rhône Valley	Red	Berry, earthy, spicy	Pizza, chicken	**
Château la Varière Bonnezeaux les Melleresses	Anjou-Saumur/Loire	Sweet	Sweet, citrus, honey	Dessert	***
Château Labégorce-Zédé	Margaux/Bordeaux	Red	Berry, smoky	Lamb	**
Château Lacombe-Noaillac	Médoc/Bordeaux	Red	Spicy, herbaceous, earthy	Pasta	**
Château Lafaurie-Peyraguey	Sauternes, Barsac/Bordeaux	Sweet	Sweet, mandarin, citrus	Cheese	***
Château Lafite-Rothschild	Pauillac/Bordeaux	Red	Complex, berry, smoky, tannic	Lamb	***
Château Lafleur	Pomerol/Bordeaux	Red	Minerally, plums, spicy	Lamb	***

FRANCE *(continued)*

Wine name	Region	Style	Flavor/Bouquet	Compatible Foods	Price Range
Château Lafon	Médoc/Bordeaux	Red	Berry, plums	Pasta	**
Château Lafon-Rochet	St-Estèphe/Bordeaux	Red	Berry, spicy, herbaceous	Lamb	**
Château Lagrange	St-Julien/Bordeaux	Red	Berry, herbaceous, tannic	Lamb	**
Château Lamotte de Haux	Premières Côtes de Bordeaux/Bordeaux	Red	Herbaceous, minerally	Beef	**
Château Lanessan	Haut-Médoc/Bordeaux	Red	Berry, tannic	Lamb	**
Château Langoa Barton	St-Julien/Bordeaux	Red	Berry, smoky	Beef	**
Château Lapeyronie	Côtes de Castillon/Bordeaux	Red	Herbaceous, minerally	Sausages	**
Château Larcis Ducasse	St-Émilion/Bordeaux	Red	Berry, smoky	Cheese	**
Château Larmande	St-Émilion/Bordeaux	Red	Plums, herbaceous, spicy	Cheese	**
Château Lascombes	Margaux/Bordeaux	Red	Herbaceous, smoky, spicy	Beef	**
Château Latour à Pomerol	Pomerol/Bordeaux	Red	Complex, spicy, herbaceous, minerally	Beef	***
Château Latour	Pauillac/Bordeaux	Red	Complex, berry, powerful, tannic	Lamb	***
Château Latour-Martillac	Pessac-Léognan/Bordeaux	Red	Berry, tannic	Beef	**
Château Laville	Bordeaux Supérieur/Bordeaux	Red	Spicy, berry	Pasta	**
Château Laville Haut-Brion	Pessac-Léognan/Bordeaux	Red	Minerally, berry, herbaceous	Game	***
Château Le Bon Pasteur	Pomerol/Bordeaux	Red	Tannic, spicy, berry	Beef	**
Château Le Bonnat	Graves/Bordeaux	White	Apples, melon, waxy, herbaceous	Fish, chicken	**
Château Le Crock	St-Estèphe/Bordeaux	Red	Spicy, herbaceous, tannic	Stew	**
Château Le Pin	Pomerol/Bordeaux	Red	Complex, powerful, tannic, spicy, herbaceous	Cold meats, stew, offal	***
Château Le Sens	Premières Côtes de Bordeaux/Bordeaux	Red	Berry, fruity	Lamb	**
Château Le Tertre Roteboeuf	St-Émilion/Bordeaux	Red	Earthy, plums, minerally, tannic	Lamb	***
Château Léhoul	Graves/Bordeaux	Red	Spicy, plums	Pizza	**
Château Léoville Barton	St-Julien/Bordeaux	Red	Berry, complex, herbaceous, smoky	Lamb	**
Château Léoville Las Cases	St-Julien/Bordeaux	Red	Complex, minerally, herbaceous, berry	Lamb	***
Château Léoville Poyferré	St-Julien/Bordeaux	Red	Berry, herbaceous, minerally	Cold meats, stew, offal	**
Château Les Arromans	Bordeaux Supérieur/Bordeaux	Red	Herbaceous, earthy	Cold meats, stew, offal	**
Château Les Carmes Haut-Brion	Pessac-Léognan/Bordeaux	Red	Spicy, herbaceous, earthy	Cold meats, stew, offal	**
Château Les Grands Chênes	Médoc/Bordeaux	Red	Herbaceous, berry	Stew	**
Château Les Jonqueyres	Premières Côtes de Blaye/Bordeaux	Red	Plums, smoky	Pasta	**
Château Les Justices	Sauternes, Barsac/Bordeaux	Sweet	Sweet, citrus	Fruit	**
Château Les Ormes-de-Pez	St-Estèphe/Bordeaux	Red	Minerally, tannic	Beef	**
Château Les Ormes-Sorbet	Médoc/Bordeaux	Red	Smoky, herbaceous	Game	**
Château Les Trois Croix	Fronsac, Canon-Fronsac/Bordeaux	Red	Earthy, berry	Cheese	**
Château Lestage Simon	Haut-Médoc/Bordeaux	Red	Berry, spicy	Cheese	**
Château Lilian-Ladouys	St-Estèphe/Bordeaux	Red	Tannic, floral, herbaceous	Game	**
Château Loubens	Ste-Croix-du-Mont/Bordeaux	Sweet	Sweet, minerally, honey	Dessert	**
Château Loudenne	Médoc/Bordeaux	Red	Tannic, berry	Cold meats, stew, offal	**
Château Loumède	Premières Côtes de Blaye/Bordeaux	Red	Herbaceous, smoky	Stew	**
Château Lynch-Bages	Pauillac/Bordeaux	Red	Berry, tannic, herbaceous	Lamb	***
Château Magdelaine	St-Émilion/Bordeaux	Red	Minerally, earthy, herbaceous	Lamb	***
Château Magneau	Graves/Bordeaux	Red	Herbaceous, plums	Stew	**
Château Maïme (Jean-Louis Sirban)	Côtes de Provence/Provence	Red	Berry, gamey	Pizza	*
Château Malartic-Lagravière	Pessac-Léognan/Bordeaux	Red	Minerally, herbaceous, tannic	Cold meats, stew, offal	**
Château Malescasse	Haut-Médoc/Bordeaux	Red	Spicy, plums	Lamb	**
Château Malescot-St-Exupéry	Margaux/Bordeaux	Red	Berry, spicy	Stew	**
Château Manos	Cadillac/Bordeaux	Red	Berry, fruity	Pasta	**
Château Maravenne (Jean-Louis Gourjon)	Côtes de Provence/Provence	Red	Berry, spicy	Cheese	**
Château Marbuzet	St-Estèphe/Bordeaux	Red	Berry, herbaceous, tannic	Cold meats, stew, offal	**
Château Margaux	Margaux/Bordeaux	Red	Complex, minerally, berry, tannic, spicy	Lamb	***
Château Marouine (Mary-Odile Marty)	Côtes de Provence/Provence	Red	Spicy, herbaceous, gamey	Game	**
Château Marquis de Terme	Margaux/Bordeaux	Red	Berry, floral	Stew	**
Château Maucaillou	Moulis/Bordeaux	Red	Berry, plums	Sausages	**
Château Maucamps	Haut-Médoc/Bordeaux	Red	Plums, herbaceous	Stew	**
Château Mayne Lalande	Listrac-Médoc/Bordeaux	Red	Herbaceous, smoky	Game	**
Château Mémoires (also Cadillac)	Loupiac/Bordeaux	Sweet	Sweet, honey	Dessert	**

FRANCE (continued)

Wine name	Region	Style	Flavor/Bouquet	Compatible Foods	Price Range
Château Mercier	Côtes de Bourg/Bordeaux	Red	Herbaceous, smoky	Pizza	*
Château Meslière Muscadet des Coteaux de la Loire	Pays Nantais/Loire	White	Minerally, citrus, zingy	Shellfish	**
Château Meyney	St-Estèphe/Bordeaux	Red	Minerally, herbaceous, tannic	Cheese	**
Château Miraval (Emmanuel Gaujal)	Côtes de Provence/Provence	Red	Berry, gamey	Lamb	**
Château Monbousquet	St-Émilion/Bordeaux	Red	Berry, herbaceous, tannic	Stew	**
Château Monbrison	Margaux/Bordeaux	Red	Berry, herbaceous	Cold meats, stew, offal	**
Château Mondésir-Gazin	Premières Côtes de Blaye/Bordeaux	Red	Herbaceous, berry	Game	**
Château Montrose	St-Estèphe/Bordeaux	Red	Minerally, complex, powerful, berry	Beef	***
Château Moulin Haut-Laroque	Fronsac, Canon-Fronsac/Bordeaux	Red	Herbaceous, berry	Beef	**
Château Moulin St-Georges	St-Émilion/Bordeaux	Red	Berry, plums	Beef	**
Château Moulin-de-Launay	Entre-Deux-Mers/Bordeaux	Red	Plums, herbaceous	Pizza	*
Château Mouton-Rothschild	Pauillac/Bordeaux	Red	Complex, berry, herbaceous, tannic, spicy	Lamb	***
Château Nairac	Sauternes, Barsac/Bordeaux	Sweet	Sweet, floral, citrus	Dessert	**
Château Nardique-la-Gravière	Entre-Deux-Mers/Bordeaux	Red	Berry, herbaceous	Pasta	**
Château Nodoz	Côtes de Bourg/Bordeaux	Red	Herbaceous, smoky	Pizza	*
Château Palmer	Margaux/Bordeaux	Red	Complex, tannic, herbaceous, berry	Cheese	***
Château Pape Clément	Pessac-Léognan/Bordeaux	Red	Berry, minerally	Stew	**
Château Patache d'Aux	Médoc/Bordeaux	Red	Herbaceous, berry	Stew	**
Château Paulet Cognac	Cognac	Brandy	Spirity, fiery	After dinner	***
Château Pavie	St-Émilion/Bordeaux	Red	Minerally, plums, herbaceous	Lamb	***
Château Pavie-Decesse	St-Émilion/Bordeaux	Red	Herbaceous, smoky	Stew	**
Château Pavie-Macquin	St-Émilion/Bordeaux	Red	Plums, berry	Pasta	**
Château Penin	Bordeaux Supérieur/Bordeaux	Red	Berry, herbaceous	Pizza	*
Château Petit-Village	Pomerol/Bordeaux	Red	Berry, spicy	Sausages	**
Château Pétrus	Pomerol/Bordeaux	Red	Complex, spicy, herbaceous, berry, tannic	Game	***
Château Phélan-Ségur	St-Estèphe/Bordeaux	Red	Spicy, earthy, herbaceous	Lamb	**
Château Pibran	Pauillac/Bordeaux	Red	Berry, spicy	Stew	**
Château Pichon-Longueville (Comtesse de Lalande)	Pauillac/Bordeaux	Red	Berry, plums, complex, tannic	Lamb	***
Château Pichon-Longueville	Pauillac/Bordeaux	Red	Berry, smoky, tannic, herbaceous	Beef	***
Château Pierre Bise Quarts de Chaume	Anjou-Saumur/Loire	Sweet	Sweet, honey	Dessert	**
Château Pipeau	St-Émilion/Bordeaux	Red	Minerally, spicy, tannic	Cold meats, stew, offal	**
Château Plaisance	Bordeaux Supérieur/Bordeaux	Red	Berry, spicy	Sausages	**
Château Pontet-Canet	Pauillac/Bordeaux	Red	Herbaceous, spicy	Cold meats	**
Château Potensac	Médoc/Bordeaux	Red	Tannic, berry	Lamb	**
Château Poujeaux	Moulis/Bordeaux	Red	Berry, herbaceous	Cheese	**
Château Poupille	Côtes de Castillon/Bordeaux	Red	Berry, spicy	Cheese	*
Château Prieuré-Lichine	Margaux/Bordeaux	Red	Berry, tannic	Lamb	**
Château Puy-Bardens	Premières Côtes de Bordeaux/Bordeaux	Red	Berry, minerally	Sausages	**
Château Puygueraud	Bordeaux-Côtes de Francs/Bordeaux	Red	Plums, berry	Pasta	**
Château Rabaud-Promis	Sauternes, Barsac/Bordeaux	Sweet	Sweet, citrus, mandarin	Dessert	**
Château Rahoul	Graves/Bordeaux	Red	Berry, herbaceous	Sausages	**
Château Ramage-la-Batisse	Haut-Médoc/Bordeaux	Red	Plums, berry	Pasta	**
Château Rauzan-Ségla	Margaux/Bordeaux	Red	Smoky, tannic	Cold meats	***
Château Rayas Châteauneuf-du-Pape	Rhône Valley	Red	Powerful, complex, berry, jam	Beef, lamb	***
Château Rayas Fonsolette Côtes du Rhône	Rhône Valley	Red	Berry, spicy, earthy, rich	Chicken, veal, pork	**
Château Rayas Pignan Châteauneuf-du-Pape	Rhône Valley	Red	Berry, jam, rich, intense	Beef, lamb	**
Château Raymond-Lafon	Sauternes, Barsac/Bordeaux	Sweet	Sweet, complex, honey	Foie gras	***
Château Rayne Vigneau	Sauternes, Barsac/Bordeaux	Sweet	Sweet, mandarin, honey	Dessert	***
Château Réal d'Or (Elphège Bailly)	Côtes de Provence/Provence	Red	Berry, spicy	Pizza	*
Château Réal Martin (Gilles Meimoun)	Côtes de Provence/Provence	Red	Berry, gamey	Stew	*
Château Reillanne (Comte G. de Chevron-Villette)	Côtes de Provence/Provence	Red	Berry, spicy	Cold meats, stew, offal	**
Château Renon	Cadillac/Bordeaux	Red	Herbaceous, fruity	Stew	**
Château Respide Médeville	Graves/Bordeaux	Red	Smoky, plums	Pasta	**
Château Reynon	Premières Côtes de Bordeaux/Bordeaux	Red	Berry, herbaceous	Stew	**
Château Rieussec	Sauternes, Barsac/Bordeaux	Sweet	Sweet, complex, honey, mandarin	Dessert	***

FRANCE *(continued)*

Wine name	Region	Style	Flavor/Bouquet	Compatible Foods	Price Range
Château Robin	Côtes de Castillon/Bordeaux	Red	Spicy, minerally	Pasta	**
Château Roc de Cambes	Côtes de Bourg/Bordeaux	Red	Fruity, berry	Cold meats, stew, offal	**
Château Rolande-la-Garde	Premières Côtes de Blaye/Bordeaux	Red	Earthy, plums	Cheese	**
Château Rollan de By	Médoc/Bordeaux	Red	Spicy, herbaceous, earthy	Beef	**
Château Romanin (Jean-André Charial)	Les Baux-de-Provence/Provence	Red	Herbaceous, spicy, gamey	Lamb	**
Château Roquefort	Bordeaux Supérieur/Bordeaux	Red	Spicy, earthy	Beef	**
Château Roubine (Philippe Riboud)	Côtes de Provence/Provence	Red	Berry, earthy	Sausages	**
Château Saint-Pierre	St-Julien/Bordeaux	Red	Plums, spicy, berry	Beef	**
Château Sigalas-Rabaud	Sauternes, Barsac/Bordeaux	Sweet	Sweet, citrus, floral	Dessert	**
Château Simone (René Rougier)	Palette/Provence	Red	Spicy, gamey	Cold meats, stew, offal	*
Château Siran	Margaux/Bordeaux	Red	Berry, plums	Cold meats, stew, offal	**
Château Smith-Haut-Lafitte	Pessac-Léognan/Bordeaux	Red	Minerally, herbaceous, tannic	Beef	**
Château Sociando-Mallet	Haut-Médoc/Bordeaux	Red	Plums, tannic	Cold meats, stew, offal	**
Château Soutard	St-Émilion/Bordeaux	Red	Plums, berry	Lamb	**
Château St Estève Viognier "Jeune Vignes"	Rhône Valley	White	Floral, stone fruit, elegant	Fish, fruits	**
Château St-Robert	Graves/Bordeaux	White	Citrus, waxy, herbaceous, vanillin	Fish, chicken	**
Château Ste Marguéritte (Jean-Pierre Fayard)	Côtes de Provence/Provence	Red	Berry, spicy	Stew	**
Château Ste Roseline (Christophe Bernard)	Côtes de Provence/Provence	Red	Minerally, spicy	Cheese	**
Château Ste-Catherine	Cadillac/Bordeaux	Red	Berry, herbaceous	Game	**
Château Ste-Marie	Entre-Deux-Mers/Bordeaux	Red	Spicy, earthy	Stew	*
Château Suau	Premières Côtes de Bordeaux/Bordeaux	Red	Herbaceous, minerally	Pasta	**
Château Suduiraut	Sauternes, Barsac/Bordeaux	Sweet	Sweet, complex, citrus	Dessert	***
Château Talbot	St-Julien/Bordeaux	Red	Berry, herbaceous, minerally	Sausages	**
Château Tayac	Côtes de Bourg/Bordeaux	Red	Plums, berry	Cold meats	*
Château Testavin (Aya Kerfridin)	Côtes de Provence/Provence	Red	Earthy, minerally	Pizza	*
Château Thieuley	Bordeaux Supérieur/Bordeaux	Red	Berry, herbaceous	Game	**
Château Thuerry (M. Parmentier)	Coteaux Varois/Provence	Red	Berry, herbaceous, spicy	Beef	**
Château Tour du Haut-Moulin	Haut-Médoc/Bordeaux	Red	Berry, spicy	Beef	**
Château Tour Haut-Caussan	Médoc/Bordeaux	Red	Berry, herbaceous	Stew	**
Château Tour-de-Mirambeau (also Bordeaux)	Entre-Deux-Mers/Bordeaux	Red	Earthy, spicy	Stew	**
Château Trocard	Bordeaux Supérieur/Bordeaux	Red	Plum, herbaceous	Cold meats, stew, offal	**
Château Troplong-Mondot	St-Émilion/Bordeaux	Red	Spicy, minerally, berry	Lamb	**
Château Trotanoy	Pomerol/Bordeaux	Red	Complex, spicy, minerally, tannic	Game	***
Château Trottevieille	St-Émilion/Bordeaux	Red	Plums, minerally	Lamb	**
Château Turcaud	Entre-Deux-Mers/Bordeaux	Red	Herbaceous, plums	Cold meats, stew, offal	*
Château Val-Joanis Cotes du Luberon	Rhône Valley	Red	Berry, spicy	Pizza, chicken	*
Château Vieux Robin	Médoc/Bordeaux	Red	Spicy, berry	Lamb	**
Château Vignelaure (David O'Brien/Hugh Ryman)	Coteaux d'Aix/Provence	Red	Berry, spicy, earthy	Pork	**
Château Villars	Fronsac, Canon-Fronsac/Bordeaux	Red	Plums, berry	Stew	**
Château-Chalon (Baud Père et Fils)	Jura	White	Complex, minerally, nutty	Chicken	**
Château-Chalon (Jean Macle)	Jura	White	Nutty, floral	Veal	**
Clair Chambertin Clos de Bèze	Gevrey-Chambertin/Burgundy	Red	Spicy, minerally, berry	Duck	***
Clair Morey St Denis en la Rue de Vergy	Morey St-Denis/Burgundy	Red	Berry, leathery	Cold meats, stew, offal	**
Clair Savigny-Les-Beaune La Dominode	Savigny-lès-Beaune/Burgundy	Red	Spicy, berry	Cold meats	**
Clairette de Die Méthode Dioise Ancestrale (Jean Claude Raspail)	Rhône Valley	Sparkling	Stone fruit, minerally, crisp	Shellfish, Asian	**
Clos Capitoro Rouge	Ajuccio/Corsica	Red	Spicy, earthy	Chicken, veal, pork	**
Clos d'Iére/Domaine Rabiéga (Lars Torstenson)	Côtes de Provence/Provence	Red	Minerally, spicy, herbaceous	Game	**
Clos de l'Abbaye Bourgueil	Touraine/Loire	Red	Berry, spicy	Cold meats, stew, offal	**
Clos de l'Oratoire	St-Émilion/Bordeaux	Red	Berry, spicy	Stew	**
Clos de la Roche (H. Lignier)	Morey St-Denis/Burgundy	Red	Spicy, gamey, complex	Cold meats	***
Clos de Vougeot (A. Gros)	Vougeot/Burgundy	Red	Gamey, leathery, spicy	Game	***
Clos Floridène	Graves/Bordeaux	White	Spicy, minerally	Shellfish	**
Clos Fourtet	St-Émilion/Bordeaux	Red	Plums, spicy	Pork	**
Clos Jean	Loupiac/Bordeaux	Sweet	Sweet, mandarin	Dessert	**
Clos l'Eglise	Pomerol/Bordeaux	Red	Berry, minerally, herbaceous, tannic	Beef	***
Clos la Neuve (Fabienne Joly)	Côtes de Provence/Provence	Red	Spicy, gamey	Lamb	**
Clos Landry Rouge	Vin de Corse/Corsica	Red	Fruity, spicy	Chicken, veal, pork	**
Clos Nicrosi Blanc	Coteaux du Cap Corse/Corsica	White	Citrus, minerally, zingy	Shellfish, fish	**
Clos Nicrosi Muscat du Cap Corse	Coteaux du Cap Corse/Corsica	White	Fruity, floral	Asian, fruits, fish	**

FRANCE (continued)

Wine name	Region	Style	Flavor/Bouquet	Compatible Foods	Price Range
Clos Roche Blanche Touraine Sauvignon Blanc	Touraine/Loire	White	Zingy, citrus, grassy	Shellfish	**
Clos Rougeard Saumur-Champigny Les Poyeux	Anjou-Saumur/Loire	Red	Minerally, earthy	Pasta	**
Clos Val Bruyère (Sophie Cerciello)	Cassis/Provence	White	Herbaceous, zingy	Salad	**
Coche Dury Corton Charlemagne	Aloxe Corton/Burgundy	White	Spicy, complex, minerally	Chicken	***
Coche Dury Meursault	Meursault/Burgundy	White	Citrus, nutty	Fish	**
Coche Dury Meursault Perrières	Meursault/Burgundy	White	Complex, citrus, spicy	Fish	**
Coche Dury Volnay Premier cru	Volnay/Burgundy	Red	Spicy, gamey	Duck	**
Colin-Deleger Chassagne Montrachet	Chassagne Montrachet/Burgundy	White	Citrus, complex, spicy	Veal	**
Colin-Deleger Puligny Montrachet Les Demoiselles	Puligny-Montrachet/Burgundy	White	Spicy, citrus, nutty	Veal	**
Corbières Château Cascadais (Philippe Courrian)	Languedoc	Red	Spicy, gamey	Pizza	*
Corbières Château Gleon Montanié Selection Combe de Berre (Jean-Pierre and Philippe Montanié)	Languedoc	Red	Berry, minerally	Stew	**
Corbières Château La Baronne Vieilles Vignes (Blanc) (Suzette Lignères)	Languedoc	White	Spicy, citrus, minerally	Lamb	**
Corbières Château La Voulte-Gasparets Cuvée Réservée (Patrick Reverdy)	Languedoc	Red	Berry, gamey	Cold meats, stew, offal	**
Corbières Château La Voulte-Gasparets Cuvée Romain Puic (Patrick Reverdy)	Languedoc	Red	Spicy, berry	Sausages	**
Corbières Dom Serres-Mazard (Annie and Jean-Pierre Mazard)	Languedoc	Red	Earthy, spicy	Game	*
Corton Charlemagne (Louis Jadot)	Aloxe Corton/Burgundy	White	Citrus, floral, tropical fruit	Chicken	***
Corton Charlemagne (Louis Latour)	Aloxe Corton/Burgundy	White	Nutty, citrus, oaky	Veal	***
Corton Charlemagne (Michel Juillot)	Aloxe Corton/Burgundy	White	Oaky, spicy, nutty	Chicken	***
Corton Perrières (Michel Juillot)	Aloxe Corton/Burgundy	Red	Smoky, berry	Cold meats, stew, offal	***
Coteaux de l'Aubance Les Fontenelles (Christian et Agnès Papin)	Anjou-Saumur/Loire	Sweet	Minerally, sweet, apples	Cheese	**
Coteaux du Languedoc Abbaye de Valmagne (Philippe d'Allaines)	Languedoc	Red	Herbaceous, spicy, earthy	Stew	**
Coteaux du Languedoc Château Saint-Martin de la Garrigue	Languedoc	Red	Berry, spicy	Pork	**
Coteaux du Languedoc Dom Clavel La Méjanelle (Pierre Clavel)	Languedoc	Red	Spicy, minerally	Stew	**
Coteaux du Languedoc Dom d'Auphilac (Sylvain Fadat)	Languedoc	Red	Earthy, berry	Sausages	*
Coteaux du Languedoc Dom de la Coste Saint-Christol (Luc and Elizabeth Moynier)	Languedoc	Red	Smoky, berry	Pasta	**
Coteaux du Languedoc Dom Peyre-Rose Clos des Cistes (Marlène Soria)	Languedoc	Red	Berry, spicy	Veal	**
Coteaux du Languedoc La Clape Château Pech Redon Selection (Christophe Bousquet)	Languedoc	Red	Spicy, earthy	Pasta	**
Coteaux du Languedoc La Clape Château Pech-Céleyran (Jacques de St Exupéry)	Languedoc	Red	Berry, earthy	Stew	*
Coteaux du Languedoc Mas Jullien Les Depierre (Olivier Jullien)	Languedoc	Red	Spicy, gamey	Lamb	**
Coteaux du Languedoc Mas Jullien Les Vignes Oubliées (Olivier Jullien)	Languedoc	Red	Smoky, spicy	Stew	*
Coteaux du Languedoc Pic St Loup Château Lascaux Noble Pierre	Languedoc	Red	Berry, spicy	Sausages	**
Coteaux du Languedoc Pic St Loup Domaine de l'Hortus (Jean Orliac)	Languedoc	Red	Gamey, earthy	Cold meats, stew, offal	**
Coteaux du Languedoc Pic St Loup Mas Bruguière	Languedoc	Red	Berry, herbaceous	Cold meats	*
Côtes d'Olt Cahors Château Les Bouysses	Southwest France	Red	Berry, earthy	Pasta	**
Côtes de Bergerac Château Court-les-Muts	Bordeaux/Southwest France	Red	Berry, spicy	Veal	**
Côtes de Duras Dom du Grand Mayne Rosé (Andrew Gordon)	Bordeaux/Southwest France	Red	Berry, earthy	Antipasto	*
Côtes de Duras Dom du Grand Mayne Rouge (Andrew Gordon)	Bordeaux/Southwest France	Red	Spicy, berry	Pasta	**
Côtes du Marmandais Cave de Cocument Tersac	Bordeaux/Southwest France	Red	Minerally, spicy	Mediterranean	**
Coulée de Serrant Savennières Becherelle	Anjou-Saumur/Loire	White	Minerally, citrus	Fish	**
Coulée de Serrant Savennières Coulée de Serrant	Anjou-Saumur/Loire	White	Minerally, spicy, citrus, complex	Chicken	***
Couprié Cognac	Cognac	Brandy	Spirity, minerally	After dinner	***
Courvoisier Cognac	Cognac	Brandy	Spirity, complex, minerally	After dinner	***
Crémant de Limoux Sieur d'Arques Grande Cuvée Renaissance	Languedoc	Sparkling	Citrus, minerally, spicy	Aperitif	**
Crémant du Jura (André et Mireille Tissot)	Jura	Sparkling	Fruity, creamy	Aperitif	**
Croizet Cognac	Cognac	Brandy	Spirity, minerally	After dinner	***
Cru Barréjats	Sauternes, Barsac/Bordeaux	Sweet	Sweet, citrus	Dessert	*
Daniel Bouju Cognac	Cognac	Brandy	Spirity, fiery, earthy	After dinner	***
Darviot-Perrin Chassagne Montrachet Blanchots	Chassagne Montrachet/Burgundy	White	Citrus, oaky, spicy	Chicken	**
De Castellane Vintage	Champagne	Sparkling	Yeasty, citrus, berry	Antipasto	**
De Cazenove Stradivarius	Champagne	Sparkling	Yeasty, citrus, berry, complex	Fish	**
De Venoge Des Princes	Champagne	Sparkling	Complex, floral, berry	Aperitif	**
De Venoge Vintage	Champagne	Sparkling	Berry, crisp	Fish	**

FRANCE *(continued)*

Wine name	Region	Style	Flavor/Bouquet	Compatible Foods	Price Range
de Courcel Pommard Rugiens	Pommard/Burgundy	Red	Spicy, gamey, earthy	Beef	***
de Montille Pommard Pézerolles	Pommard/Burgundy	Red	Berry, spicy	Game	**
de Montille Pommard Rugiens	Pommard/Burgundy	Red	Berry, spicy	Cheese	**
de Montille Puligny Montrachet Les Caillerets	Puligny-Montrachet/Burgundy	White	Spicy, citrus, minerally	Fish	**
de Montille Volnay Taillepieds	Volnay/Burgundy	Red	Spicy, gamey	Cold meats, stew, offal	**
de Suremain Monthelie	Monthelie/Burgundy	Red	Berry, plums	Pasta	**
de Villaine Bourgogne Aligoté de Bouzeron	Côte Chalonnaise/Burgundy	White	Spicy, citrus	Pasta	**
de Villaine Bourgogne Blanc	Côte Chalonnaise/Burgundy	White	Tropical fruit, citrus	Fish	**
de Vogüé Bonnes Mares	Chambolle Musigny/Burgundy	Red	Rich, complex, gamey, berry	Duck	***
de Vogüé Chambolle Musigny Les Amoureuses	Chambolle Musigny/Burgundy	Red	Gamey, silky, berry	Cheese	***
de Vogüé Le Musigny	Chambolle Musigny/Burgundy	Red	Complex, berry, silky, gamey	Duck	***
de Volontat Corbières Château les Palais Randolin	Languedoc	Red	Earthy, gamey	Beef	**
Delamain Cognac	Cognac	Brandy	Spirity, rich, complex	After dinner	***
Delamotte Vintage	Champagne	Sparkling	Berry, citrus, crisp	Shellfish	**
Delas Frères Condrieu Clos Boucher	Rhône Valley	White	Stone fruit, floral, rich	Fish, fruits	**
Delas Frères Condrieu La Galopine	Rhône Valley	White	Stone fruit, minerally, elegant	Fish, fruits	**
Denis Charpentier Cognac	Cognac	Brandy	Spirity, earthy, fiery	After dinner	***
Désiré Petit et Fils Arbois-Pupillin Vin de Paille	Jura	Sweet	Raisiny, complex, sweet	Nuts	***
Deutz Blanc de Blancs	Champagne	Sparkling	Citrus, elegant, crisp	Aperitif	**
Deutz Brut	Champagne	Sparkling	Berry, citrus, floral	Fish	**
Deutz Cuveé (William Deutz)	Champagne	Sparkling	Berry, complex, citrus	Veal	***
Deutz Vintage	Champagne	Sparkling	Berry, citrus	Fish	**
Diebolt Vintage (100% Chardonnay)	Champagne	Sparkling	Citrus, crisp	Aperitif	**
Domaine Albert Boxler Tokay Pinot Gris Grand Cru Brand	Alsace	White	Spicy, minerally	Pork	**
Domaine Albert Mann Muscat	Alsace	White	Citrus, floral	Fruit	**
Domaine Allimant-Laugner Muscat	Alsace	White	Citrus, grapey	Cold meats, stew, offal	*
Domaine Alphonse Mellot Sancerre Génération XIX	Center/Loire	White	Grassy, citrus	Fish	***
Domaine André Ehrhart et Fils Tokay Pinot Gris Cuvée Elise	Alsace	White	Floral, citrus	Veal	**
Domaine André Kientzler Muscat Grand Cru Kirchberg	Alsace	White	Floral, citrus	Fruit	**
Domaine André Kientzler Riesling Grand Cru Osterberg	Alsace	White	Zingy, floral	Veal	**
Domaine Arena Grotti di Sole	Patrimonio/Corsica	Red	Fruity, rich, complex	Beef, lamb	**
Domaine Arena Grotti di Sole	Patrimonio/Corsica	White	Stone fruit, crisp	Shellfish, fish	**
Domaine Bernard Baudry Chinon les Grèzeaux	Touraine/Loire	Red	Berry, earthy, gamey	Stew	**
Domaine Berthed-Bonet Château-Chalon	Jura	White	Nutty, spicy	Chicken	**
Domaine Berthed-Bonet Côtes du Jura Vin de Paille	Jura	Sweet	Raisiny, sweet	Nuts	***
Domaine Breton Bourgueil les Galichets	Touraine/Loire	Red	Earthy, spicy	Cold meats	**
Domaine Bruno Sorg Gewurztraminer Pfersigberg	Alsace	White	Floral, spicy	Pasta	**
Domaine Bruno Sorg Muscat Grand Cru Pfersigberg	Alsace	White	Grapey, spicy	Sausages	**
Domaine Brusset Gigondas Le Grand Montmirail	Rhône Valley	Red	Berry, vanillin, rich	Beef, lamb	**
Domaine Cady Coteaux du Layon Saint-Aubin Cuvée Volupté	Anjou-Saumur/Loire	Sweet	Sweet, citrus, honey	Dessert	***
Domaine Charles Joguet Chinon les Varennes du Grand Clos	Touraine/Loire	Red	Herbaceous, berry, spicy, complex, earthy	Lamb	**
Domaine Comte Peraldi Blanc	Ajaccio/Corsica	White	Citrus, minerally, zingy	Shellfish, fish	**
Domaine Comte Peraldi Rouge	Ajaccio/Corsica	Red	Spicy, earthy	Chicken, veal, pork	**
Domaine Couly-Dutheil Chinon Clos de l'Echo	Touraine/Loire	Red	Spicy, herbaceous, berry	Veal	**
Domaine Couronne de Charlemagne (Bernard Piche)	Cassis/Provence	White	Herbaceous, spicy, zingy	Fish	**
Domaine d'Ambinos Coteaux du Layon Beaulieu Sélection des Grains Nobles	Anjou-Saumur/Loire	Sweet	Sweet, honey	Dessert	***
Domaine d'Andezon Côtes du Rhône Syrah Veiilles Vignes	Rhône Valley	Red	Berry, jam, intense	Beef, lamb	**
Domaine de Beauregard Muscadet de Sèvre et Maine Fief du Clairay	Pays Nantais/Loire	White	Floral, fruity, zingy	Shellfish	**
Domaine de Beaurenard Châteauneuf-du-Pape Cuvée Boisrenard	Rhône Valley	Red	Jam, powerful, vanillin	Beef, lamb	**
Domaine de Bouillerot	Bordeaux Supérieur/Bordeaux	Red	Spicy, earthy	Pizza	**
Domaine de Chevalier	Pessac-Léognan/Bordeaux	Red	Berry, herbaceous, tannic, minerally	Beef	***
Domaine de Courteillac	Bordeaux Supérieur/Bordeaux	Red	Herbaceous, berry	Cheese	**
Domaine de Durban Muscat de Beaumes-de-Venise	Rhône Valley	Sweet	Floral, tropical fruit, rich	Dessert	*
Domaine de l'Arlot Nuits St Georges Clos des Forêts St Georges	Nuits-St-Georges/Burgundy	Red	Spicy, gamey, berry	Duck	**
Domaine de l'Estello (Roger Tordjman)	Côtes de Provence/Provence	Red	Berry, spicy	Stew	**
Domaine de l'Idylle Vin de Savoie Cruet Vieilles Vignes	Savoie	White	Minerally, citrus	Fish	**
Domaine de l'Oratoire St Martin Côtes du Rhône Cairanne	Rhône Valley	Red	Berry, earthy, spicy	Pizza, chicken	**
Domaine de la Bastide Neuve (Jérome Paquette)	Côtes de Provence/Provence	Red	Berry, earthy	Stew	**
Domaine de la Bigotière Muscadet de Sèvre et Maine	Pays Nantais/Loire	White	Minerally, zingy, floral	Fish	*

FRANCE (continued)

Wine name	Region	Style	Flavor/Bouquet	Compatible Foods	Price Range
Domaine de la Charbonnière Vacqueyras	Rhône Valley	Red	Berry, herbaceous, leathery, intense	Pork, beef, lamb	**
Domaine de la Gallière Touraine Mesland Cuvée (François Premier)	Touraine/Loire	Red	Berry, herbaceous, spicy	Cheese	**
Domaine de la Grangeneuve Rasteau	Rhône Valley	Sweet	Fruity, tangy	Cheese	**
Domaine de la Janasse Châteauneuf-du-Pape	Rhône Valley	Red	Berry, peppery, earthy, spicy	Beef, lamb	**
Domaine de la Janasse Côtes-du-Rhône	Rhône Valley	Red	Berry, spicy	Pizza, chicken	*
Domaine de la Lauzade (Aline Bouvier)	Côtes de Provence/Provence	Red	Earthy, gamey	Pasta	**
Domaine de la Louvetrie Muscadet de Sèvre et Maine Clos du Château de la Carizière	Pays Nantais/Loire	White	Zingy, citrus	Fish	**
Domaine de la Mordorée Châteauneuf-du-Pape Cuvée de la Reine des Bois	Rhône Valley	Red	Berry, licorice, spicy, earthy	Pork, beef	**
Domaine de la Mordorée Lirac Cuvée de la Reine des Bois	Rhône Valley	Red	Berry, licorice, herbaceous	Veal, pork, beef	**
Domaine de la Mordorée Tavel	Rhône Valley	Rosé	Berry, rich, fruity	Asian, fish	**
Domaine de la Motte Coteaux du Layon Rochefort	Anjou-Saumur/Loire	Sweet	Sweet, minerally, honey	Fruit	**
Domaine de la Perrière Chinon Blanc Confidentiel	Touraine/Loire	White	Berry, minerally, herbaceous	Veal	**
Domaine de la Renjarde Côtes du Rhône-Villages	Rhône Valley	Red	Berry, fruity, intense	Pizza, chicken	*
Domaine de la Romanée Conti Echézeaux	Vosne-Romanée/Burgundy	Red	Complex, floral, spicy, earthy	Duck	***
Domaine de la Romanée Conti La Tâche	Vosne-Romanée/Burgundy	Red	Spicy, earthy, silky, complex	Duck	***
Domaine de la Romanée Conti Le Montrachet	Puligny-Montrachet/Burgundy	White	Minerally, complex, spicy, nutty	Fish	***
Domaine de la Romanée Conti Richebourg	Vosne-Romanée/Burgundy	Red	Gamey, spicy, complex	Gamey	***
Domaine de la Romanée Conti Romanée Conti	Vosne-Romanée/Burgundy	Red	Complex, spicy, earthy, minerally	Duck	***
Domaine de la Romanée Conti Romanée St Vivant	Vosne-Romanée/Burgundy	Red	Complex, minerally, smoky, earthy	Game	***
Domaine de la Romanée Conti Grands Echézeaux	Vosne-Romanée/Burgundy	Red	Spicy, complex, minerally, berry	Lamb	***
Domaine de la Sansonnière Anjou Gamay	Anjou-Saumur/Loire	Red	Berry, crisp	Cold meats, stew, offal	**
Domaine de la Taille aux Loups Montlouis Liquoreux Cuvée Romulus	Touraine/Loire	Sweet	Honey, sweet	Dessert	***
Domaine de la Vallongue (Philippe Paul-Cavallier)	Les Baux-de-Provence/Provence	Red	Spicy, fruity	Cold meats, stew, offal	**
Domaine de Ladoucette Sancerre (Comte Lafond)	Center/Loire	White	Zingy, grassy	Cheese	**
Domaine de Marchandise (Pierre Chauvier)	Côtes de Provence/Provence	Red	Spicy, earthy	Cold meats, stew, offal	**
Domaine de Mauvan (Gaëlle Maclou)	Côtes de Provence/Provence	Red	Spicy, berry	Sausages	**
Domaine de Mont Redon (Françoise Torné)	Côtes de Provence/Provence	Red	Berry, spicy	Cheese	**
Domaine de Montbourgeau L'Etoile Blanc	Jura	White	Minerally, fruity	Fish	**
Domaine de Rocailles Vin de Savoie Apremont (Pierre Boniface)	Savoie	White	Citrus, zingy	Fish	**
Domaine de Saint-Just Saumur-Champigny Clos Moleton	Anjou-Saumur/Loire	Red	Fruity, earthy	Stew	**
Domaine de Souviou (M. Cagnolari)	Bandol/Provence	Red	Spicy, minerally, berry	Game	**
Domaine de Tanelle Cuvée Alexandra	Figari/Corsica	Red	Powerful, complex	Beef, lamb	***
Domaine de Torraccia Cuvée Oriu	Porto-Vecchio/Corsica	Red	Rich, smoky	Beef, lamb	***
Domaine de Trévallon (Eloi Durrbach)	Les Baux-de-Provence/Provence	Red	Berry, earthy	Pasta	**
Domaine des Aubuisières Vouvray sec Le Marigny	Touraine/Loire	White	Apples, citrus, minerally	Fish	**
Domaine des Baumard Anjou Blanc Clos de la Folie	Anjou-Saumur/Loire	White	Apples, citrus, minerally	Shellfish	**
Domaine des Baumard Coteaux du Layon Clos de Sainte Catherine	Anjou-Saumur/Loire	Sweet	Sweet, minerally, honey	Fruit	***
Domaine des Baumard Quarts de Chaume	Anjou-Saumur/Loire	Sweet	Sweet, honey, mandarin	Dessert	***
Domaine des Baumard Savennières Clos du Papillon	Anjou-Saumur/Loire	White	Minerally, citrus, complex	Veal	***
Domaine des Chaberts (Betty Cundall)	Coteaux Varois/Provence	Red	Spicy, gamey	Stew	**
Domaine des Corbillères Touraine Angeline	Touraine/Loire	White	Herbaceous, earthy	Fish	**
Domaine des Epinaudières Coteaux du Layon Saint-Lambert Cuvée Clément	Anjou-Saumur/Loire	Sweet	Sweet, honey, mandarin	Dessert	**
Domaine des Lambrays Clos des Lambrays	Morey St-Denis/Burgundy	Red	Earthy, plums, spicy	Lamb	***
Domaine des Marroniers Gewurztraminer	Alsace	White	Minerally, spicy	Fruit	**
Domaine des Marroniers Riesling Kastelberg	Alsace	White	Citrus, spicy	Veal	**
Domaine des Petits Quarts Bonnezeaux	Anjou-Saumur/Loire	Sweet	Sweet, honey	Nuts	**
Domaine des Roches Neuves Saumur Insolite	Anjou-Saumur/Loire	Red	Berry, spicy	Cold meats	**
Domaine des Roches Neuves Saumur-Champigny Marginale	Anjou-Saumur/Loire	Red	Gamey, berry	Pizza	**
Domaine des Sablonettes Coteaux du Layon Rablay Les Erables	Anjou-Saumur/Loire	Sweet	Sweet, citrus, honey	Cheese	**
Domaine des Thermes (M. Robert)	Côtes de Provence/Provence	Red	Gamey, spicy	Pork	**
Domaine Didier Dagueneau Pouilly-Fumé Astérôde	Center/Loire	White	Zingy, citrus, herbaceous	Mediterranean	***
Domaine Didier Dagueneau Pouilly-Fumé Pur Sang	Center/Loire	White	Minerally, citrus, spicy	Fish	***
Domaine Dominique et Vincent Richard Muscadet de Sèvre et Maine Domaine de la Haie Trois Sols	Pays Nantais/Loire	White	Minerally, citrus	Shellfish	**
Domaine Druet Bourgueil Grand Mont	Touraine/Loire	Red	Berry, gamey	Stew	**
Domaine du Caillou Châteauneuf-du-Pape	Rhône Valley	Red	Berry, floral, elegant	Beef, lamb	**

FRANCE *(continued)*

Wine name	Region	Style	Flavor/Bouquet	Compatible Foods	Price Range
Domaine du Cayron Gigondas	Rhône Valley	Red	Berry, herbaceous, elegant	Pork, beef	**
Domaine du Clos Naudin Vouvray Moelleux Réserve	Touraine/Loire	Sweet	Sweet, honey, minerally	Cheese	***
Domaine du Closel Savennières Clos du Papillon	Anjou-Saumur/Loire	White	Complex, minerally	Chicken	**
Domaine du Noble	Loupiac/Bordeaux	Sweet	Sweet, honey	Dessert	**
Domaine du Pegau Châteauneuf-du-Pape Cuvée Reservée	Rhône Valley	Red	Berry, licorice, herbaceous, rich	Beef, lamb	**
Domaine du Prieuré St Christophe Roussette de Savoie Altesse (Michel Grisard)	Savoie	White	Zingy, citrus	Fish	**
Domaine du Prieuré St Christophe Vin de Savoie Mondeuse (Michel Grisard)	Savoie	Red	Peppery, berry	Sausages	**
Domaine Eric Nicolas Jasnières Discours de Tuf	Anjou-Saumur/Loire	White	Minerally, citrus	Cheese	**
Domaine Eric Rominger Gewurztraminer Grand Cru Zinnkoepfle Les Sinneles	Alsace	White	Spicy, floral	Asian	**
Domaine Ernest Burn Tokay Pinot Gris Vendanges Tardives	Alsace	White	Sweet, complex, floral	Fruit	**
Domaine Filiatreau Saumur-Champigny Cuvée Vieilles Vignes	Anjou-Saumur/Loire	Red	Minerally, plums	Game	**
Domaine François Villard Condrieu "Poncins"	Rhône Valley	White	Minerally, earthy, stone fruit, floral	Fish, fruits	**
Domaine François Villard St Joseph	Rhône Valley	Red	Berry, earthy, peppery, rich	Pork, beef	**
Domaine Fritsch Pinot Noir Rouge de Marlenheim Barriques	Alsace	Red	Berry, gamey	Sausages	**
Domaine Fuimicicoli Rouge	Sartène/Corsica	Red	Spicy, elegant	Chicken, veal, pork	**
Domaine Gérard Millet Sancerre Fut de Chîne	Center/Loire	White	Citrus, minerally, herbaceous	Salad	**
Domaine Gérard Neumeyer Tokay Pinot Gris Grand Cru Bruderthal	Alsace	White	Floral, oily	Cheese	**
Domaine Gérard Schueller et Fils Gewurztraminer Bildstoeckle	Alsace	White	Spicy, chalky	Chicken	**
Domaine Gitton Père et Fils Sancerre Galinot	Center/Loire	White	Herbaceous, grassy	Shellfish	**
Domaine Henri Bourgeois Sanerre le M.D. de Bourgeois	Center/Loire	White	Minerally, floral	Veal	**
Domaine Henry Marionnet Touraine Gamay Les Cépages Oubliés	Touraine/Loire	Red	Berry, spicy	Game	**
Domaine Henry Pellé Menetou-Salon Clos des Banchais	Center/Loire	White	Rich, minerally, zingy	Salad	**
Domaine Hering Pinot Noir Cuvée du Chat Noir	Alsace	Red	Berry, plums	Cold meats, stew, offal	**
Domaine Huet-L'Echansonne Vouvray Clos du Bourg	Touraine/Loire	White	Minerally, citrus, apples	Fish	**
Domaine Huet-L'Echansonne Vouvray Le Haut-Lieu	Touraine/Loire	White	Minerally, citrus, zingy	Fish	***
Domaine Jacky Marteau Touraine Gamay	Touraine/Loire	Red	Spicy, gamey	Stew	**
Domaine Jean Sipp Riesling Grand Cru Kirchberg	Alsace	White	Floral, citrus	Chicken	**
Domaine Jean-Max Roger Sancerre Le Grand Chemarin	Center/Loire	White	Citrus, cold tea	Fish	**
Domaine Jean-Paul Balland Sancerre Grande Cuvée	Center/Loire	White	Zingy, citrus	Shellfish	**
Domaine Jean-Pierre Dirler Gewurztraminer Grand Cru Saering	Alsace	White	Floral, spicy	Antipasto	**
Domaine Jean-Pierre Dirler Muscat Grand Cru Spiegel	Alsace	White	Citrus, grapey, floral	Fish, pork	**
Domaine Jo Pithon Coteaux du Layon Saint-Lambert	Anjou-Saumur/Loire	Sweet	Sweet, honey, citrus	Cheese	***
Domaine Joel Taluau et Foltzenlogel Saint-Nicolas de Bourgueil	Touraine/Loire	Red	Berry, spicy	Cold meats	**
Domaine Kehren Muscat Cuvée Patricia	Alsace	White	Floral, citrus	Shellfish	**
Domaine Kirmann Sylvaner	Alsace	White	Citrus, floral	Pasta	*
Domaine la Suffrene (Cédric Gravier)	Bandol/Provence	Red	Spicy, berry	Cold meats, stew, offal	**
Domaine Laffourcade Anjou-Villages Château Perray Jouannet	Anjou-Saumur/Loire	Red	Spicy, gamey	Sausages	**
Domaine Lafran-Veyrolles (Jouve Férec)	Bandol/Provence	Red	Earthy, spicy	Cold meats	**
Domaine Leccia Blanc	Coteaux du Cap Corse/Corsica	White	Stone fruit, crisp	Shellfish, fish	**
Domaine Leccia E Crose Blanc	Coteaux du Cap Corse/Corsica	White	Rich, elegant	Shellfish, fish, cheese	**
Domaine Leccia Petra Bianca	Patrimonio/Corsica	Red	Powerful, earthy	Beef, lamb	**
Domaine Leccia Rouge	Coteaux du Cap Corse/Corsica	Red	Spicy, herbaceous	Chicken, veal, pork	**
Domaine Leflaive Bâtard Montrachet	Puligny-Montrachet/Burgundy	White	Complex, spicy, smoky	Fish	***
Domaine Leflaive Bienvenues Bâtard Montrachet	Puligny-Montrachet/Burgundy	White	Complex, citrus, nutty	Veal	***
Domaine Leflaive Chevalier Montrachet	Puligny-Montrachet/Burgundy	White	Complex, nutty, spicy, citrus	Fish	***
Domaine Leflaive Puligny Montrachet Les Combettes	Puligny-Montrachet/Burgundy	White	Complex, spicy, citrus	Veal	***
Domaine Leflaive Puligny Montrachet Les Pucelles	Puligny-Montrachet/Burgundy	White	Complex, smoky, spicy, citrus	Chicken	***
Domaine Léon Boesch Gewurztraminer Grand Cru Zinnkoepfle	Alsace	White	Floral, minerally	Cold meats, stew, offal	**
Domaine les Grands Vignes Anjou Gamay	Anjou-Saumur/Loire	Red	Berry, spicy	Mediterranean	**
Domaine les Toulons (Denis Alibert)	Coteaux d'Aix/Provence	Red	Berry, spicy	Sausages	*
Domaine Lucien Albrecht Gewurztraminer Réserve	Alsace	White	Spicy, chalky	Fish	**
Domaine Lucien Albrecht Tokay Pinot Gris Grand Cru Pfingstberg Vendanges Tardives	Alsace	White	Sweet, floral	Fruit	***
Domaine Lucien Crochet Sancerre Le Chîne	Center/Loire	White	Herbaceous, minerally, citrus	Cheese	**
Domaine Lucien Crochet Sancerre Rouge Prestige	Center/Loire	Red	Herbaceous, spicy, berry	Cold meats	**
Domaine Marcel Deiss Riesling Burg de Bergheim	Alsace	White	Floral, citrus, complex	Fish	**
Domaine Marcel Deiss Riesling Grand Cru Altenberg de Bergheim	Alsace	White	Complex, floral, minerally	Chicken	**
Domaine Martin Schaetzel Gewurztraminer Grand Cru Kaefferkopf Cuvée Catherine	Alsace	White	Chalky, spicy	Veal	**

FRANCE *(continued)*

Wine name	Region	Style	Flavor/Bouquet	Compatible Foods	Price Range
Domaine Martin Schaetzel Riesling Grand Cru Kaefferkopf Cuvée Nicolas	Alsace	White	Minerally, citrus	Pork	**
Domaine Masson-Blondelet Pouilly-Fumé Tradition Cullus	Center/Loire	White	Grassy, minerally	Salad	**
Domaine Max Aubert Châteauneuf-du-Pape Le Nonce	Rhône Valley	Red	Berry, peppery, jam	Beef, lamb	**
Domaine Max Aubert Châteuneuf-du-Pape Domaine de la Présidente	Rhône Valley	Red	Spicy, peppery, tannic	Beef, lamb	**
Domaine Meyer-Fonné Riesling Grand Cru Kaefferkopf	Alsace	White	Floral, citrus	Antipasto	**
Domaine Mittnacht Klack Tokay Pinot Gris Vendanges Tardives	Alsace	White	Sweet, oily, floral	Cheese	**
Domaine Monin Bugey Brut Méthode Traditionnelle	Bugey	Sparkling	Crisp, fruity, citrus	Aperitif	**
Domaine Monin Vin du Bugey Chardonnay	Bugey	White	Tropical fruit, citrus	Chicken	**
Domaine Ogereau Anjou Villages Prestige	Anjou-Saumur/Loire	Red	Berry, spicy, earthy	Stew	**
Domaine Ogereau Coteaux du Layon Saint-Lambert	Anjou-Saumur/Loire	Sweet	Sweet, citrus, minerally	Dessert	**
Domaine Ostertag Gewurztraminer Fronholz Vendanges Tardives	Alsace	White	Powerful, sweet, floral	Fruit	***
Domaine Ostertag Sylvaner Vieilles Vignes	Alsace	White	Floral, citrus	Cheese	**
Domaine Ostertag Tokay Pinot Gris Fronhoz	Alsace	White	Citrus, oily	Veal	**
Domaine Paul Antard Châteauneuf-du-Pape Cuvée Classique	Rhône Valley	Red	Powerful, jam, licorice	Beef, lamb	**
Domaine Paul Antard Châteauneuf-du-Pape La Côte Ronde	Rhône Valley	Red	Berry, oaky, rich	Beef, lamb	**
Domaine Paul Blanck Riesling Furstentum Vieilles Vignes	Alsace	White	Floral, citrus	Chicken	**
Domaine Philippe Tessier Cour-Cheverny	Touraine/Loire	White	Cold tea, minerally, apples	Shellfish	**
Domaine Pichot Vouvray le Peu de la Moriette	Touraine/Loire	White	Minerally, spicy	Veal	**
Domaine Pierre Aguilas Coteaux du Layon Saint-Aubin	Anjou-Saumur/Loire	Sweet	Sweet, citrus, minerally	Dessert	**
Domaine Pierre Soulez Savennières Roches-aux-Moines Chamboureau Cuvée d'Avant	Anjou-Saumur/Loire	White	Spicy, citrus, minerally	Fish	**
Domaine René Muré Gewurztraminer Schultzengass	Alsace	White	Minerally, chalky	Asian	**
Domaine René Muré Pinot Noir Clos Saint-Landelin	Alsace	Red	Berry, gamey	Cold meats	**
Domaine René Muré Riesling Grand Cru Vorbourg Clos Saint-Landelin	Alsace	White	Spicy, minerally	Asian	**
Domaine René Muré Sylvaner Clos Saint-Landelin Cuvée Oscar	Alsace	White	Floral, minerally	Fish	**
Domaine René Muré Tokay Pinot Gris Lutzeltal	Alsace	White	Floral, citrus	Fish	**
Domaine René-Noêl Legrand Saumur-Champigny Les Rogelins	Anjou-Saumur/Loire	Red	Berry, spicy	Stew	**
Domaine Retiveau-Retif Coteaux du Saumur	Anjou-Saumur/Loire	White	Medium-sweet, citrus	Fruit	**
Domaine Richou Coteaux de l'Aubance Les Trois Demoiselles	Anjou-Saumur/Loire	Sweet	Sweet, citrus, apples	Dessert	**
Domaine Rolly Gassmann Muscat Moenchreben de Rorschwihr	Alsace	White	Floral, grapey	Fruit	**
Domaine Rolly Gassmann Pinot Noir de Rodern	Alsace	Red	Smoky, berry	Duck	**
Domaine Rolly Gassmann Riesling Kappelweg de Rorschwihr	Alsace	White	Floral, spicy	Pork	**
Domaine Schlumberger Gewurztraminer Cuvée Christine	Alsace	White	Smoky, spicy	Asian	***
Domaine Schlumberger Riesling Grand Cru Kessler	Alsace	White	Floral, minerally	Pasta	**
Domaine Schlumberger Tokay Pinot Gris Grand Cru Kitterle	Alsace	White	Spicy, oily	Fish	**
Domaine Schoffit Gewurztraminer Grand Cru Rangen Clos Saint-Théobald Vendanges Tardives	Alsace	White	Sweet, powerful, chalky	Fish	**
Domaine Schoffit Tokay Pinot Gris Cuvée Alexandre	Alsace	White	Oily, spicy	Chicken	**
Domaine Schoffit Tokay Pinot Gris Grand Cru Rangen de Thann Clos Saint-Théobald	Alsace	White	Citrus, floral, oily	Fish	**
Domaine Seppi Landmann Gewurztraminer Zinnkoepfle	Alsace	White	Citrus, floral, spicy	Veal	**
Domaine Seppi Landmann Sylvaner Vallée Noble	Alsace	White	Floral, honey	Fruit	**
Domaine Seppi Landmann Tokay Pinot Gris Grand Cru Zinnkoepfle	Alsace	White	Spicy, citrus, floral	Fish	**
Domaine St André de Figuière (Alain Combard)	Côtes de Provence/Provence	Red	Berry, earthy	Pasta	**
Domaine Tempier (Jean-Marie & François Peyraud)	Bandol/Provence	Red	Complex, tannic, berry, spicy	Beef	***
Domaine Thierry Boucard Bourgueil Cuvée Marion	Touraine/Loire	Red	Spicy, berry	Game	**
Domaine Turenne (Philippe Benezet)	Côtes de Provence/Provence	Red	Earthy, berry	Cheese	**
Domaine Vacheron Sancerre Rouge	Center/Loire	Red	Berry, herbaceous	Cold meats, stew, offal	**
Domaine Vincent Pinard Sancerre Harmonie	Center/Loire	White	Zingy, herbaceous	Shellfish	**
Domaine Weinbach Riesling Grand Cru Schlossberg	Alsace	White	Complex, floral, minerally	Chicken	***
Domaine Weinbach Tokay Pinot Gris Quintessence de Grains Nobles	Alsace	Sweet	Sweet, complex, spicy	Dessert	***
Domaine Yannick Amirault Bourgueil Vieilles Vignes Petite Cave	Touraine/Loire	Red	Berry, earthy	Sausages	**
Domaine Yvon Metras Fleurie	Beaujolais	Red	Berry, floral, jam, earthy	Chicken, pork, veal, beef	**
Domaine Zind Humbrecht Gewurztraminer Hengst	Alsace	White	Complex, powerful, spicy	Veal	***
Domaine Zind-Humbrecht Gewurztraminer Grand Cru Goldert	Alsace	White	Powerful, complex, spicy	Cheese	***
Domaine Zind-Humbrecht Riesling Rangen de Thann Clos Saint-Urbain	Alsace	White	Powerful, minerally, floral	Fish	***
Domaine Zind-Humbrecht Tokay Pinot Gris Clos Jebsal Sélection de Grains Nobles	Alsace	Sweet	Sweet, complex, citrus, floral	Dessert	***

FRANCE (continued)

Wine name	Region	Style	Flavor/Bouquet	Compatible Foods	Price Range
Domaine Zind-Humbrecht Tokay Pinot Gris Grand Cru Rangen de Thann Clos Saint-Urbain	Alsace	White	Spicy, oily, powerful	Chicken	***
Domaine Zind-Humbrecht Tokay Pinot Gris Windsbuhl	Alsace	White	Spicy, oily, complex	Chicken	***
Domaines Chéreau Carré Muscadet de Sèvre et Maine Comte Saint-Hubert	Pays Nantais/Loire	White	Crisp, minerally, citrus	Shellfish	**
Dopff au Moulin Gewurztraminer Riquewihr Vendanges Tardives	Alsace	White	Sweet, floral	Fruit	***
Dopff au Moulin Riesling Riquewihr Proprieté	Alsace	White	Citrus, spicy	Fish	**
Dopff et Irion Tokay Pinot Gris Les Maquisards	Alsace	White	Spicy, citrus	Mediterranean	**
Drappier Grande Sendrée	Champagne	Sparkling	Berry, complex, powerful	Pork	***
Drappier Vintage	Champagne	Sparkling	Crisp, fruity	Fish	**
Drenga de Gaffery Cuvée des Gouverneurs	Patrimonio/Corsica	Red	Spicy, oaky	Beef, lamb	***
Drouhin Beaune Clos des Mouches	Beaune/Burgundy	White	Minerally, citrus	Fish	**
Drouhin Puligny Montrachet	Puligny-Montrachet/Burgundy	White	Citrus, minerally	Pork	**
Drouhin Vosne Romanée Petits Monts	Vosne-Romanée/Burgundy	Red	Floral, minerally, gamey	Cold meats, stew, offal	**
Ducelliers VDP Côtes de Thongue Les Chemins de Bassac Vignelongue	Vin de Pays	Red	Berry, smoky	Stew	*
Dujac Clos de la Roche	Morey St-Denis/Burgundy	Red	Complex, gamey, earthy	Duck	***
Dujac Clos St Denis	Morey St-Denis/Burgundy	Red	Earthy, minerally, berry	Beef	***
Dupuy Cognac	Cognac	Brandy	Spirity, minerally, earthy	After dinner	***
Engel Clos de Vougeot	Vougeot/Burgundy	Red	Spicy, earthy, berry	Beef	***
Engel Grands Echézeaux	Vosne-Romanée/Burgundy	Red	Berry, minerally, spicy	Duck	***
Ente Meursault	Meursault/Burgundy	White	Smoky, citrus	Pork	**
Entraygues et du Fel Jean-Marc Viguier	Southwest France	Red	Berry, spicy	Cold meats	**
Eugène Carrel et Fils Vin de Savoie Jongieux Gamay Vieilles Vignes	Savoie	Red	Spicy, berry	Pizza	**
Eugène Carrel et Fils Vin de Savoie Jongieux	Savoie	White	Zingy, citrus	Fish	**
Faiveley Corton Charlemagne	Aloxe Corton/Burgundy	White	Citrus, minerally, spicy	Veal	***
Faiveley Corton Clos des Cortons	Aloxe Corton/Burgundy	Red	Berry, gamey	Lamb	***
Faiveley Mazis Chambertin	Gevrey-Chambertin/Burgundy	Red	Earthy, minerally, berry	Beef	***
Faiveley Mercurey	Côte Chalonnaise/Burgundy	Red	Berry, earthy	Pasta	**
Faiveley Nuits St Georges Clos de la Maréchale	Nuits-St-Georges/Burgundy	Red	Minerally, earthy, berry	Beef	***
Fardel-Lubac Faugères Château Grezan Cuvée (Arnaud Lubac)	Languedoc	Red	Spicy, earthy	Stew	*
Faugères Château de la Liquière Cistus (Bernard Vidal)	Languedoc	Red	Berry, minerally	Mediterranean	*
Faugères Château des Estanilles (Michel Louison)	Languedoc	Red	Minerally, floral	Stew	**
Faugères Dom Ollier Taillefer (Alain Ollier)	Languedoc	Red	Spicy, berry	Lamb	*
Faugères Domaine Gilbert Alquier Les Bastides	Languedoc	Red	Gamey, berry	Cold meats, stew, offal	**
Faugères Domaine Raymond Roc	Languedoc	Red	Smoky, berry	Pizza	*
Fichet Meursault	Meursault/Burgundy	White	Citrus, spicy	Veal	**
Fitou Terroir de Tuchan Les Producteurs du Mont Tauch	Languedoc	Red	Berry, plums	Game	**
Fontaine-Gagnard Chassagne Morey	Chassagne Montrachet/Burgundy	White	Citrus, spicy	Pasta	**
Forest Pouilly Fuissé	Maconnais/Burgundy	White	Minerally, spicy	Fish	**
François Peyrot Cognac	Cognac	Brandy	Spirity, minerally, complex	After dinner	***
Frapin Cognac	Cognac	Brandy	Spirity, fiery, earthy	After dinner	***
Frères Couillaud VDP Jardin de la France Dom Couillaud Chardonnay	Vin de Pays	White	Tropical fruit, spicy	Chicken	*
Fronton Château Baudare (Claude Vigouroux)	Southwest France	Red	Spicy, herbaceous, berry	Cold meats, stew, offal	**
Fronton Château Montauriol	Southwest France	Red	Berry, spicy	Mediterranean	**
Fruitière Vinicole d'Arbois Arbois Savagnin	Jura	White	Citrus, spicy, zingy	Salad	**
Fruitière Vinicole d'Arbois Arbois Vin Jaune	Jura	White	Nutty, minerally, complex	Chicken	**
Fruitière Vinicole de Voiteur Côtes du Jura Vin Jaune	Jura	White	Complex, spicy, nutty	Chicken	**
Gadais Père et Fils Muscadet de Sèvre et Maine Grande Réserve du Moulin	Pays Nantais/Loire	White	Minerally, citrus, zingy	Fish	**
Gagnard-Delagrange Bâtard Montrachet	Chassagne Montrachet/Burgundy	White	Complex, nutty, minerally	Fish	***
Gagnard-Delagrange Chassagne Morey	Chassagne Montrachet/Burgundy	White	Nutty, spicy	Veal	**
Gaillac Cave de Tecou Passion	Southwest France	Red	Berry, minerally	Cold meats, stew, offal	**
Gaillac Domaine de Causse-Marines Delires D'Automne Doux (Patrice Lescarret)	Southwest France	Red	Spicy, berry	Sausages	**
Gaillac Domaine de Causse-Marines Les Greilles (Patrice Lescarret)	Southwest France	Red	Earthy, minerally	Pasta	**
Gaillac Vin D'Autan de Robert Plageoles et Fils Doux	Southwest France	White	Apples, zingy	Sausages	**
Gaillac Vin de Voile de Robert Plageoles (Robert Plageoles)	Southwest France	White	Nutty, rich	Chicken	**
Garaudet Monthelie	Monthelie/Burgundy	Red	Spicy, earthy	Sausages	**

FRANCE (continued)

Wine name	Region	Style	Flavor/Bouquet	Compatible Foods	Price Range
Gardet Vintage	Champagne	Sparkling	Berry, citrus, crisp	Shellfish	**
Gautier Cognac	Cognac	Brandy	Spirity, complex	After dinner	***
Georges Du Boeuf Morgon	Beaujolais	Red	Jam, berry, intense	Chicken, veal, pork	**
Georges Du Boeuf Moulin-à-Vent	Beaujolais	Red	Berry, earthy, minerally	Chicken, veal, pork	**
Georges Vernay Condrieu Coteaux du Vernon	Rhône Valley	White	Stone fruit, minerally, powerful	Fish, fruits	**
Gevrey Chambertin (C. Dugat)	Gevrey-Chambertin/Burgundy	Red	Berry, spicy	Beef	**
Gevrey Chambertin (D. Mortet)	Gevrey-Chambertin/Burgundy	Red	Berry, licorice	Stew	**
Gewurztraminer Grand Cru Scholnenbourg (Marc Tempé)	Alsace	White	Spicy, minerally	Asian	**
Gewurztraminer Sigillé Confrérie de Saint-Etienne (Jean-Baptiste Adam)	Alsace	White	Spicy, citrus	Fish	**
Givry (F. Lumpp)	Côte Chalonnaise/Burgundy	Red	Floral, berry	Pasta	**
Godet Cognac	Cognac	Brandy	Spirity, fiery	After dinner	***
Gosset – special bottlings such as Quatramine Centenaire/Célibris	Champagne	Sparkling	Complex, berry, yeasty, powerful	Duck	***
Gosset Brut Excellence	Champagne	Sparkling	Berry, minerally, crisp	Chicken	**
Gosset Grand Millésime	Champagne	Sparkling	Complex, berry, rich	Veal	**
Gouges Nuits St Georges Les St Georges	Nuits-St-Georges/Burgundy	Red	Earthy, berry	Game	**
Gouges Nuits St Georges Les St Porrets	Nuits-St-Georges/Burgundy	Red	Plums, berry	Cheese	**
Gouges Nuits St Georges Vaucrains	Nuits-St-Georges/Burgundy	Red	Smoky, spicy	Cheese	**
Gousseland Cognac	Cognac	Brandy	Spirity, nutty, earthy	After dinner	***
Grand Enclos du Château de Cérons	Cérons/Bordeaux	Red	Berry, spicy	Sausages	**
Grassa VDP Côtes de Gascogne Domaine du Tariquet Gros Manseng Premières Grives	Vin de Pays	White	Zingy, citrus	Shellfish	**
Grivot Clos de Vougeot	Vougeot/Burgundy	Red	Complex, earthy, berry	Lamb	***
Grivot Nuits St Georges Boudots	Nuits-St-Georges/Burgundy	Red	Spicy, gamey	Duck	***
Grivot Vosne Romanée	Vosne-Romanée/Burgundy	Red	Complex, berry	Lamb	**
Groffier Bonnes Mares	Chambolle Musigny/Burgundy	Red	Berry, gamey, spicy	Lamb	***
Groffier Chambolle Musigny Les Amoureuses	Chambolle Musigny/Burgundy	Red	Berry, spicy	Duck	***
Grossot Chablis	Chablis/Burgundy	White	Minerally, apples	Fish	**
Guffens-Heynen Pouilly Fuissé	Maconnais/Burgundy	White	Minerally, floral	Shellfish	**
Guigal Châteauneuf-du-Pape	Rhône Valley	Red	Berry, earthy, leathery, intense	Beef, lamb	**
Guigal Condrieu la Doriane	Rhône Valley	White	Stone fruit, minerally, oaky	Fish, chicken	***
Guigal Condrieu	Rhône Valley	White	Stone fruit, minerally, floral, complex	Fish, fruits	**
Guigal Côte-Rôtie Blonde et Brune	Rhône Valley	Red	Berry, smoky, rich, elegant	Beef, lamb	**
Guigal Côte-Rôtie La Landonne	Rhône Valley	Red	Berry, peppery, licorice, complex	Beef, lamb	***
Guigal Côte-Rôtie La Mouline	Rhône Valley	Red	Floral, berry, nutty, complex	Beef, lamb	***
Guigal Côte-Rôtie La Turque	Rhône Valley	Red	Berry, peppery, licorice, intense	Beef, lamb	***
Guigal Côtes du Rhône	Rhône Valley	Red	Fruity, berry, spicy	Pizza, chicken	*
Guigal Côtes du Rhône	Rhône Valley	White	Floral, stone fruit, crisp	Fish, chicken	*
Guigal Gigondas	Rhône Valley	Red	Berry, earthy, austere	Veal, pork, beef	**
Guigal Hermitage	Rhône Valley	Red	Berry, licorice, mushroom, rich	Beef, lamb	**
Guy Breton Morgon Vieilles Vignes	Beaujolais	Red	Jam, spicy, earthy	Chicken, veal, pork	**
Heidsieck & Monopole Diamant Bleu	Champagne	Sparkling	Crisp, citrus, berry	Antipasto	***
Heidsieck & Monopole Vintage	Champagne	Sparkling	Crisp, toasty, berry	Cheese	**
Hennessy Cognac	Cognac	Brandy	Spirity, fiery, minerally	After dinner	***
Henri Beurdin et Fils Reuilly Blanc	Center/Loire	White	Zingy, spicy	Cheese	**
Henriot Cuveé Baccarat	Champagne	Sparkling	Complex, elegant, citrus, berry	Fish	***
Henriot Vintage	Champagne	Sparkling	Elegant, berry, yeasty	Chicken	**
Hine Cognac	Cognac	Brandy	Spirity, minerally	After dinner	***
Hugel et Fils Gewurztraminer Sélection de Grains Nobles	Alsace	Sweet	Sweet, complex, citrus, spicy	Dessert	***
Hugel et Fils Riesling Sélection de Grains Nobles	Alsace	Sweet	Sweet, complex, powerful, floral	Dessert	***
Hugel et Fils Tokay Pinot Gris Hommage (Jean Hugel)	Alsace	White	Oily, floral	Cheese	***
Irouléguy Dom Brana (Jean et Adrienne Brana)	Landes, Gascogne and Pyrenees/Southwest France	Red	Berry, spicy	Cold meats, stew, offal	**
J. L. Chave Hermitage	Rhône Valley	Red	Complex, rich, earthy	Beef, lamb	***
J. L. Chave Hermitage	Rhône Valley	White	Powerful, floral, minerally	Fish, veal	***
J. L. Chave St Joseph	Rhône Valley	Red	Berry, minerally, complex	Pork, beef	**
J. Lassalle Blanc de Blancs	Champagne	Sparkling	Crisp, citrus, elegant	Aperitif	**
Jacquart Vintage	Champagne	Sparkling	Austere, berry, citrus	Fish	**
Jacques Selosse Extra Brut	Champagne	Sparkling	Berry, complex	Shellfish	**
Jacques Selosse Vintage	Champagne	Sparkling	Complex, berry, powerful	Game	**
Jacquesson Dégorgement Tardif	Champagne	Sparkling	Austere, berry	Shellfish	**
Jacquesson Perfection	Champagne	Sparkling	Complex, citrus, berry, dry	Cheese	***

FRANCE *(continued)*

Wine name	Region	Style	Flavor/Bouquet	Compatible Foods	Price Range
Jacquesson Signature	Champagne	Sparkling	Complex, berry, powerful	Chicken	**
Jacquesson Signature Non Dosé	Champagne	Sparkling	Dry, austere, crisp, citrus	Shellfish	**
Jadot Beaune Boucherottes	Beaune/Burgundy	Red	Berry, earthy	Cheese	**
Jadot Beaune Clos des Ursules	Beaune/Burgundy	Red	Berry, earthy	Stew	**
Jadot Chevalier Montrachet Les Demoiselles	Puligny-Montrachet/Burgundy	White	Spicy, smoky	Chicken	***
Jadot Corton Pougets	Aloxe Corton/Burgundy	Red	Berry, leathery	Duck	***
Jadot Puligny Montrachet	Puligny-Montrachet/Burgundy	White	Minerally, spicy	Veal	**
Jamet Côte-Rôtie	Rhône Valley	Red	Jam, berry, earthy, complex	Beef, lamb	**
Jasmin Côte-Rôtie	Rhône Valley	Red	Rich, complex, floral, berry, earthy	Beef, lamb	**
Javillier Meursault	Meursault/Burgundy	White	Nutty, citrus	Chicken	**
Jean Foillard Morgon	Beaujolais	Red	Berry, floral, intense	Chicken, veal, pork	**
Jean-Luc Colombo Cornas Le Terre Brûlée	Rhône Valley	Red	Berry, spicy, minerally, complex	Beef, lamb	**
Jean-Luc Colombo Côtes du Rhône les Figuieres	Rhône Valley	White	Floral, stone fruit, rich	Fish, chicken	**
Jean-Luc Colombo Muscat de Rivesettes les Saintes	Rhône Valley	Sweet	Citrus, floral, intense, zingy	Dessert	*
Jean-Noel Gagnard Chassagne Montrachet Les Caillerets	Chassagne Montrachet/Burgundy	White	Nutty, complex, spicy	Fish	**
Jean-Paul Thévenet Morgon Cuvée Cielles Vignes	Beaujolais	Red	Berry, spicy, intense	Chicken, fish, pork, pizza	**
Joblot Givry	Côte Chalonnaise/Burgundy	Red	Spicy, floral	Sausages	**
José Michel Vintage	Champagne	Sparkling	Citrus, crisp	Fish	**
Joseph Perrier Cuvée Royale	Champagne	Sparkling	Berry, citrus, floral	Aperitif	**
Joseph Perrier Josephine	Champagne	Sparkling	Complex, berry, citrus	Chicken	***
Josmeyer Gewurztraminer Les Archenets	Alsace	White	Floral, minerally	Fish	**
Josmeyer Riesling Grand Cru Hengst	Alsace	White	Floral, citrus	Veal	**
Jouffreau Cahors Clos de Gamot	Southwest France	Red	Berry, earthy	Sausages	**
Jurançon Bru-Baché L'Eminence (Claude Loustalot)	Landes, Gascogne and Pyrenees/Southwest France	Sweet	Sweet, citrus	Dessert	**
Jurançon Clos Uroulat (Charles Hours)	Landes, Gascogne and Pyrenees/Southwest France	Sweet	Sweet, honey	Fruit	**
Jurançon Dom Bellgarde Cuvée Thibault (Pascal Labasse)	Landes, Gascogne and Pyrenees/Southwest France	White	Citrus, minerally, zingy	Aperitif	**
Jurançon Dom Cauhapé Noblesse du Temps (Henri Ramonteau)	Landes, Gascogne and Pyrenees/Southwest France	Sweet	Sweet, honey	Fruit	**
Jurançon Dom Cauhapé Quintessence du Petit Manseng (Henri Ramonteau)	Landes, Gascogne and Pyrenees/Southwest France	Sweet	Sweet, citrus	Cheese	**
Jurançon Sec Clos Lapeyre (Jean-Bernard Larrieu)	Landes, Gascogne and Pyrenees/Southwest France	White	Zingy, citrus	Shellfish	**
Jurançon Sec Cuvée Marie (Charles Hours)	Landes, Gascogne and Pyrenees/Southwest France	White	Citrus, minerally, zingy	Aperitif	**
Jurançon Sec Dom Bellegarde (Pascal Labasse)	Landes, Gascogne and Pyrenees/Southwest France	White	Citrus, zingy	Aperitif	**
Jurançon Sec Dom Cauhapé Chant des Vignes (Henri Ramonteau)	Landes, Gascogne and Pyrenees/Southwest France	White	Minerally, spicy, citrus	Fish	**
Krug Clos du Mesnil	Champagne	Sparkling	Complex, citrus, yeasty, powerful	Shellfish	***
Krug Grande Cuvée	Champagne	Sparkling	Berry, complex, powerful	Fish	***
Krug Rosé	Champagne	Sparkling	Berry, complex, floral	Lamb	***
Krug Vintage	Champagne	Sparkling	Powerful, complex, berry	Game	***
Kuentz Bas Gewurztraminer Eichberg	Alsace	White	Spicy, minerally, floral	Veal	**
Kuentz Bas Riesling Grand Cru Pfersigberg	Alsace	White	Citrus, floral	Chicken	**
La Vieille Ferme Côtes du Lubéron	Rhône Valley	Red	Berry, spicy	Pizza, chicken	*
Lafarge Beaune Grèves	Beaune/Burgundy	Red	Plums, berry	Duck	**
Lafarge Volnay Clos des Chênes	Volnay/Burgundy	Red	Spicy, earthy	Stew	**
Lafarge Volnay Clos du Château des Ducs	Volnay/Burgundy	Red	Smoky, berry	Pasta	**
Langlois-Château Crémant de Loire Quadrille	Anjou-Saumur/Loire	Sparkling	Fruity, crisp, citrus	Aperitif	**
Lanson Black Label	Champagne	Sparkling	Austere, crisp, berry	Shellfish	**
Lanson Noble Cuvée	Champagne	Sparkling	Citrus, berry, complex, toasty	Chicken	***
Lanson Vintage	Champagne	Sparkling	Austere, berry, zingy	Veal	**
Laroche VDP d'Oc Chardonnay Laroche Grand Cuvée 'L'	Vin de Pays	White	Tropical fruit, citrus	Fish	**
Latour Puligny Montrachet	Puligny-Montrachet/Burgundy	White	Citrus, smoky	Chicken	**
Launois Vintage	Champagne	Sparkling	Crisp, citrus, berry	Pork	**
Laurent-Perrier Brut	Champagne	Sparkling	Crisp, citrus	Aperitif	**
Laurent-Perrier Grand Siècle Alexandra Rosé	Champagne	Sparkling	Berry, floral, melon, complex	Lamb	***
Laurent-Perrier Grand Siècle	Champagne	Sparkling	Complex, berry, floral	Fish	***
Laurent-Perrier Grand Siècle Vintage	Champagne	Sparkling	Berry, complex, yeasty	Fish	***

FRANCE (continued)

Wine name	Region	Style	Flavor/Bouquet	Compatible Foods	Price Range
Laurent-Perrier Ultra Brut	Champagne	Sparkling	Austere, dry, crisp, citrus	Shellfish	**
Laurent-Perrier Vintage	Champagne	Sparkling	Dry, citrus, berry	Antipasto	**
Le Montrachet (Baron Thenard)	Puligny-Montrachet/Burgundy	White	Complex, citrus, tropical fruit, spicy	Chicken	***
Le Montrachet (Comte Lafon)	Puligny-Montrachet/Burgundy	White	Complex, smoky, minerally	Fish	***
Le Montrachet (Marquis de Laguiche)	Puligny-Montrachet/Burgundy	White	Complex, nutty, smoky, spicy	Fish	***
Legras Cuveé St Vincent	Champagne	Sparkling	Citrus, crisp, berry	Chicken	**
Legras Présidence	Champagne	Sparkling	Berry, complex, floral	Fish	**
Leroy Auxey Duresses	Auxey Duresses/Burgundy	Red	Earthy, berry	Pasta	**
Leroy Clos de Vougeot	Vougeot/Burgundy	Red	Earthy, minerally, complex, spicy	Duck	***
Leroy Richebourg	Vosne-Romanée/Burgundy	Red	Complex, spicy, earthy	Beef	***
Leroy Romanée St Vivant	Vosne-Romanée/Burgundy	Red	Complex, spicy, minerally	Lamb	***
Leroy Savigny-Les-Beaune Narbantons	Savigny-lès-Beaune/Burgundy	Red	Minerally, floral	Stew	**
Leroy Volnay Santenots	Volnay/Burgundy	Red	Floral, smoky	Cold meats, stew, offal	**
Leroy Vosne Romanée Les Beaux Monts	Vosne-Romanée/Burgundy	Red	Spicy, earthy, minerally	Duck	***
Les Coteaux du Rieu Berlou St Chinian Berloup Schisteil	Languedoc	Red	Berry, smoky	Sausages	*
Les Coteaux du Rieu Berlou VDP d'Oc Berloup Collection	Vin de Pays	Red	Berry, herbaceous, spicy	Pasta	**
Les Vignerons de Thézac-Perricard VDP Thézac-Perricard Vin du Czar	Vin de Pays	Red	Berry, earthy	Mediterranean	*
Lilbert Vintage	Champagne	Sparkling	Crisp, berry	Cheese	**
Limoux Dom de l'Aigle Classique (Jean-Louis Denois)	Languedoc	Sparkling	Crisp, citrus, minerally	Aperitif	**
Louis Jadot Château des Jacques Moulin-à-Vent	Beaujolais	Red	Berry, vanillin, complex	Pork, veal, beef	**
Louis Jadot Domaine du Monnet Brouilly	Beaujolais	Red	Berry, spicy, earthy	Pork, veal, beef	**
Louis Latour Morgon Les Charmes	Beaujolais	Red	Jam, floral, berry, complex	Chicken, veal, pork	**
Louis Roederer Brut Premier NV	Champagne	Sparkling	Berry, citrus, minerally	Antipasto	**
Louis Roederer Cristal	Champagne	Sparkling	Complex, citrus, floral, crisp, elegant	Fish	***
Louis Roederer Cristal Rosé	Champagne	Sparkling	Berry, floral, complex	Lamb	***
Louis Roederer Rosé	Champagne	Sparkling	Floral, berry	Cheese	**
Louis Roederer Vintage	Champagne	Sparkling	Berry, citrus, complex	Fish	**
Louis Royer Cognac	Cognac	Brandy	Spirity, fiery, complex	After dinner	***
Lussac Château de la Grenière	St-Émilion/Bordeaux	Red	Herbaceous, minerally	Stew	**
Lussac Château Lyonnat	St-Émilion/Bordeaux	Red	Berry, fruity	Cold meats, stew, offal	**
Madiran Chapelle Lenclos (Patrick Ducorneau)	Landes, Gascogne and Pyrenees/Southwest France	Red	Berry, earthy	Cold meats, stew, offal	**
Madiran Château d'Aydie (Pierre Laplace)	Landes, Gascogne and Pyrenees/Southwest France	Red	Earthy, tannic	Sausages	**
Madiran Château d'Aydie Ode d'Aydie (Pierre Laplace)	Landes, Gascogne and Pyrenees/Southwest France	Red	Berry, tannic	Mediterranean	**
Madiran Château Laffitte-Teston (Jean-Marc Laffitte)	Landes, Gascogne and Pyrenees/Southwest France	Red	Berry, earthy	Mediterranean	**
Madiran Château Montus Cuvée Prestige (Alain Brumont)	Landes, Gascogne and Pyrenees/Southwest France	Red	Tannic, earthy	Stew	**
Madiran Dom de Bouscassé Vieilles Vignes (Alain Brumont)	Landes, Gascogne and Pyrenees/Southwest France	Red	Berry, tannic	Cold meats	**
Madiran Domaine Meinjarre (Alain Brumont)	Landes, Gascogne and Pyrenees/Southwest France	Red	Spicy, tannic	Antipasto	**
Maison Guy Saget Pouilly-Fumé Les Logères	Center/Loire	White	Zingy, citrus	Chicken	**
Maison Mollex Roussette de Savoie Seyssel La Taconnière	Savoie	White	Citrus, spicy	Shellfish	**
Maison Trimbach Riesling Clos Saint-Hune	Alsace	White	Citrus, floral, complex	Fish	***
Maison Trimbach Riesling Cuvée Frédéric-Emile	Alsace	White	Floral, minerally, complex	Veal	***
Maison Trimbach Tokay Pinot Gris Réserve Personelle	Alsace	White	Smoky, citrus	Chicken	**
Marc Sorrel Hermitage	Rhône Valley	Red	Berry, rich, oaky	Beef, lamb	**
Marcel LaPierre Morgon	Beaujolais	Red	Berry, rich, minerally	Chicken, veal, pork	**
Marcillac Jean-Luc Matha Cuvée Spéciale	Southwest France	Red	Spicy, peppery, berry	Game	**
Martell Cognac	Cognac	Brandy	Spirity, berry, complex	After dinner	***
Mas de Cadenet (Guy Négrel)	Côtes de Provence/Provence	Red	Berry, spicy	Pizza	*
Mas de la Dame (Marc Caysson)	Les Baux-de-Provence/Provence	Red	Berry, earthy	Sausages	**
Ménard Cognac	Cognac	Brandy	Spirity, fiery, earthy	After dinner	***
Méo-Camuzet Clos de Vougeot	Vougeot/Burgundy	Red	Minerally, berry, spicy, earthy	Duck	***
Méo-Camuzet Nuits St Georges aux Murgers	Nuits-St-Georges/Burgundy	Red	Berry, earthy	Lamb	***
Méo-Camuzet Vosne Romanée Chaumes	Vosne-Romanée/Burgundy	Red	Gamey, spicy, earthy	Cold meats, stew, offal	***
Méo-Camuzet Vosne Romanée Les Brulées	Vosne-Romanée/Burgundy	Red	Spicy, berry, gamey	Stew	***
Mercier Vintage	Champagne	Sparkling	Berry, fruity	Cheese	**
Mercurey (M. Juillot)	Côte Chalonnaise/Burgundy	Red	Spicy, berry	Sausages	**

FRANCE (continued)

Wine name	Region	Style	Flavor/Bouquet	Compatible Foods	Price Range
Merlin Macon La Roche Vineuse Vieilles Vignes	Maconnais/Burgundy	White	Minerally, tropical fruit	Mediterranean	**
Meursault (Michel Bouzereau)	Meursault/Burgundy	White	Spicy, smoky	Veal	**
Meursault Charmes (Comte Lafon)	Meursault/Burgundy	White	Nutty, spicy, complex	Veal	***
Meursault Charmes (François Jobard)	Meursault/Burgundy	White	Nutty, smoky	Chicken	**
Meursault Charmes (Rémi Jobard)	Meursault/Burgundy	White	Spicy, smoky	Fish	***
Meursault Clos de la Barre (Comte Lafon)	Meursault/Burgundy	White	Complex, minerally, nutty	Fish	***
Meursault Genevrières (Comte Lafon)	Meursault/Burgundy	White	Complex, minerally, spicy	Fish	***
Meursault Perrières (Comte Lafon)	Meursault/Burgundy	White	Citrus, spicy, minerally	Fish	***
Michel Chapoutier Condrieu	Rhône Valley	White	Floral, stone fruit, complex	Fish, fruits	**
Michel Chapoutier Côte-Rôtie	Rhône Valley	Red	Berry, herbaceous, spicy	Pork, beef	**
Michel Chapoutier Crozes Hermitage les Meysonniers	Rhône Valley	Red	Berry, spicy, earthy	Chicken, veal, pork	**
Michel Chapoutier Hermitage Chante Alouette	Rhône Valley	White	Floral, minerally, nutty, intense	Fish, chicken	**
Michel Chapoutier Hermitage La Sizeranne	Rhône Valley	Red	Berry, floral, intense, complex	Beef, lamb	**
Michel Chapoutier Hermitage Vin de Paille	Rhône Valley	Sweet	Floral, exotic, complex, rich	Dessert	***
Minervois Château Sainte-Eulalie (Isabelle Coustal)	Languedoc	Red	Berry, spicy	Pasta	*
Minervois Château Villerambert Julien (Michel Julien)	Languedoc	Red	Berry, spicy	Pizza	*
Minervois Clos Centeilles (Patricia Boyer and Daniel Domergue)	Languedoc	Red	Gamey, earthy	Pizza	*
Minervois Dom Piccinini Clos l'Angely (Jean-Christophe Piccinini)	Languedoc	Red	Gamey, berry	Cold meats, stew, offal	**
Minervois La Tour Boisée Cuvée Marie-Claude (Jean-Louis Poudou)	Languedoc	Red	Gamey, smoky	Cold meats, stew, offal	**
Moet & Chandon Brut NV	Champagne	Sparkling	Berry, earthy, yeasty	Fish	**
Moet & Chandon Dom Perignon	Champagne	Sparkling	Complex, citrus, berry, elegant, powerful	Fish	***
Moet & Chandon Dom Perignon Rosé	Champagne	Sparkling	Floral, berry, powerful, complex	Game	***
Moet & Chandon Rosé	Champagne	Sparkling	Floral, berry	Lamb	**
Moet & Chandon Vintage	Champagne	Sparkling	Berry, toasty, minerally	Chicken	**
Monbazillac Château Tirecul la Gravière (Claudie and Bruno Bilancini)	Bordeaux/Southwest France	Sweet	Sweet, honey	Dessert	**
Montagne Château Faizeau	St-Émilion/Bordeaux	Red	Plums, smoky	Beef	**
Monthelie Duresses (Comte Lafon)	Monthelie/Burgundy	Red	Berry, earthy	Cold meats, stew, offal	**
Montlouis les Lys (François Chidaine)	Touraine/Loire	Sweet	Sweet, mandarin, citrus	Dessert	***
Morot Beaune Teurons	Beaune/Burgundy	Red	Minerally, berry	Cold meats, stew, offal	**
Mugnier Chambolle Musigny Les Amoureuses	Chambolle Musigny/Burgundy	Red	Spicy, game	Game	***
Mugnier Le Musigny	Chambolle Musigny/Burgundy	Red	Berry, spicy, complex	Game	***
Mumm Cordon Rouge	Champagne	Sparkling	Fruity, sweet, berry	Cheese	**
Mumm de Crémant	Champagne	Sparkling	Citrus, yeasty, honey	Antipasto	**
Mumm Grand Cordon	Champagne	Sparkling	Berry, toasty, complex	Chicken	***
Mumm René Lalou	Champagne	Sparkling	Berry, yeasty, floral	Cheese	***
Mumm Vintage	Champagne	Sparkling	Berry, yeasty	Fish	**
Muscadet de Sèvre et Maine (Guy Bossard)	Pays Nantais/Loire	White	Minerally, floral, citrus	Shellfish	**
Muscadet de Sèvre et Maine Cuvée Expression de Granit (Guy Bossard)	Pays Nantais/Loire	White	Minerally, herbaceous, citrus	Shellfish	**
Muscadet de Sèvre et Maine Cuvée Orthogenesis (Guy Bossard)	Pays Nantais/Loire	White	Minerally, floral, citrus	Shellfish	**
Muscat Vendanges Tardives (Roger Jung et Fils)	Alsace	White	Sweet, floral	Fish	**
Nicholas Feuillatte Palmés d'Or	Champagne	Sparkling	Berry, fruity, citrus	Chicken	**
Niellon Chevalier Montrachet	Puligny-Montrachet/Burgundy	White	Citrus, smoky	Cold meats, stew, offal	***
Noël Veirset Cornas	Rhône Valley	Red	Berry, licorice, minerally	Beef, lamb	**
Nuits St Georges Hauts Pruliers (D. Rion)	Nuits-St-Georges/Burgundy	Red	Elegant, spicy	Cold meats	**
Nuits St Georges Les Cailles (R. Chevillon)	Nuits-St-Georges/Burgundy	Red	Gamey, spicy	Cold meats, stew, offal	**
Nuits St Georges Les St Georges (R. Chevillon)	Nuits-St-Georges/Burgundy	Red	Spicy, leathery	Pasta	**
Nuits St Georges Vaucrains (R. Chevillon)	Nuits-St-Georges/Burgundy	Red	Berry, spicy	Game	**
Otard Cognac	Cognac	Brandy	Spirity, complex, fiery	After dinner	***
Pacherenc du Vic-Bilh Château Montus Sec (Alain Brumont)	Landes, Gascogne and Pyrenees/Southwest France	White	Zingy, citrus	Fish	**
Pacherenc du Vic-Bilh Domaine Bouscassé Vendange Décembre (Alain Brumont)	Landes, Gascogne and Pyrenees/Southwest France	White	Citrus, minerally, zingy	Shellfish	**
Palmer Amazone	Champagne	Sparkling	Berry, citrus, complex	Game	***
Paul Bara Vintage	Champagne	Sparkling	Crisp, berry	Cheese	**
Paul Giraud Cognac	Cognac	Brandy	Spirity, complex	After dinner	***
Paul Jaboulet Aîné Côtes du Rhône Parallel Y5	Rhône Valley	Red	Berry, peppery	Pizza, chicken	*
Paul Jaboulet Aîné Crozes-Hermitage Thalabert	Rhône Valley	Red	Spicy, herbaceous, berry, complex	Veal, pork	**
Paul Jaboulet Aîné Gigondas	Rhône Valley	Red	Berry, earthy, minerally	Beef, lamb	**

FRANCE (continued)

Wine name	Region	Style	Flavor/Bouquet	Compatible Foods	Price Range
Paul Jaboulet Aîné Hermitage La Chapelle	Rhône Valley	Red	Berry, earthy, rich, complex	Beef, lamb	**
Paul Jaboulet Aîné Muscat Beaumes-de-Venise	Rhône Valley	Sweet	Powerful, mandarin, floral	Dessert	*
Paul Janin et Fils Moulin-a-Vent	Beaujolais	Red	Berry, powerful, citrus, minerally	Pork, veal, beef	**
Pernot Bâtard Montrachet	Puligny-Montrachet/Burgundy	White	Smoky, citrus	Chicken	***
Perrier-Jouet Belle-Epoque	Champagne	Sparkling	Berry, citrus, complex, toasty	Fish	***
Perrier-Jouet Belle-Epoque Rosé	Champagne	Sparkling	Floral, berry, complex	Game	***
Perrier-Jouet Blason de France	Champagne	Sparkling	Berry, complex, toasty	Fish	**
Perrier-Jouet Brut NV	Champagne	Sparkling	Crisp, citrus, berry	Antipasto	**
Perrier-Jouet Vintage	Champagne	Sparkling	Berry, minerally, complex	Fish	**
Philipponnat Clos des Goisses	Champagne	Sparkling	Berry, complex, powerful, toasty	Duck	***
Philipponnat Vintage	Champagne	Sparkling	Berry, yeasty	Chicken	**
Pierre Gaillard Côte-Rôtie "Rose Poupre"	Rhône Valley	Red	Complex, elegant, earthy	Beef, lamb	**
Pierre Peters Vintage	Champagne	Sparkling	Crisp, berry	Antipasto	**
Pierre Sparr et ses Fils Riesling Grand Cru Schoenenbourg	Alsace	White	Minerally, floral	Shellfish	**
Pinot Noir Cuvée Frédéric (Pierre Becht)	Alsace	Red	Berry, floral	Game	**
Pinot Noir Rouge d'Alsace (Louis Hauller)	Alsace	Red	Berry, gamey	Pasta	**
Piper-Heidsieck Brut	Champagne	Sparkling	Crisp, zingy, apples	Shellfish	*
Piper-Heidsieck Florens-Louis	Champagne	Sparkling	Berry, minerally, citrus	Fish	***
Piper-Heidsieck Rare	Champagne	Sparkling	Austere, berry, complex	Fish	***
Piper-Heidsieck Vintage	Champagne	Sparkling	Berry, toasty	Chicken	**
Pol Roger Blanc de Chardonnay	Champagne	Sparkling	Citrus, elegant, complex	Aperitif	**
Pol Roger Brut NV (White Foil)	Champagne	Sparkling	Berry, floral, yeasty	Shellfish	**
Pol Roger Cuvée Sir Winston Churchill	Champagne	Sparkling	Powerful, complex, berry, rich	Duck	***
Pol Roger PR	Champagne	Sparkling	Complex, berry, yeasty	Cheese	**
Pol Roger Rosé	Champagne	Sparkling	Berry, floral	Game	**
Pol Roger Vintage	Champagne	Sparkling	Berry, complex, toasty	Fish	**
Pommard Clos des Epeneaux (Comte Armand)	Pommard/Burgundy	Red	Earthy, berry, smoky	Duck	***
Pommard Saussilles (Jean-Marc Boillot)	Pommard/Burgundy	Red	Spicy, gamey, berry	Game	**
Pommery Brut	Champagne	Sparkling	Crisp, citrus	Aperitif	**
Pommery Cuvée Louise	Champagne	Sparkling	Complex, citrus, berry, elegant	Fish	***
Pommery Cuvée Louise Rosé	Champagne	Sparkling	Floral, berry, complex	Lamb	***
Pommery Flaçon	Champagne	Sparkling	Complex, berry, rich, powerful	Game	***
Pommery Summertime	Champagne	Sparkling	Floral, citrus	Aperitif	**
Pommery Vintage	Champagne	Sparkling	Citrus, berry, yeasty	Fish	**
Ponsot Clos de la Roche Vieilles Vignes	Morey St-Denis/Burgundy	Red	Spicy, gamey, berry	Game	***
Ponsot Clos St Denis	Morey St-Denis/Burgundy	Red	Berry, spicy	Game	***
Ponsot Griotte Chambertin	Gevrey-Chambertin/Burgundy	Red	Berry, gamey	Duck	***
Pouilly Fuissé (Madame Ferret)	Maconnais/Burgundy	White	Minerally, citrus	Shellfish	**
Pouilly-Fumé Cuvée Majorum (Michel Redde et Fils)	Center/Loire	White	Herbaceous, grassy, citrus	Cheese	**
Pouilly-Fumé Domaine des Riaux (Jeannot Père et Fils)	Center/Loire	White	Citrus, grassy	Fish	**
Pouilly-Fumé Les Griottines (Michel Bailly)	Center/Loire	White	Zingy, grassy	Shellfish	**
Pousse d'Or Santenay Clos des Tavannes	Santenay/Burgundy	Red	Floral, minerally	Pasta	**
Pousse d'Or Volnay Clos de la Pousse d'Or	Volnay/Burgundy	Red	Berry, spicy	Game	***
Pousse d'Or Volnay Clos des 60 Ouvrées	Volnay/Burgundy	Red	Complex, elegant, spicy	Cheese	***
Prince de Mérode Corton Bressandes	Aloxe Corton/Burgundy	Red	Spicy, berry, gamey	Game	***
Prince Hubert de Polignac Cognac	Cognac	Brandy	Spirity, fiery, complex, minerally	After dinner	***
Producteurs Plaimont Côtes de Saint-Mont (VDQS) Château de Sabazan	Landes, Gascogne and Pyrenees/Southwest France	Red	Berry, earthy	Mediterranean	**
Producteurs Plaimont Côtes de Saint-Mont (VDQS) Monastère de Saint-Mont	Landes, Gascogne and Pyrenees/Southwest France	Red	Berry, minerally	Mediterranean	**
Prunier Cognac	Cognac	Brandy	Spirity, complex, minerally	After dinner	***
Puisseguin Château Durand-Laplagne	St-Émilion/Bordeaux	Red	Berry, smoky	Stew	**
Puligny Montrachet La Truffière (Jean-Marc Boillot)	Puligny-Montrachet/Burgundy	White	Spicy, citrus, minerally	Fish	**
Pusseguin Château Guibeau-La-Fourvieille	St-Émilion/Bordeaux	Red	Berry, herbaceous	Stew	**
R.H. Coutier Vintage	Champagne	Sparkling	Crisp, berry	Cheese	**
Ramonet Bâtard Montrachet	Chassagne Montrachet/Burgundy	White	Complex, tropical fruit, smoky	Fish	***
Ramonet Chassagne Montrachet Cailleret	Chassagne Montrachet/Burgundy	White	Spicy, citrus	Pork	**
Ramonet Chassagne Montrachet Ruchottes	Chassagne Montrachet/Burgundy	White	Spicy, floral, minerally	Chicken	**
Ramonet Le Montrachet	Puligny-Montrachet/Burgundy	White	Citrus, smoky, minerally	Chicken	***
Raveneau Chablis Les Clos	Chablis/Burgundy	White	Complex, nutty, minerally	Chicken	***
Raveneau Chablis Montée de Tonnerre	Chablis/Burgundy	White	Minerally, nutty, complex	Fish	***

FRANCE (continued)

Wine name	Region	Style	Flavor/Bouquet	Compatible Foods	Price Range
Rémy Martin Cognac	Cognac	Brandy	Spirity, fiery, earthy	After dinner	***
Renaud Delile Cognac	Cognac	Brandy	Spirity, earthy	After dinner	***
Renault Cognac	Cognac	Brandy	Spirity, fiery	After dinner	***
René Rostaing Condrieu	Rhône Valley	White	Stone fruit, minerally, floral, rich	Fish, fruits	**
René Rostaing Côte-Rôtie Côte Blonde	Rhône Valley	Red	Floral, berry, elegant, intense	Beef, lamb	***
Resses et Fils Cahors Château la Caminade La Commandery	Southwest France	Red	Minerally, tannic	Stew	**
Reuilly Blanc (Jean-Michel Sorbe)	Center/Loire	White	Citrus, grassy	Shellfish	**
Ribes Fronton Château le Roc Cuvée Don Quichotte	Southwest France	Red	Herbaceous, berry	Cold meats	**
Richebourg (A. Gros)	Vosne-Romanée/Burgundy	Red	Minerally, berry, gamey	Game	***
Riesling Comtes d'Eguisheim (Léon Beyer)	Alsace	White	Citrus, apples	Shellfish	**
Riesling Grand Cru Schoenenbourg (François Lehmann)	Alsace	White	Citrus, minerally	Fish	**
Riesling Stein (Pierre et Jean Rietsch)	Alsace	White	Citrus, floral	Shellfish	**
Rigal Cahors Château Saint-Didier Parnac	Southwest France	Red	Berry, tannic	Pasta	**
Rolet Père et Fils Arbois Rouge Tradition	Jura	Red	Berry, spicy	Stew	**
Rolet Père et Fils Arbois Trousseau Memorial	Jura	Red	Berry, spicy	Veal	**
Rolet Père et Fils Arbois Vin Jaune	Jura	White	Complex, nutty	Veal	**
Roty Charmes Chambertin Très Vieilles Vignes	Gevrey-Chambertin/Burgundy	Red	Berry, earthy	Cold meats, stew, offal	***
Rouget Echézeaux (formerly H. Jayer)	Vosne-Romanée/Burgundy	Red	Gamey, berry, earthy	Beef	***
Rouget Vosne Romanée Cros Parantoux	Vosne-Romanée/Burgundy	Red	Earthy, spicy, minerally	Stew	***
Roullet Cognac	Cognac	Brandy	Spirity, complex	After dinner	***
Roulot Meursault Perrières	Meursault/Burgundy	White	Smoky, complex	Fish	**
Roulot Meursault Tesson Le Clos de Mon Plaisir	Meursault/Burgundy	White	Citrus, nutty	Veal	**
Roumier Bonnes Mares	Chambolle Musigny/Burgundy	Red	Complex, berry, silky	Game	***
Roumier Chambolle Musigny	Chambolle Musigny/Burgundy	Red	Berry, spicy	Cold meats, stew, offal	**
Roumier Chambolle Musigny Les Amoureuses	Chambolle Musigny/Burgundy	Red	Silky, gamey, berry	Game	***
Roumier Morey St Denis Clos de la Bussière	Morey St-Denis/Burgundy	Red	Complex, elegant, spicy	Cold meats	***
Roumier Ruchottes Chambertin	Gevrey-Chambertin/Burgundy	Red	Elegant, spicy, gamey	Game	***
Rousseau Chambertin Clos de Bèze	Gevrey-Chambertin/Burgundy	Red	Elegant, spicy, minerally	Duck	***
Rousseau Chambertin	Gevrey-Chambertin/Burgundy	Red	Complex, silky, berry, gamey	Game	***
Rousseau Clos de la Roche	Morey St-Denis/Burgundy	Red	Complex, silky, gamey, spicy	Cold meats, stew, offal	***
Rousseau Gevrey Chambertin Clos St Jacques	Gevrey-Chambertin/Burgundy	Red	Complex, elegant, berry, spicy	Duck	***
Roussette de Savoie Marestel (Edmond Jacquin et Fils)	Savoie	White	Citrus, zingy	Mediterranean	**
Roussette de Savoie Marestel (Noël Dupasquier)	Savoie	White	Zingy, citrus	Fish	**
Ruinart Brut	Champagne	Sparkling	Berry, yeasty	Veal	**
Ruinart Dom Ruinart	Champagne	Sparkling	Berry, citrus, elegant	Fish	***
Ruinart Dom Ruinart Rosé	Champagne	Sparkling	Floral, berry, complex	Lamb	***
Ruinart Vintage	Champagne	Sparkling	Berry, complex, toasty	Fish	**
Sack Zafiropulo Clos Ste Magdalene	Cassis/Provence	White	Zingy, cold tea, minerally	Fish	**
Saint Aubin (Marc Colin)	St-Aubin/Burgundy	White	Tropical fruit, nutty	Pasta	**
Saint Aubin Les Murgers Dents de Chien (Hubert Lamy)	St-Aubin/Burgundy	White	Citrus, spicy	Fish	**
Saint Aubin Premier Cru (G. Thomas)	St-Aubin/Burgundy	White	Minerally, citrus	Cheese	**
St Chinian Château Cazal-Viel Cuvée des Fées (Henri Miguel)	Languedoc	Red	Berry, earthy	Pork	*
St Chinian Château Maurel Fonsalade Cuvée Frédéric (Philippe and Thérèse Maurel)	Languedoc	Red	Berry, spicy	Pasta	*
St Chinian Château Milhau-Lacugue Cuvée des Chevaliers	Languedoc	Red	Smoky, earthy	Mediterranean	*
St Chinian Dom des Jougla Cuvée Signé (Alain Jougla)	Languedoc	Red	Spicy, gamey	Pizza	*
St-Georges Château St-André Corbin	St-Émilion/Bordeaux	Red	Berry, plums	Cold meats	**
St-Georges Château St-Georges	St-Émilion/Bordeaux	Red	Spicy, herbaceous, plums	Cold meats	**
Saint Romain (Alain Gras)	St-Romain/Burgundy	Red	Berry, spicy	Pasta	**
Saint-Nicolas de Bourgueil Cuvée les Graviers (Yannick Amirault)	Touraine/Loire	Red	Herbaceous, berry, spicy	Pasta	**
Salon	Champagne	Sparkling	Complex, citrus, powerful, toasty	Fish	***
Sancerre (Joseph Verdier)	Center/Loire	White	Zingy, citrus	Salads	**
Sancerre Le Chîne Marchand (Pascal Jolivet)	Center/Loire	White	Zingy, grassy	Shellfish	**
Santenay Clos des Tavannes (L. Muzard)	Santenay/Burgundy	Red	Spicy, minerally	Pizza	**
Santenay Gravières (Vincent Girardin)	Santenay/Burgundy	Red	Minerally, spicy	Sausages	**
Saumur-Champigny Le Petit Saint-Vincent (Dominique Joseph)	Anjou-Saumur/Loire	Red	Spicy, berry	Lamb	**
Saussignac Clos d'Yvigne (Patricia Atkinson)	Bordeaux/Southwest France	Sweet	Sweet, citrus	Dessert	**
Sauzet Bâtard Montrachet	Puligny-Montrachet/Burgundy	White	Complex, nutty, smoky	Chicken	***
Sauzet Puligny Montrachet Les Combettes	Puligny-Montrachet/Burgundy	White	Smoky, citrus	Chicken	***
Serafin Gevrey Chambertin Vieilles Vignes	Gevrey-Chambertin/Burgundy	Red	Berry, spicy	Game	**
Serge Dagueneau et Filles Pouilly-Fumé	Center/Loire	White	Citrus, herbaceous, minerally	Fish	**
Southcorp VDP d'Oc James Herrick Chardonnay	Vin de Pays	White	Citrus, tropical fruit	Fish	**

FRANCE *(continued)*

Wine name	Region	Style	Flavor/Bouquet	Compatible Foods	Price Range
Southcorp VDP d'Oc James Herrick Cuvée Simone	Vin de Pays	White	Tropical fruit, citrus	Veal	**
Sylvan Fessy Beaujolais-Villages	Beaujolais	Red	Berry, spicy	Fish, pork, pizza	*
Taittinger Brut NV	Champagne	Sparkling	Citrus, floral, sweet	Aperitif	**
Taittinger Comtes de Champagne	Champagne	Sparkling	Citrus, floral, complex, powerful	Shellfish	***
Taittinger Comtes de Champagne Rosé	Champagne	Sparkling	Berry, complex, powerful	Duck	***
Taittinger Vintage	Champagne	Sparkling	Citrus, elegant, floral	Fish	**
Tardieu Laurent Comes Vieilles Vignes	Rhône Valley	Red	Floral, berry, mushroom, rich	Beef, lamb	**
Thevenet Macon Clessé Cuvée Levroutée	Maconnais/Burgundy	White	Minerally, mandarin	Pasta	**
Thevenet Macon Clessé Domaine de Bon Gran	Maconnais/Burgundy	White	Citrus, minerally	Chicken	**
Tokay Pinot Gris (André Thomas et Fils)	Alsace	White	Spicy, floral	Fish	**
Tokay Pinot Gris Comtes d'Eguisheim (Léon Beyer)	Alsace	White	Floral, spicy	Mediterranean	**
Tollot-Beaut Chorey-lès-Beaune	Chorey-lès-Beaune/Burgundy	Red	Berry, minerally	Pizza	**
Vallade Fils Cognac	Cognac	Brandy	Spirity, fiery, minerally	After dinner	***
VDP Comte Tolosan Dom de Ribonnet Chardonnay	Vin de Pays	White	Melon, fruity	Fish	*
VDP Coteaux de l'Ardèche Syrah Les Vignerons Ardechois Cuvée Prestige	Vin de Pays	Red	Earthy, berry	Stew	*
VDP Coteaux des Baronnies Dom du Rieu Frais Cabernet Sauvignon (Jean-Yves Liotaud)	Vin de Pays	Red	Herbaceous, berry	Lamb	*
VDP Coteaux des Baronnies Dom du Rieu Frais Syrah (Jean-Yves Liotaud)	Vin de Pays	Red	Berry, earthy	Pizza	*
VDP Côtes Catalanes Domaine Cazes Le Credo	Vin de Pays	Red	Smoky, spicy	Cold meats	*
VDP Côtes Catalanes Domaine Cazes le Canon de Maréchal	Vin de Pays	Red	Plum, spicy	Sausages	**
VDP Côtes de Gascogne Dom de St Lannes (Michel Duffour)	Vin de Pays	Red	Berry, spicy	Cheese	*
VDP Côtes de Thongue Dom de Limbardie (Henri Boukandoura)	Vin de Pays	Red	Berry, spicy	Pizza	*
VDP Côtes de Thongue Domaine Teisserenc Cabernet de l'Arjolle	Vin de Pays	Red	Berry, earthy	Cold meats, stew, offal	*
VDP d'Oc Clos Centeilles Carignanissime (Patricia Boyer and Daniel Domergue)	Vin de Pays	Red	Herbaceous, berry	Stew	**
VDP d'Oc Domaine de Coussergues Cabernet Sauvignon	Vin de Pays	Red	Berry, herbaceous	Lamb	**
VDP d'Oc Domaine de la Baume Syrah Tête de Cuvée (B. R. L. Hardy)	Vin de Pays	Red	Earthy, spicy	Pasta	**
VDP d'Oc Domaine St Hilaire Old Vine Merlot (A. Hardy)	Vin de Pays	Red	Plum, spicy	Cold meats, stew, offal	**
VDP d'Oc Fat Bastard Chardonnay (Gabriel Meffre)	Vin de Pays	White	Tropical fruit, melon	Chicken	**
VDP d'Oc Ptomaine des Blagueurs Grenache Bonny Doon	Vin de Pays	Red	Berry, spicy	Stew	**
VDP d'Oc Utter Bastard Chardonnay (Gabriel Meffre)	Vin de Pays	White	Tropical fruit, oaky	Chicken	**
VDP de la Nièvre Dom des Granges Sauvignon (Myriam de Lesseps-Dorise)	Vin de Pays	White	Zingy, citrus	Shellfish	*
VDP des Bouches-du-Rhône Dom de Trevallon (Eloi Dürrbach)	Vin de Pays	Red	Spicy, earthy	Mediterranean	**
VDP du Gers Cave Cooperative de Plaimont Blanc	Vin de Pays	White	Citrus, minerally	Salads	*
VDP Haute Vallée de l'Aude Pinot Noir Domaine de l'Aigle (Jean-Louis Denois)	Vin de Pays	Red	Spicy, berry	Pizza	**
VDP Herault Domaine Capion Syrah (Adrian Buhrer)	Vin de Pays	Red	Spicy, earthy	Pasta	*
VDP Herault Domaine Grange des Pères	Vin de Pays	Red	Berry, spicy	Stew	**
VDP Herault Mas de Daumas Gassac (red) (Aimé Guibert)	Vin de Pays	Red	Berry, spicy, complex, tannic	Beef	***
VDP Herault Mas de Daumas Gassac (white)	Vin de Pays	White	Zingy, citrus, minerally	Fish	***
VDP Jardin de la France Dom de Bablut Chardonnay (Christophe Daviau)	Vin de Pays	White	Tropical fruit, melon	Fish	*
VDP Jardin de la France Michel Robineau Sauvignon	Vin de Pays	White	Berry, herbaceous	Shellfish	*
VDP Jardin de la France Rémy Pannier Chenin Blanc	Vin de Pays	White	Melon, apples	Aperitif	*
VDP Pyrénées-Orientales Mas Chichet Merlot	Vin de Pays	Red	Plum, spicy	Stew	*
VDP Val de Montferrand Domaine de l'Hortus Grand Cuvée (Jean Orliac)	Vin de Pays	Red	Berry, spicy	Cold meats, stew, offal	**
Verhaeghe Cahors Château de Cedre Le Prestige	Southwest France	Red	Berry, spicy, earthy	Pizza	**
Veuve Clicquot Brut	Champagne	Sparkling	Berry, yeasty	Shellfish	**
Veuve Clicquot La Grande Dame	Champagne	Sparkling	Berry, complex, minerally	Game	***
Veuve Clicquot La Grande Dame Rosé	Champagne	Sparkling	Berry, powerful, floral, rich	Lamb	***
Veuve Clicquot Vintage	Champagne	Sparkling	Berry, toasty, complex	Fish	**
Vieux Château Certan	Pomerol/Bordeaux	Red	Herbaceous, berry, spicy, minerally, tannic	Beef	***
Vieux Château Champs de Mars	Côtes de Castillon/Bordeaux	Red	Spicy, plums	Pasta	**
Vieux Château Gaubert	Graves/Bordeaux	White	Citrus, minerally	Fish	**
Vieux Télégraphe Châteauneuf-du-Pape	Rhône Valley	Red	Berry, herbaceous, spicy, rich	Beef, lamb	**
Vignerons de Buzet Buzet Château de Gueyze	Bordeaux/Southwest France	Red	Earthy, berry	Sausages	*
Villa Bel Air	Graves/Bordeaux	White	Citrus, herbaceous, vanillin	Fish, chicken	**
Vin de Savoie Mondeuse Cru Arbin Vieilles Vignes (Louis Magnin)	Savoie	Red	Peppery, spicy	Cold meats, stew, offal	**

FRANCE *(continued)*

Wine name	Region	Style	Flavor/Bouquet	Compatible Foods	Price Range
Vin de Savoie Mondeuse d'Arbin (Charles Trosset)	Savoie	Red	Peppery, fruity	Game	**
Vin de Savoie Mondeuse Vieilles Vignes (André et Michel Quénard)	Savoie	Red	Peppery, spicy	Cold meats	**
Volnay Champans (Comte Lafon)	Volnay/Burgundy	Red	Earthy, gamey	Game	***
Volnay Clos des Chênes (Comte Lafon)	Volnay/Burgundy	Red	Earthy, minerally, spicy	Lamb	***
Volnay Clos des Ducs (Marquis d'Angerville)	Volnay/Burgundy	Red	Berry, plums	Beef	**
Volnay Santenots-du-Milieu (Comte Lafon)	Volnay/Burgundy	Red	Berry, spicy	Cold meats	**
Volnay Taillepieds (Marquis d'Angerville)	Volnay/Burgundy	Red	Gamey, spicy, earthy	Cold meats	**
Vouvray Cuvée Tries de Vendange (Didier Champalou)	Touraine/Loire	White	Citrus, crispy, minerally	Chicken	**
Vouvray La Cabane Noire (Thierry Cosme)	Touraine/Loire	White	Minerally, apples, citrus	Fish	**
Yves and Matilde Gangloff Côte-Rôtie Vieilles Vignes	Rhône Valley	Red	Berry, peppery, earthy, complex	Beef, lamb	**
Yves Cuilleron Condrieu les Ayguets	Rhône Valley	White	Stone fruit, minerally, rich	Fish, fruits	**
Yves Cuilleron Condrieu les Chaillets Vieilles Vignes	Rhône Valley	White	Stone fruit, rich, floral, complex	Fish, fruits	**
Yves Guilleron Côte-Rôtie "Bassenon"	Rhône Valley	Red	Intense, earthy, minerally	Beef, lamb	**

GERMANY

Wine name	Region	Style	Flavor/Bouquet	Compatible Foods	Price Range
Adelmann Cuvée Vignette Tafelwein	Württemberg	Red	Berry, spicy	Pizza	**
Adelmann Kleinbottwarer Süssmund Riesling Spätlese Trocken	Württemberg	White	Citrus, spicy	Chicken	**
Adeneuer Spätburgunder Auslese Trocken No 1	Ahr	Red	Spicy, earthy, gamey	Sausages	**
Albert Lambrich Oberweseler Römerkrug Riesling Auslese	Mittelrhein	White	Sweet, minerally	Dessert	**
Allendorf Winkeler Jesuitengarten Riesling Kabinett	Rheingau	White	Spicy, minerally	Fish	**
Am Lump Erschendorfer Lump Riesling Eiswein	Franken	Sweet	Sweet, minerally, mandarin	Dessert	***
Am Lump Erschendorfer Lump Riesling Spätlese Trocken	Franken	White	Minerally, floral	Fish	**
Aschrott Hochheimer Hölle Riesling Kabinett	Rheingau	White	Minerally, apples	Fish	**
Bacharacher Posten Riesling Auslese (Karl Heidrich)	Mittelrhein	White	Sweet, honey	Dessert	**
Balbach Niersteiner Hipping Riesling Auslese	Rheinhessen	Sweet	Sweet, citrus	Dessert	**
Balbach Niersteiner Pettental Riesling Kabinett	Rheinhessen	White	Apples, minerally	Veal	**
Bassermann-Jordan Forster Jesuitengarten Riesling Kabinett	Pfalz	White	Minerally, floral	Fish	**
Bassermann-Jordan Forster Jesuitengarten Riesling Spätlese	Pfalz	White	Sweet, floral	Asian	**
Bassermann-Jordan Forster Ungeheuer Riesling Eiswein	Pfalz	Sweet	Mandarin, honey, sweet	Dessert	***
Bassermann-Jordan Ruppertsberger Reiterpfad Riesling TBA	Pfalz	Sweet	Complex, sweet, mandarin	Dessert	***
Bercher Chardonnay Spätlese Trocken SE	Baden	White	Melon, smoky	Veal	**
Bercher-Schmidt Oberrotweiler Käsleberg Weisser Burgunder Spätlese Trocken	Baden	White	Floral, spicy	Pasta	**
BercherBurkheimer Feuerberg Grauer Burgunder Auslese Trocken SE	Baden	White	Mandarin, citrus, minerally	Dessert	**
Bergdolt Chardonnay Spätlese Trocken	Pfalz	White	Citrus, spicy, floral	Veal	**
Bergdolt Kirrweiler Mandelberg Weisser Burgunder Spätlese Trocken	Pfalz	White	Floral, spicy	Chicken	**
Bernhard Hackenheimer Kirchberg Riesling Spätlese	Rheinhessen	White	Sweet, minerally	Cheese	**
Bernhart Schweigener Sonnenberg Grauer Burgunder Spätlese Trocken	Pfalz	White	Spicy, fruity, minerally	Pasta	**
Bernhart Schweigener Sonnenberg Spätburgunder Auslese Trocken Selection	Pfalz	Red	Berry, gamey, spicy	Fish	**
Bernkasteler Doctor Riesling Auslese (J. Wegeler Erben)	Mosel-Saar-Ruwer	White	Sweet, minerally, floral	Dessert	**
Bickel-Stumpf Frickenhäuser Kapellenberg Silvaner Spätlese Trocken	Franken	White	Floral, citrus	Pork	**
Biffar Deidesheimer Kieselberg Riesling Auslese	Pfalz	White	Sweet, citrus, floral	Dessert	**
Biffar Deidesheimer Mäushöhle Riesling Eiswein	Pfalz	Sweet	Complex, sweet, mandarin	Dessert	***
Biffar Wachenheimer Goldbächel Riesling Spätlese	Pfalz	White	Sweet, floral	Fish	**
Bischöfliche Weingüter Kaseler Nies'chen Riesling Eiswein	Mosel-Saar-Ruwer	Sweet	Mandarin, sweet, complex	Dessert	***
Blackenhorn Schliengener Sonnenstück Chardonnay Spätlese Trocken	Baden	White	Citrus, spicy, minerally	Pasta	**
Blankenhorn Schliengener Sonnenstück Riesling Eiswein	Baden	Sweet	Mandarin, sweet, complex	Dessert	***
Bopparder Hamm Feuerlay Riesling Auslese (H. Müller)	Mittelrhein	Sweet	Mandarin, sweet	Dessert	**
Bopparder Hamm Feuerlay Riesling Eiswein (August Perll)	Mittelrhein	Sweet	Complex, sweet, mandarin	Dessert	***
Bopparder Hamm Mandelstein Riesling Spätlese (Walter Perll)	Mittelrhein	White	Sweet, floral, minerally	Fruit	**
Bopparder Hamm Ohlenberg Riesling Kabinett (August Perll)	Mittelrhein	White	Zingy, citrus	Fish	**
Brauneberger Juffer-Sonnenuhr Riesling Auslese (Willi Haag)	Mosel-Saar-Ruwer	White	Sweet, complex, minerally	Dessert	**
Brauneberger Juffer-Sonnenuhr Riesling Beerenauslese (Fritz Haag)	Mosel-Saar-Ruwer	Sweet	Complex, honey, sweet	Dessert	***
Brauneberger Juffer-Sonnenuhr Riesling Kabinett (Fritz Haag)	Mosel-Saar-Ruwer	White	Floral, zingy	Fish	**

GERMANY (continued)

Wine name	Region	Style	Flavor/Bouquet	Compatible Foods	Price Range
Brenner Weisser Burgunder Trocken Selection	Rheinhessen	White	Citrus, melon	Fish	**
Breuer Rauenthaler Nonnenberg Riesling Erstes Gewächs	Rheingau	White	Citrus, floral	Fish	**
Breuer Riesling Brut	Rheingau	Sparkling	Crisp, fruity	Aperitif	**
Breuer Rüdesheimer Berg Schlossberg Riesling Erstes Gewächs	Rheingau	White	Citrus, floral	Fish	**
Breuer Rüdesheimer Bischofsberg Riesling TBA	Rheingau	Sweet	Sweet, honey	Dessert	***
Bürgerspital Randersackerer Pfülben Rieslaner Beerenauslese	Franken	Sweet	Floral, sweet, minerally	Dessert	***
Bürgerspital Würzburger Stein Riesling Spätlese	Franken	White	Sweet, citrus	Asian	**
Bürgerspital Würzburger Stein Riesling TBA	Franken	Sweet	Complex, honey, sweet	Dessert	***
Burggarten Neuenahrer Sonnenberg Spätburgunder Auslese Trocken	Ahr	Red	Berry, smoky	Cold meats, stew, offal	**
Burggarten Spätburgunder Trocken Signatur	Ahr	Red	Berry, gamey	Duck	**
Bürklin-Wolf Forster Ungeheuer Riesling Spätlese Trocken	Pfalz	White	Spicy, minerally	Veal	**
Bürklin-Wolf Wachenheimer Gerümpel Riesling Eiswein	Pfalz	Sweet	Minerally, honey, sweet	Dessert	***
Buscher Bechtheimer Stein Riesling Auslese Trocken	Rheinhessen	White	Citrus, spicy	Chicken	**
Buscher Bechtheimer Stein Spätburgunder Auslese Trocken	Rheinhessen	Red	Berry, spicy	Pasta	**
Castell Casteller Kugelspiel Rieslaner Beerenauslese	Franken	Sweet	Sweet, honey	Dessert	***
Castell Casteller Kugelspiel Silvaner Eiswein	Franken	Sweet	Sweet, mandarin	Dessert	***
Castell Casteller Schlossberg Silvaner Spätlese Trocken	Franken	White	Citrus, minerally, floral	Veal	**
Christmann Deidesheimer Hohenmorgen Riesling Beerenauslese	Pfalz	Sweet	Mandarin, sweet, complex	Dessert	***
Christmann Ruppertsberger Reiterpfad Riesling Spätlese Trocken	Pfalz	White	Citrus, floral	Chicken	**
Christmann Ruppertsberger Reiterpfad Riesling TBA	Pfalz	Sweet	Mandarin, sweet, citrus	Dessert	***
Clüsserath-Weiler Trittenheimer Apotheke Riesling Spätlese	Mosel-Saar-Ruwer	White	Sweet, citrus, minerally	Cheese	**
Crusius Traiser Bastei Riesling Spätlese	Nahe	White	Sweet, floral	Cheese	**
Crusius Traiser Rotenfels Riesling Auslese	Nahe	White	Sweet, citrus, mandarin	Dessert	**
Crusius Traiser Rotenfels Riesling Spätlese Trocken	Nahe	White	Sweet, floral	Fish	**
Darting Dürkheimer Fronhof Scheurebe TBA	Pfalz	Sweet	Sweet, mandarin	Dessert	***
Darting Ungsteiner Herrenberg Riesling Auslese	Pfalz	White	Sweet, citrus	Dessert	**
Dautel Kreation Tafelwein	Württemberg	Red	Berry, smoky	Cold meats, stew, offal	**
Dautel Chardonnay Trocken	Württemberg	White	Melon, spicy	Pizza	**
Deinhard Deidesheimer Grainhübel Riesling Auslese	Pfalz	White	Sweet, floral	Dessert	**
Deinhard Ruppertsberger Reiterpfad Riesling Eiswein	Pfalz	Sweet	Sweet, mandarin	Dessert	***
Deutzerhod Spätburgunder Auslese Trocken Grand Duc Select	Ahr	Red	Berry, spicy	Pasta	**
Diel Dorsheimer Goldloch Riesling Spätlese	Nahe	White	Citrus, sweet	Asian	**
Diel Dorsheimer Pittermännchen Riesling Auslese	Nahe	Sweet	Sweet, mandarin	Dessert	**
Domdechant Werner Hochheimer Domdechaney Riesling Spätlese	Rheingau	White	Citrus, floral	Cheese	**
Dönnhoff Niederhäuser Hermannshöhle Riesling Spätlese	Nahe	White	Sweet, floral	Asian	**
Dönnhoff Niederhäuser Hermannshöhle Riesling Spätlese Trocken	Nahe	White	Floral, apples	Chicken	**
Dönnhoff Oberhäuser Brücke Riesling Eiswein	Nahe	Sweet	Honey, sweet, complex	Dessert	***
Dönnhoff Weisser Burgunder Spätlese Trocken	Nahe	White	Citrus, melon	Chicken	**
Dr Heger Achkarrer Schlossberg Grauer Burgunder Spätlese Trocken	Baden	White	Melon, apples	Veal	**
Dr Heger Achkarrer Schlossberg Silvaner Spätlese Trocken	Baden	White	Citrus, floral	Fish	**
Dr Heger Ihringer Winklerberg Muskateller TBA	Baden	Sweet	Mandarin, sweet, honey	Dessert	***
Dr Heger Ihringer Winklerberg Riesling Auslese	Baden	White	Sweet, honey	Dessert	**
Dr Heger Ihringer Winklerberg Riesling Beerenauslese	Baden	Sweet	Complex, sweet, mandarin	Dessert	***
Dr Loosen Erdener Prälat Riesling Auslese	Mosel-Saar-Ruwer	White	Sweet, minerally, citrus	Dessert	**
Dr Loosen Erdener Treppchen Riesling Spätlese	Mosel-Saar-Ruwer	White	Sweet, zingy, smoky	Fruit	**
Dr Loosen Urziger Würzgarten Riesling TBA	Mosel-Saar-Ruwer	Sweet	Minerally, complex, sweet	Dessert	***
Dr Loosen Wehlener Sonnenuhr Riesling Kabinett	Mosel-Saar-Ruwer	White	Apples, minerally, citrus	Chicken	**
Durbacher Winzergenossenschaft Durbacher Plauelrain Riesling Auslese	Baden	White	Honey, sweet, citrus	Dessert	**
Durbacher Winzergenossenschaft Durbacher Plauelrain Riesling Auslese Trocken	Baden	White	Floral, minerally	Dessert	**
Egon Müller Scharzhofberger Riesling Auslese	Mosel-Saar-Ruwer	White	Sweet, apples, minerally	Dessert	***
Egon Müller Scharzhofberger Riesling Eiswein	Mosel-Saar-Ruwer	Sweet	Complex, honey, sweet, minerally	Dessert	***
Egon Müller Scharzhofberger Riesling TBA	Mosel-Saar-Ruwer	Sweet	Complex, mandarin, sweet	Dessert	***
Ellwanger Winterbacher Hungerberg Weisser Burgunder Auslese Trocken	Württemberg	White	Citrus, floral, spicy	Chicken	**
Emrich-Schönleber Monzinger Frühlingsplätzchen Riesling Auslese	Nahe	White	Sweet, floral	Dessert	**
Emrich-Schönleber Monzinger Frühlingsplätzchen Riesling Kabinett	Nahe	White	Minerally, apples	Veal	**

GERMANY (continued)

Wine name	Region	Style	Flavor/Bouquet	Compatible Foods	Price Range
Erbacher Hohenrain Riesling Erstes Gewächs (Jakob Jung)	Rheingau	White	Floral, citrus	Asian	**
Erben von Beulwitz Kaseler Nies'chen Riesling Kabinett	Mosel-Saar-Ruwer	White	Minerally, apples	Fish	**
F. Becker Schweigener Sonnenberg Riesling Spätlese	Pfalz	White	Sweet, citrus	Cheese	**
F. Becker Spätburgunder Tafelwein Trocken Reserve	Pfalz	Red	Berry, earthy	Cold meats, stew, offal	**
Feindert Riesling Eiswein	Württemberg	Sweet	Sweet, mandarin	Dessert	**
Finkenauer Kreuznacher Kahlenberg Riesling Auslese	Nahe	White	Sweet, citrus, minerally	Dessert	**
Forster Kirchenstück Riesling Auslese Trocken (Eugen Müller)	Pfalz	White	Citrus, spicy, floral	Fish	**
Forster Stift Riesling Eiswein (Eugen Müller)	Pfalz	Sweet	Sweet, mandarin	Dessert	***
Forster Ungeheuer Riesling Auslese Trocken (J.L. Wolf)	Pfalz	White	Citrus, spicy	Chicken	**
Franckenstein Zell-Weierbacher Abtsberg Grauer Burgunder Spätlese Trocken	Baden	White	Melon, citrus	Cold meats, stew, offal	**
Franckenstein Zell-Weierbacher Neugesetz Riesling Spätlese Trocken	Baden	White	Minerally, floral	Chicken	**
Franz Keller Grauer Burgunder Trocken	Baden	White	Citrus, minerally, floral	Asian	**
Franz Keller Spätburgunder Trocken S	Baden	Red	Berry, spicy, earthy	Pizza	**
Fröhlich Escherndorfer Lump Riesling Spätlese	Franken	White	Citrus, floral	Tropical fruit	**
Fröhlich Untereisenheimer Sonnenberg Mukateller Kabinett Trocken	Franken	White	Minerally, floral	Fish	**
Fürst Bürgstadter Centgrafenberg Rieslaner Beerenauslese	Franken	Sweet	Mandarin, sweet, honey	Dessert	***
Fürst Bürgstadter Centgrafenberg Riesling Spätlese Trocken	Franken	White	Citrus, floral	Fish	**
Fürst Bürgstadter Centgrafenberg Spätburgunder Trocken	Franken	Red	Spicy, berry, gamey	Cold meats, stew, offal	**
Fürst Bürgstadter Centgrafenberg Weisser Burgunder Spätlese Trocken	Franken	White	Melon, floral	Fish	**
Gebrüder Müller Ihringer Winlerberg Spätburgunder Spätlese Trocken	Baden	Red	Gamey, berry	Pizza	**
Gleichenstein Achkarrer Schlossberg Silvaner Spätlese Trocken	Baden	White	Minerally, floral	Fish	**
Gleichenstein Oberrotweiler Eichberg Chardonnay Spätlese Trocken	Baden	White	Citrus, melon	Chicken	**
Göhring Dalsheimer Bürgel Weisser Burgunder Auslese Trocken	Rheinhessen	White	Minerally, floral	Chicken	**
Göhring Nieder-Flörsheimer Frauenberg Riesling Spätlese	Rheinhessen	White	Sweet, floral	Fruit	**
Goswin Lambrich Oberweseler Römerkrug Riesling Eiswein	Mittelrhein	Sweet	Sweet, mandarin	Dessert	***
Goswin Lambrich Oberweseler St Martinsberg Riesling Auslese Trocken	Mittelrhein	White	Citrus, floral, minerally	Veal	**
Göttelmann Münsterer Rheinberg Riesling Spätlese	Nahe	White	Sweet, citrus	Fruit	**
Graacher Domprobst Riesling Beerenauslese (Max. Ferd. Richter)	Mosel-Saar-Ruwer	Sweet	Mandarin, sweet, complex	Dessert	***
Graacher Domprobst Riesling Beerenauslese (Willi Schaeffer)	Mosel-Saar-Ruwer	Sweet	Mandarin, sweet, honey	Dessert	***
Graacher Himmelreich Riesling Kabinett (Willi Schaeffer)	Mosel-Saar-Ruwer	White	Crisp, minerally, apples	Fish	**
Graacher Himmelreich Riesling Spätlese (J. J. Prüm)	Mosel-Saar-Ruwer	White	Floral, minerally, sweet	Cheese	**
Grans-Fassian Trittenheimer Apotheke Riesling Beerenauslese	Mosel-Saar-Ruwer	Sweet	Apples, honey, sweet	Dessert	***
Groebe Westhofener Kirchspiel Riesling Spätlese	Rheinhessen	White	Sweet, citrus	Fruit	**
Gunderloch Nackenheimer Rothenberg Riesling Auslese	Rheinhessen	White	Sweet, citrus	Dessert	**
Gunderloch Riesling Kabinett Halbtrocken Jean Baptiste	Rheinhessen	White	Apples, citrus	Chicken	**
Guntrum Oppenheimer Herrenberg Silvaner Eiswein	Rheinhessen	Sweet	Mandarin, sweet	Dessert	***
Gutsverwaltung Niederhausen-Schlossböckelheim Niederhäuser Hermannsberg Riesling Eiswein	Nahe	Sweet	Sweet, mandarin	Dessert	***
Gutsverwaltung Niederhäuser Hermannshöhle Riesling Beerenauslese	Nahe	Sweet	Sweet, honey	Dessert	***
Gutsverwaltung Schlossböckelheimer Kupfergrube Riesling Spätlese	Nahe	White	Sweet, floral	Fish	**
Hahnmühle Oberndorfer Beutelstein Chardonnay Spätlese Trocken	Nahe	White	Melon, citrus	Pasta	**
Haidle Schnaiter Burghalde Spätburgunder Auslese Trocken	Württemberg	Red	Berry, game	Cold meats, stew, offal	**
Hattenheimer Schützenhaus Riesling Auslese (Hans Lang)	Rheingau	White	Minerally, sweet, citrus	Dessert	**
Heilig Grab Bopparder Hamm Feuerlay Riesling Spätlese Trocken	Mittelrhein	White	Citrus, floral	Chicken	**
Heinemann Scherzinger Batzenberg Chardonnay Spätlese Trocken	Baden	White	Melon, minerally, citrus	Fish	**
Heinz Wagner Saarburger Rausch Riesling Auslese	Mosel-Saar-Ruwer	White	Sweet, citrus, floral	Dessert	**
Heribert Kerpen Wehlener Sonnenuhr Riesling Auslese	Mosel-Saar-Ruwer	White	Sweet, minerally, floral	Dessert	**
Hessische Staatsweingüter Kloster Eberbach Erbacher Marcobrunn Riesling Auslese	Rheingau	White	Sweet, minerally, floral	Dessert	**
Hessische Staatsweingüter Kloster Eberbach Rauenthaler Baiken Riesling Auslese	Rheingau	White	Sweet, citrus, apples	Dessert	**
Hessische Staatsweingüter Kloster Eberbach Steinberger Eiswein	Rheingau	Sweet	Mandarin, complex, sweet	Dessert	***

GERMANY (continued)

Wine name	Region	Style	Flavor/Bouquet	Compatible Foods	Price Range
Heyl zu Herrnsheim Niersteiner Brudersberg Riesling Spätlese	Rheinhessen	White	Citrus, floral, sweet	Cheese	**
Heyl zu Herrnsheim Niersteiner Hipping Weisser Burgunder Spätlese Trocken	Rheinhessen	White	Citrus, spicy	Chicken	**
Heyl zu Herrnsheim Niersteiner Pettental Riesling Auslese	Rheinhessen	Sweet	Minerally, sweet, citrus	Dessert	**
Heymann-Löwenstein Winninger Uhlen Riesling TBA	Mosel-Saar-Ruwer	Sweet	Complex, sweet, mandarin	Dessert	***
Hoensbroech Michelfelder Himmelberg Weisser Burgunder Spätlese Trocken	Baden	White	Citrus, minerally	Fish	**
Huber Chardonnay Trocken	Baden	White	Melon, citrus	Fish	**
Huber Malterer White	Baden	White	Melon, fruity	Pizza	**
Huber Spätburgunder Trocken Reserve	Baden	Red	Earthy, smoky	Game	**
Immich-Batterieberg Enkircher Batterieberg Riesling Spätlese	Mosel-Saar-Ruwer	White	Sweet, minerally, floral	Fish	**
Istein Isteiner Kirchberg Spätburgunder Auslese Trocken	Baden	Red	Spicy, berry	Game	**
J. Wegeler Erben Oestricher Lenchen Riesling TBA	Rheingau	Sweet	Complex, sweet, mandarin	Dessert	***
Johannishof Johannisberger Goldatzel Riesling Kabinett	Rheingau	White	Minerally, smoky, citrus	Veal	**
Johannishof Rüdesheimer Berg Rottland Riesling Auslese	Rheingau	White	Sweet, citrus, floral	Dessert	**
Johner Blauer Spätburgunder Trocken (S. J. Johner)	Baden	Red	Berry, spicy	Pasta	**
Johner Chardonnay Tafelwein	Baden	White	Fruity, citrus	Pasta	**
Johner Grauer Burgunder Tafelwein Trocken	Baden	White	Fruity, citrus	Pasta	**
Jost Bacharacher Hahn Riesling Auslese	Mittelrhein	White	Sweet, minerally	Dessert	**
Jost Bacharacher Hahn Riesling Kabinett	Mittelrhein	White	Zingy, minerally	Fish	**
Jost Bacharacher Hahn Riesling TBA	Mittelrhein	Sweet	Minerally, sweet, complex	Dessert	***
Juliusspital Randersackerer Pfülben Rieslaner Auslese	Franken	White	Sweet, minerally	Dessert	**
Juliusspital Würzburger Stein Riesling Beerenauslese	Franken	Sweet	Sweet, mandarin	Dessert	***
Juliusspital Würzburger Stein Riesling Spätlese Trocken	Franken	White	Minerally, floral	Chicken	**
Karlsmühle Lorenzhöfer Felslay Riesling Spätlese	Mosel-Saar-Ruwer	White	Sweet, citrus, floral	Dessert	**
Karp-Schreiber Brauneberger Juffer-Sonnenuhr Riesling TBA	Mosel-Saar-Ruwer	Sweet	Complex, sweet, mandarin	Dessert	***
Karthäuserhof Eitelsbacher Karthäuserhofberg Auslese	Mosel-Saar-Ruwer	White	Sweet, floral, citrus	Dessert	**
Keller Dalsheimer Hubacker Riesling Auslese Trocken	Rheinhessen	White	Floral, citrus	Pork	**
Keller Dalsheimer Hubacker Riesling Eiswein	Rheinhessen	Sweet	Mandarin, sweet, citrus	Dessert	***
Keller Dalsheimer Hubacker Riesling Spätlese	Rheinhessen	White	Sweet, citrus, floral	Asian	**
Keller Dalsheimer Hubacker Riesling TBA	Rheinhessen	Sweet	Complex, sweet, mandarin	Dessert	***
Kesseler Assmannshäuser Höllenberg Spätburgunder Spätlese Trocken	Rheingau	Red	Spicy, gamey, berry	Cold meats, stew, offal	**
Kesseler Rüdesheimer Berg Rottland Riesling Spätlese	Rheingau	White	Sweet, citrus	Cheese	**
Kesseler Rüdesheimer Bischofsberg Riesling TBA	Rheingau	Sweet	Complex, sweet, honey	Dessert	***
Kesselstatt Josephshöfer Riesling Spätlese	Mosel-Saar-Ruwer	White	Sweet, floral	Chicken	**
Kesselstatt Kaseler Nies'chen Riesling Spätlese	Mosel-Saar-Ruwer	White	Sweet, floral	Dessert	**
Kesselstatt Scharzhofberger Riesling Beerenauslese	Mosel-Saar-Ruwer	Sweet	Sweet, minerally, complex	Dessert	***
Kissinger Dienheimer Kreuz Riesling Spätlese	Rheinhessen	White	Sweet, smoky, citrus	Asian	**
Knipser Grauer Burgunder Tafelwein Trocken	Pfalz	White	Melon, citrus	Pizza	**
Knipser Grosskarlbacher Burgweg Spätburgunder Auslese Trocken	Pfalz	Red	Berry, spicy	Game	**
Knyphausen Erbacher Siegelsberg Riesling Eiswein	Rheingau	Sweet	Mandarin, citrus, sweet	Dessert	***
Knyphausen Kiedricher Sandgrub Riesling Spätlese	Rheingau	White	Sweet, citrus	Asian	**
Koehler-Ruprecht Grauer Burgunder Tafelwein Trocken	Pfalz	White	Fruity, melon	Chicken	**
Koehler-Ruprecht Kallstadter Saumagen Riesling Beerenauslese	Pfalz	Sweet	Honey, sweet, complex	Dessert	***
Koehler-Ruprecht Kallstadter Saumagen Riesling Spätlese	Pfalz	White	Sweet, apples, citrus	Fish	**
Koehler-Ruprecht Pinot Blanc Brut Philippi	Pfalz	Sparkling	Minerally, fruity, crisp	Aperitif	**
Königswingert Guldentaler Hipperich Riesling Auslese	Nahe	White	Sweet, mandarin, floral	Dessert	**
Königswingert Guldentaler Hipperich Riesling Spätlese Trocken	Nahe	White	Apples, minerally, floral	Veal	**
Korrell Kreuznacher St Martin Riesling Auslese	Nahe	White	Sweet, citrus	Dessert	**
Kreuzberg Dernauer Pfarrwingert Spätburgunder Auslese Trocken	Ahr	Red	Berry, gamey	Pasta	**
Kreuznacher Brückes Riesling Auslese (Paul Anheuser)	Nahe	White	Sweet, floral, minerally	Dessert	**
Krone Assmannshäuser Höllenberg Spätburgunder Spätlese	Rheingau	Red	Berry, spicy	Pork	**
Kruger-Rumpf Münsterer Dautenpflänzer Riesling Auslese	Nahe	White	Citrus, sweet	Dessert	**
Kruger-Rumpf Münsterer Pittersberg Riesling Eiswein	Nahe	Sweet	Mandarin, sweet, complex	Dessert	***
Kruger-Rumpf Münsterer Pittersberg Riesling Spätlese Trocken	Nahe	White	Floral, minerally	Chicken	**
Kühling-Gillot Oppenheimer Herrenberg Riesling Spätlese	Rheinhessen	White	Citrus, floral, sweet	Fruit	**
Kühling-Gillot Oppenheimer Sackträger Riesling Auslese	Rheinhessen	White	Sweet, mandarin	Dessert	**
Kühling-Gillot Oppenheimer Sackträger Riesling TBA	Rheinhessen	Sweet	Complex, sweet, mandarin	Dessert	***
Künstler Hochheimer Hölle Riesling Beerenauslese	Rheingau	Sweet	Honey, sweet, complex	Dessert	***
Künstler Hochheimer Kirchenstück Riesling Spätlese	Rheingau	White	Sweet, citrus, floral	Asian	**
Laible Durbacher Plauelrain Riesling Eiswein	Baden	Sweet	Mandarin, honey, sweet	Dessert	***

GERMANY *(continued)*

Wine name	Region	Style	Flavor/Bouquet	Compatible Foods	Price Range
Laible Durbacher Plauelrain Riesling Spätlese Trocken	Baden	White	Floral, citrus	Fish	**
Lämmlin-Schindler Chardonnay Spätlese Trocken	Baden	White	Citrus, melon	Fish	**
Lanius-Knab Engehöller Bernstein Riesling Beerenauslese	Mittelrhein	Sweet	Honey, sweet, complex	Dessert	***
Lanius-Knab Engehöller Bernstein Riesling Spätlese	Mittelrhein	White	Sweet, zingy, floral	Dessert	**
Le Gallais Wiltinger Braune Kupp Riesling Auslese	Mosel-Saar-Ruwer	White	Sweet, minerally, apples	Dessert	**
Leitz Rüdesheimer Berg Rottland Riesling Auslese	Rheingau	White	Floral, sweet	Dessert	**
Leitz Rüdesheimer Berg Rottland Riesling Auslese Trocken	Rheingau	White	Citrus, minerally, floral	Veal	**
Lindenhof Weisser Burgunder Brut	Nahe	Sparkling	Crisp, fruity	Aperitif	**
Lingenfelder Freinsheimer Goldberg Riesling Spätlese Trocken	Pfalz	White	Minerally, citrus, spicy	Fish	**
Lingenfelder Freinsheimer Musikantenbuckel Scheurebe Spätlese	Pfalz	White	Citrus, fruity, minerally	Pasta	**
Lorenz Bopparder Hamm Feuerlay Riesling Spätlese Trocken	Mittelrhein	White	Floral, minerally	Veal	**
Lorenz Bopparder Hamm Mandelstein Riesling Auslese	Mittelrhein	White	Sweet, honey, citrus	Dessert	**
Lötzbeyer Feilbingerter Königsgarten Riesling Eiswein	Nahe	Sweet	Complex, mandarin, sweet, minerally	Dessert	***
Lötzbeyer Norheimer Dellchen Riesling Auslese	Nahe	White	Minerally, sweet, elegant	Dessert	**
Löwenstein Homburger Kallmuth Silvaner Spätlese Trocken	Franken	White	Apples, citrus	Fish	**
Lucashof Forster Stift Riesling Eiswein	Pfalz	Sweet	Complex, mandarin, sweet	Dessert	***
Lucashof Forster Ungeheuer Riesling Spätlese	Pfalz	White	Sweet, apples, citrus	Asian	**
Mades Bacharacher Wolfshöhle Riesling Spätlese	Mittelrhein	White	Sweet, minerally, zingy	Fish	**
Männle Durbacher Kochberg Spätburgunder Trocken	Baden	Red	Berry, game	Pasta	**
Männle Durbacher Kochberg Weisser Burgunder Spätlese Trocken	Baden	White	Citrus, mandarin, melon	Fish	**
Mathern Niederhäuser Rosenberg Riesling Auslese	Nahe	White	Sweet, floral	Dessert	**
Mathern Niederhäuser Rosenheck Riesling Spätlese Halbtrocken	Nahe	White	Floral, citrus	Fish	**
Maximin Grünhäuser Abtsberg Riesling Eiswein (Maximin Grünhaus)	Mosel-Saar-Ruwer	Sweet	Sweet, mandarin	Dessert	***
Maximin Grünhäuser Abtsberg Riesling Kabinett (Maximin Grünhaus)	Mosel-Saar-Ruwer	White	Minerally, apples, floral	Fish	**
Maximin Grünhäuser Herrenberg Riesling Spätlese (Maximin Grünhaus)	Mosel-Saar-Ruwer	White	Sweet, floral, citrus	Cheese	**
Meiser Weinheimer Kirchenstück Riesling Spätlese Trocken	Rheinhessen	White	Minerally, spicy	Chicken	**
Messmer Burrweiler Schlossgarten Spätburgunder Trocken Selection	Pfalz	Red	Berry, gamey	Game	**
Messmer Burrweiler Schlossgarten Weisser Burgunder Spätlese Trocken Selection	Pfalz	White	Minerally, citrus	Chicken	**
Meulenhof Erdener Treppchen Riesling Auslese	Mosel-Saar-Ruwer	White	Sweet, floral, citrus	Dessert	**
Meyer-Näkel Dernauer Pfarrwingert Spätburgunder Spätlese Trocken	Ahr	Red	Earthy, fruity	Pizza	**
Meyer-Näkel Spätburgunder Trocken S	Ahr	Red	Spicy, berry	Pasta	**
Michel-Pfannebecker Flomborner Feuerberg Scheurebe Eiswein	Rheinhessen	Sweet	Mandarin, sweet	Dessert	***
Michel-Pfannebecker Westhofener Steingrube Riesling Auslese	Rheinhessen	White	Sweet, floral, citrus	Dessert	**
Milz-Laurentiushof Neumagener Nusswingert Riesling Spätlese	Mosel-Saar-Ruwer	White	Sweet, minerally, smoky	Chicken	**
Mosbacher Forster Freundstück Riesling Eiswein	Pfalz	Sweet	Smoky, sweet, mandarin	Dessert	***
Mosbacher Forster Pechstein Riesling Auslese	Pfalz	White	Sweet, minerally	Dessert	**
Mosbacher Forster Ungeheuer Riesling Spätlese Trocken	Pfalz	White	Citrus, apples	Pork	**
Mülheimer Helenenkloster Riesling Eiswein (Max. Ferd. Richter)	Mosel-Saar-Ruwer	Sweet	Sweet, honey	Dessert	***
Müller-Catoir Haardter Bürgergarten Muskateller Kabinett Trocken	Pfalz	White	Minerally, apples	Chicken	**
Müller-Catoir Haardter Bürgergarten Riesling Eiswein	Pfalz	Sweet	Minerally, sweet, floral	Dessert	***
Müller-Catoir Haardter Mandelring Scheurebe Eiswein	Pfalz	Sweet	Mandarin, sweet	Dessert	***
Müller-Catoir Mussbacher Eselshaut Rieslaner Auslese	Pfalz	White	Sweet, apples, honey	Dessert	**
Münzberg Weisser Burgunder Spätlese Trocken	Pfalz	White	Spicy, fruity	Chicken	**
Nägler Rüdesheimer Berg Roseneck Riesling Kabinett	Rheingau	White	Austere, minerally, citrus	Veal	**
Neipperg Neipperger Schlossberg Lemberger Trocken	Württemberg	Red	Berry, spicy	Game	**
Neipperg Schwaigerner Ruthe Riesling Spätlese Trocken	Württemberg	White	Citrus, floral	Chicken	**
Nelles Spätburgunder Trocken B52	Ahr	Red	Spicy, berry	Game	**
Nelles Spätburgunder Trocken Futura	Ahr	Red	Berry, earthy	Game	**
Niederhäuser Hermannshöhle Riesling Spätlese Trocken (Jakob Schneider)	Nahe	White	Citrus, apples	Chicken	**
Niersteiner Hipping Riesling Spätlese (Franz Karl Schmitt)	Rheinhessen	White	Sweet, floral	Dessert	**
Niersteiner Pettental Riesling Auslese (Franz Karl Schmitt)	Rheinhessen	White	Sweet, floral	Dessert	**
Ockfener Bockstein Riesling Spätlese (Heinz Wagner)	Mosel-Saar-Ruwer	White	Sweet, floral	Fish	**
Oestricher Lenchen Riesling Auslese (J. Wegeler Erben)	Rheingau	White	Sweet, citrus, floral	Dessert	**
Oestricher Lenchen Riesling Eiswein (August Eser)	Rheingau	Sweet	Complex, mandarin, sweet	Dessert	***

GERMANY *(continued)*

Wine name	Region	Style	Flavor/Bouquet	Compatible Foods	Price Range
Oppenheimer Kreuz Riesling Spätlese (Carl Koch)	Rheinhessen	White	Sweet, citrus, floral	Asian	**
P. J. Kuhn Riesling Eiswein	Rheingau	Sweet	Minerally, sweet, honey	Dessert	***
Pauly-Bergweiler Bernkasteler Alte Badstube am Doctorberg Riesling TBA	Mosel-Saar-Ruwer	Sweet	Honey, sweet, complex	Dessert	***
Pauly-Bergweiler Urziger Würzgarten Riesling TBA	Mosel-Saar-Ruwer	Sweet	Complex, honey, sweet	Dessert	***
Pfeffingen Ungsteiner Herrenberg Riesling Spätlese	Pfalz	White	Sweet, floral	Asian	**
Pfeffingen Ungsteiner Herrenberg Scheurebe Beerenauslese	Pfalz	Sweet	Mandarin, sweet	Dessert	***
Pfeffingen Ungsteiner Herrenberg Scheurebe Spätlese	Pfalz	White	Sweet, floral	Asian	**
Piesporter Goldtröpfchen Riesling Kabinett (Reinhold Haart)	Mosel-Saar-Ruwer	White	Citrus, sweet	Salads	**
Piesporter Goldtröpfchen Riesling Spätlese (Kurt Hain)	Mosel-Saar-Ruwer	White	Floral, minerally, citrus	Fish	**
Posthof Gau-Bischofsheimer Glockenberg Riesling Spätlese	Rheinhessen	White	Sweet, citrus, floral	Asian	**
Posthof Grauer Burgunder Spätlese Trocken	Rheinhessen	White	Floral, minerally	Pasta	**
Prinz Hallgartener Jungfer Riesling Auslese	Rheingau	White	Sweet, minerally, apples	Dessert	**
Prinz von Hessen Johannisberger Klaus Riesling Spätlese	Rheingau	White	Sweet, citrus	Cheese	**
Prinz zu Salm-Dalberg Wallhäuser Felseneck Riesling Auslese	Nahe	White	Sweet, citrus	Dessert	**
Prinz zu Salm-Dalberg Wallhäuser Johannisberg Riesling Spätlese	Nahe	White	Sweet, floral	Fruit	**
R. Rebholz Spätburgunder Spätlese Trocken	Pfalz	Red	Berry, spicy	Pasta	**
R. Rebholz Weisser Burgunder Spätlese Trocken	Pfalz	White	Fruity, citrus, spicy	Veal	**
Ratzenberger Bacharacher Kloster Fürstental Riesling TBA	Mittelrhein	Sweet	Complex, sweet, honey	Dessert	***
Ratzenberger Steeger Sankt Jost Riesling Auslese	Mittelrhein	White	Sweet, mandarin, minerally	Dessert	**
Rebholz Chardonnay Spätlese Trocken R	Pfalz	White	Floral, spicy	Fish	**
Rebholz Siebeldinger im Sonnenschein Riesling Spätlese Trocken	Pfalz	White	Floral, minerally	Cold meats, stew, offal	**
Reinhold Haart Wintricher Ohligsberg Riesling Spätlese	Mosel-Saar-Ruwer	White	Sweet, floral	Asian	**
Ress Hattenheimer Nussbrunnen Riesling Spätlese	Rheingau	White	Sweet, citrus, smoky	Cheese	**
Ress Oestricher Doosberg Riesling Beerenauslese	Rheingau	Sweet	Smoky, citrus, sweet	Dessert	***
Ress Oestricher Doosberger TBA	Rheingau	Sweet	Complex, sweet, honey	Dessert	***
Reverchon Filzener Herrenberg Riesling Spätlese	Mosel-Saar-Ruwer	White	Sweet, minerally, apples	Cheese	**
Riesling TBA (P. J. Kuhn)	Rheingau	Sweet	Complex, mandarin, sweet	Dessert	***
Ruck Iphofer Julius-Echter-Berg Scheurebe Spätlese Trocken	Franken	White	Floral, citrus	Veal	**
Ruck Iphofer Julius-Echter-Berg Silvaner Kabinett Trocken	Franken	White	Floral, minerally	Aperitif	**
Salwey Oberrotweiler Henkenberg Grauer Burgunder Spätlese Trocken Alte Reben	Baden	White	Citrus, floral, spicy	Fish	**
Salwey Oberrotweiler Kirchberg Riesling Spätlese Trocken	Baden	White	Floral, citrus	Cheese	**
Sankt Antony Niersteiner Auglangen Riesling Spätlese	Rheinhessen	White	Sweet, citrus	Fruit	**
Sankt Antony Niersteiner Oelberg Riesling Beerenauslese	Rheinhessen	Sweet	Mandarin, sweet	Dessert	***
Sankt Urbans-Hof Ockfener Bockstein Riesling Auslese	Mosel-Saar-Ruwer	Sweet	Citrus, minerally, sweet	Dessert	***
Sauer Erschendorfer Lump Riesling Beerenauslese	Franken	Sweet	Sweet, honey	Dessert	***
Sauer Escherndorfer Lump Silvaner Spätlese Trocken	Franken	White	Floral, citrus, minerally	Cheese	**
Schaefer Ungsteiner Herrenberg Riesling Spätlese Trocken	Pfalz	White	Minerally, spicy	Veal	**
Schaefer Wachenheimer Gerümpel Riesling Spätlese Trocken	Pfalz	White	Spicy, floral	Chicken	**
Schäfer-Fröhlich Spätburgunder Barrique	Nahe	Red	Berry, spicy	Pasta	**
Schäffer Escherndorfer Lump Riesling Spätlese Trocken	Franken	White	Floral, citrus	Chicken	**
Schales Rieslaner Auslese	Rheinhessen	White	Sweet, citrus	Dessert	**
Schales Riesling Eiswein	Rheinhessen	Sweet	Minerally, sweet, mandarin	Dessert	***
Schales Weisser Burgunder Auslese Trocken	Rheinhessen	White	Spicy, citrus	Chicken	**
Schloss Johannisberger Riesling Auslese	Rheingau	White	Minerally, sweet, citrus, floral	Dessert	**
Schloss Johannisberger Riesling Beerenauslese	Rheingau	Sweet	Complex, honey, sweet	Dessert	***
Schloss Lieser Lieser Niederberg Riesling Auslese	Mosel-Saar-Ruwer	White	Sweet, floral, honey	Dessert	**
Schloss Neuweier Neuweierer Mauerberg Riesling Spätlese Trocken Alte Reben	Baden	White	Floral, minerally	Cheese	**
Schloss Ortenberg Riesling Eiswein	Baden	Sweet	Honey, sweet, minerally	Dessert	***
Schloss Reinhartshausen Erbacher Marcobrunn Riesling Spätlese	Rheingau	White	Minerally, citrus	Fish	**
Schloss Reinhartshausen Erbacher Schlossberg Riesling Auslese	Rheingau	White	Sweet, minerally, apples, citrus	Dessert	**
Schloss Reinhartshausen Erbacher Siegelsberg Riesling Beerenauslese	Rheingau	Sweet	Mandarin, sweet, complex	Dessert	***
Schloss Saarstein Serriger Schloss Saarstein Riesling Beerenauslese	Mosel-Saar-Ruwer	Sweet	Sweet, complex, mandarin	Dessert	***
Schloss Saarstein Serriger Schloss Saarstein Riesling Spätlese	Mosel-Saar-Ruwer	White	Sweet, citrus, minerally	Fish	**
Schloss Schönborn Erbacher Marcobrunn Riesling Erstes Gewächs	Rheingau	White	Citrus, floral	Fish	**
Schloss Schönborn Erbacher Marcobrunn Riesling TBA	Rheingau	Sweet	Honey, minerally, sweet, complex	Dessert	***
Schloss Schönborn Rüdesheimer Berg Schlossberg Riesling Beerenauslese	Rheingau	Sweet	Complex, sweet, honey	Dessert	***

GERMANY *(continued)*

Wine name	Region	Style	Flavor/Bouquet	Compatible Foods	Price Range
Schloss Sommerhausen Sommerhäuser Reifenstein Scheurebe Eiswein	Franken	Sweet	Sweet, mandarin	Dessert	***
Schloss Sommerhausen Sommerhäuser Steinbach Rieslaner TBA	Franken	Sweet	Complex, sweet, minerally	Dessert	***
Schloss Sommerhausen Sommerhäuser Steinbach Riesling Spätlese Trocken	Franken	White	Floral, citrus	Chicken	**
Schlumberger Weisser Burgunder Spätlese Trocken	Baden	White	Citrus, floral	Chicken	**
Schmidt Obermoscheler Schlossberg Riesling Kabinett	Nahe	White	Minerally, apples	Shellfish	**
Schmitt's Kinder Randersackerer Pfülben Riesling Auslese	Franken	Sweet	Honey, mandarin, sweet	Dessert	**
Schmitt's Kinder Randersackerer Pfülben Riesling Kabinett	Franken	White	Zingy, minerally	Fruit	**
Schmitt's Kinder Randersackerer Sonnenstuhl Rieslaner Beerenauslese	Franken	Sweet	Sweet, honey	Dessert	***
Schneider Niersteiner Hipping Riesling Spätlese	Rheinhessen	White	Sweet, citrus	Dessert	**
Schneider Niersteiner Orbel Riesling Spätlese	Rheinhessen	White	Sweet, citrus	Asian	**
Schwegler Granat	Württemberg	Red	Berry, plums	Pasta	**
Schwegler Saphir	Württemberg	Red	Berry, earthy	Pasta	**
Seebrich Niersteiner Orbel Riesling Spätlese	Rheinhessen	White	Sweet, citrus, smoky	Fruit	**
Selbach-Oster Bernkasteler Badstube Riesling Eiswein	Mosel-Saar-Ruwer	Sweet	Sweet, minerally	Dessert	**
Selbach-Oster Zeltinger Sonnenuhr Riesling Spätlese	Mosel-Saar-Ruwer	White	Floral, sweet	Fruit	**
Selbach-Oster Zeltinger Sonnenuhr Riesling TBA	Mosel-Saar-Ruwer	Sweet	Complex, sweet, honey	Dessert	***
Siben Deidesheimer Leinhöhle Riesling Spätlese	Pfalz	White	Citrus, sweet	Cheese	**
Siegrist Grauer Burgunder Spätlese Trocken	Pfalz	White	Floral, citrus	Fish	**
Siegrist Silvaner Spätlese Trocken	Pfalz	White	Floral, spicy	Fish	**
Simon-Bürkle Zwingenberger Steingeröll Riesling Spätlese Trocken	Hessische Bergstrasse	White	Floral, minerally	Veal	**
Sitzius Langenlonsheimer Löhrerberg Riesling Spätlese	Nahe	White	Sweet, citrus, minerally	Cheese	**
Sonnenberg Neuenahrer Sonnenberg Spätburgunder Auslese Trocken	Ahr	Red	Berry, plums	Pizza	**
Staatliche Weinbau Walporzhedimer Kräuterberg Spätburgunder Auslese Trocken	Ahr	Red	Berry, smoky	Cold meats, stew, offal	**
Staatliche Weinbaudomäne Niersteiner Glück Scheurebe Beerenauslese	Rheinhessen	Sweet	Smoky, sweet, mandarin	Dessert	***
Staatliche Weinbaudomäne Oppenheimer Sackträger Riesling Auslese	Rheinhessen	White	Sweet, citrus	Dessert	**
Staatlicher Hofkeller Würzburger Stein Riesling Auslese	Franken	White	Honey, sweet	Dessert	**
Staatlicher Hofkeller Würzburger Stein Silvaner Spätlese Trocken	Franken	White	Floral, minerally	Chicken	**
Staatlicher HofkellerWürzburger Stein Riesling TBA	Franken	Sweet	Complex, mandarin, sweet	Dessert	***
Staatsweingut Bergstrasse Heppenheimer Centgericht Riesling Auslese	Hessische Bergstrasse	White	Sweet, honey	Dessert	***
Staatsweingut Bergstrasse Heppenheimer Centgericht Riesling Eiswein	Hessische Bergstrasse	White	Sweet	Dessert	***
Staatsweingut Bergstrasse Heppenheimer Steinkopf Riesling Spätlese Trocken	Hessische Bergstrasse	White	Minerally, citrus, floral	Cheese	**
Stigler Ihringer Winklerberg Riesling TBA	Baden	Sweet	Complex, citrus, sweet	Dessert	***
Stigler Ihringer Winklerberg Traminer Spätlese Trocken	Baden	White	Spicy, floral	Fish	**
Störrlein Randersackerer Sonnenstuhl Silvaner Spätlese Trocken	Franken	White	Minerally, floral	Veal	**
Strub Niersteiner Oelberg Riesling Spätlese	Rheinhessen	White	Spicy, sweet, minerally	Asian	**
Studert-Prüm Wehlener Sonnenuhr Riesling Auslese	Mosel-Saar-Ruwer	White	Sweet, citrus, minerally	Dessert	**
Tesch Laubenheimer Karthäuser Riesling Eiswein	Nahe	Sweet	Sweet, complex	Dessert	***
Tesch Laubenheimer Karthäuser Riesling Spätlese	Nahe	White	Sweet, minerally, floral	Fish	**
Urziger Würzgarten Riesling Auslese (J. J. Christoffel Erben)	Mosel-Saar-Ruwer	White	Sweet, citrus, floral	Dessert	**
Urziger Würzgarten Riesling Auslese (Robert Eymael)	Mosel-Saar-Ruwer	White	Minerally, citrus, sweet	Dessert	**
Villa Sachsen Binger Scharlachberg Riesling Beerenauslese	Rheinhessen	Sweet	Sweet, mandarin	Dessert	***
Villa Sachsen Binger Scharlachberg Riesling Spätlese	Rheinhessen	White	Sweet, floral	Cheese	**
von Buhl Forster Jesuitengarten Riesling Eiswein	Pfalz	Sweet	Complex, sweet, minerally	Dessert	***
von Buhl Forster Ungeheuer Riesling Auslese	Pfalz	White	Sweet, minerally, floral	Dessert	**
von Buhl Forster Ungeheuer Riesling TBA	Pfalz	Sweet	Mandarin, sweet, honey	Dessert	***
von Buhl Ruppertsberger Reiterpfad Riesling Spätlese Trocken	Pfalz	White	Floral, minerally	Chicken	**
von Hövel Oberemmeler Hütte Riesling Auselse	Mosel-Saar-Ruwer	White	Sweet, floral, citrus	Dessert	**
von Kanitz Lorcher Kapellenberg Riesling Beerenauslese	Rheingau	Sweet	Complex, sweet, minerally	Dessert	***
von Kanitz Lorcher Krone Riesling Spätlese	Rheingau	White	Floral, citrus	Cheese	**
Wachenheimer Gerümpel Riesling Spätlese (J. L. Wolf)	Pfalz	White	Sweet, minerally, apples	Fruit	**
Wallufer Walkenberg Riesling Spätlese Trocken (J. B. Becker)	Rheingau	White	Spicy, citrus	Chicken	**
Wallufer Walkenberg Riesling Spätlese Trocken (Toni Jost)	Rheingau	White	Floral, minerally	Chicken	**
Weegmüller Haardter Bürgergarten Riesling Eiswein	Pfalz	Sweet	Minerally, sweet, honey	Dessert	***

GERMANY *(continued)*

Wine name	Region	Style	Flavor/Bouquet	Compatible Foods	Price Range
Weegmüller Haardter Herrenletten Riesling Spätlese Trocken	Pfalz	White	Citrus, floral	Veal	**
Wegeler Erben Forster Ungeheuer Riesling Spätlese Trocken	Pfalz	White	Citrus, floral	Fish	**
Wehlener Sonnenuhr Riesling Auslese (J. J. Prüm)	Mosel-Saar-Ruwer	White	Sweet, minerally, apples	Dessert	***
Wehlener Sonnenuhr Riesling Auslese (S. A. Prüm)	Mosel-Saar-Ruwer	White	Sweet, citrus, minerally	Dessert	**
Wehlener Sonnenuhr Riesling Kabinett (S. A. Prüm)	Mosel-Saar-Ruwer	White	Minerally, apples	Veal	**
Wehrheim Birkweiler Kastanienbusch Spätburgunder Auslese Trocken	Pfalz	Red	Berry, earthy, spicy	Pasta	**
Wehrheim Birkweiler Mandelberg Weisser Burgunder Auslese Trocken	Pfalz	White	Floral, citrus	Chicken	**
Weil Kiedricher Gräfenberg Riesling Auslese	Rheingau	White	Citrus, floral, sweet	Dessert	**
Weil Kiedricher Gräfenberg Riesling Eiswein	Rheingau	Sweet	Honey, sweet	Dessert	***
Weil Kiedricher Gräfenberg Riesling TBA	Rheingau	Sweet	Complex, sweet, mandarin	Dessert	***
Weingart Bopparder Hamm Feuerlay Riesling Auslese	Mittelrhein	White	Sweet, floral	Dessert	**
Weingut der Stadt Bensheim Bensheimer Kirchberg Riesling Beerenauslese	Hessische Bergstrasse	Sweet	Sweet, complex	Dessert	***
Weingut der Stadt Bensheim Bensheimer Kirchberg Riesling Kabinett	Hessische Bergstrasse	Sweet	Zingy, floral	Fish	**
Weins-Prüm Erdener Prälat Riesling Auslese	Mosel-Saar-Ruwer	White	Minerally, floral, sweet	Dessert	**
Weins-Prüm Wehlener Sonnenuhr Riesling Kabinett	Mosel-Saar-Ruwer	White	Citrus, minerally	Fish	**
Weisser Burgunder Spätlese Trocken (Hans Lang)	Rheingau	White	Citrus, minerally	Pizza	**
Wilhelmshof Siebeldinger im Sonnenschein Weisser Burgunder Spätlese Trocken	Pfalz	White	Floral, minerally	Chicken	**
Winzergenossenschaft Achkarren Achkarrer Schlossberg Grauer Burgunder Spätlese Trocken	Baden	White	Melon, smoky	Chicken	**
Winzergenossenschaft Achkarren Achkarrer Schlossberg Ruländer TBA	Baden	Sweet	Sweet, honey	Dessert	***
Winzergenossenschaft Alde Gott Sasbachwaldener Alde Gott Grauer Burgunder Spätlese Trocken	Baden	White	Minerally, melon	Fish	**
Winzergenossenschaft Alde Gott Sasbachwaldener Alde Gott Spätburgunder Spätlese Trocken	Baden	Red	Berry, spicy	Pasta	**
Winzergenossenschaft Bischoffingen Bischoffinger Rosenkrantz Weisser Burgunder TBA	Baden	Sweet	Mandarin, sweet, honey	Dessert	***
Winzergenossenschaft Bischoffingen Bischoffinger Steinbuck Ruländer Auslese	Baden	White	Mandarin, sweet, citrus	Dessert	**
Winzergenossenschaft Britzingen Britzinger Sonnhole Grauer Burgunder Spätlese Trocken	Baden	White	Citrus, melon	Pork	**
Winzergenossenschaft Britzingen Britzinger Sonnhole Ruländer Beerenauslese	Baden	Sweet	Honey, sweet	Dessert	***
Winzergenossenschaft Königschaffhausen Königschaffhauser Hasenberg Ruländer TBA	Baden	Sweet	Sweet	Dessert	***
Winzergenossenschaft Königschaffhausen Königschaffhauser Hasenberg Weisser Burgunder Auslese Trocken	Baden	White	Mandarin, citrus	Veal	**
Winzergenossenschaft Königschaffhausen Königschaffhauser Steingrüble Spätburgunder Trocken Selection	Baden	Red	Gamey, spicy, berry	Fish	**
Winzergenossenschaft Pfaffenweiler Oberdürrenberg Grauer Burgunder Spätlese Trocken Primus	Baden	White	Citrus, minerally, spicy	Fish	**
Winzergenossenschaft Pfaffenweiler Oberdürrenberg Ruländer Eiswein	Baden	Sweet	Mandarin, sweet	Dessert	***
Winzergenossenschaft Sasbach Sasbacher Lützelberg Spätburgunder Auslese Trocken	Baden	Red	Gamey, berry	Duck	**
Wirsching Iphofer Julius-Echter-Berg Silvaner Spätlese Trocken	Franken	White	Floral, citrus	Veal	**
Wirsching Iphöfer Kronsberg Riesling Spätlese	Franken	White	Citrus, sweet	Fish	**
Wittmann Westhofener Aulerde Chardonnay TBA	Rheinhessen	Sweet	Citrus, mandarin, sweet	Dessert	***
Wittmann Westhofener Morstein Riesling Spätlese	Rheinhessen	White	Sweet, minerally, citrus	Dessert	**
Wöhrwag Philipp	Württemberg	Red	Berry, plums	Pasta	**
Wöhrwag Untertürkheimer Herzogenberg Grauer Burgunder Spätlese Trocken	Württemberg	White	Citrus, spicy	Fish	**
Wolff Metternich Durbacher Schloss Grohl Riesling Auslese	Baden	White	Minerally, smoky, sweet	Dessert	**
Wwe. H. Thanisch–Erben Thanisch Bernkasteler Badstube Riesling Kabinett	Mosel-Saar-Ruwer	White	Zingy, austere, minerally	Fish	**
Wwe. H. Thanisch–Erben Thanisch Bernkasteler Doctor Riesling Auslese	Mosel-Saar-Ruwer	Sweet	Honey, minerally, sweet, complex	Dessert	***
Zeltinger Sonnenuhr Riesling Auslese (J. J. Prüm)	Mosel-Saar-Ruwer	White	Sweet, minerally, citrus	Dessert	***
Zilliken Saarburger Rausch Riesling Eiswein	Mosel-Saar-Ruwer	Sweet	Mandarin, sweet, complex	Dessert	***
Zilliken Saarburger Rausch Riesling Spätlese	Mosel-Saar-Ruwer	White	Sweet, minerally	Asian	**

AUSTRIA

Wine name	Region	Style	Flavor/Bouquet	Compatible Foods	Price Range
Alzinger Steinertal Riesling	Wachau	White	Spicy, floral	Fish	**
Emmerich Knoll Kellerberg Riesling	Wachau	White	Floral, minerally	Shellfish	**
Emmerich Knoll Loibenberg Riesling	Wachau	White	Spicy, citrus	Salads	**
Emmerich Knoll Schütt Grüner Veltliner	Wachau	White	Floral, citrus	Chicken	**
Emmerich Knoll Schütt Riesling	Wachau	White	Floral, minerally	Fish	**
Ernst Triebaumer Marienthal Blaufränkisch	Neusiedlersee-Hügelland	Red	Earthy, tannic, oaky	Stew	**
F. X. Pichler Kellerberg Grüner Veltliner	Wachau	White	Floral, citrus	Fish	**
F. X. Pichler Kellerberg Riesling	Wachau	White	Minerally, citrus	Fish	**
F. X. Pichler Loibner Berg Grüner Veltliner	Wachau	White	Citrus, spicy, floral	Chicken	**
F. X. Pichler Steinertal Riesling	Wachau	White	Floral, citrus	Fish	**
Fred Loimer Chardonnay	Kamptal	White	Melon, minerally	Chicken	**
Freie Weingärtner Wachau (FWW) Riesling und Grüner Veltliner from Achleiten and Kellerberg.	Wachau	White	Melon, floral	Shellfish	**
Fritsch Perfektion Grüner Veltliner	Donauland	White	Crisp, citrus	Veal	**
Fritz Wieninger Grand Select Chardonnay	Vienna	White	Citrus, spicy, oaky	Chicken	**
Gross Nussberg Muskateller	South Styria	White	Minerally, grapey	Cheese	**
Heidi Schröck Ausbruch	Neusiedlersee-Hügelland	Sweet	Sweet, rich	Dessert	***
Hiedler Spiegel Weissburgunder	Kamptal	White	Citrus, fruity	Pork	**
Hirtzberger Bruck Riesling	Wachau	White	Floral, minerally	Fish	**
Hirtzberger Honivogl Grüner Veltliner	Wachau	White	Minerally, fruity	Fish	**
Hirtzberger Schön Grüner Veltliner	Wachau	White	Fruity, minerally	Asian	**
Hirtzberger Singerriedl Riesling	Wachau	White	Floral, citrus	Shellfish	**
Karl Alphart Spätrot-Rotgipfler	Thermenregion	White	Floral, spicy	Fish	**
Kollwentz Tatschler Chardonnay	Neusiedlersee-Hügelland	White	Melon, oaky	Chicken	**
Lackner-Tinnacher Grauburgunder	South Styria	White	Spicy, citrus	Veal	**
Lagler Vordersieber Grüner Veltliner	Wachau	White	Spicy, complex, floral	Chicken	**
Lang Scheurebe Trockenbeerenauslese und Eiswein	Neusiedlersee	Sweet	Sweet, honey	Dessert	***
Malat Blauburgunder	Kremstal	Red	Berry, spicy	Game	**
Mantlerhof Reisenthal Roter Veltliner	Kremstal	White	Citrus, minerally	Veal	**
Neumayer Weissburgunder	Traisental	White	Spicy, fruity	Veal	**
Nigl Riesling: Piri	Kremstal	White	Floral, citrus	Mediterranean	**
Polz Grassnitzberg Weissburgunder	South Styria	White	Minerally, spicy	Chicken	**
Polz Hochgrassnitzberg Morillon	South Styria	White	Floral, citrus	Fish	**
Polz Hochgrassnitzberg Sauvignon Blanc	South Styria	White	Grassy, crisp	Shellfish	**
Prager Riesling und Grüner Veltliner from Achleiten, Klaus and Steinriegl	Wachau	White	Citrus, minerally	Fish	**
Prieler Blaufränkisch	Neusiedlersee-Hügelland	White	Citrus, minerally	Fish	**
Proidl Riesling: Ehrenfels	Kremstal	White	Floral, spicy	Fish	**
Reinisch Reserve Blauburgunder	Thermenregion	Red	Berry, earthy	Duck	**
Retzl Bergjuwel Riesling	Kamptal	White	Floral, minerally	Salads	**
Riegersburg Sauvignon Blanc	Southeast Styria	White	Crisp, grassy	Shellfish	*
Saahs Baumgarten Weisserburgunder	Wachau	White	Spicy, citrus	Chicken	**
Saahs Im Weingebirge Riesling	Wachau	White	Floral, minerally	Aperitif	**
Saahs Steiner Hund Riesling	Wachau	White	Citrus, minerally	Salads	**
Salomon Riesling: Kögl	Kremstal	White	Floral, minerally	Fish	**
Sattlerhof Pfarrweingarten Klevner (Weissburgunder)	South Styria	White	Citrus, fruity	Chicken	**
Sattlerhof Pfarrweingarten Morillon	South Styria	White	Citrus, minerally	Pork	**
Schandl Ausbruch	Neusiedlersee-Hügelland	Sweet	Sweet, citrus, rich	Dessert	***
Schloss Gobelsburg Ried Grub Grüner Veltliner	Kamptal	White	Citrus, minerally	Fish	**
Schmidl Kuss den Pfennig Riesling	Wachau	White	Floral, spicy	Veal	**
Sepp Moser Gebling Chardonnay	Kremstal	White	Melon, citrus	Pork	**
Taubenschuss Weisser Berg Weissburgunder	Weinviertel	White	Spicy, citrus	Veal	**
Tement Grassnitzberg Weissburgunder	South Styria	White	Citrus, minerally	Fish	**
Tement Zieregg Sauvignon Blanc	South Styria	White	Crisp, zingy	Salads	**
Tinhof Blaufränkisch	Neusiedlersee-Hügelland	Red	Berry, earthy	Beef	**
Umathum Ried Haideboden	Neusiedlersee	White	Citrus, fruity, minerally	Fish	**
Wenzel Ausbruch	Neusiedlersee-Hügelland	Sweet	Rich, citrus, sweet	Dessert	***
Willi Bründlmayer Chardonnay	Kamptal	White	Tropical fruit, melon	Chicken	**
Willi Bründlmayer Grüner Veltliner: Ried Lamm	Kamptal	White	Citrus, melon	Veal	**
Willi Bründlmayer Riesling: Zöbinger Heiligenstein	Kamptal	White	Floral, minerally	Shellfish	**
Wohlmuth Muskateller	South Styria	White	Grapey, minerally	Fish	**

SWITZERLAND

Wine name	Region	Style	Flavor/Bouquet	Compatible Foods	Price Range
Bon Père Germanier Syrah Cayas	Valais	Red	Earthy, spicy	Stew	**
Bon Père Germanier Vétroz Amigne Mitis	Valais	White	Sweet, toasty	Cheese	**
Bon Père Germanier Vétroz Fendant Les Terrasses	Valais	White	Fruity, minerally	Fish	**
Caveau de Salquenen Salquenen Pinot Noir	Valais	Red	Gamey, smoky	Cold meats, stew, offal	**
Caves Châtenay-Bouvier Oeil-de-Perdrix	Neuchâtel	Red	Berry, floral	Pasta	**
Caves Orsat Primus Classicus Humagne Rouge	Valais	Red	Earthy, berry	Pasta	**
Cressier-Valentin Chardonnay (Jean-Paul Ruedin)	Neuchâtel	White	Tropical fruit, fruity, oaky	Pork	**
Dézaley L'Arbalette (Jean et Pierre Testuz)	Vaud	White	Citrus, floral	Fish	**
Domaine du Mont d'Or Johannisberg Moelleux	Valais	Sweet	Sweet, minerally, citrus	Dessert	***
Domaine du Mont d'Or Petite Arvine Sous l'Escalier	Valais	White	Minerally, citrus	Fish	**
Domaine Les Hutins Dardagny Le Bertholier Rouge	Geneva	Red	Berry, spicy	Stew	**
Domaine Les Hutins Dardagny Pinot Noir	Geneva	Red	Gamey, smoky	Duck	**
Domaine Les Hutins Dardagny Sauvignon	Geneva	White	Crisp, citrus	Shellfish	**
Domaine Louis Bovard Dézaley Medinette	Vaud	White	Fruity, melon	Veal	**
Dupraz et Fils Coteau de Lully Gamaret	Geneva	Red	Berry, gamey	Cold meats, stew, offal	**
Fendant Les Murettes (Robert Gilliard)	Valais	White	Fruity, minerally	Chicken	**
Henri Badoux et Fils Aigle Pinot Noir	Vaud	Red	Gamey, berry	Duck	**
I Vini di Guido Brivio Merlot del Ticino Riflessi d'Epoca	Ticino	Red	Plums, berry	Beef	**
Imesch Leytron Humagne Rouge	Valais	Red	Berry, earthy	Pasta	**
Imesch Petite Arvine	Valais	White	Citrus, floral	Fish	**
Les Frères Dubois Dézaley-Marsens De La Tour	Vaud	White	Citrus, spicy	Chicken	**
Les Perrières Peissy Chardonnay Futs de Chene	Geneva	White	Tropical fruit, melon	Chicken	**
Les Perrières Peissy Chasselas	Geneva	White	Minerally, citrus	Veal	**
Les Perrières Peissy Gamay	Geneva	Red	Berry, fruity	Antipasto	**
Luc Massy L'Epesses Clos du Boux	Vaud	White	Floral, minerally	Chicken	**
Provins Brindamour Malvoisie de Sierre	Valais	White	Minerally, citrus	Fish	**
Provins Corbassières Rouge	Valais	Red	Earthy, berry	Pasta	**
Provins Vieilles Vignes Blanc	Valais	White	Melon, fruity	Chicken	**
René Favre et Fils Chamoson Petite Arvine	Valais	White	Floral, citrus	Fish	**
René Favre et Fils Chamoson Pinot Noir Rénommée Saint-Pierre	Valais	Red	Berry, gamey	Duck	**
René Favre et Fils Fendant Collombey	Valais	White	Minerally, citrus	Fish	**
St-Saphorin Roche Ronde (Jean et Pierre Testuz)	Vaud	White	Floral, citrus	Pork	**
Schaffhausen Hallauer Silberkelch Riesling-Sylvaner (Hans Schlatter)	Eastern Switzerland	White	Floral, citrus	Shellfish	**
Simon Maye et Fils Chamoson Syrah	Valais	Red	Earthy, spicy	Beef	**
Tamborini Merlot del Ticino Vigna Vecchia	Ticino	Red	Spicy, plums	Beef	**
Valsangiacomo Merlot del Ticino Vigneto Roncobello di Morbio	Ticino	Red	Plums, oaky	Pasta	**
Weinbau Nussbaumer Baselbieter Kluser Pinot Gris Barrique (Basel)	Eastern Switzerland	White	Melon, citrus, oaky	Fish	**
Yvorne Château Maison Blanche	Vaud	White	Citrus, spicy	Fish	**
Zürich Truttiker Pinot Noir Barrique (Zahner)	Eastern Switzerland	Red	Berry, oaky	Game	**

ITALY

Wine name	Region	Style	Flavor/Bouquet	Compatible Foods	Price Range
Allegrini La Poja IGT	Soave Classico, Valpolicella Classico/North Central Italy	Red	Berry, licorice, spicy	Pork, lamb	***
Almondo Roero Arneis DOC Bricco delle Ciligie	Piedmont/Northwest Italy	White	Citrus, nutty, floral	Fish, chicken	**
Alto Adige Lagrein Scuro Riserva DOC Untermoserhof (Georg Ramoser)	Trentino-Alto Adige	Red	Plums, spicy	Pizza, chicken	**
Amano Primitivo IGT (Mark Shannon)	Southern Italy	Red	Berry, earthy	Chicken, veal, pork	**
Anselmi Recioto di Soave DOC I Capitelli	Soave Classico, Valpolicella Classico/North Central Italy	Sweet	Sweet, honey, nutty, minerally, rich	Dessert	**
Antinori Tignanello IGT	Tuscany	Red	Elegant, spicy, toasty	Beef, lamb	***
Barbera d'Asti Superiore DOC Montruc (Franco M. Martinetti)	Piedmont/Northwest Italy	Red	Berry, spicy, crisp	Chicken, veal	**
Barolo DOCG Vigneto Arborina (Elio Altare)	Piedmont/Northwest Italy	Red	Berry, licorice, vanillin	Beef, lamb	***
Bartolo Mascarello Barolo DOCG	Piedmont/Northwest Italy	Red	Powerful, berry, spicy	Beef, lamb	***
Bellavista Franciacorta DOCG Gran Cuvée Brut	Soave Classico, Valpolicella Classico/North Central Italy	Sparkling	Stone fruit, yeasty, minerally	Shellfish, nuts	***
Bisol Prosecco di Valdobbiadene DOC Extra Dry Vigneti del Fol	Soave Classico, Valpolicella Classico/North Central Italy	Sparkling	Citrus, minerally, crisp	Shellfish	**
Boscarelli Vino Nobile di Montepulciano DOCG Vigna del Nocio	Tuscany	Red	Rich, earthy, leathery	Beef, lamb	***
Braida Brachetto d'Acqui DOC	Piedmont/Northwest Italy	Red	Berry, crisp, floral	Pizza, chicken	**

ITALY (continued)

Wine name	Region	Style	Flavor/Bouquet	Compatible Foods	Price Range
Ca' dei Frati Lugana DOC I Frati	Soave Classico, Valpolicella Classico/North Central Italy	White	Citrus, nutty, crisp	Fish, chicken	**
Ca' del Bosco Maurizio Zanella IGT	Soave Classico, Valpolicella Classico/North Central Italy	White	Stone fruit, rich, minerally	Fish, chicken	**
Ca' Viola Dolcetto d'Alba DOC Barturot	Piedmont/Northwest Italy	Red	Berry, peppery, crisp	Pasta, chicken, pork	**
Camillo Montori Montepulciano d'Abruzzo DOC Fonte Cupa	Southern Italy	Red	Fruity, spicy	Pizza, chicken	**
Cantina Produttori San Michele Appiano Alto Adige Chardonnay DOC St Valentin	Trentino-Alto Adige	White	Apples, citrus, minerally	Fish, chicken	**
Cantina Sociale di Santadi Carignano del Sulcis DOC Tre Torri	Southern Italy	Red	Rich, plums, earthy	Veal, pork, beef	**
Cantine Lungarotti Torgiano Rosso Riserva DOC Vigna Monticchio	Central Italy	Red	Berry, earthy, leathery	Beef, lamb	**
Castel de Paolis Frascati Superiore DOC Vigna Adriana	Central Italy	White	Citrus, crisp	Shellfish, fish	**
Castello della Sala Cervara della Sala IGT	Central Italy	White	Apples, minerally	Fish, chicken	**
Cavicchioli Lambrusco di Sorbara DOC Vigna del Cristo	Emilia-Romagna	Red	Berry, fruity, crisp	Veal, pork, beef	**
Cesconi Trentino Pinot Grigio DOC	Trentino-Alto Adige	White	Stone fruit, nutty	Shellfish, fish	**
Colli di Catone Frascati Superiore DOC	Central Italy	White	Citrus, crisp	Shellfish, fish	**
Conterno Fantino Langhe Rosso IGT Monpra	Piedmont/Northwest Italy	Red	Berry, licorice, elegant	Veal, pork, beef	**
COS Cerasuolo di Vittoria DOC	Sicily	Red	Berry, spicy, earthy	Veal, pork, beef	**
Costanti Brunello di Montalcino DOCG	Tuscany	Red	Intense, berry, leathery, earthy	Beef, lamb	***
D'Ancona Passito de Pantelleria DOC Solidea	Sicily	Sweet	Sweet, floral, wax, rich	Dessert, nuts	**
D'Angelo Aglianico del Vulture DOC	Southern Italy	Red	Berry, earthy, minerally	Veal, pork, beef	**
Fattoria di Felsina Chianti Classico Riserva DOCG Rancia	Tuscany	Red	Rich, berry, spicy, complex	Beef, lamb	***
Fattoria Zerbina Albana di Romagna Passito DOCG Scacco Matto	Emilia-Romagna	Sweet	Sweet, honey, waxy, floral	Dessert	***
Fattoria Zerbina Marzieno Ravenna Rosso IGT	Emilia-Romagna	Red	Berry, spicy	Veal, pork, beef	**
Fazio Wines Torre dei Venti Rosso IGT	Sicily	Red	Berry, spicy	Veal, pork, beef	**
Feudi di San Gregorio Taurasi DOC	Southern Italy	Red	Rich, fruity, earthy	Beef, lamb	**
Firriato Santagostino Rosso IGT	Sicily	Red	Berry, spicy	Veal, pork, beef	**
Foradori Teroldego Rotaliano DOC Sgarzon	Trentino-Alto Adige	Red	Plums, jam	Chicken, veal, pork	**
Frescobaldi Nipozzano Chianti Rufina Riserva DOCG	Tuscany	Red	Berry, spicy, elegant	Beef, lamb	***
Friuli Isonzo Pinot Bianco DOC (Mauro Drius)	Friuli-Venezia Giulia	White	Apples, melon, crisp	Fish, chicken	**
Gaja Barbaresco DOCG Sori San Lorenzo	Piedmont/Northwest Italy	Red	Berry, licorice, earthy, rich	Beef, lamb	***
Gianfranco Alessandria Barbera d'Alba DOC Vittoria	Piedmont/Northwest Italy	Red	Jam, crisp, rich	Pizza, chicken	**
Girolamo Dorigo Colli Orientali del Friuli Chardonnay DOC Vigneto Ronc di Juri	Friuli-Venezia Giulia	White	Apples, butter, vanillin	Fish, chicken	**
Hofstatter Gewurztraminer DOC Kolbenhof	Trentino-Alto Adige	White	Floral, tropical fruit, spicy	Fish, pasta, Asian	**
Isole e Olena Vin Santo DOC	Tuscany	Sweet	Sweet, honey, wax, nutty	Dessert	**
Kante Carso Malvasia DOC	Friuli-Venezia Giulia	White	Floral, fruity	Asian, shellfish	**
La Monacesca Verdicchio di Matelica DOC	Central Italy	White	Stone fruit, melon	Shellfish, fish	**
La Scolca Gavi dei Gavi DOC Etichetta Nera	Piedmont/Northwest Italy	White	Stone fruit, nutty, rich	Fish, chicken	**
Le Due Terre Colli Orientali del Friuli Rosso Sacrisassi IGT	Friuli-Venezia Giulia	Red	Berry, spicy	Pizza, pasta	**
Le Pupille Morellino di Scansano DOC	Tuscany	Red	Plums, spicy	Pizza, chicken	**
Leone de Castris Salice Salentino Rosso Riserva DOC Donna Lisa	Southern Italy	Red	Powerful, earthy	Beef, lamb	**
Livio Felluga Colli Orientali del Friuli Rosazzo IGT Bianco Terre Alte	Friuli-Venezia Giulia	White	Citrus, crisp, stone fruit	Shellfish, fish	**
Maculan Breganze Cabernet Sauvignon DOC Ferrata	Soave Classico, Valpolicella Classico/North Central Italy	Red	Berry, herbaceous, toasty	Beef, lamb	**
Marco de Bartoli Moscato Passito di Pantelleria DOC Bukkuram	Sicily	White	Sweet, floral, fruity, elegant	Dessert	**
Maso Cantanghel Trentino Pinot Nero DOC	Trentino-Alto Adige	Red	Berry, spicy	Fish, chicken	**
Mastroberadino Greco del Tufo DOC	Southern Italy	White	Floral, nutty, minerally	Shellfish, fish	**
Mazzei Chianti Classico Riserva DOCG Castello di Fonterutoli	Tuscany	Red	Complex, licorice, earthy, spicy	Beef, lamb	***
Miani Colli Orientali del Friuli Sauvignon DOC	Friuli-Venezia Giulia	White	Grassy, zingy	Shellfish, cheese	**
Montepulciano d'Abruzzo DOC Riparossa (Dino Illuminati)	Southern Italy	Red	Fruity, spicy	Pizza, chicken	**
Ornellaia Poggio alla Gazze DOC	Tuscany	Red	Berry, spicy, earthy, toasty	Beef, lamb	***
Palazzone Orvieto Classico DOC Campo del Guardiano	Central Italy	White	Citrus, stone fruit, crisp	Shellfish, fish	**
Pervini Primitivo di Manduria DOC Archidamo	Southern Italy	Red	Berry, earthy	Chicken, veal, pork	**
Pieropan Soave Classico Superiore DOC La Rocca	Soave Classico, Valpolicella Classico/North Central Italy	White	Citrus, crisp, stone fruit	Shellfish, fish	**
Pierpaolo Pecorari Colli Orientali del Friuli Merlot IGT Baolar	Friuli-Venezia Giulia	Red	Plums, spicy	Veal, pork, beef	**
Planeta Chardonnay IGT	Sicily	White	Apples, minerally	Fish, chicken	**
Poderi Aldo Conterno Barolo Riserva DOCG Gran Bussia	Piedmont/Northwest Italy	Red	Complex, berry, spicy, earthy,	Beef, lamb	***
Produttori del Barbaresco Barbaresco DOCG Vigneti in Rio Sordo	Piedmont/Northwest Italy	Red	Berry, licorice, leathery, intense	Beef, lamb	***
Puiatti Collio Pinot Grigio DOC	Friuli-Venezia Giulia	White	Stone fruit, nutty, crisp	Fish, chicken	**

ITALY *(continued)*

Wine name	Region	Style	Flavor/Bouquet	Compatible Foods	Price Range
Quintarelli Amarone della Valpolicella DOCG	Soave Classico, Valpolicella Classico/North Central Italy	Red	Powerful, spicy, earthy	Pork, lamb, cheese	***
Sagrantino di Montefalco DOC (Arnaldo Caprai)	Central Italy	Red	Intense, berry, earthy, complex	Beef, lamb	**
Settesoli Nero d'Avola IGT	Sicily	Red	Plums, spicy, earthy	Beef, lamb	**
Tenuta Bonzara Colli Bolognesi Merlot DOC	Emilia-Romagna	Red	Plums, spicy	Chicken, veal, pork	**
Tenuta La Palazza Il Tornese Chardonnay IGT, Drei Dona	Emilia-Romagna	White	Apples, minerally	Fish, chicken	**
Tenuta San Guido Sassicaia DOC	Tuscany	Red	Berry, spicy, earthy, toasty	Beef, lamb	***
Tenute Capichera Vermentino di Gallura DOC	Southern Italy	White	Crisp, fruity	Shellfish, Asian	**
Teruzzi e Puthod Vernaccia di San Gimignano DOCG	Tuscany	White	Citrus, crisp	Shellfish, fish	**
Tommaso Bussola Recioto della Valpolicella Classico DOC	Soave Classico, Valpolicella Classico/North Central Italy	Red	Berry, licorice, leathery, intense	Beef, pork, lamb	**
Tre Monti Colli d'Imola Cabernet DOC Turico	Emilia-Romagna	Red	Berry, spicy	Pork, beef	**
Trebbiano d'Abruzzo DOC (Edoardo Valentini)	Southern Italy	White	Crisp, citrus, minerally	Shellfish, fish	**
Trebbiano d'Abruzzo DOC Marina Cvetic (Gianni Masciarelli)	Southern Italy	White	Crisp, fruity	Shellfish, fish	**
Turriga IGT (Antonio Argiolas)	Southern Italy	White	Fruity, nutty, elegant	Fish, chicken	**
Valpolicella Classico Superiore DOC Sant'Urbano (F. lli Speri)	Soave Classico, Valpolicella Classico/North Central Italy	Red	Berry, spicy	Pizza, chicken	**
Verdicchio dei Castelli di Jesi Classico DOC (F. lli Bucci)	Central Italy	White	Citrus, crisp	Shellfish, fish	**
Verdicchio dei Castelli di Jesi Classico Superiore DOC Casal di Serra,Umani Ronchi	Central Italy	White	Citrus, honey, crisp	Shellfish, fish	**
Vie di Romans Friuli Isonzo Sauvignon DOC Vieris	Friuli-Venezia Giulia	White	Grassy, zingy	Shellfish, cheese	**
Villa Russiz Collio Tocai Friulano DOC	Friuli-Venezia Giulia	White	Citrus, elegant	Shellfish, fish	**
Vinicola Italiana Florio Marsala Superiore Riserva DOC Vecchioflora	Sicily	Sweet	Sweet, intense, licorice, tangy	Cheese, dessert	**
Vinnaioli Jermann Vintage Tunina IGT	Friuli-Venezia Giulia	White	Rich, fruity, complex	Fish, chicken	***

SPAIN

Wine name	Region	Style	Flavor/Bouquet	Compatible Foods	Price Range
A Portella Viña Mein	Ribeiro/Galacia	White	Fruity, floral	Fish, chicken	**
A Tapada Guitian	Valdeorras/Galacia	White	Fruity, minerally	Chicken, fish	**
Abadia Retuerta Abado Retuerta Cuvée el Campanario	Castilla-León	Red	Berry, oaky	Pork, beef, cheese	***
Abadia Retuerta Abado Retuerta Cuvée el Palomar	Castilla-León	Red	Berry, oaky	Pork, beef, cheese	***
Abadia Retuerta Abado Retuerta Pago Negralada	Castilla-León	Red	Berry, oaky	Pork, beef, cheese	***
Abadia Retuerta	Castilla-León	Red	Berry, licorice	Pizza, pork, cheese	*
Abadia Retuerta Pago Valdebellon	Castilla-León	Red	Berry, oaky	Pork, beef, cheese	***
Adegas Galegas Don Pedro de Soutomaior Carballo	Rías Baixas/Galacia	White	Stone fruit, minerally	Shellfish, fish	**
Adegas Galegas Don Pedro de Soutomaior	Rías Baixas/Galacia	White	Crisp, minerally	Shellfish, fish	**
Adegas Galegas Veigadares	Rías Baixas/Galacia	White	Floral, minerally	Shellfish, fish	**
Adegas Moure Abadia da Cova	Ribeira Sacra/Galacia	White	Stone fruit, floral	Fish, chicken	**
Agapito Rico Carchelo	Jumilla/Mercia	Red	Plums, jam	Pasta, pork	**
Agapito Rico Carchelo Merlot	Jumilla/Mercia	Red	Plums, vanillin	Pork, veal, beef	**
Agapito Rico Carchelo Syrah	Jumilla/Mercia	Red	Berry, spicy	Pork, lamb	**
Agricola Falset-Murça L'Antull	Tarragona/Catalonia	Rosé	Fruity, floral	Shellfish, salads	*
Agro de Bazán Granbazan Ambar	Rías Baixas/Galacia	White	Crisp, minerally	Shellfish, fish	**
Agustí Torelló Kripta	Cava/Catalonia	Sparkling	Crisp, minerally	Cold meats, shellfish	**
Agustí Torelló Mata	Cava/Catalonia	Sparkling	Crisp, minerally	Cold meats, shellfish	**
Albet i Noya Reserva Marti	Penedès/Catalonia	Red	Plums, spicy	Pork, beef, lamb	**
Albet i Noya Syrah Colección	Penedès/Catalonia	Red	Berry, spicy	Mediterrean, pork	**
Albet i Noya Tempranillo D'Anyada	Penedès/Catalonia	Red	Berry, vanillin	Pork, beef, lamb	**
Alejandro Fernández Pesquera	Ribera del Duero/Castilla-León	Red	Plums, leathery, earthy	Lamb, beef, pork	**
Alella Vinícola Can Jonc Marfíl	Alella/Catalonia	White	Fruity, floral	Shellfish, fish, chicken	**
Alión	Ribera del Duero/Castilla-León	Red	Plums, earthy, oaky	Lamb, beef, cheese	***
Alto Aragón Enate Chardonnay	Somontano/Aragón	White	Apples, vanillin	Chicken, fish	**
Alto Aragón Enate Chardonnay-234	Somontano/Aragón	White	Apples, oaky	Chicken, fish	**
Alto Aragón Enate Reserva Especial	Somontano/Aragón	Red	Earthy, oaky	Beef, lamb, pork	**
Alto Aragón Enate	Somontano/Aragón	Rosé	Fruity, floral	Shellfish, salads	*
Alvárez y Díaz Mantel Blanco	Rueda/Castilla-León	White	Melon, apples	Fish, chicken	**
Alvárez y Díaz Mantel Blanco Sauvignon Blanc	Rueda/Castilla-León	White	Herbaceous, zingy	Shellfish, salads	**
Alvaros Palacio L'Ermita	Priorato/Catalonia	Red	Plums, oaky	Lamb, beef	***
Alvear Asunción	Montilla-Moriles/Andalucía	Fortified	Minerally, nutty	Cold meats, nuts	**
Alvear Carlos VII	Montilla-Moriles/Andalucía	Fortified	Minerally, nutty	Cold meats, nuts	**
Alvear CB	Montilla-Moriles/Andalucía	Fortified	Minerally, nutty	Cold meats, nuts	**
Alvear Pedro Ximénez 1830	Montilla-Moriles/Andalucía	Fortified	Sweet, caramelly	Dessert	**

SPAIN *(continued)*

Wine name	Region	Style	Flavor/Bouquet	Compatible Foods	Price Range
Alvear Pedro Ximénez 1927	Montilla-Moriles/Andalucía	Fortified	Sweet, caramelly	Dessert	**
Alvear Pelayo	Montilla-Moriles/Andalucía	Fortified	Minerally, nutty	Cheese, nuts	**
Alvear Solera Fundación	Montilla-Moriles/Andalucía	Fortified	Complex, nutty	Cheese, nuts	**
Angel Lorenzo Chachazo Carmín	Castilla-León	Rosé	Fruity, floral	Antipasto, salads, shellfish	**
Antaño Viña Mocen Rueda Superior	Rueda/Castilla-León	White	Spicy, fruity	Shellfish, fish	**
Antaño Viña Mocen Sauvignon	Rueda/Castilla-León	White	Herbaceous, zingy	Shellfish, salads	**
Antonio Barbadillo Eva Cream	Jeréz/Andalucía	Fortified	Sweet, nutty	Dessert, cheese	**
Antonio Barbadillo Jerez Dry Cuco	Jeréz/Andalucía	Fortified	Minerally, nutty	Nuts, cold meats	**
Antonio Barbadillo Jerez Dulce Laura	Jeréz/Andalucía	Fortified	Sweet, minerally	Nuts, cheese	**
Antonio Barbadillo Jerez Dulce Pedro Ximénez	Jeréz/Andalucía	Fortified	Sweet, caramelly	Dessert	**
Antonio Barbadillo Obispo Gascon	Jeréz/Andalucía	Fortified	Minerally, nutty	Nuts, cold meats	**
Antonio Barbadillo Principe	Jeréz/Andalucía	Fortified	Minerally, zingy	Cold meats, shellfish	**
Antonio Barbadillo Solear	Jeréz/Andalucía	Fortified	Minerally, nutty	Cold meats, nuts	**
Antonio Mascaró Mascaró Brut Monarch	Cava/Catalonia	Sparkling	Crisp, minerally	Cold meats, shellfish	**
Antonio Mascaró Mascaró	Cava/Catalonia	Sparkling	Crisp, minerally	Cold meats, shellfish	**
Aragón y Cía Araceli	Montilla-Moriles/Andalucía	Fortified	Minerally, nutty	Cheese, nuts	**
Aragón y Cía Boabdil	Montilla-Moriles/Andalucía	Fortified	Minerally, nutty	Cheese, nuts	**
Arroyo Tinto Arroyo	Ribera del Duero/Castilla-León	Red	Berry, spicy	Veal, pork, lamb	**
Ayuso Estola	La Mancha/Castilla-La Mancha	Red	Berry, earthy	Pork, veal, lamb	**
Bagordi Ecológico	Rioja/Northeast Spain	Red	Berry, spicy	Veal, pork, beef	**
Balbas Ardal	Ribera del Duero/Castilla-León	Red	Berry, spicy	Pork, lamb, beef	**
Belondrade y Lurton	Rueda/Castilla-León	White	Spicy, fruity	Shellfish, fish	**
Blancos de Castilla Marqués de Riscal Sauvignon	Rueda/Castilla-León	White	Herbaceous, zingy	Shellfish, salads	**
Blázquez (Domecq) Carta Blanca	Jeréz/Andalucía	Fortified	Minerally, nutty	Cold meats, nuts	**
Bobadilla Cream Le Merced	Jeréz/Andalucía	Fortified	Sweet, minerally	Dessert	**
Bobadilla Romántico	Jeréz/Andalucía	Fortified	Minerally, nutty	Cold meats, nuts	**
Bodega Pirineos Merlot/Cabernet-Sauvignon	Somontano/Aragón	Red	Plums, toasty, earthy	Beef, lamb, pork	**
Bretón y Cía Alba de Bretón	Rioja/Northeast Spain	Red	Berry, spicy	Veal, pork, beef	**
Bretón y Cía Dominio de Conte	Rioja/Northeast Spain	Red	Berry, licorice, oaky	Veal, pork, beef	**
Bretón y Cía Loriñón	Rioja/Northeast Spain	Red	Berry, spicy	Veal, pork, beef	**
Briego Albe Briego	Ribera del Duero/Castilla-León	Red	Berry, earthy	Lamb, beef, pork	**
Campillo Campillo	Rioja/Northeast Spain	Red	Berry, spicy	Veal, pork, beef	**
Campillo Reserva Especial	Rioja/Northeast Spain	Red	Earthy, spicy	Lamb, cheese	**
Can Rafols dels Caus Gran Caus	Cava/Catalonia	Sparkling	Crisp, minerally	Cold meats, shellfish	**
Can Vinícolas Reunidas Sot Neral	Costers del Serge/Catalonia	Red	Fruity, berry	Pizza, pasta, pork	**
Canals & Munné Brut Nature	Cava/Catalonia	Sparkling	Crisp, minerally	Shellfish, Asian	**
Casa de la Viña	Valdepeñas/Castilla-La Mancha	Red	Plums, earthy	Beef, lamb, pork	**
Castaño Hecula	Yecla/Murcia	Red	Plums, earthy	Beef, lamb, pork	**
Castaño Monastrell	Yecla/Murcia	Red	Plums, earthy	Beef, lamb, pork	**
Castell de Vilarnau Vilarnau Brut Nature	Cava/Catalonia	Sparkling	Austere, stone fruit	Shellfish, Asian	**
Castell de Vilarnau Vilarnau Vintage	Cava/Catalonia	Sparkling	Rich, nutty	Fish, pasta	**
Castell del Remei 1780	Costers del Serge/Catalonia	Red	Plums, spicy	Pork, veal, beef	**
Castelo de Medina Sauvignon	Rueda/Castilla-León	White	Herbaceous, spicy	Shellfish, fish	**
Castilla la Vieja Bornos Sauvignon	Rueda/Castilla-León	White	Herbaceous, zingy	Shellfish, salads	**
Castillo de Monjardín	Navarra	White	Fruity, floral	Fish, chicken, pasta	**
Castillo de Perelada Castillo Perelada	Empordà-Costa Brava/Catalonia	Red	Berry, spicy	Veal, pork, beef	**
Cavas Hill Brut de Brut Hill	Cava/Catalonia	Sparkling	Crisp, minerally	Cold meats, shellfish	**
Cavas Naveran Don Pablo	Penedès/Catalonia	Red	Berry, spicy	Pizza, pork, beef	**
Cavas Naveran Naveran Clos Antonia	Penedès/Catalonia	White	Fruity, floral	Fish, chicken	**
Cavas Recaredo Recaredo Brut Nature	Cava/Catalonia	Sparkling	Austere, stone fruit	Shellfish, Asian	**
Caves Catasús Casanovas Mas Xarot	Cava/Catalonia	Sparkling	Crisp, minerally	Cold meats, shellfish	**
Caves Catasús Casanovas Mas Xarot Gran Reserva	Cava/Catalonia	Sparkling	Crisp, powerful	Cold meats, cheese, fish	**
Cellers Puig i Roca Avgvstvs Merlot	Penedès/Catalonia	Red	Plums, herbaceous	Lamb, beef, pork	**
Cerrosol Doña Beatriz	Rueda/Castilla-León	White	Spicy, fruity	Shellfish, fish	**
Cerrosol Doña Beatriz Sauvignon Blanc	Rueda/Castilla-León	White	Herbaceous, zingy	Shellfish, salads	**
Clos Mogador	Priorato/Catalonia	Red	Berry, vanillin	Pork, lamb, beef	**
Codorníu Cuvée Raventós	Cava/Catalonia	Sparkling	Crisp, nutty	Cold meats, fish	**
Codorníu Gran Codorníu	Cava/Catalonia	Sparkling	Yeasty, rich	Cold meats, shellfish, nuts	**
Codorníu Jaume de Codorníu	Cava/Catalonia	Sparkling	Crisp, nutty	Cold meats, cheese, fish, pasta	**
Codorníu Non Plus Ultra	Cava/Catalonia	Sparkling	Austere, minerally	Asian, shellfish	**
Compañía Internacional de Grandes Vinos Giró Robot	Cava/Catalonia	Sparkling	Crisp, minerally	Cold meats, shellfish	**
Compañía Vinícola del Norte de España Real de Asúa	Rioja/Northeast Spain	Red	Earthy, leathery	Lamb, beef, cheese	**

SPAIN *(continued)*

Wine name	Region	Style	Flavor/Bouquet	Compatible Foods	Price Range
Compañía Vinícola del Norte de España Viña Real Oro	Rioja/Northeast Spain	Red	Plums, mushrooms	Lamb, cheese	**
Concavins Vía Aurelia Masía Les Combes	Conca de Barberà/Catalonia	Red	Berry, jam	Pork, beef	**
Condada de Haza Alenza	Ribera del Duero/Castilla-León	Red	Plums, earthy, oaky	Lamb, beef, cheese	***
Condado de Haza	Ribera del Duero/Castilla-León	Red	Plums, leathery, spicy	Lamb, beef, pork	***
Contino Graciano	Rioja/Northeast Spain	Red	Earthy, mushrooms	Lamb, beef, cheese	**
Contino	Rioja/Northeast Spain	Red	Earthy, spicy	Lamb, beef, cheese	**
Cosecheros Alaveses Artadi Pagos Viejos	Rioja/Northeast Spain	Red	Plums, earthy	Lamb, pork, beef	**
Cosecheros Alaveses Artadi	Rioja/Northeast Spain	Red	Plums, earthy	Lamb, pork, beef	**
Cosecheros Alaveses Artadi Viña El Pison	Rioja/Northeast Spain	Red	Earthy, spicy	Lamb, pork, beef	**
Costers del Siurana Dolç de L'Obac	Priorato/Catalonia	Sweet	Berry, toasty	Pork, lamb, beef	**
Cuevas de Castilla José Pariente	Rueda/Castilla-León	White	Spicy, fruity	Fish, Asian	**
Dehesa de los Canónigos	Ribera del Duero/Castilla-León	Red	Plums, spicy	Lamb, beef, pork	**
Dehesa del Carrizal	Castilla-La Mancha	Red	Berry, earthy	Lamb, beef	**
El Maestro Sierra Oloroso Viejo 1/4	Jeréz/Andalucía	Fortified	Yeasty, tangy	Cold meats, shellfish	**
Emilio Hidalgo Gobernador	Jeréz/Andalucía	Fortified	Minerally, nutty	Cold meats, nuts	**
Emilio Lustau Amontillado Escuadrilla	Jeréz/Andalucía	Fortified	Tangy, nutty	Cold meats, nuts	**
Emilio Lustau Moscatel Superior Emilín	Jeréz/Andalucía	Fortified	Sweet, rich	Fruits, dessert	**
Emilio Lustau Papirusa	Jeréz/Andalucía	Fortified	Tangy, yeasty	Nuts, cheese	**
Emilio Lustau Pedro Ximénez San Emilio	Jeréz/Andalucía	Fortified	Sweet, caramelly	Dessert	**
Emilio Lustau Península	Jeréz/Andalucía	Fortified	Minerally, nutty	Cold meats, nuts	**
Emilio Lustau Puerto Fino	Jeréz/Andalucía	Fortified	Tangy, nutty	Cold meats, nuts	**
Emilio Moro	Ribera del Duero/Castilla-León	Red	Berry, spicy	Veal, beef, pork	**
Emina	Ribera del Duero/Castilla-León	Red	Plums, spicy	Lamb, beef, pork	**
Escudero Solar de Becquer	Rioja/Northeast Spain	Red	Berry, spicy	Lamb, pork, beef	**
Explotaciones Valduero Valduero	Ribera del Duero/Castilla-León	Red	Plums, spicy	Lamb, beef, pork	**
Fariña Primero	Toro/Castilla-León	Red	Plums, spicy	Beef, lamb, pork	**
Faustino Crianza	Rioja/Northeast Spain	Red	Gamey, leathery	Cheese, lamb	*
Félix Callejo Callejo Magnum	Ribera del Duero/Castilla-León	Red	Plums, spicy	Lamb, beef, pork	**
Félix Callejo Callejo	Ribera del Duero/Castilla-León	Red	Plums, spicy	Lamb, beef, pork	**
Félix Sanz Viña Cimbron Rueda Superior	Rueda/Castilla-León	White	Spicy, fruity	Shellfish, fish	**
Félix Sanz Viña Cimbron	Rueda/Castilla-León	White	Spicy, fruity	Shellfish, fish	**
Félix Sanz Viña Cimbron Sauvignon Blanc	Rueda/Castilla-León	White	Herbaceous, fruity	Shellfish, fish	**
Ferret Ezequiel Ferret	Cava/Catalonia	Sparkling	Crisp, minerally	Cold meats, shellfish	**
Ferris J. Ferris M.	Jeréz/Andalucía	Fortified	Minerally, crisp	Cold meats, shellfish	**
Finace Allende Aurus	Rioja/Northeast Spain	Red	Plums, spicy	Beef, lamb, pork	**
Finca Allende	Rioja/Northeast Spain	Red	Plums, spicy	Beef, lamb, pork	**
Finca Luzón Castillo de Luzón	Jumilla/Mercia	Red	Plums, jam	Pasta, pork, veal	**
Finca Torremilanos Torremilanos	Ribera del Duero/Castilla-León	Red	Plums, earthy	Lamb, beef, pork	**
Francisco Domínguez Cruces-Xamfra Vi de Gel De Gewürztraminer	Penedès/Catalonia	White	Fruity, spicy	Fish, Asian	**
Fuentespina	Ribera del Duero/Castilla-León	Red	Plums, spicy	Lamb, beef, pork	**
Gabarbide Palacio de Otazu	Navarra	White	Fruity, minerally	Shellfish, fish, chicken	**
Gargalo Terra do Gargalo	Monterrei/Galacia	White	Fruity, floral	Fish, chicken	**
Garvey Ochavico	Jeréz/Andalucía	Fortified	Minerally, nutty	Cold meats, shellfish	**
Garvey Pedro Ximénez Gran Orden	Jeréz/Andalucía	Fortified	Sweet, caramelly	Dessert	**
González Byass Amontillado del Duque	Jeréz/Andalucía	Fortified	Tangy, nutty	Cold meats, nuts	**
González Byass Apóstoles	Jeréz/Andalucía	Fortified	Minerally, nutty	Cold meats, nuts	**
González Byass Matusalem	Jeréz/Andalucía	Fortified	Minerally, nutty	Cold meats, nuts	**
González Byass Noë	Jeréz/Andalucía	Fortified	Minerally, nutty	cold meats, nuts	**
González Byass Solera 1847	Jeréz/Andalucía	Fortified	Complex, nutty	Cold meats, nuts	***
Gormaz Doce Linajes	Ribera del Duero/Castilla-León	Red	Plums, spicy	Lamb, beef, pork	**
Gormaz Doce Linajes Roble	Ribera del Duero/Castilla-León	Red	Plums, spicy	Lamb, beef, cheese	**
Gracia Hermanos Gracia Oloroso Cream	Montilla-Moriles/Andalucía	Fortified	Tangy, sweet	Cheese, nuts	**
Gracia Hermanos Montearruit	Montilla-Moriles/Andalucía	Fortified	Minerally, nutty	Cheese, nuts	**
Gramona Celler Batlle	Cava/Catalonia	Sparkling	Crisp, minerally	Cold meats, shellfish	**
Gramona Tres Lustros	Cava/Catalonia	Sparkling	Crisp, minerally	Cold meats, shellfish	**
Grandes Bodegas Marqués de Velilla	Ribera del Duero/Castilla-León	Red	Plums, spicy	Lamb, beef, pork	**
Granja Fillaboa Fillaboa	Rías Baixas/Galacia	White	Minerally, floral	Shellfish, fish	**
Granja Ntra. Sra. de Remelluri Remelluri	Rioja/Northeast Spain	Red	Plums, vanillin	Lamb, beef, cheese	***
Guelbenzu Evo	Navarra	Red	Berry, spicy	Pizza, pasta, pork	**
Guelbenzu Lautus	Navarra	Red	Berry, vanillin	Pork, beef, lamb	**
Gutiérrez Colosa Campo de Guía	Jeréz/Andalucía	Fortified	Fruity, rich	Cheese, nuts	**
Gutiérrez Colosa Sangre y Trabajadero	Jeréz/Andalucía	Fortified	Fruity, rich	Cheese, nuts	**

SPAIN *(continued)*

Wine name	Region	Style	Flavor/Bouquet	Compatible Foods	Price Range
Gutiérrez Colosía	Jeréz/Andalucía	Fortified	Fruity, rich	Cheese, nuts	**
Gutiérrez de la Vega Casta Diva Cosecha Miel	Alicante/Valencia	Fortified	Fruity, rich	Dessert	*
Hacienda Monasterio Dominio de Pingus	Ribera del Duero/Castilla-León	Red	Plums, oaky	Lamb, beef, pork	**
Hacienda Monasterio	Ribera del Duero/Castilla-León	Red	Plums, spicy	Lamb, beef, pork	**
Herederos de Argüesö San León	Jeréz/Andalucía	Fortified	Minerally, nutty	Cold meats, nuts	**
Herederos de Doroteo San Juan Blasón de Costajan	Ribera del Duero/Castilla-León	Red	Plums, spicy	Lamb, beef, pork	**
Heretat Vall-Ventos Chardonnay	Penedès/Catalonia	White	Apples, vanillin	Fish, chicken, pasta	**
Herminia Viña Herminia	Rioja/Northeast Spain	Red	Plums, spicy	Beef, lamb, pork	**
Hijos de Rainera Pérez Marín La Guita Manzanilla	Jeréz/Andalucía	Fortified	Crisp, tangy	Cold meats, shellfish	**
Huertas Rodrejo	Jumilla/Mercia	Red	Plums, spicy	Pork, veal, beef	**
Infantes de Orleans-Borbón Atlantida	Jeréz/Andalucía	Fortified	Minerally, nutty	Cold meats, nuts	**
Infantes de Orleans-Borbón Fenicio	Jeréz/Andalucía	Fortified	Minerally, complex	Cold meats, nuts	**
Insulares Tenerife Viña Norte	Tacoronte-Acentejo/ Canary Islands	Red	Jam, spicy	Beef, lamb, pork	**
Irache Castillo Irache	Navarra	Red	Plums, earthy	Lamb, beef, cheese	**
Irache Prado de Irache	Navarra	Red	Plums, spicy	Lamb, beef, cheese	**
J. Ferris M. Las 3 Candidas	Jeréz/Andalucía	Fortified	Minerally, nutty	Cold meats, nuts	**
Jane Ventura Brut Nature	Cava/Catalonia	Sparkling	Austere, stone fruit	Asian, shellfish	**
Jane Ventura Finca els Camps	Penedès/Catalonia	White	Crisp, fruity	Fish, chicken	**
Jane Ventura Gran Reserva	Cava/Catalonia	Sparkling	Yeasty, minerally	Nuts, sausages, cold meats	**
Jane Ventura	Penedès/Catalonia	Rosé	Fruity, floral	Salads, Asian	**
Jaume Giró i Giró Cabernet Sauvignon	Penedès/Catalonia	Red	Plums, earthy	Lamb, beef	**
Jaume Giró i Giró Selecte Reserva	Cava/Catalonia	Sparkling	Crisp, minerally	Cold meats, shellfish	**
Jaume Serra Cabernet Sauvignon	Penedès/Catalonia	Red	Plums, leathery	Lamb, beef	**
Javier Sanz Villa Narcisa Rueda Superior	Rueda/Castilla-León	White	Spicy, fruity	Shellfish, fish	**
Javier Sanz Villa Narcisa Sauvignon Blanc	Rueda/Castilla-León	White	Grassy, zingy	Shellfish, salads	**
Jean León Cabernet Sauvignon	Penedès/Catalonia	Red	Plums, vanillin	Lamb, beef	**
Jean León Chardonnay	Penedès/Catalonia	White	Apples, buttery	Fish, chicken	**
Jean León Merlot	Penedès/Catalonia	Red	Plums, spicy	Lamb, beef	**
Jean León Petit Chardonnay	Penedès/Catalonia	White	Apples, floral	Fish, chicken	**
Joan Raventós Rosell	Cava/Catalonia	Sparkling	Crisp, minerally	Cold meats, shellfish	**
Joan Raventós Rosell Heretat Vall-Ventos Chenin	Penedès/Catalonia	White	Fruity, floral	Salads, pasta, fish	**
Joan Raventós Rosell Heretat Vall-Ventos Sauvignon Blanc	Penedès/Catalonia	White	Grassy, zingy	Salads, shellfish	**
John Harvey Bristol Cream	Jeréz/Andalucía	Fortified	Sweet, nutty	Dessert, cheese	**
José Gallego Góngora Amontillado muy Viejo Selección Imperial	Aljarafe/Andalucía	Fortified	Fruity, rich	Dessert, nuts	*
José Gallego Góngora PX Dulce Añejo Selección Imperial	Aljarafe/Andalucía	Fortified	Sweet, rich	Dessert	*
Josep M. Ferret Guasch	Cava/Catalonia	Sparkling	Crisp, minerally	Cold meats, shellfish	**
Josep María Raventós Chardonnay Raventós i Blanc	Penedès/Catalonia	White	Apples, buttery	Fish, chicken	**
Josep María Raventós i Blanc	Cava/Catalonia	Sparkling	Crisp, minerally	Cold meats, shellfish	**
Josep María Raventós i Blanc Reserva Personal Manuel Raventós	Cava/Catalonia	Sparkling	Nutty, yeasty	Asian, nuts	**
Julia Roch e Hijos Casa Castillo	Jumilla/Mercia	Rosé	Fruity, floral	Antipasto, salads, fish	**
Julia Roch e Hijos Casa Castillo Monastrell	Jumilla/Mercia	Red	Plums, earthy	Pork, veal, beef	**
Julia Roch e Hijos Casa Castillo Vendímia Selecciónada	Jumilla/Mercia	Red	Berry, earthy	Pork, lamb	**
Julian Chivite Chivite Colección 125	Navarra	White	Stone fruit, minerally	Fish, chicken, pasta	**
Julian Chivite Gran Feudo	Navarra	Rosé	Fruity, floral	Salads, Asian, fish	**
Julian Chivite Gran Fuedo	Navarra	White	Tropical fruit, apples	Salads, fish, chicken	**
Juve y Camps Gran Juve Camps	Cava/Catalonia	Sparkling	Crisp, minerally	Cold meats, shellfish	**
La Invincible Valdeazor	Valdepeñas/Castilla-La Mancha	Red	Plums, spicy	Beef, lamb, pork	**
La Rioja Alta Gran Reserva 904	Rioja/Northeast Spain	Red	Earthy, spicy	Beef, lamb, pork	***
La Rioja Alta Viña Ardanza	Rioja/Northeast Spain	Red	Plums, earthy	Beef, lamb, pork	**
La Val	Rías Baixas/Galacia	White	Minerally, floral	Shellfish, fish	**
La Val Viña Ludy	Rías Baixas/Galacia	White	Minerally, floral	Shellfish, fish	**
Lan Viña Lanciano	Rioja/Northeast Spain	Red	Plums, earthy	Beef, lamb, pork	**
Lopez Heredia Viña Bosconia	Rioja/Northeast Spain	Red	Plums, spicy	Beef, lamb, pork	**
Lopez Heredia Viña Tondonia	Rioja/Northeast Spain	Red	Plums, spicy	Beef, lamb, pork	**
López Cristobal	Ribera del Duero/Castilla-León	Red	Plums, spicy	Lamb, beef, pork	**
López Hermanos Málaga Virgen	Málaga/Andalucía	Fortified	Sweet, caramelly	Dessert, cheese	**
López Hermanos Trajinero	Málaga/Andalucía	Fortified	Sweet, caramelly	Dessert, cheese	**
Los Curros Viña Cantosan Sauvignon Blanc	Rueda/Castilla-León	White	Grassy, zingy	Shellfish, salads	**
Los Curros Yllera	Castilla-León	Red	Plums, berry	Chicken, beef, pork	**
Luberri Altun	Rioja/Northeast Spain	Red	Berry, earthy	Veal, pork, lamb	**
Luberri	Rioja/Northeast Spain	Red	Berry, spicy	Veal, pork, beef	**
Luís Cañas Recian	Rioja/Northeast Spain	Red	Plums, spicy	Beef, lamb, pork	**

SPAIN *(continued)*

Wine name	Region	Style	Flavor/Bouquet	Compatible Foods	Price Range
Luís Cañas	Rioja/Northeast Spain	Red	Plums, spicy	Beef, lamb, pork	**
M. Gil Luque Amontillado de Bandera	Jeréz/Andalucía	Fortified	Nutty, yeasty	Cold meats, nuts	**
M. Gil Luque Moscatel de Bandera	Jeréz/Andalucía	Fortified	Sweet, rich	Fruits, dessert	**
M. Gil Luque Oloroso de Bandera	Jeréz/Andalucía	Fortified	Yeasty, tangy	Cold meats, shellfish	**
M. Gil Luque Palo Cortado de Bandera	Jeréz/Andalucía	Fortified	Nutty, tangy	Cold meats, nuts	**
M. Gil Luque Pedro Ximénez de Bandera	Jeréz/Andalucía	Fortified	Sweet, caramelly	Dessert	**
Macia Batle	Binissalem/Balearic Islands	White	Fruity, floral	Fish, chicken, veal	**
Manuel de Argüeso Pedro Ximénez en Candado	Jeréz/Andalucía	Fortified	Sweet, caramelly	Dessert	**
Manuel Manzaneque Chardonnay	Sierra de Alcaraz/ Castilla-La Mancha	White	Fruity, vanillin	Chicken, fish	**
Manuel Manzaneque Finca Elez	Sierra de Alcaraz/ Castilla-La Mancha	Red	Berry, spicy	Veal, pork, beef	**
Manuel Sancho e Hijas Mont Marçal Brut Nature	Cava/Catalonia	Sparkling	Austere, minerally	Asian, shellfish	**
Marco Real Homenaje	Navarra	Red	Berry, spicy	Pizza, pork, beef	**
Marqués de Griñón Dominio de Valdepusa Cabernet Sauvignon	Toledo/Castilla-La Mancha	Red	Plums, leathery, earthy	Beef, lamb, pork	**
Marqués de Griñón Dominio de Valdepusa Syrah	Toledo/Castilla-La Mancha	Red	Berry, licorice, spicy	Veal, pork, beef	**
Marqués de Murrieta Castillo Ygay	Rioja/Northeast Spain	Red	Rich, plums, earthy, toasty	Beef, lamb, pork	**
Marqués de Murrieta Dalmau	Rioja/Northeast Spain	Red	Plums, spicy	Beef, lamb, pork	**
Marqués de Riscal Baron de Chirel	Rioja/Northeast Spain	Red	Plums, spicy	Beef, lamb, pork	**
Marqués de Riscal	Rioja/Northeast Spain	Red	Earthy, leathery	Beef, lamb, pork	**
Marqués de Victoria	Rioja/Northeast Spain	Red	Plums, spicy	Beef, lamb, pork	**
Marqués del Real Tesoro Del Principe	Jeréz/Andalucía	Fortified	Minerally, nutty	Cheese, nuts	**
Marquésa Valserrano	Rioja/Northeast Spain	Red	Plums, spicy	Beef, lamb, pork	**
Martín Códax Burgans	Rías Baixas/Galacia	White	Minerally, tropical fruit	Shellfish, Asian	**
Martín Códax Organistrum	Rías Baixas/Galacia	White	Minerally, floral	Shellfish, fish	**
Martín Códax	Rías Baixas/Galacia	White	Minerally, floral	Shellfish, fish	**
Martínez Bujanda Finca Valpiedra	Rioja/Northeast Spain	Red	Berry, licorice, oaky	Veal, pork, beef	***
Martínez Bujanda Valdemar	Rioja/Northeast Spain	Red	Plums, earthy, spicy, oaky	Beef, lamb, pork	**
Martínez Bujanda Vendímia Selecciónada	Rioja/Northeast Spain	Red	Complex, earthy	Beef, lamb, pork	***
Mas Estela Soda Vinya Selva de Mar Mas Estella Garnatxa	Empordà-Costa Brava/Catalonia	Sweet	Rich, fruity	Dessert	**
Mas Florit	Cava/Catalonia	Sparkling	Crisp, minerally	Cold meats, shellfish	**
Mas Martinet Vinicultors Clos Martinet	Priorato/Catalonia	Red	Berry, spicy	Pork, lamb, beef	**
Mas Tinell	Cava/Catalonia	Sparkling	Crisp, minerally	Cold meats, shellfish	**
Masia Bach Bach Cabernet-Sauvignon	Penedès/Catalonia	Red	Plums, earthy	Lamb, beef	**
Masia Bach Bach Chardonnay	Penedès/Catalonia	White	Apples, vanillin	Fish, chicken	**
Masroig Les Sorts	Tarragona/Catalonia	Red	Plums, spicy	Beef, lamb, pork	**
Mauro	Castilla-León	Red	Plums, spicy	Pork, beef, lamb	**
Mauro San Roman	Castilla-León	Red	Berry, spicy	Pizza, pork, beef	**
Mauro Vendímia Selecciónada	Castilla-León	Red	Plums, jam	Pork, veal, beef	**
Miguel Torres Atrium	Penedès/Catalonia	Red	Berry, spicy	Veal, chicken, pork	**
Miguel Torres Fransola	Penedès/Catalonia	White	Floral, spicy	Salads, shellfish	**
Miguel Torres Gran Coronas	Penedès/Catalonia	Red	Plums, earthy	Lamb, beef, pork	**
Miguel Torres Gran Viña Sol	Penedès/Catalonia	White	Rich, fruity	Pasta, chicken	**
Miguel Torres Grans Muralles	Conca de Barberà/Catalonia	Red	Plums, earthy	Pork, beef	**
Miguel Torres Mas la Plana Gran Coronas	Penedès/Catalonia	Red	Plums, toasty	Lamb, beef, pork	***
Miguel Torres Milmanda	Conca de Barberà/Catalonia	White	Buttery, toasty	Fish, pasta	***
Miguel Torres Viña Esmerelda	Penedès/Catalonia	White	Spicy, fruity	Shellfish, salads	**
Miguel Torres Waltraud	Penedès/Catalonia	White	Fruity, floral	Fish, chicken	**
Miquel Oliver Ses Ferritges	Pla i Llevant de Mallorca/ Balearic Islands	Red	Berry, spicy	Chicken, veal, beef	**
Molí Coloma Sumarroca Gran Brut	Cava/Catalonia	Sparkling	Crisp, minerally	Cold meats, shellfish	**
Montecillo	Rioja/Northeast Spain	Red	Earthy, gamey	Lamb, cheese	**
Muga Prado Enea	Rioja/Northeast Spain	Red	Rich, oaky	Beef, lamb, pork	***
Muga Torre Muga	Rioja/Northeast Spain	Red	Rich, oaky	Beef, lamb, pork	***
Nadal Cava Nadal Especial	Cava/Catalonia	Sparkling	Crisp, minerally	Cold meats, shellfish	**
Naveran	Penedès/Catalonia	Red	Berry, spicy	Chicken, veal, beef	**
Ntra. Sra. de la Cabeza Casa Gualda	La Mancha/Castilla-La Mancha	Red	Plums, earthy	Pork, veal, lamb	**
Ochoa Ochoa Moscatel	Navarra	Sweet	Fruity, rich	Dessert, cheese	**
Osborne y Cía Alonso el Sabio	Jeréz/Andalucía	Fortified	Minerally, nutty	Cold meats, nuts	**
Osborne y Cía Aos Solera	Jeréz/Andalucía	Fortified	Complex, rich	Cold meats, nuts	**
Osborne y Cía Bailen	Jeréz/Andalucía	Fortified	Minerally, nutty	Cold meats, nuts	**
Osborne y Cía Coquinero Dry	Jeréz/Andalucía	Fortified	Minerally, nutty	Cold meats, nuts	**
Osborne y Cía Fino Quinta	Jeréz/Andalucía	Fortified	Minerally, zingy	Cold meats, shellfish	**

SPAIN *(continued)*

Wine name	Region	Style	Flavor/Bouquet	Compatible Foods	Price Range
Osborne y Cía Moscatel Fruta	Jeréz/Andalucía	Fortified	Sweet, rich	Fruits, dessert	**
Osborne y Cía P Triangulo P	Jeréz/Andalucía	Fortified	Minerally, nutty	Cold meats, nuts	**
Osborne y Cía Pedro Ximénez 1827	Jeréz/Andalucía	Fortified	Sweet, caramelly	Dessert	**
Osborne y Cía Solera India	Jeréz/Andalucía	Fortified	Rich, nutty	Cheese, nuts	**
Osborne y Cía Very Old Dry Oloroso	Jeréz/Andalucía	Fortified	Tangy, complex	Cheese, nuts	**
Ostatu	Rioja/Northeast Spain	White	Fruity, floral	Fish, chicken	**
Pago de Carraovejas	Ribera del Duero/Castilla-León	Red	Plums, spicy	Lamb, beef, pork	**
Palacio de Fefiñanes Albariño	Rías Baixas/Galacia	White	Minerally, floral	Shellfish, Asian	**
Palacio Regio	Rioja/Northeast Spain	White	Fruity, floral	Fish, chicken	**
Palacio Reserva Especial	Rioja/Northeast Spain	Red	Plums, spicy	Beef, lamb, pork	**
Palacios Remondo 2 Viñedos	Rioja/Northeast Spain	Red	Plums, spicy	Beef, lamb, pork	**
Parxet Marqués de Alella Chardonnay	Alella/Catalonia	White	Apples, fruity	Fish, chicken	**
Parxet Marqués de Alella Clásico	Alella/Catalonia	White	Stone fruit, floral	Shellfish, fish, chicken	**
Parxet Marqués de Alella Seco	Alella/Catalonia	White	Minerally, crisp	Salads, Asian, shellfish	**
Pazo de Señorans	Rías Baixas/Galacia	White	Minerally, floral	Shellfish, fish	**
Pedro Domecq Amontillado 51-1ª	Jeréz/Andalucía	Fortified	Tangy, nutty	Cold meats, nuts	**
Pedro Domecq Botaina	Jeréz/Andalucía	Fortified	Minerally, nutty	Cold meats, nuts	**
Pedro Domecq Capuchino	Jeréz/Andalucía	Fortified	Minerally, nutty	Cold meats, nuts	**
Pedro Domecq La Ina	Jeréz/Andalucía	Fortified	Minerally, zingy	Cold meats, nuts	**
Pedro Domecq Rio Viejo	Jeréz/Andalucía	Fortified	Minerally, nutty	Cold meats, nuts	**
Pedro Domecq Sibarita	Jeréz/Andalucía	Fortified	Nutty, rich	Cheese, nuts	**
Pedro Domecq Venerable	Jeréz/Andalucía	Fortified	Complex, rich	Cheese, nuts	**
Pere Guardiola Petit Floresta	Empordà-CB	Red	Berry, spicy	Pizza, pork, chicken	**
Perez Caramés Casar de Santa Inés	Bierzo/Castilla-León	Red	Berry, spicy	Pizza, pasta, pork	**
Perez Pascuas Viña Pedrosa	Ribera del Duero/Castilla-León	Red	Berry, earthy	Lamb, beef, pork	**
Pérez Barquero Gran Barquero Amontillado	Montilla-Moriles/Andalucía	Fortified	Tangy, nutty	Cold meats, nuts	**
Pérez Barquero Gran Barquero Cream	Montilla-Moriles/Andalucía	Fortified	Sweet, nutty	Dessert, cheese	**
Pérez Barquero Gran Barquero	Montilla-Moriles/Andalucía	Fortified	Minerally, nutty	Cold meats, nuts	**
Pérez Barquero Gran Barquero Pedro Ximénez	Montilla-Moriles/Andalucía	Fortified	Sweet, caramelly	Dessert	**
Piedemonte Moscatel	Navarra	Sweet	Fruity, rich	Dessert, cheese	**
Pilar Aranda Amontillado 1730	Jeréz/Andalucía	Fortified	Tangy, nutty	Cold meats, nuts	**
Pilar Aranda La Jaca	Jeréz/Andalucía	Fortified	Minerally, nutty	Cold meats, nuts	**
Pilar Aranda Oloroso 1730	Jeréz/Andalucía	Fortified	Tangy, yeasty	Cheese, nuts	**
Pilar Aranda Palo Cortado 1730	Jeréz/Andalucía	Fortified	Tangy, minerally	Cold meats, nuts	**
Piñol L'Avi Arrufi	Terra Alta/Catalonia	Red	Berry, spicy	Beef, lamb, pork	**
Piqueras Castillo de Almansa	Almansa/Castilla-La Mancha	Red	Plums, berry	Veal, pork, beef	**
Pirineos Señorío de Lazan	Somontano/Aragón	Red	Plums, spicy	Beef, lamb, pork	**
Primicia Viña Carravalseca	Rioja/Northeast Spain	Red	Plums, earthy	Beef, lamb, pork	**
Primicia Viña Diezmo	Rioja/Northeast Spain	Red	Plums, spicy	Beef, lamb, pork	**
Raïmat Abadia	Costers del Serge/Catalonia	Red	Berry, earthy	Pork, veal, beef	**
Raïmat Cabernet Sauvignon	Costers del Serge/Catalonia	Red	Plums, leathery	Lamb, beef	**
Raïmat Casal	Costers del Serge/Catalonia	White	Floral, fruity	Fish, chicken	**
Raïmat Gran Brut	Cava/Catalonia	Sparkling	Crisp, minerally	Cold meats, shellfish	**
Raïmat Mas Castell	Costers del Serge/Catalonia	Red	Berry, earthy	Pork, beef	**
Raventós i Blanc Gran Reserva	Cava/Catalonia	Sparkling	Nutty, yeasty	Fish, pasta, nuts	**
Real Sitio de Ventosilla Pradorey	Ribera del Duero/Castilla-León	Red	Berry, vanillin	Lamb, beef, pork	**
Real Vega Ibor	Valdepeñas/Castilla-La Mancha	Red	Plums, earthy	Beef, lamb, pork	**
Remirez de Ganuza	Rioja/Northeast Spain	Red	Plums, spicy	Beef, lamb, pork	**
Rene Barbier Cabernet Sauvignon	Penedès/Catalonia	Red	Plums, toasty	Beef, lamb	**
Rene Barbier Chardonnay	Penedès/Catalonia	White	Apples, buttery	Fish, chicken	**
Reserva Mont-Ferrant Mont-Ferrant Brut Reserva	Cava/Catalonia	Sparkling	Nutty, stone fruit	Fish, Asian	**
Reyes Teófilo Reyes	Ribera del Duero/Castilla-León	Red	Plums, leathery, earthy, complex	Lamb, beef, pork	***
Ricard M. De Simon Rimarts	Penedès/Catalonia	Rosé	Fruity, floral	Salads, fish	**
Rimarts	Penedès/Catalonia	Red	Berry, spicy	Chicken, veal, beef	**
Rimarts Reserva Especial Chardonnay	Cava/Catalonia	Sparkling	Apples, minerally	Fish, pasta, salads	**
Riojanas Monte Real	Rioja/Northeast Spain	Red	Plums, earthy	Beef, lamb, pork	**
Riojanas Viña Albina	Rioja/Northeast Spain	Red	Plums, spicy	Beef, lamb, pork	**
Robles Cream Selección	Montilla-Moriles/Andalucía	Fortified	Sweet, nutty	Dessert, cheese	**
Roda I	Rioja/Northeast Spain	Red	Rich, oaky	Beef, lamb, pork	***
Roda II	Rioja/Northeast Spain	Red	Rich, oaky	Beef, lamb, pork	***
Rodero Carmelo Rodero	Ribera del Duero/Castilla-León	Red	Plums, spicy	Lamb, beef, pork	**
Roger Goulart Brut Nature	Cava/Catalonia	Sparkling	Austere, stone fruit	Asian, shellfish	**
Rotllan i Tora Amadis	Priorato/Catalonia	Red	Berry, spicy	Pork, lamb, beef	**

SPAIN *(continued)*

Wine name	Region	Style	Flavor/Bouquet	Compatible Foods	Price Range
Rotllan i Tora Balandra	Priorato/Catalonia	Red	Berry, spicy	Pork, lamb, beef	**
Roura Chardonnay	Alella/Catalonia	White	Apples, buttery	Fish, chicken, pasta	**
Rovellats Brut Nature	Cava/Catalonia	Sparkling	Austere, minerally	Asian, shellfish	**
San Salvador Galcibar	Navarra	Rosé	Fruity, floral	Salads, fish	**
Sanchez Romate Hermanos NPU	Jeréz/Andalucía	Fortified	Minerally, nutty	Cold meats, nuts	**
Sandeman-Coprimar Armada	Jeréz/Andalucía	Fortified	Minerally, sweet	Cheese, nuts	**
Sandeman-Coprimar Royal Ambrosante	Jeréz/Andalucía	Fortified	Minerally, nutty	Cheese, nuts	**
Sandeman-Coprimar Royal Corregidor	Jeréz/Andalucía	Fortified	Minerally, nutty	Cold meats, nuts	**
Sandeman-Coprimar Royal Esmerelda	Jeréz/Andalucía	Fortified	Minerally, nutty	Cheese, nuts	**
Santa Eulalia Conde de Siruela	Ribera del Duero/Castilla-León	Red	Plums, earthy	Lamb, beef, pork	**
Santa Eulalia Riberal	Ribera del Duero/Castilla-León	Red	Plums, leathery	Lamb, beef, pork	**
Segura Viudas Reserva Heredad	Cava/Catalonia	Sparkling	Powerful, minerally	Fish, pasta, Asian	**
Señorío de Condestable Finca Luzón	Jumilla/Mercia	Red	Plums, jam	Pasta, pork	**
Señorío de Nava	Ribera del Duero/Castilla-León	Red	Plums, spicy	Lamb, beef, pork	**
Sierra Cantabria Collección Privada	Rioja/Northeast Spain	Red	Plums, spicy	Beef, lamb, pork	**
Sierra Cantabria	Rioja/Northeast Spain	Red	Plums, oaky	Beef, lamb, pork	**
Signat	Cava/Catalonia	Sparkling	Crisp, minerally	Cold meats, shellfish	**
Solar de Urbezo Viña Urbezo	Cariñena/Aragón	Red	Berry, plums	Pork, lamb	**
Terras Gauda	Rías Baixas/Galacia	White	Minerally, tropical fruit	Shellfish, fish	**
Toro Albalá Don PX Gran Reserva 1972	Montilla-Moriles/Andalucía	Fortified	Complex, caramelly	Dessert	***
Toro Albalá Viejísimo Solera 1922	Montilla-Moriles/Andalucía	Fortified	Minerally, nutty	Cold meats, nuts	***
Torre de Oña Baron de Oña	Rioja/Northeast Spain	Red	Berry, oaky	Beef, lamb, pork	**
Torreblanca	Cava/Catalonia	Sparkling	Crisp, minerally	Cold meats, shellfish	**
Torreblanca Masblanc	Cava/Catalonia	Sparkling	Crisp, rich	Cold meats, shellfish	**
Union de Cosecheros de Labastida Manuel Quintano	Rioja/Northeast Spain	Red	Plums, spicy	Beef, lamb, pork	**
Union de Cosecheros de Labastida Solagüen	Rioja/Northeast Spain	Red	Plums, spicy	Beef, lamb, pork	**
Union Viti-Vinícola Gaudium	Rioja/Northeast Spain	Red	Earthy, spicy	Beef, lamb, pork	**
Uribes Madero Calzadilla	Castilla-La Mancha	Red	Berry, earthy	Lamb, beef, veal	**
Valdamor	Rías Baixas/Galacia	White	Minerally, floral	Shellfish, fish	**
Valdelana	Rioja/Northeast Spain	Red	Plums, spicy	Beef, lamb, pork	**
Valdespino PX Solera Superior	Jeréz/Andalucía	Fortified	Nutty, rich	Cheese, nuts	**
Valdespino Solera 1842	Jeréz/Andalucía	Fortified	Nutty, complex	Cheese, nuts	**
Vall de Baldomar Baldoma Selecció	Conca de Barberà/Catalonia	Red	Fruity, berry	Pizza, pork, beef	**
Vall-Lach Mas Martinet Cims de Porrera	Priorato/Catalonia	Red	Berry, earthy	Veal, pork, lamb	**
Valpincia	Ribera del Duero/Castilla-León	Red	Plums, spicy	Lamb, beef, pork	**
Vega Sicilia Único	Ribera del Duero/Castilla-León	Red	Rich, complex, plums, earthy	Lamb, beef, cheese	***
Venta D'Aubert Domus	Bajo Aragón/Aragón	Red	Jam, spicy	Pork, beef, lamb	**
Venta d'Aubert el Serrats	Bajo Aragón/Aragón	White	Floral, fruity	Fish, pasta	**
Vicente Gandia Pla Ceremonia	Utiel-Requena/Valencia	Red	Plums, spicy	Beef, lamb, pork	**
Vilella de la Cartoixa Fra Fulco	Priorato/Catalonia	Red	Berry, spicy	Pork, lamb, beef	**
Vilella de la Cartoixa Fra Fulco Selecció	Priorato/Catalonia	Red	Berry, spicy	Pork, lamb, beef	**
Vilerma	Ribeiro/Galacia	White	Fruity, floral	Fish, chicken	**
Viña Herminia Duque de Huescar	Rioja/Northeast Spain	Red	Plums, spicy	Beef, lamb, pork	**
Viñas del Vero Cabernet Sauvignon	Somontano/Aragón	Red	Plums, spicy	Beef, lamb, pork	*
Viñas del Vero Chardonnay	Somontano/Aragón	White	Apples, buttery	Chicken, fish	*
Viñas del Vero Clarión	Somontano/Aragón	White	Fruity, floral	Chicken, fish	**
Viñas del Vero Gewürtztraminer	Somontano/Aragón	White	Spicy, fruity	Asian, salads	*
Viñas del Vero Gran Vos	Somontano/Aragón	Red	Berry, spicy	Veal, chicken, pork	**
Viñas del Vero Merlot	Somontano/Aragón	Red	Plums, vanillin	Veal, pork, beef	*
Vinícola de Castilla Castillo de Alhambra	La Mancha/Castilla-La Mancha	Red	Plums, jam	Pork, lamb, beef	**
Vinícola del Priorat L'Arc	Priorato/Catalonia	Red	Berry, spicy	Pork, lamb, beef	**
Vinícola Hidalgo y Cía Napoleon Pedro Ximénez	Jeréz/Andalucía	Fortified	Sweet, caramelly	Dessert	**
Vizcarra-Ramos Vizcarra	Ribera del Duero/Castilla-León	Red	Plums, spicy	Lamb, beef, cheese	**

PORTUGAL

Wine name	Region	Style	Flavor/Bouquet	Compatible Foods	Price Range
Adega Co-op. de Lagoa Afonso XIII	Algarve/Setúbal & the South	Fortified	Spirity, powerful, complex	Nuts	**
Adega Co-op. de Portalegre	Alentejano/Setúbal & the South	Red	Berry, spicy	Mediterranean	**
Adega Co-op. de Souselas Reserva	Bairrada/The Douro to the Tagus	Red	Spicy, tannic	Game	**
Alcântara Agrícola Morgado de Sta. Catherina	Bucelas/Lisbon & Tagus Valley	White	Floral, citrus	Fish	**
Alcântara Agrícola Prova Régia Arinto	Bucelas/Lisbon & Tagus Valley	White	Zingy, floral	Pasta	**

PORTUGAL (continued)

Wine name	Region	Style	Flavor/Bouquet	Compatible Foods	Price Range
Alcântara Agrícola Quinta da Romeira Arinto	Estremadura/Lisbon & Tagus Valley	White	Crisp, citrus	Shellfish	*
Alcântara Agrícola Quinta da Romeira Sauvignon Blanc	Estremadura/Lisbon & Tagus Valley	White	Floral, crisp	Chicken	**
Aleixo Brito Caldas Quinta da Baguinha Alvarinho	Vinho Verde/The North	White	Citrus, minerally	Fish	**
António Esteves Ferreirinha Soalheiro Alvarinho	Vinho Verde/The North	White	Crisp, minerally	Shellfish	**
António Gonçalves Faria Gonçalves Faria Reserva	Bairrada/The Douro to the Tagus	Red	Berry, gamey	Stew	**
Artur Barros & Sousa Madeira range, esp. Boal & Terrantez	Madeira/Setúbal & the South	Madeira	Nutty, complex	Cheese	**
Atíade da Costa Martins Semedo Quinta da Dôna	Bairrada/The Douro to the Tagus	Red	Spicy, berry	Mediterranean	**
Atíade da Costa Martins Semedo Quinta da Rigodeira	Bairrada/The Douro to the Tagus	Red	Spicy, tannic	Cold meats, stew, offal	**
Atíade da Costa Martins Semedo Quinta da Rigodeira	Bairrada/The Douro to the Tagus	White	Citrus, minerally	Fish	**
Barbeito Madeira range	Madeira/Setúbal & the South	Madeira	Nutty, spirity, complex	Aperitif	**
Barros Almeida Port range, esp. Colheitas	Porto/The North	Port	Sweet, nutty	Chese	**
Borges & Irmã Port range	Porto/The North	Port	Sweet, spirity	Cheese	**
Borges Madeira range	Madeira/Setúbal & the South	Madeira	Complex, rich	Cheese	**
Burmester Port range, esp. Colheitas, Vintage	Porto/The North	Port	Spirity, sweet	Cheese	**
Cálem Port range, esp. Quinta de Foz	Porto/The North	Port	Spirity, sweet	Cheese	**
Casa Agrícola de Saima Casa de Saima Garrafeira	Bairrada/The Douro to the Tagus	Red	Smoky, tannic	Cold meats, stew, offal	**
Casa Agrícola de Saima Casa de Saima Garrafeira	Bairrada/The Douro to the Tagus	White	Crisp, citrus	Fish	*
Casa Burmester	Douro/The North	Red	Berry, plums	Veal	**
Casa Cadaval Cabernet Sauvignon	Ribatejano/Lisbon & Tagus Valley	Red	Berry, herbaceous	Cold meats	**
Casa Cadaval Trincadeira Preta	Ribatejano/Lisbon & Tagus Valley	Red	Spicy, smoky	Stew	**
Casa de Sezim Colheita Seleccionada	Vinho Verde/The North	White	Citrus, minerally	Shellfish	**
Casa Ferreirinha Barca Velha	Douro/The North	Red	Powerful, berry, spicy	Beef	***
Casa Ferreirinha Callabriga	Douro/The North	Red	Berry, earthy	Game	**
Casa Ferreirinha Quinta da Leda Touriga Nacional	Douro/The North	Red	Berry, tannic	Sausages	**
Casa Ferreirinha Reserva	Douro/The North	Red	Earthy, plums	Stew	**
Casa Ferreirinha Reserva Especial	Douro/The North	Red	Berry, tannic	Cold meats, stew, offal	**
Casa Ferreirinha Vinha Grande	Douro/The North	Red	Berry, spicy	Cold meats, stew, offal	**
Casal de Valle Pradinhos Valle Pradinhos	Trás-os-Montes/The North	Red	Berry, gamey	Game	*
Castas de Santar Alfrocheiro Preto	Beiras/The Douro to the Tagus	Red	Berry, spicy	Stew	**
Castas de Santar Touriga Nacional	Beiras/The Douro to the Tagus	Red	Gamey, berry	Cold meats	**
Caves Aliança Galeria Cabernet Sauvignon	Beiras/The Douro to the Tagus	Red	Berry, herbaceous	Beef	**
Caves Aliança Garrafeira	Bairrada/The Douro to the Tagus	Red	Berry, tannic	Stew	**
Caves de Murghaneira Murganheira Varosa	Távora-Varosa/The Douro to the Tagus	Sparkling	Fruity, citrus	Aperitif	**
Caves Messias Messias Reserva Touriga Nacional	Dão/The Douro to the Tagus	Red	Berry, tannic	Beef	**
Caves Messias Quinta do Cachão Tinta Roriz	Douro/The North	Red	Berry, tannic	Cheese	**
Caves Primavera Lda. Primavera Baga/Cabernet Sauvignon	Beiras/The Douro to the Tagus	Red	Berry, herbaceous	Game	**
Caves Primavera Lda. Primavera Beiras	Beiras/The Douro to the Tagus	White	Fruity, citrus, melon	Fish	**
Caves Primavera Lda. Primavera Garrafeira	Bairrada/The Douro to the Tagus	Red	Gamey, tannic	Cold meats	**
Caves Primavera Lda. Primavera Touriga Nacional	Bairrada/The Douro to the Tagus	Red	Berry, tannic	Beef	**
Caves São João Frei João Reserva	Bairrada/The Douro to the Tagus	Red	Spicy, herbaceous, tannic	Stew	**
Caves São João Poço do Lobo Cabernet Sauvignon	Beiras/The Douro to the Tagus	Red	Herbaceous, spicy, berry	Lamb	**
Caves São João Porta dos Cavaleiros Reserva Seleccionada	Dão/The Douro to the Tagus	Red	Berry, tannic	Stew	**
Caves São João Porta dos Cavaleiros Reserva Seleccionada	Dão/The Douro to the Tagus	White	Citrus, minerally	Fish	**
Caves São João Quinta do Poço do Lobo	Bairrada/The Douro to the Tagus	Red	Berry, smoky	Sausages	**
Caves São João Reserva	Bairrada/The Douro to the Tagus	Red	Earthy, spicy	Mediterranean	**
Caves Valdarcos Lda. Valdarcos Garrafeira	Bairrada/The Douro to the Tagus	Red	Berry, tannic	Cheese	**
Centro Agrícola de Tramagal, G Lda. Casal da Coelheira	Ribatejo	White	Crisp, citrus	Fish	**
Churchill Graham Port range, esp. Quinta da Gricha	Porto/The North	Port	Complex, berry, sweet	Cheese	**

PORTUGAL (continued)

Wine name	Region	Style	Flavor/Bouquet	Compatible Foods	Price Range
Churchill Port range, esp. Vintage	Porto/The North	Port	Spirity, sweet, complex	Cheese	**
Cockburn Smithes Port range, including Quinta dos Canais	Porto/The North	Port	Complex, sweet, spirity	Cheese	**
Coop. Agrícola de Santa Isidro de Pegões Vale de Judia	Terras do Sado/Setúbal & the South	White	Minerally, floral	Fish	**
Coop. de Cantanhede Marquês Marialva Baga Reserva	Bairrada/The Douro to the Tagus	Red	Berry, tannic	Cold meats, stew, offal	**
Coop. de Murça CRL Caves da Porca Garrafeira	Douro/The North	Red	Berry, spicy	Pizza	*
Coop. Regional de Monção Alvarinho Deu la Deu	Vinho Verde/The North	White	Crisp, citrus	Mediterranean	**
Croft Port range, including Delaforce	Porto/The North	Port	Spirity, sweet	Nuts	**
Da Silva Port range, esp. Colheitas	Porto/The North	Port	Sweet, spirity	Nuts	**
Domingos Alves de Sousa Quinta da Gaivosa	Douro/The North	Red	Tannic, earthy	Game	**
Domingos Alves de Sousa Quinta das Caldas	Douro/The North	Red	Smoky, plums	Pasta	**
Domingos Alves de Sousa Quinta do Vale da Raposa Tinta Cão	Douro/The North	Red	Tannic, spicy	Stew	**
Domingos Alves de Sousa Quinta do Vale da Raposa Tinta Roriz	Douro/The North	Red	Berry, spicy	Sausages	**
Domingos Alves de Sousa Quinta do Vale de Raposa Touriga Nacional	Douro/The North	Red	Berry, tannic	Veal	**
Dona Paterna	Vinho Verde/The North	White	Zingy, floral	Shellfish	**
Dow Port range, esp. Vintage	Porto/The North	Port	Rich, sweet, complex, spirity	Nuts	***
Dulcínea dos Santos Ferreirinha Sidónio de Sousa DOC Bairrada Garrafeira	Bairrada/The Douro to the Tagus	Red	Earthy, tannic	Pasta	**
Dulcínea dos Santos Ferreirinha Sidónio de Sousa Garrafeira Especial Fin de Século	Bairrada/The Douro to the Tagus	Red	Tannic, spicy	Cold meats, stew, offal	**
Dulcínea dos Santos Ferreirinha Sidónio de Sousa Reserva	Bairrada/The Douro to the Tagus	Red	Earthy, minerally	Sausages	**
Encostas de Paderne Alvarinho	Vinho Verde/The North	White	Fruity, crisp	Asian	**
Falua Tercius	Ribatejo	Red	Floral, zingy	Sausages	**
Ferreira Port range, esp. Vintage	Porto/The North	Port	Spirity, sweet	Cheese	**
Finagra Esporão Aragonês	Alentejano/Setúbal & the South	Red	Berry, spicy	Cold meats	**
Finagra Esporão Reguengos Reserva	Reguengos/Setúbal & the South	White	Fruity, citrus	Chicken	**
Finagra Esporão Reserva	Reguengos/Setúbal & the South	Red	Smoky, gamey	Lamb	**
Finagra Esporão Touriga Nacional	Alentejano/Setúbal & the South	Red	Gamey, berry	Cold meats, stew, offal	**
Finagra Esporão Trincadeira	Alentejano/Setúbal & the South	Red	Spicy, earthy	Sausages	**
Fonseca Guimaraens Dom Prior	Douro/The North	White	Crisp, floral	Mediterranean	**
Fonseca Guimaraens Port range, esp. Vintage	Porto/The North	Port	Complex, powerful, rich, sweet	Cheese	***
Fundação Eugénio de Almeida Cartuxa	Évora /Setúbal & the South	White	Floral, citrus	Fish	**
Fundação Eugénio de Almeida Cartuxa Reserva	Évora /Setúbal & the South	Red	Smoky, berry	Stew	**
Fundação Eugénio de Almeida Pêra Manca	Évora /Setúbal & the South	Red	Berry, earthy	Stew	**
Gassiot Port range, esp. Quinta da Eira Velha	Porto/The North	Port	Sweet, spirity	Cheese	**
Graham Port range, esp. Quinta dos Malvedos, Quinta del Vesúvio	Porto/The North	Port	Rich, complex, sweet, spirity	Cheese	***
Hans Kristian Jørgensen Cortes de Cima	Alentejano/Setúbal & the South	Red	Berry, gamey	Pasta	**
Hans Kristian Jørgensen Cortes de Cima Reserva	Alentejano/Setúbal & the South	Red	Earthy, plums	Veal	**
Hans Kristian Jørgensen Cortes de Cima Syrah	Alentejano/Setúbal & the South	Red	Berry, plums	Beef	**
Henriques & Henriques Madeira range	Madeira/Setúbal & the South	Madeira	Rich, nutty, complex	Nuts	**
Herdade do Mouchão Dom Rafael	Alentejano/Setúbal & the South	Red	Spicy, floral	Pasta	**
Hotel Palace do Buçaco Buçaco Reserva	Bairrada/The Douro to the Tagus	Red	Earthy, minerally	Game	**
João Portugal Ramos Antão Vaz	Alentejano/Setúbal & the South	White	Crisp, citrus	Salads	**
João Portugal Ramos Aragonês	Alentejano/Setúbal & the South	Red	Earthy, smoky	Game	**
João Portugal Ramos Marquês de Borba	Alentejo/Setúbal & the South	White	Citrus, minerally, crisp	Fish	**
João Portugal Ramos Marquês de Borba Reserva	Alentejo/Setúbal & the South	Red	Smoky, spicy	Lamb	**
João Portugal Ramos Tinta Caiada	Alentejano/Setúbal & the South	Red	Smoky, berry	Sausages	**
João Portugal Ramos Trincadeira	Alentejano/Setúbal & the South	Red	Berry, earthy	Cold meats, stew, offal	**
João Portugal Ramos Vila Santa	Alentejano/Setúbal & the South	Red	Berry, spicy	Cold meats, stew, offal	**
José Arnaldo Coutinho Quinta de Mosteirô	Douro/The North	Red	Spicy, berry	Sausages	**
José Bento dos Santos Monte d'Oiro Syrah	Estremadura/Lisbon & Tagus Valley	Red	Berry, spicy	Sausages	**
José Carlos de Morais Calheiros Cruz Quinta de Covelos Reserva	Douro/The North	Red	Earthy, tannic	Pasta	**
José Maria da Fonseca Colecção Privada Domingos Soares Franco	Terras do Sado/Setúbal & the South	Red	Berry, spicy	Cold meats, stew, offal	**
José Maria da Fonseca Domingos Soares Franco Colecção Privada	Terras do Sado/Setúbal & the South	White	Zingy, fruity	Shellfish	**
José Maria da Fonseca Garrafeira CO	Palmela/Setúbal & the South	Red	Berry, gamey	Pizza	**
José Maria da Fonseca Garrafeira RA	Palmela/Setúbal & the South	Red	Smoky, plums	Pasta	**
José Maria da Fonseca José de Sousa Mayor	Alentejano/Setúbal & the South	Red	Berry, gamey	Veal	**

PORTUGAL *(continued)*

Wine name	Region	Style	Flavor/Bouquet	Compatible Foods	Price Range
José Maria da Fonseca Moscatel de Setúbal Range, Vintage	Setúbal/Setúbal & the South	Fortified	Sweet, spirity	Cheese	**
JP Vinhos Catarina	Terras do Sado/Setúbal & the South	White	Citrus, minerally	Chicken	**
JP Vinhos Cova de Ursa Chardonnay	Terras do Sado/Setúbal & the South	White	Citrus, melon	Veal	**
JP Vinhos JP Arinto	Terras do Sado/Setúbal & the South	White	Floral, citrus	Salads	**
JP Vinhos JP Tinta Miúda	Palmela/Setúbal & the South	Red	Minerally, berry	Cold meats, stew, offal	**
JP Vinhos Má Partilha	Terras do Sado/Setúbal & the South	Red	Berry, gamey	Cold meats	**
JP Vinhos Moscatel de Setúbal Range, Vintage	Setúbal/Setúbal & the South	Fortified	Spirity, sweet	Nuts	**
JP Vinhos Tinto de Ânfora	Alentejano/Setúbal & the South	Red	Spicy, smoky	Pasta	**
Justino Henriques Madeira range	Madeira/Setúbal & the South	Madeira	Complex, nutty	Aperitif	**
Kopke Port range, esp. Quinta de São Luiz	Porto/The North	Port	Sweet, berry, spirity	Nuts	**
Leacock, Rutherford & Miles Cossart Gordon Madeira range	Madeira/Setúbal & the South	Madeira	Nutty, complex	Nuts	**
Lemos & van Zeller Quinta do Vale D. Maria	Douro/The North	Red	Spicy, berry	Cold meats, stew, offal	**
Luis Pato Quinta do Ribeirinho Baga Pé Franco	Bairrada/The Douro to the Tagus	Red	Herbaceous, floral, spicy	Cold meats	**
Luis Pato Quinta do Ribeirinho Primeira Escolha	Bairrada/The Douro to the Tagus	Red	Berry, spicy	Lamb	**
Luis Pato Vinha Barrosa	Bairrada/The Douro to the Tagus	Red	Spicy, berry	Pasta	**
Luis Pato Vinha Pan	Bairrada/The Douro to the Tagus	Red	Tannic, berry	Veal	**
Luis Pato Vinha Velhas	Bairrada/The Douro to the Tagus	Red	Spicy, berry	Game	**
Maria Alexandra Trindade Casa do Canto	Bairrada/The Douro to the Tagus	Red	Berry, tannic	Cheese	**
Maria Antónia Ferreirinha Vallado	Douro/The North	Red	Berry, tannic	Stew	**
Maria de Lourdes Osório Quinta da Ponte Pedrinha	Dão/The Douro to the Tagus	Red	Smoky, berry	Mediterranean	**
Maria Doroteia Serôdio Borges Fojo	Douro/The North	Red	Berry, spicy	Mediterranean	**
Mário Sérgio Alves Nuno Quinta das Bágeiras Especial Garrafeira	Bairrada/The Douro to the Tagus	Red	Berry, tannic	Cheese	**
Mário Sérgio Alves Nuno Quinta das Bágeiras Garrafeira	Bairrada/The Douro to the Tagus	Red	Tannic, spicy	Stew	**
Messias Port range	Porto/The North	Port	Sweet, rich	Nuts	**
Montez Champalimaud Lda. Quinta do Côtto	Douro/The North	Red	Spicy, minerally	Lamb	**
Murganheira Cerceal	Távora-Varosa/The Douro to the Tagus	White	Minerally, floral	Shellfish	**
Niepoort Passadouro	Douro/The North	Red	Spicy, earthy, tannic	Sausages	**
Niepoort Port range, esp. old tawnies, Quinta do Passadouro	Porto/The North	Port	Spirity, sweet	Cheese	**
Niepoort Port range, esp. Vintage	Porto/The North	Port	Sweet, spirity	Nuts	**
Niepoort Redoma	Douro/The North	Red	Spicy, earthy	Cheese	**
Niepoort Redoma Reserva	Douro/The North	White	Crisp, floral	Fish	**
Noval Port range, esp. Vintage, Nacional	Porto/The North	Port	Sweet, complex, rich	Cheese	***
Oliveira Madeira range	Madeira/Setúbal & the South	Madeira	Rich, complex	Nuts	**
Osborne Port range, esp. Vintage	Porto/The North	Port	Spirity, sweet	Cheese	**
Pedro Borges da Gama Quinta da Alameda Tinto Garrafeira	Dão/The Douro to the Tagus	Red	Minerally, berry	Cold meats	**
Pedro Borges da Gama Quinta da Alameda Touriga Nacional	Dão/The Douro to the Tagus	Red	Smoky, tannic	Sausages	**
Poças Port range	Porto/The North	Port	Rich, spirity	Cheese	**
Provam Alvarinho Portal do Fidalgo	Vinho Verde/The North	White	Minerally, zingy	Salads	**
Provam Vinha Antiga Alvarinho Escolha	Vinho Verde/The North	White	Minerally, floral	Shellfish	**
Quarles Harris Port range, esp. old tawnies	Porto/The North	Port	Rich, nutty, spirity	Nuts	**
Quinta da Barão Carcavelos range, Old wines	Carcavelos/Lisbon & Tagus Valley	Fortified	Spirity, berry, nutty	Nuts	**
Quinta da Covela Covela Branco Colheita Seleccionada	Minho/The North	White	Crisp, floral	Fish	**
Quinta de Azevedo	Vinho Verde/The North	White	Zingy, minerally	Veal	**
Quinta de Baixo Soc. Agrícola Lda. Quinta de Baixo Garrafeira	Bairrada/The Douro to the Tagus	Red	Berry, tannic	Cold meats, stew, offal	**
Quinta de Camarate Seco	Palmela/Setúbal & the South	White	Crisp, citrus	Shellfish	**
Quinta de Dom Carlos Arinto	Estremadura/Lisbon & Tagus Valley	White	Zingy, citrus	Veal	**
Quinta de Foz de Arouce	Beiras/The Douro to the Tagus	Red	Spicy, berry	Stew	*
Quinta de Foz de Arouce	Beiras/The Douro to the Tagus	White	Citrus, crisp	Veal	**
Quinta de Murta	Bucelas/Lisbon & Tagus Valley	White	Crisp, floral	Salads	**
Quinta de Saes Quinta da Pellada 100% Jaen	Dão/The Douro to the Tagus	Red	Berry, spicy	Stew	**
Quinta de Saes Quinta da Pellada 100% Touriga Nacional	Dão/The Douro to the Tagus	Red	Berry, tannic	Cold meats, stew, offal	**

PORTUGAL (continued)

Wine name	Region	Style	Flavor/Bouquet	Compatible Foods	Price Range
Quinta de Saes Quinta da Pellada Jaen/Touriga Nacional	Dão/The Douro to the Tagus	Red	Berry, smoky	Cold meats	**
Quinta de Saes Quinta da Pellada Tinta Roriz/Touriga Nacional	Dão/The Douro to the Tagus	Red	Berry, earthy	Stew	**
Quinta do Carvalinho Reserva/Garrafeira	Bairrada/The Douro to the Tagus	Red	Berry, minerally	Stew	**
Quinta do Côtto	Porto/The North	Port	Spirity, sweet	Cheese	**
Quinta do Crasto	Porto/The North	Port	Sweet, spirity	Cheese	**
Quinta do la Rosa Reserva (Sofia Bergqvist)	Douro/The North	Red	Earthy, gamey	Mediterranean	**
Quinta do Mouro	Alentejano/Setúbal & the South	Red	Earthy, gamey	Pork	**
Quinta do Noval Vinhos Quinta de Roriz	Douro/The North	Red	Berry, tannic	Pasta	**
Quinta do Pacheca Quinto da Pacheca	Douro/The North	Red	Plums, gamey	Cheese	**
Quinta dos Pesos Carcavelos range, Old wines	Carcavelos/Lisbon & Tagus Valley	Fortified	Spirity, powerful, rich	Cheese	**
Quinta dos Roques Alfrocheiro Preto	Dão/The Douro to the Tagus	Red	Berry, gamey	Pasta	**
Quinta dos Roques Encruzado	Dão/The Douro to the Tagus	White	Spicy, smoky	Fish	**
Quinta dos Roques Reserva	Dão/The Douro to the Tagus	Red	Berry, tannic	Cold meats, stew, offal	**
Quinta dos Roques Tinta Roriz	Dão/The Douro to the Tagus	Red	Berry, plums	Cold meats	**
Quinta dos Roques Tinto Cão	Dão/The Douro to the Tagus	Red	Spicy, gamey	Stew	**
Quinta dos Roques Touriga Nacional	Dão/The Douro to the Tagus	Red	Berry, tannic	Pasta	**
Quinta Grande	Ribatejano/Lisbon & Tagus Valley	Red	Berry, spicy	Cold meats, stew, offal	**
Ramos Pinto Duas Quintas	Douro/The North	Red	Berry, tannic	Sausages	**
Ramos Pinto Duas Quintas Reserva	Douro/The North	Red	Plums, tannic	Stew	**
Ramos Pinto Quinta dos Bons Ares	Trás-os-Montes/The North	Red	Berry, spicy	Game	**
Ramos–Pinto Port range, esp. Colheitas	Porto/The North	Port	Rich, nutty, spirity	Nuts	**
Real Companhia Velha Evel Grande Escolha	Douro/The North	Red	Berry, plums	Sausages	**
Real Companhia Velha Quinta de Sidrô Chardonnay	Trás-os-Montes/The North	White	Tropical fruit, oaky	Mediterranean	**
Roquevale Lda. Roquevale	Redondo/Setúbal & the South	White	Crisp, citrus	Shellfish	**
Roquevale Redondo	Alentejo/Setúbal & the South	Red	Berry, gamey	Veal	**
Rosa Port range	Porto/The North	Port	Sweet, rich	Cheese	**
Royal Oporto Port range, esp. old tawnies	Porto/The North	Port	Sweet, rich	Cheese	**
Rozés Port range	Porto/The North	Port	Spirity, sweet	Cheese	**
Sandeman Confradeiro	Douro/The North	Red	Berry, spicy	Cold meats, stew, offal	**
Sandeman Port range, esp. Quinta do Vau	Porto/The North	Port	Rich, sweet	Cheese	**
Silva Vinhos Madeira range	Madeira/Setúbal & the South	Madeira	Complex, nutty	Nuts	**
Smith-Woodhouse Port range, esp. Vintage	Porto/The North	Port	Rich, sweet, spirity	Nuts	**
Soc. Agrícola Baas Quintas Lda. Quinta da Fonte do Ouro	Dão/The Douro to the Tagus	Red	Berry, gamey	Pork	**
Soc. Agrícola Baas Quintas Lda. Quinta da Fonte do Ouro Touriga Nacional	Dão/The Douro to the Tagus	Red	Berry, tannic	Lamb	**
Soc. Agrícola da Herdade dos Coelheiros Tapada de Coelheiros	Alentejano/Setúbal & the South	Red	Earthy, spicy	Mediterranean	**
Soc. Agrícola da Herdade dos Coelheiros Tapada de Coelheiros Garrafeira	Alentejano/Setúbal & the South	Red	Floral, earthy	Game	**
Soc. Agrícola da Quinta do Crasto Quinta do Crasto Red	Douro/The North	Red	Berry, tannic	Game	*
Soc. Agrícola da Quinta do Crasto Quinta do Crasto Reserva	Douro/The North	Red	Berry, spicy	Cheese	**
Soc. Agrícola da Quinta do Crasto Quinta do Crasto Tinta Roriz	Douro/The North	Red	Tannic, spicy	Pasta	*
Soc. Agrícola da Quinta do Crasto Quinta do Crasto Touriga Nacional	Douro/The North	Red	Spicy, earthy	Stew	**
Soc. Agrícola da Quinta Seara d'Ordens Lda. Quinta Seara d'Ordens Garrafeira	Douro/The North	Red	Berry, spicy	Pork	**
Soc. Agrícola das Beiras Entre Serras Colheita Seleccionada	Beiras/The Douro to the Tagus	Red	Spicy, berry	Pizza	*
Soc. Agrícola das Beiras Entre Serras Touriga Nacional	Beiras/The Douro to the Tagus	Red	Berry, tannic	Pasta	**
Soc. Agrícola de Pegos Claros Lda. Pegos Claros	Palmela/Setúbal & the South	Red	Berry, spicy	Stew	**
Soc. Agrícola Faldas da Quinta da Logoalva de Cima Logoalva de Cima Syrah	Ribatejano/Lisbon & Tagus Valley	Red	Fruity, plums	Sausages	**
Soc. Agrícola Faldas da Quinta da Logoalva de Cima Quinta da Logoalva	Ribatejano/Lisbon & Tagus Valley	Red	Berry, tannic	Stew	**
Soc. Agrícola Faldas da Serra Lda. Quinta das Maias	Dão/The Douro to the Tagus	Red	Herbaceous, tannic, berry	Cold meats	*
Soc. Agrícola Faldas da Serra Lda. Quinta das Maias Jaen	Dão/The Douro to the Tagus	Red	Berry, spicy	Pork	**
Soc. Agrícola Porto da Luz/Quinta de Pancas Quinta de Pancas Cabernet Sauvignon	Estremadura/Lisbon & Tagus Valley	Red	Berry, plums	Stew	**
Soc. Agrícola Porto da Luz/Quinta de Pancas Quinta de Pancas Cabernet Sauvignon Special Selection	Estremadura/Lisbon & Tagus Valley	Red	Berry, spicy	Pasta	**
Soc. Agrícola Porto da Luz/Quinta de Pancas Quinta de Pancas	Estremadura/Lisbon & Tagus Valley	White	Minerally, fruity	Salads	**
Soc. Agrícola Porto da Luz/Quinta de Pancas Quinta de Pancas Tinta Roriz	Estremadura/Lisbon & Tagus Valley	Red	Smoky, spicy	Cold meats, stew, offal	**

PORTUGAL *(continued)*

Wine name	Region	Style	Flavor/Bouquet	Compatible Foods	Price Range
Soc. Agrícola Porto da Luz/Quinta de Pancas Quinta de Pancas Touriga Nacional Special Selection	Estremadura/Lisbon & Tagus Valley	Red	Gamey, spicy	Game	**
Soc. Agrícola Quinta do Carma Quinta do Carmo	Alentejano/Setúbal & the South	Red	Smoky, berry	Pizza	*
Soc. Agrícola Vila Velha da Vilariça Lda. Quinta das Castas Touriga Nacional	Douro/The North	Red	Spicy, earthy	Stew	**
Soc. Quinta do Portal Quinta do Portal Reserva	Douro/The North	Red	Gamey, berry	Lamb	**
Soc. Quinta do Portal Tinta Roriz	Douro/The North	Red	Earthy, spicy	Cold meats, stew, offal	**
Sociedade Agrícola da Beira Entra Serras Chardonnay	Beiras/The Douro to the Tagus	White	Citrus, fruity	Chicken	**
Sociedade Agrícola da Casa Pinheiro Lda. Quinta da Alderiz Alvarinho	Vinho Verde/The North	White	Fruity, floral	Veal	**
Sociedade Agrícola da Quinta de Santa Maria Quinta do Tamariz Loureiro Colheito	Vinho Verde/The North	White	Zingy, citrus	Mediterranean	**
Sociedade Agrícola Faldas de Serra Lda. Quinta das Maias Malvasia Fina	Dão/The Douro to the Tagus	White	Crisp, minerally, fruity	Fish	**
Sogrape Duque de Viseu	Dão/The Douro to the Tagus	White	Floral, crisp	Shellfish	**
Sogrape Duque du Viseu	Dão/The Douro to the Tagus	Red	Berry, earthy	Cold meats, stew, offal	*
Sogrape Herdade do Peso Aragonês	Alentejo/Setúbal & the South	Red	Smoky, spicy	Pizza	*
Sogrape Morgadio da Torre Alvarinho	Vinho Verde/The North	White	Fruity, zingy	Shellfish	**
Sogrape Quinta de Pedralvites	Bairrada/The Douro to the Tagus	White	Crisp, floral	Salads	*
Sogrape Quinta dos Carvalhais Alfrocheiro Preto	Dão/The Douro to the Tagus	Red	Berry, plums	Sausages	**
Sogrape Quinta dos Carvalhais Encruzado	Dão/The Douro to the Tagus	White	Fruity, floral	Salads	*
Sogrape Quinta dos Carvalhais Reserva	Dão/The Douro to the Tagus	Red	Berry, plums	Lamb	**
Sogrape Quinta dos Carvalhais Tinta Roriz	Dão/The Douro to the Tagus	Red	Berry, spicy	Pasta	*
Sogrape Quinta dos Carvalhais Touriga Nacional	Dão/The Douro to the Tagus	Red	Berry, tannic	Stew	**
Sogrape Reserva	Douro/The North	White	Minerally, citrus	Salads	**
Sophia B. Vasconcellos/Casal Branco Capucho Cabernet Sauvignon	Almeirim/Lisbon & Tagus Valley	Red	Herbaceous, berry	Cold meats, stew, offal	**
Sophia B. Vasconcellos/Casal Branco Falcoaria Almeirim	Ribatejo/Almeirim	Red	Berry, spicy	Cold meats, stew, offal	**
Taylor's Port range, esp. Vintage, Quinta de Vargellas, Quinta da Terra Feita	Porto/The North	Port	Rich, complex, powerful, sweet	Cheese	***
Venâncio da Costa Lima Garrafeira	Palmela/Setúbal & the South	Red	Berry, spicy	Stew	**
Warre's Port range, esp. Quinta da Cavadinha	Porto/The North	Port	Sweet, rich, berry, complex	Cheese	***

ENGLAND AND WALES

Wine name	Region	Style	Flavor/Bouquet	Compatible Foods	Price Range
Beenleigh Red (Sharpham Partnership)	Devon/Southwest and Wales	Red	Berry, plums, herbaceous	Veal, pork, beef	**
Biddenden Ortega	Kent/Weald and Downland	White	Floral, herbaceous	Shellfish, salads	**
Breaky Bottom Seyval Brut	Sussex/Weald and Downland	Sparkling	Citrus, crisp	Shellfish, fish	**
Breaky Bottom Seyval Dry	Sussex/Weald and Downland	White	Grassy, tangy	Shellfish, Asian	**
Chapel Down Bacchus	Kent/Weald and Downland	White	Floral, fruity, herbaceous	Shellfish, fish, Asian	**
Chapel Down Epoch I	Kent/Weald and Downland	Red	Berry, plums, spicy	Veal, pork, beef	**
Chapel Down Epoch Vintage Brut	Kent/Weald and Downland	Sparkling	Citrus, minerally	Shellfish, nuts	**
Chapel Down Schönburger	Kent/Weald and Downland	White	Stone fruit, spicy	Asian, fish	**
Chiltern Valley Dry	Oxfordshire/Thames and Chiltern	White	Fruity, floral	Asian, fish	**
Denbies Wine Estate Dornfelder/Pinot Noir	Surrey/Weald and Downland	Red	Fruity, spicy	Chicken, fish	**
Denbies Wine Estate Special Late Harvested	Surrey/Weald and Downland	Sweet	Fruity, honey, floral	Dessert	**
Denbies Wine Estate Surrey Gold	Surrey/Weald and Downland	White	Fruity, floral	Asian, fish	**
Denbines Wine Estate Pinot Blanc	Surrey/Weald and Downland	White	Stone fruit, nutty, minerally	Fish, chicken	**
Hidden Spring Dark Fields Red	Sussex/Weald and Downland	Red	Berry, spicy	Pizza, chicken	**
Nutborne Sussex Reserve	Sussex/Weald and Downland	White	Fruity, floral	Asian, fish	**
Nyetimber Classic Cuvée Vintage Brut	Sussex/Weald and Downland	Sparkling	Citrus, minerally, yeasty	Shellfish, fish	***
Nyetimber Première Cuvée Blanc de Blancs Vintage Brut	Sussex/Weald and Downland	Sparkling	Apples, citrus, minerally, yeasty	Shellfish, nuts	***
Old Luxters Dessert Wine (Chiltern Valley)	Oxfordshire/Thames and Chiltern	Sweet	Honey, waxy, floral	Dessert	**
Ridge View Estate Cuvée Merret Brut	Sussex/Weald and Downland	Sparkling	Citrus, crisp	Shellfish, fish	**
Thames Valley Vineyards Clocktower Pinot Noir	Berkshire/Thames and Chiltern	Red	Berry, spicy	Fish, chicken, pork	**
Thames Valley Vineyards Heritage Brut	Berkshire/Thames and Chiltern	Sparkling	Citrus, crisp	Shellfish, fish	**
Thames Valley Vineyards Heritage Fumé	Berkshire/Thames and Chiltern	White	Fruity, oaky	Fish, chicken	**
Three Choirs Vineyards Phoenix/Seyval	Gloucestershire/Southwest and Wales	White	Grassy, tangy	Shellfish, Asian	**
Three Choirs Vineyards Siegerrebe	Gloucestershire/Southwest and Wales	White	Citrus, spicy, tangy	Shellfish, Asian	**
Wooldings Vintage Brut	Hampshire/Wessex	Sparkling	Citrus, minerally, crisp	Shellfish, fish	**

CENTRAL EUROPE

Wine name	Region	Style	Flavor/Bouquet	Compatible Foods	Price Range
CZECH REPUBLIC					
Chateau Roudnice Pinot Noir	Bohemia	Red	Berry, gamey	Cold meats, stew, offal	**
Chateau Valtice a.s. Sylvaner Spaetlese	Moravia	White	Floral, medium-sweet	Veal	**
Lobkowicz Winery Chateau Melnik Oak-fermented Pinot Blanc	Bohemia	White	Melon, oaky	Chicken	**
Mikros-vin Gruener Veltliner	Za cihelnou/Moravia	White	Spicy, crisp	Fish	**
Novy Saldorf Znojmo Spalkovy	Moravia	Red	Berry, earthy	Pasta	**
Obce Vinselekt Pinot Blanc Kabinet	Nemcicky/Moravia	White	Melon, medium-sweet	Fish	**
St Martin Straw-Wine Blauer Portugieser	Moravia	Red	Berry, rich	Cheese	**
Velke Bilovice Ing. Frantisek Madl Sauvignon	Moravia	White	Crisp, grassy	Shellfish	*
Velke Pavlovice Radomil Aloun Neuburger Spaetlese	Moravia	White	Citrus, medium-sweet	Veal	**
Velke Pavlovice S.S.V. Andre Spaetlese	Moravia	White	Medium-sweet, floral	Fish	**
Velke Pavlovice Vinium a. s. Pinot Blanc Kabinet	Moravia	White	Melon, minerally	Fish	**
Vendule Zernosecke Vinarstvi s.r.o Riesling Kabinet	Velke Zernoseky/Bohemia	White	Floral, minerally, spicy	Salads	**
Vinne Sklepy Rodiny Vino Schaler Blauer Portugieser (port-style wine)	Moravia	Red	Berry, rich	Cheese	**
Zlechov Tramin	Moravia	White	Floral, spicy	Pork	*
Znovin Znojmo Riesling Praedikat (spaetlese equivalent)	Sobes/Moravia	White	Sweet, floral	Fish	**
SLOVAK REPUBLIC					
Ing. Vladimir Mrva Zelenec Riesling Kabinet	Slovak Republic	White	Floral, minerally	Fish	**
Pezinok Dornfelder	Slovak Republic	Red	Plums, smoky	Cold meats	**
Pezinok Palava (Muller-Thurgau x Gewurztraminer)	Slovak Republic	White	Spicy, citrus	Asian	*
Vino Nitra Barrique Cabernet Sauvignon	Slovak Republic	Red	Berry, herbaceous	Lamb	**
Vino Nitra Barrique Svatovavrinecke (St Laurent)	Slovak Republic	Red	Spicy, earthy	Cold meats, stew, offal	**
HUNGARY					
Aliscavin Borászati Rt Cabernet Franc	Szekszárd/The Southwest	Red	Plums, berry	Pork, beef, lamb	**
Aliscavin Borászati Rt Chardonnay Barrique	Szekszárd/The Southwest	White	Apples, vanillin	Fish, chicken	**
Bajor Pince Siklósi Rajnai Rizling	Villány-Siklós/The Southwest	White	Floral, fruity	Asian, shellfish	**
Balatonboglári Borgazdasági Rt Chapel Hill Cabernet Sauvignon Barrique Aged	Dél-Balaton/Lake Balaton	Red	Berry, oaky	Beef, lamb	**
Balatonboglári Borgazdasági Rt Chapel Hill Chardonnay Barrique Fermented	Dél-Balaton/Lake Balaton	White	Fruity, complex	Chicken, veal	**
Balatonboglári Borgazdasági Rt Chapel Hill Chardonnay Oaked	Dél-Balaton/Lake Balaton	White	Fruity, oaky	Chicken, veal	**
Balatonboglári Borgazdasági Rt Chapel Hill Merlot/Kékfrankos	Eger/The Northeast	Red	Plums, spicy	Pork, beef, lamb	**
Balatonboglári Borgazdasági Rt Chapel Hill Pinot Noir Rosé	Dél-Balaton/Lake Balaton	Rosé	Berry, spicy	Asian, pizza	*
Balatonboglári Borgazdasági Rt Chapel Hill Sauvignon Blanc	Dél-Balaton/Lake Balaton	White	Citrus, zingy	Shellfish, cheese	**
Balatonboglári Borgazdasági Rt Chapel Hill Sparkling Chardonnay/Pinot Noir	Dél-Balaton/Lake Balaton	Sparkling	Elegant, nutty, crisp	Shellfish, nuts	**
Bock Pince Villányi Cabernet Sauvignon	Villány-Siklós/The Southwest	Red	Plums, spicy	Pork, beef, lamb	**
Ch Pajzos és Ch Megyer Rt Aszús under the Pajzos label Disznókő Rt Aszús	Tokaj-Hegyalja	Sweet	Honey, wax, floral, nutty	Dessert	***
Danubiana Bt Gyöngyös Estate Sauvignon Blanc	Mátraalja/The Northeast	White	Grassy, melon	Shellfish, fish	**
Dreyer Domaine Viticole Vaskapu Kastély Kadarka	Mecsekalja/The Southwest	Red	Berry, spicy	Chicken, veal, pork	**
Eberhardt György Pince Mohácsi Chardonnay	Mecsekalja/The Southwest	White	Apples, minerally	Fish, chicken	**
Egerszalók Demjén Pinceszövetkezet Egri Bikavér Bull's Blood of Eger	Eger/The Northeast	Red	Rich, spicy	Pork, beef, lamb	**
Eifert és Légli Borház Légli Szőlősgyöröki Barrique Chardonnay	Dél-Balaton/Lake Balaton	White	Fruity, oaky	Chicken, veal	**
Európai Bortermelők Kft Bátáapati Estate Barrique Chardonnay	Tolna/The Southwest	White	Apples, vanillin	Fish, chicken	**
Európai Bortermelők Kft Bátáapati Estate Cabernet Sauvignon/Merlot	Tolna/The Southwest	Red	Plums, leathery	Beef, lamb	**
Európai Bortermelők Kft Bátáapati Estate Sauvignon Blanc	Tolna/The Southwest	White	Grassy, melon	Shellfish, cheese	**
Európai Bortermelők Kft Mocsényi Sauvignon Blanc	Tolna/The Southwest	White	Citrus, herbaceous	Shellfish, cheese	**
Fine Wine Borászati Vállalkozás Pécselyi Sémillon	Balatonfüred-Csopak/Lake Balaton	White	Honey, nutty	Fish, chicken, veal	**
Franz Weninger Soproni Kékfrankos Barrique	Sopron/The Northwest	Red	Fruity, peppery, oaky	Pork, beef	**
Gere Attila Villányi Cabernet Sauvignon Barrique	Villány-Siklós/The Southwest	Red	Plums, toasty	Beef, lamb	**
Gere és Weninger Kft Villányi Cabernet Sauvignon/Cabernet Franc	Villány-Siklós/The Southwest	Red	Berry, leathery, complex	Beef, lamb	**
GIA Kft Egri Barrique Chardonnay	Eger/The Northeast	White	Apples, vanillin	Fish, chicken	**
GIA Kft Egri Bikavér	Eger/The Northeast	Red	Berry, spicy	Chicken, veal, pork	**
GIA Kft Egri Kékfrankos/Blaufrankisch	Eger/The Northeast	Red	Fruity, spicy	Chicken, veal, pork	**
Györgykovács Pince Furmint	Somló/The Northwest	White	Spicy, zingy	Fish, chicken, pasta	**
Györgykovács Pince Hárslevelő	Somló/The Northwest	White	Floral, spicy	Fish, chicken	**

CENTRAL EUROPE (continued)

Wine name	Region	Style	Flavor/Bouquet	Compatible Foods	Price Range
Heimann Ferenc Szekszárdi Bikavér	Szekszárd/The Southwest	Red	Berry, spicy	Chicken, veal, pork	**
Hilltop Neszmély Rt Bin AK28 Sauvignon Blanc	Sopron/The Northwest	White	Grassy, zingy	Shellfish, cheese	**
Hilltop Neszmély Rt Hilltop Chardonnay	Tolna/The Southwest	White	Apples, butter	Fish, chicken	**
Hilltop Neszmély Rt Riverview Kékfrankos	Sopron/The Northwest	Red	Plums, peppery	Pizza, pork, beef	**
Huba Szeremley Szürkebarát	Badacsony/Lake Balaton	White	Stone fruit, nutty	Fish, chicken	**
Hungarovin Rt François President Brut	Eytek-Buda/The Northwest	Sparkling	Citrus, minerally	Shellfish, nuts	**
Lauder-Láng Pinceszét Egri Bikavér	Eger/The Northeast	Red	Berry, spicy	Chicken, veal, pork	**
Márta Wille-Baumkauff Pince Kft Aszús	Tokaj-Hegyalja	Sweet	Honey, wax, floral, nutty	Dessert	***
Ódon Pince Olaszrizling	Balatonmelléke/Lake Balaton	White	Floral, rich	Asian, fish	**
Polgár Pince Kft Villányi Cabernet Sauvignon Barrique	Villány-Siklós/The Southwest	Red	Plums, oaky	Beef, lamb	**
Royal Tokaji Wine Company Kft Aszús	Tokaj-Hegyalja	Sweet	Honey, wax, floral, nutty	Dessert	***
Szent Donatus Pincészet Kft Balatonlellei Cabernet	Dél-Balaton/Lake Balaton	Red	Plums, earthy	Beef, lamb	**
Szent Donatus Pincészet Kft Lellei Oak Aged Chardonnay	Dél-Balaton/Lake Balaton	White	Fruity, oaky	Chicken, veal	**
Szent Orbán Pince Irsai Olivér	Badacsony/Lake Balaton	White	Floral, fruity	Fruit, Asian	*
Szent Orbán Pince Olaszrizling	Badacsony/Lake Balaton	White	Floral, rich	Asian, fish	**
Szent Orbán Pince Olaszrizling Late Harvest	Badacsony/Lake Balaton	White	Floral, fruity	Asian, dessert	**
Szent Orbán Pince Szürkebarát	Badacsony/Lake Balaton	White	Stone fruit, nutty	Fish, chicken	**
Szőlőskert Szövetkezet Borászati Üzem Nagyréde Pinot Gris Reserve	Mátraalja/The Northeast	White	Stone fruit, nutty	Fish, chicken	**
Takler Pince Szekszárdi Bikavér	Szekszárd/The Southwest	Red	Berry, spicy	Chicken, veal, pork	**
Takler Pince Szekszárdi Merlot	Szekszárd/The Southwest	Red	Plums, jam	Veal, pork, beef	**
Tamás Gere Villányi Merlot/Cabernet Franc	Villány-Siklós/The Southwest	Red	Plums, berry	Pork, beef, lamb	**
Thummerer Pince Egri Bikavér	Eger/The Northeast	Red	Berry, spicy	Chicken veal, pork	**
Tiffan's Bt Cabernet Sauvignon/Cabernet Franc Grand Selection	Villány-Siklós/The Southwest	Red	Berry, leathery, earthy, rich	Beef, lamb	***
Tiffan's Bt Cabernet Sauvignon/Kékfrankos	Villány-Siklós/The Southwest	Red	Berry, spicy	Veal, pork, beef	**
Tiffan's Bt Kékoportó Vylyan Rt Villányi Kékoportó Barrique	Villány-Siklós/The Southwest	Red	Powerful, oaky	Beef, lamb	**
Tokaj Kereskedőház Rt Aszús	Tokaj-Hegyalja	Sweet	Honey, wax, floral, nutty	Dessert	***
Tokaj Oremus Kft Aszús	Tokaj-Hegyalja	Sweet	Honey, wax, floral, nutty	Dessert	***
Vida Pince Szekszárdi Cabernet Franc	Szekszárd/The Southwest	Red	Plums, berry	Pork, beef, lamb	**
Vida Pince Szekszárdi Cabernet Franc/Merlot	Szekszárd/The Southwest	Red	Berry, jam, earthy	Pork, beef, lamb	**
Vida Pince Szekszárdi Merlot	Szekszárd/The Southwest	Red	Plums, jam	Veal, pork, beef	**
Vinarium Rt Ch. Vincent Sparkling Brut	Dél-Balaton/Lake Balaton	Sparkling	Citrus, minerally	Shellfish, nuts	**
Vincze Béla Magánpincézete Egri Cabernet Franc	Eger/The Northeast	Red	Plums, berry	Pork, beef, lamb	**
Vincze Béla Magánpincézete Egri Cabernet Sauvignon	Eger/The Northeast	Red	Plums, earthy	Beef, lamb	**
Vinoland Plus Kft Villányi Pinot Noir Dobogó Vineyard	Villány-Siklós/The Southwest	Red	Berry, spicy	Fish, veal, pork	**
Vylyan Rt Villányi Cabernet Sauvignon	Villány-Siklós/The Southwest	Red	Plums, leathery	Pork, beef, lamb	**
Zwack Kft Egri Bikavér	Eger/The Northeast	Red	Berry, spicy	Chicken, veal, pork	**

SLOVENIA

Wine name	Region	Style	Flavor/Bouquet	Compatible Foods	Price Range
Agroind Vipava 1894 d.d. Barbera	Primorska	Red	Berry, savoury	Sausages	**
Agroind Vipava 1894 d.d. Cabernet Sauvignon	Primorska	Red	Berry, herbaceous	Lamb	**
Agroind Vipava 1894 d.d. Laski Rizling	Primorska	White	Floral, citrus	Shellfish	*
Agroind Vipava 1894 d.d. Rebula	Primorska	White	Minerally, citrus	Fish	**
Agroind Vipava 1894 d.d. Theodosius Extra Dry	Primorska	Sparkling	Crisp, minerally	Aperitif	**
Barbara International No 1 Cuvée Speciale	Postavje	Sparkling	Crisp, citrus	Aperitif	**
Jeruzalem Ormoz VVS d.d. Renski Rizling	Podravje	White	Floral, minerally	Fish	**
Jeruzalem Ormoz VVS d.d. Sivi Pinot	Podravje	White	Minerally, crisp	fish	*
Kapela d.d. Traminec	Podravje	White	Floral, spicy	Shellfish	**
Kemetijski Kombinat Ptuj Chardonnay	Podravje	White	Melon, citrus	Chicken	**
Kemetijski Kombinat Ptuj Lazki Rizling–Pozna Trgatev	Podravje	Sweet	Floral, sweet	Fruit	**
Kmecka Zadruga Krsko Cvicek	Postavje	Red	Berry, spicy	Game	*
Kmetijska Zadruga Chardonnay	Goriska Brda/Primorska	White	Tropical fruit, melon	Chicken	**
Kmetijska Zadruga Kraski Teran	Vinakras Sezana/Primorska	Red	Berry, spicy	Pasta	**
Kmetijska Zadruga Merlot	Goriska Brda/Primorska	Red	Plums, spicy	Sausages	**
Kmetijska Zadruga Metliska Crnina	Postavje	Red	Berry, earthy	Game	*
Kmetijska Zadruga Modri Pinot	Goriska Brda/Primorska	Red	Berry, gamey	Cold meats, stew, offal	**
Kmetijska Zadruga Smarje Pri Jelsah Modra Frankinja	Podravje	Red	Berry, spicy	Game	**
Kmetijska Zadruga Sivi Pinot	Goriska Brda/Primorska	White	Zingy, citrus	Salads	*
Kmetijski Kombinat Ptuj Rumeni Muscat	Podravje	White	Floral, citrus	Veal	**
Ljutomercan d.d. Ranina	Ljutomer/Podravje	White	Crisp, fruity	Fish	**
Radgonske Gorice d.d. Janzevec (blended wine)	Podravje	White	Citrus, floral	Pork	**
Radgonske Gorice d.d. Zlata Radgonska Penina Demi-sec	Podravje	Sparkling	Crisp, medium-sweet, fruity	Aperitif	**
Radgonske Gorice d.d. Zlata Radgonska Penina Dry	Podravje	Sparkling	Crisp, minerally	Cheese	**

CENTRAL EUROPE (continued)

Wine name	Region	Style	Flavor/Bouquet	Compatible Foods	Price Range
Skofijsko Gospodarstvo Rast d.o.o. Maribor Laski Rizling–Ledeno Vino	Podravje	Sweet	Floral, sweet	Fruit	**
Slovenske Konjice Zlati Gric Renski Rizling–Jagodni Izbor	Podravje	Sweet	Sweet, citrus	Fruit	**
Stanko Curin Kog Traminec–Ledeno Vino	Podravje	Sweet	Floral, sweet	Cheese	*
Valter Zorin Poljcane Laski Rizling–Suhi Jagodni Izbor	Podravje	Sweet	Sweet, citrus	Cheese	**
Vinag d.d. Beli Pinot	Maribor/Podravje	White	Crisp, melon	Shellfish	**
Vinag d.d. Maribor Sauvignon–Pozna Trgatev	Podravje	Sweet	Sweet, zingy	Shellfish	**
Vinag d.d. Maribor Traminec	Podravje	White	Citrus, spicy	Salads	**
Vinakoper Cabernet Sauvignon	Koper/Primorska	Red	Berry, herbaceous	Lamb	**
Vinakoper Chardonnay Prestige	Koper/Primorska	White	Tropical fruit, oaky	Chicken	**
Vinakoper Malvazija	Koper/Primorska	White	Minerally, citrus	Fish	**
Vinakoper Merlot	Koper/Primorska	Red	Berry, plums	Pork	**
Vinakoper Refosk	Koper/Primorska	Red	Berry, earthy	Cold meats, stew, offal	**
Vino Brezice d.d. Chardonnay–Jagodni Izbor	Postavje	Sweet	Sweet, melon	Fruit	**
Vino Brezice d.d. Chardonnay–Ledeno Vino	Postavje	Sweet	Sweet, melon	Fruit	**
Vino Brezice d.d. Laski Rizling–Jagodni Izbor	Postavje	Sweet	Sweet, floral	Cheese	**
Vino Brezice d.d. Laski Rizling–Ledeno Vino	Postavje	Sweet	Sweet, citrus	Fruit	**
Vreel Sauvignon	Zgornje Hoce/Podravje	White	Zingy, citrus	Shellfish	*
MONTENEGRO					
Monte Cheval Pro Corde	Plantaze Agrokombinat Podg	Red	Earthy, spicy	Cold meats, stew, offal	**
Monte Cheval Vranac	Plantaze Agrokombinat Podg	Red	Berry, plums	Sausages	**

EASTERN EUROPE

Wine name	Region	Style	Flavor/Bouquet	Compatible Foods	Price Range
BULGARIA					
Assenovgrad Merlot Reserve	Southern Region	Red	Plums, earthy	Beef	**
Azbuka Sliven Cabernet Sauvignon	Sub-Balkan Region	Red	Berry, herbaceous	Pasta	**
Controliran Svischtov Cabernet Sauvignon	Northern Region	Red	Berry, herbaceous	Cold meats, stew	**
Controliran Yantra Valley Cabernet Sauvignon	Northern Region	Red	Berry, herbaceous	Cold meats	**
Damianiza Melnik	Southwestern Region	Red	Berry, earthy	Pasta	**
Domaine Boyar Iambol Premium Reserve Merlot Gamza	Southern Region	Red	Plums, spicy	Cheese	**
Domaine Boyar Iambol Premium Reserve Merlot	Southern Region	Red	Plums, oaky	Sausages	**
Domaine Boyar Schumen Premium Cuveé Cabernet Sauvignon	Eastern Region	Red	Berry, herbaceous	Lamb	**
Domaine Boyar Schumen Premium Oak Cabernet Sauvignon	Eastern Region	Red	Berry, herbaceous, oaky	Pasta	**
Domaine Boyar Schumen Premium Oak Chardonnay	Eastern Region	White	Tropical fruit, oaky	Veal	**
Domaine Boyar Schumen Premium Oak Merlot	Eastern Region	Red	Plums, oaky	Game	**
Perushtitza Cabernet Sauvignon Rubin	Southern Region	Red	Plums, herbaceous	Lamb	**
Preslav Khan Krum Chardonnay Reserve	Eastern Region	White	Tropical fruit, oaky	Chicken	**
Russe Azbuka Merlot	Northern Region	Red	Plums, spicy	Sausages	**
Russe Chardonnay	Northern Region	White	Tropical fruit, melon	Fish	*
Russe Chardonnay Reserve	Northern Region	White	Tropical fruit, oaky	Chicken	**
Sakar Azbuka Merlot	Southern Region	Red	Plums, spicy	Cheese	**
Sakar Controliran Merlot	Southern Region	Red	Plums, spicy	Pasta	*
Sliven Cabernet Sauvignon Reserve	Sub-Balkan Region	Red	Berry, tannic, herbaceous	Lamb	**
Sliven Young Vatted Cabernet Sauvignon	Sub-Balkan Region	Red	Berry, herbaceous	Sausages	**
Stambolovo Controliran Merlot	Southern Region	Red	Berry, plums	Cold meats, stew	*
Stambolovo Merlot Reserve	Southern Region	Red	Fruit cake, berry	Lamb	**
Suhindol Cabernet Sauvignon Estate Selection	Northern Region	Red	Berry, herbaceous, tannic	Beef	**
ROMANIA					
Carl Reh Winery River Route Pinot Grigio	Romania	White	Crisp, minerally	Fish	**
Dealul-Mare Premiat Merlot	Romania	Red	Berry, spicy	Chicken, veal, pork	*
Dealul-Mare Premiat Pinot Noir	Romania	Red	Berry, earthy, leathery	Fish, chicken	*
Dealul-Mare Valley of the Monks Merlot	Romania	Red	Berry, herbaceous	Chicken, veal, pork	*
Hanwood Group Idlerock Romanian Pinot Noir	Romania	Red	Berry, gamey	Duck	**
Murfatlar Pinot Gris	Romania	White	Floral, apples	Shellfish, fish	*
Rovit Special Reserve Pinot Noir	Romania	Red	Earthy, spicy	Game	**
St Ursula Lupu Negru Cabernet Sauvignon Merlot	Romania	Red	Berry, herbaceous	Lamb	**
Tirnave Blaj Muscat Attonel	Romania	White	Floral, honey, mint	Asian, fish	**
GEORGIA					
Georgian Wines & Spirits Co Matrasa	Georgia	Red	Berry, earthy	Sausages	**
Georgian Wines & Spirits Co Pinot Noir	Georgia	Red	Berry, gamey	Cold meats, stew, offal	**

SOUTHERN EUROPE

Wine name	Region	Style	Flavor/Bouquet	Compatible Foods	Price Range
GREECE					
Ambelones Tselepos Mantinia	Mantinia/Peloponnese	White	Crisp, citrus, zingy	Shellfish, salads	**
Antonopoulos Adoli Ghis	Pàtras/Peloponnese	White	Apples, floral, complex, elegant	Fish, chicken	**
Babatzim Portogo Thessaloniki	Chalkidiki/Mainland Greece	Red	Earthy, peppery	Beef, lamb	**
Chateau Carras Cotes de Meliton	Macedonia	Red	Berry, earthy, herbaceous	Beef, lamb	**
Domaine Carras Cimnio Cotes de Meliton	Macedonia	Red	Berry, spicy	Pork, beef	**
Domaine Carras Melisanthi Cotes de Meliton	Macedonia	White	Honey, floral	Fish, chicken	**
Kostas Lazaridis Amethystos Cava	Drama/Mainland Greece	Red	Plums, berry, licorice, vanillin	Pork, beef, lamb	**
Ktima Gerovassiliou Viognier	Epanomi/Mainland Greece	White	Floral, fruity	Shellfish, Asian	**
Ktima Papaioannou Palea Klimata	Neméa/Peloponnese	Red	Berry, spicy	Veal, pork, beef	**
Nikos Lazaridis Magico Vouno	Drama/Macedonia	White	Fruity, floral, intense	Asian, fish	**
Oenoforos Asprolithi	Pàtras/Peloponnese	White	Melon, floral, honey	Shellfish, fish	**
Samos Co-op Samos Nectar	Samos/Aegean Islands	Sweet	Honey, floral, tropical fruit	Dessert	*
Semeli Chateau Semeli	Attica/Mainland Greece	Red	Rich, plums, earthy, oaky	Beef, lamb	**
Sigalas Mezzo	Santorini/Aegean Islands	White	Floral, honey, crisp	Shellfish, fish	**
MALTA					
Delicata Anchor Bay Rosé	Malta	Rosé	Fruity, berry	Antipasto	*
Delicata Chardonnay Superiore	Malta	White	Tropical fruit, citrus	Chicken	**
Delicata Fumé Blanc	Malta	White	Crisp, fruity	Shellfish	**
Delicata Golden Bay White	Malta	White	Fruity, melon	Shellfish	*
Delicata Grand Vin de Hauteville–Cabernet Sauvignon	Malta	Red	Berry, spicy	Sausages	**
Delicata Grand Vin de Hauteville–Oak Aged Chardonnay	Malta	White	Tropical fruit, oaky	Chicken	**
Delicata Green Label Dry	Malta	White	Zingy, citrus	Fish	*
Delicata Green Label Medium-Dry	Malta	White	Fruity, tropical fruit	Fish	**
Delicata Paradise Bay Red	Malta	Red	Earthy, berry	Pasta	**
Delicata Red Label Gellewza	Malta	Red	Berry, spicy	Pizza	**
Delicata Red Label Rosé	Malta	Rosé	Berry, fruity	Antipasto	*
Delicata Sauvignon Blanc	Malta	White	Zingy, grassy	Salads	**
Delicata St Paul's Bay White	Malta	White	Fruity, melon	Fish	*
Delicata Trebbiano Classico	Malta	White	Fruity, minerally	Pasta	*
Marsovin Antonin Blanc	Malta	White	Citrus, fruity	Salads	*
Marsovin Antonin Red	Malta	Red	Earthy, spicy	Pasta	*
Marsovin Cassar de Malte, Méthode Traditionelle	Malta	Sparkling	Crisp, fruity	Aperitif	**
Marsovin Cheval Franc	Malta	Red	Berry, herbaceous	Lamb	**
CYPRUS					
ETKO Despotika	Cyprus	Red	Berry, spicy	Cheese	**
ETKO Ino	Cyprus	Red	Spicy, earthy	Cold meats, stew, offal	**
ETKO Olympus	Cyprus	Red	Smoky, berry	Cold meats	**
ETKO Salera Red	Cyprus	Red	Berry, gamey	Pasta	*
ETKO Salera White	Cyprus	White	Floral, citrus	Fish	*
KEO Alkion	Cyprus	White	Crisp, citrus	Shellfish	*
KEO Cabernet Sauvignon	Cyprus	Red	Herbaceous, berry	Lamb	**
KEO Commanderie St John	Cyprus	Sweet	Sweet, honey, raisiny	Nuts	**
KEO Domaine d'Ahera	Cyprus	Red	Plums, berry	Cold meats, stew, offal	**
KEO Heritage	Cyprus	Red	Earthy, berry	Sausages	**
KEO Thisbe	Cyprus	White	Citrus, minerally	Chicken	**

AFRICA

Wine name	Region	Style	Flavor/Bouquet	Compatible Foods	Price Range
ALGERIA					
ONCV Algerian Red	Coteaux de Tlemcem/Oran	Red	Earthy, spicy	Cold meats, stew, offal	*
ONCV El Bordj Domaine El Bordj	Coteaux de Mascara/Oran	Red	Berry, spicy	Stew	**
ONCV Miliana Coteaux du Zaccar	Coteaux du Zaccar/Alger	Red	Berry, plums	Stew	**
ONCV Tlemcem Impressions	Coteaux de Tlemcem/Oran	Red	Berry, spicy	Sausages	**
ONCV Tlemcem Sand Ripples	Coteaux de Tlemcem/Oran	Red	Plums, spicy	Pasta	*

SOUTH AFRICA

Wine name	Region	Style	Flavor/Bouquet	Compatible Foods	Price Range
Alto Cabernet Sauvignon	Stellenbosch	Red	Tannic, herbaceous	Lamb	**
Axe Hill Vintage Port	Klein Karoo	Fortified	Sweet, spirity	Nuts	**
Backsberg Cabernet Sauvignon	Paarl	Red	Berry, tannic, herbaceous	Lamb	**
Backsberg Merlot	Paarl	Red	Plums, fruity	Pasta	**
Backsberg Shiraz	Paarl	Red	Earthy, tannic	Beef	**
Beaumont Natural Sweet Dessert Wine	Walker Bay	Sweet	Honey, sweet	Dessert	**
Bellingham Cabernet Franc	Franschhoek	Red	Berry, herbaceous	Lamb	**
Beryerskloof Pinotage	Stellenbosch	Red	Berry, leathery	Pizza	**
Beyerskloof Cabernet Sauvignon	Stellenbosch	Red	Berry, tannic	Lamb	**
Bloemendal Sauvignon Blanc	Durbanville	White	Citrus, grassy	Shellfish	**
Boekenhoutskloof Shiraz	Franschhoek	Red	Berry, tannic	Sausages	**
Bon Courage Red Muscadel	Robertson	Fortified	Sweet, raisiny	Nuts	**
Boplaas Port	Klein Karoo	Fortified	Sweet, raisiny	Cheese	**
Boplaas Vintage Reserve Port	Klein Karoo	Fortified	Sweet, spirity, fruity	Cheese	**
Boschendal Brut MCC	Franschhoek	Sparkling	Crisp, yeasty	Aperitif	**
Boschendal Chardonnay Reserve	Franschhoek	White	Tropical fruit, oaky, spicy	Veal	**
Boschendal Merlot	Franschhoek	Red	Berry, fruit cake	Lamb	**
Bouchard Finlayson Galpin Peak Pinot Noir	Walker Bay	Red	Smoky, berry	Duck	**
Bouwland Cabernet Merlot	Stellenbosch	Red	Herbaceous, plums	Lamb	**
Bouwland Pinotage	Stellenbosch	Red	Leathery, plums	Stew	**
Brampton Cabernet Sauvignon	Stellenbosch	Red	Berry, herbaceous	Lamb	**
Brampton Sauvignon Blanc	Stellenbosch	White	Citrus, zingy	Shellfish	**
Buitenverwachting Chardonnay	Constantia	White	Melon, citrus	Chicken	**
Buitenverwachting Christine Red Blend	Constantia	Red	Berry, smoky	Cold meats, stew, offal	**
Buitenverwachting Sauvignon Blanc	Constantia	White	Grassy, citrus	Shellfish	**
Cape Levant Pinotage	Paarl	Red	Berry, earthy	Stew	**
Clos Malverne Red Blend	Stellenbosch	Red	Berry, tannic	Pasta	**
Constantia Uitsig Reserve Chardonnay	Constantia	White	Melon, oaky	Chicken	**
Constantia Uitsig Reserve Semillon	Constantia	White	Citrus, grassy	Antipasto	**
Cordoba Crescendo Red Blend	Stellenbosch	Red	Tannic, spicy, earthy	Cheese	**
Cordoba Shiraz	Stellenbosch	Red	Earthy, tannic, berry	Beef	**
Darling Cellars Cabernet Sauvignon	Swartland	Red	Herbaceous, berry	Lamb	**
Darling Cellars Groenkloof Pinotage	Swartland	Red	Spicy, earthy	Cold meats	**
De Trafford Cabernet Sauvignon	Stellenbosch	Red	Berry, herbaceous	Lamb	**
De Trafford Chenin Blanc	Stellenbosch	White	Apples, floral	Mediterranean	**
De Trafford Merlot	Stellenbosch	Red	Berry, plums	Lamb	**
De Trafford Reserve Red Blend	Stellenbosch	Red	Berry, tannic	Beef	**
De Trafford Shiraz	Stellenbosch	Red	Berry, earthy	Cold meats, stew, offal	**
De Wetshof d'Honneur Chardonnay	Robertson	White	Melon, citrus	Fish	**
De Wetshof Finesse Chardonnay	Robertson	White	Tropical fruit, melon	Fish	**
De Wetshof Noble Late Harvest	Robertson	Sweet	Sweet, mandarin	Dessert	**
Delaire Chardonnay	Stellenbosch	White	Melon, tropical fruit	Fish	**
Delheim Cabernet Sauvignon	Stellenbosch	Red	Berry, herbaceous	Lamb	**
Delheim Gewurztraminer	Stellenbosch	White	Spicy, floral	Asian	**
Delheim Merlot	Stellenbosch	Red	Plums, berry	Pizza	**
Delheim Shiraz	Stellenbosch	Red	Earthy, tannic, berry	Beef	**
Diemersdal Pinotage	Durbanville	Red	Berry, plums	Cold meats, stew, offal	**
Diemersdal Shiraz	Durbanville	Red	Berry, tannic	Beef	**
Eikendal Chardonnay	Stellenbosch	White	Melon, citrus	Fish	**
Fairview Cabernet Sauvignon	Paarl	Red	Berry, herbaceous	Lamb	**
Fairview Shiraz	Paarl	Red	Berry, gamey	Stew	**
Genesis Cabernet Sauvignon	Stellenbosch	Red	Herbaceous, tannic	Lamb	**
Genesis Shiraz	Stellenbosch	Red	Earthy, minerally, berry	Beef	**
Glen Carlou (Reserve) Chardonnay	Paarl	White	Tropical fruit, oaky	Fish	**
Glen Carlou Chardonnay	Paarl	White	Melon, tropical fruit	Pork	**
Glen Carlou Grand Classique Red Blend	Paarl	Red	Berry, spicy	Veal	**
Glen Carlou Peter Devereux Chenin Blanc	Paarl	White	Apples, tropical fruit	Fish	**
Graham Beck Blanc de Blancs MCC	Robertson	Sparkling	Crisp, minerally, citrus	Aperitif	**
Graham Beck Pinotage	Coastal	Red	Earthy, berry	Sausages	**
Graham Beck Shiraz	Coastal	Red	Earthy, berry, spicy	Beef	**
Graham Beck The Ridge Shiraz	Robertson	Red	Berry, tannic, earthy	Cheese	**
Grangehurst CIWG Cabernet Sauvignon	Stellenbosch	Red	Berry, minerally, complex	Lamb	***
Grangehurst CIWG Pinotage	Stellenbosch	Red	Berry, earthy	Stew	**

SOUTH AFRICA (continued)

Wine name	Region	Style	Flavor/Bouquet	Compatible Foods	Price Range
Grangehurst Merlot	Stellenbosch	Red	Fruit cake, complex	Game	***
Grangehurst Red Blend	Stellenbosch	Red	Complex, tannic, berry	Beef	***
Groot Constantia Chardonnay Reserve	Constantia	White	Citrus, apples	Chicken	**
Groot Constantia Gewurztraminer	Constantia	White	Spicy, floral	Sausages	**
Groot Constantia Rhine Riesling	Constantia	White	Floral, citrus	Fish	**
Groot Constantia Shiraz	Constantia	Red	Earthy, berry	Beef	**
Hamilton Russell Chardonnay	Walker Bay	White	Melon, tropical fruit	Fish	**
Hamilton Russell Pinot Noir	Walker Bay	Red	Berry, spicy	Duck	***
Hartenberg Barrel Fermented Chenin Blanc	Stellenbosch	White	Apples, oaky	Salads	**
Hartenberg Chardonnay	Stellenbosch	White	Melon, tropical fruit	Fish	**
Hartenberg Merlot	Stellenbosch	Red	Fruit cake, plums	Lamb	**
Hartenberg Shiraz	Stellenbosch	Red	Earthy, berry	Beef	**
Hazendal Shiraz/Cabernet Red Blend	Stellenbosch	Red	Berry, tannic	Stew	**
Hidden Valley Pinotage	Stellenbosch	Red	Earthy, leathery	Stew	**
Jacobsdal Pinotage	Stellenbosch	Red	Leathery, plums	Cold meats, stew, offal	**
JC Le Roux Chardonnay MCC	Stellenbosch	Sparkling	Crisp, fruity	Aperitif	**
JC Le Roux Pinot Noir MCC	Stellenbosch	Sparkling	Yeasty, crisp	Aperitif	**
Jordan Chardonnay	Stellenbosch	White	Melon, tropical fruit	Fish	**
Jordan Merlot	Stellenbosch	Red	Berry, fruit cake	Lamb	**
Kaapzicht Pinotage	Stellenbosch	Red	Berry, plums	Stew	**
Kaapzicht Reserve Cabernet Sauvignon	Stellenbosch	Red	Berry, herbaceous	Lamb	**
Kaapzicht Reserve Pinotage	Stellenbosch	Red	Berry, earthy, complex	Stew	**
Kaapzicht Shiraz	Stellenbosch	Red	Earthy, berry, leathery	Pasta	**
Kanonkop Cabernet Sauvignon	Stellenbosch	Red	Berry, complex, herbaceous	Lamb	**
Kanonkop CIWG Pinotage	Stellenbosch	Red	Earthy, berry	Stew	**
Kanonkop Paul Sauer Red Blend	Stellenbosch	Red	Berry, complex, tannic	Lamb	**
Kanonkop Pinotage	Stellenbosch	Red	Earthy, leathery	Stew	**
Kanu Chardonnay	Stellenbosch	White	Melon, citrus	Fish	**
Karoo Die Krans Vintage Reserve Port	Klein Karoo	Fortified	Sweet, spirity, powerful	Nuts	**
Klein Constantia Rhine Riesling	Constantia	White	Floral, spicy	Fish	**
Klein Constantia Sauvignon Blanc	Constantia	White	Zingy, citrus	Shellfish	**
Klein Constantia Shiraz	Constantia	Red	Earthy, plums	Beef	**
Krone Borealis MCC	Tulbagh	Sparkling	Crisp, fruity	Aperitif	**
KWV Cathedral Cellars Cabernet Franc	Coastal	Red	Berry, herbaceous	Lamb	**
KWV Cathedral Cellars Cabernet Sauvignon	Coastal	Red	Berry, herbaceous	Lamb	**
KWV Cathedral Cellars Merlot	Coastal	Red	Berry, plums	Beef	**
KWV Cathedral Cellars Pinotage	Coastal	Red	Berry, earthy	Cold meats, stew, offal	**
KWV Cathedral Cellars Port	Coastal	Fortified	Sweet, spirity	Nuts	**
KWV Cathedral Cellars Shiraz	Coastal	Red	Berry, spicy	Beef	**
KWV Cathedral Cellars Triptych Red Blend	Coastal	Red	Earthy, minerally, spicy	Lamb	**
L'Avenir Cabernet Sauvignon	Stellenbosch	Red	Berry, herbaceous	Lamb	**
L'Avenir Chenin Blanc	Stellenbosch	White	Apples, citrus	Antipasto	**
L'Avenir CIWG Pinotage	Stellenbosch	Red	Berry, earthy	Stew	**
L'Avenir L'Ami Simon Red Blend	Stellenbosch	Red	Minerally, plums	Sausages	**
L'Avenir Pinotage	Stellenbosch	Red	Plums, earthy	Cold meats, stew, offal	**
L'Avenir Sauvignon Blanc	Stellenbosch	White	Zingy, citrus	Shellfish	**
L'Avenir Vin D'Erstelle White Blend	Stellenbosch	White	Melon, zingy	Salads	**
L'Avenir Vin de Meurveur Dessert Wine	Stellenbosch	Sweet	Sweet, citrus	Dessert	**
Laborie Cabernet Sauvignon	Paarl	Red	Berry, fruity, herbaceous	Pizza	**
Laibach Cabernet Sauvignon	Stellenbosch	Red	Berry, herbaceous	Lamb	**
Landskroon Port	Paarl	Fortified	Sweet, raisiny	Nuts	**
Lanzerac Cabernet Sauvignon	Stellenbosch	Red	Berry, herbaceous	Lamb	**
Le Bonheur Prima Red Blend	Stellenbosch	Red	Spicy, earthy	Sausages	**
Le Riche Reserve Cabernet Sauvignon	Stellenbosch	Red	Herbaceous, berry	Lamb	**
Lievland Noble Late Harvest Reserve Dessert Wine	Stellenbosch	Sweet	Honey, sweet	Dessert	**
Longridge Chardonnay	Stellenbosch	White	Melon, spicy	Fish	**
Longridge Merlot	Stellenbosch	Red	Plum, berry	Lamb	**
Meerlust Rubicon Red Blend	Stellenbosch	Red	Spicy, earthy, oaky	Beef	**
Morgenhof Chenin Blanc	Stellenbosch	White	Apples, fruity	Fish	**
Morgenhof LBV Port	Stellenbosch	Fortified	Sweet, raisiny	Nuts	**
Morgenhof Premier Selection Red Blend	Stellenbosch	Red	Earthy, berry	Cheese	**
Mulderbosch Barrel Fermented Sauvignon Blanc	Stellenbosch	White	Zingy, oaky, crisp	Pasta	**
Mulderbosch Chardonnay	Stellenbosch	White	Melon, citrus	Veal	**

SOUTH AFRICA (continued)

Wine name	Region	Style	Flavor/Bouquet	Compatible Foods	Price Range
Mulderbosch Sauvignon Blanc	Stellenbosch	White	Zingy, grassy	Shellfish	**
Mulderbosch Steen op Hout Chenin Blanc	Stellenbosch	White	Tropical fruit, spicy	Cheese	**
Nederburg Auction Cabernet Sauvignon	Paarl	Red	Berry, herbaceous	Lamb	**
Nederburg Bin R103 Red Blend	Paarl	Red	Berry, plums	Stew	**
Nederburg Bin R115 Red Blend	Paarl	Red	Spicy, berry	Beef	**
Nederburg Bin R163 Cabernet Sauvignon	Paarl	Red	Berry, herbaceous, tannic	Lamb	**
Nederburg Bin S316 Noble Late Harvest	Paarl	Sweet	Sweet, citrus	Dessert	**
Nederburg Edelkeur Dessert Wine	Paarl	Sweet	Sweet, mandarin	Dessert	***
Nederburg Eminence Dessert Wine	Paarl	Sweet	Sweet, complex, mandarin	Dessert	***
Nederburg Gewurztraminer	Paarl	White	Spicy, floral	Asian	**
Nederburg Noble Late Harvest Dessert Wine	Paarl	Sweet	Sweet, citrus	Dessert	**
Neethlinghsof Semillon Noble Late Harvest Dessert Wine	Stellenbosch	Sweet	Sweet, mandarin	Dessert	**
Neethlingshof Gewurztraminer	Stellenbosch	White	Spicy, floral	Asian	**
Neethlingshof Weisser Rielsing Noble Late Harvest Dessert Wine	Stellenbosch	Sweet	Sweet, honey	Dessert	**
Neil Ellis Cabernet Sauvignon	Stellenbosch	Red	Herbaceous, berry	Lamb	**
Neil Ellis Elgin Chardonnay	Elgin	White	Tropical fruit, melon	Fish	**
Neil Ellis Elgin Sauvignon Blanc	Elgin	White	Citrus, zingy	Shellfish	**
Neil Ellis Groenekloof Sauvignon Blanc	Darling	White	Zingy, citrus	Shellfish	**
Neil Ellis Reserve Cabernet Sauvignon	Stellenbosch	Red	Herbaceous, oaky	Cold meats	**
Neil Ellis Reserve Shiraz	Stellenbosch	Red	Berry, earthy	Cold meats, stew, offal	**
Nuy Red Muskadel Fortified Dessert Wine	Worcester	Sweet	Raisiny, nutty, complex	Cheese	**
Nuy Wit Muskadel Fortified Dessert Wine	Worcester	Sweet	Complex, raisiny	Nuts	**
Overgaauw Cape Vintage Port	Stellenbosch	Fortified	Sweet, rich	Nuts	**
Overgaauw Merlot	Stellenbosch	Red	Plums, berry	Lamb	**
Overgaauw Touirga Nacional Port	Stellenbosch	Fortified	Sweet, raisiny	Cheese	**
Paul Cluver Chardonnay	Elgin	White	Melon, citrus	Fish	**
Plaisir de Merle Cabernet Sauvignon	Franschhoek	Red	Herbaceous, tannic	Lamb	**
Pongrácz MCC	Stellenbosch	Sparkling	Crisp, fruity	Aperitif	**
Rust en Vrede Estate Red Blend	Stellenbosch	Red	Earthy, spicy	Pasta	**
Rustenberg Cabernet Sauvignon	Stellenbosch	Red	Herbaceous, berry	Lamb	**
Rustenberg Red Blend	Stellenbosch	Red	Earthy, berry	Sausages	**
Rusterberg Peter Barlow Red Blend	Stellenbosch	Red	Earthy, smoky	Cheese	**
Saxenburg Private Collection Cabernet Sauvignon	Stellenbosch	Red	Berry, herbaceous	Lamb	**
Saxenburg Private Collection Pinotage	Stellenbosch	Red	Earthy, spicy	Cold meats, stew, offal	**
Saxenburg Private Collection Sauvignon Blanc	Stellenbosch	White	Zingy, citrus	Shellfish	**
Saxenburg Private Collection Shiraz	Stellenbosch	Red	Earthy, berry	Beef	**
Saxenburg Reserve Shiraz	Stellenbosch	Red	Berry, spicy	Cold meats	***
Simonsig Chardonnay	Stellenbosch	White	Spicy, oaky, melon	Fish	**
Simonsig Frans Malan Reserve Red Blend	Stellenbosch	Red	Earthy, berry, oaky	Lamb	**
Simonsig Pinotage	Stellenbosch	Red	Earthy, spicy	Cold meats, stew, offal	**
Simonsig Red Hill Pinotage	Stellenbosch	Red	Berry, earthy	Sausages	**
Simonsig Reserve Shiraz	Stellenbosch	Red	Earthy, spicy, oaky	Beef	**
Simonsig Shiraz	Stellenbosch	Red	Berry, earthy	Pasta	**
Simonsig Tiara Red Blend	Stellenbosch	Red	Fruity, berry	Cold meats	**
Simonsig Weisser Riesling	Stellenbosch	White	Floral, citrus	Fish	**
Simonsvlei Hercules Paragon Chardonnay	Paarl	White	Melon, tropical fruit	Fish	**
Simonsvlei Hercules Paragon Shiraz	Paarl	Red	Berry, earthy	Cold meats, stew, offal	**
Slaley Shiraz	Stellenbosch	Red	Earthy, spicy	Pizza	**
Southern Right Pinotage	Walker Bay	Red	Earthy, spicy	Cold meats, stew, offal	**
Spice Route Reserve Chenin Blanc	Swartland	White	Tropical fruit, melon	Fish	**
Spice Route Reserve Pinotage	Swartland	Red	Earthy, spicy	Pasta	**
Spier IV Spears Sauvignon Blanc	Stellenbosch	White	Zingy, citrus	Shellfish	**
Springfield Life From Stone Sauvignon Blanc	Robertson	White	Zingy, citrus	Shellfish	**
Steenberg Oaked Semillon	Constantia	White	Grassy, oaky	Veal	**
Steenberg Reserve Sauvignon Blanc	Constantia	White	Citrus, tropical fruit	Salads	**
Steenberg Sauvignon Blanc	Constantia	White	Zingy, citrus	Salads	**
Steenberg Semillon	Constantia	White	Tropical fruit, fruity	Fish	**
Stellenzicht Chardonnay	Stellenbosch	White	Melon, oaky	Fish	**
Stellenzicht Reserve Semillon	Stellenbosch	White	Tropical fruit, citrus	Veal	**
Stellenzicht Syrah Shiraz	Stellenbosch	Red	Earthy, berry	Beef	**
Stellenzicht Weisser Riesling NLH Dessert	Stellenbosch	Sweet	Sweet, honey	Dessert	***
Thelema Cabernet Sauvignon	Stellenbosch	Red	Herbaceous, berry	Cheese	***

SOUTH AFRICA (continued)

Wine name	Region	Style	Flavor/Bouquet	Compatible Foods	Price Range
Thelema Chardonnay	Stellenbosch	White	Citrus, tropical fruit	Fish	**
Thelema Eds Reserve Chardonnay	Stellenbosch	White	Citrus, oaky	Veal	**
Thelema Merlot	Stellenbosch	Red	Plums, berry	Lamb	**
Thelema Reserve Chardonnay	Stellenbosch	White	Spicy, citrus, oaky	Chicken	***
Thelema Sauvignon Blanc	Stellenbosch	White	Zingy, citrus	Fish	**
Uiterwyk Estate Blend Red Blend	Stellenbosch	Red	Earthy, berry	Beef	**
Uiterwyk Merlot	Stellenbosch	Red	Smoky, berry	Pizza	**
Uiterwyk Top of the Hill Pinotage	Stellenbosch	Red	Earthy, spicy	Cold meats, stew, offal	**
Veenwouden Classic Red Blend	Paarl	Red	Berry, plums	Stew	**
Veenwouden Merlot	Paarl	Red	Plums, fruit cake	Lamb	**
Vergelegen Mill Race Red Red Blend	Stellenbosch	Red	Smoky, spicy	Sausages	**
Vergelegen Reserve Chardonnay	Stellenbosch	White	Melon, tropical fruit	Fish	**
Vergelegen Reserve Sauvignon Blanc	Stellenbosch	White	Citrus, crisp	Fish	**
Vergelegen Sauvignon Blanc	Stellenbosch	White	Grassy, citrus	Shellfish	**
Vergenoegd Cabernet Sauvignon	Stellenbosch	Red	Herbaceous, berry	Lamb	**
Vergenoegd Port	Stellenbosch	Fortified	Sweet, raisiny	Cheese	**
Vergenoegd Reserve Red Blend	Stellenbosch	Red	Smoky, earthy	Sausages	**
Villiera Bush Vine Sauvignon Blanc	Paarl	White	Grassy, tropical fruit	Salads	**
Villiera Carte d'Or MCC	Paarl	Sparkling	Austere, crisp	Shellfish	**
Villiera Chenin Blanc	Paarl	White	Apples, citrus	Pasta	**
Villiera Gewurztraminer	Paarl	White	Floral, spicy	Asian	**
Villiera Munro Brut MCC	Paarl	Sparkling	Crisp, yeasty	Aperitif	**
Villiera Sauvignon Blanc	Paarl	White	Zingy, citrus	Shellfish	**
Warwick Cabernet Franc	Stellenbosch	Red	Berry, herbaceous	Lamb	**
Warwick Chardonnay	Stellenbosch	White	Melon, tropical fruit	Fish	**
Warwick Trilogy Red Blend	Stellenbosch	Red	Earthy, smoky	Cold meats	**
Welmoed Reserve Sauvignon Blanc	Stellenbosch	White	Crisp, citrus	Salads	**
Zandvliet Chardonnay	Robertson	White	Melon, minerally	Fish	**
Zandvliet Shiraz	Robertson	Red	Berry, tannic	Beef	**
Zevenwacht Chardonnay	Stellenbosch	White	Tropical fruit, citrus	Fish	**
Zevenwacht Reserve Merlot	Stellenbosch	Red	Plums, spicy	Beef	**
Zonnebloem Pinotage	Stellenbosch	Red	Earthy, spicy	Cold meats, stew, offal	**
Zonnebloem Sémillon-Sauvignon Blanc White Blend	Stellenbosch	White	Crisp, citrus	Pizza	**

THE MIDDLE EAST

Wine name	Region	Style	Flavor/Bouquet	Compatible Foods	Price Range
ISRAEL					
Barkan Cellars Barkan Classic Cabernet Sauvignon	Samson	Red	Berry, herbaceous	Lamb	**
Barkan Cellars Cabernet Sauvignon Superieur	Galilee	Red	Berry, herbaceous	Lamb	**
Barkan Cellars Chardonnay Superieur	Galilee	White	Tropical fruit, melon	Chicken	**
Barkan Cellars Emerald Riesling Reserved	Galilee	White	Floral, crisp	Salads	**
Barkan Cellars Merlot Reserved	Galilee	Red	Plums, earthy	Cold meats	**
Baron Cellars Jonathan Tishbi Chardonnay	Shomron	White	Tropical fruit, minerally	Chicken	**
Baron Cellars Tishbi Brut NV	Shomron	Sparkling	Crisp, fruity	Aperitif	**
Baron Cellars Tishbi Estate Merlot	Samson	Red	Spicy, plums	Sausages	**
Baron Cellars Tishbi Estate Sauvignon Blanc	Galilee	White	Zingy, citrus	Fish	**
Baron Cellars Tishbi Estate Sauvignon Blanc	Shomron	White	Zingy, fruity	Fish	**
Binyamina Wine Cellars Binyamina Muscat	Shomron	White	Sweet, rich	Nuts	**
Binyamina Wine Cellars Special Reserve Merlot	Galilee	Red	Fruit cake, earthy	Sausages	**
Carmel 1998 Carmel Selected Emerald Riesling	Samson & Shomron	White	Floral, zingy, minerally	Fish	**
Carmel Merlot Private Collection	Judean Hills	Red	Plums, spicy	Stew	**
Dalton Chardonnay	Kere Ben Zimra/Galilee	White	Tropical fruit, citrus	Chicken	**
Domaine du Castel (Bordeaux Blend) Castel Grand Vin	Ramat Raziel/Judean Hills	Red	Herbaceous, plums, spicy	Sausages	**
Golan Heights Winery Gamla Cabernet Sauvignon	Golan Heights/Galilee	Red	Berry, herbaceous	Lamb	**
Golan Heights Winery Yarden Blanc de Blancs	Golan Heights/Galilee	Sparkling	Citrus, crisp	Aperitif	**
Golan Heights Winery Yarden Brut NV	Golan Heights/Galilee	Sparkling	Crisp, fruity	Aperitif	**
Golan Heights Winery Yarden Cabernet Sauvignon	Mid Golan/Galilee	Red	Berry, herbaceous	Cold meats, stew	**
Golan Heights Winery Yarden Chardonnay	Northern Golan/Galilee	White	Tropical fruit, citrus	Fish	**
Golan Heights Winery Yarden Gewurztraminer	Northern Golan/Galilee	White	Spicy, floral	Asian	**
Golan Heights Winery Yarden Katzrin Cabernet Sauvignon	Mid Golan/Galilee	Red	Herbaceous, spicy, berry	Lamb	**
Golan Heights Winery Yarden Katzrin Chardonnay	Northern Golan/Galilee	White	Tropical fruit, citrus	Fish	**
Golan Heights Winery Yarden Merlot	Mid Golan/Galilee	Red	Plums, earthy	Cheese	**

THE MIDDLE EAST (continued)

Wine name	Region	Style	Flavor/Bouquet	Compatible Foods	Price Range
Golan Heights Winery Yarden Mount Hermon Red	Golan Heights/Galilee	Red	Berry, spicy	Game	✳✳
Golan Heights Winery Yarden Muscat	Lower Golan/Galilee	White	Grapey, citrus, minerally	Mediterranean	✳✳
Golan Heights Winery Yarden Sauvignon Blanc	Golan Heights/Galilee	White	Zingy, citrus	Salads	✳✳
Margalit Cabernet Sauvignon	Galilee	Red	Herbaceous, berry	Stew	✳✳
Margalit Merlot	Galilee	Red	Plums, spicy	Sausages	✳✳
Tsora Kibbutz Tsora Sauvignon Blanc	Samson	White	Zingy, citrus	Salads	✳✳

AUSTRALIA

Wine name	Region	Style	Flavor/Bouquet	Compatible Foods	Price Range
Abbey Vale Verdelho	Western Australia	White	Citrus, tropical fruit	Chicken	✳✳
Alkoomi Blackbutt Cabernet Sauvignon	Western Australia	Red	Berry, oaky, tannic	Lamb	✳✳✳
Alkoomi Riesling	Western Australia	White	Floral	Shellfish	✳✳
Alkoomi Sauvignon Blanc	Western Australia	White	Tropical fruit	Salads	✳✳
All Saints Aleatico	North East Victoria/Victoria	Red	Fruity	Asian	✳✳
All Saints Show Reserve Tokay	North East Victoria/Victoria	Fortified	Sweet, complex	Nuts	✳✳
Allandale Chardonnay	New South Wales	White	Nutty, tropical fruit	Fish	✳✳
Amberley Cabernet Merlot	Western Australia	Red	Berry	Lamb	✳✳
Amberley Semillon Sauvignon Blanc	Western Australia	White	Tropical fruit	Shellfish	✳✳
Amberley Shiraz	Western Australia	Red	Berry, earthy	Beef	✳✳
Andrew Harris Reserve Shiraz	New South Wales	Red	Complex, berry, spicy	Beef	✳
Andrew Harris The Vision	New South Wales	Red	Oaky, complex, berry	Beef	✳✳✳
Angove's Classic Reserve Cabernet Sauvignon	Riverland/South Australia	Red	Berry, plum	Stew	✳✳
Angove's Classic Reserve Chardonnay	Riverland/South Australia	White	Tropical fruit	Pork	✳✳
Angove's Classic Reserve Shiraz	Riverland/South Australia	Red	Berry, earthy	Pasta	✳✳
Annie's Lane Contour Shiraz	Clare Valley/South Australia	Red	Berry, tannic, spicy	Beef	✳✳
Annie's Lane Riesling	Clare Valley/South Australia	White	Citrus, floral	Shellfish	✳✳
Annie's Lane Semillon	Clare Valley/South Australia	White	Tropical fruit, nutty	Antipasto	✳✳
Arrowfield Show Reserve Shiraz	New South Wales	Red	Berry, earthy	Stew	✳✳
Ashbrook Semillon	Western Australia	White	Grassy, floral	Salads	✳✳
Ashton Hills Chardonnay	Adelaide Hills/South Australia	White	Nutty, complex	Chicken	✳✳
Ashton Hills Reserve Pinot Noir	Adelaide Hills/South Australia	Red	Spicy, berry	Duck	✳✳
Ashton Hills Riesling	Adelaide Hills/South Australia	White	Citrus, floral	Shellfish	✳✳
Auldstone Cellars Late-picked Riesling	North East Victoria/Victoria	Sweet	Sweet, floral	Fruit	✳✳
Auldstone Cellars Shiraz	North East Victoria/Victoria	Red	Berry, earthy	Stew	✳✳
Baileys of Glenrowan 1920s Block Shiraz	North East Victoria/Victoria	Red	Powerful, berry, tannic	Stew	✳✳
Baileys of Glenrowan Founders Muscat	North East Victoria/Victoria	Fortified	Sweet, complex, raisiny	Nuts	✳✳
Baileys of Glenrowan Founders Tokay	North East Victoria/Victoria	Fortified	Complex, sweet, cold tea	Cheese	✳✳
Bald Mountain Chardonnay	Queensland	White	Tropical fruit	Fish	✳✳
Bald Mountain Late Harvest Sauvignon Blanc	Queensland	Sweet	Sweet, citrus	Fruit	✳✳
Balgownie Cabernet Sauvignon	Central Victoria	Red	Herbaceous, berry	Lamb	✳✳
Balgownie Shiraz	Central Victoria	Red	Berry, spicy	Beef	✳✳
Ballandean Black Label Cabernet Sauvignon	Queensland	Red	Berry, herbaceous	Lamb	✳✳
Ballandean Black Label Chardonnay	Queensland	White	Melon, tropical fruit	Fish	✳✳
Ballandean Black Label Merlot	Queensland	Red	Fruit cake, berry	Game	✳✳
Ballandean Late Harvest Sylvaner	Queensland	Sweet	Sweet, citrus	Fruit	✳✳
Ballingal Estate Botrytis Semillon	New South Wales	Sweet	Sweet, mandarin	Dessert	✳✳
Balnaves of Coonawarra Cabernet Merlot	Coonawarra/South Australia	Red	Herbaceous, berry	Lamb	✳✳
Balnaves of Coonawarra Chardonnay	Coonawarra/South Australia	White	Melon	Veal	✳✳
Bannockburn Cabernet Sauvignon	Geelong/Victoria	Red	Minerally, berry, herbaceous	Lamb	✳✳
Bannockburn Chardonnay	Geelong/Victoria	White	Nutty, complex, melon	Fish	✳✳
Bannockburn Pinot Noir	Geelong/Victoria	Red	Gamey, earthy, complex	Duck	✳✳
Bannockburn Shiraz	Geelong/Victoria	Red	Complex, spicy, berry	Beef	✳✳
Banrock Station Shiraz Cabernet	Riverland/South Australia	Red	Berry	Pizza	✳
Banrock Station Shiraz	Riverland/South Australia	Red	Berry	Pizza	✳
Banrock Station Sparkling Chardonnay	Riverland/South Australia	Sparkling	Citrus, melon	Salads	✳
Barambah Ridge Chardonnay	Queensland	White	Tropical fruit	Mediterranean	✳✳
Barossa Valley Estate E Black Pepper Shiraz	Barossa/South Australia	Red	Berry, oaky, earthy	Beef	✳✳✳
Barossa Valley Estate E Sparkling Shiraz	Barossa/South Australia	Sparkling	Oaky, plums, berry	Cold meats	✳✳
Barossa Valley Estate Ebenezer Cabernet Merlot	Barossa/South Australia	Red	Berry, tannic	Lamb	✳✳
Barossa Valley Estate Ebenezer Shiraz	Barossa/South Australia	Red	Berry, oaky, tannic	Beef	✳✳
Barwang Shiraz	New South Wales	Red	Berry, spicy	Cold meats	✳✳
Basedow Shiraz	Barossa/South Australia	Red	Berry, plum, oaky	Pasta	✳✳

AUSTRALIA *(continued)*

Wine name	Region	Style	Flavor/Bouquet	Compatible Foods	Price Range
Bass Phillip Chardonnay	Gippsland/Victoria	White	Melon, nutty	Fish	***
Bass Phillip Pinot Noir	Gippsland/Victoria	Red	Complex, berry, gamey	Duck	***
Best's Bin 0 Shiraz	Grampians & Western Victoria/Victoria	Red	Complex, earthy, berry	Beef	**
Best's Pinot Meunier	Grampians & Western Victoria/Victoria	Red	Berry, earthy	Pizza	**
Best's Pinot Noir	Grampians & Western Victoria/Victoria	Red	Spicy, berry	Game	**
Best's Thomson Family Shiraz	Grampians & Western Victoria/Victoria	Red	Berry, earthy	Beef	**
Bethany GR Shiraz	Barossa/South Australia	Red	Earthy, berry	Stew	**
Bethany Grenache Pressings	Barossa/South Australia	Red	Earthy, berry, tannic, powerful	Stew	**
Bimbadgen Semillon	New South Wales	White	Citrus	Veal	**
Blackjack Shiraz	Central Victoria	Red	Berry, earthy	Cold meats, stew, offal	**
Blass Adelaide Hills Cabernet Merlot	Adelaide Hills/South Australia	Red	Berry, spicy, oaky	Beef	**
Blass Barossa Valley Shiraz	Barossa/South Australia	Red	Berry, spicy, tannic	Beef	**
Blass Vineyard Selection Cabernet Sauvignon	Barossa/South Australia	Red	Berry, herbaceous, oaky	Sausages	**
Bloodwood Chardonnay	New South Wales	White	Tropical fruit, melon	Chicken	**
Bloodwood Ice Riesling	New South Wales	Sweet	Sweet, citrus	Dessert	**
Blue Pyrenees Estate Chardonnay	Grampians & Western Victoria/Victoria	White	Tropical fruit, melon	Veal	**
Blue Pyrenees Estate NV Reserve	Grampians & Western Victoria/Victoria	Sparkling	Crisp, citrus	Aperitif	**
Blue Pyrenees Estate Red Blend	Grampians & Western Victoria/Victoria	Red	Herbaceous, minerally, berry	Lamb	**
Bonneyview Cabernet Petit Verdot	Riverland/South Australia	Red	Berry, herbaceous	Stew	**
Bonneyview Chardonnay	Riverland/South Australia	White	Tropical fruit	Chicken	**
Bonneyview Petit Verdot Merlot	Riverland/South Australia	Red	Berry	Pasta	**
Botobolar Shiraz	New South Wales	Red	Berry, earthy	Cold meats, stew, offal	**
Bowen Estate Cabernet Sauvignon	Coonawarra/South Australia	Red	Berry, herbaceous, tannic, minerally	Lamb	**
Bowen Estate Chardonnay	Coonawarra/South Australia	White	Tropical fruit, nutty	Fish	**
Bowen Estate Shiraz	Coonawarra/South Australia	Red	Berry, spicy, tannic	Beef	**
Brangayne of Orange Reserve Chardonnay	New South Wales	White	Tropical fruit, complex	Fish	**
Brian Barry Juds Hill Cabernet Sauvignon	Clare Valley/South Australia	Red	Berry, herbaceous	Lamb	**
Briar Ridge Stockhausen Semillon	New South Wales	White	Citrus, toasty, complex	Chicken	**
Briar Ridge Stockhausen Shiraz	New South Wales	Red	Berry, earthy, leathery	Beef	**
Brokenwood Graveyard Shiraz	New South Wales	Red	Berry, complex, tannic	Beef	***
Brokenwood ILR Semillon	New South Wales	White	Complex, toasty, citrus	Pork	***
Brokenwood Semillon	New South Wales	White	Citrus	Fish	**
Brookland Valley Chardonnay	Western Australia	White	Melon, tropical fruit	Fish	**
Brookland Valley Sauvignon Blanc	Western Australia	White	Grassy, zingy	Shellfish	**
Brown Brothers Barbera	North East Victoria/Victoria	Red	Savoury, earthy	Mediterranean	**
Brown Brothers Classic Release Cabernet Sauvignon	North East Victoria/Victoria	Red	Berry, herbaceous	Lamb	**
Brown Brothers Late Harvested Noble Riesling	North East Victoria/Victoria	Sweet	Sweet, complex, citrus	Dessert	**
Brown Brothers Late Harvested Orange Muscat and Flora	North East Victoria/Victoria	Sweet	Sweet, citrus	Fruit	**
Brown Brothers Nebbiolo	North East Victoria/Victoria	Red	Earthy, berry, tannic	Pasta	**
Brown Brothers Shiraz	North East Victoria/Victoria	Red	Earthy, berry	Beef	**
Brown Brothers Very Old Liqueur Muscat	North East Victoria/Victoria	Fortified	Sweet, complex, raisiny	Nuts	**
Brown Brothers Vintage Port	North East Victoria/Victoria	Fortified	Sweet, licorice	Cheese	**
Bullers Museum Release Muscat	North East Victoria/Victoria	Fortified	Sweet, complex, raisiny	Nuts	***
Campbells Isabella Tokay	North East Victoria/Victoria	Fortified	Sweet, cold tea	Cheese	***
Campbells Merchant Prince Muscat	North East Victoria/Victoria	Fortified	Sweet, complex, raisiny	Nuts	***
Campbells The Barkly Durif	North East Victoria/Victoria	Red	Powerful, earthy, tannic	Stew	**
Canobolas-Smith Chardonnay	New South Wales	Red	Tropical fruit, nutty	Fish	**
Cape Mentelle Cabernet Sauvignon	Western Australia	Red	Berry, complex, minerally	Lamb	***
Cape Mentelle Chardonnay	Western Australia	White	Nutty, tropical fruit	Fish	**
Cape Mentelle Semillon Sauvignon Blanc	Western Australia	White	Grassy, tropical fruit	Salads	**
Cape Mentelle Shiraz	Western Australia	Red	Earthy, berry	Stew	**
Cape Mentelle Zinfandel	Western Australia	Red	Earthy, berry	Beef	**
Capel Vale Riesling	Western Australia	White	Floral	Salads	**
Capercaillie Chardonnay	New South Wales	White	Tropical fruit	Shellfish	**
Cassegrain Reserve Chambourcin	New South Wales	Red	Berry, plum	Cold meats	**
Cassegrain Reserve Chardonnay	New South Wales	White	Tropical fruit, melon	Fish	**

AUSTRALIA (continued)

Wine name	Region	Style	Flavor/Bouquet	Compatible Foods	Price Range
Cathcart Ridge Cabernet Merlot	Grampians & Western Victoria/Victoria	Red	Berry	Cold meats	**
Cathcart Ridge Shiraz	Grampians & Western Victoria/Victoria	Red	Spicy, berry	Beef	**
Chain of Ponds Amadeus Cabernet Sauvignon	Adelaide Hills/South Australia	Red	Herbaceous, berry	Lamb	**
Chain of Ponds Ledge Shiraz	Adelaide Hills/South Australia	Red	Spicy, berry	Beef	**
Chain of Ponds Riesling	Adelaide Hills/South Australia	White	Citrus, floral, zingy	Cheese	**
Chambers Rosewood Rare Muscat	North East Victoria/Victoria	Fortified	Raisiny, complex, sweet	Nuts	**
Chambers Rosewood Rare Tokay	North East Victoria/Victoria	Fortified	Complex, sweet, cold tea	Nuts	**
Chapel Hill Cabernet Sauvignon	McLaren Vale/South Australia	Red	Berry, herbaceous, complex	Lamb	**
Chapel Hill Shiraz	McLaren Vale/South Australia	Red	Berry, spicy	Beef	**
Chapel Hill The Vicar Cabernet Sauvignon Shiraz	McLaren Vale/South Australia	Red	Berry, spicy, tannic, oaky	Lamb	**
Chapel Hill Verdelho	McLaren Vale/South Australia	White	Tropical fruit	Salads	**
Charles Cimicky Merlot	Barossa/South Australia	Red	Fruit cake, berry, plum	Lamb	**
Charles Cimicky Shiraz	Barossa/South Australia	Red	Berry, plum	Stew	**
Charles Melton Nine Popes	Barossa/South Australia	Red	Berry, complex, earthy	Cold meats, stew, offal	**
Charles Melton Rose of Virginia	Barossa/South Australia	Rosé	Berry, floral	Cheese	**
Charles Melton Sparkling Red	Barossa/South Australia	Sparkling	Berry, smokey, powerful	Cold meats	**
Charles Sturt University Cabernet Sauvignon	New South Wales	Red	Berry, herbaceous	Sausages	**
Chateau Francois Semillon	New South Wales	White	Citrus, fruity	Chicken	**
Chateau Leamon Shiraz	Central Victoria	Red	Spicy, berry	Beef	**
Chateau Tahbilk Cabernet Sauvignon	Central Victoria	Red	Earthy, berry	Cold meats, stew, offal	**
Chateau Tahbilk Marsanne	Central Victoria	White	Citrus, tropical fruit	Antipasto	*
Chateau Xanadu Cabernet Reserve	Western Australia	Red	Berry, minerally, complex	Lamb	***
Chateau Xanadu Semillon	Western Australia	White	Grassy	Antipasto	**
Chatsfield Shiraz	Western Australia	Red	Berry	Stew	**
Chestnut Grove Verdelho	Western Australia	White	Tropical fruit	Veal	**
Clarendon Hills Cabernet Sauvignon	McLaren Vale/South Australia	Red	Berry, tannic, powerful	Lamb	**
Clarendon Hills Kangarilla Vineyard Old Vines Grenache	McLaren Vale/South Australia	Red	Berry, plum, powerful	Cold meats, stew, offal	***
Clarendon Hills Piggott Range Vineyard Shiraz	McLaren Vale/South Australia	Red	Spicy, berry, earthy, tannic, oaky	Sausages	***
Cleveland Winery Macedon Brut	Macedon/Victoria	Sparkling	Complex, citrus	Aperitif	**
Cleveland Winery Pinot Noir	Macedon/Victoria	Red	Spicy, berry	Game	**
Clonakilla Riesling	New South Wales	White	Citrus, floral	Asian	**
Clonakilla Shiraz/Viognier	New South Wales	Red	Berry, minerally, complex	Veal	**
Clovelly Estate Left Field Chardonnay	Queensland	White	Fruity	Chicken	**
Cobaw Ridge Chardonnay	Macedon/Victoria	White	Melon, tropical fruit	Fish	**
Cobaw Ridge Lagrein	Macedon/Victoria	Red	Berry, fruity	Antipasto	**
Cobaw Ridge Shiraz	Macedon/Victoria	Red	Earthy, berry	Beef	**
Cofield Chenin Blanc	North East Victoria/Victoria	White	Tropical fruit	Pasta	**
Cofield Late Harvest Tokay	North East Victoria/Victoria	White	Sweet, floral	Fruit	**
Cofield Sparkling Shiraz	North East Victoria/Victoria	Sparkling	Berry, plum	Cold meats	**
Coolangatta Estate Chardonnay	New South Wales	White	Tropical fruit, melon	Chicken	**
Cope-Williams R.O.M.S.E.Y. Brut	Macedon/Victoria	Sparkling	Crisp, complex, berry	Shellfish	**
Cope-Williams Willow (fortified white)	Macedon/Victoria	Fortified	Sweet, complex	Nuts	**
Coriole Diva Sangiovese Cabernet Sauvignon	McLaren Vale/South Australia	Red	Berry, herbaceous	Cold meats, stew, offal	**
Coriole Lalla Rookh Semillon	McLaren Vale/South Australia	White	Tropical fruit	Veal	**
Coriole Redstone Shiraz Cabernet Sauvignon Grenache Merlot	McLaren Vale/South Australia	Red	Berry, tannic	Stew	**
Cowra Estate Cabernet Franc Rosé	New South Wales	Rosé	Berry, fruity	Antipasto	**
Crabtree Watervale Cabernet Sauvignon	Clare Valley/South Australia	Red	Berry, herbaceous	Veal	**
Crabtree Watervale Riesling	Clare Valley/South Australia	White	Citrus, floral	Shellfish	**
Crabtree Watervale Shiraz Cabernet Sauvignon	Clare Valley/South Australia	Red	Berry, spicy	Stew	**
Crane Sparkling Chambourcin	Queensland	Sparkling	Berry, plum	Cold meats	**
Cranswick Autumn Gold	New South Wales	Sweet	Citrus, mandarin, sweet	Fruit	**
Cullen Cabernet Merlot	Western Australia	Red	Complex, minerally, berry	Lamb	***
Cullen Chardonnay	Western Australia	White	Nutty, complex, melon	Fish	**
Cullen Sauvignon Blanc Semillon	Western Australia	White	Grassy, zingy	Salads	**
D'Arenberg D'Arry's Original Shiraz Grenache	McLaren Vale/South Australia	Red	Berry, earthy	Sausages	*
D'Arenberg Peppermint Park Sparkling Chambourcin	McLaren Vale/South Australia	Sparkling	Fruit cake, berry	Cold meats	**
D'Arenberg The Footbolt Shiraz	McLaren Vale/South Australia	Red	Berry	Cold meats, stew, offal	**
D'Arenberg Twenty Eight Road Mourvedre	McLaren Vale/South Australia	Red	Berry, spicy, oaky, tannic	Stew	**
Dalwhinnie Chardonnay	Grampians & Western Victoria/Victoria	White	Complex, melon, nutty	Fish	**

AUSTRALIA (continued)

Wine name	Region	Style	Flavor/Bouquet	Compatible Foods	Price Range
Dalwhinnie Eagle Series Shiraz	Grampians & Western Victoria/Victoria	Red	Complex, spicy, berry	Beef	***
Dalwhinnie Moonambeel Cabernet	Grampians & Western Victoria/Victoria	Red	Berry, minerally, herbaceous	Lamb	**
Dalwhinnie Pinot Noir	Grampians & Western Victoria/Victoria	Red	Spicy, earthy, berry	Duck	**
David Traegar Verdelho	Central Victoria	White	Tropical fruit	Veal	**
David Wynn Patriarch Shiraz	Barossa/South Australia	Red	Berry, earthy	Beef	**
De Bortoli Black Noble	New South Wales	Fortified	Sweet, raisiny, fruit cake	Nuts	**
De Bortoli Noble One	New South Wales	Sweet	Sweet, citrus, mandarin	Dessert	**
Delatite Dead Man's Hill Gewurztraminer	Central Victoria	White	Spicy, floral	Asian	**
Delatite Riesling	Central Victoria	White	Floral	Shellfish	**
Devils Lair Cabernet Sauvignon	Western Australia	Red	Minerally, herbaceous, earthy	Lamb	**
Devils Lair Chardonnay	Western Australia	White	Melon, nutty	Fish	**
Doonkuna Estate Chardonnay	New South Wales	White	Melon, nutty	Fish	**
Doonkuna Estate Riesling	New South Wales	White	Citrus, floral	Salads	**
Dowie Doole Chenin Blanc	McLaren Vale/South Australia	White	Tropical fruit, nutty	Chicken	**
Dowie Doole Merlot	McLaren Vale/South Australia	Red	Berry, fruit cake, oaky	Lamb	**
Drayton's William Shiraz	New South Wales	Red	Berry, leathery	Stew	**
Elderton Command Shiraz	Barossa/South Australia	Red	Berry, powerful, oaky, tannic	Beef	***
Elderton Golden Semillon	Barossa/South Australia	Sweet	Sweet, mandarin, citrus	Dessert	**
Evans & Tate Redbrook Semillon	Western Australia	White	Fruity, tropical fruit	Shellfish	**
Evans & Tate Shiraz	Western Australia	Red	Earthy, minerally	Beef	**
Evans Family Hunter Valley Chardonnay	New South Wales	White	Tropical fruit, melon	Fish	**
Fox Creek JSM Shiraz Cabernets	McLaren Vale/South Australia	Red	Berry, plum	Sausages	**
Fox Creek Reserve Shiraz	McLaren Vale/South Australia	Red	Complex, berry, oaky, tannic, powerful	Beef	***
Fox Creek Vixen Sparkling Cabernet Sauvignon/Shiraz	McLaren Vale/South Australia	Sparkling	Plum, berry	Cold meats	**
Frankland Estate Isolation Ridge Shiraz	Western Australia	Red	Earthy, berry	Stew	**
Frankland Estate Olmo's Reward Bordeaux Blend	Western Australia	Red	Complex, herbaceous, berry	Lamb	**
Frankland Estate Riesling	Western Australia	White	Citrus, floral	Asian	**
Galah Wines Cabernet Sauvignon	Clare Valley/South Australia	Red	Berry	Lamb	**
Galah Wines Shiraz	Clare Valley/South Australia	Red	Berry, earthy	Pasta	**
Garden Gully Sparkling Pinot Noir	Grampians & Western Victoria/Victoria	Sparkling	Crisp, berry	Antipasto	**
Garden Gully Sparkling Red	Grampians & Western Victoria/Victoria	Sparkling	Berry, spicy	Cold meats	**
Geoff Merrill Cabernet Merlot	McLaren Vale/South Australia	Red	Berry, herbaceous	Lamb	**
Geoff Weaver Chardonnay	Adelaide Hills/South Australia	White	Complex with tropical flavour	Fish	**
Geoff Weaver Sauvignon Blanc	Adelaide Hills/South Australia	White	Zingy, grassy	Shellfish	**
Giaconda Chardonnay	North East Victoria/Victoria	White	Complex, nutty, minerally, tropical fruit	Fish	***
Giaconda Pinot Noir	North East Victoria/Victoria	Red	Earthy, gamey, spicy, complex, berry	Duck	***
Gilberts Riesling	Western Australia	White	Floral	Salads	**
Glaetzer Wines Bishop Shiraz	Barossa/South Australia	Red	Earthy, berry, tannic	Beef	**
Glenara Cabernet Sauvignon Merlot	Adelaide Hills/South Australia	Red	Herbaceous, berry	Lamb	**
Glenguin Merlot	New South Wales	Red	Berry, fruit cake	Cold meats	**
Glenguin Semillon	New South Wales	White	Citrus, toasty	Shellfish	**
Golden Grove Chardonnay	Queensland	White	Fruity	Fish	**
Goundrey Reserve Chardonnay	Western Australia	White	Melon, nutty	Chicken	**
Goundrey Reserve Shiraz	Western Australia	Red	Minerally, oaky, berry	Beef	**
Gralyn Cabernet Sauvignon	Western Australia	Red	Herbaceous, minerally	Stew	**
Gralyn Old Vine Shiraz	Western Australia	Red	Earthy, berry	Cold meats, stew, offal	**
Granite Ridge Cabernet Sauvignon	Queensland	Red	Berry, minerally, herbaceous	Lamb	**
Grant Burge Filsell Shiraz	Barossa/South Australia	Red	Berry, tannic	Stew	**
Grant Burge Meshach Shiraz	Barossa/South Australia	Red	Berry, tannic, oaky	Beef	***
Grant Burge The Holy Trinity Grenache Shiraz Mourvedre	Barossa/South Australia	Red	Earthy, berry, oaky	Cold meats, stew, offal	**
Grant Burge Zerk Semillon	Barossa/South Australia	White	Tropical fruit, oaky	Veal	**
Greenock Creek Creek Block Shiraz	Barossa/South Australia	Red	Berry, earthy, tannic	Beef	**
Grosset Gaia (Cabernet blend)	Clare Valley/South Australia	Red	Berry, herbaceous, minerally	Lamb	**
Grosset Pinot Noir	Clare Valley/South Australia	Red	Berry, spicy, gamey	Duck	**
Grosset Polish Hill Riesling	Clare Valley/South Australia	White	Citrus, floral, complex, minerally	Shellfish	**

AUSTRALIA *(continued)*

Wine name	Region	Style	Flavor/Bouquet	Compatible Foods	Price Range
Grosset Watervale Riesling	Clare Valley/South Australia	White	Citrus, floral, minerally	Fish	**
Haan Prestige Merlot	Barossa/South Australia	Red	Berry, fruit cake	Pork	**
Hamilton Hut Block Cabernet	McLaren Vale/South Australia	Red	Berry, tannic, complex	Lamb	**
Hamilton The Hills Chardonnay	Adelaide Hills/South Australia	White	Melon, complex	Chicken	**
Hanging Rock Winery Macedon Cuvee	Macedon/Victoria	Fortified	Complex, yeasty, berry, powerful	Fish	***
Hanging Rock Winery Victoria Chardonnay	Macedon/Victoria	White	Melon, tropical fruit	Fish	**
Hardys Eileen Hardy Shiraz	McLaren Vale/South Australia	Red	Berry, tannic, complex, oaky	Beef	***
Hardys Tintara Shiraz	McLaren Vale/South Australia	Red	Powerful, tannic, earthy, berry	Beef	**
Haselgrove H Botrytis Sauvignon Semillon	McLaren Vale/South Australia	Sweet	Sweet, mandarin	Dessert	**
Haselgrove H Futures Shiraz	McLaren Vale/South Australia	Red	Berry, oaky, powerful	Beef	**
Hay Shed Hill Cabernet Sauvignon	Western Australia	Red	Berry	Pasta	**
Heggies Riesling	Barossa/South Australia	White	Citrus, floral	Shellfish	**
Heggies Viognier	Barossa/South Australia	White	Tropical fruit, floral	Fish	**
Henschke Abbot's Prayer	Adelaide Hills/South Australia	Red	Berry, spicy	Lamb	**
Henschke Cyril Henschke Cabernet Sauvignon Merlot Cabernet Franc	Barossa/South Australia	Red	Berry, spicy	Lamb	**
Henschke Green's Hill Riesling	Adelaide Hills/South Australia	White	Citrus, floral	Asian	**
Henschke Hill of Grace	Barossa/South Australia	Red	Complex, berry, oaky, minerally	Beef	***
Henschke Joseph Hill Gewurztraminer	Barossa/South Australia	White	Spicy, floral	Asian	**
Henschke Julius Eden Valley Riesling	Barossa/South Australia	White	Citrus, floral	Shellfish	**
Henschke Mount Edelstone	Barossa/South Australia	Red	Complex, berry	Beef	***
Heritage Estate Shiraz	Barossa/South Australia	Red	Berry, earthy	Stew	**
Hidden Creek Nebbiolo	Queensland	Red	Berry, tannic, savory	Pasta	**
Hidden Creek Shiraz	Queensland	Red	Berry	Pizza	**
Hillstowe Buxton Sauvignon Blanc	Adelaide Hills/South Australia	White	Grassy	Shellfish	**
Hillstowe Mary's Hundred Shiraz	McLaren Vale/South Australia	Red	Berry, tannic, powerful	Beef	**
Hillstowe Udys Mill Pinot Noir	Adelaide Hills/South Australia	Red	Berry, spicy	Game	**
Hollick Cabernet Merlot	Coonawarra/South Australia	Red	Berry, herbaceous	Sausages	**
Hollick Chardonnay	Coonawarra/South Australia	White	Nutty, tropical fruit	Chicken	**
Hollick Ravenswood Cabernet Sauvignon	Coonawarra/South Australia	Red	Complex, berry, tannic, herbaceous	Lamb	***
Hollick Sparkling Merlot	Coonawarra/South Australia	Sparkling	Berry, fruit cake	Cold meats	**
Houghton Jack Mann Cabernet Sauvignon Malbec Shiraz	Western Australia	Red	Complex, berry, minerally, earthy	Lamb	***
Howard Park Cabernet Sauvignon Merlot	Western Australia	Red	Complex, herbaceous, minerally	Lamb	***
Howard Park Chardonnay	Western Australia	White	Nutty, complex, melon	Chicken	***
Howard Park Riesling	Western Australia	White	Citrus, floral, zingy	Shellfish	**
Hungerford Hill Tumbarumba Chardonnay	New South Wales	White	Melon, nutty	Fish	**
Huntington Estate Cabernet Sauvignon	New South Wales	Red	Berry, minerally, tannic	Lamb	**
Huntington Estate Reserve Shiraz	New South Wales	Red	Berry, tannic, powerful, spicy	Beef	**
Huntington Estate Shiraz	New South Wales	Red	Berry, tannic, spicy	Stew	**
Idyll Vineyard Gewurztraminer	Geelong/Victoria	White	Spicy, floral	Salads	**
Idyll Vineyard Shiraz	Geelong/Victoria	Red	Berry, peppery	Stew	**
Ingoldby Cabernet Sauvignon	McLaren Vale/South Australia	Red	Berry, tannic	Cold meats, stew, offal	*
Innisfail Vineyards Chardonnay	Geelong/Victoria	White	Tropical fruit	Fish	**
Ironbark Ridge Chardonnay	Queensland	White	Nutty, tropical fruit	Fish	**
Irvine Grand Merlot	Barossa/South Australia	Red	Berry, oaky, fruit cake	Lamb	***
Irvine Petit Meslier	Barossa/South Australia	Sparkling	Crisp, floral, fruity	Antipasto	**
Jane Brook Wood Aged Chenin Blanc	Western Australia	White	Nutty, fruity, oaky	Pork	**
Jasper Hill Emily's Paddock Shiraz	Central Victoria	Red	Berry, complex, spicy	Beef	***
Jasper Hill Georgia's Paddock Riesling	Central Victoria	White	Citrus, floral	Shellfish	**
Jasper Hill Georgia's Paddock Shiraz	Central Victoria	Red	Berry, complex, spicy	Beef	***
Jim Barry The Armagh	Clare Valley/South Australia	Red	Berry, spicy, complex, oaky, powerful, tannic	Beef	***
Jim Barry Watervale Riesling	Clare Valley/South Australia	White	Citrus, floral	Antipasto	**
Jones Winery Shiraz	North East Victoria/Victoria	Red	Berry, tannic	Stew	**
Kangarilla Road Shiraz	McLaren Vale/South Australia	Red	Berry, spicy	Beef	**
Kangarilla Road Zinfandel	McLaren Vale/South Australia	Red	Berry, plum	Stew	**
Kara Kara Sauvignon Blanc	Grampians & Western Victoria/Victoria	White	Grassy	Salads	**
Karl Seppelt Springton Cabernet Sauvignon	Barossa/South Australia	Red	Berry, herbaceous	Lamb	**
Karriview Pinot Noir	Western Australia	Red	Earthy, berry	Game	**
Katnook Estate Cabernet Sauvignon	Coonawarra/South Australia	Red	Berry, oaky, herbaceous	Lamb	**

AUSTRALIA *(continued)*

Wine name	Region	Style	Flavor/Bouquet	Compatible Foods	Price Range
Katnook Estate Chardonnay Brut	Coonawarra/South Australia	Sparkling	Crisp, citrus, fruity	Shellfish	**
Katnook Estate Chardonnay	Coonawarra/South Australia	White	Nutty, tropical fruit, melon, complex	Chicken	**
Katnook Estate Merlot	Coonawarra/South Australia	Red	Berry, fruit cake, tannic	Game	**
Katnook Estate Odyssey Cabernet Sauvignon	Coonawarra/South Australia	Red	Berry, complex, tannic, oaky, herbaceous	Lamb	***
Katnook Estate Riesling	Coonawarra/South Australia	White	Citrus, floral	Antipasto	**
Katnook Estate Sauvignon Blanc	Coonawarra/South Australia	White	Tropical fruit, zingy	Salads	**
Kay's Amery Cabernet Sauvignon	McLaren Vale/South Australia	Red	Berry, tannic	Lamb	**
Kingston Estate Cabernet Sauvignon	Riverland/South Australia	Red	Berry, plum	Pasta	*
Kingston Estate Chardonnay	Riverland/South Australia	White	Tropical fruit, melon	Chicken	*
Kingston Estate Merlot	Riverland/South Australia	Red	Berry, plum	Stew	*
Knappstein Enterprise Cabernet Sauvignon	Clare Valley/South Australia	Red	Berry, herbaceous	Lamb	**
Knappstein Enterprise Shiraz	Clare Valley/South Australia	Red	Berry, spicy	Beef	**
Knights Granite Hills Riesling	Macedon/Victoria	White	Floral, citrus	Shellfish	**
Knights Granite Hills Shiraz	Macedon/Victoria	Red	Spicy, peppery, berry	Beef	**
Knights Granite Hills Sparkling Pinot Noir Chardonnay	Macedon/Victoria	Sparkling	Crisp, yeasty	Aperitif	**
Kominos Shiraz	Queensland	Red	Berry, earthy	Sausages	**
Kulkunbulla Brokenback Chardonnay	New South Wales	White	Tropical fruit, melon	Fish	**
Kulkunbulla The Glandore Semillon	New South Wales	White	Citrus, tropical fruit	Chicken	**
Kyeema Estate Shiraz	New South Wales	Red	Peppery, spicy, berry	Pork	**
Lake's Folly Cabernet	New South Wales	Red	Berry, leathery, herbaceous	Lamb	***
Lake's Folly Chardonnay	New South Wales	White	Tropical fruit, complex	Fish	***
Lamont Barrel-Fermented Chardonnay	Western Australia	White	Melon, oaky	Fish	**
Lamont Chenin Blanc	Western Australia	White	Fruity, tropical fruit	Pasta	**
Lamont Family Reserve Premium Red Blend	Western Australia	Red	Berry	Stew	**
Lamont Verdelho	Western Australia	White	Tropical fruit	Fish	**
Lamont Vintage Port	Western Australia	Fortified	Sweet, earthy	Cheese	**
Lark Hill Chardonnay	New South Wales	White	Melon, citrus	Chicken	**
Lark Hill Riesling	New South Wales	White	Citrus, zingy	Antipasto	**
Leasingham Classic Clare Riesling	Clare Valley/South Australia	White	Citrus, floral, honey	Veal	**
Leconfield Cabernets	Coonawarra/South Australia	Red	Berry, tannic, herbaceous, complex	Lamb	**
Leconfield Merlot	Coonawarra/South Australia	Red	Berry, fruit cake	Cold meats	**
Leconfield Noble Riesling	Coonawarra/South Australia	Sweet	Sweet, citrus, melon, mandarin	Dessert	**
Leconfield Shiraz	Coonawarra/South Australia	Red	Berry, spicy, tannic	Cold meats, stew, offal	**
Leeuwin Estate Art Series Cabernet Sauvignon	Western Australia	Red	Herbaceous, minerally	Lamb	***
Leeuwin Estate Art Series Chardonnay	Western Australia	White	Complex, nutty, tropical fruit, melon	Fish	***
Lenswood Vineyards Chardonnay	Adelaide Hills/South Australia	White	Complex, melon, nutty	Fish	**
Lenswood Vineyards Pinot Noir	Adelaide Hills/South Australia	Red	Spicy, berry, complex	Duck	**
Lenswood Vineyards Sauvignon Blanc	Adelaide Hills/South Australia	White	Zingy, grassy	Salads	**
Lenton Brae Semillon Sauvignon Blanc	Western Australia	White	Grassy, zingy	Salads	**
Leo Buring Clare Valley Riesling	Clare Valley/South Australia	White	Floral	Asian	*
Leo Buring Clare Valley Shiraz	Clare Valley/South Australia	Red	Berry	Beef	**
Leo Buring Leonay Eden Valley Riesling	Barossa/South Australia	White	Citrus, floral, zingy	Fish	**
Lindemans Hunter River Reserve Porphyry	New South Wales	Sweet	Sweet, floral, citrus	Fruit	**
Lindemans Hunter River Semillon	New South Wales	White	Citrus, toasty, complex	Fish	*
Lindemans Hunter River Shiraz	New South Wales	Red	Leathery, berry	Stew	**
Lindemans Limestone Ridge Shiraz Cabernet	Coonawarra/South Australia	Red	Spicy, berry, herbaceous	Beef	**
Lindemans St George Cabernet Sauvignon	Coonawarra/South Australia	Red	Herbaceous, berry, oaky	Lamb	**
Lindemans Steven Vineyard Shiraz	New South Wales	Red	Leathery, berry, spicy	Beef	**
Lindemens Pyrus Cabernet blend	Coonawarra/South Australia	Red	Berry, spicy, tannic	Stew	**
Lowe Family Chardonnay	New South Wales	White	Melon, tropical fruit	Pork	**
Lowe Family Merlot	New South Wales	Red	Berry, earthy, fruit cake	Cold meats	**
Lyre Bird Hill Pinot Noir	Gippsland/Victoria	Red	Berry, spicy	Duck	**
Madew Riesling	New South Wales	White	Floral, citrus	Fruit	**
Maglieri Steve Maglieri Shiraz	McLaren Vale/South Australia	Red	Berry, tannic, complex	Beef	***
Magpie Estate The Malcolm	Barossa/South Australia	Red	Powerful, tannic, berry	Pizza	***
Majella Cabernet Sauvignon	Coonawarra/South Australia	Red	Berry, herbaceous, tannic	Lamb	**
Majella Mallea Cabernet Shiraz	Coonawarra/South Australia	Red	Spicy, berry, tannic, complex	Beef	**
Majella Shiraz	Coonawarra/South Australia	Red	Spicy, berry, tannic	Cold meats, stew, offal	**
Majella Sparkling Shiraz	Coonawarra/South Australia	Sparkling	Plum, berry, earthy	Cold meats	**
Malcolm Creek Cabernet Sauvignon	Adelaide Hills/South Australia	Red	Herbaceous, berry	Lamb	**

AUSTRALIA (continued)

Wine name	Region	Style	Flavor/Bouquet	Compatible Foods	Price Range
Malcolm Creek Chardonnay	Adelaide Hills/South Australia	White	Nutty, tropical	Chicken	**
Margan Family Semillon	New South Wales	White	Citrus, zingy	Shellfish	**
Margan Family Shiraz	New South Wales	Red	Berry, earthy	Cold meats, stew, offal	**
Maxwell Reserve Merlot	McLaren Vale/South Australia	Red	Fruit cake, berry, tannic	Lamb	**
Meerea Park Chardonnay	New South Wales	White	Tropical fruit	Fish	**
Mildara Cabernet Sauvignon	Coonawarra/South Australia	Red	Berry, tannic	Pasta	*
Mildara Jamiesons Run Reserve Red Blend	Coonawarra/South Australia	Red	Berry, oaky, tannic	Beef	**
Mildara Robertson's Well Cabernet Sauvignon	Coonawarra/South Australia	Red	Tannic, berry, herbaceous	Lamb	**
Mildara Robertson's Well Shiraz	Coonawarra/South Australia	Red	Berry, spicy, plum	Cold meats	**
Mildara Shiraz	Coonawarra/South Australia	Red	Berry	Pizza	*
Miranda Golden Botrytis Semillon	New South Wales	Sweet	Mandarin, sweet	Dessert	**
Mitchell Peppertree Vineyard Shiraz	Clare Valley/South Australia	Red	Berry, spicy	Beef	**
Mitchell Watervale Riesling	Clare Valley/South Australia	White	Citrus, floral	Shellfish	**
Mitchelton Blackwood Park Botrytis Riesling	Central Victoria	Sweet	Sweet, citrus	Fruit	**
Mitchelton Blackwood Park Riesling	Central Victoria	White	Citrus, floral	Fish	*
Mitchelton Marsanne	Central Victoria	White	Tropical fruit, oaky	Chicken	**
Mitchelton Print Label Cabernet Sauvignon	Central Victoria	Red	Oaky, berry	Lamb	**
Mitchelton Print Label Shiraz	Central Victoria	Red	Oaky, berry, earthy	Beef	**
Montrose Barbera	New South Wales	Red	Berry, earthy	Mediterranean	**
Montrose Black Shiraz	New South Wales	Red	Berry, earthy	Pasta	**
Moondah Brook Cabernet Sauvignon	Western Australia	Red	Herbaceous, berry	Cold meats	**
Moondah Brook Shiraz	Western Australia	Red	Earthy, berry	Stew	**
Morris Durif	North East Victoria/Victoria	Red	Earthy, tannic	Beef	**
Morris Old Premium Muscat	North East Victoria/Victoria	Fortified	Complex, sweet, raisiny	Nuts	**
Morris Old Premium Tokay	North East Victoria/Victoria	Fortified	Complex, sweet, raisiny, cold tea	Cheese	**
Morris Sparkling Durif Shiraz	North East Victoria/Victoria	Sparkling	Earthy, berry, plum	Cold meats	**
Moss Wood Cabernet Sauvignon	Western Australia	Red	Complex, minerally, berry	Lamb	***
Moss Wood Chardonnay	Western Australia	White	Nutty, tropical fruit	Fish	**
Moss Wood Semillon	Western Australia	White	Grassy, fruity	Asian	**
Mount Avoca Cabernets	Grampians & Western Victoria/Victoria	Red	Herbaceous, berry	Lamb	**
Mount Avoca Sauvignon Blanc	Grampians & Western Victoria/Victoria	White	Zingy, tropical fruit	Cheese	**
Mount Avoca Shiraz	Grampians & Western Victoria/Victoria	Red	Spicy, berry	Beef	**
Mount Horrocks Cordon Cut Riesling	Clare Valley/South Australia	Sweet	Sweet, citrus	Dessert	**
Mount Langi Ghiran Billi Billi Red Blend	Grampians & Western Victoria/Victoria	Red	Berry, earthy	Pasta	**
Mount Langi Ghiran Cabernet Merlot	Grampians & Western Victoria/Victoria	Red	Berry, minerally, herbaceous	Stew	**
Mount Langi Ghiran Pinot Grigio	Grampians & Western Victoria/Victoria	White	Tropical fruit, citrus	Antipasto	**
Mount Langi Ghiran Riesling	Grampians & Western Victoria/Victoria	White	Citrus, floral	Shellfish	**
Mount Langi Ghiran Shiraz	Grampians & Western Victoria/Victoria	Red	Complex, spicy, berry	Beef	***
Mount Pleasant Elizabeth Semillon	New South Wales	White	Citrus, complex, toasty	Fish	*
Mount Pleasant Lovedale Semillon	New South Wales	White	Complex, toasty, honey	Chicken	**
Mount Pleasant Maurice O'Shea Shiraz	New South Wales	Red	Berry, leathery	Beef	**
Mount Pleasant Rosehill Shiraz	New South Wales	Red	Berry, leathery	Stew	**
Mount Prior Vineyard Chardonnay	North East Victoria/Victoria	White	Melon, nutty	Chicken	**
Mount Prior Vineyard Durif	North East Victoria/Victoria	Red	Berry, earthy, tannic	Stew	**
Mountadam Chardonnay	Barossa/South Australia	White	Nutty, complex, tropical fruit	Fish	**
Mountadam Pinot Noir	Barossa/South Australia	Red	Gamey, berry, spicy	Duck	**
Mountview Shiraz	Queensland	Red	Berry, earthy	Pasta	**
Mountview Sparkling Shiraz	Queensland	Sparkling	Berry, plums	Cold meats	**
Mt Tamborine Cedar Creek Chardonnay	Queensland	White	Fruity, tropical fruit	Fish	**
Mt Tamborine Tehembrin Merlot	Queensland	Red	Berry, fruit cake	Stew	**
Narkoojee Vineyard Chardonnay	Gippsland/Victoria	White	Melon	Fish	**
Nepenthe Lenswood Pinot Noir	Adelaide Hills/South Australia	Red	Berry, spicy, gamey, complex	Duck	**
Nepenthe Lenswood Semillon	Adelaide Hills/South Australia	White	Tropical fruit, citrus	Antipasto	**
Nepenthe The Fugue Cabernet Sauvignon Merlot	Adelaide Hills/South Australia	Red	Herbaceous, berry	Lamb	**
Nicholson River Chardonnay	Gippsland/Victoria	White	Complex, minerally	Chicken	***
Nicholson River Semillon	Gippsland/Victoria	White	Complex	Veal	**

AUSTRALIA *(continued)*

Wine name	Region	Style	Flavor/Bouquet	Compatible Foods	Price Range
Normans Chais Clarendon Cabernet Sauvignon	McLaren Vale/South Australia	Red	Herbaceous, berry, tannic	Lamb	**
Normans Chais Clarendon Shiraz	McLaren Vale/South Australia	Red	Spicy, berry, earthy	Beef	**
Normans Chandlers Hill Chardonnay Semillon	Riverland/South Australia	White	Fruity	Asian	**
Normans Chandlers Hill Shiraz	Riverland/South Australia	Red	Berry	Pizza	**
Normans Chardonnay	McLaren Vale/South Australia	White	Tropical fruit, melon	Veal	**
Normans Lone Gum Vineyard Cabernet Merlot	Riverland/South Australia	Red	Berry, plum	Stew	*
Normans Lone Gum Vineyard Shiraz Cabernet	Riverland/South Australia	Red	Berry, earthy	Mediterranean	*
Normans Lone Gum Vineyard Unwooded Chardonnay	Riverland/South Australia	White	Melon, fruity	Salads	*
Orlando Centenary Hill Shiraz	Barossa/South Australia	Red	Berry, oaky, powerful, tannic	Beef	**
Orlando St Helga Riesling	Barossa/South Australia	White	Citrus, floral	Fish	**
Orlando Steingarten Riesling	Barossa/South Australia	White	Citrus, minerally, floral	Fish	**
Paracombe Cabernet Franc	Adelaide Hills/South Australia	Red	Herbaceous	Sausages	**
Paradise Enough Pinot Noir	Gippsland/Victoria	Red	Spicy, berry	Game	**
Parker First Growth Cabernet Sauvignon	Coonawarra/South Australia	Red	Berry, herbaceous, complex, tannic, oaky	Lamb	***
Parker Terra Rossa Cabernet Sauvignon	Coonawarra/South Australia	Red	Herbaceous, berry, spicy, tannic	Lamb	**
Passing Clouds Angel Blend Red	Central Victoria	Red	Berry	Pasta	**
Passing Clouds Graeme's Blend Red	Central Victoria	Red	Berry	Stew	**
Pattersons Pinot Noir	Western Australia	Red	Earthy, berry	Duck	**
Paul Conti Chardonnay	Western Australia	White	Melon, tropical fruit	Fish	**
Pauletts Andreas Shiraz	Clare Valley/South Australia	Red	Berry, spicy, oaky	Beef	**
Pauletts Cabernet Merlot	Clare Valley/South Australia	Red	Berry, herbaceous	Lamb	**
Pauletts Riesling	Clare Valley/South Australia	White	Citrus, floral	Fish	*
Peel Estate Chenin Blanc	Western Australia	White	Tropical fruit	Chicken	**
Peel Estate Shiraz	Western Australia	Red	Oaky, earthy	Stew	**
Pendarves Verdelho	New South Wales	White	Tropical fruit	Fish	**
Penfolds Adelaide Hills Chardonnay	Adelaide Hills/South Australia	White	Nutty, tropical fruit	Chicken	**
Penfolds Bin 707	Barossa/South Australia	Red	Berry, minerally, tannic, oaky	Lamb	***
Penfolds Eden Valley Riesling	Barossa/South Australia	White	Citrus, floral	Chicken	**
Penfolds Grandfather Port	Barossa/South Australia	Fortified	Raisins, sweet, complex	Nuts	***
Penfolds Grange	Barossa/South Australia	Red	Complex, powerful, tannic, oaky, berry, earthy	Beef	***
Penfolds Kalimna Block 42	Barossa/South Australia	Red	Complex, powerful, berry, tannic	Beef	***
Penfolds Old Vine Grenache Mourvedre Shiraz	Barossa/South Australia	Red	Berry, spicy, plum	Cold meats, stew, offal	**
Penfolds Yattarna Chardonnay	Adelaide Hills/South Australia	White	Complex, nutty, citrus, tropical fruit	Fish	***
Penley Estate Cabernet Sauvignon	Coonawarra/South Australia	Red	Berry, complex, herbaceous, tannic	Lamb	***
Penley Estate Hyland Shiraz	Coonawarra/South Australia	Red	Spicy, berry, tannic	Beef	**
Penley Estate Phoenix Cabernet Sauvignon	Coonawarra/South Australia	Red	Berry, herbaceous, tannic	Pork	**
Pepper Tree Reserve Semillon	New South Wales	White	Citrus, toasty	Pork	**
Pepper Tree Shiraz	New South Wales	Red	Leathery, tannic, berry	Stew	**
Petaluma Chardonnay	Adelaide Hills/South Australia	White	Complex, nutty, melon	Fish	**
Petaluma Croser	Adelaide Hills/South Australia	Sparkling	Crisp, yeasty, citrus, austere	Aperitif	**
Petaluma Tiers Chardonnay	Adelaide Hills/South Australia	White	Complex, nutty, tropical fruit, melon	Fish	***
Peter Lehmann Eden Valley Riesling	Barossa/South Australia	White	Citrus, floral, zingy	Shellfish	*
Peter Lehmann Reserve Riesling	Barossa/South Australia	White	Citrus, floral, complex	Chicken	**
Peter Lehmann Semillon	Barossa/South Australia	White	Tropical fruit, oaky	Veal	*
Peter Lehmann Stonewell Shiraz	Barossa/South Australia	Red	Berry, oaky, complex, tannic	Beef	**
Peter Lehmann The Mentor	Barossa/South Australia	Red	Berry, oaky, plum	Stew	**
Petersons Chardonnay	New South Wales	White	Tropical fruit	Chicken	**
Pewsey Vale Riesling	Barossa/South Australia	White	Citrus, floral, minerally	Salads	**
Pfieffer Chardonnay	North East Victoria/Victoria	White	Melon, fruity	Veal	**
Pfieffer Christopher's Vintage Port	North East Victoria/Victoria	Fortified	Sweet, licorice	Cheese	**
Pfieffer Gamay	North East Victoria/Victoria	Red	Berry	Cheese	**
Phillip Island Winery Chardonnay	Gippsland/Victoria	White	Melon, tropical fruit	Chicken	**
Picardy Pinot Noir	Western Australia	Red	Berry, complex	Duck	**
Picardy Shiraz	Western Australia	Red	Complex, berry	Beef	**
Pierro Chardonnay	Western Australia	White	Complex, nutty, melon	Chicken	***
Pierro Semillon Sauvignon Blanc	Western Australia	White	Zingy, grassy	Shellfish	**
Pike's Premio Sangiovese	Clare Valley/South Australia	Red	Berry, earthy, savoury	Mediterranean	**
Pike's Reserve Riesling	Clare Valley/South Australia	White	Citrus, floral, austere	Chicken	**

AUSTRALIA (continued)

Wine name	Region	Style	Flavor/Bouquet	Compatible Foods	Price Range
Plantagenet Cabernet Sauvignon	Western Australia	Red	Herbaceous, berry	Lamb	**
Plantagenet Omrah Chardonnay	Western Australia	White	Fruity, citrus	Salads	**
Plantagenet Riesling	Western Australia	White	Citrus, zingy	Shellfish	**
Plantagenet Shiraz	Western Australia	Red	Earthy, berry	Beef	**
Plunkett's Gewurztraminer	Central Victoria	White	Spicy, fruity	Asian	**
Plunkett's Shiraz	Central Victoria	Red	Spicy, peppery	Beef	**
Poole's Rock Chardonnay	New South Wales	White	Tropical fruit, melon	Chicken	**
Preston Peak Chardonnay	Queensland	White	tropical fruit, nutty	Chicken	**
Preston Peak Shiraz	Queensland	Red	Berry, spicy	Veal	**
Prince Albert Vineyard Pinot Noir	Geelong/Victoria	Red	Earthy, berry	Game	**
Punkett's Unwooded Chardonnay	Central Victoria	White	Citrus, melon	Salads	**
Punters Corner Cabernet Sauvignon	Coonawarra/South Australia	Red	Herbaceous, berry, tannic	Lamb	**
Punters Corner Chardonnay	Coonawarra/South Australia	White	Nutty, tropical fruit	Chicken	**
Ravenswood Lane Sauvignon Blanc	Adelaide Hills/South Australia	White	Zingy, herbaceous	Salads	**
Redbank Sally's Paddock Red Blend	Grampians & Western Victoria/Victoria	Red	Complex, berry	Stew	**
Redman Cabernet Merlot	Coonawarra/South Australia	Red	Berry, herbaceous, tannic	Stew	**
Redman Cabernet Sauvignon	Coonawarra/South Australia	Red	Berry, herbaceous	Lamb	**
Redman Shiraz	Coonawarra/South Australia	Red	Berry, tannic, spicy	Pasta	*
Renmano Chairman's Selection Reserve Chardonnay	Riverland/South Australia	White	Tropical fruit	Fish	*
Reynolds Yarraman Orange Chardonnay	New South Wales	White	Nutty, tropical fruit, complex	Fish	**
Reynolds Yarraman Semillon	New South Wales	White	Citrus, toasty	Shellfish	**
Reynolds Yarraman Shiraz	New South Wales	Red	Spicy, berry, earthy	Beef	**
Richmond Grove Cowra Chardonnay	New South Wales	White	Tropical fruit	Fish	**
Richmond Grove Eden Valley Riesling	Barossa/South Australia	White	Citrus, floral	Antipasto	**
Richmond Grove Watervale Riesling	Clare Valley/South Australia	White	Citrus, floral	Shellfish	*
Rimfire Shiraz	Queensland	Red	Berry, spicy	Beef	**
Robinsons Family Cabernet Sauvignon	Queensland	Red	Herbaceous, earthy, berry	Sausages	**
Robinsons Family Sparkling	Queensland	Sparkling	Crisp, citrus	Aperitif	**
Rochford Chardonnay	Macedon/Victoria	White	Tropical fruit, complex	Fish	**
Rochford Pinot Noir	Macedon/Victoria	Red	Spicy, berry	Game	**
Rockford Basket Press Shiraz	Barossa/South Australia	Red	Complex, berry, earthy	Beef	**
Rockford Black Shiraz	Barossa/South Australia	Sparkling	Powerful, plum, berry, earthy, complex	Cold meats	***
Rockford Dry Country Grenache	Barossa/South Australia	Red	Plum, berry, earthy	Cold meats, stew, offal	**
Romavilla Very Old Tawny Port	Queensland	Fortified	Sweet, raisiny, complex	Nuts	**
Rosemount Balmoral Syrah	McLaren Vale/South Australia	Red	Powerful, berry, spicy, oaky, complex	Beef	***
Rosemount Giant's Creek Chardonnay	New South Wales	White	Tropical fruit, citrus, melon	Chicken	**
Rosemount GSM Grenache Shiraz Mourvedre	McLaren Vale/South Australia	Red	Berry, tannic, spicy	Cold meats, stew, offal	**
Rosemount Hill of Gold Chardonnay	New South Wales	White	Tropical fruit, melon	Fish	**
Rosemount Hill of Gold Shiraz	New South Wales	Red	Berry, spicy, tannic	Beef	**
Rosemount Mountain Blue Shiraz Cabernet	New South Wales	Red	Complex, tannic, berry, spicy	Beef	***
Rosemount Orange Chardonnay	New South Wales	White	Tropical fruit, melon, complex	Fish	**
Rosemount Roxburgh Chardonnay	New South Wales	White	Melon, complex, nutty, toasty	Chicken	***
Rosemount Show Reserve Chardonnay	New South Wales	White	Melon, tropical fruit	Veal	**
Rosemount Show Reserve Semillon	New South Wales	White	Tropical fruit, citrus	Fish	**
Rothbury Estate Brokenback Chardonnay	New South Wales	White	Tropical fruit	Pork	**
Rothbury Estate Brokenback Semillon	New South Wales	White	Citrus, minerally	Fish	**
Rothbury Estate Brokenback Shiraz	New South Wales	Red	Leathery, berry	Stew	**
Rouge Homme Cabernet Sauvignon	Coonawarra/South Australia	Red	Berry, tannic, herbaceous	Lamb	**
Rouge Homme Richardsons Block Red Blend	Coonawarra/South Australia	Red	Berry, spicy, tannic	Stew	**
Rumbalara Semillon	Queensland	White	Citrus, apples	Shellfish	**
Rymill Cabernet Sauvignon	Coonawarra/South Australia	Red	Berry, herbaceous, complex, minerally, tannic	Lamb	**
Rymill Merlot Cabernets	Coonawarra/South Australia	Red	Berry, spicy	Cold meats, stew, offal	**
Rymill Pinot Noir Chardonnay Sparkling	Coonawarra/South Australia	Sparkling	Crisp, yeasty, citrus	Aperitif	**
Rymill Sauvignon Blanc	Coonawarra/South Australia	White	Grassy	Cheese	**
Rymill Shiraz	Coonawarra/South Australia	Red	Berry, spicy, earthy	Sausages	**
S. Kidman Sauvignon Blanc	Coonawarra/South Australia	White	Zingy, tropical fruit	Salads	**
S. Kidman Shiraz	Coonawarra/South Australia	Red	Berry, spicy, tannic	Beef	**
Saddlers Creek Marrowbone Chardonnay	New South Wales	White	Tropical fruit, melon	Fish	**
Salitage Pinot Noir	Western Australia	Red	Gamey, earthy	Duck	**
Saltram Mamre Brook Cabernet Sauvignon	Barossa/South Australia	Red	Berry	Stew	**

AUSTRALIA (continued)

Wine name	Region	Style	Flavor/Bouquet	Compatible Foods	Price Range
Saltram Mamre Brook Shiraz	Barossa/South Australia	Red	Berry, earthy	Stew	**
Sandalford Verdelho	Western Australia	White	Tropical fruit	Veal	**
Scarborough Chardonnay	New South Wales	White	Complex, melon, nutty	Fish	**
Scarpantoni Block 3 Shiraz	McLaren Vale/South Australia	Red	Berry, spicy	Sausages	**
Scotchmans Hill Cabernet	Geelong/Victoria	Red	Herbaceous, berry	Cold meats	**
Scotchmans Hill Chardonnay	Geelong/Victoria	White	Tropical fruit, melon	Fish	**
Scotchmans Hill Pinot Noir	Geelong/Victoria	Red	Spicy, berry	Duck	**
Scotchmans Hill Sauvignon Blanc	Geelong/Victoria	White	Tropical fruit, citrus	Cheese	**
Seaview Edwards & Chaffey Shiraz	McLaren Vale/South Australia	Red	Berry, oaky, tannic	Beef	**
Seppelt Chalambar Shiraz	Grampians & Western Victoria/Victoria	Red	Berry, earthy, fruity	Pasta	*
Seppelt DP117 Show Fino	Barossa/South Australia	Fortified	Dry, yeasty	Aperitif	**
Seppelt DP90 Show Tawny	Barossa/South Australia	Fortified	Complex, nutty, sweet	Nuts	**
Seppelt Great Western Shiraz	Grampians & Western Victoria/Victoria	Red	Earthy, complex, spicy	Stew	**
Seppelt Original Sparkling Shiraz	Grampians & Western Victoria/Victoria	Sparkling	Fruity, berry	Nuts	**
Seppelt Para Liqueur Vintage Tawny Port	Barossa/South Australia	Fortified	Sweet, raisiny	Cheese	**
Seppelt Rhymney Sauvignon Blanc	Grampians & Western Victoria/Victoria	White	Zingy	Shellfish	**
Seppelt Sheoak Riesling	Grampians & Western Victoria/Victoria	White	Floral, citrus	Shellfish	**
Seppelt Show Reserve Sparkling Shiraz	Grampians & Western Victoria/Victoria	Sparkling	Complex, spicy, berry, earthy	Cold meats	***
Seppelt Sunday Creek Pinot Noir	Grampians & Western Victoria/Victoria	Red	Berry, spicy	Cold meats	**
Sevenhill Cellars Shiraz	Clare Valley/South Australia	Red	Berry, spicy, earthy	Stew	**
Severn Brae Shiraz	Queensland	Red	Berry, spicy	Stew	**
Shaw and Smith Sauvignon Blanc	Adelaide Hills/South Australia	White	Zingy, tropical fruit, herbaceous	Shellfish	**
Skillogalee Riesling	Clare Valley/South Australia	White	Citrus, floral	Fish	**
Skillogalee Shiraz	Clare Valley/South Australia	Red	Berry, spicy	Beef	**
Skillogalee The Cabernets	Clare Valley/South Australia	Red	Berry, herbaceous	Lamb	**
Sorrenberg Chardonnay	North East Victoria/Victoria	White	Nutty, tropical fruit, complex	Chicken	**
St Hallett Eden Valley Riesling	Barossa/South Australia	White	Citrus, floral	Shellfish	**
St Hallett Old Block Shiraz	Barossa/South Australia	Red	Berry, earthy, tannic, powerful	Beef	**
Stanton & Killeen Premium Liqueur Gold Tokay	North East Victoria/Victoria	Fortified	Complex, sweet, cold tea	Nuts	***
Stanton & Killeen Special Old Liqueur Muscat	North East Victoria/Victoria	Fortified	Raisiny, complex, sweet	Nuts	***
Stanton & Killeen Vintage Port	North East Victoria/Victoria	Fortified	Sweet, licorice, berry	Cheese	**
Starvedog Lane Shiraz	Adelaide Hills/South Australia	Red	Berry, spicy	Beef	**
Stephen John Watervale Pedro Ximenez	Clare Valley/South Australia	White	Crisp, apple	Shellfish	**
Stone Ridge Chardonnay	Queensland	White	Tropical fruit, nutty	Fish	**
Stone Ridge Shiraz	Queensland	Red	Berry, earthy, spicy, tannic	Beef	**
Stuart Range Estate Goodger Chardonnay	Queensland	White	Melon, fruity	Fish	**
Summerfield Cabernet Sauvignon	Grampians & Western Victoria/Victoria	Red	Herbaceous, berry	Stew	**
Summerfield Shiraz	Grampians & Western Victoria/Victoria	Red	Berry, spicy	Cold meats, stew, offal	**
Sutherland Semillon	New South Wales	White	Citrus, toasty	Shellfish	**
Talijancich Julian James Red Liqueur	Western Australia	Fortified	Sweet, berry	Cheese	**
Taltarni Brut Tache	Grampians & Western Victoria/Victoria	Sparkling	Crisp, berry	Cheese	**
Taltarni Merlot	Grampians & Western Victoria/Victoria	Red	Berry, fruit cake	Lamb	**
Taltarni Reserve Cabernet Sauvignon	Grampians & Western Victoria/Victoria	Red	Berry, herbaceous, powerful, tannic	Lamb	**
Tamburlaine The Chapel Reserve Red	New South Wales	Red	Berry, leathery	Beef	**
Tapestry Cabernet Sauvignon	Clare Valley/South Australia	Red	Berry, herbaceous	Pizza	*
Tatachilla Clarendon Vineyard Merlot	McLaren Vale/South Australia	Red	Berry, fruit cake, spicy	Stew	**
Taylors Cabernet Sauvignon	Clare Valley/South Australia	Red	Berry	Pasta	*
The Clare Essentials Carlsfield Riesling	Clare Valley/South Australia	White	Citrus, floral	Fish	**
The Willows Semillon	Barossa/South Australia	White	Tropical fruit, nutty	Pork	**
The Willows The Doctor Sparkling Red	Barossa/South Australia	Sparkling	Berry, plum	Cold meats	**
Thistle Hill Cabernet Sauvignon	New South Wales	Red	Berry, herbaceous	Lamb	**
Tim Adams Aberfeldy Shiraz	Clare Valley/South Australia	Red	Spicy, berry, powerful	Beef	**
Tim Adams The Fergus Grenache	Clare Valley/South Australia	Red	Earthy, berry, plum	Cold meats, stew, offal	**

AUSTRALIA (continued)

Wine name	Region	Style	Flavor/Bouquet	Compatible Foods	Price Range
Tollana Botrytis Riesling	Barossa/South Australia	Sweet	Sweet, citrus	Dessert	**
Tollana Eden Valley Riesling	Barossa/South Australia	White	Citrus, floral	Asian	*
Torbreck Runrig	Barossa/South Australia	Red	Berry, earthy, tannic	Beef	**
Torbreck The Steading	Barossa/South Australia	Red	Berry, earthy, tannic, oaky, powerful	Beef	***
Tower Estate Semillon	New South Wales	White	Citrus, zingy	Fish	**
Tulloch Hector of Glen Elgin Red	New South Wales	Red	Berry, earthy	Beef	**
Turkey Flat Butcher's Block	Barossa/South Australia	Red	Berry, earthy	Beef	**
Turkey Flat Shiraz	Barossa/South Australia	Red	Berry, tannic, powerful	Beef	**
Tyrell's Rufus Stone McLaren Vale Shiraz	Clare Valley/South Australia	Red	Berry, spicy	Beef	**
Tyrell's Brokenback Shiraz	New South Wales	Red	Berry, leathery	Cold meats	**
Tyrell's Lost Block Semillon	New South Wales	White	Citrus, tropical fruit	Chicken	**
Tyrell's Moon Mountain Chardonnay	New South Wales	White	Tropical fruit, nutty	Fish	**
Tyrell's Vat 1 Semillon	New South Wales	White	Citrus, toasty, complex	Shellfish	**
Tyrell's Vat 5 Dry Red	New South Wales	Red	Berry, complex, leathery	Beef	**
Tyrell's Vat 9 Dry Red	New South Wales	Red	Berry, leathery, tannic	Stew	**
Tyrell's Vat 47 Chardonnay	New South Wales	White	Complex, tropical fruit, melon	Chicken	**
Vasse Felix Cabernet Sauvignon	Western Australia	Red	Herbaceous, oaky, berry	Lamb	**
Vasse Felix Heytesbury Chardonnay	Western Australia	White	Complex, tropical fruit, nutty	Chicken	**
Vasse Felix Heytesbury Red	Western Australia	Red	Complex, herbaceous, minerally	Beef	***
Vasse Felix Noble Riesling	Western Australia	Sweet	Sweet, citrus	Dessert	**
Vasse Felix Semillon	Western Australia	White	Grassy	Salads	**
Vasse Felix Shiraz	Western Australia	Red	Earthy, berry	Beef	**
Veritas Bull's Blood Shiraz Mourvedre Pressings	Barossa/South Australia	Red	Tannic, powerful, berry	Stew	**
Violet Cane Sparkling Shiraz	Queensland	Sparkling	Berry, earthy, plum	Cold meats	***
Violet Cane Vineyard Merlot	Queensland	Red	Fruit cake, berry	Duck	**
Virgin Hills Red Blend	Macedon/Victoria	Red	Herbaceous, minerally, berry	Lamb	**
Voyager Cabernet Sauvignon Merlot	Western Australia	Red	Herbaceous, minerally, berry	Lamb	**
Voyager Chardonnay	Western Australia	White	Tropical fruit	Chicken	**
Wa-de-lock Vineyards Chardonnay	Gippsland/Victoria	White	Melon, tropical fruit	Chicken	**
Warrenmang Vineyard Grand Pyrenees (Red Blend)	Grampians & Western Victoria/Victoria	Red	Spicy, berry	Lamb	**
Warrenmang Vineyard Late Harvest Traminer	Grampians & Western Victoria/Victoria	Sweet	Sweet, floral	Fruit	**
Water Wheel Cabernet	Central Victoria	Red	Berry, herbaceous	Lamb	**
Water Wheel Chardonnay	Central Victoria	White	Melon, tropical fruit	Fish	**
Water Wheel Shiraz	Central Victoria	Red	Spicy, berry	Cold meats, stew, offal	**
Wendouree Cellars Cabernet Sauvignon	Clare Valley/South Australia	Red	Berry, powerful, tannic	Lamb	**
Wendouree Cellars Malbec	Clare Valley/South Australia	Red	Berry, spicy, tannic	Cold meats, stew, offal	**
Wendouree Cellars Shiraz	Clare Valley/South Australia	Red	Berry, complex, spicy, tannic, powerful	Beef	**
Westend 3 Bridges Cabernet	New South Wales	Red	Berry	Pasta	**
Westend Golden Mist Botrytis Semillon	New South Wales	Sweet	Citrus, sweet	Dessert	**
Westfield Chardonnay	Western Australia	White	Melon, fruity	Chicken	**
Westfield Liqueur Muscat	Western Australia	Fortified	Sweet	Nuts	**
Whisson Lake Carey Gully Pinot Noir	Adelaide Hills/South Australia	Red	Berry, spicy	Cold meats	**
Wignalls Pinot Noir	Western Australia	Red	Gamey, earthy	Game	**
Wild Dog Winery Barrel-fermented Chardonnay	Gippsland/Victoria	White	Complex, nutty, melon	Chicken	**
Wild Dog Winery Shiraz	Gippsland/Victoria	Red	Berry, spicy	Stew	**
Wild Duck Creek Estate Alan's Cabernet	Central Victoria	Red	Berry, herbaceous	Stew	**
Wild Duck Creek Estate Black Label Reserve Cabernet	Central Victoria	Red	Herbaceous, berry	Lamb	**
Wild Duck Creek Estate Black Label Reserve Shiraz	Central Victoria	Red	Spicy, powerful	Beef	**
Wild Duck Creek Estate Duckmuck	Central Victoria	Red	Powerful, spicy, berry	Beef	***
Wild Duck Creek Estate The Blend Red	Central Victoria	Red	Berry, earthy	Stew	**
Will Taylor Clare Valley Riesling	Clare Valley/South Australia	White	Citrus, floral	Chicken	**
Wilton Estate Botrytis Semillon	New South Wales	Sweet	Sweet, citrus	Dessert	**
Windermere Sangiovese Cabernet	Queensland	Red	Berry, spicy, savoury	Pasta	**
Windermere Shiraz	Queensland	Red	Berry, spicy, tannic	Beef	**
Winewood Shiraz Marsanne	Queensland	Red	Berry, spicy	Stew	**
Wirra Wirra Chardonnay	McLaren Vale/South Australia	White	Nutty, tropical fruit, melon	Fish	**
Wirra Wirra RSW Shiraz	McLaren Vale/South Australia	Red	Berry, complex, spicy	Beef	**
Wolf Blass Black Label Cabernet Shiraz Merlot	Barossa/South Australia	Red	Berry, oaky	Lamb	***
Wolf Blass Gold Label Riesling	Barossa/South Australia	White	Crisp, citrus, floral	Fish	*
Woodstock The Stocks Shiraz	McLaren Vale/South Australia	Red	Berry, earthy, tannic	Sausages	**

AUSTRALIA (continued)

Wine name	Region	Style	Flavor/Bouquet	Compatible Foods	Price Range
Wynns Cabernet Sauvignon	Coonawarra/South Australia	Red	Berry, minerally, herbaceous, complex	Lamb	**
Wynns John Riddoch Cabernet Sauvignon	Coonawarra/South Australia	Red	Complex, berry, herbaceous, l tannic, powerfu	Lamb	***
Wynns Michael Shiraz	Coonawarra/South Australia	Red	Oaky, berry, tannic	Stew	***
Wynns Riesling	Coonawarra/South Australia	White	Floral, citrus	Shellfish	**
Wynns Shiraz	Coonawarra/South Australia	Red	Berry, spicy, tannic	Cold meats, stew, offal	*
Yalumba Oxford Landing Limited Release Merlot	Riverland/South Australia	Red	Berry, earthy	Pasta	*
Yalumba Oxford Landing Limited Release Semillon	Riverland/South Australia	White	Tropical fruit	Fish	*
Yalumba Oxford Landing Sauvignon Blanc	Riverland/South Australia	White	Fruity	Pizza	**
Yalumba Signature Cabernet Sauvignon Shiraz	Barossa/South Australia	Red	Berry, plum	Cold meats, stew, offal	**
Yalumba The Octavius	Barossa/South Australia	Red	Oaky, tannic, berry, powerful	Stew	***
Yellowglen Cuvee Victoria	Grampians & Western Victoria/Victoria	Sparkling	Crisp, yeasty	Antipasto	**
Zema Estate Cabernet Sauvignon	Coonawarra/South Australia	Red	Berry, herbaceous	Cold meats	**
Zema Estate Cluny Red Blend	Coonawarra/South Australia	Red	Berry, spicy, tannic	Beef	**
Zema Estate Family Selection Cabernet Sauvignon	Coonawarra/South Australia	Red	Tannic, berry, herbaceous	Lamb	**
Zema Estate Shiraz	Coonawarra/South Australia	Red	Berry, tannic, spicy	Sausages	**

NEW ZEALAND

Wine name	Region	Style	Flavor/Bouquet	Compatible Foods	Price Range
Alan McCorkindale Pinot Noir	Canterbury/Waipara	Red	Spicy, berry	Game	**
Alana Estate Sauvignon Blanc	Martinborough	White	Zingy, grassy	Shellfish	**
Alana Pinot Noir	Martinborough	Red	Spicy, berry, smoky	Mediterranean	***
Alana Riesling	Martinborough	White	Floral, citrus	Fish	**
Alexander Dusty Road Cabernet Franc	Martinborough	Red	Herbaceous, tannic	Cold meats, stew, offal	**
Alexander Vineyard Cabernet Sauvignon Cabernet Franc	Martinborough	Red	Herbaceous, oaky, berry	Lamb	**
Alexander Vineyard Pinot Noir	Martinborough	Red	Spicy, berry, earthy	Veal	**
Allan Scott Chardonnay	Marlborough	White	Melon, citrus	Shellfish	**
Allan Scott Riesling	Marlborough	White	Floral, spicy	Cheese	**
Allan Scott Sauvignon Blanc	Marlborough	White	Grassy, zingy	Salads	**
Alpha Domus AD Cabernet Sauvignon Merlot Malbec	Gisborne/Hawkes Bay	Red	Berry, oaky	Lamb	**
Alpha Domus AD Chardonnay	Gisborne/Hawkes Bay	White	Nutty, melon	Fish	**
Alpha Domus The Navigator (merlot/malbec/cabernet franc)	Hawkes Bay	Red	Earthy, oaky, berry	Beef	**
Ata Rangi Celebre Cabernet Sauvignon Merlot Syrah	Martinborough	Red	Berry, oaky, spicy	Lamb	**
Ata Rangi Craighall Chardonnay	Martinborough	White	Citrus, melon, oaky	Chicken	***
Ata Rangi Pinot Gris	Martinborough	White	Tropical fruit, complex	Pork	**
Ata Rangi Pinot Noir	Martinborough	Red	Spicy, gamey, berry	Cold meats, stew, offal	***
Babich Irongate Cabernet Sauvignon Merlot	Gisborne/Hawkes Bay	Red	Herbaceous, berry	Lamb	**
Babich Irongate Chardonnay	Gisborne/Hawkes Bay	White	Melon, spicy	Fish	**
Babich Mara Estate Chardonnay	Gisborne/Hawkes Bay	White	Tropical fruit, nutty	Chicken	**
Babich Mara Estate Sauvignon Blanc	Gisborne/Hawkes Bay	White	Zingy, citrus	Salads	**
Babich Marlborough Sauvignon Blanc	Marlborough	White	Zingy, citrus	Salads	**
Babich Patriarch Cabernet Sauvignon	Gisborne/Hawkes Bay	Red	Berry, earthy, herbaceous	Stew	**
Babich Patriarch Chardonnay	Gisborne/Hawkes Bay	White	Tropical fruit, citrus	Fish	**
Benfield & Delamare Cabernet Sauvignon Merlot	Martinborough	Red	Herbaceous, berry	Lamb	**
Bilancia Chardonnay	Gisborne/Hawkes Bay	White	Citrus, tropical fruit	Shellfish	**
Bilancia Merlot	Gisborne/Hawkes Bay	Red	Berry, herbaceous	Stew	**
Bilancia Pinot Gris	Gisborne/Hawkes Bay	White	Tropical fruit, citrus	Salads	**
Bilancia Reserve Pinot Gris	Gisborne/Hawkes Bay	White	Minerally, tropical fruit	Fish	**
Black Ridge Gewurztraminer	Central Otago	White	Spicy, citrus	Sausages	**
Black Ridge Pinot Noir	Central Otago	Red	Earthy, gamey	Duck	**
Black Ridge Riesling	Central Otago	White	Floral, zingy	Cheese	**
Bladen Riesling	Marlborough	White	Floral, citrus	Fish	**
Brick Bay Matakana Pinot Gris	Northland	White	Citrus, floral	Pork	**
Brookfields Gewurztraminer	Gisborne/Hawkes Bay	White	Floral, spicy	Sausages	**
Brookfields Marshall Bank Chardonnay	Gisborne/Hawkes Bay	White	Tropical fruit, citrus	Fish	**
Brookfields Pinot Gris	Gisborne/Hawkes Bay	White	Tropical fruit, melon	Chicken	**
Brookfields Reserve Cabernet Sauvignon Merlot	Gisborne/Hawkes Bay	Red	Herbaceous, berry	Pasta	**
Brookfields Riesling	Gisborne/Hawkes Bay	White	Floral, citrus	Cheese	**
Brooksfields Cabernet Sauvignon	Gisborne/Hawkes Bay	Red	Berry, oaky	Lamb	**
C. J. Pask Chardonnay	Gisborne/Hawkes Bay	White	Spicy, melon	Salads	**

NEW ZEALAND (continued)

Wine name	Region	Style	Flavor/Bouquet	Compatible Foods	Price Range
C. J. Pask Reserve Chardonnay	Gisborne/Hawkes Bay	White	Toasty, ripe, citrus	Shellfish	***
C. J. Pask Reserve Merlot	Gisborne/Hawkes Bay	Red	Plums, tannic	Mushrooms	***
Cairnbrae Chardonnay	Marlborough	White	Tropical fruit, melon	Fish	**
Cairnbrae Reserve Riesling	Marlborough	White	Citrus, minerally	Cheese	**
Cairnbrae The Stones Sauvignon Blanc	Marlborough	White	Grassy, citrus	Shellfish	**
Canterbury House Chardonnay	Canterbury/Waipara	White	Melon, tropical fruit	Fish	**
Canterbury House Pinot Noir	Canterbury/Waipara	White	Berry, spicy	Pizza	**
Canterbury House Sauvignon Blanc	Canterbury/Waipara	White	Zingy, apples	Salads	**
Chancellor Sauvignon Blanc	Canterbury/Waipara	White	Citrus, floral, zingy	Shellfish	**
Chard Farm Bragato Pinot Noir	Central Otago	Red	Berry, spicy	Game	**
Chard Farm Finla Mor Pinot Noir	Central Otago	Red	Berry, tannic	Game	**
Chard Farm Judge and Jury Chardonnay	Central Otago	White	Austere, melon, toasty	Chicken	***
Chard Farm Pinot Gris	Central Otago	White	Apples, melon	Chicken	**
Chard Farm Riesling	Central Otago	White	Citrus, floral	Fish	**
Charles Wiffen Chardonnay	Marlborough	White	Melon, tropical fruit	Fish	**
Charles Wiffen Late Harvest Riesling	Marlborough	Sweet	Sweet, mandarin, honey	Dessert	**
Charles Wiffen Riesling	Marlborough	White	Floral, spicy	Fruit	**
Church Road Chardonnay	Gisborne/Hawkes Bay	White	Citrus, oaky, spicy	Pork	**
Church Road Reserve Cabernet Sauvignon Merlot	Gisborne/Hawkes Bay	Red	Tannic, berry, smoky	Beef	***
Church Road Reserve Chardonnay	Gisborne/Hawkes Bay	White	Oaky, melon	Fish	***
Church Road Sauvignon Blanc	Gisborne/Hawkes Bay	White	Zingy, citrus	Shellfish	**
Clearview Estate Reserve Chardonnay	Gisborne/Hawkes Bay	White	Oaky, tropical fruit	Fish	***
Clearview Noble 51 Chardonnay	Gisborne/Hawkes Bay	White	Fruity, citrus	Chicken	***
Clearview Old Olive Block Cabernet Sauvignon Cabernet Franc	Gisborne/Hawkes Bay	Red	Ripe, berry, tannic	Cold meats, stew, offal	**
Clearview Reserve Cabernet Sauvignon	Gisborne/Hawkes Bay	Red	Berry, minerally	Lamb	**
Cloudy Bay Chardonnay	Marlborough	White	Melon, toasty	Fish	***
Cloudy Bay Pinot Noir	Marlborough	Red	Gamey, leathery	Duck	***
Cloudy Bay Sauvignon Blanc	Marlborough	White	Tropical fruit, zingy	Shellfish	***
Collards Chenin Blanc	Auckland	White	Apples, tropical fruit	Veal	*
Coopers Creek Reserve Cabernet Sauvignon	Gisborne/Hawkes Bay	Red	Herbaceous, berry	Stew	**
Coopers Creek Reserve Hawkes Bay Merlot Cabernet Franc	Gisborne/Hawkes Bay	Red	Plums, berry	Lamb	**
Coopers Creek Reserve Riesling	Gisborne/Hawkes Bay	White	Citrus, floral	Fish	**
Coopers Creek Swamp Reserve Chardonnay	Gisborne/Hawkes Bay	White	Melon, spicy	Veal	**
Corbans Amadeus Classic Reserve Méthode Traditionnelle	Marlborough	Sparkling	Toasty, crisp	Aperitif	**
Corbans Cottage Block Gisborne Chardonnay	Gisborne	White	Tropical fruit, melon	Chicken	**
Corbans Cottage Block Marlborough Chardonnay	Marlborough	White	Melon, tropical fruit	Fish	**
Corbans Cottage Block Noble Riesling	Marlborough	Sweet	Mandarin, honey	Fruit	**
Corbans Private Bin Amberley Riesling	Canterbury/Waipara	White	Floral, fruity	Veal	**
Corbans Private Bin Gisborne Chardonnay	Gisborne	White	Melon, citrus	Fish	**
Corbans Private Bin Marlborough Chardonnay	Marlborough	White	Melon, tropical fruit	Fish	**
Corbans Private Bin Marlborough Sauvignon Blanc	Marlborough	White	Grassy, zingy	Shellfish	**
Corbans Private Bin Noble Riesling	Marlborough	Sweet	Sweet, citrus	Dessert	**
Corbans Stoneleigh Riesling	Marlborough	White	Floral, minerally	Shellfish	**
Craggy Range Chardonnay	Gisborne/Hawkes Bay	White	Complex, minerally, spicy	Fish	***
Craggy Range Riesling	Marlborough	White	Citrus, floral, zingy, complex	Shellfish	***
Craggy Range Sauvignon Blanc	Marlborough	White	Tropical fruit, zingy	Aperitif	***
Cross Roads Talisman (up to 6 varieties)	Hawkes Bay	Red	Oaky, berry, rich	Beef	***
Daniel Le Brun Vintage Brut Méthode Traditionnelle	Marlborough	Sparkling	Toasty, complex	Aperitif	***
Danniel Schuster Pinot Blanc	Canterbury/Waipara	White	Tropical fruit, melon	Pork	**
Danniel Schuster Selection Chardonnay	Canterbury/Waipara	White	Tropical fruit, zingy	Chicken	**
Danniel Schuster Selection Pinot Noir	Canterbury/Waipara	Red	Cherry, plums, oaky	Duck	***
De Redcliffe Marlborough Riesling	Marlborough	White	Floral, citrus	Fish	**
Delegates Reserve Cabernet Sauvignon	Gisborne/Hawkes Bay	Red	Complex, berry, herbaceous	Lamb	**
Delegates Reserve Chardonnay	Gisborne/Hawkes Bay	White	Nutty, tropical fruit	Chicken	**
Delegates Reserve Merlot	Gisborne/Hawkes Bay	Red	Herbaceous, earthy	Venison	**
Deutz Blanc de Blancs Méthode Traditionnelle	Marlborough	Sparkling	Citrus, crisp	Cheese	***
Domaine Chandon Marlborough Brut Méthode Traditionnelle	Marlborough	Sparkling	Toasty, crisp, minerally	Aperitif	**
Domaine Georges Michel Chardonnay	Marlborough	White	Nutty, tropical fruit	Fish	**
Domaines Georges Michel Sauvignon Blanc	Marlborough	White	Minerally, zingy	Shellfish	**
Dry River Chardonnay	Martinborough	White	Melon, stone fruit, spicy	Shellfish	**
Dry River Craighall Botrytis Riesling	Martinborough	Sweet	Sweet, honey	Dessert	**
Dry River Craighall Riesling	Martinborough	White	Floral, citrus	Fish	**
Dry River Gewurztraminer	Martinborough	White	Spicy, floral, minerally	Chicken	**

NEW ZEALAND (continued)

Wine name	Region	Style	Flavor/Bouquet	Compatible Foods	Price Range
Dry River Pinot Gris	Martinborough	White	Melon, spicy	Fish	**
Dry River Pinot Noir	Martinborough	Red	Powerful, earthy, smoky, berry	Duck	***
Dry River Syrah	Martinborough	Red	Plums, berry, earthy	Beef	***
Duetz Marlborough Cuvée Blanc de Blancs Méthode Traditionnelle Chardonnay	Marlborough	Sparkling	Crisp, citrus, toasty	Aperitif	**
Duetz Marlborough Cuvée Méthode Traditionnelle	Marlborough	Sparkling	Austere, citrus	Fruit	**
Duetz Marlborough Pinot Noir Cuvée Méthode Traditionnelle	Marlborough	Sparkling	Crisp, berry, complex	Aperitif	**
Esk Valley Chardonnay	Gisborne/Hawkes Bay	White	Tropical fruit, melon	Fish	**
Esk Valley Merlot	Gisborne/Hawkes Bay	Red	Spicy, herbaceous	Venison	**
Esk Valley Reserve Botrytis Chenin Blanc	Gisborne/Hawkes Bay	Sweet	Sweet, apples	Dessert	**
Esk Valley Reserve Hawkes Bay Merlot Malbec Cabernet Sauvignon Cabernet Franc	Gisborne/Hawkes Bay	Red	Leathery, smoky, berry	Beef	***
Esk Valley The Terraces Malbec Merlot Cabernet franc	Gisborne/Hawkes Bay	Red	Berry, tannic, ripe	Beef	***
Fairhall Downs Sauvignon Blanc	Marlborough	White	Tropical fruit, zingy	Shellfish	**
Felton Road Block Three Pinot Noir	Central Otago	Red	Complex, berry, gamey	Duck	***
Felton Road Chardonnay	Central Otago	White	Oaky, tropical fruit	Veal	**
Felton Road Dry Riesling	Central Otago	White	Citrus, dry	Fish	**
Felton Road Riesling	Central Otago	White	Floral, sweet	Cheese	**
Fiddler's Green Riesling	Canterbury/Waipara	White	Floral	Asian	**
Forrest Estate Cornerstone Cabernet Sauvignon Merlot Cabernet Franc Malbec	Gisborne/Hawkes Bay	Red	Herbaceous, spicy	Pasta	**
Forrest Estate Sauvignon Blanc	Marlborough	White	Zingy, citrus, minerally	Shellfish	**
Forrest Merlot	Marlborough	Red	Berry, herbaceous	Lamb	**
Forrest Riesling	Marlborough	White	Floral, citrus	Aperitif	**
Forrest Semillon	Marlborough	White	Tropical fruit, grassy	Fish	**
Foxes Island Chardonnay	Marlborough	White	Citrus, spicy	Chicken	***
Framingham Classic Riesling	Marlborough	White	Floral, minerally	Fish	**
Framingham Dry Riesling	Marlborough	White	Citrus, zingy	Fish	**
Framingham Pinot Gris	Marlborough	White	Citrus, tropical fruit	Chicken	**
Framingham Reserve Late Harvest Riesling	Marlborough	Sweet	Sweet, citrus	Dessert	**
Fromm La Strada Chardonnay	Marlborough	White	Complex, nutty, tropical fruit	Veal	**
Fromm La Strada Merlot	Marlborough	Red	Berry, complex, spicy	Lamb	***
Fromm La Strada Pinot Noir	Marlborough	Red	Berry, oaky, complex	Chicken	***
Fromm La Strada Riesling Auslese	Marlborough	Sweet	Sweet, citrus, floral	Dessert	**
Fromm La Strada Riesling	Marlborough	White	Floral, citrus	Fish	**
Gibbston Valley Pinot Gris	Central Otago	White	Citrus, tropical fruit	Shellfish	**
Gibbston Valley Pinot Noir	Central Otago	Red	Spicy, berry	Game	**
Gibbston Valley Reserve Pinot Noir	Central Otago	Red	Complex, berry, earthy	Duck	***
Gibbston Valley Riesling	Central Otago	White	Citrus, zingy	Fish	**
Gibbston Valley Sauvignon Blanc	Central Otago	White	Zingy, grassy	Antipasto	**
Giesen Botrytised Riesling	Canterbury/Waipara	Sweet	Mandarin, sweet	Dessert	**
Giesen Canterbury Riesling	Canterbury/Waipara	White	Zingy, floral	Fish	**
Giesen Marlborough Sauvignon Blanc	Marlborough	White	Zingy, tropical fruit	Shellfish	**
Giesen Noble Late Harvest Riesling	Canterbury/Waipara	Sweet	Sweet, citrus	Dessert	**
Giesen Reserve Chardonnay	Canterbury/Waipara	White	Melon, tropical fruit	Chicken	**
Giesen Reserve Pinot Noir	Canterbury/Waipara	Red	Berry, earthy, gamey	Fish, veal, pork	***
Giesen Reserve Riesling	Canterbury/Waipara	White	Citrus, floral	Fish	**
Goldwater Dog Point Sauvignon Blanc	Marlborough	White	Citrus, zingy	Shellfish	**
Goldwater Esslin Merlot	Waikato/Bay of Plenty	Red	Leathery, spicy, tannic	Beef	***
Goldwater Estate Cabernet Sauvignon Merlot	Waiheke Island	Red	Berry, complex	Lamb	***
Goldwater Roseland Marlborough Chardonnay	Marlborough	White	Toasty, melon	Chicken	**
Goldwater Zell Chardonnay	Waiheke Island	White	Nutty, melon	Fish	**
Greenhough Chardonnay	Nelson	White	Citrus, melon	Fish	**
Greenhough Hope Pinot Noir	Nelson	Red	Berry, earthy	Game	**
Greenhough Sauvignon Blanc	Nelson	White	Zingy, grassy	Shellfish	**
Grove Mill Chardonnay	Marlborough	White	Melon, tropical fruit	Fish	**
Grove Mill Riesling	Marlborough	White	Floral, citrus	Shellfish	**
Grove Mill Sauvignon Blanc	Marlborough	White	Citrus, zingy	Shellfish	**
Highfield Elstree Méthode Traditionnelle	Marlborough	Sparkling	Crisp, toasty	Aperitif	**
Huia Gewurztraminer	Marlborough	White	Floral, spicy, complex	Sausages	**
Huia Méthode Traditionnelle	Marlborough	Sparkling	Toasty, complex	Fish	***
Huia Sauvignon Blanc	Marlborough	White	Tropical fruit, spicy, zingy	Shellfish	**
Huntaway Gewurztraminer	Gisborne/Hawkes Bay	White	Spicy, floral	Asian	**

NEW ZEALAND (continued)

Wine name	Region	Style	Flavor/Bouquet	Compatible Foods	Price Range
Huntaway Pinot Gris	Gisborne/Hawkes Bay	White	Melon, tropical fruit	Antipasto	**
Hunters Brut Méthode Traditionnelle	Marlborough	Sparkling	Crisp, fruity	Aperitif	**
Hunters Chardonnay	Marlborough	White	Melon, tropical fruit	Fish	**
Hunters Gewurztraminer	Marlborough	White	Floral, spicy	Asian	**
Hunters Pinot Noir	Marlborough	Red	Earthy, berry	Game	**
Hunters Riesling	Marlborough	White	Citrus, floral	Pasta	**
Hunters Sauvignon Blanc	Marlborough	White	Zingy, citrus	Shellfish	**
Huthlee Cabernet Franc	Gisborne/Hawkes Bay	Red	Berry, herbaceous	Cold meats	**
Huthlee Estate Cabernet Sauvignon Merlot	Gisborne/Hawkes Bay	Red	Herbaceous, berry	Lamb	**
Huthlee Merlot	Gisborne/Hawkes Bay	Red	Fruit cake, berry	Cold meats, stew, offal	**
Isabel Estate Chardonnay	Marlborough	White	Tropical fruit, citrus	Fish	**
Isabel Estate Pinot Noir	Marlborough	Red	Spicy, oaky, berry	Cold meats	***
Isabel Estate Sauvignon Blanc	Marlborough	White	Zingy, spicy	Shellfish	**
Jackson Estate Sauvignon Blanc	Marlborough	White	Zingy, tropical fruit	Shellfish	**
Kaituna Valley Pinot Noir	Canterbury/Waipara	Red	Berry, plum	Sausages	**
Kawarau Estate Reserve Pinot Noir	Central Otago	Red	Oaky, spicy	Cold meats, stew, offal	**
Kemble Field Chardonnay	Gisborne/Hawkes Bay	White	Melon, citrus	Fish	**
Kim Crawford Cabernet Franc	Gisborne/Hawkes Bay	Red	Berry, herbaceous	cold meats	**
Kim Crawford Marlborough Sauvignon Blanc	Marlborough	White	Tropical fruit, zingy	Shellfish	**
Kim Crawford Merlot	Gisborne/Hawkes Bay	Red	Berry, oaky, fruit cake	Game	**
Kim Crawford Tane Merlot Cabernet Franc	Gisborne/Hawkes Bay	Red	Berry, spicy	Lamb	**
Kim Crawford Unwooded Chardonnay	Marlborough	White	Melon, citrus	Fish	**
Kingsley Estate Cabernet Sauvignon	Gisborne/Hawkes Bay	Red	Berry, minerally	Beef	**
Kingsley Estate Merlot	Gisborne/Hawkes Bay	Red	Plums, berry	Venison	**
Kumeau Brajkovich Cabernet Franc	Auckland	Red	Herbaceous, berry	Cold meats	**
Kumeau Brajkovich Chardonnay	Auckland	White	Austere, citrus	Fish	**
Kumeau River Chardonnay	Auckland	White	Austere, citrus	Shellfish	**
Kumeau River Mates Chardonnay	Auckland	White	Austere, citrus, toasty	Chicken	***
Lake Chalice Botrytised Riesling	Marlborough	Sweet	Mandarin, sweet	Dessert	**
Lake Chalice Platinum Chardonnay	Marlborough	White	Melon, minerally	Chicken	**
Lawson's Dry Hills Riesling	Marlborough	White	Floral, citrus	Veal	**
Lawson's Dry Hills Sauvignon Blanc	Marlborough	White	Grassy, zingy	Shellfish	**
Lawson's Dry Hills Chardonnay	Marlborough	White	Melon, citrus	Pork	**
Lawson's Dry Hills Gewurztraminer	Marlborough	White	Floral, spicy	Asian	**
Le Brun Family No. 1 Méthode Traditionnelle	Marlborough	Sparkling	Toasty, berry, spicy	Shellfish	***
Lintz Cabernet Sauvignon Merlot	Martinborough	Red	Berry, fruity	Pasta	**
Lintz Pinot Noir	Martinborough	Red	Spicy, berry	Pizza	**
Lintz Syrah	Martinborough	Red	Earthy, berry, herbaceous	Beef	**
Lintz Vitesse Cabernet Sauvignon	Martinborough	Red	Berry, tannic, smoky	Venison	***
Margrain Merlot	Martinborough	Red	Plums, leathery	Cold meats, stew, offal	**
Margrain Pinot Gris	Martinborough	White	Citrus, tropical fruit	Pork	**
Margrain Pinot Noir	Martinborough	Red	Spicy, berry	Game	**
Margrain Riesling	Martinborough	White	Floral, citrus	Salads	**
Martinborough Pinot Gris	Martinborough	White	Zingy, apples	Fish	**
Martinborough Vineyard Chardonnay	Martinborough	White	Melon, nutty, complex	Chicken	**
Martinborough Vineyards Late Harvest Riesling	Martinborough	Sweet	Honey, mandarin, sweet	Dessert	**
Martinborough Vineyards Pinot Noir	Martinborough	Red	Spicy, earthy, berry	Game	***
Martinborough Vineyards Reserve Pinot Noir	Martinborough	Red	Oaky, berry, gamey	Duck	***
Matakana Cabernet Sauvignon Malbec Merlot Cabernet Franc	Northland	Red	Herbaceous, berry	Lamb	**
Matariki Anthology (syrah/merlot/cabernet sauvignon/ cabernet franc)	Gisborne/Hawkes Bay	Red	Smoky, berry	Cold meats	**
Matawhero Gewurztraminer	Gisborne/Hawkes Bay	White	Floral, citrus	Sausages	**
Matua Innovator Malbec	Gisborne/Hawkes Bay	Red	Earthy, berry	Cold meats, stew, offal	**
Matua Matheson Chardonnay	Gisborne/Hawkes Bay	White	Nutty, melon	Fish	**
Matua Shingle Peak Pinot Blanc	Marlborough	White	Melon, fruity	Mediterranean	**
Matua Shingle Peak Riesling	Marlborough	White	Floral, citrus	Fish	**
Matua Unwooded Chardonnay	Gisborne/Hawkes Bay	White	Stone fruit, melon	Fish	**
Matua Valley Judd Chardonnay	Gisborne/Hawkes Bay	White	Melon, berry	Chicken	**
Matua Valley Matheson Reserve Sauvignon Blanc	Gisborne/Hawkes Bay	White	Zingy, citrus	Shellfish	**
Mills Reef Elspeth Cabernet Sauvignon	Gisborne/Hawkes Bay	Red	Berry, tannic	Beef	***
Mills Reef Elspeth Cabernet Sauvignon Merlot	Gisborne/Hawkes Bay	Red	Berry, leathery	Lamb	***
Mills Reef Reserve Cabernet Sauvignon Merlot	Gisborne/Hawkes Bay	Red	Berry, smoky	Veal	**
Mills Reef Reserve Chardonnay	Gisborne/Hawkes Bay	White	Nutty, melon	Fish	**

NEW ZEALAND *(continued)*

Wine name	Region	Style	Flavor/Bouquet	Compatible Foods	Price Range
Mills Reef Traditional Method	Gisborne/Hawkes Bay	Sparkling	Crisp, fruity	Aperitif	***
Millton Barrel Fermented Chardonnay	Gisborne/Hawkes Bay	White	Nutty, spicy	Veal	**
Millton Barrel Fermented Chenin Blanc	Gisborne/Hawkes Bay	White	Melon, nutty, apples	Chicken	**
Millton Viognier	Gisborne/Hawkes Bay	White	Tropical fruit, floral	Fish	**
Milton Opou Riesling	Gisborne/Hawkes Bay	White	Citrus, zingy	Pork	**
Miro Cabernet Franc Merlot Cabernet Sauvignon	Waiheke Island	Red	Berry, tannic, oaky	Lamb	***
Mission Jewelstone Cabernet Sauvignon Merlot	Gisborne/Hawkes Bay	Red	Oaky, spicy	Beef	***
Mission Jewelstone Chardonnay	Gisborne/Hawkes Bay	White	Citrus, oaky	Fish	**
Mission Jewelstone Noble Riesling	Gisborne/Hawkes Bay	Sweet	Sweet, citrus	Dessert	**
Mission Jewelstone Pinot Gris	Gisborne/Hawkes Bay	White	Citrus, spicy	Fish	**
Mission Reserve Cabernet Sauvignon	Gisborne/Hawkes Bay	Red	Berry, spicy	Mediterranean	**
Montana Ormond Chardonnay	Marlborough	White	Melon, citrus	Veal	**
Montana Patutahi Gewurztraminer	Gisborne/Hawkes Bay	White	Zingy, spicy	Asian	**
Montana Reserve Chardonnay	Marlborough	White	Nutty, minerally, citrus	Chicken	**
Montana Reserve Merlot	Marlborough	Red	Berry, tannic, herbaceous	Lamb	**
Montana Reserve Pinot Noir	Marlborough	Red	Berry, spicy, earthy	Game	**
Montana Reserve Riesling	Marlborough	White	Floral, citrus	Veal	**
Montana Tom Cabernet Sauvignon Merlot	Gisborne/Hawkes Bay	Red	Herbaceous, minerally	Lamb	**
Morton Estate Black Label Cabernet Sauvignon	Gisborne/Hawkes Bay	Red	Berry, complex	Beef	***
Morton Estate Black Label Chardonnay	Gisborne/Hawkes Bay	White	Citrus, nutty	Fish	**
Morton Estate Black Label Merlot Cabernet Sauvignon	Gisborne/Hawkes Bay	Red	Oaky, berry, plums	Beef	***
Morton Estate Black Label Merlot	Gisborne/Hawkes Bay	Red	Oaky, tannic, tobacco	Pasta	***
Morton Estate Black Label Méthode Traditionnelle	Gisborne/Hawkes Bay	Sparkling	Toasty, austere	Aperitif	**
Morton Estate RD Méthode Traditionnelle	Gisborne/Hawkes Bay	Sparkling	Crisp, toasty	Nuts	**
Morton Estate White Label Chardonnay	Marlborough	White	Melon, floral	Chicken	**
Morton Estate White Label Marlborough Riesling	Marlborough	White	Citrus, spicy, floral	Fish	**
Morton Estate White Label Marlborough Sauvignon Blanc	Marlborough	White	Grassy, zingy	Shellfish	**
Morton White Label Hawkes Bay Chardonnay	Gisborne/Hawkes Bay	White	Melon, floral	Fish	**
Mountford Chardonnay	Canterbury/Waipara	White	Melon, tropical fruit	Pork	**
Mountford Pinot Noir	Canterbury/Waipara	Red	Berry, spicy	Duck	**
Muddy Water Pinot Noir	Canterbury/Waipara	Red	Earthy, berry	Pasta	**
Murdoch James Syrah	Martinborough	Red	Spicy, berry, earthy	Beef	**
Nautilus Chardonnay	Marlborough	White	Melon, tropical fruit	Fish	**
Nautilus Cuvée Méthode Traditionnelle	Marlborough	Sparkling	Fruity, crisp	Aperitif	**
Nautilus Sauvignon Blanc	Marlborough	White	Zingy, tropical fruit	Shellfish	**
Neudorf Brightwater Riesling	Nelson	White	Floral, citrus	Fish	**
Neudorf Moutere Chardonnay	Nelson	White	Tropical fruit, toasty, nutty	Shellfish	***
Neudorf Moutere Late Harvest Riesling	Nelson	Sweet	Mandarin, sweet	Dessert	**
Neudorf Moutere Reserve Pinot Noir	Nelson	Red	Earthy, gamey, berry	Game	***
Neudorf Nelson Chardonnay	Nelson	White	Citrus, zingy	Chicken	**
Neudorf Sauvignon Blanc	Nelson	White	Zingy, citrus, tropical fruit	Shellfish	**
Nevis Bluff Pinot Gris	Central Otago	White	Zingy, rich	Salads	**
Nga Waka Riesling	Martinborough	White	Floral, citrus	Mediterranean	**
Ngatarawa Alwyn Noble Harvest Riesling	Gisborne/Hawkes Bay	Sweet	Sweet, citrus	Dessert	**
Ngatarawa Glazebrook Cabernet Sauvignon	Gisborne/Hawkes Bay	Red	Berry, tannic	Pasta	**
Ngatarawa Glazebrook Chardonnay	Gisborne/Hawkes Bay	White	Tropical fruit, nutty	Veal	**
Ngatarawa Glazebrook Merlot Cabernet Sauvignon	Gisborne/Hawkes Bay	Red	Minerally, berry, tannic	Lamb	**
Ngatarawa Glazebrook Noble Harvest Riesling	Gisborne/Hawkes Bay	Sweet	Sweet, mandarin	Dessert	**
Nobilos Grand Reserve Chardonnay	Gisborne/Hawkes Bay	White	Melon, oaky	Fish	**
Nobilos Icon Chardonnay	Gisborne/Hawkes Bay	White	Melon, tropical fruit	Shellfish	**
Nobilos Icon Gewurztraminer	Marlborough	White	Spicy, floral, citrus	Asian	**
Nobilos Icon Riesling	Marlborough	White	Citrus, floral	Chicken	**
Obsidian Cabernet Sauvignon Merlot	Waiheke Island	Red	Tannic, berry, herbaceous	Lamb	**
Okahu Kaz Semillon	Northland/Auckland	White	Tropical fruit, citrus	Veal	**
Okahu Kaz Syrah	Northland/Auckland	Red	Earthy, berry	Beef	**
Okahu Pinotage	Northland/Auckland	Red	Berry, earthy	Pasta	**
Olssen's of Bannockburn Pinot Noir	Central Otago	Red	Fungal, berry	Pasta	**
Omaka Springs Chardonnay	Marlborough	White	Melon, fruity	Salads	*
Opihi Pinot Gris	Canterbury/Waipara	White	Tropical fruit, citrus	Mediterranean	**
Oyster Bay Chardonnay	Marlborough	White	Citrus, mandarin, oaky	Shellfish	**
Oyster Bay Sauvignon Blanc	Marlborough	White	Zingy, citrus, fruity	Shellfish	**
Palliser Chardonnay	Martinborough	White	Melon, nutty	Chicken	**
Palliser Estate Méthode Traditionnelle	Martinborough	Sparkling	Crisp, berry, citrus	Aperitif	**

NEW ZEALAND *(continued)*

Wine name	Region	Style	Flavor/Bouquet	Compatible Foods	Price Range
Palliser Estate Pinot Noir	Martinborough	Red	Gamey, berry	Game	***
Palliser Estate Riesling	Martinborough	White	Citrus, minerally	Fish	**
Palliser Estate Sauvignon Blanc	Martinborough	White	Zingy, grassy	Shellfish	**
Pegasus Bay Aria Late Picked Riesling	Canterbury/Waipara	Sweet	Sweet, mandarin	Dessert	**
Pegasus Bay Chardonnay	Canterbury/Waipara	White	Tropical fruit, melon	Fish	**
Pegasus Bay Finale Noble Chardonnay	Canterbury/Waipara	Sweet	Sweet, complex	Dessert	**
Pegasus Bay Main Divide Sauvignon Blanc	Marlborough	White	Tropical fruit, zingy	Aperitif	**
Pegasus Bay Pinot Noir	Canterbury/Waipara	Red	Gamey, earthy, berry	Game	**
Pegasus Bay Prima Donna Pinot Noir	Canterbury/Waipara	Red	Berry, smoky, complex	Duck	***
Pegasus Bay Riesling	Canterbury/Waipara	White	Citrus, zingy	Cheese	**
Pelorus Méthode Traditionnelle	Marlborough	Sparkling	Complex, toasty	Shellfish	***
Pencarrow Pinot Noir	Martinborough	Red	Earthy, berry	Game	**
Pencarrow Sauvignon Blanc	Martinborough	White	Zingy, grassy	Salads	**
Penisula Estate Cabernet Sauvignon Merlot	Waiheke Island	Red	Berry, tannic	Lamb	***
Peregrine Pinot Noir	Central Otago	Red	Spicy, berry	Sausages	**
Peregrine Riesling	Central Otago	White	Zingy, citrus	Fish	**
Perrelle Lake Hayes Grand Cuvée Méthode Traditionnelle	Central Otago	Sparkling	Crisp, citrus	Aperitif	**
Phoenix Gewurztraminer	Gisborne/Hawkes Bay	White	Spicy, floral	Asian	**
Phoenix Sauvignon Blanc	Marlborough	White	Zingy, spicy	Fish	**
Ponder Riesling	Marlborough	White	Floral, minerally	Shellfish	**
Quartz Reef Chauvet Méthode Traditionnelle	Central Otago	Sparkling	Citrus, crisp	Cheese	**
Quartz Reef Pinot Gris	Central Otago	White	Spicy, melon	Fish	**
Quartz Reef Pinot Noir	Central Otago	Red	Berry, spicy	Duck	**
Redmetal Vineyards Basket Press Merlot Cabernet Franc	Gisborne/Hawkes Bay	Red	Berry, chocolate, tannic	Beef	***
Revington Chardonnay	Gisborne/Hawkes Bay	White	Tropical fruit, zingy	Fish	**
Rippon Gewurztraminer	Central Otago	White	Spicy, floral	Asian	**
Rippon Pinot Noir	Central Otago	Red	Berry, spicy	Duck	***
Rippon Sauvignon Blanc	Central Otago	White	Zingy, citrus	Cheese	**
Rongopai Winemakers Reserve Botrytised Chardonnay	Waikato/Bay of Plenty	Sweet	Sweet, mandarin	Dessert	***
Rongopai Winemakers Reserve Botrytised Riesling	Waikato/Bay of Plenty	Sweet	Sweet, citrus	Dessert	***
Rossendale Reserve Pinot Noir	Canterbury/Waipara	Red	Berry, spicy	Pasta	**
Sacred Hill Barrel Fermented Sauvignon Blanc	Gisborne/Hawkes Bay	White	Tropical fruit, nutty	Chicken	**
Sacred Hill Basket Press Cabernet Sauvignon	Gisborne/Hawkes Bay	Red	Berry, earthy	Pasta	**
Sacred Hill Basket Press Merlot	Gisborne/Hawkes Bay	Red	Berry, plums	Venison	**
Sacred Hill Brokenstone Merlot	Gisborne/Hawkes Bay	Red	Berry, plums	Venison	**
Sacred Hill Halo Semillon	Gisborne/Hawkes Bay	White	Tropical fruit, fruity	Fish	**
Sacred Hill Rifleman's Chardonnay	Gisborne/Hawkes Bay	White	Tropical fruit, floral	Veal	**
Sacred Hill XS Noble Selection Riesling	Gisborne/Hawkes Bay	Sweet	Citrus, sweet	Dessert	**
Saint Clair Awatere Reserve Sauvignon Blanc	Marlborough	White	Grassy, zingy	Cheese	**
Saint Clair Rapaura Reserve Merlot	Marlborough	Red	Tannic, berry	Lamb	**
Saint Clair Riesling	Marlborough	White	Citrus, spicy, floral	Fish	**
Saints Chardonnay	Gisborne/Hawkes Bay	White	Citrus, spicy	Veal	**
Saints Gewurztraminer	Gisborne/Hawkes Bay	White	Floral, spicy, citrus	Asian	**
Saints Noble Riesling	Marlborough	Sweet	Mandarin, sweet	Dessert	**
Sandihurst Reserve Pinot Noir	Canterbury/Waipara	Red	Gamey, spicy	Duck	**
Seifried Barrel Fermented Chardonnay	Nelson	White	Melon, nutty	Veal	**
Seifried Gewurztraminer Ice Wine	Nelson	Sweet	Citrus, sweet	Dessert	**
Seifried Winemaker's Collection Riesling	Nelson	White	Citrus, floral	Fruit	**
Seifried Winemaker's Collection Riesling Ice Wine	Nelson	Sweet	Sweet, citrus, floral	Dessert	**
Selaks Drylands Chardonnay	Marlborough	White	Melon, nutty	Fish	**
Selaks Drylands Riesling	Marlborough	White	Floral, citrus	Veal	**
Selaks Drylands Sauvignon Blanc	Marlborough	White	Tropical fruit, zingy	Salads	**
Selaks Premium Riesling	Marlborough	White	Citrus, zingy	Chicken	**
Selaks Premium Selection Sauvignon Blanc	Marlborough	White	Zingy, grassy	Shellfish	**
Seresin Chardonnay	Marlborough	White	Nutty, melon, complex	Chicken	**
Seresin Noble Riesling	Marlborough	Sweet	Sweet, honey, citrus	Dessert	**
Seresin Pinot Gris	Marlborough	White	Tropical fruit, citrus	Fish	**
Seresin Pinot Noir	Marlborough	Red	Fungal, earthy, gamey	Duck	**
Seresin Riesling	Marlborough	White	Floral, citrus, spicy	Fish	**
Sileni Chardonnay	Gisborne/Hawkes Bay	White	Fruity, tropical fruit	Fish	**
Sileni Merlot Cabernet Sauvignon Cabernet Franc	Gisborne/Hawkes Bay	Red	Leathery, berry	Beef	***
Spencer Hill Chardonnay	Nelson	White	Melon, tropical fruit	Fish	**
Spencer Hill Tasman Bay Chardonnay	Nelson	White	Tropical fruit, citrus	Chicken	**

NEW ZEALAND *(continued)*

Wine name	Region	Style	Flavor/Bouquet	Compatible Foods	Price Range
Spencer Hill Tasman Bay Sauvignon Blanc	Nelson	White	Minerally, zingy	Shellfish	**
St Helena Reserve Chardonnay	Canterbury/Waipara	White	Tropical fruit, citrus	Chicken	**
St Helena Reserve Pinot Gris	Canterbury/Waipara	White	Tropical fruit, spicy	Salads	**
Stonecroft Gewurztraminer	Gisborne/Hawkes Bay	White	Floral, spicy	Asian	**
Stonecroft Syrah	Gisborne/Hawkes Bay	Red	Spicy, berry	Duck	***
Stoneleigh Sauvignon Blanc	Marlborough	White	Zingy, minerally	Shellfish	**
Stoneyridge Larose Cabernets (cabernet sauvignon/malbec/ merlot/cabernet franc/petite verdot)	Waiheke Island	Red	Berry, complex, tannic, oaky	Lamb	***
Stratford Chardonnay	Martinborough	White	Nutty, melon	Pork	**
Stratford Pinot Noir	Martinborough	Red	Berry, smoky	Cold meats	**
Stratford Riesling	Martinborough	White	Citrus, floral	Fish	**
Te Awa Farm Boundary (cabernet sauvignon/merlot/ cabernet franc/malbec)	Hawkes Bay	Red	Herbaceous, berry	Beef	**
Te Awa Farm Merlot	Gisborne/Hawkes Bay	Red	Berry, spicy, herbaceous	Lamb	**
Te Awa Frontier Chardonnay	Gisborne/Hawkes Bay	White	Melon, nutty	Fish	**
Te Awa Longlands Chardonnay	Gisborne/Hawkes Bay	White	Tropical fruit, spicy	Shellfish	**
Te Kairanga Reserve Chardonnay	Martinborough	White	Citrus, toasty, melon	Veal	**
Te Kairanga Reserve Pinot Noir	Martinborough	Red	Complex, berry, spicy	Duck	***
Te Mata Awatea Cabernet Sauvignon Merlot	Gisborne/Hawkes Bay	Red	Berry, herbaceous	Beef	***
Te Mata Bullnose Syrah	Gisborne/Hawkes Bay	Red	Smoky, berry	Cold meats, stew, offal	***
Te Mata Cape Crest Sauvignon Blanc	Gisborne/Hawkes Bay	White	Zingy, grassy	Salads	**
Te Mata Coleraine Cabernet Sauvignon Merlot	Gisborne/Hawkes Bay	Red	Herbaceous, berry, complex	Beef	***
Te Mata Elston Chardonnay	Gisborne/Hawkes Bay	White	Tropical fruit, nutty, toasty	Fish	***
Te Whare Ra Duke of Marlborough Chardonnay	Marlborough	White	Melon, oaky	Chicken	**
Thornbury Merlot	Gisborne/Hawkes Bay	Red	Herbaceous, plums	Venison	**
Thornbury Sauvignon Blanc	Marlborough	White	Grassy, tropical fruit	Cheese	**
Tohu Sauvignon Blanc	Marlborough	White	Zingy, tropical fruit	Shellfish	**
Torlese Gewurztraminer	Canterbury/Waipara	White	Spicy, floral	Asian	**
Trinity Hill Cabernet Sauvignon	Gisborne/Hawkes Bay	Red	Berry, tannic	Pasta	***
Trinity Hill Gimbless Road Cabernet Sauvignon Merlot	Gisborne/Hawkes Bay	Red	Smoky, tannic	Venison	***
Trinity Hill Merlot	Gisborne/Hawkes Bay	Red	Berry, leathery	Lamb	***
Trinity Hill Syrah	Gisborne/Hawkes Bay	Red	Spicy, berry, powerful	Beef	***
Trintity Hills Shepherds Croft Merlot Cabernet Franc Syrah	Gisborne/Hawkes Bay	Red	Berry, oaky	Beef	**
Trinty Hill Chardonnay	Gisborne/Hawkes Bay	White	Fruity, citrus	Cheese	**
Twin Bays Fenton Merlot Cabernet Franc	Waiheke Island	Red	Berry, herbaceous	Lamb	**
Two Paddocks Pinot Noir	Central Otago	Red	Spicy, gamey, earthy	Game	**
Unison Merlot Cabernet Sauvignon Syrah	Gisborne/Hawkes Bay	Red	Spicy, berry, oaky	Beef	**
Valli Pinot Noir	Central Otago	Red	Berry, acid, earthy	Pizza	**
Vavasour Chardonnay	Marlborough	White	Nutty, melon, minerally	Fish	**
Vavasour Dashwood Sauvignon Blanc	Marlborough	White	Zingy, tropical fruit	Fish	**
Vavasour Pinot Noir	Marlborough	Red	Gamey, berry	Duck	**
Vavasour Riesling	Marlborough	White	Citrus, floral	Veal	**
Vavasour Sauvignon Blanc	Marlborough	White	Zingy, tropical fruit	Shellfish	**
Vavasour Single Vineyard Sauvignon Blanc	Marlborough	White	Zingy, tropical fruit, citrus	Fish	**
Vidal Estate Cabernet Sauvignon	Gisborne/Hawkes Bay	Red	Tannic, berry	Stew	**
Vidal Estate Reserve Cabernet Sauvignon Merlot	Gisborne/Hawkes Bay	Red	Smoky, berry, tannic	Cold meats, stew, offal	***
Vidal Reserve Chardonnay	Gisborne/Hawkes Bay	White	Melon, toasty	Shellfish	***
Vidal Reseve Noble Semillon	Gisborne/Hawkes Bay	Sweet	Sweet, mandarin	Dessert	**
Vidal Sauvignon Blanc	Marlborough	White	Grassy, zingy	Cheese	**
Villa Maria Clifford Bay Reserve Sauvignon Blanc	Marlborough	White	Zingy, tropical fruit	Shellfish	**
Villa Maria Reserve Barrique Fermented Chardonnay	Marlborough	White	Melon, nutty, toasty	Chicken	***
Villa Maria Reserve Gewurztraminer	Gisborne/Hawkes Bay	White	Spicy, citrus	Asian	**
Villa Maria Reserve Hawkes Bay Cabernet Sauvignon Merlot	Gisborne/Hawkes Bay	Red	Berry, tannic	Beef	***
Villa Maria Reserve Hawkes Bay Chardonnay	Gisborne/Hawkes Bay	White	Nutty, citrus, tropical fruit	Fish	**
Villa Maria Reserve Marlborough Chardonnay	Marlborough	White	Melon, citrus	Pork	**
Villa Maria Reserve Marlborough Riesling	Marlborough	White	Floral, minerally	Veal	**
Villa Maria Reserve Merlot	Gisborne/Hawkes Bay	Red	Berry, minerally, herbaceous	Venison	**
Villa Maria Reserve Noble Riesling	Marlborough	Sweet	Sweet, mandarin	Dessert	***
Villa Maria Wairau Valley Reserve Sauvignon Blanc	Marlborough	White	Zingy, minerally	Shellfish	**
Vina Alta Retico Amarone-style Cabernet Franc/Merlot	Auckland	Red	Berry, plums, rich	Cheese	**
Virtu Noble Semillon	Gisborne/Hawkes Bay	Sweet	Sweet, floral	Dessert	**
Voss Estate Pinot Noir	Wairarapa/Wellington	Red	Earthy, gamey, berry	Game	**
Voss Estate Waihenga Cabernet Sauvignon Merlot	Wairarapa/Wellington	Red	Herbaceous, berry	Lamb	**

NEW ZEALAND (continued)

Wine name	Region	Style	Flavor/Bouquet	Compatible Foods	Price Range
Waiheke Vineyards Te Motu Cabernet Sauvignon Merlot	Waiheke Island/Auckland	Red	Berry, tannic	Lamb	***
Waipara Springs Riesling	Canterbury/Waipara	White	Floral, citrus	Fish	**
Waipara West Chardonnay	Canterbury/Waipara	White	Tropical fruit, melon	Chicken	**
Waipara West Pinot Noir	Canterbury/Waipara	Red	Earthy, berry	Game	**
Waipara West Riesling	Canterbury/Waipara	White	Citrus, floral	Fish	**
Walnut Ridge Pinot Noir	Wairarapa/Wellington	Red	Oaky, berry, plums	Game	**
West Brook Riesling	Marlborough	White	Floral, citrus	Chicken	**
Whitehaven Single Vineyard Reserve Sauvignon Blanc	Marlborough	White	Zingy, grassy	Shellfish	**
William Hill Gewurztraminer	Central Otago	White	Floral, spicy	Cold meats, stew, offal	**
William Hill Pinot Noir	Central Otago	Red	Earthy, berry, spicy	Pasta	**
William Hill Riesling	Central Otago	White	Floral, zingy	Fish	**
Winslow Turakrae Reserve Cabernet Sauvignon Cabernet Franc	Wairarapa/Wellington	Red	Earthy, berry, tannic	Lamb	***
Wither Hills Chardonnay	Marlborough	White	Melon, nutty	Fish	**
Wither Hills Pinot Noir	Marlborough	Red	Earthy, fungal	Game	**
Wither Hills Sauvignon Blanc	Marlborough	White	Zingy, minerally	Cheese	**

CANADA

Wine name	Region	Style	Flavor/Bouquet	Compatible Foods	Price Range
Blue Mountain Vineyard and Cellars Reserve Pinot Blanc	British Columbia	White	Stone fruit, oaky	Cheese, fish	**
Blue Mountain Vineyard and Cellars Reserve Pinot Gris	British Columbia	White	Fruity, minerally	Cheese, shellfish	**
Blue Mountain Vineyard and Cellars Reserve Pinot Noir	British Columbia	Red	Jam, vanillin	Veal, pork, beef	**
Calona Vineyards Artist Series Chardonnay	Okanagan Valley/ British Columbia	White	Butter, oaky	Fish, pasta, chicken	***
Calona Vineyards Artist Series Pinot Blanc	Okanagan Valley/ British Columbia	White	Stone fruit, complex	Pasta, fish, chicken	***
Calona Vineyards Private Reserve Cabernet Sauvignon	Okanagan Valley/ British Columbia	Red	Berry, oaky, earthy	Lamb, beef	**
Calona Vineyards Private Reserve Fumé Blanc	Okanagan Valley/ British Columbia	White	Stone fruit, citrus	Salads, shellfish, fish, cheese	**
Calona Vineyards Private Reserve Late Harvest Ehrenfelser	Okanagan Valley/ British Columbia	White	Fruity, floral	Dessert, cheese	**
Calona Vineyards Private Reserve Merlot	Okanagan Valley/ British Columbia	Red	Berry, oaky	Lamb, beef	**
Calona Vineyards Sandhill Pinot Blanc	Okanagan Valley/ British Columbia	White	Stone fruit, minerally	Shellfish, fish, chicken	**
Cave Spring Cellars Cabernet/Merlot	Niagara Peninsula/Ontario	Red	Earthy, berry	Beef, lamb	**
Cave Spring Cellars Chardonnay Reserve	Niagara Peninsula/Ontario	White	Fruity, oaky	Fish, chicken, veal	**
Cave Spring Cellars Estate Bottled Gewürztraminer	Niagara Peninsula/Ontario	White	Tropical fruit, floral	Cheese, fruit, Asian	**
Cave Spring Cellars Estate Bottled Reserve Riesling	Niagara Peninsula/Ontario	White	Fruity, minerally	Asian, shellfish	**
Cave Spring Cellars Gamay	Niagara Peninsula/Ontario	Red	Jam, berry	Pizza, Asian, chicken, veal, pork	*
Cave Spring Cellars Off Dry Riesling	Niagara Peninsula/Ontario	White	Floral, tropical fruit	Asian, cheese	*
Cave Spring Cellars Riesling Icewine	Niagara Peninsula/Ontario	White	Floral, tropical fruit	Dessert	***
Cedar Creek Estate Winery Cabernet Franc	Okanagan Valley/ British Columbia	Red	Berry, spicy	Veal, pork, chicken	**
Cedar Creek Estate Winery Chardonnay	Okanagan Valley/ British Columbia	White	Fruity, oaky	Fish, chicken, veal	**
Cedar Creek Estate Winery Reserve Chardonnay Icewine	Okanagan Valley/ British Columbia	White	Fruity, nutty	Dessert	**
Cedar Creek Estate Winery Riesling	Okanagan Valley/ British Columbia	White	Tropical fruit, floral	Asian, pasta	*
Château des Charmes Late Harvest Riesling	Niagara Peninsula/Ontario	White	Floral, stone fruit	Cheese, dessert	**
Château des Charmes Paul Bosc Riesling Icewine	Niagara Peninsula/Ontario	White	Tropical fruit, wax, floral	Dessert	***
Château des Charmes St. David's Bench Vyd. Cabernet Franc	Niagara Peninsula/Ontario	Red	Berry, oaky	Beef, pork	**
Château des Charmes St. David's Bench Vyd. Chardonnay	Niagara Peninsula/Ontario	White	Butter, oaky	Chicken, veal, fish	**
CChâteau des Charmes Sec Méthode Traditionelle	Niagara Peninsula/Ontario	Sparkling	Stone fruit, minerally	Pizza, shellfish	**
ilento Barrel Fermented Reserve Chardonnay	Niagara Peninsula/Ontario	White	Fruity, oaky	Fish, chicken	**
Cilento Late-Harvest Riesling	Niagara Peninsula/Ontario	White	Tropical fruit, floral	Dessert	**
Cilento Reserve Cabernet Sauvignon	Niagara Peninsula/Ontario	Red	Berry, oaky	Lamb, beef	**
Cilento Vidal Icewine	Niagara Peninsula/Ontario	White	Nutty, tropical fruit	Dessert	***
Colio Cabernet Franc	Lake Erie North Shore	Red	Berry, spicy	Pizza, beef, chicken	**
Colio Late Harvest Vidal	Ontario	White	Fruity, nutty	Dessert	**
D'Angelo Estate Cabernet Franc	Lake Erie North Shore	Red	Berry, spicy	Pizza, beef, chicken	**
D'Angelo Estate Select Late Harvest Vidal	Ontario	White	Fruity, nutty	Dessert	**

CANADA (continued)

Wine name	Region	Style	Flavor/Bouquet	Compatible Foods	Price Range
D'Angelo Estate Vidal Icewine	Lake Erie North Shore	White	Citrus, tropical, fruit, minerally	Dessert	***
Domaine Combret Cabernet Franc	British Columbia	Red	Berry, oaky	Beef, chicken, veal	**
Domaine Combret Chardonnay	British Columbia	White	Fruity, butter	Fish, chicken	**
Domaine Combret Riesling	British Columbia	White	Fruity	Cheese, pizza, fish	*
Domaine de Chaberton Estates Bacchus	Okanagan Valley/ British Columbia	White	Fruity	Pizza, pasta, Asian, cheese	**
Gehringer Bros. Estate Winery Auxerrois	Okanagan Valley/ British Columbia	White	Fruity, floral	Pizza, pasta, salads, chicken	*
Gehringer Bros. Estate Winery Minus 9 Ehrenfelser Icewine	Okanagan Valley/ British Columbia	White	Tropical fruit, spicy	Dessert	**
Gray Monk Estate Winery Riesling	Okanagan Valley/ British Columbia	White	Tropical fruit, floral	Asian, pasta	*
Gray Monk Estate Winery Select Late Harvest Ehrenfelser	Okanagan Valley/ British Columbia	White	Fruity, spicy	Dessert, cheese	**
Gray Monk Estate Winery Unwooded Chardonnay	Okanagan Valley/ British Columbia	White	Stone fruit, minerally	Shellfish, fish, chicken, veal	**
Hawthorne Mountain Vineyards Chardonnay	Okanagan Valley/ British Columbia	White	Butter, oaky	Fish, chicken, veal	**
Hawthorne Mountain Vineyards Chardonnay/Semillon	Okanagan Valley/ British Columbia	White	Tropical fruit, wax	Pasta, fish, chicken	**
Hawthorne Mountain Vineyards Ehrenfelser Icewine	Okanagan Valley/ British Columbia	White	Tropical fruit, floral	Dessert	***
Hawthorne Mountain Vineyards Gamay Noir	Okanagan Valley/ British Columbia	Red	Fruity, jam	Pasta, pizza, Asian, pork	*
Hawthorne Mountain Vineyards Gewürztraminer	Okanagan Valley/ British Columbia	White	Tropical fruit, floral	Asian, fish	*
Hawthorne Mountain Vineyards Lemberger	Okanagan Valley/ British Columbia	Red	Fruity, spicy	Pizza, pasta, chicken	*
Hawthorne Mountain Vineyards Merlot	Okanagan Valley/ British Columbia	Red	Berry, earthy	Pork, beef	**
Hawthorne Mountain Vineyards Riesling	Okanagan Valley/ British Columbia	White	Tropical fruit, floral	Asian, pasta	*
Henry of Pelham Family Estate Cabernet/Merlot	Niagara Peninsula/Ontario	Red	Earthy, berry	Beef, lamb	**
Henry of Pelham Family Estate Reserve Baco Noir	Niagara Peninsula/Ontario	Red	Berry, earthy	Pasta, pork	**
Henry of Pelham Family Estate Reserve Baco Noir	Ontario	Red	Jam, spicy	Pizza, pasta, pork	**
Henry of Pelham Family Estate Reserve Chardonnay	Niagara Peninsula/Ontario	White	Butter, oaky	Chicken, fish	**
Henry of Pelham Family Estate Reserve Riesling	Niagara Peninsula/Ontario	White	Floral, fruity	Asian, shellfish	**
Henry of Pelham Family Estate Riesling Icewine	Niagara Peninsula/Ontario	White	Floral, tropical fruit	Dessert	***
Henry of Pelham Family Estate Select Late Harvest Vidal	Ontario	White	Tropical fruit, nutty	Dessert	**
Henry of Pelham Family Estate Winery Barrel Fermented Chardonnay	Niagara Peninsula/Ontario	White	Fruity, oaky	Fish, chicken	**
Hernder Estate Wines Baco Noir	Ontario	Red	Fruity, spicy	Pizza, pasta, Asian	*
Hernder Estate Wines Barrel Fermented Chardonnay	Niagara Peninsula/Ontario	White	Fruity, oaky	Fish, chicken	**
Hernder Estate Wines Cabernet Franc	Niagara Peninsula/Ontario	Red	Berry, spicy	Beef, veal, pork	**
Hernder Estate Wines Icewine	Niagara Peninsula/Ontario	White	Fruity	Dessert	***
Hernder Estate Wines Select Late Harvest Vidal	Niagara Peninsula/Ontario	White	Nutty, fruity	Dessert	**
Hernder Estate Wines Select Late Harvest Vidal	Ontario	White	Tropical fruit, nutty	Dessert	**
Hester Creek Estate Winery Blanc de Noirs	Okanagan Valley/ British Columbia	Rosé	Berry, fruity	Pizza, pasta, Asian	**
Hester Creek Estate Winery Estate Pinot Blanc	Okanagan Valley/ British Columbia	White	Stone fruit, nutty	Shellfish, fish	**
Hester Creek Estate Winery Late Harvest Trebbiano	Okanagan Valley/ British Columbia	White	Fruity, citrus	Asian, fruits, dessert	**
Hester Creek Estate Winery Reserve Pinot Blanc Icewine	Okanagan Valley/ British Columbia	White	Floral, nutty	Dessert	***
Hillebrand Estates Winery Glenlake Showcase Unfiltered Cabernet Sauvignon	Niagara Peninsula/Ontario	Red	Earthy, berry	Lamb, beef	**
Hillebrand Estates Winery Harvest Riesling	Niagara Peninsula/Ontario	White	Fruity, stone fruit	Cheese, Asian	**
Hillebrand Estates Winery Trius Chardonnay	Niagara Peninsula/Ontario	White	Fruity, oaky	Chicken, veal, pasta, fish	**
Hillside Estate Winery Late Harvest Vidal	Okanagan Valley/ British Columbia	White	Nutty, stone fruit	Dessert	**
Inniskillin Okanagan Ehrenfelser Icewine	Okanagan Valley/ British Columbia	White	Tropical fruit, floral	Dessert	***
Inniskillin Okanagan Riesling Icewine	Okanagan Valley/ British Columbia	White	Stone fruit, complex	Dessert	***
Inniskillin Okanagan Vidal Icewine	Okanagan Valley/ British Columbia	White	Nutty, fruity, complex	Dessert	***

CANADA *(continued)*

Wine name	Region	Style	Flavor/Bouquet	Compatible Foods	Price Range
Inniskillin Wines Cabernet Franc	Niagara Peninsula/Ontario	Red	Berry, complex	Beef, veal, pork	**
Inniskillin Wines Culp Vyd. Chardonnay	Niagara Peninsula/Ontario	White	Stone fruit, vanillin	Fish, chicken, veal	**
Inniskillin Wines Founders' Reserve Pinot Noir	Niagara Peninsula/Ontario	Red	Berry, spicy	Pizza, veal, pork	**
Inniskillin Wines Reserve Chardonnay	Niagara Peninsula/Ontario	White	Butter, oaky	Chicken, fish	**
Inniskillin Wines Riesling Icewine	Niagara Peninsula/Ontario	White	Floral, tropical fruit	Dessert	***
Inniskillin Wines Vidal Icewine	Niagara Peninsula/Ontario	White	Nutty, tropical fruit, complex	Dessert	***
Jackson-Triggs Vintners Proprietors' Grand Reserve Chardonnay	Okanagan Valley/British Columbia	White	Butter, oaky	Fish, chicken, veal	**
Jackson-Triggs Vintners Proprietors' Grand Reserve Merlot	Okanagan Valley/British Columbia	Red	Berry, oaky, complex	Lamb, pork, beef	**
Jackson-Triggs Vintners Proprietors' Grand Reserve Riesling Icewine	Okanagan Valley/British Columbia	White	Tropical fruit, floral	Dessert	***
Jackson-Triggs Vintners Proprietors' Reserve Cabernet Sauvignon	Okanagan Valley/British Columbia	Red	Berry, earthy, oaky	Lamb, beef	**
Jackson-Triggs Vintners Proprietors' Reserve Chardonnay	Okanagan Valley/British Columbia	White	Butter, oaky	Fish, veal	**
Jackson-Triggs Vintners Proprietors' Reserve Chenin Blanc Icewine	Okanagan Valley/British Columbia	White	Tropical fruit, floral	Dessert	**
Jackson-Triggs Vintners Proprietors' Reserve Merlot	Okanagan Valley/British Columbia	Red	Berry, earthy	Lamb, beef	**
Jackson-Triggs Vintners Proprietors' Reserve Pinot Blanc	Okanagan Valley/British Columbia	Red	Stone fruit, oaky	Fish, chicken, veal	**
Jackson-Triggs Vintners Proprietors' Reserve Riesling Icewine	Okanagan Valley/British Columbia	White	Floral, tropical fruit	Dessert	***
Joseph's Estate Wines Pinot Gris	Niagara Peninsula/Ontario	White	Floral, minerally	Salads, shellfish, fish, chicken	**
Joseph's Estate Wines Vidal Icewine	Niagara Peninsula/Ontario	White	Nutty, tropical fruit, floral	Dessert	***
Kittling Ridge Estate Wines Marechal Foch	Ontario	Red	Berry, spicy	Pizza, pasta, Mediterranean	*
Konzelmann Estate Winery Late Harvest Riesling, Very Dry	Niagara Peninsula/Ontario	White	Floral, stone fruit	Asian, cheese	**
Konzelmann Estate Winery Pinot Noir	Niagara Peninsula/Ontario	Red	Berry, spicy	Chicken, veal	**
Konzelmann Estate Winery Riesling/Traminer Icewine	Niagara Peninsula/Ontario	White	Fruity, spicy	Dessert	***
Konzelmann Estate Winery Select Late Harvest Vidal	Ontario	White	Fruity, nutty	Dessert	**
Konzelmann Estate Winery Vidal Icewine	Niagara Peninsula/Ontario	White	Tropical fruit, floral	Dessert	***
Lake Breeze Vineyards Pinot Blanc	Okanagan Valley/British Columbia	White	Stone fruit, minerally	Shellfish, fish, chicken, veal	**
Lakeview Cellars Estate Winery Baco Noir	Ontario	Red	Fruity, spicy	Pizza, pasta, Asian	*
Lakeview Cellars Estate Winery Cabernet/Merlot	Niagara Peninsula/Ontario	Red	Berry, toasty	Beef, lamb	**
Lakeview Cellars Estate Winery Chardonnay Musqué	Niagara Peninsula/Ontario	White	Fruity, complex	Fish, chicken, pasta	**
Lakeview Cellars Estate Winery Vidal Icewine	Niagara Peninsula/Ontario	White	Tropical fruit, floral	Dessert	***
Lakeview Cellars Estate Winery Vinc Vyd. Reserve Chardonnay	Niagara Peninsula/Ontario	White	Butter, oaky	Fish, pasta, chicken	**
LeBlanc Estate Winery Oaked Cabernet Franc	Lake Erie North Shore	Red	Berry, vanillin	Beef, chicken, veal	**
LeBlanc Estate Winery Vidal Icewine	Lake Erie North Shore	White	Citrus, tropical fruit, minerally	Dessert	***
Magnotta Barrel Fermented Chardonnay	Niagara Peninsula/Ontario	White	Fruity, oaky	Fish, chicken	**
Magnotta Harvest Moon Vidal	Ontario	White	Fruity, floral	Cheese, fruit, dessert	**
Magnotta Limited Edition Cabernet Franc Icewine	Niagara Peninsula/Ontario	Red	Berry, mint	Cheese, dessert	***
Magnotta Limited Edition Riesling Icewine	Niagara Peninsula/Ontario	White	Floral, fruity	Dessert	***
Magnotta Limited Edition Sparkling Vidal Icewine	Niagara Peninsula/Ontario	Sparkling	Fruity, complex	Dessert	***
Magnotta Select Late Harvest Vidal	Ontario	White	Tropical fruit, nutty	Dessert	**
Magnotta Vidal Icewine	Niagara Peninsula/Ontario	White	Tropical fruit, floral	Dessert	***
Malivoire Winery Dry Late Harvest Gewürztraminer	Niagara Peninsula/Ontario	White	Tropical fruit, complex	Cheese, fruit, Asian	**
Malivoire Winery Gewürztraminer Icewine	Niagara Peninsula/Ontario	White	Tropical fruit, floral	Dessert	***
Marynissen Estate Winery Cabernet Franc	Niagara Peninsula/Ontario	Red	Berry, oaky	Beef, chicken, veal	**
Marynissen Estate Winery Merlot	Niagara Peninsula/Ontario	Red	Berry, oaky	Beef, pork	**
Marynissen Estate Winery Riesling	Niagara Peninsula/Ontario	White	Fruity, floral	Salads, Asian	*
Mission Hill Winery Grand Reserve Cabernet Sauvignon	Okanagan Valley/British Columbia	Red	Berry, leather, earthy	Lamb, beef	**
Mission Hill Winery Grand Reserve Chardonnay	Okanagan Valley/British Columbia	White	Butter, oaky	Fish, chicken, veal	**
Mission Hill Winery Grand Reserve Pinot Gris	Okanagan Valley/British Columbia	White	Nutty, floral	Pasta, fish, veal	**
Mission Hill Winery Grand Reserve Pinot Noir	Okanagan Valley/British Columbia	Red	Berry, oaky	Veal, chicken, pork	**
Mission Hill Winery Private Reserve Merlot	Okanagan Valley/British Columbia	Red	Berry, oaky	Lamb, beef	**
Pelee Island Winery Cabernet Franc	Ontario	Red	Berry, spicy	Veal, pork	**
Peller Estates Chardonnay	Niagara Peninsula/Ontario	White	Fruity, butter	Fish, chicken	**

CANADA (continued)

Wine name	Region	Style	Flavor/Bouquet	Compatible Foods	Price Range
Peller Estates Founder's Series Chardonnay	Niagara Peninsula/Ontario	White	Fruity, butter	Fish, chicken	**
Peller Estates Wines Limited Edition Pinot Gris	Okanagan Valley/British Columbia	White	Nutty, floral	Shellfish, fish, veal	**
Peller Estates Wines Trinity Icewine	Okanagan Valley/British Columbia	White	Floral, fruity	Dessert	***
Pillitteri Estates Winery Baco Noir	Ontario	Red	Fruity, spicy	Pizza, pasta, Asian	*
Pillitteri Estates Winery Barrel Aged Chardonnay	Niagara Peninsula/Ontario	White	Fruity, oaky	Fish, chicken	**
Pillitteri Estates Winery Family Reserve Cabernet Franc	Niagara Peninsula/Ontario	Red	Berry, oaky	Veal, pork, pasta	**
Pillitteri Estates Winery Riesling Icewine	Niagara Peninsula/Ontario	White	Floral, tropical fruit	Dessert	***
Pillitteri Estates Winery Select Late Harvest Riesling	Niagara Peninsula/Ontario	White	Tropical fruit, floral	Dessert	**
Pinot Reach Cellars Riesling Brut	Okanagan Valley/British Columbia	Sparkling	Citrus, complex	Antipasto, pizza, Asian	*
Poplar Grove Cabernet Franc	British Columbia	Red	Berry, oaky	Beef, chicken, veal	**
Poplar Grove Chardonnay	British Columbia	White	Fruity, butter	Fish, chicken	**
Poplar Grove Merlot	British Columbia	Red	Berry, oaky	Veal, pork, lamb, beef	**
Quails' Gate Estate Winery Family Reserve Pinot Noir	Okanagan Valley/British Columbia	Red	Berry, oaky	Pork, veal	**
Quails' Gate Estate Winery Late Harvest Botrytis Affected Optima	Okanagan Valley/British Columbia	White	Fruity, nutty	Dessert, cheese	***
Quails' Gate Estate Winery Limited Release Chenin Blanc	Okanagan Valley/British Columbia	White	Fruity, floral	Pasta, salads, fish	**
Quails' Gate Estate Winery Limited Release Dry Riesling	Okanagan Valley/British Columbia	White	Floral, tropical fruit	Shellfish, Asian	**
Quails' Gate Estate Winery Limited Release Meritage	Okanagan Valley/British Columbia	Red	Oaky, berry, complex	Lamb, beef	**
Quails' Gate Estate Winery Limited Release Old Vines Foch	Okanagan Valley/British Columbia	Red	Berry, spicy	Pizza, pasta, chicken	**
Reif Estate Winery Off Dry Riesling	Niagara Peninsula/Ontario	White	Floral, tropical fruit	Asian, cheese	*
Reif Estate Winery Reserve Chardonnay	Niagara Peninsula/Ontario	White	Butter, oaky	Chicken, fish	**
Reif Estate Winery Riesling Icewine	Niagara Peninsula/Ontario	White	Floral, tropical fruit	Dessert	***
Reif Estate Winery Select Late Harvest Vidal	Ontario	White	Tropical fruit, nutty	Dessert	**
Reif Estate Winery Vidal Icewine	Niagara Peninsula/Ontario	White	Tropical fruit, floral	Dessert	***
St. Hubertus Estate Winery Gamay Rosé	Okanagan Valley/British Columbia	Rosé	Fruity, floral	Antipasto, pizza, shellfish	*
St. Hubertus Estate Winery Oak Bay Chardonnay/Pinot Blanc	Okanagan Valley/British Columbia	White	Fruity, minerally	Pasta, fish, chicken, veal	**
St. Hubertus Estate Winery Oak Bay Pinot Meunier	Okanagan Valley/British Columbia	Red	Fruity, berry	Pizza, pasta, chicken	**
St. Hubertus Estate Winery Pinot Blanc Icewine	Okanagan Valley/British Columbia	White	Nutty, complex	Dessert	***
St. Hubertus Estate Winery Pinot Blanc/Riesling Icewine	Okanagan Valley/British Columbia	White	Floral, complex	Dessert	***
Southbrook Farms Lailey Vyd. Cabernet Sauvignon	Niagara Peninsula/Ontario	Red	Berry, leather	Beef, lamb	**
Southbrook Farms Marechal Foch	Ontario	Red	Berry, spicy	Pizza, pasta, Mediterranean	*
Southbrook Farms Pinot Gris	Niagara Peninsula/Ontario	White	Floral, minerally	Salads, shellfish, fish, chicken	**
Southbrook Farms Sauvignon Blanc	Niagara Peninsula/Ontario	White	Citrus, floral	Antipasto, salads, cheese, pasta, fish	**
Southbrook Farms Select Late Harvest Vidal	Ontario	White	Fruity, floral	Dessert	**
Southbrook Farms Triomphe Chardonnay	Niagara Peninsula/Ontario	White	Butter, oaky	Chicken, veal, fish	**
Stonechurch Vineyards Pinot Noir	Niagara Peninsula/Ontario	Red	Berry, spicy	Chicken, veal	**
Stonechurch Vineyards Vidal Icewine	Niagara Peninsula/Ontario	White	Tropical fruit, nutty	Dessert	***
Stoney Ridge Cellars Barrel Fermented Gewürztraminer Icewine	Niagara Peninsula/Ontario	White	Tropical fruit, complex	Dessert	***
Stoney Ridge Cellars Butler's Grant Vyd. Reserve Pinot Noir	Niagara Peninsula/Ontario	Red	Berry, oaky	Veal, pork	**
Stoney Ridge Cellars Cuesta Old Vines Chardonnay	Niagara Peninsula/Ontario	White	Fruity, complex	Fish, chicken, veal	**
Stoney Ridge Cellars Full Oak Chardonnay	Niagara Peninsula/Ontario	White	Fruity, oaky	Fish, chicken, veal	**
Stoney Ridge Cellars Lenko Vyd. Old Vines Chardonnay	Niagara Peninsula/Ontario	White	Butter, fruity, complex	Fish, chicken, veal	**
Stoney Ridge Cellars Reserve Chardonnay	Niagara Peninsula/Ontario	White	Butter, oaky	Chicken, fish	**
Stoney Ridge Cellars Reserve Pinot Noir	Niagara Peninsula/Ontario	Red	Berry, spicy, oaky	Pork, chicken	**
Stoney Ridge Cellars Select Late Harvest Vidal	Ontario	White	Tropical fruit, nutty	Dessert	**
Stoney Ridge Cellars Wismer Vyd. Cabernet Franc	Niagara Peninsula/Ontario	Red	Berry, oaky	Chicken, veal, pork	**
Strewn Pinot Blanc	Niagara Peninsula/Ontario	White	Stone fruit, minerally	Pasta, fish, chicken, veal	**
Strewn Riesling Sussreserve	Niagara Peninsula/Ontario	White	Citrus, fruity	Shellfish	***
Strewn Select Late Harvest Vidal	Ontario	White	Fruity, nutty	Dessert	**
Strewn Vidal Icewine	Niagara Peninsula/Ontario	White	Tropical fruit, floral	Dessert	***
Sumac Ridge Estate Cabernet Sauvignon	Okanagan Valley/British Columbia	Red	Berry, earthy, oaky	Lamb, beef	**

CANADA (continued)

Wine name	Region	Style	Flavor/Bouquet	Compatible Foods	Price Range
Sumac Ridge Estate Meritage White	Okanagan Valley/ British Columbia	White	Oaky, wax, stone fruit	Shellfish, fish, veal	**
Sumac Ridge Estate Merlot	Okanagan Valley/ British Columbia	Red	Berry, spicy	Pork, beef	**
Sumac Ridge Estate Okanagan Blush	Okanagan Valley/ British Columbia	Rosé	Berry, floral	Salads, pizza, pasta	*
Sumac Ridge Estate Pinot Blanc Icewine	Okanagan Valley/ British Columbia	White	Nutty, complex	Dessert	***
Sumac Ridge Estate Private Reserve Gewürztraminer	Okanagan Valley/ British Columbia	White	Floral, spicy	Asian, fish, cheese	**
Sumac Ridge Estate Private Reserve Pinot Blanc	Okanagan Valley/ British Columbia	White	Stone fruit, oaky	Fish, chicken, veal	**
Summerhill Estate Winery Cipes Aurora Blanc de Blancs	Okanagan Valley/ British Columbia	White	Fruity, floral	Shellfish, veal	**
Summerhill Estate Winery Gewürztraminer Reserve	Okanagan Valley/ British Columbia	White	Tropical fruit, floral	Asian, fish, cheese	**
Summerhill Estate Winery Late Harvest Riesling Icewine	Okanagan Valley/ British Columbia	White	Floral, tropical fruit	Dessert	**
Summerhill Estate Winery Pinot Blanc	Okanagan Valley/ British Columbia	White	Stone fruit, minerally	Shellfish, fish, chicken, veal	**
Summerhill Estate Winery Platinum Series Cabernet Sauvignon	Okanagan Valley/ British Columbia	Red	Berry, leather, oaky	Lamb, beef	**
Summerhill Estate Winery Platinum Series Pinot Noir	Okanagan Valley/ British Columbia	Red	Berry, spicy	Pork, veal	**
Summerhill Estate Winery Riesling Icewine	Okanagan Valley/ British Columbia	White	Floral, tropical fruit	Dessert	**
Thirty Bench Winery Reserve Cabernet Sauvignon	Niagara Peninsula/Ontario	Red	Berry, oaky	Lamb, beef	**
Tinhorn Creek Vineyards Cabernet Franc	Okanagan Valley/ British Columbia	Red	Berry, spicy	Veal, pork, chicken	**
Tinhorn Creek Vineyards Chardonnay	Okanagan Valley/ British Columbia	White	Butter, oaky	Fish, chicken, veal	**
Tinhorn Creek Vineyards Kerner Icewine	Okanagan Valley/ British Columbia	White	Spicy, fruity	Dessert	***
Tinhorn Creek Vineyards Merlot	Okanagan Valley/ British Columbia	Red	Berry, oaky	Pork, beef	**
Vineland Estates Gewürztraminer	Niagara Peninsula/Ontario	White	Tropical fruit, floral	Asian, cheese	*
Vineland Estates Reserve Riesling	Niagara Peninsula/Ontario	White	Floral, fruity	Asian, shellfish	**
Vineland Estates Semi-Dry Riesling	Niagara Peninsula/Ontario	White	Tropical fruit, floral	Asian, cheese	*
Vineland Estates Seyval Blanc	Ontario	White	Fruity, floral	Shellfish, fish, chicken	**
Wild Goose Vineyards and Winery Autumn Gold	Okanagan Valley/ British Columbia	White	Fruity, floral	Cheese, Asian	*
Wild Goose Vineyards and Winery Pinot Blanc	Okanagan Valley/ British Columbia	White	Fruity, minerally	Shellfish, fish, chicken, veal	**

UNITED STATES OF AMERICA

Wine name	Region	Style	Flavor/Bouquet	Compatible Foods	Price Range
Allegro Vineyards Cadenza (cabernet sauvignon/cabernet franc)	Pennsylvania	Red	Plums, spicy	Beef, pork, lamb	**
Amity Pinot Blanc	Willamette Valley/Oregon	White	Apples, citrus, vanillin	Fish, chicken	**
Anapamu Cellars Central Coast Chardonnay	Monterey/California	White	Buttery, rich	Fish, chicken	*
Andrew Will Pepper Bridge Cabernet	Walla Walla Valley/ Washington State	Red	Plums, toasty, rich	Beef, lamb	***
Anthony Road Wine Company Late Harvest Vignoles	New York	Sweet	Sweet, fruity	Dessert	**
Apex Ice Wine Gewurztraminer	Yakima Valley/ Washington State	White	Spicy, floral, tropical fruit	Dessert	**
Archery Arcus Estate Pinot Noir	Willamette Valley/Oregon	Red	Berry, jam, spicy	Chicken, veal, pork	***
Archery Premier Cuvée Pinot Noir	Willamette Valley/Oregon	Red	Berry, spicy, oaky	Chicken, veal, pork	***
Argyle Reserve Riesling	Willamette Valley/Oregon	White	Floral, fruity	Shellfish, fish	**
Barboursville Vineyards Pinot Grigio	Virginia	White	Citrus, floral	Shellfish, Asian	*
Bargetto Regan Vineyards Chardonnay	Santa Cruz Mountains, North Central Coast/California	White	Apples, spicy	Fish, chicken	**
Baron Herzog Lodi Zinfandel	Central Valley/California	Red	Berry, spicy	Pizza, beef, sausages	*
Basignani Winery Cabernet Sauvignon	Maryland	Red	Plums, spicy	Beef, pork, lamb	**
Baywood Cellars Lodi Vineyard Select Zinfandel	Central Valley/California	Red	Berry, spicy	Pizza, beef, sausages	*
Baywood Cellars Private Reserve California Port	Monterey/California	Fortified	Berry, jam	Dessert, nuts	*
Baywood Cellars Vineyard Select California Symphony	Monterey/California	White	Honey, floral	Salads, fruit	*
Baywood Cellars Vineyard Select Merlot	Monterey/California	Red	Plums, jam	Pizza, beef, sausages	*

UNITED STATES OF AMERICA (continued)

Wine name	Region	Style	Flavor/Bouquet	Compatible Foods	Price Range
Beaux Frères Pinot Noir	Willamette Valley/Oregon	Red	Berry, fruity, oaky	Veal, pork, beef	***
Bedell Cellars Cabernet Franc	New York	Red	Plums, spicy	Pork, beef, veal	**
Bedell Cellars Eis (Riesling Dessert Wine) Clinton Vineyards Seyval	New York	Sweet	Sweet, honey, floral	Dessert	***
Bedell Cellars Merlot	New York	Red	Plums, vanillin	Pork, beef, lamb	**
Bella Vigna Lodi Vigna Antica Zinfandel	Central Valley/California	Red	Berry, spicy	Pizza, beef, sausages	**
Bernardus Carmel Valley Marinus Meritage	Monterey/California	Red	Rich, toasty	Lamb, beef, cheese	***
Bernardus Chardonnay	Monterey/California	White	Rich, buttery	Fish, chicken, veal	***
Bernardus Sauvignon Blanc	Monterey/California	White	Rich, citrus	Shellfish, fish, cheese	**
Biff and Scooter Abroad/Livermore Valley Cellars Yolo County Orange Muscat	Central Valley/California	Sweet	Honey, floral	Dessert	*
Big White House Arroyo Seco Vineyards Viognier	Monterey/California	White	Floral, tropical fruit	Fish, salads	**
Big White House Byer Ranch Vineyard Zinfandel Port	San Francisco Bay/ Livermore Valley/California	Fortified	Fruity, rich	Dessert, nuts	**
Big White House Concannon Estate Vineyard Mourvedre	Livermore Valley, San Francisco Bay/California	Red	Plums, spicy	Pork, beef, lamb	**
Big White House Fraser Ranch Chardonnay	Livermore Valley, San Francisco Bay/California	White	Apples, buttery	Fish, chicken	**
Big White House Kurtzer Vineyard Syrah	Livermore Valley, San Francisco Bay/California	Red	Berry, spicy	Beef, lamb, pork	**
Big White House Lodi Phillips Vineyards Carignane	Central Valley/California	Red	Spicy, earthy, jam	Pizza, beef, veal, pork	*
Big White House Lodi Ripken Vineyards Roussanne	Central Valley/California	White	Floral, melon	Shellfish, salads	**
Big White House Lodi Ripken Vineyards Viognier	Central Valley/California	White	Floral, fruity	Shellfish, fruits	**
Big White House Lodi Ripken Vineyards Viognier Ice Wine	Central Valley/California	Sweet	Sweet, honey, stone fruit	Dessert	**
Big White House Lodi Von Rueten Vineyards Syrah	Central Valley/California	Red	Berry, spicy	Pork, beef, veal	**
Big White House Ruby Hills Vineyard Cabernet Sauvignon	Livermore Valley, San Francisco Bay/California	Red	Plums, spicy	Beef, lamb, pork	**
Black Sheep Amador Clockspring Vineyard Zinfandel	Sierra Foothills/California	Red	Berry, spicy	Pizza, pork, veal	*
Black Sheep Calaveras Zinfandel	Sierra Foothills/California	Red	Berry, spicy	Pizza, pork, veal	*
Black Sheep Sierra Foothills True Frogs Lily Pad White	Sierra Foothills/California	White	Floral, fruity	Shellfish, salads	*
Boeger Winery El Dorado Barbera	Sierra Foothills/California	Red	Plums, earthy	Pizza, pasta, chicken, pork	*
Boeger Winery El Dorado Merlot	Sierra Foothills/California	Red	Jam, earthy	Veal, chicken, beef	*
Boeger Winery El Dorado Muscat Canelli	Sierra Foothills/California	Fortified	Floral, fruity	Dessert, nuts	*
Bogle Vineyards California Chardonnay	Central Valley/California	White	Apples, buttery	Chicken, fish	*
Bogle Vineyards California Old Vine Cuvée Zinfandel	Central Valley/California	Red	Berry, spicy	Pizza, beef, sausages	*
Bogle Vineyards California Petite Sirah	Central Valley/California	Red	Berry, peppery	Pizza, pasta, beef	*
Bogle Vineyards Clarksburg Chenin Blanc	Central Valley/California	White	Floral, fruity	Shellfish, salads	*
Bogle Vineyards Colby Ranch Reserve Clarksburg Chardonnay	Central Valley/California	White	Butter, oaky	Chicken, fish, veal	*
Bonny Doon Vineyards Ca del Solo Big House Red	Monterey/California	Red	Plums, spicy	Pizza, pasta, beef, pork	**
Bonny Doon Vineyards Cardinal Zin Narly Old Vines Zinfandel	Contra Costa County San Francisco Bay/California	Red	Complex, spicy	Pizza, pork, veal	**
Bonny Doon Vineyards Clos de Gilroy Grenache	Santa Clara Valley, North Central Coast/California	Red	Berry, spicy	Asian, fish, pizza	*
Bonny Doon Vineyards Le Cigare Volant California	Santa Cruz Mountains, North Central Coast/California	Red	Jam, spicy	Pizza, beef, pork	**
Bonny Doon Vineyards Monterey/San Luis Obispo Syrah	Monterey/California	Red	Berry, spicy	Veal, pork, beef	**
Bonny Doon Vineyards Moscato Fior d'Arrancio Fortified Muscat	Monterey/California	Fortified	Fruity, floral	Dessert	**
Bonny Doon Vineyards Old Telegram Mourvedre	Contra Costa County San Francisco Bay/California	Red	Powerful, earthy	Beef, lamb, cheese	**
Bonny Doon Vineyards San Bernabe Vineyard Barbera	Monterey/California	Red	Spicy, earthy	Pizza, pork, veal	**
Bonny Doon Vineyards Sangiovese	Monterey/California	Red	Berry, spicy	Pizza, pasta, veal, pork	**
Bonny Doon Vineyards Vin de Glacière California Muscat	Santa Cruz Mountains, North Central Coast/California	White	Sweet, floral, complex	Cold meats, dessert	**
Boordy Vineyards Seyval	Maryland	White	Fruity, floral	Cheese, fruit, fish	*
Boyer Arroyo Seco Syrah	Monterey/California	Red	Berry, spicy	Pizza, veal, pork	**
Boyer Chardonnay	Monterey/California	White	Apples, buttery	Fish, chicken	**
Boyer Pinot Noir	Monterey/California	Red	Berry, spicy	Fish, pork, chicken	**
Breaux Vineyards Madeleine's Chardonnay	Virginia	White	Apples, buttery	Fish, chicken	**
Brewer-Clifton Sangiovese	Santa Barbara County, South Central Coast/California	Red	Powerful, spicy	Chicken, veal, pork, duck	***
Bridgeview Dry Gewürztraminer	Willamette Valley/Oregon	White	Spicy, floral	Asian, shellfish	*
Burrell School Vineyards Cabernet Sauvignon	Santa Cruz Mountains, North Central Coast/California	Red	Rich, earthy	Lamb, beef, pork, cheese	***
Burgess Cellars Lodi Zinfandel	Central Valley/California	Red	Berry, spicy	Pizza, beef, sausages	**

UNITED STATES OF AMERICA (continued)

Wine name	Region	Style	Flavor/Bouquet	Compatible Foods	Price Range
Burrell School Vineyards Chardonnay	Santa Cruz Mountains, North Central Coast/California	White	Apples, oaky	Fish, chicken	**
Cain Musque Ventana Vineyard Sauvignon Blanc	Monterey/California	White	Complex, citrus	Shellfish, fish, salads	**
Calera Central Coast Chardonnay	Monterey/California	White	Rich, tropical fruit	Fish, chicken	**
Calera Jensen Mount Harlan Pinot Noir	Monterey/California	Red	Complex, berry, spicy	Fish, pork, cheese	***
Calera Mills Mount Harlan Pinot Noir	Monterey/California	Red	Complex, berry, earthy	Fish, pork, cheese	***
Calera Mount Harlan Chardonnay	Monterey/California	White	Elegant, floral	Fish, chicken, cheese	***
Calera Mount Harlan Viognier	Monterey/California	White	Rich, floral, stone fruit	Fruits, Asian, fish	***
Calera Reed Mount Harlan Pinot Noir	Monterey/California	Red	Complex, berry, spicy	Fish, pork, cheese	***
Calera Selleck Mount Harlan Pinot Noir	Monterey/California	Red	Complex, berry, spicy	Fish, pork, cheese	***
Callaghan Buena Suerte (cabernet sauvignon/merlot/ cabernet franc)	Arizona	Red	Plums, vanillin	Veal, pork, beef	**
Camas Winery Hog Heaven White	Idaho	White	Fruity, floral	Salads, shellfish	*
Camas Winery Tej Hopped Mead	Idaho	Sweet	Sweet, honey, wax	Dessert	**
Camelot California Chardonnay	Monterey/California	White	Oaky, buttery	Fish, chicken	**
Cameron Abbey Ridge Pinot Noir	Willamette Valley/Oregon	Red	Berry, spicy	Fish, chicken, pork	**
Campus Oaks Lodi Old Vine Zinfandel	Central Valley/California	Red	Berry, spicy	Pizza, beef, sausages	**
Canoe Ridge Reserve Merlot	Columbia Valley/ Washington State	Red	Smoky, intense, plums, cloves	Beef, lamb	**
Carmel Road Chardonnay	Monterey/California	White	Oaky, buttery	Fish, chicken	**
Carmela Vineyards Barrel Ferment Chardonnay	Idaho	White	Apples, toasty	Fish, chicken	**
Carmela Vineyards Blush	Idaho	Rosé	Fruity, floral	Salads, shellfish	*
Carmela Vineyards Cabernet Franc	Idaho	Red	Berry, herbaceous	Pork, veal	**
Carmela Vineyards Lemberger	Idaho	Red	Fruity, spicy	Pizza, pasta	*
Carmela Vineyards Proprietor Grown Merlot	Idaho	Red	Berry, herbaceous	Lamb, pork, beef	**
Carmela Vineyards Riesling	Idaho	White	Floral, minerally	Shellfish	*
Carmela Vineyards Semillon	Idaho	White	Floral, wax	Fish, veal	*
Case Pinot Noir	Monterey/California	Red	Berry, spicy	Fish, pork, veal	**
Cayuse Cobblestone Vineyard Syrah	Walla Walla Valley/ Washington State	Red	Plums, smoky, spicy, oaky	Beef, lamb	**
Cedar Mountain Blanches Vineyard Cabernet Sauvignon	Livermore Valley, San Francisco Bay/California	Red	Complex, minerally	Beef, lamb, cheese	**
Cedar Mountain Cabernet Royal Dessert Wine	Livermore Valley, San Francisco Bay/California	Red	Sweet, fruity, rich	Dessert, nuts, cheese	**
Cedar Mountain Duet Cabernet Sauvignon/Merlot	Livermore Valley, San Francisco Bay/California	Red	Earthy, fruity	Lamb, beef, pork	**
Cedar Mountain Estate Chardonnay	Livermore Valley, San Francisco Bay/California	White	Crisp, rich, minerally	Fish, chicken	**
Cedar Mountain Library Reserve Cabernet Sauvignon	Livermore Valley, San Francisco Bay/California	Red	Elegant, earthy	Lamb, beef, cheese	***
Chaddsford Winery Pinot Grigio	Pennsylvania	White	Floral, nutty	Shellfish, Asian	**
Chaddsford Winery Merican (cabernet sauvignon/merlot)	Pennsylvania	Red	Plums, spicy	Beef, pork, veal	**
Chalet Débonné Pinot Gris	Ohio	White	Floral, nutty	Shellfish, fish	**
Chalone Vineyard Chalone Chardonnay	Monterey/California	White	Complex, rich	Fish, chicken	***
Chalone Vineyard Chalone Chenin Blanc	Monterey/California	White	Floral, minerally	Shellfish, fish	***
Chalone Vineyard Chalone Pinot Blanc	Monterey/California	White	Rich, nutty	Fish, chicken	***
Chalone Vineyard Chalone Pinot Noir	Monterey/California	Red	Complex, berry, spicy	Fish, pork, cheese	***
Chalone Vineyard The Pinnacles Chardonnay	Monterey/California	White	Rich, minerally	Fish, chicken	***
Chamard Vineyards Cabernet Franc	Connecticut	Red	Berry, spicy	Pork, beef	**
Chamard Vineyards Chardonnay	Connecticut	White	Apples, buttery	Fish, chicken	**
Chambourcin Presque Isle Wine Cellars Cabernet Franc/ Petite Sirah	Pennsylvania	Red	Plums, spicy	Beef, pork, veal	**
Charles B. Mitchell Vineyards El Dorado Everyday Red	Sierra Foothills/California	Red	Jam, spicy	Pizza, pork, veal	*
Charles B. Mitchell Vineyards El Dorado Malbec	Sierra Foothills/California	Red	Plum, cloves	Chicken, veal, pork	**
Charles B. Mitchell Vineyards El Dorado Semillon	Sierra Foothills/California	White	Wax, honey, citrus	Shellfish, fish	**
Charles Spinetta Winery Amador Barbera	Sierra Foothills/California	Red	Fruity, spicy	Pizza, pasta, pork	**
Charles Spinetta Winery Amador Primitivo	Sierra Foothills/California	Red	Berry, spicy	Pizza, pasta, pork	**
Charles Spinetta Winery Amador Zinfandel	Sierra Foothills/California	Red	Berry, spicy	Pizza, pork, veal	**
Chateau Christina Carmel Valley Russell's Vineyard Cabernet Sauvignon	Monterey/California	Red	Plums, toasty	Beef, lamb	**
Chateau Christina Francioni Vineyard Pinot Noir	Monterey/California	Red	Berry, spicy	Fish, chicken, pork	**
Chateau Grand Traverse Ice Wine	Michigan	Sweet	Sweet, rich, fruity	Dessert	**
Chateau Julien Chardonnay	Monterey/California	White	Apples, buttery	Fish, chicken	**
Chateau Julien Sangiovese	Monterey/California	Red	Berry, fruity	Pizza, pasta, sausages	**
Chateau Rodin Winery El Dorado Barbera	Sierra Foothills/California	Red	Plums, earthy	Pizza, pasta, pork	**

UNITED STATES OF AMERICA *(continued)*

Wine name	Region	Style	Flavor/Bouquet	Compatible Foods	Price Range
Chateau Ste Michelle Cold Creek Vineyard Riesling	Yakima Valley/ Washington State	White	Intense, floral, stone fruit	Asian, shellfish	**
Chateau Ste Michelle Reserve Merlot	Columbia Valley/ Washington State	Red	Rich, fruity, oaky	Beef, lamb	**
Chouinard Cabernet Sauvignon	Paso Robles, South Central Coast/California	Red	Jam, spicy	Beef, pork, lamb	**
Chouinard Lodi Mohr-Fry Ranch Zinfandel	Central Valley/California	Red	Berry, spicy	Chicken, veal, beef	**
Chouinard Orange Muscat	Paso Robles, South Central Coast/California	Fortified	Floral, rich	Dessert	**
Chouinard Vineyards Petite Sirah	Monterey/California	Red	Berry, peppery	Pizza, sausages, pork	**
Chouinard Vineyards San Francisco Bay Cabernet Sauvignon	Livermore Valley, San Francisco Bay/California	Red	Plums, spicy	Pork, beef, lamb	**
Chouinard Vineyards San Francisco Bay Palomares Vineyards Chardonnay	Livermore Valley, San Francisco Bay/California	White	Citrus, apples, spicy	Fish, chicken	**
Cinnabar Vineyards Cabernet Sauvignon	Santa Cruz Mountains, North Central Coast/California	Red	Plums, toasty	Lamb, beef, pork	***
Cinnabar Vineyards Chardonnay	Santa Cruz Mountains, North Central Coast/California	White	Apples, spicy	Fish, chicken	**
Clayton Lodi Petite Sirah	Central Valley/California	Red	Berry, peppery	Pizza, sausages	**
Clayton Lodi Zinfandel	Central Valley/California	Red	Berry, spicy	Pizza, pasta, beef	**
Cline Cellars Ancient Vines Zinfandel	Contra Costa County San Francisco Bay/California	Red	Rich, earthy, minerally	Lamb, beef, pork	**
Cline Cellars Cotes d'Oakley Vin Blanc	Contra Costa County San Francisco Bay/California	White	Fruity, floral	Shellfish, salads	*
Cline Cellars Cotes d'Oakley Vin Gris	Contra Costa County San Francisco Bay/California	Rosé	Berry, floral	Shellfish, cold meats	*
Cline Cellars Cotes d'Oakley Vin Rouge	Contra Costa County San Francisco Bay/California	Red	Fruity, peppery	Pizza, pasta, sausages	*
Cline Cellars Live Oak Vineyard Zinfandel	Contra Costa County San Francisco Bay/California	Red	Powerful, earthy	Lamb, beef, cheese	***
Cline Cellars Small Berry Mourvedre	Contra Costa County San Francisco Bay/California	Red	Powerful, spicy, mint	Lamb, beef, cheese	***
Cloninger Cellars Cabernet Sauvignon	Monterey/California	Red	Plums, toasty	Beef, pork, lamb	**
Cloninger Cellars Chardonnay	Monterey/California	White	Minerally, oaky	Fish, chicken	**
Cloninger Cellars Pinot Noir	Monterey/California	Red	Berry, earthy	Fish, chicken, pork	**
Clos du Val Napa-El Dorado-San Joaquin Zinfandel	Central Valley/California	Red	Berry, oaky	Beef, pork	**
Clos Tita Cabernet Sauvignon	Santa Cruz Mountains, North Central Coast/California	Red	Elegant, earthy	Lamb, beef, cheese	***
Clos Tita CV Chardonnay/Viognier	Santa Cruz Mountains, North Central Coast/California	White	Elegant, complex	Shellfish, fish	***
Clos Tita Estate Pinot Noir	Santa Cruz Mountains, North Central Coast/California	Red	Earthy, minerally	Fish, pork, cheese	***
Clover Hill Vineyards & Winery Concord	Pennsylvania	Red	Fruity, spicy	Pizza, pasta, sausages	**
Cobblestone Arroyo Seco Chardonnay	Monterey/California	White	Tropical fruit	Fish, chicken	*
Colorado Cellars Merlot	Colorado	Red	Plums, herbaceous	Lamb, beef	**
Columbia Crest Reserve Red (cabernet sauvignon/merlot/ cabernet franc/malbec)	Columbia Valley/ Washington State	Red	Plums, cloves, spicy	Beef, lamb	**
Columbia Crest Reserve Syrah (syrah/grenache)	Columbia Valley/ Washington State	Red	Berry, spicy, oaky	Chicken, veal, pork	**
Columbia Winery Red Willow Sangiovese (piccolo sangiovese/ grosso sangiovese)	Columbia Valley/ Washington State	Red	Berry, spicy, licorice, oaky	Chicken, veal, pork	**
Columbia Winery Sagemoor Cabernet Sauvignon	Columbia Valley/ Washington State	Red	Berry, herbaceous, complex, oaky	Beef, lamb	***
Concannon Vineyard Arroyo Seco Late Harvest Viognier	Monterey/California	White	Sweet, floral, honey	Dessert, fruits	**
Concannon Vineyard California Selected Vineyards Petite Sirah	Livermore Valley, San Francisco Bay/California	Red	Berry, peppery	Pizza, pork, beef	*
Concannon Vineyard Central Coast Reserve Chardonnay	Monterey/California	White	Apples, buttery	Fish, chicken	**
Concannon Vineyard Central Coast Selected Vineyard Cabernet Sauvignon	Monterey/California	Red	Plums, vanillin	Beef, pork, lamb	**
Concannon Vineyard Limited Bottling Marsanne	Santa Clara Valley, North Central Coast/California	White	Citrus, nutty	Fish, chicken	**
Concannon Vineyard Reserve Assemblage Red Meritage	Livermore Valley, San Francisco Bay/California	Red	Plums, spicy	Veal, pork, beef	**
Concannon Vineyard Reserve Assemblage White Meritage	Livermore Valley, San Francisco Bay/California	White	Citrus, honey, spicy	Shellfish, fish, chicken	**
Concannon Vineyard Reserve Petite Sirah	Livermore Valley, San Francisco Bay/California	Red	Peppery, oaky	Pork, beef, lamb	**

UNITED STATES OF AMERICA *(continued)*

Wine name	Region	Style	Flavor/Bouquet	Compatible Foods	Price Range
Concannon Vineyard San Francisco Bay Selected Vineyards Sauvignon Blanc	Livermore Valley, San Francisco Bay/California	White	Stone fruit, minerally	Shellfish, salads	*
Cooper-Garrod Cabernet Franc	Santa Clara Valley, North Central Coast/California	Red	Plums, toasty	Beef, pork, veal	* *
Cooper-Garrod Chardonnay	Santa Clara Valley, North Central Coast/California	White	Apples, toasty	Fish, chicken	* *
Coulson Eldorado Winery El Dorado Zinfandel	Sierra Foothills/California	Red	Berry, earthy	Pizza, pasta, pork	* *
Cronin Vineyards Alexander Chardonnay	Santa Clara Valley, North Central Coast/California	White	Citrus, buttery, toasty	Fish, chicken	* *
Cronin Vineyards Pinot Noir	Santa Cruz Mountains, North Central Coast/California	Red	Berry, spicy	Pork, veal	* * *
David Bruce Central Coast Pinot Noir	Monterey/California	Red	Berry, oaky, spicy	Fish, pork, veal	* *
David Bruce Chalone Pinot Noir	Monterey/California	Red	Berry, minerally	Fish, pork, veal	* * *
David Bruce Vineyards Petite Sirah	Santa Cruz Mountains, North Central Coast/California	Red	Peppery, oaky	Veal, pork, beef	* *
De Rose Cedolini Family Vineyard Cienega Valley Old Vines Zinfandel	Monterey/California	Red	Berry, spicy	Pizza, beef, pork	* *
Deaver Vineyards Amador Barbera	Sierra Foothills/California	Red	Jam, earthy	Pizza, pasta, pork	*
Deaver Vineyards Amador Sangiovese	Sierra Foothills/California	Red	Berry, spicy	Pizza, chicken, veal	*
Deaver Vineyards Amador Zinfandel	Sierra Foothills/California	Red	Berry, spicy	Beef, pork, veal	*
Deaver Vineyards Golden Nectar 150-Year-Old Vine Zinfandel Port	Sierra Foothills/California	Fortified	Fruity, rich	Dessert	* *
Delicato California Cabernet Sauvignon	Central Valley/California	Red	Plums, jam	Pizza, beef	*
Delicato California Merlot	Central Valley/California	Red	Plums, earthy	Chicken, beef	*
Delicato California Syrah	Central Valley/California	Red	Plums, spicy	Veal, beef, pizza	*
Delille Chaleur Estate Meritage blend (cabernet sauvignon/ merlot cabernet franc)	Yakima Valley/ Washington State	Red	Berry, herbaceous, toasty, elegant	Beef, lamb	* * *
Delille Charleur Estate D2 (merlot/cabernet sauvignon/ cabernet franc)	Yakima Valley/ Washington State	Red	Plums, herbaceous, vanillin	Beef, lamb	* *
Dobra Zemlja Amador Syrah	Sierra Foothills/California	Red	Plums, spicy	Pork, beef, lamb	* *
Dobra Zemlja Amador Viognier	Sierra Foothills/California	White	Elegant, floral	Shellfish, fish, fruits	* *
Domaine de la Terre Rouge Shenandoah Valley Sentinel Oak Vineyard Syrah	Sierra Foothills/California	Red	Earthy, gamey	Lamb, beef, cheese	* * *
Domaine Drouhin Cuvée Laurene Pinot Noir	Willamette Valley/Oregon	Red	Berry, jam, vanillin	Veal, pork, duck	* * *
Domaine Drouhin Pinot Noir	Willamette Valley/Oregon	Red	Berry, spicy, oaky	Chicken, veal, pork	* * *
Dr Frank's Vinifera Wine Cellars/Chateau Frank Riesling	New York	White	Crisp, floral, citrus	Shellfish, Asian	*
Dry Creek Clarksburg Chenin Blanc	Central Valley/California	White	Floral, fruity	Shellfish, salads	*
Duckwalk Vineyards Reserve Merlot	New York	Red	Plums, spicy	Pork, beef, lamb	* * *
Dunham Cabernet Sauvignon III	Columbia Valley/ Washington State	Red	Berry, herbaceous, intense, oaky	Beef, lamb	* *
Edgefield Columbia Valley Syrah	Columbia Valley/Oregon	Red	Plums, smoky	Beef, lamb	* *
Edmunds St John California Rocks and Gravel Rhone Red Blend	Sierra Foothills/California	Red	Earthy, spicy	Chicken, veal, pork	* *
Edmunds St John El Dorado Matagrano Vineyard Sangiovese	Sierra Foothills/California	Red	Complex, earthy	Beef, pork, veal	* *
Edmunds St John El Dorado Wylie-Fenaughty Syrah	Sierra Foothills/California	Red	Powerful, minerally	Lamb, beef, cheese	* * *
Elk Cove Estate Reserve Pinot Noir	Willamette Valley/Oregon	Red	Berry, spicy	Veal, pork	* *
Elliston Vineyards Cabernet Franc	Monterey/California	Red	Berry, herbaceous	Veal, beef, pork	* *
Elliston Vineyards California Captain's Claret (merlot/cabernet franc/cabernet sauvignon)	Livermore Valley, San Francisco Bay/California	Red	Plums, oaky, herbaceous	Lamb, beef, pork	* *
Elliston Vineyards Pinot Blanc	Livermore Valley, San Francisco Bay/California	White	Apples, nutty	Fish, chicken, nuts	* *
Elliston Vineyards Sunol Valley Vineyard Pinot Gris	Livermore Valley, San Francisco Bay/California	White	Floral, nutty	Shellfish, Asian	* *
Eola Hills Lodi Zinfandel	Central Valley/California	Red	Berry, spicy	Pizza, sausages, beef	*
Equinox Vintage Blanc de Blancs Méthode Champenoise	Santa Cruz Mountains, North Central Coast/California	Sparkling	Citrus, yeasty	Shellfish, Asian	* * *
Estancia Pinnacles Chardonnay	Monterey/California	White	Apples, toasty	Fish, chicken	* *
Estancia Pinnacles Pinot Noir	Monterey/California	Red	Berry, spicy	Fish, pork, Asian	* *
Evesham Unfiltered Wood Cuvée J Pinot Noir	Willamette Valley/Oregon	Red	Berry, jam, complex	Chicken, veal, pork	* * *
Eyrie Pinot Gris	Willamette Valley/Oregon	White	Honey, nutty, crisp	Chicken, fish	*
Eyrie Pinot Meunier	Willamette Valley/Oregon	Red	Plums, berry, spicy	Fish, chicken, pork	* *
Fall Creek Vineyards Meritus (merlot/cabernet malbec)	Texas	Red	Plums, herbaceous	Beef, pork, lamb	* *
Fellom Ranch Montebello Ridge Cabernet Sauvignon	Santa Clara Valley, North Central Coast/California	Red	Plums, earthy	Beef, lamb, pork	* *
Fenestra Santa Lucia Highlands Merlot	Monterey/California	Red	Complex, spicy	Lamb, beef, pork	* *
Fenestra Winery Lodi Syrah	Central Valley/California	Red	Berry, spicy	Pizza, sausages, beef	*

UNITED STATES OF AMERICA (continued)

Wine name	Region	Style	Flavor/Bouquet	Compatible Foods	Price Range
Fenestra Winery Semillon	Livermore Valley, San Francisco Bay/California	White	Honey, wax, citrus	Shellfish, fish, chicken	**
Fenestra Winery Semmonay (chardonnay/semillon)	Livermore Valley, San Francisco Bay/California	White	Complex, fruity	Fish, chicken	**
Fenestra Winery Zinfandel	Livermore Valley, San Francisco Bay/California	Red	Berry, spicy	Pizza, pork, veal	**
Ficklin Madera NV Port	Central Valley/California	Fortified	Berry, sweet	Dessert, cheese	*
Ficklin Madera Vintage Port	Central Valley/California	Fortified	Berry, sweet	Dessert, cheese	**
Fiore Winery Caronte (merlot/cabernet sauvignon)	Maryland	Red	Plums, herbaceous	Beef, pork, lamb	**
Firefall Vineyards El Dorado Sangiovese	Sierra Foothills/California	Red	Berry, spicy	Pizza, pork, pasta	**
Firefall Vineyards El Dorado Syrah	Sierra Foothills/California	Red	Fruity, spicy	Beef, pork, veal	**
Firelands Wine Co. Pinot Grigio	Ohio	White	Fruity, nutty	Shellfish, fish	**
Fitzpatrick Winery El Dorado King's Red	Sierra Foothills/California	Red	Berry, spicy	Beef, pork, veal	**
Fitzpatrick Winery El Dorado Petite Sirah	Sierra Foothills/California	Red	Berry, peppery	Chicken, veal, beef	**
Fitzpatrick Winery El Dorado Zinfandel	Sierra Foothills/California	Red	Berry, spicy	Pork, chicken, veal	**
Foley Barrel Select Chardonnay	Santa Barbara County, South Central Coast/California	White	Rich, complex, oaky	Fish, chicken	***
Folie à Deux Shenandoah Valley Fiddletown Zinfandel	Sierra Foothills/California	Red	Berry, oaky	Pork, beef	**
Fox Run Vineyards Chardonnay	New York	White	Apples, vanillin	Fish, chicken	**
Fox Run Vineyards Reserve Pinot Noir	New York	Red	Berry, spicy	Fish, pork, veal	***
Foxen Sanford & Benedict Vineyard Pinot Noir	Santa Barbara County, South Central Coast/California	Red	Complex, earthy, spicy	Fish, pork, duck	***
French Creek Ridge Vineyards Cabernet Franc	Pennsylvania	Red	Plums, spicy	Veal, pork, beef	**
Gainey Limited Selection Pinot Noir	Santa Barbara County, South Central Coast/California	Red	Rich, earthy, spicy	Fish, pork, duck	***
Galante Carmel Valley Blackjack Cabernet Sauvignon	Monterey/California	Red	Powerful, complex	Lamb, beef, pork	***
Galante Carmel Valley Rancho Galante Cabernet Sauvignon	Monterey/California	Red	Rich, smoky	Lamb, beef, pork	**
Galante Carmel Valley Red Rose Cabernet Sauvignon	Monterey/California	Red	Powerful, tannic	Lamb, beef, pork	***
Garre Vineyard and Winery California Grenache	Monterey/California	Red	Fruity, spicy	Pizza, sausages	**
Garre Vineyard and Winery Merlot	Livermore Valley, San Francisco Bay/California	Red	Plums, spicy	Pork, beef, lamb	**
Georis Winery Carmel Valley Cabernet Sauvignon	Monterey/California	Red	Powerful, tannic	Lamb, cheese	***
Georis Winery Carmel Valley Merlot	Monterey/California	Red	Powerful, tannic	Lamb, cheese	***
Glen Fiona Columbia Valley Syrah (syrah/viognier)	Columbia Valley/Washington State	Red	Berry, spicy, floral, elegant	Chicken, veal, pork	**
Gnekow Family Winery California Symphony	Central Valley/California	White	Floral, fruity	Fruit, cheese	*
Gold Hill Vineyard El Dorado Cabernet Franc	Sierra Foothills/California	Red	Plums, vanillin	Pork, veal, beef	**
Granite Springs Winery El Dorado Petite Sirah	Sierra Foothills/California	Red	Berry, peppery	Pizza, pork, pasta	**
Granite Springs Winery El Dorado Zinfandel	Sierra Foothills/California	Red	Berry, spicy	Pizza, pork, chicken	**
Gray Ghost Vineyards Cabernet Franc	Virginia	Red	Plums, spicy	Chicken, veal, pork	**
Gristina Vineyards Andy's Field Cabernet Sauvignon	New York	Red	Complex, toasty	Lamb, beef, cheese	***
Gruet Winery Blanc de Blancs	New Mexico	Sparkling	Crisp, nutty	Shellfish, cold meats	*
Guglielmo Private Reserve Petite Sirah	Santa Clara Valley, North Central Coast/California	Red	Berry, peppery	Pizza, pork, veal	**
Hahn Estates Cabernet Franc	Monterey/California	Red	Plums, spicy	Pork, beef, lamb	**
Hahn Estates Merlot	Monterey/California	Red	Plums, vanillin	Pork, beef, lamb	**
Hahn Estates Red Meritage	Monterey/California	Red	Rich, oaky	Pork, beef, lamb	***
Harpersfield Vineyard Gewurztraminer	Ohio	White	Floral, spicy	Shellfish, Asian	**
Harpersfield Vineyard Riesling	Ohio	White	Citrus, stone fruit	Shellfish, Asian	**
Hecker Pass Winery Petite Sirah Select	Santa Clara Valley, North Central Coast/California	Red	Berry, spicy	Pizza, pork, veal	**
Hedges Red Mountain Reserve (cabernet sauvignon/merlot/cabernet franc)	Yakima Valley/Washington State	Red	Fruity, oaky, rich	Beef, lamb	**
Heller Estate/Durney Carmel Valley Cachagua Cabernet Sauvignon	Monterey/California	Red	Complex, earthy	Lamb, beef, cheese	***
Heller Estate/Durney Carmel Valley Chardonnay	Monterey/California	White	Rich, minerally	Fish, chicken	***
Heller Estate/Durney Carmel Valley Chenin Blanc	Monterey/California	White	Floral, minerally	Shellfish, fish	***
Heller Estate/Durney Carmel Valley Merlot	Monterey/California	Red	Plums, toasty	Lamb, beef, pork	***
Heller Estate/Durney Carmel Valley Private Reserve Cabernet Sauvignon	Monterey/California	Red	Powerful, elegant	Lamb, beef, cheese	***
Hermann J. Weimer Vineyard Chardonnay	New Mexico	White	Apples, buttery	Fish, chicken	**
Hermann J. Weimer Vineyard Late Harvest Riesling	New Mexico	White	Sweet, floral, honey	Dessert	**
Hermann J. Weimer Vineyard Riesling	New Mexico	White	Floral, fruity	Shellfish, fruits	*
Hogue Genesis Cabernet Franc	Yakima Valley/Washington State	Red	Plums, jam, toasty	Pork, beef, lamb	**

UNITED STATES OF AMERICA (continued)

Wine name	Region	Style	Flavor/Bouquet	Compatible Foods	Price Range
Horton Vineyards Dionysius (Touriga Nacional Blend)	Virginia	Red	Berry, spicy	Veal, pork, beef	**
Horton Vineyards Norton	Virginia	Red	Fruity, spicy	Pizza, pork, pasta	**
Horton Vineyards Viognier	Virginia	White	Stone fruit, floral, minerally	Shellfish, fruits	***
Indian Creek Pinot Noir	Idaho	Red	Berry, spicy	Fish, veal, pork	**
Indigo Hills California Merlot	Central Valley/California	Red	Plums, jam	Pizza, beef, veal	*
Ingleside Plantation Vineyards Merlot	Virginia	Red	Plums, vanillin	Beef, pork, lamb	**
Ivan Tamas Cabernet Sauvignon	Livermore Valley, San Francisco Bay/California	Red	Plums, jam	Pizza, beef, chicken	*
Ivan Tamas Pinot Grigio	Monterey/California	White	Floral, spicy	Shellfish, salads	*
Ivan Tamas Sangiovese	Livermore Valley, San Francisco Bay/California	Red	Berry, licorice	Pizza, pasta, sausages	*
Ivan Tamas Trebbiano	Livermore Valley, San Francisco Bay/California	White	Floral, nutty	Shellfish, Asian	*
Ivan Tamas Zinfandel	Livermore Valley, San Francisco Bay/California	Red	Jam, spicy	Pizza, beef, chicken	*
J. Lohr Arroyo Seco Arroyo Vista Vineyard Chardonnay	Monterey/California	White	Buttery, oaky	Fish, chicken	**
J. Lohr Bay Mist White Riesling	Monterey/California	White	Floral, fruity	Fruits, shellfish	*
J. Lohr Chardonnay	Monterey/California	White	Tropical fruit, buttery	Fish, shellfish	*
J. Lohr Cypress California Chardonnay	Santa Clara Valley, North Central Coast/California	White	Apples, buttery	Fish, chicken	*
J. Lohr Lodi Cypress Zinfandel	Central Valley/California	Red	Berry, spicy	Pizza, sausages, beef	*
J. Lohr Wildflower Valdiguié	Monterey/California	Red	Fruity	Pizza, pasta	*
Jackson Cellars Zinfandel	Livermore Valley, San Francisco Bay/California	Red	Berry, spicy	Pizza, beef, pork	**
Jacuzzi Reserve Zinfandel	Contra Costa County San Francisco Bay/California	Red	Rich, fruity, tannic	Lamb, beef, cheese	***
Jade Mountain Mourvedre	Contra Costa County San Francisco Bay/California	Red	Powerful, fruity, spicy	Lamb, beef, cheese	***
Jefferson Vineyards Fantaisie Sauvage (native yeast Chardonnay)	Virginia	White	Complex, fruity	Fish, chicken	**
Jekel FOS Reserve Chardonnay	Monterey/California	White	Tropical fruit, oaky	Fish, chicken	**
Jekel Syrah	Monterey/California	Red	Berry, licorice	Pork, veal	**
Jessie's Grove Lodi Fancy Quest Old Vine Zinfandel	Central Valley/California	Red	Berry, spicy	Sausages, beef	**
Jessie's Grove Lodi Reserve Westwind Old Vine Zinfandel	Central Valley/California	Red	Berry, complex	Beef, pork	**
Jessie's Grove Lodi Spenker Vineyard Royalty Old Vine Zinfandel	Central Valley/California	Red	Rich, toasty	Beef, pork, cheese	**
Jodar Vineyard and Winery El Dorado Cabernet Sauvignon	Sierra Foothills/California	Red	Fruity, earthy	Lamb, beef, pork	**
Joel Gott Amador Dillian Ranch Zinfandel	Sierra Foothills/California	Red	Rich, fruity	Pork, beef, veal	**
Jory Winery California Chardonnay	Santa Clara Valley, North Central Coast/California	White	Apples, toasty	Fish, chicken	**
Jory Winery Syrah	Santa Clara Valley, North Central Coast/California	Red	Berry, spicy	Veal, pork, chicken	**
Joullian Carmel Valley Cabernet Sauvignon	Monterey/California	Red	Earthy, complex	Lamb, beef, cheese	***
Joullian Carmel Valley Merlot	Monterey/California	Red	Plums, earthy	Lamb, beef, pork	***
Joullian Carmel Valley Sauvignon Blanc	Monterey/California	White	Citrus, honey, toasty	Fish, pasta	**
Joullian Carmel Valley Zinfandel	Monterey/California	Red	Berry, spicy	Pork, veal, pasta	**
Joullian Chardonnay	Monterey/California	White	Rich, minerally	Fish, chicken	**
Kali-Hart Vineyard Chardonnay	Monterey/California	White	Tropical fruit	Fish, chicken	***
Kalin Cellars Semillon	Livermore Valley, San Francisco Bay/California	White	Honey, wax, citrus	Shellfish, fish, chicken	**
Karly Amador Pokerflats Zinfandel	Sierra Foothills/California	Red	Rich, fruity, smoky	Lamb, beef, cheese	***
Karly Amador Warrior Fires Zinfandel	Sierra Foothills/California	Red	Rich, fruity, smoky	Lamb, beef, cheese	***
Kathryn Kennedy California SHHH Chenin Blanc/Viognier	Santa Cruz Mountains, North Central Coast/California	White	Fruity, floral	Shellfish, Asian	**
Kathryn Kennedy Estate Cabernet Sauvignon	Santa Cruz Mountains, North Central Coast/California	Red	Elegant, powerful	Lamb, beef, cheese	***
Kathryn Kennedy Lateral Meritage	Santa Cruz Mountains, North Central Coast/California	Red	Elegant, earthy	Lamb, beef, cheese	***
Kathryn Kennedy Maridon Vineyard Syrah	Santa Cruz Mountains, North Central Coast/California	Red	Rich, tannic, spicy	Pork, veal, lamb	***
Ken Wright Canary Hill Pinot Noir	Willamette Valley/Oregon	Red	Berry, earthy, oaky	Veal, pork, beef	***
Kendall Jackson Arroyo Seco Paradise Vineyard Chardonnay	Monterey/California	White	Tropical fruit	Fish, chicken	**
Kenwood Lodi Old Vine Zinfandel	Central Valley/California	Red	Berry, spicy	Pizza, sausages, beef	*
Kestrel Signature Series Syrah	Yakima Valley/Washington State	Red	Plums, smoky	Beef, lamb	**
Koenig Vineyards Cabernet Sauvignon	Idaho	Red	Plums, spicy	Pork, beef, lamb	**
Koenig Vineyards Pinot Noir	Idaho	Red	Berry, spicy	Pork, beef, fish	**
Koenig Vineyards Zinfandel	Idaho	Red	Berry, spicy	Beef, pork	**

UNITED STATES OF AMERICA (continued)

Wine name	Region	Style	Flavor/Bouquet	Compatible Foods	Price Range
L'Ecole No 41 Barrel-fermented Semillon	Walla Walla Valley/ Washington State	White	Honey, wax, toasty	Chicken, fish	***
L'Ecole Pepper Bridge Apogée (merlot/cabernet sauvignon/ cabernet franc)	Walla Walla Valley/ Washington State	Red	Powerful, fruity, toasty	Beef, lamb	**
L. Mawby Vineyard Sparkling Wine	Michigan	Sparkling	Crisp, fruity	Fruit, Asian	**
Latcham Vineyards El Dorado Petite Sirah	Sierra Foothills/California	Red	Berry, peppery	Pizza, pork, pasta	**
Latcham Vineyards El Dorado Zinfandel Reserve	Sierra Foothills/California	Red	Berry, spicy	Pork, veal, beef	**
Lava Cap Winery El Dorado Barbera	Sierra Foothills/California	Red	Earthy, fruity	Pizza, pork, pasta	*
Lava Cap Winery El Dorado Muscat Canelli	Sierra Foothills/California	Fortified	Mandarin, honey, floral	Dessert, fruits	*
Lenz Winery Sparkling Wine	New Mexico	Sparkling	Crisp, citrus	Shellfish, Asian	**
Leonetti Merlot	Walla Walla Valley/ Washington State	Red	Powerful, tannic	Beef, lamb	***
Lincourt Pinot Noir	Santa Barbara County, South Central Coast/California	Red	Complex, spicy	Fish, pork, duck	**
Linden Vineyards Cabernet Sauvignon	Virginia	Red	Plums, toasty, herbaceous	Beef, pork, lamb	**
Livermore Valley Cellars/LVC Arcanum Red Table Wine	Livermore Valley, San Francisco Bay/California	Red	Fruity, spicy	Lamb, beef, pork	**
Livermore Valley Cellars/LVC Chenin Blanc	Livermore Valley, San Francisco Bay/California	White	Fruity, floral	Shellfish, Asian	*
Livermore Valley Cellars/LVC Graham Vineyard Zinfandel	Livermore Valley, San Francisco Bay/California	Red	Berry, spicy	Pizza, pork, veal	**
Livermore Valley Cellars/LVC One Oak Vineyard Merlot	Livermore Valley, San Francisco Bay/California	Red	Plums, spicy	Lamb, beef, pork	**
Livermore Valley Cellars/LVC Semillon/Chardonnay	Livermore Valley, San Francisco Bay/California	White	Apples, nutty, spicy	Shellfish, fish, chicken	**
Llano Estocado Cabernet Sauvignon	Texas	Red	Plums, spicy	Beef, pork, lamb	**
Lockwood Cabernet Sauvignon	Monterey/California	Red	Plums, toasty	Pork, beef, lamb	**
Lockwood Chardonnay	Monterey/California	White	Fruity, oaky	Fish, chicken	**
Lockwood Merlot	Monterey/California	Red	Plums, toasty	Pork, beef, lamb	**
Lockwood Pinot Blanc	Monterey/California	White	Apples, toasty	Fish, chicken	**
Lockwood Syrah	Monterey/California	Red	Spicy, oaky	Pork, veal	**
Lockwood Very Special Reserve Red Meritage	Monterey/California	Red	Rich, oaky	Lamb, beef, cheese	***
Logan Sleepy Hollow Vineyard Chardonnay	Monterey/California	White	Tropical fruit	Fish, chicken	**
Logan Sleepy Hollow Vineyard Pinot Noir	Monterey/California	Red	Berry, toasty	Fish, pork	**
Longoria Cuvée Blues Cabernet Franc	Santa Barbara County, South Central Coast/California	Red	Powerful, oaky	Lamb, beef, cheese	**
Lucas Lodi Chardonnay	Central Valley/California	White	Apples, minerally	Fish, chicken, pasta	*
Lucas Lodi Old Vine Zinfandel	Central Valley/California	Red	Berry, spicy	Pizza, sausages, beef	*
M. Cosentino California CigarZin Zinfandel	Central Valley/California	Red	Berry, oaky	Pork, beef	**
Madrona Vineyards El Dorado Cabernet Franc	Sierra Foothills/California	Red	Plums, spicy	Beef, pork, veal	**
Madrona Vineyards El Dorado Gewurztraminer	Sierra Foothills/California	White	Floral, spicy	Shellfish, Asian	**
Madrona Vineyards El Dorado Late Harvest Zinfandel	Sierra Foothills/California	Red	Sweet, fruity, rich	Dessert, nuts	**
Markko Vineyard Riesling	Ohio	White	Floral, fruity	Shellfish, Asian	**
Martin Ray Mariage California Chardonnay	Santa Cruz Mountains, North Central Coast/California	White	Apples, minerally	Fish, chicken	***
Mathews Cabernet Sauvignon Elerding Vineyard	Columbia Valley/ Washington State	Red	Berry, herbaceous, intense	Beef, lamb	**
McCrea Boushey Vineyard Syrah Viognier	Yakima Valley/ Washington State	Red	Berry, floral, spicy	Veal, pork, beef	**
McCrea Ciel du Cheval Vineyard Viognier	Yakima Valley/ Washington State	White	Floral, honey, stone fruit	Asian, fish	**
Mer et Soleil Central Coast Chardonnay	Monterey/California	White	Rich, buttery, toasty	Fish, chicken	***
Millbrook Vineyards & Winery Tokai	New Mexico	White	Sweet, floral, nutty	Dessert	**
Mirassou Harvest Reserve Mission Vineyard Chardonnay	Monterey/California	White	Tropical fruit	Fish, chicken	**
Mirassou Harvest Reserve Pinot Blanc	Monterey/California	White	Apples, toasty	Fish, chicken	**
Mirassou Harvest Reserve San Vincente Vineyard Chardonnay	Monterey/California	White	Tropical fruit	Fish, chicken	**
Mirassou Showcase Selection Harvest Reserve Pinot Noir	Monterey/California	Red	Berry, toasty	Fish, pork	**
Monterey Peninsula Winery Doctor's Reserve Sleepy Hollow Vineyard Chardonnay	Monterey/California	White	Tropical fruit	Fish, chicken	
Monterra San Bernabe Ranch Cabernet Sauvignon	Monterey/California	Red	Jam, toasty	Pizza, pasta, beef	*
Monterra San Bernabe Ranch Chardonnay	Monterey/California	White	Tropical fruit	Fish, chicken	*
Monterra San Bernabe Ranch Syrah	Monterey/California	Red	Jam, vanillin	Pizza, pork	*
Montevina Amador Barbera	Sierra Foothills/California	Red	Elegant, earthy	Pizza, pasta, beef, chicken, veal	*
Montevina Amador Brioso Zinfandel	Sierra Foothills/California	Red	Fruity, spicy	Pizza, pasta, beef, chicken, veal	*
Montevina Amador Sangiovese	Sierra Foothills/California	Red	Berry, spicy	Pork, chicken, veal, pizza	*
Montevina Amador Terra d'Oro Barbera	Sierra Foothills/California	Red	Earthy, spicy, oaky	Pork, veal, beef	**

UNITED STATES OF AMERICA (continued)

Wine name	Region	Style	Flavor/Bouquet	Compatible Foods	Price Range
Montevina Amador Terra d'Oro Deaver Ranch Vineyard Zinfandel	Sierra Foothills/California	Red	Complex, rich, earthy	Lamb, beef, cheese	**
Montevina Amador Terra d'Oro Sangiovese	Sierra Foothills/California	Red	Berry, oaky	Pork, veal, beef, pasta	**
Morgan Chardonnay	Monterey/California	White	Tropical fruit	Fish, chicken	**
Morgan Monterey/Sonoma Sauvignon Blanc	Monterey/California	White	Melon, citrus, toasty	Shellfish, fish, salads, cheese	**
Morgan Pinot Gris	Monterey/California	White	Floral, nutty	Shellfish, fish	**
Morgan Pinot Noir	Monterey/California	Red	Jam, spicy	Fish, pork, duck	**
Morgan Reserve Pinot Noir	Monterey/California	Red	Jam, oaky, rich	Fish, pork, duck	***
Mount Eden Edna Valley Macgregor Vineyard Chardonnay	Edna Valley, South Central Coast/California	White	Complex, oaky, tropical fruit	Fish, chicken, pasta	**
Mount Eden Santa Cruz Mountains Cabernet Sauvignon	Santa Cruz Mountains, North Central Coast/California	Red	Powerful, elegant	Lamb, beef, cheese	***
Mount Eden Santa Cruz Mountains Chardonnay	Santa Cruz Mountains, North Central Coast/California	White	Elegant, minerally	Fish, chicken	***
Mount Eden Santa Cruz Mountains Cuvée des Vielles Vignes Pinot Noir	Santa Cruz Mountains, North Central Coast/California	Red	Earthy, rich, spicy	Fish, pork, veal, cheese	***
Mount Eden Santa Cruz Mountains Old Vine Reserve Cabernet Sauvignon	Santa Cruz Mountains, North Central Coast/California	Red	Minerally, complex	Lamb, cheese	***
Mount Eden Santa Cruz Mountains Pinot Noir	Santa Cruz Mountains, North Central Coast/California	Red	Rich, complex	Fish, duck, veal	***
Mount Palomar Late Harvest Zinfandel	Temecula Valley, Southern California/California	Red	Sweet, fruity, rich	Dessert, nuts	*
Murrieta's Well Red Vendemia Meritage	Livermore Valley, San Francisco Bay/California	Red	Earthy, minerally	Lamb, beef, cheese	**
Murrieta's Well White Vendemia Meritage	Livermore Valley, San Francisco Bay/California	White	Complex, minerally	Shellfish, fish, chicken	**
Murrieta's Well Zinfandel	Livermore Valley, San Francisco Bay/California	Red	Berry, spicy	Pizza, pork, veal	**
Naylor Vineyards & Wine Cellar Vidal Ice Wine	Pennsylvania	Sweet	Sweet, honey, floral	Dessert	***
Oak Ridge Vineyards Lodi Classic Reserve Zinfandel	Central Valley/California	Red	Berry, spicy	Pizza, sausages, beef	**
Oakencroft Vineyard & Winery Chardonnay	Virginia	White	Apples, citrus, vanillin	Fish, chicken	**
Oakstone Winery El Dorado Cabernet Franc	Sierra Foothills/California	Red	Plums, spicy	Pork, veal, beef	**
Oakstone Winery El Dorado Meritage	Sierra Foothills/California	Red	Fruity, spicy	Beef, lamb, veal	**
Oasis Vineyards Cuvée D'Or (sparkling wine)	Virginia	Sparkling	Crisp, citrus	Shellfish, Asian	**
Page Mill Chardonnnay	Santa Cruz Mountains, North Central Coast/California	White	Apples, minerally	Fish, chicken	**
Palmer Vineyards Merlot	New Mexico	Red	Plums, toasty	Lamb, beef, pork	***
Palmer Vineyards Pinot Blanc	New Mexico	White	Citrus, apples, vanillin	Fish, chicken	**
Paraiso Springs Santa Lucia Highlands Chardonnay	Monterey/California	White	Apples, toasty	Fish, chicken	*
Paraiso Springs Santa Lucia Highlands Pinot Blanc	Monterey/California	White	Melon, buttery	Fish, chicken	*
Paraiso Springs Santa Lucia Highlands Pinot Noir	Monterey/California	Red	Berry, spicy	Fish, pork, cheese	**
Paraiso Springs Santa Lucia Highlands Port Souzao	Monterey/California	Fortified	Caramelly	Nuts, cheese, dessert	*
Paraiso Springs Santa Lucia Highlands Reserve Pinot Blanc	Monterey/California	White	Nutty, oaky	Fish, chicken	**
Paraiso Springs Santa Lucia Highlands Riesling	Monterey/California	White	Floral, crisp, minerally	Shellfish, fish	*
Paraiso Springs Santa Lucia Highlands Syrah	Monterey/California	Red	Spicy, smoky	Veal, pork, cheese	**
Paumonock Vineyards Assemblage (cabernet sauvignon/cabernet franc/merlot)	New Mexico	Red	Rich, oaky	Lamb, beef, cheese	***
Pavona Vineyards Paraiso Springs Vineyard Pinot Blanc	Monterey/California	White	Apples, nutty	Fish, chicken	**
Pavona Vineyards Paraiso Springs Vineyard Pinot Noir	Monterey/California	Red	Jam, spicy	Fish, pork	**
Peirano Estate Vineyards Lodi Chardonnay	Central Valley/California	White	Apples, minerally	Fish, salads	*
Peirano Estate Vineyards Lodi Old Vines Zinfandel	Central Valley/California	Red	Berry, spicy	Pizza, sausages, beef	*
Pellegrini Vineyards Cabernet Franc	New Mexico	Red	Plums, herbaceous	Veal, pork, beef	**
Pellegrini Vineyards Vintner's Pride Chardonnay	New Mexico	White	Apples, vanillin	Fish, chicken	**
Pend d'Oreille Bistro Rouge Red Table Wine	Idaho	Red	Fruity, jam	Pizza, pasta, pork	*
Pend d'Oreille Chardonnay	Idaho	White	Apples, buttery	Fish, chicken	**
Pend d'Oreille Pinot Noir	Idaho	Red	Berry, spicy	Fish, chicken, veal	**
Peninsula Cellars Chardonnay	Michigan	White	Apples, minerally	Fish, chicken	**
Perry Creek Vineyards El Dorado Nebbiolo	Sierra Foothills/California	Red	Licorice, jam	Pork, beef, lamb	**
Perry Creek Vineyards El Dorado Wenzell Vineyards Mourvedre	Sierra Foothills/California	Red	Rich, fruity, earthy	Lamb, beef, cheese	**
Perry Creek Vineyards El Dorado ZinMan Zinfandel	Sierra Foothills/California	Red	Berry, spicy	Pizza, pork, pasta	**
Phillips Vineyards California Symphony	Central Valley/California	White	Floral, fruity	Salads, fruits	*
Phillips Vineyards Lodi Cotes de Lodi Rhone Blush	Central Valley/California	Rosé	Fruity	Salads, shellfish	*
Phillips Vineyards Lodi Old Vine Carignan	Central Valley/California	Red	Earthy, spicy	Pizza, Mediterrean	*
Phillips Vineyards Lodi Syrah	Central Valley/California	Red	Berry, jam	Pizza, chicken	*
Pietra Santa California Sasso Rosso Red Table Wine	Monterey/California	Red	Rich, oaky	Pork, beef, lamb	***

UNITED STATES OF AMERICA *(continued)*

Wine name	Region	Style	Flavor/Bouquet	Compatible Foods	Price Range
Pietra Santa California Sassolino Sangiovese/Cabernet Sauvignon	Monterey/California	Red	Rich, oaky	Pork, beef	***
Pietra Santa Cienega Valley Cabernet Sauvignon	Monterey/California	Red	Rich, oaky	Pork, beef, lamb	***
Pietra Santa Cienega Valley Sangiovese	Monterey/California	Red	Rich, oaky	Veal, pork	***
Pietra Santa San Benito Dolcetto	Monterey/California	Red	Rich, oaky	Chicken, veal, pork	***
Pietra Santa San Benito Zinfandel	Monterey/California	Red	Rich, oaky	Pork, beef	***
Pindar Vineyards Cuvée Rare (Sparkling 100% Pinot Meunier)	New Mexico	Sparkling	Crisp, fruity	Shellfish, Asian	**
Plum Creek Cellars Cabernet Sauvignon	Colorado	Red	Plums, vanillin	Beef, pork	**
Ponzi Pinot Gris	Willamette Valley/Oregon	White	Citrus, nutty, crisp	Shellfish, fish	**
Ponzi Reserve Pinot Noir	Willamette Valley/Oregon	Red	Berry, spicy, toasty	Veal, pork, beef	***
Prince Michel Vineyards Chardonnay	Virginia	White	Apples, buttery, minerally	Fish, chicken	**
Quady Madera Electra Fortified Muscat	Central Valley/California	Fortified	Floral, zingy	Fruit, Asian, cold meats, dessert	*
Quady Madera Elysium Fortified Muscat	Central Valley/California	Fortified	Spicy, floral	Dessert, cheese	*
Quady Madera Essensia Fortified Muscat	Central Valley/California	Fortified	Fruity, tangy	Dessert	*
Quady Madera Starboard Port	Central Valley/California	Fortified	Berry, rich	Nuts, cheese	*
Quilceda Creek Cabernet Sauvignon	Yakima Valley/ Washington State	Red	Berry, herbaceous, oaky	Pork, beef, lamb	**
R. H. Phillips California EXP Dunnigan Hills Syrah	Central Valley/California	Red	Berry, licorice	Pizza, Mediterrerean	*
R. H. Phillips California Dunnigan Hills Night Harvest Sauvignon Blanc	Central Valley/California	White	Sweet, floral, honey	Cold meats, cheese, dessert	*
Ravenswood Lodi Zinfandel	Central Valley/California	Red	Berry, spicy	Pizza, sausages, beef	**
Renaissance North Yuba Cabernet Sauvignon	Sierra Foothills/California	Red	Berry, herbaceous	Lamb, beef, pork	**
Renaissance North Yuba Muscat	Sierra Foothills/California	Fortified	Spicy, floral, honey	Dessert, fruits	*
Renaissance North Yuba Sangiovese	Sierra Foothills/California	Red	Berry, spicy	Pizza, pork, pasta	**
Renaissance North Yuba Sauvignon Blanc	Sierra Foothills/California	White	Grassy, zingy	Shellfish, salads	**
Renaissance North Yuba Select Late Harvest Sauvignon Blanc	Sierra Foothills/California	White	Sweet, zingy, fruity	Cold meats, dessert	**
Renwood Winery Amador Clockspring Vineyard Sangiovese	Sierra Foothills/California	Red	Powerful, earthy	Pork, lamb	***
Renwood Winery Amador Colheita Vintage Port	Sierra Foothills/California	Fortified	Fruity, rich	Dessert, cheese, nuts	***
Renwood Winery Amador D'Agostini Zinfandel	Sierra Foothills/California	Red	Powerful, complex	Lamb, beef, cheese	***
Renwood Winery Amador Fred's Vineyard Chardonnay	Sierra Foothills/California	White	Rich, oaky, fruity	Fish, chicken	***
Renwood Winery Amador Grandpère Zinfandel	Sierra Foothills/California	Red	Spicy, rich, oaky	Lamb, beef, cheese	***
Renwood Winery Amador Ice Zinfandel Ice Wine	Sierra Foothills/California	Sweet	Fruity, rich	Dessert	***
Renwood Winery Amador Linsteadt Vineyard Barbera	Sierra Foothills/California	Red	Earthy, rich, oaky	Lamb, beef, cheese	***
Renwood Winery Amador Viognier	Sierra Foothills/California	White	Tropical fruit, spicy	Fish, Asian	***
Renwood Winery Sierra Foothills Syrah	Sierra Foothills/California	Red	Rich, oaky	Lamb, beef, cheese	***
Retzlaff Vineyards Cabernet Sauvignon/Merlot	Livermore Valley, San Francisco Bay/California	Red	Elegant, earthy	Lamb, beef, cheese	***
Retzlaff Vineyards Chardonnay	Livermore Valley, San Francisco Bay/California	White	Apples, minerally	Fish, chicken	**
Retzlaff Vineyards Sauvignon Blanc	Livermore Valley, San Francisco Bay/California	White	Stone fruit, minerally	Shellfish, cheese	**
Retzlaff Vineyards Trousseau Gris	Livermore Valley, San Francisco Bay/California	White	Floral, fruity	Shellfish, salads	**
Rex Hill Reserve Pinot Noir	Willamette Valley/Oregon	Red	Berry, jam, vanillin	Veal, pork, beef	***
Ridge Bridgehead Mataro	Contra Costa County San Francisco Bay/California	Red	Elegant, rich, fruity	Lamb, beef, cheese	***
Ridge California Montebello Meritage	Santa Cruz Mountains, North Central Coast/California	Red	Complex, minerally	Lamb, beef, cheese	***
Ridge Montebello Chardonnay	Santa Cruz Mountains, North Central Coast/California	White	Crisp, rich, minerally	Fish, chicken	***
Ridge Santa Cruz Mountains Chardonnay	Santa Cruz Mountains, North Central Coast/California	White	Elegant, rich	Fish, chicken	***
Ridge Santa Cruz Mountains Merlot	Santa Cruz Mountains, North Central Coast/California	Red	Complex, spicy	Lamb, pork, veal	***
Ridge Zinfandel	Paso Robles, South Central Coast/California	Red	Powerful, oaky	Veal, pork, beef	***
Robert Mondavi Coastal Monterey Merlot	Monterey/California	Red	Plums, vanillin	Pork, beef, pizza	*
Robert Mondavi Coastal Monterey Syrah	Monterey/California	Red	Berry, vanillin	Pork, beef, pizza	*
Robert Talbott Cuvée Cynthia Chardonnay	Monterey/California	White	Apples, toasty	Fish, chicken	***
Robert Talbott Diamond T Estate Chardonnay	Monterey/California	White	Tropical fruit, toasty	Fish, chicken	***
Robert Talbott Sleepy Hollow Vineyard Chardonnay	Monterey/California	White	Tropical fruit, toasty	Fish, chicken	***
Rockbridge Vineyards Meritage (merlot/cabernet sauvignon)	Virginia	Red	Plums, earthy, spicy	Lamb, beef, cheese	**
Rose Creek Vineyards Johannisberg Riesling	Idaho	White	Floral, minerally	Salads, shellfish	*
Rosenblum Carla's Reserve Zinfandel	Contra Costa County San Francisco Bay/California	Red	Rich, fruity, spicy	Pizza, beef, veal, lamb	***

UNITED STATES OF AMERICA *(continued)*

Wine name	Region	Style	Flavor/Bouquet	Compatible Foods	Price Range
Rosenblum Chateau La Paws Cote du Bone Mourvedre	Contra Costa County San Francisco Bay/California	Red	Powerful, fruity	Lamb, beef, cheese	***
Runquist Amador Z Zinfandel	Sierra Foothills/California	Red	Berry, spicy	Pizza, pork, pasta	*
Rutherford Vintners Lodi Zinfandel	Central Valley/California	Red	Berry, spicy	Pizza, sausages, beef	**
Sable Ridge Vineyards Lodi Old Vines Zinfandel	Central Valley/California	Red	Berry, spicy	Pizza, sausages, beef	**
St Amant California Zinfandel	Central Valley/California	Red	Rich, plums, earthy	Pork, lamb, beef	**
St Amant Lodi Barbera	Central Valley/California	Red	Berry, spicy, oaky	Pork, lamb, beef	**
St Amant Lodi LBV Port	Central Valley/California	Fortified	Berry, rich	Nuts, cheese, dessert	*
St Amant Lodi Mohr-Fry Ranch Old Vines Zinfandel	Central Valley/California	Red	Berry, earthy	Lamb, beef, pork	**
St Amant Lodi/Amador Syrah	Central Valley/California	Red	Rich, spicy	Mediterrerean, nuts	**
St Julian Wine Co. Semi-Dry Riesling	Michigan	White	Honey, tropical fruit	Cheese, fruits, fish	*
Ste Chapelle Cabernet Sauvignon Winemaker's Series	Idaho	Red	Plums, toasty	Beef, pork, lamb	**
Ste Chapelle Chardonnay	Idaho	White	Apples, minerally	Fish, chicken	**
Ste Chapelle Chardonnay Winemaker's Series	Idaho	White	Complex, oaky	Fish, chicken	**
Ste Chapelle Dry Riesling Winemaker's Series	Idaho	White	Floral, minerally	Shellfish, fish	**
Ste Chapelle Idaho/Washington Cabernet Sauvignon	Idaho	Red	Plums, spicy	Beef, pork, lamb	**
Ste Chapelle Idaho/Washington Merlot	Idaho	Red	Plums, herbaceous	Pork, veal, beef	**
Ste Chapelle Merlot Winemaker's Series	Idaho	Red	Plums, oaky	Beef, pork, lamb	**
Ste Chapelle Reserve Syrah Reserve Series	Idaho	Red	Berry, spicy	Sausages, beef, pork, veal	**
Sakonnet Vineyards Fumé Blanc (Vidal)	Rhode Island	White	Fruity, floral	Shellfish, fish	**
Sakonnet Vineyards Samson Brut (chardonnay/pinot noir)	Rhode Island	Sparkling	Crisp, rich	Shellfish, Asian	**
Santino Amador Moscato del Diavolo	Sierra Foothills/California	White	Sweet, floral, fruity	Shellfish, salads, fruit	*
Sarah's Vineyard Estate Chardonnay	Santa Clara Valley, North Central Coast/California	White	Complex, elegant	Fish, chicken	***
Sarah's Vineyard Estate Merlot	Santa Clara Valley, North Central Coast/California	Red	Rich, oaky	Lamb, beef, pork	***
Sarah's Vineyard Estate Pinot Noir	Santa Clara Valley, North Central Coast/California	Red	Elegant, earthy	Fish, pork, cheese	***
Savannah-Chanel Amador Muscat Canelli	Sierra Foothills/California	Fortified	Mandarin, honey	Dessert, fruit	**
Savannah-Chanel Cabernet Franc	Santa Cruz Mountains, North Central Coast/California	Red	Powerful, oaky	Lamb, beef, cheese	**
Savannah-Chanel Carignane	Santa Cruz Mountains, North Central Coast/California	Red	Berry, spicy	Pizza, pork, veal	**
Savannah-Chanel Central Coast Pinot Noir	Monterey/California	Red	Berry, oaky	Fish, pork	**
Savannah-Chanel Chardonnay	Santa Cruz Mountains, North Central Coast/California	White	Intense, spicy	Fish, chicken	**
Savannah-Chanel Laetitia Vineyards Chardonnay	Arroyo Grande, South Central Coast/California	White	Tropical fruit, oaky	Fish, chicken	**
Savannah-Chanel Late Harvest Cabernet Franc	Santa Cruz Mountains, North Central Coast/California	White	Sweet, fruity, spicy	Dessert, cheese	**
Savannah-Chanel Zinfandel	Santa Cruz Mountains, North Central Coast/California	Red	Berry, spicy	Pizza, pork, veal	**
Savannah-Chanel Zinfandel	Paso Robles, South Central Coast/California	Red	Berry, spicy	Pizza, pork, veal	**
Sawtooth Cabernet Sauvignon	Idaho	Red	Plums, earthy	Beef, lamb	**
Sawtooth Chenin Blanc	Idaho	White	Fruity, floral	Salads, shellfish	*
Sawtooth Riesling	Idaho	White	Floral, minerally	Shellfish, fruits	*
Sawtooth Semillon/Chardonnay	Idaho	White	Apples, honey	Fish, chicken	**
Scheid Vineyards Gewurztraminer	Monterey/California	White	Spicy, floral	Fruits, Asian	*
Scheid Vineyards Pinot Noir	Monterey/California	Red	Berry, spicy	Fish, pork, pizza	**
Scheid Vineyards San Lucas Chardonnay	Monterey/California	White	Apples, minerally	Fish, chicken	**
Sevenhills Merlot	Walla Walla Valley/Washington State	Red	Plums, vanillin	Beef, lamb	**
Shalestone Vineyards Legend (merlot/cabernet sauvignon/ cabernet franc)	New Mexico	Red	Plums, spicy	Beef, pork, lamb	***
Sharpe Hill Vineyard Cabernet Franc	Connecticut	Red	Berry, herbaceous	Veal, pork, beef	**
Sharpe Hill Vineyard Select Late Harvest Stonington Vineyards Rosé	Connecticut	Rosé	Sweet, fruity, floral	Cheese, fruit, dessert	**
Shenandoah Vineyards Amador Cab-Shiraz	Sierra Foothills/California	Red	Complex, earthy	Lamb, beef, pork	**
Shenandoah Vineyards Amador Sangiovese	Sierra Foothills/California	Red	Berry, spicy, earthy	Pizza, pork, pasta, beef	**
Shenandoah Vineyards Amador Vintners Selection Zinfandel	Sierra Foothills/California	Red	Powerful, spicy	Lamb, beef, pork	**
Shenandoah Vineyards Amador Zingiovese	Sierra Foothills/California	Red	Fruity, spicy	Pizza, pork, pasta, veal	*
Sierra Vista Winery El Dorado Fleur de Montagne Rhone Red Blend	Sierra Foothills/California	Red	Berry, spicy	Pizza, pork, veal	**
Sierra Vista Winery El Dorado Old Vines Zinfandel	Sierra Foothills/California	Red	Spicy, earthy	Chicken, veal, pork	**
Sierra Vista Winery El Dorado Syrah	Sierra Foothills/California	Red	Plums, spicy	Beef, chicken, pork	**

UNITED STATES OF AMERICA *(continued)*

Wine name	Region	Style	Flavor/Bouquet	Compatible Foods	Price Range
Single Leaf Vineyards El Dorado Zinfandel	Sierra Foothills/California	Red	Rich, fruity, spicy	Chicken, veal, pork	**
Smith and Hook Baroness Reserve Masterpiece Cabernet Sauvignon	Monterey/California	Red	Powerful, tannic	Lamb, beef, cheese	***
Smith and Hook Cabernet Sauvignon	Monterey/California	Red	Plums, toasty	Lamb, beef, pork	**
Smith and Hook Viognier	Monterey/California	White	Floral, honey	Shellfish, fruits	**
Sobon Estate Shenandoah Valley Cougar Hill Zinfandel	Sierra Foothills/California	Red	Complex, spicy	Lamb, beef, pork	***
Sobon Estate Shenandoah Valley Fiddletown Zinfandel	Sierra Foothills/California	Red	Rich, fruity, spicy	Lamb, beef, pork	***
Sobon Estate Shenandoah Valley Orange Muscat	Sierra Foothills/California	Fortified	Mandarin, honey, floral	Dessert, fruits	**
Sobon Estate Shenandoah Valley Rocky Top Zinfandel	Sierra Foothills/California	Red	Complex, oaky	Lamb, beef, cheese	***
Sobon Estate Shenandoah Valley Roussanne	Sierra Foothills/California	White	Grassy, melon, vanillin	Shellfish, fish, salads	**
Sokol Blosser Redlands Pinot Noir	Willamette Valley/Oregon	Red	Berry, earthy, spicy	Veal, pork, beef	**
Solis Winery Estate Sangiovese	Santa Clara Valley, North Central Coast/California	Red	Berry, spicy	Pizza, pork, veal	**
Sonora Amador Story Vineyard Old Vine Zinfandel	Sierra Foothills/California	Red	Berry, earthy, spicy	Chicken, veal, pork	**
Sonora Amador TC Vineyard Old Vine Zinfandel	Sierra Foothills/California	Red	Berry, spicy	Pizza, pork, pasta	**
Sonora Amador Winery & Port Works Old Vine Zinfandel	Sierra Foothills/California	Red	Spicy, earthy	Chicken, veal, pork	**
Sonora Sierra Foothills Vinho Tinto	Sierra Foothills/California	Red	Plums, spicy	Chicken, veal, pork	**
Sonora Sierra Foothills Vintage Port	Sierra Foothills/California	Fortified	Fruity, rich	Dessert, nuts, cheese	**
South Hills/Hegy's Chenin Blanc	Idaho	White	Fruity, floral	Salads, shellfish	*
South Hills/Hegy's Pinot Noir	Idaho	Red	Berry, spicy	Fish, veal, pork	**
Spenker Family Winery Lodi Zinfandel	Central Valley/California	Red	Berry, spicy	Pizza, sausages, beef	**
Standing Stone Vineyards Gewurztraminer	New Mexico	White	Floral, spicy	Asian, fruits	**
Stephen Kent Winery Folkhendt Vineyard Cabernet Sauvignon	Livermore Valley, San Francisco Bay/California	Red	Rich, fruity, oaky	Lamb, beef, pork	***
Stephen Ross Bien Nacido Vineyard Pinot Noir	Santa Barbara County, South Central Coast/California	Red	Rich, earthy	Fish, pork, duck	**
Stone Hill Winery Norton	Missouri	Red	Fruity	Pizza, Asian	*
Stone Hill Winery Seyval	Missouri	White	Fruity, floral	Salads, fish	*
Stony Ridge Malvasia Bianca	Livermore Valley, San Francisco Bay/California	White	Apples, melon, minerally	Shellfish, salads	**
Stony Ridge Sangiovese Robusto Dessert Wine	Livermore Valley, San Francisco Bay/California	Fortified	Fruity, rich	Dessert, nuts, cheese	**
Storr's Mann Vineyard Merlot	Santa Clara Valley, North Central Coast/California	Red	Rich, fruity	Lamb, beef, pasta	***
Storr's San Ysidro Merlot	Santa Clara Valley, North Central Coast/California	Red	Plums, toasty	Lamb, beef, pork	***
Storrs Ben Lomond Mountain Meyley Vineyard Chardonnay	Santa Cruz Mountains, North Central Coast/California	White	Elegant, tropical fruit	Fish, chicken	***
Storrs Santa Cruz Mountains Christie Vineyard Chardonnay	Santa Cruz Mountains, North Central Coast/California	White	Complex, tropical fruit	Fish, chicken	***
Storrs Santa Cruz Mountains Petite Sirah	Santa Cruz Mountains, North Central Coast/California	Red	Powerful, tannic	Lamb, beef, cheese	**
Storrs Santa Cruz Mountains Vanamanutagi Vineyard Chardonnay	Santa Cruz Mountains, North Central Coast/California	White	Tropical fruit, minerally	Fish, chicken	***
Story Winery Amador Alitia Zinfandel	Sierra Foothills/California	Red	Powerful, earthy	Chicken, veal, pork	**
Story Winery Amador Miss-Zin	Sierra Foothills/California	Red	Fruity, spicy	Pizza, pork, pasta, chicken	*
Story Winery Amador Picnic Hill Zinfandel	Sierra Foothills/California	Red	Berry, spicy	Pizza, pork, pasta, chicken	**
Story Winery Amador Sweet Mission	Sierra Foothills/California	Sweet	Sweet, fruity, tangy	Dessert, nuts, cheese	*
Sycamore Creek Johannisberg Riesling	Santa Clara Valley, North Central Coast/California	White	Fruity, floral	Shellfish, salads	*
Sylvin Farms Chardonnay	New Jersey	White	Apples, buttery	Fish, chicken	**
Talley Chardonnay	Arroyo Grande, South Central Coast/California	White	Tropical fruit, oaky	Fish, chicken	**
Talley Rincon Pinot Noir	Arroyo Grande, South Central Coast/California	Red	Berry, smoky	Fish, veal, pork	***
Taylor California Cellars Reserve Marsala	Monterey/California	Fortified	Tangy, nutty	Nuts, cheese, dessert	*
Testarossa Chalone Chardonnay	Monterey/California	White	Buttery, toasty	Fish, chicken	***
Testarossa Chalone Michaud Vineyard Viognier	Monterey/California	White	Rich, honey, floral	Shellfish, fruits	***
Testarossa Santa Lucia Highlands Cuvée Niclaire Reserve Pinot Noir	Monterey/California	Red	Berry, rich, spicy	Fish, pork, veal	***
Testarossa Santa Lucia Highlands Pisoni Vineyard Chardonnay	Monterey/California	White	Tropical fruit, toasty	Fish, chicken, pasta	***
Testarossa Santa Maria Valley Bien Nacido Vineyard Chardonnay	Santa Barbara County, South Central Coast/California	Red	Rich, fruity, oaky	Fish, pork, veal	***
Testarossa Santa Maria Valley Chardonnay	Santa Barbara County, South Central Coast/California	White	Buttery, citrus, smoky	Fish, chicken	***
Testarossa Sleepy Hollow Vineyard Pinot Noir	Monterey/California	Red	Rich, berry, earthy	Fish, pork, cheese	***

UNITED STATES OF AMERICA (continued)

Wine name	Region	Style	Flavor/Bouquet	Compatible Foods	Price Range
Thackrey Pleiades VII Old Vines Red	Contra Costa County San Francisco Bay/California	Red	Fruity, rich, spicy	Chicken, veal, beef	**
Thomas Coyne California Viognier	Central Valley/California	White	Floral, minerally	Shellfish, salads	*
Thomas Fogarty Chardonnay	Santa Cruz Mountains, North Central Coast/California	White	Apples, vanillin	Fish, chicken	**
Thomas Fogarty Gewurztraminer	Santa Cruz Mountains, North Central Coast/California	White	Floral, spicy	Shellfish, Asian	**
Thomas Kruse Brut Méthode Champenoise	Santa Clara Valley, North Central Coast/California	Sparkling	Crisp, citrus	Shellfish, Asian	**
Thomas Kruse Chardonnay	Santa Clara Valley, North Central Coast/California	White	Citrus, toasty	Fish, chicken	**
Thunder Mountain Cabernet Sauvignon	Santa Cruz Mountains, North Central Coast/California	Red	Powerful, earthy	Lamb, beef, cheese	***
Tomasello Winery Cabernet Sauvignon	New Jersey	Red	Plums, spicy	Beef, pork	**
Treleaven Wines (King Ferry Winery) Barrel Fermented Chardonnay	New Mexico	White	Apples, toasty	Fish, chicken	**
Tria Vineyards Pinot Noir	Monterey/California	Red	Fruity, vanillin	Fish, chicken, pork, pizza	*
Turley Duarte Zinfandel	Contra Costa County San Francisco Bay/California	Red	Powerful, spicy	Lamb, cheese, dessert	***
Turley Wine Cellars Lodi Spenker Vineyard Zinfandel	Central Valley/California	Red	Berry, rich	Cheese, lamb, dessert	***
Two Rivers Winery Cabernet Sauvignon	Colorado	Red	Berry, herbaceous	Beef, lamb	**
Unalii Lodi Hillside Estates Zinfandel	Central Valley/California	Red	Berry, spicy	Pizza, sausages, beef	**
Unionville Vineyards Seyval	New Jersey	White	Floral, grassy	Shellfish, salads	*
Venezio Vineyard El Dorado Zinfandel	Sierra Foothills/California	Red	Berry, spicy	Pizza, pork, pasta	**
Ventana Vineyards Barrel Fermented Dry Chenin Blanc	Monterey/California	White	Crisp, citrus	Shellfish, chicken	*
Ventana Vineyards Cabernet Franc	Monterey/California	Red	Fruity, herbaceous	Veal, pork, pizza	*
Ventana Vineyards Gold Stripe Chardonnay	Monterey/California	White	Tropical fruit	Fish, chicken	*
Ventana Vineyards Merlot	Monterey/California	Red	Plums, jam	Pizza, pork	*
Ventana Vineyards Monterey Rose	Monterey/California	Rosé	Fruity	Salads, shellfish	*
Ventana Vineyards Riesling	Monterey/California	White	Floral, fruity	Salads, shellfish	*
Ventana Vineyards Syrah	Monterey/California	Red	Jam, spicy	Pork, chicken, pizza	*
Viano Vineyards Martinez Zinfandel	Contra Costa County San Francisco Bay/Californiaa	Red	Earthy, minerally	Lamb, beef, pork	*
Vigil Lodi Mohr-Fry Ranch Old Vines Zinfandel	Central Valley/California	Red	Berry, spicy	Pizza, sausages, beef	**
Vino Noceto Amador Riserva Sangiovese	Sierra Foothills/California	Red	Berry, earthy, spicy, oaky	Pork, veal, beef	**
Vino Noceto Amador Sangiovese	Sierra Foothills/California	Red	Berry, jam, spicy	Pizza, pork, veal, pasta	*
Vino Noceto Frivolo Sparkling Malvasia Bianca/Muscat	Sierra Foothills/California	Sparkling	Fruity, crisp	Shellfish, fruits, salads	*
Vino Noceto Rosato di Sangiovese	Sierra Foothills/California	Rosé	Fruity, floral	Shellfish, salads	*
Wallersheim Wine Co. Maréchal Foche	Wisconsin	Red	Fruity, tangy	Pizza, pasta, Asian	*
Waterbrook Meritage Red Mountain (cabernet franc/merlot)	Yakima Valley/ Washington State	Red	Plums, jam, oaky	Beef, lamb	**
Waterbrook Viognier	Walla Walla Valley/ Washington State	White	Floral, honey, stone fruit	Asian, fish	**
Wente Brut Reserve Arroyo Seco Méthode Champenoise	Monterey/California	Sparkling	Crisp, citrus	Fruit, Asian, shellfish	*
Wente Central Coast Sauvignon Blanc	Monterey/California	White	Citrus, stone fruit	Shellfish, cheese	*
Wente Crane Ridge Reserve Merlot	Livermore Valley, San Francisco Bay/California	Red	Plums, oaky, earthy	Lamb, beef, pork	***
Wente Reliz Creek Reserve Arroyo Seco Pinot Noir	Monterey/California	Red	Berry, spicy	Fish, chicken, pork	**
Wente Riva Ranch Reserve Arroyo Seco Chardonnay	Monterey/California	White	Tropical fruit, minerally	Fish, chicken	**
Wente Vineyards Cabernet Sauvignon	Livermore Valley, San Francisco Bay/California	Red	Spicy, toasty	Lamb, beef, pork	**
Wente Vineyards Charles Wetmore Reserve Cabernet Sauvignon	Livermore Valley, San Francisco Bay/California	Red	Rich, elegant	Lamb, beef, cheese	***
Wente Vineyards Herman Wente Reserve Chardonnay	Livermore Valley, San Francisco Bay/California	White	Complex, oaky`	Fish, chicken	***
Westover Vineyards Je t'aime Meritage	Livermore Valley, San Francisco Bay/California	Red	Plums, spicy	Lamb, beef, pork	***
Westover Vineyards Johannisberg Riesling	Monterey/California	White	Floral, fruity	Fruit, shellfish	*
Westover Vineyards Kalthoff Vineyards Cabernet Sauvignon	Livermore Valley, San Francisco Bay/California	Red	Rich, earthy	Lamb, beef, pork	***
Westover Vineyards Late Harvest Zinfandel	Contra Costa County San Francisco Bay/California	Red	Sweet, fruity, rich	Dessert, nuts	**
Westover Vineyards San Francisco Bay Palomares Vineyards Chardonnay	Livermore Valley, San Francisco Bay/California	White	Apples, citrus, vanillin	Fish, chicken	**
Westover Vineyards San Francisco Bay Sunol Valley Vineyards Chardonnay	Livermore Valley, San Francisco Bay/California	White	Rich, fruity, minerally	Fish, chicken	**

UNITED STATES OF AMERICA *(continued)*

Wine name	Region	Style	Flavor/Bouquet	Compatible Foods	Price Range
Westover Vineyards Santa Cruz Mountains Eagles Nest Vineyards Chardonnay	Santa Cruz Mountains, North Central Coast/California	White	Apples, toasty	Fish, chicken	**
Westover Vineyards Santa Lucia Highlands Cabernet Sauvignon	Monterey/California	Red	Plums, spicy	Lamb, beef, pork	**
Westover Vineyards Thatcher Bay Merlot	Livermore Valley, San Francisco Bay/California	Red	Plums, spicy	Lamb, beef, pork	**
Westover Vineyards Zinfandel	Contra Costa County San Francisco Bay/California	Red	Berry, spicy	Chicken, veal, pork	**
Westport Vineyards Blanc de Noirs	Massachussets	Sparkling	Crisp, fruity	Fruit, Asian	**
White Hall Vineyards Cabernet Franc	Virginia	Red	Berry, spicy	Veal, chicken, pork	**
White Hall Vineyards Soliterre (Vidal Dessert Wine)	Virginia	Sweet	Sweet, honey, nutty	Dessert, nuts	**
Williamsburg Winery Gabriel Archer Reserve (cabernet sauvignon/cabernet franc/merlot)	Virginia	Red	Plums, spicy	Beef, veal, pork	**
Windwalker Vineyards El Dorado Zinfandel	Sierra Foothills/California	Red	Berry, spicy	Pizza, pasta, pork, chicken	**
Wolffer Estate/Sagpond Vineyards Merlot	New Mexico	Red	Plums, vanillin	Beef, pork, lamb	**
Wolffer Estate/Sagpond Vineyards Chardonnay	New Mexico	White	Apples, buttery	Fish, chicken	**
Woodbridge Robert Mondavi Lodi Barbera	Central Valley/California	Red	Plums, spicy	Pizza, sausages, Asian	*
Woodbridge Robert Mondavi Lodi Merlot	Central Valley/California	Red	Plums, licorice	Pizza, chicken, beef	*
Woodbridge Robert Mondavi Lodi Old Vine Zinfandel	Central Valley/California	Red	Berry, spicy	Pizza, sausages, beef	*
Woodbridge Robert Mondavi Lodi Sauvignon Blanc	Central Valley/California	White	Herbaceous, citrus	Shellfish, salads	*
Woodbridge Robert Mondavi Lodi Viognier	Central Valley/California	White	Floral, stone fruit	Fruit, salads	*
Woodward Canyon Celilo Vineyard Chardonnay	Columbia Valley/Washington State	White	Apples, buttery, vanillin	Chicken, fish	**
Woodward Canyon Charbonneau (merlot/cabernet sauvignon)	Walla Walla Valley/Washington State	Red	Berry, herbaceous, oaky	Beef, lamb	**
Woodward Canyon Merlot	Columbia Valley/Washington State	Red	Berry, plum, oaky	Beef, lamb	**

MEXICO AND SOUTH AMERICA

Wine name	Region	Style	Flavor/Bouquet	Compatible Foods	Price Range
MEXICO					
Bodegas de San Lorenzo Cabernet Sauvignon	Saltillo/Parras Valley	Red	Plums, earthy	Beef, lamb	**
Bodegas de Santo Tomás Cabernet Sauvignon	Ensenada/Baja California	Red	Plums, spicy	Pork, beef, lamb	**
Bodegas de Santo Tomás Chardonnay	Ensenada/Baja California	White	Apples, butter	Fish, chicken	**
Casa Pedro Domecq Chateau Domecq Cabernet Sauvignon	Mexico City	Red	Rich, elegant	Beef, lamb	***
Cavas de San Juan/Hidalgo Cabernet Sauvignon	San Juan del Río	Red	Plums, leathery	Beef, lamb	**
Cavas de San Juan/Hidalgo Carte Blanche	San Juan del Río	Sparkling	Crisp, stone fruit, yeasty	Shellfish, nuts	**
Cavas de Valmar Cabernet Sauvignon	Ensenada/Baja California	Red	Plums, leathery	Beef, lamb	**
L.A. Cetto Nebbiolo	Tijuana/Baja California	Red	Intense, licorice, minerally	Beef, lamb, cheese	**
L.A. Cetto Petite Sirah	Tijuana/Baja California	Red	Berry, spicy	Chicken, pork, beef	**
L.A. Cetto Zinfandel	Tijuana/Baja California	Red	Berry, spicy	Chicken, pork, beef	**
Monte Xanic Cabernet-Merlot	Enseneda/Baja California	Red	Berry, plums, earthy	Veal, pork, beef	**
Monte Xanic Chardonnay	Ensenada/Baja California	White	Apples, buttery	Fish, chicken	**
Salva Uiva Brut	San Juan del Río	Sparkling	Citrus, nutty, crisp	Shellfish, nuts	**
Vinedos San Marcos Brut	Saltillo/Parras Valley	Sparkling	Citrus, yeasty, crisp	Shellfish, nuts	**

CHILE

Wine name	Region	Style	Flavor/Bouquet	Compatible Foods	Price Range
Caliterra Cabernet Sauvignon	Central Valleys	Red	Minerally, spicy, elegant	Pork, beef	*
Caliterra Chardonnay	Central Valleys	White	Citrus, apples, crisp	Fish, chicken	*
Caliterra Merlot	Central Valleys	Red	Berry, tannic, herbaceous	Chicken, pork	*
Caliterra Merlot	Central Valleys	Red	Fruity, tannic	Chicken, pork	**
Caliterra Reserva Cabernet Sauvignon	Central Valleys	Red	Licorice, plums, minerally	Pork, beef	*
Carmen Gold Reserve Cabernet Sauvignon	Maipo Valley/Central Valleys	Red	Berry, rich, oaky	Beef, lamb	***
Carmen Petite Sirah	Maipo Valley/Central Valleys	Red	Berry, spicy, vanillin, oaky	Pork, beef, lamb	**
Carmen Reserve Chardonnay-Semillon	Maipo Valley/Central Valleys	White	Wax, honey, rich	Fish, chicken	*
Carmen Reserve Merlot	Rapel Valley/Central Valleys	Red	Elegant, plums, herbaceous	Beef, lamb	**
Carmen Reserve Sauvignon Blanc	Casablanca Valley	White	Herbaceous, crisp	Shellfish, cheese	**
Casa Donoso Reserve Cabernet Sauvignon	Maule Valley	Red	Powerful, earthy	Beef, lamb	**
Casa Donoso Reserve Chardonnay	Maule Valley	White	Buttery, toasty	Fish, chicken	**
Casa Lapostolle Cuvée Alexandré Chardonnay	Casablanca Valley	White	Buttery, fruity, oaky	Fish, chicken	**
Casa Lapostolle Cabernet Sauvignon	Rapel Valley/Central Valleys	Red	Fruity, spicy, delicate	Beef, pork	**

CHILE *(continued)*

Wine name	Region	Style	Flavor/Bouquet	Compatible Foods	Price Range
Casa Lapostolle Chardonnay	Casablanca Valley	White	Buttery, yeasty, oaky	Fish, chicken	**
Casa Lapostolle Cuvée Alexandré Cabernet Sauvignon	Rapel Valley/Central Valleys	Red	Spicy, toasty, oaky	Veal, pork, beef	**
Casa Lapostolle Cuvée Alexandré Merlot	Rapel Valley/Central Valleys	Red	Fruity, oaky, rich	Pork, beef, lamb	**
Casa Lapostolle Merlot	Rapel Valley/Central Valleys	Red	Fruity, dill, intense	Pork, beef, lamb	**
Casa Lapostolle Sauvignon Blanc	Rapel Valley/Central Valleys	White	Melon, buttery, zingy	Shellfish, fish	*
Château La Joya Gran Reserva Chardonnay	Colchegua Valley	White	Tropical fruit, oaky	Fish, chicken	*
Château La Joya Gran Reserva Merlot	Colchegua Valley	Red	Berry, oaky	Chicken, pork	*
Clos Robert Merlot	Central Valleys	Red	Berry, spicy	Pizza, chicken	*
Concho y Toro Amelia Chardonnay	Casablanca Valley	White	Buttery, toasty, tropical fruit	Fish, chicken	***
Concho y Toro Casillero del Diablo Cabernet Sauvignon	Maipo Valley/Central Valleys	Red	Fruity, minerally	Veal, pork, beef	*
Concho y Toro Casillero del Diablo Chardonnay	Casablanca Valley	White	Citrus, buttery	Shellfish, fish	**
Concho y Toro Casillero del Diablo Merlot	Maipo Valley/Central Valleys	Red	Berry, licorice, leathery	Beef, pork	*
Concho y Toro Casillero del Diablo Merlot	Rapel Valley/Central Valleys	Red	Plums, berry, herbaceous	Chicken, veal, pork	*
Concho y Toro Don Melchar Puente Alto Vineyard Cabernet Sauvignon	Maipo Valley/Central Valleys	Red	Licorice, spicy, intense	Pork, beef	***
Concho y Toro Marques de Casa Concho Peumo Vineyard Merlot	Rapel Valley/Central Valleys	Red	Earthy, austere, minerally	Beef, pork	**
Concho y Toro Trio Cabernet Sauvignon	Maipo Valley/Central Valleys	Red	Berry, spicy, oaky	Pizza, veal	*
Cono Sur Pinot Noir	Rapel Valley/Central Valleys	Red	Berry, crisp, spicy	Fish, pasta	*
Cousino Macul Antiguas Reservas Cabernet Sauvignon	Maipo Valley/Central Valleys	Red	Fruity, oaky, minerally	Beef, lamb	**
Cousino Macul Finis Terrae	Maipo Valley/Central Valleys	Red	Minerally, licorice, toasty	Beef, lamb	***
Cousino Macul Limited Release Merlot	Maipo Valley/Central Valleys	Red	Berry, earthy, leathery	Beef, lamb	**
Dallas Conté Cabernet Sauvignon	Colchegua Valley	Red	Berry, oaky	Pizza, chicken	*
De Martino Cabernet Sauvignon	Maipo Valley/Central Valleys	Red	Berry, fruity, oaky	Pork, beef	*
De Martino Prima Reserva Cabernet Sauvignon	Maipo Valley/Central Valleys	Red	Berry, oaky	Pork, beef	*
De Martino Prima Reserve Sauvignon Blanc	Maipo Valley/Central Valleys	White	Citrus, oaky	Shellfish, fish	*
De Martino Reserva de Familia Cabernet Sauvignon	Maipo Valley/Central Valleys	Red	Berry, vanillin, intense	Beef, lamb	***
Domaine Paul Bruno	Maipo Valley/Central Valleys	Red	Complex, intense	Beef, lamb	**
Doña Consuelo Viña Segú Ollé Merlot	Maule Valley	Red	Floral, berry, crisp	Pork, veal, chicken	*
Errazuriz Don Maximiano Cabernet Sauvignon	Anconcagua Valley	Red	Licorice, spicy, earthy, complex	Beef, lamb	***
Errazuriz Don Maximiano Merlot	Anconcagua Valley	Red	Fruity, earthy, oaky, rich	Beef, lamb	***
Errazuriz El Ciebo Estate Cabernet Sauvignon	Anconcagua Valley	Red	Fruity, spicy, complex	Beef, lamb	***
Errazuriz Reserva Cabernet Sauvignon	Anconcagua Valley	Red	Earthy, intense, spicy	Veal, pork, beef	**
Errazuriz Reserva Chardonnay	Casablanca Valley	White	Tropical fruit, vanillin	Fish, chicken	**
Errazuriz Wild Ferment Chardonnay	Casablanca Valley	White	Apples, buttery, complex	Fish, chicken	**
La Palma Cabernet Sauvignon	Rapel Valley/Central Valleys	Red	Fruity, spicy	Pizza, pasta	*
La Palma Gran Reserva Chardonnay	Rapel Valley/Central Valleys	White	Apples, buttery, crisp	Fish, chicken	**
La Palma Gran Reserva Chardonnay	Rapel Valley/Central Valleys	White	Apples, yeasty, vanillin	Fish, chicken	**
La Palma Gran Reserva Merlot	Rapel Valley/Central Valleys	Red	Fruity, oaky	Veal, pork, beef	**
La Palma Merlot	Rapel Valley/Central Valleys	Red	Fruity, floral	Pizza, pasta	*
La Palma Reserva Cabernet Sauvignon	Rapel Valley/Central Valleys	Red	Berry, spicy, toasty	Pork, beef	**
La Palma Reserva Merlot	Rapel Valley/Central Valleys	Red	Fruity, rich	Veal, pork, beef	**
La Playa Cabernet Sauvignon	Maipo Valley/Central Valleys	Red	Fruity, spicy, minerally	Veal, pork, beef	*
La Playa Claret	Maipo Valley/Central Valleys	Red	Fruity, herbaceous	Chicken, pork	*
La Playa Claret Maxima	Maipo Valley/Central Valleys	Red	Licorice, spicy, oaky	Veal, pork, beef	**
La Playa Estate Reserve Cabernet Sauvignon	Maipo Valley/Central Valleys	Red	Berry, spicy, toasty	Chicken, veal	*
La Playa Estate Reserve Merlot	Maipo Valley/Central Valleys	Red	Fruity, oaky, coconut	Chicken, veal, pork	**
La Playa Sauvignon Blanc	Maipo Valley/Central Valleys	White	Citrus, austere	Shellfish, cheese	*
Los Vascos Cabernet Sauvignon	Colchegua Valley	Red	Berry, oaky	Pizza, chicken	*
Los Vascos Cabernet Sauvignon	Colchegua Valley	Red	Fruity, minerally	Pizza, pasta	*
Luis Felipe Edwards Carmenere	Rapel Valley/Central Valleys	Red	Plums, berry, herbaceous	Beef, lamb	**
Luis Felipe Edwards Chardonnay	Rapel Valley/Central Valleys	White	Apples, minerally	Fish, Asian	**
Luis Felipe Edwards Pupilla Cabernet Sauvignon	Rapel Valley/Central Valleys	Red	Berry, plums, spicy	Pork, beef	**
Miguel Torres Cordillera	Maule Valley	Red	Intense, berry, spicy	Veal, beef, lamb	**
Miguel Torres Manso de Velasco Cabernet Sauvignon	Carico Valley	Red	Fruity, minerally, herbaceous	Veal, pork, beef, lamb	**
Miguel Torres Maquetra Chardonnay	Maule Valley	White	Apples, toasty	Fish, chicken	**
Miguel Torres Santa Digna Brut	Maule Valley	Sparkling	Crisp, citrus	Shellfish, nuts	**
Miguel Torres Sauvignon Blanc	Carico Valley	White	Herbaceous, zingy	Shellfish, cheese	*
Montes Alpha Cabernet Sauvignon	Carico Valley	Red	Berry, oaky, rich	Beef, lamb	***
Montes Alpha Chardonnay	Carico Valley	White	Stone fruit, buttery, vanillin	Fish, chicken	***
Montes Alpha M	Carico Valley	Red	Berry, herbaceous, complex, rich	Beef, lamb	***
Montes Alpha Merlot	Carico Valley	Red	Fruity, dill, rich	Veal, pork, beef	***
Montes Cabernet Sauvignon	Carico Valley	Red	Spicy, herbaceous	Veal, pork, beef	**

CHILE *(continued)*

Wine name	Region	Style	Flavor/Bouquet	Compatible Foods	Price Range
Montes Sauvignon Blanc	Carico Valley	White	Grassy, melon, crisp	Shellfish, Asian	**
Montes Special Cuvée Merlot	Carico Valley	Red	Berry, vanillin	Pizza, chicken	*
Pionero Cabernet Sauvignon	Central Valleys	Red	Fruity, spicy	Pizza, pasta	*
Pionero Merlot	Central Valleys	Red	Berry, crisp, spicy	Pizza, pasta	*
Pionero Sauvignon Blanc	Central Valleys	White	Citrus, crisp, herbaceous	Shellfish, cheese	*
San Carlos Malbec	Colchegua Valley	Red	Berry, spicy	Pork, veal, beef	*
Santa Alicia El Pimiento Gran Reserva Merlot	Maipo Valley/Central Valleys	Red	Fruity, plums	Pizza, chicken	*
Santa Amelia Cabernet Sauvignon	Maule Valley	Red	Berry, spicy, crisp	Pizza, chicken	*
Santa Amelia Merlot	Maule Valley	Red	Berry, austere, earthy	Pork, veal, beef	*
Santa Amelia Reserve Selection Cabernet Sauvignon	Maule Valley	Red	Fruity, vanillin	Pork, veal, beef	*
Santa Amelia Reserve Selection Chardonnay	Maule Valley	White	Grassy, citrus, crisp	Fish, pasta	*
Santa Erna Reserve Cabernet Sauvignon	Maipo Valley/Central Valleys	Red	Berry, spicy, oaky	Veal, pork, beef	**
Santa Erna Reserve Merlot	Maipo Valley/Central Valleys	Red	Berry, oaky, coconut	Chicken, veal, pork	*
Santa Marvista Reserva Cabernet Sauvignon	Central Valleys	Red	Fruity, herbaceous, austere	Chicken, veal	*
Santa Marvista Reserva Merlot	Central Valleys	Red	Plums, zingy	Pizza, pasta	*
Santa Monica Chardonnay	Rapel Valley/Central Valleys	White	Apples, crisp	Shellfish, Asian	*
Santa Monica Tierra del Sol Reserva Cabernet Sauvignon	Rancagua Valley	Red	Earthy, spicy	Pork, beef	**
Santa Monica Tierra del Sol Reserva Chardonnay	Rancagua Valley	White	Apples, wax	Fish, chicken	**
Santa Rita Casa Real Old Vines Vineyard Cabernet Sauvignon	Maipo Valley/Central Valleys	Red	Intense, fruity, tannic	Beef, lamb	***
Santa Rita Late Harvest Semillon	Maipo Valley/Central Valleys	Sweet	Honey, wax, nutty, earthy	Fish, chicken	*
Santa Rita Medalla Real Chardonnay	Casablanca Valley	White	Citrus, melon, toasty, crisp	Fish, chicken	**
Santa Rita Medalla Real Special Reserve Cabernet Sauvignon	Maipo Valley/Central Valleys	Red	Berry, herbaceous, tannic	Pork, beef, lamb	**
Santa Rita Reserva Cabernet Sauvignon	Maipo Valley/Central Valleys	Red	Fruity, toasty, tannic	Pork, beef, lamb	**
Santa Rita Reserva Sauvignon Blanc	Maule Valley	White	Grassy, zingy	Shellfish, cheese	**
Seña Red Table Wine	Anconcagua Valley	Red	Earthy, oaky, intense, elegant	Beef, lamb	***
Stony Hollow Cabernet Sauvignon	Rapel Valley/Central Valleys	Red	Berry, spicy	Pizza, chicken	*
Undurraga Cabernet Sauvignon	Colchegua Valley	Red	Fruity, jam	Pizza, chicken	*
Undurraga Chardonnay	Maipo Valley/Central Valleys	White	Apples, oaky	Fish, chicken	*
Undurraga Merlot	Colchegua Valley	Red	Berry, herbaceous, jam	Pork, veal, beef	*
Undurraga Pinot Noir	Maipo Valley/Central Valleys	Red	Berry, fruity, crisp	Fish, pork	*
Undurraga Reserva Cabernet Sauvignon	Maipo Valley/Central Valleys	Red	Fruity, berry, vanillin	Pork, beef, lamb	**
Undurraga Sauvignon Blanc	Lontue	White	Citrus, melon, zingy	Shellfish, cheese	*
Undurraga Sauvignon Blanc	Maipo Valley/Central Valleys	White	Herbaceous, citrus, oaky	Shellfish, cheese	*
Valdevisio Barrel Select Malbec	Lontue	Red	Plums, spicy	Veal, pork, beef	**
Valdevisio Caballo Loco	Lontue	Red	Complex, intense, oaky	Beef, lamb	**
Valdevisio Reserve Cabernet Franc	Lontue	Red	Berry, toasty	Veal, pork, beef	**
Valdevisio Reserve Merlot	Lontue	Red	Plums, earthy, oaky	Pork, beef, lamb	**
Veramonte Cabernet Sauvignon	Casablanca Valley	Red	Spicy, oaky, fruity	Pork, beef	*
Veramonte Chardonnay	Casablanca Valley	White	Apples, toasty, buttery	Fish, chicken	*
Veramonte Merlot	Casablanca Valley	Red	Fruity, spicy, elegant	Veal, pork	*
Veramonte Merlot	Central Valleys	Red	Spicy, berry, herbaceous, elegant	Pizza, pasta	*
Vina Calina Selección de las Lomas Merlot	Rapel Valley/Central Valleys	Red	Fruity, oaky, rich	Beef, lamb	***
Viña Aquitania Cabernet Sauvignon	Maipo Valley/Central Valleys	Red	Plums, spicy	Pork, beef, lamb	**
Viña Calina Cabernet Sauvignon	Central Valleys	Red	Berry, licorice, earthy	Beef, lamb	**
Viña Calina Cabernet Sauvignon	Rapel Valley/Central Valleys	Red	Powerful, berry, spicy	Pork, beef	*
Viña Calina Chardonnay	Rapel Valley/Central Valleys	White	Apples, crisp	Fish, Asian	*
Viña Calina Merlot	Maule Valley	Red	Fruity, herbaceous	Pizza, chicken	**
Viña Calina Selección de las Lomas Cabernet Franc	Maule Valley	Red	Fruity, toasty, elegant	Beef, lamb	***
Viña Calina Selección de las Lomas Cabernet Sauvignon	Rapel Valley/Central Valleys	Red	Spicy, fruity, intense	Pork, beef	**
Viña Calina Selección de las Lomas Chardonnay	Rapel Valley/Central Valleys	White	Citrus, oaky	Fish, chicken	**
Viña Calina Vicuña Vineyard Cabernet Sauvignon	Rapel Valley/Central Valleys	Red	Intense, fruity, toasty	Beef, lamb	***
Viña Gracia Barrique-Fermented Chardonnay	Bío-Bío Valley	White	Apples, buttery, oaky	Fish, chicken	**
Viña Gracia Chardonnay	Bío-Bío Valley	White	Apples, minerally	Fish, chicken	**
Viña Gracia Merlot	Bío-Bío Valley	Red	Plums, spicy	Chicken, veal	**
Viña La Rosa Cabernet Sauvignon	Rapel Valley/Central Valleys	Red	Plums, earthy, oaky	Pork, beef	**
Viña San Estaban Reserva Cabernet Sauvignon	Anconcagua Valley	Red	Berry, vanillin, rich	Chicken, veal, pork	*
Viña San Esteban Gran Reserva Cabernet Sauvignon	Colchegua Valley	Red	Berry, oaky, intense	Pork, veal, beef	**
Viña San Esteban Gran Reserva Cabernet Sauvignon	Colchegua Valley	Red	Plums, oaky	Pork, veal, beef	**
Viña San Esteban President's Select Cabernet Sauvignon	Colchegua Valley	Red	Fruity, herbaceous, vanillin	Pork, beef	**
Viña San Pedro Castillo de Molina Reserva Cabernet Sauvignon	Lontue	Red	Licorice, berry, oaky	Pizza, chicken	*
Viña San Pedro Castillo de Molina Reserva Chardonnay	Lontue	White	Fruity, buttery, toasty	Fish, chicken	*
Viña Santa Carolina Chardonnay-Sauvignon Blanc	Colchegua Valley	White	Citrus, crisp, tropical fruit	Shellfish, Asian	*

CHILE (continued)

Wine name	Region	Style	Flavor/Bouquet	Compatible Foods	Price Range
Viña Santa Carolina Reserva Merlot	Maule Valley	Red	Berry, vanillin	Pork, veal, beef	*
Viña Tarapaca Chardonnay	Maipo Valley/Central Valleys	White	Apples, buttery, citrus	Fish, chicken	*
Viña Tarapaca La Isla Sauvignon Blanc	Maipo Valley/Central Valleys	White	Tropical fruit, crisp	Asian, fish	*
Viña Tarapaca Reserva Merlot	Maipo Valley/Central Valleys	Red	Fruity, spicy, elegant	Chicken, veal	*
Viña Tarapaca Reserva Merlot	Maipo Valley/Central Valleys	Red	Licorice, fruity, oaky	Chicken, veal, pork	*
Viña Tarapaca Zauala	Maipo Valley/Central Valleys	Red	Earthy, minerally, oaky	Beef, lamb	***
Viñedos J. Bouchon Chicureo Cabernet Sauvignon	Maule Valley	Red	Plums, berry, spicy	Pizza, chicken	*
Vista Sur Merlot	Central Valleys	Red	Plums, spicy	Chicken, pork, beef	**
Viu Manent Reserva Cabernet Sauvignon	Colchegua Valley	Red	Berry, elegant, herbaceous	Veal, pork, beef	**
Viu Manent Reserve Chardonnay	Colchegua Valley	White	Citrus, vanillin, elegant	Fish, chicken	**
Viu Manent Reserve Fumé Blanc	Colchegua Valley	White	Minerally, oaky, herbaceous	Shellfish, fish	*
Viu Manent Reserve Oak-Aged Malbec	Colchegua Valley	Red	Berry, toasty, zingy	Pork, beef	**
Walnut Crest Estate Selection Chardonnay	Casablanca Valley	White	Buttery, oaky	Fish, chicken	*

ARGENTINA

Wine name	Region	Style	Flavor/Bouquet	Compatible Foods	Price Range
Alamos Ridge Chardonnay	Mendoza	White	Apples, butter, spicy	Fish, chicken	*
Alamos Ridge Malbec	Mendoza	Red	Berry, plums, spicy	Chicken, veal, pork	*
Altos de les Hormigas Malbec	Mendoza	Red	Berry, spicy	Pizza, beef	*
Balbi Cabernet Sauvignon	Mendoza	Red	Berry, herbaceous, minerally	Pork, beef	**
Balbi Chardonnay	Mendoza	White	Citrus, minerally, zingy	Shellfish, fish	**
Balbi Malbec	Mendoza	Red	Berry, spicy	Pizza, chicken	**
Balbi Malbec-Syrah	Mendoza	Red	Floral, berry, fruity	Pizza, chicken, fish	*
Barral y Roca Malbec	Mendoza	Red	Berry, herbaceous, spicy	Pork, beef	**
Bodegas Curton Tempranillo-Malbec	Mendoza	Red	Berry, spicy	Pizza, beef	**
Bodegas Escorihuela Don Miguel Gascón Malbec	Mendoza	Red	Berry, licorice, rich	Pork, beef, lamb	*
Bodegas Escorihuela Don Miguel Gascón Viognier	Mendoza	White	Tropical fruit, minerally, austere	Fish	**
Bodegas Etchart Arnaldo B Etchert Reserva	Cafayate	Red	Minerally, berry, herbaceous	Pork, beef, lamb	**
Bodegas Etchart Cafayate Chardonnay Barrel Fermented	Cafayate	White	Citrus, butter, toasty	Fish, chicken	**
Bodegas Etchart Rio de Plata Merlot	Mendoza	Red	Berry, spicy	Pizza, chicken	*
Bodegas Etchart Torrontes	Cafayate	White	Floral, tropical fruit	Asian, shellfish	*
Bodegas Norton Privada	Mendoza	Red	Earthy, spicy	Beef, lamb	**
Canale Malbec	Rio Negro	Red	Berry, earthy	Pork, beef, lamb	**
Catena Agrelo Vineyards Cabernet Sauvignon	Mendoza	Red	Berry, fruity, vanillin	Chicken, veal, pork	**
Catena Agrelo Vineyards Chardonnay	Mendoza	White	Fruity, oaky, butter	Fish, chicken	**
Catena Alta Malbec	Mendoza	Red	Complex, rich, earthy, oaky	Beef, lamb	***
Catena Lunlunta Vineyards Malbec	Mendoza	Red	Plums, fruity, rich, oaky	Beef, lamb	***
Correas Syrah-Sengiovese	Maipu	Red	Berry, earthy, crisp	Pizza, chicken	*
Correca Cabernet Sauvignon	Maipu	Red	Berry, minerally	Pizza, beef	*
Covisan Syrah Artuel Valley	San Rafael	Red	Berry, mint, rich	Pork, lamb	*
Etchart Arnaldo Etchert Reserve	Cafayate	Red	Fruity, earthy, spicy	Beef, lamb	**
Finca Flinchman Dedicado	Maipu	Red	Berry, earthy, oaky	Beef, lamb	**
Finca Flinchman Reserva	Maipu	Red	Berry, herbaceous, oaky	Beef, lamb	**
Graffigna Barbera	San Juan	Red	Berry, spicy	Pizza, chicken	**
Graffigna Cabernet Sauvignon	San Juan	Red	Plums, spicy, elegant	Chicken, pork, beef	**
Graffigna Cabernet Sauvignon-Merlot	San Juan	Red	Plums, spicy, oaky	Pork, beef, lamb	**
Graffigna Chardonnay	San Juan	White	Apples, butter, elegant	Fish, chicken	**
Graffigna Chardonnay-Sauvignon	San Juan	White	Apples, melon, spicy	Fish, chicken	**
Graffigna Malbec	San Juan	Red	Berry, spicy	Veal, pork, beef	**
Graffigna Pinot Gris-Semillon	San Juan	White	Floral, fruity, zingy	Shellfish, Asian	**
Graffigna Shiraz-Cabernet Sauvignon	San Juan	Red	Berry, licorice, oaky	Pork, beef, lamb	**
Grove Street Cabernet Sauvignon	Mendoza	Red	Berry, herbaceous, vanillin	Pizza, beef	**
Hos de Medrano Viña Hormigas Reserva Malbec	Mendoza	Red	Fruity, intense, toasty	Pork, beef, lamb	***
Infinitus Malbec-Syrah	Patagonia	Red	Rich, berry, spicy	Veal, pork, beef	***
La Agricola Montepulciano	Mendoza	Red	Berry, earthy	Beef, lamb	*
Lavaque Cabernet Sauvignon	Mendoza	Red	Berry, earthy, leathery	Beef, lamb	**
Lavaque Cabernet Sauvignon-Merlot	Mendoza	Red	Berry, spicy, herbacous	Pork, beef, lamb	*
Lavaque Pinot Noir	Mendoza	Red	Spicy, leathery, oaky	Fish, pork	*
Mariposa Tapiz Merlot	Mendoza	Red	Berry, spicy	Chicken, pork	**
Mariposa Tapiz Reserve Malbec	Mendoza	Red	Berry, tannic	Beef, lamb	**
Michel Torino Don David Cabernet Sauvignon	Mendoza	Red	Berry, dill, oaky	Beef, lamb	**

ARGENTINA (continued)

Wine name	Region	Style	Flavor/Bouquet	Compatible Foods	Price Range
Norton Barbera	Mendoza	Red	Berry, spicy	Pizza, chicken	*
Norton Privada	Mendoza	Red	Berry, herbaceous, oaky	Pork, beef	**
Proviar Castel Chandon	Mendoza	Red	Berry, plums, spicy	Chicken, veal, pork	**
Proviar Chardonnay	Mendoza	White	Apples, minerally	Fish, chicken	**
Putini Malbec	Mendoza	Red	Plums, spicy	Pork, beef	**
Q Merlot	Mendoza	Red	Intense, plums, dill, toasty	Beef, lamb	**
Q Tempranillo	Mendoza	Red	Rich, berry, spicy, dill	Beef, pork	**
Rafael Malbec-Tempranillo	Mendoza	Red	Rich, plums, berry, leathery	Chicken, veal, pork	*
San Telmo Merlot	Mendoza	Red	Fruity, spicy	Chicken, pork	*
Santa Julia Malbec-Cabernet Sauvignon	Mendoza	Red	Berry, spicy, minerally	Veal, pork, beef	*
Santa Julia Oak Reserve Cabernet Sauvignon	Mendoza	Red	Berry, spicy, leathery	Beef, lamb	*
Santa Julia Oak Reserve Chardonnay	Mendoza	White	Citrus, yeast, toasty	Fish, chicken	*
Santa Julia Oak Reserve Malbec	Mendoza	Red	Berry, vanillin	Pizza, chicken	*
Santa Julia Sauvignon Blanc	Mendoza	White	Herbaceous, vanillin	Shellfish, fish	*
Santa Julia Tempranillo	Mendoza	Red	Berry, minerally	Pizza, chicken	*
Santa Julia Torrontes	Mendoza	White	Citrus, floral, fruity	Shellfish, Asian	*
Santa Silva Barbera	Mendoza	Red	Berry, spicy	Pizza, chicken	**
Trapiche Fond de Cave Chardonnay	Mendoza	White	Apples, smoky, toasty	Fish, chicken	**
Trapiche Iscay Merlot-Malbec	Mendoza	Red	Rich, toasty, powerful	Veal, pork, beef	***
Trapiche Medalla Cabernet Sauvignon	Mendoza	Red	Berry, oaky, austere	Beef, lamb	**
Trapiche Medalla Chardonnay	Mendoza	White	Tropical fruit, toasty	Fish, chicken	**
Trapiche Medalla Merlot	Mendoza	Red	Berry, oaky, tannic	Veal, pork, beef	**
Trapiche Medalla Red	Mendoza	Red	Berry, minerally, oaky	Veal, pork, beef	**
Trapiche Oak Cask Cabernet Sauvignon	Mendoza	Red	Fruity, oaky	Pizza, beef	*
Trapiche Oak Cask Chardonnay	Mendoza	White	Apples, spicy	Fish, chicken	*
Trapiche Oak Cask Malbec	Mendoza	Red	Berry, oaky	Chicken, pork	*
Tri Vento Malbec	Mendoza	Red	Berry, elegant	Pizza, chicken	*
Trumpeter Cabernet Sauvignon	Maipu	Red	Berry, dill, oaky	Pizza, beef	*
Trumpeter Merlot	Tupungato	Red	Plums, spicy, toasty	Pizza, beef	*
Valentin Bianchi Cabernet Sauvignon	San Rafael	Red	Rich, spicy, oaky	Pork, beef	**
Valentin Bianchi Elsa Malbec	San Rafael	Red	Berry, fruity, vanillin	Pizza, beef	*
Valentin Bianchi Elsa Semillon Chardonnay	San Rafael	White	Citrus, minerally	Shellfish, fish	*
Valentin Bianchi Famiglia Bianchi Cabernet Sauvignon	San Rafael	Red	Intense, earthy, spicy, toasty	Beef, lamb	***
Valentin Bianchi Malbec	San Rafael	Red	Powerful, earthy	Beef, lamb	**
Valentin Bianchi Sauvignon Blanc	San Rafael	White	Citrus, minerally, crisp	Shellfish, fish	**
Valle del Condor Malbec	Mendoza	Red	Berry, spicy, rich	Pork, beef	**
Viñas de Medrano Cabernet Sauvignon	Mendoza	Red	Berry, plums, spicy	Pizza, beef	*
Viñas de Medrano Malbec	Mendoza	Red	Plums, earthy, spicy	Beef, lamb	*
Vinterra Cabernet Sauvignon	San Juan	Red	Herbaceous, vanillin	Pizza, beef	*
Vinterra Chardonnay	San Juan	White	Butter, wax, apples	Fish, chicken	*
Vinterra Malbec	San Juan	Red	Berry, vanillin	Pizza, chicken	*
Vinterra Merlot	San Juan	Red	Berry, vanillin	Pizza, beef	*
Weinert Cabernet Sauvignon	Mendoza	Red	Berry, earthy, toasty	Beef, lamb	**
Weinert Carrascal	Mendoza	Red	Earthy, minerally	Beef, lamb	**
Weinert Cevas de Weinert Gran Vino	Mendoza	Red	Mushroom, earthy, austere	Beef, lamb	**
Weinert Malbec	Mendoza	Red	Berry, gamey, leathery	Pork, beef, lamb	**

Glossary

Steve Charters MW

a.b.v. "Alcohol by volume," the standard form of measuring the alcohol level in a wine, given as a percentage.

AC Initials of *Appellation Controlée.*

Acid The component of substances which gives them a sharp, tangy taste. Lemons, for example, are very acidic. Acidity, mainly in the form of tartaric acid, is a key component of wine.

Acidification The process of adding acidity to juice or wine to make it taste fresher and prevent damage from bacteria and oxygen.

Adega (Portuguese) A cellar or winery.

Aguardiente (Spanish) A popular high-proof grape spirit produced by the continuous still method.

Air-bag press A cylindrical press which works by expanding a rubber bladder under air pressure. As the bladder expands it squeezes the grapes in the press, producing juice.

Alcohol by volume *see* a.b.v.

Appellation A term used to describe a demarcated wine region, one where the boundaries of the region are mapped out. The term is originally French. *See also Appellation Controlée.*

Appellation Controlée (AC) (French) A demarcated wine region in France. For example, only wine made in the specifically defined area around Bordeaux can claim to be from the Bordeaux appellation. French appellation laws also prescribe various viticultural and wine-making practices for each AC.

Aromatic Literally a wine with a noticeable smell, but often used to describe wines with a very floral or spicy nose.

Artisanal Wine made by an artesan: the "crafted" result of small-scale (probably quite traditional) production.

Auslese (German) One of the *Prädikats* of German wine law, literally meaning "selected harvest." In practice, a wine with greater must weight than is normal for German wines, and probably with noticeable sweetness and a hint of botrytis.

Autolysis The process resulting from the decomposition of dead yeast cells following fermentation. It gives a creamy texture and

yeasty aromas to wine. It is especially important for sparkling wine which has undergone second fermentation by the traditional method.

Autolytic characters The aroma and flavor characters resulting from autolysis in sparkling wines.

Balance The relationship among the factors that make up the structure of a wine—the acid, residual sugar, tannin, alcohol, weight, texture and fruit intensity—when tasting it.

Barrel-aging The process of aging wine in a barrel (usually of new or newish oak) rather than in a large tank and/or the bottle.

Barrica (Spanish) *see Barrique.*

Barrique (French) A term originally used in Bordeaux but now commonly used worldwide for a barrel of 225 liters (60 gallons).

Base wine The wine, fermented dry, that will undergo a second fermentation to become sparkling wine.

Battonage (French) The stirring of yeast lees in barrel. It encourages the uptake of lees flavors in the wine, and prevents some faults developing in the wine.

Baumé (French) One of the methods of quantifying sugar levels in grape juice; the others are brix and *oeschle*. This method is used in France and Australia. One degree *baumé* is roughly equal to one percent of alcohol in the resulting wine.

Beerenauslese (**BA**) (German) One of the *Prädikats* of German wine law, literally "selected berries." This category implies the selection of botrytized grapes, to make intense and sweet wine.

Biodynamic A system of cultivation which is related to organic viticulture. It is based around viewing the soil as a living organism which should not be treated with inorganic substances. The system has a complex dogma, which is dismissed as superstition by some, but it has been adopted by some of the leading producers in France and elsewhere.

Bladder press *see* Air-bag press.

Bodega (Spanish) This word has many meanings: cellar, wine producer, merchant, store selling wine, tavern.

Bodeguero (Spanish) Proprietor of a *bodega.*

Botrytis Latin term for fungus, encompassing all the rots which can affect grapes and damage

the resulting wine. In one form, however—noble rot—it does not harm the grapes, but produces a complex and sweet wine, commonly referred to as "botrytized."

Bottle shock The term for the impact of bottling on wine: the wine can become less aromatic or tasty in the few weeks after bottling.

Brix One of the methods of quantifying sugar levels in grape juice; the others are *baumé* and *oeschle*. This method is used by winemakers in the USA and New Zealand as one component of assessing grape ripeness.

Cane The woody growth developing from vine shoots: it both produces the vine leaves and carries the bunches of grapes.

Canteiro (Portuguese) The eaves of the Madeira houses under which the island's great vintage wines must age for a minimum of 20 years in cask.

Carbonic maceration The process of starting to ferment juice in unbroken grapes, using enzymes rather than yeast; a full yeast fermentation follows once the alcohol level in the grapes reaches about 4 percent. It is traditionally used in Beaujolais, producing fruity wines with low tannin.

Cap The mixture of skins, stalks and other matter which accumulates at the top of fermenting red must.

Cava Spanish sparkling wine made in a number of regions by the traditional method.

Chaptalization The process of adding sugar to fermenting must to increase the resulting alcoholic strength of the wine.

Charmat A method of inducing the second fermentation, and thus creating sparkling wine, in large pressure tanks. This method reduces the production costs usually associated with the traditional method.

Clairet Deep rosé wine that is produced in Bordeaux.

Climat (French) A term used particularly in Burgundy for a vineyard site, defined by its mesoclimate as well as by its soil.

Clos (French) A walled vineyard.

Colheita (Portuguese) A tawny port which is not a blend of different years but which is "dated," that is, from a single vintage.

Concentration The intensity and focus of flavor in a wine.

Condition The state of a wine being drunk; whether or not it has any faults.

Cordon A permanent branch of a vine, usually trained along a wire.

Cork taint A wine fault caused generally by the interaction of mold (originating from the cork) with chlorine compounds, causing a loss of fruit flavor and—to a greater or lesser extent—a damp, hessian-like smell on the wine.

Crianza (Spanish) The term for aging, and for the youngest official category of a wood-matured wine (used particularly in Rioja, and some other regions, such as Ribera del Duero).

Crossing A new variety produced by adding the pollen of one variety to the flowers of another and planting the resulting grape seeds. Müller-Thurgau is probably the most utilized crossing in the world. Note the difference between a crossing and a hybrid.

Cru (French) Literally "growth." Practically, this is difficult to translate, but usually it is used in a qualitative context, as in "premier cru"—"first growth"—which is a high-quality wine.

Cuvée (French) Derived from the term for a tank, this word now refers to a particular selection of wine. In Champagne it is the first selection of juice on pressing—the best for making sparkling wine.

Deacidification The process of reducing the acid level in wine, normally by malolactic fermentation or the addition of various compounds which cause acidity to deposit out.

Demarcation The process of defining the exact geographical limits of a wine region. *See also* Appellation.

Disgorgement The action of expelling frozen yeast lees from a bottle of wine which has undergone second fermentation, to ensure that the wine is not cloudy.

En primeur (French) The first sale of wine in Bordeaux from each vintage, in which wine is sold to the customer while the wine is still in barrels in the châteaux' cellars.

Enology The science of wine production.

Enrichment The process of increasing the alcohol level of the wine, usually by chaptalisation, to modify its structure.

Estufa (Portuguese) The method of heating madeira which accelerates its development; it gives madeira its characteristic style by caramelising the sugars in the wine.

Ethyl alcohol Scientific classification of the predominant type of alcohol in wine. Often popularly referred to as ethanol.

Extract The dry matter which would remain were you to evaporate the liquid from a wine. The higher the sugar-free extract, the more flavor, body and phenolic components there are in the wine. However, over-extraction can cause a wine to be unbalanced, especially if it results in excessive phenolics.

Feinherb (German) A term denoting an off-dry wine.

Fermentation The chemical process involved in converting sugar to alcohol and carbon dioxide, brought about by the activity of yeast.

Filtration The process of removing unwanted matter (even matter as small as bacteria or yeast cells) from a wine by various methods of straining.

Finesse The term used to describe elegant delicacy in a wine.

Fining The process of removing undesirable particles (usually proteins or phenolics) dissolved in the wine.

Fortification The addition of spirit (normally grape spirit) to wine. This is normally done during fermentation, to a point where yeast cells die and fermentation stops. Wines produced in this way are referred to as "fortified."

Fractional blending The process whereby when some wine is extracted from a cask for bottling it is replaced by wine from a more recent blend, which in turn may be replaced by a yet more recent blend, and so on until wine from the current vintage is added to the youngest blend. The process is used particularly in the making of sherry.

Garrafeira (Portuguese) A wine which has been subject to additional aging—three years for red wine and one year for white—for that type of wine. Wines labeled "Garrafeira" are generally considered to be of better quality.

Generoso (Spanish and Portuguese) Fortified wine.

Glycerol A heavy liquid, which is related to alcohol, which may impart hints of sweetness to a wine.

Gran Reserva (Spanish) This term is used to denote a wine that has had extra aging. Specifically, this means two years in cask and three years in bottle for red wines; and rather less for whites.

Grand vin (French) Literally "big wine": this can be interpreted as a great, serious, or important wine. Also used in Bordeaux for the main wine (not the second wine) made by a château.

Granvas (Spanish) Sparkling wine made by either the tank method or the charmat method.

Green harvesting The process of removing some bunches on a vine to reduce the yield and enhance the ripening process in the bunches which remain.

Guyot-trained A method of training a vine which uses a new cane or canes each year to provide shoots and ultimately fruit; it is unlike cordon training, which uses a permanent branch.

Halbtrocken (German) Literally "half dry": in practice, a medium dry wine.

Harmony The sense of integration and equilibrium one gets when tasting a wine which is in balance.

Herbaceous A wine which tastes rather herbal, or of dried grass. Sometimes used in a derogatory way.

Hybrid A new vine produced from two parents, generally one *Vitis vinifera* (which provides almost all the grape varieties used for making wine) and the other a native American species. This was done to combine the best aspects of both varieties, and to increase the vines' resistance to phylloxera (in Europe in the late nineteenth century), but the hybrids produced poor wine; only a few, such as seyval blanc and chambourcin, make acceptable wine.

Jeropiga (Portuguese) Grape juice prevented from fermenting by fortification. Usually used to sweeten fortified wines.

Joven afrutado (Spanish) A young wine made to emphasize overt fruity characters.

Jug wine US wine of mediocre quality produced in bulk and sold cheaply.

Kabinett (German) The most basic of the *Prädikats* of German wine law, but still usually of higher quality than basic QbA wine. These are very light wines.

KWV Initials (from the name in Afrikaans) of the Cooperative Wine Growers' Association of South Africa.

Lagar (Portuguese) A shallow basin in which the grapes used for port can be trodden to release their juice and extract phenolics while fermentation takes place.

Late disgorgement A form of champagne which remains on its yeast lees in the bottle for many years. The champagne is then disgorged shortly before sale. The lees allow the champagne to age slowly, and may also impart further flavor complexity.

Lees The term literally means any debris that falls out of wine (including skins, pips etc), but it is often used to refer to the dead yeast cells deposited at the end of fermentation, (also known as yeast lees). *See also* Autolysis; *Battonage.*

Length The amount of time the taste of wine lingers in the mouth after it has been swallowed. A long wine is generally a wine of high quality.

Levada (Portuguese) An irrigation trench used in Madeira to take water to the vineyards.

Low cropping Vines which are managed in order to produce lower yields (and therefore, theoretically, higher quality yields). Also called crop thinning.

Maceración carbonica (Spanish) *see* carbonic maceration.

Maceration The process of leaving must or wine with grape skins during or after fermentation in order to increase the taking up of phenolics.

Maderization A process by which wine is made to taste like madeira: oxidation is sped up by the addition of heat. The term is sometimes used pejoratively, to indicate excessive oxidation and consequent unpleasant taste.

Malolactic fermentation The conversion by bacteria of crisp malic acid into softer lactic acid, making the wine fuller. It is commonly used in making red wines, but only with discretion in whites.

Mercaptans A wine fault stemming from a sulfur compound that causes an unpleasant garlic-like smell, and which is impossible to shift.

Meritage (USA) A trademarked name for wine based on a blend of the traditional red Bordeaux varieties—primarily cabernet sauvignon, cabernet franc, and merlot. Most Meritage is made in California.

Méthode ancestrale (French) A traditional way of making sparkling wine which involves stopping the fermentation by chilling, leaving a wine that is fizzy, slightly sweet and cloudy (from the yeast lees). It is mainly used for Blanquette de Limoux.

Méthode champenoise (French) The traditional method of making sparkling wine as utilized in Champagne.

Méthode traditionelle (French) *see* Traditional method.

Methyl alcohol A form of alcohol found in wine, but is much less important than ethyl alcohol. PIt is more popularly known as methanol.

Método tradicional (Spanish) *see* Traditional method.

Minerally A tasting term used to describe wine flavors which are not fruity, oaky or floral, but which may be more reminiscent of sucking on a pebble.

Mistelle (French) Grape juice which has been prevented from fermenting by fortification with spirit.

Moelleux (French) Sweet, but not luscious.

Mousse The bubbles on the surface of a sparkling wine. The term is also used to describe the feel of the bubbles in the mouth.

Must The liquid that is fermenting—neither pure juice nor finished wine.

Muzzle The wire restraint which contains the cork of a sparkling wine.

Négociant (French) A wine merchant.

Nematodes Microscopic insects which may damage a vine or, more dangerously, carry a disease which will infect the vine.

Noble A contraction of "noble rot," referring to wine which has undergone the beneficial effects of botrytis.

Nose A term used to describe the smell of a wine.

Oechsle One of the methods of quantifying sugar levels in grape juice; the others are *baumé* and brix. It is commonly used by winemakers in Germany and Central Europe as one component of assessing grape ripeness.

Organoleptic An adjective referring to the process of tasting.

Oxidation The dulling of the color, aroma and flavor of a wine which results from too much air contact.

Palate A term used to describe the taste of wine.

Passerillage (French) Concentrating the sugars in grapes by leaving them to hang on the bunches and partially dehydrate.

pH The scientific measurement of acidity and alkalinity. Water (which is neutral) has a pH of 7. A pH of less than that means a substance is acidic (at a pH of 1 it would be very highly acidic), and a pH above 7 means the substance is alkaline. Wine generally has a pH between 2.9 and about 3.6 (sometimes a little higher).

Phenolics Substances extracted from the skins of grapes which provide the coloring (anthocyanins) and texture (tannins) for red wine.

Power A tasting term referring to the combined weight and flavor intensity of the wine—and possibly the impact of its alcohol as well.

Prädikat (German) Literally a "distinction," given to QmP wines: essentially a marker of the sugar level and an indicator of the likely style of the wine. The term is used in Germany and Austria.

Pumping over A method of increasing phenolic extraction from black grapes by pumping must from the bottom of a tank and spraying it over the cap at the top.

Punching down A method of increasing phenolic extraction from black grapes by pressing the cap down into the must, thus increasing contact between the cap and the liquid.

Qualitätswein bestimmter Anbaugebiete (QbA) (German) Literally "quality wine from a region": the most basic level of quality wine in Germany and Austria.

Qualitätswein mit Prädikat (QmP) (German) Higher in quality than QbA in Germany and Austria, QmP wines are defined using an additional categorization, which is based essentially on the wine's must weight (sugar level). *See also* Kabinett; *Spätlese; Auslese; Beerenauslese; Trockenbeerenauslese.*

Racking The process of moving wine from one container to another, generally leaving some deposit behind. Sometimes, though not invariably, some aeration is involved.

Recioto (Italian) A sweet wine made from dried grapes, most famously from the Soave and Valpolicella regions.

Reduction The process of maturing wine in an environment with no oxygen contact. As the oxygen dissolved in the wine is used up, further oxidation cannot occur. This environment helps preserve freshness in wine, but in certain environments off-odors can develop.

Reserva (Spanish) Red wine that has been aged for at least a year in cask and two years in bottle. White wines age for a shorter period. These wines are generally of higher quality than ordinary wines.

Residual sugar Sugar which remains in the finished wine after fermentation has been completed, giving some sweetness to it.

Riddling The process (in the traditional method) of slowly shaking the yeast lees to the neck of the bottle ready for disgorgement.

Saignée (French) The process of "bleeding off" some red must at the start of fermentation in order to achieve a greater concentration of phenolics.

Second fermentation The means of adding the fizz (in the traditional method), by adding additional yeast and sugar to base wine in a bottle or tank, then capping it in order to trap the resulting carbon dioxide.

Set The point, after the vine has flowered, when the fertilized flower heads begin to turn into minute berries.

Shy-bearing A vine which does not produce much fruit.

Solera system A system of fractional blending, used mainly with sherry, which allows younger wine to gradually be blended with, and refresh, older wine.

Sorting tables Tables set up at harvest on which grapes can be sorted before crushing, to remove any of unacceptable quality. *See also triage.*

Spätlese (German) One of the *Prädikats* of German wine law, literally "late picked."

Spritzig (German) Wine which has a prickle of carbon dioxide, without being fully sparkling.

Stabilization The process of ensuring that wine has no components which may give rise to haze, deposits or further microbial activity once bottled.

Structure In tasting, the relationship between the elements sensed in the mouth (sugar, acidity, tannin, alcohol, bitterness, weight and texture), as well as the flavor intensity of the wine.

Sur lie (French) Literally "on lees": a wine which has been matured for some time on its yeast lees.

Süssreserve (German) Literally "sweet reserve": unfermented grape juice or grape concentrate added to the wine before bottling to sweeten it.

Table wine In Europe, this is the legal classification of the most basic wine, which distinguishes it from "quality" wine. In some European Union countries, this can now refer to blended wines, called European table wines.

Tafelwein (German) *see* Table wine.

Tannin A phenolic compound which gives a textural character to (mainly red) wine—"furring" the teeth and gums in much the same way that stewed tea does. In balance within the wine, it is an essential part of the structure of red wine.

Texture A tasting term for the tactile sensation of wine in the mouth: this relates particularly to tannin.

Traditional method The production of sparkling wine by the induction of a second fermentation in a bottle, which is then riddled and undergoes disgorgement.

Triage (French) The sorting of grapes during vintage to discard those of unacceptable quality. With botrytized wines, *triage* is used to delay the picking of grapes which have not yet adequately developed noble rot.

Trockenbeerenauslese (**TBA**) (German) One of the *Prädikats* of German wine law, literally "selected dried berries": the name implies selection of botrytized grapes, to make very intense and sweet wine. This is the pinnacle of German and Austrian sweet wine, and commands extremely high prices.

Vaslin press A cylindrical press which works by pulling together two plates from either end of the cylinder, thus squeezing the grapes contained between the plates.

Vendange (French) Harvest.

Vendange tardive (French) Late harvest. The term is used in Alsace, and equates to the German *spätlese*.

Veraison (French) A critical stage in the ripening process, when black grapes start to attain their color, and white grapes cease to be intense green and become translucent. From this point the grape size expands noticeably and the sugar content starts to increase dramatically.

Verband Deutscher Prädikats und Qualitätsweingüter (**VDP**) A German growers' association that requires its members to meet far higher production and quality standards than those demanded by the wine laws.

Vigor Vines may have more or less vigor. A certain amount implies a healthy vine, but excessive vigor may result in too much foliage, which shades the bunches and may impede ripening. Some vines are naturally more vigorous than others.

Vin de pays (French) A category of table wine which is nevertheless allowed to state a region of origin. Its production—particularly its yield—is more controlled than that of table wine (although without the constraints imposed by the appellation system), in an attempt to produce better wine.

Vino joven afrutado (Spanish) Young, fruity wine.

Vin doux naturel (French) Literally, "a wine that is naturally sweet," but used to describe a kind of fortified wine where spirit is added to grape juice rather than to wine. In various forms this is made across much of the south of France, either from grenache or muscat.

Vintage The year in which the grapes used to produce wine were picked.

Vitis vinifera (Latin) Botanical classification for the wine vine. Almost all varieties used to make wine are members of this species.

Weight The apparent feeling of heaviness (or otherwise) which a wine gives when in the mouth. It is related to the alcohol content of the wine.

Winkler–Amerine heat summation scale A system of viticultural climate classification for California, based on the average environmental temperature. Growing zones are graded into regions (I–V) using monthly averages of temperatures over 50° Fahrenheit (10°C) during the vine's growing season. Daily temperature surpluses are averaged then multiplied by the number of days per month. Accumulations of heat are measured in degree days. The fewer the degree days, the cooler the region.
  I. Less than 2,500 degree days: Bordeaux, Reims, Carneros, Edna Valley.
  II. 2,501–3,000 degree days: Asti in Piedmont, Auckland, St. Helena in Napa Valley.
  III. 3,001–3,500 degree days: Calistoga in Napa Valley, Ukiah in Mendocino.
  IV. 3,500–4,000 degree days: Capetown, Florence.
  V. More than 4,000 degree days: Perth, San Joaquin Valley.

Index

Italic page numbers refer to maps. **Bold** page numbers refer to major geographic sections. Pictures have not been indexed. Vineyards are indexed under their full names, including the words Château and Domaine.

In general Italian names are entered in the index under *de*, *di* and *della*. Spanish names are entered under the main part of the name, with the *de* inverted. French names are entered under *Du*, *La* and *Le*, but *de* is inverted. Afrikaans names are entered under prefixes, but German names are usually entered under the name following the prefix. It is important to check all possible positions in the index, as common usage of specific names sometimes differs from the general rules.

This index was created by Glenda Browne, a Registered Member of the Australian Society of Indexers.

Captions for the photographs in the introductory pages of each chapter.

France
62–63: The Château Latour vineyards in fall, Paulliac, Bordeaux. 65: Plowing with a horse in the Rhône Valley; At work in the Tain-Hermitage vineyards, Rhône Valley; Vineyards above the town of Tain with the Rhône in the background.

Germany
222–23: Looking down to Berkastel from the Doktor vineyard, Mosel. 225: An ivy-clad house in the Mosel Valley; Grape pickers, Mosel; Trittenheim, Mosel.

Austria
264: The alpine village of Karten. 265: Fertilizing vines with old grapeskins; Picking riesling at Wolkersdorf.

Switzerland
272: Terraced vineyards, Sion, Valais. 273: Pickers near Sion, Valais; Pickers taking a break, Lavaux.

Italy
278–79: Vineyards from Abbey Risazzo Manzano, Colli Orientale del Friuli. 280: Rows of vines, Barbaresco, Piedmont; River Arno, Florence, Tuscany. 281: Mounted police in Florence, Tuscany.

Spain
334–35: A shepherd tending to his sheep, Costa Brava. 337: Vines near Cirauqui, Navarra; The Rio Vero in Aragon.

Portugal
376–77: Flat-bottomed port boats *(barcos rabelos)*, Douro. 379: Treading grapes, Quinta do Noval Douro Valley; Braganca castle.

England and Wales
400: Vineyards and winery buildings in Wootton Vineyard, Shepton Mallett, Somerset. 401: Big Ben, London; Hunters, South Downs, East Sussex.

Central Europe
406-07: Tsantali vineyard and winery, Macedonia. 409: Wine tasting by an enologist at Vino Nitra, South Slovakia; Stari Grad harbor, Hvar Island, Dalmatia, Croatia.

Eastern Europe
422–23: Rkatsiteli grapes, Russe, Northern region, Bulgaria. 424: Church interior, Bulgaria; Vines, Melnik, Southwestern region, Bulgaria.

Southern Europe
434–35: Fields near Zeebug in the center of Malta. 436: Tending vines in Greece. 437: Oak wine barrels, Turkey; a typical white-washed home in Greece.

Africa
448: Vineyards, Celliers de Meknes, M'Tir, Morocco. 449: Bab El Kheims Gate, Meknes, Morocco.

South Africa
454–55: Vineyards under the Windhoek Mountain, Western Cape. 457: Harvesting sauvignon grapes, Bouchard-Finlayson winery, Overberg; Winery nestling at the foot of a mountain.

The Middle East
482: Elevated view of Ciinsault vines on terra rossa soil, Bekaa Valley, Lebanon. 483: Worker transferring wine, Israel; Byblos, Lebanon.

Asia
488–89: Pruning trellised grapes, China. 490: Dragon boat at the Summer Palace, China. 491: Chardonnay vines and bougainvillea, Champagne Maharashtra, India.

Australia
500–501: Gum tree and vines at Chapel Hill, McLaren Vale. 502: An outside tasting area at Leasingham, Clare Valley; Penfolds' grand Kaiser Stuhl Winery in South Australia.

New Zealand
576–77: A view from Rippon Vineyard across a lake, Otago, South Island. 578: Mills Reef Winery, Waikato/Bay of Plenty; Winemaker.

Canada
630–631: Poplar grove, Naramata Bench, Okanagan Valley, BC. 633: Moose warning sign, Quebec; Café in old quarter, Quebec.

United States of America
654–55: Green vistas and fertile farmlands in Pennsylvania, part of the Atlantic Uplands. 656: Showing the flag; Eberle vineyards, Paso Robles, California. 657: Vines in full leaf.

Mexico and South America
744: Settling tanins in Santa Barbara, Baja California; Shrine to Santa Barbara. 745: Preparing new vineyards for planting, Casa Madero, Baja California, Mexico.

Chile
754: Bodega, Errazuriz Panquehuf, Aconcagua Valley, Chile. 755: Tending grape vines; Irrigation at Errazuriz Panquehue, Aconcagua Valley.

Argentina
772: Road from Salta to Cafayate, Salta. 773: Cabernet Sauvignon harvest, Finca Flichman, Mendoza; Loading grapes, Proviar Vineyards, Mendoza.